1 MONTH OF
FREE
READING

at

www.ForgottenBooks.com

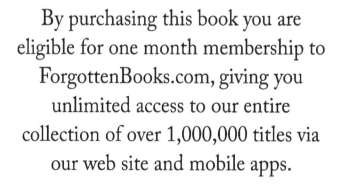

By purchasing this book you are eligible for one month membership to ForgottenBooks.com, giving you unlimited access to our entire collection of over 1,000,000 titles via our web site and mobile apps.

To claim your free month visit:
www.forgottenbooks.com/free894342

ISBN 978-0-266-82058-1
PIBN 10894342

This book is a reproduction of an important historical work. Forgotten Books uses
state-of-the-art technology to digitally reconstruct the work, preserving the original format
whilst repairing imperfections present in the aged copy. In rare cases, an imperfection in
the original, such as a blemish or missing page, may be replicated in our edition. We do,
however, repair the vast majority of imperfections successfully; any imperfections that
remain are intentionally left to preserve the state of such historical works.

THE

R OF THE REBELLION:

A COMPILATION OF THE

OFFICIAL RECORDS

OF THE

UNION AND CONFEDERATE ARMIES.

———

PREPARED, UNDER THE DIRECTION OF THE SECRETARY OF WAR, BY

The late Lieut. Col. ROBERT N. SCOTT, Third U. S. Artillery

PURSUANT TO ACTS OF CONGRESS.

———

SERIES I—VOLUME XXVI—IN TWO PARTS.

PART I.

EPORTS..............UNION AND CONFEDERATE.
ORRESPONDENCE..UNION.

WASHINGTON:
GOVERNMENT PRINTING OFFICE.
1889.

PREFACE.

y an act approved June 23, 1874, Congress made an appropriation
enable the Secretary of War to begin the publication of the Official
ords of the War of the Rebellion, both of the Union and Confed-
e Armies," and directed him "to have copied for the Public Printer
eports, letters, telegrams, and general orders not heretofore copied
rinted, and properly arranged in chronological order."

ppropriations for continuing such preparation have been made from
to time, and the act approved June 16, 1880, has provided "for
printing and binding, under direction of the Secretary of War, of
00 copies of a compilation of the Official Records (Union and Con-
rate) of the War of the Rebellion, so far as the same may be ready
publication, during the fiscal year"; and that "of said number,
0 copies shall be for the use of the House of Representatives, 2,000
ies for the use of the Senate, and 1,000 copies for the use of the
cutive Departments." *

his compilation will be the first general publication of the military
rds of the war, and will embrace all official documents that can be
ined by the compiler, and that appear to be of any historical value.

Volumes I to V distributed under act approved June 16, 1880. The act approved
1st 7, 1882, provides that—
The volumes of the Official Records of the War of the Rebellion shall be distributed
llows: One thousand copies to the Executive Departments, as now provided by
  One thousand copies for distribution by the Secretary of War among officers of
Army and contributors to the work. Eight thousand three hundred copies shall
nt by the Secretary of War to such libraries, organizations, and individuals as
be designated by the Senators, Representatives, and Delegates of the Forty-
ith Congress. Each Senator shall designate not exceeding twenty-six, and each
esentative and Delegate not exceeding twenty-one of such addresses, and the
mes shall be sent thereto from time to time as they are published, until the pub-
ion is completed. Senators, Representatives, and Delegates shall inform the
tary of War in each case how many volumes of those heretofore published they
forwarded to such addresses. The remaining copies of the eleven thousand to
iblished, and all sets that may not be ordered to be distributed as provided
n, shall be sold by the Secretary of War for cost of publication with ten per
added thereto, and the proceeds of such sale shall be covered into the Treasury.
vo or more sets of said volumes are ordered to the same address the Secretary of
shall inform the Senators, Representatives, or Delegates, who have designated
ame, who thereupon may designate other libraries, organizations, or individuals.
Secretary of War shall report to the first session of the Forty-eighth Congress
 volumes of the series heretofore published have not been furnished to such
ries, organizations, and individuals. He shall also inform distributees at whose
nce the volumes are sent."

The publication will present the records in the following order of arrangement:

The **1st Series** will embrace the formal reports, both Union and Confederate, of the first seizures of United States property in the Southern States, and of all military operations in the field, with the correspondence, orders, and returns relating specially thereto, and, as proposed is to be accompanied by an Atlas.

In this series the reports will be arranged according to the campaigns and several theaters of operations (in the chronological order of the events), and the Union reports of any event will, as a rule, be immediately followed by the Confederate accounts. The correspondence, &c., not embraced in the "reports" proper will follow (first Union and next Confederate) in chronological order.

The **2d Series** will contain the correspondence, orders, reports, and returns, Union and Confederate, relating to prisoners of war, and (so far as the military authorities were concerned) to State or political prisoners.

The **3d Series** will contain the correspondence, orders, reports, and returns of the Union authorities (embracing their correspondence with the Confederate officials) not relating specially to the subjects of the *first* and *second* series. It will set forth the annual and special reports of the Secretary of War, of the General-in-Chief, and of the chiefs of the several staff corps and departments; the calls for troops, and the correspondence between the national and the several State authorities.

The **4th Series** will exhibit the correspondence, orders, reports, and returns of the Confederate authorities, similar to that indicated for the Union officials, as of the *third* series, but excluding the correspondence between the Union and Confederate authorities given in that series.

ROBERT N. SCOTT,
Major Third Art., and Bvt. Lieut. Col.

WAR DEPARTMENT, *August* 23, 1880.

Approved:

ALEX. RAMSEY,
Secretary of War.

THE

R OF THE REBELLION:

A COMPILATION OF THE

OFFICIAL RECORDS

OF THE

NION AND CONFEDERATE ARMIES.

ADDITIONS AND CORRECTIONS

TO

SERIES I—VOLUME XXVI.

be inserted in the volume. For explanation see General
Index volume, Serial No. 130, page XXVIII.)

PUBLISHED UNDER THE DIRECTION OF

The Hon. ELIHU ROOT, Secretary of War,

BY

BRIG. GEN. FRED C. AINSWORTH,

CHIEF OF THE RECORD AND PENSION OFFICE, WAR DEPARTMENT,

AND

MR. JOSEPH W. KIRKLEY.

Mr. JOHN S. MOODEY, Indexer.

WASHINGTON:
GOVERNMENT PRINTING OFFICE.
1902.

TEXT.

PART 1.

Page 3. For *16-20, 1863*, read *14-20, 1863*, and in same line for *Expedition* read *Expeditions.* Insert the following: *Oct. 28, 1863.—Mutiny of Vidal.*

Page 222. Address, for *H. T. Wade, jr.*, read *H. F. Wade, jr.*

Pages 265, 267, 269, 271. Headline, for *Tribodeaux* read *Thibodeaux.*

Page 633. Third Brigade, after *175th New York*, erase *Col. Michael K. Bryan.*

Page 634. Banks to Gardner, second line, insert * after *11th instant* and add footnote, * *See Series II, Vol. 6, p. 104.*

Page 874. In note, for *1884* read *1864.*

Page 896. Under *Port Hudson, La.*, for *Col. Lorenzo D. Sargent* read *Lieut. Col. Lorenzo D. Sargent.*

Page 900. Third Brigade, for *Col. Abraham Bassford* read *Maj. Abraham Bassford.*

Page 901. Eighth line, bottom, for *Fifth Infantry, California Volunteers*, read *Fifth U. S. Infantry.*

Pages 933-1039. Strike out foot-note *No circumstantial reports on file*, wherever it occurs.

Page 940. For *Banks, Nathaniel F.*, read *Banks, Nathaniel P.*

PART 2.

Page 127. First line, first word, for *vive* read *vide.*

Page 130. Maury to Cooper, third line, for *First Confederate Battalion* read *Battalion, First Confederate.*

INDEX.

Insert all words and figures in *italics* and strike out all in [brackets]. An asterisk (*) following a correction indicates that "Additions and Corrections" to the text should be consulted. References are to parts of volume.

	Part.
A. G. Brown, Steamer, *328*	1
Adams, *J. Q.* [William]	2
Alabama Troops.	
Cavalry—Companies	
[Amos', *39*]	2
Allen, Henry W.	
Correspondence with War Dept., C.S., 173	2
[For correspondence, see Jefferson Davis].	2
Antelope, Schooner [Steamer]	1
Arkansas Troops (C.).	
Infantry—Battalions:	
Jones', B., 1st [[8th]]	1, 2
Atchafalaya *River,* La	1
Bagley [Bagaly], Steamer	1
Bell, J. H., C. S. S., *298, 336* [Belle, C. S S., 298, 336]	2
Bell, *Jesse M.* [Lieutenant]	2
Bellot, De *Menier* [Mermes] & Co.	2
Benavides, *Cristoval* [Christobal]	1, 2
Bernes [Barnes], George	2
Berwick, *Oscar D.* [O.]	1
Bickham, *M* [A. C.]	1
Bisbie [Bisbee], D. T	2
Block, *David* [——]	2

	Part.
Bonaparte, Charles L. N., 143, 144, 148, 315	2
Borgne, Lake, La.	
Affair on, Nov. 22, 1863, 3	1
Boyce, *Henry* [Judge]	2
Brott, *George F.* [——]	1
Brown, A. G., Steamer, *328* [Brown, Steamer, 328]	1
Brown, J. M., Steamer, *642* [Brown, I. M., Steamer, 642]	1
Brown, R. B , *741* [Brown, R. W., 741]	1
Bryan, Michael K , [633]*	1
Burk, *E A.* [Burke, E]	2
Cahawba [Cahawha], U. S. S., [298]	1
Campbell, *J.* [——]	1
Carmichael, *A.* [Major]	2
Carter, *Haley M.* [Lieutenant-Colonel]	2
Carter, *J. C.* [Major]	2
Cayuga, U. S. S., 298	1
Clifton, *U. S S.* [C. S. S.]	2
Cole, *George H. T.* [Captain]	1
Comstock, Joseph J., *jr*	1
Confederate Troops.	
Infantry—[Battalions: 1st, 130]*	2
Infantry—Regiments: 1st, *130**	2

Part.

enant] 2

:. S., [173] 2
.... 1
t, Major] 2
tain] 1
.J 1
:o.onel] 1
.... 1
.... 2
ner] 1
Harris 2

.... 2
Florida, C. S. Steamer,
.... 1
amer 2
', 552 1
'. 1
eneral] 1
arza, General] 2
ner] 2
:hooner [Steamer] 2
:ommodore] 1
[(Captain)], 895 [Gros-
M. (Colonel), 895] 1
ne (C.).
to District, 40 2

:nt of the Gulf, 40 2
nses designated as, 40] 2
, 1864, 40.............. 2
. S S. Marmora [567] 1
.......•................ 1
.... 2
.] 1
—] 2
'William] 2
i] 1

:giments:
.... 1
911; B, 894, 911; F, 911,
)11; I, 531; K, 75, 894;
4] 1
, 336 2
r, 642 [I. M. Brown,
.... 1
l. Cav.), 24............. 1
7. S. C. T.), [24]........ 1

', General, 573]........ 2
uo de [De La Fuente,
.... 2
.S. [Corvette] 1
uys, Drouyn de l'].... 1

h Waldemar [William]
.... 2
District of 2
;h], Joseph M 1
)hn W................. 1
'; Gunboat No. 2, [567] 1
her [Charles] G. 2

Part

Mississippi and E. Louisiana, 3d Dist., Dept.
of (C.).
Organization, strength, etc., of troops, 98 ... 2
Montgomery, William W., 68 [Montgomery,
William M., 68] 2
Mullins [Mullens], M 1
Mutiny.
Camp Hubbard, Thibodeaux, La.; Aug 29-
30, 1863, 262-273 1
Galveston, Tex., Aug. 10-13, 1863, 241-248... 1
Jackson, Fort, La , Dec. 9, 1863, 456-479 . . . 1
Terrell's Texas Cavalry, Sept. 11, 1863, 2 1
Vidal, Adrian J., Oct. 28, 1863, 447-452 1
Mutiny.
Galveston, Tex., Aug 10, 1863, 170, 171...... 2
Terrell's Texas Cavalry, 237, 238, 278, 280. • 2
Vidal, Adrian J., 397...................... 2
N W. Thomas, Steamer, 296, 299, 300 1
Natchez, Miss.
Expeditions, etc.
Red River, La., Oct. 14-20 [16-20], 1863 .. 1
Neal, Arthur [Sailing-master].......... 1
Neal, Arthur [———] 2
Newbury [Newberry], S S 1
New Ironsides, U. S. S., 180 2
New National, Steamer 1
Oldham, Williamson [William] S 2
Peebles [Peeples], Richard Rogers 2
Pierce, Charles J. [———].................. . 2
Planet, Steamboat [Schooner]............... 1
Pocahontas, U. S S , 89; Pocahontas, Steamer,
[89]................................... 1
Pringle, J. S , Steamer...................... 1
Ramsay, Francis [Frank] M. 1
Red River, La.
Expeditions [Expedition], etc., Oct. 14-20
[16-20], 1863............................ 1
Rio Grande Expedition, etc., Oct. 27-Dec. 2,
1863.
Reports of
Taylor, Richard (33d Tex. Cav) 1
Rogers, L. M [Major] 2
Sampson, Henry [———] 1
Schmitt [Schmidt], Louis 1
Shipley, Samuel D , 207, 209; Shipley, Alex-
ander N., Mentioned, [207, 209]........ 1
Smith, Joseph, 612, 827, 901 [Smith, J (Major),
612, 827, 901]......................... 1
Stone, Charles P.
Relieved from command of troops at New
Orleans, 832 1
Taggart, Samuel L 1
Taylor, Richard (Maj. Gen.).
Mentioned, [433, 434, 440-443] 1
Reports of
[Rio Grande Expedition and operations
on the coast of Texas, Oct. 27-Dec. 2,
1863, 443]............................. 1
Taylor, Richard (33d Tex. Cav.).
Mentioned, 433, 434, 440-443 1
Report of Rio Grande Expedition, etc., Oct.
27-Dec. 2, 1863, 443 1
Tennessee Troops (C.).
Artillery, Heavy—Regiments:
1st (Batteries), G (Fisher)............... 1, 2
Artillery, Light—Regiments:
1st (Batteries), B (Rock City) 1, 2

4 ADDITIONS AND CORRECTIONS.

Part

Tensas Bayou, La.
   Skirmish at, Aug. 10, 1863, 2 1
Terrazas, *Luis* [Governor] 1
Texas.
   [Adjutant and Inspector General's Office,
   State of. Correspondence with John
   B. Magruder, 170] 2
Texas Troops (C.).
   Artillery, Heavy—Batteries.
     Howe's, *563, 565* 2
   Artillery, Heavy—Regiments.
     1st, *281* 2
   Cavalry—Regiments
     2d *Partisan* [6th] 1, 2
   Infantry—Regiments.
     11th, *402* 2
Thompson, A. A. [H.] 2
Throckmorton, *James W.* [Major] 2
Tucker, *Philip C.* [Major] 2

Part.

Uraga, *José L.* [General] 1
Van Denbergh [Vandenburgh], Robert S. ... 1
Van *Tuyl* [Puyl], Benjamin T 1
Vidal, Adrian *J.* [I.] 1
Vidaurri [Vidauri], Santiago 1
Virginia, C. S. S. (*U. S. Frigate Merrimac*), *891* 1
Walker, *James* [J. W.] 2
Walthersdorff [Waltersdorff], A 2
War Department, C S.
   Correspondence with
     Allen, H. W., 173 2
     Davis, Jefferson, [173] 2
[Western Louisiana, District of.
   See Louisiana, Western, District of] 2
Weston, *James M.* [Captain] 2
Williams, William H., *895* [Williams, Fred-
   erick A., *895*] 1
Wright, A. U. [W.] 2

CONTENTS.

CHAPTER XXXVIII.

Page.

ions in West Florida, Southern Alabama, Southern Mississippi, Louis-
(excluding those connected with the siege of Vicksburg), Texas, and
Mexico. May 14–December 31, 1863................................... 1–920

CONTENTS OF PRECEDING VOLUMES.

VOLUME I.

CHAPTER I.　　　　　Page.
)perations in Charleston Harbor, South
Carolina. December 20, 1860–April 14,
1861.................................... 1–317

CHAPTER II.
The secession of Georgia. January 3–26,
1861.................................... 318–325

CHAPTER III.
The secession of Alabama and Mississippi.
January 4–20, 1861 326–330

CHAPTER IV.
)perations in Florida. January 6–August
31, 1861................................. 331–473

CHAPTER V.　　　　　Page.
The secession of North Carolina. Janu-
uary 9–May 20, 1861..................... 474–488

CHAPTER VI.
The secession of Louisiana. January 10–
February 19, 1861 489–501

CHAPTER VII.
Operations in Texas and New Mexico.
February 1–June 11, 1861 502–636

CHAPTER VIII.
Operations in Arkansas, the Indian Territory, and Missouri. February 7–May 9,
1861.................................... 637–691

VOLUME II.

CHAPTER IX.　　　　　Page.
)perations in Maryland, Pennsylvania, Virginia, and West Virginia. April 16–July 31, 1861.. 1–1012

VOLUME III.

CHAPTER X.　　　　　Page.
)perations in Missouri, Arkansas, Kansas, and Indian Territory. May 10–November 19, 1861.. 1–749

VOLUME IV.

CHAPTER XI.　　　　　Page.
)perations in Texas, New Mexico, and
Arizona. June 11, 1861–February 1, 1862. 1–174

CHAPTER XII.
)perations in Kentucky and Tennessee.
July 1–November 19, 1861 175–565

CHAPTER XIII.　　　　　Page.
Operations in North Carolina and Southeastern Virginia. August 1, 1861–January 11, 1862.............................. 566–721

VOLUME V.

CHAPTER XIV.　　　　　Page.
)perations in Maryland, Northern Virginia, and West Virginia. August 1, 1861–March 17, 1862. 1–1106

VOLUME VI.

CHAPTER XV.　　　　　Page.
perations on the coasts of South Carolina,
Georgia, and Middle and East Florida.
August 21, 1861–April 11, 1862.......... 1–435

CHAPTER XVI.　　　　　Page.
Operations in West Florida, Southern Alabama, Southern Mississippi, and Louisiana. September 1, 1861–May 12, 1862. 436–894

VOLUME VII.

CHAPTER XVII.　　　　　Page.
perations in Kentucky, Tennessee, N. Alabama, and S. W. Virginia. Nov. 19, 1861–Mar. 4, 1862. 1–946

VOLUME VIII.

CHAPTER XVIII.   **Page.**

Operations in Missouri, Arkansas, Kansas, and Indian Territory. Nov. 10, 1831– April 10, 1862.   1–834

VOLUME IX.

CHAPTER XIX.   Page.

Operations in Southeastern Virginia. January 11–March 17, 1862   1–71

CHAPTER XX.

Operations in North Carolina. January 11–August 20, 1862   72–480

CHAPTER XXI.   **Page.**

Operations in Texas, New Mexico, and Arizona. February 1–September 20, 1862   481–730

VOLUME X—IN TWO PARTS.

CHAPTER XXII.

Operations in Kentucky, Tennessee, North Mississippi, North Alabama, and Southwest Virginia. March 4–June 10, 1862.

Page.

Part I—Reports...   1–927
Part II—Correspondence, etc   1–642

VOLUME XI—IN THREE PARTS.

CHAPTER XXIII.   *

The Peninsular Campaign, Virginia. March 17–September 2, 1862.

Page.

Part I—Reports, March 17–June 24...   1–1077
Part II—Reports, June 25–September 2   1–994
Part III—Correspondence, etc..   1–691

VOLUME XII—IN THREE PARTS.

CHAPTER XXIV.

Operations in Northern Virginia, West Virginia, and Maryland. March 17–September 2, 1862.

Page.

Part I—Reports, March 17–June 25...   1–818
Part II—Reports, June 26–September 2..   1–820
Part III—Correspondence, etc...   1–966

VOLUME XIII.

CHAPTER XXV.

Page.

Operations in Missouri, Arkansas, Kansas, the Indian Territory, and the Department of the Northwest, April 10–November 20, 1862   1–981

VOLUME XIV.

CHAPTER XXVI.

Page.

Operations on the coasts of South Carolina, Georgia, and Middle and East Florida. April 12, 1862–June 11, 1863..   1–1025

VOLUME XV.

CHAPTER XXVII.

Operations in West Florida, Southern Alabama, Southern Mississippi (embracing all operations against Vicksburg, May 18–July 27, 1862), and Louisiana, May 12, 1862–May 14, 1863, and operations in Texas, New Mexico, and Arizona, September 20, 1862–May 14, 1863.................   1–1135

VOLUME XVI—IN TWO PARTS.

CHAPTER XXVIII.

ions in Kentucky, Middle and East Tennessee, North Alabama, and Southwest Virginia.　June 10–October 31, 1862.

Page.
I—Reports 1–1168
II—Correspondence, etc 1–1017

VOLUME XVII—IN TWO PARTS.

CHAPTER XXIX.

Operations in West Tennessee and Northern Mississippi.　June 10, 1862–January 20, 1863.

Page.
I—Reports 1–817
II—Correspondence, etc 1–916

VOLUME XVIII.

CHAPTER XXX.

Page.
tions in North Carolina and Southeastern Virginia.　August 20, 1862–June 3, 1863 1–1104

VOLUME XIX—IN TWO PARTS.

CHAPTER XXXI.

tions in Northern Virginia, West Virginia, Maryland, and Pennsylvania.　September 3–November 14, 1862.

Page.
I—Reports, September 3–20 1–1108
II—Reports, September 20–November 14; Correspondence, etc., September 3–November 14 1–739

VOLUME XX—IN TWO PARTS.

CHAPTER XXXII.

tions in Kentucky, Middle and East Tennessee, North Alabama, and Southwest Virginia.　November 1, 1862–January 20, 1863.

Page.
I—Reports 1–997
II—Correspondence, etc 1–516

VOLUME XXI.

CHAPTER XXXIII.

Page.
tions in Northern Virginia, West Virginia, Maryland, and Pennsylvania.　November 15, –January 25, 1863 1–1152

VOLUME XXII—IN TWO PARTS.

CHAPTER XXXIV.

ations in Missouri, Arkansas, Kansas, the Indian Territory, and the Department of the Northwest.　November 20, 1862–December 31, 1863.

Page.
I—Reports 1–926
II—Correspondence, etc 1–1168

VOLUME XXIII—IN TWO PARTS.

CHAPTER XXXV.

Operations in Kentucky, Middle and East Tennessee, North Alabama, and Southwest Virginia. January 21–August 10, 1863.

		Page.
Part	I—Reports	1–858
Part	II—Correspondence, etc.	1–986

VOLUME XXIV—IN THREE PARTS.

CHAPTER XXXVI.

Operations in Mississippi and West Tennessee, including those in Arkansas and Louisiana connected with the Siege of Vicksburg. January 20–August 10, 1863.

		Page.
Part	I—Reports, January 20–May 15, including the "General Reports" for whole period, January 20–August 10	1–787
Part	II—Reports, May 16–August 10	1–699
Part III—Correspondence, etc.		1–1070

VOLUME XXV.—IN TWO PARTS.

CHAPTER XXXVII.

Operations in Northern Virginia, West Virginia, Maryland, and Pennsylvania. January 26–June 3, 1863.

		Page.
Part	I—Reports	1–1119
Part	II—Correspondence, etc.	1–862

Sunday.	Monday.	Tuesday.	Wednesday.	Thursday.	Friday.	Saturday.		Sunday.	Monday.	Tuesday.	Wednesday.	Thursday.	Fr...	
....	....	....	ᵘ	1	2	3	July...	....	....	....	1	2		
4	5	6	7	8	9	10		5	6	7	8	9	1	
11	12	13	14	15	16	17		12	13	14	15	16	1	
18	19	20	21	22	23	24		19.	20	21	22	23	£	
25	26	27	28	29	30	31		26	27	28	29	30	£	
..	....	....	....	...	...	....	Aug...	....	....	....	....	....	·	
1	2	3	4	5	6	7		2	3	4	5	6		
8	9	10	11	12	13	14		9	10	11	12	13	1	
15	16	17	18	19	20	21		16	17	18	19	20	£	
22	23	24	25	26	27	28		23	24	25	26	27	£	
....	....	....	....	...	...	....		30	31	....	....	....	·	
1	2	3	4	5	6	7	Sept...	....	....	1	2	3		
8	9	10	11	12	13	14		6	7	8	9	10	1	
15	16	17	18	19	20	21		13	14	15	16	17	1	19
22	23	24	25	26	27	28		20	21	22	23	24	25	£6
29	30	31	....	...	..	....		27	28	29	30	....	....	....
..	....	....	1	2	3	4	Oct...	....	....	....	1	2	3	
5	6	7	8	9	10	11		4	5	6	7	8	9	10
12	13	14	15	16	17	18		11	12	13	14	15	16	17
19	20	21	22	23	24	25		18	19	20	21	22	23	24
26	27	28	29	30	....	....		25	26	27	28	29	30	31
..	....	....	....	...	1	2	Nov...	1	2	3	4	5	6	7
3	4	5	6	7	8	9		8	9	10	11	12	13	14
10	11	12	13	14	15	16		15	16	17	18	19	20	21
17	18	19	20	21	22	23		22	23	24	25	26	27	28
24	25	26	27	28	29	30		29	30	....	....	....	....	
31	....	....	....	...	..	....	Dec...	....	....	1	2	3	4	5
..	1	2	3	4	5	6		6	7	8	9	10	11	12
7	8	9	10	11	12	13		13	14	15	16	17	18	19
14	15	16	17	18	19	20		20	21	22	23	24	25	26
21	22	23	24	25	26	27		27	28	29	30	31	....	....
28	29	30	....	...	..	....								

RATIONS IN WEST FLORIDA, SOUTHERN ALA-BAMA, SOUTHERN MISSISSIPPI, LOUISIANA,* TEXAS, AND NEW MEXICO.

May 14–December 31, 1863.

PART I.

PORTS ················· Union and Confederate.
RRESPONDENCE, ETC·· Union.

SUMMARY OF THE PRINCIPAL EVENTS.†

14, 1863.—The army of General Banks *en route* from Alexandria for operations against Port Hudson, La.
Scouts from Merritt's Plantation, on the Clinton road, La.
Skirmish at Boyce's Bridge, Cotile Bayou, La.
16, 1863.—Skirmish at Tickfaw Bridge, La.
17, 1863.—Operations on west side of the Mississippi River, near Port Hudson, La.
18, 1863.—Affair near Cheneyville, La.
18–19, 1863.—Operations about Merritt's Plantation, and on the Bayou Sara
road, La.
20, 1863.—Skirmish near Cheneyville, La.
21–26, 1863.—Operations on the Teche road, between Barre's Landing and
Berwick, La.
21–July 8, 1863.—Siege of Port Hudson, La.
22, 1863.—Steamer Louisiana Belle attacked near Barre's Landing, Bayou
Teche, La.
Skirmish at Bayou Courtableau, La.
25, 1863.—Skirmish at Centreville, La.
27, 1863.—Skirmish near Lake Providence, La. (operations against Vicksburg).
30, 1863.—Affair at Point Isabel, Tex.
1, 1863.—Skirmish at Berwick, La.
3, 1863.—Engagement near Simsport, La. (operations against Vicksburg).
4, 1863.—Affair at Lake Saint Joseph, La. (operations against Vicksburg).
Skirmish at the Atchafalaya, La.
6, 1863.—Skirmish near Richmond, La. (operations against Vicksburg).

'or reports of those events in Louisiana immediately connected with operations
nst Vicksburg, see Series I, Vol. XXIV, Parts I and II.
†f some of the minor conflicts noted in this "Summary," no circumstantial reports
in file.

June   7, 1863.—Attack on Milliken's Bend and Young's Point, La. (operations against Vicksburg).

7–July 13, 1863.—Operations in Louisiana, west of the Mississippi River.

9, 1863.—Action near Lake Providence, La. (operations against Vicksburg).

15, 1863.—Action near Richmond, La. (operations against Vicksburg).

16, 1863.—Skirmish on the Jornada del Muerto, N. Mex.

20, 1863.—Reconnaissance from Young's Point to Richmond, La. (operations against Vicksburg).

24, 1863.—Skirmishes at Mound Plantation and near Lake Providence, La. . (operations against Vicksburg).

29, 1863.—Skirmish at Mound Plantation, La. (operations against Vicksburg).

30, 1863.—Attack on Goodrich's Landing, La. (operations against Vicksburg).

July   4, 1863.—Skirmish with Indians near Fort Craig, N. Mex.

7–Aug. 19, 1863.—Operations against Navajo Indians in New Mexico.

10, 1863.—Skirmish with Indians at Cook's Cañon, N. Mex.

18, 1863.—Skirmish with Indians on the Rio Hondo, N. Mex.
Skirmish at Des Allemands, La.

19, 1863.—Skirmish with Indians on the Rio de las Animas, N. Mex.

22, 1863.—Brashear City, La., reoccupied by Union forces.

24, 1863.—Skirmish with Indians at Cook's Cañon, N. Mex.

29, 1863.—Skirmish with Indians at Conchas Springs, N. Mex.

Aug.   3, 1863.—Skirmish at Jackson, La.

7, 1863.—The Thirteenth Army Corps assigned (from the Department of the Tennessee) to Department of the Gulf.
Maj. Gen. Cadwallader C. Washburn, U. S. Army, temporarily in command of the Thirteenth Army Corps.

10, 1863.—Skirmish at Bayou Tensas, La.

10–13, 1863.—Mutiny at Galveston, Tex.

10–26, 1863.—The Thirteenth Army Corps transferred from Vicksburg and Natchez, Miss., to Carrollton, La.

18, 1863.—Skirmish with Indians at Pueblo Colorado, N. Mex. •

20, 1863.—Maj. Gen. William B. Franklin, U. S. Army, assumes command of the Nineteenth Army Corps.

20–Sept. 2, 1863.—Expedition from Vicksburg, Miss., to Monroe, La., including skirmishes (24th) at Bayou Macon and at Floyd.

20–Dec. 16, 1863.—Operations against Navajo Indians in New Mexico.

29–30, 1863.—Mutiny at Camp Hubbard, Thibodeaux, La.

Sept.   1– 7, 1863.—Expedition from Natchez, Miss., to Harrisonburg, La., including skirmishes (2d) at Trinity and (4th) near Harrisonburg, and capture of Fort Beauregard.

2, 1863.—Affair with Zapata's banditti, near Mier, Mexico.

4–11, 1863.—The Sabine Pass (Texas) Expedition.

7, 1863.—Skirmish at Morgan's Ferry, on the Atchafalaya, La.

8– 9, 1863.—Skirmishes on the Atchafalaya, La.

11, 1863.—Mutiny in Terrell's Texas Cavalry.

12, 1863.—Skirmish at Stirling's Plantation, near Morganza, La.

13–Oct. 2, 1863.—Scouting near Lake Ponchartrain, La.

14, 1863.—Attack on Vidalia, La.

15, 1863.—Maj. Gen. E. O. C. Ord, U. S. Army, resumes command of the Thirteenth Army Corps.

15–Oct. 5, 1863.—Scout from Fort Wingate to Ojo Redondo (Jacob's Well), N. Mex.

19, 1863.—Skirmish on the Greenwell Springs road, near Baton Rouge, La.

20, 1863.—Skirmish at Morgan's Ferry, on the Atchafalaya, La.

23, 1863.—Affair opposite Donaldsonville, La.

24-29, 1863.—Expeditions from Carrollton and Baton Rouge to New River and
     to the Amite River, La.
  25, 1863.—Operations in the vicinity of Baton Rouge, La.
  27-29, 1863.—Expedition from Goodrich's Landing to Bayou Macon, La
  29, 1863:—Action at Stirling's Plantation, on the Fordoche, La.
3-Nov. 30, 1863.—Operations in the Teche Country, La.
   5, 1863.—Skirmish on the Greenwell Springs road, La.
  12, 1863.—Attack on blockade-runner under the walls of Fort Morgan, Ala. *
16-20, 1863.—Expedition from Natchez, Miss., to Red River, La.
  20, 1863.—Maj. Gen. Cadwallader C. Washburn, U. S. Army, assumes com-
     mand of the Thirteenth Army Corps.
  26, 1863.—Maj. Gen. Napoleon J. T. Dana, U. S. Army, assumes command
          of the Thirteenth Army Corps.
  27-Dec. 2, 1863.—The Rio Grande expedition, and operations on the coast
       of Texas.
  —, 1863.—Skirmish with Indians on the Gila, N. Mex.
   8, 1863.—Skirmish at Bayou Tunica, or Tunica Bend, La.
   9, 1863.—Skirmish near Indian Bayou, La.
       Skirmish near Bayou Sara, La.
  16, 1863.—Expedition from Vidalia to Trinity, La.
  17, 1863.—Skirmish at Bay Saint Louis, Miss.
  18-21, 1863.—Operations against United States gunboats and transports near
       Hog Point, Mississippi River.
  22, 1863.—Affair on Lake Borgne, La.
  30, 1863.—Skirmish near Port Hudson, La.
   3, 1863.—Affair at Saint Martinsville, La.
   9, 1863.—Mutiny at Fort Jackson, La.
  10-19, 1863.—Descent upon Confederate Salt-Works in Choctawhatchie Bay.†
  29, 1863.—Skirmish on Matagorda Peninsula, Tex.

GENERAL REPORTS.

.—Maj. Gen. Henry W. Halleck, General-in-Chief, U. S. Army, of operations
   in the Departments of the Gulf and of New Mexico, December 16, 1862-
   November 10, 1863.
.—Maj. Gen. Nathaniel P. Banks, U. S. Army, of operations in the Department
   of the Gulf, December 16, 1862-December 31, 1863.
.—Synopsis of operations in the Department of New Mexico, May 16-December
   28, 1863.

No. 1.

rt of Maj. Gen. Henry W. Halleck, General-in-Chief, U. S. Army,
operations in the Departments of the Gulf and of New Mexico, De-
nber 16, 1862-November 10, 1863.

HEADQUARTERS OF THE ARMY,
Washington, D. C., November 15, 1863.

R : In compliance with your orders, I submit the following summary
ilitary operations since my last annual report:

*   *   *   *   *   *   *

DEPARTMENT OF THE GULF.

ajor-General Banks took command of the Department of the Gulf
he 16th of December. Almost immediately on assuming command,

be United States gunboat Kanawha, Lieut. Commander W. K. Mayo, and the
er Eugenie, Lieut. H. W. Miller, engaged. See Annual Report of the Secretary
e Navy, December 5, 1864.
or report of Acting Ensign Edwin Crissey, U. S. Navy, see Annual Report of the
tary of the Navy, December 5, 1864.

he ordered a detachment of troops to Galveston, Tex., to occupy that place, under the protection of our gunboats. Colonel [Isaac S.] Burrell, with three companies of the Forty-second Massachusetts Volunteers, the advance of the expedition, arrived at that place on the evening of the 24th of December. On consultation with the commander of the blockading force, he landed his men upon the wharf and took possession of the city.

On the 1st of January, before the arrival of the remainder of our forces, the rebels made an attack by land with artillery and infantry, and by water with three powerful rams. Colonel Burrell's command of 260 men were nearly all killed and taken prisoners, the Harriet Lane captured, and the flag-ship Westfield was blown up by her commander to prevent her falling into the hands of the enemy. The rebels also captured the coal transports and a schooner. The commanders of the Harriet Lane and the Westfield and a number of other naval officers and men were killed. The remainder of the expedition did not leave New Orleans till December 31, and arrived off Galveston on the 2d of January, the day after our forces there had been captured and destroyed by the enemy. Fortunately they did not attempt to land, and returned to New Orleans in safety. It is proper to remark that this expedition was not contemplated or provided for in General Banks' instructions.

On the 11th of January, General Weitzel, with a force of infantry and artillery, aided by the gunboats under Lieutenant-Commander Buchanan, crossed Berwick Bay, and attacked the rebel gunboat Cotton in the Bayou Teche. This gunboat, being disabled by the fire of our naval and land forces, was burned by the rebels.

The loss of General Weitzel's command in this expedition was 6 killed and 27 wounded. A number were killed and wounded on our gunboats, and among the former Lieutenant-Commander Buchanan.

On learning the capture of the Queen of the West by the rebels above Port Hudson, and their movements in Red River and the Teche, Admiral Farragut determined to run past the enemy's batteries, while the forces at Baton Rouge made a demonstration on the land side of Port Hudson. The demonstration was made, and, March 14, Admiral Farragut succeeded in passing the batteries with the Hartford and Albatross. The Monongahela and Richmond fell back, and the Mississippi grounded, and was blown up by her commander. Had our land forces invested Port Hudson at this time, it could have been easily reduced, as its garrison was weak. This would have opened communication by the Mississippi River with General Grant at Vicksburg. But the strength of the place was not then known, and General Banks resumed his operations by the Teche and Atchafalaya.

In the latter part of March, Colonel [Thomas S.] Clark was sent with a small force up to Ponchatoula, and destroyed the railroad bridge at that place. He captured a rebel officer and 4 privates, and three schooners loaded with cotton. His loss was 6 wounded. At the same time General [F. S.] Nickerson was sent to the Amite River to destroy the Jackson Railroad. He proceeded as far as Camp Moore, captured 43 prisoners, a considerable amount of cotton, and destroyed valuable rebel manufactories.

In his operations up the Teche and Atchafalaya, General Banks encountered the enemy, under Sibley, Taylor, and Mouton, at several points, and defeated them in every engagement. Butte-à-la-Rose was captured, with a garrison and two heavy guns, by the gunboats under Lieut. Commander Cooke, of the navy. General Banks reached Alexandria on the 8th of May, the enemy retreating toward Shreveport and

,o Texas. In this expedition, General Banks reports the capture of 00 prisoners, 22 pieces of artillery, 2 transports, and a large amount public property. We destroyed 3 gunboats and 8 transports. Our n loss in the different engagements with the enemy was "very ght," numbers not given. General Banks now returned to the Mississippi River, crossed his ny to Bayou Sara, where he formed a junction May 23 with General ɪgur's forces, from Baton Rouge. The latter had an engagement th the enemy on Port Hudson Plains on the 22d, in which he lost 19 led and 80 wounded. Port Hudson was immediately invested. While alting the slow operations of a siege, General Banks made two un-cessful assaults. Finally, on the 8th of July, the place uncondition-y surrendered. We captured 6,233 prisoners, 51 pieces of artillery, teamers, 4,400 pounds of cannon powder, 5,000 small-arms, 150,000 ɪnds of ammunition, &c. Our loss from the 23d to 30th May, includ- the assault of the 27th, as reported, was about 1,000.

eing re-enforced from General Grant's army on the termination of ᴇ Mississippi campaign, General Banks sent an expedition under neral Franklin to occupy the mouth of the Sabine River, in Texas. reached the entrance to the harbor on the 8th of September, and the ɴboats engaged the enemy's batteries; but two of them, the Clifton 1 Sachem, being disabled and forced to surrender, the others re-ated, and the whole expedition returned to Brashear City. The cers and crew of the gunboats, and about 90 sharpshooters who re on board, were captured, and our loss in killed and wounded was out 30. After a long delay at Brashear City, the army moved for-rd by Franklin and Vermillionville, and, at last account, occupied elousas.

     *   *   *   *   *

DEPARTMENT OF NEW MEXICO.

he troops in this department have been principally employed ring the past year on the Indian frontier, and in opening and in arding roads to the newly discovered gold mines ɪn Arizona. The ulous richness of these mines has attracted large numbers of miners d traders from California and Mexico, and this hitherto barren Ter-ory will soon become a wealthy and populous State.

     *   . *   *   *   *

ll of which is respectfully submitted.

                             H. W. HALLECK,
                                 General-in-Chief.

on. E. M. Stanton, *Secretary of War.*

No. 2.

port of Maj. Gen. Nathaniel P. Banks, U. S. Army, of operations in he Department of the Gulf, December 16, 1862–December 31, 1863.**

                        NEW YORK, *April 6, 1865.*

n. E. M. Stanton,
     Secretary of War, Washington, D. C.:

ɪʀ: I have the honor to transmit a report of the military operations my command in the Department of the Gulf in 1862, 1863, and 1864.

See also siege of Port Hudson, p. 43, the Sabine Pass Expedition, p. 286, and the Grande Expedition, &c., p. 396.

It is prepared by direction of the Adjutant-General. Being absent from the records, I have been unable to state as fully and as much in detail as could be desired the history of the different campaigns.

After the campaign of Port Hudson, the troops were engaged immediately and continuously, and the officers were, for that reason, unable to make detailed reports of the operations of their respective commands.

I have been unable, therefore, to name the officers who deserve the consideration and favor of the Government for distinguished services, of whom there are many, and I shall ask leave to submit an additional report upon that subject.

The details of the Port Hudson campaign are drawn from such publications and dispatches of the time as have been within my reach.

Any error that may occur will be corrected at the earliest possible moment.

With much respect, your obedient servant,

N. P. BANKS,
Major-General, Commanding.

NEW YORK,
April 6, 1865.

SIR: The military objects contemplated by the orders which I received upon assuming command of the Department of the Gulf, dated November 8, 1862, were: The freedom of the Mississippi; an expedition to Jackson and Marion after the fall of Vicksburg and Port Hudson; and the occupation of the Red River country as a protection for Louisiana and Arkansas and a basis of future operations against Texas.

I assumed command of the department December 16, 1862. The 18th of December, Brig. Gen. Cuvier Grover, with 10,000 men, was ordered to take possession of Baton Rouge, then held by the enemy. This was the first step toward the reduction of Port Hudson.

The Island of Galveston, Tex., had been captured in October, and was then occupied or held by the navy. Information had been received, previous to my arrival in New Orleans, of a contemplated attack for the recovery of that position by the enemy. Upon consultation with Rear-Admiral D. G. Farragut and Major-General Butler, both of whom recommended the measure, the Forty-second Massachusetts Volunteers, Colonel Burrell commanding, was sent to occupy the island, in support of the navy. Brig. Gen. A. J. Hamilton, who had been commissioned as Military Governor of Texas, and who accompanied my expedition to New Orleans, with a large staff, also pressed my occupation of Texas with the greatest earnestness, and it was in deference, in a great degree, to his most strongly expressed wishes, that the expedition was undertaken, though it was fully justified by the information which had been received of a proposed attack by the enemy, as well as by the advice of the naval and military authorities of the department. Three companies of this regiment, under command of Colonel Burrell, arrived at Galveston Island on December 27, 1862, and, by the advice of the naval officers, landed on the 28th.

On the morning of January 1, 1863, they were attacked by about 5,000 of the enemy, who gained possession of the island by a bridge from the mainland, which had been left unimpaired during the entire occupation of the island by our forces. The naval forces were attacked at the same time by the cotton-clad gunboats of the enemy, which resulted in the capture of our land force, numbering 260 men, including their officers, the steamer Harriet Lane, two coal transports, and a schooner, and the steamer Westfield was blown up by its commanding officer. The losses in killed and wounded were but slight. The balance of the regiment did not arrive at Galveston Island until January 2, the day after the attack. Upon the discovery of the condition of affairs by the capture of one of the rebel pilots, they returned to New Orleans.

This attack upon our forces had been in contemplation for a long time. It succeeded solely because the bridge connecting the island with the mainland had been left in possession of the enemy. Had the troops sent for its occupation arrived a day or two earlier, or in sufficient time to have destroyed the bridge, the attack would have been defeated.

The possession of this island and its military occupation would have been of great importance to the Government in all operations in that part of the country. It would have held a large force of rebel troops in the vicinity of Houston, enabled us to penetrate the territory of Texas at any time, or to concentrate our forces on the Mississippi, and rendered unnecessary the expedition of 1864 for the re-establishment of the flag in Texas.

Colonel Burrell and his men remained in captivity more than a year, and, after much suffering, were exchanged in the spring of 1864.

It is true, as stated by Major-General Halleck in his report of November 15, 1863, as General-in-Chief of the Army, that "this expedition was not contemplated or provided for in General Banks' instructions." But, having undoubted information of an immediate attack by the enemy, and of the purpose entertained by General Butler to re-enforce the navy by a detachment of land troops, as well as the direct approval of this purpose by Admiral Farragut, as commander of the naval forces in the Gulf, it would have been inexcusable, if not criminal, had I declined to maintain the occupation of so important a position, when so slight a force was required, upon the ground that it was not contemplated or provided for in my instructions. I regarded the loss of Galveston in its consequences, though not in the incidents immediately attending its capture, as the most unfortunate affair that occurred in the department during my command. Galveston, as a military position, was second in importance only to New Orleans or Mobile.

The defensive positions of the enemy in the department were Port Hudson, on the Mississippi, which was strongly fortified, and held by a force of not less than 18,000 men; on the Atchafalaya the water communications toward Red River were defended by strong works at Butte à-la-Rose, and on Bayou Teche by strong land fortifications near Pattersonville, called Fort Bisland, extending from Grand Lake on the right to impassable swamps on the left of the Bayou Teche. Butte à-la-Rose was defended by the gunboats of the enemy and a garrison of 300 to 500 men, and Fort Bisland, on the Teche, by a force of 12,000 to 15,000 men, distributed from Berwick Bay to Alexandria and Grand Ecore, on Red River. These positions covered every line of communication to the Red River country and the Upper Mississippi.

The first object was to reduce the works at Port Hudson. This could be done by an attack directly upon the fortifications, or by getting possession of the Red River, for the purpose of cutting off supplies received by the garrison from that country.

My command, upon my arrival at New Orleans, with the troops that accompanied me, was less than 30,000. There were fifty-six regiments, of which twenty-two regiments were enlisted for nine months only, the terms of service of a part expiring in May, a part in July, and all in August. None of the regiments or men had seen service, and few had even handled a musket.

The military positions held by our forces extended from the Floridas to Western Texas, on the Gulf, and upon the Mississippi from its mouth to Port Hudson. Key West, Pensacola, and Ship Island, on the Gulf, . were strongly garrisoned, and threatened constantly with attack by the enemy. Forts Jackson and Saint Philip, and English Bend, on the lower river; New Orleans, Bonnet Carré, Donaldsonville, Plaquemine, and Baton Rouge, on the upper river; and Forts Pike and Macomb, on Lake Pontchartrain, leading to the Gulf, and Berwick Bay, were open to the incursions of the enemy, and, necessarily, strongly held by our forces. None of these could be evacuated, except the town of Pensacola, leaving a garrison in the permanent works at the navy-yard. All these positions were constantly threatened by an active and powerful enemy, who could concentrate at any point he pleased. That at Galveston had been captured by a force of not less than 24 men to 1. It was deemed inexpedient, with but slight knowledge of the condition of affairs, in the absence of any absolute necessity, to greatly weaken or expose any position then in our possession.

After garrisoning these numerous posts, the strongest force I could command for permanent offensive operations against Port Hudson did not exceed 12,000 or 14,000. It was impossible to attack so strong a position, garrisoned by a force so much larger, with any chance of success. Attention was, therefore, turned west of the Mississippi to the Atchafalaya and Teche, with a view of getting command of these waters, by which our gunboats could reach Red River, and communicate with the forces, naval and military, at Vicksburg, and cut off the supplies of the enemy west of the Mississippi. The first effort to accomplish this was made in an unsuccessful endeavor to open the Bayou Plaquemine, which communicated with the Atchafalaya near Butte-à-la-Rose.

The command of Brigadier-General Weitzel, on Berwick Bay, had been increased the first and second weeks in January to 4,500 men, with a view to operations upon the Teche, for the purpose of destroying the works and dispersing the forces of the enemy on that bayou.

On January 11, he made a successful invasion of the Teche country, repulsed the forces of the enemy, and destroyed the gunboat Cotton. This relieved Berwick Bay from the danger of an attack by the enemy's most formidable gunboat, in case our forces, naval and military, moved up the Atchafalaya toward Butte-à-la-Rose. An attempt was then made to get possession of Butte-à-la-Rose, by combining the command of Weitzel, moving up the Atchafalaya, with that of General Emory, moving from the Mississippi by Bayou Plaquemine, their forces joining near Butte-à-la-Rose.

This attempt failed on account of the complete stoppage of Bayou Plaquemine by three years' accumulation of drift-logs and snags, filling the bayou from the bed of the stream, and rendering it impenetrable to our boats, and requiring the labor of months to open it for navigation. The troops were engaged in this work the most of the month of February.

During these operations on Bayou Plaquemine and the Atchafalaya, news was received of the capture by the enemy of the steamers Queen of the West and De Soto, which had run past the batteries at Vicksburg. This event was deemed of sufficient importance by Admiral Farragut to demand the occupation of the Mississippi between Port Hudson and Vicksburg, by running the batteries on the river at Port Hudson, in order to destroy these boats and cut off the enemy's communication by the Red River with Vicksburg and Port Hudson, thus accomplishing, by a swifter course, the object of our campaign west of the river.

The army was called upon to make a demonstration against the fortifications at Port Hudson, while the fleet should run the batteries upon the river. All the disposable force of the department was moved to Baton Rouge for this purpose early in March.

On March 13, the troops moved out to the rear of Port Hudson, about 12,000 strong. The pickets of the enemy were encountered near Baton Rouge, and a considerable force in the vicinity of Port Hudson, which was quickly driven in. The army reached the rear of the works on the night of the 14th, and made a demonstration as for an attack on the works the next morning.

The arrangement between the admiral and myself was that the passage of the batteries by the navy should be attempted in the gray of the morning, the army making a simultaneous attack on the fortifications in the rear; but affairs appearing to be more favorable to the fleet than was anticipated, the object was accomplished in the evening and during the night of the 14th. Naval history scarcely presents a more brilliant act than the passage of these formidable batteries.

The army returned to Baton Rouge the next day, the object of the expedition having been announced in general orders as completely accomplished. Our loss in this affair was very slight, the enemy not resisting us with any determination until we were in the vicinity of their outer works. Col. John S. Clark, of my staff, received a wound while closely reconnoitering the position of the enemy, which disabled him from further participation in the campaign.

Pending these general movements, a force, under command of Col. Thomas S. Clark, of the Sixth Michigan Volunteers, was sent out from New Orleans to destroy the bridge at Ponchatoula, and a small force, under Col. F. S. Nickerson, of the Fourteenth Maine Volunteers, to destroy the enemy's communication by the Jackson Railroad and the bridges on the Amite River. Both these objects were successfully accomplished.

. Endeavors were made at this time to collect at Baton Rouge a sufficient force to justify an attack upon Port Hudson, either by assault or siege; but the utmost force that could be collected for this purpose did not exceed 12,000 or 14,000 men. To withdraw the force of Weitzel from Berwick Bay would open the La Fourche to the enemy, who had 10,000 or 15,000 men upon the Teche, and the withdrawal of the forces from New Orleans would expose that city to the assault of the enemy from every point. The strength of the enemy at Port Hudson was then believed to be from 18,000 to 20,000. It is now known with absolute certainty that the garrison on the night of March 14 was not less than 16,000 effective troops.

The statement of the General-in-Chief of the Army, in his report of November 15, 1863, that, had our forces invested Port Hudson at this time it could have been easily reduced, as its garrison was weak, was without any just foundation. Information received from Brig. Gen. W. N. R. Beall, one of the officers in command of Port Hudson at this time, as well as from other officers, justifies this opinion. It was inadvisable, therefore, to make an attack upon Port Hudson, either by assault or siege, with any expectation of a successful issue. Operations, therefore, on the waters west of the Mississippi were immediately resumed. While at Baton Rouge, an attempt was made to force a passage to the upper river, across a point of land opposite to Port Hudson. This was successfully accomplished after some days, but without establishing communication with the admiral, who had moved to the Red River. In one of these expeditions the chief signal officer and a party of his men were taken prisoners opposite Port Hudson.

Orders were given on March 25 to take up the line of march to Brashear City. The rebel steamers Queen of the West and Webb were reported at Butte-à-la-Rose, on the Atchafalaya, and it was understood that the enemy, supposing my command to be fixed at Port Hudson, threatened to move at once upon the La Fourche and New Orleans. Weitzel reached Brashear City on April 8, and Grover and Emory on the 9th and 10th. They commenced crossing Berwick Bay on the 9th. It was a very slow process, on account of the want of transportation, but Weitzel and Emory succeeded in crossing by dark on the 10th, their transportation and supplies being sent over the same night and the following morning. General Grover arrived on the 10th, in the evening, and his command was immediately put on board the transports of my command, and sent up the Atchafalaya and Grand Lake, to turn the enemy's position, landing his force at Indian Bend, above Fort Bisland. It was estimated that his movement and landing would require about twelve hours, but the difficulties of navigating unknown rivers made his voyage longer than was anticipated. His boats could not come within 1¼ miles of the shore on account of shoal water, and he was obliged to use flatboats to land his men and artillery. After Grover's departure, we advanced directly upon Franklin, a distance of 20 miles, encountering small bodies of the enemy during the march.

On the 13th, we had advanced within 400 yards of his works, on both sides of the Bayou Teche, driving him to his fortifications and destroying the gunboat Diana, which he had captured from us a short time before. This battle lasted the whole day. We captured many prisoners. Our troops were ready for an assault upon the works in the evening, but it not being certain that Grover had reached the position assigned him for the purpose of intercepting the retreat of the enemy, it was deferred until the morning of the 14th.

During the night, the enemy, learning of Grover's successful landing, sent a large part of his force to attack him at Irish Bend. The fight was very severe. The enemy was defeated, but Grover was unable to get into such position as to cut off his retreat.

Early on the following morning, the balance of the enemy's forces evacuated Fort Bisland, which was immediately occupied by our troops, and we pursued the enemy with great vigor, capturing many prisoners. The enemy's forces in this affair were commanded by Generals Taylor, Sibley, and Mouton. They retreated toward Opelousas, making a strong resistance at Vermillion Bayou, from which position they were quickly driven. The gunboats in the meantime had encountered the steamer Queen of the West on Grand Lake, destroying her, and capturing her officers and crew.

We reached Opelousas April 20, the enemy retreating toward Alexandria in disorder, and destroying the bridges in his flight. The same day the gunboats, under command of Lieut. Commander A. P. Cooke, assisted by four companies of infantry, captured the works at Butte-à-la-Rose, which contained two heavy guns and a large quantity of ammunition, and was garrisoned by a force of 60 men, all of whom were captured.

These works constituted the key of the Atchafalaya, and, being in our possession, opened the way to Red River.

On May 2, we established communication with Admiral Farragut, at the mouth of Red River, through the Atchafalaya, by the gunboat Arizona, Captain Upton commanding, accompanied by Capt. R. T. Dunham, of my staff.

On May 5, our headquarters at Opelousas were broken up, and the troops moved for Alexandria, a distance of from 90 to 100 miles, making this march in three days and four hours. Moving rapidly to the rear of Fort De Russy, a strong work on Red River, we compelled the immediate evacuation of that post by the enemy, and enabled the fleet of gunboats, under Admiral Porter, to pass up to Alexandria without firing a gun. The army reached Alexandria May 9, in the evening, the navy having reached there the morning of the same day. The enemy continued his retreat in the direction of Shreveport.

In order to completely disperse the forces of the enemy, a force under Generals Weitzel and Dwight pursued him nearly to Grand Ecore, so thoroughly dispersing him that he was unable to reorganize a respectable force until July, more than five weeks after we had completed the investment of Port Hudson.

During these operations on the Teche we captured over 2,000 prisoners and twenty-two guns; destroyed three gunboats and eight steamers; captured large quantities of small-arms, ammunition, mails, and other public property, and the steamers Ellen and Cornie, which were of great service to us in the campaign.

A letter from General Taylor, commanding at Fort Bisland, was captured with an officer of the Queen of the West, which informed us that the enemy had contemplated an attack upon our forces at Brashear City, April 12, the day before the assault was made by us upon Fort Bisland, and a subsequent dispatch from Governor Moore to General Taylor was intercepted by General Dwight, in which Taylor was directed, in case he was pursued beyond Alexandria, to fall back into Texas with such of his forces as he could keep together. The purpose of the enemy in retreating up the Teche was to draw off toward Texas, on our left flank, for the purpose of cutting off our supplies by the Teche. But the capture of Butte-à-la-Rose enabled us to open a new line of communication through the Atchafalaya and Courtableau direct to Washington and Barre's Landing, within 6 miles of Opelousas; and upon reaching Alexandria we were enabled to establish a third line of communication by the Atchafalaya and Red Rivers. These were interior waters, wholly inaccessible to the enemy, and made perfectly safe lines of communication during our occupation of that country.

While at Brashear City, I had received a dispatch from Admiral Farragut, by Mr. Gabaudan, his secretary, informing me that General Grant would send 20,000 men by May 1 through the Tensas, Black, and Red Rivers, for the purpose of uniting with us in the reduction of Port · Hudson. It was felt that this re-enforcement was necessary, and would secure the speedy reduction of that position.

On reaching Alexandria, I received two dispatches from General Grant, one dated April 23, stating that he could spare us a re-enforcement of 20,000 men, if we could supply them, and the other, dated May 5, proposing to send one army corps to Bayou Sara by May 25, and asking that I should then send all the troops I could spare to Vicksburg after the reduction of Port Hudson.

To both of these plans I consented, and answered that we could supply them from New Orleans, and that this force would insure the capture of Port Hudson; but I was afterward informed by a dispatch, dated Auburn, May 10, which I received May 12, that he had crossed the Mississippi, landing his forces at Grand Gulf, and was then in close pursuit of the enemy, under such circumstances that he could not re-

trace his steps nor send me the forces he had contemplated, and requesting me to join his command at Vicksburg.

This change in his plans was a cause of serious embarrassment. There
were three courses open to my command : First, to pursue the enemy to
Shreveport, which would be without public advantage, as his army had
been captured or completely routed; secondly, to join General Grant at
Vicksburg; and, thirdly, to invest Port Hudson with such forces as I
had at my command.

It was impossible for me to move my forces to General Grant at
Vicksburg for want of sufficient water transportation. I had barely
steamers enough to put my troops across Berwick Bay and the Atchafalaya, and on the morning after the passage of the bay, when
our forces had turned the enemy's position, and the troops under Emory
and Weitzel had advanced directly upon his works, there was not a
single boat of any kind left with which I could communicate with
Brashear City across the bay. It seemed impossible for me at that time
to transport any portion of my troops and artillery to General Grant
without leaving my trains and 6,000 fugitive negroes, who had come
within our lines, to the chances of capture by the enemy. Besides, it
was perfectly clear that, in the event of the movement of my forces to
Vicksburg, unless that post should immediately fall, the rebel garrison
at Port Hudson, then 16,000 to 18,000 strong, would prevent our communication with New Orleans, and, in the event of any disaster by
which we should be detained at Vicksburg, would hold that city at its
mercy. The force west of the Mississippi, which I had dispersed, would
reorganize by re-enforcements from Texas, and move directly upon the
La Fourche and Algiers, opposite New Orleans, both of which were
nearly defenseless. This was so apparent to my mind that I felt that
a compliance with the request of General Grant would result in the loss
of my trains, the recapture of the negroes who were following the army,
and the probable loss of New Orleans. This conclusion was justified by
the subsequent invasion and occupation of the west bank of the river,
and a most desperate attack by the Louisiana and Texas forces, 12,000
strong, on the works at Donaldsonville, June 28. I therefore concluded to move immediately against Port Hudson, and to take my
chances for the reduction of that post.

To avoid mistake, I directed Brig. Gen. William Dwight to report our
condition to General Grant in person and solicit his counsel. General
Dwight returned with the advice that I attack Port Hudson without
delay, and that he would give me 5,000 men, but that I should not wait
for them.

My command moved from Alexandria on May 14 and 15, a portion
going down the river, and the remainder marching by land to Simsport,
crossing the Atchafalaya at that point with great difficulty, by means
of our transports and the steamers we had captured, and from thence
moved down the right bank of the Mississippi to Bayou Sara, crossing
the Mississippi at that point on the night of the 23d, and moving directly
upon the enemy's works at Port Hudson, a distance of 15 miles, on
May 24.

Maj. Gen. C. C. Augur, commanding the forces at Baton Rouge, about
3,500 men, had been directed to effect a junction with our forces in the
rear of Port Hudson. He encountered the enemy at Plains Store,
about 4 miles from Port Hudson, repulsing him with a loss of 150
killed, wounded, and prisoners, and effected a junction with the rest of
our forces on the 25th.

Our right wing, under Generals Weitzel, Grover, and Dwight, who

ꞏsucceeded General Emory, encountered the enemy outside of his works on the afternoon of the 24th, and, after a very sharp fight, drove him ꞏ to his outer line of intrenchments.

On the 25th, the junction of all the forces having been completed, the works of the enemy were invested. Preparations were immediately made for an assault. Rumors had been circulated for several days previous that the enemy had abandoned the position, and it was impossible to obtain definite information of his strength. ꞏ It was generally supposed, however, that the force had been greatly diminished, and that an assault would result in its capture.

A very thorough preparation was made on the 25th and 26th, and on May 27 a desperate attack upon the works was made, Generals Weitzel, Grover, and Dwight commanding our right, General Augur the center, and General T. W. Sherman the left. The plan of attack contemplated simultaneous movements on the right and left of our lines. The attack upon the right commenced with vigor early in the morning. Had the movement upon the left been executed at the same time, it is possible the assault might have been successful. But the garrison was much stronger than had been represented, and the enemy was found able to defend his works at all points.

The conduct of the troops was admirable, and most important advantages were gained, which contributed to the success of all subsequent movements. At one time our advance had reached the interior line of the enemy, but were unable to hold their position. Nothing but the assault would have satisfied the troops of the presence or strength of the enemy and his works.

Our loss in this engagement was 293 killed and 1,549 wounded. We were unable to estimate with accuracy the loss of the enemy, but it was very severe. In one regiment, the Fifteenth Arkansas, out of 292 officers and men, the loss sustained during the siege, according to a history of the defense by a rebel officer, was 132, of whom 76 fell on May 27. The force of the enemy within the fortifications numbered from 7,000 to 8,000, with 2,500 cavalry in our rear at Clinton, and a small force on the west side of the river, commanding a point opposite the enemy's batteries, making altogether between 10,000 and 11,000 men engaged in the defense of the position, inside and outside the works.

The operations in the Teche country, with the losses sustained in battle and sickness occasioned by rapid and exhausting marches, had reduced my effective force to less than 13,000, including Augur's command. Of these, twenty regiments were nine-months' men, whose terms began to expire in May, and all expired in August. This was not an adequate force for the capture of the place. There ought not to have been less than 3 to 1 for this purpose. The force that we had anticipated receiving from General Grant, promised in the several communications to which I have referred, would have enabled us, on the 27th, beyond any question, to have completed the capture of the works and garrison, when we could have immediately moved to Vicksburg to aid him in his attack on that place, without exposing New Orleans or any other post on the Lower Mississippi to capture by the enemy.

On the night of the 27th, the army rested within rifle-shot of the enemy's works, and commenced the construction of works of defense. The enemy's interior line extended from 4 to 5 miles, from river to river. The line occupied by us necessarily covered from 7 to 8 miles. Our greater length of line made the enemy equal, if not superior, in numbers in any attack that could be made by us upon them.

From the night of May 27 until June 14, we occupied this line. Another partially successful assault was then made. An incessant and harassing fire was kept up upon the enemy night and day, leaving him without rest or sleep.

On June 10, a heavy artillery fire was kept up, and at 3 o'clock on the morning of the 11th we endeavored to get within attacking distance of the works, in order to avoid the terrible losses incurred in moving over the ground in front of the works; but the enemy discovered the movement before daybreak. A portion of the troops worked their way through the abatis to the lines, but were repulsed with the loss of several prisoners.

On June 14, a second general assault was made at daylight. A column of a division was posted on the left, under General Dwight, with the intention of getting an entrance to the works by passing a ravine, while the main attack on the right was made by the commands of Grover and Weitzel. Neither column was successful in fully gaining its object, but our lines were advanced from a distance of 300 yards to distances of from 50 to 200 yards from the enemy's line of fortifications, where the troops intrenched themselves and commenced the construction of new batteries. On the left, an eminence was gained which commanded a strong point held by the enemy, called the citadel, and which, later, enabled us to get possession of a point of the same bluff upon which the citadel was constructed, within 10 yards of the enemy's lines. This day's work was of great importance; but it was now felt that our force was unequal to the task of carrying the works by assault, and the slower, but more certain, operations of the siege were commenced.

The fighting had been incessant night and day for a period of twenty-one days and nights, giving the enemy neither rest nor sleep. During these operations the nine-months' men, whose terms had expired or were about to expire, were dissatisfied with their situation, and unwilling to enter upon duty involving danger. Great embarrassment and trouble was caused by the conduct of some of these troops, one regiment, the Fourth Massachusetts, being in open mutiny.

The siege operations were pursued with the greatest vigor. On the right, we had completed our saps up to the very line of the enemy's fortifications. On the left, a mine had been prepared for a charge of 30 barrels of powder, in such position as would have made the destruction of the citadel inevitable.

Communication had been regular with General Grant at Vicksburg during the progress of the siege, and on July 6 we received information of the surrender of that post. Maj. Gen. Frank. Gardner, in command. of the post, asked for an official statement of the report of the capture of Vicksburg, which had been circulated throughout his command, and I sent him a copy of that portion of the official dispatch of General Grant relating to the surrender of Vicksburg, and received on the night of July 6 a request that there might be a cessation of hostilities, with a view to an agreement of terms of a surrender. This was declined. He then made known officially his determination to surrender the post and garrison. A conference was appointed to agree upon the terms, which resulted in the unconditional surrender of the works and garrison, which was formally executed on July 8, and our troops entered and took possession of the works on the morning of the 9th.

General Gardner, in commending the gallantry of his men for their unwearied labors in the defense, which all our troops readily acknowledged, stated emphatically, as if he desired to be understood, that his surrender was not on account of the fall of Vicksburg or the want of ammunition or provisions, but from the exhaustion of his men, who had been without rest for more than six weeks, and who could not resist another attack. Though they might have held out a day or two longer, the attempt would have been at the expense of a useless effusion of blood.

During the investment and siege of Port Hudson, the enemy west of the Mississippi had been concentrating, and on June 18 one regiment of infantry and two of cavalry, under command of Colonel [J. P.] Major, captured and burned two of our small steamers at Plaquemine, taking 68 prisoners, mostly convalescents of the Twenty-eighth Maine Volunteers. The same force then passed down the river and Bayou La Fourche, avoiding Donaldsonville, and attacked our forces on the 20th at La Fourche Crossing, on the Opelousas Railway, cutting off communication between Brashear City and New Orleans. They were, however, finally repulsed, but renewed their attack on the 21st, which resulted in their again being repulsed, leaving 53 of their dead upon the field and 16 prisoners in our hands. Our loss was 8 killed and 16 wounded.* Reenforcements were sent from New Orleans, but the enemy did not renew the attack. Our forces were under command of Lieut. Col. Albert Stickney, Forty-seventh Massachusetts Volunteers. Subsequently they fell back to Algiers.

Orders had been sent to Brashear City to remove all stores, and hold the position, with the aid of the gunboats, to the last; but the enemy succeeded in crossing Grand Lake by means of rafts, and surprised and captured the garrison June 22 [23], consisting of about 300 men, two 30-pounder Parrott guns, and six 24-pounders. The enemy, greatly increased in numbers, then attacked the works at Donaldsonville, on the Mississippi, which were defended by a garrison of 225 men, including convalescents, commanded by Maj. J. D. Bullen, Twenty-eighth Maine Volunteers. The attack was made at 4.30 in the morning of June 28, and lasted until daylight. The garrison made a splendid defense, killing and wounding more than their own number, and capturing as many officers and nearly as many men as their garrison numbered. The enemy's troops were under command of General [Thomas] Green, of Texas, and consisted of the Louisiana troops, under General Taylor, and 5,000 Texas cavalry, making a force of 9,000 to 12,000 in all, in that vicinity. The troops engaged in these operations left but 400 men in New Orleans. The vigor and strength of the enemy in these several attacks show that, with the aid of the garrison at Port Hudson, New Orleans could not have been defended had my command been involved in the operations against Vicksburg.

Upon the surrender of Port Hudson, it was found that the enemy had established batteries below on the river, cutting off our communication with New Orleans, making it necessary to send a large force to dislodge them. The troops, exhausted by the labors of the long campaign, including nine-months' men and the regiment of colored troops, which had been organized during the campaign from the negroes of the country, did not number 10,000 effective men. It was impossible to drive the enemy from the river below, and leave troops enough at Port Hudson to maintain the position and guard between 6,000 and 7,000 prisoners. For these reasons, the privates were paroled and the officers sent to New Orleans.

On July 9, seven transports, containing all my available force, were sent below against the enemy in the vicinity of Donaldsonville. The

---

* But see report of Lieutenant-Colonel Stickney, p. 192.

country was speedily freed from his presence, and Brashear City was recaptured July 22.

During the siege, the colored troops held the extreme right of our line on the river, and shared in all the dangers of May 27 and of June 14, sustaining, besides, several desperate sorties of the enemy, particularly directed against them, with bravery and success. The new regiments of General Ullmann's brigade, which had been raised during the campaign, also shared the labors of the siege and the honors of the final victory.

Col. B. H. Grierson, commanding the Sixth and Seventh Regiments of Illinois Cavalry, arrived at Baton Rouge in April, from La Grange, Tenn., and joined us with his force at Port Hudson, covering our rear during the siege and rendering most important services. His officers and men were constantly on duty, regardless of toil and danger. They covered our foraging parties, dispersed the cavalry forces of the enemy, which they concentrated, and contributed in a great degree to the reduction of the post. Our deficiency in cavalry made his assistance of the utmost importance. With the exception of this command, much reduced by long journeys, our mounted force consisted chiefly of infantry mounted on the horses of the country, collected during the campaign.

The co-operation of the fleet, under Rear-Admiral Farragut, on the waters west of the Mississippi, as well as at Port Hudson, was harmonious and effective, and contributed greatly to the success of our arms. A battery of heavy guns was established in the rear of the works by one of the officers of the navy, the fire of which was most constant and effective.

The signal corps, under command of Captain [W. W.] Rowley, and subsequently under Captain [W. B.] Roe, and the telegraphic corps, under Captain Bulkley, rendered every assistance possible to these branches of the service. By means of signals and telegraphs, a perfect communication was maintained at all times, night and day, between the fleet and the army and with the different portions of the army.

The rebels admitted, after the close of the siege, that they had lost in killed and wounded during the siege 610 men; but they underrated the number of prisoners and guns they surrendered, and their loss in killed and wounded was larger than was admitted by them. It could not have been less than 800 or 1,000 men. Five hundred were found in the hospitals. The wounds were mostly in the head, from the fire of sharpshooters, and very severe.

A small portion of the troops composing the garrison at Port Hudson were ordered to Vicksburg, to strengthen the command of General Pemberton, subsequent to the attack in March. This gave rise to the report that the place had been evacuated, and it was only after the unsuccessful assaults of May 27 and June 14 that the strength of the fortifications and garrison was appreciated, and all parties were satisfied that our force was insufficient to effect the capture by assault. The uncertainty as to the movements of Johnston's command, which was known to be in the rear of Vicksburg, and the constant expectation that some part of his force would attack us in the rear, made it necessary that every consideration should be disregarded which involved the loss of time in our operations, and the general systematic attacks upon the works of the enemy were executed at the earliest possible moment after the necessary preparations had been made.

The siege lasted forty-five days, of which twenty-one days was incessant and constant fighting. It was conducted constantly with a view to the capture of the garrison as well as the reduction of the post.

When the proposition of General Gardner to suspend hostilities with a view to consider terms of surrender was received, there were 6,408 officers and men on duty within the lines; 2,500 in the rear of the besieging forces and on the west bank of the river, opposite Port Hudson, and 12,000 men, under Generals Green and Taylor, between Port Hudson and Donaldsonville, who had, by establishing their batteries on the west bank of the river, effectually cut off our communication with New Orleans, making 21,000 men actively engaged in raising the siege at the time of its surrender.

The besieging force was reduced to less than 10,000 men, of which more than half were enlisted for nine months' service, and a few regiments of colored troops organized since the campaign opened from the material gathered from the country. The position assailed was, from the natural defenses of the country, as well as from the character of the works constructed, believed by the enemy to be impregnable. The besieging army, to reach the position, had marched more than 500 miles, through a country where no single line of supplies could be maintained, against a force fully equal in numbers, fighting only in intrenchments, and gathering material for re-enforcing its regiments in the country through which it passed. There are but few sieges in the history of war in which the disparity of forces has been more marked, the difficulties to be encountered more numerous, the victory more decided, or the results more important.

Every officer and man who discharged his duty in that campaign, whether living or dead, will leave an honored name to his descendants, and receive hereafter, if not now, the grateful and well-merited applause of his country. The results of the surrender of Vicksburg and Port Hudson were the permanent separation of the rebel States east and west, and the free navigation of the Mississippi, thus opening communication between the Northern and Southern States occupied by our forces, and an outlet for the products of the Upper Mississippi Valley to the markets of the world.

The two armies that had fought each other with such resolute determination fraternized on the day of the surrender without manifestations of hostility or hatred. A common valor had given birth to a feeling of mutual respect.

Brig. Gen. T. W. Sherman was seriously wounded in the assault of May 27, and Brigadier-General Paine on June 14. Among those killed during the siege were Colonel Bean, of the Fourth Wisconsin; Colonel Holcomb, of the First Louisiana; Col. D. S. Cowles, of the One hundred and twenty-eighth New York; Lieutenant-Colonel Rodman, of the Thirty-eighth Massachusetts; Lieutenant-Colonel Lull, of the Eighth New Hampshire; Colonel Smith, of the One hundred and sixty-fifth New York Zouaves; Colonel Chapin, of the One hundred and sixteenth New York; Major Haffkille and Captain Luce, of the Engineers; Lieutenant Wrotnowski, and many other gallant officers whose names, in the absence of official records, it is not in my power to give, who gave their lives to the cause of liberty and their country.

In this campaign we captured 10,584 prisoners, as follows: Paroled men at Port Hudson, exclusive of the sick and wounded, 5,953—officers, 455; captured by Grierson at Jackson, 150; First [Arkansas Battalion] and Fifteenth Arkansas captured May 27, 101; on board steamers in Thompson's Creek, 25; deserters, 250; sick and wounded, 1,000; captured at Donaldsonville, June 28, 150; captured west of the Mississippi, 2,500; in all, a number fully equal to the force to which the garrison surrendered. We also captured 73 guns, 4,500 pounds of powder, 150,000 rounds of ammunition, 6,000 small-arms, 4 steamers, 20,000 head of horses, cattle, and mules, 10,000 bales of cotton, and destroyed the enemy's salt-works at New Iberia, 3 gunboats, and 8 steam transports. The cattle, horses, mules, cotton, and other products of the country were sent to New Orleans, turned over to the quartermaster, and, except such as could be used by the army in kind, were applied to the support of the Government.

August 5, a dispatch was received and published, from the General-in-Chief of the Army, congratulating the troops on the crowning success of the campaign, for whom was reserved the honor of striking the last blow for the freedom of the Mississippi River, and announcing that the country, and especially the great West, would ever remember with gratitude their services.*

[THE TEXAS EXPEDITION.†]

After the surrender of Port Hudson, I joined with General Grant in recommending an immediate movement against the city of Mobile. My views upon the question were expressed in several dispatches in July and August. With such aid as General Grant had offered and subsequently gave me, a speedy capture of that city seemed to be reasonably certain.

On the 15th of August, 1863, I was informed by a dispatch, dated the 6th of that month, that there were important reasons why our flag should be established in Texas with the least possible delay, and instructing me that the movement should be made as speedily as possible, either by sea or land. I was informed by a dispatch dated the 12th of August, and which I received on the 27th of August, that the importance of the operations proposed by me in a previous dispatch against the city of Mobile was fully appreciated, but there were reasons other than military why those directed in Texas should be undertaken first; that on this matter there was no choice, and that the views of the Government must be carried out. I was advised in a dispatch, dated the 10th of August, that the restoration of the flag to some one point in Texas could be best effected by the combined naval and military movements upon Red River to Alexandria, Natchitoches, or Shreveport, and the occupation of Northern Texas. This line was recommended as superior for military operations to the occupation of Galveston or Indianola, but the final selection was left to my judgment.

The difficulties attending a movement in the direction of Shreveport—a route which had been thoroughly explored in the spring campaign of 1863—satisfied me that it was impracticable, if not impossible, for the purposes entertained by the Government. The selection of the line of operations having been submitted to me, I made immediate preparations for a movement by the coast against Houston, selecting the position occupied by the enemy on the Sabine as the point of attack. This point was nearest to my base of supplies. It was immediately connected by the Gulf with Berwick Bay, of which we had full possession, and by the river, and also by railway from the bay, with New Orleans.

If suddenly occupied, I regarded it certain, as the enemy's forces were then disposed, that we could concentrate and move upon Houston by land with 15,000 to 17,000 men before it would be possible for the enemy to collect his forces for its defense. The occupation of Houston would

---

* See General Orders, No. 57, Headquarters Department of the Gulf, August 5, 1863, p. 671.
† See letter of transmittal, p. 5.

place in our hands the control of all the railway communications of Texas; give us command of the most populous and productive part of the State; enable us to move at any moment into the interior in any direction, or to fall back upon the Island of Galveston, which could be maintained with a very small force, holding the enemy upon the coast of Texas, and leaving the Army of the Gulf free to move upon Mobile, in accordance with my original plan or whenever it should be required. The expedition sailed from New Orleans on the 5th day of September. Its organization and command had been intrusted to Maj. Gen. W. B. Franklin. The gunboats assigned to the expedition by Admiral Farragut were under command of Captain Crocker, a skillful and brave officer. He was thoroughly acquainted with the waters of the Sabine Pass, having been stationed there for many months, and was anxious to participate in the expedition. The forces were organized for operations upon land. The gunboats were intended to assist and cover their debarkation and movements upon the coast. At various points, between the Sabine and Galveston, a landing was practicable and safe. Unless the weather or the forces of the enemy should intervene, nothing could prevent a successful debarkation of troops at some point upon the coast.

General Franklin's instructions were verbal and written. He was directed to land his troops 10 or 12 miles below Sabine Pass, or at some other point on the coast below, and proceed by a rapid movement against the fortifications constructed for the defense of the Pass, unless the naval officers should find, upon reconnaissance, that the works were unoccupied, or that they were able to take them without delay. Nothing was wanting to secure the success of the expedition. The troops were in good condition, the weather fine, the sea smooth, and the enemy without suspicion of the movement. Instead, however, of moving below the Pass and effecting a landing of the troops, General Franklin states in his report that it was determined that Captain Crocker should enter the Pass and make an attack directly upon the works. The gunboats (originally lightly constructed merchant vessels) were unable to make any impression upon the works. They soon run aground in the shallow water and narrow channel of the Pass, under the guns of the fort, and were compelled to surrender. The enemy's position was occupied and defended by less than 100 men. The troops under General Franklin made an unsuccessful, and, as it appeared afterward, a feeble effort to land within the bay, after the loss of two gunboats, and returned to New Orleans without attempting a landing below upon the coast in rear of the works. Had a landing been effected, even after the loss of the boats, in accordance with the original plan, the success of the movement would have been complete, but as it regarded the occupation of Sabine Pass and operations against Houston and Galveston, the enemy had at this time all his forces in that quarter, and less than 100 men on the Sabine.

The failure of this expedition having notified the enemy of our purposes, it was impracticable to repeat the attempt at that point. The instructions of the Government being imperative, I then endeavored, without delay, to carry out my instructions by a movement toward Alexandria and Shreveport, or, if possible, across the southern part of Louisiana to Niblett's Bluff. The attack upon Sabine Pass was made on the 8th of September. The fleet returned on the 11th; on the 13th, orders were given for the overland movement. The troops were rapidly transferred to the Teche Bayou, and organized for this expedition, but it was soon found impracticable, if not impossible, to enter Texas in that direction. The country between the Teche and the Sabine was without supplies of any kind, and entirely without water, and the march across that country of 300 miles with wagon transportation alone, where we were certain to meet the enemy in full force, was necessarily abandoned. A movement in the direction of Alexandria and Shreveport was equally impracticable. The route lay over a country utterly destitute of supplies, which had been repeatedly overrun by the two armies, and which involved a march of 500 miles from New Orleans and nearly 400 miles from Berwick Bay, with wagon transportation only, in a country without water, forage, or supplies, mostly upon a single road, very thickly wooded, and occupied by a thoroughly hostile population.

Being satisfied that it was impossible to execute the orders of the Government by this route for these reasons, which were stated in my several dispatches, I decided, as the only alternative left me for the execution of the orders of the Government, to attempt the occupation of the Rio Grande, which I had suggested on the 13th September as an alternative if the land route was found impracticable. Leaving the troops opposite Berwick Bay upon the land route into Texas, I organized a small expedition, the troops being placed under command of Maj. Gen. N. J. T. Dana, and sailed on the 26th of October, 1863, for the Rio Grande. A landing was effected at Brazos Santiago, which was occupied by the enemy's cavalry and artillery, the 2d day of November. The enemy was driven from his position the next day, and the troops ordered forward to Brownsville, 30 miles from the mouth of the river. Colonel Dye, of the Ninety-fourth Illinois Volunteers, commanding the advance, occupied Brownsville on the 6th day of November, where, a few hours after his arrival, I made my headquarters. Major-General Dana was left in command of this post. As soon as it was possible to provide for the garrison and obtain transportation for the navigation of the river, which occupied four or five days, I moved, with all the troops which could be spared from that point, for the purpose of occupying the passes on the coast between the Rio Grande and Galveston, intending to complete my original plan by the occupation of Galveston from the coast below instead of above. Point Isabel was occupied on the 8th [6th] of November. By the aid of steamers, obtained on the Rio Grande with the consent of the Mexican Government, we were enabled to transport troops to Mustang Island. The troops were under the command of Brig. Gen. T. E. G. Ransom, who carried the enemy's works commanding Aransas Pass, after a gallant assault, capturing 100 prisoners and the artillery with which the place was defended. The troops instantly moved upon Pass Cavallo, commanding the entrance to Matagorda Bay, and which was also defended by strong and extensive fortifications and a force of 2,000 men, artillery, cavalry, and infantry, who could be re-enforced in any emergency from Houston and Galveston. The troops were under command of Maj. Gen. C. C. Washburn, then commanding the Thirteenth Corps.

Fort Esperanza was invested, and, after a most gallant action, the enemy blew up his magazine, partially dismantled his defenses, and evacuated the position, the major part of his men escaping to the mainland by the peninsula near the mouth of the Brazos.

The occupation of Brownsville, Brazos Santiago, the capture of the works and garrison at Aransas Pass, and the defeat of the enemy and the capture of his works at Fort Esperanza by our troops, left nothing on the coast in his possession but the works at the mouth of Brazos River and on the Island of Galveston, which were formidable, and defended by all the forces of the enemy in Texas. The command of General Magruder had been withdrawn from different parts of the State and concentrated on the coast between Houston, Galveston, and Indianola, in consequence of our movement against the works at Sabine Pass, the occupation of the Rio Grande, and the capture of the works constructed for the defense of Aransas Pass and Pass Cavallo, on the Texas coast. To carry the works at the mouth of Brazos River, it was necessary to move inland and to attack the enemy in the rear, in which we necessarily encountered the entire strength of the rebel forces, then greatly superior in number to ours.

Preparations were made for more extended operations on the mainland from Indianola at Matagorda Bay or on the peninsula connecting with the mainland at Brazos River, and notice given to the War Department of the plan of operations, with the request for an increase of the forces for extended operations in Texas, if it was found expedient. The troops on the Teche, under command of Major-General Franklin, would have been transferred to the coast in such force as to make certain the occupation of Houston or Galveston. From this point I intended to withdraw my troops to the Island of Galveston, which could have been held with perfect security by less than 1,000 men, which would have left me free to resume my operations, suggested in August and September, against Mobile. The Rio Grande and the Island of Galveston could have been held with 2,000 or 3,000 men. This would have cut off the contraband trade of the enemy at Matamoras and on the Texas coast. The forces occupying the Island of Galveston could have been strengthened by sea at any moment from Berwick Bay, connecting with New Orleans by railway, or with New Orleans by the river, compelling the enemy to maintain an army near Houston, and preventing his concentrating his forces for the invasion of Louisiana, Arkansas, or Missouri.

The occupation of the Rio Grande, Galveston, and Mobile would have led to the capture or destruction of all the enemy's river and sea transportation on the Gulf coast, and left the west gulf blockading squadron, numbering one hundred and fifty vessels and mounting four hundred and fifty guns, free to pursue the pirates that infested our coast and preyed upon our commerce.

The army would have been at liberty to operate on the Mississippi or to co-operate with the Army of the Tennessee, by the Alabama River and Montgomery, in the campaign against Atlanta.

These general views are substantially expressed in my dispatches of the 12th and 30th December, 1863.

If successfully accomplished, it would have enabled the Government to concentrate the entire forces of the Department of the Gulf, as occasion should require, at any point on the river or coast against an enemy without water transportation or other means of operation than by heavy land marches, or to move by land into the rebel States east or west of the Mississippi. The winter months offered a favorable opportunity for such enterprise.

I remain, your obedient servant,

N. P. BANKS,
Major-General of Volunteers.

The SECRETARY OF WAR, *Washington, D. C.*

ADDENDA.

GENERAL ORDERS, }   HDQRS. DEPARTMENT OF THE GULF,
No. 25.   }   *New Orleans, February 19, 1864.*

I. The following-named regiments and batteries of the Nineteenth Army Corps will immediately have inscribed upon their colors the

names of the several actions set opposite their names, wherein they
have borne a distinguished part, as follows :

12th Maine Volunteers, Irish Bend, Port Hudson.
14th Maine Volunteers, Baton Rouge, Port Hudson.
8th Vermont Volunteers, Cotton, Bisland, Port Hudson.
26th Massachusetts Volunteers, La Fourche.
30th Massachusetts Volunteers, Baton Rouge, Plains Store, Port Hudson, Cox's
    Plantation.
31st Massachusetts Volunteers, Bisland, Port Hudson.
38th Massachusetts Volunteers, Bisland, Port Hudson.
12th Connecticut Volunteers, Georgia Landing, Cotton, Bisland, Port Hudson.
13th Connecticut Volunteers, Georgia Landing, Irish Bend, Port Hudson.
75th New York Volunteers, Cotton, Bisland, Port Hudson.
90th New York Volunteers, Port Hudson.
91st New York Volunteers, Port Hudson.
110th New York Volunteers, Bisland.
114th New York Volunteers, Bisland, Port Hudson.
116th New York Volunteers, Plains Store, Port Hudson, Cox's Plantation.
128th New York Volunteers, Port Hudson.
131st New York Volunteers, Port Hudson.
133d New York Volunteers, Bisland, Port Hudson.
156th New York Volunteers, Bisland, Port Hudson.
159th New York Volunteers, Irish Bend, Port Hudson.
160th New York Volunteers, Cotton, Bisland, Port Hudson.
161st New York Volunteers, Plains Store, Port Hudson, Cox's Plantation.
162d New York Volunteers, Bisland, Port Hudson.
165th New York Volunteers, Port Hudson.
173d New York Volunteers, Port Hudson.
174th New York Volunteers, Plains Store, Port Hudson, Cox's Plantation.
175th New York Volunteers, Bisland, Port Hudson.
176th New York Volunteers, La Fourche.
1st Louisiana Volunteers, Port Hudson.
2d Louisiana Volunteers, Plains Store, Port Hudson, Cox's Plantation.
1st New Hampshire Cavalry,* Georgia Landing, Bisland, Port Hudson.
3d Massachusetts Cavalry, Company L, Georgia Landing, Port Hudson.
4th Wisconsin Cavalry, Bisland, Clinton, Port Hudson.
1st Louisiana Cavalry, Companies A, B, C, Georgia Landing, Cotton, Port Hudson.
6th Michigan Artillery, Baton Rouge, Cotton, Port Hudson.
1st Indiana Heavy Artillery, Baton Rouge, Cotton, Bisland, Port Hudson.
Battery A, 1st U. S. Artillery, Cotton, Bisland, Port Hudson.
Battery F, 1st U. S. Artillery, Bisland, Port Hudson.
Battery L, 1st U. S. Artillery, Port Hudson.
Battery C, 2d U. S. Artillery, Irish Bend, Port Hudson.
Battery G, 5th U. S. Artillery, Port Hudson.
1st Maine Battery, Georgia Landing, Cotton, Bisland, Port Hudson, Cox's Planta-
    tion.
1st Vermont Battery, Port Hudson.
2d Vermont Battery, Plains Store, Port Hudson.
2d Massachusetts Battery, Baton Rouge, Port Hudson.
4th Massachusetts Battery, Baton Rouge, Cotton, Port Hudson.
6th Massachusetts Battery, Baton Rouge, Georgia Landing, Cotton, Bisland, Port
    Hudson.
13th Massachusetts Battery, Port Hudson.
18th New York Battery, Bisland, Port Hudson.
21st New York Battery, Port Hudson.
25th New York Battery. La Fourche.

II. The following are the dates at which the above named actions
took place:
Baton Rouge, August 5, 1862.
Georgia Landing, October 27, 1862.
Cotton, January 14, 1863.
Bisland, April 12 and 13, 1863.
Irish Bend, April 14, 1863.
Plains Store, May 21, 1863.

_____

* The Eighth New Hampshire.

Clinton, June 3, 1863.
La Fourche, June 21, 1863.
Port Hudson: Invested, May 24, 1863; assaulted, May 27 and June 14, 1863; surrendered, July 7, 1863.
Cox's Plantation, July 13, 1863.
By command of Major-General Banks:

RICHARD B. IRWIN,
Assistant Adjutant-General.

No. 3.

Synopsis of operations in the Department of New Mexico, May 16–December 28, 1863.

GENERAL ORDERS, } HDQRS. DEPARTMENT OF NEW MEXICO,
   No. 3.   }   *Santa Fé, N. Mex., February* 24, 1864.

The following notices of combats with hostile Indians in New Mexico, and synopsis of Indian depredations, as well as operations generally against them, during the year 1863, are published for the information of all concerned.

Perhaps not over one scout in four which was made against the Indians during that period was at all successful, but no notice is made except of scouts which had results for or against us. This fact is stated to convey a better idea of the labor of the troops:*

*   *   *   *   *   *   *

May 16.—On the night of the 15th the Navajoes stole from Jemez 6 head of horses.

May —.—Charles T. Hayden, citizen, reports that the Indians attacked his train near the line of Chihuahua. They were defeated, with a loss of 11 killed, including the renowned Copinggan; 3 horses were captured in this fight.

May —.—Capt. T. T. Tidball, Fifth Infantry, California Volunteers, with 25 of his company and a small party of citizens, attacked a rancheria in Cajon de Arivaypa, killing over 50 Indians, wounding as many more, taking 10 prisoners, and capturing 60 head of stock, with the loss of only 1 man, Thomas McClelland. The party marched five days without lighting a fire, maintaining silence, hiding by day and traveling by night, over a country hitherto untrod by white men.

June —.—Maj. Joseph Smith, commanding Fort Stanton, reports that the Indians attacked the expressmen on the 21st of June, near the Gallinas, and compelled them to abandon their mules and express matter, and take to the mountains. The mules and express lost.

June 24.—Major Morrison reports an attack on Lieutenant Bargie and escort, on the Jornada, in which Lieutenant Bargie, while fighting gallantly, was killed. The conduct of Sergeants Piña and Urlibarra, and the two prisoners they had in charge, is highly praised.

June 26.—Major Morrison reports further in regard to the fight on the Jornada that Private Lucero, First New Mexico Volunteers, was killed.

June 20.—Capt. A. H. Pfeiffer, wife, and 2 servant girls, with escort of 6 men of the First New Mexico Volunteers, were attacked by a

* For portion of order here omitted, see Series I, Vol. XV, pp. 227–231.

party of Apache Indians, numbering 15 or 20, at a hot spring near Fort McRae. The captain was bathing at the time, when the Indians made a rush upon the party, killing two men, Privates N. Quintana and Mestas. Captain Pfeiffer was wounded in his side by an arrow, and Private Dolores received two shots in his right arm and hand. A citizen named Betts, who was with Captain Pfeiffer, was also wounded. The remainder of party, except the women, succeeded in reaching Fort McRae unharmed, and reported facts to Major Morrison, commanding post. He immediately started in pursuit with 20 mounted men, but did not succeed in overtaking the Indians. Mrs. Pfeiffer and the' servant girls were found in the trail, badly wounded. Mrs. Pfeiffer and one of the servants have since died; the other doing well. Loss in this affair, 2 privates killed, 2 women mortally wounded, 1 officer, 1 private, 1 woman, and a citizen wounded; 7 horses and 2 mules taken by the Indians. Indian loss unknown.

June 27.—Maj. Joseph Smith, commanding Fort Stanton, reports the loss of part of his herd of horses and mules, stolen by Indians. An infantry company sent in pursuit.

June 28.—Lieut. W. H. Higdon, Fifth Infantry, California Volunteers, reports that on his way from Fort Stanton to Santa Fé, near Gallinas Springs, he found the bodies of Privates N. Quintana, of Company A, First New Mexico Volunteers, and John Hinkley, of Company A, Fifth California Volunteers, who had been murdered by the Indians. The Indians had evidently wounded Private Quintana, tied him to a stake, and burned him. Some legal-tender notes and several letters were found near the body of Hinckley.

July 2.—Lieutenant-Colonel Chaves reports that Capt. Rafael Chacon, First New Mexico Volunteers, with 22 men, was sent in pursuit of a band of Indians who had stolen some horses and oxen from Fort Wingate. The oxen were recaptured near the post. The troops followed the trail of the Indians for three days, and finally overtook them, when a sharp fight ensued. The Indians fought with great bravery, but were finally driven from their cover, and fled. The conduct of Sergeant Antonio José Trezquez in this affair is highly spoken of by Captain Chacon. Indian loss unknown; troops, 1 private wounded.

July 4.—Capt. N. J. Pishon reports that, with 27 men of his company, D, First Cavalry, California Volunteers, he pursued a party of 8 Indians who had driven off 104 Government mules from Fort Craig, overtook them a few miles from the post, and killed 4 Indians and recovered all the mules. Capt. Julius L. Barbey, who accompanied the command, was shot through the wrist by an arrow. Privates Jackson and Bancroft were also slightly wounded.

July 12.—Capt. A. H. French, First Cavalry, California Volunteers, with 27 men of his company, attacked and routed, near Fort Thorne, a band of Apache Indians, supposed to number 60 warriors. Indian loss, 10 killed and 4 horses captured. Sergeant Walsh and Farrier Burns were wounded.

July 11.—Sergeant E. W. Hoyt, of Company D, First Infantry, California Volunteers, with 3 men of Company B and 3 men of Company D, First Infantry, California Volunteers, having in charge 4 wagons *en route* to Las Cruces, was attacked by Indians in Cook's Pass, and forced to abandon 3 wagons and 19 mules, and had 4 men slightly wounded. Four Indians are known to have been killed and a number wounded. Sergeant Hoyt acted with the greatest coolness in this affair.

July 19.—Lieut. Juan Marques, First New Mexico Volunteers, while returning from Horse Head crossing of the Pecos with 15 men of Company A, First New Mexico Volunteers, was attacked at the Rio Hondo by about 50 Indians while in camp at that point. The Indians gained possession of the camp, but were finally driven across the river, carrying with them their wounded. They soon after recrossed the river, and charged on the herd, but were again driven back with loss. In this charge Private José Chaves was killed. For several hours the fight was continued. The Indian force rapidly increased, and at last numbered some 200. The ammunition gave out, and the soldiers were ordered to break their rifles and make their escape, which they did. Lieutenant Marques reports the conduct of the following-named men as worthy of mention : Corporals [Blass] Brigaloa, and José Y. Gonzales, and Privates Santiago Torres, G. Romero, Antonio Archuleta, José D. Tresquez, and Jesus Lopez. All the public animals, including 10 mules, were lost in this affair. Indian loss, 6 killed.

July 22.—Capt. F. P. Abreü, First New Mexico Volunteers, and Capt. Emil Fritz, First Cavalry, California Volunteers, with a detachment of New Mexico and California volunteers, left Fort Stanton for the Rio Pecos, to overtake and chastise the Indians who had attacked Lieutenant Marques. After following the Indians for 45 miles, Captain Fritz came upon their camp, and captured 2 horses, 6 mules, and all the plunder of the camp. The Indians made their escape.

July 30.—Lieut. W. H. Higdon reports that on the 30th of July, *en route* from Fort Union to Fort Stanton, he saw about 75 Indians driving a large herd of sheep, judged to number 20,000. Believing his party too small to attack so large a band of Indians, they were allowed to pass unmolested.

July 24.—Lieut. John Lambert, Fifth Infantry, California Volunteers, reports that the Indians attacked a detachment under his command in Cook's Cañon. At the first fire, Sergeant Hance, of Company H, Fifth Infantry, was wounded in his shoulder and hand; soon after, Private Queen, of Company F, was mortally wounded. Two wagons were abandoned to the Indians, also 12 mules. Private Queen died before the fight ended.

July 19.—Lieutenant-Colonel McMullen's ambulance was attacked by Indians near Paraje, and Asst. Surg. E. L. Watson, First Infantry, California Volunteers, and Private Johnson, Company G, First Infantry, California Volunteers, were killed. The escort killed two Indians and wounded others. Colonel McMullen's horse was captured by the Indians. Our loss, 1 commissioned officer and 1 private killed; 1 horse lost. Indian loss, 3 killed and — wounded.

August 4.—Lieut. B. Stevens, First New Mexico Volunteers, reports that, when returning from Cuvero to Fort Wingate, he came upon a party of Navajo Indians, 7 men and 2 boys ; took them prisoners, and placed them in the guard-house at Fort Wingáte.

August 6.—M. Steck, superintendent of Indian affairs, reports that a portion of the Utahs, Mohuaches, and Tabahuaches had killed 9 Navajoes and captured 22 horses.

August 6.—Capt. E. H. Bergmann reports that a party of Company I, First New Mexico Volunteers, in charge of a herd of beef-cattle, were attacked by a body of Navajoes on the 22d of July, near Conchas Springs. The party consisted of Sergt. José Lucero and Privates Juan F. Ortiz and José Banneras, who fought the Indians from 11 a. m. until after sundown, killing and wounding several of them. The Indians succeeded in killing Sergeant Lucero and Private Ortiz. Private Banneras, being severely wounded by eight arrow shots, gathered up the muskets and pistols of his dead comrades and threw them into the springs. The Indians fractured his skull with rocks and left him for dead, but he recovered toward morning and made his way to Chaperito. The Indians drove off the cattle. (Number not stated.)

Captain Bergmann, learning that the Indians had driven off 10,000 sheep, mounted 30 men, and endeavored to intercept them at the crossing of the Pecos. Corporal Martinez came close to their rear, and succeeded in killing 2 and wounding several. The corporal destroyed their camp utensils and captured 3 beeves.

August 11.—M. Steck, superintendent Indian affairs, reports that the Utahs have, during the last ten days, killed 30 Navajoes, and captured and brought in 60 children of both sexes, and captured 30 horses and 2,000 sheep. On the 11th instant, 4 Utahs came in with three scalps and 6 captives. Total, 33 killed, 66 captured, and 30 horses and 2,000 sheep taken.

August 19.—Col. Christopher Carson reports that he left camp near Cañon Bonita, August 5, 1863, on a scout for thirty days. On the first day out, sent Sergeant Romero with 15 men after 2 Indians seen in the vicinity; he captured one of their horses; the Indians made their escape. On the night of the 4th instant, Captain Pfeiffer captured 11 women and children, besides a woman and child, the former of whom was killed in attempting to escape and the latter accidentally. Captain Pfeiffer's party also captured two other children, 100 sheep and goats, and 1 horse. The Utes captured in the same vicinity 18 horses and 2 mules, and killed 1 Indian. Captain Pfeiffer wounded an Indian, but he escaped. On the 16th, a party who were sent for some pack-saddles brought in 1 Indian woman. At this camp the brave Major Cummings, First New Mexico Volunteers, was shot through the abdomen by a concealed Indian and died instantly. One of the parties sent out from this camp captured an Indian woman. Total Indians killed, 3; captured, 15; wounded, 1; 20 horses, 2· mules, and 100 sheep and goats captured. Troops, 1 commissioned officer killed.

August 19.—Capt. Henry A. Greene, First Infantry, California Volunteers, having received information that a party of Indians with a large herd of sheep had crossed the Rio Grande on the morning of the 8th instant, mounted 20 men, and started in pursuit, and, after following their trail for nearly 200 miles, came upon them, and opened fire. The Indians fled, and the command recovered 1,600 to 1,800 sheep, and drove them to Fort Craig.

August 24.—Capt. W. Craig reports that a party of 16 Indians attacked his herders near Fort Union, and drove off 18 Government mules.

August 27.—Capt. V. Dresher, First Infantry, California Volunteers, reports the horses and mules at Fort West were stampeded by Indians; animals not recovered; Indians not pursued; 26 mules and 1 horse lost.

August 29.—Capt. Henry A. Greene, First Infantry, California Volunteers, reports that the Indians attacked the mail stage on the Jornada, near the Point of Rocks, and captured 7 mules. As soon as the information was received, 15 mounted men were sent in pursuit, and 9 men detailed to escort the stage through. The mounted party, on coming in view of the Rio Grande, saw 3 Indians on the bank; the balance of the band were back in the brush; the 3 Indians were fired upon; one of them fell, but recovered again. A part of the command, under Lieutenant Fountain, charged across the river; the Indians ran and concealed themselves. The party then dismounted, and commenced to skirmish through the bushes. While on this duty, Private George S. Dickey was mortally wounded by the only shot fired by the Indians during the affair. Dickey saw an Indian jump into the river, and shot him; the Indian turned after being shot, and gave Dickey the wound which caused his death. Indian loss, 1 killed; 3 wounded. Our loss, 1 private killed.

August —.—Col. Christopher Carson, with his command, left Pueblo, Colo., on the 20th day of August, for Cañon de Chelly with the main force, secreting 25 men, under Captain Pfeiffer, in the cañon, to watch for Indians. Soon after, 2 Indians were seen approaching the cañon, and were fired upon, and, although badly wounded, succeeded in getting away. On the same day the advance guard pursued and killed an Indian. On the 31st the command returned to Fort Canby. Indian loss: 1 killed, 2 wounded.

August 27.—Two Navajo Indians, prisoners, attempted to escape from the guard-house at Fort Defiance; one was killed by the guard and the other mortally wounded. One killed, 1 wounded.

August 31.—Lieutenant-Colonel Chaves, commanding Fort Wingate, reports that a large party of Navajoes attacked the escort to the wood wagons about 5 miles from the post, wounding Private Luciano Pais and driving off 12 mules. The Indians were pursued but not overtaken. Our loss: 1 man wounded, 12 mules taken.

August 23.—Capt. R. Chacon, First Cavalry, New Mexico Volunteers, left Fort Wingate with 40 enlisted men, on a scout after Indians. On the 27th, when near the Salt Lakes, the party espied a band of Navajoes, and succeeded in killing 2 and capturing 8. On the same day, one of the Indians, in attempting to escape, was killed by the soldier who had him charge. On the 28th, the party attacked 150 Indians, who fled in all directions. The party here captured 7 children and recovered a captive Mexican boy named Agapito Apodaca; killed 3 Indians and captured 1,500 head of sheep and goats, 17 head of horses, mules, burros, and colts. On this scout there were 6 Indians killed, 14 captured, 1 Mexican boy rescued, 1,500 head of sheep, 17 horses, mules, burros, and colts captured.

August 27.—Capt. T. T. Tidball, Fifth Infantry, California Volunteers, commanding Fort Bowie, reports that the Apache Indians ran off 6 horses and 1 mule from that post.

September 8.—Capt. Joseph P. Hargrave, First Infantry, California Volunteers, reports that he left Fort Wingate on the 22d of August, on an expedition against the Navajoes. On the 26th August he saw 40 Indians on the Little Colorado; charged on them, but they fled before the troops got within gunshot of them. At this place captured 500 head of sheep. On the 30th of August the mules belonging to command (number unknown) were driven off by Indians. A party of mounted men were sent in pursuit, but failed to overtake them.

September 5.—M. Steck, superintendent of Indian affairs, reports that a party of Utahs have killed 9 Navajoes and captured 40 children, and that the Pueblo Indians have killed a Navajo warrior, and that the Governor of Jemez had killed 1 Navajo. Indian loss: 11 killed, 40 captured.

September 5.—Capt. J. H. Whitlock, Fifth Infantry, California Volunteers, reports that he found an Indian camp, surprised it, and captured 2 mules, 1 Sharp's carbine, 1 United States blanket, and 1,000 pounds of mescal. Burned the camp, including all that pertained to it. On the 8th of September, found Indians in force, and had a spirited fight with them for fifteen minutes. One man and the guide severely wounded, and 1 horse killed. Indian loss unknown. Our loss: 1 soldier and 1 citizen wounded and 1 horse killed.

September 8.—The Indians made an attack on Puertecito de las Salinas. Three Mexicans who went in pusuit of them were killed.

September 26.—Capt. Henry A. Greene, the indefatigable, commanding Fort McRae, learning that a band of Indians with 10 head of stock had crossed the Rio Grande near the Rio de los Allamosa, and that Corporal Argust with 3 men had gone in pursuit, immediately mounted 8 men, and started for the town of Allamosa. Arriving at this point, 18 mounted Mexicans joined his party. The whole party then traveled to. Cañada Palomas Crossing. At this point the stock was found, having been abandoned by the Indians. Corporal Argust, and Privates Daniel D. Tompkins, Alonzo C. Mullen, and William Lockhart, are highly praised by Captain Greene for their zeal and energy on this occasion.

September 27.—Lieut. P. A. J. Russell, First Infantry, California Volunteers, with 4 mounted men and a party of Pueblo Indians, started from Valles Grande on the trail of a band of Navajoes, who had stolen a lot of stock from the Pueblos. The trail was followed into the town of Jemez, where the party recaptured 125 head of sheep and 2 horses; killed 8 Navajoes, and took 20 women and children prisoners.

September 28.—Baltasar Montaño, citizen, reports the result of a campaign against the Navajoes as follows: Two Indians killed, 5 wounded, 11 or 12 animals captured, 2 horses and 1 mule lost.

October 5.—Colonel Carson reports that on the 22d of September his command pursued a party of Indians, but owing to the broken-down condition of his animals they only succeeded in capturing 1. On the 2d day of October, discovered a small Indian village which had just been abandoned; this was destroyed; 19 animals captured, 7 of which got away. Three men left camp to hunt up the animals which had escaped; they did not return until after the command had returned to Fort Canby; they state that they were attacked by a party of Indians when within 5 miles of the post, 1 of whom they killed. One of the men, named Artin, was severely wounded, and the Indians captured his mule. On the 3d day of October, Lieutenant Postle discovered an Indian, pursued him, and wounded him in three places; the lieutenant was slightly wounded by the Indians. Indian loss, 1 killed, 1 wounded, and 1 captured; 12 animals captured. Our loss, 1 officer and 1 private wounded, and 1 mule lost.

October 5.—Ramon Luna, agent for the Pueblo Indians, reports that the Pueblos, in a recent campaign against the Navajoes, killed 22 of them, captured 51 prisoners, 1,200 sheep, and 40 mules; some of the mules had the U. S. brand.

October 6.—Maj. Edward B. Willis, First Infantry, California Volunteers, left Fort Wingate on the 15th day of September, on an expedition against the Indians, with 40 men each of Company, H, First Infantry, California Volunteers, and Company F, First New Mexico Volunteers. At the Cienega Amarilla the command captured 1 horse and 1 mule; at Jacob's Well found a few Indians, and captured 2 of them. At this point found and destroyed several fields of pumpkins and watermelons. The command then returned to Fort Wingate. Major Willis, in his report, says: " I cannot speak in too high terms of the officers and men of this command; no men could be more anxious to do their duty, or more cheerfully incur the hardships of a campaign; after a march of 25 or 30 miles, the whole command would cheerfully volunteer and march the whole night on the slightest prospect of doing any service." Two Indians, 1 horse, and 1 mule captured.

October 13.—Two wagons which had been sent about a mile from Fort Canby for wood, in charge of a non-commissioned officer and 5 men, were attacked by the Indians. The escort and the teamsters ran at the first fire, leaving the wagons and teams in possession of the Indians; 10 mules were lost, 2 mules and the wagons were left. One of the soldiers, in his hurry to escape, left his musket at the wagons; the Indians carried it off.

October 15.—The train of Miguel Romero, hay contractor, was attacked by Indians while on its way from hay camp to Fort Canby; the non-commissioned officer in charge of the escort was wounded, and 1 teamster severely wounded. The Indians drove off 5 mules and 1 pony.

October 16.—Lieut. Thomas Henderson, First Cavalry, New Mexico Volunteers, reports that while *en route* from Fort Stanton to Santa Fé, he met 3 Indians with a lot of mules near the Buffalo Spring. The Indians, on being discovered, abandoned 19 mules and escaped.

October 18.—Lieutenant Dowlin, First Cavalry, New Mexico Volunteers, reports that a party under his command killed 2 Indians near the Laguna Negra.

October 22.—Capt. Rafael Chacon with his company pursued a band of Indians, who had run off stock near Fort Wingate, and captured from them 2 mules and 2 horses.

October 25.—Lieut. Charles H. Fitch, on an Indian scout, captured 2 horses and 1 mule.

October 21.—Lieut. Nicholas Hodt, First New Mexico Volunteers, with 40 men, left Fort Canby October 21, on a scout against the Indians. On the 22d, saw a party of Indians, who succeeded in escaping to the mountains; near Cañada, Colo., the command captured 1 woman.

October 31.—Lieut. E. E. Latimer, First Cavalry, California Volunteers, left Fort Union with a detachment of 9 men for Fort Sumner, having in charge 21 Indian prisoners. On the night of November 4, while encamped at the mouth of Gallinas River, 16 of the Indians succeeded in making their escape. They were pursued but not recaptured.

November 9.—A party of Mexicans passed through Fort Wingate on the 1st instant in pursuit of Indians; at the Sierra Negra the party had a fight with a band of Navajoes; killed 5 and took 16 prisoners. About 2 leagues from Sierra, the party had another fight with the Indians; killed 2 and took 2 prisoners. At the Sierra de Chusea had a skirmish with the Indians, and captured 24 prisoners, 20 horses and mules, and 25 sheep and goats. Indian loss: Killed, 7; prisoners, 42; 20 horses and mules, and 25 sheep and goats captured.

At Carriso Springs the party came upon a band of Indians, numbering from 200 to 300, with several thousand head of stock. The captain of the party being fearful of losing his prisoners, allowed this band to pass unmolested. .

November 4.—Capt. A. L. Anderson reports that while in camp on the Gila River, near the Pinal Mountains, the Indians crept to within range of his picket line, and discharged several volleys of arrows at the animals, sentinels, and the men sleeping near. Four horses were so badly wounded that it became necessary to kill them. A squad of men was left concealed in the camp, and, after the column had marched, they succeeded in killing one of a party of Indians who approached them. Indian loss, 1 killed. Our loss, 4 horses killed.

November 5.—Capt. Henry A. Greene, commanding Fort McRae, reports that a band of Indians crossed the Rio Grande near the Rio Plumas, with several hundred sheep, on the 4th of November. As soon as the information was received at Fort McRae, Captain Greene mounted 7 men, and started for the point it was reported the Indians had crossed. Arriving there, he found that the men at the vedette station had already started in pursuit. Captain Greene took up the trail, and, on the 5th instant, overtook the men from the station. After traveling with them for 150 miles, Captain Greene returned to Fort McRae, leaving Sergeant Rhodes and Corporal Argust to follow the trail. On the 12th November, Sergeant Rhodes returned, and reported that he overtook the Indians about 225 miles from the Rio Grande, and, after a sharp skirmish, routed them, and recovered 170 sheep. Private Atkinson was wounded by an arrow in this affair. The sergeant and the men who were with him are highly commended by Captain Greene. Indian loss, 1 killed and 4 wounded. Captain Greene states that the Indians could not have crossed the river with the sheep within 2 miles of Lieutenant Whittemore's camp had that officer used proper vigilance. Our loss, 1 private wounded.

November 5.—Lieut. Nicholas Hodt, First Cavalry, New Mexico Volunteers, left Fort Canby October 27, on a scout after Indians. Result of this scout, 4 Government mules worn out and shot.

November —.—E. Montoya, brigadier-general, New Mexico Militia, reports that Captain Tafolla overtook a party of Indians near the Sierra del Datil, and took from them 26 head of cattle, 4 burros, and 3 horses.

November —.—E. Montoya reports that his party attacked a band of Indians at the Three Brothers, and recovered 42 head of cattle—no Indians killed.

November 15.—Colonel Carson, with his command, left Fort Canby for the country west of the Oribi villages, for the purpose of chastising the Navajo Indians inhabiting that region. On the 16th, a detachment under Sergt. Andres Herrera overtook a small party of Indians, 2 of whom were killed and 2 wounded; 50 sheep and 1 horse were captured. Colonel Carson speaks in high terms of the zeal and energy displayed by Sergeant Herrera.

On the 25th, the command captured 1 boy and 7 horses, and destroyed an encampment; on the same day captured 1 woman and 1 child, and about 500 head of sheep and goats, 70 horses, and destroyed an Indian village. On the 3d of December, surprised an Indian encampment, capturing 1 horse and 4 oxen. The Indians escaped. Indian loss, 2 killed, 2 wounded, 3 captured; 550 sheep and goats, 9 horses, and 4 oxen captured.

November 27.—Roman A. Baca reports that he left Cebolletta with a party of 116 mounted Mexicans, and traveled in a northwesterly direction for six days; when about 50 miles from Chusca, on the sixth day out, the party encountered about 200 Indians; killed 6, and took 3 prisoners, who are now in the custody of Lieutenant Stevens. The party also captured 3 Indian ponies.

November 30.—L. M. Baca, judge of probate, reports that on the night of the 27th November, 3 miles from La Joya, the people at that place captured from 61 Navajoes 1,907 head of sheep.

November 30.—Lieut. J. Laughlin, while *en route* from Fort Wingate to Los Pinos, on the night of November 30, surprised a party of 6 or 7 Indians at the Rio Puerco; the Indians fled, leaving 70 head of cattle, which were taken to Los Pinos and turned over to the owner.

On the 4th of November, 10 head of cattle belonging to the command at Valles Grande were driven off by the Indians.

On the 9th day of November, José Ignacio Valencia, in charge of a herd of sheep, had a fight with the Indians at Cañoncitas of the Conchas; 1 Indian was killed.

December 1.—Capt. Henry A. Greene, First Infantry, California Volunteers, receiving information that a band of Indians had crossed the Jornada with 200 sheep, took 7 men of his company and started on their trail. The party overtook the sheep on the summit of the Sierra Caballo, on the east side of the Rio Grandé. The sheep were taken to Fort McRae.

December 16.—Maj. Henry D. Wallen, Seventh U. S. Infantry, commanding Fort Sumner, reports that on the morning of the 16th instant Mr. Labadie and Rev. Mr. Fialon reported to him that a large number of Indians, with an immense herd of sheep, were at the Carretas. The officers and men of Company D, Fifth, and Company C, Seventh Infantry, were awakened and prepared to take the field, with two days' rations. A lieutenant with 8 mounted men of Company B, Second Cavalry, California Volunteers, was also got in readiness; Mr. Labadie, Mr. Fialon, and 30 Apache Indians also started in pursuit. The party left the post at 5.30 a. m. for the Carretas. The mounted men and Indian agent with the Indians outstripped the party on foot, and took up the Navajo trail on the west bank of the Pecos River. At 35 miles northwest from Fort Sumner, they overtook the Navajoes, in number about 130, 10 mounted and 20 armed with rifles. A severe contest ensued, in which the Navajoes lost 12 killed and left on the field, and a number killed and wounded who were carried off; 1 prisoner taken, all the sheep recovered, amounting to 5,259; 13 burros, 4 rifles, 1 horse, their provisions, blankets, 150 pairs of moccasins, and nearly all the effects taken from Mr. Labadie's train.

Major Wallen calls the attention of the general commanding to the gallant conduct of Mr. Labadie, Privates Loder and Osier, of Company B, Second Cavalry, California Volunteers, Ojo Blanco and Cadetta, the chiefs of Apaches; Alazan, an Apache, who was badly wounded, and the Apaches generally, who rendered signal service.

Lieutenant Newbold with 3 men pursued the flying Navajoes 3 miles beyond the scene of action, but, owing to the exhausted condition of his animals, was obliged to desist from farther pursuit.

The Navajoes, just before reaching the Pecos, were alarmed by some pistol-shots discharged from a wagon train, and abandoned 4,630 sheep, which were secured by the Mexicans attached to the train.

Lieutenant McDermott, with 10 mounted men and 6 Apaches, was sent to collect the herd and bring it to the post. Before reaching the camp, Alazan, the Apache named above, died.

December 16.—Thirty-five Navajo Indians were sent to Fort Sumner this day; this party gave themselves up at Fort Wingate as prisoners of war.

December 20.—First Lieut. D. Montoya, First Cavalry, New Mexico Volunteers, in accordance with instructions received from Colonel Carson, left Fort Canby in pursuit of a party of Navajo Indians. On the second day out, marched through a heavy snow-storm. On the third day, came upon an Indian encampment, attacked it, and succeeded in killing 1 Indian and capturing 13 women and children, besides a lot of Navajo blankets, moccasins, &c. Near the Pueblo Colorado the command pursued 2 Indians (man and woman), and wounded the Indian and captured the woman.

Lieutenant Montoya recommends to the notice of the colonel commanding the good conduct and soldierly bearing of First Lieut. C. M. Hubbell and First Sergt. Antonio Nava, of Company C, First Cavalry, New Mexico Volunteers, who were severely wounded in the last affair. Corporal Marquez, of Company C, was particularly conspicuous on this scout; he was also wounded. Sergt. José M. Ortiz was also very active in pursuing and engaging the Indians.

December 7.—Lieut. Benj. Stevens reports that he saw 3 Mexicans near Cebolletta, having 3 Indian captives in their possession. The whole party were taken prisoners by him. The Mexicans soon after made their escape. The captives were sent to Fort Sumner.

December 22.—Capt. John Thompson, First Cavalry, New Mexico Volunteers, left Fort Canby with 100 men on a scout after Indians. On the 26th, at Mesa la Baca, sent out Sergeant Romero with 30 men, who came upon a party of Indians ; killed 1 and captured 12. On the same day, a party under Sergeant Dorsette discovered 2 Indians ; wounded 1 and captured the other. Indian loss : 1 killed, 13 captives, and 1 wounded.

On the 6th of December the Navajoes ran off some cows from the Pueblo Santa Ana. The Indians of the pueblo went in pursuit, recovered their stock, and killed 2 Navajoes.

On the 11th of December, José Ma. Martin, with a party of Mexicans, went in pursuit of Navajoes who had been stealing stock. The stock was recovered and 2 Indians killed.

On the 28th December, the people of San Miguel and Pueblo overtook and surprised a party of Indians, and recovered a lot of cattle and took the arms of the Indians.

The zeal and energy shown by the officers and soldiers, and the fortitude with which they have encountered hunger, thirst, fatigue, and exposure in their pursuit of hostile Indians within this department during the past year, are deserving of the highest admiration. Not less is this due to those parties who were so unfortunate as not to overtake the Indians than to those who came up with them. All toiled and suffered alike. The gallantry which every one has shown when there was an opportunity to close with the enemy proves that that virtue among the troops in New Mexico is common to all.

The alacrity with which citizens of New Mexico have taken the field to pursue and encounter the Indians is worthy of all praise. Many of them have been conspicuous for their courage; and all have shown a settled determination to assist the military in their efforts to rid the country of the fierce and brutal robbers and murderers who for nearly two centuries have brought poverty to its inhabitants and mourning and desolation to nearly every hearth throughout the Territory.

The department commander congratulates the troops and the people on the auspicious opening of the year 1864. For one hundred and eighty years the Navajo Indians have ravaged New Mexico; but it is confidently expected that the year 1864 will witness the end of hostilities with that tribe. Then New Mexico will take a stride toward that great prosperity which has lain within her grasp, but which hitherto she has not been permitted to enjoy.

By command of Brigadier-General Carleton:

BEN. C. CUTLER,
Assistant Adjutant-General.

RECAPITULATION.

Month	Taken from Indians.					Taken by Indians.				Citizens.		Indians.			Commissioned officers.		Enlisted men.	
	Sheep.	Horses.	Mules.	Cattle.	Burros.	Sheep.	Horses.	Mules.	Cattle.	Killed.	Wounded.	Killed.	Wounded.	Captured.	Killed.	Wounded.	Killed.	Wounded.
1863.																		
January														248			1	
January														100				
January												20	15				1	1
January												1						
January			34									9						
January		3										11	1					
February						4,000												
February	2,000					2,000						3						
February 25						6,000												
March									310									
March														15				
March	2,300					2,300			7						1		1	
March												28						
April									70	1		3						1
May											2							
May									12									
May		7										1						
May							6											
May		3										11						
May				50								1	50	10				
June									2						1			
June																		
June							7	2		2	2					1	2	1
June																	2	
July																		1
July			104						104			4				1		2
July		4										10						2
July									19			4						4
July									10			6					1	
July									1			2				1	1	
July		2	6						12					9			1	1
August												9						
August		22										2						
August				3		10,000						33		66			2	1
August	2,000	30										3	1	15	1			
August	100	20	2															
August	1,800		18															
August							1	26				1	3				1	
August								7				1	2					
August												1	1					1
August																		
August									12									
August	1,500	17										6		14				
August							6	1										
September	500																	
September												11		40				
September																		1
September											1							
September				10						3								
September	125	2										8		20				
September												2	5					1
October												1		1	1			
October	1,200		40									22		51				
October		1	1											2				
October									10									1
October		1	5															
October 16			19										1					
October												2						
October		2	2															
October		2	1															
October						89												
October																1		
November	25	20										7		42				
November	170											1						1
November												1	4					
November			3	26	4													
November				42														
November	550	9		4								2	2	3				
November		3										6		3				
November	1,907																	

RECAPITULATION—Continued.

Month.	Taken from Indians.					Taken by Indians.				Citizens.		Indians.			Commissioned officers.		Enlisted men.	
	Sheep.	Horses.	Mules.	Cattle.	Burros.	Sheep.	Horses.	Mules.	Cattle.	Killed.	Wounded.	Killed.	Wounded.	Captured.	Killed.	Wounded.	Killed.	Wounded.
1863.																		
November			70															
November										10								
November												1						
December.....	200																	
December....												2						
December....	9,889	1			13							12		1				
December....												2						
December....														35				
December....												1	1	13				
December....												1	1	14				2
	24,266	152	2C2	215	17	24,389	21	205	402	16	4	301	87	703	3	4	14	21

Official:

CYRUS DE FORREST,
Aide-de-Camp.

MAY 14, 1863.—Scouts from Merritt's Plantation, on the Clinton road, La.

Reports of Col. Nathan A. M. Dudley, Thirtieth Massachusetts Infantry, commanding Third Brigade, First Division, Nineteenth Army Corps.

CAMP ON MERRITT'S PLANTATION,
May 14, 1863.

SIR: Colonel Grierson, with his command, has just returned from a scout on the Clinton road. He left camp with about 350 men, taking two of his small pieces with him. Crossing the road leading from Alexander's plantation to the Clinton Plank road, near White's Bayou, passed Colonel Messer's camp, *en route* to Clinton, until reaching a point about 1½ miles west of Red Wood Creek, when his advance came upon the pickets of the enemy. He drove them back into the rifle-pits which they had constructed on the west side of Red Wood Bridge. Here they made considerable of a stand, firing with rifles. As no infantry tracks were discovered after crossing, Colonel Grierson is of the opinion that the rifle-pits were occupied by dismounted cavalry. He fired several shots from his light guns, which soon [drove] them out. After crossing the bridge, four companies, two mounted and two dismounted, proceeded on about 1 mile, at which point the advance party met fully an equal force of cavalry to his own. At this place they discovered on the road the tracks of what was supposed to be four pieces of artillery. This supposition was strengthened by information gained on the road. One company of infantry was down on the road as a support to the rebel picket last night.

Colonel Grierson goes to town this evening. He expressed a great desire to take his command with him.

I trust the commanding officer will not reduce the force under my command. I have to guard the Springfield Landing, Bayou Sara, and Clinton roads, and I do not think I have a man to spare.

The Illinois troops can recruit here better, in my opinion, than at Baton Rouge.

I am, sir, respectfully, your obedient servant,

N. A. M. DUDLEY,
Colonel and Acting Brigadier-General, Commanding.

Capt. [GEORGE B.] HALSTED,
Assistant Adjutant-General.

CAMP ON MERRITT'S PLANTATION,
May 14, 1863.

SIR : I have the honor to report the return of the two other scouts sent out, which I referred to in my communication of this morning. Captain Godfrey, with his company of Louisiana cavalry, made the junction at the Plains with Capt. J. D. Angeley, Company C, Sixth Illinois Cavalry, at the time appointed, and succeeded, after a short skirmish, in which the enemy lost 2 killed and 5 wounded, in capturing 16 prisoners, 30 guns, and 20 horses.

Lieutenant Morse, First Louisiana Cavalry, and Lieutenant ——, of the Seventh Illinois Cavalry, accompanied these parties, and are complimented by Captain Godfrey and Lieutenant Angeley.

I am, sir, respectfully, your obedient servant,

N. A. M. DUDLEY,
Colonel and Acting Brigadier-General, Commanding.

Captain HALSTED,
Assistant Adjutant-General.

MAY 14, 1863.—Skirmish at Boyce's Bridge, Cotile Bayou, La. .

REPORTS.

No. 1.—Brig. Gen. Godfrey Weitzel, U. S. Army.
No. 2.—Col. Sidney A. Bean, Fourth Wisconsin Infantry.

No. 1.

Report of Brig. Gen. Godfrey Weitzel, U. S. Army.

HEADQUARTERS UNITED STATES FORCES,
Murdock's Plantation, * *May* 19 [18], 1863.

SIR : I have the honor to report that I arrived here with my whole command at 10.30 a. m. to-day. I left Alexandria yesterday morning at 4 o'clock. The gunboats remained until 12. My rear guard has up to this time seen or heard nothing of an enemy. I await further orders here.

On last Thursday, while in command at Alexandria, I received information that the enemy to the number of 200 or 300 had returned to Cotile Bayou, and were constructing breastworks of cotton at Judge Boyce's bridge. I sent two companies of cavalry to reconnoiter their

---

* At junction of the Huffpower and Bayou Boeuf.

position. This reconnaissance attacked the enemy, and found him to number about 1,000 dismounted cavalry, with several pieces of light artillery. Our force, upon falling back, was pursued by the enemy a short distance. As soon as they were out of range of their breastworks, our forces turned upon them, charged them, and drove them pell-mell back behind their breastworks.

Our loss, 1 man wounded and several horses killed. Three dead bodies of the enemy were found in the field and buried. It is known that their loss was much greater. On the following day I sent the whole cavalry force, with one piece of Nims' battery, and about 200 of the Seventy-fifth New York, on the gunboat Switzerland, to attack the enemy.

As soon as this force appeared in sight, the enemy fled in three directions, closely pursued by our cavalry. His main body then took position behind Cane River, and up to the time of our departure only a few of his pickets had ventured down to Cotile Bayou.

The breastworks of the enemy were found to consist of two strong parallel lines of cotton bales about 200 yards apart. We captured 6 prisoners belonging to Colonel [W. P.] Lane's Texas regiment, which left Texas two weeks ago yesterday. On the same day that this affair occurred, but a little earlier in the day, Sergeant Mallory and 9 men of Perkins' cavalry were in the pine woods after horses; in a short time they found themselves surrounded by a large force of the enemy. They seized every negro they met as a guide; in this way they gave the enemy the slip, and brought with them into camp 15 negro guides, each mounted upon a fine horse.

I am, sir, very respectfully, your obedient servant,

G. WEITZEL,
Brigadier-General, U. S. Volunteers.

Lieut. Col. RICHARD B. IRWIN,
Assistant Adjutant-General, Department of the Gulf.

No. 2.

Report of Col. Sidney A. Bean, Fourth Wisconsin Infantry.

[Printed in Series I, Vol. XV, p. 346.]

MAY 17, 1863.—Operations on west side of the Mississippi River, near Port Hudson, La.

Report of Lieut. Col. M. B. Locke, First Alabama Infantry.

MAY 18, 1863.

CAPTAIN: Yesterday at 1 o'clock I received an order through Lieutenant-Colonel [M. J.] Smith, chief of heavy artillery, from the major-general commanding, directing that I prevent the enemy above from communicating with the fleet below. I immediately ordered Companies C, D, and E, of my regiment, numbering, respectively, 25, 45, and 48 men, to proceed across the river. My means of transportation being so limited, I could only send about 25 men over at a time in the skiffs; consequently, I directed Captain [J. T.] Stubbs, commanding Company C, to proceed across in the first boat, and take position at the junction of the State with the False River levee, and, if the enemy should land before I could reach him, to defend that point as long as it was practicable.

Immediately after arriving at his position, he very unexpectedly observed a cavalry force of the enemy at the dike, the point where the road crosses False River, running to Waterloo, variously estimated from 100 to 250.

So soon as the enemy observed him, he divided his force, and attacked him in front; dismounted and deployed the other party to right, for the purpose of flanking Stubbs and cutting off his retreat. This movement on the part of the enemy caused Captain Stubbs to fall back behind the river levee running east. He then held the enemy in check until nearly surrounded; was forced to fall back again to the levee running from the main river levee to the wood-pile below the Hermitage. Just at this time I arrived with about 15 men, and held the enemy in check, the firing soon ceasing.

During the time Captain Stubbs was falling back, he kept up a brisk skirmish with the enemy, contesting every inch of ground. The force I had over here being so small, and the enemy being so strongly posted, I deemed it imprudent to attack him until the balance of my troops arrived. Accordingly, so soon as all came up (which was about 4.30 o'clock), I advanced; but my pickets informed me the enemy's pickets had just retired. I pushed on to the dike, and was there informed by citizens that the main body of the enemy had been gone about one hour, driving with them all the cattle belonging to the Government and many belonging to private individuals, besides capturing Lieutenant [D. M. C.] Hughes and about 20 or 25 men of his command; also Captain [William H.] Pruett, Lieutenant [A. F.] Crymes, and 3 men of my regiment, who were posted over here to fire the wood in case the enemy's ships should attempt to pass at night; those latter were fishing at the dike at the time the enemy came upon them. I then decided to pursue the enemy and endeavor to recapture the cattle, and proceeded about 2 miles, but was informed by citizens that it was impossible to overtake him, and almost impracticable to travel on foot over the road he went—a very dim road from the dike to Winter's place, near the fleet below. I returned to the dike, and shall use every effort to prevent a repetition of such an affair, as well as to prevent any communication between the two fleets.

The only casualty in my command was 1 man in Captain Stubbs' company slightly wounded. The enemy's loss is unknown, except that 1 man and 2 horses are known to have been killed.

The enemy informed the citizens that he would return to-day to get the sheep left, and a courier has just arrived, informing me that 600 cavalry, landed and encamped at Morganza last night, would come in this direction to-day.

I have but about 120 men, and would respectfully suggest that the two companies of my regiment (Companies H and F) who have been assigned to policing the river be sent over to me, with the exception of a sufficient detail to man the boat, kept on duty all the while.

I am, very respectfully, your obedient servant,

M. B. LOCKE,
Lieutenant-Colonel, Commanding.

Capt. T. F. WILLSON,
Assistant Adjutant-General.

MAY 18, 1863.—Affair near Cheneyville, La.

Report of Brig. Gen. Godfrey Weitzel, U. S. Army.

HEADQUARTERS UNITED STATES FORCES,
Murdock's Plantation, May 19, 1863.

SIR: Since my dispatch of yesterday,* the enemy's cavalry has appeared. Lane's Texas regiment was encamped at Lloyd's bridge (13 miles above here) last night. Their pickets extended below Cheneyville. I attacked the outpost with two companies of my cavalry last night, and drove the whole in on the main body, capturing 2 prisoners. A deserter also came in. Prisoners and deserters also say that the cavalry force is all following. Orders were sent back to bring all their troops back to Alexandria on their transports. Would it not be well to send some gunboats up the river to stop this? Would it also not be well to keep a watch at Moreauville to prevent any cavalry making a raid along the Mail road?

I am, sir, very respectfully, your obedient servant,
G. WEITZEL,
Brigadier-General, U. S. Volunteers, Commanding.

Lieut. Col. RICHARD B. IRWIN,
Assistant Adjutant-General, Department of the Gulf.

MAY 18-19, 1863.—Operations about Merritt's Plantation, and on the Bayou Sara road, La.

Reports of Col. Nathan A. M. Dudley, Thirtieth Massachusetts Infantry, commanding Third Brigade, First Division, Nineteenth Army Corps.

CAMP ON MERRITT'S PLANTATION, LA.,
May 19, 1863.

CAPTAIN: I am in receipt of your communication dated 10 o'clock last night, which did not reach me till 8 o'clock this morning. The enemy last night made an attack on my cavalry pickets, driving them in within half a mile of my main camp; at the same time an attempt was made to get in on my rear with an infantry force, each of which failed. The force in front was large. They attempted at three or four different points, but found each picketed. From information gained from parties that came in this morning, and the experience of last night, I think it expedient, in the absence of the major-general commanding, that Holcomb's battery and at least one regiment of infantry, two, if possible, should be added to my present immediate force. They had better start at once, in order to reach me in time to be posted across the bayou on my left toward the Springfield Landing road before dark.

Let them march with only rubber blankets and two days' uncooked rations. Camp kettles can be brought out in wagons.

I am, sir, respectfully, your obedient servant,
N. A. M. DUDLEY,
Colonel and Acting Brigadier-General, Commanding.

Captain HALSTED,
Assistant Adjutant-General.

---

* See p. 35.

BIVOUAC ON BAYOU SARA ROAD,
May 19, 1863—8.30 p. m.

Sir : This afternoon I made a reconnaissance in full force 7½ miles to the front, beyond the Plains Store; sending a cavalry force to insure the safety of my left flank round by the Springfield and Port Hudson roads, which made a junction with my main force at the north end of the Plains. We found the enemy's pickets strongly posted on both roads, but they retreated as we advanced. I threw my Sawyer guns to the front, supported by the Thirtieth Massachusetts Infantry and 400 cavalry, to a point within 2 miles of the works of the enemy, and fired a dozen shells into them; waited some two hours, but could not tempt them into a brush.

The men enjoyed the scout much. They begged to be allowed to go ahead and draw the fire of the enemy's guns. I have never seen more reliable enthusiasm exhibited. The result of this scout will guarantee a quiet night's rest to the troops, at any rate. Gardner's pickets have been very impudent for the last three days.

Hoping soon to see the general with a good force come up the road, I remain, truly, your obedient servant,

[N. A. M. DUDLEY,]
Colonel, and Acting Brigadier-General.

Captain HALSTED, *Assistant Adjutant-General.*

MAY 20, 1863.—Skirmish near Cheneyville, La.

Report of Brig. Gen. Godfrey Weitzel, U. S. Army.

HEADQUARTERS UNITED STATES FORCES,
Murdock's Plantation, La., May 20, 1863—3.15 p. m.

Sir : I have the honor to report that this morning the enemy attacked my pickets. Colonel Bean, in command of the advance guard, repulsed the enemy, and pursued him with his whole force, consisting of the cavalry, mounted infantry, and Twelfth Connecticut Volunteers. Captain Barrett, with 17 non-commissioned officers and privates of his company, was in the advance. When within about 1½ miles of Cheneyville, Major Robinson, in command of the rest of his cavalry, halted the column. Captain Barrett, rather too daringly, still continued to advance, and, after passing a sugar-house, a force of about 150 rebel cavalry jumped out, and cut him off from the rest of the command. Captain Barrett moved before them, intending to cross the Cheneyville Bridge and come down on the west bank of the bayou; but when he arrived at the bridge, he found it held by a force of 600 of the enemy. He was then compelled to surrender. One or two of his non-commissioned officers escaped. Sergeant Haley was killed. The rest were taken prisoners. The enemy lost 2 killed, 2 wounded, and 2 taken prisoners. The prisoners are of [E.] Waller's battalion, Texas cavalry. They left Natchitoches on Tuesday ; came through the pine wood, not passing near Alexandria. They say the force immediately in my front is Lane's regiment, Waller's battalion, about 200 of Sibley's brigade, and a battery of artillery, and that the rest of their force is moving down.

I am, sir, very respectfully, your most obedient servant,

G. WEITZEL,
Brigadier-General, Commanding U. S. Forces.

Lieut. Col. RICHARD B. IRWIN, *Assistant Adjutant-General.*

May 21-26, 1863.—Operations on the Teche road, between Barre's Landing and Berwick, La.

Report of Col. Joseph S. Morgan, Ninetieth New York Infantry, commanding Provisional Brigade.

BRASHEAR CITY, LA., May 28, 1863.

SIR: I have the honor to report for the information of the major-general commanding Department of the Gulf, that, in compliance with his orders, I embarked my regiment on board of transports at this place and proceeded to Barre's Landing, La., where I reported to Colonel Chickering, commanding forces at that post. By his orders, the infantry and artillery, then at that post, were provisionally brigaded, and placed under my command for the purpose of convoying a train of contrabands and army stores to Brashear City.

In accordance to his orders, the convoy took up the line of march on the morning of May 21 instant, in the following order: The Forty-first Massachusetts Volunteers in advance, supported by one piece of Nims' battery, and one regiment of infantry, via the Teche road. The first day's march we made 25 miles, and averaged for the three succeeding days 18 miles. Nothing of importance transpired until the evening of the 23d May, when a private, named Loomis, of the Ninetieth New York Volunteers, was reported to be shot by a planter named Wilcoxen, the circumstances of which are substantially as follows: The quartermaster of the regiment had gone to the plantation for the purpose of obtaining sugar sufficient for the use of the men that evening. Loomis was engaged in loading the sugar into the wagon when he was shot by Wilcoxen, who immediately made his escape across the bayou. Upon obtaining information of these facts, and in accordance with a recommendation of a board of commission appointed to investigate the matter, I ordered a detachment of mounted infantry to the place, to arrest all persons found thereon, in compliance with which they arrested the wife of Wilcoxen, whom I have brought to this place, and hold as a hostage until Wilcoxen delivers himself up, or she be released by order of the major-general commanding. Secreted upon her person was found a loaded revolver, and in the house several fire-arms, which were brought away, and have been turned in to the proper authorities.

Apprehending, from information received, that I should be attacked at the bridge across the Teche at Saint Martin's, I ordered an additional regiment up to support Colonel Chickering and prevent the burning of the bridge, which I had been informed was the intention of a band of guerrillas, known to be in the vicinity, under Colonel [V. A.] Fournet. However, everything passed off quietly until the evening of Monday, 25th instant. The train had encamped some 5 or 6 miles below Franklin, when word was sent to me that the rear guard, under command of Lieutenant Wood, of the One hundred and tenth New York Volunteers, had been attacked by guerrillas near Franklin. I immediately proceeded to the ground, and found the report correct; and, I regret to say, found Lieutenant Wood mortally, and several of the men slightly, wounded. I ordered the infantry up, together with one piece of Nims' battery. The infantry quickly deployed in fighting order. The guerrillas also deployed in line as skirmishers, but could not stand our advance, and took shelter in an old sugar-house near by. I then ordered Lieutenant Snow, of the battery, to shell them out, which was done. I have since learned they lost 4 in killed, we taking also 1 prisoner.

Previous to the attack, several officers of the One hundred and seventy-fifth New York Volunteers had gone back to Franklin to visit some friends there, and have not yet reported. It is supposed they were taken prisoners by Fournet. Feeling myself not justified in hazarding the safety of the immense train in my charge by attempting any further movement against this band of guerrillas in the night, I ordered a night march of the entire command, and arrived to within 11 miles of Berwick at 4 o'clock a. m. of the 26th instant, where I made a halt, having marched 40 miles in twenty-two hours.

I cannot give too much praise to both officers and men of my command for their conduct upon all occasions; and am proud to say that no instance has come to my knowledge of any outrage upon the property or person of any of the inhabitants upon the line of march. No property has been taken other than that required for the use of the troops and animals.

From the best information I can obtain, I have computed the number of contrabands in the train at 5,000; horses and mules at 2,000; cattle, 1,500. The train extended some 8 miles in length, all of which I am pleased to say have been safely transferred across the bay to this place. I regret to inform you that Lieutenant Wood, of the One hundred and seventy-fifth [One hundred and tenth] New York Volunteers, wounded by guerrillas at Franklin, has since died of his wounds; also that Private Lawson, of the Ninetieth New York Volunteers, was accidentally shot dead during the march. Private Loomis, of the Ninetieth New York Volunteers, shot by Wilcoxen, is still living, but no hopes are entertained of his recovery. Lieutenant Curtis, of the One hundred and seventy-fifth New York Volunteers, and Corporal Brewer, of the One hundred and sixty-second New York Volunteers, went back to Franklin upon a reconnaissance, and have not since been heard from.

Trusting the above will meet with the approval of the major-general commanding, I have the honor to be, sir, most respectfully, your obedient servant,

JOS. S. MORGAN,
Col. Ninetieth New York Vols., Comdg. Provisional Brigade.

Lieut. Col. RICHARD B. IRWIN, **A. A. G.**, *19th Army Corps.*

MAY 21–July 8, 1863.—Siege of Port Hudson, La.

SUMMARY OF THE PRINCIPAL EVENTS.

May   21, 1863.—Action at Plains Store.

         23, 1863.—Skirmishes on the Springfield and Plains Store roads.

         25, 1863.—Capture of the Confederate steamers Starlight and Red Chief.
                  Skirmish at Thompson's Creek.

         27, 1863.—First assault.

June 3– 8, 1863.—Expedition to Clinton.

         11, 1863.—Capture of Confederate outposts.

         14, 1863.—Second assault.

         16, 1863.—Raid on the Union lines.

         26, 1863.—Capture of Union outposts.

July   2, 1863.—Affair at Springfield Landing.

        8, 1863.—Surrender of Port Hudson.

REPORTS.*

No. 1.—Maj. Gen. Nathaniel P. Banks, U. S. Army, commanding Department of the Gulf.

No. 2.—Returns of Casualties in the Union forces.

---

* See also General Halleck's report, p. 3.

No. 3.—Lieut. Col. Richard B. Irwin, Assistant Adjutant-General, U. S. Army, of affair at Springfield Landing.

No. 4.—Capt. John C. Palfrey, U. S. Corps of Engineers, of operations July 5–6.

No. 5.—Capt. William B. Roe, Sixteenth Michigan Infantry; Chief Signal **Officer, of** operations April 9–July 8.

No. 6.—Lieut. John C. Abbott, Thirteenth Connecticut Infantry, Acting Signal Officer, of operations June 2–July 25.

No. 7.—Lieut. Milton Benner, Second Pennsylvania Heavy Artillery, Acting Signal Officer, of operations May 23–June 5.

No. 8.—Lieut. John W. Dana, Twelfth Maine Infantry, Acting Signal Officer, of operations June 29–July 3.

No. 9.—Lieut. Stephen M. Eaton, Twelfth Maine Infantry, Acting Signal Officer, of operations March 13–July 11.

No. 10.—Lieut. Thomas S. Hall, Twenty-eighth Maine Infantry, Acting Signal Officer, of operations April 10–July 16.

No. 11.—Lieut. Joseph L. Hallett, Thirty-first Massachusetts Infantry, Acting Signal Officer, of operations May 12–July 9.

No. 12.—Lieut. George R. Herbert, One hundred and fifty-ninth New York Infantry, Acting Signal Officer, of operations May 27–June 13.

No. 13.—Lieut. Amos M. Jackson, Twenty-fourth Maine Infantry, Acting Signal Officer, of operations May 18–June 15.

No. 14.—Lieut. John F. Jencks, Twenty-sixth Connecticut Infantry, Acting Signal Officer, of operations May 22–June 19.

No. 15.—Lieut. James H. Rundlett, Fiftieth Massachusetts Infantry, Acting Signal Officer, of operations May 24–July 7.

No. 16.—Lieut. E. H. Russell, Ninth Pennsylvania Reserves, Acting Signal Officer, of operations May 24–July 11.

No. 17.—Col. N. A. M. Dudley, Thirty-first Massachusetts Infantry, commanding Third Brigade, First Division, Nineteenth Army Corps, of action at Plains Store.

No. 18.—Col. Thomas S. Clark, Sixth Michigan Infantry, commanding First Brigade, Second Division, of the assault June 14.

No. 19.—Col. Thomas G. Kingsley, Twenty-sixth Connecticut Infantry, of the first assault.

No. 20.—Lieut. Col. Joseph Selden, Twenty-sixth Connecticut Infantry, of the first assault.

No. 21.—Capt. Francis S. Keese, One hundred and twenty-eighth New York Infantry, of the first assault.

No. 22.—Lieut. Col. Justus W. Blanchard, One hundred and sixty-second New York Infantry, of affair at Springfield Landing.

No. 23.—Brig. Gen. Halbert E. Paine, U. S. Army, commanding Third Division, of the expedition to Clinton.

No. 24.—Maj. James P. Richardson, Thirty-eighth Massachusetts Infantry, Third Brigade, of operations May 22–July 12.

No. 25.—Capt. Apollos Comstock, Thirteenth Connecticut Infantry, Third Brigade, Fourth Division, of the assault June 14.

No. 26.—Brig. Gen. Godfrey Weitzel, U. S. Army, commanding Provisional Division, of operations June 7–11.

No. 27.—Lieut. Col. Frank H. Peck, Twelfth Connecticut Infantry, of the assault May 27.

No. 28.—Col. Benjamin H. Grierson, Sixth Illinois Cavalry, commanding Cavalry Brigade, of operations June 3-7.

No. 29.—Col. Edward Prince, Seventh Illinois Cavalry, of the capture of the Confederate steamers Starlight and Red Chief.

No. 30.—Lieut. Col. Augustus W. Corliss, Second Rhode Island Cavalry, of affair at Springfield Landing.

[o. 31.—Lieut. Commander Edward Terry, U. S. Navy, commanding Naval Battery, of operations May 30–July 8.

[o. 32.—Statement of Confederate organizations paroled at Port Hudson.

[o. 33.—Capt. C. M. Jackson, Acting Assistant Inspector-General, C. S. Army, of the surrender of Port Hudson.

[o. 34.—Returns of Casualties in the Confederate forces (incomplete).

[o. 35.—Capt. Louis J. Girard, C. S. Army, Chief of Ordnance, Third Military District.

[o. 36.—Brig. Gen. W. N. R. Beall, C. S. Army, commanding brigade.

[o. 37.—Capt. John R. Fellows, Assistant Inspector-General, C. S. Army, of skirmish at Thompson's Creek, and assault on the works at Port Hudson.

[o. 38.—Col. David Provence, Sixteenth Arkansas Infantry, of the capture of Union outposts, and casualties to July 8.

[o. 39.—Col. O. P. Lyles, Twenty-third Arkansas Infantry, of operations May 31–July 3.

No. 40.—Lieut. Col. P. F. De Gournay, Twelfth Louisiana Artillery Battalion, of operations May 24–July 2.

No. 41.—Col. I. G. W. Steedman, First Alabama Infantry, of operations May 25–July 7.

No. 42.—Col. W. B. Shelby, Thirty-ninth Mississippi Infantry, of operations June 8.

No. 43.—Maj. Thomas H. Johnston, First Mississippi Infantry, of operations July 2–3.

No. 44.—Lieut. E. A. Toledano, Watson (Louisiana) Battery, of operations May 24.

No. 45.—Lieut. Col. J. H. Wingfield, Ninth Louisiana Battalion Partisan Rangers.

No. 46.—Col. W. R. Miles, Louisiana Legion, of operations May 21–July 7.

No. 47.—Lieut. Col. Frederick B. Brand, Miles' (Louisiana) Legion, of operations June 24–27.

No. 48.—Col. John L. Logan, Eleventh Arkansas Infantry, of operations May 21–July 8.

No. 1.

Reports of Maj. Gen. Nathaniel P. Banks, U. S. Army, commanding Department of the Gulf.*

HDQRS. DEPT. ᴏF THE GULF, NINETEENTH ARMY CORPS,
Before Port Hudson, La., May 30, 1863.

GENERAL: Leaving Simsport, on the Atchafalaya, where my command was at the date of my last dispatch, I landed at Bayou Sara at 2 o'clock on the morning of the 21st. A portion of the infantry was transported by steamer, and the balance of the infantry, artillery, cavalry, and wagon train moving down on the west bank of the river, and from this to Bayou Sara.

On the 23d, a junction was effected with the advance of Major-General Augur and Brigadier-General Sherman, our line occupying the Bayou Sara road, at a distance of 5 miles from Port Hudson. Major-General Augur had an encounter with a portion of the enemy on the Bayou Sara road, in the direction of Baton Rouge, which resulted in the repulse of the enemy with heavy loss.

On the 25th, the enemy was compelled to abandon his first line of works. General Weitzel's brigade, which had covered our rear in the march from Alexandria, joined us on the 26th, and on the morning of the 27th a general assault was made upon the fortifications. The artillery opened fire between 5 and 6 o'clock, which was continued with animation during the day.

At 10 o'clock a. m. Weitzel's brigade, with the division of General

---

* See also General Reports, p. 5.

Grover, reduced to about two brigades, and the division of General Emory, temporarily reduced by detachments to about a brigade, under command of Colonel Paine, with two regiments of negro troops, made an assault upon the right of the enemy's works, crossing Sandy Creek and driving him through the wood into his fortifications. The fight lasted on this line until 4 o'clock, and was very severely contested. On the left, the infantry did not come up until later in the day, but at 2 o'clock an assault was opened upon the works on the center and left of center by the divisions under Major-General Augur and Brigadier-General Sherman. The enemy was driven into his works, and our troops moved up to the fortifications, holding the opposite sides of the parapet with the enemy. On the right, our troops still occupy this position. On the left, after dark, the main body, being exposed to a flank fire, withdrew to a belt of wood, the skirmishers remaining close upon the fortifications.

The works are defended by a garrison much larger than generally represented. There appears to be no want of ammunition or provisions on the part of the enemy. The fortifications are very strong, and surrounded by a most intricate tract of country, diversified by ravines, woods, plains, and cliffs, which it is almost impossible to comprehend without careful and extended reconnaissances.

Six regiments, under command of Colonel Chickering, were detailed at Alexandria to guard the train from that point and from Opelousas. These troops will be here to-morrow, and strengthen our force some 3,000 men. My effective force on the day of the assault was about 13,000; that of the enemy, within the works, ten regiments, of between 500 and 600 each—in all, about 8,000 men—with mounted infantry outside the works in our rear (2,200), consisting of the Ninth and Eleventh Regiments of Arkansas troops.

In the assault of the 27th, the behavior of the officers and men was most gallant, and left nothing to be desired. Our limited acquaintance with the ground and the character of the works, which were almost hidden from our observation until the moment of approach, alone prevented the capture of the post.

We occupy the enemy night and day with harassing attacks of infantry and artillery, giving him no rest or sleep. Numerous prisoners and deserters, who are captured or come in, report that the men are dispirited and depressed. We wait only the arrival of our troops and the completion of more perfect reconnaissances to renew our assault, and have strong hopes that it will be successful. No time will be lost.

To avoid possible failure in carrying this important post, I have notified General Grant by one of his staff officers, who was present on the day after the assault, of the details of our position and our strength, and have asked him, if it be possible, to send us 5,000 or 10,000 men, with whose aid we could accomplish its reduction in a single day. I understand the pressing circumstances of his position, but hope that he may be able to assist us in this emergency. We want only men. With the reduction of Port Hudson we can join him without delay with at least 15,000 men and a finely appointed siege train of artillery, which he greatly needs. We shall not, however, delay our operations or postpone effective movements for the reduction of the post on account of this application to him for aid.

On the extreme right of our line I posted the First and Third Regiments of negro troops. The First Regiment of Louisiana Engineers, composed exclusively of colored men, excepting the officers, was also engaged in the operations of the day. The position occupied by these troops was one of importance, and called for the utmost steadiness and bravery in those to whom it was confided. It gives me pleasure to report that they answered every expectation. In many respects their conduct was heroic. No troops could be more determined or more daring. They made during the day three charges upon the batteries of the enemy, suffering very heavy losses and holding their position at nightfall with the other troops on the right of our line. The highest commendation is bestowed upon them by all the officers in command on the right. Whatever doubt may have existed heretofore as to the efficiency of organizations of this character, the history of this day proves conclusively to those who were in condition to observe the conduct of these regiments that the Government will find in this class of troops effective supporters and defenders. The severe test to which they were subjected, and the determined manner in which they encountered the enemy, leaves upon my mind no doubt of their ultimate success. They require only good officers, commands of limited numbers, and careful discipline, to make them excellent soldiers.

Our losses from the 23d to this date, in killed, wounded, and missing, are nearly 1,000, including, I deeply regret to say, some of the ablest officers of the corps. I am unable yet to repeat them in detail.

I have the honor to be, with much respect, your obedient servant,

> N. P. BANKS,
> *Major-General, Commanding.*

Major-General HALLECK,
Commander-in-Chief, U. S. Army, Washington, D. C.

> HEADQUARTERS DEPARTMENT OF THE GULF,
> *Before Port Hudson, June 14, 1863.*

GENERAL: I have the honor to inform you that, having silenced all the enemy's artillery, completely invested the place, and established my batteries within 350 yards, I yesterday opened a vigorous cannonade for an hour, and at its expiration made a formal demand on General Gardner for the surrender of the garrison. He replied that his duty required him to defend the place, and therefore he declined to surrender. Accordingly the necessary arrangements were made to assault the works at daylight this morning, after a cannonade and bombardment lasting during the night, renewed with vigor just previous to the attack. The attack was in three columns. One, of a division under Brigadier-General Dwight, was intended to gain entrance to the enemy's works on the extreme left; a feigned attack was to be made with vigor by Major-General Augur in the center, and the main attack was to be made by the right wing, under Brigadier-General Grover. Neither column was successful in gaining the work, but our troops gained advanced positions within from 50 to 200 yards from the works. These we shall hold and intrench to-night. The enemy made several attempts to open with artillery, but was almost immediately silenced. I believe our losses are not heavy except in officers. I regret to say that that gallant officer, Brig. Gen. Halbert E. Paine, fell, severely but it is thought not dangerously wounded, while leading the Third Division to the attack. I am still confident of success.

Very respectfully, your most obedient servant,

> N. P. BANKS,
> *Major-General, Commanding.*

Major-General HALLECK,
General-in-Chief, U. S. Army.

HDQRS. DEPT. OF THE GULF, NINETEENTH ARMY CORPS,
Before Port Hudson, La., June 29, 1863.

GENERAL: Affairs here are progressing steadily to a favorable con-clusion. The battery erected on our extreme left, at about 300 yards of the citadel, breached the parapet of the citadel, drove the enemy out of a troublesome rifle-pit, and destroyed a gallery, which is believed to have been a part of a mine. Under cover of its fire, our approach on the extreme left has been pushed up to the citadel, and General Dwight makes an attempt to enter it to-night.

The sap on General Grover's front has been pushed to within 13 feet of the ditch in the re-entrant of the priest-cap. The sap-roller rolled into the ditch last night.

An *élite* storming party has been organized, made up of about 850 volunteers from the whole force, under the command of Col. H. W. Birge, Thirteenth Connecticut, who has been engaged some days in preparing the column for its work.

The number of deserters increases steadily. There have been 30 to-day. The beef-cattle of the garrison have all been killed, either for food or by our fire, and the salt meat has all been eaten. The men who deserted to-day after dinner have had no meat, and were told they would get no more, and that mule meat was to be issued hereafter.

I have seen a copy of the Port Hudson Herald of the 28th, containing the news of the arrival at that place of an officer from General Joe Johnston with dispatches. General Gardner publishes a general order, of date the 27th, assuring the garrison that General Johnston will soon relieve Vicksburg, and then send re-enforcements here, and declaring his purpose to defend the place to the last extremity.

On the 18th instant a force of the enemy (stated by some of our pris-oners who were released on parole to be one regiment of infantry, two of cavalry, and a battery of artillery, under the command of Col. James P. Major, formerly of our service) captured and burned the steamers Anglo American and Sykes at Plaquemine, taking 68 prisoners, of whom 5 were citizens. The prisoners consisted mainly of some convalescents belonging to the Twenty-eighth Maine.

The same force then passed down the river and Bayou La Fourche, and, avoiding Donaldsonville, struck the Opelousas Railway at Terre Bonne Station on the 20th instant, cutting off communication between Brashear City and New Orleans.

The same day they attacked and were repulsed by our forces at La Fourche Crossing, consisting of the One hundred and seventy-sixth New York and Twenty-third Connecticut, lacking two companies, which had been concentrated to meet the attack, under the command of Lieut. Col. Albert Stickney, Forty-seventh Massachusetts.

The attack was renewed on the afternoon of 'the 21st, and again re-pulsed in a manner very creditable to the troops engaged and to their commander. With less than 1,000 men, he drove back the greatly su-perior force of the enemy, who retired, leaving 53 of his dead on the field and 16 prisoners in our hands. Our loss was 8 killed and 16 wounded.

The Twenty-sixth Massachusetts and Ninth Connecticut were sent down from New Orleans in a special train that night, and the Fifteenth Maine, which had opportunely arrived from Pensacola, followed the next morning. No further attack was made.

The steamer Saint Mary's, sent round from New Orleans, with orders from General Emory to the troops at Brashear to hold out to the last, met at Southwest Pass the gunboat Hollyhock, returning from Berwick Bay, with the unpleasant news that the enemy, having crossed the lake on rafts in considerable force, succeeded, on the 22d instant, in surprising and capturing the small garrison of Brashear—although as fully warned of their danger as any orders could warn them—taking at the same time about 300 prisoners, two 30-pounder Parrott and six 24-pounder guns, a small train of cars, and everything else at the place.

Early yesterday morning Donaldsonville, garrisoned by but 225 men, including convalescents, under the command of Maj. J. D. Bullen, Twenty-eighth Maine, was attacked by a large force of the enemy, under the command of Brig. Gen. Thomas Green, of Texas.

The attack began at 1.30 a. m., and lasted till daylight. The defense was most gallant. The brave garrison defended their interior line with desperation, and finally repulsed the enemy with great slaughter, killing and wounding more than their own number, and taking prisoners twice as many officers and nearly as many men as they had.

The enemy retreated some 5 miles, and General Green sent in a flag, asking permission to bury his dead, singularly enough accompanied by an apology for his failure—that he was unfortunate in not getting his men into the skirmish, owing to the rashness of his commanders.

I sent down Brigadier General ——— last night with the First Louisiana Volunteers and two sections of Closson's battery, and General Emory sent up two companies from New Orleans.

The gunboats Winona, Princess Royal, and Monongahela rendered great assistance in the defense of Donaldsonville, and they have since been joined by the Genesee.

Our forces on the railway have fallen back upon Algiers. The forces of the enemy now occupying the La Fourche and operating upon our communications consist of all the troops in Western Louisiana, under Major-General Taylor, and about 5,000 cavalry, sent by Magruder from Texas. Their whole force is from 9,000 to 12,000. The fall of Port Hudson will enable us to settle that affair very speedily.

The dispositions of Brigadier-General Emory were well made and with the greatest promptitude, and our only misfortune at Brashear is due entirely to the carelessness and disobedience of subordinates.

In these operations but 400 soldiers could be left in New Orleans to protect the depots of this army and all our vital interests in a large city occupied by a population essentially hostile, and liable, from its position, to sudden attacks from several quarters.

The consequences that would have followed the movement of the enemy upon the La Fourche, had my command moved to Vicksburg, leaving Port Hudson and its garrison in my rear, are obvious—New Orleans would have fallen. A few more days must decide the fate of this place. I regard its fall as certain.

Our losses in the attack were as follows:

Officers and men.	Killed.	Wounded.	Missing.	Total.
May 27:				
Officers	15	90	2	107
Men	278	1,455	155	1,888
Total	293	1,545	157	1,995
June 14:				
Officers	21	72	6	99
Men	182	1,245	180	1,607
Total	203	1,401	188	1,805

The discrepancy between the totals consists of 13 killed and 84 wounded and missing; total 99 reported in one instance without distinguishing between officers and men. Many who were at first reported missing are now known to have been killed.

I have the honor to be, general, your most obedient servant,

N. P. BANKS,
Major-General, Commanding.

Maj. Gen. H. W. HALLECK,
General-in-Chief, Washington, D. C.

HDQRS. DEPT. OF THE GULF, NINETEENTH ARMY CORPS,
Before Port Hudson, La., July 6, 1863.

GENERAL: Since my dispatch of the 29th ultimo was written, the siege has been progressing rather slowly, indeed, but with all the rapidity attainable under the circumstances. Our approaches are pushed up to the ditch at the citadel on our extreme left, and in front of the right priest-cap, where the assault of the 14th was made.

On the morning of the 4th, when the right sap was within 10 feet of the ditch, the enemy sprung a small mine, and extended the approach into the ditch. Both on the right and left we are now engaged in pushing mines to blow up the parapet, and the enemy is clearly counter-mining. The column of stormers is fully organized and ready. A few days more must decide this operation, and, I have no doubt, in our favor.

By the arrival of Col. Kilby Smith yesterday, with dispatches from General Grant, I have news from the forces before Vicksburg to June 30. Affairs there are evidently in much the same condition as here. Colonel Smith was particularly struck with and remarked upon the coincidence. The most important piece of intelligence brought by the colonel is of the inactivity of Johnston's army, and of his apparent inability to raise the siege.

From the reports of General Emory, dated the 3d and 4th instant, copies of which and my replies I have the honor to inclose, you will see that the enemy has thrown more force into the La Fourche, and is actively engaged in annoying our communications and menacing New Orleans. I have urgently requested Admiral Farragut to patrol the river, so as to prevent the success of any attempt of the enemy to cross the river, either in force or by detachments, and partially, at least, to frustrate the attempt to cut off communication with the city. I inclose a copy of my note to the admiral.

As matters stand, the enemy will do us some harm in the La Fourche and cause us considerable annoyance on the river; but I consider it certain that Port Hudson will fall before New Orleans is seriously endangered, and that the close of this operation will enable us to make short work of the other; but I cannot refrain from reflecting what would have been the condition of affairs had this command, leaving the hostile garrison of Port Hudson in our rear, marched to Vicksburg, where General Grant has already, as he states, "a very large force—much more than can be used in the investment of the rebel works." When General Emory concentrated his little command at La Fourche Crossing, to repel the enemy's advance there, there were just 400 soldiers in and around New Orleans. I think General Emory overestimates the force in the La Fourche when he puts it at 13,000, and believe that the whole force of the enemy there consists of Taylor's army, of about 4,000 men, which we defeated on the Teche, and a re-enforcement of from 3,000 to 5,000 cavalry or mounted infantry from Texas. The infantry garrison of Port Hudson and the cavalry force which is hovering on our rear numbered, united, when we arrived here, at least 7,000. Against a combined attack of these forces on both sides of the river, New Orleans could not have been defended.

I shall request General Grant to send me at least —— thousand men as soon as he can possibly spare them, in order that we may secure what we shall so hardly have gained. I am confident, general, of a speedy and favorable result.

Very respectfully, your most obedient servant,

N. P. BANKS,
Major-General, Commanding.

Maj. Gen. H. W. HALLECK,
General-in-Chief, Washington, D. C.

[Inclosure No. 1.]

HEADQUARTERS DEPARTMENT OF THE TENNESSEE,
Near Vicksburg, Miss., June 30, 1863.

Maj. Gen. N. P. BANKS,
Commanding Department of the Gulf:

GENERAL: Feeling a great anxiety to learn the situation at Port Hudson, I send Col. Kilby Smith to communicate with you. Colonel Smith has been here during the entire siege of Vicksburg, and can inform you fully of the position of affairs at this place. I confidently expected that Vicksburg would have been in our possession before this, leaving me able to send you any force that might be required against Port Hudson. I have a very large force—much more than can be used in the investment of the rebel works—but Johnston still hovers east of Black River. Whether he will attack or not, I look upon now as doubtful. No doubt he would, however, if I should weaken my force to any extent. I have sent into Louisiana to learn the movements of Kirby Smith, but, as yet, hear nothing definite.

Should it be my good fortune, general, to get into Vicksburg while you are still investing Port Hudson, I will commence immediately shipping troops to you, and will send such number as you may indicate as being necessary. The troops of this command are in excellent health and spirits. There is not the slightest indication of despondency among either officers or men.

Hoping to hear favorable news from your field of operations by the return of Colonel Smith, I remain, very respectfully, your obedient servant,

U. S. GRANT,
Major-General.

[Inclosure No. 2.]

HEADQUARTERS DEFENSES OF NEW ORLEANS,
New Orleans, La., July 3, 1863.

Major-General BANKS,
Commanding Nineteenth Army Corps:

GENERAL: The time has come when I think it imperatively necessary that you send me re-enforcements. The enemy are in force at Des Allemands Bayou, on the Vacherie road, and at Whitehall Saw-mill. The Iberville has been fired into and disabled, and is now coming down in tow of the Sallie Robinson. I do not think you have one moment to lose in sending re-enforcements. Transports will have to be convoyed by gunboats. The enemy have sent a flag of truce from Des Alle-mands Bayou, saying they have 1,200 prisoners they wish to deliver. Where they came from I do not know. They have already sent in 50 by the way of the fort at Donaldsonville. These men have used such seditious language that the commanding officer at the United States barracks has been obliged to put them in confinement.

The navy is all above, except the Pensacola and Portsmouth, and the New London, which is about being completed and sent to Texas.

Just as I finished the above, the Zephyr, with my aide-de-camp, Lieutenant French, returning from Donaldsonville, where I was compelled to send re-enforcements, has also been fired into, receiving two solid shots.

As I before informed you, the attempt to raise a force here is a failure. The enemy's plan is to cut your communications, and then march on this city.

Very respectfully, your most obedient servant,
W. H. EMORY,
Brigadier-General, Commanding.

[Inclosure No. 3.]

HDQRS. DEPT. OF THE GULF, NINETEENTH ARMY CORPS,
Before Port Hudson, La., July 5, 1863.

Brig. Gen. W. H. EMORY, *Comdg. Defenses of New Orleans, La.:*

GENERAL: Your dispatch of July 3, I received by the hand of Captain Porter last evening at 5 o'clock. It is impossible for me to send to you re-enforcements in such numbers as to change the condition of affairs in New Orleans. I do not think, however, that the city is in peril. Some inconveniences and annoyances must necessarily ensue from the operations of the enemy while the bulk of our forces are engaged at this point. We shall, however, be released in a few days.

The navy must patrol the river, and prevent, as far as possible, the formation of any position which shall imperil our communication with the city; but it is not possible to prevent a chance shot being fired into our boats occasionally. This occurred constantly on the river while our troops were in New Orleans in force, and cannot be prevented, except by such operations as will result in expelling the enemy altogether from the country bordering upon the river. I am confident that this will be effected in a few days.

The prisoners referred to in your letter are doubtless the garrison and convalescents captured at Brashear City. This was a most discreditable affair to the officers in command. It would have been impossible, with any watchfulness whatever, for the enemy to have prepared his rafts and crossed the waters above that city without such notice as to have enabled them to escape. They had a railroad at their command and transports and gunboats on the water. The seditious language said to have been used by the prisoners I do not understand.

Affairs here are progressing favorably, but slowly, and in a few days will result in a successful issue. The behavior of Major Bullen and the troops under his command at Donaldsonville was most creditable, and has greatly encouraged the spirit of the army. It is a compensation for the disgrace that rests upon Brashear. I will communicate with you again to-morrow.

I have the honor to be, with much respect, your obedient servant,
N. P. BANKS,
Major-General, Commanding.

[Inclosure No. 4.]

HEADQUARTERS DEFENSES OF NEW ORLEANS,
New Orleans, La., July 4, 1863.

Major-General BANKS,
Commanding Nineteenth Army Corps:

GENERAL : The paroled prisoners have come in, and my information is as nearly positive as human testimony can make it that the enemy are 13,000 strong, and they are fortifying the whole country as they march from Brashear to this place, and are steadily advancing.

I respectfully suggest that, unless Port Hudson be already taken, you can only save this city by sending me re-enforcements immediately and at any cost. It is a choice between Port Hudson and New Orleans. The attempt to raise troops here is futile. There are at least 10,000 fighting men in this city (citizens), and I do not doubt, from what I see, that these men will, at the first approach of the enemy within view of the city, be against us to a man.

I have the honor to be, &c.,

W. H. EMORY,
Brigadier-General, Commanding.

[Inclosure No. 5.]

HDQRS. DEPT. OF THE GULF, NINETEENTH ARMY CORPS,
Before Port Hudson, La., July 5, 1863.

Brig. Gen. W. H. EMORY,
Commanding Defenses of New Orleans, La. :

GENERAL : The commanding general has this moment received your dispatch of the 4th instant, by the hands of First Lieutenant Woodrow, Seventeenth Infantry, acting aide-de-camp. The general directs me to say that operations here can last but two or three days longer at the outside, and then the whole command will be available to drive back the enemy, who is now annoying our communications and threatening New Orleans. We are to-day effecting the passage of the ditch in front of the right priest-cap. When this operation is decided, the commanding general will re-enforce you with the utmost promptitude, and with a large force; but he regards New Orleans as safe, if the navy does its duty in preventing the passage of the river. The general deems your force, though obviously too small, large enough to hold the works on the right bank of the river and to keep New Orleans quiet. Much, in his opinion, very much, will depend upon the management of affairs in the city quietly and with a firm hand.

The people of New Orleans understand, or ought to understand, well that their conduct upon this occasion will be the measure of their treatment hereafter by the military authorities of the United States.

Very respectfully, your obedient servant,

RICHARD B. IRWIN,
Assistant Adjutant-General.

[Inclosure No. 6.]

HDQRS. DEPT. OF THE GULF, NINETEENTH ARMY CORPS,
Before Port Hudson, La., July 5, 1863.

Rear-Admiral D. G. FARRAGUT,
Commanding, &c. :

Your letter of July 2 I received at 5 o'clock last evening. It had been delayed by some mischance upon its way hither. A subsequent letter, relating to the same subject, was received and has been answered.

The result at Donaldsonville was very gratifying, and I feel greatly indebted to the officers of the navy for the assistance they gave and the distinguished part they played in this most creditable affair.

General Emory writes me, July 3, that the rebels have fired upon our transports from a point some few miles below Donaldsonville. They have disabled the Iberville, which was towed back to New Orleans, and put some shots through one or two other vessels. I desire you, if possible, to patrol the river with the gunboats, so that our communication may be kept open for a few days longer. This is very important. General Emory is much alarmed for the safety of New Orleans, but I cannot think the city in any danger. It is impossible for me just now to send him the re-enforcements he requires, but, although their movements will occasion some inconvenience, I am quite satisfied that there is no imminent peril.

We have no news from Grant. Affairs in the north are becoming interesting.

We are progressing favorably, but not as rapidly as I could wish, with our movements here. Three or four days more will bring our affairs to a successful issue. I shall be delighted to see you again.

I have the honor to be, with much respect, your obedient servant,
N. P. BANKS,
Major-General, Commanding.

—

HDQRS. DEPT. OF THE GULF, NINETEENTH ARMY CORPS,
Before Port Hudson, La., July 8, 1863.

GENERAL: I have the honor to report that the garrison of Port Hudson surrendered this afternoon upon the terms stated in the accompanying copy of the articles of capitulation—terms which, you will perceive, are those of an unconditional surrender. We shall take formal possession at 7 o'clock to-morrow morning.

I inclose a copy of the correspondence preliminary to the surrender.

Very respectfully, your most obedient servant,
N. P. BANKS,
Major-General, Commanding.

Maj. Gen. H. W. HALLECK,
General-in-Chief, Washington, D. C.

[Inclosure No. 1.]

HEADQUARTERS,
Port Hudson, La., July 7, 1863.

Maj. Gen. N. P. BANKS,
Comdg. U. S. Forces, near Port Hudson, La.:

GENERAL: Having received information from your troops that Vicksburg has been surrendered, I make this communication to ask you, to give me the official assurance whether this is true or not; and, if true, I ask for a cessation of hostilities, with a view to consider terms for surrendering this position.

I remain, general, very respectfully, your obedient servant,
FRANK. GARDNER,
Major-General, Commanding C. S. Forces,

[Inclosure No. 2.]

HDQRS. DEPT. OF THE GULF, NINETEENTH ARMY CORPS,
Before Port Hudson, La., July 8, 1863—1.15 a. m.

Maj. Gen. FRANK. GARDNER,
Comdg. C. S. Forces, Port Hudson, La.:

GENERAL: In reply to your communication, dated the 7th instant, by flag of truce, received a few moments since, I have the honor to inform you that I received yesterday morning, July 7, at 10.45 o'clock, by the gunboat General Price, an official dispatch from Maj. Gen. Ulysses S. Grant, U. S. Army, whereof the following is a true extract:

HEADQUARTERS DEPARTMENT OF THE TENNESSEE,
Near Vicksburg, Miss., July 4, 1863.

Maj. Gen. N. P. BANKS, *Comdg. Department of the Gulf:*

GENERAL: The garrison of Vicksburg surrendered this morning. Number of prisoners, as given by the officers, is 27,000; field artillery, one hundred and twenty-eight pieces, and a large number of siege guns—probably not less than eighty.

I am, general, very respectfully, your obedient servant,

U. S. GRANT,
Major-General.

I regret to say that, under present circumstances, I cannot consistently with my duty consent to a cessation of hostilities for the purpose you indicate.

Very respectfully, your most obedient servant,

N. P. BANKS,
Major-General, Commanding.

[Inclosure No. 3.]

HEADQUARTERS, *Port Hudson, La., July* 8, 1863.

Maj. Gen. N. P. BANKS, *Comdg. U. S. Forces, near Port Hudson, La.:*

GENERAL: I have the honor to acknowledge the receipt of your communication of this date, giving a copy of an official communication from Maj. Gen. U. S. Grant, U. S. Army, announcing the surrender of the garrison of Vicksburg.

Having defended this position as long as I deem my duty requires, I am willing to surrender to you, and will appoint a commission of three officers to meet a similar commission appointed by yourself at 9 o'clock this morning, for the purpose of agreeing upon and drawing up the terms of surrender; and for that purpose I ask for a cessation of hostilities. Will you please designate a point outside of my breastworks where the meeting shall be held for this purpose?

I am, general, very respectfully, your obedient servant,

FRANK. GARDNER,
Major-General, Commanding C. S. Forces.

[Inclosure No. 4.]

HEADQUARTERS UNITED STATES FORCES,
Before Port Hudson, La., July 8, 1863—4.30 a. m.

Maj. Gen. FRANK. GARDNER, *Comdg. C. S. Forces, Port Hudson, La.:*

GENERAL: I have the honor to acknowledge the receipt of your communication of this date, stating that you are willing to surrender the garrison under your command to the forces under my command, and that you will appoint a commission of three officers to meet a similar commission appointed by me at 9 o'clock this morning, for the purpose of agreeing upon and drawing up the terms of the surrender.

In reply, I have the honor to state that I have designated Brig. Gen. Charles P. Stone, Col. Henry W. Birge, and Lieut. Col. Richard B. Irwin as the officers to meet the commission appointed by you. They will meet your officers at the hour designated, at a point near where the flag of truce was received this morning. I will direct that active hostilities shall entirely cease on my part until further notice, for the purpose stated.

Very respectfully, your most obedient servant,

N. P. BANKS,
Major-General, Commanding.

[Inclosure No. 5.]

Articles of capitulation proposed between the commissioners on the part of the garrison of Port Hudson, La., and the forces of the United States before said place, July 8, 1863.

ARTICLE I. Maj. Gen. F. Gardner surrenders to the United States forces under Major-General Banks the place of Port Hudson and its dependencies, with its garrison, armament, munitions, public funds, and material of war, in the condition, as nearly as may be, in which they were at the hour of cessation of hostilities, viz, ·6 a. m., July 8, 1863.

ART. II. The surrender stipulated in Article I is qualified by no condition, save that the officers and enlisted men composing the garrison shall receive the treatment due to prisoners of war, according to the usages of civilized warfare.

ART. III. All private property of officers and enlisted men shall be respected and left to their respective owners.

ART. IV. The position of Port Hudson shall be occupied to-morrow at 7 a. m. by the forces of the United States, and its garrison received as prisoners of war by such general officer of the United States service as may be designated by Major-General Banks, with the ordinary formalities of rendition. The Confederate troops will be drawn up in line, officers in their positions, the right of the line resting on the edge of the prairie south of the railroad depot, the left extending in the direction of the village of Port Hudson. The arms and colors will be piled conveniently, and will be received by the officers of the United States.

ART. V. The sick and wounded of the garrison will be cared for by the authorities of the United States, assisted, if desired by either party, by the medical officers of the garrison.

CHAS. P. STONE,
Brigadier-General.
W. R. MILES,
Colonel, Comdg. Right Wing of the Army, Port Hudson, La.
WM. DWIGHT,
Brigadier-General.
I. G. W. STEEDMAN,
Colonel, Commanding Left Wing.
HENRY W. BIRGE,
Colonel, Commanding Third Brigade, Grover's Division.
MARSHALL J. SMITH,
Lieutenant-Colonel, and Chief of Heavy Artillery.

Approved:

FRANK. GARDNER,
Major-General.
N. P. BANKS,
Major-General, Commanding.

HDQRS. DEPT. OF THE GULF, NINETEENTH ARMY CORPS,
Port Hudson, La., July 10, 1863.

SIR: I have the honor to inform you that with the post there fell into our hands over 5,500 prisoners, including 1 major-general and 1 brigadier-general, 20 pieces of heavy artillery, 5 complete batteries, numbering 31 pieces of field artillery, a good supply of projectiles for light and heavy guns, 44,000 pounds of cannon powder, 5,000 stand of small-arms, 150,000 rounds of small-arms ammunition, besides a small amount of stores of various kinds.

We captured also two steamers, one of which is very valuable, and will be of great service at this time.

Upon the surrender, I found it necessary to move at once every available man to Donaldsonville, to dislodge the enemy, who had temporarily obstructed our communication with New Orleans, and to drive his forces from the La Fourche district, where he was in considerable numbers. My transportation was wholly insufficient for its duty, and our supplies limited. I was also compelled to garrison this post for the present by the nine-months' regiments, most of which are of opinion that their term of service has already expired, and the colored regiments. It became thus very difficult to remove, to supply, or to guard my prisoners. I decided, therefore, after the post had surrendered unconditionally, to release the non-commissioned officers and privates upon their parole. These paroles will be taken with more than the usual formalities. The consolidated list will be signed by the men themselves, by Major-General Gardner, and by the officer who receives the parole, and each man will be furnished with a duplicate parole signed by himself, his regimental commander, and the paroling officer. The men will then march out and disperse to their several homes. The officers will be kept in confinement until further orders.

Trusting that my course in this matter will be approved by you and by the Department, I have the honor to be, general, very respectfully, your most obedient servant,

* N. P. BANKS,
Major-General, Commanding.

Maj. Gen. H. W. HALLECK,
General-in-Chief, Washington, D. C.

—

HEADQUARTERS DEPARTMENT OF THE GULF,
New Orleans, La., August 17, 1863.

SIR: I beg leave to inclose a copy of a dispatch, which I had the honor of addressing to you on the 10th ultimo, relative to the parole of the Confederate prisoners surrendered to me at Port Hudson.

In further explanation of the manner in which these men were paroled, I have also the honor to inclose a copy of the form used.* Each man signed in presence of his officers duplicate paroles in this form. Major-General Gardner approved in duplicate the rolls so signed for each regiment, company, and detachment. The United States provost-marshal signed them in duplicate as paroling officer. One copy of these consolidated paroles was retained by the paroling officer, and is now on file at these headquarters; one copy was delivered to Major-General Gardner, according to previous agreement entered into at his own request, in order that, to quote his own reason, he might forward them to

---

* Form omitted.

the War Department of the Confederate States. In addition to this, each man signed an individual parole, which was retained by himself, having the same caption as the consolidated rolls, varying only in the substitution of the singular for the plural.

These individual paroles were signed, first, by the prisoner; secondly, by the regimental or battery commander; thirdly, by the United States provost-marshal as paroling officer. They were made out and given to the prisoners at the request of Major-General Gardner, who assigned as a reason for this request that the men themselves were anxious to have them, in order, as he said, that the conscript officers might not pick them up and send them to duty.

These forms having been gone through with, the men were marched beyond our lines in organized bodies, under charge of their own non-commissioned officers, in pursuance of orders issued to them in circular form by Major-General Gardner, and were discharged from their imprisonment at points which had been mutually agreed upon between General Gardner and myself. From that time they were to be governed by the circular orders from General Gardner, above referred to, embracing in their provisions all the usual arrangements for subsistence and transportation.

It is important to observe in this connection that the commissioners appointed by Major-General Gardner to draw up the articles of capitulation urged so strongly the paroling of the garrison that our commissioners submitted the point to me for instructions. I directed them to decline entering into conditions, and to state to the enemy's commissioners that I would give my reply on that point after the surrender. This was done.

Immediately after the formal surrender, I informed General Gardner personally that I had concluded to agree to his proposition, and release his men on parole. It is certain that Major-General Gardner, the commander of the opposing army, considered that he was acting for and binding his Government according to the terms of the cartel.

I have the honor to be, general, very respectfully, your most obedient servant,

N. P. BANKS,
Major-General, Commanding.

Maj. Gen. H. W. HALLECK,
General-in-Chief, Washington, D. C.

ADDENDA.

GENERAL ORDERS, } HDQRS. DEPT. OF THE GULF, 19TH A. C.,
    No. 49.   }   *Before Port Hudson, June 15, 1863.*

The commanding general congratulates the troops before Port Hudson upon the steady advance made upon the enemy's works, and is confident of an immediate and triumphant issue of the contest. We are at all points upon the threshold of his fortifications. One more advance and they are ours!

For the last duty that victory imposes, the commanding general summons the bold men of the corps to the organization of a storming column of 1,000 men, to vindicate the flag of the Union and the memory of its defenders who have fallen! Let them come forward!

Officers who lead the column of victory in this last assault may be assured of the just recognition of their services by promotion, and every officer and soldier who shares its perils and its glory shall receive a medal fit to commemorate the first grand success of the campaign of 1863 for the freedom of the Mississippi. His name will be placed in general orders upon the Roll of Honor.

Division commanders will at once report the names of the officers and men who may volunteer for this service, in order that the organization of the column may be completed without delay.

By command of Major-General Banks:

RICH'D B. IRWIN,

Assistant Adjutant-General.

· *Officers and men who volunteered for storming party at Port Hudson, La., under General Orders, No. 49, Headquarters Department of the Gulf, June 15, 1863.*

STAFF.

Capt. Duncan S. Walker, assistant adjutant-general.
Lieut. Edmund H. Russell, Ninth Pennsylvania Reserves, acting signal officer.

TWELFTH CONNECTICUT.

Capt. Lester E. Braley, Co. G.
Lieut. A. Dwight McCall, Co. G.
Lieut. George A. Harmount (adjutant).
Private Charles J. Constantine, Co. A.
Sergt. John Mullen, Co. B.
Private Charles Duboise, Co. B.
Corporal John Moore, Co. C.
Private George T. Dickson, Co. C.
Private Willoughby Hull, Co. C.
Private William Putnam, Co. C.
Private Christopher Spies, Co. C.
Private George W. Watkins, Co. C.
Private John P. Woodward, Co. C.
Sergt. Alexander Cohn, Co. D.
Private George Kohler, Co. D.
Private Reuben Miles, Co. D.

Private Frederick C. Payne, Co. D.
Private William P. Smith, Co. E.
Sergt. Charles E. McGlaflin, Co. G.
Sergt. Andrew H. Davison, Co. G.
Corpl. John T. Gordon, Co. G.
Private Oliver C. Andrews, Co. G.
Private James Dunn, Co. G.
Private Patrick Fitzpatrick, Co. G.
Private Patrick Franey, Co. G.
Sergt. John W. Phelps, Co. H.
Corpl. Joseph W. Carter, Co. H.
Corpl. Charles E. Sherman, Co. H.
Private Edwin Converse, Co. H.
Private Warren Gammons, Co. H.
Private William Lenning, Co. H.
Private Melvin Nichols, Co. H.

THIRTEENTH CONNECTICUT.

Capt. Apollos Comstock (commanding regiment).
Capt. Charles D. Blinn, Co. C.
Capt. Homer B. Sprague, Co. H.
Capt. Dennison H. Finley, Co. G.
Capt. Charles J. Fuller, Co. D.
Lieut. Perry Averill, Co. B.
Lieut. Frank Wells, Co. I.
Lieut. Charles E. Tibbets, Co. A.
Lieut. William F. Norman, Co. K.
Lieut. Charles Daniels, Co. K.
Lieut. Charles H. Beaton, Co. E.
Lieut. John C. Kinney, Co. A.
Lieut. Louis Meisner, Co. I.
Lieut. Newton W. Perkins, Co. C.
Corpl. Francis J. Wolff, Co. A.
Corpl. Christopher Fagan, Co. A.
Corpl. Andrew Black, Co. A.
Private William Bishop, Co. A.
Private Walter Egan, Co A.
Private John Fagan, Co. A.
Private Francis J. Gaffuay, Co. A.
Private Edward Lantry, Co. A.
Private John Maguire, Co. A.
Private Henry Morton, Co. A.
Private Loren D. Penfield, Co. A.
Sergt. George E. Fancher, Co. B.

Sergt. George H. Pratt, Co. B.
Sergt. Alonzo Wheeler, Co. B.
Corpl. Francis E. Weed, Co. B.
Corpl. Roswell Taylor, Co. B.
Corpl. Isaac W. Bishop, Co. B.
Private George M. Balling, Co. B.
Private John J. Brown, Co. B.
Private William E. Casey, Co. B.
Private Balthazar Emmerich, Co. B.
Private Peter Gentien, Co. B.
Private Dennis Hegany, Co. B.
Private William W. Jones, Co. B.
Private John Klein, Co. B.
Private Benjamin L. Mead, Co. B.
Private John Mohren, Co. B.
Private Charles Nichols, Co. B.
Private Victor Pinsaid, Co. B.
Private George Prindle, Co. B.
Private Morant J. Robertson, Co. B.
Private Sidney B. Ruggles, Co. B.
Private Louis Schmeidt, Co. B.
Private Frederick L. Sturgis, Co. B.
Sergt. John N. Lyman, Co. C.
Sergt. John Maddox, Co. C.
Private Chauncey Griffin, Co. C.
Private Joseph H. Pratt, Co. C.
Private Mortimer H. Scott, Co. C.

Private Joseph Taylor, Co. C.
Private Daniel Thompson, Co. C.
Corpl. Edward Alton, Co. D.
Private John Dillon, Co. D.
Private John Fee, Co. D.
Private Jos. A. Gardner, Co. D.
Sergt. Nicholas Schue, Co. E.
Sergt. Richard Croley, Co. E.
Corpl. Robert C. Barry, Co. E.
Corpl. Leonard L. Dugal, Co. E.
Private Jacob Brown, Co. E.
Private Frederick Hanns, Co. E.
Private George W. Howland, Co. E.
Private Michael Murphy, Co. E.
Private Charles F. Oedekoven, Co. E.
Private F. F. F. Pfieffer, Co. E.
Private Andrew Reagan, Co. E.
Private Frederick Schuh, Co. E.
Private August Wilson, Co. E.
Private James Cosgrove, Co. F.
Private Patrick Leach, Co. F.
Private Henry E. Phinney, Co. F.
Sergt. Charles B. Hutchings, Co. G.
Sergt. John W. Bradley, Co. G.
Sergt. Francis Huxford, Co. G.
Corpl. Moses Gay, Co. G.
Corpl. Louis Feotish, Co. G.
Corpl. Edmund Bogue, Co. G.
Private Timothy Allen, Co. G.
Private George I. Austin, Co. G.
Private John Brand, Co. G.
Private Octave Ceressolle, Co. G.
Private Charles Culver, Co. G.
Private James Gay, Co. G.
Private Albert Hopkins, Co. G.
Private John Hunt, Co. G.
Private Henry A. Hurlburt, Co. G.
Private Asahel Ingraham, Co. G.
Private Jeremy T. Jordan, Co. G.
Private Michael Kearney, Co. G.
Private Joseph Kemple, Co. G.
Private William M. Maynard, Co. G.
Private John McKeon, Co. G.
Private Daniel Moore, Co. G.
Private Timothy O'Connell, Co. G.

Private Henry Robinson, Co. G.
Private Anton Schlosser, Co. G.
Private Martin J. Sbaden, Co. G.
Private Martin Sheer, Co. G.
Private Charles Sidders, Co. G.
Private John Snarman, Co. G.
Private Sebree W. Tinker, Co. G.
Sergt. William H. Huntley, Co. H.
Sergt. Dennis Doyle, Co. H.
Sergt. Herman W. Bailey, Co. H.
Private Philo Andrews, Co. H.
Private Niram Blackman, Co. H.
Private John Blake, Co. H.
Private Frank Patterson, Co. H.
Private George H. Twitchell, Co. H.
Sergt. Abner N. Sterry, Co. I.
Sergt. Samuel Taylor, Co. I.
Sergt. E. Sauter, Co. I.
Private Michael Burke, Co. I.
Private James Dillon, Co. I.
Private Thomas McGee, Co. I.
Sergt. Miles J. Beecher, Co. K.
Sergt. George A. Winslow, Co. K.
Sergt. Charles E. Humphrey, Co. K.
Corpl. Herman Saunders, Co. K.
Corpl. Herbert C. Baldwin, Co. K.
Corpl. John Nugent, Co. K.
Corpl. Robert Hollinger, Co. K.
Private John Bennett, Co. K.
Private Benjamin E. Benson, Co. K.
Private Frank C. Bristol, Co. K.
Private William Call, Co. K.
Private George Clancy, Co. K.
Private William J. Cojer, Co. K.
Private Thomas Duffy, Co. K.
Private Edward Ellison, Co. K.
Private Thomas Griffin, Co. K.
Private Patrick Mahoney, Co. K.
Private Thomas Morris, Co. K.
Private Richard O'Donnell, Co. K.
Private George C. Russell, Co. K.
Private Bernard Stanford, Co. K.
Private John Storey, Co. K.
Private Bartley Tiernon, Co. K.

TWENTY-FIFTH CONNECTICUT.

Lieut. Henry C. Ward (adjutant).
Lieut. Henry H. Goodell, Co. F.

Sergt. Maj. Charles F. Ulrich.
Private Samuel Schlesinger, Co. F.

FIRST LOUISIANA.

Capt. J. R. Parsons, Co. I.
Lieut. C. A. Tracy, Co. I.
Sergt. Michael H. Dunn, Co. I.
Sergt. James York, Co. I.
Sergt. George McGraw, Co. I.
Corpl. Henry Carle, Co. I.
Corpl. John Emperor, Co. I.
Corpl. Jos. A. Scovell, Co. I.
Corpl. John Lower, Co. I.
Private Charles Baker, Co. I.
Private Richard Balshaw, Co. I.
Private Patrick Brennan, Co. I.

Private Jos. Briggs, Co. I.
Private Leonard Demarquis, Co. I.
Private John Fahy, Co. I.
Private John Hunt Co. I.
Private Henry Kathra, Co. I.
Private Alex. Kiah, Co. I.
Private James Manahan, Co. I.
Private John Reas, Co. I.
Private Joseph Reaman, Co. I.
Private Jerry Rourke, Co. I.
Private James Smith, Co. I.

SECOND LOUISIANA.

Capt. William Smith, Co. H.
Private Lewis Diemert, Co. A.

Private Henry Mayo, Co. A.
Private Frederick A. Nurmon, Co. A.

Sergt. Albert Sadusky, Co. B.
Corpl. John Hoffman, Co. B.
Private James Clinton, Co. B.
Private Michael Dunn, Co. B.
Private Barney McClosky, Co. B.
Private William Rocher, Co. B.
Private James Sullivan, Co. B.
Sergt. Andrew Harrigon, Co. C.
Private James Donovan, Co. C.
Private John Fry, Co. C.
Private Daniel Theale, Co. C.
Private William Wilkie, Co. C.
Private Leon Paul, Co. D.
Private Joseph Dupuy, Co. F.
Private William Gallagher, Co. F.
Private George Tyler, Co. F.
Private Eugene Gallagher, Co. G.
Sergt. Theodore Lederick, Co. H.
Sergt. Benjamin C. Rollins, Co. H.

Corpl. Jacob Stall, Co. H.
Private John Brennan, Co. H.
Private Patrick Devine, Co. H.
Private John Eldridge, Co. H.
Private Patrick Garrity, Co. H.
Private Louis Harrell, Co. H.
Private John Hayes, Co. H.
Private Louis Icks, Co. H.
Private John Lane, Co. H.
Private Thomas R. Blakely, Co. I.
Private Louis L. Drey, Co. I.
Private James Mariner, Co. I.
Private Francis McGahay, Co. I.
Private Edwin Rice, Co. I.
Corpl. Otto Fouche, Co. K.
Private Henry Gordon, Co. K.
Private George Seymore, Co. K.
Private Paul E. Trosclair, Co. K.

FIRST LOUISIANA NATIVE GUARDS.*

Sergt. Joseph Frick, Co. C.
Sergt. Charles Dugué, Co. C.
Sergt. Ernest Legross, Co. C.
Corpl. Arthur Meyé, Co. C.
Private Camile Cazainier, Co. C.
Private Valcour Brown, Co. C.
Private Edmond Champanel, Co. C.
Private Eugene Degruy, Co. C.
Private Clement Galice, Co. C.
Private Louis Lacraie, Co. C.
Private Pierre Martiel, Co. C.
Private Joseph Moushaud, Co. C.
Private Armand Roche, Co. C.
Private Francois Severin, Co. C.
Private Henry Smith, Co. C.
Private J. Baptiste Smith, Co. C.
Private Martin White, Co. C.
Private Robert Lotsum, Co. G.
Private Joseph Lewis, Co. G.
Corpl. Jules Frits, Co. H.
Private Jacques Auguste, Co. H.
Private Henry Bradford, Co. H.
Private Joseph Carter, Co. H.
Private Isidore Charles, Co. H.
Private Emile Chatard, Co. H.
Private Frederick Derinsbourg, Co. H.
Private Francis Fernandez, Co. H.

Private Arthur Guyot, Co. H.
Private Samuel Hall, Co. H.
Private John Howard, Co. H.
Private Joseph Jackson, Co. H.
Private Richard John, Co. H.
Private Joe Joseph, Co. H.
Private Auguste Lee, Co. H.
Private Henry Lee, Co. H.
Private Oscar Pointoiseau, Co. H.
Private Joseph Patterson, sr., Co. H.
Private Joseph Patterson, jr., Co. H.
Private Perry Randolph, Co. H.
Private James Richards, Co. H.
Private Benjamin String, Co. H.
Private Ralemy Walse, Co. H.
Sergt. John J. Cage, Co. I.
Sergt. John W. Berweeks, Co. I
Corpl. Thomas Alexander, Co. I.
Private Charles Branson, Cq. I.
Private Alexander Jones, Co. I.
Private William McDowell, Co. I.
Private Collin Page, Co. I.
Private Thomas Redwood, Co. I.
Private William Wood, Co. I.
Private George Burke, Co. K.
Private Ed. Madison, Co. K.
Private Charles Smith, Co. K.

THIRD LOUISIANA NATIVE GUARDS.†

Private Abram Frost, Co. A.
Private Henry Marshel, Co. A.
Sergt. Wade Hambleton, Co. C.
Corpl. Massalla Lofra, Co. C.
Corpl. William Mack, Co. C.
Corpl. E. Thominick, Co. C.
Private Daniel Anderson, Co. C.
Private —— Bracton, Co. C.
Private William Dallis, Co. C.
Private Jack Dorson, Co. C.
Private William Finick, Co. C.

Private Solomon Fleming, Co. C.
Private William Green, Co. C.
Private George Joseph, Co. C.
Private Victor Lewis, Co. C.
Private —— Saunders, Co. C.
Private —— Taylor,‡ Co. C.
Private —— White,§ Co. C.
Sergt. Thomas Jefferson, Co. E.
Private W. Henry, Co. E.
Private Benjamin Johnson, Co. E.
Private Joseph Miller, Co. E.

* The whole regiment "expressed their willingness to go, but, supposing you did not want them all, I have selected from the volunteers named picked men who are ready any moment you may call upon them."—*Lieut. Col. C. J. Bassett to Col. J. A. Nelson, June 18, 1863, transmitting above list.*

† Capt. Charles W. Blake, commanding regiment, reported that the whole regiment expressed their willingness to go, but that those above named had been selected.

‡ Richard, or Hinson; both in Co. C.   § George, or Thomas; both in Co. C.

Private Thomas Simmons, Co. E.
Private J. W. Thomas, Co. E.
Private Edward Brown, Co. H.
Private Isaac Gillis, Co. H.
Private ―― Johnson, Co. H.
Private Silas Huff, Co. H.
Private Lewis Paulin, Co. H.
Private John Ross, Co. H.

Private J. Smith,* Co. H.
Private Silas Dicton, Co. I.
Private Loudon McDaniel, Co. I.
Private John Taller, Co. I.
Private Isaac Twiggs, Co. I.
Private George Washington, Co. I
Private ―― Williams,t Co. I.

TWELFTH MAINE.

Capt John F. Appleton, Co. H.
Lieut. Daniel M. Phillips, Co. H.
Lieut. Marcellus L. Stearns, Co. E.
Private John Cooper, Co. A.
Private Isaac R. Douglass, Co. A.
Private Almon L. Gilpatrick, Co. A.
Private John Weller, Co. A.
Sergt. Seymour A. Farrington, Co. E.

Corpl. Henry S. Berry, Co. E.
Private Edgar G. Adams, Co. E.
Private Oliver D. Jewett, Co. E.
Private Nathan W. Kendall, Co. E.
Private James Powers, Co. E.
Sergt. William M. Berry, Co. H.
Private James W. Smith, Co. I.

THIRTEENTH MAINE.

Lieut. Joseph B. Corson.

FOURTEENTH MAINE.

Lieut. Col. Charles S. Bickmore.
Maj. Albion K. Bolan.
Sergt. Maj. Charles W. Thing.
Capt. George Blodgett. Co. K.
Lieut. John K. Laing, Co. F.
Lieut. I. Frank Hobbs, Co. G.
Lieut. Warren T. Crowell, Co. K.
Lieut. Merrill H. Adams, Co. B.
Lieut. William H. Gardiner, Co. G.
Lieut. Charles E. Blackwell, Co. I.
Sergt. Jos. F. Clement, Co. A.
Sergt. George C. Hagerty, Co. A.
Corpl. William C. Townsend, Co. A.
Corpl. Otis G. Crockett, Co. A.
Corpl. Alva Emerson, Co. A.
Private Peter Beauman, Co. A.
Private Wilson Bowden, Co. A.
Private Richard J. Colby, Co. A.
Private Seth P. Colby, Co. A.
Private Peter Misher, Co. A.
Private Irvin Morse, Co. A.
Private Edwin Ordway, Co. A.
Private Albert Webster, Co. A.
Sergt. John Dougherty, Co. B.
Sergt. James Shehan, Co. B.
Private Benjamin Douglass, jr., Co. B.
Private James Elders, Co. B.
Private George N. Larrabee, Co. B.
Private John Dailey, Co. C.
Private Simon Beattie, Co. E.

Sergt. Jos. W. Grant, Co. F.
Corpl. William F. Jenkins, Co. F.
Private Edward Bethum, Co. F.
Private William E. Merryfield, Co. F.
Private Horace Sawyer, Co. F.
Sergt. Archelaus Fuller, Co. G.
Corpl. Edward Bradford, Co. G.
Private Samuel Conuelly, Co. G.
Private Ezra A. Merrill, Co. G.
Sergt. Calvin S. Gordon, Co. H.
Corpl. Louis C. Gordon, Co. H.
Private John Cunningham, Co. H.
Sergt. C. Pembroke Carter, Co. I.
Sergt. Samuel T. Logan Co. I.
Sergt. John S. Smith, Co. I.
Corpl. John Hayes, Co. I.
Private William R. Hawkins, Co. I.
Private Jos. Preble, Co. I.
Private Albert B. Meservey, Co. I.
Private Benjamin F. Roleson, Co. I.
Sergt. William Muller, Co. K.
Sergt. Alex. Wilson, Co. K.
Sergt. Bazel Hogue, Co. K.
Corpl. John Moore, Co. K.
Corpl. William Darby, Co. K.
Private Daniel Conners, Co. K.
Private George Waterhouse, Co. K.
Private Julius Wendlandt, Co. K.
Private Charles Wilkerson, Co. K.
Private Elliott Witham, Co. K.

TWENTY-FIRST MAINE.

Capt. James L. Hunt, Co. C.
Capt. Samuel W. Clarke, Co. H.
Private J. Mink, Co. A.
Private Otis Sprague, Co. A.
Private Sewell Sprague, Co. A.
Private Joel Richardson, Co. B.
Private Andrew P. Watson, Co. B.
Private John H. Brown, Co. C.
Private John E. Heath, Co. C.

Private Charles T. Lord, Co. C.
Private George F. Stacey, Co. C.
Private William N. Tibbetts, Co. C.
Corpl. Galen A. Chapman, Co. D.
Corpl. Alonzo L. Farrow, Co. D.
Private David O. Priest, Co. D.
Private Charles S. Crowell, Co. D.
Private David B. Cole, Co. E.
Private Melville Merrill, Co. E.

* Jacob, or James; both in company.
t David, Esau, Isaac, Samuel, Henry, or Johnson; all in Company I.

Private William Douglass, Co. F.
Private Gustavus Hiscock, Co. F.
Corpl. Minot D. Hewett, Co. G.
Private Leander Woodcock, Co. G.
Private Frederic Goud, Co. H.

Private Thomas Wyman, Co. H.
Private John B. Morrill, Co. I.
Private James S. Jewell, Co. K.
Private Frank S. Wade, Co. K.

TWENTY-SECOND MAINE.

Capt. Isaac W. Case, Co. H.
Capt. Henry L. Wood, Co. E.
Lieut. George E. Brown, Co. A.
Private Van Buren Carle, Co. B.

Private Daniel McPhetres, Co. B.
Sergt. Samuel S. Mason, Co. F.
Private Timothy N. Erwin, Co. G.
Private Amaziah W. Webb, Co. K.

TWENTY-FOURTH MAINE.

Sergt. George E. Taylor, Co. H.

Private James Hughes, Co. H.

TWENTY-EIGHTH MAINE.

Private James N. Morang, Co. E.

THIRD MASSACHUSETTS CAVALRY.

Col. Thomas E. Chickering.
Capt. Francis E. Boyd, Co. H.
Lieut. William T. Hodges, Co. C.
Lieut. Henry S. Adams (adjutant).
Lieut. David P. Muzzey, Co. G.
Lieut. Charles W. C. Rhoads, Co. H.
Sergt. Maj. William S. Stevens.
Private Ferdinand Rolle, Co. A.
Sergt. Nathan G. Smith, Co. C.
Sergt. Horace P. Flint, Co. C.
Private Joseph Elliott, Co. C.
Private Edward Johnson, Co. C.
Corpl. Patrick Dunlay, Co. G.
Private Simon Daly, Co. G.
Private Peter Donahue, Co. G.

Private James Gallagher, Co. G.
Sergt. William Wildman, Co. H.
Sergt. John Kelly, Co. H.
Corpl. William S. Caldwell, Co. H.
Corpl. Randall F. Hunuewell, Co. H.
Corpl. William P. Pethie, Co. H.
Corpl. Charles Miller, Co. H.
Corpl. William R. Davis, Co. H.
Private Edwin T. Ehrlacher, Co. H.
Private Gros Granadino, Co. H.
Private Eli Hawkins, Co. H.
Private Patrick J. Monks, Co. H.
Private John Veliscross, Co. H.
Private George Wilson, Co. H.

THIRTEENTH MASSACHUSETTS BATTERY.

Private Cesar Du Bois.

Private John V. Warner.

TWENTY-SIXTH MASSACHUSETTS.

Lieut. Seth Bonney, Co. F.

THIRTIETH MASSACHUSETTS.

Capt. Edward A. Fiske, Co. D.
Lieut. Thomas B. Johnston, Co. H.
Lieut. Nathaniel K. Reed, Co. C.
Lieut. Ferdinand C. Poree, Co. C.
Sergt. W. H. H. Richards, Co. B.
Corpl. George E. Coy, Co. B.
Corpl. Thomas Courtney, Co. B.
Private James M. Brown, Co. B.
Private Andrew Cole, Co. B.
Private George Towey, Co. B.
Private Martin Hassett, Co. B.
Sergt. Luther H. Marshall, Co. C.
Private William McCutcheon, Co. C.
Private Charles B. Richardson, Co. C.
Private George Sutherland, Co. C.
Sergt. George H. Moule, Co. D.
Sergt. John E. Ring, Co. D.

Corpl. Charles D. Moore, Co. D.
Private James Boyce, Co. D.
Private William Kenny, Co. D.
Private Horace F. Davis, Co. E.
Sergt. John Leary, Co. G.
Corpl. Michael Mealey, Co. F.
Sergt. John Leary, Co. G.
Sergt. Willard A. Hussey, Co. H.
Private John Battles, Co. H.
Private John Higgins, Co. H.
Private Paul Jesemaughn, Co. H.
Private William F. Cavanagh, Co. H.
Private John Welch, Co. H.
Private John Wilson, Co. H.
Sergt. Samuel, Ryan, Co. I.
Sergt. Thomas A. Warren, Co. F.

THIRTY-FIRST MASSACHUSETTS.

Capt. Edward P. Hollister, Co. A.
Capt. Samuel D. Hovey, Co. K.
Lieut. Luther C. Howell (adjutant).
Lieut. James M. Stewart, Co. A.
Private Chester Bevens, Co. A.
Private Patrick Carnes, Co. A.

Private Frank Fitch, Co. A.
Private William Thorington, Co. A. •
Private Peter Valun, Co. A.
Private Ethan H. Cowles, Co. B.
Private William J. Coleman, Co. K.
Private Maurice Lee, Co. K.

THIRTY-EIGHTH MASSACHUSETTS.

Lieut. Frank N. Scott, Co. B.

FORTY-EIGHTH MASSACHUSETTS.

Private Michael Roach, Co. G.

FORTY-NINTH MASSACHUSETTS.

Lieut. Edson T. Dresser, Co. F.
Private James W. Bassett, Co. A.
Private William E. Clark, Co. A.
Private Willard L. Watkins, Co. A.
Private George Dowley, Co. B.
Private Henry E. Griffin, Co. B.
Private Conrad Heins, Co. B.
Corpl. Thomas H. Hughes, Co. D.
Private Peter Come, Co. D.

Private Edwin N. Hubbard, Co. D.
Private Franklin Allen, Co. H.
Private George Knickerbocker, Co. H.
Corpl. John Kelley, Co. I.
Private Zera Barnum, Co I.
Private Philander B. Chadwick, Co. K.
Private Thomas Maloney, Co. K.
Private Albert F. Thompson, Co. K.

FIFTIETH MASSACHUSETTS.

Private James Miller, Co. B.

Corpl. E. S. Tubbs, Co. G.

FIFTY-THIRD MASSACHUSETTS.

Private Peter T. Downs, Co. G.

Private Peter Dyer, Co. H.

SIXTH MICHIGAN.

Private Robert Atwood, Co. A.
Private John R. Cowles, Co. A.
Private James E. Root, Co. A.
Sergt. Lester Fox, Co. C.
Sergt. Albert B. Chapman, Co. C.
Corpl. William A. Porter, Co. C.
Private Walter B. Hunter, Co. C.
Private Joseph W. Rolph, Co. C.
Corpl. Charles St. John, Co. D.
Private Peter Dorr, Co. D.
Private Tobias Porter, Co. D.
Sergt. Frederick Buck, Co. E.
Sergt. William L. Leinrie, Co. E.
Corpl. Harry S. Howard, Co. E.
Corpl. William Kelly, Co. E.
Corpl. Henry Rhodes, Co. E.
Private John Austin, Co. E.
Private Daniel Fero, Co. E.
Private William Hogue, Co. E.
Private James R. Johnson, Co. E.
Private Augustus Jones, Co. E.
Private William Rapsher, Co. E.

Private Jacob Urwiler, Co. E.
Private Alfred E. Day, Co. F.
Private George W. Sparling, Co. F.
Sergt. George H. Harris, Co. G.
Corpl. Peter A. Martin, Co. G.
Corpl Francis M. Hurd, Co. G.
Private George W. Dailey, Co. G.
Private Freeman Hadden, Co. G.
Private John W. McBride, Co. G.
Private Robert Payne, Co. G.
Private Charles E. Plummer, Co. G.
Private Enoch T. Simpson, Co. G.
Private Osborn Sweeney, Co. G.
Private Theodore Weed, Co. G.
Sergt. A. C. Whitcomb, Co. H.
Private Henry B. Dow, Co. H.
Private George A. Benet, Co. I.
Corpl. Levi. A. Logan, Co. K.
Corpl. John H. Wisner, Co. K.
Private Simon P. Boyce, Co. K.
Private David H. Servis, Co. K.
Private Francis E. Todd, Co. K.

EIGHTH NEW HAMPSHIRE.

Capt. Jos. J. Ladd, Co. D.
Lieut. Dana W. King, Co. A.

Private John Riney, Co. B.

SIXTEENTH NEW HAMPSHIRE.

Capt. John L. Rice, Co. H.
Lieut. Edgar E. Adams, Co. F.
Lieut. Edward J. O'Donnell, Co. C.
Corpl. Daniel C. Dacey, Co. A.
Private Edward J. Wiley, Co. B.

Corpl. Clinton Bohannon, Co. C.
Private Asa Burgess, Co. C.
Corpl. William A. Rand, Co. K.
Private Rufus L. Jones, Co. K.

SEVENTY-FIFTH NEW YORK.

Private Edson V. R. Blakeman, Co. B.
Private Levi Coppernoll, Co. B.

Private Lenox Kent, Co. B.
Private Martin Norton, Co. I.

NINETIETH NEW YORK.

Capt. Honore De La Paturelle, Co. E.
Sergt. Henry M. Crydenwise, Co. A.
Corpl. John Neill, Co. F.
Private Martin McNamara, Co. F.
Private John McCormick, Co. F.
Private James Proctor, Co. F.

Private George Wilson, Co. G.
Private Christopher Autenreith, Co. K.
Private John Heron, Co. K.
Private Amos Maker, Co. K.
Private Nelson Root, Co. K.

NINETY-FIRST NEW YORK.

Private Samuel Webster, Co. A.
Sergt. James A. Shattuck, Co. B.
Private James T. McCollum, Co. B.
Sergt. Edward R. Cone, Co. C.

Corpl. Platt F. Vincent, Co. C.
Private Edwin De Frate, Co. C.
Corpl. Charles E. Bowles, Co. E.
Private Jos. C. Wallace, Co. E.

ONE HUNDRED AND SIXTEENTH NEW YORK.

Corpl. Frank Bentley, Co. A.
Private Isaac Colvin, Co. A.
Private Andrew Cook, Co. A.
Private Daniel Covensparrow, Co. A.
Private Philip Linebits, Co. A.
Private Jacob Bergtold, Co. B.
Private Sylvester Glass, Co. B.
Corpl. George W Hammond, Co. C.
Private Henry D. Daniel, Co. C.
Private Charles Fisher, Co. C.
Private Frederick Hilderbrand, Co. C.
Private Christian Grawi, Co. D.
Private William W. McCumber, Co. D.
Private Cornelius Fitzpatrick, Co. E.
Private James Gallagher, Co. E.

Private Theodore Hansell, Co. E.
Private Thomas Maloney, Co. E.
Private Henry C. Miller, Co. E.
Private Frederick Webber, Co. E.
Corpl. Joshua D. Baker, Co. F.
Private Jacob Demerly, Co. F.
Private Frederick Jost, Co. G.
Private William Martin, Co. G.
Private Samuel Whitmore, Co. G.
Private Jacob Tschole, Co. H.
Private Jacob Zumstein, Co. H.
Private Philip Mary, Co. I.
Corpl. Albert D. Prescot, Co. K.
Private Nicholas Fedick, Co. K.

ONE HUNDRED AND TWENTY-EIGHTH NEW YORK.

Capt. Francis S. Keese, Co. C.
Sergt. Theo. W. Krafft, Co. C.
Sergt. Freeman Skinner, Co. A.
Corpl. Milo P. Moore, Co. A.
Private Jos. M. Downing, Co. A.
Private John N. Hague, Co. A.
Private James Mosherman, Co. A.
Private Jos. C. Mosher, Co. A.
Private Freeman Ostrander, Co. A.
Sergt. Charles W. McKown, Co. C.
Sergt. Henry A. Brundage, Co. C.
Sergt. John H. Hagar, Co. C.
Corpl. Clement R. Dean, Co. C.
Corpl. David H. Haunaburgh, Co. C.
Corpl. Elijah D. Morgan, Co. C.
Corpl. George F. Simmons, Co. C.

Private Albert Cole, Co. C.
Private George Cronk, Co. C.
Private Edward Delamater, Co. C.
Private Albert P. Felts, Co. C.
Private Charles Murch, Co. C.
Private Daniel Neenan, Co. C.
Private George A. Norcutt, Co. C.
Private John R. Schriver, Co. C.
Private John L. Delamater, Co. D.
Private William Platto, Co. D.
Private Charles P. Wilson, Co. D.
Corpl. Charles Brower, Co. F.
Private Charles F. Appleby, Co. I.
Private Stephen H. Moore, Co. I.
Corpl. Sylvester Brewer, Co. K.
Private Thomas Rice, Co. K.

ONE HUNDRED AND THIRTY-FIRST NEW YORK.

Lieut. Eugene H. Fales, Co. C.
Lieut. Eugene A. Hinchman, Co. H.
Lieut. James O'Connor, Co. F.
Lieut. Louis F. Ellis, Co. I.
Lieut. James E. McBeth, Co. K.
Private William Burris, Co. B.
Private Charles Cameron, Co. B.
Private Nicholas Hansler, Co. B.
Private George E. Stanford, Co. B.
Sergt. Robert W. Reid, Co. C.

Corpl. Jonas Cheshire, Co. C.
Corpl. Edward Northrup, Co. C.
Corpl. Isaac Ogden, Co. C.
Private Henry Ayres, Co. C.
Private Richard M. Edwards, Co. C.
Private Theodore Kelley, Co. C.
Private Charles W. Weeks, Co. C.
Private Jacob Hohn, Co. I.
Private Ferdinand Nesch, Co. I.

ONE HUNDRED AND THIRTY-THIRD NEW YORK.

Capt. James K. Fuller, Co. C.
Lieut. Richard W. Buttle, Co. D.
Lieut. Henry O'Connor, Co. I.
Private Nicolas Pitt, Co. B.
Private Nelson Beane, Co. C.
Private Patrick Boyne, Co. C.
Private Joseph Finn, Co. C.
Private Peter Hudson, Co. C.
Private James G. Kelly, Co. C.
Corpl. John Eisemann, Co. D.
Private Patrick Callanan, Co. E.
Private Cyrus Tooker, Co. F.

Sergt. George Giehl, Co. G.
Private Jos. J. Burke, Co. G.
Private George Schleifer, Co. G.
Private James Brennan, Co. I.
Private John H. Dawson, Co. I.
Private John H. Gale, Co. I.
Sergt. George Hamel, Co. K.
Corpl. William Stratton, Co. K.
Private Patrick Costello, Co. K.
Private Henry Hodinger, Co. K.
Private Philip Ready, Co. K.

ONE HUNDRED AND FIFTY-SIXTH NEW YORK.

Private Philip Lewis, Co. B.
Sergt. John D. Fink, Co. F.
Sergt. Charles B. Western, Co. K.
Sergt. Henry Abbott, Co. K.
Corpl. Ivan Netterberg, Co. K.
Corpl. Isaac W. Fullager, Co. K.

Private Charles Gay, Co. K.
Private August Leonhardt. Co. K.
Private Neil Neilson, Co. K.
Private Samuel Onderkirk, Co. K.
Private Charles Stump, Co. K.
Private Jos. von Matt, Co. K.

ONE HUNDRED AND FIFTY-NINTH NEW YORK.

Capt. Robert McD. Hart, Co. F.
Lieut. Alfred Greenleaf, jr., Co. B.
Lieut. Duncan Richmond, Co. H.
Private George W. Hatfield, Co. B.
Private Amos Hark, Co. B.
Private Hugh McKenny, Co. B.
Private John Taylor, Co. B.
Sergt. Michael Hogan, Co. C.

Private Christian Schnack, Co. C.
Sergt. James T. Perkins, Co. E.
Private John Thorp, Co. E.
Sergt. Gilbert S. Gullen, Co. F.
Private Bartholomew Toser, Co. F.
Private James Brazier, 2d, Co. I.
Private George W. Schofield, Co. I.

ONE HUNDRED AND SIXTIETH NEW YORK.

Lieut. Col. John B. Van Petten.
Asst. Surg. David H. Armstrong.
Lieut. William J. Van Deusen, Co. A.
Lieut. Robert R. Seeley, Co. I.
Private Oscar Curtis, Co. B.
Private A. C. Hammer, Co. C.
Private Jos. S. Insley, Co. C.
Private Henry F. McIntyre, Co. C.
Private George Matthies, Co. C.
Private John O'Lahey, Co. E.

Private Michael Hill, Co. E.
Private John Long, Co. E.
Sergt. B. F. Maxson, Co. G.
Sergt. Elon P. Spink, Co. G.
Sergt. Samuel Kriegelstein, Co. G.
Sergt. Jacob McDowell, Co. K.
Sergt. Michael Hewett, Co. K.
Private Arthur Clarkson, Co. K.
Private Lewis Kraher, Co. K.
Private John M. Raince, Co. K.

ONE HUNDRED AND SIXTY-FIRST NEW YORK.

Maj. Charles Strawn.
Lieut. William B. Kinsey (adjutant).
Capt. Benjamin T. Van Tuyl, Co. A.
Corpl. Clark Evans, Co. A.

Private William Jolley, Co. A.
Private Cornelius Osterhout, Co. A.
Private James Anderson, Co. B.
Sergt. Lewis E. Fitch, Co. C.

Corpl. Mahlon M. Murcur, Co. C.
Private Edgar L. De Witt, Co. C.
Private Henry W. Mead, Co. C.
Private George Oliver, Co. C.
Private Charles Spaulding, Co. C.
Sergt. Dennis Lacy, Co. D.
Sergt. Bradford Sanford, Co. D.
Private James E. Borden, Co. D.
Private Luman Philley, Co. D.
Private Thomas A. Sawyer, Co. D.

Private John Van Dousen, Co. D.
Private Madison M. Collier, Co. E.
Sergt. Baskin Freeman, Co. F.
Private Charles Robinson, Co. F.
Sergt. DeWitt C. Amey, Co. H.
Corpl. Samuel Robinson, Co. H.
Private John F. Young, Co. H.
Sergt. Silas E. Warren, Co. K.
Private Charles A. Herrick, Co. K.

ONE HUNDRED AND SIXTY-SECOND NEW YORK.

Capt. William P. Huxford, Co. G.
Lieut. John H. Van Wyck, Co. G.
Lieut. William Kennedy, Co. E.
Sergt. John McCormick, Co. A.
Private Thomas Barry, Co. A.
Sergt. John E. Burke, Co. B.
Sergt. Henry Landt, Co. C.
Sergt. Frederick Schellhaas, Co. C.
Private Anton Bleistein, Co. C.
Private William F. Eisele, Co. C.
Private John Engel, Co. C.
Private Alex. Herrman, Co. C.
Private Leo Kalt, Co. C.
Private Conrad Siegle, Co. C.
Sergt. Theodore Churchill, Co. D.
Corpl. Thomas McConnell, Co. D.
Sergt. James Stack, Co. E.
Sergt. George W. Keiley, Co. E.
Corpl. John McLaughlin, Co. E.
Corpl. George W. Waite, Co. E.
Corpl. James Ball, Co. E.
Private Thomas Clarey, Co. E.
Private Peter Corbett, Co. E.
Private Thomas Duff, Co. E.

Private Daniel W. Dunn, Co. E.
Private Patrick Ginety, Co. E.
Private Daniel Grey, Co. E.
Private Lawrence Halley, Co. E.
Private George Larmore, Co. E.
Private James McCall, Co. E.
Private Patrick Sweeny, Co. E.
Corpl. Gustave Normann, Co. F.
Private John G. Thalmann, Co. F.
Sergt. George W. Gibson, Co. G.
Sergt. Edmund Nourse, Co. G.
Private William Ferguson, Co. G.
Private William Keating, Co. G.
Corpl. Edward Murphy, Co. I.
Private Joseph Martines, Co. I.
Private Maxamillian Miller, Co. I.
Private James Brady, Co. K.
Private Peter Cherry, Co. K.
Private Eugene Deitrich, Co. K.
Private John Frazer, Co. K.
Private Jos. Gitey, Co. K.
Private Flemming Knipe, Co. K.
Private John McDonald, Co. K.
Private Lewis Young, Co. K.

ONE HUNDRED AND SIXTY-FIFTH NEW YORK.

Capt. Felix Agnus, Co. A.
Capt. Henry C. Inwood, Co. E.
Lieut. Gustavus F. Linguist, Co. C.
Sergt. Walter T. Hall, Co. A.
Sergt. William T. Sinclair, Co. A.
Sergt. John Fleming, Co. A.
Sergt. John W. Dickins, Co. A.
Corpl. Richard Baker, Co. A.
Corpl. Josiah C. Dixon, Co. A.
Corpl. George E. Armstrong, Co. A.
Private James E. Barker, Co. A.
Private Peter S. Beaucamp, Co. A.
Private Samuel Davis, Co. A.
Private Gustav Druckhammer, Co. A.
Private David Lewis, Co. A.
Private George McKinney, Co. A.

Private George A. Metzel, Co. A.
Private Elias H. Tucker, Co. A.
Private John H. Valk, Co. A.
Private Edward Vass, Co. A.
Private Patrick H. Matthews, Co. B.
Private John Cassidy, Co. C.
Private Robert Hobbey, Co. C.
Private Laurentz Lange, Co. C.
Private John Laughtman, Co. C.
Corpl. James F. Campbell, Co. D.
Private Thomas Belcher, Co. E.
Private John Feighery, Co. E.
Private Stephen Gillen, Co. E.
Private Edwin A. Shaw, Co. E.
Private William Vero, Co. E.

ONE HUNDRED AND SEVENTY-THIRD NEW YORK.

Private Alex. Hendrickson, Co. C.

ONE HUNDRED AND SEVENTY-FOURTH NEW YORK.

Lieut. Edward Marrener, Co. I.
Lieut. Latham A. Fish, Co. E.
Lieut. Eugene S. Ennson, Co. C.
Lieut. Charles Emerson, Co. I.

Sergt. Morris Lancaster, Co. A.
Corpl. Louis Hageman, Co. A.
Private William Cooper, Co. A.
Private John Cullen, Co. A.

Private John Maloney, Co. A.
Corpl. George Anderson, Co. B.
Sergt. John Gray, Co. C.
Private John G. Kuhfuss, Co. C.
Private Ernst Schmidt, Co. C.
Sergt. John Kenney, Co. E.
Corpl. Joseph H. Murphy, Co. E.
Private Thomas Williams, Co. E.
Private Thomas Fletcher, Co. G.
Private Henry D. Lasher, Co. G.
Private Charles N. Thompson, Co. G.
Sergt. Charles Gardner, Co. H.
Private Thomas Carroll, Co. H.

Private William Johnson, Co. H.
Private Henry Jones, Co. H.
Private Cornelius Mohoney, Co. H.
Private Joseph Messmer, Co. I.
Private Henry Pooler, Co. I.
Private Richard Schottler, Co. I.
Sergt. Charles Draner, Co. K.
Private Frederick Bandka, Co. K.
Private William Heinrichs, Co. K.
Private Edward Kuhlmann, Co. K.
Private Julius Ladiges, Co. K.
Private Frederick Nilsen, Co. K.

ONE HUNDRED AND SEVENTY-FIFTH NEW YORK.

Lieut. Seigmund Sternberg, Co. I.
Sergt. Maj. Abraham Loeb.
Private Frank Markham, Co. A.
Corpl. Timothy Allen, Co. B
Private Otto Dornback, Co. C.
Private Richard O'Gorman, Co. C.

Private Patrick Mannering, Co. D.
Sergt. William O'Callaghan, Co. E.
Sergt. James Hillis, Co. E.
Private John O'Conner, Co. E.
Corpl. Philip Daub, Co. K.

ONE HUNDRED AND SEVENTY-SEVENTH NEW YORK.

Sergt. John D. Brooks, Co. A.
Corpl. Percy B. S. Col' f.o. A.
Private Seymour D. Carpenter, Co. A.
Private John J. Gallup, Co. A.
Private Thomas J. Garvey.
Private William Hemstreet, Co. A.
Private John Housen, Co. A.
Private Barney Lavary, Co. A.
Private Richard C. Main, Co. A.
Private Adam Milliman, Co. A.
Private Henry von Lehman, Co. A.
Corpl. George A. McCormick, Co. B.
Private Eben Halley, Co. B.

Private David N. Kirk, Co. B.
Private Charles M. Smith, Co. B.
Private Samuel H. Stevens, jr., Co. B.
Private John Gorman, Co. C.
Private Moses De Coster, Co. D.
Private Charles W. Lape, Co. E.
Corpl. Alonzo G. Ludden, Co. G.
Private S. W. Meisden, Co. G.
Private Elias Nashold, Co. G.
Private Jeddiah Tompkins, Co. G.
Private Russell W. Cooneys, Co. H.
Private George Merinus, Co. I.

EIGHTH VERMONT.

Sergt. Byron J. Hurlburt, Co. F.
Corpl. Edward Saltus, Co. F.
Private George N. Fanenf, Co. F.
Private David Larock, jr., Co. F.
Private Abner Niles, Co. F.

Corpl. Abner N. Flint, Co. G.
Private Seymour N. Coles, Co. G.
Private Lyman P. Luce, Co. G.
Private Andrew B. Morgan, Co. H.
Private Patrick Bolan, Co. I.

FOURTH WISCONSIN.

Private Patrick Pigeon, Co. A.

—

I. PUBLIC RESOLUTION No. 7.

RESOLUTION expressive of the thanks of Congress to Maj. Gen. Nathaniel P. Banks, and the officers and soldiers under his command at Port Hudson.

Resolved by the Senate and House of Representatives of the United States of America, in Congress assembled, That the thanks of Congress are hereby tendered to Maj. Gen. Nathaniel P. Banks, and the officers and soldiers under his command, for the skill, courage, and endurance which compelled the surrender of Port Hudson, and thus removed the last obstruction to the free navigation of the Mississippi River.
Approved January 28, 1864.

No. 2.

Returns of Casualties in the Union forces.

[Compiled from nominal lists, returns, &c.]

AT PLAINS STORE, LA., MAY 21, 1863.

Command.	Killed.		Wounded.		Captured or missing.		Aggregate.
	Officers.	Enlisted men.	Officers.	Enlisted men.	Officers.	Enlisted men.	
2d Louisiana		2		11		1	14
30th Massachusetts			1	3			4
48th Massachusetts		2		7		11	20
49th Massachusetts			1	4		1	6
116th New York*		11	1	43		1	56
Total		15	3	68		14	100

AT PORT HUDSON, LA., MAY 23-JULY 8, 1863.

NINETEENTH ARMY CORPS.

Maj. Gen. NATHANIEL P. BANKS.

FIRST DIVISION.

Maj. Gen. CHRISTOPHER C. AUGUR.

First Brigade.

(1) Col. EDWARD P. CHAPIN.†
(2) Col. CHARLES J. PAINE.

Command.	Killed.		Wounded.		Captured or missing.		Aggregate.
	Officers.	Enlisted men.	Officers.	Enlisted men.	Officers.	Enlisted men.	
2d Louisiana		32	5	103		4	144
21st Maine	1	14	3	60	1	9	88
48th Massachusetts	1	8	7	46			62
49th Massachusetts	1	17	10	73		1	102
116th New York	2	18	4	101		5	130
Total First Brigade	5	89	29	383	1	19	526

Second Brigade.

Brig. Gen. GODFREY WEITZEL.‡

Command.	Killed.		Wounded.		Captured or missing.		Aggregate.
	Officers.	Enlisted men.	Officers.	Enlisted men.	Officers.	Enlisted men.	
Staff	1						1
12th Connecticut		18	5	78			101
75th New York		10	4	88	1	4	107
114th New York	1	10	4	56		2	73
160th New York		2	4	35			41
8th Vermont	1	24	4	128		9	166
Total Second Brigade	3	64	21	385	1	15	489

Third Brigade.

Col. NATHAN A. M. DUDLEY.

Command.	Killed.		Wounded.		Captured or missing.		Aggregate.
	Officers.	Enlisted men.	Officers.	Enlisted men.	Officers.	Enlisted men.	
30th Massachusetts			1	18			19
50th Massachusetts			1	4			5
161st New York		3		14			17
174th New York		2		9		3	14
Total Third Brigade		5	2	45		3	55

* Lieut. Charles Borusky, One hundred and sixteenth New York, died of wounds received in this action.

† Killed May 27.

‡ Weitzel also appears as commanding the right wing, the Fourth Division, and as general of the trenches, &c., and Col. Stephen Thomas is reported on same records as commanding the brigade.

AT PORT HUDSON, LA., MAY 23–JULY 8, 1863—Continued.

Command.	Killed.		Wounded.		Captured or missing.		Aggregate.
	Officers.	Enlisted men.	Officers.	Enlisted men.	Officers.	Enlisted men.	
Artillery.							
1st Indiana Heavy		4	1	10		7	22
1st Maine Battery		1		19			20
6th Massachusetts Battery				1			1
18th New York Battery				3			3
1st United States, Battery A		3	1	12		3	19
5th United States, Battery G		2		2			4
Total artillery		10	2	47		10	69
Unattached.							
1st Louisiana Engineers, Corps d'Afrique	1	7		26		19	53
1st Louisiana Native Guards	2	32	3	92			129
3d Louisiana Native Guards	1	9	1	37	1	2	51
1st Louisiana Cavalry		5		6		19	30
2d Rhode Island Cavalry			1	5		2	8
Total unattached	4	53	5	166	1	42	271
Total First Division	12	221	59	1,026	3	89	1,410
SECOND DIVISION.							
Brig. Gen. THOMAS W. SHERMAN.*							
Staff				2			2
First Brigade.							
(1) Brig. Gen. NEAL DOW.†							
(2) Col. DAVID S. COWLES.‡							
(3) Col. THOMAS S. CLARK.							
Staff			1				1
26th Connecticut	1	14	9	151		1	176
6th Michigan	1	19	5	124			149
15th New Hampshire		17	3	55		2	77
128th New York	2	21	3	97	1	5	129
162d New York	1	5	3	47		3	59
Total First Brigade	5	76	24	474	1	11	591
Third Brigade.							
Brig. Gen. FRANK S. NICKERSON.							
14th Maine		5	5	23			33
24th Maine				13			13
28th Maine		3	1	8			12
165th New York	1	15	7	80		3	106
175th New York	1	5	5	38		2	51
177th New York	1	3	2	17			23
Total Third Brigade	3	31	20	179		5	238
Artillery.							
1st Vermont Battery		1		6			7
Total Second Division	8	108	46	659	1	16	838

* Wounded May 27, and was succeeded by Brig. Gen. George L. Andrews, chief of staff. Brig. Gen. Frank S. Nickerson assumed command May 28, and Brig. Gen, William Dwight May 30,
† Wounded May 27,
‡ Killed May 27,

AT PORT HUDSON, LA., MAY 23–JULY 8, 1863—Continued.

Command.	Killed.		Wounded.		Captured or missing.		Aggregate.
	Officers.	Enlisted men.	Officers.	Enlisted men.	Officers.	Enlisted men.	
THIRD DIVISION.							
(1) Brig. Gen. HALBERT E. PAINE.*							
(2) Col. HAWKES FEARING, Jr.							
Staff	......	......	1	......	......	......	1
First Brigade.							
(1) Col. TIMOTHY INGRAHAM.							
(2) Col. SAMUEL P. FERRIS.							
28th Connecticut	2	5	1	43	1	10	62
4th Massachusetts	1	7	3	57	......	......	68
110th New York	1	4	2	21	......	9	37
Total First Brigade	4	16	6	121	1	19	167
Second Brigade.							
(1) Col. HAWKES FEARING, Jr.							
(2) Maj. JOHN H. ALLCOT.							
8th New Hampshire	4	26	7	191	2	28	258
133d New York	1	22	5	85	......	2	115
173d New York	2	11	6	72	......	1	92
4th Wisconsin†	3	46	9	108	1	52	219
Total Second Brigade	10	105	27	456	3	83	684
Third Brigade.							
Col. OLIVER P. GOODING.							
31st Massachusetts	......	13	2	47	......	......	62
38th Massachusetts	2	13	5	85	......	3	108
53d Massachusetts	2	15	7	92	......	5	121
156th New York	......	3	2	25	......	......	30
Total Third Brigade	4	44	16	249	......	8	321
Artillery.							
4th Massachusetts Battery...............	......	......	......	2	......	......	2
1st United States, Battery F	......	1	......	......	......	2	3
2d Vermont Battery	......	......	......	2	......	......	2
Total artillery.............	......	1	......	4	......	2	7
Total Third Division	18	166	50	830	4	112	1,180
FOURTH DIVISION.							
Brig. Gen. CUVIER GROVER.							
First Brigade.							
Col. JOSEPH S. MORGAN.							
1st Louisiana	1	30	3	86	......	3	123
22d Maine	......	4	2	17	1	5	29
90th New York.........................	......	7	1	42	......	......	50
91st New York	2	19	8	112	......	8	149
131st New York	1	20	2	86	2	8	119
Total First Brigade	4	80	16	343	3	24	470

* Wounded June 14.
† Includes losses at Clinton, June 3.

AT PORT HUDSON, LA., MAY 23–JULY 8, 1863—Continued.

Command.	Killed.		Wounded.		Captured or missing.		Aggregate.
	Officers.	Enlisted men.	Officers.	Enlisted men.	Officers.	Enlisted men.	
Second Brigade.							
Col. WILLIAM K. KIMBALL.							
24th Connecticut		14	6	46			66
12th Maine		10	2	57		1	70
52d Massachusetts		8	2	12		2	24
Total Second Brigade		32	10	115		3	160
Third Brigade.							
Col. HENRY W. BIRGE.							
13th Connecticut	1	6	3	20		1	31
25th Connecticut		5	4	35		2	46
26th Maine		5	1	11		5	22
159th New York		17	1	53		2	73
Total Third Brigade	1	33	9	119		10	172
Artillery.							
2d Massachusetts Battery				2		3	5
1st United States, Battery L				2			2
2d United States, Battery C				1			1
Total artillery				5		3	8
Total Fourth Division	5	145	35	582	3	40	810
CAVALRY.							
Col. BENJAMIN H. GRIERSON.							
6th Illinois		1		6	1	5	13
7th Illinois				4			4
1st Louisiana		5		16		19	40
3d Massachusetts	1	1		5		2	9
14th New York		2		6		20	28
Total cavalry *	1	9		37	1	46	94
CORPS D'AFRIQUE.							
6th Infantry		1		1			2
7th Infantry		2		3			5
8th Infantry		5	1	5		1	12
9th Infantry		2					2
10th Infantry	1	4		2		3	10
Total Corps d'Afrique	1	14	1	11		4	31
Total Nineteenth Army Corps	45	663	191	3,145	12	307	4,363

OFFICERS KILLED.

CONNECTICUT.

Lieut. Joseph Strickland, 13th Infantry.   Capt. David D. Hoag, 28th Infantry.
Capt. John L. Stanton, 26th Infantry.   Lieut. Charles Durand, 28th Infantry.

LOUISIANA.

Col. Richard E. Holcomb, 1st Infantry.   Lieut. John H. Crowder, 1st Native
Lieut. J. B. Butler, 1st Engineers, Corps   Guards.
d'Afrique.   Maj. Adam Haffkille, 3d Native Guards.
Capt. Andrew Cailloux, 1st Native Guards.

* These losses occurred mainly at Clinton, June 3 and 4.

MAINE.

Lieut. Aaron W. Wallace, 21st Infantry.

MASSACHUSETTS.

Lieut. Solon A. Perkins, 3d Cavalry (at Clinton, La.).
Capt. William H. Bartlett, 4th Infantry.
Lieut. Col. William L. Rodman, 38th Infantry.
Lieut. Frederick Holmes, 38th Infantry.

Lieut. Col. James O'Brien, 48th Infantry.
Lieut. Col. Burton D. Deming, 49th Infantry.
Capt. George H. Bailey, 53d Infantry.
Lieut. Alfred R. Glover, 53d Infantry.

MICHIGAN.

Lieut. Frederick J. Clark, 6th Infantry.

NEW HAMPSHIRE.

Lieut. Col. Oliver W. Lull, 8th Infantry.
Lieut. George W. Thompson, 8th Infantry.

Lieut. Luther T. Hosley, 8th Infantry.
Lieut. Joseph Wallis, 8th Infantry.

NEW YORK.

Capt. Henry S. Hulbert, 91st Infantry.
Lieut. Sylvester B. Shepard, 91st Infantry.
Lieut. Valorus Randall, 110th Infantry.
Capt. Charles E. Tucker, 114th Infantry.
Col. Edward P. Chapin, 116th Infantry.
Lieut. Timothy J. Linahan, 116th Infantry.
Col. David S. Cowles, 128th Infantry.
Lieut. Charles L. Van Slyck, 128th Infantry.
Lieut. Nathan O. Benjamin, 131st Infantry.

Lieut. Benjamin F. Denton, 133d Infantry.
Maj. James H. Bogart, 162d Infantry.
Lieut. Charles R. Carville, 165th Infantry.
Capt. Henry Cochen, 173d Infantry.
Lieut. Morgan Shea, 173d Infantry.
Col. Michael K. Bryan, 175th Infantry.
Lieut. James Williamson, 177th Infantry.

VERMONT.

Lieut. Stephen F. Spalding, 8th Infantry.

WISCONSIN.

Col. Sidney A. Bean, 4th Infantry.
Lieut. Edward A. Clapp, 4th Infantry.

Lieut. Gustavus Wintermeyer, 4th Infantry.

UNITED STATES VOLUNTEERS.

Capt. John B. Hubbard, assistant adjutant-general.

Lieut. Benjamin Wadsworth, 10th Infantry, Corps d'Afrique.

OFFICERS MORTALLY WOUNDED.

CONNECTICUT.

Capt. Jedediah Randall, 26th Infantry.
Lieut. Martin R. Kenyon, 26th Infantry.

Lieut. Harvey F. Jacobs, 26th Infantry.

LOUISIANA.

Lieut. Martin V. B. Hill, 1st Infantry.
Lieut. Joseph N. Moulton, 2d Infantry.

Lieut. James E. Coburn, 2d Infantry.

MAINE.

Lieut. John C. Fulton, 14th Infantry.
Lieut. Charles L. Stevens, 14th Infantry.

Capt. Henry Crosby, 22d Infantry.

MASSACHUSETTS.

Lieut. James McGinniss, 48th Infantry.
Lieut. Isaac E. Judd, 49th Infantry.
Capt. George S. Bliss, 52d Infantry.

Capt. Jerome K. Taft, 53d Infantry.
Lieut. Josiah H. Vose, 53d Infantry.

NEW YORK.

Maj. George W. Stackhouse, 91st Infantry.
Col. Elisha B. Smith, 114th Infantry.
Lieut. David Jones, 116th Infantry.
Lieut. Col. Thomas Fowler, 156th Infantry.
Lieut. Stephen C. Oakley, 162d Infantry.
Lieut. John Neville, 162d Infantry.
Lieut. Col. Abel Smith, jr., 165th Infantry.
Maj. A. Power Gallway, 173d Infantry.
Lieut. Samuel H. Podger, 173d Infantry.
Capt. Harmon N. Merriman, 177th Infantry.

WISCONSIN.

Capt. Levi R. Blake, 4th Infantry.
Lieut. Daniel B. Maxson, 4th Infantry (at Clinton, La.).

No. 3.

Report of Lieut. Col. Richard B. Irwin, Assistant Adjutant-General, U. S. Army, of affair at Springfield Landing.

HEADQUARTERS DEPARTMENT OF THE GULF,
Before Port Hudson, July 3, 1863.

SIR: I have the honor to report that, in compliance with instructions, I visited Springfield Landing early this morning for the purpose of making an investigation of the circumstances attending the affair at that place of yesterday morning. I inclose a sketch,* rude but pretty accurate, of the locality. As the result of my inquiries, I respectfully report that, as nearly as can be ascertained, the enemy's cavalry, in some force, having surprised the picket of the One hundred and sixty-second New York, stationed on the old Springfield Landing road, made a dash at the Landing by that road, at half past 8 or 9 o'clock yesterday morning; that he approached to within 150 yards of the road and to within about 30 yards of the negroes before any alarm was given; that from that distance he charged upon the squad of 30 armed negroes who were guarding some quartermaster's stores belonging to Ullmann's brigade; that these colored troops, being thus taken completely by surprise, and being in their tents, rushed to the adjoining woods; that the enemy, setting fire, by means of turpentine, to the quartermaster's stores, divided into at least three parties, sending, first, 50 men straight down the road to the Landing; second, another force of about 50 men among the negro huts in the rear of the young cottonwood grove on the right of the road; and third, a force, said to be about 100 men, up the road toward the hill.

The first detachment dashed down the road toward the river, turned sharp to the right, along the trail which keeps the edge of the young cottonwood, and made toward the ordnance depot, the quartermaster's office, provost-marshal's office, and sutler's shop. The officers and employés in that neighborhood rushed on board the Suffolk, which put out into the stream, and steamed up to the head of Profit's Island. The provost-guard, consisting of 32 men, commanded by Capt. A. J. Hersey, Sixteenth New Hampshire, made fight from behind the levee, and drove the enemy off, killing 3, including a captain, and wounding 5 of their number. Captain Hersey's loss was 3 wounded, 3 prisoners, and 1 missing. The second force did no harm beyond terrifying the negroes. It was joined by the first detachment passing through the young cottonwood grove by the trail in rear of the provost-marshal's

---

* Not found.

office. The post commissary, Lieutenant Darling, hastily arranging a few boxes and barrels in form of a breastwork, and rallying some men, opened fire upon the enemy's rear and flank. By this time the One hundred and sixty-second New York, Lieut. Col. J. W. Blanchard commanding, had got under arms, and moved at double-quick through the trail from the commissary stores to the elbow of the levee. On arriving at the levee, the two detachments of the enemy above named, united as described, being at X [on sketch], the regiment was rapidly thrown forward into line, and opened fire upon them. They immediately retreated in some confusion toward old Springfield Landing. Lieutenant-Colonel Blanchard followed them as far as the point of woods, and then, replacing his captured picket, returned, and formed line behind the levee, his left resting on the road, and thus remained until evening. In this affair we lost 1 severely and 1 slightly wounded.

The third detachment went up the road to the hill, and took prisoners (afterward paroling) 4 of the picket at that place watching the approach from above. Two others of that picket are missing, and the remaining 9 escaped and came safely into camp. Where this detachment met the Second Rhode Island Cavalry, and what happened then, I cannot yet learn. By 11 o'clock all was quiet. Our losses were, in all, 5 wounded, 12 prisoners, and 3 missing, and a full supply of clothing, camp and garrison equipage for nearly 1,000 men burned. A negro is supposed to have been drowned. Two plantation wagons were broken, and a number of mules got loose in the stampede of teamsters. Colonel Blanchard furnished the following pickets: 5 men by day and 15 at night, under an officer, near the old house on the old Springfield Landing road; 15 men on top of the hill by day, 25 at night, watching the approach from above; 3 mounted men at night at old Springfield Landing.

I attribute the surprise entirely to the negligence of the picket in allowing itself to be taken without a shot by an enemy who could not approach within 100 yards without being in sight. The pickets were, in my opinion, well posted. With any show of fidelity on their part, the surprise must have failed. The regimental commander visited them at 11 p. m. and 4 a. m. the night before, and says they were attentive; certainly I found them so to-day. I directed Lieutenant-Colonel Blanchard to post a picket of 5 men near the old house, and a reserve of 10 men about 100 yards this side, at a slight bend in the road, and to connect them by two vedettes as well as by patrols. Two colored sentinels, very wide awake, are posted in the middle of the field, about 200 yards from the main road. While I was at the Landing this afternoon, at about 1.30, the contrabands, seeing Lieutenant Sayles with 20 men coming from the same direction as yesterday's raiders, raising a wild cry of " Rebels!" "The rebs is comin'!" rushed in a frantic, terror-stricken mass of men, women, and children, with loud cries, toward the river. At the bluff they were stopped by the bayonets of the Sixteenth New Hampshire, which formed with great promptitude behind the levee. The One hundred and sixty-second New York got under arms at once, came up at double-quick, and in about five minutes was in line at the road, but by this time the alarm was over. Two negroes rushed into the river and were drowned. This affords a pretty fair idea, I think, of the alarm of yesterday. I respectfully recommend—

1. That the ammunition boat Suffolk be anchored in the stream, either above or below the chute.

2. That all the officers north of the main road be removed to the south side, where they will not be cut off from the troops, as they were

yesterday by the enemy and to-day by an impenetrable crowd of contrabands.

3. That all the able-bodied contrabands at Springfield Landing, needed for work there, be enrolled, organized, and kept for that purpose; that all such who are not needed for work there be turned over to Colonel Hodge for work on the approaches; and that all non-effective men and all the women and children be sent immediately to New Orleans.

4. That the cottonwood grove be cleared at once and entirely of all negroes, and policed.

5. That the camp of the One hundred and sixty-second New York be then moved to the levee, and that the regiment there encamp in line of battle, arms stacked, left resting on the main road. The sentinels of the police guard are then in plain sight of the reserves of the outposts.

6. If the contrabands cannot be sent to New Orleans at once, I suggest that they be moved to Profit's Island at once, for I am satisfied that no military post can exist in the constant fear of such a tumult as I witnessed to-day.

7. That the 50 men of the One hundred and sixty-second New York, whom General Dwight has detached to picket the road leading from his commissary store to the Plains, be immediately relieved, and returned to their regiment.

I shall make the conduct of the Second Rhode Island Cavalry the subject of a special investigation to-morrow.

Very respectfully, your most obedient servant,
RICH'D B. IRWIN,
Assistant Adjutant-General.

Maj. Gen. N. P. BANKS,
Commanding Department of the Gulf.

No. 4.

Reports of Capt. John C. Palfrey, U. S. Corps of Engineers, of operations July 5–6.

BEFORE PORT HUDSON,
July 6, 1863.

COLONEL: I have the honor to submit the following report of the work in the trenches yesterday:

The work in front of Captain Bainbridge's battery advanced about 20 yards. The parallel before priest-cap was extended to the left about 11 yards. The zigzag was filled with sand-bags, to protect the work on a shaft. The heavy rain of the night prevented much work. The shaft to run obliquely under enemy's salient was commenced. This was directed, instead of a vertical shaft with enveloping galleries, as shorter though more dangerous.

The embrasure for Parrott guns in parallel not finished, and progressing slowly.

Left cavalier finished and occupied. Right one nearly finished, and injured constantly by enemy's 24-pounder gun. To-morrow morning the following working parties should report as follows, at 6 a. m.:

One hundred men in rear of Captain Bainbridge's battery, to work on approach in front of that position.

Three hundred men at Captain Cox's battery, to work on main approach of General Grover.

One hundred men at navy battery, to finish covered approach to Captain Mack's battery.

Two hundred men to Colonel Johnson, at his camp near Slaughter's house.

These men may be either white or black.

Respectfully,

JOHN C. PALFREY,
Captain of Engineers.

Lieut. Col. RICHARD B. IRWIN,
Assistant Adjutant-General.

BEFORE PORT HUDSON,
July 7, 1863.

COLONEL: I have the honor to submit the following report of the work done in the trenches yesterday :

The sap in front of Captain Bainbridge's battery was advanced about 42 feet.

The parallel of General Grover's main approach was extended to the left about 65 feet. This was attempted at evening by a flying sap, and some difficulty was experienced in making the workmen stay in so very dangerous a situation. No work was done in the zigzag approach. The shaft toward the salient of priest-cap was carried about 27 feet in. A new approach was started from the parallel toward the south salient of priest-cap. The cavaliers were finished, except plank steps for the marksmen to stand on, the timber for which was received. The embrasure for gun on left of cavalier was completed, and gun was to go in last night.

To-morrow it is proposed to continue approach in front of Captain Bainbridge's battery ; to continue parallel to the left, and boyaux toward south salient of priest-cap, and shaft toward enemy's salient ; to put steps in cavaliers, and complete, as far as possible, steps and loopholes in parallel ; to clear out and widen approach to Captain Mack's battery, and start an approach from there to lead into our parallel near priest-cap ; to make a parallel in front of Colonel Johnson's approach.

For this the following working parties should report at 6 a. m. on the 8th, as follows :

One hundred men in rear of Captain Bainbridge's battery.

Three hundred men at Captain Cox's battery.

Two hundred men at the navy battery.

Two hundred men at headquarters of Colonel Johnson, Twenty-first Maine Volunteers.

I also respectfully request that 500 colored troops may make 2,000 fascines, and collect them at the material depot near Captain Cox's old battery.

Respectfully submitted.

JOHN C. PALFREY,
Captain of Engineers.

Lieut. Col. RICHARD B. IRWIN,
Assistant Adjutant-General.

No. 5.

*Report of Capt. William B. Roe, Sixteenth Michigan Infantry, Chief
Signal Officer, of operations April 9–July 8.*

NEW ORLEANS, LA.,
August 20, 1863.

COLONEL: I have the honor to submit the following report, accompanied by the individual reports of each acting signal officer, of the
operations of the signal detachment serving with the army in this department, from April 9, 1863, to the time of the surrender of Port Hudson to the United States forces under Major-General Banks, July 8,
1863:

As Captain Rowley (who was in command of the corps until April 29)
did not make a report of the operations of the corps in the Teche campaign, I will submit the report of the detachment under my charge at
Baton Rouge during the time that Captain Rowley and party were operating with the army on the Teche; also the official reports of each officer
in his detachment, which will show the amount of duty performed by
the corps, and by each officer, during the whole campaign.

On the 8th of April, I received orders from General Augur, commanding at Baton Rouge, to report to Captain Alden, of the U. S. S. Richmond, for temporary duty. Accordingly, on the 9th, I proceeded with
a party, consisting of Lieut. George R. Herbert, of the signal corps, and
Lieutenants Tenney and Dean, of the Thirtieth Massachusetts Volunteers, to the point opposite Port Hudson, and, with the help of a party
from the U. S. S. Genesee, we succeeded by the use of small boats (as
the country was flooded by a crevasse) to so far penetrate the swamp
as to convince ourselves that we could communicate with the admiral,
who was to be down on the 15th, by means of boats, if signals should
fail. •

In the meantime the masts of the Richmond were raised to such a
height that, on the 15th, we were able to signal over the trees with the
admiral's ship above the batteries of Port Hudson. We also sent a
party across the point with mail, dispatches, &c. (See Captain Alden's
report, a copy of which is inclosed;* also reports of Lieut. S. M. Eaton,
who was on duty on the Hartford, and Lieut. John C. Abbott, who
was on duty on the Richmond.) Much valuable information was transmitted by signals between the two ships, which it would have been almost
impossible to have obtained in any other way.

From the 15th of April until the fall of Port Hudson, constant communication was held between the two ships by signals.

On the 29th of April, Capt. William W. Rowley's term of service having expired, I was placed in command of the corps by special orders
from headquarters Department of the Gulf, and immediately entered
upon the discharge of my duties. Lieut. Joseph L. Hallett was placed
in charge of the detachment at Baton Rouge, which consisted of 6 officers, one of whom was in charge of the signal telegraph train.

On the 19th of May, in obedience to orders from Major-General Banks,
I accompanied him to the headquarters of the army, then at Simsport,
La., and ordered the remainder of the party to proceed by first train to
same point.

Immediately on my arrival, May 21, I received orders from yourself
to place an officer on the U. S. S. Hartford. Accordingly, Lieut. Ros-

---

* Not found.

well C. Harris was sent on board, and Lieut. Thomas S. Hall reported for duty to General Grover, who was then on the move toward Bayou Sara.

On the morning of the 23d, headquarters moved to Bayou Sara, and on 24th received orders from yourself to place an efficient officer on board the Hartford, in place of Lieut. R. C. Harris (who was unable to work the station, it being so elevated), in obedience to which Lieut. S. M. Eaton was ordered to her. The same day, Lieut. Thomas S. Hall was relieved from duty with General Grover, and Lieuts. John C. Abbott and R. C. Harris were ordered on duty with him. I found that communication with the Hartford, Richmond, and thence to General Augur, could be obtained by establishing a station at Bayou Sara. Accordingly, Lieutenant Hall was placed upon the Episcopal church, and communication was established. Lieutenant Hallett and his party were at this time with General Augur in the rear of Port Hudson, and had communication from Springfield Landing to the Richmond by signals, and from same point to General Augur's headquarters by means of signal telegraph train.

May 23, headquarters moved to a point near Port Hudson, and on the 24th I had verbal communication with Lieutenant Hallett, who was with General Augur.

On the 26th, Lieuts. E. H. Russell and John W. Dana were ordered to report to General Weitzel for duty, and my attention was directed to establishing stations, so as to have communication between the different headquarters—a task which I found to be very difficult, as the country was very thickly wooded, and our lines were not far enough advanced to warrant me in establishing stations very near the batteries. Consequently the corps did not prove of much service during the first assault; still, the officers acted as aides to the different generals with whom they were attached, and communication was held with the fleet above and below the batteries by means of signal telegraph train to Springfield Landing, and thence by signals to the fleet.

May 30, communication was opened with the Richmond from the tree-tops on the right and left of our lines. On the 31st, I ordered Lieut. John C. Abbott to the Richmond, to assist Lieut. A. M. Jackson, there being four stations to communicate with from that ship.

At this time communication was established from the commanding general's headquarters direct to the Richmond, Hartford, and Springfield Landing, it being so arranged that the stations were at or near the headquarters of Generals Grover and Dwight.

Many official messages were sent from the headquarters to the Richmond and Hartford. (Please see reports of Lieutenants Eaton, Abbott, and Jackson.)

On the day of the second assault, signal communication was held between the headquarters of Major-General Banks in the center, and General Dwight on the left of our line, by which the commanding general could be informed at any time of the progress of General Dwight. (For a copy of messages, see reports of Lieutenants Hall and Rundlett.) The line from the general's headquarters to the ships was kept in working order until Port Hudson surrendered.

On the 29th of June, Lieutenant Dana was ordered to the left, to communicate with Lieutenant Eaton (whose station was in a barn, from which could be seen most of the enemy's guns on the river front), for the purpose of directing the shots from our guns on the left upon those of the enemy. (Please see report of Lieutenant Dana on directing shots.) The signal telegraph train proved of great service, and from May 28 to the time that I was ordered to deliver the wire to Captain **Bulkley,** June 5, two hundred and fifty-five official messages were sent, **many of** which were sent from Springfield Landing to the fleet by Lieutenant Jencks, signal officer at that point. The country being so level and thickly wooded, it was almost impossible to establish stations; still, in our main line there were ten stations, eight of which were in tree-tops or on masts of vessels. Three stations of observation, which were also in tree-tops, and three stations which are not described, were likewise built in trees, and were abandoned for the reason of their being in range of the enemy's sharpshooters. In fact, all the main stations were within range of the enemy's guns. Some officers were driven from their stations, but in every case returned again as soon as the firing was over.

All the officers and men in the detachment have shown a willingness to comply in every particular with the orders given them, and, in many instances, have shown a determination to do all in their power to promote the efficiency of the corps.

I inclose the reports of each officer, also a map showing the stations, the dotted lines showing over which points the signals were worked.*

My desire and determination is to have the corps in this department as good as any in the service, and know if we have the countenance and confidence of the commanding generals we shall be of great service in the army and to the country.

I have the honor to be, colonel, very respectfully, your obedient servant,

WM. B. ROE,
Captain, and Chief of Signal Corps, Department of the Gulf.

Lieut. Col. RICHARD B. IRWIN,
Assistant Adjutant-General, Department of the Gulf.

No. 6.

Report of Lieut. John C. Abbott, Thirteenth Connecticut Infantry, Acting Signal Officer, of operations June 2–July 25.

NEW ORLEANS, LA.,
July 27, 1863.

SIR: In obedience to Captain Roe's orders, I proceeded to the signal station on the U. S. S. Richmond, where I have been in communication with four stations, viz:· Lieutenant Eaton's, on the Hartford; Lieutenant Russell's, on the right of the line of our army; Lieutenant Hall's, on the left; and Lieutenant Jencks, at Springfield Landing.

The following is a correct transcript of messages sent and received by me from June 2, 1863, to July 25, 1863, inclusive:

U. S. S. HARTFORD, *June* 2.
Commodore PALMER:

Send prisoners, and tell Colonel Benedict to send contrabands and mules.
FARRAGUT,
Admiral.

JUNE 4.
Admiral FARRAGUT:

The enemy number their water batteries 1, 2, from up the river down. The main magazine is behind Battery No. 6, and about 200 to 500 yards back from the river.
BANKS,
General.

---

* Map omitted.

JUNE 5.

Captain ALDEN:

I desire you to fire one of your rifle pieces upon the rebel pivot gun.

GROVER,
General.

One message omitted here by mistake.

JUNE 6.

Admiral FARRAGUT:

·The shelling of the mortar-boats on Thursday night was reported to have seriously inconvenienced the enemy. Beef-cattle killed, and wounded many, and rendered a regimental camp untenable. The bulk of the shot passed a little to the left and beyond the main magazine. The sleep of half of the garrison was prevented.

BANKS,
General.

JUNE 6.

General BANKS:

I have him under my control. The minute he opens, I silence him.

FARRAGUT,
Admiral.

JUNE 6.

Admiral FARRAGUT:

Your note of yesterday received. The sextant has arrived; it will be taken care of and returned safely. Much obliged with your offer in regard to the boats in Bayou Sara. We heard of their safety yesterday, but would like particulars. Thanks for the hand-grenades.

BANKS,
General.

JUNE 9.

General BANKS:

Hammering and building is reported at the mouth of Thompson's Creek. Can you account for it?

FARRAGUT,
Admiral.

JUNE 9.

Admiral FARRAGUT:

We have men near by the creek, and will report to you. All going well.

BANKS,
General.

SPRINGFIELD LANDING, *June* 9.

Admiral FARRAGUT:

Colonel Prince has been to-day to the mouth of Thompson's Creek, on the east bank, and reports neither hearing nor seeing anything of the enemy in that neighborhood. Our picket line is complete to the captured steamboats, whence it is extended by frequent patrols beyond the steamboats to the river. The crossing of Thompson's Creek is reported impracticable. We burned the enemy's store-house this afternoon.

BANKS,
General.

JUNE 9.

Admiral FARRAGUT:

Opened fire at 11 a. m. from the heavy guns and mortars, and fired· slowly during the day, with good range and excellent effect, driving the enemy away from the parapet. Our fire was, except in one or two·cases, unanswered. The navy guns were admirably served. Please keep up your mortar fire during the whole of the night. We shall fire slowly all night. We will send you a report of the operations at the mouth of Thompson's Creek this evening.

BANKS,
General.

JUNE 10.

Admiral FARRAGUT:

Please send to Springfield Landing 500 blank cartridges, 50 shrapnel, 500 shell, and 50 solid shot for the 9-inch navy guns. Please let me know when they will be there.

BANKS,
General.

JUNE 10.

General BANKS:

The ammunition you asked for will be at Springfield Landing at 5 p. m.

ALDEN,
Captain.

JUNE 12.

Admiral FARRAGUT:

Your letter is received; will send an answer about charges desired for the navy guns.

BANKS,
General.

JUNE 12.

General BANKS:

Your request will be attended to.

FARRAGUT,
Admiral.

JUNE 13.

Admiral FARRAGUT:

Please send an order to the company of sharpshooters from the Arizona, said to be ashore at Saint Francisville, to join their regiment at once.

BANKS,
General.

JUNE 13.

General BANKS:

Commodore Palmer sent me word, and I sent it to you, that the sharpshooters of the Arizona had joined their regiment some time before the Arizona went up the river to Natchez, but will send over by the first opportunity.

FARRAGUT,
Admiral.

SPRINGFIELD LANDING, *June* 13.

Admiral FARRAGUT:

Dispatches to General Grant delivered in person. Chief engineer asks, Can you give Captain Baker four 30-pounder Parrott guns, and what kind of carriages?

J. T. BARKER,
Captain and Engineer.

JUNE 13.

Capt. J. T. BARKER, *Engineer:*

The admiral has no 30-pounder Parrott guns here. It is understood there is a large number belonging to the army at New Orleans in store.

T. A. JENKINS,
Captain, and Chief of Staff.

JUNE 13.

Admiral FARRAGUT:

Colonel —— informs me that you told him that you had received orders not to fire; if so, it must be a great mistake in some of my dispatches. Please continue the fire of your mortars all night. We shall fire all night, also.

BANKS,
General.

JUNE 13.

Admiral FARRAGUT:

Please send as many shrapnel as you can spare for the 9-inch navy guns. General Gardner answers that his duty requires him to defend the place, and he declines to surrender,

BANKS,
General.

General BANKS:

Ammunition for the naval battery just received, and will be sent this a. m. to Springfield Landing.

T. A. JENKINS,
Captain, and Chief of Staff.

JUNE 14.

Admiral FARRAGUT:

Getting very short of ammunition. Please send us as much Dahlgren ammunition as you can spare, to the extent of 800 rounds, chiefly shell and shrapnel. Can you spare any 20-pounder Parrott ammunition?

BANKS,
General.

SPRINGFIELD LANDING, *June* 15.

Lieutenant SCHLEY:

Send me as many 5-second fuses as you can possibly spare to Springfield Landing, care of General Arnold, chief of artillery.

E. TERRY.

JUNE 15.

General BANKS:

Sir: From information received, I think an attack will be soon made upon my forces by a large force of cavalry. If the enemy does not attack me to-day, I shall move my force to the lower fleet, for the purpose of getting a safe position and near supplies.

C. H. SAGE,
Colonel, Commanding.

JUNE 15.

General BANKS:

I can deliver in New Orleans one thousand 30-pounder Parrott shot or shell, and six hundred 20-pounder Parrott shot or shell. If wanted, telegraph to Commodore Morris for it to be sent in an army transport.

FARRAGUT,
Admiral.

SPRINGFIELD LANDING, *June* 17.

Admiral FARRAGUT:

Can you send me two surgeons, as wounded are coming in very fast, and I am short-handed?

J. C. FISHER,
Medical Director.

JUNE 17.

J. C. FISHER, *Medical Director:*

I have but one surgeon.

FARRAGUT,
Admiral.

U. S. GUNBOAT WINONA,
Donaldsonville, June 18.

Admiral FARRAGUT:

SIR: The enemy is in force near Plaquemine—cavalry, infantry, and artillery. The force that made this morning's raid numbered 300. It seems they intended attacking this place. I at once proceeded here as quickly as possible.

The commanding officer expects an attack. With the assistance of a gunboat, the fort can be held, in my opinion, against any force the rebels can bring.

A. W. WEAVER,
Lieutenant-Commander.

JUNE 20.

Commodore PALMER:

The admiral has sent a pilot for one of your vessels. Shall I send him over? We have a few letters for your fleet. All quiet here and below.

JAMES ALDEN,
Captain.

Admiral FARRAGUT:

Please open fire with your mortars only at 11 p. m., and cease firing at exactly 10 a. m. Throw your shell as nearly as possible in the center of the works.

BANKS,
General.

JUNE 28.

General BANKS:

I sent the Genesee, a powerful gunboat, at daylight this morning to Donaldson-ville, with Lieutenant Harwood on board.

ALDEN,
Captain.

JUNE 28.

Captain ALDEN:

The commanding general requests that you spare your tug to take ammunition from Springfield Landing to Donaldsonville. Please answer.

RICH'D B. IRWIN,
Assistant Adjutant-General.

General BANKS:

About 6,000 contrabands here. Please send a steamer for them. Have ceased firing on account of troops being in direct line of fire.

JAMES ALDEN,
Captain.

JULY 7.

Colonel IRWIN:

The Hebe will be at Essex's berth at sunset. Admiral gone down the river. I follow at once on Saint Mary's.

C. EMERSON,
Acting Assistant Adjutant-General.

JULY 8.

Admiral FARRAGUT:

Bands will play, and we shall fire a salute of one hundred guns from right to left at noon; will be glad to have you participate.

N. P. BANKS.

I have the honor to be, very respectfully, your obedient servant,

JOHN C. ABBOTT,
Second Lieut. Thirteenth Conn. Vols., Acting Signal Officer.

Lieut. GEORGE R. HERBERT,
Acting Adjutant, Signal Corps.

No. 7.

Report of Lieut. Milton Benner, Second Pennsylvania Heavy Artillery,
Acting Signal Officer, of operations May 23–June 5.

HDQRS. SIGNAL TELEGRAPH TRAIN, DEPT. OF THE GULF,
Springfield Landing, June 10, 1863.

SIR: I have the honor to submit the following report of operations of the signal telegraph train from May 23 to June 5, inclusive:

On the 23d ultimo, in accordance with instructions from Major-General Augur, the wire was run out on the Springfield road from Springfield

Landing (our depot for supplies) to a point on that road where it connects with the Bayou Sara road, and about 1 mile from Placion Church, near Barnes' Cross-Roads. Communications from the telegraph station near the Cross-Roads were conveyed to their destinations by orderlies detailed for that purpose by General Augur. The line was in good working order until June 5, when I was directed by the chief signal officer to turn my wire over to Captain Bulkley, of the United States Military Telegraph, for temporary use, and the same to be worked by his instruments. Up to the time of writing, the wire remains in his possession.

I inclose copies of a few messages only, as it would require too much space and time to give you complete files of all transmitted. The following shows the operations for each day so long as the wire was worked by my instruments:

May 23 :
    Number of messages 10
    Number of words 370
    Average number of words.. 37
May 24 :
    Number of messages 14
    Number of words 461
    Average number of words.. 33
May 25 :
    Number of messages 18
    Number of words 580
    Average number of words.. 32
May 26 :
    Number of messages 6
    Number of words 136
    Average number of words.. 22
May 27 :
    Number of messages 12
    Number of words 421
    Average number of words.. 35
May 28 :
    Number of messages 20
    Number of words 813
    Average number of words.. 40
May 29 :
    Number of messages 18
    Number of words 700
    Average number of words.. 39
May 30 :
    Number of messages 28
    Number of words 1,124
    Average number of words.. 44
May 31 :
    Number of messages 15
    Number of words 505
    Average number of words.. 33
June 1 :
    Number of messages 14
    Number of words 382
    Average number of words.. 27
June 2 :
    Number of messages 22
    Number of words 612
    Average number of words.. 27
June 3 :
    Number of messages 27
    Number of words 591
    Average number of words.. 21
June 4 :
    Number of messages 30
    Number of words 702
    Average number of words.. 23

June 5:
    Number of messages 11
    Number of words 425
    Average number of words 38

RECAPITULATION.

Number of messages 245
Number of words 7,822
Average number of words 31

    Respectfully submitted.
      Your obedient servant,

MILTON BENNER,
Acting Signal Officer.

[Inclosures.]

HEADQUARTERS UNITED STATES FORCES,
Near Port Hudson, May 23, 1863.

To Signal Officer in command of Signal Telegraph, near Placion Church:

    SIR: The following good news has just been received from Colonel Grierson:

> We are half a mile north of the railroad. Have met General Grover with his division. General Banks is 3 miles back. News from General Grant is glorious. He cut Johnston's forces to pieces, capturing sixty-one pieces of artillery. He has Vicksburg hemmed in so they cannot use their siege guns.

C. C. AUGUR,
Major-General, Commanding.

    Send the above dispatch to the fleet.

G. B. HALSTED,
Assistant Adjutant-General.

HEADQUARTERS FIRST DIVISION,
Plains Store, May 24, 1863—6 p. m.

Captain ALDEN,
    Commanding the Richmond:

    General Banks is up with his forces, and we close in around the fort this morning, and will probably open upon them in the course of the day.

    The general wishes me to say that he will keep the admiral informed of the progress of affairs.

C. C. AUGUR,
Major-General, Commanding.

HEADQUARTERS DEPARTMENT OF THE GULF,
Riley's, before Port Hudson, May 26, 1863—Noon.

Rear-Admiral FARRAGUT, U. S. Navy,
    Flagship Hartford:

    ADMIRAL: The commanding general is at the front. I will forward your dispatch to him immediately; meanwhile, I take the liberty of stating our position early this morning: Sherman on the left, in advance of the enemy's first line of rifle-pits, having his pickets at the front edge of a skirt of woods, separated from the enemy's main line of works by an open plain. His position is in front of the school-house. Augur next, on the roads from the Plains to Port Hudson, and well advanced. Grover on the Jackson Railroad, holding the front edge of a wood which is within from 200 to 400 yards of the apparent center of the works, and in plain sight and easy range of them. Weitzel, with his own brigade, Dwight's, and Paine's (Emory's division), reduced to about a brigade, on the right, near where the Telegraph road from Port Hudson to Bayou Sara crosses Big Sandy Creek.

This morning everybody except Grover has closed. up, and Grover cannot close up without taking the works in front of him.

Thus the place is completely invested. I understand that the commanding general's intention is to make the decisive attack to-morrow morning, but upon this point I do not speak officially or decidedly, as everything, of course, depends upon circumstances, which an hour might totally change.

I have the honor to be, sir, with great respect, your most obedient servant,

RICH'D B. IRWIN,
Assistant Adjutant-General.

No. 8.

Report of Lieut. John W. Dana, Twelfth Maine Infantry, Acting Signal Officer, of operations June 29–July 3.

NEW ORLEANS, LA.,
July 27, 1863.

SIR: I have the honor to report that on the 29th of June, 1863, I was ordered to open communication with the mortar battery on the left of our line at Port Hudson with Lieutenant Eaton, whose station was in a barn on the opposite side of the river, from which he could see the. enemy's river [batteries], with the aim of directing fire of our guns and mortars upon enemy's batteries.

The following is a correct transcript of messages sent and received by me while there:

JUNE 29, 1863.

Sent. "How shall the mortars fire to hit the gun on wheels behind the citadel? How many yards is it?"
Received. "Three hundred and fifty. The gun is not there."
Sent. "Where is it?"
Received. "Eight hundred [yards] on the verge of the bank."
Sent. "Is it a rifled gun, about 1.28-pounder?"
Received. "Yes."
Sent. "Eight hundred yards from here?"
Received. "Yes."
Sent. "Watch a shot fired at it from here. How was that?"
Received. "Try it again at 500 yards."
Received. "Neither shell exploded. F. L. L."
Sent. "Did they fall in the river?"
Received. "No. F. L. L."
Sent. "Watch now."
Received. "Splendid range; fire 100 yards short of last shot; that did not explode; could not see where it fell."
Sent. "Will try it again; keep watch."
Received. "That fell 150 yards short; range good."
Sent. "Was not fired at it; watch now. Did you see that?"
Received. "No, did not; can seldom see them unless they burst."
Sent. "Will cease firing for the present. Can you see the rebs in the citadel?"
Received. "No; but scores of them on this side."
Sent. "Direct fire at them. Orders are to cease firing for the present."
Received. "Will they permit you to direct fire of one of the Parrotts?"
Sent. "They only bear on the citadel, and all firing has ceased."

During this day we were directing the fire of the mortars.

. On July 1, we were again at the same station, and the following are the messages received and sent:

Sent. "Can you see the gun that is firing now?"
Received. "The rebels from opposite me are firing."
Sent. "Are they together?"
Received. "No; one is 600 yards, the next 1,000 yards, and the next 1,200 yards from your battery."
Sent. "On the river bank?"
Received. "Yes, within 50 yards of it."
Sent. "How was that shell from here?"
Received. "Don't know. Can direct fire of your guns, if you are ready."
Sent. "Ready now; firing at second gun; watch now."
Received. "Your last shot was very good; a little to the right."
Sent. "How was that?"
Received. "F. L. L. and 100 yards short."
Sent. "Have rebel shell done any damage to our battery on right bank?"
Received. "Can't say."
Sent. "Send a man to find [out], if not too dangerous. Watch fire of these mortars particularly. How was that?"
Received. "Did not explode?"
Sent. "How far to gun nearest citadel?"
Received. "Six hundred yards."
Sent. "Chart says 85 yards from here.'
Received. "O. K."
Sent. "Will fire at it."
Received. "Fell 200 yards short; range good."
Received. "The fifth gun in our battery hit the lower rebel piece last shot. Tell them to F. L. L. and a hair lower. Just hit it again."
Sent. "See last shot?"
Received. "It was 10 feet to the left."
Sent. "I mean the mortar shot."
Received. "Struck in the citadel, 200 yards short."
Sent. "How is this one?"
Received. "One hundred and fifty yards short."
Received. "One Parrott on this bank is disabled."
. Sent. "How?"
Received. "Hit by a shot."
Sent. "Yes, but how badly disabled, and hit in what part?"
Received. "The carriage was hit underneath. No great damage done. Last shot was 100 yards too short."
Sent. "General Stone wants to know if any damage has been done to rebel guns."
Received. "Our fifth gun has hit the breastwork of the big rifle four times. Its fire is splendid. Can dismount it soon. No other damage done."
Sent. "You say your fifth gun?"
Received. "Yes, from the left."
Sent. "Is the carriage of our Parrott gun too much disabled to be immediately repaired?"
Received. "The sixth gun has just made a glorious shot. I think not; believe they are working on it; am not sure. Let the sixth gun fire 16 feet more to the left."
Sent. "How now about the fifth and sixth guns?"
Received. "No. 6 gun is the bully boy."
Sent. "Can you give it any direction to make it any more bully?"
Received. "Last shot was a little to the right."
Received. "Fire sixth immediately. Rebs are fixing rifle; sixth can stop them."
Sent. "Report immediately any damage done to our guns."
Sent. "Have ceased firing until rebs open again. Did fifth and sixth have good aims?"
Received. "Yes, they have knocked half the earthworks over before the rifle."
Sent. "Can they now hit it with same aim?"
Received. "Yes."
Sent. "Will fire at rifle. Now report every shot."
Received. "S. S. E. I mean from guns just fired. I must know what guns are to fire."
Sent. "Only one in this battery. Cannot see your signals at all because of smoke and darkness. Now can see."
Received. "Do you know which gun is firing? Is it fifth or sixth."
Sent. "Neither; 'tis a navy Dahlgren, which I want you to direct the fire of."
Received. "O. K."

SAME STATION, JULY 2, 1863.

Received. "No. 1 fires a shade too low."
Sent. "Report everything important in regard to battery on right bank."
Received. "Whatever I know."

Lieutenant SLACK:
Please ask Captain Closson to send me to-day twenty boxes spherical case and twenty boxes shells.

BRADLEY,
Lieutenant.

Received. "Big rifle is just disabled by our Parrott."
Sent. "How badly ; any need of big battery firing at it any more ?"
Received. "The gun has pitched forward."
Sent. "We are firing at gun in ravine behind the citadel. How was that ?"
Received. "I can't see any mounted within 1,000 yards of citadel. How was that ?"
Received. "One thousand yards. I should like to direct the fire of guns No. 9 or 10."
Received. "The last mortar shell fell 70 yards from the disabled gun. Two fine guns lowest down on the river bank are firing at our Parrotts."
Sent. "You can direct the fire of No. 9; 'tis a 24-pounder siege gun. Will wait for your report after each shot. Did you see last shot ?"

Lieutenant BRADLEY:
Cease firing for the present, and withdraw your section from the bank.

RICHARD ARNOLD,
Brigadier-General.

Received. "Last shot was 10 yards to the right."
Sent. "How was last shot from howitzer ?"
Received. "The last shot but one was 10 yards to the right. The last shot of all was splendid; only 3 feet to the right."
Received. "Good shot ; . F. L. L."
Received. "F. L. L. That shot struck the breastwork 8 feet to the right of the gun, F. L. L., and a little lower."
Sent. "And the last ?"
Received. "Had good range, but was 100 yards short."
Received. "That burst short."
Received. "The last shot was 10 yards to the right. This shot was capital ; a fraction high."
Received. "Last shot was 10 yards to right."
Sent. "Cannot get it any farther to the left. Where is the second rebel gun ; can't it fire at that ? How was the last shot ?"
Received. "A little too high."
Received. "The lower gun is 45 yards from river ; the second gun is a little farther up and 400 yards from him; last shot a little too high."
Sent. "Are we firing at lower or second gun ?"
Received. "The howitzer is firing at the second gun, the other to your right of both. The howitzer's shells go 2 feet over the gun every time."
Received. "Last shot was too high ; little too high again."
Received. "Can't they or won't they depress that gun ?"
Sent. "Won't, I guess ; was that any better, and that ?"
Received. "Both, and forever too high."
Sent. "Cease signaling."
Received. "Cease signaling."

On the 3d, I was again at the battery, but no firing was done during the day. Did not go again.

I have the honor to be, very respectfully, your obedient servant,
JOHN W. DANA,
Second Lieutenant, and Acting Signal Officer.

Lieut. GEORGE R. HERBERT,
Adjutant Signal Corps, Department of the Gulf.

No. 9.

Report of Lieut. Stephen M. Eaton, Twelfth Maine Infantry, Acting Signal Officer, of operations March 13–July 11.

NEW ORLEANS, LA.,
July 15, 1863.

SIR : I have the honor to submit the following report of signal duty performed by me while on and attached to the U. S. S. Hartford, on the Mississippi River, between Port Hudson and Vicksburg, from March 13 to July 11, 1863:

In compliance with Special Orders, No. 24, Headquarters Signal Corps, Baton Rouge, La., March 13, 1863, I reported for duty the same day, with Lieutenants Jencks and Abbott, and with our respective parties, to Admiral Farragut, on flagship Hartford.

In furtherance of orders on the subsequent day, Lieutenant Jencks and party were transferred to the iron-clad Essex, and Lieutenant Abbott and party to U. S. S. Richmond.

At 9 p. m. of Saturday, March 14, the fleet, in line of battle, by pairs, and lashed together, advanced to run the gauntlet of the Port Hudson batteries.

After a gallant and stubborn fight, the Hartford and her consort, the Albatross, succeeded, and came to anchor at midnight above the fortifications, and well out of range.

My efforts the next morning to communicate with the unsuccessful vessels below from the mast-head were to no purpose. The intervening woods were too high, and the admiral declined my proposal to cross the Point.

At 10 a. m. we sailed for Red River and Vicksburg. Had a sharp engagement at Grand Gulf on the 19th, and five separate engagements with the Warrenton batteries, from March 20 to March 30.

During these ten days, I exchanged signals repeatedly with certain of Admiral Porter's officers.

On the 15th of April, the Hartford steamed down within view of Port Hudson, and anchored. I immediately opened communication with the Richmond, distant, by the river, 10 miles ; in an air-line, 6 miles. Here signal station had been raised to a height of 160 feet. My station was 135 feet high. The following is a correct transcript of the messages sent and received, then and afterward, by me :

U. S. S. HARTFORD,
April 15, 1863—11 a. m.

All well. Gabaudan arrived safely at Baton Rouge, missing the upper fleet.

Queen of the West was captured in Grand Lake April 14. Captain [E. W.] Fuller and crew prisoners at Berwick Bay. The enemy evacuated his works at Centreville last night, but will probably be captured, as he is between Emory and Grover. Leaving his guns and ammunition.

T. W. SHERMAN,
Brigadier-General.

Can send a party to you across the Point in skiffs, coming out at lower mouth of False Run.

JAMES ALDEN.

Sent. " Who are you, and what ship ? "
Abbott. " The Richmond."

Captain ALDEN :

I want my secretary and dispatches if they can be sent me safely. I wish to return to Red River to-morrow morning. Answer.

FARRAGUT,
Admiral.

Gabaudan starts immediately with a party. Send a boat to meet them at lower mouth False River, to dike, half a mile up the river.

ALDEN,
Captain.

How is Captain McKinstry? Is Cummings dead? We are all well, but want the news.

FARRAGUT,
Admiral.

Cummings died on the 17th. The captain is doing well. Drop down half a mile, and wait half an hour.

ALDEN.

Sent. "Steam ahead 300 or 400 yards, and watch my flag."
Received. "Cease signaling."
Sent. "Cease signaling."

4 P. M.

Received. "Have you sent your boat? It is time the party had arrived."
Sent. "The boats are here. Cease signaling."
Received. "Has the party arrived?"

Yes. The officers return to-morrow morning. Send the mail early in the morning. Cease signaling.

FARRAGUT,
Admiral.

Received. "All right. Cease signaling."

APRIL 16—a. m.

Captain ALDEN:
The mail has gone over. Has it arrived? I will return here on Thursday.

D. G. F.

The mail has arrived. Shall we send you ship's letters? We have many official letters for the admiral.

ALDEN.

Send the letters, but not papers, at once.

D. G. F.

Three or four river steamers are seen almost daily at Port Hudson, bringing stores. They are probably now in Thompson's Creek.

J. A.

The party with letters has started. We hear firing below, and are going down. Cease signaling.

J. A.

Sent. "Cease signaling."

APRIL 20.

Admiral FARRAGUT:
We marched on Opelousas at 6 a. m. Can be in Alexandria the last week of the month. Can gunboats meet me there? Have burned three gunboats and many transports. Captured 2,000 prisoners with best officers of army and navy, and am still pursuing. When will Grant be down?

BANKS,
General.

Any news from the north?

FARRAGUT,
Admiral.

Received. "Attack made on Charleston the 7th instant. Nothing reliable since. Rebels look glum. Fox, in a letter to Smith, says: 'We feel no regret at the attempt, for the unflinching qualities displayed make us forget Galveston.'"

Captain ALDEN:
Can you send my mail?

FARRAGUT.

We have no letters of importance. Hear you have five more gunboats.

ALDEN.

Sent. "Did Swann return safely?"

Yes. Circassian reports all well on the coast of Texas. The Brooklyn will go to Ship Island to repair. Pocahontas' boilers are worn out. Shall I order a survey, and, if condemned, shall I order her north? I have ordered the court of inquiry, at

Pensacola, on Commodore Hitchcock, about the Florida's escape. I have ordered him north with the Susquehanna as soon as his court is over, as ordered by the Secretary of the Navy.

HENRY W. MORRIS,
Commodore.

General BANKS :

Glad to learn your successes. Unless gunboats come from Vicksburg, I have none that could pass Fort De Russy, at Gordon's Landing. I can hear nothing from Grant until the five boats below Vicksburg arrive. Port Hudson on half rations. Troops discontented. Enemy sent to Arkansas for troops for Taylor. Nothing to impede communication with me in the Atchafalaya.

D. G. FARRAGUT,
Admiral.

Sent. "Cease signaling."

Received. "Cease signaling."

APRIL 24—8 a. m.

Captain ALDEN :

As you have the guides, send one immediately. I will have a force at the Landing. My letters will explain everything.

Will send immediately.

JAMES ALDEN.

I have 15 or 20 contrabands I must send over. No place for them. Can I do it safely ?

D. G. F.

If you have skiffs to send with them, you can.

J. A.

Tell Mr. Schley to send my valise and a few shirts.

GABAUDAN.

Our party has started.

JAMES ALDEN.

GABAUDAN :

Did you get your message in time ? Love to Watson and Kimberly.

SCHLEY.

Have you all the dispatches now ?

EATON.

Received. "All right. Have you been re-enforced by gunboats; and how many have passed Vicksburg ?"

Captain ALDEN :

Glad the Department approves our conduct. Efforts cannot always command success.

D. G. FARRAGUT.

When shall I look for you again ?

ALDEN.

I hope to be down again on Saturday, the 2d.

D. G. F.

Are you 23 ?

EATON.

Received. "Yea."

Sent. "Any other officer with you ?"

Received. "No; I called you a long time last night. Did you not see me ?"

Sent. "All the time ; but the admiral objected to my answering. Danger of fire."

Let us know when Swann arrives. Until then cease signaling.

D. G. F.

What firing took you down river last Thursday ?

D. G. F.

Practiced with the heavy guns at Baton Rouge.

J. A.

Sent. "Swann is here. O. K."

Let us know when they return.

ALDEN.

Sent. "They have just started."
Received. "My station is very shaky. I wish you always to give it time to get still before you answer. The flagman and myself occupy the same box (23).
Sent. "O. K."

ADMIRAL:
When do you go up?

ALDEN.

Immediately.

D. G. F.

Sent. "Cease signaling."
Received. "C. S."

U. S. S. HARTFORD,
Opposite Mouth of Red River, May 4—1 a. m.
Soon after midnight of May 4 an alarm beat to quarters. A large fleet was discovered descending the Mississippi. We exchanged messages.

PORTER,
Admiral.

IRON-CLAD BENTON.

My compliments.

FARRAGUT,
Admiral.

I will be on board immediately.

PORTER.

NEAR PORT HUDSON,
May 5—12.30 p. m.
Captain ALDEN:
Did Swann get over safely? I am in communication with Banks and Grant. Porter arrived Sunday night with four iron-clads, and is now up Red River.

FARRAGUT,
Admiral.

Swann is here. Large lot of corn at lower mouth of False River. Two regiments of Illinois cavalry, from Tennessee, reached Baton Rouge on the 2d. Left the 27th. They came down the Jackson and New Orleans Railroad, destroying much of it; all the bridges, cars, and locomotives. Heard heavy firing on the 29th at Grand Gulf. Lost 1 man killed, 5 wounded. Now is the time to take Port Hudson.

A.

Sent. "Are you Abbott?"
Received. "No. Jackson."

Captain ALDEN:
I hope to be at New Orleans last of the week. Order up the mortar-boats, the Essex, and Genesee. Shell Port Hudson every night at a different hour, for an hour or two, until the Hartford passes down.

FARRAGUT.

We will not communicate across the Point. Too much risk.

FARRAGUT.

McDermot killed at Sabine Pass, on shore at the light-house. Boat's crew taken. Read escaped with his boat's crew, himself wounded. Tell Porter that there are three steamboats up Thompson's Creek.

J. A.

SCHLEY:
Please send my coat and valise to Van.

GABAUDAN.

Sent. "Cease signaling."
Received. "Cease signaling."

MAY 6—6.30 a. m.

Captain ALDEN:

Cannot say when the Hartford will return, but not until to pass below Port Hudson.

FARRAGUT.

Sent. "Porter has captured Grand Gulf. Took nine big guns. Grant is behind Grand Gulf with 30,000 men. Has captured 500 prisoners and one battery. Hopes to bag all."
Received. "Very windy. Be brief."
Sent. "We are off. Cease signaling."
Received. "Cease signaling."

On the 8th of May, Admiral Farragut and staff went to New Orleans by way of the Atchafalaya. I accompanied him. Reported for duty again to General Banks at his headquarters at Bayou Sara about midnight, May 23, 1863. Immediately ordered to the Hartford.

U. S. S. HARTFORD,
Near Port Hudson, May 24—10.30 a. m.

Admiral FARRAGUT:

I have nothing from General Banks since yesterday morning, when he had joined Augur at Newport.

PALMER,
Commodore.

We are in communication with him, and they now invest Port Hudson. Wait for a reply from the admiral. Do not send a message till I answer your call.

JACKSON.

Sent. "I am Eaton. Was signaling to Hall at Bayou Sara. He can see you. Can't you see him? Look a little to the left of me. Where is the admiral?"

U. S. S. MONONGAHELA.

Commodore PALMER:

Hold on and watch events, and be ready to take advantage of them.

D. G. FARRAGUT.

Admiral FARRAGUT:

I have now in the Mississippi the Albatross, Arizona, and Sachem, the two latter at Bayou Sara. I have the Estrella on the Atchafalaya. The Pittsburg I sent yesterday to report to Captain Walker, to assist in blockade of Red River. General Grant has been everywhere successful. We hope Vicksburg by this time has fallen. I have received about 120 tons of coal for all of us. Hope to get 100 more from the army. I have sent over an officer with a communication for you.

J. S. PALMER,
Commodore.

Commodore PALMER:

To fire from above on the batteries would injure our troops more than the enemy, perhaps.

ALDEN,
Captain.

Received. "I cannot see to read, but will send you a message. General Banks' troops are on the Point. Augur is a mile from the forts, and the rest near."
Sent. "Cease signaling."

(In communication with Bayou Sara station.)

MAY 25—7.30 a. m.

Sent. "Where is General Weitzel?"
Received. "He has just passed here."
Sent. "How long since?"
Received. "About two hours ago. Weitzel's brigade is here. He passed to the front himself with one aide at 6 this morning."
Sent. "Who are you?"
Received. "Dana. 'Tis very smoky; use large flag. I leave soon with Weitzel's brigade. Hall remains here."
Sent. "Would I were with thee! The guns of the army seem to be shelling Port Hudson."
Received. "Too hard on eyes. Cease signaling."
Sent. "Cease signaling."

(In communication with U. S. S. Richmond.·)

Admiral FARRAGUT:

General Banks requests me to shell the west side of Thompson's Creek at midnight, to prevent any attempt of the enemy to escape over that side. You can understand the firing.

PALMER,

Commodore.

Sent. "Cease signaling."
Received. "Cease signaling."

MAY 26—6.30 a. m.

Any news from the army?

PALMER,

Commodore.

Received. "Shall leave Port Hudson soon. Closely invested. Paine on the north, then Grover, then Augur, and Sherman on the south. Will assault when practicable. Every one confident of success" (2314).

Sent. "Lieutenant Watson starts for your side at 9 a. m. Let General Banks know there is signal communication between us. Cease signaling."

Received. "Cease signaling."

(In communication with Bayou Sara station.)

9.35 A. M.

Received. "It is impossible to call up Jackson."

Sent. "I signaled with him this morning and called your attention. Is Stephens with you?"

Received. "He is."

Sent. "Keep good watch of me."

Received. "Can see you better in the foretop."

(In communication with U. S. S. Richmond.)

3.05 P. M.

Admiral FARRAGUT:

Grierson's cavalry have captured the two steamers in Thompson's Creek.

PALMER.

Sent. "Can't you read well."

Received. "'Tis very windy, and shakes us."

General BANKS:

A lieutenant of Grierson's cavalry is here, and says the enemy cannot escape across Thompson's Creek and between Fancy Point and the river. They must take the Bayou Sara road, if they escape at all. Should you wish me to fire again at night in the direction indicated in your note, throw up a rocket half an hour before I am to begin. Send me the news.

PALMER,

Commodore.

MAY 27—6.15 a. m.

Commodore PALMER:

The light artillery opens at daylight, the heavy at 6 a. m. Port Hudson will be ours to-day. The ships will cease firing when the artillery ceases.

BANKS,

General.

Sent. "Cannot read when in motion. Cease signaling."
Received. "Cease signaling."

12.15 P. M.

Commodore PALMER:

All is going well with the army. They push the rebels hard on the right. Do not fire again.

ALDEN,

Captain.

Sent. "Do you see this tree?"
Received. "Yes."
Sent. "Well, you are at times hidden behind it. Look often when you signal."
Received. "I will. Cease signaling."
Sent. "S. C."

(In communication with Bayou Sara station.)

MAY 28—7.50 A. M.

Sent. "Has Rich returned from New Orleans?"
Received. "He has not been here."
Sent. "Let Commodore Palmer know when any gunboat arrives from the Atchafalaya."
Received. "I will do so."
Sent "Any news from Grant or from our army?"
Received "I heard yesterday that Captain Hubbard was killed."
Sent. "Any more news? Work faster."
Received. "We get none. Cease signaling."

(In communication with U. S. S. Richmond.)

8.40 A. M.

Sent. "The commodore is hungering and thirsting for news. Keep him posted."
Received "An assault was made yesterday. Generals Sherman and Dow wounded. The lower batteries opened on the 'bummers' this morning, but were silenced."
Sent "Was the army loss heavy?"
Received. "I know no more. Cease signaling."

(In communication with Bayou Sara station.)

6.30 P. M.

The Sachem or the Arizona will take position opposite Bayou Sara to-night, near the right bank, and shell the enemy if he appears, which will be a signal to us. Kirby Smith is said to be marching down on that side. Report any alarm immediately to us.

PALMER,
Commodore.

MAY 29—7.10 A. M.

Sent. "What had you to send last night?"
Received. "Nothing. They reported you calling. Our loss the day before yesterday was heavy. They were burying the dead yesterday. Cease signaling.".
Sent. "General Grant will have Vicksburg within a week."

3.28 P. M.

Did the Arizona go up the river last night? What gunboats are now at Bayou Sara?

PALMER, .
Commodore.

Received. "The Arizona is just starting. The Sachem is here."
Sent. "Any news?"
Received. "None. Both of my men are sick. I am doing my own flagging."
Sent. "You flag first rate. Has Rich come yet?"
Received. "No. I expect to leave here to-morrow. Cease signaling."
Sent. "Cease signaling."

(In communication with U. S. S. Hartford.)

MAY 30—10.52 A. M.

Sent. "Are you working with another?"
Received. "Yes; with Russell, near Thompson's Creek."
Sent. "Done with him?"
Received. "Yes."
Sent. "Had got ready to land on the point opposite Port Hudson and open communication with Russell. Tell him to look for me at 4 p.'m. If advisable, the Hartford may drop down enough to see him. No news for the commodore? Cease signaling."
Received. "No. Cease signaling."

(In communication with U. S. S. Richmond.)

MAY 31—10.50 A. M.

ROE or DANA:

I was on the point opposite Port Hudson yesterday afternoon. Tell General Banks or Weitzel that I wish to repeat my trip and bring my notes to-night, for examination. A battery of Parrotts there would be a thorn in their side. Roads good; levee high; range short. Answer.

EATON.

JUNE 1—3 p. m.

General BANKS :

An orderly, with dispatches for the Hartford, reached Bayou Sara last night. Not waiting for transportation, he started down by land, and has not yet arrived.

EATON,
Lieutenant.

JUNE 2—1 p. m.

Commodore PALMER :

Send prisoners, and tell Colonel Benedict to send contrabands and mules.

D. G. FARRAGUT.

Sent. " What of the fight this morning ? "
Received. " Trees are in the way. Cease signaling."
Sent. " Cease signaling."

The Mississippi, which for a fortnight had been falling rapidly, had now, subsided 20 feet. Signal communication with the Richmond was intercepted. To restore it, I began cutting a track through a dense and heavy growth of timber 4 miles deep.

On the 19th of June I opened communication with a new station inland, about 6 miles distant, directly in the rear of Port Hudson, and on a line toward General Banks' headquarters.

Sent. " Anything official ? "
Received. " No. Use white flag. Can you see my flag well ? "
Sent. " I have no other flag. Till 5 p. m., cease signaling."

The new station being visible to both the Hartford and Richmond, communication between us was again resumed.

(In communication, by repeating, with the U. S. S. Hartford.)

JUNE 20—11.20 a. m.

Commodore PALMER :

The admiral has sent a pilot for one of your vessels. Shall I send him over ? We have a few letters for your fleet. All quiet here and below.

ALDEN,
Captain, Senior Officer present.

General BANKS :

Commodore Palmer is about to send a gunboat to Vicksburg. Has the general any commands ?

EATON.

(In communication with U. S. S. Richmond.)

Captain ALDEN :

Send me pilot and letters.

PALMER,
Commodore.

(In communication with General Banks' headquarters.)

Commodore PALMER :

The general only wishes you to send word to General Grant that he is confident of success.

RICH'D B. IRWIN,
Assistant Adjutant-General.

JUNE 21—11 a. m.

Anything from Vicksburg ?

DANA.

No. 'Tis rumored on shore that it's taken.

EATON.

JUNE 28—8.50 a. m.

Two orderlies with dispatches from Commodore Palmer are said to have been captured last night at Bayou Sara. Ask Colonel Irwin if it is so.

EATON.

Can you get over the Point at 11 a. m. ?

DANA.

Sent. "On what part of it ?"
Received. "Little this side, to find a lookout to direct the fire of our batteries."
Sent. "I'll go, but 'tis a fool's errand."

OPPOSITE PORT HUDSON,
June 29—8 a. m.

Wait a moment. Am waiting for orders.

DANA.

Sent. "From whom ?"
Received. "General Dwight. Move a little to the left. How shall the mortars fire to hit the gun on wheels behind the citadel ? How many yards is it ?"
Sent. "Three hundred and fifty. The gun is not there."
Received. "Where is it ?"
Sent. "Fire 800 yards on the verge of the bank. No ; fire 600 yards."
Received. "Is it a rifled gun—about 62-pounder ?"
Sent. "Yes."
Received. "Six hundred yards from here ?"
Sent. "Yes."
Received. "Watch a shot fired at it from the mortar. How was that ?"
Sent. "Try it at 500 yards. Neither shell exploded. Fire little to left."
Sent. "Splendid range. Fire 100 yards short of last shot."
Sent. "That did not explode. Could not see where it fell."
Received. "Will try it again ; keep watch."
Sent. "That fell 100 yards short. Range good.
Received. "Did you see that ?"
Sent. "No ; did not explode. Can only see the shells when they burst."
Received. "Will cease firing for the present. Can you see the rebs or the citadel ?"
Sent. "Not in the citadel, but scores of them on this side of it."
Received. "Direct our fire at them."
Sent. "All right."

Orders have come to cease firing until further orders. Is it best to remain ? The captain commanding the battery will not profit by our instructions. Must see some one higher in authority.

DANA.

Sent. "Will they permit you to direct the fire of one of the Parrotts ?"
Received. "They only bear on the citadel, and all firing has ceased. Shall we go home ?"
Sent. "If you can do nothing with those important artillerists, we will vamose."
Received. "I can do nothing. Will send you word if you are to come. Cease signaling."

JUNE 30—3 p. m.

Captain ROE :
It is necessary for Main to leave the Hartford. What are your orders ?

EATON.

JULY 1—8 a. m.

EATON :
Go to your lower station [as soon] as possible. Will be in the same position opposite.

DANA.

OPPOSITE PORT HUDSON,
July 1—11 a. m.

Received. "Can you see that gun that is firing now ?"
Sent. "Rebel guns opposite me are firing."
Received. "Are they together ?"
Sent. "No. One is 600, the next 1,000, and the next 1,100 yards from your battery."
Received. "On the river bank ?"
Sent. "Yes, within 50 yards of it,"

Received. "How was that shell from her?"
Sent. "Don't know. I can direct one of your guns, if you are ready."
Received. "Ready now. Firing at second gun. Watch." ·
Sent. "Your last gun made a good shot. Little too far to the right."
Received. "Watch our mortar. How was that?"
Sent. "Fire little to left and 100 yards short."
Received. "Have rebel shells done any damage to our battery on right bank of the river?"
Sent. "Can't say."
Received. "Send a man to find out, if not too dangerous. Watch fire of these mortars particularly."
Received. "How was that?"
Sent. "Did not explode; fire again."
Received. "How far is that gun next to citadel?"
Sent. "Six hundred yards."
Received. "Chart says 85 yards from church. Will fire at it."
Sent. "Good range. Fell 200 yards short."
Received. "O. K. Who are the navy chaps with you?"
Sent. Dr. King and three others. Fifth gun in our battery hit the lower rebel gun last shot. Tell them to F. L. L. and a hair lower. Have just hit it again."
Received. "See last shot?"
Sent. "'Twas 10 feet to the left."
Received. "I mean the mortar shell."
Sent. "Struck in the citadel 200 yards short."
Received. "How is this?"
Sent. "One hundred and fifty yards short."
Sent. "One Parrott on this bank is disabled."
Received. "How?"
Sent. "Hit by rebel shells."
Received. "Yes, but how badly disabled, and hit in what point?"
Sent. "The carriage was hit underneath. No great damage. Last shot 1,000 yards short."
Received. "General Stone wants to know if any damage has been done to the rebel guns."
Sent. Our fifth gun has hit the breastwork of the big rifle four times. Its fire is splendid. Can dismount it soon. No other damage."
Received. "You say our fifth gun?"
Sent. "Yes, from the left."
Sent. "Our sixth gun just made a glorious shot."
Received. "Is the carriage of our Parrott too much disabled to be immediately repaired?"
Sent. "Think not. Believe they are at work on it. Let the sixth gun fire 10 feet more to the left."
Received. "How now about the fifth and sixth guns?"
Sent. "The sixth gun is the bully boy."
Received. "Can you give it any directions to make it more bully?"
Sent. "Last shot was little to the right."
Received. "Fearfully hot here. Several men sunstruck. Bullets whiz like fun. Have ceased firing for awhile, the guns are so hot. Will profit by your directions afterward."
Sent. "The rebels are firing that rifle. No. 6 can stop them."
Received. "Tell Charles to be more careful about his motions. Report immediately any damage to our guns. How is No. 6 now? Have just ceased firing until rebels open again. Did fifth and sixth have good aims?"
Sent. "Yes; they have knocked half the earthworks over before that big rifle."
Received. "Can they now hit it with same aim?"
Sent. "Yes."
Received. "Will fire at rifle now; report any shot."
Sent. "I must know which guns are to fire."
Received. "Only one in this battery."
Sent. "Is it fifth or sixth?"
Received. "Neither; it is a navy Dahlgren which I want you to direct the fire of."
Received. "Be there again to-morrow morning at 6 a. m. Cannot see. C. S."

OPPOSITE PORT HUDSON,
July 2—6 a. m.

Received. "Are you ready?"
Sent. "No. One gun fires a shade too low."
Received. "Report everything important in regard to batteries on right bank."

Lieutenant SLACK, *Mortar Battery:*

Please ask Captain Closson to send me to-day twenty boxes of spherical case and twenty boxes shells.

BRADLEY,
Lieutenant.

Received. "Report shells from mortar."

Sent. "Big rifle is just disabled by our Parrott."

Received. "How badly? Is any gun of big battery firing at it now?"

Sent. "The gun has pitched forward. No."

Received. "We are firing at the gun in ravine behind the citadel. How was that?"

Sent. "Can't see any gun mounted within 1,000 yards of the citadel. Should like to direct fire of No. 9 or 10; is it possible? Last mortar shell fell 70 yards short of the disabled rifle."

Received. "What do you propose to fire at with No. 9 or 10?"

Sent. "Two fine guns, the lowest on river bank, and now firing at our Parrotts."

Received. "You can direct the fire of No. 9 or a 24-pounder. Will wait for your report after each shot. What was last shot?"

Sent. "Forty yards to the right. That shell burst little short. Range first rate."

Lieutenant BRADLEY:

Cease firing for the present, and withdraw your section from the bank.

RICHARD ARNOLD,
Brigadier-General.

Sent. "Last shot but one was 50 yards to the right; last shot was splendid, only 3 yards to right. F. L. L. Cease signaling."

Sent. "F. L. L."

Received. "How was last shot from howitzer?"

Sent. "That shot touched the breastwork 8 feet to the right of the gun. F. L. L. and little lower."

Received. "And the last?"

Sent. "Had good range, but was 100 yards short."

Sent. "That burst short."

Sent. "Last shot was 100 yards to the right. This shot was capital; a fraction high. Last shot was 50 yards to the right."

Received. "It can't get any farther to the left. Where is the second rebel gun?"

Sent. "The lowest gun is 75 yards from the river; second gun is a little farther up, and 40 yards from the river."

Received. "How was that?"

Sent. "Little too high. Last shot little too high."

Received. "Are we firing at the lower or second gun?"

Sent. "Howitzer is firing at second gun; the others fire to your right of both S. O. E. very little."

Sent. "Howitzer's shell goes 6 feet over the gun every shot; last shot was too high; little too high again. Can't they, or won't they, depress that gun?"

Received. "Won't, I guess."

Received. "Was that shot any better, and that?"

Sent. "Both and forever too high."

Received. "We will vamose now. Come again to-morrow."

Sent. "Nine a. m. will do, will it not?"

Received. "Yes; cease signaling."

OPPOSITE PORT HUDSON,
July 3—9 a. m.

The record of this day's work is so long and monotonous that I omit it. One day is almost literally the counterpart of another. The firing of our heavy batteries yesterday, under the guidance of our signals, was accurate and destructive.

(In communication with General Banks' headquarters.)

JULY 7—11 a. m.

General BANKS:

I am detaining the General Price here to take Colonel Smith back to Vicksburg. If he intends returning, pray send him at once.

PALMER,
Commodore.

Commodore Palmer:
    General Banks is writing dispatches ₁to General Grant, which I will send in a few moments. Colonel Smith remains here.

RICH'D B. IRWIN,
Assistant Adjutant-General.

JULY 8—p. m.
Commodore Palmer, *Hartford:*
    Port Hudson has surrendered, and will be formally turned over to us at 7 o'clock to-morrow morning. Please keep a bright lookout to-night.

N. P. BANKS,
Major-General.

(In communication with U. S. S. Richmond.)

10.20 A. M.
Commodore Palmer:
    Please send my clerk immediately. Let him stop at Colonel Sayre's, and ask him how many teams he can send me. Have him bring a horse for me.

W. F. MEREDITH.

Mr. Meredith:
    You can let your stores remain if they are in safety. I shall probably be down this afternoon. Port Hudson surrenders to-day. I send your clerk over.

J. S. PALMER,
Commodore.

(In communication with General Banks' headquarters.)

General Banks:
    We are short of coal here, and the transports have had steam up all day. Coal is scarce. Shall I let the fire go down?

J. S. PALMER,
Commodore.

12 M.
Commodore JAMES S. PALMER, *Hartford:*
    You have authority to pass down by Port Hudson whenever you please. Please order our transports to go to Point Pleasant Landing to-night. The general requests you to keep one gunboat above to watch the place and the river to-night, and to place one at his disposal to take dispatches to Vicksburg.

RICH'D B. IRWIN,
Assistant Adjutant-General.

To seal Red. River, thereby cutting off the supplies of both Port Hudson and Vicksburg, the Hartford came to anchor at its mouth April 1, 1863.

An attack at night with a fleet of rams and gunboats was angrily threatened by the enemy for six weeks. With my flagman, I volunteered to ascend the river several miles each night in a skiff, thoroughly equipped with rockets, to announce his approach.

We ʼserved upon this nocturnal picket, relieved at times by the regular officers· and men of the flagship, until the arrival of Admiral Porter's iron-clads, after the reduction of Grand Gulf.·

I have the honor to add that to the performance of this and our more legitimate signal duty Admiral Farragut awarded official mention and approval in his communications to the. Secretary of the Navy.

My flagmen were Charles P. Eaton and Orville S. Sanborn. They were in eight sharp engagements while on the Hartford. They stood at their posts at a time when veteran sailors crouched and crawled and hid. Each of them, during the sickness of the other, has divided the day with myself, and stood single, unrelieved watches of twelve consecutive hours. Both were intrusted by Commodore Palmer with important errands, and Eaton was selected to carry the original dispatches from General Grant to General Banks announcing the surrender of Vicksburg. They are brave, intelligent, and trusty men.

I have the honor to be, very respectfully, your obedient servant,
S. M. EATON,
First Lieutenant Twelfth Maine, Acting Signal Officer.

Lieut. GEORGE R. HERBERT,
Adjutant, Signal Corps, Department of the Gulf.

·———

No. 10.

Report of Lieut. Thomas S. Hall, Twenty-eighth Maine Infantry, Acting Signal Officer, of operations April 10–July 16.

PORT HUDSON, LA.,
July 16, 1863.

SIR: In obedience to orders, I have the honor to report the following transcript of messages sent and received by me from April 10 to July 16, inclusive:

JUNE 4—4 p. m.

Admiral FARRAGUT:
The enemy number their batteries 1, 2, &c., from up river down. The magazine is behind battery No. 6, and from 300 to 500 yards back from the river.
N. P. BANKS,
Major-General, Commanding.

JUNE 5—4.15 p. m.

Admiral FARRAGUT:
SIR: General Emory reports that he sent the Cornie to Bayou Sara, and that she found the three steamers there safe. Please inform Commodore Palmer.
N. P. BANKS,
Major-General, Commanding.

JUNE 6—2.30 p. m.

Admiral FARRAGUT:
The shelling by the mortar-boats on Thursday night is reported to have seriously inconvenienced the enemy. Beef-cattle killed, several wounded, and a regimental camp rendered untenable. The bulk of the early fire passed a little to the left of and beyond the magazine. The sleep of half the garrison was prevented.
N. P. BANKS,
Major-General, Commanding.

JUNE 6—2.30 p. m.

General BANKS:
I have him under my control. The minute he opens, I silence him. I am glad to know I hurt him.
FARRAGUT,
Admiral.

JUNE 6—4 p. m.

Admiral FARRAGUT:
Your note of yesterday received. The sextant has arrived. It will be taken care of, and returned safely. Am much obliged with your offer in regard to the boats in Bayou Sara. We heard of their safety yesterday, but would like particulars. Thanks for the hand-grenades.
N. P. BANKS,
Major-General, Commanding.

JUNE 7—10.30 a. m.

General BANKS:
Hammering and building is reported at the mouth of Thompson's Creek. Can you account for it?
FARRAGUT,
Admiral.

JUNE 7—2.30 p. m.
Admiral FARRAGUT:

We have men near by the creek, and will report to you. All going well.
N. P. BANKS,
Major-General, Commanding.

JUNE 9—6 p. m.
Admiral FARRAGUT:

Opened fire at 11 a. m. from the heavy guns and mortars, and fired slowly during the day with good range and excellent effect, driving the enemy away from the parapet. Our fire was, except in one or two instances, unanswered. The navy guns were admirably served. Please keep up your mortar fire during the whole of the night. We shall fire slowly all night.
N. P. BANKS,
·· *Major-General, Commanding.*

JUNE 9—6.30 p. m.
Admiral FARRAGUT:

Will send you a report of the operations at the mouth of Thompson's Creek this evening.
N. P. BANKS,
Major-General, Commanding.

JUNE 10—1.30 p. m.
Admiral FARRAGUT:

Please send to Springfield Landing 500 blank cartridges, 250 shrapnel, and 50 solid shot for the 9-inch navy guns. Please let me know when they will be there.
N. P. BANKS,
Major-General, Commanding.

JUNE 10—3.15 p. m.
General BANKS:

The ammunition you asked for will be at Springfield Landing at 5 p. m.
ALDEN,
Captain.

Admiral FARRAGUT:

Your letter received ; will send an answer about charges for navy guns.
N. P. BANKS,
Major-General, Commanding.

JUNE 12—8 a. m.
General BANKS:

Your request will be attended to
. FARRAGUT,
Admiral.

JUNE 13—9 a. m.
General BANKS:

Commodore Palmer sent me word, and I send it to you, that the sharpshooters of the Arizona had joined their regiment some time before the Arizona went up the river to Natchez; but I will send by the first opportunity.
FARRAGUT,
Admiral.

JUNE 13—5 p. m.
Admiral FARRAGUT:

Please send as many shrapnel as you can spare for the 9-inch guns. General Gardner answers that his duty requires him to defend the place, and therefore he declines to surrender.   •
N. P. BANKS,
Major-General, Commanding.

JUNE 14—7 a. m.
General DWIGHT:

Send me a report every half hour, or oftener, if you can.
N. P. BANKS,
Major-General, Commanding.

JUNE 14—7.30 a. m.

General BANKS:

Our skirmishers and sharpshooters are within 30 rods of the parapet. A ravine between them and the parapet, full of fallen timber, raked by artillery on my right and left.

DWIGHT,
General.

JUNE 14—8 a. m.

General BANKS:

I cannot advance farther until the skirmishers silence the field batteries.

DWIGHT,
General.

JUNE 14—9 a. m.

General BANKS:

Our artillery is trying to silence that of the enemy. Our infantry is very quiet. Nothing of importance.

DWIGHT,
General.

JUNE 14—9.13 a. m.

General BANKS:

General Dwight is preparing to renew the attack; should prefer to do so at same time with General Grover. When can Grover do so ?

G. A. FISKE, JR.,
Aide-de-Camp.

JUNE 14—1 p. m.

Colonel IRWIN, *Assistant Adjutant-General:*

All quiet but sharpshooting. As the First and Second Brigades cannot retire, General Dwight cannot assault again at present. Shall throw up rifle-pits after dark.

G. A. FISKE, JR.,
Lieutenant, and Aide-de-Camp.

JUNE 14—6.30 p. m.

Admiral FARRAGUT:

Getting very short of ammunition. Please send as much Dahlgren ammunition as you can spare, to the extent of 800 rounds, chiefly shell and shrapnel. Can you spare any 20-pounder Parrott ammunition ?

N. P. BANKS,
Major-General, Commanding.

JUNE 26—4 p. m.

Captain HALSTED, *Assistant Adjutant-General:*

I would respectfully request that Lieutenant-Colonel Bickmore, of the Fourteenth Maine Volunteers, be relieved from the storming party, in order to take command of his regiment, Colonel Porter, of the same, being under arrest.

DWIGHT,
General.

JUNE 27—8 a. m.

General BANKS:

The rebels opened sharply with 10-inch shell and rifle shells during the fog this morning; did no damage. I caused four guns to be turned on them, and they have ceased firing. The citadel has gone in. The second Dahlgren has been mounted, and will be at work in half an hour.

CHAS. P. STONE,
Brigadier-General.

JULY 11 [?]—7.30 a. m.

General BANKS:

I have ceased firing on account of the troops being in range of my shelling.

ALDEN,
Captain.

JULY 11 [?]—7.30 a. m.*
The RICHMOND:
What boats came down, and what news did they bring?
IRWIN,
Colonel, Assistant Adjutant-General.
The Sachem brought dispatches for the admiral. No news.
JOHN C. ABBOTT,
Lieutenant.
Very respectfully, your obedient servant,
THOMAS S. HALL,
. *First Lieut. 28th Maine Volunteers, Acting Signal Officer.*
Lieut. GEORGE R. HERBERT, ·
Adjutant, Signal Corps, Department of the Gulf.

No. 11. .

Report of Lieut. Joseph L. Hallett, Thirty-first Massachusetts Infantry, Acting Signal Officer, of operations May 12–July 9.

HEADQUARTERS SIGNAL CORPS,
Port Hudson, La., July 10, 1863.
SIR: I have the honor to report that—*
* • * * * * *
May 10, I received Special Orders, No. 3, dated New Orleans, April 30, directing me to proceed at once to Baton Rouge, and take charge of the detachment of the signal party at that place.
May 12, I obtained transportation at Alexandria on the steamer Union, and left the same day for Brashear City, via Red River, Atchafalaya, and Grand Lake, thence to New Orleans by the Opelousas Railroad. At New Orleans I embarked with my party on the steamer Nassau, and arrived at Baton Rouge on Sunday, the 17th. I immediately reported to Maj. Gen. C. C. Augur, commanding United States forces at Baton Rouge. Agreeably to verbal orders from Maj. Gen. C. C. Augur, I made a reconnaissance with a detachment of the Seventh Illinois Cavalry on the 20th to Springfield Landing, for the purpose of opening communication with the fleet below Port Hudson and the army encamped in rear of the rebel batteries on the Bayou Sara road. Finding it impracticable to signalize direct from General Augur's headquarters to the fleet on account of the forest of lofty trees, I ordered First Lieut. John F. Jencks to establish a signal station at Springfield Landing, to communicate with Second Lieut. A. M. Jackson, acting signal officer on the U. S. S. Richmond, and Second Lieut. John N. Main, acting signal officer on the iron-clad Essex. I also gave orders to First Lieut. Milton Benner, in charge of the signal telegraph train, to lay the wire of his train from Lieutenant Jencks' station to the junction of the Springfield and Port Hudson roads. ,
The distance from Springfield Landing to the fleet is 3 miles; from Springfield Landing to the junction of the Springfield and Port Hudson roads, 4½ miles.
The station at Springfield Landing was established on the 21st of May. The telegraph was completed to the junction of the Springfield and Port Hudson roads on the evening of the 22d, and communication opened with the fleet on the morning of the 23d.

----

* Portion here omitted relates to operations, April 9–May 14, in West Louisiana, and is printed in Series I, Vol. XV, p. 363.

The reports of Lieutenants Benner and Jencks will show that these stations have been of good service in keeping the army and navy instructed in each other's movements during the siege of Port Hudson, and have transmitted a large number of official messages.

First Lieut. Thomas S. Hall was relieved from duty on the gunboat, and reported to me at General Augur's' headquarters on the 31st of May. Lieutenant Harris reported to me, by order of Capt. W. B. Roe, on the 21st of June.

Signal stations were established on the left of our line, 5 miles above Springfield Landing, to communicate with the fleet above and below Port Hudson; also with the left wing, commanded by Brigadier-General Dwight; the right, by Brigadier-General Grover; the center, by Major-General Augur; and with Major-General Banks' headquarters, 2 miles in rear of the center. Communication was established through these stations from Major-General Banks' headquarters to Springfield Landing. Lieutenants [H. C.] Dane and Main were in charge of C station; Lieutenant Hall, D station, both stations on the left; Lieut. James H. Rundlett, E station, on the right; Lieutenant Harris, F station, on the center; and Lieut. John W. Dana, A station, at Major-General Banks' headquarters. Owing to heavy woods and the peculiar position of the enemy's works in and around Port Hudson, we were obliged to build stations in tall trees, within easy range of the rebel batteries.

The enemy frequently opened on the stations with solid shot and shell, which was a source of some annoyance when sending and receiving messages. E station was shelled on the 5th of June, and the officer in charge obliged to leave it for the time being. He returned to his post after the enemy had ceased firing, and, on the 6th, built another station near the first, but less exposed to the enemy.

On the 14th of June, in compliance with verbal orders from Capt. William B. Roe, I reported for signal duty to Brigadier-General Dwight. A station for signaling with the right and center was built in a point of woods on the left, near General Dwight's headquarters. We were about to open communication, when our position was discovered by the enemy, and the station was shelled by his artillery. It being so near the rebel breastworks, and the firing so rapid and close, we were obliged to fall back to D station. The enemy attempted to shell this station, but the range was very poor. Communication was kept open from this point during the day.

Stations C, D, and E, overlooking the fort, have been of great benefit in discovering the movements and position of the enemy, and directing the fire of our artillery.

I am happy to report that the officers and enlisted men deserve credit for faithfulness in the discharge of their duties, and that no casualties have occurred to any of the party. Communication was kept open with the fleet above and below Port Hudson and Springfield Landing, to and from Major-General Banks' headquarters, until the surrender of Port Hudson.

In conformity with orders from Capt. William B. Roe, of the 9th of July, the officers were relieved from their stations, and reported to him at headquarters of the signal corps, Port Hudson, La.

I am, sir, very respectfully, your obedient servant,

JOS. L. HALLETT,
First Lieutenant Thirty-first Mass. Vols., Acting Signal Officer.

Lieut. GEORGE R. HERBERT,
Acting Adjutant, Signal Corps, Department of the Gulf.

No. 12.

Report of Lieut. George R. Herbert, One hundred and fifty-ninth New York Infantry, Acting Signal Officer, of operations May 27–June 13.

NEW ORLEANS, LA.,
July 28, 1863.

SIR : I have the honor to transmit the following report of official messages sent and received by me during the recent campaign at Port Hudson and vicinity.

The messages were all sent from General Banks' headquarters. On the 27th of May, Lieutenant Hallett and myself proceeded to open communication with the gunboat Richmond, lying below Port Hudson, which was accomplished, but did not send or receive any official messages. For several days I assisted in building stations, and on the 1st of June communication was opened all along the line, consisting of six stations.

JUNE 4.

Admiral FARRAGUT :

The enemy number their water batteries 1, 2, &c., from up river down. The magazine is behind battery No. 6, and about 300 to 500 yards back from the river.
N. P. BANKS.

General BANKS :

I have him under my control. The minute he opens, I silence him.
D. G. FARRAGUT.

JUNE 5.

Admiral FARRAGUT :

General Emory reports that he sent the Cornie to Bayou Sara, and that she found the three steamers there safe. Please inform Commodore Palmer.
N. P. BANKS.

JUNE 6.

Admiral FARRAGUT:

The shelling by the mortar-boats on Thursday night is reported to have seriously inconvenienced the enemy. Beef-cattle killed, several men wounded, and a regimental camp rendered untenable. The bulk of the early fire passed a little to the left of and beyond the main magazine. The sleep of half the garrison was prevented.
N. P. BANKS,
Major-General, Commanding.

JUNE 6.

Admiral FARRAGUT :

Your note of yesterday received. The sextant has arrived. It will be taken care of, and returned safely. Am much obliged for your offer with regard to the boats in Bayou Sara. We heard of their safety yesterday, but would like particulars. Thanks for hand-grenades.
N. P. BANKS,
Major-General, Commanding.

JUNE 9. ·

Admiral FARRAGUT :

Opened fire at 11 a. m. from the heavy guns and mortars, and fired slowly during the day, with good ranges and excellent effect, driving the enemy away from the parapet. Our fire was, except in one or two instances, unanswered. The navy guns were admirably served. Please keep up your mortar fire during the whole of the night. We shall fire slowly all night. Will send you report of the operations at the mouth of Thompson's Creek this evening. ·
N. P. BANKS,
Major-General, Commanding.

JUNE 10.

Admiral FARRAGUT:

Please send to Springfield Landing 500 blank cartridges, 250 shell, and 50 solid shot for the 9-inch navy guns. Please let me know when they will be there.

N. P. BANKS,
Major-General, Commanding.

JUNE 10.

General BANKS:

The ammunition you asked for will be at Springfield Landing at 5 p. m.

ALDEN,
Captain.

JUNE 11.

Captain ALDEN:

Your letter received. The general's request was for 200 shrapnel; you mention 50 only. We need them very much.

RICH'D B. IRWIN,
Assistant Adjutant-General.

JUNE 11.

Admiral FARRAGUT:

Your letter received. Will send an answer about charges of powder for navy guns.

N. P. BANKS,
Major-General, Commanding.

JUNE 13.

Admiral FARRAGUT:

Please send as much shrapnel as you can spare for the 9-inch navy guns. General Gardner answers that his duty requires him to defend the place, and therefore he declines to surrender.

N. P. BANKS,
Major-General, Commanding.

JUNE 13.

General BANKS:

Your request will be attended to.

FARRAGUT,
Admiral.

JUNE 13.

Admiral FARRAGUT:

Please send an order to the company of sharpshooters from the Arizona, said to be ashore at Saint Francisville, to rejoin its regiment at once.

N. P. BANKS,
Major-General, Commanding.

JUNE 13.

General BANKS:

Commodore Palmer sent me word, and I send it to you, that the sharpshooters of the Arizona had joined their regiment some time before the Arizona went up the river to Natchez; but I will send by the first opportunity.

D. G. FARRAGUT,
Admiral.

Having been ordered to New Orleans on account of sickness, the above is all the report I have to make.

I have the honor to be, very respectfully, your obedient servant,

GEO. R. HERBERT,
Second Lieut. 159th New York Regiment, Acting Signal Officer.

Capt. WILLIAM B. ROE,
Chief Signal Officer, Department of the Gulf.

No. 13.

Report of. Lieut. Amos M. Jackson, Twenty-fourth Maine Infantry, Act-
, *ing Signal Officer, of operations May 18–June 15.*

NEW ORLEANS, LA.,
June 27, 1863.

SIR: I have the honor to submit the following report of duties performed by me as signal officer on board the U. S. S. Richmond from
May 18, 1863, to June 15, 1863, the report from May 1 to May 18 having
been submitted to Lieutenant Jencks, then in command of the signal
party at Baton Rouge, La.

The following is a correct copy of the messages sent and received by
me within the time mentioned above:

MAY 18.

Captain ALDEN:
Shall I use the mortars to-night?

FROM THE ESSEX. .

Captain CALDWELL:
Yes.

ALDEN,
Captain.

Captain CALDWELL:
When do you open?

JAMES ALDEN,
Captain.

Captain ALDEN:
·At 12.

CALDWELL,
Captain.

MAY 19.

Captain ALDEN: :
Sharp artillery firing heard in the rear of Port Hudson and abreast of us; about
thirty shots in each place. ˙ From good authority.

CALDWELL,
Captain.

MAY 19.

Captain ALDEN:
. Firing continued very heavy, with musketry at intervals.

CALDWELL,
Captain.

MAY 22.

Lieutenant MAIN:
Report on board the ship immediately with man and kit.

JAMES ALDEN,
Captain.

Captain ALDEN:
Colonel Grierson is one-half mile north of the railroad; has met General Grover
with his division. General Banks is 3 miles back. News from·Grant good; he cut
Johnston's forces to pieces at Jackson, capturing sixty-one guns; he has Vicksburg
so hemmed in they cannot use their siege guns.·

C. C. AUGUR.

MAY 24.

Admiral FARRAGUT:
I have nothing from Banks since yesterday morning.

PALMER,
Commodore.

MAY 24.

Commodore PALMER:

Hold on and watch events, and be ready to take advantage of them.

D. G. FARRAGUT,
Admiral.

MAY 24.

Commodore PALMER:

To fire on the batteries from above would injure our troops more than the enemy, perhaps.

JAMES ALDEN,
Captain.

MAY 24.

Admiral FARRAGUT:

I have now in the Mississippi the Albratross, the Arizona, and the Sachem, the latter at Bayou Sara; I have the Estrella in the Atchafalaya; the Pittsburg was to report to Captain Walker yesterday, to assist him.

PALMER,
Commodore.

MAY 24.

Commodore PALMER:

Banks has forces on the Point. Augur is within 1 mile of the forts. The rest are near.

JAMES ALDEN,
Captain.

U. S. S. HARTFORD,
May 24.

General Grant has been every way successful. I hope Vicksburg by this time is ours. I have sent an officer over with dispatches for you. Any news from the army?

PALMER,
Commodore.

MAY 24.

Admiral FARRAGUT:

General Banks requests me to shell the west side of Thompson's Creek at midnight, to prevent any attempt of the enemy to escape on that side. You will understand the firing.

PALMER,
Commodore.

MAY 24.

Admiral FARRAGUT:

I have received a dispatch from Colonel Chandler, quartermaster, Brashear, requesting me to ask you what disposition is to be made of the coal towed around by the Anglo-American. He says they cannot get in. He has no boats to send for them, and asks if they had not better come back. Please let me know.

A. N. SHIPLEY,
Assistant Quartermaster.

MAY 26.

Admiral FARRAGUT:

Grierson's cavalry captured the two steamers on Thompson's Creek.

PALMER,
Commodore.

MAY 26.

General BANKS:

A lieutenant of Grierson's cavalry is here, and says the enemy cannot escape between Fancy Point and the river. They must take the Bayou Sara road if they escape at all. Should you want me to fire in the direction indicated in your note, send up a rocket half an hour before I am to begin.

PALMER,
Commodore.

MAY 27.

Commodore PALMER:

The light artillery will open at daylight. The heavy guns at 6 p. m. Port Hudson will be ours to-day. The ships will cease firing when the artillery ceases.

BANKS,
General.

MAY 27.

Commodore PALMER:

All is going well with the army; they push the rebels hard on the right Do not fire again.

ALDEN,
Captain.

MAY 30.

Admiral FARRAGUT:

The shells fired from the mortar fleet at the batteries at 1 o'clock this morning fell on the right of our lines; five-eighths of a mile to west, with same range, and you will hit the enemy's forts, or 100 yards to left, and you will hit their rifle-pits.

G. WEITZEL,
General.

MAY 30.

Admiral FARRAGUT:

General Weitzel says continue the firing as we direct.

STATION AT THOMPSON'S CREEK,
May 31.

Capt. WILLIAM B. ROE:

I was on the point opposite Port Hudson yesterday p. m. Tell General Banks or General Weitzel I would like to repeat my trip, and bring my notes for examination to-night. A battery of Parrott guns would be a thorn in their side. Roads good, levee high, range short.

S. M. EATON,
Lieutenant.

MAY 31.

Admiral FARRAGUT:

Let the mortars fire on that gun which shot at us last night.

WEITZEL,
General.

JUNE 1.

General BANKS:

An orderly reached Bayou Sara last night with dispatches for the Hartford. Not waiting transportation, he started by land, and has not yet arrived.

S. M. EATON,
Lieutenant.

JUNE 2.

Admiral FARRAGUT:

If possible, I will send the Parrott guns to your side. It offers a good position. We are getting in position for a vigorous attack, and are confident of success. We are getting the large guns up to-day. I will keep you well informed, and am sorry so few messages reach you.

N. P. BANKS,
General,

JUNE 2.

General BANKS:

Your telegrams about Parrott guns for the Point received. Do not think it safe. Have written fully.

D. G. FARRAGUT,
Admiral.

JULY [JUNE] 2.

Admiral FARRAGUT:

The steamer Crescent is here. She will return in the morning to New Orleans.

JOHN WATTERS.

JUNE 2.

Admiral FARRAGUT:

I beg you to bring the mortars to bear while daylight lasts—to bear on a circle of 200 yards in diameter, a circle about 800 yards south of the church. Let the shell fall near this point and it will destroy their magazine. It is just in rear of the first clump of trees between the tower and your position.

N. P. BANKS,
General.

JUNE 9.

Admiral FARRAGUT:

We opened fire at 11 a. m. from heavy guns and mortars. Fired slowly during the day, with good range and excellent effect, driving the enemy away from the parapet. Our fire was, except in one or two instances, unanswered. Please keep up your mortar fire during the whole of this night. We shall fire slowly all night.

N. P. BANKS,
General.

JUNE 9.

Admiral FARRAGUT:

I will send you a report of the operations at the mouth of Thompson's Creek this evening.

BANKS,
General.

JUNE 9.

Admiral FARRAGUT:

The range of your guns is too great to-night. Some of the shells explode between the enemy's works and General Grover's front.

N. P. BANKS,
General.

JUNE 10.

Admiral FARRAGUT:

Does the Arizona need the company of sharpshooters which we put on board? They were set ashore at Saint Francisville. Steamer arrived from the north, date to the 24th. No news. Gold, 144. Twenty rebels ran out to sea by Pass à l'Outre.

BANKS,
General.

JUNE 10.

General BANKS:

Sharpshooters not needed on the Arizona. News from General Grant, to the 27th, good. Rebels gone to sea is another Fox case. Captain and crew of the Fox arrived in New Orleans, and should be arrested.

D. G. FARRAGUT,
Admiral.

JUNE 10.

Admiral FARRAGUT:

You can have as much ice as you can stow by sending for it. The ice vessel has to be lightened to be got out of this place for Baton Rouge.

JOHN WATTERS.

JUNE 10.

Admiral FARRAGUT:

Please send the sharpshooters not required on the Arizona to these headquarters. Orders have been sent to General Bowen, at New Orleans, to arrest captain and crew of the Fox.

N. P. BANKS,
General.

JUNE 10.

Admiral FARRAGUT:

Colonel Prince reports no raft built at the mouth of Thompson's Creek, or any indications of the escape of the enemy; the east side is very swampy, and can be traveled only on foot. A reconnoitering party was sent down the east bank of Thompson's Creek as far as Sandy Creek, which is 340 yards from the mouth of

Thompson's Creek. Colonel Prince saw our camp at Fausse Point, and the commanding officer there could observe everything transpiring at the mouth of Thompson's Creek. Please ask him to do so.

N. P. BANKS.

JUNE 11.

Admiral FARRAGUT:

The captain and engineer of the Fox have been arrested, and the engineer discharged on $10,000 bail, at the request of his friend, Hon. Mr. Flanders.

N. P. BANKS,
General.

SPRINGFIELD STATION, June 12.

One hundred and seventy contrabands and paroled prisoners and some army horses await transportation at Springfield.

D. G. FARRAGUT.

JUNE 12.

Admiral FARRAGUT:

The enemy's commissary stores have been removed to point near the railroad landing. Cannot the guns and the mortars of the fleet be brought to bear on it?

CHAS. P. STONE,
Brigadier-General.

REMARKS.

May 22.—At 11 a. m. the Hartford appeared across the point opposite Port Hudson, and the signal officer on board of her called me. I answered him, requesting him to wait, as I was not ready. He continued to call me, not recognizing my answer. I answered repeatedly, without a reply from him. First, having left the glass a few moments to arrange something about my station, on returning I found him sending a message, of which, of course, I got very little. I then waited to have the sails furled, as they shook my station badly, before calling for a repeat. I then found him calling me, and answered again and again, but could get no recognition. At 2 p. m. Captain Alden moved the ship ahead, to give a better view if possible. While under way, the opposite station called. I answered, requesting him to wait until we were at anchor, but he attempted to send a message, which I could not read while in motion. Soon after we came to anchor it began to rain, which obstructed the view till dark. I called with torches in the evening, but received no reply.

May 22.—The station at Springfield Landing was established, with which Lieutenant Main communicated while on board the Richmond. He being ordered off May 29, I took charge of both stations.

May 30.—Another station opened communication with us near the mouth of Thompson's Creek. Having these three stations to watch, it sometimes occurred that more than one called at the same time, which caused embarrassment and delay.

June 2.—I opened communication with a station in the woods on the left of our line. Lieutenant Abbott arrived, and from that date took charge of the station communicating with the Hartford, and Lieutenant Hall's station, communicating with Springfield Landing and Thompson's Creek. The latter station was abandoned; date not known. I discovered it accidentally, after watching needlessly for several days, and calling without reply.

June 15.—I was obliged to leave my station on account of illness.

Very respectfully, your obedient servant,

A. M. JACKSON,
2d Lieut. Twenty-fourth Maine Vols., and Actg. Signal Officer.

Lieut. GEORGE R. HERBERT,
Adjutant of Signal Corps.

No. 14.

Report of Lieut. John F. Jencks, Twenty-sixth Connecticut Infantry, Acting Signal Officer, of operations May 22–June 19.

NEW ORLEANS, LA.,
August 10, 1863.

SIR: I have the honor to report that, in obedience to orders received from Lieut. J. L. Hallett, acting signal officer, dated May 22, 1863, I proceeded to Springfield Landing with men, horses, and signal equipments, and established a station communicating with Lieut. A. M. Jackson, acting signal officer, whose station was on the U. S. steam sloop of war Richmond, and with Lieut. Milton Benner, commanding signal telegraph train. Accompanying this paper please find a copy of the messages sent and received by me while in charge of the station.

On account of sickness, on the 25th of June I received orders from Capt. William B. Roe to report at Baton Rouge, which order was complied with immediately.

On the 13th of July, by orders received from Lieut. J. L. Hallett, acting signal officer, I proceeded to Port Hudson and relieved Lieut. Thomas S. Hall, whose station was in communication with Lieut. John C. Abbott, on the U. S. steam sloop of war Richmond. The weather being bad, no official messages were sent or received while I was in charge of the station. On the 19th of July, I received orders from Lieut. J. L. Hallett, at Donaldsonville, La. I proceeded the same date by steamboat North America, and reported according to orders. On the 20th of July, I received orders from Lieut. E. H. Russell to take charge of the party then in his charge, as he had orders to report to New Orleans. The time that I was there, no stations were established. On the 29th of July, by orders from General Grover, then in command of the troops in Donaldsonville, I reported by telegraph to the chief of signal corps for orders, but not receiving any, on the 3d day of August I proceeded to Baton Rouge. On the 5th of August, by orders from Lieut. J. L. Hallett, I was ordered to report with horses and equipments to Capt. William B. Roe, at New Orleans, as soon as transportation could be procured, which was done on the 8th of August, arriving there on the 9th.

I am, sir, very respectfully, your obedient servant,
JOHN F. JENCKS,
First Lieut. Twenty-sixth Conn. Vols., and Actg. Signal Officer.
Lieut. GEORGE R. HERBERT,
Adjutant, Signal Corps, Department of the Gulf.

Messages referred to in foregoing report.

MAY 22, 1863.
General BANKS:

A force of cavalry will leave at daylight for Bayou Sara, May 23.
C. C. AUGUR,
Major-General.

Capt. JAMES ALDEN:

Colonel Grierson is one-half mile north of the railroad. He has met General Grover with his division. General Banks is 3 miles back. The news from Grant is good. He has cut Johnston's forces to pieces at Jackson, capturing sixty-one pieces of artillery. He has Vicksburg hemmed in so they cannot use their siege guns.
C. C. AUGUR,
Major-General.

MAY 23, 1863.

Major-General AUGUR:

The admiral has arrived, and would like to know the condition of things and how he can serve you.

JAMES ALDEN,
Captain, U. S. Navy.

Capt. JAMES ALDEN:

General Banks is up with his forces, and we close in around them this morning; will probably open fire upon them in the course of the day. The general wishes me to say that he will keep the admiral informed of the progress of affairs.

C. C. AUGUR,
Major-General.

MAY 24, 1863.

Admiral FARRAGUT:

General Banks wishes to inform you that our forces are in possession of the point opposite Port Hudson. Our troops are somewhat above, and retired, but they command the point. They captured a signal officer and 6 men last night. I am a mile from the fortifications. Grover is on his way to the same. Sherman is close at hand.

C. C. AUGUR,
Major-General.

: MAY 24, 1863.

Admiral FARRAGUT:

I have received a dispatch from Colonel Chandler, assistant quartermaster at Brashear City, requesting me to ask you what disposition is to be made of the coal towed around by the Anglo-American. He says they cannot get in. He has no boats to send for them, and asks if they had not better return.

A. N. SHIPLEY,
Assistant Quartermaster.

Capt. JAMES ALDEN:

Can the tug take me to Baton Rouge and return, on important business?

JOHN H. RAUCH,
Medical Director.

J. H. RAUCH, Medical Director:

Yes; will send her down soon.

JAMES ALDEN,
Captain, U. S. Navy.

JUNE 4, 1863.

Admiral FARRAGUT:

I beg of you to bring your mortars to bear immediately while daylight lasts—your mortars to bear upon a circle of 200 yards diameter, the circle about 800 yards south of the church. Let the mortar shell fall in a circle of 200 yards in that vicinity. One shell near this point will destroy the magazine. It is just in rear of first clump of trees looking up toward the town from your position.

N. P. BANKS,
Major-General.

Admiral FARRAGUT:

Colonel Prince has been to-day to the mouth of Thompson's Creek, on the east bank, and reports neither seeing nor hearing anything of the enemy in the neighborhood. Our picket line is complete to the captured steamboats, whence it is extended by frequent patrols beyond the steamboats to the river. The crossing of Thompson's Creek is reported impracticable. We burned the enemy's store-house this afternoon.

N. P. BANKS,
Major-General, Commanding.

JUNE 9, 1863.

Admiral FARRAGUT:

The range of your guns is rather too great to-night, some of the shells exploding between the enemy's works and General Grover's front.

N. P. BANKS,
Major-General.

JUNE 10, 1863.

Admiral FARRAGUT:

Does the Arizona need the company of sharpshooters which we put on her? They have been set ashore at Saint Francisville. Steamer Locust Point is in from the north; dates to the 24th. No news. Gold, 144. Tow-boat Boston captured at Pass à l'Outre last [night] by 20 rebels, and run out to sea.

N. P. BANKS,
Major-General, Commanding.

Major-General BANKS:

The sharpshooters are not needed on the Arizona. News from Grant, to the 27th, good. Rebels gone to sea is another Fox case. Captain and crew of the Fox have arrived in New Orleans, and should be arrested.

D. G. FARRAGUT,
Admiral.

Admiral FARRAGUT:

You can have as much ice as you can store by sending for it. The ice vessel has got to be lightened to be sent out of this place to Baton Rouge.

JOHN WATTERS,
Lieutenant-Commander.

Admiral FARRAGUT:

Please send the sharpshooters not needed on the Arizona to these headquarters. Orders have been sent to General Bowen, at New Orleans, to arrest the captain and crew of the Fox.

N. P. BANKS,
Major-General, Commanding.

Admiral FARRAGUT:

Colonel Prince reports no raft being built at the mouth of Thompson's Creek, and no indications there of any effort on the part of the enemy to escape. The ground on the west side is very swampy and can only be traversed by men on foot. A recon-noitering party, sent down the east bank, went as far as the mouth of Sandy Creek, which is about 340 yards above the mouth of Thompson's Creek, but met no pickets. Colonel Prince saw our camp at Fausse Point, and thinks the commanding officer there would be able to observe everything transpiring at the mouth of Thompson's Creek. Please ask him to do so.

N. P. BANKS,
Major-General, Commanding.

W. S. SCHLEY, *Executive Officer of the Richmond:*

Send as many 5-second fuses as you can possibly spare to Springfield Landing, in care of Colonel Arnold, chief of artillery.

E. TERRY.

JUNE 11.

Admiral FARRAGUT:

Captain and engineer of the Fox have been arrested, and one discharged on $10,000 bail, at the request of his relative, the Hon. Mr. Flanders.

N. P. BANKS,
Major-General, Commanding.

JUNE 10.

Admiral FARRAGUT:

Colonel Benedict informs me that you had orders not to fire. It must have been a great mistake in some of my dispatches. Please continue the fire of your mortars the whole night. We shall fire, also.

N. P. BANKS,
Major-General, Commanding.

Admiral FARRAGUT:

The enemy's commissary store has been removed to the bank of the river near the railroad landing. Cannot the guns and mortars of the fleet be brought to bear upon it?

CHAS. P. STONE,
Brigadier-General.

Admiral FARRAGUT:

Dispatches to General Banks delivered in person. Chief engineer asks, Can you give him four 30-pounder Parrott guns, and on what kind of carriages ?

J. S. BAKER,
Captain and Engineer.

J. S. BAKER, *Engineer :*

The admiral has no 30-pounder Parrott guns here. It is understood a large number belonging to the army are at New Orleans, in store.

T. A. JENKINS,
Captain, and Chief of Staff.

JUNE 13, 1863.

'General BANKS :

Ammunition for the naval battery just received, and will be sent to Springfield Landing this a. m.

T. A. JENKINS,
Captain, and Chief of Staff.

JUNE 14, 1863.

Admiral FARRAGUT:

The telegraph operator here was ordered to the front this morning. We have no communication with General Banks' headquarters. Officers coming in report Weitzel inside the enemy's works. The front was defeated in an assault. This is what I can learn here at Springfield Landing.

JOHN WATTERS,
Lieutenant-Commander.

JUNE 15, 1863.

Commanding Officer of the Lower Fleet :

From information received, I think' an attack will be made upon my force by a large force of cavalry. If the enemy does not attack me to-day, I shall move my force to the lower fleet, for the purpose of getting a safe position and near supplies.

C. H. SAGE,
Colonel, Commanding.

Send this to General Banks.

D. G. FARRAGUT.
Admiral.

JUNE 15, 1863.

Major-General BANKS :

I can deliver in New Orleans 1,000 30-pounder Parrott shot or shell, and 600 20-pounder Parrott shot or shell. If wanted, telegraph to Commodore Morris for it to be sent in any army transport.

D G. FARRAGUT,
Admiral.

JUNE 17, 1863.

Admiral FARRAGUT :

Can you send me two surgeons, as the wounded are coming in very fast and I am short-handed ?

J. C. FISHER,
Medical Director.

JAMES C. FISHER,
Medical Director :

I have but one surgeon.

D. G. FARRAGUT,
Admiral.

U. S. GUNBOAT WINONA,
Springfield Landing, June 19, 1863.

Admiral FARRAGUT :

SIR : The enemy is in force near Plaquemine—cavalry, infantry, and artillery. The force that made this morning's raid numbered 300. It seems they intended attacking this place. I at once proceeded here as quick as possible. The commanding officer expects an attack. With the assistance of a gunboat the fort can be held, in my opinion, against any force the rebels can bring.

> A. W. WEAVER,
> *Lieutenant-Commander, U. S. Navy.*

This is respectfully submitted by—

> JOHN F. JENCKS,
> *First Lieut. 26th Conn. Vols., and Acting Signal Officer.*

Lieut. GEORGE R. HERBERT,
Adjutant, Signal Corps, Department of the Gulf.

No. 15.

*Report of Lieut. James H. Rundlett, Fiftieth Massachusetts Infantry,
Acting Signal Officer, of operations May 24–July 7.*

> NEW ORLEANS, LA.,
> *July 27,* 1863.

SIR: I have the honor to report to you the following signal duty as having been performed by me since the 24th of May, 1863:

May 24, I was ordered by Lieutenant Hallett, commanding detachment at Baton Rouge, to report to Springfield Landing without delay. I proceeded from there to the headquarters of General Augur, and was then ordered by Lieutenant Hallett to report to Acting Brigadier-General Dudley's headquarters for duty.

June 1, having opened communication with the headquarters of General Augur, sent the following messages:

> JUNE 1.

General AUGUR:

Please ask Captain Holcomb the range of the three last spherical case shots I fired after I received his message.

> DUDLEY,
> *Colonel.*

> JUNE 1.

Colonel DUDLEY:

I did not see them.

> HOLCOMB,
> *Captain.*

Was now ordered by Lieutenant Hallett to build a station on Griffith's plantation, on a line of communication between the headquarters of General Banks and the U. S. sloop of war Richmond.

> JUNE 4.

Admiral FARRAGUT:

The enemy number their water batteries 1, 2, &c., from up-river down. The magazine is behind battery No. 6, 500 yards back from the river.

> N. P. BANKS.

> JUNE 6.

General BANKS:

I have got the enemy under my control. The minute he opens, I silence him. I am glad I hurt him.

> D. G. FARRAGUT.

> JUNE 9.

General BANKS:

Hammering and building is reported at the mouth of Thompson's Creek. Can you account for it?

> D. G. FARRAGUT.

JUNE 10.

Admiral FARRAGUT:

Please send to Springfield Landing 500 blank cartridges, 250 shrapnel, 200 shell, and 50 solid shot for the 9-inch navy guns. Please let me know when they will be there.

N. P. BANKS,
Major-General.

JUNE 10.

General BANKS:

The ammunition you asked for will be at Springfield Landing at 5 p. m.

ALDEN,
Captain.

JUNE 11.

Admiral FARRAGUT:

Your letter received. Will send answer about charges of powder desired for navy guns.

N. P. BANKS,
Major-General, Commanding.

JUNE 11.

Captain ALDEN:

Your letter received. The general's request was for 200 shrapnel. You mentioned 50 only. We need them very much.

RICH'D B. IRWIN,
Assistant Adjutant-General.

JUNE 13.

Admiral FARRAGUT:

Please send an order to the company of sharpshooters from the Arizona, said to be ashore at Saint Francisville, to rejoin their regiment at once.

RICH'D B. IRWIN,
Assistant Adjutant-General.

JUNE 13.

General BANKS:

Commodore Palmer sent me word, and I send it to you, that the sharpshooters of the Arizona had joined their regiment some time before the Arizona went up the river to Natchez; but I will send by the first opportunity.

FARRAGUT,
Admiral.

JUNE 13.

Admiral FARRAGUT:

Please send us as much shrapnel as you can spare for the 9-inch navy guns. General Gardner answers that his duty requires him to defend the place, and therefore he refuses to surrender.

N. P. BANKS,
Major-General, Commanding.

JUNE 13.

Admiral FARRAGUT:

Please commence firing, with mortars only, at 11 p. m., and cease exactly at 2 a. m. Throw your shell as nearly as possible in the center of the works.

N. P. BANKS.

JUNE 14.

General BANKS:

Our artillery are trying to silence that of the enemy. Infantry very quiet. Nothing of importance.

DWIGHT,
General.

JUNE 14.

General BANKS:

General Dwight is preparing to renew the attack; should prefer to do so at the same time with General Grover. When will General Grover do so?

FISKE,
Lieutenant, Aide-de-Camp.

JUNE 14.

General DWIGHT:

General Grover's column is reported ready, and will move forward at once to the assault.

By order of Major-General Banks:

RICH'D B. IRWIN,
Assistant Adjutant-General.

JUNE 14.

General BANKS:

Our skirmishers and sharpshooters are within 20 rods of the parapet; a ravine between them and the parapet is full of fallen timber, and raked by artillery on my right and left.

DWIGHT,
General.

JUNE 14.

General DWIGHT:

Grover seems to be attacking now.

RICH'D B. IRWIN,
Assistant Adjutant-General.

JUNE 14.

General BANKS:

General Dwight cannot advance farther until the skirmishers silence the field batteries.

DWIGHT,
General.

JUNE 14.

General BANKS:

The Parrotts have made them haul back from their guns; none now in sight of them.

CHAS. P. STONE,
Brigadier-General.

JUNE 14.

Colonel IRWIN:

All quiet but sharpshooting. As the First and Second Brigades cannot retire, General Dwight cannot assault again at present. Shall throw up rifle-pits at dark.

FISKE,
Lieutenant, Aide-de-Camp.

JUNE 20.

Commodore PALMER:

General Banks wishes to say to General Grant that he has perfect confidence of success.

RICH'D B. IRWIN,
Assistant Adjutant-General.

JUNE 20.

General BANKS:

I hear that Vicksburg has fallen, and that 20,000 fresh troops are in the rear. Is it true?

ALDEN,
Captain.

JUNE 26.

Captain ALDEN:

It is a rumor, and can be traced to no reliable source.

RICH'D B. IRWIN,
Assistant Adjutant-General.

JUNE 29.

Captain ALDEN:

The commanding general requests you to spare your tug, if possible, to take ammunition from Springfield Landing to Donaldsonville. Please answer.

RICH'D B. IRWIN,
Assistant Adjutant-General.

JUNE 29.

RICHARD B. IRWIN:
Yes.

ALDEN,
Captain.

JULY 1.

General BANKS:
About 6,000 contrabands here; please send a boat to take them.

ALDEN,
Captain.

JULY 7.

Admiral FARRAGUT:
Bands will play, and we shall fire salute of one hundred guns from right and left at noon. I shall be glad if you will participate with us.

N. P. BANKS,
Major-General, Commanding.

JULY 7.

General BANKS:
I am detaining the General Price to take Colonel Smith back to Vicksburg. If he intends returning, pray send him at once.

PALMER,
Commodore.

JULY 7.

Commodore PALMER:
General Banks is writing dispatches to General Grant. I will send them in a few minutes. Colonel Smith remains.

RICH'D B. IRWIN,
Assistant Adjutant-General.

JULY 7.

Commodore PALMER:
Your officer has arrived. Have you dispatches yet?

RICH'D B. IRWIN,
Assistant Adjutant-General.

· Very respectfully, your obedient servant,
JAMES H. RUNDLETT,
Second Lieut. Co. K, Fiftieth Mass. Vols., and Actg. Signal Officer.

Lieut. GEORGE R. HERBERT,
Adjutant of Signal Corps.

No. 16.

Report of Lieut. E. H. Russell, Ninth Pennsylvania Reserves, Acting Signal Officer, of operations May 24–July 11.

NEW ORLEANS, LA.,
July 27, 1863.

SIR: I have the honor to present the following report of signal duty performed by me at the siege of Port Hudson, La., beginning on the 24th of May, 1863, and ending on the 11th of July, 1863:

On the 24th of May, 1863, I reported for duty to Capt. William B. Roe, acting chief signal officer at headquarters Department of the Gulf, above Port Hudson, La.

I was directed to report on the 26th of May to Brig. Gen. G. Weitzel, commanding a division of the right wing of our forces before Port Hudson.

On the morning of the 27th of May, I reported again to Brigadier-- General Weitzel, shortly after the commencement of the assault made by our right wing. As the country was so densely wooded as to render signaling impracticable, I made myself useful whenever I could as acting aide. On the 28th and 29th of May, no communication was maintained by signals.

On the 30th of May I opened communication with the U. S. sloop of war Richmond (then lying below Port Hudson) from the top of a tree on the extreme right of our line. Second Lieut. A. M. Jackson, acting signal officer, was at that time in charge of the station on the Richmond. The distances between the stations were from 3 to 5 miles.

The following official messages were sent and received between the 30th of May and the 6th of June, when the station was discontinued,' ᵢ as unnecessary, by the general commanding the right wing:

Admiral FARRAGUT:
Let the mortars now fire on the gun which shot at us last night.
WEITZEL,
General.

Brigadier-General WEITZEL:
The mortars cannot reach the gun.
FARRAGUT, ·
Admiral.
11 A. M.

General BANKS:
An orderly reached Bayou Sara last night with dispatches for the Hartford. Not waiting for transportation, he went by land, and has not yet arrived.
FARRAGUT,
Admiral.

The above are all the official messages which appear upon my de-fective minutes of the work done upon this station. No signaling was required upon the right wing after the station was discontinued.

Second Lieut. John W. Dana and Second Lieut. R. C. Harris assisted me in the duties of the station.

I subjoin a rough sketch* of the country across which we communi-cated.

On the 8th of July, Port Hudson surrendered to our troops. · On the 11th of July, in obedience to orders, I reported' to Brigadier-General Grover for duty, and proceeded with him to Donaldsonville.

Very respectfully, your obedient servant,
E. H. RUSSELL,
First Lieut. Ninth Pa. Reserve Corps, and Acting Signal Officer.

Lieut. GEORGE R. HERBERT,
Adjutant of Signal Corps, Department of the Gulf.

No. 17.

Report of Col. N. A. M. Dudley, Thirty-first Massachusetts Infantry, · commanding Third Brigade, First Division, Nineteenth Army · Corps, of action at Plains Store.

CAMP AT THE PLAINS STORE, May 23, 1863. ·

SIR:·I have the honor to report that in compliance with General Orders, No. 1, dated headquarters United States forces, camp on· Mer-

---

* Sketch omitted.

ritt's plantation, May 20, 1863, the following forces under my command left camp at 6 a. m. of the 21st:

Third Brigade, First Division, consisting of Thirtieth Massachusetts Volunteers, Lieut. Col. W. W. Bullock; Second Louisiana Volunteers, Col. C. J. Paine; One hundred and sixty-first New York Volunteers, Col. G. T. Harrower; One hundred and seventy-fourth New York Volunteers, Lieut. Col. B. F. Gott, accompanied by Captain Godfrey's squadron of cavalry, four pieces of light artillery, Battery G, Fifth U. S. Artillery, Lieutenant Rawles; and one section of the Eighteenth New York Battery, under Sergt. D. W. McConnell, proceeded up the Bayou Sara road to the opening of the first plain, when the advance came upon a considerable picket force of the enemy's, which was dispersed by Godfrey's cavalry. The column continued its march until near the clearing on the west side of the plains, about three-fourths of a mile from the Plains Store, when a brisk skirmish was opened by Captain Fiske's and Lieutenant Johnston's companies of the Thirtieth Massachusetts Volunteers, which were thrown out onto the edge of the woods in front of the enemy's battery position. One section of Light Battery G was placed in position on the Bayou Sara road, which engaged the rebel battery for fully half an hour under a heavy fire, but failed to silence it; another section of the same battery and the section of the Eighteenth New York were brought up, and even this increased fire did not succeed in permanently silencing the fire of the enemy.

The section of the Eighteenth New York, by direction of Major-General Augur, was withdrawn, and replaced by four pieces of the Second Vermont Battery, Captain Holcomb. The pieces of Lieutenant Rawles were moved to the right, and Holcomb's sections took the position on the left of the road, the latter supported by the One hundred and seventy-fourth New York, and the right pieces supported by four companies of the Thirtieth Massachusetts. The Second Louisiana Volunteers, supported by the One hundred and sixty-first New York Volunteers, moved through the woods on the right, with a view of getting on the ———— of the enemy's battery, which they succeeded in doing. The skirmish fire of these regiments, with the three companies of the Thirtieth Massachusetts Volunteers, rendered good service and materially contributed toward driving the enemy from their position. Previous to this latter disposition, Captain Ferris' company had been sent over on the right flank of the column, where it engaged the enemy's skirmishers, having 1 lieutenant and 1 man wounded. This company took several prisoners, and completely cleared the woods at this point. The concentrated fire of this force drove the enemy from their position. At this juncture, my command was immediately ordered to move to the front and take position near the Plains Store. One section of Light Battery G, under command of Lieutenant Beck, was placed on the Port Hudson road, the other on the Bayou Sara road, where it remained until the renewed attack in the afternoon on the right flank, when I was ordered to support Holcomb's battery, which had been put in position on Bayou Sara road, about 250 yards to the front of the junction of the Port Hudson road. This was gallantly done by Lieutenant-Colonel Gott's regiment, One hundred and seventy-fourth New York Volunteers. At the same time this heavy firing was going on in front of the One hundred and seventy-fourth, I was ordered to send up the Port Hudson road a section of artillery. Lieutenant Beck responded promptly to this call, and held his position until abandoned by his support. Having had two swing horses and drivers killed, he was compelled to retire, leaving one piece for a short time behind, when the men of the reserve pieces joined their comrades, and succeeded in bringing off the piece. Holcomb's battery having whipped the enemy in front,. the several corps took up their positions assigned them for the night on the field from which they had driven the enemy.

The following is the amount and character of ammunition expended by the three sections of artillery attached to my brigade: 45 rounds solid shot, 22 rounds spherical case, 58 rounds shell, 8 rounds canister.

It would be useless to attempt to bestow any special compliment on any individual of my immediate command for their conduct during the engagement; all seemed to vie with each other in carrying out promptly and to the letter any order given. Lieut. Col. Charles Everett, Second Louisiana, and First Lieutenant Norcross, Thirtieth Massachusetts, were severely wounded while gallantly engaging the enemy's skirmishers in front. I am specially indebted to the members of my staff, Captains Speed and Whittier, Lieutenants Dean, Skinner, and Loring, for their prompt and efficient services in transmitting orders from point to point, frequently under a heavy cross-fire of canister and shell. Annexed is a list of killed, wounded, and missing of this brigade and the corps attached.*

I am, sir, your obedient servant,

[N. A. M. DUDLEY,]
Colonel, and Acting Brigadier-General.

Capt. G. B. HALSTED, Assistant Adjutant-General.

No. 18.

Report of Col. Thomas S. Clark, Sixth Michigan Infantry, commanding First Brigade, of the assault June 14.

BEFORE PORT HUDSON, LA., June 16, 1863.

CAPTAIN: I have the honor to transmit the following report of the casualties, &c., of this command during the engagement of the 14th instant:

Agreeably to orders received from the general commanding the division, I ordered the Sixth Michigan Volunteers and Fourteenth Maine Volunteers to the extreme left, for the purpose of storming the enemy's works on the river, which I afterward found they could not accomplish, owing to the nature of the ground.

Returning to the Mount Pleasant road, I deployed my skirmishers, supporting them by the One hundred and twenty-eighth New York Volunteers, Colonel Smith commanding. They were immediately followed by the Fifteenth New Hampshire Volunteers and Twenty-sixth Connecticut Volunteers, whom I brought forward in column of companies on the main road; but I was compelled to deploy them, as the enemy were pouring into us a well-directed fire of shot and shell. As the field would not permit of their being deployed but for a short distance, I was again obliged to form them into columns by companies. I mention this latter circumstance more particularly, as the several movements ordered were executed with alacrity and with a coolness and precision which is deserving of special praise. In the interim, the skirmishers, under the immediate command of Captain Wilkinson, of the One hundred and twenty-eighth New York Volunteers, were steadily advancing toward the enemy's works, but were unable to go nearer than 300 yards of the parapet.

The main column came up in good order until they arrived at a deep ravine, which had been rendered almost impassable by felled trees and

----

* See revised statement, p. 67.

a dense growth of chaparral. The enemy had also planted a battery, which kept up a raking and destructive fire upon our forces while they were endeavoring to cross it.

Here I found it necessary that the men should be cautioned that they must use every means in their power to go forward under such cover as the bushes and trees in the vicinity afforded. The enemy's sharp-shooters had thrown bags of sand on the parapet, placed in such manner as to permit of their picking off our men without exposing themselves.

After communicating with and learning the wishes of the general commanding, I fell back, and established the headquarters about 350 yards from the enemy's parapet, which enabled me to watch their move-ments as well as to direct those of the skirmishers and advanced parties.

Owing to the advanced position of the brigade, I did not deem it advisable to draw them off before dark, as by so doing it would have occasioned a useless loss of life without any important advantage ac-cruing from it. About 7 o'clock in the evening I drew off my men, together with the dead and wounded, without further loss, leaving the sharpshooters and skirmishers to hold the ground from which we had driven the enemy in the earlier part of the day.

Both officers and men conducted themselves in a manner worthy of American soldiers. The nine-months' troops have demonstrated by their gallant conduct that they can be relied on in any emergency. The Fourteenth Maine Volunteers were not in the engagement. Our loss in killed, wounded, and missing is not heavy, considering the ad-vantages possessed by the enemy, and the number of the natural and artificial obstacles which our forces had to surmount.

I append a list of the number of the killed, wounded, and missing; the missing, since heard of, were killed, and could not be found at the time.

Command.	Killed.	Wounded.	Missing.	Total.
6th Michigan	......	8	......	8
15th New Hampshire	......	25	7	32
128th New York	1	20	......	21
26th Connecticut	......	61	12	73
14th Maine	......	1	......	1
Total	1	115	19	135

Respectfully submitted.

THOS. S. CLARK,
Colonel, Commanding First Brigade, Second Division.

Capt. WICKHAM HOFFMAN, *Assistant Adjutant-General.*

No. 19.

Report of Col. Thomas G. Kingsley, Twenty-sixth Connecticut Infantry, of the first assault.

CONVALESCENT HOSPITAL, *Baton Rouge, La., June 3, 1863.*

SIR: I have the honor to make to you the following report of the killed, wounded, and missing of the Twenty-sixth Regiment Connecticut

Volunteers at the battle near Port Hudson, on Wednesday the 27th day of May, 1863 :

The regiment is in General Dow's brigade and in the Second Division, commanded by General Sherman. We were ordered to make an assault upon the works, and to do it in four lines. The first line was formed by the Sixth Michigan; second, Fifteenth New Hampshire; third, Twenty-sixth Connecticut; fourth, One hundred and twenty-eighth New York. In advancing in line of battle, we encountered three high parallel fences, and, in getting over them, much confusion ensued, and before we could get into line the enemy opened on us with shell, shot, grape, and canister, mowing our men down by scores. As our men advanced, the ranks were thinned, until, after one hour's fighting, our men were compelled to seek shelter behind stumps, logs, &c. Generals Sherman and Dow were both wounded and carried from the field.

The Twenty-sixth brought off the wounded and did not leave the field until past 8 p. m. This is the first time the regiment has been under the enemy's fire, and permit me to say that, with the exception of two or three, they did honor to themselves and credit to their State.

. I am in the hospital, badly wounded (not fatally), and have not the opportunity of giving so full a statement of the nature of the wounds as I should like.

I think the lieutenant colonel may make a report also.

I am, most respectfully, your obedient servant,

T. G. KINGSLEY,
Colonel Twenty sixth Regiment Connecticut Volunteers.

ADJUTANT-GENERAL, UNITED STATES.

No. 20.

Report of Lieut. Col. Joseph Selden, Twenty-sixth Connecticut Infantry, of the first assault.

IN THE FIELD, NEAR PORT HUDSON,
May 31, 1863.

GENERAL: I inclose a list of killed, wounded, and missing in this regiment, resulting from our participation in the attack on Port Hudson, on the afternoon of May 27, 1863.*

The attempt was made to take the rebel batteries and intrenchments by storm. Our regiment was formed in line of battle with the Sixth Michigan and One hundred and twenty-eighth New York Regiments in front of us, and the Fifteenth New Hampshire in our rear. The brigade was ordered forward on the double-quick. Four fences intervened between us and the intrenchments, which greatly impeded our advance. In passing these fences, the different regiments were thrown into confusion and became somewhat mixed up. On entering the field, a perfect shower of grape, shot, and canister met us, severely wounding Generals Sherman and Dow, and cutting down officers and men by scores. Still, we advanced, and for more than two hours held the ground, and when obliged to fall back, it was not in disorder. I rallied our men, and formed the regiment near the entrance of the field, and we held the ground occupied by our brigade during the day. This being the first time the regiment had been under fire, I must be permitted to say that

---

* Embodied in revised statement, p. 68.

they conducted themselves with great gallantry and bravery, for the truth of which assertion I have but to point to the record inclosed.

Very respectfully, your most obedient servant,

JOSEPH SELDEN,
Lieutenant-Colonel, Commanding Twenty-sixth Connecticut Vols.

General J. D. WILLIAMS,
Adjutant-General, Hartford, Conn.

No. 21.

Report of Capt. Francis S. Keese, One hundred and twenty-eighth New York Infantry, of the first assault.

BEFORE PORT HUDSON, *May* 31, 1863.

SIR: I have the honor to transmit the following report of the part taken by this regiment in the battle of Wednesday, May 27:

During the early part of the day, Companies H, I, and G, under my immediate command, were stationed on the Port Hudson road, deployed as skirmishers and sharpshooters. At 1.30 p. m. moved to the position occupied by the Vermont battery, in line of woods facing the rebel earthworks. From there we moved forward, and formed line of battle with the remainder of the regiment, under command of Col. D S. Cowles. We moved to the charge about 2.10 p. m., the One hundred and twenty-eighth being the rear regiment of the brigade. The whole regiment, except Companies A and C, were in the fight. These two companies were deployed on the right as sharpshooters. Several fences broke the line of battle at the time of the charge, throwing the troops into considerable confusion and disorder. A deep gully upon the right of the road also operated disadvantageously. Col. D. S. Cowles boldly led forward his regiment in face of a galling fire, and after Generals Sherman, yourself, and Clark, of the Sixth Michigan Volunteers, were wounded, the command of the brigade devolved upon him. He was mortally wounded while rallying his men, and died upon the field of battle. Throughout the entire engagement he displayed signal coolness and courage, and showed himself every inch a soldier. After his death, the command of the regiment devolved upon myself, I being the senior officer upon the field. All the men of this command fought nobly, and boldly advanced to the charge in spite of the great disadvantages under which they labored. The officers performed their duty boldly, and were to be seen in front of their men, cheering them on. Where all the officers performed their duty so well, it would be invidious to distinguish.

The regiment retreated about 4.30 p. m., but afterward many again advanced to the front, and, from behind stumps and logs, kept up an incessant fire upon any of the enemy who showed themselves above the parapet. Capt. Arthur De Wint, Company F, was wounded in the arm while in charge of the advance guard or storming party. Lieut. Charles L. Van Slyck, Company E, was killed during the early part of the engagement, while nobly cheering on his men. The bodies of many of our dead were found within a short distance of the rebel earthworks, while none retreated until the command was given to that effect.

I am sir, respectfully, your obedient servant,

FRANCIS S. KEESE,
Captain, Comdg. 128th New York Volunteers.

Brig. Gen. NEAL DOW,
Comdg. First Brig., Second Div., Nineteenth Army Corps.

No. 22.

Report of Lieut. Col. Justus W. Blanchard, One hundred and sixty-second New York Infantry, of affair at Springfield Landing.

SPRINGFIELD LANDING, LA.,
July 2, 1863.

GENERAL: I beg leave to inform you the rebels made an attack on the post at about 8.30 a. m., about 150 to 200 strong. The attack was very vigorous on some negro troops, who retreated, allowing the rebels to set fire to the commissary stores, which were mostly destroyed. I brought my regiment to the scene of action, and drove them back in double-quick. They were again repulsed on our right and on our left, losing 3 or 4 killed, a number wounded, and 2 prisoners. We have 2 of my regiment and 3 of the negro regiment wounded, 1 negro killed. All is now quiet.

I am, very respectfully, your obedient servant,
J. W. BLANCHARD,
Commanding 162d New York Vols. and this Post.

Brigadier-General DWIGHT.

P. S.—I fear a portion of our pickets have been taken prisoners.

[Indorsement.]
JULY 2, 1863.

Respectfully forwarded. Our troops did not behave well. The officers refused to volunteer to bring a dispatch to the headquarters of the commanding general.

WILLIAM DWIGHT,
Brigadier-General, Commanding.

No. 23.

Report of Brig. Gen. Halbert E. Paine, U. S. Army, commanding Third Division, of the expedition to Clinton.

PORT HUDSON, LA.,
June 9, 1863.

COLONEL: The troops placed under my command for the expedition to Clinton marched at 4 a. m. on Friday last, and encamped that night at the Redwood Bayou Bridge. The excessive heat prostrated a large number of officers and men, who were sent back to headquarters in the evening. On Saturday morning we marched to the Comite Bridge, encamped there during the day, and at midnight marched toward Clinton. The cavalry entered the town at daylight Sunday morning, the infantry being about 3 miles in the rear. The enemy had moved their stores during the three preceding days, and the last of their troops had left on Saturday.

Colonel Grierson burned the cotton-mill, railroad depot, and railroad bridge. The information obtained as to the number, character, and destination of these troops was very conflicting. Your own estimate (1,500 to 2,000) is probably correct. Most of them are mounted. They appear to have four pieces of indifferent artillery, and will, I think, at present rendezvous at or near Liberty, Miss. In my opinion, Colonel Grierson would have routed them on Wednesday last but for their immense advantage of position.

The whites and blacks gave us various reports as to their objects— that they designed to attack Baton Rouge simultaneously with our attack on Port Hudson; that they intended a raid on our train near Springfield Landing; that they expected to get in the rear of my command; that they contemplated a junction with General Kirby Smith, who was said to be crossing the river at Natchez, with a view to relieve Port Hudson; that they were fortifying Whiteside; that the force was collected for General Johnston, to be used in an attack upon the Army of the Gulf, New Orleans, &c.

Some of the inhabitants seemed altogether despondent; others exhibited in their demeanor, as well as language, great confidence that their army would fall upon us before the capture of Port Hudson. We marched back to the Comite River on Sunday morning, encamped there during the day, marched in the evening to Redwood Bayou, where we encamped during the night, and on Monday morning (the 8th instant) returned to Port Hudson.

No casualties occurred except such as resulted from the intense heat.

Most respectfully, your obedient servant,

HALBERT E. PAINE,
Brigadier-General.

Lieut. Col. RICHARD B. IRWIN,
Assistant Adjutant-General.

ADDENDA.

SPECIAL ORDERS, } HDQRS. DEPT. OF GULF, 19TH ARMY CORPS,
No. 131. } *Before Port Hudson, June 4, 1863.*

I. Brigadier-General Grover, commanding the right wing, will immediately detail one brigade of infantry, 2,000 strong, and two sections of Napoleon guns, under the command of Brig. Gen. Halbert E. Paine, for special service. Brigadier-General Paine will at once report in person at these headquarters for instructions. The men will take three days' rations in their haversacks.

*   *   *   *   *

By command of Major-General Banks.

[RICH'D B. IRWIN,]
Assistant Adjutant-General.

HDQRS. DEPT. OF THE GULF, 19TH ARMY CORPS,
Before Port Hudson, June 5, 1863.

Brig. Gen. H. E. PAINE,
Commanding Expedition :

GENERAL: The commanding general directs me to communicate the following instructions for your guidance :

The force under your command consists of a full brigade and two sections of artillery from your own division, and all of Colonel Grierson's cavalry brigade, including a section of Nims' battery, excepting the necessary detachments for picket duty. The object of your expedition is to attack and disperse the force of the enemy, supposed to be from 1,500 to 2,000 strong, which has been collected at Clinton.

The details of this operation are left to your discretion, with the single direction that it is essential that the object shall be accomplished as speedily and as thoroughly as possible. If practicable, a part of the cavalry may be sent, after your main purpose is accomplished, to break up the rendezvous of the enemy near Woodville.

Having executed the foregoing instructions, you will rejoin this command without delay.

Please report frequently.

Very respectfully, your obedient servant,
RICH'D B. IRWIN,
Assistant Adjutant-General.

No. 24.

Report of Maj. James P. Richardson, Thirty-eighth Massachusetts Infantry, Third Brigade, of operations May 22–July 12.

BATON ROUGE, LA.,
July 14, 1863.

SIR: In regard to the operations of the Thirty-eighth Regiment Massachusetts Volunteers before Port Hudson, I have the honor to report that the regiment landed with the rest of the army at Bayou Sara on the 22d May last, and marched for Port Hudson on the same day, where they arrived in the evening of the 23d, and rested in order of battle near a sugar-house. On the 24th, it moved forward about three-quarters of a mile, and rested for the night. On the 25th, the regiment was ordered to Thompson's Creek, to support the Eighteenth New York Battery. During the day we had a slight skirmish with the enemy; in which we lost 2 killed and 1 wounded. We remained in support of the battery until the 27th, when we were ordered to report to General Paine. The enemy was attacked and driven back through the woods into his works, and an assault ordered. We went forward in column of companies very near to the works, but in consequence of the severe fire of the enemy, sheltered behind his works, it was found to be impracticable to enter, and the regiment sought such shelter as the ground afforded until night, when it was withdrawn. During the day, Lieutenant-Colonel Rodman, who was in command of the regiment, was shot through the heart and instantly killed. The loss of the regiment during the day, in addition to the above, was 3 killed and 12 wounded. In the evening of the same day, the regiment went on picket duty at the front, where it remained for three days constantly under the fire of the enemy. On the 28th, 1 corporal was wounded in the arm. On the 30th, I joined the regiment and reported for duty, having been absent sick since the regiment left Opelousas on the 5th May. The regiment had just been relieved from picket duty. At night we went on picket again, where we remained until the 4th of June. During that time we had 1 killed and 1 wounded. On the 4th of June, we were moved in the rear of Battery F, where we remained until the next morning, when we were ordered to march under General Paine.

We started at 4 a. m. toward Clinton, and marched till about 11.30 o'clock, and halted at a sugar-house for two hours. On starting again, the heat was so intense that several men were sunstruck, and another halt was made in the woods until 6 p. m. In the evening we marched till about 10 o'clock, and rested in the woods.

On the morning of the 6th, at 6 o'clock, we started and marched to

Comite River, and rested until midnight, when we marched for Clinton, arriving near that place about 4.30 a. m. It being ascertained that the enemy had fled, we returned to Comite River, and rested until 6 a. m., when we marched till 9 p. m., and rested near Redwood Bayou. On the morning of the 8th we marched at 4 o'clock, and arrived in camp before Port Hudson at 10 a. m. We rested till evening, then marched about 2 miles, and went into camp.

On the 13th of June, we formed with the rest of the Third Division in order of battle for an assault upon the enemy's works. The next morning, on the 14th, at daylight, our regiment was deployed as skirmishers, and, under the lead of General Paine, went forward on the double-quick, under a very severe fire from the enemy. We reached the ditch and some of the men crossed it; one got inside the works and was taken prisoner. We took position where we could beat away the enemy and compel him to keep concealed behind his works, and waited for the storming column, which was to follow us, but the column did not come, and we remained under the works all day, subjected to a broiling sun. At night we were ordered back to our camp. Our loss in this affair was, commissioned officers, 1 killed and 5 wounded; enlisted men, 7 killed and 77 wounded, and 2 missing.

On the 19th, the regiment was again sent to the front, to support Battery F, where it remained until the surrender of Port Hudson on the 8th of July, during which time 2 men were wounded.

Upon the surrender of the enemy, we were designated as one of the regiments to take possession of the fort. At 4 p. m. we marched for that purpose to the left, near the headquarters of General Augur, where we were ordered to wait until morning. At 12.30 o'clock we received orders to march immediately for Plains Store, which we did, arriving there at a little before daylight on the morning of the 9th. Remained there until the 11th, when we marched at 5.30 p. m., in charge of a train of artillery and baggage, for Baton Rouge, where we arrived early on the morning of 12th July.

All of which is respectfully submitted.

J. P. RICHARDSON,
Major, Comdg. Thirty-eighth Massachusetts Volunteers.

Col. O. P. GOODING,
Comdg. Third Brig., Third Div., Nineteenth Army Corps.

No. 25.

Report of Capt. Apollos Comstock, Thirteenth Connecticut Infantry, Third Brigade, Fourth Division, of the assault June 14.

BEFORE PORT HUDSON,
June 14, 1863.

GENERAL: I have the honor to report the action taken by the Thirteenth Connecticut Volunteers in the engagement of the 14th instant, before Port Hudson, as follows:

As per order, we moved from our position in rear of Duryea's battery at 2.30 a. m. to the Jackson road, and rested near the bridge, on the right of said road (going toward Port Hudson), in rear of the rifle-pits, where the remaining regiments of the brigade joined us. At daylight we were ordered forward, and moved to the plateau beyond the rifle-pits, and rested on left of the road, in rear of First Brigade. At 7 a. m. we were ordered to support the First Brigade as they moved on the enemy's works. The Thirteenth held the right of our brigade, and, following by the flank along the ravine, close in rear of the First, the regiment filed into line, the right forming under cover of a ridge of ground, about 100 yards from the enemy's works. As there was not room enough to form the whole regiment in line there, I ordered Lieutenant Gardner, acting adjutant, to take the five left companies, pass through a ravine, and form in line under cover of another ridge, on the left of the ravine and nearly parallel with the right. Soon after, Lieutenant Gardner was wounded, as also Captain Grosvenor, Company I. Still, the left moved steadily to the position referred to. At this point Colonel Holcomb, commanding First Brigade, fell, while leading his command to the charge, and his right gave way. I ordered my right to advance to their support, which they did under a very heavy fire from the enemy's works. Lieutenant Strickland, commanding Company F, fell here, killed instantly. Still they maintained the position nobly. At this time I ordered the regiment to file around the left of this position, and move forward through a ravine to a height which overlooked the enemy's works, and not more than 20 or 30 yards from them. As this was the nearest point I could reach without a direct assault of the enemy's works, which we had no instructions to do, I concluded to maintain that position and await orders. A regular detail of sharpshooters was kept at work on the brow of the height till sunset, when a strong picket was ordered to occupy it, which we did till about 10 p. m., when we were relieved, and ordered to our old position which we left on the morning of the action.

We lost 22 killed and wounded, which I have reported, with name, rank, and company in full.

Very respectfully, your obedient servant,

A. COMSTOCK,
Captain, Commanding Thirteenth Connecticut Volunteers.

HORACE J. MORSE,
Adjutant-General, State of Connecticut.

No. 26. *

Reports of Brig. Gen. Godfrey Weitzel, U. S. Army, commanding Provisional Division, of operations June 7–11.

HEADQUARTERS FOURTH DIVISION,
Before Port Hudson, La., June 8, 1863—5.30 a. m.

SIR : In compliance with instructions, I have the honor to report that nothing of importance has occurred in the Second Brigade, First Division, since last report.

The First Brigade, Fourth Division, reports incessant musketry firing all night, particularly at the mortar battery, where the soldiers were at work felling trees. The enemy was very attentive. Several shells also passed over and near the battery; also over brigade headquarters; 1 man wounded.

Owing to a report which reached brigade headquarters about 8 o'clock last evening, that the enemy was moving, and that some of the pickets could hear distinctly the words, " Hurry up," &c., the pickets were doubled and every precaution used which could guard against a surprise. The enemy appeared by the sound to be moving guns from the rear to the neighborhood of his rifle-pits, and the noise of a mill could be heard all night. The Second Brigade, Fourth Division, reports one regiment on duty with Brigadier-General Paine, two regiments in reserve near the cross-roads, with the exception of 100 men detailed from these two regiments for fatigue duty at the mortar battery.

By command of Brigadier-General Weitzel:

E. E. GRAVES,
First Lieutenant, and Acting Assistant Adjutant-General.

Brigadier-General GROVER,
Commanding Right Wing.

—

HEADQUARTERS FOURTH DIVISION,
Before Port Hudson, La., June 11, 1863.

SIR: I have the honor to report the Second Brigade, First Division as follows:

That at 12 midnight a line of skirmishers, consisting of seventeen companies, extending from right to left at intervals of about 2 yards, each to advance out of cover upon the position of the enemy, with orders to fire rapidly and feel it thoroughly, moved out from half to two-thirds the distance toward the parapet of the works in front, but found the fire of the enemy so hot that they were compelled to lie down for protection while receiving it. The Twelfth Connecticut skirmishers, under Captain Clark, seized the cover of a ravine and moved close in upon the enemy, firing rapidly, as ordered, until Captain Clark and Captain Granniss and a number of men were wounded. Captain Roche, with his company, received the fire in his front, and then led his company up on to the parapet, when he was shot in the heel from within, and his followers all shot down.

There being no advance on our immediate left, this regiment and the Seventy-fifth New York were exposed to a raking fire, and the same was the case on our right, where our line was a long way advanced beyond any other. There being no fair prospect of taking the enemy's works without an advance of reserves, I ordered the troops to remain as they were until, as daylight came, it became necessary to withdraw them to save them. The force opposed to us is not heavy, but thoroughly posted, but it is the opinion of all the officers of the skirmishers that it can be driven out by an advance of our whole force, though with considerable loss.

I regret to add that the loss in killed and wounded is large, as follows: Killed, 2; wounded, 41; missing, 6; aggregate, 49.

Among the wounded, besides the captains mentioned before, is Lieutenant-Colonel Peck, slightly wounded in hand by splinter from a shell which exploded over brigade headquarters. This was from the only cannon fired at us, and came from the battery directly in front of the mortar battery.

The First Brigade, Fourth Division, report as follows:

The brigade commenced the advance against Port Hudson at 12 midnight.

The One hundred and thirty-first New York advanced half the distance between the position occupied yesterday and the enemy's works, which they now hold.

No full report has been received of casualties; so far, report 4 wounded.

The Twenty-second Maine advanced under a heavy fire through the ravine, but, owing to the obstructions and heavy fire from the enemy's breastworks, could not maintain their position, and were ordered to fall back, leaving two companies in the ravine, and cannot ascertain their whereabouts as yet. The companies that succeeded in retiring were ordered to support the Ninety-first New York, which was at daylight holding an exposed position within 75 yards of the enemy's breastworks. They have since retired, and are now occupying their old position. They report 8 wounded, certain; not able yet to make a full report. The Twenty-second Maine report 6 officers and 53 privates missing. The Second Brigade, Fourth Division, in reserve near the cross-roads.

By command of Brigadier-General Weitzel:

E. E. GRAVES,
Captain, and Acting Assistant Adjutant-General.

Capt. J. HIBBARD, Jr.,
Assistant Adjutant-General, Right Wing.

No. 27.

Report of Lieut. Col. Frank H. Peck, Twelfth Connecticut Infantry, of the assault May 27.

IN THE FIELD NEAR DONALDSONVILLE,
July 10, 1863.

SIR: I have the honor to submit the following report of the operations of this regiment since the 25th day of May, 1863, on which day we arrived in rear of the belt of woods, a mile or near in depth, which encircles the fortifications of Port Hudson:

At 5 o'clock on the morning of the 27th, our brigade advanced in line through the woods, driving in the enemy's skirmishers, and reaching the clearing in front shortly after 6. We were received, as we emerged, with volleys from artillery and infantry. I received orders from General Dwight, temporarily in command of our brigade, to advance to the front and left, and silence the artillery, which was firing grape and canister into our lines.

We moved by the flank, under a heavy fire, past four pieces, and took up a suitable position. Three companies were sent forward as skirmishers, and soon came upon the skirmishers of the enemy, whom they drove before them. A detachment was sent from inside the works, which attempted to turn our flank.

Our left being entirely unsupported, I sent one company, which succeeded by sharp fighting in repelling the attack. The entire regiment was finally engaged, and by noon had succeeded in driving the enemy inside the parapet, and in a short time afterward had silenced four pieces of artillery, two of which, being field pieces, were withdrawn, the other two (mounted *en barbette*), the two wings of the regiment relieved each other in guarding till late in the day. Our line did not halt until it reached the parapet, and at one time the extreme right had succeeded in scaling the work, but, for want of harmonious support of other corps, were compelled to rest satisfied with holding the position. The day closed with an armistice, when we were relieved by another regiment, and rejoined our brigade upon the right of the center. From this time until June 10 'the regiment was on duty day and night as sharp-shooters, behind hastily constructed works of logs and earth, and within about 150 yards of the enemy's breastworks. On the night of June 10, four companies were ordered to be thrown forward as skirmishers, to form part of a continuous line around the works, with the design of compelling the enemy to disclose the position of his artillery. Orders were also given by the brigade commanders to scale and occupy the works, if possible. Companies A, B, F, and K were sent out and advanced, at the signal arranged, through a deep intervening ravine, obstructed by fallen trees and underbrush. They received a volley from the enemy as they came up, but pressed on to the base of the parapet. The regiment on our right and left failed to support us, thus giving the enemy an opportunity to concentrate their troops against us with terrible effect. Company G was afterward ordered forward to cover the withdrawal of our men. Skirmishing was continued until daylight, when they were recalled, bringing in most of the killed and wounded. The casualties of this night were greater in proportion to the number engaged than in any other single engagement during the entire siege. The gallantry of the officers and men cannot be too highly praised. They received conspicuous mention from our division commander.

On the 14th of June, a general attack was made upon the entire front of the fortifications. For the sake of secrecy, the position selected for the assault had not been announced. At 1 a. m. we received orders to move. A guide was sent from headquarters to conduct us to our position in the line. He was joined afterward by a staff officer, through whose unfortunate ignorance we were led three times the necessary distance through the woods, and at one time were rendered most anxious.

He was shortly joined by a third, and with their combined aid reached the point selected before daylight. We advanced immediately to the front through a covered way, passing in our way the Ninety-first New York, with hand-grenades, and the Twenty-fourth Connecticut, with sacks of cotton, and deployed as skirmishers to the left, the Seventy-fifth New York being deployed upon our right. The line was advanced cautiously, the men availing themselves of the irregularities of the ground for cover until our right rested upon the line of a ridge no more than 50 yards from the priest-cap. At other points the line advanced even nearer. A sharp fire was kept up on both sides until noon, when the original plan of operations was abandoned. The regiment was withdrawn after dark in perfect order, and returned to its former position. Lieut. Theodore Clark, of Company F, deserves mention for conspicuous courage during this engagement. The regiment from this time until the final surrender was engaged as before. On the night of the 8th of July, for the first time since we advanced to the front, we were permitted to sleep without an uninterrupted accompaniment of artillery and musketry. On the 9th, with martial music and flying colors, we marched into Port Hudson. That evening we took transports, and arrived at this place on the 10th. I inclose a list of casualties.*

I am, sir, your obedient servant,

FRANK H. PECK,
Lieutenant-Colonel, Commanding Regiment.

Brig. Gen. HORACE J. MORSE,
Adjutant-General [State of Connecticut.]

---

* Embodied in revised statement, p. 67.

No. 28.

*Reports of Col. Benjamin H. Grierson, Sixth Illinois Cavalry, command-
ing Cavalry Brigade, of operations June 3–7.*

HEADQUARTERS FIRST CAVALRY BRIGADE,
June 2, 1863.

COLONEL: I am informed that there are a number of Sharps' carbines in New Orleans. About half of my command are armed with the
Union and Smith's carbines, the ammunition for which we are unable
to obtain. I would respectfully ask, if there are any of the Sharps'
carbines in New Orleans, that about 500 be ordered to be sent here immediately, that I may turn over the Union and Smith's, and thus the
more effectively arm my command.

The following detachments have reported to me and are now under
my orders: 300 men of the Fourth Wisconsin Mounted Infantry; 150
men of the Forty-first Massachusetts Mounted Infantry; three companies of the Fourteenth New York Cavalry; two companies of the Second Massachusetts Cavalry; one company of the First Louisiana Cavalry; one section Nims' battery.

I would respectfully report to the general commanding that I shall
move at daylight to-morrow morning, June 3, with all the effective force
of the Sixth and Seventh Illinois Cavalry, Second Massachusetts Cavalry, Fourth Wisconsin Mounted Infantry, the section of Nims' and my
own light batteries, leaving the Fourteenth New York and First Louisiana Cavalry and Forty-first Massachusetts Mounted Infantry to picket
the roads in our absence.

Respectfully, your obedient servant,
B. H. GRIERSON,
Colonel, Commanding Brigade.

Lieut. Col. RICHARD B. IRWIN,
Assistant Adjutant-General.

—

HEADQUARTERS CAVALRY,
Eight miles west of Clinton, June 3, 1863.

GENERAL: I have just received a report that [J. L.] Logan was 4
miles from Plains Store, on the Clinton road, this morning before breakfast, and was said to be going toward Port Hudson. He left his camp
near Clinton at midnight last night.

I shall push on to Clinton and endeavor to destroy his camp, and
should the information prove true, I will immediately proceed toward
Plains Store and fall in his rear.

I send you the negro boy who gave me the information, and you can
get it from him as I received it.

Respectfully, your obedient servant,
B. H. GRIERSON,
Colonel, Commanding Brigade.

Major-General BANKS.

—

BEFORE PORT HUDSON,
June 12, 1863.

COLONEL: I have the honor to report that, in obedience to instructions from the major-general commanding, I started at 5 o'clock on

the morning of June 3 with my command, composed of the Sixth and
Seventh Illinois Cavalry, the Second Massachusetts, two companies
First Louisiana, also two companies Fourth Wisconsin Mounted In-
fantry, and one section of Nims' battery, in all about 1,200 strong.

Taking the Jackson road, we proceeded without interruption to within
3 miles of Jackson, where I detached Captain Godfrey, with 200 men of
the Massachusetts and Louisiana cavalry, to go by way of Jackson,
while with the main column I proceeded on the direct road to Clinton.
Captain Godfrey dashed into Jackson, captured and paroled a number
of prisoners, convalescents and stragglers; thence, taking the Clinton
road, rejoined the column 2 miles from Jackson. Proceeding on, we encountered and drove in their pickets 6 miles from Clinton, capturing 1
man and 4 horses. We did not again encounter the enemy until we arrived at the Comite River, 1 mile from Clinton, where the advance guard
were fired upon from ambush. Pushing across the bridge over this
stream, and two following ones, we arrived at a small plain, where we
encountered a considerable force of the enemy ambushed on either side
of the road. I immediately dismounted the whole of the Seventh Illinois Cavalry, which was in advance, deployed them as skirmishers, and
drove the enemy to Pretty Creek, where their whole force was posted in
a strong position.

I immediately dismounted the Fourth Wisconsin, and deployed them,
with the Seventh Illinois, along the bank of Pretty Creek, and brought
up a section of the 2-pounder guns and a section of Nims' battery, which
I placed in position on the right and left of the road in the plain. One
battalion of the Seventh Illinois had already been posted on our right
flank across the railroad, and I now posted the two companies of the
Second Massachusetts Cavalry, commanded by Lieutenant Perkins, to
guard our left flank. It soon became evident that the enemy in our
front far outnumbered us, besides having a strong position, while we,
in addition to the disparity of numbers, were posted in a dense swamp,
to and from which we had access to the open country in our rear only
through a narrow defile leading across five narrow bridges.

A portion of the Seventh Illinois Cavalry, who were in the front, were
armed with the Smith carbine, the ammunition for which we had been
unable to obtain in this department, and their ammunition becoming
exhausted, they were obliged to fall back. I immediately sent Captains
Godfrey and Yeaton with the two companies of the First Louisiana Cavalry to take their place. The troops in the front held their ground, and
pressed the enemy nobly against a great disadvantage both in numbers
and position.

It soon became evident that the enemy was throwing a portion of his
forces to the right and left, probably with a view of turning our flanks.
Observing this, I brought up the Sixth Illinois Cavalry, which had
composed the rear guard during the march, and, dismounting, posted
them to the right and left as a still further guard to our flanks. It soon
became evident that the enemy's numbers and position were too strong
for us to carry, and, our ammunition becoming scarce, I decided to fall
back. Acting upon this design, I ordered the section of Nims' battery,
which had been brought up, but, owing to the lowness of the ground,
could obtain no advantageous position, to fall back to the brow of a
hill nearly a mile in our rear, and there come into battery until further
orders. I then withdrew the Fourth Wisconsin and First Louisiana,
and such of the Seventh Illinois as still remained in the front, they
tearing up a bridge as they returned, and posted the Second Massachusetts and First Louisiana in a bayou on the right and left of the road,

to hold the enemy in check until the infantry could mount their horses and withdraw from the swamp, after which they were ordered to fall back, mount, and retreat. In the meantime I had one battalion of the Sixth Illinois Cavalry and two guns of our little battery organized to bring up the rear.

The section of Nims' battery, most of the Seventh Illinois, the Fourth Wisconsin, the Second Massachusetts, and Yeaton's company of Louisiana cavalry had all withdrawn and gained a good position on the high ground in our rear, when the enemy with a yell charged in solid masses upon our front and left flank. Captain Godfrey's company, from some unknown cause, had not obeyed the order to fall back and mount after the infantry had withdrawn, and, when the enemy charged, they found him still dismounted; and his horses having gone to the rear, he took to the bushes and along the railroad, where the enemy, coming in upon his left, cut off a number of his men. The 2-pounder battery poured canister into the column advancing on our front with telling effect, until those on our left had come within 50 yards of the guns, when they were limbered to the rear, and the battalion of the Sixth Illinois falling in between them and the enemy, beat back the advancing host, and retreated slowly and in good order from the narrow defile.

Having crossed the last bridge, they filed to the right and left of the road, and, forming in the edge of the timber, awaited the approach of the enemy until they had advanced within easy range, when they poured volley after volley into them, repulsing them with considerable loss. Under cover of the consternation created in the ranks of the enemy, this battalion fell back to the brow of the hill, where the light battery and a line of battle had already been formed.

The enemy, recovering from his repulse, again advanced to the bridge, recrossed, but was met by volley after volley of canister from our little guns and from the line formed on either side of the road to support them. Being again repulsed, and this time with fearful loss, they did not deem it prudent to follow us farther, and my command being by this time almost destitute of ammunition, I withdrew and returned to camp, arriving about 12 m.

Our loss in this engagement was 8 killed, 28 wounded, and 15 missing; that of the enemy between 20 and 30 killed, over 60 wounded, and about 20 taken prisoners.

The officers and men all acted with the utmost coolness and bravery. Among the slain was the lamented Lieutenant Perkins, a brave and gallant young officer, commanding a squadron of the Second Massachusetts Cavalry.

The action lasted between three and four hours, and we succeeded in bringing off all but 3 of our dead and 7 wounded.

On the morning of the 5th, we again started for Clinton, in connection with a brigade of infantry and a battery of artillery, under General H. E. Paine, taking a road leading from the Bayou Sara and Baton Rouge road to the Clinton Plank road at Olive Branch. We encamped on the night of the 5th at Redwood Creek. On the 6th, made an easy march to the Comite River, 9 miles from Clinton, where we halted until 12 m., when we again marched, reaching Clinton at early daylight on the morning of the 7th. The enemy had pickets at Olive Branch and again at the Comite, but fired and fled upon our approach.

Arriving at Clinton, we found that the enemy, hearing of our approach, had left the day before, taking the Jackson road until within 2 miles of Jackson, when they moved off toward Liberty. We found in the town two hospitals, containing 7 of our own men wounded and about 20 sick and wounded of the enemy. All their sick and wounded which could be moved, to the number of several hundred, were sent to Osyka the day before.

We paroled about 30 prisoners, destroyed the railroad depot, machine-shops, a locomotive, woolen and cartridge manufactories, a large quantity of ammunition, several hundred hides, and much other Government property which in their haste the enemy failed to take away. We also destroyed all the bridges on the road leading toward Jackson, over the Comite River and the numerous small streams and bayous in the vicinity.

Having accomplished as nearly as possible the object of the expedition, we returned to the Comite River, where we rested until 5 p. m., and from thence returned to camp, arriving about 9 p. m.

I would also report that since the arrival of my command in this department, we have been operating in the vicinity of Baton Rouge and before Port Hudson, under Major-General Augur. We succeeded in cutting the railroad and telegraph between Port Hudson and Clinton, and the command took an active part in the engagement at Plains Store on the 21st of May, and in the numerous other skirmishes in which the forces have been engaged. Since the arrival of Major-General Banks and the investment of Port Hudson, besides the engagements herein reported, we have been employed under his immediate command in picketing and patrolling the approaches in the rear of our army.

Our loss since entering the Department of the Gulf has been small in men but heavy in animals, having had in the two Illinois regiments between 75 and 100 horses killed and badly wounded.

Most respectfully, your obedient servant,

B. H. GRIERSON,
Colonel, Commanding Brigade.

Lieut. Col. RICHARD B. IRWIN,
Assistant Adjutant-General, Department of the Gulf.

—

HDQRS. CAVALRY DIVISION, SIXTEENTH ARMY CORPS,
Memphis, Tenn., September 1, 1863.

COLONEL: I have the honor herewith to inclose copy of the official report of the expedition which, under my command, marched from La Grange, Tenn., April 17, to Baton Rouge, La.,* where we arrived May 2, 1863.

The original report was sent from Baton Rouge, La., to General Grant, at his request. I would further report that, in pursuance of instructions from Maj. Gen. C. C. Augur, we left Baton Rouge on the 12th of May, and proceeded toward Port Hudson, with the order to endeavor to destroy the railroad and telegraph between that point and Clinton, La. This we succeeded in accomplishing at a point within 5 miles of the stronghold of the enemy. After this the command lay in front of Port Hudson, and was engaged in reconnaissances to ascertain the strength and position of the enemy's works until the 21st of May, when we were engaged, in connection with Major-General Augur's division, in a battle with the enemy at Plains Store. The cavalry took an active part in this engagement, which lasted several hours, part of the time being dismounted to support batteries. Our loss was only 1 man slightly wounded, 1 taken prisoner, and over 20 horses killed. On the

---

* See Series I, Vol. XXIV, Part I, p. 521.

23d, by order of Major-General Augur, we proceeded toward Bayou Sara, ·
and formed a junction with Major-General Banks, who had landed at
that point the day before. A complete investment of Port Hudson was
immediately accomplished, and my command was employed under the
· immediate direction of General Banks in picketing and patrolling the
approaches to Port Hudson, in the rear of our army. On the 3d of June,
I was sent with my command and an additional force of about 500 men
to endeavor to dislodge a body of the enemy, about 2,500 strong, which,
under Colonel Logan, had taken position at Clinton, La., about 25 miles
distant. I started at daylight in the morning, and reached Clinton .
about 3 p. m. Driving in the enemy's pickets, we engaged them, though
far outnumbering us, for four hours, until our ammunition becoming
exhausted, we were obliged to withdraw, which we did in good order,
and returned to camp, where we arrived. about midnight. Our loss in
this engagement was 8 killed, 28 wounded, and 15 missing.

On the 5th, we again started for Clinton, in connection with a brigade
of infantry and battery of artillery, arriving at daylight on the morning
of the 7th. We found that the enemy, hearing of our approach, had
left the day before. We ascertained that the losses of the enemy in the
engagement of the 3d have been much heavier than our own, amounting in the aggregate to upward of 100.

On the 16th instant [ultimo] I received and accepted my appointment
as brigadier-general of volunteers.

Port Hudson having surrendered on the 8th of July, in accordance
with Special Orders, No. 174, headquarters Department of the Gulf,
copy of which is herewith inclosed, marked A,* I left that place on the
18th instant, and arrived at Vicksburg on the evening of the 19th.
Having reported to Major-General Grant, in pursuance of Special Orders, No. 195, headquarters Department of the Tennessee, copy of which
is herewith inclosed, marked B,† we left that place on the 20th, and
arrived in Memphis on the evening of the 23d, where I reported with
my command to Maj. Gen. S. A. Hurlbut.

All of which is respectfully submitted.

B. H. GRIERSON,
Brigadier-General of Volunteers.

Lieut. Col. HENRY BINMORE, *Assistant Adjutant-General.*

No. 29.

*Reports of Col. Edward Prince, Seventh Illinois Cavalry, of the capture
of the Confederate steamers Starlight and Red Chief.*

STEAMER STARLIGHT, *May 25, 1863.*

SIR: I have taken possession of the only· two steamboats on the
creek, and shall hold them without further orders until they are destroyed by myself or the enemy.

I will undertake to keep the enemy from crossing Thompson's Creek
with the force at my disposal.

Respectfully,

EDWARD PRINCE,
Colonel, Commanding Expedition.

Lieutenant WOODWARD,
Assistant Adjutant-General, First Brigade, Cavalry Division.

----

* See p. 645.   † Omitted.

BEFORE PORT HUDSON,
May 30, 1863.

SIR: I report through you to the colonel commanding brigade that, in pursuance of his orders, I reported on the 25th May to Colonel Paine, and was assigned to the duty of capturing the steamboats lying under the guns of Port Hudson, on Thompson's Creek, which I effected by a surprise, with 200 men of my own regiment and two companies of infantry of the Thirty-first Massachusetts, and the left section of the First Maine Battery. I took the liberty of disobeying the instructions of the department commander as to the destruction of the boats, as I found that I could place them where a light guard would be sufficient, and also found that in case of necessity they could be very easily run out into the Mississippi River and up to the upper fleet. For this I received the unqualified approval of the commanding general. In pursuance of orders, I turned over the steamboats to an infantry guard, with about 25 prisoners of war. The names of the steamboats are Starlight and Red Chief; both in perfect running order, and worth about $75,000.

Respectfully,

EDWARD PRINCE,
Colonel, Seventh Illinois Regiment Cavalry.

Lieutenant WOODWARD,
Assistant Adjutant-General, First Brigade, Cavalry Division.

No. 30.

Report of Lieut. Col. Augustus W. Corliss, Second Rhode Island Cavalry, of affair at Springfield Landing.

BEFORE PORT HUDSON, LA.,
July 2, 1863.

SIR: I have the honor to report that, in obedience to an order received from you this morning at 2 a. m., I marched with 88 men to report to General Dwight. I arrived at his headquarters at about 4 a. m., and was met by an officer, who said he was about to start to meet me. He informed me that the mail of the division had been captured by a party of rebel cavalry; that Captain Godfrey, of the Louisiana cavalry, knew where they were, and would join me, and aid in cutting them off and capturing them.

We met Captain Godfrey, with about 15 men, near the Springfield road. He informed the staff officer that the mail had not been captured, but there was a body of rebel cavalry near the church on the Baton Rouge road. The staff officer ordered me to proceed to Springfield Landing, and then to scout the roads east as far as the main road to Baton Rouge.

I arrived at Springfield Landing at about 7.30 o'clock, and found everything quiet. I started on my return at about 8 o'clock, and had proceeded about 1½ miles, when a messenger came to me, and informed me that the rebel cavalry were at the Landing. I at once ordered an officer to proceed down the road rapidly and gain what information possible; at the same time turned the head of my column about, and started to return. At this time we received a scattering volley from the enemy. I replied, and, I am quite sure, with effect. I ordered my men into column of fours, and charged on the enemy. They fell back on their main body, and then the whole force fired at us and charged. They greatly outnumbered us, and we fell back, driving the train on the road back toward Port Hudson.

The dust in the road was so thick that we could not distinguish friend from foe. They followed us for some distance, firing rapidly. When about 3 miles from the Landing, Captain Beach came to the rear, and informed me that the enemy was in our front. I ordered a charge through them, but found they had fled. At this time I saw on my right, about 300 yards from the road, a line of about 400 dismounted rebels advancing, with skirmishers deployed toward the road. They did not fire at me, probably supposing us to be their own men. After passing them, we saw nothing more of the enemy.

At the time of the first attack, I sent a messenger to your headquarters, and in a few moments sent two more. As we were turning to go back to the Landing, I saw 2 officers in a buggy, one of whom I am informed was Major-General Augur. He told me to save the train; and then drove rapidly away in the direction of Port Hudson.

I have missing now 2 lieutenants, prisoners; 4 enlisted men; 1 enlisted man killed, and 6 enlisted men wounded.

I have the honor to be, your obedient servant,
                                     A. W. CORLISS,
     Lieut. Col., Comdg. Second Regiment Rhode Island Cavalry.
Maj. Gen. N. P. BANKS.

No. 31.

Report of Lieut. Commander Edward Terry, U. S. Navy, commanding Naval Battery, of operations May 30–July 8.

                              HASTINGS-ON-THE-HUDSON,
                                    September 5, 1863.

SIR: I have the honor herewith to inclose the report of Lieutenant-Commander Terry, and the testimonials given that officer and Ensigns Shepard and Swann, for the energy, zeal, and skill displayed at the naval battery at the siege of Port Hudson by the army and navy, which I hope will be placed upon record for their future benefit.

Very respectfully, your obedient servant,
                                     D. G. FARRAGUT,
                                          Rear-Admiral.
Hon. GIDEON WELLES,
     Secretary of the Navy, Washington, D. C.

                         [Inclosure.]

                    Letter of Capt. T. A. Jenkins.

                              U. S. S. RICHMOND,
                              New Orleans, July 30, 1863.

ADMIRAL: I transmit herewith the report of Lieutenant-Commander Terry, and two letters from the officer of the army charged with the artillery employed in reduction of Port Hudson.

Lieutenant-Commander Terry and the officers and men under his command at the naval batteries before Port Hudson received from the army the highest commendations, and it affords me great pleasure to place in your hands a detailed report setting forth the important services rendered on shore by the navy during the siege of that stronghold of the enemy.

I am, very respectfully,

THORNTON A. JENKINS,
Captain.

Rear-Admiral D. G. FARRAGUT,
  · *Commanding West Gulf Blockading Squadron.*

[Sub-Inclosure No. 1.]

Report of Lieut. Commander Edward Terry.

U. S. S. RICHMOND,
Below Port Hudson, July 10, 1863.

SIR : I have the honor to submit the following report of the operations of the naval battery under my command in position before Port Hudson:

On the 30th May, in obedience to an order from the admiral, I proceeded on shore, to report to General Banks as the commanding officer of the battery of 9-inch guns. The latter referred me to Brigadier-General Arnold, chief of artillery, from whom I learned that the guns were at Springfield Landing. After several days' delay, owing to want of transportation, they were brought to a position near the battery. On June 4, Acting Ensign R. P. Swann, Master's Mates Cox and Bourne, and three guns' crews (51 men) from the Richmond, and Ensign E. M. Shepard, with one gun's crew of 17 men from the Essex, landed and encamped one-half mile in the rear of the battery. June 5, shifted camp to ravine 500 yards in the rear of battery. From that date until June 9 engaged in slinging, transporting, and mounting guns and stowing magazine. Considerable delay on account of platforms not being furnished. June 9, 11 a. m., unmasked the battery, which was 748 yards from the enemy's works, and opened fire upon the latter. Sharp musketry fire from the enemy. Continued firing all day at intervals of two and one-half minutes, and all night at intervals of five minutes. June 10, firing all day; dismounted one of the enemy's guns. Enemy's sharpshooters somewhat troublesome. On the 12th instant, set fire to some of the buildings within their lines; firing slowly all night and rapidly at daylight. On the 13th, firing all night at intervals of ten minutes. At 11 a. m., artillery opened all along their lines, firing rapidly for one hour. At meridian, General Grover demanded the surrender of the place. A refusal was the reply. At 5 p. m., dismounted a light gun. On the 14th instant, at 2 a. m., opened a heavy artillery fire all along the line, after which an unsuccessful attack was made by the infantry; disabled a light gun. On the 15th and 16th, firing slowly; 17th, no firing; flag of truce. On the 18th, firing briskly all day. Removed one gun to a battery on the left; sent Mr. Swann to take charge of it, Mr. Bourne accompanying him. Occasional gun fired from the battery on the right, but with no rapid or continued firing subsequent to that date. On the 25th, the battery on the left opened fire on the enemy's works. About 3.30 p. m. John Williams, third, seaman, was mortally wounded, and John McNalley and William Kelcher slightly. On the 27th, another 9-inch gun was removed from the right battery to the left. At 5 p. m. William Kelcher, stationed in the left battery, was severely wounded. On the 28th, at 10 a. m., the battery on the left opened fire; the rebels replied with two heavy guns. On the 29th, firing slowly all day, the enemy reply-ing with two heavy guns. June 30, July 1, 2, and 3, firing at long in-tervals. On the 2d, I received orders from Captain Alden to return on board, to take charge of the ship, the latter going north on a leave of absence.

On the evening of the 2d, turned over the command of the battery on the left to Mr. Swann, and the battery on the right to Mr. Shepard. The two guns transferred to the left were placed in a seventeen-gun battery, 340 yards from the enemy's works, commanded by an officer of the Regular United States Artillery, but, at Captain Alden's request, I still maintained a supervision over all the guns manned by seamen, visiting the battery on the left every day.

The battery on the right was on the right of the center (General Augur's command). The officers rendered me every assistance in their power, especially Messrs. Shepard and Swann, the latter displaying the same zeal, energy, and fearlessness which have characterized his con-duct in every action on board this vessel. I would also recommend to your favorable notice Acting Master's Mate Edmund L. Bourne, who, although but a short time on board of a man-of-war, rendered most valuable assistance in mounting guns, and afterward in directing their fire. Mr. Swann, with whom he was associated on the left, speaks of his services as invaluable.

The men, as a body, with very few exceptions, which were sent on board the ship, behaved in the most creditable manner, working on two or three occasions all day and night without a murmur, although some of the work which we were obliged to do we expected would be com-pleted before our arrival. One of the gun carriages in the battery on the left was struck on the breast and forward axle-tree fourteen times by musket-balls, showing the accuracy of the enemy's fire.

Mr. Swann reports that subsequent to the 2d of July there was no firing of consequence.

I am, very respectfully, your obedient servant,
EDWARD TERRY,
Lieutenant-Commander, U. S. Navy.

Capt. THORNTON A. JENKINS,
Commanding Richmond.

[Sub-Inclosure No. 2.]

OFFICE CHIEF OF ARTILLERY, NINETEENTH ARMY CORPS,
Port Hudson, July 10, 1863.

The Officer Commanding Naval Forces below Port Hudson :

SIR: Upon the return to you for duty of the detachment from the naval force which has assisted in the reduction of Port Hudson, I am requested by Brigadier-General Arnold, chief of artillery, to express to you his thanks, and to acknowledge the service rendered by the naval battery commanded by Lieutenant-Commander Terry and Ensigns Shepard and Swann. Their duties were discharged with the most dis-tinguished zeal and skill, and they have gained a right to the thanks of the army. The commanding general will be most happy to convey, through you, to those officers these expressions, and the chief of artil-lery takes pleasure in acknowledging his obligations.

By order of Brigadier-General Arnold, chief of artillery:

I have the honor, sir, to be, very respectfully,
S. S. NEWBURY,
Assistant Chief of Artillery.

[Sub-Inclosure No. 3.]

OFFICE CHIEF OF ARTILLERY, NINETEENTH ARMY CORPS,
Port Hudson, July 10, 1863.

R. P. SWANN,
  Acting Master, U. S. Navy:

SIR: I am directed by the brigadier-general, chief of artillery of this army, to express to you his thanks for the eminent services of yourself and command during the siege of Port Hudson.

It was your fortune to occupy for many days the most prominent position among the batteries, and the skill and efficiency with which your guns were served merits and receives, through the officers, the thanks of the army.

Nothing more than the naval battery, and none of the guns of that battery more than your own, has contributed to the successful termination.

From the time that you assumed command of the naval forces on shore to this day, your promptitude, zeal, and value has been marked. Your fire has been most effective, and the conduct of your whole command beyond praise.

By order of Brigadier-General Arnold, chief of artillery :

I have the honor, sir, to be, very respectfully,

S. S. NEWBURY,
  Assistant Chief of Artillery.

No. 32.

Statement of Confederate organizations paroled at Port Hudson.*

1st Alabama, Col. I. G. W. Steedman.
49th Alabama, Maj. T. A. Street.
Maury (Tennessee) Artillery.†
1st [8th] Arkansas Battalion, Lieut. Col. B. Jones.
10th Arkansas, Maj. C. M. Cargile.
11th and 17th Arkansas (detachment).
12th Arkansas, Col. T. J. Reid, jr.
14th Arkansas, Lieut. Col. Pleasant Fowler.
15th Arkansas, Col. Ben. W. Johnson.
16th Arkansas, Col. David Provence.
18th Arkansas, Lieut. Col. W. N. Parish.
23d Arkansas, Col. O. P. Lyles.
4th Louisiana (detachment), Capt. Chas. T. Whitman.
9th Louisiana Batt'n (Infantry), Capt. T. B. R. Chinn.
9th Louisiana Battalion (Partisan Rangers), Maj. J. De Baun.
12th Louisiana Heavy Artillery Battalion, Lieut. Col. P. F. De Gournay.
30th Louisiana (detachment), Capt. T. K. Porter.

Miles' (Louisiana) Legion, Col. W. R. Miles.
Boone's (Louisiana) battery, Capt. S. M. Thomas.
Watson (Louisiana) battery, Lieut. E. A. Toledano.
1st Mississippi, Lieut. Col. A. S. Hamilton.
39th Mississippi, Col. W. B. Shelby.
Claiborne (Mississippi) Light Infantry, Capt. A. J. Lewis.
1st Mississippi Light Artillery (three batteries).‡
English's (Mississippi) battery, Lieut. P. J. Noland.
Seven Stars (Mississippi) Artillery, Lieut. F. G. W. Coleman.
1st Tennessee Heavy Artillery,† Company G, Capt. James A. Fisher.
1st Tennessee Light Artillery,† Company B, Lieut. Oswald Tilghman.
Improvised Tennessee Battalion,§ Capt. S. A. Whiteside.

---

* As shown by the parole rolls.
† Attached to De Gournay's Twelfth Louisiana Heavy Artillery Battalion.
‡ Abbay's, Bradford's, and Herod's. Remainder of regiment surrendered at Vicksburg.
§ Composed of details from the Forty-first, Forty-second, Forty-eighth, Forty-ninth, Fifty-third, and Fifty-fifth Tennessee Regiments.

No. 33.

*Report of Capt. C. M. Jackson, Acting Assistant Inspector-General,
C. S. Army, of the surrender of Port Hudson.*

JULY 9, 1863.

Port Hudson surrendered yesterday at 6 a. m. Our provisions were exhausted, and it was impossible for us to cut our way out, on account of the proximity of the enemy's works.

Our casualties during the siege are 200 killed and between 300 and 400 wounded. About 200 men have died from sickness. At the time of surrender, there were only 2,500 men for duty. I came out through the enemy's lines about an hour after the surrender, and tried to ascertain the strength of General Banks' army, but did not succeed ; but from my own observation, I am led to believe his force to be 25,000 or 30,000 men.

C. M. JACKSON,
Acting Asst. Insp. Gen. to Maj. Gen. Frank. Gardner.

General JOSEPH E. JOHNSTON.

No. 34.

Returns of Casualties in the Confederate forces (incomplete).

AT PLAINS STORE.

Officers and men.	Killed.	Wounded.	Total.
Commissioned officers	4	3	7
Non-commissioned officers		4	4
Privates	8	29	37
Total	12	36	48

OFFICERS KILLED.—Lieuts. Irvin Pierce and H. J. Gorman, First Mississippi Artillery; Lieuts. M. G. Crawford and G. J. Wilson, Miles' Legion.

SIEGE OF PORT HUDSON.

Officers and men.	Killed.	Wounded.	Total.
Commissioned officers	15	48	63
Non-commissioned officers	27	49	76
Privates	134	350	484
Total	176	447	623

OFFICERS KILLED.—Lieut. William Hemingway, Twelfth Arkansas Infantry; Capt. Q. T. Stokely, and Lieuts. W. H. Harrison and P. H. Pruett, Tenth Arkansas Infantry ; Lieut. E. M. Spain, Sixteenth Arkansas Infantry ; Lieut. J. B Edrington, First Mississippi Artillery; Lieut. Thomas Frank, First Alabama Infantry ; Lieut. T. M. Bond, Ninth Louisiana Battalion (Partisan Rangers) ; Lieut. Thomas B. Cooke. First Tennessee Artillery. (List incomplete.)

Number died in hospital are included in the body of the report among the wounded.

J. R. BARNETT,
Chief Surgeon Third District.

No. 35.

*Report of Capt. Louis J. Girard, C. S. Army, Chief of Ordnance,
Third Military District.*

RICHMOND, VA.,
January 24, 1864.

GENERAL: Inclosed please find-report of Ordnance Department that
I have not been able to give you at New Orleans, nor to send you from
New York, as requested, but hope that it may reach you at once on
your arrival, as I leave it at War Department, thinking that the best
disposition to make of it under the circumstances.

. I have the honor to be, very respectfully, your obedient servant,
LOUIS J. GIRARD,
Captain, and Chief of Ordnance.
[Major-General GARDNER.]

RICHMOND, VA., *January* 24, 1864.

SIR: In accordance with your order, dated May 20, 1863, I manufactured a siege carriage for the 12-pounder rifled cannon which we
had from gunboat on Amite River, and placed it on the breastworks.

On the 21st, we removed two 24-pounder smooth-bores from the river
defenses to the breastworks.

On the 22d, we removed two 24-pounder rifled pieces, taking them from
barbette carriage on siege carriage.

On the 26th, three of these guns were dismounted by the fire of the
enemy. On the same night the damage done to the carriages was repaired and the guns remounted.

On the 27th, one 24-pounder smooth-bore was entirely disabled and
two others dismounted. The damage done was repaired during the night
and the guns remounted during the next day. I then commenced to
manufacture a siege carriage for a 32-pounder navy gun, which carriage
was completed in two days and the gun in position. On the same day
I removed one more 24-pounder from the river to the rear. These guns
during the siege were dismounted and remounted twenty-one times.
Having made so much alteration in our river defenses, 1 removed the
30-pounder Parrott from Battery 2 to Battery 11; the 32-pounder rifle
from Battery 3 to Battery 11; one 42-pounder from Battery 3 to Battery
1, and took the 8-inch howitzer from the low battery on the bluff, placing
it on a pivot carriage, so as to be enabled to operate with it on land as
well as on river defenses. At the same time the 10-inch columbiad was
dismounted, with carriage chassis, truck-wheel, and axle-tree broken.
Remained a week to repair it.

On June 14, three of our guns were dismounted. At the request of
Col. B. [W.] Johnson, Fifteenth Arkansas, I fixed some 13-inch mortar
shell outside the fortification, to be burst at the approach of the enemy.
A few days after, we placed some fourteen others outside our fortifications at different places, arming the men with hand-grenades.

On June 20, I found the ammunition would be short, having shot
away most all of our shells for heavy artillery. Some men were detailed
to pass through the different encampments picking up bullets, cannon
shell of all sizes, and mortar shell for 8 and 10 inch. The bullets were
melted and remolded, and from 4,000 to 5,000 Enfield cartridges were
daily manufactured, which kept the men supplied with ammunition.
The artillery ammunition was refixed and used by our artillery, the
smaller size shell being fixed for hand-grenades, and the shell of large

caliber, which we could not use with our ordnance, were fixed to roll down upon the enemy's works.

On July 1, as the enemy was mining our works, I was requested by the chief engineer to direct the counter-mine. I fixed and placed my mining battery, and the counter-mine was successfully blown up on the morning of July 4. The ammunition for artillery was of inferior manufacture, many of the 8 and 10 inch shell being cast so that the hollow was too small to contain the bursting charge. The fuses were fixed so that the most of the 10-second and 14-second burst at the muzzle of the gun, the friction-primers being entirely unserviceable.

At the surrender, besides the arms used by the men, there were 600 flint-lock muskets, unserviceable without repairs; 30,000 Enfield cartridges manufactured during the siege; 30 pieces light artillery, with 2,500 rounds, mostly solid shot; 10,000 pounds of powder, including the lot directed to Lieutenant-General [E. K.] Smith, of the Trans-Mississippi Department; 12 heavy ordnance, with 100 solid shot to the gun.

All of which is most respectfully submitted.

Very respectfully, your obedient servant,

LOUIS J. GIRARD,
Captain, and Chief of Ordnance, Port Hudson, La.

Maj. Gen. FRANK. GARDNER,
    Commanding, Port Hudson, La.

No. 36.

Reports of Brig. Gen. W. N. R. Beall, C. S. Army, commanding Brigade.

PORT HUDSON, LA.,
June 8, 1863.

SIR: I have just received your communication containing instructions from the major-general commanding that I shall send 80 men from my line to relieve the Ninth Louisiana Battalion [Partisan Rangers], on Colonel Miles' line; that this battalion cannot be trusted on outpost or picket duty; that they are deserting, &c., and that I must put them where they can be watched and shot down in case they desert.

I would respectfully call the attention of the major-general commanding to the following facts: With my brigade I was assigned a certain portion of the breastworks to defend. Since the enemy have appeared in our front, more than one-third of my best troops have been taken from me and moved to the left, where they now are, under the command of a junior officer. This I did not object to, as the interests of the service seemed to require such an assignment; but now that 80 men on the right are found who are worse than no men at all, I do object to having men taken from my line, which is so thinly guarded that I am constantly fearing that the enemy may storm the works, and 80 soldiers "that cannot be trusted" put in their stead. I do not think that is doing me justice, and if I am to take the 80 men from the line, cannot say that the chance to hold it against the enemy is even a good one. I have no place to assign these 80 men where they can be watched and fired upon should they attempt to desert, and the only place where this can be done is the guard-house, and I would recommend that they be sent there for safe-keeping. I cannot guard them on my line. I had far rather not have them than to have them. I ask that 80 men from the left be sent to take the place of these men. If the major-general will only pass along my line, he will see how few men I have to guard a long and important front. Every day that I pass along it, my apprehensions are greatly increased. I am, respectfully,

W. N. R. BEALL,
Brigadier-General.

Lieut. J. S. LANIER, *Acting Assistant Adjutant-General.*

—

HDQRS. BEALL'S BRIG., *Jackson Road, June* 14, 1863.

GENERAL: The men have repulsed several charges on this line. The First Mississippi is scarce of caps; can you send me any? I am trying to get them from the regiments on the right. Our loss thus far small; that of the enemy large. Most of our guns (artillery) are disabled on this line. Fire of artillery from enemy very severe.

Respectfully,

W. N. R. BEALL,
Brigadier-General.

[Major-General GARDNER.]   —

HDQRS. BEALL'S BRIG., *Port Hudson, La., June* 14, 1863.

MAJOR: The loss of the First Mississippi Regiment in to-day's engagement is very severe—18 killed and about 14 wounded. The command is much reduced. Cannot the 100 men ordered to Colonel [B. W.] Johnson for duty be returned to the regiment?

Very respectfully,

W. N. R. BEALL,
Brigadier-General.

Maj. T. F. WILLSON,
Assistant Adjutant-General, Third Military District.

[Inclosure.]

Report of Casualties in Beall's brigade up to June 1, 1863.*

Command.	Killed.	Wounded.	Missing.	Total.
1st Alabama, Company K	2	2	......	4
49th Alabama	3	18	11	32
10th Arkansas	14	20	49	83
12th Arkansas	3	11	......	14
15th Arkansas	12	39	30	81
16th Arkansas	2	3	......	5
23d Arkansas	7	28	5	40
1st Arkansas Battalion	1	1	......	2
12th Louisiana Artillery Battalion, Company D	......	6	......	6
Watson (Louisiana) Battery	2	10	......	12
1st Mississippi	5	13	1	19
39th Mississippi	2	4	......	6
1st Mississippi Light Artillery Battalion	11	33	......	44
1st Tennessee Artillery Battalion, Company B	2	2	......	4
1st Tennessee Artillery Battalion, Company G	2	4	......	6
Total	68	194	96	358

Respectfully submitted.

W. N. R. BEALL,
Brigadier-General.

[Major-General GARDNER.]

* These casualties are probably included in Surg. J. R. Barnett's returns.

HEADQUARTERS BEALL'S BRIGADE,
Port Hudson, La., June 17, 1863.

GENERAL: The dead, 160, and 1 wounded man have been delivered. There are signs of many having been buried by the enemy.

General Paine was wounded in three places—in the leg, side, and shoulder—and lay all the day of the fight near our breastworks; he will lose a leg. There are hundreds of guns near the breastworks, also any number of hand-grenades.

I am, general, respectfully, &c.,

W. N. R. BEALL,
Brigadier-General.

Major-General GARDNER,
Commanding.

—

HEADQUARTERS BEALL'S BRIGADE,
[Port Hudson,] July 7, 1863.

GENERAL: The works of the enemy opposite the First Mississippi are very strong and extensive, and enable him to throw a force in our ditch without our being able to use sharpshooters on them. These facts will, I think, enable him to throw a force of men inside of our works without our being able to drive him back, unless heavy re-enforcements are brought from other points of the line. ·

To do this will be to leave said points unguarded, and to permit the enemy to come over there also.

There is more discontent among the men within the last few days than I have discovered before, and I very much fear that the officers are at the bottom of it.

If you have any directions to give me in reference to use of the troops in case the enemy get over the works, I should like to have them, as I do not think that his attack will be delayed much longer, as his works are very formidable, and, to appearances, nearly completed.

But one company of the Tenth Arkansas has reported—the others refuse, so I am told.

I am, general, very respectfully, &c.,

W. N. R. BEALL,
Brigadier-General.

Major-General GARDNER.

———

No. 37.

Reports of Capt. John R. Fellows, Assistant Inspector-General, C. S. Army, of skirmish at Thompson's Creek, and assault on the works at Port Hudson.

HEADQUARTERS BEALL'S BRIGADE,
May 25, 1863.

GENERAL: I have the honor to state that this afternoon a body of cavalry of the enemy appeared in the open field to the left of Troth's Mills, and were fired upon by the guns on Colonel [W. R.] Miles' line. The shots evidently did execution, and caused a very rapid retreat of the enemy. About an hour after they disappeared, a small party, bearing a white flag, came in the lower part of the field. Colonel Miles sent a flag to meet them, but before it had advanced far, the Federals and flag fell back in the woods, bearing with them what we are well convinced was dead or wounded. All of our officers and men witnessed the base expedient thus resorted to to remove their wounded and killed from the field of their cowardly flight under a flag of truce.

I am general, very respectfully,

JNO. R. FELLOWS,
Captain, and Assistant Inspector-General.

Brigadier-General [W. N. R.] BEALL.

[JUNE] —, 1863.

. GENERAL: Enemy have advanced three times on the works, and have been repulsed with loss. We shot down their flag in the last attack, and it has not since been raised. They are forming a fourth line. Have no fear as to matters here. We are perfectly able to maintain our line without further help. My horse has run off; can you send me another? Two men killed and 1 wounded here, all in the artillery.

Respectfully,

JNO. R. FELLOWS,
Captain, and Assistant Inspector-General.

[Brigadier-General BEALL.]

No. 38.

Reports of Col. David Provence, Sixteenth Arkansas Infantry, of the capture of Union outposts, and casualties to July 8.

JUNE 27, 1863.

GENERAL: Yesterday morning works of the enemy were discovered about 200 yards to my front, and some 300 in advance of any of the neighboring works of the enemy. I was unable to comprehend the design of these works. I therefore directed Lieutenant-Colonel [J. M.] Pittman to send out a brave and cautious man to examine them. Accordingly, Private Mieres was sent out, who passed beyond the works to the right of them, so that he could get a view of them from the enemy's side. He reported the works connected with the woods by a deep ravine, and that they were occupied by some 15 or 20 men. A short time before nightfall, Colonel Pittman sent out Sergt. J. W. Parker, the result of whose reconnaissance was substantially the same as that of Private Mieres. Feeling that I would not be able to post our pickets without the loss of life, or else discontinue pickets altogether, I determined to take the works and destroy them. I directed Colonel Pittman to call for 30 volunteers from the Sixteenth Arkansas for the execution of this order, and place them under a proper officer. Many of the men and large numbers of the officers volunteered. The accompanying is a list of those finally chosen and allowed to go,* to which list, if proper, I might add the names of several commissioned officers. The whole were placed under the command of Lieut. A. S. McKennon. At nightfall they were placed outside of our works, at a point south and west of the enemy's works. At the same time a number of our men, at a point considerably to the left of Lieutenant McKennon, were directed to make a noise and engage the enemy at the battery in

---

*Not found.

conversation, with the view of directing attention from the point of approach. This was done, and a lively and noisy conversation ensued. While this was going on, Lieutenant McKennon approached to within about 30 yards of the enemy's works, when he gave the order to charge. In an instant the work was in our possession. The enemy fired but once, and then at a great elevation. After the works were in our possession, the men, with the assistance of others from the regiment, tore down the works and scattered the sand-bags, bringing many of them into camp. Besides destroying the works, 7 prisoners were taken, and several were killed and wounded. We had only 1 man hurt, who was knocked down by one of the enemy as he was leaping into the works. Some 12 or 14 guns were also brought in.

We finally posted our pickets, and were only annoyed during the night by occasional volleys fired from the woods.

Respectfully, &c.,

D. PROVENCE,
Colonel, Commanding.

[Brigadier-General BEALL.]

—

HEADQUARTERS LEFT WING, BEALL'S BRIGADE,
July 8, 1863.

CAPTAIN: The following is a report of the casualties of this command: First Mississippi Regiment, Major [Thomas H.] Johnston commanding, Private W. D. Striclan, Company F, killed; Forty-ninth Alabama, Major [T. A.] Street commanding, Private James Terrel, Company A, wounded slightly; first section Watson Battery, Lieutenant [J. E.] Norés commanding, none. Recapitulation—killed, 3; wounded, 3.

Respectfully submitted.

D. PROVENCE,
Colonel, Commanding.

Capt. BEALL HEMPSTEAD,
Assistant Adjutant-General.

———

No. 39.

Reports of Col. O. P. Lyles, Twenty-third Arkansas Infantry, of operations May 31–July 3.

PORT HUDSON, LA.,
May 31, 1863.

MAJOR: The enemy has dismounted our large gun and wounded 5 men. I think by getting a new wheel ———. The shots thrown upon the enemy's intrenchments with our gun before it was dismounted did good work.

O. P. LYLES,
Colonel, Commanding Right Wing.

[Maj. T. F. WILLSON,
Assistant Adjutant-General.]

—

PORT HUDSON, LA.,
June 30, 1863.

MAJOR: On yesterday I succeeded in burning the cotton of the enemy that he was rolling before him. He approached within a few yards of the works, when Captain Lindsey, of the Twelfth Arkansas, threw brands of fire on him, and destroyed his cotton. Early in the night last night, the enemy approached, and attempted a sort of feeble charge, throwing a few hand-grenades into my trenches, but did no harm. I repulsed him and drove him off, killing a considerable number of his men. I am sure he was quite demoralized—so much so that his sharpshooters fell entirely back out of range. Later in the night his sharpshooters returned, and killed and wounded several of my men (new men of my regiment, Twenty-third Arkansas, who were not acquainted with the place). He is now rolling before him a hogshead filled with sticks. I must arrest his progress before 3 p. m., or he will throw his hand-grenades into my trenches again. I am certain I can stop him. I now have Major [E. L.] Black, with 125 men of Twenty-third Arkansas, on the extreme right. Colonel [W. N.] Parish, with the Eighteenth Arkansas, came just before daylight this morning. I think I could have held the place even without this re-enforcement, and feel sanguine that I can with it. I will hold it.

I am, major, very respectfully, &c.,

O. P. LYLES,
Colonel, Commanding Right Wing.

Maj. T. F. WILLSON,
Assistant Adjutant-General.

——

JUNE 30, 1863.

MAJOR: It is the Twenty-third Arkansas that I want. The Eighteenth Arkansas has gone to General Beall. The little fight, think, has pretty well blown over, though he is still making demonstrations. He got in my trenches and got 1 officer. I whipped him (the enemy) out again, killing some. Watch on General Beall's line; I think they intend something there.

O. P. LYLES,
Colonel, Commanding Right Wing.

[Maj. T. F. WILLSON,
Assistant Adjutant-General.]

——

PORT HUDSON,
June 30, 1863.

MAJOR: I said to you that the enemy charged me on the extreme right. So he did, and a few of his men got into my trenches. I killed 6 in my trenches, and as to the number outside killed and wounded, I do not know, but his loss must be considerable. It was rather a small business, as usual (I mean his charge). He took 1 captain and 3 of my men out of my trenches, and killed 1, making my loss 5 in the aggregate. I repulsed him very handsomely, and all is now quiet. I can repulse him every time, and will do it. During the skirmish, I discovered he was marching a large force toward General Beall's line, and hence the suggestion to watch in that direction. The Twenty-third Arkansas has not got here yet, but it will, no doubt, soon be here. I sent the Eighteenth Arkansas off long before night.

I am, major, very respectfully, &c.,

O. P. LYLES,
Colonel, Commanding Right Wing.

Maj. T. F. WILLSON,
Assistant Adjutant-General.]

PORT HUDSON, LA., *July* 1, 1863.

MAJOR: I am unable as yet to check the enemy in his march with his trenches. I am of opinion that he will reach my trenches to-night. He has shelled my troops at the extreme right very much to-day, with the view, I think, of trying to demoralize them, so as to storm my rifle-pit to-night. He has almost ruined my rifle-pit with his artillery. I am wide awake.

Respectfully, &c.,

O. P. LYLES,
Colonel, Commanding Right Wing.

[Maj. T. F. WILLSON,
Assistant Adjutant-General.]

—

PORT HUDSON, LA., *July* 3, 1863.

MAJOR: All is well down here in the Devil's Elbow. Last night was unusually quiet. The enemy keeps coming with his trench. I think he is filing a little to the right. I am ready for him; let him come. I can whip him in four minutes if he shows himself. I do not think his trench will do him any good. I can hold the point, and intend to do it.

This little report is made simply to inform you that I am still in life and spirits.

I am, major, very respectfully, &c.,

O. P. LYLES,
Colonel, Commanding Right Wing.

Maj. T. F. WILLSON, *Assistant Adjutant-General.*

P. S.—We throw our hand-grenades on him, &c.

———

No. 40.

Reports of Lieut. Col. P. F. De Gournay, Twelfth Louisiana Artillery Battalion, of operations May 24–July 2.

HEADQUARTERS LEFT WING, HEAVY BATTERIES,
Port Hudson, May 24, 1863.

COLONEL: During the two hours and a half bombardment by the enemy's mortar and gunboats, the batteries of this command fired twenty-four shots with little effect, being at very long range. One of the shots from Captain [W. B.] Seawell's battery struck the Monongahela in the bow. Our batteries were struck many times, but with no damage. The gun-carriage at Battery 10 was slightly injured, but not enough to disable it.

I have to deplore the following casualties among the men armed as infantry at the breastworks on the extreme right, viz: Killed, Corporal [William] Zengle and Private [Adolph] Hildman, of Company **A**, Twelfth Louisiana Battalion; Private [John] Haindel, Company E, Twelfth Louisiana Battalion. Wounded, Private [John] Fink, Company A, Twelfth Louisiana Battalion.

I am, colonel, respectfully, your obedient servant,

P. F. DE GOURNAY,
Lieutenant-Colonel, Commanding.

Lieut. Col. M. J. SMITH,
Chief of Heavy Artillery.

HEADQUARTERS LEFT WING, HEAVY BATTERIES,
Port Hudson, May 24, 1863.

MAJOR: I have to report the following casualties among the men of my command armed as infantry, and stationed at the breastworks on the extreme right: Killed, Corporal [William] Zengle and Private [Adolph] Hildman, of Company A, and Private [John] Haindel, of Company E, Twelfth Louisiana Battalion. Wounded, Private [John] Fink, Company A, Twelfth Louisiana Battalion. These casualties resulted from a single bomb-shell. The gun carriage at Battery No. 10 was slightly injured, but not disabled. I have no other damages to report, although the batteries were struck quite often by fragments of bomb and rifle shells.

I am, very respectfully, your obedient servant,
P. F. DE GOURNAY,
Lieutenant-Colonel, Commanding Left Wing, Heavy Batteries.

Maj. T. F. WILLSON,
Assistant Adjutant-General.

—

HEADQUARTERS LEFT WING, HEAVY BATTERIES,
Port Hudson, May 29, 1863.

COLONEL: I had the Parrott gun and the rifled 24-pounder trailed and pointed yesterday, and bearings marked, so that they could be directed at the mortar-boats during the night. At 11.30 the mortars commenced bombarding, when our guns replied, firing at the flash, deliberately and slowly. We fired in all nineteen shots, and this morning the mortar fleet is below the Point, having fallen back during the darkness that preceded daybreak. I owe this result in great part to the excellent management of Lieutenant [L. A.] Schirmer, whom I had placed in charge of the Parrott gun. During the fight the bursting of a bomb-shell in the rear of the battery wounded 3 men of Company D, Twelfth Louisiana Battalion; 1 seriously. No damage to the works.

I am, colonel, very respectfully, your obedient servant,
P. F. DE GOURNAY,
Lieutenant-Colonel, Commanding Left Wing, Heavy Batteries.

Lieut. Col. M. J. SMITH,
Chief of Heavy Artillery.

—

HEADQUARTERS LEFT WING, HEAVY ARTILLERY,
Port Hudson, June 5, 1863.

MAJOR: During the furious bombardment by the enemy's mortar-boats this afternoon, a shell struck the gun (32-pounder rifled) at Battery No. 10, breaking the screw. The damage is easily repaired, and the gun can be used to-night. Another shell fell in the camp near Battery No. 9, killing 1 man instantly. The mortar-boats have moved to-day nearer the Point, probably on account of the river falling steadily. They are not much nearer to us, but in better view. For several days they have been using occasionally extra charges of powder, by which they have attained greater range, and thrown shells beyond Battery No. 6. I will take advantage of their new position, and attack them to-morrow with the Parrott gun (30-pounder) and the rifled 24-pounder and 32-pounder.

I am, major, respectfully, your obedient servant,

P. F. DE GOURNAY,
Lieutenant-Colonel, Commanding Left Wing, Heavy Batteries.

Maj. T. F. WILLSON,
Assistant Adjutant-General.

—

HEADQUARTERS LEFT WING, HEAVY BATTERIES,
Port Hudson, June 10, 1863.

COLONEL: The communication to General Gardner from several officers of the right wing, land defenses, asking that more heavy guns should be placed on that wing, is before me, and I have the honor to submit my opinion, as requested by you. As regards the 8-inch shell gun, the only one from my command alluded to, I cannot see the practicability of its removal to the lines. It is a barbette gun, and a battery would have to be constructed, which would involve delay and labor; it would, besides, deprive the river defenses of one of the few effective guns they have with which to contend against the superior armament of the fleet.

If this gun were placed in Battery No. 8, on a columbiad pivot carriage, as agreed lately, it might be brought to bear on the enemy's land batteries, while still retaining its position on the river.

Such is the case with the 30-pounder Parrott and rifled 24-pounder, which commands both the river and land. These two guns will support any battery on the right wing whenever, by previous understanding, it wishes to open. By so doing, they will probably attract the fire of the fleet, but such a consideration can have no weight. If we calculate the number of guns of the enemy, and bow to their superiority, we are lost.

We have to fight them when and as we can, and trust to God and our own fortitude for the result. There is nothing to warrant the opinion that with two heavy guns on the line we can silence all their batteries, and, in my opinion, the removal of the 8-inch shell gun would give certain prejudice and barely probable benefit.

These remarks are my candid opinion, but should the general order any of the guns of my command to be moved to other positions, he may rest assured that· we will fight them as long as they will stand. Should he wish the 24-pounder and 30-pounder Parrott to open to-morrow on the enemy's batteries, I will have it done. We could effect nothing at night with these guns, as the enemy's batteries are concealed from view, and we must be guided by the smoke of their guns.

I am, colonel, respectfully,

P. F. DE GOURNAY,
Lieutenant-Colonel, Commanding Left Wing, Heavy Batteries.

Lieut. Col. M. J. SMITH,
Chief of Heavy Artillery.

—

HEADQUARTERS LEFT WING, HEAVY BATTERIES,
Port Hudson, June 11, 1863.

COLONEL: During the firing from the ships this morning, the 24-pounder rifled gun at Battery 11 was struck by a shell near the vent, ·

and a small piece of metal broken off. No serious damage, however, and the gun can be worked with safety.

Yours, respectfully,

P. F. DE GOURNAY,
Lieutenant-Colonel, Commanding Left Wing, Heavy Batteries.

Lieut. Col. M. J. SMITH, *Chief of Heavy Artillery.*

—

HEADQUARTERS LEFT WING, HEAVY BATTERIES,
Port Hudson, June 12, 1863.

COLONEL: The 30-pounder Parrott gun was disabled about an hour ago by a solid shot from a land battery, nearly opposite, that had just opened for the first time. The shot struck the gun near the muzzle, cutting off a piece and splitting the gun. Two other successive shots broke the axle and a wheel, making the piece a complete wreck. The piece was just being placed in position to fire, and was not yet in battery when struck. Sharpshooters now line the hill opposite, and keep up a steady fire when our men show themselves. Amid this sad disaster, I have the consolation to report that none of my cannoneers were hurt.

Respectfully, your obedient servant,

P. F. DE GOURNAY,
Lieutenant-Colonel, Commanding Left Wing, Heavy Batteries.

Lieut. Col. M. J. SMITH, *Chief of Heavy Artillery.*

—

HEADQUARTERS LEFT WING, HEAVY BATTERIES,
Port Hudson, June 26, 1863.

MAJOR: The enemy opened fire from their land batteries and the fleet (including mortar-boats) at 3.45 o'clock this afternoon, to which the guns on this wing replied, and soon brought on a spirited artillery fight. The mortar-boats ceased firing after two hours and a half, the gunboats four hours. No damage was done to our guns and no man hurt at the batteries. The works at Battery No. 11 were badly torn up by the enemy's fire, which seemed to be, in great part, concentrated on that point. So terrific was the fire at that battery, that it was found impossible to man the siege 24-pounder rifled gun without an almost certainty that it would be dismounted. The guns engaged on the extreme left were the rifled 32-pounder, which fired fourteen shots; the 8-inch shell gun, which fired six shells with excellent effect on the enemy's principal works, after which it unfortunately got disabled by the accidental giving way of the elevating screw—the damage is now being repaired; the rifled 24-pounder barbette, which fired 27 Reid shots at the mortar-boats, many shots taking effect on the boats and also on the Essex.

From the center, the 10-inch and 8-inch columbiads of this command were also engaged, first with the fleet, and subsequently, with much better effect, firing on the enemy's works. I cannot yet report the number of shots fired from these two guns.

I beg leave to make most honorable mention of Lieut. L. A. Schirmer, of my command, for an act of heroic bravery. The flag of [W. R.] Miles' Legion was hoisted on the extreme left (Battery 11), and was shot down. Lieutenant Schirmer seized it, fixed it to a light pole, and, jumping on the parapet, planted the flag-staff amid a shower of bullets. Again and again the flag was shot down, and each time the gallant lieutenant raised it, waved it defiantly, and planted it firmly, regardless of the volleys of the enemy's sharpshooters. He escaped unhurt after re-peating thrice this gallant feat, that called forth the enthusiastic cheers of the brave men who lined our works.

There is still occasional firing, and it is probable that the attack will be renewed to-night, preparatory to an attempt to charge the works in the morning. The men are in excellent spirits and will do all their duty.

I am, major, respectfully, your obedient servant,

P. F. DE GOURNAY,
Lieutenant-Colonel, Commanding Left Wing, Heavy Batteries.

Maj. T. F. WILLSON, *Assistant Adjutant-General.*

—

HEADQUARTERS LEFT WING, HEAVY BATTERIES,
Port Hudson, La., July 2, 1863.

MAJOR: Capt. Felix Le Bisque, Company B, Twelfth Louisiana Battalion, died yesterday in the general hospital, after a protracted illness.

My batteries were again engaged to-day with the enemy's guns recently placed on the opposite side of the river. The 32-pounder rifled gun at Battery No. 10 was dismounted by a shot cutting down the cheeks. The gun is not injured. Captain [W. N.] Coffin, commanding, was slightly wounded. We are unable to say what damage was inflicted on the enemy.

I am, sir, very respectfully, your obedient servant,

P. F. DE GOURNAY,
Lieutenant-Colonel, Commanding Left Wing, Heavy Batteries.

Maj. T. F. WILLSON, *Assistant Adjutant-General.*

———

No. 41.

Reports of Col. I. G. W. Steedman, First Alabama Infantry, of operations May 25–July 7.

HEADQUARTERS LEFT WING,
Port Hudson, La., May 26, 1863.

MAJOR: I have the honor to report the following casualties of my command in yesterday's engagement, viz:

Command.	Killed.	Wounded.	Missing.	Total.
1st Mississippi...	......	4	4	8
1st Alabama	2	8	1	11
15th Arkansas	2	5	1	8
Wingfield's cavalry...	1	1	......	2
Captain [A. J.] Lewis' company*.............................	......	......	1	1
Captain [R. T.] English's company..........................	......	1	......	1
Watson Battery†..	......	2	......	2
39th Mississippi	......	4	1	5
Total	5	25	8	38

* Four horses killed.   † Three horses wounded.

I am, very respectfully, your obedient servant,

I. G. W. STEEDMAN,
Colonel, Commanding Left Wing.

Maj. T. F. WILLSON, *Assistant Adjutant-General.*

[HEADQUARTERS LEFT WING], 12 *o'clock*.

All seems to have quieted in my front. I can learn of no mischief done our men or works. Enemy either made an attempt to charge Lieutenant-Colonel [M. B.] Locke's front (in corner of bull-pen), or made a bold effort to push forward his lines. Whatever his intention, he has been defeated, and gained nothing. Can hear his wounded groaning along our lines. I feel comparatively easy as to balance of night. The enemy has a battery 400 yards in front of slaughter-pen. He fired only two guns (small, I think). The enemy is evidently extending his lines toward our left. Has been cutting timber there. Also reported cutting in front of Lieutenant-Colonel Locke. Have ordered artillery on Commissary Hill to fire shell slowly among them if it prove true. I doubt the correctness of the report. Have well guarded the space between my left and Colonel [W. B.] Shelby's right.

Respectfully,

I. G. W. STEEDMAN,
Colonel First Regiment Alabama Volunteers.

Major [T. F.] WILLSON,
Assistant Adjutant-General.

HEADQUARTERS LEFT WING,
June 10, 1863.

SIR: Two companies of my regiment, Captains [J. F.] Whitfield and [James D.] Meadows, are in charge of siege guns on various parts of the field works. I think either company sufficient for the purpose. Please inquire, and, if possible, order one of the companies to report to Major Knox, near Commissary Hill, to-night at dark. We are in great need of them.

The troops on my line are promiscuously mixed. I am satisfied this will not do. I want a battalion or regiment in charge of each portion of the lines, and its officers responsible for its safety, defense, &c. By giving me Colonel Lyles' regiment, Twenty-third Arkansas, and Fourteenth in place of Eighteenth Arkansas, Lieutenant-Colonel Parish, I can arrange this to my satisfaction.

This changing of troops will not do. The men will not work on lines which they are not compelled to remain in. I am maturing arrangements to send scouts out to-night. I will present my plan by night. Am selecting my men. Think I can arrange it.

Respectfully,

I. G. W. STEEDMAN.

Major WILLSON,
Assistant Adjutant-General.

HEADQUARTERS LEFT WING,
June 11, 1863—Sun-up.

I supposed, until daylight this morning, that the firing in my front was simply from a weak line of sharpshooters, who took up the fire because the firing was going on on the right, but I learn now that the enemy attempted an advance in my whole front, extending one-quarter to a mile left of Slaughter house. At daylight we found the enemy had actually pushed into our lines, and were sheltering themselves from rain in the Slaughter house. As soon as discovered, our troops attacked them, capturing a lieutenant and scattering the whole party back into the abatis, where they are now sheltering in the abatis. I have sent two companies of the best men in the Thirty-ninth Mississippi to effectually drive them out. My only uneasiness is from an unreliable regiment which occupies the threatened point. They are within 300 yards of a battery of six guns and two mortars. It is impossible to remove them to-day. I can only re-enforce as necessity demands. The reference to the regiment is an official secret. It is the Tenth Arkansas. I have had to conciliate them. We cannot do otherwise now. My great troubles resulted from this cause. I was luckily in the trenches occupied by them during all the night fight. I have not been able to close my eyes during the night. I am well this morning. Colonel [W. B.] Shelby's left is quiet and has been all night. I have no report from the right of my line since dark last night. No casualties reported.

It is of vital importance that the 32-pounder be mounted as early as possible. The enemy, I think, will attempt an advance, if at all, under cover of this heavy battery opposite slaughter-pen. The trouble in the Tenth Arkansas prevented my getting all my regiments in permanent positions as I wanted. I am compelled to wait until night again, and then be governed by circumstances. Remember the secret as to this regiment. If this matter is stirred or talked, I fear we will have a mutinous regiment, but with caution I think I can assuage them until they are all right. Will send the prisoners soon.

Respectfully,

I. G. W. STEEDMAN,
Colonel, Commanding Left Wing.

Major [T. F.] WILLSON,
Assistant Adjutant-General.

———

HEADQUARTERS LEFT WING,
Port Hudson, June 11, [1863.]

MAJOR: From all appearances the enemy are preparing for demonstration in my front, and more particularly in front of the slaughter-pen. I have made all my dispositions, and am ready to use at best advantage the force at my disposal. If the attack is made at the point I most suspect, Colonel Shelby's troops will be principally engaged, assisted by the left wing of the Eighteenth Arkansas, posted round about the battery at Bennett's house.

I have but one piece of artillery in such position that it can be used, and this open and exposed to the fire of the enemy's heavy battery. The enemy's battery now consists of four mortars and not less than six guns. The remaining two pieces of artillery in our battery at Bennett's can be used if the attack extends into the bull-pen.

Our men seem to be vigilant, and in as good moral condition as the mud and slop and surrounding circumstances will admit. A few shells fired from now till morning by Colonel Smith at the enemy's battery would be of great assistance in case of an attack. I would suggest the importance of this.

Respectfully, yours, ·

I. G. W. STEEDMAN,
Colonel, Commanding Left Wing.

Major WILLSON,
Assistant Adjutant-General.

[First indorsement.]

Referred to Colone. Smith, who will fire hourly at the enemy's battery, and change the range to the left a little.

Respectfully,

FRANK. GARDNER,
Major-General.

[Second indorsement.]

GENERAL: I shall commence firing, though I think it will have the effect of causing the enemy's guns to get our range and position, and stir them out sooner than they intended to start. I have been on the watch to get the first intimation of a general attack from the enemy, and should have opened as I deemed best. The firing of these guns, unless a general attack, I do not approve of, as the concentration of the enemy's fire from all directions upon this center will do our guns far more harm than we can possibly do the enemy.

Respectfully,

MARSHALL J. SMITH,
Chief of Heavy Artillery.

HEADQUARTERS LEFT WING,
June 11, 1863.

SIR: Please say to the general that I found the Tenth Arkansas on the lines yesterday when I took the command of this line. They had relieved the Twelfth Arkansas the night before. This plan of changing troops, except from necessity, is ruinous. I shall dispose of the regiments on this line to the best of my discretion, and keep them there. I gave such orders as I thought proper to effect this end last night, and all was moving smoothly until the Tenth Arkansas hesitated in its obedience to my order, and delayed the movement until the fight opened, so the whole movement was defeated. It is not the men of the regiment who are troublesome—they have no officers. I feel no doubt, though, in reconciling everything to-day.

Say to the general that I feel remarkably well this morning, and feel no uneasiness as to my health.

Please give me a summary of information gained from the captured lieutenant, especially all relating to my position here and the character of the movement last night. My scouts left promptly after dark last night, and I think got out safely.

Respectfully,

I. G. W. STEEDMAN,
Colonel, Commanding Left Wing.

Lieutenant [A.] DUPRÉ,
Aide-de-Camp.

P. S.—I have just learned that we have driven the enemy back to his old position of yesterday. At daylight, about one company of the enemy was discovered 100 yards in front of our siege guns. We gave them a double charge of grape and canister. The whole company threw down their arms and fled in the utmost confusion. I think we can get the guns to-day.

HEADQUARTERS LEFT WING,
Port Hudson, La., June 15, 1863.

MAJOR: From concurrent testimony of officers on all parts of my line, I am satisfied that there was an extensive movement of wagons and artillery, and perhaps a large body of troops, from some point on my right out on the Jackson road. About 1 or 2 o'clock they apparently either halted or went out of hearing, as they could not be distinctly heard afterward. There was in my immediate front and on the enemy's line no change that we are aware of. I am inclined to think that if this line is attacked at all, the principal effort will be made on the extreme left, across the bridge. Two pieces of artillery were stationed there yesterday afternoon across the creek, and sharpshooters have appeared all around that position; at least two white regiments have been seen maneuvering about the bridge.

I would urge the importance of having all our heavy guns ready to assist in meeting any demonstration there. Those guns, if properly served, will be equal to any number of troops that can be brought to bear upon that point.

I am, captain, very respectfully, your obedient servant,

I. G. W. STEEDMAN,
Colonel, Commanding Left Wing.

Major WILLSON,
Assistant Adjutant-General.

—

HEADQUARTERS LEFT WING,
June 20, 1863.

MAJOR: After heavy skirmishing this evening, the enemy ordered a charge upon our works on the hill in front of Colonel [W. B.] Shelby, but failed to charge. Colonel Shelby reports no loss. Loss of the enemy unknown.

Fearing an assault in the morning, I have ordered Lieutenant [J. P.] Caldwell, with a 6-pounder brass piece, to move to-night from the arsenal, and report to Colonel Shelby on the left, and at the same time ordered Colonel Shelby to prepare a pit in readiness for the gun.

Very respectfully, your obedient servant,

I. G. W. STEEDMAN,
Commanding Left Wing.

Maj. T. F. WILLSON,
Assistant Adjutant-General.

—

HEADQUARTERS LEFT WING,
June 25, 1863.

MAJOR: All quiet on this line except occasional sharpshooting. The enemy are working at no point except in front of Colonel [B. W.] Johnson, extending his rifle-pits to within 150 yards.

About 12 o'clock to-day a shell from the enemy exploded an ammunition chest in the limber at a gun between Colonel Johnson's camp and the mill. The gun was masked. The shot must have been a stray one, or the position of the gun must have been given by deserters. I have made inquiries on all parts of my line to-day concerning the firing that was heard last night. All agreed that there was considerable firing from 10 o'clock till daylight. Some artillery officers say there seemed to be as many as two batteries firing. Some difference of opinion as to the direction of the firing; some say that it was up the river; the majority say that it was in the direction of Jackson, La. I have some reports that the same firing has been heard to-day. This firing has awakened new hopes among the troops.

I am, major, very respectfully, your obedient servant,

I. G. W. STEEDMAN,
Colonel, Commanding Left Wing.

Maj. T. F. WILLSON,
Assistant Adjutant-General.

HEADQUARTERS LEFT WING,
June 29, 1863.

MAJOR: The troops on the left wing are posted at the works in the following order, from right to left: Colonel Johnson's Fifteenth Arkansas, and Captain [M. C.] Peel's company, Eighteenth Arkansas; one brass 12-pounder howitzer, Captain [A. J.] Herod; two Blakely guns, two 6-pounders, First Lieutenant [E. B.] Thompson commanding; First Alabama, Major Knox commanding; Eighteenth Arkansas, Lieutenant Colonel Parish commanding; Tenth Arkansas, Lieutenant-Colonel [E. L.] Vaughan commanding; one 24-pounder siege gun (rifle); one 12-pounder howitzer and one 6-pounder gun, Lieutenant Toledano commanding; Thirty-ninth Mississippi, Colonel Shelby commanding; Wingfield Battalion, Major De Baun. At different points in Colonel Shelby's line are two 6-pounder guns, Captain Herod; one 6-pounder gun, Watson Battery, Lieutenant Caldwell commanding; one 6-pounder gun of Lieutenant Brown's ordnance department.

Accompanying find rough draught, giving the relative position of troops, batteries, &c.*

I am, sir, very respectfully,

I. G. W. STEEDMAN,
Colonel, Commanding Left Wing.

Major WILLSON,
Assistant Adjutant-General.

—

HEADQUARTERS LEFT WING,
June 29, 1863.

MAJOR: I am greatly mortified and disappointed to report that about half of the Eighteenth Arkansas Regiment, 50 men, have refused to move to the right, as ordered, saying they have worked hard to fortify their present position, &c. The lieutenant-colonel commanding is willing to go with the willing ones. I have repeated the order, and directed him to leave those who are so lost to duty and State pride under command of a suitable officer, and proceed with the balance immediately, and report to Colonel Lyles. I have a hope that all may consent to go upon mature reflection. If you can say to them that they only go temporarily, and will be sent back as soon as the emergency is over, I think all will go. Reply soon.

I am, respectfully, &c.,

I. G. W. STEEDMAN,
Colonel, Commanding Left Wing.

Major WILLSON,
Assistant Adjutant-General.

---

* Sketch omitted.

HEADQUARTERS LEFT WING,
June 30, 1863.

MAJOR: About 80 men of the Eighteenth Arkansas are still in the trenches on this line. I have ordered them to move at once to the right, and join their regiment. They are under command of a lieutenant. I have sent the order by Captain [W. F.] Owen (the best officer in the regiment). I have ordered that a complete list of those who disobey the order be sent in immediately. I think, and sincerely hope, that they may go. But, major, assure the general that, if they continue in this disobedience, our safety demands an immediate trial and execution of the most guilty parties. To hesitate will be to imperil the whole army ; this spirit is spreading, and, unless arrested, will lose Port Hudson to us on the first vigorous attack of the enemy.

When the regiment reached their position designated in the order last night, they could find no one to report to, and remained there for three hours without a position.

Your communication of last night (saying that this regiment should be returned as soon as the emergency passed) was forwarded to them. Your communication of this morning says the change must be permanent, and cooks must be moved, &c. I fear the results. I have given the order to move cooks, &c. I would suggest that if there is any safe position in which the regiment could be held in reserve, where they could be comfortable, &c., it might prevent trouble. I learn that there is serious prejudice in the Eighteenth against Colonel Lyles. Perhaps an intimation to the colonel to be cautious in his orders to them might avoid difficulties. But, major, some Arkansas soldier will *have to be shot by court-martial* before they are convinced that they have to obey orders irrespective of their own feelings. *I have lost confidence in their reliability in emergencies.* They are under no discipline.

In case any of those men refuse to go this morning, I will forward the list of names at once, and ask that a general court-martial be called immediately.

I am, captain, very respectfully, &c.,
I. G. W. STEEDMAN,
Colonel, Commanding Left Wing.

Major WILLSON,
Assistant Adjutant-General. •

P. S.—What damage and loss on the right yesterday and last night, and how do matters stand down there ?

HEADQUARTERS LEFT WING,
July 3, 1863.

MAJOR • The enemy opened a new gun upon our battery at Bennett's house this afternoon. The gun is located in the edge of the bull-pen, about 250 or 300 yards from our battery. It fired a number of shots at our siege gun.

Our gun opened, and at the third fire silenced the enemy's gun. We cannot say whether it was dismounted or simply ceased firing. The sharpshooting was directed mainly on the batteries, and caused by the artillery fire. Unless we can silence the gun, it will annoy us very seriously, and cripple the battery in an assault.

I visited Colonel [B. W.] Johnson's camp last night. The enemy have run a zigzag ditch to within 75 yards of his parapet. I see no way of stopping it unless by a sortie up one of the ravines, under cover of darkness. All quiet elsewhere.

I am, respectfully,

I. G. W. STEEDMAN,
Colonel, Commanding Left Wing.

Major [T. F.] WILLSON,
Assistant Adjutant-General.

HEADQUARTERS LEFT WING,
July 7, 1863.

MAJOR: In accordance with instructions from headquarters this morning, I have arrested Lieutenant-Colonel Vaughan, Tenth Arkansas, and placed Captain [S. M.] Shelton, senior officer, in command.

I can hear no bad effect resulting from rumors of to-day. I have tried to guard against it as much as possible.

· I am, major, very respectfully, your obedient servant,

I. G. W. STEEDMAN,
Colonel, Commanding.

Major WILLSON,
Assistant Adjutant-General.

Abstract from muster-roll of First Alabama Volunteers, Col. I. G. W. Steedman, April 20–November 30, 1863.

The enemy commenced investing Port Hudson on May 19. The First Alabama Regiment was immediately withdrawn from the west side of the river after a slight skirmish with the enemy's cavalry, in which we drove them off without loss on our side.

On May 21, the regiment was ordered about three-quarters of a mile in front of northern defenses of Port Hudson. With occasional assistance from the Tenth Arkansas and Fifteenth Arkansas, the regiment held [General Godfrey] Weitzel's division, United States Army, in check for six days.

On the morning of May 27, we were forced back to the line of defense. On the night before, the line of defense being only partially fortified north of Port Hudson, the regiment had rolled logs and piled rails, thus making a sort of breastwork. This work was assaulted with great force by the enemy on the morning of May 27. The enemy acted with gallantry, but were repulsed with great slaughter. At the time of this assault the acting quartermaster, adjutant, and sergeant-major were on duty with Colonel [I. G. W.] Steedman, commanding left wing defenses; Colonel [M. B.] Locke commanded Tenth Arkansas and battalion First Mississippi; Major [Samuel L.] Knox commanded First Alabama, two companies provost-guards, and a section from each of two batteries of artillery; the assistant surgeon, ordnance sergeant, and commissary sergeant on duty with Major Knox; the surgeon in charge of hospital, and the acting commissary of subsistence at camp—by order of General Gardner.

The fine discipline and bouyant spirits of the regiment were conspicuous during the entire siege. In their exposed position they were assaulted incessantly, almost day and night, but never successfully.

No. 42.

Report of Col. W. B. Shelby, Thirty-ninth Mississippi Infantry, of operations June 8.

HEADQUARTERS LEFT WING,
June 8, 1863.

MAJOR: Some day or two since I was ordered by the major-general commanding to send back from the Twelfth Arkansas Regiment, which occupied a position in the trenches on my right, 1 field officer and 110 men, leaving me 100 men of that command. Since that time this number has dwindled down to not exceeding 40 men. This force is too small to occupy the position, and I respectfully request that, if possible, they may be re-enforced.

I take the liberty of submitting to the major-general commanding the propriety of mounting a single piece in the point of woods near the house occupied by Major Bennett, with a view of driving the mortars from the position they now have on my front. The shelling from the mortars was so heavy this morning as to compel Lieutenant [E. A.] Toledano and men to temporarily abandon his pieces, and the men near the slaughter-pen are subjected to a very heavy fire from them. Something ought to be done, if possible, to draw the enemy from this position. My pickets report the enemy as fortifying on this side of the creek, near the bridge.

I am, major, very respectfully, your obedient servant,

W. B. SHELBY,
Colonel, Commanding Left Wing.

Maj. T. F. WILLSON,
   Assistant Adjutant-General.

No. 43.

Report of Maj. Thomas H. Johnston, First Mississippi Infantry, of operations July 2-3.

JULY 3, 1863.

From indications all day yesterday, last night, and this morning, the enemy must be massing a heavy force at some point on our right. There seems to be a movement of infantry, cavalry, artillery, ambulances, and wagons. I am not prepared to say whether this force, or any part of it, has been taken from my front, or whether they are re-enforcing from elsewhere.

The enemy are still actively engaged in pushing forward their works in my vicinity. Had a serious accident from the hand-grenades last night—2 men mortally wounded (1 since dead) by the explosion accidentally of some of the grenades.

Respectfully,

THOS. H. JOHNSTON,
Major First Mississippi Regiment, Commanding.

Lieutenant-Colonel [A. S.] HAMILTON,
   Commanding Left, Beall's Brigade.

[Indorsement.]

Respectfully referred to Major-General Gardner. The hand-grenades which were fired were fired by being ignited by a person who had lighted the fuse of a hand-grenade, and was about throwing it at the enemy. I do not think that the movement of troops in different directions is other than the ordinary reliefs passing back and forth.

WM. N. R. BEALL,
Brigadier-General.

———

No. 44.

Report of Lieut. E. A. Toledano, Watson (Louisiana) Battery, of operations May 24.

MAY 24, 1863.

I have the honor to make the following report of operations during the day:

One section (two guns), commanded by Lieutenant [J. P.] Caldwell, has been stationed during the day in the woods north of Wingfield's cavalry camp; has not been in action during the day. One section (two guns), commanded by Lieutenant [J. E.] Norés, at the left of the breastworks, has been in action twice during the day, once to silence a battery of the enemy in the point of woods adjoining, and once to dislodge the enemy's sharpshooters—both objects fully accomplished. This section has fired in all 60 rounds of spherical case and 5 of solid shot. A third section of two guns, commanded by Serg. Maj. H. L. Nichols, stationed near the railroad, on the fortification, has not been in action at all during the day. No casualties of any kind have occurred in the battery during the day.

E. A. TOLEDANO,
Lieutenant, Commanding.

Captain [BEALL] HEMPSTEAD,
Assistant Adjutant-General.

———

No. 45.

Reports of Lieut. Col. J. H. Wingfield, Ninth Louisiana Battalion Partisan Rangers.

PORT HUDSON,
May 24, 1863.

MAJOR: I herewith furnish a report of the operations of my command during Saturday, May 23. The report is as full as the circumstances of the moment will permit me to make. I hope it will be satisfactory to the major-general commanding.

I am, captain, very respectfully, your obedient servant,
J. H. WINGFIELD,
Lieutenant-Colonel, Commanding.

MAJOR: Early yesterday morning I informed the major-general commanding that the enemy had left their encampment at the ford on Thompson's Creek, and were advancing in the direction of Mrs. Newport's. I immediately ordered a picket of 10 men, under Lieutenant [A. C.] Bickham, of Company K, to the gate at Captain Chambers' plantation, on the Bayou Sara road.

At about 12 o'clock I received intelligence that the enemy's cavalry had driven my picket, and that they had fallen back to the gin-house on Mr. Flowers' plantation, which fact I dispatched to the major-general commanding. Half an hour later, I received information that the enemy's cavalry, some 50 to 100 strong, had made its appearance in the upper field of Neville's plantation, and were in the house now occupied by Mr. Aburger. Upon receiving this intelligence, I immediately ordered Capt. O. P. Amacker, of Company E, and Lieut. J. B. Dunn, of Company D, with 50 men, to Neville's field; also Captain [William] Turner, of Company K, and Captain [E. S.] Morgan, of Company G, with detachments from Companies B and F, and [E. A.] Scott's, respectively commanded by Lieutenants [B. B] Starnes, [J.] Barnett, and [M.] McQueen, above ' Mrs. Huston's field, near Captain Chambers' gate, where the enemy was reported to be. Immediately thereafter Colonel [I. G. W.] Steedman arrived at my encampment with a battalion of the First Alabama Volunteers and a section of Watson Artillery.

The First Alabama, now under Lieutenant-Colonel [M. B.] Locke, deployed itself as skirmishers in the woods in front of the left wing of the breastworks leading into Neville's field. I sent Captain [G. W.] Lewis, of Company C, and his men as flankers to the right wing of this battalion, the left wing being protected by Captain Turner, in the advance. This disposition of my battalion protected the left and right of Colonel Steedman's forces—the left and advance commanded by Captain Turner, and the right and its advance under Captain Amacker.

Captain Turner reports that, upon his arrival at the position assigned him, he found the enemy's cavalry, estimated from 1,000 to 1,200 strong, drawn up in line of battle in Mrs. Huston's field. On their discovering his position, the enemy fired upon him, he answering with considerable effect, causing the enemy to fall back out of range. The enemy, having reformed, charged Captain Turner three times, but were repulsed each time, after which they withdrew from Mrs. Huston's field in the direction of the Bayou Sara road, Captain Turner retaining his position until this morning, when he was ordered to withdraw. Captain Turner had no loss.

Captain Amacker reports having met the enemy in Neville's field. He skirmished with them some time, driving them from Mr. Aburger's house, and then across the field into the woods bordering on the Jackson road. Again was the enemy driven from the woods, Captain Amacker occupying the position, and placing a picket in a commanding position at the edge of the woods. Having accomplished the desired object, he withdrew his force. It is impossible to state the enemy's loss. Several horses were killed, and the saddles and other paraphernalia were recovered from them. Captain Lewis with his company, acting as flankers, remained at their post during the entire day.

During the whole day I suffered no loss, excepting 1 man of Company E, who was thrown from his horse while charging the enemy and had his arm badly sprained. The enemy must have suffered considerably, though I cannot estimate their loss.

It is with pleasure that I must make special mention of the gallant conduct of Captains Turner, Amacker, and Morgan in the manner in which they carried out the instructions given them and the promptness with which they kept me informed of the movements of the enemy. It is also gratifying to me to be able to report that both officers and men engaged behaved with the utmost coolness and bravery, and, by their conduct, drove ten times their number.

The operations of my pickets on the Springfield road and on the Plains Store road deserve being mentioned, as the enemy during the day attempted to drive them back.

Major James De Baun and Captain J. J. Slocum, of Company **A**, were ordered by me to inspect the various posts, and they report that Lieutenant [T. M.] Bond, in command at Springfield, had two or three skirmishes during the day, in which the enemy were each time repulsed; that Lieutenant [E.] McCain, at Plains Store, had also several skirmishes with the advance of the enemy, repulsing them, and retaining his position.

Very respectfully submitted.

[J. H. WINGFIELD,
Lieutenant-Colonel, Commanding.]

Maj. T. F. WILLSON,
Assistant Adjutant-General.

ADDENDA.

GENERAL ORDERS, }   HEADQUARTERS,
    No. 47.   }   *Port Hudson, La., May 23, 1863.*

It is with much pleasure the major-general commanding announces to the troops a successful skirmish of Colonel Wingfield's Partisan Rangers with the whole force of the enemy's cavalry, in which the enemy were several times repulsed, and finally driven back with considerable loss.

These examples of heroic conduct are cheering to us all, and will convince the enemy that we are determined to defend this post to the last.

By command of Maj. Gen. Frank. Gardner:

T. FRIEND WILLSON,
Assistant Adjutant-General.

MAY 25, 1863.

GENERAL: The enemy again drove back my pickets stationed at Sandy Creek, where the telegraph wires are placed.

Lieutenant [C. C.] Harris, of Company G, commanded that post. The ground is very open on this side of the creek, and the men necessarily much exposed.

They have not yet crossed the creek. I am skirmishing with them now. I regret to inform you that First Lieutenant Harris was killed, and in consequence of the open country at the ford, it was impossible to remove his body, the enemy being ambushed across the river, the timber being such as to enable them to do so.

I would be much pleased, general, to recover the body of Lieutenant Harris, if possible.

I am, general, your obedient servant,

J. H. WINGFIELD,
Lieut. Col., Comdg. Ninth Louisiana Battalion Partisan Rangers.

Major-General GARDNER.

———

No. 46.

*Reports of Col. W. R. Miles, Louisiana Legion, of operations May 21–
July 7.*

HEADQUARTERS MILES' LEGION,
Port Hudson, May 22, 1863.

MAJOR: With 400 infantry and a battery of my command, I moved out yesterday on the Plains road, in obedience to orders. About 2½ miles from this place my skirmishers fell in with an advance party of the enemy, fired on them, emptied three saddles, and drove the rest rapidly back. A short distance beyond, his cavalry were seen drawn up in considerable force. Our artillery opened a well-directed fire, and the cavalry retreated rapidly. We advanced, firing shell and shrapnel at intervals, until near Plains Store, where my skirmishers found the enemy's infantry with some artillery, and had a sharp contest with them. The line was quickly formed and ordered to advance. It moved forward steadily, and was soon engaged in close and deadly conflict. The contest raged with great fury for nearly an hour, when I discovered we were overpowered by greatly superior numbers, and my line was being pressed back. I at once ordered a section of Captain [R. M.] Boone's battery to advance up the Plains Store road, to a point where it could deliver a raking fire on the enemy's right flank. The order was promptly obeyed, and the fire was so effective as to completely check his movements, enabling me to withdraw the command at leisure and in good order, bringing off 23 of my wounded, this being all I could furnish transportation for.

In this affair both infantry and artillery behaved with great coolness and courage, and deserve much praise for their soldierly bearing.

I have no means of knowing the exact number of the enemy we encountered. It was quite large, however, and very much exceeded our own, the prisoners captured by us stating it to consist of fifteen regiments of infantry, besides artillery and a large cavalry force.

Our loss in killed, wounded, and missing is 89. It is impossible to state with accuracy the number of killed and wounded. I only know of 8 killed and 23 wounded. The enemy, however, report having buried 40 of our dead, and say they are in possession of a number of our wounded.

I am, major, very respectfully, your obedient servant,

W. R. MILES,
Colonel, Commanding Legion.

Maj. T. F. WILLSON,
Assistant Adjutant-General.

ON THE FIELD,
May 24, 1863.

I beg leave to report that no attack or menace has been made on my line to-day. The shelling from guns and mortars, however, has been extraordinarily furious, and I regret to say that 3 men have been killed and 3 others slightly wounded by them. The casualties occurred in Maj. Anderson Merchant's battalion.

I am, general, very respectfully,

W. R. MILES,
Colonel, Commanding.

Maj. T. F. WILLSON,
Assistant Adjutant-General.

—

ON THE FIELD,
May 25, 1863.

I beg leave to report that, at an interval of about two hours, two advances have been made on our lines to-day—the first by infantry and cavalry, and the second by cavalry alone—both times in considerable force, and both times were driven back hurriedly, the latter time in great confusion and in full run.

.A short time after the second repulse, a flag of truce was observed near the place from which the enemy was driven. I sent Captain [R. M.] Hewitt and Lieutenant [B. W.] Clark to meet it. Before they reached the ground, the flag moved off. They could plainly see litters, bearing off either wounded or dead. It occurs to me that this is a plain violation of the white flag. I dared not fire upon it, and yet it may have been made use of to carry off wounded who otherwise would have become our prisoners. If it can be used for one illicit purpose it may be for another; and its sanctity will be destroyed; I therefore beg leave to call Major-General Gardner's atention to it.

I am, major, very respectfully,

W. R. MILES,
Colonel, Commanding, &c.

Maj. T. F. WILLSON,
Assistant Adjutant-General.

—

ON THE FIELD,
May 27, 1863.

About half an hour by sun this morning the enemy opened an infernal fire on our lines. With occasional lulls, the cannonade continued until about 2 p. m., when I learned the enemy had formed in line of battle, and was advancing on General Beall's center and left. Without waiting for official notification, I at once pushed forward to his support every man I could spare. My men had barely got their position when the enemy opened fire, advancing with infantry and artillery. He was repulsed three several times, and has now retired. I am holding the field, General Beall's forces having gone to the left. What the enemy's loss is it is impossible to say. Subordinate commanders not having handed in their reports, it is impossible to give an accurate list of casualties. I will supply the omission hereafter.

Respectfully, &c.,

W. R. MILES,
Colonel, &c.

Maj. T. F. WILLSON,
Assistant Adjutant-General.

—

ON THE FIELD,
May 28, 1863.

The enemy opened his accustomed cannonade at an early hour this morning, the mortar fleet and gunboats below chiming in, and for some time shell and solid shot fell thick along the line. Between 10 and 11 o'clock I received notice that Major-General Banks had asked for a truce, to allow him the opportunity to bury his dead and care for his wounded, who covered the ground where the fights occurred yesterday. The various precautionary orders connected therewith were received, promptly communicated, and vigilantly enforced. I observed no disposition on the part of the enemy to violate the truce during the day. Ten prisoners were taken by my men and sent to headquarters this morning.

Lieutenant [W. W.] Carloss, thought to have been mortally wounded yesterday evening, is improving, and will, I think, recover. The wounds received by others are slight, with one exception. We had none killed. ·

I am, respectfully, &c., your obedient servant,

W. R. MILES,
Colonel, &c.

Maj. T. F. WILLSON,
Assistant Adjutant-General.

ON THE FIELD,
May 30, 1863.

During last night the fleet shelled us without intermission, but without result. We have only been fired at during the day by a few skirmishers. No one hit. It is the first day of calm since the 24th.

I am very respectfully, &c.,

W. R. MILES,
Colonel, &c.

Maj. T. F. WILLSON, .
Assistant Adjutant-General.

ON THE FIELD,
May 31, 1863.

This morning the enemy's sharpshooters, deployed in front of a part of my lines under cover, opened an irregular fire, which has been kept up all day. The cannonade, directed at my redans and an attempted enfilade of the works, has been quite vigorous at times, never entirely ceasing. About 4 o'clock this evening, the fleet below commenced shelling furiously, and kept it up two hours and a half.

Last night the fleet shelled us from 11 o'clock until sun-up this morning; all this resulting in wounding 1 man. I have sent 200 men to relieve that number of Colonel [I. G. W.] Steedman's men, on the left. Since their arrival there this evening, I learn 2 of them have been wounded severely.

I am, major, very respectfully, your obedient servant,

W. R. MILES,
Colonel, &c.

Maj. T. F. WILLSON,
Assistant Adjutant-General.

—

ON THE FIELD,
June 1, 1863.

The fleet indulged in its customary shelling last night, and at intervals to-day. The enemy's batteries for the last twenty-four hours have been steadily playing on our front, attempting at times to enfilade the works. No serious result. Sharpshooters, as usual, have been plying their vocation on both sides. So far as can be learned, no immediate attempt will be made to carry the works by assault, the enemy not having recovered from the effects of his last attempt upon us.

W. R. MILES,
Colonel, &c.

Maj. T. F. WILLSON,
Assistant Adjutant-General.

. ON THE FIELD,
June 3, 1863.

Just after writing my report of yesterday, 2 men of the legion were wounded here by the enemy's sharpshooters. I have learned that the detachment of the legion holding Colonel Steedman's position has had 1 man killed to-day and 5 wounded.

The fleet last night shelled us slowly, without inflicting any injury; and the batteries, though playing on us all day, have not injured a man or affected the works. The enemy is at work in front of the outer works in Gibbon's field. It is impossible to tell precisely what he is doing; most probably digging rifle-pits and preparing a place for his artillery.

I am, major, very respectfully, &c.,

W. R. MILES,
Colonel, &c.

Maj. T. F. WILLSON,
Assistant Adjutant-General.

—

ON THE FIELD,
June 6, 1863.

The batteries and fleet for some two hours this forenoon gave us a very heavy fire. The battery heretofore stationed at the mouth of Troth's lane moved off this evening in the direction of the river below; and the battery near Hunt's house, with eight wagon-loads of stores, moved off also about the same hour and in the same direction. Unless these movements are a ruse, it is evident the enemy is moving off a large portion, if not all, of his forces. I have no casualties to report for the day.

I am, major, very respectfully, &c.,

W. R. MILES,
Colonel, &c.

Maj. T. F. WILLSON,
Assistant Adjutant-General.

ON THE FIELD,
June 7, 1863.

Early this morning a large body of infantry marched from the river at Troth's, through the lane out toward the works. [R. M.] Boone's battery fired several shots at the column as it passed, and a number of them were seen to fall. They double-quicked out of range, and got under cover.

During the day the enemy has been discovered working steadily in the edge of the woods nearly midway between where his batteries that were taken off yesterday evening were formerly posted. It looks as if he is preparing a place for a large battery. Late this evening several companies of troops have been seen passing from the woods toward Troth's. They were fired upon by Lieutenant [H. W.] Coleman, and made to pass by in haste and some confusion. I will send out a scout between midnight and day to examine the woods between my right and Troth's, for the purpose of learning the enemy's numbers there, and what he is doing.

The fleet shelled us last night, and a battery back of Slaughter's late residence, in front of General Beall's lines, has been firing on us through the day. No casualty.

The batteries near Hunt's house and the mouth of Troth's lane that were removed yesterday evening have not yet reappeared. No artillery visible in front of my lines.

I am, major, very respectfully, your obedient servant,

W. R. MILES,
Colonel, &c.

Maj. T. F. WILLSON,
    Assistant Adjutant-General.

ON THE FIELD,
June 8, 1863.

Late yesterday evening, after writing my report, I had 1 man killed by the enemy's sharpshooters. Between 1 and 2 o'clock this morning, the enemy in force made an advance on my left and center. He was handsomely repulsed, and did not renew the attack. During the night, two pieces of artillery were placed in position near Hunt's house, and have saluted us several times since. My scouts, sent out in the woods between the Troth road and the river, report a strong force of the enemy there, and say they are engaged in digging rifle-pits and throwing up earthworks. Should you desire to. send any one outside the lines for information, the two young men who acted for me, I think, would successfully accomplish the mission. The fleet shelled us, as usual, during the night.

I am, major, very respectfully, your obedient servant,

W. R. MILES,
Colonel, &c.

Maj. T. F. WILLSON,
    Assistant Adjutant-General.

—

ON THE FIELD,
June 9, 1863.

The enemy has brought back his Parrott and Whitworth guns to my front, and, in addition, has planted two light 8-inch mortars and one 8-inch gun, with all of which he has been delivering an energetic fire since about 11 o'clock this morning, wounding 1 man severely. It seems a miracle that we have escaped thus, for the 8-inch gun has an enfilading fire along several hundred yards of my left.

This gun is placed in the point of woods between Hunt's and Slaughter's, and is beyond the range of my small pieces. I sent word to that effect to Brigadier-General Beall, and requested him to order some of his guns opposite to open on it, in the hope of either silencing it or deranging its fire. For some good reason, doubtless, nothing of the sort has been done.

I beg leave respectfully to suggest that it is of very great importance to pay some attention to this big gun, as it is by all means the ugliest acquaintance we have yet made. The shelling by the fleet last night was not very severe.

I am, major, very respectfully, your obedient servant,

W. R. MILES,
Colonel, &c.

Maj. T. F. WILLSON,
    Assistant Adjutant-General.

ON THE FIELD,
June 10, 1863.

The mortars of the fleet, the mortars of the land batteries, the Parrott and Whitworth guns, opened on us at dusk yesterday evening, and kept up a furious fire through the night. The practice was good and the scenic effect splendid. At 2 o'clock this morning the 8-inch shell gun joined in, and delivered her raking fire along my entire left. Three men were wounded severely during the night. Lieutenant-Colonel [M. J.] Smith's fire was without effect on these pieces, his range being short and his aim inaccurate. Lieutenant-Colonel Smith's guns can only do good by moving one or more of them out to the line. It is for you to determine whether it is politic and practicable to place in position on the outer line his 8-inch gun and 42-pounder. They might silence the enemy's heavy batteries. They are of no value, except for river defense, where they now are.

During the entire day the enemy have been shelling my lines. The men, I am proud to say, bear it like heroes, and I think will make good the defense against any assault.

I am, major, very respectfully, your obedient servant,

W. R. MILES,
Colonel, &c.

Maj. T. F. WILLSON,
Assistant Adjutant-General.

ON THE FIELD,
June 11, 1863.

In addition to the casualties mentioned in my report of yesterday, I have to add four more who were not reported to me until after my report was sent in. None of the wounds serious, however. Last night, on my extreme right, where Lieutenant-Colonel [Fred. B.] Brand commands, my picket was surprised, Lieutenant [J. A.] Taylor, in command of it, seriously wounded, 9 privates and 2 non-commissioned officers captured.

To-day, Capt. R. M. Boone (Boone's battery), while at his post directing his guns, was seriously wounded in the thigh. One other man has been wounded to-day.

The enemy has opened some additional guns on me to-day, placed in a new position between Troth's road and the river. He has kept up a tremendous fire during the day from all his guns and mortars, and the small number of casualties would seem to indicate that a special Providence is protecting us.

I am, major, very respectfully, your obedient servant,

W. R. MILES,
Colonel, &c.

Maj. T. F. WILLSON,
Assistant Adjutant-General.

—

ON THE FIELD,
June 12, 1863.

Last night the guns and mortars from the fleet, as well as the guns and mortars from the numerous batteries on shore, kept up a brisk fire upon us, resulting in no loss of life, or wound, even. During the day their fire has slackened considerably—I would fain hope tapering to its final end.

Neither of the 24-pounder guns are yet mounted on my lines, and if no more attention shall be given in directing the labor of the large nightly details I am called on to furnish than has been bestowed heretofore, it is a mere matter of conjecture when they will be put in position.

No casualties reported during the day. The 30-pounder Parrott gun at the extreme right has been dismounted to-day by the enemy's land batteries.

I am, major, very respectfully, your obedient servant,

W. R. MILES,
Colonel, &c.

Maj. T. F. WILLSON,
Assistant Adjutant-General.

—

ON THE FIELD,
June 13, 1863.

Very early this morning we were quite severely cannonaded. Later on in the forenoon the most tremendous affair of the siege came off. From the fleet in the river and from every gun in position on shore came the quick flash and angry roar of threatening annihilation. The air grew thick with smoke and hoarse with sound. After some hours spent in this manner, it became apparent the enemy was making preparations for a charge. General Beall's line being most threatened, I sent one battalion to his support, keeping the balance of my force in position to repel an attack should one be made on my own line, or move to the further support of General Beall. No attack was made on me; and, after trying several times to bring their lines to the assault, the enemy beat a hasty retreat. Nothing but a few of his sharpshooters approached the breastworks, and the neighborhood soon grew too hot for them. How many of them were killed and wounded I do not know. Of the battalion sent by me to General Beall's support, 2 men were severely wounded. Besides these, I have lost on my lines to-day 1 man killed and 1 wounded. Yesterday, on the extreme right, where Lieutenant-Colonel [Fred. B.] Brand commands, there were of the pickets 1 man killed, 1 wounded, and 5 captured.

I am, major, very respectfully, your obedient servant,

W. R. MILES,
Colonel, &c.

Maj. T. F. WILLSON,
Assistant Adjutant-General.

—

ON THE FIELD,
June 14, 1863.

About 4 a. m. the enemy opened a terrible fire from all his guns along the line, from the extreme right to the extreme left. It was kept up till 8 o'clock, varying in intensity, but always severe. At an early hour I could distinguish the rattle of small-arms toward the left, and for a time thought no demonstration was intended against my position, but was soon undeceived. In regular line of battle, the enemy attempted an advance through the open field upon my left. A few shots from the artillery and a few rounds from the infantry caused him to fall back. He then moved toward the woods on his left, where, being joined by addi-'tional forces, he attempted to carry the advanced work near the Troth road. He was allowed to pass one regiment unmolested down the hill into the ravine at the base of the work. Thinking no opposition was meant, perhaps, he started a second regiment down the same road, which was also allowed to make its march unmolested about half-way down the hill, when, at the same moment, the advancing regiment was opened upon by a section of [R. M.] Boone's battery and the stationary one by the infantry. Stupefied and bewildered, these regiments scarcely attempted to reply, but broke in confusion, and in disorder hurried from the conflict. Though his infantry amounted to many reg-iments, these two were all that came within the range of our pieces.

The casualties of the.day are 4 killed and 11 wounded.

Failing in his general attack of the morning, the enemy has distrib-uted a large number of sharpshooters all along the line, who, throughout the day, have been unwearying in their work. I regret to add that Lieu-tenant [B. W.] Clark, of my staff, discovered last night a considerable space of the breastwork next to my left not only without men to resist an attack, but even without a guard or picket. I sent one company to guard the work during the night.

I am, major, very respectfully, your obedient servant,

W. R. MILES,
Colonel, &c.

Maj. T. F. Willson,
    Assistant Adjutant-General.

—

ON THE FIELD,
June 15, 1863.

The fleet shelled us last night. The land batteries have fired on us at intervals throughout the day, and the sharpshooters have been more than ordinarily energetic, productive of no casualty, however. Opposite my extreme right, the enemy is busily engaged in throwing up a new chain of rifle-pits, which we are unable to prevent.

I am, major very, respectfully, your obedient servant,

W. R. MILES,
Colonel, &c.

Maj. T. F. Willson,
    Assistant Adjutant-General.

—

ON THE FIELD,
June 16, 1863.

The fleet last night shelled us at its accustomed time and in about the usual quantity. The batteries to-day have been active, but not extremely vigorous. The sharpshooters, particularly on the extreme right, have displayed more energy and perseverance than on any day heretofore. The casualties of the day are 1 killed and 3 wounded. No evidence of any extraordinary demonstration by the enemy.

I am, major, very respectfully, your obedient servant,

W. R. MILES,
Colonel, &c.

Maj. T. F. Willson,
    Assistant Adjutant-General.

ON THE FIELD,
June 17, 1863.

The ordinary shelling of the fleet last night was productive of nothing except its noise.   There has been but little firing from the land batteries to-day, resulting in severely wounding 1 man.   The sharpshooters on parts of my line have been very active, but have hit no one to-day. The works on the hill opposite to my right are progressing rapidly. I have no means of stopping them.

I am, major, very respectfully, your obedient servant,
W. R. MILES,
Colonel, &c.

Maj. T. F. WILLSON,
Assistant Adjutant-General.

HEADQUARTERS RIGHT WING,
June 24, 1863.

The fleet was again quiet last night.   The land batteries have fired at intervals during the day.   Sharpshooting as usual, resulting in the killing of 1 man.   The enemy's works on my right continue to progress rapidly toward completion.   They threw up a parallel and traverse last night, the parallel distant about 150 yards from the brow of the hill upon which Battery No. 11 is placed.   The enemy's fatigue parties have been driven from their work several times during the day by shells thrown from Captain [S. M.] Thomas' pieces in the outer work on the Troth road.   He has instructions to fire at distant intervals during the night, to prevent any further work, if possible.

I am, major, respectfully, &c.
W. R. MILES,
Colonel, &c.

Maj. T. F. WILLSON,
Assistant Adjutant-General.

ON THE FIELD,
July 6, 1863.

So far as I can discover, the enemy has made no material progress on the right.   His ditch seems to be taking a different direction.   The heavy guns of his batteries on both sides of the river, during parts of the day, have been served with much activity, while his sharpshooters in swarms have hailed their bullets on our lines.   I have to report 1 lieutenant (Ninth Louisiana Battalion Partisan Rangers) killed and 1 lieutenant (Twenty-third Arkansas) seriously wounded by them.   Your order of to-day, directing me to retire the whole of Major [Anderson] Merchant's command, has been obeyed, as well as that other order directing me to make a permanent detail of 9 men from my command, to report for duty to the provost-marshal.   In obeying these orders, however, I beg leave most respectfully to say that I think the public interest is greatly jeopardized thereby.   Of the 125 men of Major Merchant's command originally given to me, the last is now taken away, and I am required to send away 9 men in addition.   This leaves me with less than 400 muskets to defend over 1¼ miles of breastworks.   I have at least one-third of the entire line, and less than one-sixth of the fighting force to defend it with.   Besides, when the center and left were in danger in the early part of the siege, the labor and blood of my command were freely contributed to sustain them. Now that the right is sorely pressed, and more vigorously menaced than any other part of the lines, I hardly think it just to me, or right in view of the public interest, to reduce my men to so low an ebb. Let me be understood: I will hold my line as long as a man stands up; but in justice to the men, who are worked and fought without rest day or night, I earnestly request that enough be left with me to give them an occasional respite of a day.

I am, major, very respectfully, your obedient servant,

W. R. MILES,
Colonel, &c.

Maj. T. F. WILLSON,
Assistant Adjutant-General.

ON THE FIELD,
July 7, 1863.

Sharpshooting, though less active to-day than yesterday, has been quite brisk. One man of the legion killed. The cannonading has been irregular; at no time very severe, and productive of no result. The enemy still works with the spade in close proximity to my rifle-pits, but it is impossible to fathom his designs. His tower grows and his ditch lengthens, one day in one direction, another day in another. This morning all his land batteries fired a salute, and followed it immediately with shotted guns, accompanied by vociferous yelling. Later in the day the fleet fired a salute also. What is meant we do not know. Some of them hallooed over, saying that Vicksburg had fallen on the 4th instant. My own impression is that some fictitious good news has been given to his troops in order to raise their spirits; perhaps with a view of stimulating them to a charge in the morning. We will be prepared for them should they do so.

I am, major, very respectfully, your obedient servant,

W. R. MILES,
Colonel, &c.

Maj. T. F. WILLSON,
Assistant Adjutant-General.

No. 47.

Reports of Lieut. Col. Frederick B. Brand, Miles' (Louisiana) Legion, of operations June 24–27.

HEADQUARTERS RIGHT WING,
June 25, 1863.

SIR: I assumed command of right wing last night, as per order through Captain [R. M.] Hewitt. I left Major [J. T.] Coleman in command of my right. Lieutenant [James] Freret, of Engineer Corps, commenced a ditch in front of Battery 11, to place sharpshooters in, but did not finish it. The enemy advanced about 10 yards last night with their trench.

I keep up an occasional fire from Captain [S. M.] Thomas' guns. I discovered that they had a bale of cotton, which they advanced as required; but watching the moment that they moved the bale, I gave them a volley of musketry which drove them in altogether. To-night I shall keep up the shooting as during the last night and to-day.

I am, major, very respectfully, your obedient servant,

FRED'K B. BRAND,
Lieutenant-Colonel, Commanding Right Wing.

Maj. T. F. WILLSON,
Assistant Adjutant-General.

P. S.—All quiet along my line.

———

HEADQUARTERS RIGHT WING,
June 26, 1863.

SIR: I have to report that I prevented the work of the enemy last night. He has now four bales to work behind, but has made very little progress. The sharpshooters have been very active on my right. At 3 p. m. the fleet opened, and at the same time four field pieces and one or two mortars from the large breastworks. I have not yet received my reports from the different commanders as to casualties, but so soon as they come in, I will make a full report. All quiet on my left. I have sent a working party down to the right to repair damages, if any. I fear that I shall have to report the loss of many a brave man.

I remain, major, your most obedient servant,

FRED'K B. BRAND,
Lieutenant-Colonel, Commanding Right Wing.

Maj. T. F. WILLSON,
Assistant Adjutant-General.

———

HEADQUARTERS RIGHT WING,
June 26, 1863.

SIR: I have to report that the enemy have torn up my breastwork a great deal. They are throwing at intervals 8 and 10 pounder mortar shells into Battery 11. My casualties are Captain [C. R.] Purdy (Fourth Louisiana), 1 private ([Calvit] Roberts' battery), and 3 privates (Miles' Legion) killed, and but 10 wounded. Colonel [M. J.] Smith assisted me very much by throwing shell into the enemy's works. I have three companies in Battery 11 armed with muskets, which I think is enough, but have only a few buck cartridges. All my officers and men behaved well. Major [J. T.] Coleman is in good spirits and a very hot place. I feel certain that I will hold out.

I remain, your most obedient servant,

FRED'K B. BRAND,
Lieutenant-Colonel, Commanding Right Wing.

Maj. T. F. WILLSON,
Assistant Adjutant-General.

———

HEADQUARTERS RIGHT WING,
June 27, 1863.

SIR: I have to report that the batteries in my front have been keeping up a very sharp fire all along my right, injuring my breastworks a great deal. My sharpshooters are at work with effect. My casualties are 2 killed and 2 wounded.

I have ordered the four companies of my left wing under charge of Major [J. T.] Coleman. I have but a very small reserve on the right, but will hold every man ready to move.

I remain, sir, your most obedient servant, &c.,

FRED'K B. BRAND,
Lieutenant-Colonel, Commanding Right Wing.

Maj. T. F. WILLSON,
Assistant Adjutant-General.

P. S.—Since writing the above report, I have the honor to report that Captain [C. W.] Cushman, Thirtieth Louisiana, and Lieutenant [J. D.] Conn, Fourth Louisiana, have come forward with their companies, amounting to about 45 men, all volunteers, to act as the reserve or anything else.

No. 48.

Reports of Col. John L. Logan, Eleventh Arkansas Infantry, of operations May 21–July 8.

NEAR MRS. NUTTENELL'S, BAYOU SARA ROAD,
May 21, 1863—6 p. m.

GENERAL: I am in enemy's rear with 300 cavalry and mounted men, and 300 infantry. General Augur's division has all passed up. I would strike him, but my force is too weak. I have no information from Plains Store excepting that the enemy occupy the place. My dispatch from Colonel [F. P.] Powers was received too late to strike the enemy on his right flank; besides, they came in too great numbers for Colonel Powers, and forced him back to the railroad before I could get here. I shall keep on his right flank, and strike as opportunity offers.

In a little skirmish this evening, I captured 2 prisoners, [who informed] me that Augur's entire division has passed up, including two brigades of infantry, four batteries, and about 700 or 800 cavalry, commanded by Grierson. I think for the present I had better move the most of my force to Clinton.

I am, general, very respectfully, your obedient servant,

JNO. L. LOGAN.
Major-General GARDNER.

HEADQUARTERS,
Olive Branch, May 22, 1863.

GENERAL: I find that the small pieces of artillery are not of much service; besides, I have no ammunition for them. I must have more ammunition for the pieces I have (6-pounder smooth-bore and 12-pounder howitzers), and I really think that I ought to have Roberts' entire battery. The enemy have a great deal of artillery, and, unless I have a sufficiency to cope with them, I cannot accomplish much. I am determined to annoy the enemy and hurt him at every favorable point and opportunity, on his flanks and in his rear. I am concentrating my force, as much so as I can, leaving for the present, on the Plank road and the roads toward the Comite, a small picket to watch the movements of the enemy. I send Quartermaster-Sergeant Mack with this dispatch, who will take charge of anything you desire to send to me, and bring it to my command to-night.

All quiet on Plank road; think most of the force has crossed to the Bayou Sara road. Enemy still reported at Plains Store; am going to see.

Very respectfully, your obedient servant,
JNO. L. LOGAN,
Colonel, Commanding.

Major-General GARDNER.

—

HEADQUARTERS,
Clinton, La., May 29, 1863.

GENERAL: Your dispatches, per courier, for General Frank. Gardner, were brought to my headquarters on 25th instant. Every effort has been made to get them through, but without success. The dispatches ordering the evacuation of Port Hudson * were also received by me and sent through. Major-General Gardner was then completely invested, and to have attempted to cut his way through the lines of the enemy, 20,000 strong, well posted, with a large cavalry force at hand, would have been attended with very great loss; besides, I doubt his being able to get through at all. If he had, the line of retreat would have been so long we must have suffered greatly before we could have reached Jackson.

I have had no communication from General Gardner since the 24th. On that night he intended to come out, if possible, and ordered me to place my forces so as to assist him, which I did. I think he found it impossible to cut his way through, and has, perhaps, concluded to remain to defend the place as long as he can, hoping to be relieved by re-enforcements. I am at this place with a small command of cavalry and mounted infantry, 1,200 men, doing all I can to aid General Gardner by dashing upon the enemy's lines, destroying his wagon train, &c., drawing the enemy's troops from Port Hudson. I cannot do a great deal, but am determined to do all that can be done with the means at my command. I have so far prevented the enemy's making raids into the country. Can we get re-enforcements? To relieve General Gardner is certainly very important; besides, I think it of very great importance to hold our position at Port Hudson as well as the New Orleans, Jackson and Great Northern Railroad.

The country along the Mississippi River and east of it for 50 miles is a very wealthy one; there is a large amount of stock in it, and the people are doing everything they can for our cause—raising large crops of corn and potatoes for the army. A re-enforcement of 8,000 or 10,000 men, thrown in Banks' rear, will drive him from Port Hudson in five days. I am informed that Lieut. Gen. E. K. Smith is now at or near the mouth of Red River with 10,000 men. If he would come down and cross at Port Hudson, under cover of our guns, Port Hudson would be relieved at once. Dispatches sent via Natchez, Miss., would reach Lieutenant-General Smith. Pardon me for making these suggestions.†

I am, general, very respectfully, your obedient servant,
JNO. L. LOGAN,
Colonel Eleventh Arkansas, Comdg. Outposts, Port Hudson.

[General JOSEPH E. JOHNSTON.]

---

* See order, May 19, Part II, p. 9.
† See Taylor to Logan, June 15, Part II, p. 53.

CLINTON, LA., *June 3*, 1863.
VIA OSYKA, *June 6*.

GENERAL: The enemy attacked us this evening at 2 o'clock, 2,000 strong. After an engagement of three hours, we repulsed them and drove them from the field. Our loss, 20 killed and wounded. Enemy's loss, 20 killed, 50 wounded, and 40 prisoners. No further news from General Gardner.

JNO. L. LOGAN,
Colonel, Commanding.

General JOSEPH E. JOHNSTON.

—

HEADQUARTERS,
Ten Miles north of Clinton, June 7, 1863.

GENERAL: The enemy is moving a column of cavalry, infantry, and artillery, 4,000 strong, upon Clinton. I have met his cavalry and whipped it, but, of course, will have to retire before a heavy column of infantry and artillery. I will range around through the country, and, when an opportunity offers, strike his cavalry. Banks has lost very heavily at Port Hudson, but seems determined to take the place. He has dug rifle-pits and made breastworks of cotton along our entire line of works. I have annoyed him a great deal with my little force in his rear, and he seems very uneasy for fear a heavy force will be thrown in his rear. He has already burned the Manchac Bridge, that he rebuilt, for fear of being flanked.

As I have already stated, a small re-enforcement sent here will not only raise the siege of Port Hudson, but drive the enemy from the country, and, I believe, from Baton Rouge. Ten thousand men, I am confident, could accomplish all this. I hope you will pardon me for urging this matter, but the relief of General Gardner, and the importance of holding Port Hudson and protecting a large section of the finest country that we have in the Confederacy, leaving out the importance of the position as regards future movements upon New Orleans, compels me to ask for these re-enforcements. The people in this country are doing all they can for the support of our army—raising large crops of corn and potatoes. The re-enforcements I ask for can be subsisted entirely upon this country for thirty days, at least.

There is a large amount of stock in the way of beef-cattle, mules, and horses, that will fall in the hands of the enemy if we leave here. Please let me hear from you, as soon as possible, by telegraph to Osyka. Should the enemy occupy Clinton and Jackson, it will be useless for me to remain longer, as I can be of no service to General Gardner.*

I am, general, very respectfully, your obedient servant,

JNO. L. LOGAN,
Colonel, Commanding Brigade of Cavalry and Mounted Infantry.

General JOSEPH E. JOHNSTON.

—

CAMP NEAR CLINTON,
June 16, 1863.

I made a dash upon the enemy's lines yesterday morning at daylight. Captured two of his camps, took 100 prisoners, including 1 major, 2

---

* See Johnston to Logan, June 8 and 9, Part II, p. 40.

captains, and 3 lieutenants, many wagons, teams, salt, arms, and negroes. My loss nothing. Enemy's loss in killed and wounded 10 to 15. Colonel Logan has arrived and will take command.

JNO. L. LOGAN,
Colonel, &c.

Col. B. S. Ewell, *Assistant Adjutant-General.*

—

CAMP NEAR CLINTON,
July 1, 1863.

A party of my scouts down near Port Hudson captured Brig. Gen. Neal Dow, Federal Army, last night at 9 o'clock. He will be forwarded to your headquarters at once.

JNO. L. LOGAN,
Colonel.

Col. B. S. Ewell, *Assistant Adjutant-General.*

—

JACKSON, *July* 3, VIA MONTGOMERY, [*July*] 6, 1863.
(Received at Richmond, July 9.)

Following dispatch just received:

General JOSEPH E. JOHNSTON:

On morning of 2d, at daylight, I surprised and captured Springfield Landing, the enemy's depot for landing supplies, 7 miles below Port Hudson, 6 miles in their lines. Burned their commissary and quartermaster's stores, destroyed 100 wagons, killed and wounded 140, captured 35 prisoners, paroling 22 of them. My loss, 4 killed and 10 wounded; and engaged brigade of the enemy, and held him in check until the work was done, and then retired.

JNO. L. LOGAN,
Colonel, Commanding, &c.

T. B. LAMAR,
Assistant Adjutant-General.

General S. COOPER.

—

HEADQUARTERS NEAR JACKSON, LA.,
July 8, 1863.

COLONEL: Inclosed please find a communication from Brigadier-General Green, commanding cavalry brigade, &c., west of the Mississippi River, which I forward at once for your information. The young man states to me that General Taylor has two brigades of infantry, two of cavalry, and a sufficient amount of artillery, including some 12-pounder Parrotts, and that they were mounting two 24-pounder smooth-bore pieces; that transports could not pass their batteries, but that gunboats continue to pass by, running near the east shore of the river.

I have answered the communication, and urged General Green to hold his present position and cut off enemy's supplies, and at the same time open communication with General Gardner, and provision the garrison at Port Hudson by swimming beeves across the river.

I hope from this statement you will understand the position, &c. Being on the move, I write in great haste.

I am, colonel, very respectfully, your obedient servant,

JNO. L. LOGAN,
Colonel, Commanding Brigade.

Col. B. S. Ewell,
Assistant Adjutant-General.

[Inclosure.]

HEADQUARTERS FIRST TEXAS CAVALRY BRIGADE,
Assumption Church, on La Fourche, July 5, 1863.

To any Confederate Officer commanding on the east of the Mississippi.

I send my young volunteer aide-de-camp, Leander McAnelly, of the Fifth Texas Cavalry, to communicate with any Confederate force on the east of the Mississippi.

We have a sufficient force on this side, of cavalry, infantry, and artillery, to hold it against any force the Yankees can bring against us. If a force on the east, below Donaldsonville, could hold their own on the river, we can stop the supplies to Banks' army, and force him to raise the siege of Port Hudson. We will, I am confident, be able to whip his army in the open field should he move on this side.

McAnelly will give you full details.

THOMAS GREEN,
Brigadier-General, Commanding First Cavalry Brigade.

MAY 22, 1863.—Steamer Louisiana Belle attacked ·near Barre's Landing, Bayou Teche, La.

Report of Capt. George S. Merrill, Fourth Massachusetts Infantry.

BRASHEAR CITY, *May* 23, 1863.

COLONEL : I have the honor to submit the following report concerning the recent guerrilla attack upon a detachment of this regiment:

On Wednesday, the 20th instant, by orders from headquarters, I was directed to report with 50 members of my company (B) to Colonel Chandler, assistant quartermaster, on board steamer Louisiana Belle. My subsequent orders from Colonel Chandler were to proceed with the steamer, principally as a guard against guerrilla attacks while taking freight. We reached Washington about sunset on the 21st, and, after stationing a guard, commenced loading with cotton. Our forces had been entirely withdrawn from the town, and the inhabitants, in our limited intercourse, received us with evident lack of friendship. At 10 p. m., from reports brought in by some of my guards of suspicious movements, and after a personal investigation, I became fearful of a night attack by a band of guerrillas, and thereupon doubled the number of my sentries, and adopted other extra precautions to guard against the apprehended surprise. The night passed quietly, our freight being stowed by midnight.

At 6 a. m. on the 22d we started down the bayou. When about 1 mile above Barre's Landing, I observed 3 horsemen some distance in advance (on the left bank, coming down), leisurely riding along the road. They were well mounted, and carried arms, blankets, and canteens. No sooner did the steamer come within their sight than they put spurs to their horses and galloped out of our view, in the direction of Barre's Landing. While passing this point, a citizen came toward the bank and warned us against a band of guerrillas, who, he stated, were located just below. I immediately ordered my men to put on their full equipments, and hold themselves in readiness to repel any attack should we be molested. A mile and a quarter, I judge, from the Landing had been passed without indications of any foe, and my men, without, however, removing equipments or putting aside arms, were on the upper deck eating breakfast, when, at a sharp turn in the bayou, where the stream is quite narrow, we were greeted with a murderous volley from the dense woods on the left bank. Captain Alexander, in command of the steamer, who was on the hurricane deck, fell, mortally wounded by this fire; one of the pilots, two of the deck-hands, and ten of my own men were also wounded. The shots of the enemy, who were fully concealed, seem to have been directed principally at the pilot-house, which was completely riddled by ball and buck-shot, and which diversion of fire alone prevented a much greater sacrifice among those on board. The principal pilot, who was unharmed, escaped to the engine-room below. The boat, now manageless, ran forcibly upon, and the bows became entangled in, a fallen tree on the left bank, while the stern, forced round by the strong current, caught upon the opposite bank, the wheel becoming wedged into the branches of an overhanging tree. Upon these apparent evidences of the success of their attack, the guerrillas sent up loud shouts of triumph, and called upon us to surrender. The position of the boat was such that it was impossible to land our force and clear the woods, even had that course been advisable, under the severe fire we must have sustained from the ambushed band.

Immediately ordering my men behind such shelter as the boat afforded, we briskly returned the fire of our foes, who were fully concealed by the foliage, and succeeded in so far driving them back and silencing their volleys as to enable us to force the bow of the boat into the stream, and extricate ourselves from the position. Meanwhile the pilot had arranged a temporary steering apparatus below, by which we succeeded in moving very slowly down the bayou. The guerrilla band followed, or rather kept in advance of us, each turn of the bayou or stoppage of the steamer (which, owing to the insufficient facilities for pilotage and steerage, caught occasionally against either bank) being made the occasion for a fresh volley from their pieces. We kept up a smart fire into the woods in advance and beside us, and had the satisfaction of seeing the fire of our foes lessen and grow weaker with each successive volley, while a number who ventured into sight were made to bite the dust before the rifle-shots of my men.

Just after extricating the steamer from its first position of danger, we were fired upon from the doorway of a house on the opposite (right) bank, where a white flag was flying, and which house, I am informed, had been guarded by a detail from the Forty-first Massachusetts while that regiment was stationed at the Landing.

From the time of the first attack, 8.15 a. m., during an hour and a half, we were pursued and continually fired upon by this cowardly band, until, at the distance of some 5 miles from the point of their first ambush, the overflowage of water impeding their progress, the pilot was able to resume in safety his customary position, and the miscreants gave us no further annoyance.

The master of the steamer lived nearly four hours from the time of receiving his wounds; one in the head and the other, most severe, in his side. Of the men under my command, 10 were wounded, 2 dangerously in the back; 1 dangerously in the neck, back, arm, leg, and foot; 1 seriously in both legs; the others in less degree.

Much credit is due to the pilot for his successful efforts in managing the boat after the pilot-house became untenable. Of my own men, I may say they behaved with all the coolness and courage I could have desired, freely braving danger, and risking personal exposure whenever it would lend to the discomfiture of our opponents. The attacking party, I judge, numbered some 30 ; so far as seen were mainly in citizens' dress, and, from all the attendant circumstances, were, I am well satisfied, principally or wholly citizens of Washington.

With much respect, colonel, your obedient servant,

GEO. S. MERRILL,
Captain Company B, Fourth Massachusetts.

Lieut. Col. E. T. COLBY,
Commanding Fourth Massachusetts Regiment.

MAY 30, 1863.—Affair at Point Isabel, Tex.

Report of Col. James Duff, Thirty-third Texas Cavalry.

HEADQUARTERS LINE OF THE RIO GRANDE,
Fort Brown, May 31, 1863.

SIR: I have the honor to report for the information of the general commanding [H. P. Bee], that on yesterday morning about 6 o'clock our launches, each carrying one gun and 35 to 40 men, from the U. S. frigate Brooklyn, effected a landing at Point Isabel. On discovering the approach of the boats, Lieutenant [J. B.] Ammons, of the Thirty-third Texas Cavalry, in command of a small detachment of 11 men at the Point, burned the schooner Eager, lying at the wharf loaded with merchandise, and retired a short distance. The Yankees fired a few rounds at our troops without any effect, and, taking possession of a small schooner which has for some time been in charge of the custom-house officers, re-embarked and left. In their haste to get off, they ran the stolen schooner aground and set her on fire.

Lieutenant Ammons approached the boats sufficiently close to get a shot at the party; with what success he is unable to report.

I regret that the detachment of my command at Point Isabel was so small and so badly armed as to entirely preclude an engagement with the enemy, and I would earnestly ask that steps be taken to more thoroughly arm my regiment. I am placed in a position where the services of every man in my command are required, and it is absolutely necessary that the means be placed at my disposal to render them efficient.

I have the honor to be, colonel, your obedient servant,

JAMES DUFF,
Colonel Thirty-third Regiment Texas Cavalry, Commanding.

Lieut. E. R. TARVER, *Aide-de-Camp.*

JUNE 1, 1863.—Skirmish at Berwick, La.

Reports of Brig. Gen. William. H. Emory, U. S. Army, commanding Defenses of New Orleans.

HDQRS. DEFENSES OF NEW ORLEANS, *June* 1, 1863.

The following telegram has just been received from the quartermaster at Brashear City :

GENERAL : The advanced guard of [Alfred] Mouton attacked our guards at Berwick at 10 o'clock. Re-enforcements were sent at once across the bay, and, after a few rounds from the 12-pounder howitzers in our possession, the rebels left.

We expect to be troubled for some time to come, as our force here is quite light. Mouton is reported as being 2,000 strong. This place will be defended to the last. The negro troops will be sent this p. m.

I have the honor to be, with much respect, your obedient servant,

THOS. S. DENNETT,
Captain, and Assistant Quartermaster.

I have ordered all our sick brought this side, and have telegraphed to Colonel Holmes to know the exact state of the case, and why he does not telegraph himself.

W. H. EMORY,
Brigadier-General, Commanding.

Lieutenant-Colonel IRWIN.

 —

HEADQUARTERS DEFENSES OF NEW ORLEANS,
New Orleans, June 1, 1863.

I have just received this further report from commanding officer at Brashear City:

A force of guerrillas, about 200, at Berwick, attacked us this forenoon, and were driven back. We are all moving our hospital as fast as possible. We expect an attack on the road at Bayou Bœuf to-night. Shall take all measures to repel the foe.

C. W. WORDIN,
Lieutenant-Colonel, Commanding.

W. H. EMORY,
Brigadier-General, Commanding.

Lieutenant-Colonel IRWIN.

JUNE 7–JULY 13, 1863.—Operations in Louisiana, west of the Mississippi.

SUMMARY OF THE PRINCIPAL EVENTS.

June   16, 1863.—Demonstration on Waterloo.
    18, 1863.—Skirmish at Plaquemine.
    19, 1863.—Raid on Bayou Goula.
    20, 1863.—Capture of Thibodeaux.
    20–21, 1863.—Engagement at La Fourche Crossing.
    21, 1863.—Skirmish at Brashear City.
    23, 1863.—Capture of Brashear City.†
    24, 1863.—Skirmish at Chacahoula Station.
              Capture of Union forces at Bayou Bœuf Crossing.
    28, 1863.—Attack on Donaldsonville.
July   7–10, 1863.—Attacks on Union gunboats and transports on the Mississippi.
    12–13, 1863.—Engagement on the La Fourche (Cox's Plantation, etc.), near Donaldsonville.

REPORTS.*

No. 1.—Brig. Gen. William H. Emory, U. S. Army, commanding Defenses of New Orleans, of operations June 7–28.
No. 2.—Capt. Albert Stearns, One hundred and thirty-first New York Infantry, Provost-Marshal, of skirmish at Plaquemine.
No. 3.—Lieut. Col. Albert Stickney, Forty-seventh Massachusetts Infantry, of engagement at La Fourche Crossing.

---

* See also General Reports, pp. 3–34, and Banks' reports of June 29 and July 6, pp. 46, 48.
† See reports of Col. John A. Keith, Appendix, p. 911.

No. 4.—Capt. John A. Grow, Twenty-fifth New York Battery, of operations June 20-25, including engagement at La Fourche Crossing.
No. 5.—Lieut. Col. Richard Fitz Gibbons, Ninth Connecticut Infantry, of skirmish at Chacahoula Station.
No. 6.—Maj. Henry M. Porter, Seventh Vermont Infantry, of attack on Donaldsonville.
No. 7.—Lieut. Charles Emerson, One hundred and seventy-fourth New York Infantry, Acting Assistant Adjutant-General, of attack on the steamboat Saint Mary's, July 8.
No. 8.—Brig. Gen. Cuvier Grover, U. S. Army, of the engagement on the La Fourche (Cox's Plantation, etc.), near Donaldsonville.
No. 9.—Col. Nathan A. M. Dudley, Thirtieth Massachusetts Infantry, commanding Brigade, of engagement on the La Fourche, near Donaldsonville.
No. 10.—Maj. Gen. Richard Taylor, C. S. Army, commanding District of Western Louisiana, of operations June 23–July 13.
No. 11.—Brig. Gen. Alfred Mouton, C. S. Army, of operations June 22–July 4.
No. 12.—Col. James P. Major, C. S. Army, commanding Cavalry Brigade, of operations June 10-24.
No. 13.—Capt. T. A. Faries, Louisiana Battery, of attacks on gunboats and transports on the Mississippi River, July 7-10, and operations near Donaldsonville, July 12-13.
No. 14.—Maj. Sherod Hunter, Baylor's (Texas) Cavalry, commanding Mosquito Fleet, of the capture of Brashear City.
No. 15.—Brig. Gen. Thomas Green, C. S. Army, commanding Cavalry Brigade, of operations June 22–July 13.

No. 1.

Reports of Brig. Gen. William H. Emory, U. S. Army, commanding Defenses of New Orleans, of operations June 7–28.

HEADQUARTERS DEFENSES OF NEW ORLEANS,
June 23, 1863.

COLONEL : The fight at La Fourche Crossing the afternoon of the 21st was a most creditable thing to our troops and to Colonel Stickney, who commanded them.   With less than 1,000 men, he was attacked by Colonel Major's whole force, four regiments of Texans, and artillery. He repulsed them, leaving 53 of the enemy's dead upon the field, and 16 prisoners.   His wounded he carried off, and we have no means of knowing.   Our loss was 8 killed and 16 wounded.

Colonel Cahill, with the re-enforcements, is now looking after the enemy.   All of enemy's men are mounted, and it is difficult, if not impossible, to catch them without cavalry.   Colonel Cahill reports continuous and heavy firing both in the direction of Donaldsonville and Brashear.   It cannot be both ; it must be Brashear City.

The enemy's forces are all composed of troops fresh from Texas. They report this as the advance of Magruder's army.   Doubtful ; but, as they passed so near you, it would be well to send over some cavalry to ascertain if this be so.

The enemy captured a parcel of sick in Thibodeaux, whose presence there was utterly unknown to me.   By whom left there, or by what authority, I have no knowledge.

W. H. EMORY,
Brigadier-General, Commanding.

Lieutenant-Colonel IRWIN,
Assistant Adjutant-General.

HEADQUARTERS DEFENSES OF NEW ORLEANS,
June 29, 1863.

GENERAL : Our victory at Donaldsonville was a brilliant affair; 100 of the enemy killed; wounded not known; prisoners, 120, including 1 lieutenant-colonel, 2 majors, 3 captains, and 5 lieutenants.

W. H. EMORY,
Brigadier-General, Commanding.

Major-General BANKS.

HEADQUARTERS DEFENSES OF NEW ORLEANS,
June 30, 1863.

COLONEL: The telegrams sent to headquarters have faithfully represented to you every movement made by our troops in the defense of the Opelousas Railway, Brashear City, and Donaldsonville. But it may be proper for me to give a connected history of events.

Brashear City was not in the list of what was turned over to me as the Defenses of New Orleans, but the critical condition of affairs there, and the inexperience of the officer in command, compelled me to assume control. On the 1st of June, I ordered Berwick City to be evacuated.

On the 7th, learning the troops at Brashear were in great disorder, especially the convalescents, and that the place was threatened by the enemy and the lieutenant-colonel there in command having requested to be relieved, I sent Lieutenant-Colonel Stickney, Forty-seventh Massachusetts, the only officer available, to assume command. I also applied to Commodore Morris for a gunboat to be sent there, with which request he complied, at great inconvenience to the naval service.

Stickney at once commenced to put affairs in a proper condition, drove the enemy's pickets from the opposite bank of the river, and ascertained the enemy to be in considerable force.

On the 10th, after consulting with the general commanding, I ordered Fort Chêne to be abandoned, as we had not force enough to hold it.

On the 17th, I warned Colonel Stickney that the enemy were planning a raid down the La Fourche, and on the 18th directed him to destroy every boat and scow he could find. I also re-enforced Donaldsonville, ordered it to be held to the last extremity, and asked Commodore Morris to send a gunboat there, which was done.

On the 20th, learning the enemy were moving down the La Fourche in some strength, I directed Colonel Stickney, after guarding well his communications with Brashear, especially Bayou Bœuf, to proceed with all his available force to La Fourche Crossing. I also detached Colonel Cahill from this city to proceed to the support of Colonel Stickney with all the troops he could collect, leaving in this city only 250 men under Lieutenant-Colonel Stedman, Forty-second Massachusetts. A part of Colonel Cahill's command, the Twenty-sixth Massachusetts, under Lieutenant-Colonel Sawtell, united with Stickney that day, but before they had all got together, with a force of not more than 600 men, they repulsed very superior forces of the enemy, inflicting considerable loss, and in a manner which reflects the highest credit upon Lieutenant-Colonel Stickney and the men under his command.

The enemy withdrew, it was believed, in the direction of Brashear, intending to attack that place. Colonel Cahill, with his reserve, was immediately ordered forward to fall upon their rear. To overtake them was difficult, if not impossible, we having scarcely a squadron of cavalry and they at least three regiments of cavalry and twelve pieces of light artillery, and having also burned the bridge over the Chacahoula, from which place, however, they were immediately driven, and a party sent, under Colonel Colburn, railway superintendent, with men and material, to repair the bridge. I had previously sent round the Saint Mary's, with orders to the commanding officer at Brashear to hold out to the last extremity, and that I would soon send him assistance.

On the 22d, the Fifteenth Maine arrived very opportunely from Pensacola. I sent it immediately to the support of Colonel Cahill, moving toward Brashear.

On the 23d, I had the honor to receive a telegram from General Banks, directing me not to risk too much for Brashear; to have the gunboat take off the men and guns, and evacuate the place if I could not hold it. On the same day I had already ordered the railway to be repaired, and that Colonel Cahill should push on toward Brashear as the only means of its relief. At this time I had no idea of any other force attacking Brashear than that just repulsed from La Fourche.

On the 24th, I reiterated my order not to retire from La Fourche, but to press on to Brashear, repairing the railway. Soon after, I received the following telegrams from Colonel Cahill:

LA FOURCHE, *June* 24, 1863.

Major Morgan, at Thibodeaux, reports 7,000 of the enemy moving down the Bayou La Fourche.

CAHILL,
Colonel, Commanding.

LA FOURCHE, *June* 24, 1863.

The enemy is advancing on both sides the Bayou La Fourche in large force, 4 miles above. My trains have not yet arrived.

CAHILL,
Colonel, Commanding.

At the same time that I received these two telegrams, the Saint Mary's returned from Brashear with the sad intelligence of the fall of that place, and that it was taken by a force brought from the opposite side of the river. Accounts received before this satisfied me that the force which had previously been threatening Brashear amounted to about 5,000 men, whom I naturally supposed the same force which had made the raid through the La Fourche country. But prisoners captured by Lieutenant-Colonel Stickney disclosed the fact that the troops which attacked him at the crossing were an altogether independent force.

It came direct from Texas, was commanded by Colonel Major, consisted of five regiments and twelve pieces of artillery, crossing the Atchafalaya opposite Port Hudson, drove in your pickets, and came down across the Plaquemine at Indian Village. Besides Major's troops, Taylor has been re-enforced by the brigades of [J. W.] Speight and Spade [?], and I estimated their united forces at from 9,000 to 12,000 men. The whole of my force now assembled amounted to but 1,600 men. Under these circumstances, I considered any attempt to recover Brashear hopeless, and withdrew my small force to this city.

I send you copies of the reports made by such officers as escaped from Brashear City. The works at that place were nothing but water batteries, open behind, and the place was taken by a party landing from Flat Lake and attacking in the rear. It appears the gunboat was too frail in its structure to be of any service, and I am sorry to say it also appears that the 400 convalescents whom I had ordered to be left there, with instructions that they should be armed and organized for the defense of the place, were neither armed nor organized, and did little or nothing for its defense.

Two companies, however, sent there by your order, belonging to the Twenty-third Connecticut, and also the battery of the Twenty-first Indiana, fought bravely.

In this connection, I turn with pleasure to the occurrences which took place immediately after at Donaldsonville. On the 27th, I received notice that Donaldsonville was threatened. I ordered the place to be held at every cost, sent up re-enforcements under Major Clark, and communicated the information to Admiral Farragut, who sent up an additional gunboat; both arrived in time. At half past 1 on the morning of the 28th, the enemy made a furious assault upon the little fort, and continued the attack till daybreak, when they were finally repulsed, losing 100 killed, 120 prisoners, including several officers of rank, and many wounded, of which we have no account. Too much praise cannot be given to Major Bullen and his command, as well as to the officers and men who manned the gunboats that participated in repelling the attack. Our loss was only 16 killed and wounded.

I have the honor to be, your obedient servant,

W. H. EMORY,
Brigadier-General, Commanding.

Lieutenant-Colonel IRWIN, *Assistant Adjutant-General.*

HEADQUARTERS DEFENSES OF NEW ORLEANS,
July 21, 1863.

SIR: I inclose you herewith the report of Lieutenant-Colonel Stickney* of the action at La Fourche on June 23 [20 and 21], which should have accompanied my report of June 30, but, although dated July 1, it only reached me yesterday morning.

This affair was very creditable to Colonel Stickney and the troops engaged, and I take great pleasure in forwarding his report. I regret that the murder of Major Bullen, a few days after the brilliant defense at Donaldsonville, and before he made his report, has been the reason why no detailed account of that affair has been sent. About the time of his murder, re-enforcements came from above, and a report from the next in command may have gone through Lieutenant-Colonel Hadlock, who commanded those re-enforcements. If so, it was irregular, and I request, if there is no objection, that I may be furnished with a copy of said report, as much dissatisfaction—no doubt unfounded—exists with those engaged in the defense with what is understood to be, from some source or another, the official report of the affair. I refer more particularly to the complaints made by the officers of the navy, who had three gunboats in the fight, and whose presence undoubtedly aided materially, if they did not absolutely prevent the capture of the place.

I am, very respectfully, your obedient servant,

W. H. EMORY,
Brigadier-General.

Lieut. Col. RICHARD B. IRWIN, *Assistant Adjutant-General.*

HEADQUARTERS DEFENSES OF NEW ORLEANS,
July 23, 1863.

COLONEL: Owing to the death of Major Bullen, I received no report of the defense of the fort at Donaldsonville, and the only report of that

---

* See p. 192.

battle which has been received by me is from Maj. H. M. Porter, which has been this day received, and which I herewith inclose.* ·

I am sorry the report is not more in detail, that I might signalize the officers and men of both the army and navy† who took part in this heroic and brilliant defense. The men were composed of two reduced companies of the Twenty-eighth Maine, and a party of convalescents from various regiments, hastily drawn together in this city and sent up by me to meet the emergency.

In addition to the Princess Royal, commanded by Captain Woolsey, and the Winona, commanded by Captain Weaver, justly mentioned by Major Porter as having distinguished themselves in the action, I beg the privilege of mentioning Captain Waters, of the Kineo, and the officers and crew of that ship, who rendered me the greatest assistance in enabling me to place the proper ammunition in that fort, and instructing the men, all of whom were infantry, totally unpracticed in artillery, in the use of the guns.

These 180 men, with the three gunboats, repelled an assault of the enemy, numbering 5,000, capturing 130 prisoners, including 1 lieutenant colonel, 1 major, 2 captains, and 5 lieutenants, all of whom were delivered to me in this city, and killing and wounding at what is estimated at 350 of the enemy, among them Colonel [Joseph] Phillips and several other officers known to be of high rank. By this repulse, combined with that at La Fourche, under Colonel Stickney, the enemy were checked in their movement upon this city and the attempt to cut communication between General Banks and his supplies.

I am, very respectfully, your obedient servant,

W. H. EMORY,
Brigadier-General, Commanding.

Lieutenant-Colonel IRWIN,
    Assistant Adjutant-General.

(Copy to Admiral Farragut.)

———

No. 2.

Report of Capt. Albert Stearns, One hundred and thirty-first New York Infantry, Provost-Marshal, of skirmish at Plaquemine.

NEW ORLEANS, LA.,
    June 19, 1863. ·

GENERAL: I have to inform you that the town of Plaquemine was attacked about 6.30 a. m. on the 18th instant by about 300 Confederate cavalry. They succeeded in capturing Lieutenant Witham and 22 men of the Twenty-eighth Regiment Maine Volunteers, whose names are annexed.‡ I and 13 of my men succeeded in making our escape. Upon the approach of the cavalry, they were fired upon by my men, killing 1 man, and, as I have since learned, wounding 2 others, but their force was such that further resistance was useless, and the place was surrendered to them. Upon gaining possession of the town, they immediately proceeded to Bayou Plaquemine, where the steamboat Lasykes was aground, fired upon and wounded 1 man who was on board, and then set her on fire. They also captured the officers and crew of the steamboat Anglo-American, wounding 1 of her men, and then set her

---

* See p. 202.   † See Emory to Farragut, July 21, p. 650.   ‡ Names omitted.'

on fire; both vessels were a total loss. I think a small steamboat, called the Belfast, was also captured, as she went down the Bayou Plaquemine the previous evening to get a load of molasses, about 4 miles from the river. The boat belonged to Edward Pilcher, of New Orleans. They also burned about 80 bales of cotton that were ready for shipment.

At about 9.15 a. m. the gunboat Winona, commanded by Captain [Aaron W.] Weaver, came down from Baton Rouge, and having heard, when 5 miles above, of the capture of the town, immediately commenced to throw shell, upon which the main body of the enemy left. I then made my way to the levee; hailed Captain Weaver, and procured a boat to take me and the 13 men on board. We also had the 2 wounded men placed on board the La Fourche, and sent along with my dispatches to Baton Rouge.

At about 11 a. m. we learned that a portion of the cavalry had returned. Captain Weaver immediately threw shell into that portion of the town where they were supposed to be. After about 90 rounds had been fired, I went on shore with my men, assisted by a squad from the boat, and marched through the town without finding any of the enemy, but we learned that they were in considerable force about 4 miles back, and under the command of Col. C. D. [Joseph] Phillips.

A man named A. Grass was arrested for having guided the enemy into and about the town. He admitted to me that he had done so, but says that he was compelled by threats to show them around the place. He lives near Indian Village, and has never taken the oath of allegiance. I left him in charge of Captain Weaver. Upon returning to the boat, Captain Weaver proceeded to Donaldsonville, to warn them of danger and to assist in case of attack; also, to leave the men who had escaped with me.

I am inclined to think that there is a force of from 5,000 to 8,000 men between Plaquemine and Simsport; also, that they have several cannon. It was generally believed, from remarks dropped by Confederate officers, that General Green was approaching with a brigade to occupy the town or to operate against Donaldsonville.

We lost about 35 Enfield rifles and a very small amount of commissary stores.

I remain, very respectfully, your obedient servant,
ALBERT STEARNS,
Captain, Provost-Marshal, Iberville Parish.

Brig. Gen. JAMES BOWEN,
Provost-Marshal-General, Department of the Gulf.

No. 3.

Report of Lieut. Col. Albert Stickney, Forty-seventh Massachusetts Infantry, of engagement at La Fourche Crossing.

CONGO SQUARE,
July 9, 1863.

COLONEL: I have the honor to report that, in accordance with Special Orders, No. 16, from your headquarters, I proceeded to Brashear City on June 7 last, and assumed command of the forces there. I found things in a very disorganized condition, and immediately proceeded to put the place in the best state for defense that I could, and to obtain all possible intelligence of the force and designs of the enemy in that vicinity. I reported to you from time to time the operations at that post, and at the same time made what preparations were in my power for defending any other threatened points on the line of the Opelousas Railroad.

On the morning of June 20, at about 4 o'clock, I received a telegram from you, informing me that the enemy were advancing in force on La Fourche Crossing, and ordering me to send re-enforcements to that point. Judging that there was no danger of any attack at Brashear City, for a day or two, at least, and thinking that affairs at La Fourche required my presence there, I left Major Anthony, Second Rhode Island Cavalry, in command of Brashear City, and went to La Fourche Crossing immediately, with such forces as I could spare from Brashear, intending to return as soon as possible to my former station.

I reached La Fourche about 6 a. m., with 75 men of the Twenty-third Connecticut Volunteers and 115 men of the One hundred and seventy-sixth New York Regiment, 46 men of the Forty-second Massachusetts, and two pieces of artillery, one 6-pounder gun and one 12-pounder howitzer. I had ordered Captain Blober, with his company of First Louisiana Cavalry, on the day previous to scout the country as far certainly as Napoleonville, and farther, if possible with safety, and to send immediately any intelligence of the enemy he might obtain. He went only a mile or two beyond Labadieville, and returned with no intelligence whatever of any force on the Bayou La Fourche. He also reported that gentlemen from Napoleonville gave no information of any force in that direction. After my arrival at La Fourche, I sent out Captain Blober and his command again to scout the country above Thibodeaux. They returned on the afternoon of the 20th, reporting that they had been closely pursued by the enemy, and had lost 2 of their men. The force of the enemy advanced very rapidly on Thibodeaux that day, being almost entirely composed of mounted men and artillery, and captured nearly all the infantry stationed there and in the vicinity on the plantations, amounting to about 100 men. They were 47 men of the Twelfth Maine, with 2 lieutenants, convalescents, whom I had sent from Brashear City; 40 others, convalescents, from Brashear; about 10 men of Company D, One hundred and seventy-sixth New York Regiment, and a very few men who had been stationed as guards on plantations. Captain Blober's company was mostly composed of new recruits, and, in consequence, undrilled and undisciplined. Had their scouting been properly done, there was no necessity whatever of the infantry force at Thibodeaux being captured. They had only to retreat this side of the bridge over Bayou La Fourche, and then march down under cover of the levee. The enemy rested two or three hours in Thibodeaux before coming down to La Fourche Crossing, and the infantry once reaching the bridge could have defended themselves against merely their advance guard.

On the afternoon of Saturday, I received an order to send back two companies to Brashear, but, as the enemy were then advancing down the bayou to the crossing, I did not dare at that moment to weaken my force by sending them away. I sent a train back to Terre Bonne to bring down to La Fourche the company and one piece of artillery there stationed. The enemy succeeded in capturing 1 commissioned officer of the company at Terre Bonne, the others of the company escaping on the train and arriving safely at La Fourche. Immediately afterward the railroad and telegraph were cut at Terre Bonne, and the place occupied by cavalry.

About 5 o'clock in the afternoon my pickets were driven in, and the cavalry of the enemy immediately afterward appeared in our front. I do not know how large their force was at that time, but judge it to have been under 100.

Our position was as follows: The levee of the Bayou La Fourche is about 12 feet high; the railroad crosses the bayou over the top of the levee, nearly in a direction perpendicular to that of the bayou, and is about 12 feet above the level of the surrounding country. For 5 or 6 miles to the east of La Fourche Crossing a carriage-road runs up and down the bayou on both sides, close to the levee, passing under the railroad on both sides of the bayou. We were on the east side of the bayou and north of the railroad, our front being parallel with the railroad, extending about 150 yards from the levee, and being about 200 yards from the railroad. From the right of our front, I had a line of defense running perpendicular to and resting upon the railroad. I was obliged to have my front farther from the railroad than it otherwise would have been, on account of trees standing which could not be cut down. The country around was level, affording full play for the artillery, and was covered with tall grass, which I subsequently had cut down, as it concealed, in a measure, movements in our front.

A short time before our pickets were driven in, I had ordered a detachment of about 50 men, of the Twenty-third Connecticut Volunteers, under command of Major Miller, to lie down in the tall grass on both sides of the road along the levee, about 450 yards in advance of our main line. After the first fire of the enemy, I found Major Miller some distance to the rear of his command, crouching in the high weeds on the levee. I ordered him under arrest, and put in command of this detachment the next senior officer, who faithfully executed my order.

The remainder of the infantry was drawn up in line along our front and the extreme left of our right flank, with the exception of a company of convalescents, under Captain Fletcher, Twenty-sixth Maine, who were at the railroad bridge. Captain Blober's cavalry was posted so as to guard against the turning of our right flank. The artillery was posted as follows: A 12-pounder gun on the railroad, at the point where it crosses the left bank of the bayou; two 12-pounder howitzers and one 6-pounder gun on our front, one of the howitzers·being placed on the extreme right, so that its fire could be directed to the front or right flank.

After the cavalry of the enemy drove in our pickets, they continued to advance until fired upon by the detachment of the Twenty-third Connecticut Volunteers. A few volleys were exchanged without loss on our side, when our men fell back, and took position on the right flank. As the enemy were now in easy range, we opened upon them with shell and solid shot, the 12-pounder gun on the bridge doing the most execution. They stopped, seemingly surprised to find such preparations for their reception, and in a few minutes retired toward Thibodeaux, carrying with them the few that were killed or wounded by our fire.

Soon after the disappearance of the enemy, I sent a flag of truce to obtain permission to move our hospital stores and sick from the hospital, which was in front of our lines and exposed to our fire. The flag of truce went toward Thibodeaux before meeting the pickets of the enemy, who refused to comply with my request. I, however, succeeded in moving safely all the contents of the hospital to our rear, and just after dark burned the building, lest it should interfere with the effectiveness of our fire, and that, at the same time, the light might enable me to perceive the movements of the enemy. For the same reason I had a building fired on the other side of the bayou, anticipating that the Confederates might come down on that side and attempt to cross the railroad bridge.

Up to this time, Saturday evening, June 20, our forces amounted to about 502 men, as follows: 195 of the Twenty-third Connecticut; 154 of the One hundred and seventy-sixth New York; 46 of the Forty-second Massachusetts; 37 of the Twenty-sixth Maine; 50 men in Captain Blober's cavalry, and about 20 artillerists, mostly of the Twenty-first Indiana.

The men were kept under arms, at their several posts, ready to repel an attack at any moment. Pickets were thrown out on the front to a distance of about 400 yards, and squads of cavalry scouted on our right and rear.

About 11 p. m. of the 20th, Lieutenant-Colonel Sawtell, of the Twenty-sixth Massachusetts, arrived with five companies (306 men). As he was the senior officer, I offered him the command, which he refused. I then ordered his regiment into line on the front, to relieve the men posted there. During that night no demonstrations were made by the enemy.

On the following morning, Captain Grow, of the Twenty-fifth New York Battery, reached La Fourche Crossing, with one section of his battery, about 30 men, one gun of which I ordered into position on the extreme left of our front on the Bayou road, and the other within our lines, so that it could be moved to our front or right flank as occasion should require. We had begun throwing up slight earthworks, but they were at no point over 2 feet in height, and extended only a few yards in either direction from the angle formed by our two fronts. At different times during the morning reconnoitering cavalry of the enemy appeared in our front and at some distance on the right, but only came within fire of our outposts.

A little after noon, a heavy rain commenced and continued until about 6.30 p. m., thoroughly drenching the men, who were in line a greater part of the time. This was necessary, as I could not depend upon their falling into position with sufficient alacrity at the least warning.

About 4 p. m. the infantry and cavalry of the enemy, about 150 strong, engaged our outposts and pickets, but made no attempt to advance on our main force. An intermittent fire was kept up for an hour and a half, when the enemy retired, and our pickets again resumed their places.

At 6.30 p. m. the Confederates again came in view, and this time in large force. Our position was much the same as on the previous night, except that two companies of the Twenty-sixth Massachusetts were on our front, two on our right flank, and the remaining one protecting the field piece on the bridge. The artillery was all posted as before described. The enemy advanced rapidly, and soon compelled the pickets to fall back on the main line, which they reached in rather a straggling condition at our left wing.

Just about dusk the enemy opened upon us with one field piece (which appeared to be a 12-pounder howitzer), throwing shell and solid shot, when I ordered the reserve piece of the Twenty-fifth New York Battery to take such a position on the right as would enable them to reply to this piece. The howitzer of the enemy soon ceased firing, whether compelled by the shots of our piece or the bad quality of their ammunition I am unable to say. Prisoners subsequently stated that they had other guns in position, which the rain prevented their using. All this time our artillery had been constantly firing, using shell for the most part; but the infantry did not, as yet, reply to the straggling bullets which came from the enemy. The moisture of the atmosphere held the smoke of the cannon so close to the ground that it was almost impossible to ascertain the distance or numbers of the enemy, or on what ponit he would mass his force.

At about 7 p. m. their loud shouts indicated that they were charging in our front. I immediately ordered the infantry to fire by rank and the artillery to use canister. Having no canister for the 6-pounder gun, we used in it packages of musket ammunition.

Notwithstanding a most rapid but accurate fire on our part, the enemy, who had dismounted before charging, advanced boldly up to our lines, firing continually as they came. Our infantry became nervous, and no longer fired by rank, but at will. At the same time a strong attempt was made to turn our right flank. This was prevented (though at one time they seemed on the point of success) by the enfilading fire of our reserve piece and the speedy rally of the men there posted. The attack of the enemy was principally directed against our guns, and the cannoneers of two pieces became panic-stricken and fled. These were the guns of the Twenty-fifth New York Battery, on the Bayou road, and the 12-pounder howitzer at the angle of our front and right flank. The contest over these pieces was hand-to-hand. The enemy were driven off at the point of the bayonet.

At length, at about 8 p. m., the Confederates, growing weary of a fight so unequal in its results, hastily retreated toward Thibodeaux, leaving a great number of their dead and wounded near our lines.

Our actual force during the fight amounted to 838 men, of whom only about 600 were engaged, the remainder being posted as a guard to the field piece on the bridge and to protect our right. This was necessary, because the darkness rendered it impossible to see the enemy's movements, and few of the troops were steady enough to trust them to make any rapid movement in the excitement of action. The actual force of the enemy engaged in the charge on our lines I estimate at about 600 men.

Our loss was as follows

Command.	Killed.	Wounded.	Total.
23d Connecticut	2	16	18
26th Massachusetts	3	10	13
176th New York	2	12	14
42d Massachusetts	1	3	4
Total	8	41	49

The enemy were engaged during the night in carrying away their killed and wounded who were outside of our lines, and the following morning 53 of their dead were counted inside of our pickets. When we entered Thibodeaux, Tuesday morning, nearly 60 wounded were found in the hospitals, from which I conclude that their loss in killed and wounded must have been 300, taking 50 as the number of their killed, and reckoning the ratio of killed to wounded as 1 to 4.

The men who charged upon our lines belonged mostly to the Second Texas Mounted Rangers, Colonel [Charles L.] Pyron, claimed to be the oldest regiment in the Confederate service, and that they had never before been beaten in action. Their wounded in our hands thought that our troops must be Regulars, so steadily did they stand at their posts. But I regret to say that the train in waiting on the track left at the commencement of the fight without orders, carrying away some cowardly soldiers, and that during the battle some few left their ranks and sought shelter near and behind the railroad.

Had the enemy brought up his reserve, which was in line at no great distance, at the time the cannoneers deserted their guns, or had he made his attack on the right flank with equal force and with the same persistent energy as was displayed upon our front, perhaps the result might have been different, although our troops, for the most part, stood manfully under so close a fire. Our men remained in line under arms the whole night, but there was no further attack.

The next morning a flag of truce came in, requesting permission to bury their dead and carry away their wounded. This was granted, on condition that all the wounded men outside the camp lines should be paroled; that none of their drivers should come within our outposts, and that all wounded should be retained who were within our camp. As they agreed to these conditions, our drivers were engaged with the ambulances of the enemy during the morning in carrying to Thibodeaux the dead and wounded.

About 11 a. m. Colonel Cahill arrived with the Ninth Connecticut Volunteers, a detachment of the Twenty-sixth Massachusetts, and the other section of the New York Battery, and took command of the forces at La Fourche. Major Morgan, commanding the One hundred and seventy-sixth New York Regiment, through the action encouraged his men, and to him is due, in a great degree, the fine conduct that they showed. Captain Jenkins, commanding the Twenty-third Connecticut, displayed the greatest bravery and coolness. A Confederate officer seized him by the throat, demanding a surrender. The assault was immediately returned in precisely the same manner, when one of Captain Jenkins men bayoneted the Confederate.

Lieutenant Starr, of the Twenty-third Connecticut, was the only commissioned officer injured in the action. He was wounded in the thigh, and afterward died in consequence of amputation and ensuing weakness.

I desire particularly to mention Sergt. John Allyn, Company A, Forty-seventh Massachusetts Regiment, who has been with me since I was ordered to Brashear City, and has at all times rendered the most valuable service, going on dangerous scouts, once inside the enemy's lines, and showing at all times the greatest courage and remarkably sound judgment. His thorough knowledge of the country and habit of reporting facts only were of the greatest assistance to me.

Very respectfully,

ALBERT STICKNEY,
Lieutenant-Colonel, Commanding Forces at La Fourche.

Lieut. Col. W. D. SMITH,
Acting Assistant Adjutant-General.

No. 4.

Report of Capt. John A. Grow, Twenty-fifth New York Battery, of operations June 20–25, including engagement at La Fourche Crossing.

METARIE RACE COURSE, *July 5, 1863.*

SIR: An indisposition has prevented me from sending you an account of the movements of my battery since the 20th ultimo at an earlier period; but trusting even at this late day that it may not be without interest to you, I send you the inclosed statement. There may be much in it which you may desire to remedy.

On the 20th day of June I received orders to proceed at once to La Fourche Crossing. The order having been received at about 4 p. m., my battery, with all the baggage, was taken across the river and put on board the cars by 1 a. m. (night); the train left at 4 a. m. On reaching Boutte Station, I found Colonel Cahill stationed at that place with his regiment. He ordered me to leave one section of my battery with him, and to proceed myself with the other section to the La Fourche Crossing. I reached that place about 10 a. m. of the 21st. My battery was soon unloaded and the pieces parked. I reported to Lieutenant-Colonel Stickney. He ordered out one of my pieces to shell a sugar-house, which I did most successfully, the distance being only about 1,700 yards; the shells, however, from some cause, refused to explode.

At 6.30 p. m. the scouts came in, announcing the rebels coming down in force.

In about 10 minutes my section was ready to move. While giving my attention to something else for a few minutes, Lieutenant-Colonel Stickney ordered off one of my pieces to take position on the left, in the Bayou road, to commence firing canister before any enemy could be seen. The position which he assigned was given before I had the least knowledge of its whereabouts—it was only by the firing of the piece that I could discover its position. I immediately rode to it, and found it stationed in the above road, about 2 rods in advance of our line of battle, in a most exposed position, and without any adequate support, and the piece was firing canister without stint. By this time, however, the enemy had formed in line of battle, and were rapidly advancing. The rebels now opened on us with a howitzer, with shell and solid shot, but at too great a distance to seriously affect us any further than to frighten our infantry. The other piece having been left for me to use as I should see proper, during the progress of the battle, as soon as the enemy opened on us with shell, I rode over to our right, and ordered my reserved piece into position to the rear of our front, and to the right of our right flank, and opened on the enemy's piece with fuse shell at 1,600 yards, very fortunately getting the range of the piece the first fire. The enemy's gun was silenced with the third shell. At this time the rebels were charging on our lines and were making a strong effort to turn our right flank. My piece being in position to enfilade their lines of attack on our flank, I ordered my piece to open on them with canister. The first fire was most disastrous and deadly on their ranks. Among the number who fell at our first discharge of canister was a rebel colonel and his horse. After ten or twelve discharges of canister, the rebels fell back to the front, and finally made a hasty retreat, a large majority creeping off from the field on their hands and knees, so destructive was our fire.

As soon as we had ceased firing, I learned that, on the last charge of the rebels, the support of my left piece had fled, and that my sergeant gave the order to limber to the rear, when the horses became unmanageable, and ran away and left the piece. The sergeant was evidently frightened badly—that piece, if properly managed, could have been made the most effective piece in the field. The Bayou road was scarcely 14 feet wide, with a levee 10 feet high on the left, and a ditch on the right, grown up with a thick growth of bushes on either side. The piece controlled the road. After clearing the road of the enemy, the piece could have been turned so as to have raked the whole assaulting line of the enemy on our front. The sergeant allowed that golden opportunity to slip, and left his piece in the road. The moment the fact came to my knowledge, in order to mortify the sergeant of that piece, I sent my sergeant with his limber and brought it off. The men at my piece behaved most gallantly—so much so, I have mentioned them in my report to Colonel Cahill.

General, you may recollect, when last up to Apollo stables, that I had a deserter in confinement awaiting trial, and that on my desiring to withdraw the charges and try him again, you ordered him brought out and talked to him. General Emory shortly afterward ordered his release. He acted as No. 5 at the piece under my charge, and fully redeemed himself. The action lasted an hour and a quarter. For some reason or other, the enemy was not pursued by our cavalry. We had a company of cavalry of about 80 in number. We lost, I believe, 9 killed and 30 wounded; the enemy lost about 70 killed and over 200 wounded. The force on our side engaged did not exceed 400, but that of the rebels exceeded 800. At 12 p. m. that night I saw Colonel Stickney, and advised him to retreat to Boutte Station, as the rebels had within 5 miles not less than 2,000 effective men, and, without any re-enforcements, he must evidently overcome us. I forgot to mention that we had one 18-pounder brass piece, called the Saint Mary's gun, two 12-pounder howitzers, and one 6-pounder brass piece, all in position, which were well managed during that fight. The next forenoon was occupied with a flag of truce, which the enemy sent up asking the privilege of burying his dead. While this was pending, Colonel Cahill arrived with his forces. We were then about 1,100 strong, and, through the strength of our position, we could effectually defend our position against 2,000 rebels. The arrival of Colonel Cahill was distinctly seen by the rebels, and that night they commenced to retreat. On the next morning we made a forced reconnaissance to Thibodeaux, and found that all the rebels had left the country. On Monday afternoon, the 22d, the Fifteenth Maine regiment arrived, making us at least 1,700 strong. On this reconnaissance was this regiment, with 140 men of the One hundred and seventy-sixth New York, and my battery. Finding no enemy, all returned but the One hundred and seventy-sixth New York, who were left in possession of the town. With the forces which we had, we could successfully resist an attacking force of the enemy of 3,000.

On the 24th, in the afternoon, negroes and white men came flying into camp, reporting that the rebels were advancing, 3,000 strong, with eleven pieces of artillery, and that they were within 5 miles of Thibodeaux.

The next report that came was that the rebs, finding that the One hundred and seventy-sixth New York, with a section of my battery, were holding the bridge at Thibodeaux, had changed their course, and were advancing on the other side of the Bayou La Fourche.

At this juncture I received orders to take my caissons off the field and to load them up. Not knowing whether this meant an advance or a retreat, I went to one of the colonel's aides, and told him that it was necessary for me to know, in order to determine what to take with me. I was told to take everything. Colonel Cahill had telegraphed for cars, and they were hourly expected, and should have been all at the depot at 6 p. m. Matters began to look ominous. There was one locomotive here, but the colonel sent that off a distance of about 5 miles with a company of the Twenty-third Connecticut to guard the railroad track; that, with the other trains failing to arrive, created a perfect panic.

At 8 p. m. no trains arrived. The telegraph is in full operation. Major Morgan, of the One hundred and seventy-sixth New York, is ordered to burn the Thibodeaux Bridge, and to retreat to La Fourche Crossing. General Emory orders that if we do not have time to get everything off, to destroy rather than leave it.

I had crossed my caissons, forge, and battery wagons, and about 15 of my horses. Colonel Cahill ordered all of my horses that were not loaded up, to retreat to Raceland Station, via the Bayou road. The panic increased; the colonel was anxious for my battery. I told him I could manage that well enough, because, if we were too hard pressed, I could retreat to Raceland Station. He ordered me to retreat at once. I ordered out of the field my two pieces, my own horses being loaded in the cars. I occupied a seat on one of the limber chests, and proceeded with the pieces to the station, where I arrived about two hours before Colonel Cahill, who, it seems, had set out on foot at the time I left, leaving his aides to manage the retreat. Up to this time not a soul of our own forces had seen or heard of an enemy. On our arrival at the station, I found that all the trains had gone forward to La Fourche Crossing, which, by the railroad, is 9½ miles distant and 12 by the Bayou road. At 7 a. m. of the 25th, the trains began to arrive with the soldiers, stores, and baggage from the Crossing. At the time I left, the railroad bridge had been fired and had just commenced to burn. Up to the time the trains left, no enemy had been seen. What I deplore more than all else is the destruction of the brass pieces; the 18-pounder and the 12-pounder howitzers were spiked and thrown into the bayou, and the 6-pounder had its trunnions knocked off, and was spiked and its carriage burned.

At about 10 p. m. of the 24th, the colonel's aides seemed to be possessed with the besom of destruction. My horses that were in the cars were turned out loose, and my harness and saddles were thrown promiscuously on the platform, and every infantry officer was making a grab for a saddle and a horse. I had, fortunately, left force enough to look after my property, who made a timely discovery enough to take care of it before it was lost. My private horses had been appropriated, and it was with difficulty that my sergeant could make the possessors give them up. The horses were gathered up, harnessed and saddled, and sent by the Bayou road to the station. Before Major Morgan fell back from Thibodeaux, Lieutenant Southworth sent up to the depot one of his pieces and his two caissons; as soon as they arrived, the colonel's aides ordered all the ammunition in the chests to be thrown into the bayou, amounting to 350 rounds, and personally carried out the order, and then ordered the piece, with the two caissons in that condition, to proceed by the Bayou road to the station, without a round of ammunition to defend itself.

My battery was ordered to this place, where I have been ever since; my horses stand hitched to their pieces; the men sleep by them every night. I inclose you a rough draught of the field of action.*

I find that it is quite a detriment to have fine battery horses. I have to exercise the utmost vigilance to keep them from being stolen. The whole brigade seem to be of the opinion that I can furnish all of the officers with saddle-horses and saddles. I am even ordered to furnish adjutants and officers of the day with horses to ride. It has become a source of annoyance to me; perhaps it is all right.

If I venture my own views, general, with reference to our "retreat,"

---

* Not found.

I trust you will not consider it amiss or an act of insubordination, as I should express it to no one else.

In the first place, there was no necessity of a retreat, because we were strong enough to hold our position.

In the second place, if the reports were true with respect to the advance of the enemy, my battery should have been retained until the last, as a matter of safety. The situation of the depot was such that my battery could have defended it against all the force that the rebels could bring to bear against it, and all the guns and stores could have been loaded up and sent off; when my battery, and the cavalry as an escort, could have retreated on the Bayou road to the station.

Two thousand men, with one battery, can march back to La Fourche Crossing and never fight a battle, and, with the aid of a good gunboat, retake Brashear City. I am satisfied that the enemy are not 2,000 strong.

I have not written this in a spirit of criticism, for I do not feel that I am competent to do that. But, general, you will always find the Twenty-fifth Battery prompt to do its duty, and ever rendering a good account of itself, while I am in command.

I am, general, your most obedient servant,

JOHN A. GROW,
Captain, Comdg. Twenty-fifth Battery New York Vols.

Brig. Gen. RICHARD ARNOLD,
Chief of Artillery.

No. 5.

Report of Lieut. Col. Richard Fitz Gibbons, Ninth Connecticut Infantry, of skirmish at Chacahoula Station.

NEW ORLEANS, LA.,
June 27, 1863.

GENERAL: I have the honor to submit the following report of the movements of Companies C, E, G, I, and K, of the Ninth Regiment of Connecticut Volunteers, ordered to guard a train while repairing the track on the New Orleans, Opelousas and Great Western Railroad:

Left La Fourche Crossing at 8 a. m. on the 24th June, 1863. Arrived at Terre Bonne Station, distance, 4 miles ; detached Company I, Capt. Elliot M. Curtis commanding, to watch the cross-roads leading into the place; repaired the track 1 mile beyond the last-named station; then proceeded toward Chacahoula Station; arrived at a point within 1 mile of the station, where we found a bridge burning; commenced rebuilding this bridge. Between this bridge and the station was a very heavy swamp, both sides of the track, thickly wooded.

I immediately sent out Captain Wright, Company G, to skirmish up toward the station, together with Lieutenant Payne, Company C, Lieutenant McKeon, Company E, and Lieutenant Fitz Gibbons, with a sufficient force to support him. On arriving within sight of the station, a very sharp fire was opened upon our forces, which was briskly returned. I then ordered up Company C, Capt. John G. Healy, and also Company E, Capt. Terrance Sheridan ; Company K, Capt. Thomas Healy, and part of Company G, was kept in reserve. My forces being obliged to confine their operations to the railroad track, the enemy being posted in considerable force in an open country in front, under cover of some small buildings and fences, I considered it prudent to return after engaging him one hour ; I also heard the gun fired from La Fourche Crossing as a signal to return.

Sergt. Peter Donnelly and Private Charles Reynolds, of Company C, were taken prisoners of war, and on the 26th of June, 1863, were paroled at La Fourche Crossing, La. Our loss was 3 wounded.

*   *   *   *   *   *   *

We arrived at Raceland at daylight next morning, where we halted until the afternoon of the 25th instant, when we were ordered to take a train of cars for Algiers, and the same night reached Lafayette Square, our former quarters, where we now are.

I am, general, very respectfully, your obedient servant,
RICHARD FITZ GIBBONS,
Lieut. Col., Comdg. Ninth Regiment Connecticut Volunteers.

HORACE J. MORSE,
Adjutant-General, State of Connecticut.

No. 6.

Reports of Maj. Henry M. Porter, Seventh Vermont Infantry, of attack on Donaldsonville.

DONALDSONVILLE,
June 28, 1863.

GENERAL : The enemy attacked us at 1.30 o'clock this morning, and fought until daylight. We expect another attack, and need 400 or 500 more men very much. We have taken 120 prisoners, some of them officers. One colonel, 1 major, and 1 lieutenant were known to be killed. Our loss, 5 or 6 killed and a few wounded.

Princess Royal, Kineo, and Winona are here. I think we can hold the place, but we need more men. Our troops fought splendidly.

Your obedient servant,
H. M. PORTER,
Major, and Provost-Marshal, Commanding Post.
General EMORY.

—

OFFICE OF PROVOST-MARSHAL,
Donaldsonville, July 1, 1863.

GENERAL : I take the liberty to respectfully submit to you a few facts in regard to the brilliant victory achieved by the army and navy at this place on the morning of the 28th of June.

About 4.30 p. m. of the 27th, General Green, commanding the rebel forces, sent a message, under a flag of truce, to Major [Joseph D.] Bullen, Twenty-eighth Maine Regiment, commandant of the post, requesting permission to notify the women and children within 3 miles of the fort to remove, or that Major Bullen should so notify them. Major Bullen replied that he would have the women and children removed.

I immediately sent both telegrams and couriers up and down the river for more gunboats, the Princess Royal only being here.

At 1.30 o'clock on the morning of the 28th, the enemy, about 5,000 strong, attacked both the fort and the gunboat with infantry and artillery, and continued fighting until 4.30 a. m. They fought with great desperation, but were nobly driven back by the combined efforts of the garrison and the gunboats.

The great number of rebel dead and dying revealed by the morning light, lying on the very banquette of the fort, showed very plainly how hot and warmly contested had been the fight on shore, and the many dead and wounded at a distance proved how effective had been the services of the large guns upon land and water.

There were but 180 men in the fort, and this was the first engagement for most of them. Nobly did both officers and men acquit themselves.

This was also the first engagement of the Princess Royal, commanded by Captain [M. B.] Woolsey, and with great coolness and daring did both officers and men perform their duties.

The Winona, commanded by Captain [A. W.] Weaver, came to our aid at 3.30 a. m., and gallantly did she assist in bringing to a successful issue this closely contested battle.

Our loss on shore: Killed, 1 lieutenant,* 1 sergeant, and 6 privates; wounded, 2 lieutenants, 3 sergeants, 2 corporals, and 6 privates. On the Princess Royal, 1 killed and 2 wounded.

Enemy's loss probably 350 killed and wounded; 1 colonel, 1 major, and 2 lieutenants known to be killed, and 4 lieutenants wounded. One hundred and thirty prisoners were taken; among them were 1 lieutenant-colonel, 1 major, 2 captains, and 5 lieutenants.

Hoping and believing that if the rebels attack us again they will meet with an equally warm reception, I am, sir, with great respect, your obedient servant,

H. M. PORTER,
Major, and Provost-Marshal.

Brig. Gen. W. H. EMORY,
    Commanding, New Orleans.

———

No. 7.

Report of Lieut. Charles Emerson, One hundred and seventy-fourth New York Infantry, Acting Assistant Adjutant-General, of attack on the steamboat Saint Mary's, July 8.

NEW ORLEANS,
July 8, 1863.

SIR : I have the honor to report my arrival here this morning, and the delivery of the dispatches to General Emory and Colonel Holabird. General Emory said that he wished to send a dispatch to General Banks by me, and this I am expecting. Also, for your information, I have the honor to report that the steamer Saint Mary's was fired upon by artillery at three places on her way down this a. m.

First, about 8 miles below Donaldsonville. Here by about four light pieces, say 12-pounders; the gunboats accompanied her by this battery.

Second, at College Point. Here, so far as I could judge, by only a single piece (light), but also at this point she was exposed to quite a severe fire of riflemen.

Third, at Fifty-five Mile Point. Here I should think that from four to six pieces bore upon her, mostly rifled (though all light pieces, none

---

* Lieut. Isaac Murch, Twenty-eighth Maine.

heavier than 3-inch or 12-pounder). Here she was struck five times, a conical shell and a spherical case shot bursting in her, with no damage to life or any of consequence to the ship.

Very respectfully, your most obedient servant,

C. EMERSON,
Second Lieut. 174th New York Infantry, and Actg. Asst. Adjt. Gen.

Colonel IRWIN,
Assistant Adjutant-General.

No. 8.

Report of Brig. Gen. Cuvier Grover, U. S. Army, of engagement on the La Fourche (Cox's Plantation, &c.), near Donaldsonville.

HEADQUARTERS UNITED STATES FORCES,
Donaldsonville, La., July 14, 1863.

SIR: I have the honor to report that yesterday, in the afternoon, the enemy attacked General Weitzel's advance guard, consisting of Dudley's brigade, supported by one other brigade, and drove them back nearly a mile, capturing two 6-pounder rifled pieces, with two limbers and 7 rounds of ammunition. The enemy supposed to be about 800 strong, with three or four pieces of artillery. Weitzel's loss about 120; from 30 to 40 killed.

A simultaneous attack was made upon the advance guard of my division, on the opposite side of the bayou, consisting of my First Brigade, commanded by Colonel [Joseph S.] Morgan, by a force of not over 400. Colonel Morgan fell back without cause, losing 30 or 40 pickets captured, 4 or 5 killed, and 15 or 20 wounded. Colonel Morgan behaved badly, and I shall cause an investigation into his conduct. I should have reported this last night, but I was unable to get the full particulars till it was too late.

The gunboats had not left New Orleans yesterday. The admiral promised to send the Sachem last night or this morning to Brashear City, and the Arizona as soon as she arrived from above. There ought to be more boats than that sent around. There should be four or five, at least. Six 20-pounders will be enough, I think.

Everything is quiet this morning. Enemy's loss in the affair of yesterday not known. Could not have been great.

I am, sir, very respectfully, your obedient servant,

C. GROVER,
Brigadier-General, Commanding.

Lieut. Col. RICHARD B. IRWIN,
Assistant Adjutant-General, Nineteenth Army Corps.

P. S.—Since writing the above, I have gained such other information as practicable. I think that the unnecessary and unauthorized falling back of Colonel Morgan was the cause of the loss of the two pieces on the other side of the bayou, though it is by no means certain. The enemy's loss was probably about equal to ours. An officer, under a flag of truce to collect killed and wounded, would not state their loss, but said it was less than ours.

I think more gunboats should be sent to Brashear City, and that if more cannot be sent now, the Sachem should be detained till at least four are ready to move.

ADDENDA.

Return of Casualties in the Union forces engaged on the Bayou La Fourche (Cox's Plantation), near Donaldsonville, La., July 13, 1863.

[Compiled from nominal list of casualties, returns, &c.]

Command.	Killed.		Wounded.		Captured or missing.		Aggregate.
	Officers.	Enlisted men.	Officers.	Enlisted men.	Officers.	Enlisted men.	
1st Louisiana	......	3	......	14	......	13	30
2d Louisiana	......	7	......	21	......	9	37
30th Massachusetts	......	8	2	37	......	1	48
48th Massachusetts	......	1	......	9	2	21	33
49th Massachusetts	......	1	1	6	......	14	22
90th New York	......	2	1	20	......	48	71
116th New York	1	5	....	18	......	20	44
131st New York	......	2	......	10	1	42	55
161st New York	......	7	1	38	......	7	53
174th New York	1	17	1	28	......	7	54
1st Maine Battery...................................	......	1	1	14	......	1	17
6th Massachusetts Battery........................	......	......	......	1	......	......	1
Total........................	2	54	7	216	3	183	465

OFFICERS KILLED.—Capt. David W. Tuttle, One hundred and sixteenth New York; Lieut. De Van Postley, One hundred and seventy-fourth New York.

GENERAL ORDERS, } HDQRS. DEPARTMENT OF THE GULF,
  No. 67.   }   *New Orleans, September 10, 1863.*

I. Before a general court-martial convened at New Orleans, La., pursuant to Special Orders, No. 184, current series, from these headquarters, and of which Brig. Gen. William Vandever is president, was arraigned and tried Col. Joseph S. Morgan, Ninetieth Regiment New York Volunteers.

CHARGE 1ST.—Misbehavior before the enemy.

Specification 1st.—In this, that he, Col. Joseph S. Morgan, Ninetieth Regiment New York Volunteers, while in command of the First Brigade, Fourth Division, Nineteenth Corps, in face of the enemy, having been placed in position on advance guard by his superior officer, Col. H. W. Birge, temporarily commanding the Fourth Division, and having been ordered by his said superior officer to hold that position, did, without just cause, fail to obey said order, and did shamefully abandon his post or position, thereby exposing the advance guard on the other side of the Bayou La Fourche to a destructive cross-fire from the ground he was ordered to cover.   This on the Bayou La Fourche, near Donaldsonville, La., on or about the 13th day of July, 1863.

Specification 2d.—In this, that he, Col. Joseph S. Morgan, Ninetieth Regiment New York Volunteers, while in command of the First Brigade, Fourth Division, Nineteenth Corps, in face of the enemy, when unnecessarily abandoning a position which he was ordered by his superior officer to hold, and ground he was ordered to cover, did neglect and fail to call in his skirmishers, thereby shamefully abandoning them to capture by the enemy.   This on the Bayou La Fourche, near Donaldsonville, La., on or about the 13th day of July, 1863.

CHARGE 2D.—Drunkenness on duty.

Specification.—In this, that he, Col. Joseph S. Morgan, Ninetieth Regiment New York Volunteers, while in command of the First Brigade, Fourth Division, Nineteenth Corps, in face of the enemy, did become so drunk as to be utterly unfit for duty, thereby exposing his command to disaster, and disgracing his position before his whole command. This on Bayou La Fourche, near Donaldsonville, La., on or about the 13th day of July, 1863.

To all of which charges and specifications the accused pleaded "Not guilty."

The court, after mature deliberation on the evidence adduced, finds the accused as follows:

Of the 1*st specification* of 1ST CHARGE, "Guilty," except as to the words his "superior officer," in the fifth line; also the word "his," in the seventh line; also the word "superior," in the eighth line.

Of the 2*d specification* of 1ST CHARGE, "Not guilty."

Of the 1ST CHARGE, "Guilty."

Of the *specification* of the 2D CHARGE, "Guilty."

Of the 2D CHARGE, "Guilty."

And does therefore sentence him, Col. Joseph S. Morgan, Ninetieth Regiment New York Volunteers, to be cashiered, and utterly disqualified from holding any office or employment under the Government of the United States."

*   *   *   *   *   *   *

VII. The major-general commanding disapproves of the proceedings, findings, and sentence in the case of Col. Joseph S. Morgan, Ninetieth Regiment New York Volunteers, the evidence appearing too conflicting and unsatisfactory. The execution of the sentence is suspended until the pleasure of the President can be known.

*   *   *   *   *   *

By command of Major-General Banks:

G. NORMAN LIEBER,
Acting Assistant Adjutant-General.

WAR DEPARTMENT, JUDGE-ADVOCATE-GENERAL'S OFFICE,
Washington, D. C., June 20, 1885.

Lieut. Col. R. N. SCOTT,
In Charge Publication Office War Records, 1861–'65:

COLONEL: In reply to yours of to-day, I have the honor to inform you that it appears from the proceedings in the case of Col. Joseph S. Morgan, Ninetieth New York Infantry, that the record was returned by this office to Major-General Banks, the reviewing officer, October 10, 1863, with instructions that, "as the proceedings, findings, and sentence had been disapproved, no sentence remained for the action of the President. The proceedings against the accused were therefore terminated, and he should be released."

General Banks thereupon, on October 26, 1863, ordered the accused to be released and returned to duty.

Very respectfully,

G. NORMAN LIEBER,
Acting Judge-Advocate-General.

No. 9.

Report of Col. Nathan A. M. Dudley, Thirtieth Massachusetts Infantry, commanding Brigade, of engagement on the La Fourche, near Donaldsonville.

BIVOUAC NEAR DONALDSONVILLE, LA.,
July 15, 1863.

CAPTAIN: I have the honor to submit the following report of the reconnaissance made by the Third Brigade, on the 12th and 13th instant, by order of Brigadier-General Weitzel, commanding division:

Besides my own brigade, which consisted of the Thirtieth Massachusetts Volunteers, One hundred and sixty-first and One hundred and seventy-fourth New York Volunteers, there were temporarily assigned me two sections of the Sixth Massachusetts Battery, First Lieutenant Phelps commanding, and Captain Barrett's company of cavalry.

At 3 p. m. on the 12th instant, I sent in advance, down the right side of Bayou La Fourche, a small force of cavalry, followed by four companies of infantry, under Captain Shipley, Thirtieth Massachusetts Volunteers, the balance of the force following in order by the flank, with cavalry scouts constantly out on my right.

Previous to starting, I had an interview with Colonel and Acting Brigadier-General Morgan, commanding brigade, Emory's division, who stated that he was ordered to follow down the opposite side of the bayou with his brigade. We arranged signal flags, to be used in case of necessity, before separating.

The advance skirmishers had not proceeded more than 1 mile before the enemy opened a brisk fire upon them, driving in the cavalry to the infantry support. The enemy's pickets being well supported by a dismounted force, in full view, I ordered Lieutenant Phelps to bring up one of his pieces, and, after four or five shots, they fell back, keeping up a fire from both sides of the bayou as we advanced. When about 1 mile from Kock's plantation, I halted till Colonel Morgan came up on the opposite side, when the two columns moved forward nearly abreast up to Kock's residence, when I made the following disposition of my forces: One section of Phelps' battery I placed on the road fronting down the bayou, supported on the left by two companies of infantry, on the right by the One hundred and seventy-fourth and One hundred and sixty-first New York Volunteers, the latter under Colonel Harrower and the former in command of Major Keating. These two regiments were in line of battle, the right of the One hundred and sixty-first extending down a broad lane, with a clear field in front about 100 yards wide. Three-fourths of a mile to the right I posted two companies from the One hundred and sixty-first, to prevent a surprise on that flank. With strong pickets on the roads running down the bayou, and at right angles to it, with mounted vedettes in front, I felt certain of no surprise.

The Thirtieth Massachusetts Volunteers were posted as a reserve near Kock's house, in line of battle, with the exception of two companies, which were stationed with pickets out on the flanks, at the junction of a plantation road and the Bayou road, with the remaining section of Phelps' battery. By this disposition, I had command of both roads running to the right; protection to my rear and front, with Colonel Morgan's command on the left. This was my arrangement of the force for the night of the 12th.

About 6 o'clock in the evening, the enemy opened a brisk skirmish in front, and exchanged a few shots with our artillery.

Expecting an attack at daylight on the morning of the 13th, I had my whole force under arms at 3 a. m. About 4.30 o'clock they advanced in considerable force, compelling my pickets to retire a short distance. I immediately re-enforced them, and ordered the section in rear to the front, placing it in advance of the position occupied by the One hundred and seventy-fourth New York Volunteers during the night. The section in the road was thrown forward, and placed in an angle of the levee, supported by the One hundred and seventy-fourth Regiment.

Finding that the enemy were trying to flank me on the right; that they had considerable force on the left of the bayou; that they had thrown several hundred sharpshooters into the tall cornfields immediately in front, and by their rapid firing they developed a superior force of artillery, I deemed it prudent to request of the commanding general re-enforcements, which very promptly brought up Colonel Paine's brigade, and First Maine Battery, under command of First Lieutenant Haley. Withdrawing the section of Sixth Massachusetts Battery, I replaced it by the rifles of the First Maine, transferring the former to a position alongside of the other section of the same battery to the right.

The fire from the enemy at this time had partially slackened, and I directed Lieutenant Haley to advance a second section about 300 yards to another angle in the levee. This effectually silenced the enemy's fire for over two hours and a half. Colonel Paine's infantry was up to this time held in reserve some distance in the rear.

During the forenoon, I had communications with Colonel Morgan, who assured me that one of his regiments occupied the first sugar-house on his front; that his pickets were half-way between it and another sugar-house nearly half a mile nearer the enemy's pickets.

About 1.30 p. m. the enemy commenced a rapid cannonade at several points, followed up almost instantly by a warm musketry fire from cornfields in the front, down the Bayou road, and from the left side of the bayou, from behind the levee. Lieutenant Haley nobly fought his two advanced pieces until ordered to retire, which movement he successfully executed under a cross-fire from three different points. The other section was not so fortunate; only one piece was brought off, notwithstanding every effort was made on the part of the supports to save it, as the casualties in a space of 20 yards around the piece give sufficient proof; 16 dead belonging to the Thirtieth Massachusetts and the One hundred and seventy-fourth New York Volunteers, and some 20 wounded, with 8 horses killed, were found in the evening by our flag of truce. Most gallantly did Major Keating, of the One hundred and seventy-fourth New York, and his two companies, aided by Captain Fiske, of the Thirtieth Massachusetts, and his company, vainly strive to retrieve this gun.

The fire that caused this sacrifice came principally from the south side of the bayou, and nearly opposite the battery, where it was expected our own troops were stationed. At this crisis, I moved Colonel Harrower's regiment, the One hundred and sixty-first New York Volunteers, to the front, in order to cover the withdrawal of the three pieces of the Sixth Massachusetts Battery, which I ordered to be taken to the rear by detail. This regiment I specially watched, as it covered my rear in falling back to take up a new position, which I had decided to do. I would like to refer specially to the cool and determined manner in which this regiment, under its brave colonel, retraced its steps, but where all behaved so admirably, I cannot for fear of injustice particularize.

Previous to making these preparations to fall back on a line just in rear of Kock's plantation, where I felt certain I could hold my position against any force the enemy had, I directed Colonel Paine to place his whole brigade in line of battle on the Plantation road, which runs at right angles with the bayou at this point, with instructions to hold this line while the force in front fell back and formed in his rear. These dispositions were all made before a single regiment or company excepting those belonging to the pickets moved to the rear.

This was the state of affairs when the general commanding the division arrived on the field and ordered the whole force to gradually fall back on this point, which order was executed without any panic or excitement on the part of the troops that were under my observation.

Had I had any means of protecting my left flank, I feel confident that our loss would have been very much less, and the service would not have to mourn the loss of so many of its gallant soldiers. Among this number was Second Lieut. De Van Postley, One hundred and seventy-fourth New York Volunteers, who was killed while endeavoring, with Lieutenant Haley, Captains Shipley, Fiske, and Lieutenant Barker, of the Thirtieth Massachusetts, with Captain Van Denbergh, of the One hundred and seventy-fourth New York and others, to save one of the First Maine Battery pieces.

I am unable to account for the loss of the Napoleon gun belonging to the Sixth Massachusetts Battery. It was reported disabled early in the morning, and I directed it to be sent to the rear for repairs. It was taken 1 mile to the rear of our advance, nearly remounted, and, notwithstanding the artificers had fully one hour to withdraw it, they failed to do so.

Captain Barrett, of the Louisiana Cavalry, with his company, was efficient and prompt in giving me information constantly of the change of position of the rebels.

Captains Speed and Whittier, with Lieutenants Dean and Loring, of my staff, each rendered most valuable service during the day in the transmittal of orders and obtaining information of the movements of the enemy.

I have made this report more full than may seem necessary, but I was anxious, under the circumstances, that the general commanding might know the exact disposition made of the forces assigned to my command.

I am, sir, respectfully, your obedient servant,

N. A. M. DUDLEY,
Colonel, and Acting Brigadier-General, Commanding Brigade, &c.

Capt. W. W. CARRUTH,
Assistant Adjutant-General.

No. 10.

Reports of Maj. Gen. Richard Taylor, C. S. Army, commanding District of Western Louisiana, of operations June 23–July 13.

HEADQUARTERS DEPARTMENT TRANS-MISSISSIPPI,
Shreveport, La., June 29, 1863.

GENERAL: I have the honor to inclose herewith Major-General Taylor's report of his operations in Lower Louisiana. It having been found impracticable to do anything toward the relief of Port Hudson by operations opposite, General Taylor has, pursuant to the plan of operations, made a demonstration east of the La Fourche and on the Lower Mississippi, with the hopes that his operations may induce or compel General Banks to raise the siege of Port Hudson.

I remain, general, very respectfully, your obedient servant,

E. KIRBY SMITH,
Lieutenant-General, Commanding.

General S. COOPER,
Adjutant and Inspector General, C. S. Army, Richmond, Va.

[Indorsement.]

EXECUTIVE DEPARTMENT, C. S. A.,
Richmond, Va., July 21, 1863.

Captain [R. G. H.] KEAN:

Please submit this letter at once to the honorable Secretary. The President requests his immediate attention. As the messenger to General E. K. Smith leaves this afternoon, any action to be taken at the War Department must be prompt.

Very respectfully,

BURTON N. HARRISON,
Private Secretary.

—

HEADQUARTERS DISTRICT OF WESTERN LOUISIANA,
Brashear City, June 23, 1863.

GENERAL: I have the honor to inform you that we stormed the position of the enemy this morning. We crossed Berwick Bay in skiffs, stormed the forts, drove off the enemy's gunboats, and captured over 1,000 prisoners, ten heavy guns (among them the siege piece I was forced to abandon in my retreat in April), two trains of cars, with engines complete, large numbers of small-arms, ordnance, &c., and thousands of dollars in stores.

I received a dispatch from Colonel [J. P.] Major last evening. He had reached Thibodeaux on the 21st, having carried all before him. I determined to act at once to secure co-operation with him. Our loss is small, as the forts were stormed with the bayonet, the men being forbidden to load. I am using every exertion to forward on the troops to form a junction with Major.

Respectfully, your obedient servant,

R. TAYLOR,
Major-General.

Brigadier-General [W. R.] BOGGS, *Chief of Staff.*

—

HEADQUARTERS DISTRICT OF WESTERN LOUISIANA,
Brashear, June 24, 1863.

GENERAL: This morning at dawn we formed a junction with Colonel Major at the Bœuf, 7 miles from this, capturing all between us. Colonel Major lost 31 killed and 18 wounded. He captured 500 prisoners, 2,000 negroes, 1,000 horses and mules, burned three large sea steamers in the Mississippi, and took four fine heavy guns. He has distinguished himself above praise, and I desire him to receive his promotion. He has most richly earned it.

The quantity of quartermaster's and commissary and ordnance stores captured at this place exceeds belief. I have taken steps to secure everything, and shall transfer all surplus by the Teche to New Iberia. The enemy have fortified this bay so well that I trust a few days will make it secure to us. I push on to the La Fourche this evening.

Respectfully, your obedient servant,

R. TAYLOR,
Major-General.

Brigadier-General BOGGS,
Chief of Staff.

—

HEADQUARTERS DISTRICT OF WESTERN LOUISIANA,
Alexandria, June 27, 1863.

GENERAL: I left Brashear City late on Wednesday night (24th instant), having made all the dispositions which were practicable, and arrived here a few hours ago. The receipt of the communication from General [C. Le Doux] Elgee, volunteer aide-de-camp of my staff (a copy of which was forwarded to you), conveying the views and messages from General Johnston, induced me to hasten to this point, for the purpose of making such arrangements as are called for by the information contained in that communication.

I have also received a report from Major-General [J. G.] Walker, in which he states that the unhealthiness of the locality in which his division has been operating has produced much sickness among his troops, which is daily increasing, and the effective men of the command are greatly reduced in number. Should the fall of Vicksburg occur, as predicted by General Johnston, Port Hudson must, of course, speedily follow, and thus a junction between the troops in the Washita and Upper Mississippi Valleys and those in the La Fourche would be attended with great difficulty. It is true that the fall of those places might endanger the command in the La Fourche, but deeming it of great importance that the forces in my command should be concentrated, and believing that results of great interest can be accomplished by such concentration, I have ordered Major-General Walker's division to proceed immediately to Berwick Bay; thence I shall send it into the La Fourche country..

Before the lieutenant-general commanding called my attention to the views of the War Department, and communicated his own relative to operating upon the enemy's line of communication above Vicksburg, I had determined upon the same plan. The reasons herein stated have, of course, rendered the change of the disposition of troops necessary. I feel confident that if Vicksburg should not fall shortly, the operations of our forces on the Mississippi coast between Baton Rouge and New Orleans will relieve Port Hudson. I had hoped that the communication from General Johnston, through General Elgee, would have induced the lieutenant-general commanding to visit this point, as a personal interview would be of great importance. I shall leave on to-morrow for Berwick Bay.

The property captured is much greater in quantity and value than I at first reported. Over 5,000 new Enfield and Burnside rifles were taken, with a very large supply of ammunition therefor. Several 30-pounder Parrott guns, on siege carriages, were captured among the heavy pieces. The supply of ammunition for field pieces which was captured is not large, and I would respectfully inform you that a much larger supply is needed than is now on hand. The value of commissary and quartermaster's stores (including shoes and clothing) exceeds in value, at cost prices, $2,000,000, as estimated by the quartermasters and commissaries whom I placed in charge of them. With the small-arms alluded to, if the lieutenant-general commanding deems the two regiments of [J. W.] Speight's brigade, which were detained in Shreveport, in fit condition to be put in the field, I could arm them with these rifles and equip them completely. I would particularly like to have [A. M.] Alexander's regiment put in the field with Colonel Speight.

I shall not accumulate stores at this point, but shall make the line from Vermillionville to Niblett's Bluff the base of operations in the lower portion of the State, so that if disasters at Vicksburg and Port Hudson should occur, I could retreat along that line into Texas.

I would respectfully suggest that fortifications should be constructed at some eligible point a short distance below Shreveport, on Red River.

Very respectfully, your obedient servant,

R. TAYLOR,
Major-General, Commanding.

Brig. Gen. W. R. BOGGS,
Chief of Staff.

—

HEADQUARTERS DEPARTMENT OF THE TRANS-MISSISSIPPI,
Shreveport, La., July 16, 1863.

GENERAL: I have the honor to transmit herewith a report made by Major-General Taylor of his recent operations. Upon the receipt of this report, I wrote to General Taylor (on the 12th instant)* as follows:

*   *   *   *   *   *   *

The fall of Vicksburg, which now seems to be a certainty, has important bearing on your movements. Could we retain possession of the Mississippi, the occupation of New Orleans should be hazarded at all risks. The loss of Vicksburg entails the loss of Port Hudson and the Mississippi. Any occupation of New Orleans can now only be temporary. You inflict a severe blow upon the enemy by destroying the stores collected there, but to throw yourself into the city in the hopes of holding it would be placing your command in a *cul-de-sac*, from which there could be no extrication. I yesterday inclosed you a copy of instructions to General [J. G.] Walker. I do not think any serious occupation of Louisiana will be attempted by the enemy this summer. Monroe and Alexandria may be the objective points of their campaign; still, you should endeavor to make such disposition of your command as will defend the upper valley of Red River; its occupation in force by the enemy loses us its supplies, and endangers the wheat-growing region of Texas. It cuts the department in two, and renders the concentration of the troops from Arkansas difficult, if not impracticable.

*   *   *   *   *   *   *

With much respect, I am, general, your most obedient servant,

E. KIRBY SMITH,
Lieutenant-General.

General S. COOPER,
Adjutant and Inspector General, C. S. Army.

[Inclosure.]

HEADQUARTERS DISTRICT OF WESTERN. LOUISIANA,
Brashear, July 4, 1863.

GENERAL: I have the honor to report my arrival at this point from the front, having returned for the day to inspect the progress of our defenses. Two heavy guns have been placed in position in each of the forts commanding the entrances into the bay. An additional gun at each fort will be in readiness to-night. These forts are Berwick and Chêne, constructed by Maj. Gen. M. L. Smith, and abandoned after

---

*See Smith to Taylor. July 12, 1863, Part II, p. 109.

the fall of New Orleans. I purpose making the place as, strong as the means at my disposal will permit, as the bay is the key to this whole section. The railroad has been repaired, and the first train passed to Thibodeaux to-day. The telegraph will soon be in operation from Bayou des Allemands to New Iberia, and I hope to find wire to extend the line to Alexandria. The events since my last report are as follows:

On the 24th ultimo, we drove the enemy from Raceland Station so rapidly-that he abandoned four field pieces, one of them being the 12-pounder gun left disabled at Bisland on April 13 last.

On the 28th, the advance on the railroad reached Bayou des Alle-mands, where the enemy abandoned another field piece.

On the 1st instant, we held Boutte Station, 20 miles from New Or-leans. I am now pushing for the Barataria Canal, behind which the enemy have been routed. Defensive works were erected along this canal before the fall of New Orleans, and I shall make a close recon-naissance in person before I attack in front. A boat expedition through Lake Washa can turn these works, and I shall probably adopt this route if I decide to strike at the city. Brigadier-General Green, with his own and [James P.] Major's brigades, pushed up the La Fourche to-ward Donaldsonville, the vicinity of which point they reached on the 26th ultimo. General Green dispatched thence to General Mouton, at Thibodeaux, that an examination of the enemy's fort induced him to withhold an attack, as he could plant his guns on the river below Don-aldsonville, to interrupt the enemy's transports. He represented the fort in the angle between the river and bayou mounting five guns, manned by 300 or 400 men, surrounded by a 16-foot ditch, with stock-ades running to the bayou and river. Five gunboats lying near. Gen-eral Mouton approved of General Green's course in declining to attack, as appears from his indorsement on the report. This reached me *en route* from Franklin. On arriving here, however, I learned Green had made the attack on the morning of the 28th, and been repulsed with severe loss. At Thibodeaux, General Mouton informed me our loss had been 276 officers and men. In the absence of official report from Gen-eral Green, General Mouton cannot account for the change of purpose shown in attacking.

Our men seem to have acted with the most heroic daring. They stormed the work, overthrew the garrison, and captured the guns, when the fleet in the river opened on both parties and forced us to retire, with the above very heavy loss. In forwarding the report of General Green I will show all the facts, more especially as I will be near the scene to-morrow.

Meanwhile a column has been pushed down the river below Saint Charles Court-House, some 20 miles from New Orleans, finding no enemy. Colonel Major is on the river, 10 miles from Donaldsonville, with six rifled guns, and expects to prevent transports, at least, from passing. One of my scouts has returned from the city with journals up to the 1st. The city is greatly excited. Enemy have worked night and day to remove negroes and stores from Algiers to the other side. A steamer for New York was stopped, all her passengers put ashore, and she was sent to Pensacola to bring the garrison to New Orleans. She returned with about 600 men. I hope to hear this evening on my return to Thibodeaux more news from the city. I may succeed in establishing important relations there, so as to justify a *coup*. A party has been sent over the river to cut the telegraph from Baton Rouge and gather intelligence. Another party for the same purpose has been sent to Plaquemine, on this side. Banks' army is undoubtedly much reduced by casualties and sickness, and, I have no doubt, disheartened. As rapidly as space can be overcome, everything is pressed to the front. The necessity of garrisoning the bay and holding the line from it to Donaldsonville (80 miles), as well as the railroad and the cut-offs leading from the La Fourche to the river above and below, consumes much of my little army.

I have so far succeeded in my purposes. The enemy have been driven from the La Fourche region, with the exception of the ground on which the fort at Donaldsonville stands. Berwick Bay, the key to the Attakapas, is in our hands, and we have a powerful artillery on the river between Banks and his base—New Orleans. We have paroled over 2,000 non-commissioned officers and privates, and recaptured most of the stolen property carried off in the late raid. If any opportunity, however slight, offers, I will throw myself into New Orleans, and make every effort to hold it, leaving my communications to take care of themselves. I trust the lieutenant-general commanding will not feel disappointed at these results. At all events, I have used every exertion to relieve Port Hudson, and shall continue to the last.

The copy of a communication from General Johnston to the lieutenant-general commanding, of the 26th ultimo, forwarded by Lieutenant and Aide-de-Camp [E.] Cunningham, reached me this morning. I feel pained at the contents. The first communication of General Johnston, of which I received a copy, stated that he had a force with which he hoped to relieve Vicksburg, but that he could not separate his troops to relieve Port Hudson, and desired the attention of the lieutenant-general commanding to the latter point. The next communication from General Johnston was through one of my staff, General [C. Le Doux] Elgee, a copy of which was sent to department headquarters. General Johnston had no suggestions to make, but seemed to approve the instructions I had left for the guidance of the troops opposite Vicksburg. In the late communication a tone of complaint seems to prevail that nothing has been accomplished on this side of the river. The troops opposite Vicksburg never numbered 4,000 effective, although 8,000 is assumed to be the number in this communication. It is to be presumed that the difficulty of communication prevents us from hearing what efforts the army under General Johnston has made to relieve Vicksburg. As this army is some 25,000 or 30,000 strong, and has no Mississippi River to cross, I certainly accord most heartily with the suggestion that the lieutenant-general in person should take the field. In the present critical state of the campaign, his presence would be of great utility.

I beg leave to add, with great respect, that if all the forces in Arkansas were thrown upon Helena, and firmly established there, with adequate artillery, more could be done to relieve Vicksburg than by any other move on this side of the river.

Respectfully, your obedient servant,

R. TAYLOR,
Major-General, Commanding.

Brigadier-General BOGGS,
Chief of Staff.

—

HEADQUARTERS DISTRICT OF WESTERN LOUISIANA,
La Fourche, July 13, 1863.

GENERAL: I have the honor to announce a brilliant success gained by a portion of my forces, under the command of Brigadier-General [Thomas] Green, over [Generals Godfrey] Weitzel and [William] Dwight.

The enemy, over 4,000 strong, advanced to-day 6 miles from Donaldsonville, where he was met by General Green, with his own and a part of [James P.] Major's brigade (in all 1,200 men), and driven from the field, with a loss of 500 in killed and wounded, some 300 prisoners, three pieces of artillery, many small-arms, and the flag of a New York regiment. The gallant and noble Green, dismounting from his horse, placed himself at the head of his old regiment, captured the enemy's guns, and drove his forces into the fort and under the guns of the fleet. In the generalship and daring of the commander, and in the devotion of the troops, this action will compare favorably with any I have witnessed during the war.

Respectfully, your obedient servant,

R. TAYLOR,
Major-General.

Brig. Gen. W. R. Boggs,
  •   *Chief of Staff.*

No. 11.

Report of Brig. Gen. Alfred Mouton, C. S. Army, of operations June 22–July 4.

HEADQUARTERS FORCES SOUTH OF RED RIVER,
Thibodeaux, La., July 4, 1863.

MAJOR : In obedience to instructions from Maj. Gen. R. Taylor, commanding District of Western Louisiana, on June 22, after surmounting difficulties amounting to almost impossibilities, I succeeded in collecting some thirty-seven skiffs and other row-boats near the mouth of the Teche, with a view to co-operate from the west side of the Atchafalaya with Colonel Major's command, then on the La Fourche. An expedition, numbering 325 gallant volunteers from the different regiments under my command, under the gallant Maj. Sherod Hunter, of [George W.] Baylor's regiment, started at 6 p. m. to turn the enemy's stronghold at Brashear City. General Thomas Green, with the Fifth Texas Mounted Volunteers, the Second Louisiana Cavalry, [E.] Waller's Texas Battalion, and the Valverde and [W. H.] Nichols' batteries, advanced under cover of night to opposite the enemy's camp. The Seventh Texas, Lieutenant-Colonel [P. T.] Herbert commanding ; the Fourth Texas, Lieutenant-Colonel [G. J.] Hampton, and Baylor's regiment were thrown across the Atchafalaya to Gibbon's Island during the night. General Green was to attract the enemy's attention and fire, while the troops on Gibbon's Island were to be thrown across to the support of Major Hunter as soon as the boats returned from the latter's landing point, in rear of the enemy's position.

Everything remained quiet, and the enemy were aware of our purpose only when awakened by the shots from the Valverde Battery. The enemy's whole attention was drawn to General Green's position, the land batteries concentrating their fire upon him, while their gunboats shamefully retreated in the beginning of the action.

At about 6.30 a. m. of the 23d, the shouts from Hunter's party were heard in the rear of the railroad depot. Our gallant men charged the enemy's guns one after the other, and, when they arrived near the main fort (Buchanan), the garrison surrendered without a struggle. The enemy surrendered a force of over 1,200 men, strongly posted and intrenched, and eleven heavy guns (all protected by a gunboat), to a force of 320 men.

Our loss was 2 killed and 18 wounded.

The amount of quartermaster's, commissary, and ordnance stores is very large. Our troops crossed the bay as rapidly as possible, but were delayed on account of want of transportation. Nothing larger than skiffs could be had.

As rapidly as possible, General Green was ordered to the Bayous Ramos and Bœuf, to capture those of the enemy who had escaped, and also prevent them from burning the bridges, locomotives, and cars. Unfortunately they had already destroyed the railroad and wagon bridge over the Ramos and had retired to the Bœuf.

Our troops pushed on, and at daylight of the 24th the enemy surrendered to a scouting party under the command of General Green's daring scout [Leander] McAnelly. The force consisted of 435 officers and men, three siege guns, and a 12-pounder gun. At this point General Green's and Colonel Major's commands connected. Their troops were pushed forward to Thibodeaux and La Fourche Railroad crossing, capturing 25 Federal sick and wounded and four pieces of light artillery.

On the 27th, the troops marched to Donaldsonville.

On the 28th, at 1 a. m., the fort (Butler) was attacked, and at daylight, after the most desperate struggle, we were repulsed with 260 casualties.

Too much cannot be said of the gallantry and devotion of the brave men who stormed this stronghold.

Colonel [Joseph] Phillips, Lieutenant-Colonel [D. W.] Shannon, and Major [Alonzo] Ridley are among the missing. They fell in a desperate hand-to-hand fight, but I hope they are only wounded.

As one of the main objects of this campaign was to take possession of the Mississippi, I immediately threw, by roads passing through plantations, troops on the river bank.

I have the honor to report that on the 3d instant the Federal transport Iberville was badly crippled by Colonel [W. P.] Hardeman's regiment and the rifled section of [O. J.] Semmes' battery.

To-day one section attacked the flag-ship Monongahela. The work is going on bravely.

While General Green and Colonel Major were marching upon Donaldsonville, Major [H. H.] Boone, with Waller's battalion and [C. L.] Pyron's regiment, pushed on to Raceland, and thence to the Des Allemands, at which latter place the enemy had abandoned a piece of artillery and burned the railroad bridge. Major Boone, with his usual energy, swam some of his horses, and pushed on, driving the enemy from Boutte Station; but his force being small, he had to return to the Des Allemands.

This, major, covers the whole field of operations on the west side of the bay. The other part of the operations, under the accomplished and gallant soldier, Colonel Major, will be found in his inclosed report.

The conduct of General Green, Colonel Major, Major Hunter, and the officers and men under them, is beyond all praise, and deserves the thanks of the country.

I beg leave to tender my thanks to the officers of my staff for their energy and faithful performance of the arduous duties imposed upon them: Maj. Louis Bush, assistant adjutant-general; Lieut. A. J. Watt, aide-de-camp; Capt. A. Schreiber, ordnance officer; Maj. R. W. Sanders, assistant quartermaster, and Capt. M. T. Squires, chief of artillery, who were with me all the time.

I will again in this report particularly mention Private Alfred Fusilier, to whose indomitable energy and devotion to duty I owe mostly the successful collecting of boats for Major Hunter's expedition.

Accompanying this report please find those of General Green, Colonel Major, and Major Hunter.

I am, major, very respectfully, your obedient servant,

ALFR. MOUTON,
Brigadier-General, Commanding.

Maj. E. Surget,
Assistant Adjutant-General, District of Western Louisiana.

[Indorsement.]

HEADQUARTERS DISTRICT OF WESTERN LOUISIANA,
Thibodeaux, July 6, 1863.

The zeal, energy, and ardor manifested by Brigadier-General Mouton, commanding forces south Red River, merit the highest praise.

The conduct of Brigadier-General Green fully justified the high expectations which I had formed, based upon the previous services of this officer in the field under my own observation.

R. TAYLOR,
Major-General, Commanding.

No. 12.

Report of Col. James P. Major, C. S. Army, commanding Cavalry Brigade, of operations June 10–24.

HEADQUARTERS SECOND CAVALRY BRIGADE,
Near Napoleonville, June 30, 1863.

MAJOR: I have the honor to submit the following report of the operations of my brigade since June 10:

Pursuant to orders received from your headquarters, dated 8th instant, I left Washington on the 10th, and arrived at Morgan's Ferry, on the Atchafalaya, on the 11th. I was detained there one day in making preparations to cross the river, the entire command, owing to conflicting orders, not arriving until 14th, and on the 15th I moved for Hermitage; arrived within 5 miles the same night; found the bridge burned across Bayou Sara; halted until daylight; then moved on Waterloo, 4 miles above Hermitage. The enemy were re-enforced from Banks' army at Port Hudson. I made demonstrations of an attack during the day. At night drove in the enemy's pickets, and under cover of darkness withdrew my force, leaving a strong picket force in the rear, and moved for Grossetête [Bayou].

On 17th, went down Grossetête [Bayou] to Rosedale; fed horses and men. At dark started for Indian Village; arrived at 2 a. m. on 18th; crossed [Joseph] Phillips' regiment, who made a dash into Plaquemine, taking 87 prisoners, burning 3 fine steamers, 2 steam flats, 100 bales of cotton, and capturing a large quantity of commissary stores. There were no facilities for crossing Bayou Plaquemine; it took until 5 p. m. to cross entire brigade.

At 6 p. m. started down Mississippi River, and at daylight on 19th arrived at Bayou Goula. In marching down the bank of the river, three large gunboats passed the column, but did not discover us. As an attack on them would have given our locality, which I was anxious to conceal. I allowed them to pass unmolested.

At Bayou Goula took commissary and quartermaster's stores; destroyed Federal plantations; recaptured over 1,000 negroes, stolen by Banks from planters living in Saint Landry and Rapides Parishes; found them starving and in great destitution; kept the men, and left women and children. Heard that a Federal force was intrenched in strong works at Donaldsonville, and conceiving that if I took the place it would be at a great sacrifice of life, and unable to hold it against the gunboats, and believing I could operate to better advantage on the river below in cutting off Banks' supplies from New Orleans, I made a feint on the fort, and at dark sent a portion of Lane's and Phillips' regiments, under Colonel [W. P.] Lane, through the swamp direct to Thibodeaux, with instructions to take the place, possession of the railroad, and cut the telegraph wires.

At midnight I withdrew the remaining force, and moved for Thibodeaux; found that the Cut-off road had been blockaded by Federals, and pronounced entirely impracticable for artillery. Sent a party of negroes with a guard, under Lieutenant [J. A. A.] West, of [O. J.] Semmes' battery, to open it, and by 10 o'clock on the 20th passed my entire column through. I moved on to the La Fourche, striking it 6 miles below Donaldsonville. Here made another feint on the fort, and at night moved down the La Fourche. At Paincourtville received a dispatch from Colonel Lane, stating he had captured the town, taking 140 prisoners and a large amount of stores, also a small force at Terre Bonne Station, and that there was a force in strong position, with artillery, at La Fourche Crossing. I pushed on, and arrived at Thibodeaux at 3.30 a. m. on the 21st. Pickets reported re-enforcements from New Orleans during the night, and at sun-up reported the enemy advancing. I posted Pyron's regiment, West's battery, and two squadrons cavalry on the east bank La Fourche, and moved them down toward the railroad bridge. Lane, [B. W.] Stone, and Phillips were posted at Terre Bonne Station, and they were moved forward to La Fourche Crossing. The enemy fell back, and my pursuit was checked by one of the heaviest rains I ever saw fall. It rained until 5 p. m., and having only 30 rounds of ammunition to the man when I started, and not over 100 cartridge-boxes in the entire command, my ammunition was nearly all ruined, and I found myself with an enemy in front, rear, and on the flank, with only 3 rounds of ammunition to the man. I directed Pyron, as soon as it stopped raining, to strengthen his picket and feel the enemy, find his position, and test his strength, giving him some discretion in the matter. He advanced his picket, driving the enemy into his stronghold, and then charged his works, taking 4 guns, and causing a great many of the Federals to surrender. But night had come on; it was very dark, the ammunition nearly all gone, and just at that moment a train with about 300 fresh men arrived from New Orleans, and Pyron was forced to retire from a position won by a daring assault, unequaled, I think, in this war. Had I known his intention to assault the works, I could have sent him such re-enforcements as would have insured success. Pyron's strength in the attack was 206. The enemy's force, reported by themselves, was over 1,000.

The next day (22d) it rained again, and finding it impossible to dry my ammunition, and not hearing anything from our forces at Berwick Bay; knowing that I had only one avenue by which to connect with General Green's brigade, and that the enemy were intrenched on the route at Bayou Bœuf and at Brashear City; that their forces at those points were greater than mine, besides the advantage of position, and, in consequence, I would be compelled to cut my way to Berwick Bay, unless General Green cut toward me, I therefore refrained from attacking with my whole force the enemy at La Fourche Crossing, although I could certainly have demolished him, and the temptation was great to revenge the death of those gallant men who fell in Pyron's assault. I then gave the order to march on Brashear City. The movement began at nightfall. Making demonstrations of a night attack, and opening a heavy fire on their position with my artillery, I withdrew my force, and commenced marching at 9 p. m., moving all night.

I arrived at Chacahoula Station just before dawn on the 23d, and at the same instant heard with no little pleasure the cannonade at Brashear. I rested my command two hours, feeding the horses and men, and arrived at Bayou Bœuf at 4.20 p. m., having driven in the pickets of the enemy for 6 miles. I at once took possession of the east bank (the enemy being intrenched on the opposite bank), made a reconnaissance of his position, and began crossing at 2 a. m. on the 24th.

At daylight had Lane and Stone entirely surrounding the fort, while Phillips, Pyron, and the artillery were posted in front on the eastern bank. Just as I had arranged to open from my batteries, I discovered a white flag flying from a large house near the crossing, and, on sending to inquire the reason, was surprised to learn that the fort had surrendered to General Mouton, whose advance was 5 miles off on Bayou Ramos, a scouting party under General Green's intrepid scout, [Leander] McAnelly, being the only force of their command near, and to him the flags were delivered. The colonel (Federal), however, on my asking to what force he had surrendered, said to mine, supposing it to be a portion of Mouton's, who had made a previous demand for surrender, and, seeing McAnelly, had sent to him a white flag. I mention this merely to show that, although the flags were delivered to others, the surrender was in fact to my force, and the gallant General Green waived the honor of the capture to me.

The prisoners here captured were 275; four guns, ammunition, small-arms, commissary and quartermaster's stores, and about 3,000 negroes.

Too much praise cannot be awarded to the gallant band who comprise the Second Cavalry Brigade, who, without murmur, shared in the trials and hardships incident to so extended and rapid a march through country occupied by the enemy, passing many sleepless nights and fasting days, subsisting through the entire march on one ration per day, and averaging but three hours of rest in every twenty-four.

To the citizens on the route I have to acknowledge many favors, who generously furnished the infantry with transportation until I mounted them upon animals captured from the plantations cultivated by the Federal authorities.

This command, composed of infantry, artillery, and cavalry, marched 176 miles in four days, an average of 44 miles per day. It moved in an orderly manner, never depredating on private property, and bore the hardships without a murmur. It is, however, with sorrow that I have to report the death of the noble men who fell in the charge under the gallant Colonel [C. L.] Pyron, at La Fourche, and under Colonel Phillips at Plaquemine, of which casualties I will make a detailed report.

To the members of my staff, Captains [Henry F.] Wade, jr., and [H. H.] Zacharie, I am indebted for a hearty co-operation throughout the trip; also to Lieutenant [J. A. A.] West, for his efficiency in his department. The services of Captain Ratliffe, volunteer aide, were invaluable, owing to his thorough knowledge of the country and indefatigable exertions.

Volunteer Aides Major McGoffin and Captain Duzenberry also rendered me great service.

JAS. P. MAJOR,
Colonel, Commanding Second Cavalry Brigade.

Maj. LOUIS BUSH, *Assistant Adjutant-General.*

[Indorsement.]

HEADQUARTERS DISTRICT OF WESTERN LOUISIANA,
Thibodeaux, July 6, 1863.

The conduct of Colonel Major during the service herein mentioned has been above all praise. He has shown energy, industry, and capacity which render him fit for any command, and I respectfully recommend and request that his command as colonel commanding brigade may be made permanent, as I am sure the interests of the service and the country will be promoted by his promotion.

R. TAYLOR,
Major-General, Commanding.

No. 13.

Reports of Capt. T. A. Faries, Louisiana Battery, of attacks on gunboats and transports on the Mississippi River, July 7–10, and operations near Donaldsonville, July 12–13.

IN THE FIELD, ASSUMPTION PARISH, LA.,
Allemand Plantation, July 10, 1863.

SIR: I have the honor to report that the rifle section of this battery, two 3-inch Parrott guns, under First Lieut. B. F. Winchester, took position at Battery No. 1, on Gaudet's plantation, right bank of the Mississippi River, Saint James Parish, about 12 miles below Donaldsonville, where embrasures were cut through the levee (some 12 feet high) on the morning of the 7th instant, at 2 a. m.; and at 9 a. m. engaged a sloop of war, said to be the Genesee, and one gunboat convoying a small steam tug, bound up. This section fired five time-fuse shell and eight solid shot with effect, as I learned through parties from Donaldsonville subsequently that a captain, second lieutenant, and 7 men were killed or wounded.

At 3 a. m. on the morning of the 8th of July instant, the rifle section fired two solid shot and three shell at two gunboats convoying a transport going down the river, making four hits. Same day, at 5 a. m., fired seven shell (time-fuse) and ten solid shot at two gunboats, bound up, making fifteen hits. The Mississippi River at this point is about 2,000 yards wide.

On July 9, constructed platforms and cut embrasures at intervals of 100 to 150 feet for two 6-pounder bronze smooth-bore guns, two 12-pounder bronze field howitzers of this battery, and one heavy 12-pounder bronze field gun of [F. O.] Cornay's (Louisiana) battery, the last under Lieutenant [O. H.] Jones.

At 8.30 p. m., the night being dark and misty on the river, with occasional lightning, causing objects on the water to appear obscure, opened with the seven pieces on a fleet of nine vessels, composed of gunboats and transports, including the iron-clad Essex and a sloop of war; to cover the passage of transports, a gunboat was apparently lashed on each side of a transport, which last were evidently well loaded with men and material, bound down. All the vessels on the right of their column approached my position with shotted guns, as they all instantly answered my fire by a broadside from their whole line, all of which passed over us.

The two 3-inch rifles fired eight time-fuse shell and six solid shot. The heavy firing from this fleet of vessels (many of them armed with 8, 11, and 15 inch guns) prevented the effect of the shots from the rifle section being accurately observed. Most of them, however, were hits.

The 12-pounder field gun, under Lieutenant Jones, fired six spherical case and four solid shot, making seven hits, and, by the sound, doing considerable damage to the vessels of the enemy.

The 12-pounder howitzer section, under Second Lieut. O. Gaudet, fired eight shell, five of which took effect.

The section of 6-pounder bronze smooth-bore guns, under Lieut. S. R. Garrett, fired fourteen solid shot, making fourteen hits.

On the morning of July 10, at 1.30 a. m., the seven guns at Battery No. 1 opened on the U. S. gunboat New London, bound down.

The rifle section under First Lieut. B. F. Winchester fired ten shell and fourteen solid shot, he having run his guns out over the levee on to the *batture*, enabling the cannoneers to fire more rapidly and longer at the same object. Most of these shot struck this vessel, one of them cutting her steam pipe or cylinder, when a rocket was sent up from her, which proved to be a signal for assistance.

Lieutenant Jones' 12-pounder field gun fired three spherical case and two solid shot, making two hits.

The 12-pounder howitzer section under Lieut. O. Gaudet fired one shell, which took effect.

The 6-pounder section, under Lieut. S. R. Garrett, fired two solid shot, one of which struck her.

The cavalry pickets above had neglected to notify me of her approach. The sky was so overcast with clouds it was difficult to make out floating objects. The new moon, which had been obscured most of the night, shed a feeble light, when, about the time stated, the cannoneers who were on guard at the pieces reported this vessel almost abreast of my position. This will account for so few shots being fired by the five smooth-bore pieces, all of which were posted above the rifle section.

The New London proved to be a bark-rigged vessel, carrying a heavy rifled gun amidships and two 20-pounder Parrott rifles, one on her bow and the other in her stern. She replied but feebly to our guns. It was subsequently ascertained that she was acting as a dispatch boat for the army, carrying important information from Vicksburg or Port Hudson to New Orleans. As soon as she was disabled, one or more boats were lowered, and she was towed or drifted into the left bank of the river, nearly 2 miles below this battery. At this time, information was received by Lieutenant-Colonel [Isham] Chisum, commanding the scouts, and my only support, several companies of B. W. Stone's Texas Cavalry, that the enemy was landing a force just above my position (which proved to be false). I was ordered to retire to the heavy timbered woods, over 4 miles in my rear, and back of the cane fields on the river, where the Cut-off or Vacherie road entered the swamp. While the teams were being fed in this road, I received orders to return to my position at Battery No. 1. But for this false report of the enemy on my flank, which occasioned the loss of over five hours of most valuable time, I am satisfied this vessel could have been destroyed and lost to the enemy.

At 9.30 a. m. the seven guns were again in position at the levee. The New London was seen tied up to the bank, at Godberry's plantation, on the opposite bank, some distance below Battery No. 1. I immediately ordered embrasures to be cut for the two rifled pieces and the heavy 12-pounder bearing directly on her broadside. Before half of this work could be done, the Genesee sloop of war and iron-clad Essex appeared, coming from below. The Genesee covered the New London with her larger hull, and she was soon after lashed to her for the purpose of towing away. Meanwhile the Essex, to cover these preparations, approached my position, and, when nearly opposite, opened on us with 11 and 15 inch guns, firing slowly, either to draw my fire, or because it was so-evident her heavy projectiles had very little effect on a 12-foot Mississippi River levee—the best of earthworks. The sloop and gunboats being out of range of most of my guns, I considered it useless to waste my light projectiles on the iron sides of the Essex, which may be regarded as fortunate, as I received orders soon after she commenced firing to retire in the direction of Assumption Church, on Bayou La Fourche, as speedily as possible, as our flank was now really threatened by a strong force on the River road, coming from Donaldsonville (where General Weitzel had arrived with one or more Federal brigades from Port Hudson). Not receiving any reply to her fire, the Essex retired slowly, firing at long intervals, until she rejoined the Genesee and New London below, where the three vessels were lashed together and steamed down the river. I then limbered up, and retired to the Cut-off road leading to Assumption Church, before referred to, and reached this place, 4 miles above the church, at 4 p. m. to-day, with the six pieces of my battery, Lieutenant Jones, with his 12-pounder, having rejoined Cornay's battery, with General Mouton's infantry, below the church.

Lieutenant [Henry] Angel, commanding a section of Captain [Thomas] Gonzales' (Texas) battery, which was in position at Battery No. 1 on the 7th and 8th instant, above the rifle section, after the firing on the 8th of July, in which it participated, was withdrawn, and ordered to report to Brig. Gen. T. Green, commanding Texas Cavalry Brigade, on the left or west bank of Bayou La Fourche. I received no report of the shots fired by this section. I have no casualties to report.

I am, very respectfully, your obedient servant,

T. A. FARIES,
Captain, Commanding Battery.

Capt. H. T. WADE, Jr.,
Chief of Artillery, Major's Brigade, Texas Cavalry.

IN THE FIELD, BAYOU LA FOURCHE, LA.,
Near Assumption Church, July 14, 1863.

SIR: I have the honor to report that on Sunday night, the 12th instant, the rifle section of this battery, under First Lieut. B. F. Winchester, moved forward up the Bayou road, and at 8.30 o'clock that night reached Kock's lower plantation, and reported to Colonel Lane, commanding the force of Texas cavalry in front, on the east bank of the bayou.

At 4.30 a. m. on Monday, the 13th of July instant, moved forward toward Donaldsonville, and at 5 a. m. opened with shell on the enemy's skirmishers in a grove and thicket at Wilson's, driving them out; again advanced with the cavalry, and, shelling Hewitt's sugar-house, drove the enemy from that shelter. This section was here under a very severe fire from four pieces of the enemy on the west or right bank of Bayou La Fourche. The Confederate line on that side of the bayou had not advanced as rapidly as our line on the east bank, which subjected this section and its support of dismounted cavalry to a fire on their flank from infantry and four field howitzers of the enemy, who were protected by the levee on the opposite bank. This continued until about 9 a. m., when Lieutenant Garrett, with his section of 6-pounder smooth-bore guns, took position to the right of the road, just below Kock's upper sugar-house, then occupied by the enemy's infantry. A rapid fire with solid shot and spherical case from the two 6-pounders caused them to abandon this shelter hastily. This section then returned to the Bayou road, and in front of Hewitt's plantation was fired on from the opposite bank of the bayou. Lieut. S. R. Garrett immediately returned the fire, and drove this force from the shelter of the levee on the right bank.

At 10 a. m. the left section, two 12-pounder field howitzers, under Lieut. O. Gaudet, was moved forward, relieving Lieutenant Garrett, the Bayou road being the only way of advancing, and only two pieces could occupy it at the same time in battery. The howitzers were engaged with the enemy's skirmishers on both banks of the bayou and their artillery on the left bank from 11 a. m. up to 3 p. m., firing and moving forward by hand for long distances, the road between the levee and fences making it impracticable to limber up promptly. Defective friction primers prevented the pieces of the right and left sections from firing with their accustomed rapidity. About 3.30 p. m. we passed the abandoned camp of the ——— Kentucky (Federal) Regiment. A short distance above, halted for some time, the enemy on both sides of the Bayou La Fourche having been driven to the Mississippi River, under the guns of several gunboats and Fort Butler, on the west bank of the bayou.

About 5 p. m. received orders to retire, and moved down the bayou to Assumption Church, where the guns were parked for the night.

The conduct of the officers and men of the three sections was most creditable. The rifle section fired seventy-five time-fuse shell and one solid shot. Casualties, 1 man slightly wounded. The howitzer section fired twenty-eight shell and spherical case. Casualties, 1 man slightly wounded. The center section fired fifty-three spherical case and ten solid shot. No casualties. One horse killed. Total casualties, 2 men slightly wounded.

I am, very respectfully, your obedient servant,

T. A. FARIES,
Captain, Commanding Battery.

Capt. H. F. WADE, Jr.,
Chief of Artillery, Major's Brigade, Texas Cavalry.

No. 14.

Report of Maj. Sherod Hunter, Baylor's (Texas) Cavalry, commanding Mosquito Fleet, of the capture of Brashear City.

BRASHEAR CITY, *June* 26, 1863.

GENERAL: I have the honor to report to you the result of the expedition placed under my command by your order June 20.

In obedience to your order, I embarked my command, 325 strong, on the evening of June 22, at the mouth of Bayou Teche, in forty-eight skiffs and flats, collected for that purpose. Proceeding up the Atchafalaya into Grand Lake, I halted, and muffled oars and again struck, and, after a steady pull of about eight hours, reached the shore in the rear of

Brashear City. Here, owing to the swampy nature of the country, we were delayed some time in finding a landing place; but at length succeeded, and about sunrise commenced to disembark my troops, the men wading out in water from 2 to 3 feet deep to the shore, shoving their boats into deep water as they left them. Thus cutting off all means of retreat, we could only fight and win. We were again delayed here a short time in finding a road, but succeeded at length in finding a trail that led us by a circuitous route through a palmetto swamp, some 2 miles across, through which I could only move in single file.

About 5.30 we reached open ground in the rear of and in full view of Brashear City, about 800 yards distant. I here halted the command, and, after resting a few minutes, again moved on, under cover of a skirt of timber, until within 400 yards of the enemy's position, where I formed my men in order of battle. Finding myself discovered by the enemy, I determined to charge at once, and, dividing my command into two columns, ordered the left (composed of Captains [J. P.] Clough, of [Thomas] Green's regiment [Fifth Texas Cavalry]; [W. A.] McDade, of Waller's battalion; [J. T.] Hamilton, of [L. C.] Rountree's battalion, and [J. D.] Blair, of Second Louisiana Cavalry) to charge the fort and camp below and to the left of the depot, and the right (composed of Captains [James H.] Price, [D. C.] Carrington, and [R. P.] Boyce, all of [G. W.] Baylor's Texas cavalry) to charge the fort and the sugar-house above and on the right of the depot; both columns to concentrate at the railroad buildings, at which point the enemy were posted in force and under good cover, each column having nearly the same distance to move, and would arrive simultaneously at the point of concentration. Everything being in readiness, the command was given, and the troops moved on with a yell. Being in full view, we were subjected to a heavy fire from the forts above and below, the gun at the sugar-house, and gunboats below town, but, owing to the rapidity of our movements, it had but little effect. The forts made but a feeble resistance, and each column pressed on to the point of concentration, carrying everything before them. At the depot the fighting was severe, but of short duration, the enemy surrendering the town.

My loss is 3 killed and 18 wounded; that of the enemy, 46 killed, 40 wounded, and about 1,300 prisoners. We have captured eleven 24 and 32 pounder siege guns; 2,500 stand of small-arms (Enfield and Burnside rifles), and immense quantities of quartermaster's, commissary, and ordnance stores, some 2,000 negroes, and between 200 and 300 wagons and tents.

I cannot speak too highly of the gallantry and good conduct of the officers and men under my command. All did their whole duty, and deserve alike equal credit from our country for our glorious and signal victory.

I am, sir, very respectfully, your obedient servant,

SHEROD HUNTER,
Major, Baylor's (Texas) Cavalry, Commanding Mosquito Fleet.
Brig. Gen. ALFRED MOUTON,
Commanding South Red River.

[Indorsement.]

HEADQUARTERS DISTRICT OF WESTERN LOUISIANA,
Thibodeaux, July 6, 1863.

I would respectfully call the attention of the lieutenant-general commanding to the gallantry and meritorious services of Major Hunter and the officers commanding the detachments which composed his expedition, and earnestly suggest that they may be brought to the notice of the Government.

R. TAYLOR,
Major-General, Commanding.

No. 15.

Reports of Brig. Gen. Thomas Green, C. S. Army, commanding Cavalry Brigade, of operations June 22–July 13.

HEADQUARTERS FIRST CAVALRY BRIGADE,
Near Panco, on the La Fourche, June 30, 1863.

GENERAL: Early in this month I was ordered by you to the Lower Teche, for the purpose of reconnoitering the enemy at Brashear, and to collect together and fit up light boats preparatory to making a descent upon the enemy, if practicable. While engaged in the execution of these orders, you came down and assumed command, ordering me to advance toward the bay.

On the night of the 22d instant, in accordance with orders, I moved to Cochran's sugar-house, 2 miles distant from the bay, with the Fifth Texas, Second Louisiana Cavalry, and Waller's battalion, and the Valverde and a section of Nichols' batteries, leaving our horses at that place. I advanced the troops above mentioned on foot before daylight to the village of Berwick, opposite the enemy's encampment.

At the dawn of day, finding the enemy quiet and asleep, I opened fire upon him from the Valverde Battery. The first shot exploded in the center of his encampment, causing the greatest confusion, the distance being only about 900 yards. We fired about 40 or 50 shots from our battery into the enemy before he replied to us at all. The first shot from the enemy was fired on us from his gunboat, which was at anchor in the bay a short distance below our position. After daylight the gunboat advanced toward us as if to contest with our battery the position we occupied on the water's edge, but a few well-directed shots from the Valverde Battery drove the boat 1 mile below, where she opened on us with her heavy guns. About the same time several batteries from the opposite shore opened on us. The shot of the enemy was so well directed that we found it necessary several times to shift the position of our guns and caissons. The heavy gun on shore which first opened fire on us from the principal fort above Brashear, with the garrison of that fort, was brought down nearly opposite my position, and opened fire on me. With the running of the gunboat, and drawing out this heavy gun and most of the garrison from Fort Buchanan, left the waters above free to the approach of Major [Sherod] Hunter's command in our little flotilla to Tiger Island. Major Hunter, who had moved under your orders from the mouth of the Teche during the night of the 22d on board our Mosquito Fleet, landed, unperceived and unsuspected by the enemy, above their defenses, and, making his way through the swamp, about 7 o'clock on the morning of the 23d attacked the enemy in his rear while I was occupying him in front, completely surprising and routing him.

The enemy surrendered their defenses and the town of Brashear to Major Hunter about 7.30 o'clock on the morning of the 23d. Major Hunter's command consisted of about 300 men from Baylor's, the Fifth Texas, and Waller's battalion, and Second Louisiana Cavalry (picked men). After crossing a part of the troops, I was ordered to pursue the enemy to the Bœuf. During the evening of the same day, I had quite an animated skirmish with him at the Ramos, where he had burned both the railroad and public bridges, and was well fortified on the east bank; but, finding that I had flanked him with a part of my command on the east side of the Bœuf, he hastily retreated. I threw a small detachment over the Ramos on the night of the 23d, and moved them as close as possible to the enemy on the Bœuf. Colonel Major's command being behind the enemy, and it being difficult for him to escape, about 400 strong surrendered to us about daylight on the morning of the 24th.

Our troops during the three days' campaign did their duty with great alacrity, and behaved with gallantry on all occasions.

Very respectfully, your obedient servant,

THOMAS GREEN,
Brigadier-General, Commanding First Cavalry Brigade.

Brigadier-General MOUTON,
Commanding, &c.

—

FORD AND DAVENPORT PLANTATION,
Saturday, June 27, 1863.

SIR: I have been all the morning collecting together all the information relative to the situation and strength of the defenses of Donaldsonville. After traveling all night, we arrived here at sunrise this morning, 8 or 9 miles from Donaldsonville. I learn from citizens that the fort contains from 300 to 500 Yankees, and that there are five gunboats there now. The approach to the fort is through an open plain 900 yards, and the ditch around it is 16 feet wide and 12 feet deep, making it impossible to scale, except by having strong plank or suitable ladders. I have had a full consultation (which, by the by, is not the best thing to be governed by). They think that an attempt to storm will be attended with great loss and no adequate benefit, even if successful; and this is my opinion. The object of the expedition—being to annoy and take, if possible, the enemy's transports—can be better and more safely done by taking a position below Donaldsonville. I am making a bridge of sugar-coolers at this camp to cross one regiment, intending to swim the horses. I will push that regiment close upon Donaldsonville, throwing pickets up on the river. I am about sending another regiment down on this side near the fort, throwing pickets above, where the river can be seen. My pickets above and below will be able to see what number of gunboats there are at the fort, and I propose to fix the bridge during the day so that I can get artillery on the Mississippi. With one rifle section I can make the transports coming up retreat.

Come down and take command. I want you badly, as I do not know fully what your views are, and would not like to take any steps in conflict with them. Until I came down here, I had no idea of the position, strength, or feasibility of taking the fort, or the value when taken. I think now the fort can be rendered nugatory by taking a. position below it. Adopting the latter view will induce the Yankees very probably to abandon the fort or come out and fight us. Come down as soon as you can.

Yours,

[THOMAS] GREEN.

General MOUTON.

HEADQUARTERS DISTRICT OF WESTERN LOUISIANA,
Thibodeaux, July 6, 1863.
Respectfully forwarded. The reply of Brigadier-General Mouton, approving the views of General Green as to turning the fort, was not received by the latter officer until the attack had been made.

R. TAYLOR,
Major-General, Commanding.

—

HEADQUARTERS FIRST CAVALRY BRIGADE,
Camp on La Fourche, near Paincourtville, July 3, 1863.
MAJOR : In accordance with the order of General Mouton, commanding, of the 26th ultimo, dated at Thibodeaux, commanding me to take possession of the Federal fort at Donaldsonville, I took up the line of march from Thibodeaux about 8 o'clock at night, with [W. P.] Hardeman's, [D. W.] Shannon's, and [P. T.] Herbert's regiments, of my brigade, and [W. P.] Lane's, [B. W.] Stone's, and [Joseph] Phillips' regiments, of Colonel [James P.] Major's brigade, and [O. J.] Semmes' battery. After marching the entire night, I encamped within 9 miles of the fort about sunrise the next morning.

. During the 27th, I rested our jaded troops and horses, getting all the information which could be procured in relation to the situation of the fort, its force, defenses, &c. I placed a pontoon bridge across the La Fourche, made of sugar-coolers, and crossed over Stone's regiment to the east of the bayou, and ordered him to advance toward Donaldsonville on that bank, and attract the attention of the enemy, and, if possible, to attack him on that side. With the balance of the command, I advanced during the night of the 27th to within 1½ miles of the fort, where I dismounted the command. Having determined on the plan of attack, I called the officers commanding regiments together, and explained to them specifically the position each one was to occupy in the assault.

Major Shannon, of the Fifth Texas Mounted Volunteers, was to perform a circuit around the fort, reach the Mississippi 1 mile above, and advance down the levee to the stockade of upright timbers set in the ground between the levee and the water's edge, and there make an entrance. Colonel Hardeman, with the Fourth Texas Mounted Volunteers, was to move up the Bayou road along the levee of the La Fourche, and as soon as he heard the fire opened by Shannon, or a fire opened by the enemy, to assault the fort at the water's edge, along the stockade, and simultaneously with Shannon to make an entrance through the stockade, and with Shannon assault the garrison within, hand to hand. Both Shannon and Hardeman were charged that they were expected to take the fort, while Phillips, Lane, and Herbert, with their regiments, were to envelop the works, moving up around them to the brink of the ditch, shooting down the cannoneers and their supporters from the ramparts at a distance of only 16 or 18 feet.

After a full explanation to the commanding officers of regiments of the plan of attack, and furnishing Shannon and Hardeman with guides, and the head of the column of the three regiments which were to envelop the fort, I moved Shannon and Hardeman forward. Waiting a short time for Major Shannon to perform the circuit around the fort to the Mississippi above, I moved the column which was to envelop the ditch, with Colonel Major at the head. Before this column had advanced to the place intended for it preparatory to the assault, Major Shannon, of the Fifth

Texas, encountered the pickets of the enemy, and a fire from above was opened upon him by the artillery of the fort and from the two gunboats in the river. He advanced down the levee of the Mississippi next to the water's edge to the stockade (of upright timbers) behind the levee, driving the enemy from the stockade and firing upon them through their own port-holes. He pushed a portion of his men over their works, the men helping each other over; the balance of his men moved around the stockade through the water, which was shallow, into the fort. Hearing the small-arms of Major Shannon amid the roar of artillery, I ordered an advance of the whole line. Colonel Phillips, at the head of the column under Colonel Major, made a circuit of the fort, and, with most of his men and officers, made an entrance into the fort with Shannon, of the Fifth. Colonel Herbert, with the Seventh, enveloped the ditch as directed. The fight was desperately contested on every part of the ground. Colonel Hardeman, with the Fourth Texas, being unable to control his guide, was delayed in his attack on the stockade on the La Fourche side until nearly daylight, but his casualties show with what determined courage that veteran regiment stood its ground after it came into action. By some mistake, Colonel Lane's regiment did not get into action; he was waiting for and expecting a guide, while I supposed and was informed that he was at the head of the column under Colonel Major. There is no blame attached to Colonel Lane for the mistake.

The attack on the fort was made at 2 a. m., being before daylight, for the purpose of preventing the gunboats from seeing our advance. The columns of attack of Shannon above and Hardeman below were expected to move along under the levee, sheltered from the artillery and musketry of the fort, until they reached the stockade, the weeds on the margin of the water, as I was informed, preventing a full view of them by the gunboats.

Shannon succeeded in making the entrance with little or no loss, and he and Colonel Phillips (entering on the same side) would doubtless have succeeded in capturing the works had it not been for the existence of a ditch fronting and inside the levee, of which I had no knowledge or information. All my guides (and some of them resided within 2 miles of the fort) assured me that when we got through the stockade, between the levee and the river, we had an open way into the fort without impediment other than the bayonets of the enemy. We were not repulsed and never would have been until we found, after getting into the stockade, there was yet a ditch to cross, running in front of and parallel with the river, and no means whatever on hand to cross it. At this ditch a most desperate fight ensued between the commands of Shannon and Phillips and the enemy. Our men here used brick-bats upon the heads of the enemy, who returned the same. Captain [Ira G.] Killough and Lieutenant [W. S.] Land, and other officers and men, were wounded on their heads with bricks thrown by the enemy, which had first been thrown by our men. There never was more desperate courage displayed than was shown by our men engaged in this assault. The enemy have been shown an example of desperate courage, which will not be without its effect. But for the false information in relation to that part of the fort fronting the river, it would most certainly have fallen into our hands. Had we known of the existence of this ditch, we would have been prepared to have crossed it.

We fought from 2 a. m. until daylight without intermission, and our dead and wounded show the desperation of the assault. The garrison contained between 500 and 600 Federals. Our assaulting party engaged was about 800 strong.

At daylight I sent in a flag of truce, asking permission to pick up our wounded and bury our dead, which was refused, as I expected. My object in sending a flag so early was to get away a great number of our men who had found a little shelter near the enemy's works, and who would have been inevitably taken prisoners. I must have saved 100 men by instructing my flag of truce officer as he approached the fort to order our troops still there away.

We mourn the·fall of many of our bravest and best officers and men. Among the former are Major Shannon, Captain [D. H.] Ragsdale, Lieutenants [James A.] Darby and [James F.] Cole, of the Fifth ; Major [Alonzo] Ridley, of Phillips' regiment, and Lieutenant [N. D.] Cartwright, of the Fourth, and others.

The fort was much stronger than it was represented to be, or than we expected to find it. Had it fallen into our hands, I am satisfied, with a little work on it, we would have held it against all the gunboats below Port Hudson. Its capture and occupation would doubtless have caused great uneasiness and inconvenience to the Federal army besieging that fortress. In this view, much risk was justified in its attempted capture.

I cannot say too much in commendation of the officers and men who were engaged in this assault. Colonel Major, commanding the Second Cavalry Brigade, led the head of the column enveloping the fort, carrying his men to the ditch amid a storm of shot and shell in the most dauntless manner, where he was himself wounded.

The conduct of the lamented Shannon and his officers, Colonel Phillips and his officers, and Colonel Herbert and his officers, and, in fact, all the officers whose conduct came under my observation, is above all praise.

My own staff came fully up to my expectations. Capt.· C. B. Sheppard, my aide-de-camp, and my volunteer aides, W. G. Wilkins and Leander McAnelly, rendered me good service, and behaved themselves, as they had on many former occasions done, with coolness and courage.

I herewith submit a list of casualties. Full reports, showing the killed, wounded, and missing, are inclosed.

Respectfully submitted.

· THOMAS GREEN,
Brigadier-General, Commanding.

Maj. LOUIS BUSH,
Assistant Adjutant-General, Thibodeaux.

[Indorsement.]

HEADQUARTERS DISTRICT OF WESTERN LOUISIANA,
Thibodeaux, July 6, 1863.

Respectfully forwarded. Personal observation satisfies me that if the guide of [W. P.] Hardeman's regiment had not failed to conduct it to the fort, its capture would have been accomplished. No engagement during this war has illustrated more signally the desperate valor of Confederate troops than the attack on this position.

· Although the attack may have been in some respects an unwise one, I am not disposed to attach the slightest censure to so gallant a soldier as General Green, whose disposition it is to attack the enemy wherever he finds him.

R. TAYLOR,
Major-General, Commanding.

Report of Casualties in the First and Second Cavalry Brigades.

Command.	Killed.	Wounded.	Missing.	Aggregate.
4th Texas Cavalry	2	23	3	28
5th Texas Cavalry	12	38	49	99
7th Texas Cavalry	6	35	34	75
Phillips' regiment	19	18	21	58
Stone's regiment	1			1
Lane's regiment				
Total	40	114	107	261

THOMAS GREEN,
Brigadier-General, Commanding.

—

HEADQUARTERS GREEN'S BRIGADE,
Assumption Church, on La Fourche, July 14, 1863.

MAJOR: After the assault on Fort Butler of the 28th ultimo, three regiments of my brigade—the Fourth, Fifth, and Seventh Texas Cavalry—were occupied in watching the movements of the enemy at Donaldsonville, while the cavalry brigade of Colonel [James P.] Major was ordered to the Mississippi River, between the Vacherie road, leading from Thibodeaux, and the Barteau road, leading from Assumption Church, a distance of about 20 miles, on the banks of the Mississippi. Several batteries were sent to the river with Colonel Major, numbering in guns about eighteen or twenty, which kept up an almost continuous fire on the enemy's gunboats and transports by day and by night from the levee of the river. Several of the enemy's boats were crippled—some badly. This interruption of the navigation of the river caused great uneasiness on the part of the enemy, and on July 11 at least ten transports came down from Port Hudson to Donaldsonville, crowded with troops.

On the 12th, several other boats came down with troops. In view of this threatened advance in force on us by the enemy, I ordered Colonel Major's brigade and artillery to withdraw from the river to the La Fourche, for the purpose of concentrating on each side of the bayou as near as possible to the enemy, which order met with your approbation. Major's brigade, consisting of [W. P.] Lane's, [B. W.] Stone's, [George W.] Baylor's, and [Joseph] Phillips, regiments, not over 800 effective men present, with two sections of [T. A.] Faries' battery, were placed on the right ascending bank of La Fourche, and three regiments of my brigade ([W. P.] Hardeman's, commanded by Lieutenant-Colonel [G. J.] Hampton; [A. P.] Bagby's, commanded by Lieutenant-Colonel [P. T.] Herbert, and [H. A.] McPhaill's, being the Fourth, Fifth, and Seventh Texas Cavalry, one section of [Thomas] Gonzales' battery, under Lieutenant [Henry] Angel, not over 750 effective men) were posted on the left ascending bank, opposite the brigade of Colonel Major. There had been warm skirmishing for several days near Donaldsonville between our troops on the Upper La Fourche and the enemy on both sides of the bayou.

On the morning of July 13, the enemy advanced down the bayou on both sides toward Thibodeaux in large numbers, their principal force being on the right descending bank. About 9 o'clock in the morning, the enemy pressed us with artillery and an unusually large force of skirmishers, and, not being able to ascertain his precise strength with skirmishers on account of the large cornfields crossing the whole valley, I concluded to feel him a little more heavily, and, if a favorable opportunity offered, to make an assault on his advancing columns. Accordingly, after checking the enemy's advance by heavily re-enforcing our skirmishers, I made dispositions for an attack. Calling Colonel Lane, who commanded Major's brigade, from the other side of the bayou, I gave him the necessary instructions for his operations on that side. Immediately after the return of Colonel Lane to his command, I commenced the attack on the left ascending bank of the bayou, and soon found the enemy deployed entirely from the La Fourche to the swamp across the broad valley. Not having troops enough on the left ascending bank to front the entire line of the enemy, I attacked his two wings with the largest part of my force. Captain [H. A.] McPhaill, with a par⁺ o the Fifth and a small detachment of the Seventh, moved upon the bayou, attacking the enemy's artillery and carrying it in gallant style, killing most of his gunners and terribly cutting to pieces his infantry supporters. At the same time, Colonel Hampton, with the Fourth Texas, was charging gallantly the enemy's right wing and turning it, while Colonel Herbert, through the fields, with the Seventh Regiment and a part of the Fifth, was driving in their center in splendid style. The enemy frequently rallied in the ditches across the fields, but one of their flanks or the other was invariably turned by us at every stand they made, and a fire poured down the ditches, while Colonel Herbert, with his command, moved upon them in front, and thus we drove them for about 4 miles and almost to the walls of the fort. Each stand they attempted to make was more feeble than the preceding. The ground over which we fought was strewed with the dead and wounded of the enemy, while our loss was very inconsiderable. There were over 500 of the enemy killed and wounded, of whom 200 were left dead on the field, and about 250 prisoners. We captured a large number of the most improved small-arms, principally Enfield rifles. We captured also three pieces of artillery, one of which was a very superior rifled gun, besides ammunition, provisions, tents, and wagons, teams, and much other camp equipage.

In this battle the prisoners represented that we fought the brigades of Generals Weitzel and Dwight on the right descending bank of the La Fourche, and a part of the command of General [Cuvier] Grover on the other side. The whole of this battle was a succession of charges, and I have never before witnessed such determined valor as was displayed by our troops. They frequently charged upon the enemy in line of battle, and delivered their fire upon them at 25 paces, with the coolness of veterans. The victory on our part was a signal one, and the rout of the enemy complete.

Where gallantry displayed by our officers and men was so universal, I cannot make distinctions. The regiments under the command of Colonel Lane, on the opposite side of the bayou, behaved with gallantry. That portion of Colonel Lane's own regiment which was dismounted moved up the bayou along the levee, and gallantly co-operated with our troops on the left descending bank. In this action the enemy were so roughly handled that they attempted no further movements from Donaldsonville during our stay on the La Fourche.

Our loss did not exceed 3 killed and 30 wounded, 6 mortally, while that of the enemy in killed, wounded, and prisoners was little less than 1,000. This great disparity of loss is most wonderful, and can only be accounted for on the ground of the enemy's panic in our first impetuous charge, which was kept up during the action, giving them little time to rally and to collect together their broken forces.

I remained in the vicinity of the enemy for two days after the battle of the 13th, and until ordered to move toward the bay, during which time the enemy remained quietly in and around the fort, making no demonstrations toward us whatever, and not even following us with their pickets.

This victory completely paralyzed the enemy in our rear, and enabled us to move from the La Fourche after the fall of Vicksburg and Port Hudson without molestation.

Respectfully submitted.

THOMAS GREEN,
Brigadier-General, Commanding.

Maj. LOUIS BUSH,
Assistant Adjutant-General, Vermillionville.

[Indorsement.]

HEADQUARTERS DISTRICT OF WESTERN LOUISIANA,
Alexandria, August 9, 1863.

Respectfully forwarded. In a previous report I took occasion to express my high appreciation of the conduct of Brigadier-General Green and his command in this action.

R. TAYLOR,
Major-General.

JULY 7–AUGUST 19, 1863.—Operations against Navajo Indians in New Mexico.

Reports of Col. Christopher Carson, First New Mexico Cavalry, commanding expedition.

HEADQUARTERS DEPARTMENT OF NEW MEXICO,
Santa Fé, N. Mex., September 5, 1863.

GENERAL: I have the honor to inclose for the information of the War Department copies of the following enumerated communications relating to operations against the Navajo Indians in this department:

I. Letter from Col. Christopher Carson, First New Mexico Volunteers, commanding Navajo expedition, dated Camp at Pueblo Colorado, N. Mex., July 24, 1863, to these headquarters.

II. Letter from Colonel Carson, commanding Navajo expedition, dated Camp at Pueblo Colorado, N. Mex., July 24, 1863, to these headquarters.

III. Letter from myself to Colonel Carson, commanding expedition against the Navajoes, dated August 18, 1863.

IV. Letter from Colonel Carson, commanding Navajo expedition, dated Camp at Pueblo Colorado, N. Mex., August 19, 1863.

I am, general, very respectfully, your obedient servant,

JAMES H. CARLETON,
Brigadier-General, Commanding.

Brig. Gen. LORENZO THOMAS,
Adjutant-General of the Army, Washington, D. C.

[Inclosures.]

I.

HEADQUARTERS NAVAJO EXPEDITION,
Camp at Pueblo Colorado, N. Mex., July 24, 1863.

SIR : I have the honor to report that in obedience to General Orders, No. 15, current series, Headquarters Department of New Mexico, I left camp near Los Lunas, N. Mex., July 7, 1863, en route to Pueblo Colorado, N. Mex., with Companies D, K, L, and M, First New Mexico Volunteers, the only companies of the expedition which had arrived at the place of rendezvous up to that time.

I arrived at Fort Wingate on the 10th instant, where I remained three days receiving supplies and some necessary articles of outfit for my command. Having ascertained that there were two trains with supplies for my command shortly to arrive at this post, I directed that Companies B and C, First New Mexico Volunteers, should remain at the post until their arrival, to escort them to the depot. They have not yet joined. Left Fort Wingate on the 14th, and arrived at Ojo-del-Oso on the night of the 16th. Owing to a scarcity of water on the route, my animals suffered a good deal, and many of the mules were completely broken down and unable to travel. I therefore concluded to give them a rest, and remained in camp on the 17th, 18th, and until 2.30 p. m. on the 19th instant. There were two small fields of wheat near to the camp, which I had fed to the animals. On the 17th, I found some wheat at a spring about 2 miles west of camp, which I sent for. The wheat found at the camp and at the west spring amounted to about 40,000 pounds, and, with the grass, which at this place was abundant and of good quality, put my animals in good condition.

I was joined at this place on the 19th by Captain [Asa B.] Carey, chief quartermaster, and Lieutenant Cook, chief commissary, with a supply train, escorted by Captain Sena's company, C, First New Mexico Volunteers, but as his animals also needed rest, I left him behind for this purpose. I arrived with my command at Fort Defiance on the 20th instant, where I found a large quantity of wheat, say 100,000 pounds, which was also fed to the public animals. The Utah Indians had preceded us on this day's march; killed 1 man (Navajo), and captured 20 sheep. Shortly after encamping, I was joined by 19 Ute warriors, who had been operating against the Navajoes on their own account. They report having met a party of Utes returning to their country, having 11 captives, women and children; and that there are two other parties now in this country; they themselves saw no Navajoes. I have hired 5 of this party as spies. I remained at Fort Defiance on the 21st. On the 22d I left for this place with the board appointed to select a site for Fort Canby, taking with me the field and staff, and 70 men of the command, and the Ute Indians. About one-third the distance from Defiance, I left the command and pushed on with the Utes. When about 9 miles from this point, and on the Rio de Pueblo Colorado, we came on a small party of Navajoes, and killed 3 men. From a Pah-Ute woman captured, I ascertained that a strong party of Navajoes, with a large herd of sheep, cattle, and horses, were at a pond of water about 35 miles west of here, and would remain there all night. I immediately determined to pursue them with the command as soon as possible after its arrival. It reached here about 5 p. m., and at 7.30 p. m. I started. At 5 o'clock next morning, 23d, I arrived at the water only to find that the Navajoes with their stock had left the previous evening. I followed their trail for two hours, and until many of the horses had given out, and only returned on my own conviction, supported by the superior knowledge of Kan-a-at-sa, that it would be impossible to overtake them without having to travel some 90 miles without water, and this my horses could not do.

On my return route, the Ute Indians killed 8 Navajoes, making a total of 12 killed since my arrival in this country.

I arrived at this place with the party yesterday evening at 5 o'clock, having been nearly thirty-six hours continuously in the saddle. The remainder of the command left behind at Fort Defiance arrived here yesterday at 4 o'clock in the afternoon, also Captain Carey and Lieutenant Cook.

I would respectfully call the attention of the general commanding the department to the valuable services rendered by the Ute Indians, and earnestly request that I may be authorized to send an officer to their country to employ at least 30 more Utes as spies for the expedition.

I am, sir, very respectfully, your obedient servant,

C. CARSON,
Colonel First New Mexico Vols., Comdg. Navajo Expedition.

ASSISTANT ADJUTANT-GENERAL,
Headquarters Department of New Mexico, Santa Fé, N. Mex·

II.

CAMP AT PUEBLO COLORADO, N. MEX.,
July 24, 1863.

DEAR GENERAL: I send by Captain Cutler the official report of the operations of my command since leaving Los Lunas, but in it have made no mention of the women and children captured by the Utes (4 women and 17 children). It is expected by the Utes, and has, I believe, been customary, to allow them to keep the women and children and the property captured by them for their own use and benefit, and as there is no other way to sufficiently recompense these Indians for their invaluable services, and as a means of insuring their continued zeal and activity, I ask it as a favor that they may be permitted to retain all that they may capture. I make this request the more readily as I am satisfied that the future of the captives disposed of in this manner would be much better than if sent even to the Bosque Redondo. As a general thing, the Utes dispose of their captives to Mexican families, where they are fed and taken care of, and thus cease to require any further attention on the part of the Government. Besides this, their being distributed as servants through the Territory causes them to lose that collectiveness of interest as a tribe which they will retain if kept together at any one place. Will you please let me know your views on this matter as soon as possible, that I may govern my conduct accordingly?

The Utes more than come up to the expectations I had formed of their efficiency as spies, nor can any small straggling parties of Navajoes hope to escape them. I trust you will grant me permission to send Captain Pfeiffer to their villages to employ some more of them. I am very badly off for guides, and intend to employ some Zuñi Indians as such in a few days, when I shall visit their village.

The Navajoes have planted a large quantity of grain this year. Their wheat is as good as I have ever seen. Corn is rather backward, and not so plentiful.

I have directed Major Cummings to send out a party to-morrow to bring in all the grain on this creek, which will amount to over 75,000 pounds of wheat and a large amount of corn. The latter, when dried, will answer for fodder for the animals in the winter. I would have permitted all the grain in this vicinity to have ripened, but that it is hoped you will change the location of the depot, there being neither grass, timber, nor anything like a sufficiency of water any place in this neighborhood for this purpose.

I forwarded with Captain Cutler the resignations of Chaplain Taladrid and Captain McCabe, and request that you will accept them, as well as all others which I may forward you, as I do not wish to have any officer in my command who is not contented or willing to put up with as much inconvenience and privations for the success of the expedition as I undergo myself. I respectfully urge that, in the event of your accepting the resignation of Captain McCabe, Lieutenant Brady be promoted to the vacant captaincy.

Respectfully, yours,

C. CARSON,
Colonel First New Mexico Volunteers.

Brig. Gen. JAMES H. CARLETON,
Commanding Department of New Mexico, Santa Fé.

—

III.

HEADQUARTERS DEPARTMENT OF NEW MEXICO,
Santa Fé, N. Mex., August 18, 1863.

COLONEL: I have the honor to acknowledge the receipt of your letter of the 24th ultimo, in relation to the disposition to be made of captured Navajo women and children, and to say in reply that all prisoners which are captured by the troops or employés of your command will be sent to Santa Fé by the first practicable opportunity after they are, from time to time, brought in as prisoners. There must be no exception to this rule. Here the superintendent of Indian affairs and myself will make such dispositions as to their future care and destination as may seem most humane and proper. All horses, mules, or other stock which the troops or employés under your command may capture belong to the United States, and will be reported to department headquarters. The horses and mules will be turned over to your chief quartermaster, who will have them carefully branded U. S., and used in the public service. These he will account for on his property returns. But to stimulate the zeal of the troops and employés who have captured horses and mules from the Navajoes, or who may hereafter make such captures from those Indians, a bonus of $20 apiece will be paid to their captors as prize-money on the delivery to the chief quartermaster of every sound, serviceable horse or mule. These will be accounted for as purchased. All sheep captured will be turned over to the chief commissary of your expedition. These will be taken up on the returns of provisions; will be properly marked; will be killed, from time to time, and issued as fresh meat to the troops and employés. The chief commissary is authorized to pay the captors of such sheep $1 per head as prize-money, and as an encouragement to renewed exertions. Every lot captured will at once be reported to department headquarters. The sheep paid for as here set forth will be taken up as purchased.

All other property captured from the Indians will be reported, when orders will be given as to what disposition shall be made of it.

I am, colonel, very respectfully, your obedient servant,

JAMES H. CARLETON,
Brigadier-General, Commanding.

Col. CHRISTOPHER CARSON,
Comdg. Expedition against the Navajoes, Fort Canby, N. Mex.

IV.

HEADQUARTERS NAVAJO EXPEDITION,
Camp at Pueblo Colorado, N. Mex., August 19, 1863.

CAPTAIN: I have the honor to report that on the 5th instant I left my camp, 7 miles south of Cañon Bonito, with Companies B and H, First New Mexico Volunteers, dismounted, and D, G, K, and M, mounted (total strength, twelve companies, and 4 field and staff officers, and 333 enlisted men), on a scout for thirty days.

Companies G and H arrived at Defiance on the 2d instant with their horses in very poor condition. Those of Captain Pfeiffer's company (H) were so broken down that I was reluctantly obliged to dismount his men, and leave his horses at Defiance to recruit. All of my animals showed plainly the want of grain, none of which they have had since leaving the Rio Grande, excepting such as was found growing—the property of the Navajoes.

After leaving camp, I took a direction south, toward Zuñi, intending to visit that village. procure some guides, thence to scour the country to the Moqui and Oribi villages, and return by the Cañon de Chelly. When about two hours from camp, we found and destroyed about 70 acres of corn. Three hours afterward encamped in wheat and corn fields. The wheat, about 15 acres, was fed to the animals, and the corn, about 50 acres, was destroyed. Sent Sergeant Romero, of Company D, with 15 men after 2 Indians seen in this vicinity. He captured one of their horses. Distances between camps, about 15 miles.

On the night of the 4th instant, I detached Captain Pfeiffer, with Lieutenant Fitch, with 100 enlisted men, 25 of whom were mounted, and the Ute Indians, to examine the country to the right and left of the line of march.

On the 6th, after traveling about 17 miles, I found part of his detail encamped, having in charge 11 women and children, 5 of whom were taken by Captain Pfeiffer's detail, besides a woman and child, the former of whom was killed in attempting to escape, and the latter accidentally, and 100 head of sheep and goats. When I arrived, Captain Pfeiffer, with the balance of his party, were out scouting. He returned about 12 o'clock at night with 2 children and 1 horse, captured. About an hour before reaching camp, found and destroyed 5 acres of corn.

Next morning I sent to Fort Defiance, with an escort of 10 men, the 7 prisoners captured by Captain Pfeiffer, with directions to the commanding officer to forward them by the first convenient opportunity to Fort Wingate, and to request the commanding officer of that post to forward them to Los Pinos.

Continued the direction toward Zuñi on the 7th, until, within about 15 miles from the village, we captured 5 Moqui Indians, who, when questioned, stated that there were Navajoes with large herds in the vicinity of their villages. I immediately changed the direction west for Moqui, and, after traveling some distance, encamped in a rain-storm. On the 8th instant it commenced raining before we left camp, and continued steadily until 2 p. m.; at 1 p. m. we encamped. Distance traveled, about 18 miles. Shortly after leaving camp on the 9th, destroyed about 12 acres of corn, marched about 15 miles, and encamped. At 5 p. m. I left this camp with Companies D, G, and K, 75 men of Companies H and M, dismounted, and 30 mounted men of Company M, and the Utes. Took but 1 pack animal to each company, and three days' cooked rations for the men; the remainder of the pack animals were left with Captain Everett's company, to follow up next day. Marched all night, and arrived at 10 a. m. next morning at a cañon a little west of Moqui. Here the Utes took 2 women and 3 children prisoners, and Captain Berney's company (D) captured 25 head of horses; there were also captured 100 sheep and goats. While Captain Berney was after the horse herd, Captain Pfeiffer, with 30 cavalry, pursued and captured 1,000 head of sheep and goats; some of the Utes captured in the same vicinity 18 horses and 2 mules, and killed 1 Indian. Captain Pfeiffer severely wounded an Indian, but he contrived to secrete himself in the rocks.

The Utes here left the command to return to their homes, ostensibly because they could not get the herds captured by Captains Berney and Pfeiffer, as they stated that it was the understanding with the general that they were to receive all the stock captured during the campaign. The real cause, however, was the fact that they had now sufficient stock and captures. Marched about 3 miles farther west to spring in cañon, and encamped on table-land above; horses very much broken down. At retreat, Lieutenant Hubbell and a private of Company M are missing. Some Moqui Indians report the death of the Indian wounded by Captain Pfeiffer, and say that he was not only one of the most powerful, but the worst chief of the nation. I intended to remain at this camp on the 11th, but as Lieutenant Hubbell and the private had not yet come in, I made a detail of 50 men to accompany me in search of him. Just as I had the detail ready to start, an Oribi Indian brought me word that a party of Navajoes, with large herds, had passed their village, 12 miles distant, just as he left with the information. I increased the detail to 100 men, under Captain Thompson, who volunteered to accompany me, and followed in pursuit. I continued it a distance of 25 miles without overtaking them, when night came on; I could no longer keep the trail. I then encamped, and it being useless to continue the pursuit, returned next day. During my absence, and while Major Morrison was in command, 7 public mules strayed from the camp and were taken by the Navajoes. On inquiry, I found that Major Morrison is blameless. The pack train arrived shortly after my departure from camp, as did also Lieutenant Hubbell and the soldier, the mules nearly broken down for want of water. On my return, I directed the command, excepting that portion which was with me, to proceed immediately to some springs, reported by the Indians as but a short distance off, the water at this camp having become insufficient. Next morning I proceeded to join them, and found them encamped in a cañon about 12 miles west of Moqui, where there was an abundance of good water and grass; fed to animals about an acre of corn found here. I laid over on the 14th to recruit my animals. At about 2 a. m. on the morning of the 15th, the camp was aroused by the whooping of a 'party of Navajoes, who made an unsuccessful attempt to drive off our herd. They retired after a few volleys from our pickets. Owing to the darkness, it is not known whether any of them were injured by our fire. After leaving this camp, took northeast direction, so as to strike this stream some distance south of the Pueblo Colorado. While *en route* on the 16th, destroyed about 50 acres of corn; several of my animals gave out and were shot.

17th.—Sent a party this morning to bring in some pack-mules which were left behind yesterday. They returned this evening with the packs, and 1 woman captured.

This forenoon I arrived at this camp, rendered memorable by the death of the brave and lamented Maj. Joseph Cummings, who fell, shot through the abdomen by a concealed Indian. At the time of his death he was almost alone, having with him an unarmed citizen, and, having left the command some time previous, contrary to my positive instructions, his death is the result of his rash bravery. I sent his body to Defiance this morning. I sent, at dark yesterday evening (dismounted), two parties of 40 men each, to examine the country in the vicinity. Before leaving the valley, one of the parties captured a woman, who was sent into camp. This morning the parties returned without having seen any Indians.

Captain Deus captured 5 horses yesterday. To-day I have sent to Defiance to recruit all the animals unable to travel, retaining only about 60.

From all I could learn from the Moqui Indians, and the captives taken, the majority of the Navajoes, with their herds, are at the Little Red River, and this is confirmed by my own observation. My next scout will probably be in that direction, and will, I trust, be more successful.

I am, captain, very respectfully, your obedient servant,

C. CARSON,
Colonel, Commanding

Capt. BENJ. C. CUTLER,
Asst. Adjt. Gen., Hdqrs. Dept. of New Mexico, Santa Fé.

AUGUST 3, 1863.—Skirmish at Jackson, La.

REPORTS.

No. 1.—Brig. Gen. George L. Andrews, U. S. Army, commanding at Port Hudson
No. 2.—Col. John L. Logan, Eleventh Arkansas Infantry.

No. 1.

Report of Brig. Gen. George L. Andrews, U. S. Army, commanding at Port Hudson.

HEADQUARTERS,
Port Hudson, August 6, 1863.

SIR: I have the honor to report that on the 2d instant I sent Lieut. M. Hanham, Sixth New York Volunteers, with a detachment of 250 infantry (colored), 50 cavalry (Third Massachusetts), and one section of the Second Vermont Battery, to Jackson, La., to collect negroes for the Twelfth Regiment Infantry, Corps d'Afrique.

Lieutenant Hanham was directed to keep his scouts and spies well out from the town, to get timely notice of the approach of the enemy in force, and to keep up frequent communication with this post.

He collected 50 negroes on Monday. Nothing unusual occurred until about 3 p. m. Monday (August 3), when some rumors were heard of the advance of Logan's force. The troops were at once drawn up to receive them, but the accounts were so vague that Lieutenant Hanham decided before withdrawing to send out additional scouts to learn the true state of the case.

Unfortunately several of these scouts were captured, in some instances, it is reported, through the aid of so-called citizens, and others were cut off and unable to return to the town.

The attack commenced on the part of Logan's force at about 5 p. m., with little warning from the scouts, but the detachment was prepared, and seems to have received the attack with commendable steadiness, for the most part.

A detachment from the Sixth Regiment Infantry, Corps d'Afrique, under Lieutenant Royce, is especially mentioned for steadiness and good conduct. The artillery and cavalry also rendered excellent service.

After a conflict of some length, finding the enemy in greatly superior numbers, the detachment retreated with no great loss at first, and would probably have brought off its artillery but for the accident of having a guide shot at a critical moment, which caused the route intended to have been followed to be lost and a new one to be taken, through which it was impracticable to bring artillery.

The enemy's force, according to the report of prisoners, was about 800, It is supposed, however, to have been considerably greater. The detachment returned to this post at about midnight.

Lieutenant Hanham is reported to have behaved most gallantly, and was slightly wounded. The enemy acknowledge a loss in killed and wounded of about 40. We took 6 prisoners, including 1 lieutenant.

Our loss, which will probably be somewhat diminished by the arrival of stragglers, now stands as follows. The proportion of killed and wounded of the number is not known:

Command.	Officers.	Enlisted men.	Total.
3d Massachusetts Cavalry	......	14	14
2d Vermont Battery	*1	14	15
1st Regiment Infantry, Corps d'Afrique	1	21	22
3d Regiment Infantry, Corps d'Afrique	......	11	11
6th Regiment Infantry, Corps d'Afrique	3	13	16
Total	5	73	78

* Wounded.

Two guns, two caissons, and 16 horses belonging to Second Vermont Battery.

Six wagons and 24 mules from the quartermaster's department.

The information here was that Logan was above Natchez with his force, and, from the accounts of the prisoners, it appears that he actually left that neighborhood only two days before this affair.

He had just arrived within 4 miles of Woodville, to which place he was probably led by the report of a raid made a few days ago by some of General Grant's forces, who burned the factory at that place, and was on his way back toward Natchez, and intending, it was supposed, to go nearly to Jackson, Miss., when he received intelligence that our forces were in Jackson, La., and at once marched on that place.

Considering the advantages given by fortune to the rebel forces on this occasion, their success appears to me not very remarkable.

It is reported that 1 or 2 of the colored soldiers who fell into the hands of the rebels have been hung, and it is certain that some of the prisoners were severely beaten. The rebels have refused to give any information concerning the officers or men of the colored troops who are in their hands. I have sent two flags of truce to the enemy at Jackson, one to inquire about our wounded and one to demand explanations from General [Colonel] Logan with regard to the treatment of colored soldiers when prisoners of war.

To the latter I have received no reply yet, General [Colonel] Logan having left Jackson with nearly all his force, leaving only a small cavalry force in the town.

I learn that our wounded belonging to the white troops are well cared for, but fear such is not the case with colored troops. The rebels hold an assistant surgeon of one of the colored regiments, and refuse to give any account of him. I have accordingly confined all the rebel surgeons at this post, and, while awaiting General [Colonel] Logan's answer to my demand for an explanation concerning his treatment of colored soldiers of this command, I have confined the rebel prisoners now at this post.

Respectfully, your obedient servant,

GEO. L. ANDREWS,
Brigadier-General Volunteers, Commanding.

Lieutenant-Colonel IRWIN,
Assistant Adjutant-General.

No. 2.

Report of Col. John L. Logan, Eleventh Arkansas Infantry.

NEAR JACKSON, LA.,
August 4, 1863.

GENERAL: I met the enemy at Jackson, La., yesterday evening, whipping him handsomely, driving him from the town, capturing two Parrott guns, horses, ten wagons with commissary stores, killing, wounding, and capturing not less than 100 Yankees and a large number of negroes in arms. The enemy fled in the greatest confusion, leaving his dead and wounded behind him. It was a complete rout. His force was about 600 infantry (mixed colors), 150 cavalry, and two pieces of artillery. My force not so large—about 500. Our loss in killed and wounded 12.

Your dispatch of the 28th ultimo just received, and the instructions will be carried out.

I am, general, very respectfully, your obedient servant,

JNO. L. LOGAN,
Colonel, Commanding Cavalry.

Lieutenant-General HARDEE,
Commanding Army of the West.

P. S.—What disposition shall I make of negroes captured in arms? Port Hudson is garrisoned by 7,000 Yankee troops and armed negroes. The troops that came down the river some time since went up Black River on transports,

AUGUST 10–13, 1863.—Mutiny at Galveston, Tex.

REPORTS.

No. 1.—Lieut. Col. E. F. Gray, Third Texas Infantry.
No. 2.—Col. X. B. Debray, Twenty-sixth Texas Cavalry, commanding Second Brigade, Second Division.
No. 3.—Col. P. N. Luckett, Third Texas Infantry, commanding First Brigade, Second Division.
No. 4.—General Orders, No. 139, Headquarters District of Texas, New Mexico, and Arizona.

No. 1.

Report of Lieut. Col. E. F. Gray, Third Texas Infantry.

GALVESTON,
August 4, 1863.

SIR: I would respectfully and earnestly call the attention of the general commanding to the character of the provisions being issued to the troops of this regiment, and, I presume, to all at this post.

The only issue now given consists of beef, molasses, and corn-meal. The latter, even when good, is exceedingly heating in its effects on the blood, and when, added to this, it is sour, dirty, weevel-eaten, and filled with ants and worms, and not bolted (and the troops without the means of sifting it themselves), it becomes wholly superfluous to add that it is exceedingly unwholesome.

The daily increasing number on the sick reports fully demonstrates by the character of the diseases that the food is one if not the chief cause producing it.

Were this character of food, or even worse, the only kind which could be procured by the commissary department, I have no hesitation in saying the troops, actuated by true patriotism, would not complain. But, sir, when such is not the case, and it is a fact well known among the troops that large supplies of good and wholesome flour are in depot at Columbus and Harrisburg, I cannot but consider their murmurs in some measure just and not without reason, for I feel satisfied that wholesome food can be obtained with but little exertion.

It is with regret that I feel myself forced into the position of a complainant, but I deem it one of the first duties of a commander to watch with zealous care the welfare of those under his command, and I could not feel that I had discharged my duty to them should I 'fail to make these representations, which I believe it only necessary to do to have them corrected.

Accompanying this communication I send a sample of the corn-meal issued to this regiment. A casual examination will satisfy you of its unwholesomeness.

I have the honor to be, very respectfully, your obedient servant,

E. F. GRAY,
Lieutenant-Colonel Third Texas Infantry, Comdg. Regiment.

Lieut. R. M. FRANKLIN,
Actg. Asst. Adjt. Gen., Second Brig., Second Div., Galveston, Tex.

No. 2.

Reports of Col. X. B. Debray, Twenty-sixth Texas Cavalry, commanding Second Brigade, Second Division.

GALVESTON, *August* 11, 1863.

SIR : ·It is my painful duty to report to the brigadier-general commanding the sub-district the fact that the Third Regiment of Texas Infantry yesterday afternoon refused to drill and to obey the orders of their officers, evincing tumultuous and riotous evidences of insubordination. The fact was reported to me by Major [J. H.] Kampmann, their commanding officer, who stated that he had used every effort to quell the disturbance and induce the men to return to their duty.

I was at the time at the drill-ground of my regiment, superintending their drill, but feeling that it was all-important to crush this movement in the most summary manner, I ordered my regiment to their quarters to procure ammunition, directing them to rendezvous on Broadway, where also I had ordered Captain [O. G.] Jones to bring his light battery. Colonel [H. M.] Elmore had received instructions to get his three companies under arms and proceed to a point assigned him.

At about the usual hour the Third Regiment repaired to the parade ground (the court-house square) for dress-parade. As the parade was about concluding, I advanced at the head of my column and appeared. on the parade, the cavalry being stationed with loaded carbines on either flank, while the artillery, supported by Elmore's companies, advanced, took position immediately in the front, unlimbered, and loaded with canister. I then advanced to the front of the regiment, and addressed a few words to these misguided men, assuring them that military discipline must be observed and respected, no matter at what cost of life, and that I was there determined and able so to preserve it. I then ordered, " Stack arms," which they did, though somewhat slowly ; and after having marched them from their muskets, over which I placed a guard, and have since turned in to the post ordnance officer, directed Major Kampmann to march them to their quarters, placing a sufficient guard around the premises, and to allow no man to leave his said quarters under any pretext.

These orders were promptly carried out, and I am happy to be able to state that the men behaved in a quiet and orderly manner during the night. This morning the regiment drilled without arms the two hours which they had formerly done, but which I had of late discontinued, at the special request of the officers of this regiment, owing to the heat at that time of day, and comported themselves with order and propriety. I still keep them within their quarters, when not on drill, except the daily guard, which I am compelled still to make from this regiment, having no other to call upon; these latter mount guards without arms and receive the arms of the old guard at the guard-house, and in turn, next morning, turn over the arms to the detail relieving them.

The causes of this movement I am not yet able positively to state, but I have ordered a board of inquiry, which will be held without delay, and thoroughly investigate the whole matter, and endeavor to ascertain, if possible, the ringleaders. The movement was general, with the exception of one company (Company C), but I am convinced was brought about, as is always the case, by a few men having influence with the mass, and there are doubtless many who already regret the part they have taken. I am informed that this is not the first time this regiment has behaved in this way when they wished to gain a point, and that on such previous occasion or occasions it has ended by a compromise between the officers and men, a course which, of course, I would never consent to adopt.

The rest of the garrison behaved well on the occasion, obeying all my orders with alacrity, and would, I feel sure, had the painful necessity occurred, have used their weapons with fearful accuracy and determination upon this self-willed, rebellious body of men.

I did not send word for [Joseph J.] Cook's regiment, from the fact that they were at their drill-ground in the city, without ammunition, and it would have occupied far too much time to send them out to the various forts for their cartridges, and await their return.

So soon as the court of inquiry have examined into this painful business, and made their report, I will forward a copy thereof to the brigadier-general commanding division.

I have the honor to be, very respectfully, your obedient servant,

X. B. DEBRAY,
Colonel, and Acting Brigadier-General.

Capt. A. N. MILLS,
Assistant Adjutant-General, Houston.

—

GALVESTON,
August 12, 1863.

SIR: I write hastily, through Dr. Holland, to state that the garrison of Galveston is in a most deplorable state of discipline. The day before yesterday Luckett's regiment refused to drill. I disarmed them. Yesterday Cook's regiment refused to leave the batteries which they now hold. To attack them, I have but 150 men in Elmore's regiment, these even of doubtful disposition, and my regiment, armed with indifferent musketoons. They are, however, steady, and I am at every moment apprehending a collision between the men of Cook's regiment and them. Threats have been uttered.

I have no force to guard the ordnance armory, where the guns of Luckett's regiment have been deposited. The sappers and miners, I am just informed, refuse to work, claiming six months' pay due.

The alleged cause is the want of bread, the corn-meal now issued to the men being old and weevil-eaten, and indeed of inferior and detestable quality. No flour on hand to be issued. The true cause, I believe, I can trace to seeds of discontent spread by bad citizens, the exciting speeches lately made here by political aspirants, and the talk of paroled prisoners from Vicksburg, who are, indeed, very demoralized and dissatisfied.

Brigadier-General Luckett arrived here yesterday; he has to-day issued an order promising good rations, and suspending drill until further orders. I wish the compromise may bring matters to a better standing, although I doubt it, and, if so, it will be only for a few days. The arrival of [N. C.] Gould's regiment and [W. H.] Griffin's battalion here would only add fuel to the conflagration.

My position here is difficult, having to depend exclusively upon my regiment, about 300 men, who, as I have stated above, are obnoxious to the balance of the garrison.

I have the honor to be, very respectfully, your obedient servant,

X. B. DEBRAY,
Colonel, and Acting Brigadier-General.

Capt. EDMUND P. TURNER,
Assistant Adjutant-General.

HEADQUARTERS SECOND BRIGADE, SECOND DIVISION,
Galveston, August 12, 1863.

SIR : In pursuance of my promise to inform you from day to day of the existing state of affairs in the garrison since the late disturbance, I have the honor to report that I have diligently endeavored to ascertain the cause of the mutinous feeling among the men, and, so far as I can learn, it is principally owing to the bad quality of the food issued to them. This, the original cause, has, I doubt not, been seized upon by some few designing men, who are using it in order to suit their own bad purposes, and will, I fear, unless checked in one way or another, end in open and general revolt.

I had endeavored some time since to remedy this evil with respect to the bad quality of flour and meal, but without success, each new supply arriving being worse than the last. As to the actual condition of the flour and meal sent to this garrison, there can be but one opinion; it is very bad, and utterly unfit to be issued; the flour is sour, and the meal sour and absolutely filled with weevils and worms.

I regret to be compelled to state that mutiny was yesterday pretty generally developed in Cook's regiment, although more of a negative than demonstrative character, of the light artillery. Jones' battery, I am informed, are inclined to sympathize with the malcontents.

Elmore's regiment continues to perform their duty as usual, but, from information that I have received, I cannot with any certainty count upon them in case of a collision.

The cavalry, from all that I can gather from their officers and from personal observation, are loyal, and will stand by their officers and colors to the last extremity.

Brigadier-General Luckett, arriving last evening, has assumed command,* and it is, therefore, at present, out of my province to make further report.

I have the honor to remain very respectfully, your obedient servant,
X. B. DEBRAY,
Colonel, and Acting Brigadier-General.

Capt. A. N. MILLS,
Assistant Adjutant-General, Houston.

[Indorsement.]

Respectfully forwarded for the information of the commanding general. Inclosure marked No. 1 also forwarded.
P. N. LUCKETT,
Acting Brigadier-General.

[Inclosure No. 1.]

GALVESTON,
August 12, 1863.

Capt. A. N. MILLS,
Assistant Adjutant-General:

In the communication sent to-day by General Debray, General Luckett wishes the words "has assumed command, &c.," erased before it is forwarded to General Magruder.
WM. K. FOSTER,
Captain, and Acting Assistant Adjutant-General.

---

* See Inclosure No. 1, following.

No. 3.

Report of Col. P. N. Luckett, Third Texas Infantry, commanding First Brigade, Second Division.

GALVESTON.
August 13, 1863.

SIR : On the morning of the 11th instant 1 learned through a telegram from Galveston that a mutiny had broken out at that place the evening before, and that the Third Regiment of Infantry had been disarmed. I immediately proceeded in person by that morning's train to Galveston, and found, upon consultation with the officers, that great discontent and dissatisfaction pervaded almost the entire garrison, and that the afternoon before, the 11th instant, the Third Regiment of Infantry had, at the usual hour for drilling, refused to turn out for that purpose. The officers used every effort to induce them to do so, but without effect, as the men replied they were willing to do all their garrison and other duties, but were too weak to drill four hours a day, &c.

This state of things was promptly reported to Brigadier-General Debray, who caused the regiment to be surrounded by Debray's regiment of cavalry, Elmore's regiment of infantry, and two light batteries at the evening or dress parade. These dispositions being made, the men were ordered to stack their arms, which they did promptly and without a word, and were marched to their quarters, and were guarded in them by Company D, Third Regiment of Infantry, Captain [J. B.] Hicks, whose men had turned out to drill.

The afternoon of that day, the 11th instant, it was stated that Cook's regiment of artillery would also refuse to drill, and at the usual hour Brigadier-General Debray visited the batteries, and found all but two of the companies at their posts, but that Company C, at Fort Magruder, were in a state of mutiny and refused to drill, as also Company ——, at Fort Bankhead.

The burden of the complaints made by the men was the character of the rations issued by the commissary department, these consisting of corn-meal, molasses, and fresh beef; the two first represented to be sour, dirty, and unwholesome.

Some of the men also complained and wished for furloughs, stating they had not been permitted to visit their families, though they had been in the service for nearly two years. The opinion of a large majority of the officers being given that there was really no disloyal sentiment amongst the men, and also that three-fourths of the daily guard was detailed from the Third Regiment of Infantry, as usual, Brigadier-General Debray reporting that this was the case because he could not perform the garrison duty without them; and Lieutenant-Colonel Gray feeling well satisfied that the Third Regiment could be relied upon, I directed Brigadier-General Debray to issue an order for their arms to be restored to them. I also issued an order suspending further drills until a better class of provisions could be obtained, and have caused a board of officers to be appointed to ascertain the extent of the disaffection and the causes. Until that board has made its report, I can give no more positive statement of the affair than a mere expression of opinion, based upon the verbal statements of the officers, to the effect that it was only intended as an expression of dissatisfaction at the quality of their food, and the amount of duty required of them during the extreme hot weather, and was not prompted by any disloyalty to our cause, but that they took this course to bring their complaints forward, thinking that thereby they would insure more prompt attention.

They all seem sensible that they adopted an improper mode of expressing their grievances, and many are thoroughly ashamed. I must, in justice to Brigadier-General Debray, state that his course was prompt and efficient, and I fully indorse his action, as I feel he could not have done less under the circumstances as they were presented to him. At the time General Debray disarmed the regiment, he was not aware of the extent of the dissatisfaction, which fact has had great influence on my course of action, a full report of which will be forwarded when I receive the reports of a board I have ordered.

Brigadier-General [W. R.] Scurry arrived here this evening. At present I see no cause of alarm.

I have the honor to be, your obedient servant,

P. N. LUCKETT,
Acting Brigadier-General, First Brigade, Second Division.

Capt. EDMUND P. TURNER,
Assistant Adjutant-General.

No. 4.

General Orders, No. 139, *Headquarters District of Texas, New Mexico, and Arizona.*

GENERAL ORDERS, } HDQRS. DIST. TEX., N. MEX., AND ARIZ.,
No. 139.   }   ·Galveston, August 24, 1863.

The commanding general received with feelings of deep mortification the intelligence of the mutinous and insubordinate conduct of a portion of the troops guarding the city and island of Galveston. He could hardly believe that the gallant men who so nobly supported him on the 1st of January, and shed so bright a halo of glory around our holy cause, could, within a few months, be so unmindful of their high obligations and so unjust to themselves and the fair fame of their regiments as to exhibit a spirit of Insubordination from such petty motives as dissatisfaction with their rations and indisposition to drill or a desire for furloughs.

The devoted soldiers of Texas, who have illustrated every battle-field in Virginia, Tennessee, Mississippi, and New Mexico by their heroism; who have lived for weeks on insufficient and uncooked food; who have borne with scanty clothing the snows and frosts of a rigorous climate, to which they had not been accustomed, without a murmur; who, leaving this State as cavalry, have drilled with little intermission from morning till night to perfect themselves as infantry; who have sacrificed every private preference to insure success against the common enemy, will hear with incredulity, and then believe with anguish, the tale which reflects such dishonor and disgrace upon their comrades left behind to defend their beloved State, their aged parents, their faithful wives and helpless children.

The major-general commanding, while condemning, will be just to his troops, and takes great pleasure in making it known that, while some few of them have been misled by bad and thoughtless men, no trace of disaffection or disloyalty has made its appearance among them; they have been ready to meet the enemy at any moment, and to ·" welcome him with bloody hands to hospitable graves."

Instead of taking the necessary means to inform the commanding general of the causes of their discontent, which, when properly presented, he would have promptly remedied, some few of the garrison of Galveston indicated a disposition to take the matter into their own hands. This the commanding general cannot too strongly condemn, nor can he too fully indorse the course pursued by Acting Brigadier-General Debray to reduce the insubordinate to obedience, whilst he is far from casting any censure on the course pursued by other officers in affairs which soon became so deplorably complicated. Indeed, the loyalty and devotion of the officers in their trying positions, with one or two exceptions (now the subjects of investigation), assure the commanding general that we will triumph over the domestic enemies of the country, if there be any, as we have done over those who have invaded our soil.

The very steps taken by those who originated or participated in this insubordination are calculated to defeat the object they had in view, for the commanding general will never yield to force even that which his sense of justice and propriety would have dictated. At the moment when this spirit exhibited itself, but before he had the least suspicion of dissatisfaction, the commanding general was perfecting a plan, to be laid before the lieutenant-general commanding the department, by which he hoped to obtain, by means of cotton, the full ration of coffee for all the troops on this side of the Mississippi, and to improve the ration in other respects.

Whether the lieutenant-general commanding will allow it under present circumstances is a matter of doubt. At all events the commanding general announces to the army under his command that the most perfect obedience of all orders will be exacted from the troops, both officers and men, on the one hand, whilst every attention will be paid to their comfort, their health, and rights, under the regulations, on the other hand.

Drills will be resumed at once, under such regulations as Brigadier-General Debray may direct.

The enemy not·developing his plans immediately after the fall of Vicksburg, no furloughs could with propriety be granted. Judging from movements made within the last few days by the enemy, the commanding general is of opinion that furloughs to a limited extent, and regulated by orders, can now be granted with comparative safety. These orders and regulations will be published within a few days, and the commanding general expects those who have for a moment forgotten their duties to the country and themselves to prove by their future conduct that they are still worthy of the confidence of their officers, of the country, and of their more faithful comrades.

In conclusion, the commanding general cannot too highly express his appreciation of the steadiness, patriotism, and fidelity exhibited during the late excitement by Debray's gallant regiment, by [W. G.] Moseley's light artillery, by the greater portion of the companies commanded by Captains Jones and [George R.] Dashiell, and the companies of Elmore's regiment remaining on the island, and by a portion of Cook's heavy artillery, and a small portion of the Third Texas Infantry. The country has cause to thank them, their commanding general thanks them in orders, and, above all, when they look back in after years to the events of this glorious struggle for liberty and independence, they will feel a just pride in having performed all their duties as faithful patriot soldiers, who were willing not only to shed their blood in the service of their country, but to endure every hardship and discomfort. without a murmur for her sake.

By command of J. Bankhead Magruder, major-general, commanding.
W. T. CARRINGTON,
Lieutenant, and Acting Assistant Adjutant-General.

Commanding officers of regiments, battalions, or separate companies will have this order read to their commands and filed in the adjutant's office. No newspaper will publish.

By command of J. Bankhead Magruder, major-general, commanding.
W. T. CARRINGTON,
Lieutenant, and Acting Assistant Adjutant-General.

AUGUST 20-SEPTEMBER 2, 1863.—Expedition from Vicksburg, Miss., to Monroe, La., including skirmishes (24th) at Bayou Macon and at Floyd.

Report of Brig. Gen. John D. Stevenson, U. S. Army, commanding Expedition.

HDQRS. THIRD DIVISION, SEVENTEENTH ARMY CORPS,
Vicksburg, Miss., September 3, 1863.

GENERAL: In pursuance of your written instructions of date August 20, 1863, I assumed command of the expedition designated by you as the Louisiana Expedition, consisting of the Third Division, Seventeenth Army Corps; Third Brigade, Sixth Division, Seventeenth Army Corps; Bolton's and Sparrestrom's batteries; the howitzer section of the Eighth Michigan Battery, and Major Osband's battalion of cavalry.

On the 20th of August, the entire command was embarked on steamboats, and transported to Goodrich's Landing, Carroll Parish, La., where it was debarked on the morning of the 21st of August. Resting until 4 a. m. of the 22d, we commenced the march in direction of Monroe, La. Pushing the command forward with all rapidity, we arrived at Monroe on the 27th instant. In the course of the march we first encountered the pickets of the enemy on the Bayou Tensas, they retiring before our cavalry advance. At Bayou Macon, some show of a stand was made, but, being soon driven from their position by the command of Major Osband, the ford of the bayou was taken possession of, and held until the advance of the infantry column reached the ford. I then directed Major Osband to push forward with his command to the town of Floyd, which he did with great promptness with a part of his command. Finding the place occupied by rebel cavalry, he charged into the town, and, after a sharp skirmish, drove the enemy from the place, with the loss to them of a number of prisoners, and to his command of 1 enlisted man severely wounded. In the meantime, a portion of his command, being detached for that purpose, surprised the camp of a company of rebel cavalry south of the ford, destroying the camp, capturing 7 prisoners, the tents, and transportation of the force. The march from Floyd to Monroe was uninterrupted, with the exception of frequent feints of defense on the part of the enemy, they invariably fleeing on the approach of the command. The military results of the expedition were the breaking up of the several camps at Floyd, Delhi, Monticello, Oak Ridge, and Monroe, and the precipitate flight of the enemy beyond the Washita River, in the direction of Shreveport. From the best information of the force of the enemy, when aggregated, the whole being under the command of Brig. Gen. P. O. Hébert, I estimate their nominal strength at 4,000 men, all cavalry, with two pieces of artillery. I do not think the effective force exceeded 1,000, many of the men being unfit for duty on account of sickness. At Oak Ridge, and also at Monroe, we found a number of hospitals established, all of them crowded with sick. In the town of Monroe, the enemy abandoned a small amount of commissary stores and forage. I found the inhabitants well disposed, and many expressions of satisfaction at the occupancy of the place by the Federal Army. The evidences of residuary loyalty were marked, and, in my judgment, only require the certainty of the establishment of Federal authority to assume the form of open declaration of attachment to the Federal Government, with demonstrative acts of loyalty for its maintenance.

I found two small earthworks thrown up by the enemy on the west bank of the Washita, immediately opposite the town; they were not occupied. Three miles west of these works about 5,000 bales of Confederate cotton had been collected and stored. This the enemy burned as they retired. I found the country in a high state of cultivation, with immense crops of corn and cotton maturing, and vast numbers of cattle fattening in the cane-brakes and swamps. I have no doubt but that forage and beef could be secured from this country in sufficient quantities to supply the department for the ensuing winter. The cotton crops of the past two years are ginned and baled on the plantations. So far as I could learn, no cotton has been burned west of Bayou Macon. I think I do not overestimate the cotton in this region that could be taken possession of by the Government in fixing the amount at 50,000 bales.

The railroad, known as the Vicksburg and Shreveport Railroad, is not operated beyond Monroe. The rolling-stock is limited—five engines and about fifty freight and two or three passenger cars. The road is in running order to Delhi. Some small portion of the machinery of each engine was removed, to prevent the use of the road, but could easily be supplied. I did not consider the destruction of road or rolling-stock a military necessity, it being of no value for military purposes to the enemy. I therefore left them undisturbed.

I remained at Monroe one day and night, and, having fully accomplished the objects of the expedition, as expressed in your letter of instruction, commenced my return march on the 28th ultimo, reaching the Mississippi River on the morning of the 2d instant. Embarking the entire command on boats provided for that purpose, have returned the entire command to their respective commands at this post. The distance accomplished by the command was 152 miles marching, and about the same distance on boats. The endurance and spirit of the command during the entire expedition were of the highest order. It affords me much pleasure to bring to your special notice the fact that the march throughout the entire distance was marked by comparatively no acts of vandalism or plunder, the whole command treating all the inhabitants with the utmost forbearance and consideration, giving them no cause of complaint. To all the officers of the command I am indebted for the promptness and efficiency with which they discharged their several duties, and to it attribute the success of the expedition.

Respectfully,

JOHN D. STEVENSON,
Brigadier-General, Commanding.

Maj. Gen. J. B. McPHERSON,
Commanding Seventeenth Army Corps.

AUGUST 20–DECEMBER 16, 1863.—Operations against Navajo Indians
in New Mexico.

REPORTS.

No. 1.—Col. Christopher Carson, First New Mexico Cavalry.
No. 2.—Capt. Rafael Chacon, First New Mexico Cavalry.
No. 3.—Capt. Joseph P. Hargrave, First California Infantry.
No. 4.—Maj. Henry D. Wallen, Seventh U. S. Infantry.

No. 1.

Reports of Col. Christopher Carson, First New Mexico Cavalry.

HEADQUARTERS NAVAJO EXPEDITION,
Fort Canby, N. Mex., August 31, 1863.

CAPTAIN: I have the honor to report, for information of the general
commanding, that, on the morning of the 20th instant, the command
left Pueblo Colorado to make an examination of the country north of
that place, including the neighborhood of the Cañon de Chelly. About
5 miles from camp found and destroyed about 10 acres of good corn;
at the night camp, some 10 miles farther, found a patch of corn, which
was fed to the animals.

On the 21st instant, returned on the route of the previous day, about
2 miles, to the Cañon Cito de los Trigos, which I had explored the night
previous. This cañon runs to northeast and southwest, with a small
stream of clear water running through it; its sides are nearly perpendicular, averaging 150 feet high; its width about 300 feet; it is about 3
miles in length; found large quantities of pumpkins and beans, the latter quite ripe, and about 50 acres of corn. Left this cañon about 4 o'clock
p. m., and returned to the camp of the 20th, taking with me packed on
the animals all the grain not previously consumed by them or destroyed
by the command. When leaving the cañon, I secreted 25 men, under
Captain Pfeiffer, in two parties, believing that the Indians who owned
this farm would return as soon as the troops had left. In this I was
not disappointed, as but a short time elapsed before 2 Indians came
to the fields. They were allowed to pass the first party, but, before getting in range of the second party, it fired on them. They were now
between the two parties, when a chase ensued, and, although badly
wounded, I am sorry to say the Indians escaped.

While *en route* on the 22d, discovered the bodies of 2 Indians killed
by a party of Utes some short time since. About 10 o'clock a. m., the
command arrived at a large bottom, containing not less than 100 acres
of as fine corn as I have ever seen. Here I determined to encamp, that
I might have it destroyed. Just as the advance guard reached the
cornfield, they discovered a Navajo, whom they pursued and killed.
He slightly wounded 1 horse, with an arrow, in the neck. Lieutenant
Fitch was in charge of the guard.

At 8 a. m. on the 23d, arrived at the west opening of Cañon de Chelly,
but could find no water; about 12 miles farther found abundance of
running water and good grass, and encamped. I made a careful examination of the country on this day's march, particularly in the immediate neighborhood of Cañon de Chelly, and am satisfied that there are
very few Indians in the cañon, and these of the very poorest. They
have no stock, and were depending entirely for subsistence on the corn
destroyed by my command on the previous day, the loss of which will

cause actual starvation, and oblige them either to come in and accept emigration to the Bosque Redondo, or to fly south to Red River to join the wealthy bands now there. I am inclined to think they will adopt the first of these courses.

On the 24th, I encamped on a bottom of very fine grass, which my animals were very much in need of. My guide informed me that General Canby encamped here with his command for several days when on his campaign of 1860, at which time the Indians were very numerous and bold, coming in sight of the troops in large numbers on the high mesas to the left of the route. Now there is not one to be seen, nor has there been any in this vicinity for a long time.

On the 25th, changed the direction of the line of march to northeast; we had heretofore been traveling due north; marched 15 miles; good grass and water.

On the 26th, traveled about 12 miles in southeast direction over a fine stock-raising country.

On the 27th, about 12 miles from the camp of the previous evening, crossed the stream that runs through the eastern opening of the Cañon de Chelly; encamped on a branch of this stream 4 miles farther on. I am of the opinion that in a very short time both these streams could be turned off, were it necessary to do so, and thus compel any Indians who might take refuge in that stronghold to abandon it for want of water; general direction of this day's march east-southeast.

August 28, left camp at 6 a. m.; marched about 12 miles to camp; direction southeast.

On the 29th, left camp at 6 a. m.; when about 7 miles out, I sent a detachment, composed of Companies D and H, to a wheat field 5 miles east of the line of march, where they killed an Indian; marched 3 miles farther and encamped; sent at night two detachments, one under Captain Everett toward Cañon de Chelly, and one under Lieutenant Dowlin to examine mountains east of the day's route; both parties returned next day. The party under Lieutenant Dowlin discovered 1 Indian mounted, but owing to the excitability of 3 of the men, he discovered the party in time to effect his escape; his horse was captured, having a wound in his back, caused by a ball passing through the saddle, and which, I think, must have injured the rider. Captain Everett saw no Indians or signs.

On the 31st, I arrived at this post.

On the 8th instant, an employé of the quartermaster's department at this post, named Hoffsletter, captured and brought into post an Indian, who stated that he came in to have a talk with his white brethren; his statement not being believed by the post commander, he was confined. While attempting to escape on the night of the 12th instant, he was killed.

I respectfully call the attention of the general commanding to Major Blakeney's report of the killing of 1 Indian and the capture of 3 others, 2 of whom escaped. From all I can learn, these Indians came in with a flag of truce, and I cannot but regret that they were not better received (when received at all), and kept until my arrival. The Indian who was here on my arrival is about seventy years of age, and is called Little Foot. I have examined him, and he states that he came from the salinas southwest of Zuñi to Chusco, where his people live, and that he came here to make arrangements to comply on the part of his people with the wishes of the general commanding, and that his people were destitute, and were ready to go to the Bosque Redondo, or anywhere else the general was disposed to send them. I believe him to have spoken in good faith, and have set him at liberty, giving him twelve days to return with his people, at which time he promises to be here.

In summing up the results of the last month's scout, I congratulate myself on having gained one very important point, viz, a knowledge of where the Navajoes have fled with their stock, and where I am certain to find them. I have also gained an accurate knowledge of a great portion of the country, which will be of incalculable benefit in our future operations. I have ascertained that a large party of Navajoes are on Salt River, near the San Francisco Mountains, among the Apaches, and within easy striking distance of Pima villages. I would respectfully suggest that a force operating against them from that point would greatly facilitate the entire subjugation of the Navajo nation.

I am about to send the command just returned to the camp 7 miles south of this post, where they will remain a few days to recruit their animals and refit, previous to proceeding to Red River.

Very respectfully, your obedient servant,

C. CARSON,
Colonel First New Mexico Volunteers, Commanding.

Capt. BENJ. C. CUTLER,
Asst. Adjt. Gen., Hdqrs. Dept. of New Mexico, Santa Fé, N. Mex.

—

HEADQUARTERS NAVAJO EXPEDITION,
Fort Canby, N. Mex., October 5, 1863.

CAPTAIN: I have the honor to report, for the information of the general commanding, my arrival at this post to-day, off a scout of twenty-seven days.

On the 9th ultimo, I left camp at the Cienega Amarilla, 7 miles south of this post, with Companies D, G, H, K, L, and M, numbering 10 officers and 395 enlisted men and 192 horses.

On the 11th, I arrived at Zuñi, where I met Surveyor-General Clark and escort returning from the newly discovered mines. From Captain Pishon, First Cavalry, California Volunteers, who was in command of the escort, I learned that he had seen no fresh trails of Navajoes on the Little Colorado; but nevertheless I determined to examine that section of country, with a view to future operations, and hoping that by proceeding some distance below, where the road leaves the river, I might surprise some party, who, calculating upon the fact that no previous expedition had penetrated that portion of the country, would be there with their herds in fancied security. The Governor of Zuñi furnished 3 men as guides to the river, and I was accompanied by about 20 others, who desired thus to show their friendship to the whites and their enmity to the Navajoes. That they are not on friendly terms with the Navajoes, and are desirous to aid us in every possible manner, I am fully satisfied, not alone from their professions, but from having seen the dead bodies of some Navajoes, whom they had recently killed in an engagement, and from other facts which have come under my observation. They have a considerable quantity of corn, which they are willing to sell to the Government, and my chief quartermaster is making the necessary arrangements for its purchase.

I encamped 4 miles southwest of their village, and remained in camp until 4 p. m. next day, when I started, traveling all night, and arriving at next water (Jacob's Well), 35 miles from Zuñi, about 3 a. m. on the 13th.

The grass in this vicinity was not good, and in the afternoon I moved to a spring 9 miles farther. Before leaving camp, I sent some infantry with the Zuñi Indians to examine the mountains south and east of our route. From these springs the road to the Little Colorado leads for 30 miles over the finest grass country I have ever seen; but there is no permanent water.

Encamped about 7 p. m. on the edge of an arroyo, where we found some water-holes; little water and very muddy. Moved camp next day 2 miles to some more holes of same description. Here I left the packs and infantry, under Capt. F. McCabe, directing him to proceed to the river next day, it being but 15 miles distant, while I proceeded with the mounted men of my command to examine the country northwest of our line of march. I left camp at sundown, under the guidance of an enlisted man of Company M, who professed knowing the country. About 10 p. m. found my guide ignorant of our whereabouts, and encamped. About 4 p. m. next day, found some very muddy rainwater, and encamped; about 40 miles since previous evening. I saw no indications of Indians. On the 17th, joined the pack train on the river, having marched about 35 miles. Learned from Captain McCabe that the Zuñi Indians had returned to the village, having taken about 50 head of sheep and goats from the Navajoes. The 3 guides returned with them. On the 22d, some fresh signs reported by my spies. I sent forward in the evening Captains Pfeiffer and Deus and Lieutenants Hodt, Hubbell, and Postle, with 126 enlisted men, with directions to march all night, so as to get to the Rapids near daylight. I myself followed up next morning with the remainder of the command. On the 24th, was joined by Captain Pfeiffer's party. At the Rapids they saw and pursued 7 Navajoes with about 15 horses; but, owing to the broken-down condition of our horses, the Indians escaped. They captured 1 child. I examined the river thoroughly a distance of 85 miles from where the California road first strikes it, and am satisfied that no Indians have been on the river within this distance since last spring, excepting this party of 7 seen by Captain Pfeiffer. On the 25th, commenced our return march on the river. On the 27th, I selected the best of the animals (horses and mules), and, with 7 officers and 148 enlisted men, determined to explore the country from the Colorado north to Fort Canby.

The remainder of the command, under Capt. J. Thompson, I directed to return to the post by easy marches on the route we came. Marched 15 miles up the river, and encamped until 6.30 p. m., when we left the river.

On the 30th, about 60 miles from the river, we arrived at our fourth camp of the previous scout, when en route for Moqui. At quarter to 7 a. m., on the 2d instant, halted in a small cañon to breakfast, and to rest and water the animals. Saw fresh Indian signs, and had the country in the vicinity examined; discovered a small village, which had just been abandoned. This I had destroyed. We found in it 6 saddles and bridles, 1 rifle, some blankets and other property, which we destroyed. The parties I sent out captured 19 animals, part of which were wild mares; 7 of the latter got away, and, with my broken-down animals, I was unable to recover them. No Indians were discovered. Three men left the camp, without my knowledge, to hunt up the mules. They did not again join the command until its arrival at this post, where they arrived yesterday evening. They were attacked by a party of Indians when within 5 miles of this post, one of whom they killed. One of the men named Artin, a private of Company G, being a little in advance, was very severely wounded, though it is expected he will recover. The Indians captured his mule.

On the 3d of October, I arrived at the Jara, about 8 miles south of the Pueblo Colorado. Lieutenant Postle here discovered an Indian, whom he pursued with 6 men. Being in advance of his party, he overtook the Indian, whom he wounded in three places, when he was himself slightly wounded by the Indian.

Captain Thompson's command has not yet arrived, but is expected on the 7th instant.

This scout, I am sorry to say, was a failure as regards any positive injury inflicted on the Navajoes; but the fatigues and hardships undergone by my command are fully compensated for by increased knowledge of the country, and of the haunts of the Navajoes with their stock.

I would respectfully call the attention of the general commanding to the fact that since leaving the river the animals of my command have had but five days' rations of corn; that since that time they have been almost constantly in the field, and operating in a country where grass has only been found at long intervals, and where the supply of water is uncertain and too irregular for marching columns. The only exception to this has been while east of Cañon de Chelly and on the Little Colorado; and that at no time since their arrival in this country have they been in an efficient condition for field service. The result of all this is, that I cannot again this winter take the field with a mounted force; and as I believe the animals to be too poor to stand the rigors of a winter at this place, I respectfully suggest the economy of having them wintered on the Rio Grande. I am now about to operate in detached parties on foot, which plan of campaign I shall continue during the winter. One party of 75 men will leave this post to-morrow morning.

Little Foot did not come in as promised, and I shall send a party immediately to hunt him up at Chusco.

I am, captain, very respectfully, your obedient servant,

C. CARSON,
Colonel First New Mexico Cavalry, Commanding Expedition.

Capt. BENJ. C. CUTLER.
Asst. Adjt. Gen., Hdqrs. Dept. of New Mexico, Santa Fé, N. Mex.

—

HEADQUARTERS DEPARTMENT OF NEW MEXICO,
Santa Fé, N. Mex., December 20, 1863.

Brig. Gen. LORENZO THOMAS,
Adjutant-General, U. S. Army, Washington, D. C.:

GENERAL: Inclosed herewith please find the official report of Colonel Carson's last scout after the Navajo Indians. I beg to call the attention of the War Department to what he says of the destitute condition of that peaceable and gentle tribe of Indians known as the Moquis.

A copy of a private letter from Maj. Henry D. Wallen, U. S. Army, commanding at Fort Sumner, N. Mex., will be found inclosed herewith.* It gives an interesting account of the feelings, condition, and prospects of the Apache and Navajo Indians gathered together at that point.

I am, general, very respectfully, your obedient servant,

JAMES H. CARLETON,
Brigadier-General, Commanding.

---

* See letter of December 11, 1863, p. 844.

HEADQUARTERS NAVAJO EXPEDITION,
Fort Canby, N. Mex., December 6, 1863.

CAPTAIN: I have the honor to report, for the information of the department commander, that on the 15th ultimo I left this post with Companies C, D, G, H, and L, First Cavalry, New Mexico Volunteers, dismounted, for the purpose of exploring the country west of the Oribi villages, and, if possible, to chastise the Navajoes inhabiting that region.

On the 16th, I detached 30 men, with Sergt. Andreas Herrera, of Company C, First Cavalry, New Mexico Volunteers, on a fresh trail which intersected our route. The sergeant followed the trail for about 20 miles, when he overtook a small party of Navajoes, 2 of whom he killed, wounded 2, and captured 50 head of sheep and 1 horse. *En route* the party came on a village lately deserted, which they destroyed. The energy and zeal displayed by the sergeant and his party on this occasion merit my warmest approbation.

On the 21st, arrived at the Moqui village. I found on my arrival that the inhabitants of all the villages, except the Oribi, had a misunderstanding with the Navajoes, owing to some injustice perpetrated by the latter. I took advantage of this feeling, and succeeded in obtaining representatives from all the villages, Oribi excepted, to accompany me on the war-path. My object in insisting upon parties of these people accompanying me was simply to involve them so far that they could not retract—to bind them to us, and place them in antagonism to the Navajoes. They were of some service, and manifested a great desire to aid in every respect. While on this subject, I would respectfully represent that these people, numbering some 4,000 souls, are in a most deplorable condition, from the fact that the country for several miles around their villages is quite barren and is entirely destitute of vegetation. They have no water for purposes of irrigation, and their only dependence for subsistence is on the little corn they raise when the weather is propitious, which is not always the case in this latitude. They are a peaceable people; have never robbed nor murdered the people of New Mexico, and are in every way worthy of the fostering care of the Government. Of the bounty so unsparingly bestowed by it on the other Pueblo Indians, aye, even on marauding bands, they have never tasted, and I earnestly recommend that the attention of the Indian Bureau be called to this matter. I understand that a couple of years' annuities for the Navajoes, not distributed, are in the possession of the superintendent of Indian affairs at Santa Fé, and I consider that, if such an arrangement would be legal, these goods would be well bestowed on these people.

Before my arrival at Oribi, I was credibly informed that the people of that village had formed an alliance with the Navajoes, and on reaching there I caused their governor and another of their principal men to be bound, and took them with me as prisoners. The first day's march from their village I unbound them, and during the time they were with me they conducted themselves well. From the Oribi village I marched my command 65 miles, with but one halt of two hours, and at 2 a. m. on the 24th I arrived at a running stream, a tributary of the Little Colorado. Next day my command captured 1 boy and 7 horses and destroyed an encampment. The mounted party, while out scouting that day, had 2 horses give out, and when the riders were returning to camp they passed 3 concealed Indians, one of whom fired off his rifle in the air and then rode toward them. On his approach, the soldiers were going to shoot him, but owing to his gesticulating they allowed him to draw nigh. He had 2 rifles on his saddle, both of which the soldiers took, after which they allowed him to depart as he came. One of the rifles was recognized by the Moquis as belonging to Manuelita, a chief of great influence. It is more than probable that the Indian, whoever he was, desired to have an interview with me, but was deterred by the hostile attitude of the soldiers.

On the 25th, we captured 1 woman and child, about 500 head of sheep and goats, and 70 head of horses, and destroyed another Indian encampment. There were 5 Indians with this herd, but on our approach they fled. About 3 miles from their encampment the spies gave us the information. The mounted party and a few of the officers immediately rode forward. Captain McCabe, Lieutenant Dowlin, Mr. J. C. Edgar, myself, and Lieutenants Murphy and Montoya, with those of the mounted party, were the first to arrive at the herd, but only in time to see the Indians climbing the very steep side of the cañon of the Little Colorado, where their herd was, and out of our reach. The conduct of the above-named gentlemen on this occasion is worthy of commendation. Had our horses been in a fit condition, there is no doubt but that we would have been enabled to overhaul these Indians, but they were unable to travel sufficiently quick, owing to the fact that they had been the three days previous without sufficient rest, and with but little grass. I encamped on the table-lands of the river, and that night sent out spies, who, on their return, informed me that the Navajoes were in the vicinity. At daylight next morning I sent out two parties of 50 men each, under the command of Captains Pfeiffer and McCabe, to examine the localities indicated by the spies as occupied by the Navajoes. The parties returned to camp late at night without having found any Indians, although they found every indication of where they had recently been; in some places the fires were still burning. From this place to where the Navajoes went is three days' march, without water, as I am informed by a Mexican boy taken captive some time since by the Navajoes and recaptured by Captain McCabe. This my animals could not stand, and I was reluctantly obliged to let them go unmolested. Our camp of this day is about 25 miles northwest of the San Francisco Mountains.

On my return to Moqui, I took a different route from the one I came, but on neither route is water to be found for a distance of at least 50 miles. While en route on the morning of the 3d instant, I descried at a distance the smoke of an Indian encampment. I took with me the mounted party and 50 infantry, with the hope of being able to surprise them. After a rapid march of about 8 miles, we came to the valley, at the opposite side of which were the Indians, but being obliged to descend a steep hill in view of the Indians (of whom there were 5), they managed to escape. They left behind them their shields, clothing, &c., and we captured 1 horse and 4 oxen.

I arrived yesterday at this post, and as soon as the animals are sufficiently rested, I shall send a command to examine the Cañon de Chelly, and the smaller cañon which intersects it. Were I not of the opinion that but few, if any, Navajoes are in the cañon, I should have paid it a visit long since, but of that I convinced myself while in that vicinity in September. To the Zuñi Indians, whom I employed as spies, I am greatly indebted for the zeal and ability displayed by them, particularly their governors, Mariano and Salvadore, the latter of whom acted as my interpreter with the other Indians.

The boy who was taken by us on the 24th ultimo I allowed to go off, that he might communicate to the Navajoes the intentions of the general commanding in regard to them, of which I took particular pains to inform him.

It is quite possible that, owing to the extended operations of our armies elsewhere, those of my command may be overlooked, but I will venture to assert that no troops of the United States have ever before been called upon to endure as many hardships as did the men of my command on this scout, and I am proud to say that all was borne with the utmost cheerfulness, both of officers and men.

Inclosed I have the honor to transmit a report of Maj. F. P. Abreü, commanding at this post, and reports of other officers of his command.*

I am, captain, very respectfully, your obedient servant,

C. CARSON,
Colonel First Cavalry, New Mexico Vols., Comdg. Expedition.

Capt. BENJ. C. CUTLER,
Asst. Adjt. Gen., Hdqrs., Dept. of New Mexico, Santa Fé, N. Mex.

No. 2.

Report of Capt. Rafael Chacon, First New Mexico Cavalry.

FORT WINGATE, N. MEX.

SIR : In conformity with Orders, No. 72, from these headquarters, I started for the Navajo country on the 23d of August last, with 40 enlisted men, and Second Lieut. Martin Quintana, of my company.

August 23.—Went to Cebolletta, and encamped for the night; wood, water, and grass in abundance; distance, 18 miles.

August 24.—From this point I started about 1 o'clock in the morning in a southwesterly direction, and stopped to rest at an arroyo, which was full of rain-water; distance, 18 miles. I left this point and camped for the night in the Llano de los Beteados, same general direction; abundance of rain-water in holes, also of grass, but no wood; total distance traveled to-day, 35 miles. As yet no fresh sign of Indians.

August 25.—Left this place during the night, still keeping the same direction, and traveled for about 12 miles, and found a lagoon of water, and rested. In the afternoon I left this place, and reached the Rito Quemado where I encamped for the night, with abundance of water, grass, and wood; total distance traveled, 33 miles. No Indians seen.

August 26.—Left the Rito Quemado during the night, pursuing the same general direction, and, after traveling about 15 miles, arrived at La Cañada de José Largo, where I rested for three or four hours. From this point I returned to the Rito Quemado in a northwesterly direction, and encamped in the valley of the Quemado, without water; abundance of grass and wood; distance traveled, 34 miles.

August 27.—From this point I left during the night and traveled in a westerly direction, and stopped to rest at the Salt Lakes of Zuñi (salinas), and rested for a few hours in order to water the horses and mules. After my animals were somewhat refreshed, I left this place, and soon as we got on the high ground we espied some Navajoes, whom we immediately pursued, and we succeeded in killing 2 and capturing 1 full-grown Indian, 2 grown women, and 5 small children. The man (Indian) informed me that on the head of the Colorado Chiquito there were over 2,500 Navajo Indians trading with the Coyote Apaches, and that he was on

----

* Not found.

his way from Jemes with powder and lead, for the purpose of trading with the Navajoes. He also informed me that the Navajoes residing in Jemes are continually trading powder and lead with these Indians (the warlike); he himself had in his possession a very fine rifle, and an abundance of powder and lead.

During the night of the same day, I dispatched a sergeant, with 15 men, in order to attack some Navajo huts which the captive Indian promised to show to us. Upon arriving at the place, they discovered that the Indians had all fled; the captive also attempted to escape, but did not succeed, as he was killed by one of the soldiers who had him in charge. On this day I traveled in various directions, and at night I encamped at a lagoon full of rain-water, about 18 miles south of the Salt Lakes; there was also an abundance of grass and wood. Total distance traveled, about 26 miles.

August 28.—I left this place about 3 o'clock in the morning toward Cienega Amarilla, nearly due west. At this point I found a great many Indians, but they got sight of us and fled. They traveled all day in an easterly direction, and during the night took a westerly direction, making a sort of triangle. I remained all day at the Cienega Amarilla, and kept my spies out, in order that they might see the direction of the dust. During the night I left this place, and, after traveling about four hours, arrived within 2 miles of where the Indians were. Attacked at day-break, but although they exceeded the number of 150, they immediately fled in all directions. We here captured 7 children, and recovered a captive Mexican boy named Agapito Apodaca from Ticolote; also 1,500 head of sheep and goats, 17 head of horses, mules, burros, and colts. We killed 2 men and 1 squaw during the skirmish; and I ordered all their equipage which we captured to be burned. There were some old guns and pistols which were captured, which were also burned, as they were not worth the trouble to pack them. At this place there is no water.

August 29.—From this place I took a southeasterly direction, in order to strike the Colorado Chiquito as soon as possible, as my animals were sadly in want of water; arrived at the Colorado Chiquito, I met Captain Hargrave, First Infantry, California Volunteers, with his company ; we camped together at this place, distant from the Cienega Amarilla about 25 miles. During the night, I sent off 20 mounted men up the river, in order to see if they could discover anything of Indians; they returned the next day, and reported nothing in sight except the tracks.

August 30.—From this place we traveled down the river, in order to strike the Zuñi road. On our return to the fort, we encamped on the river that night, 8 miles distant from our last camp.

August 31, *September* 1 *and* 2.—During these three days made about 67 miles, and camped at Peñas Negras, about 4 miles east of Zuñi, and Captain Hargrave camped at Zuñi; abundance of wood, water, and grass.

September 3.—From last camp I marched to the Pescado Spring and encamped; distance about 12 miles. Captain Hargrave, who had overtaken me and passed me in the morning before I left camp, had his mules driven off by the Indians. Immediately upon my arrival, I sent off 10 men (mounted) in pursuit, but they returned on the next day, reporting that they had not been able to overtake the mules, as they had been divided into bands, and also as a large part of their horses gave out entirely. It is my opinion that the Zuñi Indians had a hand in this robbery, and my opinion is further strengthened by what Jesus Alriso says about the matter, viz, that when he and the soldiers were on the trail in pursuit, a lot of Zuñi Indians who were pretending to be guiding them, would run across the trail, and also in different directions excepting the one in which the trail went, thereby apparently trying to mislead them—at any rate to delay them until night would come on—and our men then would not be able to follow the trail on account of the darkness; and it is also more than probable that even if·Navajoes did steal them, they were in their town (at the Pescado) with the Zuñis when Captain Hargrave's company arrived.

September 4, 5, 6, and 7.—Traveled by the old Zuñi road toward the fort, and arrived without any further difficulty, excepting that during the 6th I missed one of my men, and, after inquiring about him, I learned that he had not been seen since the night before, while we were on the march. I sent back 4 men from the Aqua Fria in search of him, but they were unable to find him. He since arrived at the post, and appears to be somewhat out of his head. He reports that this side of Inscription Rock he was pursued by a large number of Indians, and when he discovered they were gaining on him, he threw himself off his horse, and hid himself among the rocks, and in this way he escaped.

During my entire trip none of my men were either wounded or sick, and I am happy to say that of the property I took with me I have lost but 1 horse. The total number of Indians killed is 6 men and 2 women; captured 14 captives, large and small, and rescued 1 Mexican captive; also 1,500 head of sheep and goats and 17 head of horses, mules, burros, and colts.

Respectfully submitted.

RAFAEL CHACON,
Captain First New Mexico Volunteers.

Lieut. Col. J. F. CHAVES,
First New Mexico Vols., Comdg. Officer, Fort Wingate, N. Mex.

No. 3.

Report of Capt. Joseph P. Hargrave, First California Infantry.

FORT WINGATE, N. MEX., *September 8, 1863.*

SIR: I have the honor to report that, pursuant to Orders, No. 72, current series, from headquarters Fort Wingate, dated August 21, 1863, I left this post on the 22d ultimo with 44 men of my company (C), First Infantry, California Volunteers, on our expedition against the Navajoes. According to instructions, I proceeded to the Zuñi villages with wagons; reached that place on the 25th, a distance of 75 miles. At Zuñi, I left the wagons, extra animals, and stores in charge of a guard, consisting of Sergeant Boone and 3 men, and started the next morning, 26th instant, with pack-mules for the Little Colorado, going via the Ojo Venado; reached the river on the 28th, the distance being about 65 miles.

The next morning started up the river, keeping well into the hills to avoid being seen. Having gone about 10 miles, saw a party of Indians on the river, perhaps 40 in number. We approached cautiously and unobserved to within about 2,000 yards, and seeing that, from the nature of the ground, it was impossible to get closer without coming in plain view, we made a run for them, but as they had not unsaddled their horses, they mounted and got off before we got within gunshot of them. We pursued them several miles, but to no purpose; they, being well mounted, soon left us in the distance.

We then scoured the country for several miles around, and captured about 500 head of sheep; saw a few Indians, but failed to get within shooting distance. In the afternoon met and joined Capt. R. Chacon, First New Mexico Volunteers, whom I deem the proper person to report the further proceedings of the expedition.

I am, sir, very respectfully, your obedient servant,
J. P. HARGRAVE,
Captain First Infantry, California Volunteers.
[Lieut. Col. J. F. CHAVES,]
Commanding Officer, Fort Wingate, N. Mex.

No. 4.

Report of Maj. Henry D. Wallen, Seventh U. S. Infantry.

HEADQUARTERS DEPARTMENT OF NEW MEXICO,
Santa Fé, N. Mex., December 23, 1863.

GENERAL: Please find inclosed herewith a report of Maj. Henry D. Wallen, Seventh U. S. Infantry, commanding Fort Sumner, N. Mex., of a fight which took place within 35 miles of that post between parties sent out from the post and 130 Navajo Indians. The result was, 12 Navajoes were left dead upon the field, and 1 was taken prisoner. Many were doubtless wounded, but these were borne away. Our people recaptured 9,889 sheep and a good deal of other property.

I beg to call your attention to the conduct of Lieutenant Newbold, Fifth U. S. Infantry, who led the handful of cavalry; and also to the conduct of Mr. Lorenzo Labadie, Indian agent, and to the gallant chaplain of Fort Sumner, the Rev. Mr. Fialon. These two gentlemen, at the head of 30 Mescalero Apache Indians from the reservation at Fort Sumner (Apaches who one year ago were our mortal enemies), did most all the work, as they were fortunate in being the first to encounter the Navajoes.

Captain Bristol and Lieutenant McDermott, Fifth U. S. Infantry, at the head of their companies, manifested the utmost zeal and alacrity on this occasion, but were unable to get up in time to participate in the affair. It was a handsome little battle on the open plains.

The Apache chiefs, Cadette and Blanco, were very distinguished. One of their braves, named Alazau, was mortally wounded.

I beg to have authority to issue a suit of clothes to each of these 30 Apaches who took part in this fight. The Government should give them some token of its appreciation of such fidelity and gallantry. They volunteered for the service, and fought without the hope of reward.

I am, general, very respectfully, your obedient servant,
JAMES H. CARLETON,
Brigadier-General, Commanding.
Brig. Gen. LORENZO THOMAS,
Adjutant-General, U. S. Army, Washington, D. C.

HEADQUARTERS,
Fort Sumner, N. Mex., December 18, 1863.

CAPTAIN: I have the honor to report to the general commanding the department that about 4 o'clock on the morning of the 16th instant, Mr. Labadie, Indian agent, and the Rev. Mr. Fialon, chaplain of the post, reported to me that a large number of Navajo Indians, with an immense herd of sheep, were at the Carretas. I immediately had the officers of Company D, Fifth, and Company C, Seventh Infantry, awakened, and their companies prepared to take the field, with two days' rations in haversacks. Lieutenant Latimer, with 8 mounted men of Company B, Second Cavalry, California Volunteers (all the cavalry at the post), was also got in readiness. Mr. Labadie, Mr. Fialon, and about 30 Apache Indians also started in pursuit. The companies left the post at 5.30 a. m., for the Carretas. The mounted party and the Indian agent, with his Indians, outstripped the party on foot, having taken up the Navajo trail on the west bank of the Pecos River, and about 10 miles from the post. At a distance of 35 miles in a direct line, a little north of west from Fort Sumner, they overtook the Navajoes, in number about 130, 10 mounted and 20 armed with rifles, and 5,259 sheep. A severe contest ensued, in which the Navajoes lost 12 killed and left on the field, and a number killed and wounded who were carried off, 1 prisoner taken, all the sheep recovered, amounting to 5,259, 13 burros, 4 rifles, 1 horse, their provisions, blankets, moccasins (150 pairs), and pretty much all the effects taken from Mr. Labadie's train *en route* to this place.

I beg respectfully to call the attention of the commanding general to the gallant conduct of Mr. Labadie, Privates Loder and Osier, of Company B, Second Cavalry, California Volunteers, Ojo Blanco, and Cadette, the chiefs of the two bands of Apaches on the reservation, Alazau, an Apache, who was badly wounded, and the Apaches generally, who rendered signal service.

Lieutenant Newbold, with 3 men, pursued the flying Navajoes for 3 miles beyond the scene of action, but from the great number of the enemy and the exhausted condition of his horses, was obliged to desist .from farther pursuit. His zeal on this occasion was highly commendable.

The infantry, under command of Captain Bristol and Lieutenant McDermott, Fifth Infantry, marched rapidly in heavy sand and snow about 24 miles, when word was sent to Captain Bristol from the front that farther pursuit by the infantry would be unnecessary, when he returned to the fort.

I am under obligations to the chaplain, Rev. Mr. Fialon, for riding back alone in the night from the battle-ground in order to secure conveyance for the wounded Apache. At daylight on the 17th, the surgeon with an ambulance was dispatched to bring in the wounded man ; but before reaching the camp the Indian had died.

The Navajoes, just before reaching the Pecos, were alarmed by some pistol-shots discharged from a wagon train that left the post that morning, and abandoned 4,630 sheep, which were secured by the Mexicans attached to the train.

On the morning of the 17th, I dispatched Lieutenant McDermott, with 10 mounted men and 6 Apaches, to collect the herd and bring it to the post, that the sheep may be properly distributed; and I await instructions from the commanding general with regard to the distribution of both herds of sheep, 9,889 in all.

Delgadito, the chief of the peace party of Navajoes now at the post, called on me this morning, and expressed his pleasure that the " Ladrones" (as he termed them) had been chastised, and begged that I would permit him on the next occasion to join the scouting party with some of his men.

I am, captain, very respectfully, your obedient servant,
H. D. WALLEN,
Major Seventh U. S. Infantry, Commanding.

Capt. BENJ. C. CUTLER,
Asst. Adjt. Gen., Dept. of New Mexico, Santa Fé, N. Mex.

AUGUST 29–30, 1863.—Mutiny at Camp Hubbard, Thibodeaux, La.

Proceedings of a Military Commission, and Correspondence.

PROCEEDINGS OF A MILITARY COMMISSION ASSEMBLED AT THIBO-
DEAUX, LA., SEPTEMBER 5, 1863, BY VIRTUE OF THE FOLLOWING
ORDERS:

GENERAL ORDERS, } HDQRS. DEFENSES OF NEW ORLEANS,
　　No. 46.　　 } 　　*New Orleans, La., September 4,* 1863.

A military commission, consisting of Co1. E. L. Molineux, One hundred and fifty-ninth New York Volunteers, Lieut. Col. Charles A. Burt,
One hundred and fifty-ninth New York Volunteers, Lieut. Col. J. Tarbell, Ninety-first New York Volunteers, Maj. W. M. Rexford, One hundred and thirty-first New York Volunteers, and Capt. George H. Wheaton, One hundred and thirty-first New York Volunteers, is appointed
to meet at Camp Hubbard, to inquire into the cause of the mutiny, its
course and suppression, in the First Louisiana Cavalry.

This investigation will be prompt, and sit without regard to day or
hour.

By command of Col. E. G. Beckwith, commanding Defenses of New
Orleans:

W. D. SMITH,
Lieutenant-Colonel, and Acting Assistant Adjutant-General.

THIBODEAUX, LA., *September* 5, 1863.

The court met pursuant to the above order at Thibodeaux, La., Saturday, September 5, 1863, and after being duly sworn (the members by
the recorder and the recorder by the president), proceeded to the examination of witnesses.

Lieut. Col. HARAI ROBINSON, being duly sworn, deposes and says:

My name is Harai Robinson. I am lieutenant-colonel of the First Louisiana Cavalry. I was charged with the execution of Special Orders, 209; Paragraph VIII,
Department of the Gulf (a copy of which is hereunto annexed, marked A). I was
delayed in the execution of the order by having to send to Donaldsonville for the stragglers and Government property, and to allow the officers of the late Second Rhode
Island Cavalry necessary time to make out descriptive lists of the men and inventories
of public property. They informed me none wished to remain; none wished to apply
for commissions in the First Louisiana Cavalry. They did not hesitate in telling me
that in their opinion I should never be able to do anything with their men. They
further said to me that, as they understood Special Orders, 209, Paragraph VIII,
Department of the Gulf, they themselves were already discharged the service. In
reply to which I intimated to them that certainly no certificates of honorable discharge would be given them if they permitted the men that they had there present
to desert before they were consolidated, or failed scrupulously to turn over to the
regimental quartermaster of the First Louisiana Cavalry all public property.

The officers of the Second Rhode Island Cavalry had full control of their men up to
August 29, when they informed me that all their papers were ready. On this day,
at 4 p. m., the First Louisiana Cavalry assembled for dress-parade. The officers of the
Second Rhode Island Cavalry were instructed to form their line in front of and facing
the First Louisiana Cavalry, 40 yards distant.

Special Orders, 209, Paragraph VIII, Department of the Gulf, was then for the first
time read by the adjutant to the First Louisiana Cavalry, the First Louisiana Cavalry
being at ordered arms. I turned with my staff to the Second Rhode Island Cavalry,
the commanding officer of which had to receive a peremptory order before the men
or the officers were brought to a salute. The adjutant of the First Louisiana Cavalry
was then instructed by me to read to them Special Orders, 209, Paragraph VIII, Department of the Gulf. Instantaneously, and as if by accord, a tumultuous and general
"No, no," was uttered from one end of the line to the other. I then assumed command
of them in person, ordered sabers to be presented. After hesitating and wavering, they
executed the order. Sabers were then ordered to be carried and returned. Men ordered

to dismount, and form ranks as preparatory to fighting on foot. A detachment of the First Louisiana Cavalry was then sent to relieve the horse-holders and to take the horses from the ground.

In order to divide the late Second Rhode Island Cavalry into five different squads, five non-commissioned officers from each company were placed at intervals of 10 paces from each other, on a line at right angles with right company guides. The roll was called by the first sergeants; the men were placed as directed on the left of the non-commissioned officers, in which manner they were marched off, and formed on the left of the different companies of the First Louisiana Cavalry. Orders were given by me to each of the officers of the First Louisiana Cavalry after the parade was dismissed that the men should not leave the camp of the companies to which they had been assigned.

On the following morning (August 30, 1863), Lieut. Thomas Maher, regimental commissary and acting regimental quartermaster, who was charged with the reception of the property from the Second Rhode Island Cavalry, informed me that it was impossible for him to proceed with the work, as horses, after he had received them, were being cast loose from the picket rope by the enlisted men of the late Second Rhode Island Cavalry, who were also carrying off other public property.

To investigate the matter, I went myself to the camp of the late Second Rhode Island Cavalry, and found, as near as I could judge, all the enlisted men who had been assigned to the First Louisiana Cavalry the evening previous assembled in groups, sitting on the ground in the center of the camp. I rode up to them, and quietly ordered them to take up their packs and join their respective companies. Not a man offered to obey the order. Two of them arose, and used the following language, or words to this effect: "Colonel, we have made up our minds that, as we enlisted in the Second Rhode Island Cavalry, we will, by God, serve in no other. We will not go. Do as you like; but, by God, we won't serve." A murmur of assent ran through the crowd, but not a man moved.

I immediately ordered out the First Louisiana Cavalry, one company mounted, three on foot. The mounted company was ordered to encircle the camp, and the three on foot to form a line facing the mutineers. I then rode up to the mutineers, taking with me a German interpreter, who, after I had addressed them myself in English, Spanish, and French, and ordering them to join the companies to which they had been assigned, communicated the same order to them in German. Not a man of the mutineers stirred. I then told them emphatically that if they did not rise up and form line, I should order them to be fired on. They then arose, and I picked out the two ringleaders, one of whom had used mutinous and seditious language the evening previous at the consolidation. Some decisive action was necessary. Some of the late Rhode Islanders had deserted the same morning. Their character was notorious for lawlessness and want of discipline. Nearly three of the companies present of the First Louisiana Cavalry were recruits who had not been a month in camp. I knew that no guard could hold these Rhode Islanders in camp. Imprisonment they did not fear. It was reported to me that they courted being sent to some place of confinement in a body, and I was certain that nothing but fear would prevent them from turning into a band of marauders, which would completely demoralize the First Louisiana Cavalry, cause the orders of the department to fall to the ground, and make military law and discipline a farce. I chose severe and instantaneous measures. I ordered two companies of the First Louisiana Cavalry, on foot, to form line on the wings and at right angles with the line of mutineers. I wrote the following penciled order in the saddle, appointing Adjt. E. Hall provost-marshal, and placed the third company at his disposal:

"First Lieutenant Hall, adjutant of the First Louisiana Cavalry, is hereby appointed provost-marshal of the day, and is charged as such with the execution of Private Richard Murphy, Boston *alias* Richard Smith, and of Private Frederick Freeman, *alias* William Davis, mutineers—a military necessity.

"HARAI ROBINSON,
"*Lieutenant-Colonel, Commanding First Louisiana Cavalry.*"

In accordance with this order, and within half an hour of the calling out of the First Louisiana Cavalry to suppress the mutiny, the two ringleaders, Privates Richard Murphy, *alias* Dick Smith, and Frederick Freeman, *alias* William Davis, were shot to death in front of the whole command.

By the JUDGE-ADVOCATE:

Question. Were the 2 men who were shot the men who used the mutinous language?

Answer. They were. The smaller of the two having also used seditious language the evening previous.

Question. Did you hear the seditious language used the evening pre-vious to the execution, or was it reported to you?

Answer. I heard it. It was addressed to me personally

Question. What was the purport of it?

Answer. "We have been cheated into this. Had we known it, we would not have been here." The attitude, at the same time, being insolent and defiant.

Question. Have you a copy of Special Orders, 209, Headquarters Department of the Gulf?

Answer. I have.

Colonel Robinson here produced the order, a copy of which is appended hereto.

Question. State more definitely in regard to the execution. How were they shot, by whom, &c.?

Answer. The mutineers and two companies of the First Louisiana Cavalry, on foot, formed three sides of a square, the mutineers forming the base. On a line perpendicular with the center of the base, and some 20 feet beyond the wings, Company F, First Louisiana Cavalry, at the time composed of about 20 men, was divided into two platoons, one commanded by Lieutenant Masicot, the other by the orderly sergeant. The men to be executed were severally placed at 10 paces in front of the center of each platoon. The adjutant of the regiment charged with their execution had them blindfolded, took their two names and last requests, and offered them time to pray; after all of which, at a signal from him, each platoon fired successively.

By the COURT:

Question. Has that part of the First Louisiana Cavalry which was formerly the Second Rhode Island Cavalry, since the execution of two of its members, shown any disposition to mutiny?

Answer. None in the least.

Question. Have they since that time obeyed all orders and shown a disposition to conduct themselves as good soldiers?

Answer. They have, in every sense; vying with their new associates in the faithful performance of their duty and neatness of personal appearance.

Question. During the particulars of the arrest and execution of the two men described by you, were you present all the while, and was the arrest and execution in obedience to your order and direction?

Answer. I was present all the while, and everything that was done was in obedience to my orders.

Question. What was the personal appearance, condition of the arms, &c., of the Second Rhode Island Cavalry at the time of the consolidation?

Answer. Appearance bad. Condition of the arms such that they cannot be used. They appear not to have been cleaned since issued.

Capt. FRANCIS M. IVES, First Louisiana Cavalry, being duly sworn, deposes and says:

My name is Francis M. Ives. I am a captain in the First Louisiana Cavalry. On the afternoon of the 29th of August, 1863, the regiment (Second Rhode Island Cavalry) was formed for consolidation with the First Louisiana Cavalry. The Special Orders, 209, Paragraph VIII, was read to them. After the adjutant was through reading, the regiment in a body called out "No!" The men were dismounted and assigned to the various companies of the First Louisiana Cavalry, and were marched to the quarters of the First Louisiana Cavalry. After having taken their names, they were dismissed in order to get their clothing, and ordered to report immediately back, which they failed to do. On the morning of the 30th, Colonel Robinson ordered each company commander of the First Louisiana Cavalry to send a guard and bring up the men assigned to them from the Second Rhode Island Cavalry. Before any of the guard reached the Rhode Island camp, Colonel Robinson went there and ordered the men to the camp of the First Louisiana Cavalry. They refused to obey in a body. The colonel recalled the guard of the First Louisiana Cavalry, and ordered all the companies to fall in under arms, stating to me at the same time that the Second Rhode Island Cavalry were in mutiny.

One company was mounted. He marched us to the camp of the Second Rhode Island Cavalry, and formed us in front and on both flanks of their camp. The colonel then told them that those men who wished to obey the order should rise and form line in the center, and that in case they refused he would have them shot where they stood. He repeated this in English, French, and Spanish, so that all could understand. Most all of them came. He then directed the adjutant to march them out and form them in line facing from our camp, with one company of the First Louisiana on each flank. Company F, of our regiment, was then detailed for the execution of two of the mutineers. The adjutant was appointed provost-marshal by the colonel, for the carrying out of the order for the execution. The men were then executed. The men of the Second Rhode Island Cavalry were then called out by name, and ordered to report to the company to wnich they had been assigned the previous evening, which they did, and have been doing duty with said companies since.

By the COURT:

Question. Did you hear any insubordinate language from any of the men of the Second Rhode Island Cavalry during the act of consolidation on the 29th or during the proceedings of the 30th of August? If so, state what.

Answer. I did. They said they were willing to serve in the First or Third Rhode Island Cavalry, but they would "be damned if they would do any duty in the First Louisiana Cavalry, under Colonel Robinson." That they would endure any punishment imposed upon them, but would not serve. This on the 29th of August.

Question. Do you know of any other facts than what you have here stated to the court as to the origin of the mutiny in the Second Rhode Island Cavalry?

Answer. The consolidation of the two regiments is the only cause I know of.

Question. Did you hear any mutinous language on the 29th from either of the men who were executed?

Answer. I did not know either of the men by sight or name; therefore could not say.

By the JUDGE-ADVOCATE:

Question. When the colonel ordered the men to their companies, and most of them went, were the two who were executed of their number?

Answer. I do not know, but I think not.

Lieut. EDWARD B. HALL, adjutant First Louisiana Cavalry, being duly sworn, deposes and says:

My name is Edward B. Hall. I am the adjutant of the First Louisiana Cavalry.

By the JUDGE-ADVOCATE:

Question. Was there a mutiny among certain enlisted men belonging to the Second Rhode Island Cavalry when consolidated with the First Louisiana Cavalry?

Answer. There was.

Question. Was it general?

Answer. It appeared to be.

Question. What, in your opinion, led to the mutiny?

Answer. It was a dislike on the part of the enlisted men to the consolidation with the First Louisiana Cavalry.

Question. What caused this dislike?

Answer. I know of no cause. Nothing special.

Question. What acts of mutiny took place?

Answer. On the afternoon of the 29th of August, after I had read the order for the consolidation, there was a universal "No! no!" running down the line. On the morning of the 30th, they left the companies to which they had been assigned, and gathered together in a group by themselves in their former camp. As I was coming out of my tent, I met Colonel Robinson. He said he wished me to accompany him, as he anticipated trouble with the Rhode Island men. I accompanied him to their camp. I rode with him to where they were assembled. He warned them that if any man refused to obey his order he would do it at his peril, as he should inflict summary punishment upon them. He ordered them to form in line; but a few obeyed, the remainder remained where they were, sitting or lying on the ground.

Question. Was there any mutinous language used at this time?

Answer. I heard three or four of them talking with their associates, but could not distinguish what they said, but should judge from their actions that they were urging them to mutiny. Colonel Robinson called one of the men up to him, and said: "You are the spokesman for these men this morning, and are urging them to mutiny. Do you refuse to obey my order?" The man replied, "Not more than the rest do." Colonel Robinson then ordered me to turn him over to the guard.

Question. Was Special Orders, 209, Paragraph VIII, read to the men so that all could understand it?

Answer. I think every man understood it.

Question. Were the orders of Colonel Robinson given in a cool, soldierly manner?

Answer. They were.

Question. How long a time elapsed from the commencement of the mutiny on the 30th until it was quelled?

Answer. From what I saw of it, I should say not over half an hour.

Question. What quelled it?

Answer. Shooting two of the ringleaders on the spot.

Question. Did the men, after the execution of these two, return to the companies to which they were assigned, and have they since that time obeyed all orders promptly and without murmur?

Answer. They have.

Question. Did you hear either or both of the men who were executed refuse to obey orders?

Answer. I did. On the 29th, one of them said he would do no duty in a Louisiana regiment, "he'd be damned if he would," and other expressions of a similar nature. The other was the man spoken of as spokesman on the 30th.

Whereupon the court adjourned to meet on Sunday, the 6th instant, at 8 a. m.

SUNDAY, *September* 6, 1863.

The court met pursuant to adjournment, all present, and continued the examination of witnesses.

JULES A. MASICOT, second lieutenant Company F, First Louisiana Cavalry, being duly sworn, deposes and says:

My name is Jules Masicot. I am second lieutenant of Company F, First Louisiana Cavalry.

By the JUDGE-ADVOCATE:

• Question. Were you present at the camp of the First Louisiana Cavalry on the 29th and 30th August, 1863?

Answer. I was.

Question. Was Special Orders, 209, Paragraph VIII, read to the First Louisiana Cavalry and to the Second Rhode Island Cavalry? If so, by whom, and was it read so that the men of both regiments could hear and understand it?

Answer. It was read by Adjutant Hall, and in such a manner that all could hear and understand it.

Question. Was there any mutinous language used by the Second Rhode Island Cavalry during or immediately after the reading of the order? If so, state what.

Answer. There was. The men in a body answered, "No, no! Rhode Island forever!"

Question. Were there any acts of mutiny in the Second Rhode Island Cavalry on the morning of the 30th? If so, what were they?

Answer. There was. Colonel Robinson ordered the men of the Second Rhode Island to fall in the rear of our column, threatening at the same time, if they disobeyed, he would shoot them on the spot. All obeyed with the exception of two.

Question. Were Colonel Robinson's orders given in a cool, soldierly manner?

Answer. They were.

Question. What was done after the Second Rhode Island fell in, with the exception of the two spoken of?

Answer. The colonel ordered the adjutant to take the Second Rhode Island and form them in line facing from our camp, and two companies of the First Louisiana Cavalry on each flank of them, so as to form three sides of a square. I was ordered then to march my company below the square. The two men who had not fallen in were then brought forward, and executed by my company, by order of Colonel Robinson.

CHARLES WALTON, private First Louisiana Cavalry, being duly sworn, deposes and says:

My name is Charles Walton. I am a private in the First Louisiana Cavalry.

By the JUDGE-ADVOCATE:

Question. Were you present with your regiment at the time the order of consolidation was read to the First Louisiana and Second Rhode Island Cavalry?

Answer. I was.

Question. Did you hear any mutinous language used by the Second Rhode Island Cavalry during or immediately after the reading of the order? If so, what?

Answer. Yes. A general shout of "No!" along the line.

Question. Do you know of any acts of mutiny in the Second Rhode Island on the following morning?

Answer. No. I was on duty. Two prisoners were turned over to the guard by the colonel.

SIDNEY E. IRVING, sergeant-major First Louisiana Cavalry, being duly sworn, deposes and says:

My name is Sidney E. Irving. I am the sergeant-major of the First Louisiana Cavalry.

By the JUDGE-ADVOCATE:

Question. Were you present at the time the order of consolidation was read to the First Louisiana and the Second Rhode Island Cavalry?

If so, was it read so that the men of both commands could hear and understand it?

Answer. I was present at the time. It could be heard distinctly.

Question. What was your position at that time?

Answer. Sergeant, acting as lieutenant, commanding a company in Second Rhode Island Cavalry.

Question. Did you hear any mutinous language used by the men of the Second Rhode Island Cavalry during or immediately after the reading of the order? If so, state what.

Answer. I did. I heard several of the men say they would not do any duty in the First Louisiana Cavalry. They would go to Ship Island, or submit to any punishment rather than serve their term of enlistment in the Louisiana Cavalry.

Question. Did the officers of the First Louisiana Cavalry do all in their power on the evening of the 29th to suppress the mutiny and get the men to submit peacefully and go to the companies to which they had been assigned?

Answer. They did.

Question. Were you present during the proceedings of the following morning?

Answer. I was.

Question. State what took place.

Answer. A majority, nearly all of the Rhode Island men, were in their camp, sitting on the ground. The lieutenant-colonel of the First Louisiana Cavalry sent a cavalry guard of his regiment and surrounded them. He then marched the balance of his men on foot, forming line fronting the Rhode Island men. He rode up to the Rhode Island men, and told them in three different languages that all those who wished to obey orders and do their duty as soldiers must fall in line. A majority of the men fell in line. I was ordered away by Colonel Robinson to look up some men. I was absent some three minutes. When I returned, they had all fallen in, with the exception of 3 men, one of whom he ordered to fall in, which order was obeyed. Both regiments were then formed in three sides of a square. The two men were placed in the square under guard, their arms tied behind them, a handkerchief was tied over their eyes; they were placed a short distance in front of the guard. The adjutant then spoke with each man some little time. He then motioned, and the guard fired, and the men were shot successively.

The court having heard and examined the evidence, which is above written, after mature deliberation thereon, make the following findings, to wit:

I. The origin of the mutiny in the Second Rhode Island Cavalry was the reading of the order of consolidation with the First Louisiana Cavalry, on the 29th day of August, 1863.

II. The course of said mutiny was from the reading of Special Orders, No. 209, Paragraph VIII, Headquarters Department of the Gulf, consolidating the Second Rhode Island Cavalry with the First Louisiana Cavalry, on the 29th day of August, 1863, to the time of the arrest and execution of the two men of the Second Rhode Island Cavalry on the 30th day of August, 1863.

III. The suppression of the mutiny was in the prompt and efficient manner in which the ringleaders were executed by order of Lieut. Col. H. Robinson, First Louisiana Cavalry.

EDWARD L. MOLINEUX,
Colonel and Presiding Officer.
GEO. H. WHEATON,
Captain and Recorder.

[Indorsement.]

HEADQUARTERS DEPARTMENT OF THE GULF,
New Orleans, October 23, 1863.

It is probable that order could have been maintained in the regiment without the application of capital punishment to the two men executed; but the conduct of the Second Rhode Island Cavalry was such that it is impossible to say how soon the mutiny would have been repeated.

Severe measures were required with them: The commanding general regrets the necessity for the execution, but is unable, with his knowledge of the facts, to say that it was not justifiable in consideration of all the circumstances of the case.*

N. P. BANKS,
Major-General, Commanding.

APPENDIX A.

WAR DEPARTMENT, ADJUTANT-GENERAL'S OFFICE,
Washington, September 4, 1863.

Major-General BANKS,
Commanding Department of the Gulf, New Orleans, La.:

GENERAL: I have the honor to inclose you herewith a copy of Special Orders, 209, Headquarters Department of the Gulf, transferring the enlisted men of the Second Rhode Island Cavalry to the First Louisiana Cavalry, and mustering out of service the commissioned officers of the regiment.

I am directed by the Secretary of War to request an early report as to the authority upon which said order was based.

I am, general, &c.,

THOMAS M. VINCENT,
Assistant Adjutant-General.

[Inclosure.]

SPECIAL ORDERS, }   HDQRS. DEPARTMENT OF THE GULF,
No. 209.   }   *New Orleans, August 24, 1863.*

*   *   *   *   *   *   *

VIII. The enlisted men of the Second Rhode Island Cavalry are transferred to the First Louisiana Cavalry, and will be assigned to companies by the commanding officer of the latter regiment.

The officers of the Second Rhode Island Cavalry are hereby mustered out of the service. Such of them as desire to remain in the service may, upon proving themselves fitted for and deserving of commissions in the First Louisiana Cavalry, before a board to be appointed by its regimental commander, be appointed to fill vacancies. Lieutenant-Colonel Robinson, First Louisiana Cavalry, is charged with the execution of this order.

By command of Major-General Banks:

G. NORMAN LIEBER,
Acting Assistant Adjutant-General.

---

* The findings of the court and indorsement of the commanding general were published in Special Orders, No. 266, Headquarters Department of the Gulf, October 24, 1863.

STATE OF RHODE ISLAND, EXECUTIVE DEPARTMENT,
Providence, September 4, 1863.
Hon. E. M. STANTON,
Secretary of War:

SIR: I have the honor to inform you that I received this a. m. an extract from Special Orders, No. 209, Paragraph VIII, Headquarters Department of the Gulf, dated August 24, 1863.

By this order—

The enlisted men of the Second Rhode Island Cavalry are transferred to the First Louisiana Cavalry, and will be assigned to companies by the commanding officer of the latter r egiment.

The officers of the Second Rhode Island Cavalry are hereby mustered out of the service.

This order cannot do otherwise than conflict with our ideas of right and justice.

These officers so summarily mustered out were commissioned by the Governor of Rhode Island, and, even should they be re-appointed, they would lose rank by date of commission, while the men who enlisted in a Rhode Island regiment lose all their identity with their native State, and are coolly thrust into a new organization, and "assigned to companies by its commanding officer."

I do, therefore, in justice to the Rhode Island men enlisted in that regiment, and to the regiments now being raised here, most respectfully but urgently request that the order in question be revoked by your Department, and the Second Rhode Island Cavalry be allowed to maintain its name and organization.

I am, sir, your most obedient servant,
JAMES Y. SMITH,
Governor of Rhode Island.

—

WAR DEPARTMENT, ADJUTANT-GENERAL'S OFFICE,
Washington, September 6, 1863.
GOVERNOR OF RHODE ISLAND,
Providence, R. I.:

SIR: I have the honor to acknowledge the receipt of your letter of the 4th instant, in relation to the action of Major-General Banks, disbanding the Second Rhode Island Cavalry.

In reply, I am directed by the Secretary of War to inform you that the matter has already been brought to the notice of this Department, and to inclose you copy of letter to General Banks on the subject.

I am, sir, &c.,
THOMAS M. VINCENT,
Assistant Adjutant-General.

—

STATE OF RHODE ISLAND, EXECUTIVE DEPARTMENT,
Providence, November 7, 1863.
Hon. E. M. STANTON,
Secretary of War, Washington, D. C.:

SIR: On the 4th of September last I wrote you, requesting the immediate disapproval by your Department of the order of Major-General Banks, by which our Second Cavalry was consolidated and the officers mustered out of service. Your reply was a copy of a letter requesting

General Banks to state by whose authority he issued the order in question, and that is the last we have heard of it.

Now this is a matter, sir, which cannot be lightly dropped and thought no more of. The order was an act of injustice to the men and an injustice to Rhode Island, and should be immediately revoked, or your Department should take the matter in hand, and have the men of the Second Cavalry transferred by special order to our First Cavalry, which is in need of those very men that are now disgraced by being torn from their own organization and placed in one which is in every way distasteful to them. Yet these men are volunteers. I will ask your own judgment; should they be treated so? Do not drafted men even receive better treatment?

I have understood, officially, that two men of the Second Cavalry were shot by order of Colonel Robinson, of the Louisiana cavalry, for simply remonstrating against the order of consolidation.

I feel it my duty to inform you, sir, that our people consider the order in question of much injury to the service, and an outrage to Rhode Island.

What assurances can we give officers or recruits from this State that they will be protected in their rights if they are to be so summarily dealt with, without even a show of justice?

In conclusion, allow me to say that the order issued by Major-General Banks was in direct opposition to a protest from this department, to which he paid no attention otherwise than by sending a copy of the said order.

An early reply will be considered a favor.

I have the honor to be, sir, very respectfully, your most obedient servant,

JAMES Y. SMITH,
Governor of Rhode Island.

[Indorsement.]

NOVEMBER 16, 1863.

General Banks' report, inclosed, shows the necessity of his order, and I think it should be allowed to stand, at least for the present.

H. W. HALLECK,
General-in Chief.

—

WAR DEPARTMENT, ADJUTANT-GENERAL'S OFFICE,
Washington, November 17, 1863.

GOVERNOR OF RHODE ISLAND,
Providence, R. I.:

SIR: I have the honor to acknowledge the receipt of your letter of the 7th instant, in relation to the consolidation of the Second Rhode Island Cavalry by Maj. Gen. N. P. Banks, commanding Department of the Gulf.

In reply, I am directed to inclose herewith a copy of the report of the general, made in answer to the orders of this Department, and to invite the attention of Your Excellency to the remarks of the General-in-Chief indorsed thereon.

I am, sir, &c.,

THOMAS M. VINCENT,
Assistant Adjutant-General.

[Inclosure.]

HEADQUARTERS DEPARTMENT OF THE GULF,
New Orleans, October 16, 1863.
THOMAS M. VINCENT,
Assistant Adjutant-General, Washington, D. C.:

SIR: I have the honor to acknowledge the receipt of your letter, making inquiries concerning the consolidation of the Rhode Island with the New York Cavalry, and asking my authority for the order.

I had no authority for this act whatever, except such as the necessity of my situation gave me. The Rhode Island cavalry was enlisted from New York chiefly, and had very good officers and some good men; but the organization was mostly composed of men entirely beyond control. Their depredations and robberies were frightful. One or two men on the march to Alexandria were shot for offenses of this character. They were wholly worthless as soldiers. When we reached Port Hudson, and they were deprived of the power of depredation by the circumscribed limits occupied, they gave us still greater trouble by the erroneous reports made in regard to the movements of the enemy. Our camp was continually in a disturbed and disordered condition from the false representations made by these men. We submitted to it as long as it could be endured, and changed it only when the safety of my command required it. The officers of the regiment, who are Rhode Island men, acknowledged their inability to control their men, and resigned their commissions on that account. Some correspondence had taken place with the Governor of Rhode Island in regard to their consolidation, which had been talked of long before, but it was not effected until it was represented by the officers from Rhode Island that it would not be objected to by the Governor of that State. Upon the resignation of the officers, with this representation, and under the exigency which I have described, the remnant of the regiment, consisting of only 100 or 200 men, was consolidated with à New York regiment for the purpose of bringing it into some discipline and protecting us against, first, their depredations, and, secondly, against the panics that their reports occasioned.

I have the honor to be, with much respect, your obedient servant,
N. P. BANKS,
Major-General, Commanding.

[Indorsement.]

WAR DEPARTMENT, ADJUTANT-GENERAL'S OFFICE,
October 28, 1863.

Respectfully submitted to the General-in-Chief. It is recommended that no further action be taken in this matter until a copy of General Banks' letter is forwarded to the Governor of Rhode Island.
E. D. TOWNSEND,
Assistant Adjutant-General.

—

WAR DEPARTMENT, ADJUTANT-GENERAL'S OFFICE,
•   Washington, D. C., December 5, 1863.
Major-General BANKS,
Commanding Department of the Gulf, New Orleans, La.:

GENERAL: I have the honor to inform you that the action, by Special Orders, No. 209, current series, from your headquarters, in transferring the enlisted men of the Second Rhode Island Cavalry to another organization, has been approved by the General-in-Chief. A copy of your report giving reasons for the transfer, with the General-in-Chief's indorsement thereon, was forwarded to the Governor of Rhode Island. Since its receipt, the Governor has requested by letter (copy herewith)* that the enlisted men of the Second may be transferred to the Third Cavalry upon its arrival in your department.

For the reasons given by His Excellency, I am directed to request that the change may be made by a special order, to be issued from your headquarters.

The Governor has been notified as to the action.

The Third Cavalry will start for your department at an early day.

I have the honor, &c.,

THOMAS M. VINCENT,
Assistant Adjutant-General.

SEPTEMBER 1–7, 1863.—Expedition from Natchez, Miss., to Harrison-burg, La., including skirmishes (2d) at Trinity and (4th) near Harrison-burg, and capture of Fort Beauregard.

REPORTS.

No. 1.—Brig. Gen. Marcellus M. Crocker, U. S. Army, commanding Expedition.
No. 2.—Col. Cyrus Hall, Fourteenth Illinois Infantry, commanding Brigade.
No. 3.—Brig. Gen. Walter Q. Gresham, U. S. Army, commanding Brigade.
No. 4.—Col. A. G. Malloy, Seventeenth Wisconsin Infantry (Mounted).
No. 5.—Col. Horace Randal, Twenty-eighth Texas Cavalry, commanding Brigade.
No. 6.—Lieut. Col. George W. Logan, Chalmette (Louisiana) Regiment.

No. 1.

Report of Brig. Gen. Marcellus M. Crocker, U. S. Army, commanding Expedition.

HEADQUARTERS UNITED STATES FORCES,
District of Natchez, Miss., September 10, 1863.

COLONEL: Of the expedition to Harrisonburg, I have the honor to report as follows:

The expedition consisted of the following troops: The Second Brigade, Fourth Division, Col. C. Hall, Fourteenth Illinois, commanding; the Third Brigade, Fourth Division, General W. Q. Gresham commanding; Company F, Second Illinois Artillery, and the Fifteenth Ohio Battery, with the Seventeenth Wisconsin Infantry (mounted), commanded by Colonel Malloy.

On the 1st instant, the Seventeenth Wisconsin crossed the river at this place at daylight, with orders to proceed without delay to Trinity; the Third Brigade crossed with the Fifteenth Ohio Battery, and moved toward Trinity about 6 miles; the Second Brigade, with Company F, Second Illinois Artillery, crossed, and encamped on the bank opposite Natchez.

On the 2d instant, General Gresham moved with his command within 3½ miles of Trinity. Colonel Hall moved to and across Cross Bayou, 16 miles from Natchez. In the meantime Colonel Malloy had moved to Trinity, as directed, and, after a slight skirmish with the

---

* Omitted.

enemy, had captured a small steamer, the Rinaldo, but had, for reasons best known to himself, burned the boat, and fallen back to General Gresham. Upon the advance of General Gresham toward Trinity, he again moved toward the town, and early on the morning of the 3d instant he crossed the river with a portion of his regiment in flats, and took possession of the place.

The Black River at Trinity was found to be about 800 feet wide; we crossed by making flats of the pontoons. First, the regiment of mounted infantry, then General Gresham's command, then Colonel Hall's command.

The mounted infantry was then ordered to move to the junction of the Alexandria and Trinity roads; General Gresham to move as near that point as he could. The day having been entirely consumed in crossing, Colonel Hall encamped about 1 mile from Trinity.

When I found that it was impossible to lay the pontoon at Trinity, I ordered the troops to take two days' rations in haversacks, and that transportation sufficient only to carry the ammunition should cross, and left two regiments of Colonel Hall's command to guard the crossing and the train left there.

On the morning of the 4th, General Gresham, with part of the regiment of mounted infantry and his brigade, started in the direction of Harrisonburg, but receiving reports from that portion of the mounted men sent out on the Alexandria road that the enemy was approaching from that direction in large force, the brigade was halted and formed in line of battle, this causing a delay of several hours.

On coming up to the Third Brigade, accompanied by Colonel Hall, after a little time spent in reconnoitering, I ordered the whole command to move to Harrisonburg, where we arrived between 10 and 11 a. m.

The fort (Beauregard) and the town had been evacuated that morning. The enemy had burned all his commissary stores, and the fire was burning in all the casemates and over the magazines, and a very large amount of ammunition had been destroyed. They had left eight guns in the works, four 32-pounders, and four 6-pounder brass pieces. The 32-pounders we spiked and disabled as much as possible, and left them in the burning casemates. One of the 6-pounder brass guns was in a casemate that had been fired and caved in so that it could not be gotten out; another was in a detached work, so that it could not be gotten out without great labor, which we had not the tools to perform. Both these pieces were rendered useless.

The two remaining pieces Lieutenant Gilman, of Colonel Hall's staff, placed upon a flat, and succeeded in boating to Trinity, from which place we brought them safely in. They had also burned a large quantity of small-arms. We completed the work of destruction on the fort as well as possible, and destroyed a large quantity of ammunition stored in the jail and court-house; also some corn and provisions stored in the town; and at 4 p. m. started back toward Trinity, Colonel Hall in advance.

Before leaving, I sent Colonel Malloy out on the Natchitoches road, where he destroyed a grist-mill that had been used in grinding meal for the fort, with a quantity of commissary stores that had been removed from the town. He also burned 57 bales of cotton, marked "C. S. A." On the 5th instant, the whole command recrossed the Black at Trinity. On the 7th, the command recrossed the Mississippi at Natchez, without anything of interest occurring on the march.

On the expedition we captured 20 prisoners of war, who are now here confined, besides a number of suspicious persons, the most of whom have been released. I send herewith reports of the brigade commanders; also sketch of the fort, made by Captain Cadle, of my staff.* The conduct of the troops on the march was generally excellent, and they returned in good health and spirits.

Fort Beauregard and the post at Harrisonburg were commanded by Lieutenant-Colonel Logan, and garrisoned by an irregular force of conscripts—artillery, cavalry, and infantry—of from 150 to 500.

Very respectfully, your obedient servant,

M. M. CROCKER,
Brigadier-General, Commanding.

Lieut. Col. WILLIAM T. CLARK, A. A. G., *Seventeenth Army Corps.*

No. 2.

Report of Col. Cyrus Hall, Fourteenth Illinois Infantry, commanding Brigade.

HDQRS. SECOND BRIG., FOURTH DIV., 17TH ARMY CORPS,
Near Natchez, Miss., September 7, 1863.

CAPTAIN: In compliance with an order from division headquarters, dated September 7, 1863, I have the honor to submit the following report of the part taken by my command (consisting of the Fourteenth, Fifteenth, Forty-sixth, and Seventy-sixth Regiments Illinois Infantry, and Captain Powell's company (F), Second Regiment Illinois Artillery, the battery belonging to General Ransom's command, but detached for the expedition) in the late expedition to Harrisonburg, La.:

I received orders on the morning of the 1st instant to cross the river (Mississippi) with my command, which orders were complied with, and I encamped upon the west bank of the river, near Vidalia, for the night.

I started on the morning of the 2d instant, at daylight, on the road leading to Trinity, the Third Brigade being in advance of my command. I reached the ferry at Cross Bayou about 5 p. m., and by 9 o'clock had succeeded in crossing my entire command to the west side, at which time and place I went into camp.

On the next day (3d instant) I started for Trinity; reached the river (Black) at 11 a. m. At 3.20 p. m. I received orders from Brigadier-General Crocker to cross the river with my two largest regiments and Powell's battery, leaving the remaining portion of my command on the east side of the river; at 4.45 p. m. the detachment was in motion, and, passing through the town, marched to a point about 1 mile west of the town, where I encamped.

On the succeeding morning (4th instant) I started at daylight, taking the Alexandria road. I reached the junction of the Harrisonburg road at 8.30 a. m., where I found the Third Brigade, under command of Brig. Gen. W. Q Gresham, in line of battle. I was then ordered by Brigadier-General Crocker to take position on the left of the Third Brigade, which I did, and remained in that position until ordered by General Crocker to take up the line of march and follow the Third Brigade in the direction of Harrisonburg. This I did, reaching Harrisonburg between the hours of 12 and 1 p. m., at which place we remained until ordered to return at 4 p. m. to the Junction, where I encamped.

Early next morning (5th instant) I started, and, reaching Trinity, crossed Black River, and was resting in camp at 10.30 a. m. Here I

---

* Sketch not found.

was rejoined by the two regiments of my command which had been left to guard the pontoons and the crossing. At 1 p. m. I was again on the road, marching that afternoon to Cross Bayou, and ferrying over by 9 p. m. At that time I went into camp, remaining until morning (6th instant), when I again moved eastward, reaching the river (Mississippi), the infantry crossing and moving out to the camps before dark, the baggage following as fast as the limited transportation would permit. The command had thus made a march of 88 miles in five days, without loss of life or limb.

Two of the brass guns captured at Harrisonburg were brought in through the exertions of Captain (then Lieutenant) Gilman, of the Fifteenth Illinois Infantry, acting provost-marshal of this brigade, for which he is deserving much credit. The health of the command was excellent, and the men in good spirits and elated by the success of the expedition.

. The report of the number and names of officers and men remaining in camp, and the cause of their so doing, will be transmitted as soon as reports can be had of regimental commanders.

I have the honor to be, sir, very respectfully, your obedient servant,

CYRUS HALL,
Colonel, Commanding Brigade.

Capt. W. H. F. RANDALL,
Asst. Adjt. Gen., Fourth Div., Seventeenth Army Corps.

No. 3.

Report of Brig. Gen. Walter Q. Gresham, U. S. Army, commanding Brigade.

HDQRS. THIRD BRIG., FOURTH DIV., 17TH ARMY CORPS,
Natchez, Miss., September 7, 1863.

CAPTAIN: I have the honor to submit the following report of the part taken by my command, consisting of the Twelfth Wisconsin, Col. George E. Bryant; Fifty-third Indiana, Lieut. Col. William Jones; Twenty-eighth Illinois, Lieut. Col. Richard Ritter; Thirty second Illinois, Maj. George H. English, and Spear's (Fifteenth Ohio) battery, Lieutenant Burdick, in the expedition to Harrisonburg, La.:

On Tuesday, the 1st instant, in pursuance of orders from Brigadier-General Crocker, I crossed the Mississippi River with my command, and moved out on the Trinity road to Lake Concordia, and bivouacked for the night.

At daylight on the morning of the 2d instant, my command was on the march on the Trinity road, and at 9.30 a. m. I arrived at Cross Bayou, and commenced ferrying by means of a small flat. At 10 a. m. Colonel Malloy, of the Seventeenth Wisconsin Mounted Infantry, arrived at the bayou, and reported that he had left Black River, opposite Trinity, at 5 a. m. that morning, in consequence of having skirmished with the enemy, and expended all, or nearly all, of his ammunition. At 3 p. m. my entire command was on the west side of the bayou, including the transportation of the Seventeenth Wisconsin and the pontoon train, which had been placed in my charge by General Crocker. At 3.20 p. m. I resumed the march (Colonel Malloy having gone in advance), and halted at sunset within 3 miles of Trinity, having marched 23 miles.

' At 5.35 a. m. of the 3d instant my command was moving, and at 6.30 a. m. it was at Black River, opposite Trinity. By 10 a m. Captain ———— had three pontoon boats in readiness, and I crossed my command, leaving all my transportation on the east side of the river, excepting one ambulance and one ammunition wagon to each regiment. Here I received orders from General Crocker to press on to Harrisonburg by the left-hand road.

Leaving Trinity at 3.50 p. m., I marched until 7.40 p. m., and halted 9 miles north of Trinity and 2 miles south of the junction of the Trinity and Alexandria roads. I received a message at 11 p. m. from Colonel Malloy, stating that he was at the junction with his command, and that the enemy, from 2,000 to 4,000 strong, was approaching from the west on the Alexandria road. Upon the receipt of this intelligence, I sent an order to Colonel Malloy to send four companies of his command out on the Alexandria road, with instructions to obtain information of the strength and whereabouts of the enemy, if he should be found; and I moved with my command over a difficult road to the junction, where I arrived at 3 a. m. on the 4th instant, and formed in line of battle across the Alexandria road. I remained in this position until 6.20 a. m., and not hearing from the reconnoitering party, I determined to leave Colonel Malloy to look to the rear, and move on to Harrisonburg. When within 3 or 3½ miles of Harrisonburg, I was overtaken by a courier from Colonel Malloy, with information that he, Malloy, had encountered the enemy, 4,000 strong, on the Alexandria road, 5 miles from the junction, and that he was skirmishing with him and gradually falling back. I immediately countermarched my command, and arrived at the junction at 7.45 a. m., and formed in line of battle as before. About this time General Crocker arrived, and I reported to him what had transpired.

About 8.30 a. m. Colonel Hall arrived with the Second Brigade, and formed on my left. I remained in this position until I received orders from General Crocker to resume the march in the direction of Harrisonburg, at which place I arrived at 11.40 a. m., and rested until 5 p. m., when I received orders from General Crocker to return to Natchez by the same route, following the Second Brigade. About dark I halted at a point 2 miles west of Harrisonburg, and rested until 5 a. m. next morning, the 5th instant, and resumed the march, arriving at Trinity at 11.30 a. m., when I received orders from General Crocker to cross the river, and remain on the opposite side until the mounted infantry arrived and the pontoons were ready to be taken up, which I did. After crossing Black River, I marched 4 miles, and halted at 6 p. m. on the Tensas River.

At an early hour on the morning of the 6th instant, my command was on the march, and at 6.30 p. m. I halted near Vidalia. Have marched 94 miles in less than five days. On the morning of the 7th instant, I recrossed the Mississippi, and returned to my old camp.

Considering the excessive heat and the obstacles encountered in crossing rivers and bayous, the expedition is remarkable for the length of time in which it was made. It affords me pleasure to be able to say that, although the march was fatiguing and arduous, the men endured it with a fortitude and patience characteristic of good soldiers.

I have the honor to be, very respectfully, your obedient servant,

W. Q. GRESHAM,
Brigadier-General.

Capt. W. H. F. RANDALL,
Asst. Adjt. Gen., Fourth Div., Seventeenth Army Corps.

No. 4.

Report of Col. A. G. Malloy, Seventeenth Wisconsin Infantry (Mounted).

HEADQUARTERS WISCONSIN MOUNTED INFANTRY,
September 9, 1863.

CAPTAIN: I have the honor to submit the following report of the part taken by my command in the late expedition to Harrisonburg, La.:

On the morning of the 1st instant, pursuant to orders, I crossed the Mississippi River at this point with my command, and moved forward to Trinity, capturing on the way two of the enemy's outposts. The prisoners informed me that a re-enforcement of 2,000 men were advancing to the relief of Harrisonburg. I arrived at Trinity at 8 p. m., and bivouacked on the east side of Black River. About 10 o'clock the Confederate steamer Rinaldo appeared in sight coming down the river, and tied up on the Trinity side. I at once sent three companies, Captain Apker commanding, to intercept the steamer in case she should attempt to escape, and at the same time dispatched a party of 20 men, Captain Crane commanding, 6 miles up Bayou Tensas, to procure a flat-boat with which to cross the river. About 11 p. m. the enemy became aware of our presence through their pickets on this side of the river. On the alarm being given, the steamer at once loosed from the shore, and attempted to escape up the river. Not observing the orders of Captain Apker to round to, he poured into her two well-directed volleys, when the captain ran her ashore on the opposite side, and abandoned her with his crew. About 12 p. m. Captain Crane and party returned with the flat-boat for which they had been dispatched, and at once crossed the river in the face of the enemy's fire, seized the steamer, and drove the enemy, who were for the most part concealed, back through the town, Captain Crane sustaining a loss of 4 men wounded, 1 mortally. I then had the steamer brought across the river, and discovered that her steam-pipe had been pierced in a number of places by our balls. Having been engaged in constant skirmishing during the entire night, expending over 3,000 rounds of ammunition, and not knowing on what road their re-enforcements were advancing, I deemed it prudent to open communication with the commanding general.

I therefore burned the steamer and returned to Cross Bayou. After replenishing my ammunition, I at once moved back to my former bivouac opposite Trinity. At daylight on the morning of the 3d, I observed a number of people on the opposite side of the river, and ordered them to send across a skiff. They not complying with my command, 2 men of my regiment, Corporal Brunson and Private Thomas Healey, of Company F, volunteered to swim the river and procure a skiff. This they did successfully, though fired upon by the concealed enemy, but a few well-directed volleys by a company which I had stationed on this side of the river soon cleared the opposite shore. I then crossed my entire command. About 2 p. m., by order of the general commanding, moved forward toward Harrisonburg, soon meeting the enemy, and having a running fight with them for 9 miles, with the loss of 1 man from my command. Night coming on, I was obliged to desist. Bivouacked at the junction of the Trinity and Alexandria roads. At this place, capturing a courier, I learned that a force of between 3,000 and 4,000 men, a portion of [J. G.] Walker's division, were advancing on the Alexandria road, 8 miles from my place of bivouac. Believing the information to be reliable, I immediately sent a dispatch to General Gresham, who arrived with his command. At 2 a. m. the general ordered me to send three of my companies out on the Alexandria road to reconnoiter and feel the enemy. The companies were sent out under the command of Maj. D. D. Scott. On advancing about 4 miles, they became engaged with the enemy, driving them 1½ miles through their main camp, which was known by the large number of fires, amounting to fifty or more. At this moment I came up with the balance of the regiment, and ordered two companies to advance as skirmishers. After marching 1 mile or more, passing through their deserted camp, and finding no enemy, I recalled the skirmishers, and marched toward Harrisonburg, joining the general commanding on his entrance into the town. At 3 p. m. I received orders to destroy a mill and commissary stores, on the Natchitoches road. Arriving at the place where the stores were supposed to be, I found 8 Confederate soldiers, whom I captured, but no stores. After destroying the mill and 57 bales of Confederate cotton, I returned to Natchez, arriving here the evening of the 7th.

I feel under special obligations to Major Scott, Captains Crane, Apker, Beaupre, and Lieut. Dela Hunt, for their promptness and ready obedience and gallantry in the execution of orders. I would also mention, as deserving of notice, my 2 guides, Messrs. Dougherty and Norris, for their assistance during the expedition. I captured in all about 25 prisoners.

Repectfully, your obedient servant,

A. G. MALLOY,
Colonel, Comdg. Seventeenth Wisconsin Mounted Infantry.

Capt. W. H. F. RANDALL,
Asst. Adjt. Gen., Fourth Div., Seventeenth Army Corps.

No. 5.

Reports of Col. Horace Randal, Twenty-eighth Texas Cavalry, commanding Brigade.

HEADQUARTERS RANDAL'S BRIGADE,
Sulphur Springs, La., September 5, 1863—9.40 a. m.

MAJOR: I have the honor to report that the enemy, near 5,000 strong, met me yesterday morning at the break of day 12 miles this side of Fort Beauregard, thus cutting off the possibility of a junction with the forces at the fort under Lieutenant-Colonel [George W.] Logan. I drove in his pickets, and withdrew my command, having deceived the enemy. My retreat was followed up to the junction of the upper and lower Alexandria roads. I have heard of no farther advance on either road in the direction of Alexandria.

Lieutenant-Colonel Logan abandoned the fort between 2 and 3 o'clock yesterday morning, retiring by Centreville and Natchitoches road. He saved four pieces of artillery. He is now near Little River, at Gillmore's Ferry, where he will cross to-day.

I retired by the Alexandria road for two reasons—to protect Colonel Logan, and to prevent a flank movement upon my rear. If it is designed that I should retire to Alexandria, I have rations; otherwise I will forward my trains. Colonel Logan will join me to-morrow. I will continue my march toward Alexandria, crossing the river to-day, unless otherwise ordered. I have sent out scouts to ascertain the position of the enemy on the roads leading from this place to the Washita River. Three different persons have seen the enemy's camp near Trinity, and all report them 16,000 strong. I will learn everything I can, and have reports made without delay. I will make a full report so soon as I reach my desk and have time.

Respectfully, your obedient servant,

HORACE RANDAL,
Colonel, Commanding Brigade.

Major [E.] SURGET,
Assistant Adjutant-General.

—

HEADQUARTERS RANDAL'S BRIGADE,
Camp on Little River, La., September 6, 1863.

MAJOR: In obedience to Special Orders, No. 223, district headquarters, I left the vicinity of Alexandria on the morning of the 1st instant; crossed Little River on the 2d, and on the 3d marched to Brushy Bridge, 10 miles west of Harrisonburg, where the command slept on their arms until 4 o'clock on the morning of the 4th instant.

The enemy having driven in Lieutenant-Colonel [G. W.] Logan's pickets on the evening of the 3d, and occupied the approaches to Harrisonburg, thus rendering a night march in the face of an enemy whose strength greatly outnumbered mine hazardous in the extreme, the total absence of cavalry left me no other alternative than to rest until light.

In the meantime Colonel Logan's confidential scout came to me from Colonel Logan, informing me that he could not hold the fort until morning; that 1,100 men would be of no assistance to him in resisting the enemy, and that it would be useless for me to attempt to reach him if I had not more than 1,100 muskets, and that he would evacuate the fort some time during the night. His scout further stated that the enemy's strength was between 10,000 and 15,000, composed of artillery, infantry, and cavalry.

On the 3d, the enemy advanced on the Alexandria road, and formed line of battle east of the Brushy Bridge, in a strong position, behind open fields exposed to the fire of his artillery, with the approaches to his position strongly ambuscaded. My advanced pickets on the night of the 3d were within 400 yards of the enemy's lines, and the opposing forces passed the night within 800 yards of each other, the enemy outnumbering me five to one, with the additional advantage of artillery and cavalry.

At 4.30 o'clock on the 4th, my pickets received the first fire from the enemy's advance. Captain Flynn's battalion of sharpshooters were thrown forward, and drove in the enemy's skirmishers. Wishing to evade a battle, I formed on his right, forcing him to change his front. In the meantime I had occupied the hills immediately in my rear, · giving me the advantage in position where I wished to receive the attack, which the enemy declined, preferring to face me through his ambuscade.

The object of the expedition having failed, the superior strength of the enemy and the remoteness of any assistance, and the facility with which the enemy could gain my rear, induced me to retire to the line of Little River, where I am now encamped.

I have compared all the reports as to the enemy's strength and composition, and conclude as follows: Eight pieces of artillery, 400 cavalry, and 15,000 infantry west of the Washita, and one brigade of infantry east of that stream. Their cavalry (200 strong) are reported by a citizen 7 miles west of Harrisonburg, on the Alexandria road. There seems to be no intention to advance in the direction of Alexandria as yet.

Loss of the enemy in the skirmish, 3 killed; wounded, not known. None of my men were injured.

The cavalry force that I have should be increased, as it is not strong enough to perform the required duties; besides, a force of cavalry could inflict serious injury upon the enemy and keep him within narrow limits.

I will remain in this vicinity until further orders. Lieutenant-Colonel Logan is now on the Alexandria road leading to Gillmore's Ferry, on Little River. .

I am, major, very respectfully, your obedient servant,

HORACE RANDAL,
Colonel, Commanding Brigade.

Major [E.] Surget,
Assistant Adjutant-General.

[Indorsement.]

HEADQUARTERS DISTRICT OF WESTERN LOUISIANA,
Alexandria, La., September —, 1863.

Respectfully forwarded. A brigade of infantry with a battery has been sent forward this morning to re-enforce Colonel Randal. Major's brigade will reach this [place] to-night, and will immediately push on to the point. I hope to receive some reliable information to-day.

R. TAYLOR,
Major-General, Commanding.

No. 6.

Reports of Lieut. Col. George W. Logan, Chalmette (Louisiana) Regiment.

GILLMORE'S FERRY, LITTLE RIVER,
September 5, 1863—11 a. m.

MAJOR: I evacuated Fort Beauregard at 3 a. m. yesterday and destroyed the works. Find it impossible for General [Colonel Horace] Randal to re-enforce me, and, in accordance with his advice, I have been endeavoring to form a junction with him, but have been unable to do so, so far. I hope to join him to-morrow on the Alexandria road, 16 miles from Alexandria.

Having only 40 effective men in garrison, I have only been able to save all our wagons, horses, and mules, and four of my best pieces of artillery (three 3-inch rifles and one 12-pounder howitzer).

All day on the 3d instant our cavalry engaged the advance guard of the enemy on the Hawthorn road, with a view to check his progress and prevent his intercepting the forces of General [Colonel] Randal, then advancing to our relief, but they were not successful.

I am, very respectfully, your obedient servant,

GEO. WM. LOGAN,
Lieutenant-Colonel, Commanding.

Maj. E. Surget,
Assistant Adjutant-General, Alexandria, La.

—

NATCHITOCHES ROAD, 40 MILES FROM ALEXANDRIA,
Rapides Parish, La., September 6, 1863.

CAPTAIN: I wrote you last on the 2d instant by Captain Purvis. On the 3d, before day, the Yankees in very heavy force crossed the river at Trinity, and engaged all of the cavalry, some 80 in number, which I had taken away from the Tensas River lines and kept ready for the purpose of disputing their advance. They fell back slowly before the overwhelming force of the enemy advancing by the Upper Trinity, or otherwise called the Hawthorn road.

Colonel [Horace] Randal (with his brigade to re-enforce me and take command, as per order sent me by General Taylor) had been communicating with me for several days; reached the Brushy Bridge, 10 miles from the fort, on the evening of the 3d instant; had advised me if I discovered that the Abolitionists were in heavy force to save what guns I could and form a junction with him, he being destitute of cavalry and artillery and needing them. The enemy are probably 15,000 strong, and have been following him up to last accounts, when he was encamped within 5 miles of them. I could not feel assured of the very heavy force of the enemy until the afternoon of the 3d, at dark. They had steadily but slowly succeeded in driving in my cavalry, not only to the junction of the Hawthorn road with the Alexandria and Harrisonburg road, at a point half-way between us and our re-enforcements on the road, thus cutting off communication between Colonel Randal and myself, but pressed on nearly 2 miles nearer to the fort.

From desertion and sickness, having only about 40 men in garrison fit for duty, and they being much disheartened under the strain, I called a council of all the commissioned officers of the fort, and, in accordance with their unanimous advice, given in secret council on the 3d, I determined to evacuate, save as many of the guns as possible, and, by rapid march, attempt a junction with Colonel Randal, as suggested by him the previous day. Having had the horses for all except four pieces of artillery sent off some 20 miles to a place of security on the Natchitoches road the previous day, where I expected and intended to stand a siege, and having too few men to lift the 30-pounder Parrott rifle out of position into a wagon which I had kept prepared for it, I was unable to save anything more than all the Government horses, mules, and wagons, and the 3-inch rifled guns and 1 howitzer (12-pounder). I was obliged to move at night, as it was necessary to pass within 2½ miles of the enemy, in force, and without a moment's delay.

After determining my course, I commenced the evacuation at 1 a. m. on the 4th, passed within short distances of the enemy several times with impunity, and have ever since been trying to reach Colonel Randal, with whom I have been in daily communication.

He engaged them on the morning of the 4th with his skirmishers. I have crossed the Little River at Gillmore's Ferry, having traveled 26 miles on the 4th to Centreville, 24 miles yesterday, and 8 this morning since daylight to this hour (9.30 a. m.), when I halted the rear guard for the purpose of writing this letter, which heretofore I have been unable to do. I now fear, from what I can hear of the road, that I will be unable to overtake Colonel Randal until he reaches Alexandria, as I will have to travel some 98 miles, while he has had the direct road of 60 miles, only 50 of which he had to make.

My last accounts of the enemy were that they were in great force some 10 or 11 miles from Fort Beauregard, on the Alexandria road, and supposed to be still pursuing Colonel Randal and advancing upon Alexandria in force—15,000 or 16,000 strong. I am continuing this route by order of Colonel Randal, and hope to be not much behind him in reaching Alexandria. I expect to encamp to-night within 20 miles of Alexandria, on the road from that place to Winfield.

I neglected to state previously that I remained with Lieutenants

Moore, Parker, Nichols, and a few others, at the fort until 4.15 a. m. on the 4th instant, when I superintended personally the destruction of the casemates, commissary, guns, &c., by fire and explosion.

I am, very respectfully, your obedient servant,

GEO. WM. LOGAN,
Lieutenant-Colonel, Comdg. Garrison, Fort Beauregard.

Capt. ISAAC N. DENNIS,
Assistant Inspector General, Vienna, La.

P. S.—I dispatch this by Private Isaac Ross, of Captain McCall's cavalry company, who will give you more news of our condition, &c.

[Indorsement.]

HEADQUARTERS DISTRICT OF WESTERN LOUISIANA,
Alexandria, September 10, 1863.

Respectfully forwarded. Lieutenant-Colonel Logan, having reached this point, was ordered to send in his report direct. It has not passed through Brigadier-General Hébert, and I am therefore not yet aware what orders were issued by that officer. The fact of the horses having been sent from the fort in anticipation of a siege appears to have been the cause of so little public property being saved. All the heavy guns and one brass field piece have been left in the fort by the enemy, also caissons and other property, to secure and bring off which steps are now being taken. Having no duty to assign Colonel Logan to, I have ordered him to report to the lieutenant-general commanding.

R. TAYLOR,
Major-General, Commanding.

SEPTEMBER 2, 1863.—Affair with Zapata's Banditti near Mier, Mexico.

REPORTS.

No. 1.—Maj. Gen. John B. Magruder, C. S. Army, commanding District of Texas, New Mexico, and Arizona.
No. 2.—Brig. Gen. Hamilton P. Bee, C. S. Army, commanding First Division, Army of Texas.
No. 3.—Maj. Santos Benavides, Thirty-third Texas Cavalry.

No. 1.

Report of Maj. Gen. John B. Magruder, C. S. Army, commanding District of Texas, New Mexico, and Arizona.

HEADQUARTERS DISTRICT OF TEXAS, &C.,
Sabine Pass, September 29, 1863.

GENERAL: I have the honor herewith to transmit, for the information of the lieutenant-general commanding, a copy of the communication from Brigadier-General Bee, inclosing the official report of Maj. Santos Benavides, of the Thirty-third Texas Cavalry, of his engagement and defeat of the Zapata banditti. This band of depredators has long been a source of annoyance and danger on the Rio Grande frontier, and the

brilliant achievement of the forces under Major Benavides is deserving ɪ'
of the highest commendation.

I am, general, very respectfully, &c.

J. BANKHEAD MAGRUDER,
Major-General, Commanding.

Brig. Gen. W. R. BOGGS,
Chief of Staff.

No. 2.

*Report of Brig. Gen. Hamilton P. Bee, C. S. Army, commanding First
Division, Army of Texas.*

HEADQUARTERS FIRST DIVISION, ARMY OF TEXAS,
Fort Brown, Tex., September 11, 1863.

SIR: I have the honor to inclose a copy of the official report of Maj.
Santos Benavides, Thirty-third Cavalry, of his engagement with a
party of robbers in Mexico, headed by the notorious outlaw Zapata,,
from which it will be seen that we shall be no more troubled with this
emissary of the Lincoln Government, who has for so long disturbed the
peace of this frontier, and at one time actually crossed the Rio Grande
into Texas with the flag of the United States. I especially recommend
Major Benavides for his untiring energy and patriotism, and would respectfully suggest that the general commanding recognize officially the
distinguished services of Major Benavides, and the firm, unyielding
support which the companies of Laredo, commanded by Captains Refugio and Christobal Benavides (all Mexicans), have ever given to our
cause.

Should E. J. Davis ever invade the Rio Grande with his regiment of
refugees and outlaws, he will miss his friend Zapata, who had the power
to do us great injury. I have great hopes that there will be no more
trouble on this line, and congratulate myself that this final blow has
been struck on the eve of my leaving the Rio Grande, and was the
legitimate result of my labors here, which gave the right of our troops
to cross into Mexico for just such purposes.

With great respect, your obedient servant,

H. P. BEE,
Brigadier-General, Provisional Army.

Capt. EDMUND P. TURNER,
Assistant Adjutant-General, Houston.

No. 3.

Report of Maj. Santos Benavides, Thirty-third Texas Cavalry.

HEADQUARTERS LINE OF THE RIO GRANDE,
Carrizo, Tex., September 3, 1863.

SIR: I respectfully submit the following report:

On the evening of the 1st instant, I received an official communication
from the first alcalde of Guerrero, stating that a detachment of troops
from that town had been attacked and routed by a party of outlaws,

under lead of Zapata. I at once set out from this post with a part of Capt. C. Benavides' company (H), and went to Clareño, and there took a part of Captain [Thomas] Rabb's company (D), and crossed the Rio Grande, and went to the point where the Guerrero soldiers and banditti had their skirmish, and, finding nobody there, took the trail of Zapata's party, and followed it to within a short distance of Mier, when, about 9 o'clock of the 2d instant, I found the camp of the banditti.‑ I directed the non‑commissioned officers of Company H to select the leaders of the banditti, all of whom were known to them, and without delay attack the scoundrels. After a short fight they were all dispersed, and on account of the thickness of the chaparral, and our want of knowledge of the country, many escaped.

We found dead of the enemy 10, among whom were all the officers, viz, Octaviano Zapata, who claimed the rank of colonel; Monico Salmas, captain; Manuel Villareal and Guillermo Viño, lieutenants. The balance were unknown to us. We fortunately suffered no casualties, which was remarkable, for the camp was in the bottom of a ravine, which our men were obliged to enter in single file, under a sharp fire from the thieves.

My force consisted of 3 lieutenants and 39 men from Company H, and 2 lieutenants and 35 men from Company D.

The officers and men without exception showed great gallantry. Lieutenant [R. F.] Haskins, of Company D, especially distinguished himself. Corpl. Natividad Hererra, of Company H, deserves especial mention for his courage and gallantry, for that after his carbine was discharged, finding that there was danger of the escape of Zapata before he could reload, attacked him, and gave him his death‑blow with the butt of his gun, although Zapata had a loaded pistol and was firing at the corporal all the time.

I have the honor to be, very respectfully, your obedient servant,

SANTOS BENAVIDES,
Major Thirty-third Texas Cavalry, Commanding.

Lieut. Çol. WILLIAM O. YAGER,
Acting Assistant Adjutant-General, C. S. Provisional Army.

SEPTEMBER 4–11, 1863.—The Sabine Pass (Texas) Expedition.

REPORTS.*

No. 1.—Maj. Gen. Nathaniel P. Banks, U. S. Army, commanding Department of the Gulf.

No. 2.—Capt. William B. Roe, Chief Signal Officer, Department of the Gulf.

No. 3.—Maj. Gen. William B. Franklin, U. S. Army, commanding Expedition.

No. 4.—Brig. Gen. Godfrey Weitzel, U. S. Army, commanding First Division, Nine‑teenth Army Corps, with Itinerary of the Division for September, 1863.

No. 5.—Itinerary of the First Brigade, Third Division, Nineteenth Army Corps, Brig. Gen. Frank S. Nickerson, U. S. Army, commanding, for September, 1863.

No. 6.—Acting Volunteer Lieut. Frederick Crocker, U. S. Navy.

No. 7.—Maj. Gen. John B. Magruder, C. S. Army, commanding District of Texas, New Mexico, and Arizona, with congratulatory orders and proclamation.

No. 8.—Col. Leon Smith, C. S. Army, commanding Marine Department, Texas.

---

* For reports of Commodore Henry H. Bell, Lieut. Commander William H. Dana, and Acting Masters Charles W. Lamson and Howard Tibbetts, U. S. Navy, see Annual Report of the Secretary of the Navy, December 7, 1863.

No. 9.—Capt. F. H. Odlum, Cook's (Texas) artillery.
No. 10.—Lieut. R. W. Dowling, Company F, Cook's (Texas) artillery.
No. 11.—Thanks of the Confederate Congress to Captain Odlum, Lieutenant Dowling, *
    and the men under their command.

No. 1. •

*Reports of Maj. Gen. Nathaniel P. Banks, U. S. Army, commanding Department of the Gulf.**

•   NEW ORLEANS, *September* 5, 1863.

. GENERAL : I have the honor to report that Major-General Franklin has sailed on the expedition to Sabine Pass, Tex.

Owing to the limited means of transportation at my disposal in this department, especially of steamers capable of navigating the Gulf of Mexico, the start has been delayed much beyond the time I had hoped and expected, but I believe rumor has been kept entirely at fault, and that the blow will fall on the enemy in a quarter unexpected by them.

Using all our transportation, it has been impossible to send in the first line more than about 5,000 infantry, with three field batteries and two heavy Parrott batteries. Such of the navy gunboats as can enter the Pass were assembled in Berwick Bay, and telegraphic communication having now been established between the Southwest Pass of the Mississippi and Berwick Bay, the sailing of the transports from the one point and the gunboats from the other was made with such interval as to bring the two at the same time, or nearly the same, off Sabine Pass.

As an exposition of the intended operations, I inclose a copy of my instructions to Major-General Franklin. As soon as the first line shall have disembarked, all the transports of light draught will come to Berwick Bay, whither I have ordered the First Division of the Thirteenth Army Corps to be ready for embarkation. Three-fourths of that division are already at a point a few miles distant from Brashear City. The transports of heavier draught will return to this place, where troops of the Thirteenth Army Corps will be ready to embark. •

The day before yesterday, information was sent me by the naval officer in command near Morgan's Bend, on the Mississippi River, that the rebels were establishing there four field batteries to annoy our transports. I have dispatched the Second Division, Thirteenth Army Corps, to that quarter, directing the commander (General Herron) to co-operate with the gunboat, and to capture or destroy the rebel force in that vicinity, which, by various accounts, numbers from 900 to 1,500 men of the three arms.

General Herron will be able to accomplish this object and return in time to take part in the Texas expedition, and will doubtless have returned before transportation will be ready for him.

I have reliable information to-day from Galveston (August 14), which gives the force of Magruder at that point as 2,300 men, in a very demoralized condition. The refugee is highly intelligent, and states that our attack on Texas is expected in the direction of Vermillionville, La., and Niblett's Bluff.

Very respectfully, I am, general, your obedient servant,

                                        N. P. BANKS,
                                    Major-General, Commanding.
Maj. Gen. H. W. HALLECK,
    Commanding U. S. Army, Washington, D. C.

---

* See also General Reports, pp. 18-21. ·

HDQRS. DEPT. OF THE GULF, 19TH ARMY CORPS,
New Orleans, August 31, 1863.

Maj. Gen. WILLIAM B. FRANKLIN,
Commanding Nineteenth Army Corps:

GENERAL: You are hereby assigned to the following duty:

1. You will please embark the First Brigade, First Division, and the Third Division, Nineteenth Army Corps, with the artillery which has been assigned to the First and Third Divisions, and that portion of the First Indiana Heavy Artillery, temporarily assigned to your command, at Baton Rouge.

You will embark the Reserve Brigade, Nineteenth Army Corps, which has been ordered to report to you at Algiers, and the Texas cavalry, and a battalion of the First Engineer Regiment, at this place.

On account of the limited means of transportation available at this time, you will not be able to embark the whole of the artillery of the division named, but the remainder, with wagons, camp equipage, &c., will be sent to you as soon as possible.

2. As soon as the embarkation shall have been effected, you will assemble all the transports at some convenient point on the river below this city, and will there have a personal conference with the commodore commanding the West Gulf Squadron, and with Acting Volunteer Lieutenant Crocker, U. S. Navy, who, it is understood, will command the co-operating naval force.

You will arrange with them the detail of your contemplated movements, it being well understood that the gunboats will immediately precede the transports and cover the landing of the troops; but at the same time you will please bear constantly in mind the fact that there are important reasons, in addition to those of a purely military character, for the immediate occupation of some important point in the State of Texas where the Government of the United States can permanently maintain its flag.

A landing, if found impracticable at the point now contemplated, should be attempted at any place in the vicinity where it may be found practicable to attain the desired result.

3. After coming to a complete understanding with the naval commanders, you will proceed to Sabine Pass, Tex., and if you find that the navy has succeeded in making the landing feasible, you will disembark your whole force as speedily as possible, occupy the strongest position to be found, and immediately commence strengthening it by means of your engineer force.

4. After making your landing, you will make a careful examination of the country in your front, and if you can safely proceed as far as the railroad from Houston to Beaumont, you will seize and hold some point on that line. Beaumont is probably the preferable point, but the exact position [is left] to your own judgment and professional skill after your arrival on the line.

5. After seizing such point on the railroad, you will make reconnaissances in the direction of Houston, so as to learn the position and force of the enemy, but you are not expected, with the force you take with you, to occupy any point farther west than the one selected by you on the railroad, unless you find that no enemy appears in force.

6. You will communicate with me as fully and as frequently as possible, giving all the information necessary to guide me in determining the

amount and character of the force to be added to your command for further operations, which will be immediately forwarded.

Very respectfully, I am, general, your most obedient servant,

N. P. BANKS,
Major-General.

—

HEADQUARTERS DEPARTMENT OF THE GULF,
New Orleans, September 13, 1863.

GENERAL: It is with regret that I am obliged to report that the effort to effect a landing at Sabine Pass was without success.

The immediate cause of the failure was the misapprehension of the naval authorities of the real strength of the enemy's position, and the insufficient naval force with which the attempt was made.

It represented, however, the entire naval power that the department affords for an enterprise of this character. No vessel drawing over 6 feet of water can pass the bar at the mouth of the Sabine. This reduced the number of boats able to enter to four, the Clifton, Sachem, Arizona, and Granite City. These were all old boats of decayed frames and weak machinery, constantly out of repair, even when engaged in the ordinary service of the river.

The naval authorities most familiar with the Sabine, which has been constantly under blockade, believed that this force would be sufficient. They supposed the battery at the Pass to mount but two guns, and were perfectly confident of being able, if the enemy was not so far apprised of our movements as to be able to concentrate their forces, to silence the guns without delay. It proved, however, that the battery mounted six heavy guns, three of which are believed to be 9-inch, one a 7 or 8 inch rifle, and the others to be mounted on siege carriages. To these were added a light battery and two gunboats.

The army, of course, relied confidently on the information furnished by the officers familiar with the ground. It would have been wiser to have tested the strength of the enemy's position, as might easily have been done by the gunboats stationed at that point forcing their fire, but the desire to avoid arousing suspicion of our movement, the pressure of the Government for prompt action, and the entire confidence of the naval authorities in their information, led to the course adopted.

The attack would have been successful as it was had the boats been adapted to the waters in which they engaged.

The action opened on Tuesday, the 8th instant, at 3 p. m., and lasted about one hour. The Clifton and Arizona were early grounded, and the Sachem disabled by a chance shot, before the Granite City reached the scene of action, and the Clifton and Sachem, being under the guns of the fort, were obliged to surrender.

The Arizona and Granite City, with all the transports and troops inside the bar, got off during the evening.

The Clifton is represented to have made a most gallant fight. General Weitzel, with 500 men on board the transport General Banks, was following close upon the Clifton when she commenced the attack, with an intention to land at Old Battery Point, about half a mile below the fort, and suppress the fire of the enemy's gunners. This would have been accomplished had not the Clifton grounded exactly between him and the point selected for the landing, and the attempt was abandoned only when the Clifton and Sachem had surrendered, and the Arizona was seen to be aground and helpless. Being deprived of all aid of the gunboats, the troops [transports] fell back to a position outside the bar.

Our loss is limited to the two gunboats, the officers and crew, and about 90 men, who were on board the boats as sharpshooters; these were captured. The killed and wounded, it is believed, will not exceed 30. The troops and remaining gunboats returned to Berwick Bay and New Orleans on the 11th instant.

In all respects the co-operation of the naval authorities has been hearty and efficient. Fully comprehending the purposes of the Government, they entered upon the expedition with great spirit. Commodore Bell gave all the assistance in his power, and Captain Crocker, of the Clifton, now a prisoner, deserves especial mention for his conspicuous gallantry.

Were it not for the very serious and lamentable deficiency of light-draught boats in this department, to which I have so often called the attention of the Government, I should consider the loss of the two boats as unimportant, except as to their armament. That of the Clifton was important.

The boats were unreliable for any service, on account of their decay and weakness both of hull and machinery.

It gives me great pleasure to say that both in the preparation and conduct of the expedition, General Franklin, his officers, and men exhibited the best spirit, and satisfied every expectation that could reasonably have been required of them. The failure is to be attributed solely to the misfortune attending the gunboats, and the impossibility of managing them in the shoal waters of the Sabine. Had it not been for this incurable unfitness for the work in hand, the gallant spirit exhibited by both navy and army would have insured the entire success of the enterprise. It would have placed our army between Taylor, Magruder, and Kirby Smith, and given us with certainty the immediate control of Texas.

I have the honor to inclose full reports by Generals Franklin and Weitzel, which will give in detail the operations of the army and navy, and embrace some precedent neglect on the part of the advance naval boats to which I have not adverted. The only incident of serious moment, tending to disclose to the enemy our plans, that occurred, was the desertion of an engineer while the gunboats were at Berwick Bay. This is believed to have been the only advance information they obtained.

Immediately upon the receipt of information of the failure at Sabine, and before the return of the troops, I commenced preparations for an overland movement from Brashear City via Vermillionville and Niblett's Bluff.

Had we the requisite naval force or transportation, I would renew the attempt on the Sabine, or strike at the Rio Grande. But we have neither.

It is impossible to move up the Red River at this season, except by most tedious marches, on account of the low stage of water. The entrance to the Atchafalaya is now covered by a dry sand-bar, which extends entirely across the bed of the river.

I have constantly borne in mind your suggestion as to a movement from Alexandria or Shreveport, but the low stage of the water makes it impracticable at this season.

The march to the Sabine will be difficult, but the men are full of energy and can accomplish it. It will enable us to disperse or destroy the enemy, leaving nothing in our rear but guerrillas to harass or threaten our position on the river.

If successful, we shall establish communication with the coast at Calcasieu, the Sabine, and Galveston, dispersing or destroying as we move, with the aid of the blockading vessels or transports and gunboats, the army of the enemy.

I have received your dispatch, notifying me that re-enforcements from the north are impossible at present. Appreciating fully the pressure upon the Government at this time, I cheerfully yield, of course, to the necessity which governs the action, but I earnestly urge you to give us all the aid possible from General Grant's army. I repeat in this dis- patch, what I have urged in former dispatches in aid of this application, that I shall not lock up large forces in unimportant or non-effective positions. I can return to him the whole of his force, if necessary, as soon as the expedition is over, and still maintain my department.

I have now in arms 12,000 blacks. I hope to increase the force to 25,000 or 30,000 at once. I think I can promise without failure from 2,000 to 5,000 white troops, raised in this department, but though avail-able for its defense by and by, they cannot serve us now.

If we can add from 30,000 to 40,000 troops to the effective force of the army from this department alone, I think we present a very just and strong claim to the temporary assistance we ask at your hands, and this I believe. To succeed in this, however, we require some assistance in the work we have in hand.

Solicitous that my action in all these important affairs may meet the approval of the Government, I remain, general, with considerations of high respect, yours, &c.,

N. P. BANKS,
Major-General, Commanding.

Major-General HALLECK, *Commander-in-Chief, U. S. Army.*

—

HEADQUARTERS DEPARTMENT OF THE GULF,
New Orleans, October 22, 1863.

SIR: Dispatches from the General-in-Chief impress me with the belief that my plan of action in the movement to the Sabine Pass is not per-fectly understood by the Government. It was not intended for the oc-cupation of Sabine City, nor was it, indeed, the purpose to land at that point except it could be done without serious resistance. The landing contemplated and referred to in the orders given to General Franklin, as an alternative for that of Sabine Pass, was upon the coast, 10 or 12 miles below. Had the landing been accomplished either at the Pass or below, a movement would have been immediately made for Beau-mont from the Pass, or for Liberty if the landing had been made below, and thence directly to Houston, where fortifications would have been thrown up, and our line of communication and supplies immediately established at the mouth of the Brazos River, west of Houston, until we could have gained possession of Galveston Island and City. I should have had in ten days from the landing 20,000 men at Houston, where, strongly fortified, they could have resisted the attack of any force that it was possible to concentrate at that time. Houston would have been nearly in the center of the forces in and about Louisiana and Texas, commanding all the principal communications, and would have given us ultimately the possession of the State. The inclosed sketch illustrates the intended routes.

The movement to the Sabine was made upon the reports furnished by the naval officers, who were perfectly confident of their success in being able to destroy the enemy's guns. The grounding of two boats, and the withdrawal of the other two boats, caused the failure to effect a landing and the return of the army. In my judgment, the army

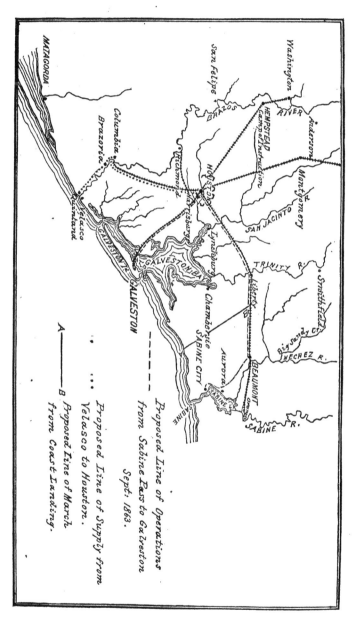

should not have returned, but should have continued to the point indicated for landing upon the coast, as contemplated in the instructions. This would have been done but for the withdrawal of the two boats that were free after the loss of the Sachem and the Clifton. The expedition sailed from the Mississippi on the 4th of September, and returned to the Mississippi on September 11. It was impossible to repeat the attempt, the failure having given notice to the enemy of our purposes, and enabled him to concentrate his forces against us. I therefore directed the movement of the troops across Berwick Bay, with a view to an overland movement into Texas. The deficiency of transportation, the removal of the numerous obstructions to the navigation of the Teche, and the difficulty of obtaining supplies, made it impracticable for us to reach Opelousas until this date.

We are now in position for a movement westward into Texas and northward to Northeastern Texas, by the way of Shreveport. The resources of the whole of this country are completely and thoroughly destroyed by the enemy. To the Sabine, we have a march from Opelousas and Vermillionville of between 100 and 200 miles, without water, without supplies, and without other transportation than by wagons. At Niblett's Bluff, on the Sabine, we shall encounter all the possible force of the enemy in the State of Texas, and a powerful enemy hanging upon our rear throughout the whole march, which is now waiting for us between Alexandria and Opelousas. From the Sabine to Houston is 100 miles, making altogether a march of from 250 to 300 miles. By the way of Alexandria and Shreveport to Marshall, which is the nearest point on the other route, we have a march of from 350 to 400 miles in that direction, without other communication than by wagon train, and through a country utterly depleted of all its material resources. Either of these routes present almost insuperable difficulties. It is not good policy to fight an absent enemy in a desert country, if it can be avoided.

While the army is preparing itself for one or the other of these movements, I propose to attempt a lodgment upon some point on the coast from the mouth of the Mississippi to the Rio Grande. The gunboat Tennessee was dispatched by Commodore Bell for this purpose on the 29th. A careful and intelligent engineer, Captain Baker, accompanied the expedition. The Tennessee returned to New Orleans on the 16th instant. The report was most favorable for operations upon the Gulf coast, and the difficulties, although great, much less than those presented upon either of the land routes, by the way of Niblett's Bluff to Houston, or to Alexandria, Shreveport, and Marshall, and, if it is successful, the results must be far more important than could be obtained by getting possession of the town of Marshall in Northeastern Texas. I have therefore determined to make an expedition for the purpose of landing between Sabine and the Rio Grande, most probably at the latter point. The expedition will sail to-morrow morning (23d) at 9 o'clock. The troops, about 3,500 in number, are under the command of Major-General Dana. I accompany the expedition myself, and am confident of its success. The earliest possible communication will be made to you of its results. This expedition will produce exactly the same results as that by the Sabine Pass; it is only reversing the order of procedure, beginning at the Rio Grande and moving eastward, instead of at the Sabine, moving westward.

I have the honor to be, with much respect, your obedient servant,

N. P. BANKS,
Major-General, Commanding.

The PRESIDENT OF THE UNITED STATES, *Washington, D. C.*

No. 2.

Report of Capt. William B. Roe, Chief Signal Officer, Department of the Gulf.

' NEW ORLEANS, LA.,
February 2, 1864.

SIR: I have the honor to submit the following report of duty performed by the signal corps in the department during the Sabine Pass expedition:

September 1, 1863.—I received orders from General Banks to report with my whole force to Maj. Gen. William B. Franklin, commanding Nineteenth Army Corps, for duty. On the above date I reported to General Franklin, and received orders to place officers on the following vessels: Lieut. S. M. Eaton, with General Weitzel, on Belvidere; Lieut. Thomas S. Seabury, with General Emory, on Crescent. Lieut. John W. Dana was placed on board the U. S. gunboat Clifton, and Lieut. Henry C. Dane on the U. S. gunboat Sachem. I accompanied General Franklin on the steamer Suffolk.

The expedition left New Orleans on the evening of September 4, and arrived at the mouth of Southwest Pass early the next morning. After organizing the expedition, we set sail for Sabine Pass, Tex. Arrived at our destination at 11 a. m., September 7. None of the gunboats or transports that preceded us were in sight until about 6 p. m., when the entire fleet, convoyed by the gunboats, were in view. No signal communication was held between the Suffolk and transports during the voyage out; still, the officers with Generals Weitzel and Emory rendered much valuable service during the voyage.

September 8, 3.30 p. m.—The gunboats atacked the fort at Sabine Pass. Lieutenants Dane and Dana were subjected to very severe fire from the enemy's works, they having occupied a very exposed position, to enable them to communicate with each other and also with General Franklin.

During the engagement, constant communication by signals was held between the two gunboats Sachem and Clifton, and also between General Franklin's headquarters and the gunboats. During the thickest of the engagement, the signal flags were distinctly seen transmitting orders between the fated gunboats.

At 4 p. m. the gunboats were compelled to surrender, and the 2 officers and 4 enlisted men were taken prisoners, together with the entire crews of the vessels.

Immediately upon their surrender, orders were sent by signals to the different generals to get under way and move to the mouth of the Mississippi River, and await orders.

General Franklin arrived at the mouth of the river on the morning of September 11. Orders were signaled to Generals Weitzel and Emory to encamp their troops at Algiers, where we arrived at 11 p. m., September 11.

My station on the Suffolk kept me so busy that I found it impossible to keep a correct copy of the messages sent and received. However, during the time over 100 official messages were sent and received.

Lieut. Thomas S. Seabury is entitled to much credit for the faithful manner in which he performed his duty ; also by staying on board the steamer Crescent, when others abandoned her, and greatly assisting in getting her off the bar.

Lieutenant Eaton also performed his duties with great promptitude.

The brave and gallant conduct of Lieutenants Dane and Dana can hardly be overestimated. Never have I seen signal officers subjected to as hot a fire as were they, and in no case were they found absent from their post of duty. I respectfully recommend that they each receive battle-flags, with appropriate inscriptions thereon, as a partial reward for their gallant conduct at Sabine Pass on the 8th of September, 1863.

I have the honor to be, very respectfully, your obedient servant,

WM. B. ROE,
Captain, and Chief of Signal Corps, Department of the Gulf.

Maj. G. B. DRAKE,
Assistant Adjutant-General, Department of the Gulf.

No. 3.

Reports of Maj. Gen. William B. Franklin, U. S. Army, commanding Expedition.

HEADQUARTERS NINETEENTH ARMY CORPS,
On board the Steamship Suffolk, September 11, 1863.

GENERAL: I have the honor to report that, in obedience to your orders of the — instant, [31st ultimo,]* I embarked the troops of my command at the points indicated.

On Friday, [September 4,] at 5 p. m., Brigadier-General Weitzel started from New Orleans with about 1,000 infantry, one battery of 30-pounder Parrott guns, and one of 20-pounder, of First Indiana Artillery, in the steamers Belvidere, Banks, Landis, and Saint Charles. The remainder of the force, with few exceptions, embarked during Friday night, and arrived at the mouth of the river during all of Saturday.

General Weitzel's instructions were to proceed as far as off Berwick Bay, in company with the gunboat Arizona, when he was to be joined by Lieutenant-Commander Crocker, U. S. Navy, with the gunboats Clifton and Sachem; thence they were to proceed in company to Sabine Pass, off which they expected to arrive during Sunday night. On Monday morning, at daylight, they were to enter the mouth of Sabine River. The gunboats were to engage and silence the rebel battery, and General Weitzel's troops were to co-operate, and were to hold a position on shore until the arrival of the other troops. Unfortunately the gunboat Granite City, which had been dispatched to the Pass several days before to carry Captain Crocker's pilot, who was well acquainted with the channel of the Pass, and who was to place a light to enable him to run in at daylight, did not arrive at the Pass until Monday afternoon; also, on Sunday night there were no blockaders off the Pass. The consequence was, that Captain Crocker missed Sabine Pass on Sunday night; imagined that he had run past it; ran back, and at daylight on Monday morning was off Calcasieu Pass, the next opening to the eastward, instead of being ready to run into Sabine Pass.

On Monday morning, about 11 o'clock, I arrived off Sabine Pass at the head of the fleet of transports, crossed the bar, and was about to run in, when, seeing nothing to indicate the presence of our people, I recrossed the bar. It was not until late in the afternoon that I ascer-

---

* See inclosure to Banks' report of September 5, p. 287.

tained definitely that nothing had yet been done.   I then learned that Captain Crocker now intended to make the attack on Tuesday morning, and that he had dispatched a gunboat to warn me to keep back, in order that the enemy might not see the transport fleet, but the gunboat only stopped some of the rear vessels of the fleet, missing the leading vessels entirely.

By this series of misfortunes, the attack, which was intended to be a surprise, became an open one, the enemy having had two nights' warning that a fleet was off the harbor, and, during Monday, a full view of most of the vessels composing it; besides, twenty-four hours of valuable time and good weather were uselessly consumed.

After consultation with Captain Crocker on Monday night, it was determined that the Clifton should go into the harbor at daylight, and make a reconnaissance, and that further operations should be determined by the report received from Captain Crocker.

He went in, made his reconnaissance, and signaled for the other vessels to come in.   I therefore sent all of the transports which it was supposed could cross the bar, and found the greatest difficulty in getting over any vessels drawing more than 6 feet.   About 10 o'clock, 700 infantry, one battery of field artillery, and eight heavy guns were inside of the bar, and a transport, with 700 infantry, was hopelessly aground. A tug drawing 6 feet was sent to her assistance, but had to return, not being able to reach her.

In company with General Weitzel and Captain Crocker, I made a reconnaissance of the Texas shore; small boats grounded in mud about 125 feet from the shore.

The shore itself is a soft marsh, and parallel to it, and about 50 feet inside of it, is a narrow strip of sand, on which is a road.   This road strikes the water and high ground about one-half mile below the fort, at which point there is an old fort.   Sailors wading sank into the mud above their knees; soldiers loaded with muskets and rations would have sunk to their middle.

The fort completely commands the road and the channels of the entrance, and contains six guns, three of which are, in my opinion, 9-inch guns, one a 7 or 8 inch rifled gun, and·two others on siege carriages.

The channel divides about 1,000 yards below the fort, and the two channels unite at a short distance above it.

As there were four gunboats available for the attack, the following plan was adopted in conjunction with Captain Crocker: Three of the gunboats were to move up the channel to the point of separation; there two of them, the Sachem and the Arizona, were to take the channel to the right, and were to pass the fort by that channel, drawing its fire.   The Clifton was to take the left-hand channel, moving slowly up, and, when about half-a mile distant, was to go at full speed, within grape and canister range, and engage the fort at close quarters.   General Weitzel was to keep near the Clifton with a boat containing 500 infantry, who were to land as soon as the Clifton began to go at full speed at the old fort; from there they were to advance upon the fort as skirmishers, endeavoring to drive the enemy from his guns, while the Clifton engaged the fort at close quarters.   The fourth gunboat, the Granite City, was to support this movement.

While the arrangements necessary to carry out this plan were being made, the troops that were in the transport aground on the bar were brought in, to be in readiness to assist General·Weitzel's movement in case of necessity.

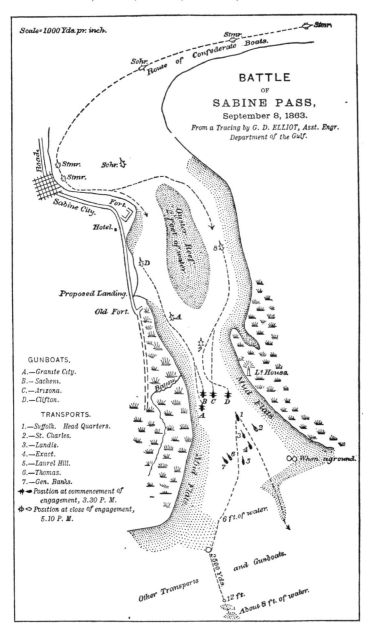

Scale= 1000 Yds. pr. inch.

BATTLE
OF
SABINE PASS,
September 8, 1863.
From a Tracing by G. D. ELLIOT, Asst. Engr.
Department of the Gulf.

GUNBOATS.

A.—Granite City.
B.— Sachem.
C.—Arizona.
D.—Clifton.

TRANSPORTS.

1.—Suffolk. Head Quarters.
2.—St. Charles.
3.—Landis.
4.—Exact.
5.—Laurel Hill.
6.—Thomas.
7.—Gen. Banks.
Position at commencement of
 engagement, 3.30 P. M.
Position at close of engagement,
 5.10 P. M.

The movement of the gunboats commenced at 3 o'clock, and progressed according to the plan for about thirty minutes, when the fort opened on the Sachem and Arizona, and in a few minutes put a shot through the boilers of the Sachem, killing and wounding many of her officers and men. She soon afterward hoisted a white flag. The Arizona was during part of this time aground.

The Clifton steamed slowly up her channel, firing slowly, and finally lay with her broadside toward the fort, engaged at close quarters. A shot went through her steam-pipe shortly afterward, disabling her, but she fought gallantly for ten minutes more, when she, too, surrendered.

As soon as she hoisted the white flag, the Arizona and Granite City steamed over the bar; the Arizona grounded, but got off during the night.

General Weitzel's report, herewith inclosed, shows why that part of the engagement assigned to him could not be carried out.

After the engagement, my situation was as follows: I was in the mouth of the Sabine Pass with seven transports. These contained 1,200 infantry, which could be landed; twelve guns and fifty wagons, which could not be landed. The enemy had a heavy battery of six guns, two gunboats, and a field battery within 6 miles, and was being rapidly re-enforced. We had nothing to protect us, except the fire from the guns on our transports, which would have been of little use against the enemy's gunboats.

The enemy's battery commanded the whole landing, and he could, with his battery and gunboats, have destroyed us at any time.

The remainder of my force was outside the bar in vessels, all of which had to be lightened, and at least three days would have been required to land it.

The stock of fresh water was nearly exhausted, and the animals were already on short allowance of water; the men were living on uncooked rations, and there was no fuel on shore for cooking.

No fresh water could be obtained unless the fort was in our possession, and the day's experience had taught me that no attack which I could make with the troops which I had been able to get across the bar could possibly succeed. It would have been absurd to have attempted to have passed the fort with the troops already inside of the bar, there being but one means of access to Sabine City, and this commanded for 1½ miles by six heavy guns and whatever field artillery the enemy might have. There was no time to send to New Orleans to get instructions, and I therefore concluded to recross the bar and return to the mouth of the Mississippi.

I arrived at the mouth of the Mississippi this morning, having left Sabine Pass on the 9th instant, and believe there have been no losses except those reported by General Weitzel, and 200,000 rations thrown overboard from the Crescent (the grounded transport), to get her off the bar, where she would have been taken by the enemy, and 200 mules thrown overboard from the Laurel Hill, a steamer which had 'lost her smoke-stacks on account of the heavy sea. The loss of the mules will be investigated, as they were thrown overboard without orders from any responsible officer.

Very respectfully, your obedient servant,

W. B. FRANKLIN,
Major-General, Commanding.

Maj. Gen. N. P. BANKS,
Commanding Department of the Gulf, New Orleans, La.

HEADQUARTERS NINETEENTH ARMY CORPS,
Algiers, La., September 14, 1863.

GENERAL: I omitted to state in my report of the late expedition to Sabine Pass that on Monday, the 7th instant, I was boarded by an officer from the gunboat Cayuga, who informed me that his vessel was on a cruise in that part of the Gulf. He also informed me that he had been off the Pass near daybreak of that morning.

His vessel accompanied us during the remainder of the voyage to the Pass, and staid near us until we left.

Commodore Bell noticed this omission in my report, and asked me to make this correction, which I do with pleasure.

Another omission is, I should have mentioned that a field battery of the enemy fired into Captain Crocker's vessel, the Clifton, while she was engaged with the fort. I learned this from General Weitzel after the report was written.

I shall be glad if a copy of this letter be furnished to Commodore Bell.

Very respectfully, yours,

W. B. FRANKLIN,
Major-General, Commanding Nineteenth Corps.

Maj. Gen. N. P. BANKS,
Commanding Department of the Gulf, New Orleans, La.

No. 4.

Report of Brig. Gen. Godfrey Weitzel, U. S. Army, commanding First Division, Nineteenth Army Corps, with Itinerary of the Division for September, 1863.

ON BOARD STEAMER SUFFOLK,
September 11, 1863.

SIR: I have the honor to report the following as the part my command took in the expedition to Sabine Pass:

I left New Orleans at 7 p. m. on the 4th instant, on the steamer Belvidere, and made the Southwest Pass at 11 a. m. on the 5th instant, accompanied by the steamers General Banks, Saint Charles, and I. C. Landis, under convoy of the U. S. gunboat Arizona.

At 7 a. m. on the 6th instant, was joined off Berwick Bay by the U. S. gunboats Clifton and Sachem, and, after furnishing the three boats with the sharpshooters they requested, we sailed for Sabine Pass at 3.30 a. m. on the 7th instant.

I was informed that Captain Crocker, of the U. S. gunboat Clifton, had discovered that we were westward of Sabine Pass, and had ordered the boats to turn back.

At about 7 a. m. Captain Crocker came aboard of my vessel, and reported to me that he had been mistaken, and that we were off Calcasieu River, about 30 miles to the eastward of Sabine Pass.

After consultation, we concluded it would be best to try and stop the rest of the expedition at the point we were, and then attempt to dash on the enemy's works on the next morning. We were unsuccessful in this, as the general commanding the corps had passed us. Two of my transports, the General Banks and Saint Charles, were disabled, and required some time for repairs; as soon as these repairs were made, at about 5 p. m., we started for the Pass, and reported to the general com-manding at about 9 p. m.

I was ordered on the next morning to put the troops from the Belvi-dere on the Thomas, and follow the gunboats over the bar. I did this, after a reconnaissance of the landing and the enemy's works and posi-tion had been made, and after consultation with Captain Crocker, com-manding the Clifton and the gunboat fleet.

I was ordered to place 500 men on the transport General Banks, to follow up the rear gunboat as soon as the attack was commenced, and to land the men at the Old Battery Point, with orders to advance on the enemy's works, and keep down the fire of the enemy's gunners while the gunboats were engaged.

At 3.45 p. m. the gunboats advanced to the attack; I followed, ac-cording to orders, the last gunboat, the Granite City. Before the Granite City came near to the position assigned her, to cover my land-ing, the Sachem had been disabled, the Clifton was aground, and, un-fortunately, in exact range of my proposed point of landing. I had just given orders to attempt the landing, nevertheless, when I saw the colors of the Clifton had been struck and the white flag raised on the Sachem, and saw that the Arizona was aground. A few moments afterward I was ordered to retire, and then again to go outside and anchor in rear of the Crescent. Later in the night I received orders to go with my vessels, with the troops arranged as they had been, to the Southwest Pass, Mississippi River, which I did after considerable de-lay in towing the Laurel Hill (disabled), and arrived at that point at about 7 a. m. this day.

There were 2 officers and 75 men of the Seventy-fifth New York Vol-unteers on the Clifton as sharpshooters. Six of them escaped. On the Sachem there were 1 officer and 25 men from the One hundred and sixty-first New York Volunteers. How many were killed and wounded I do not know.

My total loss is, therefore, 3 officers and 94 men.

I am, captain, very respectfully, your obedient servant,

G. WEITZEL,
Brig. Gen., Comdg. First Division, Nineteenth Army Corps.

Capt. WICKHAM HOFFMAN,
Assistant Adjutant-General, Nineteenth Army Corps.

———

*Itinerary of the First Division, Nineteenth Army Corps, for September, 1863.**

September 1.—Brig. Gen. G. Weitzel assumed command at Baton Rouge, La.

September 2.—The First Brigade moved from Baton Rouge by steamers to New Orleans.

September 4.—The First and Third Brigades, and Company A, First Artillery, embarked on transports, and sailed at 5 p. m.

September 5.—At 6 a. m. arrived at Southwest Pass. Sailed at 9 a. m., steering westward, under convoy of gunboat Arizona.

September 6.—At 6 a. m. arrived off Berwick Bay; joined by gunboats Clifton and Sachem; 1 officer and 25 sharpshooters on Sachem, and 2 officers and 75 sharpshooters on Clifton, and steamed westward.

---

* From "Record of Events," on division return.

September 7.—Convoy having missed the entrance to Sabine Pass, during the early morning the squadron returned to Lake Calcasieu, and anchored at 10 a. m., joined by Brigadier-General Emory's fleet. Steamed for Sabine Pass at 4 p. m.; arrived at 9 p. m.

September 8.—At 7 a. m. arrived at Sabine Pass. Transferred the Seventy-fifth New York Volunteers from steamer Belvidere to river steamer Thomas. At 8 a. m. steamed for bar. During the day a selected party was placed on board the steamboat Banks, to attempt a landing.

At 3 p. m. the gunboats opened fire upon the rebel battery. The Sachem having been exploded and Clifton grounded, it was found impossible to land troops. At 6 p. m. troops returned to transports. Ordered to proceed to Southwest Pass. At 9 a. m. *en route* for Southwest Pass.

September 11.—At 6 a. m. arrived at the mouth of Mississippi River, and anchored at the head of the passes. At 3 p. m. sailed for New Orleans.

September 12.—Arrived at New Orleans; troops ordered into camp at Algiers.

September 15.—The Third Brigade proceeded by rail to Brashear City.

September 16.—The First Brigade and Battery L proceeded by rail to Brashear City.

September 17.—Crossed Berwick Bay, and encamped at Berwick City.

September 20.—Moved to Washington Smith's plantation, and encamped, joined by the First Maine Battery.

September 26.—At 4 a. m. moved to Tarleton's plantation; marched 10 miles, and encamped at 10 a. m.

September 28.—Two regiments and Battery L, First Artillery, under command of Colonel Love, moved to head of Bayou Lallie road, to support cavalry reconnaissance.

September 29.—Colonel Love's command returned to camp at Tarleton's.

September 30.—In camp at Tarleton's plantation.

No. 5.

Itinerary of the First Brigade, Third Division, Nineteenth Army Corps, Brig. Gen. Frank S. Nickerson, U. S. Army, commanding, for September, 1863.[*]

September 2.—This brigade left Baton Rouge, La., on transports Pocahontas, Belvidere, and North America. The last-named vessel being condemned as unseaworthy, the One hundred and tenth and One hundred and sixty-second New York Volunteers and Fourteenth Maine Regiments were transferred to the Robert C. Winthrop, at New Orleans, and the brigade, under command of Brigadier-General Nickerson, constituted part of the expedition to Sabine Pass which sailed from New Orleans on September 4.

September 12.—It returned to Algiers, La.

September 17.—It proceeded, under command of Brig. Gen. J. W. McMillan, by the Opelousas Railroad, to Brashear City.

September 18.—It marched to its present camp, Bisland.

---

[*] From " Record of Events," on brigade return.

No. 6.

*Report of Acting Volunteer Lieut. Frederick Crocker, U. S. Navy.**

HOUSTON, TEX.,
September 12, 1863.

SIR : By permission of the provost-marshal-general of Texas, I have the honor to make a concise report concerning the capture of the Clifton and Sachem, and the failure of our attack on the fort at Sabine, passing the failure of the Granite City to anchor off the bar and show the concerted signal, whereby we lost the advantage of surprise, and other failures.

On the night of the 7th instant, the whole fleet anchored off the bar, and at daylight the next morning I crossed the bar in the Clifton to reconnoiter. I found a cotton-clad gunboat, and a very strong looking battery situated where I expected to find it, and, after attempting to draw their fire without success, fell back, and signalized for the whole fleet to cross the bar, which was done.

I then went on board General Franklin's ship to arrange for the attack, which was finally decided as follows : While the Clifton was shelling the battery with short-fuse shells, the Sachem and Arizona were to advance up the Louisiana channel, and thus compel the enemy to change the training of his guns, when the Clifton was to advance rapidly up the Texas channel, and endeavor to obtain a position near enough to the battery to enable the sharpshooters to pick off the enemy's gunners. The Granite City was to start with the Clifton, and, following her up the Texas channel, take up a position just above the Old Battery, and cover the landing of troops at that place from the transport General Banks, which troops were to advance rapidly up the bank toward the enemy, and support the Clifton, should she, as was expected, ground near the battery.

It was 4 o'clock in the afternoon before General Franklin was ready to co-operate, by which time the smoke of several steamers was discovered coming down the lake.

The arrangements of the army being at last completed, the Clifton took up her position in the Texas channel, and began to shell the enemy. The Sachem started up the Louisiana channel, followed by the Arizona, and, after grounding slightly, entered the channel fairly, and joined in the action as they moved up. The Granite City and the General Banks, with their anchors up, lay ready to follow. At the second discharge from the enemy's guns, the Clifton, with a full head of steam, steamed rapidly up the Texas channel toward the battery. When the Clifton was about half-way up to the battery, I noticed with great surprise that the Granite City and the General Banks were still lying, drifting across the tide, making no attempt to follow. At the same time a shot from the enemy struck the Sachem's boiler, disabling her instantly and silencing her fire ; but, depending upon the support of all the others, the Clifton kept on her course. In a short time, however, her wheel rope was shot away, and she grounded sooner than was expected, and in such a position that only three of her guns could bear on the battery ; and with three we kept up the fight, making every effort to get the vessel afloat ; but before we succeeded, a shot passed through her boiler and machinery, disabling her completely.

Until this time every man stood to his post, and the fight was pro-

---

* Found in the files of the District of Texas, New Mexico, and Arizona.

gressing favorably; but the steam drove all the sharpshooters off the upper deck. Many, thinking the vessel was about to blow up, jumped overboard. At the same time the enemy got our range, and their fire began to tell severely. The vessel twice caught fire, and the men were falling fast. My executive officer (Acting Master Robert Rhodes) fell, mortally wounded. Two other officers received wounds, and the men noticing that no support was near, many of them became unsteady. Enough of them remained, however, to keep up a very effectual fire, which was being done with the faint hope that we might yet be supported, when I was met by two of my officers, and informed by one of them that he had hauled down the flag, and that we could not fight any more. With great indignation, I ordered it hoisted again, and all to stand to their guns; but the example had become contagious; with few exceptions, the men had left their guns and were taking to the water. At the same time a shot from the enemy disabled one of my three guns, and the lock of another broke, the remnant of the crew firing it with a hammer.

Under these circumstances, and seeing that the Arizona failed to push on; the Granite City and General Banks to make the slightest attempt to support me; the enemy's fire becoming more and more deadly; deserted by all but a few brilliant exceptions, I deemed it my duty to stop the slaughter by showing the white flag, which was done, and we fell into the hands of the enemy.

While the fight was thus progressing, the commander of the Sachem sent to the Arizona an order to advance and take him in tow; but it was not obeyed. The Arizona lay astern nearly silent until the termination of the fight, when she turned and fled.

The conduct of the commanders of the Arizona and Granite City, or of my officer who hauled down the flag, I am not now called upon to characterize; nor that of General Franklin in failing so utterly to cooperate; but I trust my Government will soon place me in a position to ask an inquiry into the facts.

I cannot conclude without bearing testimony to the gallant manner in which the commanding officer of the Sachem carried out, so far as he could, his part of the programme.

I am, very respectfully, your obedient servant,
FREDERICK CROCKER,
Acting Volunteer Lieutenant, Commanding Expedition.

Commodore H. H. BELL,
Comdg. West Gulf Squadron, off New Orleans, La.

No. 7.

Reports of Maj. Gen. John B. Magruder, C. S. Army, commanding District of Texas, New Mexico, and Arizona, with congratulatory orders and proclamation.

HEADQUARTERS DISTRICT OF TEXAS, &C.,
Houston, September 9, 1863.

SIR: I beg leave to state that on yesterday morning about 6 o'clock the enemy appeared off Sabine Pass with a force of twenty-seven vessels. Some of them approached, coming inside the bar, and commenced shelling the fort.

The necessity for additional forces on the northern frontier, connected with the fact that several companies of [W. H.] Griffin's battalion, which was stationed on the Sabine Pass, were becoming restless under the depredations reported to have been committed by the Indians and others in the section of country in which these companies were raised, induced me to order them to Millican, and hold at that point four companies of this battalion, leaving a force of 200 men to man the fort at the Pass. The enemy has, perhaps, compelled them to retire and occupy the fort. This, however, if it has occurred, could not have been prevented by these four companies remaining at Sabine Pass, inasmuch as the whole of the force at that place could not have stood against so large a force of the enemy. I have the honor to state that I have ordered all the troops which have arrived at Millican, under my orders, to Beaumont and Orange, to prevent the enemy, if possible, from ascending the Sabine River, or from occupying the important position of Beaumont, and thus securing the railroad. The troops ordered to Sabine and vicinity are as follows: The Third Regiment Texas Infantry, Gould's regiment, four companies of Griffin's battalion, Jones' company of light artillery, and a battalion of light artillery, consisting of Captains Nichols' and Gonzales' batteries. Besides the 200 men already there, there are four companies of Elmore's regiment in the vicinity of the Pass. The only other regiment at my disposal, Colonel Buchel's, has been ordered by me to Beaumont.

I have the honor to be, very respectfully, your obedient servant,

J. BANKHEAD MAGRUDER,
Major-General, Commanding.

Brig. Gen. W. R. BOGGS,
Chief of Staff.

—

BEAUMONT,
September 10, 1863.

SIR : I have the honor to announce a second brilliant victory over the enemy's fleet, gained at Sabine Pass on the evening of the 8th instant, resulting in the capture of two fine gunboats, the Clifton and the Sachem, with a full supply of ordnance stores, eighteen heavy guns, 200 prisoners, among them Commander Frederick Crocker, commanding the expedition, the loss of the enemy being over 50 killed and wounded, while on our side not a man was hurt.

This gallant achievement was won by the little garrison at Fort Grigsby (44 men), commanded by Lieut. R. W. Dowling, supported by a small force, the whole under command of Capt. F. H. Odlum. Though attacked by five of the enemy's gunboats, the little fort, mounting but three guns of small caliber, maintained its fire until the two gunboats mentioned were forced to surrender, while the other fled over the bar (one of them being badly crippled), to join the discomfited fleet of twenty-two more vessels which witnessed the contest.

This victory, even in the face of a formidable expedition which still threatens the coast, is announced with the more satisfaction from the fact that the two vessels captured were among those which disgracefully fled under a flag of truce from the scene of triumph of Texan valor at Galveston in January last.

J. BANKHEAD MAGRUDER,
Maj. Gen., Comdg. Dist. of Texas, New Mexico, and Arizona.

Brig. Gen. [W.] R. BOGGS,
Chief of Staff.

HEADQUARTERS DISTRICT OF TEXAS, &C.,
Beaumont, Tex., September 10, 1863.

SIR: I have the honor to state that the enemy has withdrawn and disappeared from Sabine Pass.

It is supposed that the expedition, estimated at 15,000 men, commanded, as it is represented by the Federal prisoners, by Major-General Franklin in person, has gone up the Calcasieu. If this be true, he can approach to within 20 miles of Niblett's Bluff, and thus take possession of the place. I can, I hope, fortify against him on the Texas side, at the mouth of the Sabine, but cannot do so on the Louisiana side.

Should the enemy succeed in getting possession of Niblett's Bluff, which I shall do my best to prevent, the army of General Taylor will, in my opinion, be extricated with difficulty. In view of this, and of the defense both of Louisiana and Texas, I beg that Lieutenant-General Smith will order Major-General Taylor to assemble his forces at Niblett's Bluff. I shall send a courier direct to General Mouton, and request that he move his command as rapidly as possible to Niblett's Bluff.

If these troops are concentrated at that point, with such assistance as I may be able to give, after diverting the 2,000 State cavalry from Bonham, at which point I·had ordered them to assemble, I hope we may be able to crush the enemy; but, in my opinion, unless such steps are taken, he will invade Texas from Louisiana, and, reaching the heart of the State, get possession of Houston, which will necessitate the fall of Galveston.

I have the honor to state that I received last night letters from Mrs. General Bankhead, inclosing letters from Brigadier-General [S. P.] Bankhead, stating that he had united with Brigadier-Generals [William] Steele and [D. H.] Cooper, and though in search of the enemy, none could be found. In consideration of these facts, I hope the lieutenant-general commanding will see fit to direct Major-General Taylor to move his forces and place them as indicated above. The depots of supplies from Vermillionville to Niblett's Bluff have been established in accordance with Major-General Taylor's request, and thus the movements may be easily effected.

The fort at the mouth of the Pass was defended by only 40 men. Lieutenant Dowling, of Cook's regiment of artillery, commanded the fort, and Captain Odlum, of the same company, commanded the post. This small force, in the presence of a fleet of 15,000 of the enemy, drove off one gunboat, captured two others, thirteen pieces of cannon, and 340 prisoners, who are now here.

This seems to me to be the most extraordinary feat of the war, and I beg that the lieutenant-general commanding will notice the conduct of Captain Odlum, Lieutenant Dowling commanding, and men of the Davis Guards.

Commodore Leon Smith and Capt. W. S. Good, of the ordnance department, arrived at the fort during the engagement, passing through the enemy's fire to reach it. Both deserve great credit for their gallantry.

Commodore Leon Smith, seizing the flag, stood with it upon the ramparts, and stimulated the men by his example and words.

·I cannot too highly commend this sensible, heroic, and useful officer to the commander-in-chief, nor speak too highly of the services of Captain Good, who not only manufactures projectiles and ammunition of all kinds, but also is casting excellent brass cannon. This district could do little or nothing without him.

He declines to appear before the board of examiners for the ordnance [service], and I beg the lieutenant-general to recommend his appointment as major or captain of ordnance, without an examination, as has been done in some cases in the armies east of the Mississippi.

I have the honor to be, very respectfully, your obedient servant,.
J. BANKHEAD MAGRUDER,
Major-General, Commanding.

Brig. Gen. W. R. BOGGS,
Chief of Staff.

—

HDQRS. DIST. OF TEXAS, NEW MEXICO, AND ARIZONA,
Sabine Pass, September 27, 1863.

GENERAL : I have the honor herewith to transmit my official report of the recent brilliant engagement at this place, resulting in the capture of the enemy's gunboats Sachem and Clifton, accompanied by the flags of the captured vessels. This remarkable victory, in the face of 15,000 of the enemy's land forces and several other gunboats, entitles the gallant little garrison to the favorable consideration of the Department, and will, I trust, be promptly noticed and rewarded by the honorable Secretary of War. We are menaced with another attack, and though the force at my disposal is very small, I trust I shall be able to follow up the success which has hitherto attended our arms on the Texas coast. I also inclose copies of my orders in relation to the victory. The report I had previously made to Lieutenant-General [E. Kirby] Smith.

Very respectfully, your obedient servant,
J. BANKHEAD MAGRUDER, ·
Major-General, Commanding District.

General S. COOPER,
Adjutant and Inspector General, Richmond, Va.

HDQRS. DIST. OF TEXAS, NEW MEXICO, AND ARIZONA,
Sabine Pass, Tex., September 27, 1863.

GENERAL : A fleet of twenty-two steam transports, largest size, with five war steamers, attempted to pass into this river on the 8th instant. The number of troops is estimated by the coolest men and stated by prisoners to be 15,000 picked men, mostly of Grant's army. The transports could not pass unless the war steamers reduced our fort of six 32-pounder guns.

Lieutenant [R. W.] Dowling, in immediate command of the fort, directed his men not to return the fire of the enemy, as our guns were of short range.

The enemy at length approached with his war steamers, four in number, backed by the whole fleet of transports, to a point well within our range, when Lieutenant Dowling, of the Davis Guards, opened upon the advanced ships of war, and in some thirty-five minutes two surrendered, with over 300 prisoners, and another left in a crippled condition. The fleet then backed out and sailed east.

This seems to me to be the most extraordinary feat of the war, and I beg that the Department will notice the conduct of Captain [F. H.] Odlum, Lieutenant Dowling, commanding, and the men of the Davis Guards.

Commodore Leon Smith and Capt. W. S. Good, of the ordnance department, arrived at the fort during the engagement, passing through the enemy's fire to reach it. Both deserve great credit for their gallantry. Commodore Smith, seizing the flag, stood with it upon the ramparts, and stimulated the men by his example and words. I cannot too highly commend this sensible, heroic, and useful officer to the commander-in-chief, nor speak too highly of the services of Captain Good, who not only manufactures projectiles and ammunition of all kinds, but also is casting excellent brass cannon. This district could do little or nothing without him.

I arrived the day after at Beaumont, a strategic point, with a portion of the troops from the interior, and have since concentrated 2,500 men here, and greatly strengthened the works at this place. I expect their return soon with iron-clads, and hope to be prepared to meet them successfully. Had they got in, they would have proceeded at once to Niblett's Bluff, cut us off from Major-General Taylor, and probably advanced on Houston. Now it will be more difficult. The prisoners all stated that they were bound for Houston, and will yet get there. I trust, however, my dispositions of the available forces under my command will thwart them, although very small in number.

I am, general, very respectfully, your obedient servant,

J. BANKHEAD MAGRUDER,
Major-General, Commanding.

General S. COOPER,
Adjutant and Inspector General, Richmond, Va.

[Inclosure.]

GENERAL ORDERS, } HDQRS. DIST. OF TEX., N. MEX., AND ARIZ.,
No. 154.   }   *Houston, Tex., September 9, 1863.*

I. The major-general commanding has the satisfaction of announcing to the army a brilliant victory won by the little garrison of Sabine Pass against the fleet of the enemy. Attacked by five gunboats, the fort, mounting but three guns of small caliber, and manned by the Davis Guards, Lieut. R. W. Dowling, assisted by Lieutenant [N. H.] Smith, of the Engineers, supported by about 200 men, the whole under command of Capt. F. H. Odlum, steadily resisted their fire, and at last forced the surrender of the two gunboats, Clifton and Sachem, badly crippling another, which, with the others, escaped over the bar. The result of this gallant achievement is the capture of two fine gunboats, fifteen heavy guns, over 200 prisoners, among them the commodore of the fleet, and over 50 of the enemy killed and wounded, while not a man was lost on our side or a gun injured.

II. The enemy's fleet, with his land forces, is still off the coast, no doubt intending a landing at the first favorable moment. He may endeavor to retrieve his losses at Sabine by an attack upon the works at other points on the coast. Should this be-the case, the major-general commanding confidently expects to receive from his troops at these points as cheering a report as that which he now communicates to the army from the defenders of the Sabine. ·

III. The result of the engagement had with the enemy's fleet on the coast of Texas proves that true pluck and resolution are qualities which make up for disparity of metal and numbers, and that no position defended with determination can be carried by the enemy's gunboats alone. Should any of the forts on the coast or the forces on land be attacked, the troops need but remember the success of their comrades at Sabine, emulate their courage and skill, and victory will be the result.

By command of Maj. Gen. J. Bankhead Magruder :

EDMUND P. TURNER,
Assistant Adjutant-General.

HDQRS. DIST. OF TEX., N. MEX., AND ARIZONA,
Beaumont, September 10, 1863.

To the Men of Texas :

FELLOW-CITIZENS : Almighty God in His divine mercy has given us another signal victory over our enemies. A handful of determined men, in the face of 15,000 of the enemy's troops and a powerful fleet of gunboats, have for the present defeated their landing, capturing two and crippling two others of the gunboats, with eighteen pieces of artillery and over 300 prisoners.

Fellow-citizens, I need your assistance. Form yourselves into companies, and assemble at Beaumont with your arms as rapidly as possible. Those passing through Houston will be furnished transportation, ammunition, and rations, by reporting to Lieut. Col. J. D. McAdoo, assistant adjutant-general State troops. The enemy will return to the attack upon the works at Sabine Pass, and threatens vengeance for his defeat. Let us meet him like men resolved to conquer or die.

Men of Texas, I know I do not call upon you in vain. Shall it be said that your State was invaded and you hastened not to the aid of your brethren in the field? Let the mothers, wives, and daughters of Texas, remembering the outrages and tyranny their sisters of the South have met at the hands of the foe, urge every man to do his duty and tarry no longer from the field. The gray-haired sires and women of Texas have the courage to defend their homes from local danger if the able-bodied men will march to meet the enemy and contest every inch of ground which leads to plantations and homes to be desolated by his vandal hand.

Business men and planters, the time has come for you to turn aside from your daily pursuits and rally to the defense of your country. Wait not until the enemy has wrested from you the fruits of years of toil, or ravaged the fields upon which you rely for a sustenance.

Old Texans, men of the days of '36, men of the Republic, you have grasped the rifle and trusty knife before at the call of danger. Come now, and the men who love you for your deeds of valor, the youths who would emulate your example, will follow you. Many of your comrades are in the ranks. Form with them a wall of fire and steel against which the foe shall press in vain.

J. BANKHEAD MAGRUDER,
Major-General, Comdg. Dist. of Texas, New Mexico, and Arizona.

No. 8.

Report of Col. Leon Smith, C. S. Army, commanding Marine Department, Texas.

SABINE PASS,
September 8, 1863.

SIR : After telegraphing the major-general this morning before leaving Beaumont, I took a horse, and proceeded with all haste to Sabine,

from which direction I could distinctly hear a heavy firing. At 3. p. m.
I arrived at the Sabine Pass, and found the enemy off and inside the
bar, with nineteen gunboats and steamships and three sloops of war,
carrying, as well as I can judge, about 15,000 men. After learning the
state of affairs, I proceeded with Captains [F. H.] Odlum and [W. S.]
Good to the fort, where I found Lieutenants [R. W.] Dowling and N. H.
Smith, with 42 men, defending the fort. During the day until 3 p. m.
our guns were not opened on the enemy, as the range was too distant,
the officers coolly holding their fire until the enemy had approached
near enough to reach them; but the enemy arriving within good range,
our batteries were opened, and gallantly replied to a galling and most
terrific fire from the enemy. As I entered the fort, the gunboats Clifton,
Arizona, Sachem, and Granite City, and several others came boldly up
to within 1,000 yards, and opened their batteries, which were gallantly
and effectively replied to by the Davis Guards, commanded by Captain
Odlum and Lieutenant Dowling. For one hour and a half a most terrific
bombardment of grape, canister, and shell was directed upon our devoted,
heroic little band within the fort. The shot struck in every direction,
but, thanks be to God, not one of that noble Davis Guards was hurt.

Too much credit cannot be rendered Captain Odlum and his gallant
lieutenant (Dowling), who displayed the utmost heroism in the discharge of the duty assigned him—the defense of the fort.

The Davis Guards, one and all, God bless them. The honor of the
country was in their hands, and they nobly sustained it. Every man
stood at his post, notwithstanding the murderous fire that was poured
upon us from every direction.

In consequence of the small number of officers, Lieut. N. H. Smith, of
the Engineer Corps, was placed in command of two 32-pounders, and
displayed the utmost gallantry and ability in the discharge of that duty.

I would also mention the conduct of Captain [R. V.] Cook and 30 men,
of Company D, Griffin's battalion; Lieutenant [Joseph M.] Chasten, of
Company F, and his men (Griffin's battalion), both of whom rushed
immediately to the scene of danger, to participate in this gallant affair.

Lieutenant [Joseph O.] Cassidy and men of Company B, [A. W.]
Spaight's battalion, also behaved like soldiers of Texas—gallantly and
nobly—their position being on board the steam gunboat Uncle Ben,
which boat run down to the Sachem and brought her into port.

I would also recommend the gallant conduct of Lieutenant [N. H.]
Smith, of Company B, Spaight's battalion; also Lieutenant [Charles]
Harris, of Captain [Andrew] Daly's company, his command acting as
scouts and couriers.

I would also mention the energy displayed by Lieutenant-Colonel
[L. A.] Abercrombie, of [H. M.] Elmore's regiment, stationed at Orange
and Niblett's Bluff, in conjunction with Capt. L. C. Irwin, of the Marine
Department; Capt. John Payne, commanding gunboats on Sabine River;
Capt. G. Hall, commanding gunboat Uncle Ben, in hastening forward
re-enforcements from Orange and Niblett's Bluff, and coming themselves
to participate in the defense of this post; also to Capt. John Price, of
the steamer Florilda, and his officers, who assisted in placing the re-
enforcements at disposal in time to effectually intimidate the enemy
from further attack.

The result of this battle, which lasted from 3.30 till 5 p. m., is the
capturing the steamer Clifton, carrying eight guns, and the gunboat
Sachem, carrying five guns, our prisoners numbering nearly 400, and
the driving off outside the bar most of the enemy's fleet in a crippled
condition, comprising twenty sail in all.

To-night we expect an attack, and we have distributed our little band in various quarters ready for the onset. I have the gunboat Sachem alongside the wharf, and am taking off her guns. I shall go to the Clifton in half an hour, and as she is hard aground, I will endeavor to save her guns, and will, at high tide in the morning, try and get her into the dock.

Killed and wounded of the 42 men, praises be to God, none on our side.

I have the honor to be, very respectfully, your obedient servant,

LEON SMITH,
Commanding Marine Department, Texas.

Capt. EDMUND P. TURNER,
Assistant Adjutant-General.

No. 9.

Reports of Capt. F. H. Odlum, Cook's (Texas) Artillery.

HEADQUARTERS,
Sabine Pass, September 8—7.30 a. m.

SIR: I have the honor to report that the enemy opened fire this morning at 6.30 o'clock from one of their steamers, and withdrew at 7.30 o'clock, after firing twenty-six shell. One shot struck the parapet, but did no material damage. One shell struck within the works, but no one hurt. The shell is believed to be an 11-inch shell. Their shots are all good, but doing no damage. I issued orders to Lieutenant [R. W.] Dowling, commanding Fort Griffin, to reserve his fire until the steamers were within range, and then to aim at their wheel-houses, so as to cripple them, which I believe will answer very well. Lieutenant Dowling is carrying out my orders strictly. The gunboat Uncle Ben will act according to circumstances. I have only three companies to keep the enemy at bay. I am under the impression they will try to take us by sea and land. There are six steamers within the bar, apparently holding a consultation. If possible, I hope the commanding general will send troops here at once. I am determined to hold the Pass, if possible. There are twenty-one vessels outside the bar.

Yours, very respectfully,

F. H. ODLUM,
Captain Cook's Artillery, Commanding Sabine Pass.

Capt. A. N. MILLS,
Assistant Adjutant-General.

—

HEADQUARTERS,
Sabine Pass, Tex., September 9, 1863.

SIR: I have the honor to report that on the 8th instant our fight commenced just below the old fort, at 6.30 a. m., by the enemy's steamer Clifton opening fire on us, giving us about twenty-six shot and shell, all within range, and most of them falling close to the fort, one shell exploding within the fort, and one striking the parapet on the south angle without doing material damage. They withdrew at 7.30 a. m., without receiving any reply from us.

At 11 o'clock, ordered the gunboat [Uncle] Ben to steam down near the fort, for the purpose of making a feint, and showing the enemy she was all right. They honored her with three shots, which all passed over and clear of us, after which all remained quiet until about 3 p. m., when eight of the enemy's boats commenced moving up the Pass, four or five of the foremost firing constautly on the fort with shot and shell, grape and canister, hailing them in and all around the fort. We retained our fire at the fort until the first three of them got within close and easy range, when we opened on them fast and heavy, and waked them up with astonishment, as they afterward said, for they had taken our guns for wooden imitations from our holding fire so long. About the fifth shot took good effect in the boiler of the Sachem, the foremost of the fleet, blowing her up and silencing her. Next, and very soon after, the Clifton was served in the same way, and also silenced, and in the meantime the third was being badly peppered and crippled, and began falling back, when the balance of the ascending fleet took warning and fright, and all got back to the bar. The first two, hoisting a white flag, surrendered unconditionally.

We captured two steamers, carrying thirteen guns, of which the Sachem had five—one a 30-pounder rifled Parrott, an excellent gun in fine order, and four 32-pounders. The Sachem is a propeller.

The Clifton, a regular steamship, carried eight guns, of which two are rifled 32-pounder Parrotts, two 9-inch Dahlgrens, and four 32-pounder smooth-bores, all in good order. Besides these we captured a quantity of small-arms of different kinds, together with a large lot of ammunition and naval stores of various descriptions, and also a good store of provisions and medicines.

Neither of the vessels are materially damaged, and can be easily repaired, and each is worth over $500,000 apiece. We have them both safe and anchored at the Pass. The crews on both vessels number about 180, of whom about 18 were killed, several wounded, and the balance prisoners.

Our loss was, strictly and positively, nobody hurt. Not a single man received even a scratch, and the fort but very slightly injured, and the contents entirely uninjured.

On the whole, it is a glorious and honorable little affair, considering the very small handful of men then at the post and the powerful and formidable appearance of the enemy. The men are in high spirits, and elated with the result, and eager for another attack. It does really seem that Providence has kindly favored us in this affair.

I don't think it amiss here to add that the glory and honor, with the sanction of God, in this little victory is ascribed not only by me, but by all that witnessed it, entirely and exclusively to the Davis Guards, in command of First Lieut. R. W. Dowling, commanding the battery, assisted by Lieutenant [N. H.] Smith, of the engineering department, who volunteered his services on the occasion, the company being short of commissioned officers. They all acted nobly and bravely, and acquitted themselves with honor.

Captains [R. V.] Cook's and [Charles] Bickley's companies, of Griffin's battalion, arrived just in time to assist in bringing in the vessels and prisoners. The three companies of Elmore's regiment, under command of Lieutenant-Colonel [L. A.] Abercrombie, unfortunately did not arrive in time to participate in the engagement.

I have the honor to be your most obedient servant,

F. H. ODLUM,
Captain, Cook's Artillery, Commanding Sabine Pass.

Capt. A. N. Mills, ·
Assistant Adjutant-General.

No. 10.

Report of Lieut. R. W. Dowling, Company F, Cook's (Texas) Artillery.

FORT GRIFFIN, *Sabine Pass, September* 9, 1863.

CAPTAIN: On Monday morning, about 2 o'clock, the sentinel informed me the enemy were signaling, and, fearing an attack, I ordered all the guns at the fort manned, and remained in that position until daylight, at which time there were two steamers evidently sounding for the channel on the bar; a large frigate outside. They remained all day at work, but during the evening were re-enforced to the number of twenty-two vessels of different classes.

On the morning of the 8th, the U. S. gunboat Clifton anchored opposite the light-house, and fired twenty-six shell at the fort, most of which passed a little over or fell short; all, however, in excellent range, one shell being landed on the works and another striking the south angle of the fort, without doing any material damage. The firing commenced at 6.30 o'clock and finished at 7.30 o'clock by the gunboat hauling off. During this time we had not replied by a single shot. All was then quiet until 11 o'clock, at which time the gunboat Uncle Ben steamed down near the fort. The U. S. gunboat Sachem opened on her with a 30-pounder Parrott gun. She fired three shots, but without effect, the shots all passing over the fort and missing the Ben. The whole fleet then drew off, and remained out of range until 3.40 o'clock, when the Sachem and Arizona steamed into line up the Louisiana channel, the Clifton and one boat, name unknown, remaining at the junction of the two channels. I allowed the two former boats to approach within 1,200 yards, when I opened fire with the whole of my battery on the foremost boat (the Sachem), which, after the third or fourth round, hoisted the white flag, one of the shots passing through her steam-drum. The Clifton in the meantime had attempted to pass up through Texas channel, but receiving a shot which carried away her tiller rope, she became unmanageable, and grounded about 500 yards below the fort, which enabled me to concentrate all my guns on her, which were six in number—two 32-pounder smooth-bores; two 24-pounder smooth-bores; two 32-pounder howitzers. She withstood our fire some twenty-five or thirty-five minutes, when she also hoisted a white flag. During the time she was aground, she used grape, and her sharpshooters poured an incessant shower of Minie balls into the works. The fight lasted from the time I fired the first gun until the boats surrendered; that was about three-quarters of an hour. I immediately boarded the captured Clifton, and proceeded to inspect her magazines, accompanied by one of the ship's officers, and discovered it safe and well stocked with ordnance stores. I did not visit the magazine of the Sachem, in consequence of not having any small boats to board her with. The C. S. gunboat Uncle Ben steamed down to the Sachem and towed her into the wharf. Her magazine was destroyed by the enemy flooding it.

During the engagement I was nobly and gallantly assisted by Lieut. N. H. Smith, of the Engineer Corps, who, by his coolness and bravery, won the respect and admiration of the whole command. This officer deserves well of his country.

To Asst. Surg. George H. Bailey I am under many obligations, who, having nothing to do in his own line, nobly pulled off his coat, and assisted in administering Magruder pills to the enemy, and behaved with great coolness.

During the engagement the works were visited by Capt. F. H. Odlum, commanding post; Maj. [Col.] Leon Smith, commanding Marine Department of Texas.

Capt. W. S. Good, ordnance officer, Dr. Murray, acting assistant surgeon, behaved with great coolness and gallantry, and by them I was enabled to send for re-enforcements, as the men were becoming exhausted by the rapidity of our fire; but before they could accomplish their mission, the enemy surrendered.

Thus it will be seen we captured with 47 men two gunboats, mounting thirteen guns of the heaviest caliber, and about 350 prisoners. All my men behaved like heroes; not a man flinched from his post. Our motto was "victory or death."

I beg leave to make particular mention of Private Michael McKernan, who, from his well-known capacity as a gunner, I assigned as gunner to one of the guns, and nobly did he do his duty. It was his shot struck the Sachem in her steam-drum.

Too much praise cannot be awarded to Maj. [Col.] Leon Smith for his activity and energy in saving and bringing the vessels into port.

I have the honor, captain, to remain, with great respect, your most obedient servant,

R. W. DOWLING,
First Lieut., Comdg. Co. F, Cook's Art., Fort Griffin, Sabine Pass.

Capt. F. H. ODLUM,
Commanding Post.

No. 11.

Thanks of the Confederate Congress to Captain Odlum, Lieutenant Dowling, and the men under their command.

Resolved, That the thanks of Congress are eminently due, and are hereby cordially given, to Captain Odlum, Lieut. Richard W. Dowling, and the 41 men composing the Davis Guards, under their command, for their daring, gallant, and successful defense of Sabine Pass, Tex., against the attack made by the enemy on the 8th of September last, with a fleet of five gunboats and twenty-two steam transports, carrying a land force of 15,000 men.

Resolved, That this defense, resulting, under the Providence of God, in the defeat of the enemy, the capture of two gunboats, with more than 300 prisoners, including the commander of the fleet; the crippling of a third gunboat, the dispersion of the transports, and preventing the invasion of Texas, constitutes, in the opinion of Congress, one of the most brilliant and heroic achievements in the history of this war, and entitles the Davis Guards to the gratitude and admiration of their country.

Resolved, That the President be requested to communicate the foregoing resolutions to Captain Odlum, Lieutenant Dowling, and the men under their command.

Approved February 8, 1864.

SEPTEMBER 7, 1863.—Skirmish at Morgan's Ferry, on the Atchafalaya, La.

Report of Maj. Gen. Francis J. Herron, U. S. Army.

HDQRS. SECOND DIVISION, THIRTEENTH ARMY CORPS,
Morgan's Bend, September 8, 1863.

GENERAL: I arrived below this place night before last, but could not learn anything definite from the commander of the Neosho. By reconnoitering yesterday with the cavalry, the main body of the enemy was discovered to be at Morgan's Ferry, on the Atchafalaya, 3,000 strong, under Brigadier-General Green. I sent out a portion of one brigade, under Colonel Day, to look after the party hovering about this place. He skirmished with them during the entire afternoon, driving them back toward the main body. His loss is 6 wounded; that of the enemy 2 killed, 10 or 12 wounded, and about the same number prisoners in our hands. The enemy has possession of all the roads leading back from the river, and it is impossible to get around them without marching 55 or 60 miles. I leave at daylight with the balance of my command to join Colonel Day, and will attack Green at once. He shows fight, and says he will meet us at Morgan's Ferry, and I propose to accommodate him. Small bodies of the enemy are constantly hovering near us on the south, firing on our pickets, &c.

I communicated yesterday with Captain Ramsay, commanding gunboat lying off the mouth of Red River. He says the enemy have two transports in use on the Atchafalaya, and that mounted parties of Green's command are moving through the country south of Red River.

On the east side of the river 4,000 cavalry, under Logan, Posey [Powers?], and [John S.] Scott, are annoying the planters and firing upon boats. They range from Port Hudson to Fort Adams.

Among the captures yesterday is one John A. Stevenson, of New Orleans, who is an agent of the Confederate Government, buying cotton as basis for their loan. He had considerable Confederate money and drafts, and printed contracts for a large amount of cotton.

I cannot learn that the enemy have over eight pieces of artillery. Will report further to-night.

Very respectfully, your obedient servant,

F. J. HERRON,
Major-General, Commanding.

Brig. Gen. CHARLES P. STONE,
Chief of Staff.

SEPTEMBER 13–OCTOBER 2, 1863.—Scouting near Lake Pontchartrain, La.

Report of Lieut. C. M. Allen, Second Arkansas Cavalry.

CAMP NEAR RAYMOND, MISS.,
October 9, 1863.

SIR: In obedience to orders from Col. F. Dumonteil, commanding brigade in your absence, I left camp on the morning of September 13 with a squad of 6 men, for the purpose of scouting in that portion of Louisiana bordering on Lake Pontchartrain, and extending from there to the Mississippi, (Saint Tammany, Livingston, and Ascension Parishes).

On the morning of the sixth day from camp, I crossed the Amite River at Scriver's Ferry by swimming, and proceeded to the Mississippi River, where I encountered 9 of the enemy's scouts and vedettes, whom I captured, together with their arms, accouterments, and 4 led horses. They reported to me that their camp consisted of about 40 men from the Fourteenth New York Cavalry, and was located opposite Donaldsonville. Dispatching a guard of 5 men with the prisoners, with orders to drop back to the Amite Swamp, I, with 1 man, proceeded down the river some 5 miles. I found the crops in fine condition, particularly the cane, which our enemies are rapidly making preparations to grind, almost every plantation being occupied and farmed by Federal authority. I also found the stock of mules and horses quite heavy on all the places. Finding that I could procure no more information that would be valuable to our cause, I returned, and recrossed the Amite River. From there I proceeded to Madisonville, Saint Tammany Parish. From citizens whom I met on my route to that place I learned that a general system of contraband trade was being carried on with the enemy in cotton, cattle, &c., which was fast demoralizing the people in that section, and from further information received I judge there must be at least 1,200 or 1,500 conscripts and deserters secreted in the three parishes above named. An occupation of that country for a short period by a small body of efficient cavalry would, I am certain, soon compel a great portion of such men to return to their duty, and if the death penalty were enforced in some of the most flagrant cases of spoliators and depreciators of our currency, it would have the most salutary effect.

From Madisonville I commenced my return to camp, where I arrived on the 2d instant. I would respectfully suggest that, in my opinion, a squadron or battalion of cavalry could now deal the enemy an effective blow by a rapid dash on the coast, burning the sugar-mills, outhouses, &c., on the plantations occupied by them. A great many fine horses and mules could also be secured, with clothing, blankets, provisions, &c. A good crossing can be effected at the French Settlement, there being one or two good flats there.

I learn from reliable information that the enemy had completed the bridge over South Pass Manchac, and were working a large force of laborers on this side, repairing the road. Their object, no doubt, will be to complete the road as high up as Ponchatoula or Tickfaw Stations, which at once would place them in position to drain that whole country of cotton, cattle, &c. A small body of men could at any time cross Lake Maurepas, and destroy railroad track, and train, which is now making daily trips to Pass Manchac from New Orleans.

Very respectfully,

C. M. ALLEN,
Lieutenant Company C, Second Arkansas Cavalry.

Col. JOHN L. LOGAN,
Comdg. Brigade Cavalry and Mounted Infantry.

SEPTEMBER 14, 1863.—Attack on Vidalia, La.

Report of Brig. Gen. Marcellus M. Crocker, U. S. Army.

HEADQUARTERS UNITED STATES FORCES,
Natchez, Miss., September 15, 1863.

COLONEL: I have the honor to report that, on the morning of the 14th instant, a force of rebel cavalry, numbering from 150 to 200, made an attack upon our forces stationed at Vidalia, opposite this city. There were stationed there at the time a small detachment of Colonel Farrar's regiment of negroes, partially armed with shotguns, and about 40 men of the Thirtieth Missouri Infantry, besides the company of pontoniers under Captain Lochbihler. The enemy cut their way through the negro pickets, and appeared, almost without warning, in the camp of the pontoniers, and commenced cutting loose the mules, shooting the men, and pillaging the tents. Their firing gave notice to Colonel Farrar, of the

Thirtieth Missouri, who at once advanced with his 40 men, and gallantly attacked the rebels, driving them from the very start, so that they had no time to drive off the mules or do any damage to the pontoon train. General Gresham, commanding the post, sent over as fast as possible, with very limited means of transportation, the Ninety-fifth Illinois Infantry, the First Kansas, and the Seventeenth Wisconsin Mounted Infantry, and afterward the Eleventh Illinois Infantry.

The Seventeenth Wisconsin and the First Kansas were sent in pursuit of and moved against the enemy, who were retiring, with occasional skirmishing, across Cross Bayou, 16 miles in the direction of Trinity, where they came upon the main body of the enemy, about 800 strong. This force, I am informed this morning (the 15th instant), is recrossing the Black River at Trinity.

The mounted infantry has been ordered to return, as they are considered entirely insufficient for any successful pursuit, as they are badly mounted and badly armed, and of very little use for any purpose whatever.

The force of the enemy is estimated at about 800, all cavalry. They are direct from Alexandria. Their object seemed to have been to capture the negroes recruited for Colonel Farrar's regiment, and to destroy the pontoon train. The negroes, however, had all been transferred to this side of the river, except those doing picket duty, and the pontoon train was awaiting transportation.

Colonel Farrar, with the few men under him, attacked the enemy so vigorously that he had not time to accomplish his object, but was in full retreat twenty minutes after his first appearance.

I regret to say that 2 men of the pontoniers were killed, 2 were wounded, and 4 are missing. Captain Lochbihler, commanding pontoniers, was so severely wounded that his right arm had to be amputated. One of our men was also killed in the pursuit. The extent of the damage done the enemy is not known. One of their lieutenants and several men were killed in the first attack and left in our hands. We also captured 9 horses and several prisoners.

Great praise is due Colonel Farrar for the promptness, coolness, and courage with which he attacked the enemy with his small number of men. As the various detachments sent out have not yet returned, I am unable to send you an accurate statement of the casualties, but think I have stated the most of them. I will send a full report as soon as I receive the necessary information.

Very respectfully, your obedient servant,

.   M. M. CROCKER,
                                  Brigadier-General, Commanding, &c.

Lieut. Col. W. T. CLARK,
    Assistant Adjutant-General, Seventeenth Army Corps.

SEPTEMBER 15–OCTOBER 5, 1863.—Scout from Fort Wingate to Ojo
    •   Redondo (Jacob's Well), N. Mex.   •

Report of Maj. Edward B. Willis, First California Infantry.

FORT WINGATE, N. MEX., *October* 6, 1863.

CAPTAIN: I have the honor to report that, in accordance with orders received from Lieutenant-Colonel Chaves, I left this post on Tuesday, the 15th ultimo, with 40 men each of Companies H, First Infantry, California Volunteers, and F, First New Mexico Volunteers, for an expedition against the Navajo Indians. I proceeded from this post direct to a rancheria in the vicinity of the Sierra Datil, about 100 miles from here; but on my arrival at that point found it had been attacked two days before by a party of about 300 Pueblo Indians, who had killed the chief, Barboncito, with 16 others, and captured 44 squaws and children, and about 1,000 head of sheep, losing themselves 2 men. This had scattered the Navajoes from this vicinity. While I was here, the Indians passed close by me, with 200 or 300 head of horses and a large quantity of sheep; but, having no mounted men, I was unable to overtake them. They passed north, and I was informed were going to the Sierra Chusca.

I then proceeded about 50 miles south to the Cienega Amarilla. In this vicinity there were signs of having been large lots of stock, principally horses, but they were driven off on our arrival, and we were not able to overtake them. We succeeded in taking 1 horse and 1 mule at this place.

After searching this country thoroughly, I marched, in accordance with my orders, to the Little Colorado River, which stream I reached at the point of its issue from the Sierra Blanca. I proceeded down the river, examining the country for about 40 miles, everything in that vicinity showing that the Indians had left there. I directed the command by way of the Venado Spring to the Ojo Redondo, or Jacob's Well, on Beale's wagon-road to California.

At this point I found few Indians, capturing 2. I also found large fields of corn, watermelons, and pumpkins, which I destroyed; also a large rancheria, which was burned by us.

From this place I returned to Fort Wingate, having been absent twenty-one days, and traveling with infantry companies very nearly 400 miles.

I cannot speak in too high terms of the officers and men of this command. No men could be more anxious to do their duty, or more cheerfully incur the hardships of a campaign. After a march of 25 to 30 miles, the whole command would cheerfully volunteer and march the whole night on the slightest prospect of doing any service.

In passing Zuñi, I found those Indians had declared war against the Navajoes, and at the time I was there were having a war-dance over some scalps taken by them. Their chiefs requested from me that, in case of the Government making a peace with the Navajoes, they should be informed of it, as they intended to continue fighting them until this happened.

It is the opinion of all who have facilities for gaining information that I have conversed with that the Navajo tribe have been more severely punished this summer than ever before. They have been closely hunted in almost every direction by the troops, and of late by the Zuñi, Apache, and Pueblo Indians.

In the large scope of country over which I have traveled during the past month, every evidence tends to show that in that section they have no longer permanent abiding places, but are fleeing from one part to another, in a continual state of fear.

I am, captain, respectfully, your obedient servant,

EDWARD B. WILLIS,
Major First Infantry, California Volunteers, Comdg. Post.

Capt. BENJ. C. CUTLER,
Asst. Adjt. Gen., Dept. of New Mexico, Santa Fè, N. Mex.

SEPTEMBER 23, 1863.—Affair opposite Donaldsonville, La.

Report of Lieut. Col. W. D. Smith, Aide-de-Camp.

NEW ORLEANS,
September 23, 1863—10.30 p. m.

I have the honor to leave copy of telegram just received:

DONALDSONVILLE, VIA BONNET CARRÉ,
September 23.

Lieut. Col. W. D. SMITH:

The rebel cavalry, 200 or 300 strong, made a descent on Captain Metcalf's company, Fourteenth New York Cavalry, last night at 1 o'clock, opposite this place. They were completely surprised. Captain Metcalf and about 10 men, and also Mr. Allen, the telegraph operator, were taken prisoners. Do not know how many were taken up the river on telegraph line. Will write you particulars as soon as I get them. Have saved all the papers and instrument belonging to telegraph office.

W. O. FISKE,
Colonel, Commanding.

We also have information at headquarters Defenses of New Orleans that about 1,500 mounted men are in that region. This having to be sent to Bonnet Carré before telegraphing here, accounts for the late hour of receipt. I know of nothing I can do this evening, but if you wish to see me any time to-night, your servant will find me at 19 Rampart street, this side of canal.

Your obedient servant,

W. D. SMITH,·
Lieutenant-Colonel.

GENERAL STONE.

SEPTEMBER 24–29, 1863.—Expeditions from Carrollton and Baton Rouge to New River and to the Amite River, La.

REPORTS.

No. 1.—Brig. Gen. Stephen G. Burbridge, U. S. Army, commanding Fourth Division, Thirteenth Army Corps.
No. 2.—Itinerary of the First Brigade, Fourth Division, Thirteenth Army Corps, for September, 1863.
No. 3.—Col. Oliver P. Gooding, Thirty-first Massachusetts Infantry, commanding at Baton Rouge, La.

No. 1.

Report of Brig. Gen. Stephen G. Burbridge, U. S. Army, commanding Fourth Division, Thirteenth Army Corps.

CARROLLTON, LA.,
September 30, 1863.

COLONEL: In pursuance to instructions from corps headquarters, asking for a report of my recent operations against the enemy on New River and the country on the Amite, I respectfully submit as follows:

On the evening of the 24th instant, I was directed by Major-General Ord to proceed up the Mississippi River with 1,500 infantry, one battery of light artillery, and the Sixteenth Regiment Indiana Volunteer Infantry, mounted, to a point near Donaldsonville, and debark on the left bank of the river, destroy, capture, or break up the enemy under Logan, as well as force the evacuation of all the space between the Mississippi River and Lakes Maurepas and Pontchartrain.

In obedience to these instructions, I directed Colonel Owen, commanding First Brigade, Fourth Division, to prepare his command for the expedition, and at 8 o'clock the expedition was ready for embarking. In consequence of the boats detailed for transporting the troops not arriving promptly, much delay was occasioned. At 8.35 o'clock, I received a dispatch from General Stone saying that all the boats were on the way, but at 12 o'clock only three had arrived. Supposing that the other boat would soon report, I embarked with the Eighty-third Ohio, and pushed forward to have all arranged at Donaldsonville by the time the remainder of the forces should arrive. Colonel Owen was left in command, with instructions to follow on as rapidly as possible.

I arrived at Donaldsonville at 7 a. m., September 25, and delivered orders to Captain Carnahan for additional cavalry force. The captain immediately reported with about 120 men, but as the Glasgow did not arrive at Carrollton until about 4 a. m. on the 25th, Colonel Owen was not able to join me with the remaining forces until 4 p. m. As soon as he arrived, I debarked the infantry and artillery at a point about 4 miles below Donaldsonville, called Manning's, and proceeded into the interior about 10 miles, to New River, and encamped for the night at a point called Lannaries.

The cavalry and mounted infantry was put in charge of Colonel Lucas, Sixteenth Indiana, and directed to debark about 9 miles above Donaldsonville, proceed by way of Dutch Store, cross Bayou Manchac at Hampton's Ferry, thence to the Amite, cross at Bennett's Ferry, and join me at Galveston, by approaching it from the rear. Upon learning from reliable scouts and citizens that there was no enemy in that vicinity, and that the party of the enemy who had recently visited the neighborhood of Donaldsonville had passed thirty-six hours in my advance, I did not deem it necessary to move the infantry and artillery farther into the interior. So, on the morning of the 26th, I sent forward all the mounted force at my command to meet Colonel Lucas at Galveston, and deliver him instructions to proceed to Civique's, 5 miles below, on the Amite, destroy that bridge, and rejoin me at my camp on New River.

Colonel Lucas followed his instructions with promptness and zeal, and met the mounted force sent forward at Galveston. He was not able to cross the Amite at Galveston, and was compelled to proceed to Civique's, on the east side of the river. At 10 p. m. I received a dispatch from him, saying that there was no enemy heard of or seen in that country; that the bridge has been destroyed; that he could not cross there; and that he would return by way of Bennett's Ferry, and rejoin me as soon as possible.

Upon receiving this dispatch, I at once directed the infantry and artillery to return to the Mississippi at Manning's, and sent forward couriers ordering the transports to meet me there.

At 6 a. m. on the 27th, all the infantry and artillery had arrived safely back on the Mississippi. About 10 a. m., 27th, I dispatched to General Stone, chief of staff, asking for instructions, and was directed to return. Thereupon I immediately embarked with the Eighty-third Ohio, and returned, leaving Colonel Owen to bring back the remaining forces as soon as Colonel Lucas rejoined him. I arrived at my headquarters, Carrollton, at 10 p. m.

At 1 a. m. Colonel Lucas arrived at Manning's, much exhausted, having marched 150 miles. The cavalry forces from Donaldsonville were sent back to their place of encampment at Donaldsonville, and at 4 p. m. Colonel Owen reported at Carrollton with the remainder of the expedition.

The only enemy heard of in that country was the party of about 80, who had visited the vicinity of Donaldsonville. Citizens reported a camp of 300 or 400 on the Ponchatoula River. We found the roads passable; citizens disposed to be peaceable, and thriftless. Many paroled prisoners from Vicksburg and others who had abandoned the rebel service were met. Some horses and mules were impressed, but mostly to supply the places of those broken down by heavy marching.

I am, very respectfully, your obedient servant,

S. G. BURBRIDGE,
Brigadier-General, Commanding Expedition.

Col. WALTER B. SCATES,
Assistant Adjutant-General, Thirteenth Army Corps.

No. 2.

*Itinerary of the First Brigade, Fourth Division, Thirteenth Army Corps, for September, 1863.**

September 1.—Colonel Lucas, in command of the First Brigade, Fourth (late Tenth) Division, Thirteenth Army Corps, recently arrived from Vicksburg, and is now encamped at Carrollton, La., continuing a regular system of drill, especially in the bayonet exercise. General Lawler has been commanding the division since General Smith's assignment to duty at Columbus, Ky.

September 7.—Colonel Owen, having recovered from illness, reports for duty, and resumes command of the brigade.

September 11.—The brigade quartermaster, Captain Friedley, resumes his duties, having been absent on leave.

September 18.—The Sixteenth Indiana Volunteers permanently detached from the brigade, to act as mounted infantry.

September 20.—General Burbridge assumes command of the division.

September 24.—The First U. S. Infantry attached to the brigade for the purpose of making its reports and drawing supplies, but remains on duty at corps headquarters. The brigade ordered on an expedition to Ascension Parish, La. Embarked on steamers Meteor, Kennett, Empress, and Glasgow.

September 25.—About 2 p. m. landed nearly opposite Donaldsonville. The brigade marched to New River, about 10 miles.

September 26.—On New River until evening, the cavalry being sent forward. The rebels having dispersed, the infantry and artillery of the brigade marched during the night to the east bank of the Mississippi, opposite Donaldsonville, La.

September 27.—Embarked, awaiting the cavalry of the expedition, viz, the Fourth Illinois and Sixteenth Indiana.

September 28.—Our boat conveyed the Fourth Illinois Cavalry to Donaldsonville, and took the Sixteenth Indiana, with infantry and artillery, to Carrollton Landing. Here an order was met for the artillery to remain on board, be conveyed to Algiers, La., and thence by railroad to Brashear City, La., which was carried out. The infantry regiments of the brigade, at the date of this return, [September 30,] remain in camp near Carrollton, La., 4 miles from the city of New Orleans.

---

* From brigade returns,

No. 3.

Report of Col. Oliver P. Gooding, Thirty-first Massachusetts Infantry, commanding at Baton Rouge, La.

BATON ROUGE,
September 29, 1863.

GENERAL: Lieutenant Earl, of the Fourth Wisconsin Cavalry, in command of a squad of 40 men, marched last night as far as the Amite, and returned this morning with 14 prisoners, with their horses, arms, and equipments. Among them were two notorious guerrilla chiefs, one known as Colonel Hunter and the other as Captain Penny.

Major-General Herron brings the news that Logan is at Morganza Bend, on this side of the river, about 7 miles below Morganza, with from 2,000 to 3,000 men and four pieces of artillery.

General Herron will arrive in New Orleans to-day.

It is presumed that Logan's force have all been ordered to Liberty, Miss.

O. P. GOODING,
Colonel, Commanding.

Brig. Gen. CHARLES P. STONE,
Chief of Staff, New Orleans.

SEPTEMBER 29, 1863.—Action at Stirling's Plantation, on the Fordoche, La.

REPORTS.

No. 1.—Maj. Gen. Nathaniel P. Banks, U. S. Army, commanding Department of the Gulf, including skirmish on the Teche, October 3.

No. 2.—Maj. Gen. N. J. T. Dana, U. S. Army, commanding Second Division, Thirteenth Army Corps.

No. 3.—Maj. John Bruce, Nineteenth Iowa Infantry.

No. 4.—Abstracts from "Record of Events" on the several returns of the Second Division, Thirteenth Army Corps, for September, 1863.

No. 5.—Brig. Gen. Alfred Mouton, C. S. Army, commanding Sub-District Southwestern Louisiana.

No. 6.—Brig. Gen. Thomas Green, C. S. Army.

No. 1.

Report of Maj. Gen. Nathaniel P. Banks, U. S. Army, commanding Department of the Gulf, including skirmish on the Teche, October 3.

HEADQUARTERS DEPARTMENT OF THE GULF,
New Orleans, October 4, 1863.

GENERAL: I have the honor to inclose to you a report of Captain Palfrey,* in charge of the works at Fort Jackson, showing their progress.

The guns have arrived, and the workmen are busily engaged in constructing platforms for them, which will soon be ready.

---

* Omitted.

General Herron's division at Morganza suffered the loss of about 400 men, captured the early part of this week. The enemy's force consisted of two brigades, under the command of General Green. The troops were much advanced and made a most gallant defense, but were overpowered by numbers.

The enemy sent in a flag of truce, with a request for permission to bury their dead. Their loss was considerable in killed and wounded, and we have some prisoners, among others the colonel of one of the regiments.

A skirmish took place yesterday between the advanced cavalry on the line of the Teche, under Colonel Davis, and about 200 of the enemy's cavalry.

The enemy was quickly repulsed, losing one gun, which was captured by us; and the loss of the officer in charge of the gun, who was killed. We suffered no loss.

Our whole force is now moving upon New Iberia. I have suffered much anxiety on account of the dilatory movements of the troops, but it has been impossible to hasten them. In my next dispatch, I trust to give you more favorable information.

N. P. BANKS,
Major-General, Commanding.

Maj. Gen. H. W. HALLECK,
    General-in-Chief, U. S. Army, Washington, D. C.

No. 2.

Reports of Maj. Gen. N. J. T. Dana, U. S. Army, commanding Second Division, Thirteenth Army Corps.

MORGANZA, LA.,
September 29, 1863—8 p. m.

SIR: The advanced force stationed at Bayou Fordoche was attacked about noon to-day on all sides simultaneously by General Green, with probably three brigades. The cavalry escaped, but the Nineteenth Iowa and Twenty-sixth Indiana, amounting to about 500 men, with two guns, were captured. They are reported to have made a gallant defense and to have suffered greatly. I have taken some prisoners, including a colonel.

N. J. T. DANA,
Major-General.

Brig. Gen. CHARLES P. STONE,
    Chief of Staff.

—

HDQRS. SECOND DIVISION, THIRTEENTH ARMY CORPS,
Morganza, La., September 30, 1863.

COLONEL: I have the honor to report that I assumed command of the detachment here at noon on the 28th instant, Major-General Herron leaving at that time. The troops were stationed at this point on the river, with an advanced detachment 7 miles out on the direct road to the Atchafalaya River, being the nearest place where water could be obtained. This detachment was composed of a part of the Nineteenth

Iowa Infantry, commanded by Captain Adams, 320 men; a part of the Twenty-sixth Indiana Infantry, Lieutenant-Colonel Rose, 346 men; one section of Battery E, First Missouri Light Artillery, Second Lieut. E. S. Rowland, 28 men; detachments of Sixth Missouri, Second and Thirty-sixth Illinois Cavalry, under Major Montgomery, 160 men. The whole being under command of Lieut. Col. J. B. Leake, Twentieth Iowa Infantry.

Lieutenant-Colonel Leake's instructions from Major-General Herron were to keep the country well reconnoitered; to keep his cavalry constantly out; to push daily reconnaissances toward the Atchafalaya, where a considerable force of the enemy were posted, and frequently to push his advances up to the river, and annoy the enemy's pickets and drive them in. The morning after I assumed command (yesterday), I dispatched a courier with an escort to Lieutenant-Colonel Leake, with orders, &c.; two wagons loaded with knapsacks belonging to his command were sent out with a small infantry guard.

The weather had been stormy during the preceding afternoon and night, and the rain was still drenching and the road bad. Soon after noon, a messenger came back from the wagons, with information that the road was in possession of a strong force of the rebels, about half-way to Lieutenant-Colonel Leake's camp; that the guard had skirmished with them, and had held their ground, but that heavy infantry firing was heard on the road in their front, supposed to be Lieutenant-Colonel Leake clearing the road. I immediately ordered Colonel Black, Thirty-seventh Illinois Infantry, to march with his regiment to open the communication, and to assume command of his own and Lieutenant-Colonel Leake's troops, and be governed by circumstances, pursuing the enemy and punishing him as much as possible.

The road was bad and heavy for marching, and the rain was drenching, and when Colonel Black had proceeded 3 miles, he met Major Montgomery with his cavalry detachment, and from him and stragglers he learned that the enemy had attacked Lieutenant-Colonel Leake's command on all sides at once; had surprised him by coming through the cane and corn fields of the country, as well as by the road, and by first opening the attack in the rear, and being dressed in United States uniforms.

Major Montgomery's command checked the enemy, and escaped with the loss of 5 men missing, and brought off 6 prisoners; but as the enemy was pushed in between his force and the infantry, he failed to effect a junction, but supposed the infantry force had been captured.

Colonel Black took a strong position in line of battle, and remained there till after dark, when, at 7 o'clock, an officer bearing a flag of truce from the enemy made his appearance with the following dispatch:

BAYOU FORDOCHE,
September 29, 1863.

Major-General HERRON,
    Or Commander of Forces at Morganza:

GENERAL: I send to you a flag of truce by Captain Breaux, the object of which he will explain. Considering it an act of humanity, the brigadier-general commanding has instructed me to send you this message: That you have many wounded and dead, which he cannot bury or care for, and, if it meets with your approval, hostilities will be suspended for twenty-four hours, to allow you to take care of the wounded and dead. The general also instructs me to say that he has left your surgeons and steward to attend on them.

By order of Brig. Gen. Thomas Green:
    Very respectfully,

W. B. RATLIFF,
Captain, Commanding Post.

To which the following reply was made:

MORGANZA, LA.,
September 29, 1863—7.30 p. m.

Capt. W. B. RATLIFF, .
Commanding Post at Bayou Fordoche:

Your dispatch and flag of truce, addressed to Major-General Herron, is this moment received, and I am instructed by Major-General Dana, who now commands the United States forces here, to reply that, for the reasons stated, he accepts the proposition of Brigadier-General Green for a suspension of hostilities for twenty-four hours, the time to commence at daylight to-morrow morning, and he will immediately send out some surgeons and medical supplies, with such vehicles as can be procured to bring in the wounded, and will also send out a burial party at daylight.

Very respectfully, your obedient servant,

WM. HYDE CLARK,
Assistant Adjutant-General.

From the information gathered, it now appears that rebel Brigadier-General Green with his own and Colonel Major's brigade of cavalry (dismounted), and with General Mouton's and Colonel Speight's brigade of infantry (four brigades in all of foot), with about 350 cavalry, and certainly one (Semmes') and probably two batteries of artillery, crossed the Atchafalaya at Morganza Ferry during the afternoon and night of the 28th. Their effective force is variously stated at from 3,500 to 7,000 men, and from six to twelve guns. They took different roads and by-paths, and at about 1 p. m. yesterday attacked our advance on all sides, and, after a gallant resistance, finally overpowered and broke it up, and captured most of the infantry force and the section of artillery with it.

In fairness to Lieutenant-Colonel Leake, who is wounded and a prisoner in the hands of the rebels, I refrain from passing judgment on him in the harsh terms in which this surprise would appear to make it my duty to do. Bearing heretofore a high reputation as an officer and a gentleman, and selected by a discriminating commander from a knowledge of his qualities to fulfill his delicate task, it is to be sincerely hoped that an investigation will, on his return, place him in a satisfactory light. Of one thing I feel sure—that, after being surprised, they fought as officers and men gallantly, and even after all hope was gone they broke into squads, and endeavored singly to make their escape, in which many succeeded. They sustained the high reputation of veteran soldiers.

We have captured 1 lieutenant-colonel and 9 prisoners. Our loss is, commissioned officers, 2 killed and 4 wounded; enlisted men, 12 killed and 29 wounded; total, 47.*

It is impossible to obtain a correct statement of the number taken prisoners, as stragglers are coming in every hour, and having laid out all night in the rain and without food since yesterday morning, they scatter themselves among the camps for food and rest, and do not report. At present there are about 500 men and officers missing. This will, however, in my opinion, be much diminished by stragglers coming in, and as others who are already in report themselves. A correct list of killed and wounded accompanies this report, and a list of prisoners will be sent as soon as possible.

Very respectfully,

N. J. T. DANA,
Major-General.

Lieut. Col. WALTER B. SCATES,
Assistant Adjutant-General, Thirteenth Army Corps.

---

* But see revised statement, p. 325.

HDQRS. SECOND DIVISION, THIRTEENTH ARMY CORPS,
Morganza, October 2, 1863.

COLONEL: I reported to you in my dispatch of the 29th ultimo the particulars of the affair at Bayou Fordoche, where a detachment composed of portions of the Nineteenth Iowa and Twenty-sixth Indiana Volunteer Infantry and a section of artillery were surprised and cut up by four brigades of the enemy.

The suspension of hostilities, which, at the solicitation of the rebel commander, I consented to, to enable me to bring in my wounded, expired at daylight yesterday morning. The night of the 29th and the day of the 30th were spent in bringing in our dead and wounded. The former were buried here yesterday, and the latter will be sent to New Orleans by the first boat.

At daylight yesterday morning I sent out the cavalry force, supported by the Thirty-seventh Illinois Volunteer Infantry, all under command of Colonel Black, of that regiment, with orders to push a reconnaissance as much beyond the battle-field as prudence would allow, to push back the pickets of the enemy, to gather whatever information he could, and to make efforts to capture some prisoners, and bring in any public property which the enemy might have been unable to carry off.

The work was well done, and it is believed, though not positively ascertained, that the enemy's force has recrossed the Atchafalaya, with the exception of about 400 or 500 men.

At a distance of 3 miles from here, the detachment was met by a flag, with a demand for a suspension of hostilities, to enable the rebel commander to care for his wounded.

This I refused, and the reconnaissance was pushed forward between 8 and 9 miles, some distance beyond the battle-field. Nineteen rebels badly wounded were found in a building near the field. One of our caissons was found destroyed by all the spokes being cut, but we brought in a limber and some muskets and ammunition.

The detachment in returning was located, by my order, 2½ miles from here, with the cavalry half a mile in the front. The recent rain has supplied water.

In the afternoon yesterday I sent out an officer of my staff with about 20 mounted men to reconnoiter the road from here to New Texas Landing, and the direct road from there to Bayou La Tenache. He found the enemy's pickets about 3½ miles out that road, about 5 miles from here.

I have directed a portion of the cavalry to drive them back to-day and ascertain if there is anything behind them. My effective cavalry force is reduced to less than 100, and the country here is so difficult to patrol and affords so much cover that it would require five times that number to keep it properly reconnoitered, considering the perfect knowledge our enemy has of it.

I am satisfied that the enemy met with severe punishment in the affair of Fordoche. His loss was not less than 30 killed and 70 wounded, and some of the rebels at the field hospital placed the number as high as 50 killed and 80 wounded.

Respectfully, your obedient servant,

N. J. T. DANA,
Major-General, Commanding.

Lieut. Col. WALTER B. SCATES,
Assistant Adjutant-General, Thirteenth Army Corps.

Return of Casualties in the Union forces engaged at Stirling's Plantation, on Bayou Fordoche, near Morganza, La., September 29, 1863.

[Compiled from nominal list of casualties, returns, &c.]

Command.	Killed.		Wounded.		Captured or missing.		Aggregate.
	Officers.	Enlisted men.	Officers.	Enlisted men.	Officers.	Enlisted men.	
26th Indiana	......	3	1	15	9	209	237
19th Iowa	2	8	3	20	11	199	243
20th Iowa (commander of forces engaged only)	......	......	......	......	1	......	1
2d Illinois Cavalry	......	......	......	2	......	2	4
6th Missouri Cavalry	......	......	......	......	......	5	5
1st Missouri Light Artillery, Battery E	......	3	1	3	......	18	25
Total	2	14	5	40	21	433	515

NOTE.—Lieuts. Silas Kent and John W. Roberts, Nineteenth Iowa, killed, and Capt. Andrew M. Taylor. Nineteenth Iowa, mortally wounded.

No. 3.

Report of Maj. John Bruce, Nineteenth Iowa Infantry.

HDQRS. NINETEENTH IOWA VOLUNTEER INFANTRY,
Brownsville, Tex., October 15, 1863.

GENERAL : I have the honor to submit to you a report of the part taken by my regiment in the engagement at Stirling's farm, fought on the 29th of September, 1863, in Point Coupée Parish, Louisiana.

On the 5th day of September, the Second Division, Thirteenth Army Corps, commanded by Major-General Herron, of which command the Nineteenth Iowa formed a part, embarked on board transports, and proceeded up the river to disperse a force under General Taylor, which was then on the west side, below the mouth of Red River, seriously threatening the navigation of the Mississippi. On the 8th day of September, the division was halted near Morganza, La.; landed, and proceeded to the interior; met the enemy's pickets about 2 miles from the river, drove them in, and drove the rebels back 10 miles across the Atchafalaya. I was left with my regiment and two pieces of artillery to protect the transports at the river. The division returned to the transports on the 11th.

On the 12th, the Nineteenth Iowa, Twenty-sixth Indiana, and two pieces of artillery, the whole under command of Lieutenant-Colonel Leake, of the Twentieth Iowa, were ordered out to feel the enemy. We met the enemy's pickets —— of a mile from the river, drove them in, and soon found the enemy in considerable force. We skirmished with them, and drove them back across the Atchafalaya. We then fell back to Stirling's farm, 7 miles in the interior from where the transports lay. From this point our advance and pickets skirmished almost daily with the advance of the enemy.

On the 29th, the enemy, having received re-enforcements, turned our right, and attacked us in the rear, cutting off our retreat. He at the same time attacked us on the front. My regiment was first called into action, mèt the enemy boldly, and, at short range, delivered a deadly volley, which compelled him to fall back. He, however, rallied again in overwhelming force, and, after a firm and desperate struggle, in which we were well supported by the Twenty-sixth Indiana, we were completely overpowered and compelled to surrender; many of our men, however, refusing to give up until the guns were taken from their hands by the rebels. The rebels were commanded by General Green in person, and consisted of three brigades—in all, a force of 5,000 men. Our entire force there was about 500 men. My regiment had only about 260 men in the action, many having been left sick in convalescent camps at Carrollton, La. They were not on the expedition.

The fight was short but deadly, considering the numbers engaged, the cane and high weeds concealing the lines until they approached within pistol-shot. Many of our men escaped, and came straggling into camp for two days afterward.

In the action we had 2 officers and 8 enlisted men killed; wounded, 1 officer (since dead) and 16 enlisted men, and 11 officers and 203 enlisted men taken prisoners.* The loss in the Twenty-sixth Indiana was not so much as ours. The enemy's loss was 50 killed in the field and many more wounded.

Great credit is due to the officers and men of my regiment, who fought bravely and desperately against fearful odds. The rebel officers acknowledged it was to them a dearly bought victory, and were much chagrined at finding so small a capture after so vigorous a resistance.

I was not in the engagement, having been ordered to New Orleans a few days prior. The regiment was at the time commanded by the senior captain, William Adams, Company E, who was taken prisoner.

I am, very respectfully, your obedient servant,

JOHN BRUCE,
Major, Commanding Nineteenth Iowa Volunteer Infantry.

Adjt. Gen. N. B. BAKER,
Davenport, Iowa.

No. 4.

Abstracts from "Record of Events" on the several returns of the Second Division, Thirteenth Army Corps, for September, 1863.

DIVISION RETURN.

September 1.—Division in camp at Carrollton, La., and there remained until September 4, when it was reviewed by Maj. Gen. U. S. Grant, and ordered to be prepared to march immediately.

September 5.—Embarked on transports, leaving the Thirty-eighth Iowa Infantry and all the sick, convalescents, and sufficient men to guard the camp and property, behind. It moved without tents, knapsacks, or woolen blankets, and sailed up the river, arriving at Morgan's Bend on the 7th instant. A detachment of cavalry (about 200), under Major Montgomery, accompanied the expedition.

September 8.—In the morning, the cavalry and Second Brigade were ordered out on a reconnaissance toward the Atchafalaya River, under

---

* But see revised statement, p. 325.

command of Colonel Day, who met the enemy's pickets, and afterward found the enemy in some force, and, after some light skirmishing, drove them across the Atchafalaya River, and fell back 3 miles until morning.

September 9.—The First Brigade, under Major-General Herron, started out and joined Colonel Day, when Major-General Herron proceeded in force to the Atchafalaya to·reconnoiter; arrived about 4 p. m., and immediately began skirmishing with the enemy. Having ascertained position, &c., and orders being not to bring on an engagement, retired to the Mississippi. Marched 30 miles. Lost 1 killed, and 1 officer and 2 men wounded.

September 12.—The cavalry force was ordered to the front to keep a close watch on the enemy, and the Nineteenth Iowa, Twenty-sixth Indiana, and a section of Battery E, First Missouri Light Artillery, were sent out some 7 miles in front, to strongly picket the country and support the cavalry, all commanded by Lieut. Col. J. B. Leake, Twentieth Iowa, where all remained, as ordered by department headquarters, watching and harassing the enemy. The rest of the division present on the expedition lay on the levee of the Mississippi, without tents, blankets, or change of clothing, with nothing transpiring of importance, until the 28th instant, when, Major-General Herron having received a leave of absence, Major-General Dana was assigned to the command of the division.

September 29.—In the morning, the enemy, having crossed the river in force, surrounded Colonel Leake's command, and, after a desperate engagement, captured the largest portion of his men, with the section of artillery. Our loss is: Commissioned officers killed, 2; wounded, 4. Enlisted men killed, 11; wounded, 30; missing, about 350. It is impossible to obtain correct reports of the missing, as parts of each regiment are in Carrollton, and all regimental and company books are there.*

September 30.—Division still at Morgan's Bend.

RETURN OF THE FIRST BRIGADE, COL. WILLIAM M'E. DYE COMMANDING.

September 1.—Brigade yet encamped at Carrollton, La., but in readiness to move on short notice.

September 5.—Orders received to embark immediately, in the lightest possible marching order, leaving all baggage and transportation. The Thirty-eighth Iowa Volunteer Infantry, being unfit for active field service, was ordered into convalescent camp at Carrollton. Left Carrollton at 3.30 p. m., and arrived at Port Hudson, La., at 8 a. m. on the 6th. Remained here until about midnight, and went from thence to McCollum's Landing.

September 10.—Brigade moved out to Atchafalaya River, 12 miles. Remained there until 3 a. m. of the 11th, and arrived at Morganza at 3 p. m., the transports having moved up during the night to this place.

September 12.—At 4 p. m. troops embarked and the transports dropped down to McCollum's Landing.

September 14.—Lieut. Col. J. B. Leake was placed in command of a detachment from the division, comprising the Twenty-sixth Indiana Volunteer Infantry, one section of Battery E, detachment of mounted infantry from Twentieth and Thirty-fourth Iowa and Thirty-seventh Illinois, of the First Brigade, and ordered to proceed to the vicinity of Atchafalaya Bayou, to watch the movements of the enemy, the balance of the brigade remaining at McCollum's Landing until the 20th; then

---

* But see revised statement, p. 325.

embarked and moved up to Morganza; there disembarked and bivouacked on the banks of the river.

September 27.—Steamer Brown arrived with the baggage of the command. Health of the troops generally good.

RETURN OF THE SECOND BRIGADE, COL. H. M. DAY COMMANDING.

September 1.—Brigade in camp at Carrollton, near New Orleans, La.
September 4.—Corps reviewed by Maj. Gen. U. S. Grant.
September 6.—Brigade embarked for up the Mississippi, by order, of Major-General Herron, arriving at McCollum's Landing, near Port Hudson, La.
September 8.—The Ninety-first and Ninety-fourth Illinois, and Twentieth Wisconsin Infantry, Battery B, First Missouri Artillery, was ordered out on a reconnaissance by General Herron toward Atchafalaya River, under command of Colonel Day. When the command arrived at the wood, about 10 miles out, skirmishing commenced between Major Montgomery's cavalry (which formed part of the expedition) and the enemy, with cavalry, artillery, and infantry, back and across the river, some 5 miles in all. At 9 o'clock the force arrived at the river, when, a few shells being thrown across, the enemy replied quite sharply. Seeing the enemy posted on the other side of the river, which was unfordable, after a short artillery practice the command was withdrawn, to await orders and the advantage of daylight.
September 9.—Colonel Day was joined by the First Brigade. Major-General Herron arriving, assumed command of forces. Capt. Joseph A. James, Company B, Ninety-first Illinois, was slightly wounded by a piece of shell; also several men. One corporal killed on picket.
September 10.—Forces marched back to McCollum's Landing.
September 12.—The Nineteenth Iowa was ordered out in the advance, 7 or 8 miles, where it is now.
September 20.—The division moved to Morganza, La., 3 miles above McCollum's Landing, and went into camp.
September 26.—Colonel Bertram, with 100 men of the Twentieth Wisconsin Infantry, went in search of guerrillas up the river, on board tinclad No. 8, and captured 2 prisoners, a safe, with about $4,800 Confederate States money, and a few shotguns and muskets.
September 29.—The Nineteenth Iowa and Twenty-sixth Indiana, of the First Brigade, were attacked by General Green's forces, C. S. Army, and nearly all captured, with a heavy loss in officers and men. There are at Carrollton some 10 officers and 350 men. Owing to the absence of the officers of the regiment, no correct report can be made.
September 30.—All the remainder of the brigade in camp at Morganza, La.

———

No. 5.

Report of Brig. Gen. Alfred Mouton, C. S. Army, commanding Sub-District Southwestern Louisiana.

HDQRS. SUB-DISTRICT SOUTHWESTERN LOUISIANA,
Opelousas, October 4, 1863.

MAJOR: Conceiving it probable that a favorable opportunity would offer on General Green's front to surprise and attack the enemy, on the

19th ultimo, and on several occasions subsequently, I instructed General Green to make every preparation for such a movement. Accordingly, the proper steps were taken, and the requisite re-enforcements having been sent to General Green, the final order to attack was given on September 25. These orders were carried out with marked ability and activity, and I now have the honor of submitting the reports of the various commands engaged, which establish a complete success, and the capture of a large number of prisoners.

To Brigadier-General Green and the officers and men under his command too much praise cannot be awarded.

I am, major, very respectfully, your obedient servant,

ALFR. MOUTON,
Brigadier-General, Commanding.

Maj. WILLIAM M. LEVY,
Assistant Adjutant and Inspector General.

[Indorsement.]

HEADQUARTERS DISTRICT OF WESTERN LOUISIANA,
Moundville, October 6, 1863.

Respectfully forwarded. The conduct of Lieutenant-Colonel [J. E.] Harrison, commanding Speight's brigade, and the gallant Major [H. H.] Boone, severely wounded in the engagement, is especially deserving of mention. The recognition of Major Boone's gallantry by the Government would be of service to the troops. General Green has fully met the expectations formed from his previous services.

R. TAYLOR,
Major-General.

No. 6.

Report of Brig. Gen. Thomas Green, C. S. Army.

HEADQUARTERS FORCES ON ATCHAFALAYA,
Camp McBride, La., October 2, 1863.

MAJOR: I have the honor herewith to tender a full report of the action on September 29 at the Fordoche Bridge and Mrs. Stirling's place, on the Fordoche, 6 miles from Morganza.

At midnight on September 26, a communication was addressed to Colonel [J. P.] Major, commanding Major's brigade (encamped on Big Cane), to send one of his best regiments to Lyons' Ferry, on the Atchafalaya, on the following day (the 27th), and to cross at that ferry and march to Livonia by the night of the 28th, and on the morning of the 29th to move up to the Fordoche, near the bridge on the Morganza State road. This order was promptly complied with, Colonel Major sending Phillips' regiment, commanded by Major [George M.] Frazer, of the Arizona battalion.

On the 27th, the necessary orders were issued to the several commands to make preparations on the 28th for an advance upon the enemy. The means of crossing the Atchafalaya consisted at this time of two small ferry-flats, carrying together 18 horses or 80 footmen.

The crossing commenced at 3 p. m. on the 28th, Waller's and Rountree's battalions leading with their horses, followed by Semmes' battery, all of which were successfully crossed before dark. Speight's and Mouton's brigades of infantry were next in order, the Fourth, Fifth, and

Seventh Regiments Texas Mounted Volunteers (dismounted) crossing last. All were safely landed on the east bank of the Atchafalaya about 1 a. m. on the 29th. The rain commenced falling at dark on the evening of the 28th, and continued with only temporary cessation until the night of the 30th.

At daylight on the morning of the 29th, the troops were ready for the march. Colonel Henry Gray, commanding Mouton's brigade, was ordered to take up his line of march (Speight's brigade having been added to his command, together with 15 mounted men from Waller's battalion, under command of Lieutenant [R. N.] Weisiger) by a trail through the swamp, which intersected the Morganza State road some 4 miles from that place, and between the enemy's forces at Morganza and their advance at Mrs. Stirling's and the Fordoche Bridge. Colonel Gray was ordered to attack the enemy's advance at once on reaching the intersection of road, which he did by ordering Speight's brigade, under command of Lieutenant-Colonel [J. E.] Harrison, to the attack (see accompanying reports*). The balance of the troops, consisting of Waller's and Rountree's battalions of cavalry, Semmes' battery, the Fourth, Fifth, and Seventh Regiments Texas Mounted Volunteers (dismounted), took up their line of march by the main State road to Fordoche Bridge, which point was reached about 11 o'clock. An advance of cavalry was sent forward to the bridge, and were fired upon by the enemy's pickets at that place. Skirmishing continued here for half an hour, when the firing was heard from the rear at Mrs. Stirling's. With one section of the battery, under command of Lieutenant [J. A. A.] West, and the Fourth and Fifth Regiments, I deployed through a plowed field, and opened with the artillery upon the quarters at Mr. Catlett's, where a portion of the enemy's cavalry were stationed, and at the same time ordered Major [H. H.] Boone, with the two sections of battery and the Seventh Regiment, to move rapidly down the road to the bridge, all of which was done, the dismounted men of the Fourth and Fifth moving at a double-quick across the plowed field to the quarters, but the enemy's advance of cavalry had fallen back to their headquarters, 1 mile farther on, at a Mr. Norwood's house. The sections of artillery united at the bridge, and the whole command proceeded with great rapidity toward the house. Majors Boone and Rountree made a dashing charge upon the enemy's cavalry, drawn up in line of battle near the house, and scattered them with such effect that they were not seen afterward, having retreated through a lane and turn rows to a road leading around the rear of plantations, which was unknown to me.

During these transactions, the firing from the rear had continued with slight interruption, and Major Boone was ordered to take his own command and Rountree's battalion and charge the enemy at Mrs. Stirling's, which he did most gallantly, charging the enemy's battery and receiving two severe wounds. This charge closed the fight, the enemy surrendering in detachments as they retreated and were overtaken by our troops.

The result of the victory consists of 433 non-commissioned officers and privates and 29 officers prisoners, two 10-pounder Parrott guns in fine order, with caissons complete, 2 new ambulances and 1 hospital wagon, new, filled with medical stores, and 2 stand of regimental colors belonging to the Nineteenth Iowa and Twenty-sixth Indiana Volunteers. Many small-arms and accouterments were saved, and every man with an inferior weapon was supplied with a good and efficient one.

---

* Not found.

Maj. W. L. Robards, chief of ordnance, was with me on the field and doing all to secure the fruits of the victory that could be done.

The wounded were sent rapidly to the rear, under the direction of Chief Surg. George Cupples, who had made every preparation, and by his active supervision saved the lives and conduced greatly to the comfort of the wounded. Too much praise cannot be awarded to him for his efficiency.

After burying the dead, the line of march was taken up for Morgan's Ferry, Colonel [Henry] Gray, with Mouton's brigade, having been called in, and Phillips' regiment of cavalry sent forward toward Morganza to repulse and check the enemy should they attempt to advance. The artillery reached the bank of the Atchafalaya at 7 p. m., and commenced crossing. Owing to the state of the banks, and that only one ferry-flat could be used, it was nearly daylight before their crossing was completed. Many of the infantry and dismounted men fell by the roadside, completely exhausted; but all were safely crossed the morning of the 30th. A small steamboat having arrived, was used in crossing the infantry.

I cannot award too much praise to the troops under my command for their rapid movements under the discouraging effects of a heavy rain and roads knee-deep in mud, and their willingness and enthusiasm to attack the enemy.

Col. Henry Gray, with his command, proceeded to the point designated in his orders with all the speed possible, having to pass through the swamp by a trail which was pointed out to him by Lieutenant [E. A.] Carmouche and Private Newsome, whose services were invaluable as guides. Colonel Gray was also accompanied by General [J. L.] Lewis as volunteer aide, rendering him efficient service.

To Lieutenant-Colonel [J. E.] Harrison, commanding Speight's brigade, and Colonels [J. W.] Speight and [F. H.] Clack and Major [John W.] Daniel, who led their commands most gallantly to the attack, all honor is due; and to the officers of their several commands, who displayed great coolness in the action. Many of their men had never been under fire before, but moved like veterans up to the enemy under a heavy fire, and succeeded in driving them from house to house up to the levee, when Major [H. H.] Boone's charge was made.

The heavy loss sustained by Speight's brigade shows the desperate nature of the conflict, and it is not out of place to mention here, even where all distinguished themselves, the gallant bearing and activity of Lieutenant [John B.] Jones, assistant adjutant-general of Speight's brigade.

The charges made by Majors Boone and [L. C.] Rountree stand forth to be recorded in the annals of history. The lamented Lieut. W. F. Spivey, of Company I, Rountree's battalion, was killed in the charge. We deplore his loss, he being one of the most energetic officers in the brigade, and of tried courage and discretion.

Col. A. P. Bagby, of the Seventh Texas Mounted Volunteers, in command of Green's brigade, brought his men most handsomely to the charge, and kept them in hand ready for any emergency, and by his activity rendered most efficient service.

Col. J. P. Major's command, consisting of two regiments and the Pelican Battery, were stationed on the west bank of the Atchafalaya, to protect the crossing and act as a reserve in case of necessity. Colonel Major accompanied and gave great assistance to me, acting in his usual gallant style, and to his staff officers I am indebted for prompt action when called upon.

My own personal staff, Lieutenant [E. R.] Wells, acting assistant adjutant-general; Captain [C. B.] Sheppard, aide-de-camp; Captains Calvitt and [Leander] McAnelly, volunteer aides-de-camp, were active and efficient and rendered me excellent service.

The gallant dead have proven their devotion to our cause, and the wounded in their silent sufferings have shown that fortitude which a good cause alone could have endued them with.

Notwithstanding the severe march, the troops are ready and anxious to again meet the invader upon our soil.

Below I respectfully submit a statement of the losses sustained in the action.

I am, major, very respectfully, your obedient servant,

THOMAS GREEN,
Brigadier-General, Commanding.

Maj. Louis Bush,
Asst. Adjt. Gen., Sub-District Southwestern Louisiana.

[Inclosure.]

Command.	Killed.		Wounded.		Missing.		Aggregate.
	Officers.	Men.	Officers.	Men.	Officers.	Men.	
Speight's brigade	3	20	5	69	......	7	104
Monton's brigade	......	1	1	6	......	3	11
Waller's battalion	......	......	1	1	......	......	2
Rountree's battalion	1	1	......	2	......	......	4
Total	4	22	7	78	......	10	121

OCTOBER 3–NOVEMBER 30, 1863.—Operations in the Teche Country, La.

SUMMARY OF THE PRINCIPAL EVENTS.

Oct.   3, 1863.—The Union forces, under command of Maj. Gen. William B. Franklin, advance from Berwick Bay and New Iberia.

4, 1863.—Affair at Nelson's Bridge, near New Iberia.

9–10, 1863.—Skirmishes at Vermillion Bayou.

14–15, 1863.—Skirmishes at Carrion Crow Bayou.

16, 1863.—Skirmish at Grand Coteau.

18, 1863.—Skirmish at Carrion Crow Bayou.

19, 1863.—Skirmish at Grand Coteau.

21, 1863.—Skirmishes at Opelousas and Barre's Landing.
Occupation of Opelousas by the Union forces.

24, 1863.—Skirmish at Washington.

30, 1863.—Affair near Opelousas.

31, 1863.—Skirmish at Washington.

Nov.   1–17, 1863.—The Union forces retire from Opelousas to New Iberia.

2, 1863.—Skirmish at Bayou Bourbeau.

3, 1863.—Engagement at Bayou Bourbeau, near Grand Coteau.
Skirmish at Carrion Crow Bayou.

5, 1863.—Skirmish at Vermillionville.

8, 1863.—Skirmish at Vermillionville.

Nov.   11, 1863.—Skirmishes at Carrion Crow and Vermillion Bayous.
　　　12, 1863.—Operations about Saint Martinsville.
　　　18, 1863.—Skirmish at Carrion Crow Bayou.
　　　20, 1863.—Skirmish at Camp Pratt.
　　　23, 1863.—Affair at Bayou Portage, Grand Lake.
　　　25, 1863.—Affair at Camp Pratt;
　　　　　　Skirmish near Vermillion Bayou.
　　　30, 1863.—Skirmish at Vermillion Bayou.

REPORTS.

No. 1.—Organization of the troops under the immediate command of Maj. Gen. William B. Franklin, U. S. Army, operating in the Teche Country, La., October 31, 1863.

No. 2.—Maj. Gen. William B. Franklin, U. S. Army, commanding forces in the field.

No. 3.—Capt. William A. Pigman, Forty-sixth Indiana Infantry, Chief Signal Officer.

No. 4.—Maj. Gen. E. O. C. Ord, U. S. Army, commanding Thirteenth Army Corps, of engagement at Bayou Bourbeau.

No. 5.—Maj. Gen. Cadwallader C. Washburn, U. S. Army, commanding detachment Thirteenth Army Corps, of operations October 23–November 3, including engagement at Bayou Bourbeau.

No. 6.—Brig. Gen. Stephen G. Burbridge, U. S. Army, commanding Fourth Division, of engagement at Bayou Bourbeau, and operations (November 12) about Saint Martinsville.

No. 7.—Col. Joshua J. Guppey, Twenty-third Wisconsin Infantry, First Brigade, of engagement at Bayou Bourbeau.

No. 8.—Abstracts from "Record of Events" on the several returns of the Thirteenth Army Corps, for October and November.

No. 9.—Col. Lewis Benedict, One hundred and sixty-second New York Infantry, commanding First Brigade, Third Division, Nineteenth Army Corps, of skirmishes November 11.

No. 10.—Itinerary of the Nineteenth Army Corps, October 1–November 18.

No. 11.—Brig. Gen. Albert L. Lee, U. S. Army, commanding Cavalry Division, Department of the Gulf, of skirmish at Camp Pratt and affair at Bayou Portage.

No. 12.—Lieut. William Marland, Second Massachusetts Battery, of engagement at Bayou Bourbeau.

No. 13.—Col. John G. Fonda, One hundred and eighteenth Illinois Infantry, (Mounted), commanding Cavalry Brigade, of engagement at Bayou Bourbeau, and skirmishes November 11.

No. 14.—Lieut. Col. Harai Robinson, First Louisiana Cavalry, of engagement at Bayou Bourbeau.

No. 15.—Col. Thomas J. Lucas, Sixteenth Indiana Infantry, commanding Cavalry Brigade, of affair at Bayou Portage.

No. 16.—Col. Charles J. Paine, Second Louisiana Infantry, commanding Cavalry Brigade, of affair at Bayou Portage.

No. 17.—Abstracts from "Record of Events" on the several returns of the Cavalry Division, for October and November.

No. 18.—Daily Memoranda for Adjutant-General's Office, Department of the Gulf, October 9–14.

No. 19.—Lieut. Gen. E. Kirby Smith, C. S. Army, commanding Trans-Mississippi Department.

No. 20.—Maj. Gen. Richard Taylor, C. S. Army, commanding District of Western, Louisiana.

No. 21.—Brig. Gen. Alfred Mouton, C. S. Army, commanding Sub-District of Southwestern Lousiana, of affair at Nelson's Bridge, &c.

No. 22.—Brig. Gen. Thomas Green, C. S. Army, commanding Cavalry Division, of engagement at Bayou Bourbeau.

No. 1.

Organization of the troops under the immediate command of Maj. Gen. William B. Franklin, U. S. Army, operating in the Teche Country, La., October 31, 1863.*

THIRTEENTH ARMY CORPS.

(Detachment.)

Maj. Gen. CADWALLADER C. WASHBURN.*

FIRST DIVISION.†

Brig. Gen. MICHAEL K. LAWLER.

First Brigade.	*Second Brigade.*
Col. HENRY D. WASHBURN.	Col. CHARLES L. HARRIS.
33d Illinois, Col. Charles E. Lippincott.	21st Iowa, Lieut. Col. Salue G. Van Anda.
99th Illinois, Col. George W. K. Bailey.	22d Iowa, Maj. Ephraim G. White.
8th Indiana, Lieut. Col. Charles S. Parrish.	23d Iowa, Col. Samuel L. Glasgow.
18th Indiana, Lieut. Col. William S. Charles.	11th Wisconsin, Maj. Jesse S. Miller.

Third Brigade.

Col. LIONEL A. SHELDON.

49th Indiana, Col. James Keigwin.
69th Indiana, Lieut. Col. Oran Perry.
7th Kentucky, Lieut. Col. John Lucas.
22d Kentucky, Lieut. Col. George W. Monroe.
16th Ohio, Maj. Milton Mills.
42d Ohio, Maj. William H. Williams.
120th Ohio, Maj. Willard Slocum.

Artillery.‡

2d Illinois, Battery A, Lieut. Herman Borris.
1st Indiana Battery, Lieut. Lawrence Jacoby.
7th Michigan Battery, Lieut. George L. Stillman.
1st Wisconsin Battery, Lieut. Daniel Webster.

---

* On October 20, Major-General Washburn, owing to the illness of Maj. Gen. E. O. C. Ord, assumed command of the Thirteenth Army Corps; and on or about same date Major-General Franklin must have assumed command of the combined forces. On October 26, Maj. Gen. N. J. T. Dana assumed command of the Thirteenth Army Corps, but Washburn continued in command of that portion above indicated.

† Lawler assigned to command October 19. Colonel Washburn succeeded Col. David Shunk in command of First Brigade October 12. The Third and Fourth Brigades consolidated September 23, under Lawler's command, and Sheldon succeeded him as brigade commander October 19. The division near New Iberia.

‡ According to corps return, both the Illinois and Michigan batteries were left at Carrollton.

THIRD DIVISION.*

Brig. Gen. GEORGE F. MCGINNIS.

First Brigade.

Brig. Gen. ROBERT A. CAMERON.

11th Indiana, Col. Daniel Macauley.
24th Indiana, Col. William T. Spicely.
34th Indiana, Lieut. Col. Robert B. Jones.
46th Indiana, Col. Thomas H. Bringhurst.
29th Wisconsin, Lieut. Col. William A. Greene.

Second Brigade.

Col. JAMES R. SLACK.

47th Indiana, Lieut. Col. John A. Mc-Laughlin.
24th Iowa, Lieut. Col. John Q. Wilds.
28th Iowa, Col. John Connell.
56th Ohio, Col. William H. Raynor.

Artillery.†

2d Illinois, Battery E, Lieut. Emil Steger,
1st Missouri, Battery A, Lieut. Charles M. Callahan.
2d Ohio Battery, Lieut. William H. Harper.
16th Ohio Battery, Capt. Russell P. Twist.

FOURTH DIVISION.‡

Brig. Gen. STEPHEN G. BURBRIDGE.§

First Brigade.

Col. RICHARD OWEN.

60th Indiana, Capt. Augustus Goelzer.
67th Indiana, Lieut. Col. Theodore E. Buehler.
83d Ohio, Col. Frederick W. Moore.
96th Ohio, Lieut. Col. Albert H. Brown.
23d Wisconsin, Col. Joshua J. Guppey.

Second Brigade.

Col. WILLIAM J. LANDRAM.

77th Illinois, Col. David P. Grier.
97th Illinois, Lieut. Col. Lewis D. Martin.
130th Illinois, Maj. John B. Reid.
19th Kentucky, Lieut. Col. John Cowan.
48th Ohio, Capt. Joseph W. Lindsey.

Artillery.

Chicago Mercantile Battery, Capt. P. H. White.
17th Ohio Battery, Capt. Charles S. Rice.

NINETEENTH ARMY CORPS.‖

Maj. Gen. WILLIAM B. FRANKLIN.

Escort.

14th New York Cavalry, Company B, Capt. J. B. Ayres.

FIRST DIVISION.¶

Brig. Gen. GODFREY WEITZEL.

First Brigade.

Col. GEORGE M. LOVE.

30th Massachusetts, Lieut. Col. William W. Bullock.
116th New York, Maj. John M. Sizer.
161st New York, Lieut. Col. William B. Kinsey.
174th New York, Lieut. William L. Watkins.

Third Brigade.

Col. ROBERT B. MERRITT.

12th Connecticut, Lieut. Col. Frank H. Peck.
75th New York, Capt. Henry B. Fitch.
114th New York, Col. Samuel R. Per Lee.
160th New York, Lieut. Col. John B. Van Petten.
8th Vermont, Maj. Henry F. Dutton.

---

* McGinnis assigned to command of the division September 13, and Cameron assigned to First Brigade October 8.   The division at Opelousas.

† According to corps monthly return.   The division return accounts only for the Missouri battery, and on September 9, by corps orders, the other batteries were ordered to the convalescent camp at New Orleans, and, on September 29 they were reported as at Carrollton.   The Second Ohio was at Greenville and the Sixteenth Ohio at Carrollton, October 31.

‡ At Barre's Landing and Franklin ; the Ninety-seventh and One hundred and thirtieth Illinois detached at New Iberia, under command of Col. Nathaniel Niles.

§ Assigned to command of the division September 18, vice Lawler, transferred to First Division.

‖ Headquarters at Opelousas.   The Fourth Division in the Defenses of New Orleans and La Fourche District.

¶ About Opelousas and New Iberia ; the Second Brigade (Col. O. P. Gooding commanding) at Baton Rouge ; Battery A, First U. S. Artillery, at New Orleans.

Artillery.

1st Maine Battery, Capt. Albert W. Bradbury.
6th Massachusetts Battery, Lieut. Edw. K. Russell.

THIRD DIVISION.*

Brig. Gen. CUVIER GROVER.

First Brigade.	*Second Brigade.*
Col. LEWIS BENEDICT.	Brig. Gen. JAMES W. McMILLAN.
110th New York, Col. Clinton H. Sage.	14th Maine, Col. Thomas W. Porter.
162d New York, Col. Lewis Benedict.	26th Massachusetts, Col. Alpha B. Farr.
165th New York (six companies), Lieut. Col. Gouverneur Carr.	8th New Hampshire, Lieut. Col. George A. Flanders.
173d New York, Col. Lewis M. Peck.	133d New York, Col. Leonard D. H. Currie.

Artillery.

4th Massachusetts Battery, Capt. George G. Trull.
1st United States, Battery F, Lieut. Hardman P. Norris.

ARTILLERY RESERVE.

Capt. HENRY W. CLOSSON.

25th New York Battery, Capt. John A. Grow.
1st United States, Battery L, Capt. Henry W Closson.

CAVALRY DIVISION.†

Brig. Gen. ALBERT L. LEE.

First Brigade.	*Second Brigade.*
Col. JOHN G. FONDA.	Col. JOHN J. MUDD.
118th Illinois,‡ Capt. Arthur W. Marsh.	2d Illinois (seven companies), Lieut. Col. Daniel B. Bush, jr.
1st Louisiana (nine companies), Lieut. Col. Harai Robinson.	3d Illinois (five companies), Capt. Robert H. Carnahan.
6th Missouri (seven companies), Maj. Bacon Montgomery.	15th Illinois, Company F, Capt. Joseph Adams.
14th New York (six companies), Lieut. Col, John, W. Cropsey.	36th Illinois, Company A, Capt. George A. Willis.
	1st Indiana, Company C, Capt. James L. Carey.
	4th Indiana, Company C, Capt. Andrew P. Gallagher.

Not brigaded.

87th Illinois,‡ Lieut. Col. John M. Crebs.
16th Indiana,‡ Col. Thomas J. Lucas.
2d Louisiana,‡ Col. Charles J. Paine.
2d Massachusetts Battery, Capt. Ormand F. Nims.

---

*At Opelousas and Vermillion Bayou. McMillan relieved Brig. Gen. W. H. Emory (going on sick leave), September 17, in command of the division, and was relieved by Brigadier-General Grover, October 6.

†Organized September 14, under command of Brigadier-General Lee. The Third Massachusetts at Port Hudson, the First Texas on the Texas expedition, and the Fourth Wisconsin at Baton Rouge.

‡ Infantry mounted.

No. 2.

Reports of Maj. Gen. William B. Franklin, U. S. Army, commanding forces in the field.

HEADQUARTERS NINETEENTH ARMY CORPS,
Carrion Crow Bayou, October 11, 1863.

GENERAL: My advance arrived here about 11 a. m., the enemy falling back before them.

There is no doubt that the rebel Generals Mouton, Major, and Green passed here yesterday, bound north. Their object must have been to get information from their spies, or to select a place to fight. They left this house early this morning.

Yesterday five or six guns (bronze) passed north; two of them were left here to defend the passage of the bayou, but they were taken away this morning. We fired eight shots, and the force that was here immediately left.

I encamp the command beyond the bayou. The stream is wooded, but the water is only in pools. I cannot tell before to-morrow whether it will be sufficient; I think it will be. I anticipate no danger here.

Very respectfully, yours,

W. B. FRANKLIN,
Major-General, Commanding Nineteenth Corps.

Brig. Gen. CHARLES P. STONE,
Chief of Staff.

P. S.—The force of the artillery was all mounted, probably 1,000 men.

—

HEADQUARTERS NINETEENTH ARMY CORPS,
Carrion Crow Bayou, October 12, 1863—9 a. m.

GENERAL: I sent a message by signal to you half an hour since, stating that there was nothing new during the night, excepting a little picket firing, and that reconnaissance will be made in front and on the flanks as far as possible. Scouts will also be sent out for information.

General Weitzel informs me that he has reliable information that the enemy's force in our front does not exceed 10,000 men, consisting of Walker's division, Green's, Major's, and Mouton's brigades. I do not know his informant.

Very respectfully, yours,

W. B. FRANKLIN,
Major-General, Commanding Nineteenth Corps.

Brig. Gen. CHARLES P. STONE,
Chief of Staff, Department of the Gulf.

—

HEADQUARTERS NINETEENTH ARMY CORPS,
Carrion Crow Bayou, October 12, 1863—9.15 a. m.

GENERAL: The short-handedness of some of the field batteries in this corps can be corrected in some degree by the substitution of negro drivers for the drivers of battery wagons and forges and afterward of caissons. I therefore respectfully request authority to make these changes as they may become necessary, and that I may have authority to direct the quartermasters to pay the teamsters the ordinary wages of negro teamsters, with the regulation issues of provisions and clothing, whatever they may be.

It may, perhaps, be preferable to have men detailed from negro regiments for this service, but they do not seem to be available at present, and it is now that they are required.

Very respectfully, yours,

W. B. FRANKLIN,
Major-General, Commanding Nineteenth Army Corps.

Brig. Gen. CHARLES P. STONE,
Chief of Staff.

— ·

HEADQUARTERS DEPARTMENT OF THE GULF,
Vermillion Bayou, October 14, 1863.

GENERAL: I have the honor to forward the following dispatch just received from Major-General Franklin:

HEADQUARTERS NINETEENTH ARMY CORPS,
October 14, 1863—6 p. m.

I have received General Banks' order detaching Colonel Davis' regiment, and have issued it. He will obey it as soon as his pickets can be withdrawn. I do not think that I need another division of infantry, but this is an uncomfortable place, as the enemy is continually trying to find a weak point in our lines with his cavalry. Cavalry is what we need here. I hear of a rebel camp some 8 miles to the rear and right, near Vermillion Bayou. I do not consider the information reliable, but as General Ord is sending out that way, it may be well to ascertain.

Respectfully, yours,

W. B. FRANKLIN,
Major-General, Nineteenth Army Corps.

I send the above for your information. Copy sent to Major-General Ord.

Very respectfully, your obedient servant,
[J. SCHUYLER CROSBY,]
Acting Assistant Adjutant-General.

Maj. Gen. N. P. BANKS.

—

HEADQUARTERS DEPARTMENT OF THE GULF,
Vermillion Bayou, October 15, 1863.

GENERAL: I have just received the following dispatch from Major-General Franklin by signal telegraph:

The enemy has fallen back from his position. I shall hold it if the other division is sent up.

Very respectfully, your obedient servant,
[J. SCHUYLER CROSBY,]
Acting Assistant Adjutant-General.

Maj. Gen. N. P. BANKS.

—

HEADQUARTERS DEPARTMENT OF THE GULF,
New Orleans, October 17, 1863.

GENERAL: The following dispatch is just received from the front:

VERMILLIONVILLE,
October 16, [1863]—3.40 p. m.

. The enemy made an attack on our pickets this morning about 10 o'clock, but without any result. We may expect such attacks as long as we stay here. My casualties: None killed, 6 wounded. I understand that Generals Mouton, Green, and Colonel

Major were all here. Colonel Davis estimated enemy's force at 2,500. There were three generals, and I think 1,000 would be nearer the estimate. The enemy's casualties were the same as ours. The theory of the attack, I think, is that they thought we were a rear guard protecting a movement to the westward, and thought they could easily beat us, and probably take us. As soon as they saw infantry, they left, and our artillery helped to send them off. I have a pretty strong but very extensive position, reaching to 3 miles beyond the bayou.

W. B. FRANKLIN,
Major-General, Commanding Nineteenth Army Corps.

This is the latest report we have, being received at 4 o'clock this morning, the 17th.

I remain, with much respect, your obedient servant,

N. P. BANKS, ·
Major-General, Commanding.

Maj. Gen. H. W. HALLECK,
General-in-Chief, U. S. Army, Washington, D. C.

CARRION CROW BAYOU,
October 17, 1863.

GENERAL: General Ord was yesterday too ill to attend to duty. The order of the commanding general, issued just before he left for New Orleans, seemed to be based upon the feasibility of opening water communication with Barre's Landing. Is it his intention that we shall move before that is determined? Colonel Chandler telegraphs me that General Washburn will be ready to move in two days. My train, I understand, is on its way from New Iberia; may be here to-morrow. Enemy very pertinacious and annoying. Mouton, Green, and Major were with the attack on Wednesday.

Very respectfully,

W. B. FRANKLIN,
Major-General, Commanding Nineteenth Army Corps.

· Brig. Gen. CHARLES P. STONE,
Chief of Staff, New Orleans.

HEADQUARTERS NINETEENTH ARMY CORPS,
October 20, 1863—10 a. m.

GENERAL: My dispatch of yesterday should read, "New Iberia is to be held and Barre's Landing." My dispatch of this morning will explain that I am taking means to get hold of Barre's Landing, if possible, before the Red Chief arrives.

W. B. FRANKLIN,
Major-General, Commanding Nineteenth Army Corps.

Brig. Gen. CHARLES P. STONE,
Chief of Staff, New Orleans.

—

OPELOUSAS,
October 21, 1863—12 m.

GENERAL: The head of my column has arrived here. The enemy made a stand about 3 miles out. They had nine regiments of cavalry, two battalions of infantry, and three or four guns. A little shelling drove them away. I leave at once for Barre's Landing, and shall encamp near there to-night with the infantry. Part of the cavalry will go there to-night.

Respectfully,

W. B. FRANKLIN,
Major-General, Commanding Nineteenth Army Corps.

Brig. Gen. CHARLES P. STONE,
Chief of Staff, New Orleans

—

HEADQUARTERS TROOPS IN THE FIELD,
Bayou Barricroquant, October 23, 1863—12 m.

GENERAL: I have already announced to the commanding general my arrival at this place. My troops hold Opelousas and Barre's Landing. On account of a violent storm now raging, movements must be delayed some time, and I shall act according to my best judgment. I cannot say in this dispatch what I intend to do. Shall be very glad to get definite instructions. Forage is very scarce here and higher up. There seems to be no chance of the boat's arrival. The trains could not possibly move to-day.

Respectfully,

W. B. FRANKLIN,
Major-General, Commanding Troops in the Field.

Brig. Gen. CHARLES P. STONE,
Chief of Staff.

—

HEADQUARTERS TROOPS IN THE FIELD,
October 24, 1863—5 p. m.

GENERAL: I have received a dispatch from you, directing that two good regiments, now in the Teche Basin, shall report without delay to the Defenses of New Orleans. I have, therefore, ordered General Washburn to send two of his regiments back for that purpose. I do not consider that I have any control over the forces at New Iberia or at Franklin. They do not report to General Washburn and did not to General Ord.

This morning I sent out a reconnaissance, consisting of the whole cavalry command. It has gone 9 miles beyond Washington, and has met and dispersed a small body of the enemy. It is the opinion of General Lee, who is in command, that the whole force is retreating as fast as it can march toward Alexandria. It consisted of cavalry and infantry. They retreated northward on both sides of the bayou. It is useless, therefore, to march this large force any farther with any expectation of getting a fight from the enemy. There is absolutely nothing within reach. General Washburn's force, with the exception of what he left at Vermillion, in obedience to orders received from department headquarters, and that left on the Teche, New Iberia, and Franklin, is now here; also the train, with fifteen days' supplies.

We hold Barre's Landing, the line from there to Opelousas. The train is 2 miles in rear of Opelousas, and, by sending back a strong force with each train, I presume that we may be fed here. But there is very little forage in the country, and a move somewhere must soon be made. The forage question is important, and I think that we must get nearer to New Iberia or the Mississippi River.

I respectfully reiterate my request for definite instructions, believing that I have demonstrated that there is no enemy in front who can be attacked by this expedition, and also that'it is impossible to stay here long. I shall stay here, if possible, until I receive an answer to this dispatch.

Very respectfully, yours,

W. B. FRANKLIN,
Major-General, Commanding.

Brig. Gen. CHARLES P. STONE,
Chief of Staff, Department of the Gulf, New Orleans.

—

HEADQUARTERS TROOPS IN THE FIELD,
Bayou Havroquant, October 26, 1863—9 a. m.

GENERAL: I received yesterday and this morning the duplicate dispatch of the 22d instant from the commanding general. A division will be sent to New Iberia in a few days. Two regiments of that division will at once be sent to New Iberia, to replace two other regiments, which will be ordered to go to New Orleans. I think I shall hold my advance in the vicinity of Carrion Crow Bayou, as by taking that position I can get forage more easily, and the supply of provisions can be kept up. I do not quite understand from the dispatch whether the commanding general wishes me to keep up that supply, or whether I shall let the wagons be emptied. I shall take measures to have the supply kept up, however, and in the meantime will be glad to be informed on that point. Colonel Chandler has written Colonel Holabird and Captain Vallance to get things in readiness for keeping us supplied from New Iberia.

There is difficulty in sweeping the country between the Teche and Mississippi from this point as a base. The bayous are hard to cross, and a rain makes the road impracticable. New Iberia would be a better point to start from than any point farther to the front. I doubt whether there are many good horses in the country. I, however, have sent out a cavalry force this morning in that direction.

Very respectfully, yours,

W. B. FRANKLIN,
Major-General, Commanding.

Brig. Gen. CHARLES P. STONE,
Chief of Staff, New Orleans.

—

HEADQUARTERS TROOPS IN THE FIELD,
November 1, 1863.

GENERAL: I have received the two communications from you and that from the commanding general. I have been obliged to return to this place, Carrion Crow Bayou, on account of scarcity of forage and doubt about supplies. The roads are getting exceedingly bad. One of the objects which you suggest will be attained by building a bridge across the Mermenton. As soon as possible this will be done. Please order the telegraph laid to Vermillion, where I go with the Nineteenth Corps to-morrow, leaving the Thirteenth here. The cavalry will be divided between the posts.

W. B. FRANKLIN,
Major-General, Commanding.

Brig. Gen. CHARLES P. STONE,
Chief of Staff, New Orleans.

HEADQUARTERS TROOPS IN THE FIELD,
November 2, 1863.

GENERAL: I yesterday acknowledged by telegraph your two notes of the 28th ultimo, and that of the commanding general of the 25th. I also acknowledge that of the 29th from you. Ever since the march up the Teche began, I have heard of José Cavriere and his men. I have sent for him three times, and while our force was at Opelousas he had ample time to come in. But neither he nor any of his men came. Perhaps the fact that the country in that vicinity is infested with small guerrilla bands, and that these people did not believe that we intend to hold the country, may have kept them from coming in, but the fact is patent that none of them came. I judge, however, from what I see and hear, that there is a better chance of success than there was above, and am to-morrow to have an interview with, I think, the men whose names you mentioned in your letter. The scout company, commanded by Captain Armstrong, has, I believe, about 15 members. I will give you my impressions of the expected conversation as soon as I have had it.

I shall send out a cavalry force in the direction of the Mermenton as soon as possible, and, if I consider it feasible or safe, shall send a division of infantry there with bridge train, or at any rate with materials for building a bridge.

We are gathering cattle in plenty, but horses and mules are very scarce. The Mermenton trip may open some stores of the latter.

The troops are now distributed as follows: Three brigades of the Thirteenth Corps at Carrion Crow Bayou, one brigade of that corps and one brigade of cavalry about 3 miles in front of that bayou, the two divisions of the Nineteenth Corps at this place, with one brigade of cavalry, one regiment mounted infantry, and the Engineer Regiment and heavy artillery. The 30-pounders of that artillery are very heavy to pull now. It would not answer to send them back at present, I know, but if it rains any more they cannot be taken. The roads south and east of Opelousas were nearly impassable yesterday, and it rained last night. Between this place and Carrion Crow they are better, but the marching is heavy. I think the impression is strong that we are going to Texas by the route from here.

Colonel Chandler leaves for New Iberia and Brashear to-morrow. I am much crippled by losing him, on account of the disorganized condition of the Thirteenth Corps, but I understand how necessary he must be at Brashear.

Very respectfully, yours,

W. B. FRANKLIN,
Major-General, Commanding.

Brig. Gen. CHARLES P. STONE,
Chief of Staff, Department of the Gulf.

—

HEADQUARTERS TROOPS IN THE FIELD,
Vermillion Bayou, November 3, 1863.

GENERAL: General Washburn's division is now at New Iberia. He informs me that it numbers about 4,500 men. There are two batteries, of six guns each, on the Teche, one at New Iberia with General Washburn's division, and one distributed between there and Franklin. General Lawler commands this division, and General Washburn is dissatisfied with General Dana's assumption of the command of the corps, and wishes to go back to his division. I have, however, left him at Carrion Crow Bayou, in command.

Yesterday the enemy attacked him in some force, but were driven back to 1½ miles from Opelousas, where they made a stand in the woods. There General Burbridge maneuvered to draw them out, but was unable to do it. They finally retired. It was another attempt to learn our forces and intentions, but was unsuccessful. I inclose a dispatch for you, which, by some oversight, the messenger did not take at the time it was written.

The artillery and infantry now at New Iberia are about what you ask for. The 200 cavalry can be sent whenever they are required.

W. B. FRANKLIN,
Major-General, Commanding.

Brig. Gen. CHARLES P. STONE, <i>Chief of Staff.</i>

—

HEADQUARTERS TROOPS IN THE FIELD,
November 3, 1863.

GENERAL: I inclose you a note from Major-General Washburn,* which was the first information that I received of his Carrion Crow fight. Upon this was based my telegraphic dispatch on the subject to you. The detailed reports have not yet come in, but I hope to get them to-day. General Washburn has gone down to take command of his division.

Burbridge's division, which will be at New Iberia to-day, is only about 1,100 strong. I think that unless there are indications of the enemy near Franklin, it will be well to move at least one regiment from there to New Iberia. If you think this move good, please order it, as I have received no reports from that post.

General Lee goes out to-morrow on the Texas road with a heavy force. Yesterday a large wagon train was reported as moving from the north-ward toward the southwest. It will be investigated to-morrow. The enemy has been very quiet since we have been here, though large bodies of mounted men have made their appearance in the vicinity.

The force here now is McGinnis' division and the two of the Nineteenth Corps—a small force to hold my position. Should any more infantry be ordered away, a good deal of artillery must go with it, as the amount of artillery with me was predicated somewhat on the small amount in the Thirteenth Corps. I hope, therefore, that no more troops will be taken from here, unless it be the intention to evacuate this position.

The cavalry, since General Lee's arrival, is beginning to do well. He has arranged it in three brigades of about 700 men each. He is much in want of staff officers of all kinds. Please send all that you can.

Very respectfully, your obedient servant,
W. B. FRANKLIN,
Major-General, Commanding.

Brig. Gen. CHARLES P. STONE, <i>Chief of Staff.</i>

—

HEADQUARTERS TROOPS IN THE FIELD,
Vermillion, November 5, 1863.

GENERAL: Have received your dispatch of to-day. I think that Green was in command, but that part of Walker's force was present—infantry, not mounted. The force of the enemy was probably 2,000

---

* See Washburn's reports, pp. 355–359.

mounted men, infantry and cavalry, and one brigade of Walker's—say 2,000. It was a discreditable surprise on our part. Yesterday a flag of truce went out at the invitation of the enemy, to bring in our wounded in their hands and return theirs in ours. I judge from the officer's information who went out with it that there is not yet a large force in our front, but one is gathering. I have brought all my force to this place, and will give them a fight here if they will accept, which I do not believe.

New Iberia is exposed to a raid from Opelousas, and a mounted force has been sent up the Teche 20 miles to examine that matter. The road between here and Carrion Crow has become exceedingly unsafe for small parties.

W. B. FRANKLIN,

Major-General, Commanding.

Brig. Gen. CHARLES P. STONE,

    Chief of Staff, New Orleans, La.

HEADQUARTERS TROOPS IN THE FIELD,

November 10, 1863—9 a. m.

General Lee went out 18 miles toward the Mermenton yesterday. He captured 1 lieutenant and 4 men of a Texas regiment that I had not heard of before. They are just from Niblett's Bluff. They report four blockade-runners, just unloaded, direct from New Orleans in the Mermenton. The names of two are Antelope and Derby. The lieutenant says that he lately saw the Harriet Lane fully equipped for sea.

I think that the force of the enemy is increasing in our front. The guerrillas are in our rear between here and Iberia. They captured a signal officer yesterday.

The blockade-runners were loaded with flour and salt meat.

W. B. FRANKLIN,

Major-General.

General CHARLES P. STONE,

    Chief of Staff, New Orleans, La.

P. S.—General Lee was attacked by about 300 of the enemy, but he drove them off easily.

HEADQUARTERS TROOPS IN THE FIELD,

Vermillion, November 11, 1863—2.30 p. m.·

I have heard from General Lee. He went to Carrion Crow Bayou, and there found the enemy, as he reports, in line of battle, with all three arms, in force greatly exceeding his. He has, therefore, fallen back. There has been a good deal of cannonading, but not much else. All are coming in now. I have a brigade and battery about 1 mile in front of the town to protect Lee, should he have to fall back in a hurry. The result shows that the enemy is in some force, and is waiting for something—what, I cannot tell. Will it be proper for me to send a noncommissioned officer from each regiment for the men's overcoats?

W. B. FRANKLIN,

Major-General, Commanding.

General CHARLES P. STONE,

    Chief of Staff, New Orleans, La.

HEADQUARTERS TROOPS IN THE FIELD,
November 11, 1863—8 p. m.

General Lee and force have returned. The enemy followed his rear very closely with cavalry and artillery. But we damaged them with our artillery more than they did us. He estimates the force that he saw deployed in front of Carrion Crow Bayou as 4,000 infantry and 3,000 cavalry, and three batteries. Our casualties are about 15. Captain Marsh, One hundred and eighteenth Illinois Mounted Infantry, killed; also 1 or 2 men.

W. B. FRANKLIN,
Major-General, Commanding.

Brig. Gen. CHARLES P. STONE,
Chief of Staff, New Orleans, La.

—

HEADQUARTERS TROOPS IN THE FIELD,
Vermillion, November 13, 1863—3 p. m.

GENERAL: Yesterday at dusk the enemy withdrew his pickets from our front. He returned again this morning with a large observing force, but I think that it is a rear guard, and that we have ceased to amuse him. This morning a brigade of cavalry, with two guns, went to Saint Martinsville and above. Has seen no enemy.

I think of sending the heavy guns to New Iberia to-morrow.

The question of overcoats and blankets for the men of this command is becoming a very serious one. The want of them is affecting the health of the men. They were stored before we started for Sabine, when a short campaign was expected.

W. B. FRANKLIN,
Major-General, Commanding.

Brig. Gen. CHARLES P. STONE,
Chief of Staff, New Orleans.

—

HEADQUARTERS TROOPS IN THE FIELD,
November 13, 1863—4 p. m.

With the large force of cavalry of the enemy, he can make it very uncomfortable for us between here and New Iberia, and, besides, he can get to New Iberia by the right before I can. I think it will be well to make that point our extreme one. What do you think of this, or does your dispatch mean the Teche proper? That is, do you consider Vermillion a part of the Teche country?

W. B. FRANKLIN,
Major-General, Commanding.

Brig. Gen. CHARLES P. STONE,
Chief of Staff, New Orleans, La.

P. S.—The forage question at this point will soon become important.

—

HEADQUARTERS TROOPS IN THE FIELD,
Vermillion, November 14, 1863—3 p. m.

Have you received my message of 4 p. m. yesterday? The work that my cavalry does here is exceedingly hard, and, although I can easily fight any large cavalry movement in my rear, you will see by an examination of the map that if the enemy get between me and New Iberia in force, it will embarrass me much to fight them.   There are rumors of Magruder and Price re-enforcing in front of me, and although I do not credit them, I nevertheless believe that the enemy is yet stronger than he has been.   I only fear him in my rear.   My position here is good against double my number.   Rifle-pits and abatis make me entirely safe in front, but my rear is exceedingly weak.

W. B. FRANKLIN,
Major-General, Commanding.

Brig. Gen. CHARLES P. STONE,
Chief of Staff, New Orleans, La.

NEW IBERIA, LA.,
November 17, 1863—11.30 a. m.

I left Vermillion yesterday morning at daylight, and encamped at Camp Pratt.   I came from there here this morning.   I destroyed the Vermillion Bridge.   The enemy made no show of opposition to our crossing.   One or two mounted men came to the bayou, and fired on us after we were over.

W. B. FRANKLIN,
Major-General, Commanding Troops in the Field.

Brig. Gen. CHARLES P. STONE,
Chief of Staff, New Orleans, La.

HEADQUARTERS TROOPS IN THE FIELD,
New Iberia, November 18, 1863—1.30 p. m.

Have received your dispatch referring to Green's movement.   It, of course, may be so, but there is, nevertheless, quite a large cavalry force of the enemy at Camp Pratt.   They drove in a force of 250 of our cavalry, sent there to reconnoiter, this morning.   I have the cavalry out in all directions now.   The officer in command of the Camp Pratt expedition estimates what he saw there at 600, and others were coming up from Vermillion with great dust.   However, it is very dusty, and a small force, judged by the dust, looks large.

W. B. FRANKLIN,
Major-General, Commanding.

Brig. Gen. CHARLES P. STONE,
Chief of Staff, New Orleans, La.

HEADQUARTERS TROOPS IN THE FIELD,
New Iberia, November 20, 1863—8 a. m.

I have just heard from General Lee.   He surprised the enemy at Camp Pratt, finding there the Seventh Texas [Cavalry], Colonel [A. P.] Bagby.   He has taken 100 prisoners, killed and wounded several, and our loss is nothing, he thinks.   It is his impression that this is an advanced post of a force at Vermillion.   Until he comes in, I cannot tell upon what he bases that supposition.

W. B. FRANKLIN,
Major-General, Commanding.

Brig. Gen. CHARLES P. STONE,
Chief of Staff, New Orleans, La.

HEADQUARTERS TROOPS IN THE FIELD,
New Iberia, November 20, 1863—11.30 a. m.

The affair this morning at Camp Pratt was very handsome and complete. The cavalry went out the Abbeville road, and struck the Vermillion road about 1 mile in rear of Camp Pratt. A brigade of infantry (Cameron's) and four guns went out on the Vermillion road. Both bodies arrived about daylight, shot the vedettes, and came upon the the enemy entirely by surprise, surrounding him entirely.

The regiment is the Sixth [Seventh] Texas [Cavalry], commanded by Colonel Bagby. He, however, now commands a brigade at Vermillion. The lieutenant-colonel (P. T. Herbert) was absent and the major escaped. The prisoners are 12 commissioned officers and 100 men, precisely.

The cavalry went as far as half-way to Vermillion, dispersed the Second Louisiana Cavalry (rebel), and have now returned. The result shows there is not much force this side of Vermillion. About 25 of Bagby's regiment escaped.

W. B. FRANKLIN,
Major-General, Commanding.

Brig. Gen. CHARLES P. STONE,
Chief of Staff, New Orleans, La.

—

HEADQUARTERS TROOPS IN THE FIELD,
New Iberia, November 24, 1863.

For the last three days the telegraph wire has been cut at several places. Yesterday it was repaired, but was cut immediately after the repair was finished.

Yesterday morning, before daylight, three parties of our cavalry arrived at Dauterive's Landing, and at a camp of conscripts and guerrillas near there. The camp was entirely surprised, and we captured 3 officers and 30 men, besides a quantity of arms and horses. Two of the rebels were killed. Our loss was nothing. One object of the expedition was to catch Major [St. L.] Dupeire, who is raising the rebel battalion to which these prisoners belong, but he had left the house where his wife was staying about an hour before we surrounded it. Parties have been out after the persons who cut the wire, but none have been caught yet.

Very respectfully, yours,

W. B. FRANKLIN,
Major-General, Commanding.

Brig. Gen. CHARLES P. STONE,
Chief of Staff, New Orleans.

—

HEADQUARTERS TROOPS IN THE FIELD,
New Iberia, November 24, 1863.

GENERAL: As the present campaign has given me some experience as to the best manner of holding this section of the country, I beg leave respectfully to submit my views on the subject, for the consideration of the general commanding the department.

I find that an infantry force is very hard to move on account of the scarcity of supplies, and, when moved, is of but little use. The enemy is nearly entirely mounted, and if he pursues the course hereafter which he has adopted for this campaign, the system of warfare will be merely that of annoyance. In no case will he risk a general battle, unless his forces are superior to ours and he certain of success. He has it in his power to hover on all sides of an infantry force, producing an annoyance the severity of which cannot be appreciated unless it be felt.

The only way of meeting this method of warfare is to keep a large force mounted. This force should be the main body of the army, and the infantry should be subordinate to it. In fact, I doubt whether any infantry be necessary at all. The artillery should be horse artillery, and there should be a liberal allowance of it, say three batteries.

All of the infantry should be mounted whose unexpired terms of service will justify the labor of teaching them to be cavalry, and about one-half should be mounted infantry, the remainder cavalry.

Such towns as are to be held should have works thrown up which will command them. These works should be provisioned and watered, so as to be independent of the country outside, and should be able to stand a short siege, and be protected against a *coup de main*. They should be held by strong garrisons, with good artillery. The question as to whether the animals belonging to the mounted force which I have indicated can be fed in the country is a grave one. But it belongs to the subject of holding the country at all. I do not think that the enemy can be perfectly driven from this country until some course like that here suggested be adopted.

Respectfully, your obedient servant,

W. B. FRANKLIN,
Major-General, Commanding.

Brig. Gen. CHARLES P. STONE,
Chief of Staff.

—

HEADQUARTERS TROOPS IN THE FIELD,
New Iberia, November 24, 1863.

Night before last the cavalry surprised a rebel camp near Bayou Portage, captured 3 officers, 30 men, 1 flag, and killed 2 men. The camp was entirely broken up. Some horses and mules were taken. There has been nothing new since then. Would have informed you before, but telegraphic communication has continually been broken by hostile parties in our rear.

W. B. FRANKLIN,
Major-General, Commanding.

Brig. Gen. CHARLES P. STONE,
Chief of Staff, New Orleans, La.

P. S.—Have written you by to-day's boat.

—

HEADQUARTERS TROOPS IN THE FIELD,
November 25, 1863—9.15 a. m.

Have received your dispatches relative to movements of the enemy. Some of the prisoners asked us if we had taken any of Magruder's men yet, from which I infer that they thought he was on his way here, but I have had no other indication that he has been expected at Vermillion. No troops have passed through Saint Martinsville. They may, however, have crossed the Teche higher up. One of the prisoners spoke of Mouton being on Bayou Grele, east of the Atchafalaya, but I thought that was the movement toward mouth of Red River.

This morning I have sent out to Vermillion Bayou. I think it would take Magruder two weeks, or perhaps longer, to march 20,000 men from Niblett's Bluff to Vermillion. There are two long bridges to build, perhaps three.

I will let you know as soon as I hear anything from the front. I have sent ɪ large force.

W. B. FRANKLIN,
Major-General, Commanding.

Brigadier-General STONE,
Chief of Staff, New Orleans, La.

—

HEADQUARTERS TROOPS IN THE FIELD,
New Iberia, November 25, 1863.

I have just had a report from General Lee, who commanded the cavalry reconnaissance this morning. He has driven the enemy across Vermillion Bayou, the Fourth Texas [Cavalry] and Second Louisiana [Cavalry], taking 4 officers and 68 men. He burned the bridge. Major's brigade was there. He heard nothing of Magruder. My headquarters guard has also taken 11 guerrillas to-day.

W. B. FRANKLIN,
Major-General, Commanding.

Brig. Gen. CHARLES P. STONE,
Chief of Staff, New Orleans, La.

—

HEADQUARTERS TROOPS IN THE FIELD,
November 25, 1863.—7.15 p. m.

The regiments at Vermillion are, Fourth, Fifth, and Seventh Texas [Cavalry], Hardeman's, Green's, and Bagby's, forming Bagby's brigade; Stone's, Phillips', Baylor's, W. G. Vincent's, and one other, whose colonel's name begins with B, but whose name I cannot make out, forming Major's brigade. This is all the force at Vermillion. The prisoners say that they understand that Magruder is at the Mermenton, but they are not well posted, and speak from rumor, or else they have been stuffed. The cavalry to-day made a saber charge, killed 7 or 8 of the enemy, wounded sundry others, and had no loss on our side.

I mistook General Lee's dispatch; the bridge was not burned. He pursued them to the bridge.

W. B. FRANKLIN,
Major-General.

Brig. Gen. CHARLES P. STONE,
Chief of Staff, New Orleans, La.

—

HEADQUARTERS TROOPS IN THE FIELD,
November 25, 1863—9.30 p. m.

Have received your dispatch of 9 p. m. I shall keep a sharp lookout for Magruder. Can hold this position against a largely superior force, but cannot vouch for my communications. Had intended to go back to Olivier's if I were sure that such force were coming. There, could hold on for a long time against anything, but the trouble will be more from want of forage than from the enemy. There is a ditch in front of

Olivier's that makes it a strong position on this side the bayou; the other side is not so strong.

I do not believe that Magruder is coming here, or I think we would have heard more of him by this time.

W. B. FRANKLIN,
Major-General, Commanding.

Brig. Gen. CHARLES P. STONE,
Chief of Staff, New Orleans, La.

HEADQUARTERS TROOPS IN THE FIELD,
New Iberia, November 26, 1863—1 p. m.

Information has been brought to me from a source which I consider not very reliable, though meaning well, corroborating what you sent me about Magruder; that is, that his force is concentrating on Vermillion Bayou; that it began to arrive yesterday evening, and that it is 20,000 strong. The information which you sent me got out about here, and, after all, it may be the source of this rumor. The idea is, that 1,200 men are to be east of the Teche, and that the main force is to move from Vermillion in this direction. I find that the ditch in front of Olivier's can be easily turned on the left about 1 mile from the bayou. I rather think that their tactics will be to turn us, and make us fall back by that means.

I have sent out to-day for some more guerrillas, said to be on other · side of bayou

W. B. FRANKLIN,
Major-General.

Brig. Gen. CHARLES P. STONE,
Chief of Staff, New Orleans, La.

HEADQUARTERS TROOPS IN THE FIELD,
New Iberia, November 26, 1863—7.30 p. m.

To-day 200 cavalry have gone near Vermillion Bayou and encamp there to-night. They sent two parties of 6 men over the bayou, to go to the Texas roads west, and see if they can learn anything of Magruder's movements. I will probably hear of them to-morrow evening.

Another party is down the bayou, on the other side, after guerrillas. I do not know of any point this side of Franklin where a better stand can be made than here. Of course, shall take the best position possible, if the news about Magruder turns out to be true. I only keep about six days' supplies on hand, and can move my whole force, I think, with twelve hours' notice. I cannot credit the Magruder news. But may he not be on the Mississippi River, or rather his force?

W. B. FRANKLIN,
Major-General.

Brig. Gen. CHARLES P. STONE,
Chief of Staff, New Orleans, La.

—

HEADQUARTERS TROOPS IN WESTERN LOUISIANA,
November 27, 1863—2.30 p. m.

The expeditions yesterday were not successful. The parties could not cross the bayou as was expected. They, however, went to Abbeville,.and there learned from citizens that there had been no movement of troops of any kind from the westward. I am convinced, therefore, that no movement from Texas has been made in this direction. No troops of the enemy were seen at Camp Pratt this morning, as the expedition returned.

Is it possible to send me any one who has rank and intelligence enough for chief quartermaster? No one here is fit for the place.

W. B. FRANKLIN,
Major-General.

Brig. Gen. CHARLES P. STONE,
Chief of Staff, New Orleans, La.

—

HEADQUARTERS TROOPS IN THE FIELD,
New Iberia, November 28, 1863—3 p. m.

The expedition to Vermillion Bayou has returned, but found it absolutely impossible (as they represent) to cross horses over the bayou between Vermillion and Abbeville. From all the information they could gather, I infer that no troops have come from the west, and that those at Vermillion have gone northward; how far, I cannot tell. I send another expedition to Vermillion on Monday, and will give you the result.

W. B. FRANKLIN,
Major-General, Commanding.

Brig. Gen. CHARLES P. STONE,
Chief of Staff, New Orleans, La.

—

HEADQUARTERS TROOPS IN WESTERN LOUISIANA,
November 28, 1863.

I have just received a communication from Brigadier-General Green, commanding rebel forces at Vermillion, dated yesterday or to-day, proposing an exchange of prisoners upon the cartel now in force, upon the ground that all of our prisoners in their hands are without blankets, many without shoes, and indifferently supplied with clothing of all kinds, whose sufferings during the winter it will be impossible for them to alleviate. General Taylor directs General Green to use all exertions consistent with the dignity of his position to perfect some arrangement for exchanging man for man.

I respectfully ask instructions, and recommend that the arrangements for exchange be commenced.

W. B. FRANKLIN,
Major-General, Commanding.

Brig. Gen. CHARLES P. STONE,
Chief of Staff, New Orleans, La.

—

HEADQUARTERS TROOPS IN WESTERN LOUISIANA,
New Iberia, November 29, 1863.

I have sent a letter by flag of truce to General Taylor, offering to exchange man for man, if he will commence the exchange without reference to regiments or corps, and proposing to him to send clothing and blankets to our prisoners, provided he will permit the delivery, the

United States to pay reasonable expenses for freight and handling. I also asked him to turn over to me 4 prisoners, with their arms and accouterments, who were taken during this campaign while acting as safeguards.

Can the clothing and blankets, say 700 suits and 1,000 blankets, be at once furnished?   .

W. B. FRANKLIN,
Major-General.

Brig. Gen. CHARLES P. STONE,
Chief of Staff, New Orleans, La.

HEADQUARTERS TROOPS IN WESTERN LOUISIANA,   ·
November 30, 1863—6.30 p. m.

The cavalry has returned from the Vermillion expedition. It had a skirmish, in which 1 man was wounded, and we took 1 prisoner. Rebel loss in killed and wounded not known. The prisoner states that there are two cavalry brigades at Vermillion, Bagby's and Major's, under command of Green. Green himself went to Opelousas yesterday. Another expedition is out toward Petite Anse, and, I understand, has captured 12 prisoners. I have not heard definitely, however, and will not assert it until I hear more.

The prisoner left Texas four weeks ago, and says Magruder was then south of Galveston.

·   W. B. FRANKLIN,
Major-General, Commanding.

Brig. Gen. CHARLES P. STONE,
Chief of Staff, New Orleans, La.

No. 3.

Report of Capt. William A. Pigman, Forty-sixth Indiana Infantry, Chief Signal Officer.

HDQRS. SIGNAL DETACHMENT, NINETEENTH ARMY CORPS,
New Iberia, La., December 28, 1863.

SIR: I have the honor herewith to submit the following report of the operations of the signal detachment attached to the command of Maj. Gen. W. B. Franklin:

Upon .the. advance of the United States forces from Vermillionville, La., to Carrion Crow Bayou, October 11, 1863, in accordance with instructions from the general commanding, a line of signals was established as rapidly as the army advanced, and communication was open with headquarters Department of the Gulf on the following day. The line continued in successful operation until October 21, 1863, at which time the army advanced to Opelousas.

On the 15th of October, during the skirmish between the Federal and Confederate forces, Lieut. F. A. Irvin, Lieut. C. M. Roberts, and Lieut. George R. Herbert accompanied Capt. W. B. Roe to the scene of action, and, I have reason to believe, rendered valuable assistance by reporting the movements and positions of the enemy.

During the time that the army was encamped at Carrion Crow Bayou, there were transmitted, through the line of signals, forty-one official messages from Carrion Crow to Vermillionville, and fifty-nine official messages were received at Carrion Crow.   On the morning of October 21, the line was broken up.

Lieut. J. L. Hallett, with 3 enlisted men, who were on duty at an intermediate station, were captured by the enemy.   The officers who were on duty at headquarters signal station accompanied the army in its advance to Opelousas.   Several messages were sent during the skirmish which occurred on that day.

As soon after the arrival of the army at Opelousas as was practicable, a line was established communicating between headquarters near Barre's Landing, on the Bayou Courtableau, and General Grover, who remained at Opelousas.

Although the line continued in operation but eight days, a large amount of official business was transacted through it.   Thirty-seven messages were sent and received.

On the 31st of October, orders were received to discontinue the line, and move toward Vermillionville on the following morning.

On the 2d of November we reached Vermillionville, and on the 3d established communication, by means of signals and signal telegraph, with Maj. Gen. C. C. Washburn, commanding Thirteenth Army Corps, then encamped on Carrion Crow Bayou.   This line was an important one, but, owing to roving parties of the enemy, could not be kept in successful operation.   It was discontinued on the evening of November 5, and the signal telegraph wire was taken up and removed within the lines.

Although communication was no longer practicable, the Catholic church in Vermillionville was still occupied as a signal lookout, and used as a station, communicating by means of signals with headquarters.   From the church a fine view of the surrounding country could be had.

During the day almost every movement of the enemy within 5 miles of our lines could be distinctly seen, and reports were promptly sent to headquarters.   Valuable information was furnished by the signal officer on the church to Brigadier-General Lee, commanding cavalry, and also to the officer in charge of outposts during the time the army remained at Vermillionville.

The following is a list of the signal officers engaged at different times during the recent operations of this detachment: First Lieut. W. P. Miner, First Lieut. J. L. Hallett, First Lieut. F. D. Butterfield, First Lieut. F. A. Irvin, First Lieut. W. A. Harris, First Lieut. G. W. Bailey, and Second Lieut. W. F. Warren.   To each and all of the above-named officers, as also to the enlisted men of this detachment, credit is due for the promptness and efficiency which characterized their actions while in the discharge of the duties incumbent upon them.

The health of this detachment has been, throughout the present campaign, uniformly good.

In regard to the present condition of this detachment, I will here state that everything is in readiness for active service.

I have the honor to remain, very respectfully, sir, your most obedient servant,

WILL. A. PIGMAN,
Captain, and Chief Signal Officer, Nineteenth Army Corps.

Maj. WICKHAM HOFFMAN,
Assistant Adjutant-General, Nineteenth Army Corps.

No. 4.

Report of Maj. Gen. E. O. C. Ord, U. S. Army, commanding Thirteenth Army Corps, of engagement at Bayou Bourbeau.

HEADQUARTERS THIRTEENTH ARMY CORPS,
New Orleans, La., January 18, 1864.

SIR: I have the honor to inclose sub-reports, just received, of the affair at Bayou Bourbeau, November 3, 1863.

Disparaging remarks having appeared in a large part of the public newspapers upon the management of this affair by Major-General Washburn, I beg to call attention to the report of that officer, to that of General Burbridge, Colonel Guppey, Twenty-third Wisconsin Volunteers, and the order of march of Major-General Franklin, by which it will be seen that General Washburn was at his prescribed post, with his command, on the morning of the attack, and that it was owing to his zeal and diligence that the rear guard, when attacked, were re-enforced promptly, and the enemy driven away discomfited. Lieutenant-Colonel Buehler, whom General Washburn reports guilty of conduct attributable to cowardice or incompetency, will be brought before a commission for examination for competency as soon as he joins the corps. He is at present, I am unofficially informed, at a camp of paroled or exchanged prisoners somewhere in this department.

I am, sir, very respectfully, your obedient servant,
E. O. C. ORD,
Major-General of Volunteers, Comdg. Thirteenth Army Corps.

Brig. Gen. LORENZO THOMAS,
Adjutant-General, U. S. Army, Washington, D. C.

[Inclosure.]

GENERAL ORDERS, }   HDQRS. NINETEENTH ARMY CORPS,
No. 22.   }   *Barricroquant Bayou, La., October* 31, 1863.

I. The troops of this command will move to-morrow in the direction of Carrion Crow Bayou.

II. 1. General Washburn's command will start at 6 a. m.

2. General Grover's division will follow the trains of General Washburn's command.

3. Indiana artillery and Reserve artillery.

4. The Engineer Regiment and pontoon train.

5. Ammunition train.

6. General Grover's train.

7. General Weitzel's train.

8. General Weitzel's division.

9. Colonel Fonda's cavalry, who will bring up the rear and collect all stragglers.

III. General Burbridge will move toward Carrion Crow Bayou at 6 a. m., by the Teche road. Colonel Mudd will move in his rear.

IV. General Washburn will encamp on the north side of Carrion Crow Bayou; Generals Grover and Weitzel on the south side, on the right and left of the road, respectively, and General Burbridge and the cavalry will encamp at their old camp ground, on the bayou, 2 miles north of Carrion Crow Bayou. The Indiana siege and Reserve artillery, the ammunition train, the Engineer Regiment, and the pontoon train will encamp on the south side of Carrion Crow Bayou.

V. The camps will face toward Opelousas.

VI. Commanding officers will see that a sufficient infantry guard is sent with each train.

By order of Major-General Franklin:

WICKHAM HOFFMAN,
Assistant Adjutant-General.

No. 5.

Reports of Maj. Gen. Cadwallader C. Washburn, U. S. Army, commanding detachment Thirteenth Army Corps, of operations October 23–November 3, including engagement at Bayou Bourbeau.

HEADQUARTERS THIRTEENTH ARMY CORPS, .
Opelousas, La., October 24, 1863.

GENERAL: In obedience to the orders of General Franklin, I left Vermillion Bridge yesterday morning, but, learning through General Ord that Major-General Dana was to start the day before from New Orleans to take command of this corps, I left two regiments of infantry and one regiment of mounted infantry at the bridge, to hold the point until General Dana should arrive, when they were to report to him. Your dispatch of yesterday, ordering me to hold Vermillion in large force, in view of the failure of the boats to get up the Courtableau, I did not receive until this morning at this place. I much regret that I did not receive the order sooner, as it would have saved my command from marching through the terrible storm of yesterday. The troops at Vermillion Bridge, I think, are ample to hold the point, as there is no force of any magnitude anywhere near. Our cavalry advanced to and occupied Washington this morning, the rebels retreating before them. They are not supposed to be in any force within 25 or 30 miles of here.

I was at General Franklin's headquarters this morning, near Barre's Landing. The bar at mouth of Courtableau has only 1 foot of water upon it.

Your dispatch to General Franklin, ordering him to send two regiments from the Teche Basin back to New Orleans, he has referred to me, and asked me to designate the regiments. Neither of us understand whether you mean that we shall send troops back from here, or from the troops now on the Teche, at Franklin, or Iberia. I have asked for further information by telegraph, which will continue in operation to Vermillion Bridge so long as the force remains there.

The report of the capture of General Mouton, which I sent you, was untrue. It was a militia general, by name of [James] Trudeau, that was captured.

Respectfully, your obedient servant,

C. C. WASHBURN,
Major-General.

Brig. Gen. CHARLES P. STONE, *Chief of Staff.*

—

HEADQUARTERS THIRTEENTH ARMY CORPS,
Carrion Crow Bayou, November 2, 1863.

GENERAL: We have had a pretty lively time to-day. The enemy made a determined attack this morning upon our cavalry, killing 1 man and wounding 2 others. General Burbridge at once rallied, and pursued them. They formed in line, about 1,000 strong, on the same ground they formed upon, the day you entered Opelousas. They were driven away, and took refuge in the woods. Maneuvering for a long time to draw them out, we failed to do so, and finally commenced, to fall back. They then swung round, and formed a line in the prairie on our left, and charged down, about 1,500 strong.

Twice they attempted a charge, and as often the plain was swept by our artillery, and they retired, and finally, about 3 p. m., withdrew altogether. I think their move to-day was to endeavor to develop our strength.

I directed as little to be exposed to view as possible. After, they made their last and most formidable display, I ordered a part of the troops here up, but they had only moved a mile or two when it became apparent that they would not be wanted, and they returned to camp. I shall expect fighting every day that I remain here, and probably we may have to meet their entire force if we stay long enough for them to concentrate it. I do not apprehend that we shall need any help, though I wish we had more cavalry.·

Should you send out to the Mermenton, would it not be advisable to send a good force? They, no doubt, think that we are covering a move in that direction, and as soon as they know that troops are going that way, they, very likely, will dispatch the force now in our front across by the direct road from Opelousas to the Mermenton Crossing, and if our force there should be small, they might be handled roughly.

If you do not make that move, but will send here Colonel Mudd and his cavalry, Colonel Lucas with his mounted infantry, and any other cavalry you can scare up, we will make a strong effort to capture some of their force before we leave here.

I had a captain of the Twenty-fourth Iowa Infantry shot to-day under circumstances of great atrocity. He was out with a foraging party, west of here, and saw a party of men in the prairie, about half a mile away, dressed in blue uniforms. He supposed them to be our soldiers, and rode alone toward them, and the parties were seen to salute each other as he came near them, and the first knowledge he had that he was approaching enemies was given by a rifle-ball through his heart. They robbed him of his clothing, watch, and pistol, and fled.

I presume the enemy has come back to his old camp this side of Opelousas. There is little chance to catch any of his men, unless we can get in his rear. If I had 2,000 cavalry, I believe that I could make a move at night that would entrap some of them, but, knowing the country as they do, and with fleet horses, the chance is not the best.

Respectfully, yours

C. C. WASHBURN,
Major-General.

Major-General FRANKLIN, *Commanding Forces in the Field.*

HDQRS. DETACHMENT THIRTEENTH ARMY CORPS,
Vermillion Bridge, November 7, 1863.

MAJOR: I inclose herewith report of Brigadier-General Burbridge in regard to the battle of Grand Coteau on the 3d instant; also of Lieutenant-Colonel Robinson, commanding Second Louisiana Cavalry, and statements of Captain Sims, Sixty-seventh Indiana, and Lieutenant Gorman, First Louisiana Cavalry,* who were wounded and taken

---

* Statements of Sims and Gorman not found.

prisoners, but who were supposed to be privates, and were delivered over under a flag of truce with other wounded.

On the 27th instant [ultimo] the First Division of this corps, under Brigadier-General Lawler, moved from Opelousas back to New Iberia, with a view of being where they could be moved rapidly to Brashear City, should circumstances require it; that left at Opelousas the Third Division, under General McGinnis, and one brigade of the Fourth Division, under General Burbridge, at Barre's Landing, 8 miles east of Opelousas and east of the Bayou Teche, near its junction with the Courtableau.

On the morning of the 1st instant, by order of Major-General Franklin, the troops of the Third Division were ordered to march and encamp at Carrion Crow Bayou, while General Burbridge with the troops under his command were ordered to march down the Teche and cross it, and move via Grand Coteau, where the road from Vermillion to Opelousas crosses Muddy Bayou, about 3 miles from Carrion Crow Bayou, in the direction of Opelousas, and go into camp there on the north side of the bayou. Colonel Fonda, with about 500 mounted infantry, was also ordered to encamp near him. The troops all moved, and went into camp as ordered. The Nineteenth Corps on the same day moved back to Carrion Crow Bayou, and on the following day to Vermillionville, leaving the Third and First Brigades of the Fourth Division of the Thirteenth Corps to hold the position before named. The position of the troops on the morning of the 3d instant was then as follows: Brigadier-General Burbridge, with one brigade of the Fourth Division, about 1,200 strong, with one six-gun battery of 10-pounder Parrotts, and Colonel Fonda, with about 500 mounted infantry and a section of Nims' battery, on the north side of Muddy Bayou, and the Third Division, General McGinnis commanding, 3,000 strong, with one battery, at Carrion Crow Bayou, 3 miles in the rear of General Burbridge. The two bayous before named run in an easterly direction, nearly parallel with each other, and along the stream there is a belt of timber about 150 yards in width, while between the two is smooth, level prairie. To the right of General Burbridge's position was an extensive and dense tract of woods, while on his front and left the country was high, open prairie.

About 9 o'clock of the morning of the 3d, I received a note from General Burbridge, saying the enemy had shown himself in some force. I immediately ordered out the Third Division, and just as I got them into line I received another note from General Burbridge, saying that the enemy had entirely disappeared. Ordering the division to remain under arms, I rode rapidly to the front, and learning from General Burbridge and Colonel Fonda that all was quiet, and that such troops of the enemy as had shown themselves had all fallen back, I started to return to my headquarters near the Third Division. When I arrived about midway between the two camps, I heard a rapid cannonade. Sending two members of my staff to the rear to bring up the Third Division, I rode back to the front, and, crossing the bayou and passing through the timber to the open ground, I soon discovered that we were assailed with terrible energy by an overwhelming force in front and on both flanks. Many of the troops had broken and were scattered over the field, and the utter destruction or capture of the whole force seemed imminent. The attack on the right through the woods was made by infantry, and though our troops fought most gallantly on that wing, were obliged to give way before overwhelming numbers. Here it was that we lost most of our men in killed and wounded.

The Twenty-third Wisconsin, Colonel Guppey commanding, Ninety-sixth Ohio, Lieutenant-Colonel Brown commanding, Sixtieth Indiana, commanded by Captain Goelzer, and Seventeenth Ohio Battery, [Captain] Rice commanding, fought with the greatest desperation, holding the enemy in check for a considerable length of time, but for which our entire train with our artillery would have been captured. As it was, General Burbridge was enabled to bring off every wagon and all Government property, with the exception of one 10-pounder Parrott gun, which was captured just as it was crossing the bayou, the horses having been shot.

The bringing off of the section of Nims' battery, commanded by Lieutenant Marland, after the regiment sent to its support had surrendered, extorted the admiration of every beholder.

While the fight was proceeding, the Third Division came up on the double-quick, but by the time they had reached the middle of the prairie, and 1½ miles from the scene of action, General Burbridge's command had been driven entirely out of the woods, while the rebel cavalry, in great force, charged through the narrow belt of timber on the left, and were coming down on his rear. By this time the Third Division had come within range, formed in line, and commenced shelling them, which immediately checked their farther advance, while General Burbridge, who had again gotten his guns into position, opened a raking cross-fire upon them, when the whole force of the enemy retreated to the cover of the woods. Our whole force was deployed in line of battle, and moved as rapidly as possible through the woods, driving the enemy out of it, who retreated rapidly. I moved the troops up on their line of retreat about 1½ miles, while the cavalry pursued about 3 miles. My men having been brought up at a double-quick, were very much exhausted, and it was not possible to pursue farther.

Our losses are 26 killed, 124 wounded, and 566 missing.* The loss of the enemy in killed was about 60; number of wounded not known, as they carried all but 12 off the ground, but wounded officers who were taken prisoners represent the number of wounded as being very large. We took 65 prisoners.

Brigadier-General McGinnis, being very ill, was not able to be on the field. The troops of the division behaved admirably, under the command of Brigadier-General Cameron, of the First, and Colonel Slack, of the Second Brigade. The action of General Burbridge was gallant and judicious from the time I first saw him until the close of the engagement. The conduct of the Sixty-seventh Indiana Infantry was inexplicable, and their surrender can only be attributed to the incompetency or cowardice of the commanding officer. They had not a single man killed. Our mounted force, under Colonels Fonda and Robinson, though very small, behaved very handsomely.

I left at Carrion Crow Bayou, to hold that position, three regiments of the Third Division, viz, the Eleventh Indiana, Twenty-ninth Wisconsin, and Twenty-fourth Iowa, with one section of artillery. It was fortunate that I did so, for while the fight was proceeding with General Burbridge's command, Colonel [George W.] Baylor, of the First Texas Mounted Rifles [Second Regiment Arizona Brigade], swept round on our left, and attacked the camp at Carrion Crow Bayou, but they were driven off, with a loss of 3 killed. We lost none. I refer particularly to the report of General Burbridge for the names of those deserving honorable mention.

---

* But see revised statement, p. 359.

On the 4th instant the enemy sent in a flag of truce, proposing to give up such of our wounded as they had, not having the means to take care of them. I sent for and received 47. They refused to give up our wounded officers, among them Colonel Guppey, of the Twenty-third Wisconsin, a most gallant and meritorious officer. Though wounded, I am pleased to learn that his wound is not severe, and that all our prisoners were being well treated.

As to the force of the enemy engaged, opinions are conflicting, but, from the best data I have, I judge them to have been from 6,000 to 7,000, the whole under the command of Brigadier-General Green.

Respectfully, yours,

C. C. WASHBURN,
Major-General, Commanding.

Maj. WICKHAM HOFFMAN,
Assistant Adjutant-General.

A D D E N D A.

Return of Casualties in the Union forces engaged at Bayou Bourbeau, or Buzzard's Prairie, near Grand Coteau, La., November 3, 1863.

[Compiled from nominal list of casualties, returns, &c.]

Command.	Killed.		Wounded.		Captured or missing.		Aggregate.
	Officers.	Enlisted men.	Officers.	Enlisted men.	Officers.	Enlisted men.	
60th Indiana		4	1	29	2	95	131
67th Indiana			2	9	13	187	211
28th Iowa				2			2
48th Ohio						1	1
83d Ohio				4	1	51	56
96th Ohio		11	1	32	5	67	116
23d Wisconsin		6	1	36	4	81	128
4th Indiana Cavalry, Company C						1	1
1st Louisiana Cavalry (detachment)		3	1	7		27	38
14th New York Cavalry (detachment)				2	1	2	5
2d Massachusetts Battery (detachment)						2	2
17th Ohio Battery		1		2		22	25
Total		25	6	123	26	536	716

No. 6.

Reports of Brig. Gen. Stephen G. Burbridge, U. S. Army, commanding Fourth Division, of engagement at Bayou Bourbeau, and operations (November 12) about Saint Martinsville.

HDQRS. FOURTH DIVISION, THIRTEENTH ARMY CORPS,
Near Vermillion Bayou, La., November 7, 1863.

MAJOR: Pursuant to instructions from Major-General Washburn, I respectfully submit the following report of the engagement near Bayou Carrion Crow, on the 3d instant:

My camp was situated about 3 miles from Bayou Carrion Crow, near the head of a small bayou which runs in the direction of Opelousas through a ravine 1 mile wide. Upon each side was an extensive prairie. After skirmishing all day on the 2d with the enemy, and having on several occasions that day seen his lines—fully 2,500 strong—I felt sure he would attempt to harass me on the following day. This conviction was made more sure by 6 of the First Louisiana Cavalry deserting from the reserve pickets Monday night (2d), and going over to the enemy. Early on the morning of the 3d, our outposts were driven in, and a heavy force seen on our front and left. This intelligence was sent to General Washburn promptly; our lines formed, the artillery gotten into place, and a few well-directed rounds from the artillery and some maneuvering soon made him retire. About 10 o'clock a. m. but few of the enemy could be seen. I directed the troops then to retire to camp, but hold themselves ready to fall in at a moment's warning. Sent a dispatch to Major-General Washburn that the enemy had nearly all retired out of sight, and, after reconnoitering my left in person, returned to my headquarters.

After the enemy had disappeared, at about 10 o'clock, I sent out a forage train, in charge of the Eighty-third Ohio, in the direction of Grand Coteau. In the present attitude of our situation, with a large body of rebel cavalry hovering around us, I did not deem it safe to risk a train out with a less number than 200, which was about the strength of the Eighty-third Ohio.

At 12.30 p. m. I received a message from Colonel Fonda, One hundred and eighteenth Illinois Mounted Infantry, that the enemy was approaching with heavy columns of cavalry and infantry, supported by artillery. I at once dispatched to that effect to General Washburn, and ordered the infantry and artillery to get ready for action. The rebel infantry approached through a ravine from the direction of Opelousas. Upon the left, across the prairie, a heavy column of cavalry could be seen moving upon me in line of battle. I directed one of my largest regiments, the Sixty-seventh Indiana, about 260 strong, one section of Nims' battery, and one section of the Seventeenth Ohio Battery, to take a position on my left. I then posted about 150 cavalry on their left, and directed the whole to guard against an attack on my rear and left. My remaining three regiments, the Eighty-third Ohio being out guarding foraging trains, and four pieces of artillery (Seventeenth Ohio Battery), I posted so as to meet the rebel infantry in the ravine. The cavalry, under Colonel Fonda, One hundred and eighteenth Illinois, was intrusted with guarding my right.

The enemy in overwhelming numbers were pressing me, and I feared that I could not hold my position until re-enforcements could be brought up. I directed my teams to be moved to the rear. After engaging the enemy a short time in front, I discovered them attempting to flank me on the right. His line in front being about three times as long as mine, and his cavalry bearing down upon my left, I found it necessary to extend my lines to the right, in order that I might not be completely surrounded. I now directed the Sixty-seventh Indiana (Lieutenant-Colonel Buehler) and the forces placed, to guard my left, while I advanced my right. Colonel Buehler, from a misapprehension of my orders, or some other cause, failed to commence his movements until I had dispatched a third time to him. He was by this time almost surrounded by ten times his number of cavalry, and he with almost his whole regiment were taken prisoners. The artillery played upon the enemy until it was almost surrounded, but succeeded in withdrawing, excepting one piece of the Seventeenth Ohio Battery and its caisson, which had its horses killed.

My left now being totally gone, and the enemy's cavalry pressing heavily upon me, I gradually fell back through the ravine, so as to cover my train. The Eighty-third Ohio, which had been ordered back from the foraging expedition as soon as the action began, came up just as we were abandoning the ravine. Seeing that re-enforcements were coming up, so as to secure my left, I formed the Eighty-third Ohio upon the plain, upon which my shattered forces now rallied. My artillery was placed upon the left and the cavalry on the right. Here we checked the enemy until our support had come fully up, when the enemy retired. As soon as we could distribute ammunition to the men, we advanced upon the enemy in the woods. General Cameron, upon my left, seeing that the enemy was disposed to offer but little more resistance, a cavalry charge was ordered through the ravine, and nearly 100 prisoners were captured. After pursuing the enemy a short distance beyond the ravine, we returned, picked up our wounded and dead, and fell back to Carrion Crow Bayou.

The forces engaged on our side in this affair were the Sixtieth Indiana, Sixty-seventh Indiana, Eighty-third and Ninety-sixth Ohio, and Twenty-third Regiment Wisconsin Infantry, numbering 1,040 effective men; the One hundred and eighteenth Illinois Mounted Infantry, First Louisiana Cavalry, and detachment Fourteenth New York Cavalry, numbering 460 men; the Seventeenth Ohio Battery, and one section Nims' battery, numbering 125 men; total, 1,625.

The enemy engaged me with about 3,500 infantry in front and not less than 2,500 cavalry and a battery of artillery on my left. In killed and wounded he suffered much more than I did, 42 of his dead being left upon the field and buried by our forces, besides quite a number that he carried away. I am led to the conclusion that I have placed an exceedingly moderate estimate upon his forces, as well as the punishment we inflicted, by the statements, herewith respectfully submitted, of Captain Sims, Sixty-seventh Indiana, and Lieutenant Gorman, First Louisiana Cavalry, who were captured and returned with our wounded. Our losses were: Killed, 26; wounded, 124; missing, 566. We lost also 36 horses, one 10-pounder Parrott gun, and 1 caisson. Most of our camp equipage and all our supply trains and ammunition were saved.

The engagement began at 12.30 p. m. and continued until nearly 3 p. m. Every inch of the ground was contested through the entire ravine, and both officers and men displayed the utmost coolness and bravery. Colonel Guppey and Captain Bull, Twenty-third Regiment Wisconsin; Colonel Owen, commanding brigade, and Lieutenant Richardson, his acting assistant adjutant-general; Lieutenant-Colonel Brown, Ninety-sixth Ohio; Captain Rice, Seventeenth Ohio Battery; Colonel Fonda, One hundred and eighteenth Illinois; Lieutenant-Colonel Robinson, First Louisiana Cavalry, and Lieutenant Marland, commanding section of Nims' battery, deserve an honorable mention in that day's contest. Colonel Guppey, for rallying his men once after he was shot down; Lieutenant Richardson, acting assistant adjutant-general, for taking the advance until his horse was shot under him; Captain Rice, for standing by his battery until the last moment, and Lieutenant-Colonel Robinson, for heading a brilliant cavalry charge, all deserve the very highest approbation. The section of Nims' battery, Lieutenant Marland commanding, did more than its whole duty. I am indebted to Captain [Richard] Vance, Major [Victor] Vifquain, Surgeon [Frederick] McGrew, Captain [William B.] Lebo, and Lieutenants [Thomas J.] Elliott, [John M.] Shields, [Silas] Baldwin, and [John S.] Van Vliet, of my staff, for assisting in the execution of my orders.

S. G. BURBRIDGE,
Brigadier-General.

Maj. WILLIAM H. MORGAN,
Assistant Adjutant-General, Thirteenth Army Corps.

HDQRS. FOURTH DIVISION, THIRTEENTH ARMY CORPS,
New Iberia, La., November 12, 1863—5.30 p. m.

GENERAL : The enemy fired upon a boat about 3 o'clock this evening. There were about 60 of them. I have cavalry and infantry over the bayou after them. When last heard of, my forces were close upon the rebels. Three men were wounded on the boat; no serious damage done to it. I have not heard from Saint Martinsville to-day. One hundred of the Seventy-fifth New York were sent there to-day, and directed to return by way of the junction of the Vermillion, and New Iberia and Vermillion and Saint Martinsville roads.

I will report as soon as they come in.

S. G. BURBRIDGE,
Brigadier-General.

Major-General FRANKLIN.

—

HDQRS. FOURTH DIVISION, THIRTEENTH ARMY CORPS,
New Iberia, La., November 12, 1863.

MAJOR : My scouts are all in; they report about 500 men in Saint Martinsville, mostly operating against our boats below. The party who attacked the boat escaped in the direction of Saint Martinsville. All confirm the report that there is a general rendezvous, near Saint Martinsville, of 500 French guerrillas, under Major Dupeire. My cavalry chased the party below here until nearly sundown, and left them near Saint Martinsville. Two boats have arrived since my last dispatch. Lieutenant-Colonel [V. A.] Fournet, who has resigned out of the Confederate service, was arrested by my scouts at Saint Martinsville to-day. I will send him to you in the morning if you do not order otherwise. The bridge at Saint Martinsville has been destroyed; there is another 4 miles above that place.

S. G. BURBRIDGE

Major HOFFMAN,
Assistant Adjutant-General.

—

HDQRS. FOURTH DIVISION, THIRTEENTH ARMY CORPS,
New Iberia, La., November 14, 1863—11 a. m.

Contrabands coming in report that Price and Magruder are on the way to re-enforce the rebels in your front. They say that the rebels know that re-enforcements have been sent to Texas. Reports say that the rebels are building a bridge on Bayou Vermillion, in the neighborhood of Abbeville. Could they not cross at Perry's Bridge? Could they not also pass down in the rear of Saint Martinsville, and get below me? I have not sufficient cavalry here to watch both points. I will send 100 cavalry out this evening; they will camp 1 mile this side of Saint Martinsville; scout beyond to-morrow.

The Treasury Department has an agent here. He thinks it best to ship all cotton and sugar to New Orleans, and have claims investigated there. All abandoned property is claimed by speculators. Major Cowan, First Louisiana Cavalry, has shipped 76 bales of cotton and 82 hogsheads of sugar. Nothing from below to-day.

S. G. BURBRIDGE,
General, Commanding.

Major HOFFMAN,
Assistant Adjutant-General, Nineteenth Army Corps.

ADDENDA.

DEPARTMENT OF THE GULF,
Vermillion, November 14, 1863.

If you get anything definite about Price and Magruder re-enforcing the rebels in my front, I shall be glad to know it; my position here is good against double my number. I have sent to see about the Abbe-ville Bridge, but I do not believe it; Perry's Bridge is destroyed, to the best of my knowledge and belief. If the rebels get below you on the other side of the Teche, in force, they will never get above you again. Colonel Fournet, with Mr. Béreaud, will see you to-morrow morning. I wish you to investigate the case of the former as soon as possible, letting me know result. Major Cowan's papers ought to show whether he has authority to ship sugar. Demand to see them.

W. B. FRANKLIN,
Major-General.

Brigadier-General BURBRIDGE,
Commanding.

—

HDQRS. FOURTH DIVISION, THIRTEENTH ARMY CORPS,
New Iberia, La., November 15, 1863—7.30 p. m.

MAJOR: My scouts are just in, and they report that they were in Saint Martinsville this morning. They went miles above on this side the bayou; saw several small squads of guerrillas on the other side the bayou, and exchanged shots with some of them. They bring in 2 prisoners, and say there is a camp of several hundred this side and to the right, all across the bayou. Negroes reported to the guard on the boat that came up to-day that a considerable number of guerrillas were below me on the bayou, but the guard saw none. Two pieces of artil-lery came up to-day. Negroes coming in say that rebel citizens are jubilant over the arrival of Price and Magruder's re-enforcements. My scouts from Saint Martinsville to-day say they heard cannonading in your direction. I am working soldiers, citizens, negroes, and specula-tors, and will finish my works to-morrow. If you will give me the escort that came with the train this evening, I will send out all my mounted force to Saint Martinsville, and attack that camp to-morrow night. I can send with that additional force about 500 or 600.

S. G. BURBRIDGE,
Brigadier-General.

[Major HOFFMAN, *Assistant Adjutant-General.*]

———

No. 7.

Report of Col. Joshua J. Guppey, Twenty-third Wisconsin Infantry,
First Brigade, of engagement at Bayou Bourbeau.

NEW ORLEANS, LA.,
January 9, 1864.

SIR: I was taken prisoner in the engagement which took place be-tween First Brigade, Fourth Division, of the Thirteenth Army Corps, and the rebel forces near Bayou Bourbeau on the 3d of November last, and have been unable to make a report concerning it prior to this date. I now submit that report, and address it to you, for the reason that the officers in command of the brigade on that day are not now on duty with it.

The brigade was encamped on a prairie, having in its rear a narrow belt of timber, through which the Bayou Bourbeau ran. Our camp faced the west, and about 4 miles in rear of it was the Carrion Crow Bayou, on which the main body of the United States forces were stationed. The land between the belt of timber on the Bourbeau and the Carrion Crow was prairie.

The approaches to our position were as follows:

First. By the road leading from Opelousas, which, in its southerly course, struck the right end of our camp. This road ran near the edge of the timber, and on the west side of it, and almost cornering with the front of our camp on the right there was a field stretching to the west, and inclosed with the ordinary ditch and wood fence. Through this field cavalry could not be moved with much rapidity.

Second. By the open prairie in our front. The enemy, approaching us from the direction of Opelousas, could go to the west of the field I have named, and come in on our front.

The Sixtieth Indiana, the Ninety-sixth Ohio, the Eighty-third Ohio, the Sixty-seventh Indiana, and the Twenty-third Wisconsin constituted the infantry force of the brigade, and they were encamped from right to left in the order named. The Seventeenth Ohio Battery formed a part of the brigade, and was in camp with it. Each of the infantry regiments numbered about 200 men.

We had an infantry picket in our front and a cavalry force watching the road from Opelousas and the country adjoining it. What the numbers of the latter may have been I cannot state.

We knew that the enemy was in our front, for he had followed us from Opelousas and Barre's Landing, when our forces had returned from those places on the 1st of November, and had commenced skirmishing with our pickets early the next morning. We knew that his cavalry force was about 4,000, for he had displayed it on the prairie in front of the Carrion Crow Bayou on the 15th of October, in an attack on the Nineteenth Army Corps, on which day Brigadier-General Burbridge marched General Cameron's and our brigade from Vermillionville to Carrion Crow as the advance of the Thirteenth Army Corps. But it was not supposed that the enemy had any infantry near our camp.

We were thus situated, with regard to the main body of our force, and thus advised of the strength of the rebel cavalry hovering around our brigade, when the morning of the 3d of November opened with alarms and skirmishing along the picket lines. The regiments were soon in line of battle, and the battery was ready for work. The enemy, however, retired from our picket lines, and, after the brigade had been under arms some hours, the men were permitted to stack arms and return to their quarters, but were directed to keep on their equipments and be ready to fall in at a moment's notice. After the alarm had subsided, the Eighty-third Ohio Volunteers, with the wagons of the brigade, were sent out on a foraging expedition.

Two paymasters were in camp paying off the troops, and my regiment was engaged in voting for State officers, yet, when the order was again given to "fall in," the line of battle was formed in a few moments. This was about noon.

The four regiments of infantry in the camp and the battery were disposed as follows: The Sixtieth Indiana and four pieces of artillery were moved to the north, on the Opelousas road, and took position between the field and Bayou Bourbeau. The Ninety-sixth Ohio Volunteer Infantry followed as a support. The Sixty-seventh Indiana, with two pieces of the battery, were sent out on the prairie in front of the camp, and to the west of the field. The Twenty-third Wisconsin was ordered to remain in front of the camp, and its colonel was directed to cover the camp, or move in support of the other troops, as occasion might require.

Firing soon commenced in the direction taken by the Sixtieth Indiana, and, after changing front forward on first company, I moved my regiment in line of battle from the left to the right end of the camp, so as to be nearer to the troops engaged. The firing from the direction of the Sixtieth Indiana, both of musketry and artillery, became very heavy and well sustained, and, in a short time, I saw that our force was falling back. I then learned that the Sixtieth Indiana and the artillery with it had encountered a brigade of infantry, accompanied by artillery and cavalry.

Up to this time no one supposed that the enemy had any infantry within striking distance of us, and I may state here that I was informed while I was a prisoner that the rebel infantry had been marched from Opelousas that morning, and put into action without an instant's rest.

The attacking force of the enemy was so heavy that the Sixtieth Indiana and the pieces of the battery with it were compelled to give way. The Sixtieth Indiana broke ranks, I am told, and its men ran into the ranks of the Ninety-sixth Ohio Volunteer Infantry, who were in their rear, and broke them.

It was about this time that General Burbridge, waving his hat as he dashed up, ordered me to take position in a ravine between the right of the camp and the bayou. I put my regiment in the designated position as quickly as possible, and ordered my men to lie down, so that the Sixtieth and Ninety-sixth could pass over them. Many of the Ninety-sixth were here rallied by their gallant commander, Lieutenant-Colonel Brown, and placed in my line. I ordered the men not to fire a gun till I gave the command.

At the moment I entered the ravine, the Eighty-third Ohio returned to camp with the baggage wagons, and artillery firing commenced on the prairie, where the Sixty-seventh Indiana was. I knew that if General Green's cavalry division was sweeping in across the prairie, as I doubted not it was, our condition was desperate enough. With one look at the Sixty-seventh, another at the Eighty-third, then in front of our camp, and another toward General Burbridge, who was trying to form the flying men in rear of my regiment, I turned by attention again to the advancing infantry of the enemy, and gave the order to fire as soon as it was within good rifle-range. Never was an order more coolly obeyed or better followed up. In ten minutes the regiment in my front was so doubled up that its men were 10 or 12 deep, and all mixed up, but still gallantly advancing. Two other regiments were also in the enemy's line, one to the right and the other to the left of that in my front, and each stretching beyond my flanks, and giving me a heavier fire than I could return. I then sent to General Burbridge for the Eighty-third Ohio, but he did not send it to our position. At this time I was wounded just below the left knee.

Failing to get re-enforcements, I maintained the fight as best I could for awhile; but I soon saw the long line of rebel cavalry (about 3,000 in number) charging across the prairie toward and around the camp, unchecked by the Sixty-seventh Indiana; in fact, the latter had then surrendered, as I afterward learned. Seeing that this cavalry would be in rear of me if I held my position longer, I commenced falling back toward the point held by General Burbridge while he was covering the removal of the train—fighting enough as we went to check the rapid advance of the rebel infantry. None of my men would have been taken prisoners if the cavalry had not by this time begun to get in our rear. While we were thus falling back, my wounded limb became powerless, and I turned over the command of my regiment to Lieutenant-Colonel Hill, and attempted, with the assistance of Lieutenant Stanley, to get off the field, but the enemy's cavalry was too near me, and the lieutenant and myself were taken prisoners by it. Afterward it took about 80 of my men, and among them many of the wounded. As soon as the enemy found that the baggage train was out of their reach, and that General Burbridge was prepared to renew the battle on the prairie, in rear of the Bayou Bourbeau, they left the field, hurried along by the shells from our artillery, and taking with them the prisoners they had captured.

Owing to the absence of men on picket duty, I took into battle only about 160 men. Of these, 10 were killed and 30 wounded, being a loss in killed and wounded of 1 to 4 of the men engaged. I have the satisfaction of knowing, however, that the enemy suffered much more in killed and wounded than we did. The regiment in my immediate front lost, its colonel informed me, 54 in killed and wounded, and the others nearly the same. His cavalry also lost considerably. The officers and men of my regiment fought most gallantly; but this report is so extended already, that I must refrain from naming particular cases of good conduct.

I close with saying that our disposition at first was against a cavalry attack, and I think we could have driven the cavalry if it had been unaided by infantry. As it was, three of our regiments were used against the rebel infantry—unfortunately, only one at a time—and this left only two regiments to act against the cavalry.

The enemy numbered over 5,000. Three of his mounted regiments acted as infantry, in support of his infantry proper. He felt sure that he would capture our wagons and baggage and our artillery; but Captain Rice's battery and two sections of Nims' battery, which acted with us, were capitally handled, and the rebels captured but one gun. All the wagons, well loaded with baggage, were brought off safe.

Respectfully, your obedient servant,

J. J. GUPPEY,
Colonel, Comdg. Twenty-third Regt. Wisconsin Vol. Infantry.

Capt. A. B. SHARPE,
Assistant Adjutant-General, Thirteenth Army Corps.

No. 8.

Abstracts from "Record of Events" on the several returns of the Thirteenth Army Corps, for October and November, 1863.

CORPS RETURN.

October 3.—The First, Third, and Fourth Divisions, Thirteenth Army Corps, marched from Berwick City, La., by way of Franklin and New

Iberia, to Vermillion Bayou, arriving October 10.   One brigade of the Fourth Division was left at Franklin.

October 20.—On account of the illness of General Ord, General Washburn assumed command, and moved forward to Opelousas.

October 26.—General Ord went on sick leave, and General Dana assumed command of the troops.   The Second Division, under command of General Dana, embarked from New Orleans for Texas.

October 27.—The First Division moved on its return to New Iberia, arriving October 29.

RETURN OF THE FIRST DIVISION.

October 23.—Marched [from Vermillion Bayou] for Opelousas, arriving the 24th.   Remained in camp until the 27th, when orders were received returning the division to New Iberia.   The return march was accomplished in three days, the division reaching Iberia the 30th, where it has since been encamped.   No events of special importance have transpired thus far in the campaign.

October 28.—The Fifty-fourth Indiana Volunteers, Col. Fielding Mansfield commanding, sent to New Orleans, by order of Major-General Banks.   The term of service of this regiment expires in the month of November, it being one of the one-year regiments from that State.   The One hundred and eighteenth Illinois Volunteers detached from the division October 3, to be mounted, by order of Major-General Banks.

RETURN OF THE FIRST BRIGADE, THIRD DIVISION.

October 16.—Marched to Buzzard Prairie; enemy drove in our grand guard, but would not attack.

October 21.—Left Buzzard Prairie; skirmished with the enemy and drove them through Opelousas, La., and encamped at Barre's Landing, 8 miles beyond the latter place.   On our return march, arrived at Opelousas same day, where we are now [October 31] in camp.

November 1.—Left Opelousas, La., and marched to Carrion Crow Bayou.

November 2.—Moved out to the front to re-enforce General Burbridge. The Fourth Division returned the same day.

November 3.—Again re-enforced General Burbridge's division, which had quite a spirited engagement at the front.   This brigade took very little part in the action, the enemy retiring on perceiving us re-enforce the Fourth Division.

November 5.—Moved to Camp Pratt, La.

November 17.—Moved to New Iberia, La.

November 20.—Marched to Camp Pratt, and, in connection with General Lee's Cavalry Division, surprised and captured a rebel outpost, consisting of 13 officers and 98 non-commissioned officers and privates, and returned the same day.   The whole distance marched during the month, 57 miles.

November 30.—Still in camp at New Iberia, La.

RETURN OF THE FOURTH DIVISION.

October 10.—Marched [from vicinity of New Iberia] to Vermillion Bayou, 24 miles, where we remained until the 14th, when we moved up to Carrion Crow Bayou.

October 15.—Took the advance, and skirmished with the enemy.
October 16.—Established our camp on Bayou Bourbeau.
October 21.—Moved against Opelousas; had the advance; enemy offered but little resistance; drove the enemy through the town, and established our camps beyond and to the right of Opelousas, at Barre's Landing, on Bayou Courtableau, where we remained during the rest of the month.

RETURN OF THE SECOND BRIGADE, FOURTH DIVISION

October 7, *Wednesday.*—Marched from Berwick City.
October 9, *Friday.*—Having marched to within 3 miles of New Iberia, received orders to leave two regiments (Ninety-seventh and One hundred and thirtieth Illinois, in command of Colonel Niles, of One hundred and thirtieth Illinois), and move back with balance of command and occupy this post.
October 11, *Sunday.*—Made Camp Franklin, La.

No. 9.

Report of Col. Lewis Benedict, One hundred and sixty-second New York Infantry, commanding First Brigade, Third Division, Nineteenth Army Corps, of skirmishes November 11.

VERMILLION BAYOU,
November 11, 1863.

CAPTAIN: I have the honor to report that, in obedience to orders from headquarters, I marched my command about 1 mile north of Vermillionville, and took position commanding two roads leading east and west. Captain Trull, with his battery, reported to me, and took position, where the whole force remained until Captain Baker, of General Franklin's staff, brought me an order from General Lee to move forward to his support, as a superior force of cavalry and infantry was in his front, threatening him. I moved forward until I learned that he was retreating; then retired. Receiving a request to select a good position, where my men would be concealed, I did so, and waited. Our cavalry retreated to our rear, when the enemy advanced to the mouth of the road opening on the plain, and our artillery opened upon them with some effect. After an artillery duel of some twenty minutes, their forces disappeared, and I received orders to retire. I did so, and again took position, in obedience to orders from General Lee, in a ditch near Vermillionville; but no enemy appearing, I was ordered to return to this camp.

Our loss is as follows: One hundred and tenth [New York], 1 killed, 3 wounded; One hundred and sixty-second [New York], 1 wounded; One hundred and seventy-third [New York], 1 wounded; One hundred and sixty-fifth [New York], none. Total, 1 killed, 5 wounded; all of whom were brought from the field.

I have the honor to be, your most obedient servant,

LEW. BENEDICT,
Colonel, Commanding.

Capt. DUNCAN S. WALKER,
  Asst. Adjt. Gen., Third Division, Nineteenth Army Corps.

No. 10.

Itinerary of the Nineteenth Army Corps, October 1–November 18, 1863.*

October 1.—In camp at Bisland, La.
October 3.—Marched to Franklin, La.; 12 miles.
October 4.—Marched to Sorrel's plantation; 11 miles.
October 5.—Marched to Olivier's, near New Iberia; 13 miles.
October 8.—Marched to near Vermillion Bayou; 15 miles.
October 9.—Crossed Vermillion Bayou; 8 miles. Slight skirmish; enemy retired.
October 11.—Marched to Carrion Crow Bayou; 10 miles.
October 15.—Enemy deployed on our front at daylight; skirmish; enemy driven from the grounds. Our loss was 7 killed and wounded. Two brigades of the Thirteenth Corps reported in the evening.
October 17.—Headquarters moved to bayou, 2 miles to the front.
October 19.—Reconnaissance in force. Skirmish with the enemy on bayou, 4 miles in advance. Our force retires.
October 21.—Marched to Opelousas; 8 miles. Enemy checks our cavalry at the railroad crossing, 2 miles south of Opelousas; retreats, on infantry coming up. We occupy Opelousas and Barre's Landing, 8 miles from Opelousas.
October 24.—Cavalry reconnaissance to Moundville. Enemy in small force, and retreats.
October 31.—In camp at Bayou Barricroquant, La., near Barre's Landing.
November 1.—Fell back to Carrion Crow Bayou; 16 miles.
November 2.—Fell back to Vermillion Bayou; 11 miles.
November 3.—In camp at Vermillion Bayou.
November 4.—First Division to Carrion Crow Bayou.
November 5.—First Division fell back to Vermillion Bayou.
November 6–10.—In camp at Vermillion Bayou.
November 11.—Skirmish; our loss about 20; the enemy's rather more.
November 12–15.—In camp.
November 16.—Fell back to Camp Pratt; 13 miles.
November 17.—Fell back to New Iberia; 5 miles.
November 18–30.—In camp.

No. 11.

Reports of Brig. Gen. Albert L. Lee, U. S. Army, commanding Cavalry Division, Department of the Gulf, of skirmish at Camp Pratt and affair at Bayou Portage.

IN THE FIELD, NEAR NEW IBERIA, LA.,
November 22, 1863.

GENERAL: I have respectfully to report that on the 20th November, our front having been on the previous day severely annoyed by the cavalry of the enemy, learning that he occupied in some force Camp Pratt, a point 6 miles north of your camps, I attempted, under your direction, his surprise and capture. At 2 a. m. the First Brigade of this di-

---

* Compiled from "Record of Events" on the corps returns.

vision, Col. T. J. Lucas, Sixteenth Indiana, commanding the Third Brigade, Col. C. J. Paine, Second Louisiana, commanding, and a section of Nims' Second Massachusetts Horse Artillery, all under command of Colonel Lucas, moved out 4 miles on the road leading west from Iberia, and thence north across the prairie until opposite the flank and in rear of the enemy's camp, reaching this position, undiscovered, shortly before dawn. At 4 a. m., with 300 cavalry and another section of Nims' battery, and supported by the First Brigade of Infantry of the Third Division, Thirteenth Army Corps, under command of General Cameron, I moved out on the road leading directly from Iberia to Camp Pratt. Just before day, at a point 1 mile south of Camp Pratt, my advance came on the enemy's pickets, wounded and captured 1, and drove the remainder in. I at once charged their camp with cavalry, the infantry moving rapidly as a support. The enemy made a lively skirmish, but at this moment, as previously ordered, the command of Colonel Lucas closed rapidly on their flanks and rear, and, in a quarter of an hour, almost the entire force of the enemy were prisoners. A few escaped through the adjoining woods. We found that their force consisted of the Seventh Texas Cavalry, Colonel Bagby. The colonel was not with the regiment. Our captures amounted to 12 commissioned officers, 101 enlisted men, 100 horses and equipments, and about 100 stand of arms of all kinds. This constituted the effective force of the regiment, which they have claimed was the flower of their cavalry. The rebels lost 1 killed and 3 wounded; our loss was nothing. I have to mention with commendation the promptness and skill displayed by Col. T. J. Lucas in conveying his command during a night of intense darkness to the rear of the enemy, and effecting so decided and perfect a co-operation with my attacking force in front. Col. C. J. Paine, commanding Third Brigade, Lieut. Col. H. Robinson, First Louisiana Cavalry, and Maj. Bacon Montgomery, Sixth Missouri Cavalry, are worthy of special mention for their gallant conduct on this occasion. The infantry were, by the rapidity of events, denied any participation in the skirmish, but were eager and prompt in their conduct. The prisoners have been transferred to your provost-marshal.

I have the honor to be, respectfully, your obedient servant,

A. L. LEE,
Brigadier-General, Chief of Cavalry, Department of the Gulf.

Major-General FRANKLIN,
   Commanding U. S. Forces near New Iberia, La.

IN THE FIELD, NEAR NEW IBERIA, LA.,
November 24, 1863.

GENERAL: I would respectfully report that, learning a detachment of the enemy were in camp near Grand Lake, 16 miles northeast from this point, I sent on the night of the 22d instant detachments of the First, Second, and Third Brigades, of this division—in all, 650 strong—to effect their capture; Col. T. J. Lucas, commanding First Brigade, was in charge. Leaving camp at 10 p. m., the forces moved to a point on Bayou Portage, near Grand Lake, and succeeded in surprising the camp of a detachment of the First Louisiana Mounted Zouaves, under command of Major Dupeire, C. S. Army. Four commissioned officers, 31 privates, 25 horses, and about 50 stand of arms, and the colors of the battalion, were captured. I send herewith the reports of Colonel

Lucas and Colonel Paine. The prisoners were transferred to your provost-marshal, and the colors are transmitted with this report.

I am, general, respectfully, your obedient servant, .

A. L. LEE,
Brigadier-General, Chief of Cavalry, Department of the Gulf.

Major-General FRANKLIN,
Commanding U. S. Forces, near New Iberia, La.

No. 12.

Report of Lieut. William Marland, Second Massachusetts Battery, of engagement at Bayou Bourbeau.

CARRION CROW BAYOU, LA., *November* 4, 1863.

GENERAL: In pursuance to your orders, I have the honor to make the following report of the part taken in the action at this place on the 3d of November by the section under my command :

In obedience to orders received on the evening of the 2d of November, I harnessed up at 4 a. m. on the 3d; remained so until 11 a. m., when I was ordered to unharness; the pickets firing all the while. At about 12.45 p. m. the firing became general. Hearing the cavalry buglers blow "Boots and saddles," I began to harness up on my own responsibility, and was attacked in camp before I could get harnessed. The enemy being within 400 yards of me, I opened on them with canister and percussion shell, which checked their advance and drove them to the right. I limbered to the front, and advanced to the fork of the road, which is about 100 yards; went into battery, and fired a few shot until all my support had left me. Finding it too warm, I limbered to the rear, and moved about 300 yards. Finding the enemy in my rear and on the right, I fired to the right about fifty shots, and was charged upon on three sides A regiment came up on my left as support, fired one volley, and left.

The enemy then opened two pieces of artillery on me at about 300 yards, killing 1 horse and disabling one caisson wheel. The cavalry still advancing, and no infantry to be seen, when they got within 30 yards I limbered up and started for the woods; here I ordered my cannoneers to draw their revolvers, and had quite a brisk fight; had another horse killed, 2 men missing (1 sergeant and 1 private); went through the woods, the enemy coming out in front and rear of men. As the bridges constructed across the bayou for the passage of our troops were held by the enemy, it was necessary to charge through, which was accomplished, notwithstanding a cavalryman had mired and was taken prisoner near where the section crossed. I got through the enemy's lines without loss, and came up to the Forty-sixth Indiana Regiment, and formed on their right. Colonel Bringhurst told me he would support me, and I went back through the woods with General Cameron's command, driving the enemy in disorder, who left their dead and wounded on the field. I then returned to camp with General Cameron's brigade.

I am, sir, very respectfully, your most obedient servant,

WM. MARLAND,
First Lieutenant, Commanding Section.

Brig. Gen. RICHARD ARNOLD,
Chief of Artillery, Department of the Gulf.

No. 13.

Reports of Col. John G. Fonda, One hundred and eighteenth Illinois Infantry (mounted), commanding Cavalry Brigade, of engagement ·at Bayou Bourbeau, and skirmishes November 11.

HEADQUARTERS FIRST CAVALRY BRIGADE,
Carrion Crow Bayou, November 3, 1863.

GENERAL : I respectfully submit the following as my report of the part taken by the cavalry under my command in the action of to-day :

In anticipation of an attack at daybreak this morning, I had the horses saddled and the men in readiness at 4 a. m. The enemy not appearing, however, at 8 a. m. I sent 200 of the First Louisiana Cavalry to guard a forage train going in the direction of Grand Coteau, and took 80 men of the One hundred and eighteenth Illinois Mounted Infantry to reconnoiter our front. Advancing directly west about 1 mile, I discovered what appeared to be a strong line of pickets.

I had not been here long when you came out with two pieces of artillery and some infantry. After firing upon the enemy some time with the artillery, they seemed to retire. I then advanced about 2 miles into the prairie without discovering any force. All appeared to have gone to our right.

I returned to camp, with 80 men that I had with me, at 10 a. m. Between this time and noon there was some firing on the picket line. At noon I was informed by the officer of the picket that a heavy column of the enemy was coming down the Opelousas road. I immediately ordered all the cavalry to saddle, and within fifteen minutes they were in line in front of the camp.

The forage train had just returned. I ordered the forage thrown out . of the wagons, and the camp equipage to be loaded and driven to the rear.

We had not been in line long when the enemy, in strong force, attempted to turn our right flank. I immediately ordered all the cavalry to dash across the bridge, and form on the south side of the bayou. The One hundred and eighteenth Illinois was dismounted and sent forward as skirmishers, the First Louisiana Cavalry, Colonel Robinson, advancing with them. The enemy did not succeed in turning our flank.

I now ordered the First Louisiana Cavalry to recross the bridge, which they did, and gallantly charged the enemy, who were then in our camp, cut his line in two, and drove those on the right from that part of the field. While making this charge, my horse, having been hit once before, was shot, and fell to the ground. My men were moving rapidly against the enemy on the right, and, by the time that I had recovered from my fall, I found myself entirely alone, and exposed to the fire of those on the left. I was compelled to escape on foot. My men recrossed the bayou below the bridge, and were again formed into ·line in the prairie, on the south side of the timber.

About 2 p. m. the whole command moved forward again, and drove the enemy entirely out of the timber.

Colonel Robinson, with a portion of his regiment, now pushed forward into the prairie in pursuit of the enemy's cavalry. They were retreating too rapidly, however, to be cut off or overtaken.

The forces under my command consisted of the First Louisiana Cavalry, 300 men; Fourteenth New York Cavalry, 80 men, and 80 of the One hundred and eighteenth Illinois Mounted Infantry ; in all, 460 men.

The loss sustained is as follows, viz: First Louisiana Cavalry, 1 com-missioned officer killed, 3 men killed, 7 men wounded, and 27 men missing; Fourteenth New York Cavalry, 4 missing, two of whom are known to be wounded and in the hands of the enemy; also lost 3 horses, and 12 wounded; total loss in killed and wounded and missing, 42.

It affords me great pleasure to state that the officers and men under my command have shown themselves on this, as well as other occasions, brave and gallant soldiers; and, although it was well known to them that they were fighting an enemy outnumbering us, yet no man has hesitated to attack them whenever I have ordered.

I have the honor to be, general, your most obedient servant,

JOHN G. FONDA,
Colonel, Commanding First Cavalry Brigade.

General BURBRIDGE,
Commanding Fourth Division, Thirteenth Army Corps.

—

HDQRS. SECOND BRIGADE, CAVALRY DIVISION,
Vermillion Bayou, November 12, 1863.

CAPTAIN: I have the honor to submit the following report of the operations of this brigade yesterday:

In accordance with previous orders, the cavalry under my command, consisting of 230 men of the Second Illinois, 115 of the Third Illinois, and 110 of the One hundred and eighteenth Illinois Mounted Infantry, were in line at division headquarters at daylight.

I was ordered to take the advance, and move out on the Opelousas road after passing the town of Vermillion. One squadron of Second Illinois Cavalry was sent forward as advance guard, and one squadron of same regiment sent to the right, with orders to move on that flank at about a half mile from the main column. We had not gone far when the enemy's pickets were discovered; they fell back to a lane, to what appeared to be their reserve. Thinking they might make some resistance, I sent forward another squadron of the Second Illinois. Nothing further of importance occurred on the march out. When within 2 miles of Carrion Crow Bayou, I was ordered to halt. A portion of the Third Illinois was ordered to the right, and the One hundred and eighteenth Illinois to dismount and sent to support Nims' battery; the remaining portion of the Second and Third Illinois were formed in column of companies. After remaining here about half an hour, General Lee ordered me to move back. The led horses of the One hundred and eighteenth were sent to the rear. Colonel Mudd, with Second Illinois, moved next.

The Third Illinois were called in, and the skirmishers ordered to fall back slowly. We had not gone far when the enemy began to annoy our rear. Captain Evans, with one platoon of the One hundred and eighteenth. was sent back to assist the flankers. The enemy's force continuing to accumulate, I sent back another squadron of the One hundred and eighteenth Illinois. When we had moved back about 4 miles, Capt. A. W. Marsh, who was in command of the One hundred and eighteenth, was killed. About this time the enemy attempted to make a charge on us, and at first I feared they would succeed, but I am happy to say that I was able to hold our men in their places, and the enemy was kept in check. They followed us to where we found their pickets in the morning, continually rushing up in the most daring manner, and annoying us with a galling fire. Soon after this, I passed inside of our infantry line, and moved all the cavalry to the right and rear.

After remaining here a short time, General Lee ordered me to send the

Third Illinois forward and to the right. Two squadrons of the Second Illinois were sent forward, and two to the left. Shortly after they were all withdrawn, and Colonel Mudd, with the Second Illinois, reported to General Lee. I was ordered to camp with the remaining portion of the command. A report of the killed and wounded has already been furnished.

 With great respect, your obedient servant,

JOHN G. FONDA,
Colonel, Commanding Brigade.

Capt. F. W. EMERY, *Assistant Adjutant-General.*

No. 14.

Report of Lieut. Col. Harai Robinson, First Louisiana Cavalry, of engagement at Bayou Bourbeau.

VERMILLION BAYOU, *November 5, 1863.*

MAJOR: Pursuant to instructions from Major-General Washburn, I forward this report of conclusions formed by me from conversation with the enemy's officers during yesterday's truce, and from report of First Lieutenant Gorman, First Louisiana Cavalry, wounded and taken prisoner in the late action, and who was returned yesterday among the wounded as a private soldier.

FLAG OF TRUCE.

Lieutenant-Colonel [G. J.] Hampton and Lieutenant [G. B.] Crain, bearers of the flag of truce, belonged to Colonel Bagby's [Hardeman's] Mounted Texas Regiment, which, with another Texas regiment (about 850 strong each), attacked on foot General Burbridge's front, while three other regiments, mounted, with the Valverde Battery, were sent around to attack our left and left flank. I saw two of these regiments moving around toward Opelousas after my last charge through the woods. Three regiments of Texas infantry, from Walker's division, commanded by Colonel [O. M.] Roberts, with one battery, moved down the Opelousas road, and attacked us on the right flank, all under command of General Green (officers would not admit that any other general was present). A number of ambulances came with them. This infantry has been a long time in service, and the officers boasted that it never had been under fire before. The regiments were full. This infantry was encamped at Moundville, 2 miles above Washington, since reconnaissance made by General Lee; that General Mouton (or some other general) has a division of Louisiana infantry for which Texas has a profound contempt.

 Green commands one brigade of Texas cavalry and Major another.

REPORT OF LIEUTENANT GORMAN.

Lieutenant Gorman was sent by me, according to directions of Colonel Fonda, with his squad on the right of our infantry regiment sent up through the woods on our right flank; was slightly wounded in the head in the commencement of the skirmishing and stunned for some time. His squadron was driven back, and he fell into the hands of the enemy; was taken out into the Opelousas road at the point where the reserve of our pickets had been stationed (about half a mile from General Burbridge's infantry camp). He saw enemy's infantry in two lines of battle within distance of 300 yards. These lines extended from within the woods as far as he could see in the open field toward the prairies; thinks there were about 3,500 men; did not see enemy's battery (it must have been in front line and behind him). He could not see from where he was the two dismounted regiments attacking our front; saw General Taylor between the two lines at the edge of the woods, cheering up the men; did not see General Green; afterward saw both of these generals visiting the hospital at Opelousas; was marched off to Mrs. Rodgers' plantation, where the enemy had established a hospital; saw fourteen regular ambulances and at least thirty plantation, and family vehicles on the road; the drivers of the latter were citizens, asking for enemy's wounded. Before arriving at Mrs. Rodgers' plantation, saw about 400 rebel cavalry strike off in a line leading to Grand Coteau; shortly after getting into the road, saw and counted 30 of the enemy's dead laid side by side (we buried more than 30 yesterday; I had 20 buried in one trench); this makes enemy's killed over 60. At Mrs. Rodgers' plantation, Lieutenant Gorman met a battery of six brass guns, called Saint Mary's [Cornay's], in position, and supported by 400 cavalry, and more cavalry off to the west of it. Lieutenant Gorman was allowed to remain only a few minutes at Mrs. Rodgers' plantation, and was hurried off to Opelousas, where he saw 200 men, provost-guard; no other troops. He bivouacked with some 300 other United States prisoners at General Green's camp near the church. In the morning was sent to the Court-House Hospital (rebel), to have his wounds dressed; he remained there until yesterday afternoon, when he was sent back with the rest of our wounded. He heard no movement of troops passing through Opelousas, although 600 were said to have passed this way the first night he was there. During the night he lay next to the church, soldiers were coming in by twos and threes, inquiring for their friends. These men said Watkins' camp was 2 miles this side Alexandria, but Lieutenant Gorman saw no camp-fires. Last night, returning (the ambulance at our pickets at 11 p. m.), Lieutenant Gorman counted nine camps, largest about one brigade, between Opelousas and Mrs. Rodgers' plantation. (I infer the smaller camps to have been cavalry.) The last night at least 600 mounted men were in line on either side of the road within a quarter of a mile of our pickets. The enemy admitted to him that they had 6,000 men in action.

   Very respectfully, your obedient servant,
                          HARAI ROBINSON,
          Lieutenant Colonel, Commanding First Louisiana Cavalry.
   Major MORGAN, *A. A. G., Thirteenth Army Corps.*

No. 15.

Report of Col. Thomas J. Lucas, Sixteenth Indiana Infantry, command-
   ing Cavalry Brigade, of affair at Bayou Portage.

   HEADQUARTERS FIRST BRIGADE, CAVALRY DIVISION,
          In the Field, near New Iberia, La., November 24, 1863.
   SIR: I have the honor to submit the following report of the operation of the forces under my command during the night of the 22d and
23d of November, 1863:
   In accordance with verbal instructions from General Lee, I moved
across the pontoon bridge with 200 of my brigade at 10 p. m., and struck
the Saint Martinsville road, Colonel Mudd's command joining me about
6 miles from town. I proceeded to the road leading to Dauterive's Landing, where I halted until Colonel Paine's command of 250 men joined me.
I sent Colonel Mudd down the road leading to Dauterive's Landing, with

instructions to lengthen his lines along the left, skirting the road. On account of the fog, at the fork of the road he took the wrong direction, and reached the lake some 3 miles below the point indicated, failing to connect with me, though I have no doubt he made all possible exertion, to co-operate with me. Leaving a force sufficient to hold the position at this cross-road, the strongest position to be found in that locality, I proceeded with my immediate command 1 mile farther, and took the road to the right, leading to the bridge across the bayou which connects with Grand Lake. At about half a mile I halted, and thoroughly searched all the dwellings, outhouses, and buildings on two adjoining plantations, which were said to be the lurking places of Major Dupeire and Captain Neville, but to no purpose. They were there during the early part of the evening, but had escaped.

Upon being joined by Colonel Paine's command, and 20 men under a lieutenant of Colonel Mudd's command, I proceeded down the road until near the bayou, when I halted. After sending Colonel Paine across the bridge to take a road leading to the rebel camp, I procured a guide, who showed me a lower road leading to the right of the rebel camp, where I crossed the bayou on a submerged bridge, sending in the meantime a lieutenant and 20 men to search a house on this side of the bayou, where they captured 4 prisoners. It was now daylight, and, hearing a few shots fired, I hurried forward, and found Colonel Paine already in possession of the rebel camp. He had advanced rapidly upon them, capturing a portion of their pickets. The woods were thoroughly scoured in all directions, but, owing to the swamps and the nature of the country, some of them escaped. After burning their camp, I started back toward our camp.

On reaching the road leading to Dauterive's Landing, I found that nothing had been learned at this point from Colonel Mudd, but afterward learned that he had captured Captain [B. D.] Dauterive and 8 others. As it was raining very hard, after sending a party to look for Colonel Mudd, I started for camp, which I reached at 3 p. m., November 23.

We captured 4 officers and about 30 men, a quantity of arms, mostly shotguns, and quite a number of horses. I complied with all of the general's orders, except proceeding to the saw-mill, which I deemed unnecessary upon receiving information from the guides.

All of which is respectfully submitted.

T. J. LUCAS,
Colonel, Commanding First Brigade, Cavalry Division.

Capt. F. W. EMERY, A. A. G., Cavalry Division.

No. 16.

Report of Col. Charles J. Paine, Second Louisiana Infantry, commanding Cavalry Brigade, of affair at Bayou Portage.

HEADQUARTERS THIRD BRIGADE,* CAVALRY DIVISION,
Near New Iberia, La., November 24, 1863.

SIR: I have the honor to report that, in obedience to verbal orders received from General Lee, commanding Cavalry Division, my command

---

* Organized November 7; to consist of Company F, Fifteenth Illinois; Company C, First Indiana; Company C, Fourth Indiana; the Second Louisiana Infantry (mounted), seven companies of the Sixth Missouri, and six companies of the Fourteenth New York.

of 250 men from my brigade marched at 11 p. m., November 22, and halted about 12 miles out for two hours, where a lieutenant and 20 men of the Second Illinois Cavalry reported for duty to me. I then marched at 3.30 a. m., November 23, slowly and carefully beating the fields on both sides with flankers, under Captain Carey, First Indiana Cavalry, to the bridge over Bayou Portage, just beyond which I captured 6 soldiers, fatigue party, with forage train.

· I marched down the bayou about 5 miles, and came on the enemy's pickets, about 10 strong. My advanced guards charged them and captured some; the rest took to the woods and escaped. The advance guard, which I then strengthened to 50 men, under Major [Bacon] Montgomery, Sixth Missouri, galloped half a mile farther into the enemy's camp, and captured many of them before they could escape to the woods. I scoured the woods with cavalry and infantry for 2 miles, picking up a few prisoners; burned the camp, with everything but the guns and property of use to us, which I brought away, including a number of horses; several of the enemy escaped, but, excepting some of their pickets, it is believed, none with arms.

I captured 25 enlisted men and 1 officer of Dupeire's battalion; 2 officers Eighteenth Louisiana; 28 in all, who have all been turned over to division provost-marshal. Two of the enemy were killed; none of our men were hurt; also the banner of the battalion, and the letter of presentation of same, with the papers of Major Dupeire, all of which have been turned over to General Lee. The camp was that of Major Dupeire, Confederate Zouaves.

I am, captain, very respectfully, your obedient servant,

CHARLES J. PAINE, •
Commanding Cavalry, Third Brigade.

Capt. F. W. EMERY,
Assistant Adjutant-General, Cavalry Division.

No. 17.

Abstracts from "Record of Events" on the several returns of the Cavalry Division, Department of the Gulf, for October and November.

DIVISION RETURN.

·The First Texas Cavalry and the First Louisiana Cavalry, then composing the First Brigade, Col. E. J. Davis commanding, and a portion of the Second Brigade, formed the advance [October 3], under Major-General Franklin, moving up Bayou Teche to Bayou Bourbeau. At Vermillion Bayou and Carrion Crow Bayou sharp engagements took place between the cavalry force of the enemy, numerically much superior to Colonel Davis' command, resulting in slight loss to our force. Forty prisoners were captured in these affairs. From Carrion Crow Bayou the First Texas Cavalry was ordered to New Orleans, to take part in the Texas expedition.

October 19.—General Lee took command in the field of the First and Second Brigades, and had the advance of the army in its movements to Opelousas and Barre's Landing. The enemy retreated before the advancing army, his cavalry force of 3,000 composing the rear guard, and making moderate resistance. General Franklin directed a reconnaissance from Barre's Landing and Opelousas to Washington and beyond, if possible. General Lee pushed 9 miles north of Washington with 1,500 cavalry, and discovered the movements and force of the enemy, the rebel rear guard of infantry and cavalry making steady resistance. Two thousand infantry of the enemy, near Moundville, left their camps in face of the reconnoitering force.

From October 15 to October 31, one-half of the small cavalry force was constantly in the saddle, engaged in scouts of greater or less extent. The Sixteenth Indiana Mounted Infantry was stationed near Vermillionville, guarding the communications of the army. The Second Louisiana and Eighty-seventh Illinois Mounted Infantry are at New Iberia, being mounted. Battery B, Massachusetts Light Artillery, was with the cavalry in the advance, doing fine service. The Fourth Wisconsin and Third Massachusetts Cavalry were at Baton Rouge and Port Hudson, respectively, engaged in outpost duty.

November 1.—The army under General Franklin fell back from Opelousas and Barre's Landing, the cavalry in the field serving as rear guard.

November 3.—Colonel Fonda's brigade, in the affair at Bayou Bourbeau or Grand Coteau, distinguished itself by gallant charges; 40 prisoners were taken by the cavalry.

November 7.—The cavalry was strengthened by mounting infantry, and newly brigaded.

November 11.—General Lee took from near Vermillion Bayou the First and Second Brigades, and developed the strength of the enemy at Carrion Crow Bayou, 16 miles distant. The reconnaissance was thoroughly successful, the enemy displaying cavalry, artillery, and infantry. On the return, the enemy pressed in superior force, both in rear and flank, but were successfully resisted. He followed to within 3 miles of Vermillionville, where lines were formed, and the First Brigade, Third Division, Nineteenth Army Corps, co-operating, the enemy was driven back in confusion.

November 20.—With a portion of each brigade, General Lee moved from New Iberia early in the morning, at daybreak surprised and surrounded a rebel outpost of 120 men at Camp Pratt, 6 miles above, wounding 2 men, and capturing 12 commissioned officers and 101 enlisted men of the Seventh Texas Cavalry.

November 23.—At daybreak an expedition under Colonel Lucas surprised the camp of Dupeire's battalion, near Grand Lake, and captured 4 officers and 31 enlisted men. The horses, arms, and the colors of the battalion were also taken.

November 25.—Moved from New Iberia to Camp Pratt on a reconnaissance. Colonel Fonda moved to within 5 miles of Vermillion Bayou with a portion of the Second and Third Illinois Cavalry, when, meeting a superior force of the enemy, he charged them, and, after a 5 miles' run, succeeded in capturing, under the guns of the enemy, in force on the opposite bank, 1 commissioned officer and 68 enlisted men.

RETURN OF THE FIRST BRIGADE.

October 19.—Colonel Fonda assumed command of the brigade. On the same day had a skirmish with the rebels on the Opelousas road.

October 21.—Broke up camp and moved on Opelousas. Heavy skirmishing most of the way. The Fourteenth New York Cavalry joined the brigade.

October 22.—Three hundred men marched in the direction of Ville Platte, and drove in the enemy's pickets.

October 24.—The whole brigade moved on Washington, and 300 men marched 6 miles beyond, and drove the enemy before them.

October 26.—Drove in the enemy's pickets on the Ville Platte road.

October 28.—Made a reconnaissance west of Opelousas.

October 30.—Thirty-two men of the First Louisiana Cavalry, while on a scout west of Opelousas, were attacked by a superior force. Lost 13 men, prisoners.

October 31.—Drove the enemy out of Washington.

November 7.—The brigade was reorganized.*

November 9.—Made a reconnaissance nearly to Indian Bayou. Skirmished with a small body of the enemy.

November 11.—Made a reconnaissance to Carrion Crow Bayou. Found the enemy in force, and fell back, skirmishing, to Vermillionville, where a very brisk skirmish ensued, in which we were victorious.

November 16.—Moved from Vermillion Bayou to Camp Pratt; bivouacked, and next morning moved to this place.

November 20.—Went to Camp Pratt, and surprised and captured 12 officers and 100 men.

November 23.—At daylight, surprised the camp of the Yellow Jacket Battalion [Fournet's], and captured 3 officers and 30 privates.

November 25.—Found a small force of the enemy at Camp Pratt, and, after a running fight of 10 miles, captured 8 officers and 70 men.

RETURN OF THE SECOND BRIGADE.†

October 1.—Troops in good condition.

October 4.—Three hundred men, under Lieutenant-Colonel Bush, reported to Colonel Davis, commanding First Brigade, with two days' rations.

October 10.—Moved to Vermillion.

October 21.—Marched to Barre's Landing, on Bayou Courtableau, flanking the enemy at Opelousas. The same day had a skirmish with the Fifth Texas Cavalry. Lost 8 men killed, wounded, and missing. Lieutenant-Colonel Bush joined me. Has had several skirmishes. Lost 4 in killed, wounded, and missing.

October 31.—Troops in good condition for service. No sour flour nor spoiled bacon issued. Hard bread and first-rate contraband beef in plenty.

November 1.—Marched from Opelousas, La., to Bayou Bourbeau, a distance of 10 miles.

November 2.—Skirmish.

November 3.—Battle of Grand Coteau, or Carrion Crow Bayou.

November 5.—Moved camp to Vermillion Bayou.

November 11.—Made a reconnaissance to Carrion Crow Bayou; sharp skirmishing on return march. Captain Marsh, of the One hundred and eighteenth Illinois, was killed.

November 16.—Moved camp to New Iberia.

November 20.—The brigade formed a part of an expedition to Camp Pratt; took 110 prisoners.

November 21.—Skirmish.

November 25.—With 200 men of the Second and Third Illinois Cavalry, took 67 prisoners near Vermillion Bayou.

---

* Under command of Colonel Lucas, and consisting of the Eighty-seventh Illinois and Sixteenth Indiana Infantry Regiments (mounted), and the First Louisiana Cavalry.

† Reorganized November 7, under command of Colonel Fonda; to consist of the Second and Third Illinois Cavalry, and the One hundred and eighteenth Illinois Infantry, mounted.

No. 18.

Daily Memoranda for Adjutant-General's Office, Department of the Gulf, October 9–14.

NEW ORLEANS.

October 9.—At 5 p. m. yesterday, the major-general commanding, with staff, arrived at Madame Olivier's plantation, on banks of Bayou Teche, about 3 miles below New Iberia. Further navigation of the bayou interrupted by wreck of steamer Hart, burned by the rebels during last campaign, to prevent her falling into our hands.

Dispatches received from Major-General Franklin on arrival of the boat, stating that he had awaited at Madame Olivier's plantation the arrival of the general commanding until 2 p. m., and had then left for the advance of his forces, some 12 miles beyond New Iberia, in the direction of Vermillion. There had been some skirmishing with the enemy's cavalry, which had been steadily driven back.

All the Nineteenth Army Corps had passed New Iberia, and one brigade of Washburn's division has gone forward.

Chief of staff telegraphed to assistant adjutant-general, New Orleans, special orders for Generals Asboth and P. St. George Cooke; first to go to Pensacola; latter to Baton Rouge; also in reference to artillery for Port Hudson.

Instructions sent to General Franklin, approving his intention to move on to Vermillion Bayou. Orders given to Major-General Ord to send forward the remaining brigade of First Division, Thirteenth Corps, at 6 a. m. following morning, viz, to-day. Steamer A. G. Brown, which brought the general and staff up, ordered back to Brashear to bring up supplies.

Orders sent to Major-General Dana, through acting assistant adjutant-general, New Orleans, to bring his force away from Morgan's Bend to Carrollton, and prepare his division to take the field. Orders sent to Capt. R. T. Dunham, assistant adjutant-general, to report by telegraph whether or not light iron-clads or tin-clads could be expected, and to report at headquarters in the field without delay.

At daybreak, received dispatch from Major-General Franklin, reporting his cavalry advance at Bayou Vermillion; enemy in some force. Dispatch dated 1.30 a. m. to-day stated that the enemy had been driven by our cavalry in skirmish, and had fallen back across bridge and burned it; that he should move forward and dislodge him. Orders given to Major-General Ord to place one good brigade at Franklin. Dispatch received from Captain Dunham, stating that Admiral Porter had sent three tin-clads, but did not think it best to send any iron-clads, during low stage of water. Telegram sent to acting assistant adjutant-general, New Orleans, to have any tin-clads which might arrive sent at once to Berwick Bay, for co-operation with troops in the field.

At 11 a. m. commanding general and staff left to join General Franklin; stopped at wreck of Hart, and witnessed explosion of charge under her boilers, which was highly successful, and threw them clear of the bed and nearly on shore. Charge placed and exploded by Captain Bulkley. Continued route; passed New Iberia, and, when about half-way to Bayou Vermillion, received dispatch from General Franklin, stating that he held the end of the bridge over Bayou Vermillion and could hold it, and that the cavalry was crossing at a ford above; some skirmishing; continued on, and arrived at bayou, General Franklin's headquarters, at 3.30 p. m.

Sent back dispatch by hands of Major Wilson to Major-General Ord, desiring him to move forward at 6 a. m. to-morrow, with the force with , him, leaving one strong regiment and 100 cavalry at the head of navigation on the Teche.

The general and staff accompanied Generals Franklin and Weitzel to the Bayou Bridge. Found Weitzel's division holding position of bridge, with one regiment across; Grover's division holding position of ford, about 1 mile above, where the cavalry had passed. Slight bridge had been constructed, on which Generals Banks, Franklin, and Stone passed. Chief of staff rode forward to junction of roads leading respectively from ford and bridge to town, and found that point well held by Colonel Davis' cavalry. Village in sight; rode forward, and made slight reconnaissance; could see only a dozen or fifteen cavalry in outskirts of village. General Franklin commenced laying down two pontoon bridges at position of burnt bridge, capable of crossing artillery with safety. Casualties reported during the day: 1 major and 1 private wounded.

At 8 p. m. received dispatches from General Lee, chief of cavalry, giving notice of sending 200 mounted infantry and mountain howitzer battery to-morrow to Brashear. Also notice that steamer Red Chief had arrived at Brashear, and is partly loaded, and that Hancox had left Brashear with barge in tow having 100,000 rations—well.

Orders to General Lee to make preparations to come up. These orders sent to New Iberia to telegraph.

Memoranda closed at 8.30 p. m., October 9.

October 10.—Last night, between sunset and 9 p. m., two pontoon bridges were thrown across Vermillion Bayou, near the site of the late bridge on main road, by order of Major-General Franklin, and one brigade of Weitzel's division, Nims' light battery, and one field battery were thrown over the bayou before 10 p. m.

The enemy made no demonstrations during the night. Early this morning the cavalry under Colonel Davis and a section of Nims' battery advanced. Two shells from Nims' guns scattered the small force displayed near the village of Vermillionville, and our cavalry pursued the fugitives 1½ miles beyond the village. Cavalry outposts were gradually advanced during the day, with a little random firing between our advance and small bodies of the enemy's cavalry, until to-night we hold the road for 5 miles beyond Vermillionville, on the way to Opelousas.

The Nineteenth Corps crossed the bayou, and encamped on the north side before noon to-day. Washburn's division, Thirteenth Corps, came up during the morning, and crossed immediately, camping on the left of Weitzel. About noon, the chief of staff, with part of headquarters escort, visited the advanced pickets, and reconnoitered those of the enemy 5 miles beyond Vermillion. The only force displayed seemed to be about 20 cavalry, although our pickets reported that they had seen about 80. The escort was fired upon as it advanced, but no damage done.

General headquarters established in lawn before the house of Mr. Basil Crow, near the bridge. General Franklin's headquarters in rear of Governor Mouton's mansion. Good order was maintained in Vermillionville by a provost-guard from Weitzel's division. Major-General Ord arrived about 5 p. m.; left two divisions of his corps about 10 miles in rear, and reported with his headquarters train, in obedience to instructions. There was left at the head of navigation on Bayou Teche a force of two regiments and 100 cavalry. One hundred cavalry, under Colonel Mudd, were sent by orders from these headquarters this morning from New Iberia to Saint Martinsville, where a small force of the enemy's cavalry was seen yesterday, reported 60 strong.

The people in this parish represent that they are heartily tired of Texan rule, and it is indicated that if the Government will furnish a basis of protection, a mere point of support, they will make armed resistance to another invasion by the Confederates.

This evening, 6 o'clock, Nineteenth Army Corps and Davis' cavalry brigade ordered to march to-morrow to Carrion Crow Bayou, on Opelousas road.

Memoranda closes at 7 p. m.

October 11.—Memoranda yesterday closed at 7 p. m. Nothing of importance occurred during the night. There was some uneasiness felt at headquarters by reason of not hearing of arrival of boats at New Iberia with provisions.

General Burbridge's division (Fourth), Thirteenth Army Corps, arrived at Vermillion Bayou early in the evening.

The Nineteenth Army Corps commenced its forward movement at sunrise, and at 9 a. m. was clear of the town of Vermillion, with no stragglers in sight. Some depredations reported on the part of the Thirteenth Army Corps. Two regiments of the First Division, Thirteenth Corps, moved to the right, and occupied position held until this morning by Weitzel's division. An Illinois regiment of mounted infantry arrived, and was ordered to report to Major-General Ord.

A reconnaissance was thrown out from headquarters of department, under Major Fullerton, to examine the country on the right as far as Breaux Bridge, and ascertain whether the enemy are in any force in that direction.

Major-General Franklin, at 12.30 p. m., reported his presence at Bayou Carrion Crow, the enemy having fallen back before him without fighting. Generals Mouton and Green, with about 1,000 men, left this morning the position now held by Franklin.

Hon. Albert Voorhees, judge of the supreme court of Louisiana, reported himself in camp, in compliance with his parole given yesterday to Major Fullerton, at Saint Martinsville. The general ordered him to New Orleans, and directed that his parole should be taken to report at New Iberia, and that he should be allowed to take his family with him.

The general commanding made preparations to go to New Orleans, and directed that orders should be given to the corps quartermasters to seize all the available horses in this part of the country within reach of our forces for the purposes of the army. He also directed that the troops shall move forward toward Washington as rapidly as they can be securely furnished with supplies.

Memoranda closes at 5.30 p. m.

October 12.—The major-general commanding left headquarters after dark last night, with escort of an officer and 16 men of headquarters cavalry, and accompanied by Lieutenant [Charles S.] Sargent, aide-de-camp, for New Orleans, via New Iberia. General Ord notified that command of troops in the field devolved upon him. Major Fullerton returned from his scout to Breaux Bridge, bringing 2 prisoners, privates of Second Louisiana (rebel) Cavalry. He found no force of the enemy in that region. General Franklin sent in 4 prisoners from the front at Carrion Crow Bayou. They were closely examined by the chief of staff, and sent to provost-marshal Thirteenth Army Corps. Several cases of depredations on the citizens by men straggling from camps reported, and measures adopted to prevent continuance of such conduct.

This morning Lieutenant-Colonels Small and Chandler arrived. General Arnold received orders to proceed to New Orleans, and undertake the supervision of the command of the permanent works near New

Orleans. He left at 2 p. m. for New Iberia, accompanied by Lieutenant Ramsay. General Franklin was duly notified of General Banks' departure.

General Ord reported to the chief of staff that he was ill, and desired that he would give all necessary orders. About noon it was reported that Colonel Lucas, instead of reporting to General Ord, had gone on and reported to General Franklin, so that our flank had been uncovered all night and half the day. Chief of staff immediately signaled to General Franklin, and Colonel Lucas was sent back. His command was posted north of Vermillionville, with orders to watch and scout the roads leading north and west from that village, and a portion of the line toward General Franklin. Trains arrived bringing seven days' provisions for Thirteenth Army Corps, and trains reported on the way bringing additional for the Nineteenth Corps. A great deal of straggling and marauding on the part of soldiers reported, and stringent orders were given by General Ord to his division and brigade commanders to prevent it.

Captain Dunham arrived in camp about 4 p. m., bringing papers from assistant adjutant-general's office, New Orleans, of 10th; acted on, and ordered sent back.

Arrival in New Orleans of Colonel Dwight and Major Carpenter reported by acting assistant adjutant-general, and orders asked for given.

At 7.30 p. m., General [John G.] Pratt and his nephew, his aide decamp, of State of Louisiana service, arrived as prisoners, sent in by General Franklin. Allowed them to remain on parole at Mr. Crow's residence for the night, to be sent down to New Orleans to-morrow.

Memoranda closes at 8 p. m.

CHAS. P. STONE,
Brigadier-General, Chief of Staff.

—

VERMILLION BAYOU.

October 13.—Reports from General Franklin state all quiet in his front; slight skirmishing with the enemy's cavalry. Major Elfield, assistant engineer to Major Houston, sent out on a reconnaissance to Breaux Bridge, with an escort of 6 mounted men from Colonel Mudd's command. He returned at 4.30 p. m., reporting that he proceeded as far as Breaux Bridge, finding that the bridge had been burned, but could be repaired, requiring new timber, as the abutments still stand.

He saw at the distance a few mounted men of the enemy, but no force had been there in two or three days.

. The small bridges over the gullies have been torn up, but can be repaired in a few hours. He reports he saw no picket or scout of ours, except the one stationed 1½ miles beyond Lafayette, and reports that there would be no difficulty for either cavalry or infantry of the enemy to approach this place by the way of Newton Bridge, and suggested the propriety of establishing a picket at the latter place. Reported to Major-General Ord.

Brigadier-General Stone, chief of staff, left here at 12.45 p. m. for New Orleans, via New Iberia, escorted by 6 men and a non-commissioned officer of the headquarters cavalry. Captain Dunham accompanied him to New Iberia, and was to return in the morning.

Orderly arrived at 5 p. m., with dispatches from New Iberia for Major Houston and Colonel Chandler.

A citizen came in this evening from Saint Landry Parish, and reports that the enemy are between Washington and Holmesville; the most of their wagons and baggage have been sent on toward Alexandria; force said to be about 10,000 men, under Generals Green, Walker, and Mouton; has traveled 25 miles on our left flank, and has seen no armed men of the enemy on the route. He thinks their whole force will fall back on Alexandria, if pressed by our advance.

Until Sunday the enemy had a regular line of couriers established between Vermillion and Opelousas and the Texas line; says the Texans have driven off almost all the negroes to Texas. Governor Moore and Kirby Smith said to be at Shreveport; estimates the whole force of the enemy in this State at 25,000. Seventy-five wagons arrived with supplies; 30 men and 1 officer ordered to escort a part of this train to General Franklin's command. Notes close at 8 p. m.

October 14.—Two negroes came in, reporting that there was a force of 300 mounted men of the enemy on the Teche, in the neighborhood of Breaux Bridge, waiting for an opportunity for our main force to pass this point, in order that they might attack our supply trains coming forward. Communicated this to General Ord, in the absence of the major-general commanding.

General Ord sent a force of infantry and mounted men to ascertain the fact, and capture the party, if possible.

In obedience to a telegram received from headquarters Department of the Gulf, at New Orleans, Major Houston, chief engineer, left here at 3 p. m. for New Orleans; Major Elfield ordered to act as chief engineer of these headquarters in Major Houston's absence.

At 5 p. m. the signal officer reported heavy firing in the direction of General Franklin's force. At 9 p. m. received a dispatch from Major-General Franklin, stating that Colonel Davis, First Texas Cavalry, would be sent to New Orleans as soon as his picket could be withdrawn (in obedience to instructions received from the major-general commanding, through General Ord); reports also that the enemy have a force on our right flank, near Vermillion Bayou, and that he does not need any more infantry, but cavalry, as the enemy are endeavoring to find some weak point in our line to make an attack. This dispatch communicated to General Ord at 9.20 p. m., and also a copy to the major-general commanding at New Orleans. Received some rebel prisoners from the Nineteenth Corps and forwarded them to General Ord.

The One hundred and eighteenth Illinois Mounted Infantry arrived this evening, and encamped opposite these headquarters.

Memoranda closed at 9.30 p. m.

J. SCHUYLER CROSBY,
Acting Assistant Adjutant-General.

No. 19.

Report of Lieut. Gen. E. Kirby Smith, C. S. Army, commanding Trans-Mississippi Department.

HEADQUARTERS DEPARTMENT OF THE TRANS-MISSISSIPPI,
Shreveport, La., November 8, 1863.

I have the honor to inclose the last dispatch received from General Taylor, announcing a successful attack of General Green upon the enemy's retreating column.

I would respectfully call the attention of the Department to General Taylor's late operations in Lower Louisiana. Cautious, yet bold; always prepared for and anticipating the enemy; concentrating skillfully upon his main force, holding it in check, and crippling its movements; promptly striking his detached columns, routing and destroying them, the enemy have been completely foiled in the objects of their campaign, and have fallen back for a new plan and a new line of operations. General Taylor has been ably assisted by his subordinates, and in this connection I would respectfully urge upon His Excellency the President the immediate appointment of general officers to his command. Not only will its efficiency be increased, but the services of the officers merit the promotion.

Brig. Gen. Thomas Green, commanding the Cavalry Division, should be made major-general for his repeated successes throughout the operations in Lower Louisiana. He is a rising officer, and has displayed greater ability and military genius than any officer of his grade in the department. Col. A. P. Bagby, commanding Green's brigade, with Col. J. P. Major, Col. Horace Randal, and Col. J. W. Speight, each commanding brigades, should be promoted to brigadier-generals.

I am, general, respectfully, your obedient servant,

E. KIRBY SMITH,
Lieutenant-General, Commanding.

General S. COOPER, *Adjutant-General, C. S. Army.*

[Indorsements.]

DECEMBER 22, 1863.

Respectfully submitted to Secretary of War. The want of proper returns from the Trans-Mississippi Department makes it impossible to determine here the wants of general officers for the various commands there, consistent with a proper organization agreeably to acts of Congress. According to these acts, general officers can be appointed to the command of army corps, divisions, and brigades. From the last returns of that department received here, dated June 1, 1863, it appears that Brigadier-General Green, who is recommended within for advancement to major-general, was commanding a cavalry brigade of four regiments, and Colonels Randal and Speight, also recommended within for advancement to brigadiers, were then commanding brigades. Col. J. P. Major, who is likewise recommended within for brigadier, was long since appointed brigadier, to report to Major-General Taylor, and the returns show that he was commanding a brigade before he was thus appointed. I have written to General Smith to require a full return of the brigades and divisions of his command, and for the names and rank of the general officers in his command, with a view of ascertaining whether these late recommendations of his can be legally sustained by appointment.

S. COOPER,
Adjutant and Inspector General.

DECEMBER 29, 1863.

Respectfully submitted to the President. General Green might, I think, be at once promoted, as a major-general in addition is probably wanted. The other promotions might await the answer to General Cooper's inquiry.

J. A. SEDDON,
Secretary of War.

SECRETARY OF WAR:

It is deemed better to wait for the present a reply from General Smith.

J. D. [JEFFERSON DAVIS.]

No. 20.

Reports of Maj. Gen. Richard Taylor, C. S. Army, commanding District of Western Louisiana.

HEADQUARTERS DISTRICT OF WESTERN LOUISIANA,
Alexandria, October 6, 1863.

COLONEL: By direction of Major-General Taylor, I have the honor to inclose the accompanying copy of a letter from General Mouton,* and the pass given by Major-General Franklin, from which you will perceive the condition of affairs below. I also quote the following from General Taylor's letter:

> There is no doubt that the enemy is advancing in very large force. Whether it is his intention to march to the Red River Valley before going to Texas has not yet been developed, but to-day or to-morrow will decide what he means.

You know he can strike out by the road from Vermillionville, or from New Iberia, via Abbeville, to Niblett's Bluff. I shall gradually and quietly remove surplus stores from this point. There are some 470 or 480 Federal prisoners, captured by General Green, who will be started for Shreveport to-morrow morning.

Very respectfully, your obedient servant,
E. SURGET,
Assistant Adjutant-General.

Col. S. S. ANDERSON,
Assistant Adjutant-General.

[Indorsement.]

HDQRS. DEPARTMENT OF THE TRANS–MISSISSIPPI,
Shreveport, La., October 9, 1863.

Respectfully forwarded to Major-General Magruder for his information.

By order of Lieut. Gen. E. Kirby Smith:
S. S. ANDERSON,
Assistant Adjutant-General.

—

HEADQUARTERS DISTRICT OF WESTERN LOUISIANA,
Opelousas, October 11, 1863—2 a. m.

GENERAL: I have just returned from the front near Vermillionville. We had some brisk skirmishing at the Bayou Vermillion to-day, inflicting some loss to the enemy. The bayou being low and fordable in many places, the enemy succeeded in forcing a passage by bringing up heavy masses at different fords. The enemy moves with the greatest caution. Nothing can induce his cavalry to separate 500 yards from his infantry supports. Franklin, with his corps (the Nineteenth) is at Vermillionville, and a large part of the Thirteenth Corps is in close proximity. I think a fair estimate of Franklin's strength is 10,000. The Thirteenth Corps is believed to be larger. The priest from Abbeville to-day reports that he met on the 10th, on the road from New Iberia to Abbeville, a force of some 2,000 mounted men, escorting a pontoon train.

---

* See Report No. 21, p. 393.

If this be the case, the enemy are going the west road to Niblett's, cross-ing the Vermillion and Mermenton at the lower ferries, and using these streams and the Calcasieu to run in supplies to their column by light craft. He may then move his masses well together, and render it impos-sible for me to bring him to action without encountering an overwhelm-ing force. He could entirely abandon one base as soon as another was reached. Could General Magruder send a force to the Calcasieu, or even this side, he could not only materially delay the enemy's move-ments, but might very likely capture a fleet of supplies or destroy a pontoon train. Such a force could always fall back on Niblett's as its base. The conformation of the country prevents me from sending a force for the purpose indicated, as the enemy, marching by the west road, throws me on my exterior lines.

I will communicate to this effect to General Magruder, and respect-fully request that the lieutenant-general commanding will do so in addi-tion, if he approve the views expressed.*

Respectfully, your obedient servant,

R. TAYLOR,
Major-General.

Brig. Gen. W. R. BOGGS,
Chief of Staff.

HEADQUARTERS DISTRICT OF WESTERN LOUISIANA,
Opelousas, October 11, 1863.

GENERAL: I have just returned from the front of my army, and have clearly ascertained the position of the enemy, and am enabled to esti-mate his (approximate) strength. Franklin's Army Corps (Nineteenth), with one brigade of the Thirteenth Corps (Washburn's), is above the Ver-million Bridge, about 1½ miles below Vermillionville, with his advance from 6 to 7 miles above Vermillionville. Washburn's corps is within easy supporting distance of Franklin. I think Franklin's strength is about 10,000; the Thirteenth is somewhat larger.

The priest from Abbeville to-day reports that he met on the 10th, on the road from New Iberia to Abbeville, a force of some 2,000 mounted men, escorting a pontoon train. If this be the case, the enemy are going by the Coast road to Niblett's Bluff, crossing the Vermillion and Mer-menton at the lower ferries, and using these streams and the Calcasieu to run in supplies to their column by light craft. He may then move his masses well together, and render it impossible for me to bring him to action without encountering an overwhelming force. He could entirely abandon one base as soon as another was reached. If you can send a force to the Calcasieu, or even this side of that stream, you cannot only materially delay the enemy's movements, but might very likely capture a fleet of supplies or destroy a pontoon train. Such a force could always fall back on Niblett's Bluff as its base. The conformation of the country prevents me from sending a force for the purpose indicated, as the enemy, marching by the Coast road, throws me on very exterior lines. I will endeavor from time to time to advise you of all the move-ments of the enemy which I can ascertain. When I received your com-munication relative to sending Major Rountree's cavalry to you, it was impossible to do so, as it was then across the Atchafalaya, with the ex-pedition under General Green which terminated so successfully. At

---

* Copy transmitted by Smith to Magruder, October 15, 1863.

present I cannot send it to Texas, but will do so at the earliest moment when the movement can be effected.*

I remain, general, very respectfully, your obedient servant,

R. TAYLOR,
Major-General, Commanding.

Maj. Gen. J. B. MAGRUDER,
  Comdg. District of Texas, Arizona, and New Mexico.

HEADQUARTERS DISTRICT OF WESTERN LOUISIANA,
Washington, October 20, 1863.

GENERAL: Yesterday evening the enemy threw forward a heavy force of all arms, and drove in our advance pickets. General Green promptly re-enforced, and a very brisk skirmish ensued. I reached the front at dusk, and found that the enemy had been driven back, leaving some dead on the field. We lost 3 killed and some wounded; the exact number I have not yet had a report of. Green contested the ground with his usual obstinacy, and prevented the enemy from gaining a knowledge of his position, which seems to have been the object of his advance. All quiet so far this morning (8 a. m). I returned from the extreme front after midnight, the enemy having retired to his previous encampment. A scouting party returned on yesterday from between New Iberia and Abbeville. They report all quiet on the Texas roads; no evidence of a movement in that direction; also that Banks had reached New Iberia, and that the enemy's whole army was in my immediate front. They report, in addition, that scouts of General Magruder were met by them at Mermenton Crossing.

I feel anxious about the Red River obstructions. Major [H. T.] Douglas has not as yet communicated with me. The uncertain purposes of the enemy necessarily prevent any work for the time as low as the Rapids. I think every preparation should be made to obstruct the river above.

Respectfully, your obedient servant,

R. TAYLOR,
Major-General.

Brig. Gen. W. R. BOGGS,
  Chief of Staff.

HEADQUARTERS DISTRICT OF WESTERN LOUISIANA,
Washington, October 21, 1863—9 a. m.

GENERAL: I have the honor to report that the dispositions of the enemy indicate an advance in force to-day. A column is moving up also on the Teche road, to strike the Courtableau below Washington, and turn the left of my position in front of Opelousas. This, with the largely superior force of the enemy, will compel me to move to the north of Washington. Fifty pieces of artillery, including seven 20 and 30 pounder Parrotts, 1,500 cavalry, and 20,000 infantry, have passed New Iberia in this direction. Five hundred army wagons, prepared with water-tanks, large stores of marching rations, accompany them. General Ord has taken command of the Thirteenth Corps, and Banks is now present with the troops. Officers and men all say Texas is the objective point

---

* See Magruder to Taylor, October 18, Part II, p. 335.

of the movement. No water expedition is in contemplation from Berwick Bay. Three regiments and four pieces of artillery have been left at Franklin, and a strong guard at New Iberia. All the remainder are in my front. If the enemy follows me north of the Courtableau without detaching to the west, then Northern Texas, and not Niblett's, will be his object.

Respectfully, your obedient servant,

R. TAYLOR,
Major-General.

Brigadier-General Boggs,
Chief of Staff.

—

HEADQUARTERS DISTRICT OF WESTERN LOUISIANA,
Washington, October 22, 1863.

GENERAL: I have the honor to report that, on yesterday morning, the advance of the enemy along his whole line compelled me to withdraw from Opelousas. The enemy's advance of some 5,000 up the Teche road turned our position at Opelousas. This I was prepared to expect. After some skirmishing in front of Opelousas, in which we lost 2 killed, General Green withdrew to Washington, inflicting some loss on the enemy. The expedition sent by General Green, under Colonel [W. G.] Vincent, Second Louisiana, to the enemy's rear, on the 13th, returned last night, bringing 1 lieutenant and 7 men of the signal corps, captured near Vermillion. The lieutenant had on him a signal book, with copies of many important dispatches between Franklin, Ord, and Banks. The latter was with the enemy on the 8th instant, but subsequently returned to New Orleans. It appears from these dispatches that some thousand wagons crossed Berwick Bay; that the reserve artillery at Baton Rouge has been ordered to the army; that the enemy are increasing their cavalry. The last dispatch from Banks to Franklin, of the 20th, directs him to establish and hold the best line he can, and wait for the Red Chief to arrive. This is a very small, light steamer, that is intended to navigate the Courtableau. I have taken measures to destroy her if she comes up.

On the 7th instant, Banks telegraphs:

It is my wish that the advance should be made sufficiently [strong] to cover the Courtableau. I am sure of the safety of Barre's Landing; that being accomplished, the base of supplies can be changed.

Now, Barre's Landing is 12 miles below Washington, on the Courtableau, and is where the Teche communicates with it. A change of base of supplies from Barre's Landing must mean Simsport—at least, that is what I suppose—for the time. No appearance of a movement west, and Barre's Landing is entirely out of the direction of Texas.

Then, all conclusions point to a farther advance in this direction. From different sources of information, I find the first plan of the enemy was to secure Sabine Pass with Franklin's expedition, which consisted of 5,000 men, or the two brigades of Weitzel and Emory. As soon as Sabine Pass was secured, Ord, with a heavy force, then at Ship Island, was to re-enforce Franklin at Sabine Pass. Washburn, with 13,000 men, was sent to Berwick Bay, to drive me from the Teche as soon as Franklin succeeded. At the same time, Herron's division was sent to Morganza, to cross in my rear and prevent me from reaching Red River and Shreveport, while Franklin, by guarding the Sabine River, would prevent me from reaching Texas. The failure of Franklin to reach Sabine Pass, and the defeat of Herron's division at the Fordoche, have defeated this notable scheme. Franklin, Ord, and Herron have all joined Washburn below, as have the troops from Port Hudson and Baton Rouge, excepting small garrisons.

The withdrawal of Lee's cavalry from Mississippi having relieved the enemy of all apprehension on the east bank of the river, I shall watch the Texas road closely, as well as Simsport and the Atchafalaya. The enemy are just advancing on this place from Barre's Landing. From Opelousas also they are moving—2 p. m.

Respectfully, your obedient servant;

R. TAYLOR,
Major-General.

Brig. Gen. W. R. BOGGS,
Chief of Staff.

—

HEADQUARTERS DISTRICT OF WESTERN LOUISIANA,
Bayou Bœuf, October 23, 1863—9 p. m.

GENERAL: I have just returned from a visit to the front, near Washington. The enemy have a large force at Barre's Landing, 12 miles below Washington, on the Courtableau, and are preparing to bridge that bayou, when they will take the road—a perfectly practicable one—by Big Cane, striking the Bayou Bœuf at its junction with the Huff-power. I have just heard, indirectly, from Colonel Major, that the enemy are advancing in large force on the road leading by Chicot to Alexandria and Natchitoches. As this last mentioned is the shortest one to both those places, I have sent a staff officer to verify the report, and, if correct, I shall at once fall back, so as to make that road. I think that all thought of the enemy moving to Texas now may be dismissed, unless after first marching up the valley of Red River to Shreveport. I have directed all the sick and others which are at Alexandria to be removed at once to Natchitoches.

Very respectfully, your obedient servant,

R. TAYLOR,
Major-General, Commanding.

· Brig. Gen. W. R. BOGGS,
Chief of Staff.

—

HEADQUARTERS DISTRICT OF WESTERN LOUISIANA,
Bayou Bœuf, October 25, 1863.

GENERAL: Yesterday morning the enemy advanced some 5 miles above Washington, on the Bœuf road. We were drawn up to oppose them or fight; the enemy, however, declined, and returned to Washington.

Last night, Colonel Major captured 23 of the Thirteenth Corps below Opelousas. We have beaten the enemy in a number of skirmishes, taking prisoners. He, however, declines any serious engagement unless he has his whole force in hand. No movement toward the west. All the recent prisoners say the expedition is going to Alexandria and Shreveport. I have moved the main body of my forces to the Huff-power, as we have entirely consumed the forage on the Lower Bœuf. In addition, I can throw more cavalry on the prairies to the enemy's left, not having the Big Cane road to guard. I have just received another communication from General Magruder, urging me to move at once to Niblett's Bluff. He thinks a large force is at Ship Island, to co-operate with the expedition in my front. Ord, who was at Ship Island, is with the army here, and I think no movement on Texas is possible. My pickets are still up to Washington, where the enemy have now a very heavy force.

Respectfully, your obedient servant,

R. TAYLOR,
Major-General.

Brig. Gen. W. R. Boggs,
Chief of Staff.

—

HEADQUARTERS DISTRICT OF WESTERN LOUISIANA,
Opelousas, November 4, 1863.

GENERAL: The enemy in my front are retreating to Berwick Bay. Yesterday we overtook their rear guard 9 miles below this place, and defeated them completely, capturing one gun and some 600 prisoners. It was a portion of the Thirteenth Corps, from Vicksburg. I have just received positive information from New Orleans that an expedition of some 5,000 men is near the Balize, in the river, with Banks in person in command. The last rumors point to Mobile as the objective point, to relieve Rosecrans, but I have nothing but rumors. The expedition to Texas by land is abandoned, and you, of course, can judge what point of Western Texas is most likely to be attacked. The vessels at the Balize are all sea transports.

Your obedient servant,

R. TAYLOR,
Major-General.

Maj. Gen. J. B. Magruder,
Commanding Texas, &c.

—

SHREVEPORT, LA.,
November 7, 1863.

We take the following from the Caddo Gazette Extra, November 7, 1863:

The following official letter from General Taylor to General Boggs has been given us for publication:

"WASHINGTON, LA.,
"*November 5,* [1863.]

"GENERAL: In my previous report, I had the honor to inform you that, learning of the enemy's movements in retreat, General [Thomas] Green, with his division of cavalry and three regiments of infantry, was ordered to pursue and harass the retreat.

"On the 2d, the enemy withdrew from Opelousas, Colonel [J. P.] Major, with his brigade, skirmishing briskly with the enemy all day and delaying his movements. Late in the day, General Green pursued him with Green's brigade, commanded by Colonel [A. P.] Bagby, and the three regiments of infantry, with the Valverde Battery. General Green made his preparations for attacking the following morning. The enemy's rear guard was encamped on the Bourbeau, 7 miles below Opelousas.

"Green attacked with his usual energy; captured one Parrott gun, their camp, with all its contents, and over 600 prisoners, including 2 colonels, 1 lieutenant-colonel, 10 captains, and 17 lieutenants. After routing the enemy and holding his camp for two hours, heavy re-enforcements, under [W. B.] Franklin, came up, and forced Green to withdraw to the vicinity of Opelousas, which he did, bringing off the gun and prisoners. The force engaged and whipped proved to be Washburn's division of the Thirteenth Corps, from Vicksburg, and numbered about 4,000. A force of equal or superior strength came to their assistance.

"Our loss in all, perhaps, 100, including 30 killed. The enemy's camp was burned before leaving it, and his dead and wounded left on the field. His loss in killed and wounded was very severe, and is not included in the computation of prisoners above.

"R. TAYLOR,
" Major-General."

[Indorsement.]

HEADQUARTERS DISTRICT OF ARKANSAS,
November 8, 1863. '

General [J. S.] MARMADUKE:

GENERAL: The preceding statement was telegraphed to Camden from Shreveport, and forwarded to these headquarters by General [J. F.] Fagan.

Respectfully,

J. F. BELTON,
Lieutenant-Colonel, and Assistant Adjutant-General.

—

HEADQUARTERS DISTRICT OF WESTERN LOUISIANA,
Bayou Bœuf, November 7, 1863.

GENERAL: I have the honor to forward herewith the report of Brigadier-General Thomas Green of the action of the 3d instant, near Opelousas. Too much praise cannot be given to General Green and the troops engaged. The exact moment when a heavy blow could be given was seized in a masterly manner. I have so frequently had occasion to commend the conduct of General Green, that I have nothing to add in his praise, except that he has surpassed my expectations, which I did not think possible. This officer has within the past few months commanded in three successful engagements—on the La Fourche, on the Fordoche, and near Opelousas—two of which were won against heavy odds. His sphere of usefulness should be enlarged by his promotion to a major-general. He is now commanding a division of cavalry, and I respectfully urge that he be promoted. I also beg leave to repeat the recommendation previously forwarded for the promotion of Colonel Major. This officer has for some months been in command of a brigade, and has shown marked energy and ability. On the 3d instant he led a brilliant and effective charge on the enemy's line.

Respectfully, your obedient servant,

R. TAYLOR,
Major-General.

Brig. Gen. W. R. BOGGS,
Chief of Staff.

[Indorsement.]

HDQRS. DEPARTMENT OF THE TRANS-MISSISSIPPI,
Shreveport, November 24, 1863.

Respectfully forwarded, with the request that the attention of His Excellency the President may be called to the recommendation of Major-General Taylor in the cases of Brigadier-General Green and Colonel Major.

E. KIRBY SMITH,
Lieutenant-General, Commanding.

No. 21.

*Report of Brig. Gen. Alfred Mouton, C. S. Army, commanding Sub-
District of Southwestern Louisiana, of affair at Nelson's Bridge, &c.*

CAMP PRATT, LA.,
October 4, 1863—7.30 p. m.

GENERAL : I have the honor to report the enemy at New Iberia. We
left the town at sundown. Colonel Vincent ambuscaded them at Nelson's Bridge, and their advance driven in, leaving the road full of dead
and wounded. I will move this command, say about 250 men, beyond
the Vermillion after midnight to-night, leaving only men enough to
observe and get on their flank, so as to find out their exact strength.
They are in large force. Colonel Major cannot reach the Vermillion
before to-morrow night. I have sent him orders to cut across the country, and cross the Vermillion at Mouton's Bridge, 6 miles above the
public bridge. I cannot do anything except watch their movements
and ascertain their force. A prisoner taken this evening states the
enemy have seven regiments cavalry, a very large quantity of artillery,
among them the siege Parrotts. He says he has always heard there
were 75,000 men under General Franklin ; they are going to Texas. The
expedition by water was given up. General Banks is in New Orleans.
General Grant, he says, is expected, having gone to Mobile. He says
their camps extended from near Berwick Bay to near Franklin, showing these by their force. The prisoner is an American, rather intelligent, and gave the names and numbers of the cavalry regiments, and
was made to repeat them, so as to see whether he was telling the truth.
His statement was consistent in every instance. I hope to meet Colonel
Major to-morrow, before the enemy reaches that point.
  I am, general, very respectfully, your obedient servant,
                                        ALFR. MOUTON,
                                  Brigadier-General, Commanding.
Maj. Gen. RICHARD TAYLOR,
   Commanding District of Western Louisiana.

No. 22.

*Report of Brig. Gen. Thomas Green, C. S. Army, commanding Cavalry
Division, of engagement at Bayou Bourbeau.*

HEADQUARTERS DIVISION OF CAVALRY,
Opelousas, November 4, 1863.

MAJOR : After having retired from Opelousas, October 20, with the
division of cavalry under my command, before the advancing enemy, in
three columns, to wit, Major's brigade up the Chicot road, and Bagby's
and the artillery up the Bœuf and Big Cane roads, to a point where
forage could be procured for our horses, only a few days' rest intervened when my scouts reported that the enemy had fallen back from
the vicinity of Opelousas and Barre's Landing, at which places they
had encamped in considerable force. Upon this information being conveyed to the major-general commanding, I was ordered to pursue and
harass the enemy with my division of cavalry and three regiments of
infantry, then on outpost duty, to wit, Colonel [O. M.] Roberts' Eleventh Texas, Colonel [W. H.] King's Eighteenth Texas, Colonel [J. W.]

Speight's Fifteenth Texas (the latter commanded by Lieutenant-Colonel [James E.] Harrison), and three sections of artillery.

In pursuance of orders, I took up the line of march in the direction of Opelousas on the 1st instant, and overtook the rear guard of the enemy on Bayou Bourbeau, 7 miles below that place, consisting of two brigades of infantry, commanded by General Burbridge, of the Thirteenth Army Corps, and three regiments of cavalry and two batteries. After having sufficiently reconnoitered the position of the enemy, I determined to attack him, and made my dispositions accordingly. Colonel Roberts, in command of the three regiments of infantry before mentioned, was assigned to the command of our left wing, and was directed to sweep down the Bellevue road and occupy the timber below the enemy on the bayou, and assail his right flank. Colonel [J. P.] Major, with his brigade of cavalry, constituted our right wing, while Colonel [A. P.] Bagby, with his brigade of cavalry, occupied our center. Two of his regiments (the Fourth and Fifth) were dismounted, and acted as infantry for the occasion, supporting our artillery, which consisted of a rifle section of Daniel's battery and a section of the Valverde, commanded, respectively, by Lieutenants [Samuel M.] Hamilton and [P. G.] Hume, both sections being placed for the occasion under the command of Lieutenant Morse. These dispositions having been made, and the brigade commanders occupying the ground assigned to them, I ordered an immediate advance.

About 11 a. m. of the 3d instant, Colonel Roberts drove in the enemy's skirmishers on his right flank, and commenced the attack. Our infantry was engaged for half an hour before our cavalry and dismounted troopers, with the artillery, were closely engaged on our right and center. Our infantry was most stubbornly resisted by the enemy, but they gallantly and steadily moved forward, without for a moment faltering, under a most terrific fire of artillery and musketry. Our artillery was brought up within 400 yards of a line of the enemy's infantry, in front of their encampment, and fired a few shots into them, but about this time the cavalry, under Colonel Major, on our extreme right, dashed into the left flank of the enemy, while Colonel Bagby, with Herbert's regiment and Waller's battalion, mounted, and Hardeman's and McNeill's regiments, dismounted, charged them in front, the cavalry making, on a partially concealed foe, the most brilliant charge on record. Our gallant infantry, under their brave officers, had given the enemy such a chastisement on his right flank, pushing him back to his encampment, that the whole Federal force gave way as soon as the engagement became general and close.

The victory was complete, the fruits of which are about 250 of the enemy killed and wounded, 100 of whom are estimated to have been killed, and over 600 prisoners, 32 of whom were officers. Prisoners were taken from the following regiments: Sixtieth and Sixty-seventh Indiana, Twenty-third Wisconsin, Eighty-third and Ninety-sixth Ohio, First Louisiana Cavalry, and two batteries. Besides a large quantity of improved small-arms and accouterments, three pieces of artillery fell into our hands. We only had horses, however, to bring off one fine Parrott gun and caisson, most of the horses of the enemy's guns being killed. Two hours after our victory, General Weitzel, of the Nineteenth (U. S.) Army Corps, came up with a division of infantry of three brigades from Carrion Crow Bayou, 3 miles distant, and two regiments of cavalry. Deeming it imprudent to fight this large additional force, after a warm skirmish, I withdrew slowly and without loss, the enemy not attempting to follow me.

I cannot say too much for the gallantry of the officers and men under my command in this action. It was above all praise. I have never before witnessed good conduct in battle so universal.

I am greatly indebted to my own staff for their efficiency. Captain Hart, who always distinguishes himself in battle, was placed under the command of Colonel Roberts, to assist him on our left, and for his conduct I refer you particularly to the report of Colonel Roberts.* Captain [C. B.] Sheppard, of my old military family, was (as ever before in battle) gallant and useful. I cannot say too much in praise of Acting Assistant Adjutant-General [E. R.] Wells. My engineer, Captain Ellis, and Lieutenant [J.] Avery, and Volunteer Aide-de-Camp (for the occasion) George [T.] Madison, were also very useful and efficient.

I herewith submit a statement of casualties. A full list of names as soon as procured will be forwarded.

To Chief Surgeon George Cupples great praise is due in using the limited means at his command in alleviating the sufferings of our noble soldiers and his great and untiring activity in the discharge of all his duties.

Owing to the breaking down of the horses in section of Semmes' battery, it did not arrive in time to participate in the action.

I am, very respectfully, your obedient servant,

THOMAS GREEN,
Brigadier-General, Commanding Cavalry Division.

Maj. E. SURGET,
Assistant Adjutant-General, District of Western Louisiana.

[Inclosure.]

Command.	Killed.	Wounded.	Missing.
11th Texas Infantry, Col. O. M. Roberts commanding	4	15	32
15th Texas Infantry, Lieutenant-Colonel Harrison commanding	7	22	5
18th Texas Infantry, Colonel King commanding	10	40	4
Lane's (Texas) cavalry, Major [W. P.] Sautley commanding			8
Madison's (Texas) cavalry, Colonel [George T.] Madison commanding	1	4	2
Stone's (Texas) cavalry, Lieutenant-Colonel [Isham] Chisum commanding		6	1
4th Texas Cavalry, Colonel [W. P.] Hardeman commanding		4	2
5th Texas Cavalry, Colonel [H. C.] McNeill commanding		6	1
7th Texas Cavalry, Lieutenant-Colonel [P. T.] Herbert commanding		2	
Waller's battalion cavalry, Captain [W. A.] McDade commanding		3	
Rifle section Daniel's battery, Lieutenant [S M.] Hamilton commanding		1	
Total	22	103	55

OCTOBER 27–DECEMBER 2, 1863.—The Rio Grande Expedition, and operations on the coast of Texas.

SUMMARY OF THE PRINCIPAL EVENTS.

Oct. 27. 1863.—Expedition, under command of Major-General Banks, U. S. Army, sails from the mouth of the Mississippi River.

Nov. 2, 1863.—Brazos Island occupied by the Union forces.

6, 1863.—Brownsville and Point Isabel occupied by the Union forces.

17, 1863.—Capture of Confederate battery at Aransas Pass.

22–30, 1863.—Expedition against and capture of Fort Esperanza, Matagorda Island.

* Not found.

Nov.   23, 1863.—Skirmish at Cedar Bayou.
      23–Dec. 2.—Expedition to Rio Grande City.

REPORTS.*

No. 1.—Maj. Gen. Nathaniel P. Banks, U. S. Army, commanding Department of the
     Gulf.
No. 2.—Maj. Gen. N. J. T. Dana, U. S. Army, commanding Thirteenth Army Corps.
No. 3.—Maj. Gen. Cadwallader C. Washburn, U. S. Army, commanding First Divis-
     ion, of expedition against and capture of Fort Esperanza.
No. 4 —Col. Henry D. Washburn, Eighteenth Indiana Infantry, commanding First
     Brigade, of expedition against and capture of Fort Esperanza.
No. 5.—Col. [John] Charles Black, Thirty-seventh Illinois Infantry, First Brigade,
     Second Division, of expedition to Rio Grande City.
No. 6.—Maj. John Bruce, Nineteenth Iowa Infantry, Second Brigade, of the occupa-
     tion of Brownsville, &c.
No. 7.—Brig. Gen. T. E. G. Ransom, U. S. Army, commanding Third Brigade, of the
     capture of Confederate battery at Aransas Pass, and expedition against
     and capture of Fort Esperanza.
No. 8.—Abstracts from "Record of Events" on the several returns of the Thirteenth
     Army Corps, for October, November, and December, 1863.
No. 9.—Maj. Gen. John B. Magruder, C. S. Army, commanding District of Texas,
     New Mexico, and Arizona.
No. 10.—Brig. Gen. Hamilton P. Bee, C. S. Army, commanding First Division, Army
     of Texas, of operations November 1–21.
No. 11.—Col. James Duff, Thirty-third Texas Cavalry, of operations October 28–
     November 8.
No. 12.—Capt. Richard Taylor, Thirty-third Texas Cavalry, of operations November
     2–3.
No. 13.—Capt. Henry T. Davis, Thirty-third Texas Cavalry, of operations Novem-
     ber 2–3.
No. 14.—Col. W. R. Bradfute, C. S. Army, commanding Coast, of operations Novem-
     ber 23–29.
No. 15.—Maj. John Ireland, Eighth Texas Infantry, of operations November 23.

No. 1.

*Reports of Maj. Gen. Nathaniel P. Banks, U. S. Army, commanding
Department of the Gulf.†*

HEADQUARTERS DEPARTMENT OF THE GULF,
New Orleans, November 7, 1863.

GENERAL: I have just received the following dispatch from the major-general commanding the department, viz:

HEADQUARTERS ON FLAG-SHIP McCLELLAN,
Off Brazos, November 2.

Brig. Gen. CHARLES P. STONE,
    Chief of Staff:
   The flag of the Union floated over Texas to-day at meridian precisely. Our enter-
prise has been a complete success. Make preparations for movements as directed.
Details to-morrow.

N. P. BANKS,
Major-General, Commanding.

(Similar dispatch to President of the United States on November 3, 1863.)

---

* For reports of Commodore Henry H. Bell and Commander James H. Strong, U. S.
Navy, see Annual Report of the Secretary of the Navy, December 5, 1864.
  † See also Sabine Pass Expedition, p 286, and Banks' general report, p. 18.

In accordance with the instructions of the major-general commanding, troops will concentrate at Brashear and Berwick as rapidly as transportation can be provided for them on the returning and other disposable steamers.

I have the honor to be, general, very respectfully, your obedient servant,

CHAS. P. STONE,
Brigadier-General, Chief of Staff.

Maj. Gen. H. W. HALLECK,
.   *Washington, D. C.*

HEADQUARTERS DEPARTMENT OF THE GULF,
Flag-ship McClellan, off Brazos Santiago, November 4, 1863.

GENERAL : I have the honor to report that on November 2, at meridian, the flag of the Union was raised on Brazos Island, which is now in our possession. It was occupied by a small force of rebel cavalry, which fled at our disembarkation without serious resistance. We left New Orleans on Monday, the 26th, at 12 o'clock, having been detained three days in the river beyond the time fixed for our departure in my last dispatch by a violent storm.

On Friday, the 30th, off Aransas Pass, we encountered a severe gale, which lasted through the day, and separated several of the transports from the fleet.

The flag-ship reached the rendezvous, latitude 27°, Sunday morning, reconnoitered the Brazos and Boca Chica, and, returning to the fleet, resumed the voyage, and arrived off Brazos Santiago at 5 o'clock Sunday evening. The sea was high and the wind very strong; a landing seemed impossible, but energetic preparations were made, and on Monday, the 2d instant, at meridian precisely, the first transport, General Banks, crossed the bar in safety, and was immediately followed by other transports. We have since been engaged in discharging those too heavy to cross the bar.

Three naval vessels, the Monongahela, Owasco, and Virginia, left New Orleans as convoy for the fleet. The Virginia was disabled on the 29th off Aransas, and did not reach the Brazos until Sunday evening. The Monongahela and Owasco were separated from the fleet during the gale, keeping in company with the dispersed transports, and reached the mouth of the Brazos Tuesday morning. The force consists of the Second Division, Thirteenth Army Corps, to which are added the Thirteenth and Fifteenth Regiments Maine Volunteers; First Texas Cavalry and the First and Sixteenth Regiments, Corps d'Afrique,* numbering in all about 4,000 men, under the immediate command of Major-General Dana, who has superintended the disembarkation.

The recent movements in the Teche country, and the late attack upon the Sabine, have drawn all the forces from Western to Eastern Texas. But for this, the landing we have effected would have been impossible. Our success is complete, and, if followed up, will produce important results in this part of the country. It is my purpose, after getting possession of the Rio Grande, to secure the important passes upon the coast as far as Pass Cavallo. To effect this object, I shall move a portion of the troops under General Franklin, at Vermillionville, to this point.

---

* The First Engineers and Sixteenth Infantry.

I earnestly entreat that we may be strengthened in our force by the return of so many conscripts, at least, as will fill up our regiments. I am certain that in New England and the West men will readily volunteer for service in Texas, if it is permitted.

Unless we are strengthened, we may have to abandon the great advantage we have gained. We shall commence our movement to the Rio Grande to-day.*

I have the honor to be, with much respect, your most obedient servant,

N. P. BANKS,
Major-General, Commanding.

Maj. Gen. H. W. HALLECK,
General-in-Chief, U. S. Army, Washington, D. C.

ADDENDA.

Strength and composition of the Rio Grande Expedition, October 31, 1863.

Command.	Present for duty.		Aggregate present.	Aggregate present and absent.	Pieces of field artillery.
	Officers.	Men.			
Staff and pioneers	15	89	114	115	....
First Brigade	74	1,174	1,511	2,606	10
Second Brigade	82	1,667	2,075	3,468	6
Corps d'Afrique	16	416	467	499	....
1st Texas Cavalry	16	205	249	310	....
Total*	203	3,551	4,416	6,998	16

* Does not account for the Fifteenth Maine.

SECOND DIVISION, THIRTEENTH ARMY CORPS.

Maj. Gen. N. J. T. DANA.

First Brigade.

Brig. Gen. WILLIAM VANDEVER.

37th Illinois, Col. [John] Charles Black.
91st Illinois, Col. Henry M. Day.
26th Indiana, Col. John G. Clark.
34th Iowa, Col. George W. Clark.
38th Iowa, Maj. Charles Chadwick.
1st Missouri Artillery, Battery E, Capt. Joseph B. Atwater.
1st Missouri Artillery, Battery F, Capt. Joseph Foust.

Second Brigade.

Col. WILLIAM McE. DYE.

94th Illinois, Col. John McNulta.
19th Iowa, Maj. John Bruce.
20th Iowa, Maj. William G. Thompson.
13th Maine, Lieut. Col. Frank S. Hesseltine.
20th Wisconsin, Col. Henry Bertram.
1st Missouri Artillery, Battery B, Capt. Martin Welfley.

Attached.

15th Maine, Lieut. Col. Benjamin B. Murray, jr.
1st Engineers, Corps d'Afrique, Col. Justin Hodge.
16th Infantry, Corps d'Afrique, Col. Matthew C. Kempsey.
1st Texas Cavalry, Col. Edmund J. Davis.
Pioneer Company, Capt. Alden H. Jumper.

* See Halleck to Banks, November 19, p. 806.

HEADQUARTERS DEPARTMENT OF THE GULF,
Brownsville, Tex., November 6, 1863—10 p. m.

GENERAL: The Ninety-fourth Illinois Volunteers, the advance of my command, reached the neighborhood of Brownsville last evening, and entered the town this morning at 10 o'clock.

A battery of the First Missouri Light Artillery, and the Thirteenth Maine Volunteers, entered the town at 3 p. m. I arrived with my staff at 12 o'clock, making my headquarters ·at Brownsville. The enemy evacuated the town at our approach, burning the United States barracks, and destroying large quantities of property which they could not remove.

The conflagration extended to one or two squares of the town in the neighborhood of the barracks, which were also destroyed. The troops of General Bee's command gave themselves up to plunder and violence, which excited the citizens to a considerable degree of resistance. General José Maria Cobos, who has been a resident of this town since ·March last, having been banished from Mexico at the time of the evacuation of the Spanish and English authorities, excited by the violence of the rebel troops and the conflagration, received permission from the authorities of Brownsville to organize the people for the purpose of resisting the depredations of the rebels and the suppression of the conflagration. This occurred on the 4th of November. On the evening of the 5th, after the arrival of our troops, Cobos crossed the· river with the men under his command, and took possession of Matamoras, imprisoning the Military Governor of Tamaulipas, Señor Don Manuel Ruiz, and all his associate officers. To-day, at 10 o'clock, he issued a proclamation to the army, and another to the people of Matamoras, copies of which are herewith inclosed.

Cobos is a Spaniard by birth, forty-five years of age, and emigrated to this country from Spain at thirteen or fourteen. He has been twenty years in the Mexican army, always supporting the Mexican Government, but a partisan of the Church party. He has held commission as general of division for five years, is well educated, has much influence with the army, particularly with that portion in the interior of Mexico, and is in all respects an able man. He has never resided much in this part of the country. Since March he has been a· resident of Brownsville.· He is represented by his friends to be adverse to the French interests. They say his purpose is, if the French attack Matamoras, to resist them in the attempt, and to withdraw into the interior with his forces, and to continue the contest as guerrillas against their Government. ·

He was in Mexico and here the companion and friend of Miramon, and is supposed to favor the same general policy.

The friends of Cobos represent Miramon as being devoted to the interests of Mexico against those of France, but, from considerations of policy; to be affiliating with the French authorities at the same time for the purpose of gaining time and strength. This is the representation of the friends of Cobos.

My impression, from all that I can gain, and notwithstanding what is herein stated, is that the tendency of Cobos' movement is to the benefit of France. He is a desperate man, and seized Matamoras at this particular moment for the purpose of putting himself and friends in possession of power or property to treat with any party that can best subserve his and their interests. I am unable to see how it can end otherwise than in a coalition with France. Still, his friends declare that he is adverse to the French interests, and seeks only an improved theory, and an efficient organization of the Mexican forces against their invaders. They represent the Juarez Government to be unpopular with the people, and universally unacceptable to the army.

If Cobos is successful, this will be the tendency of his movement, but it may be changed by events as they transpire from day to day. Associated with Cobos is General Cortinas, a Mexican, thoroughly hostile to the French interests, of great influence with the Mexican people, although an uneducated man, and of not very prepossessing manners. He has for several years resided in Tamaulipas, and two years since organized a revolutionary movement against the Texan authorities of this country. It was unsuccessful, and he has since resided in Mexico. His friends count him as in the interests of the United States Government, and we have relied upon his assistance in raising Mexican troops, if it should be necessary.

Don Manuel Ruiz, the deposed Military Governor of Tamaulipas, whose headquarters were at Matamoras, is unquestionably a friend of the United States. He had, before the occurrence of this revolution, made such arrangements in regard to the use of steamers to assist us in our movements as puts this question beyond possibility of doubt. His overthrow cannot be considered otherwise than as a very serious misfortune to our Government.

This is the condition of things as they stand to-night. Cobos has from 500 to 700 armed men.

The citizens of Matamoras seemed to have been paralyzed by the suddenness of this movement, and were unprepared at the moment to resist.

Anticipations of an *émeute* to-night are confidently expressed by Mexican citizens who are in Brownsville.

The best informed persons I have seen represent Spain to be hostile to the French movement on this continent, and all those of Spanish descent, I am credibly informed, share earnestly that feeling of the mother country.

The reason they assign for this course of Spain and the Spanish residents of this country is, that Mexico having been colonized and fostered by the Spanish nation, although it has since attained an independent position, they are unwilling to see its influence and its power pass to the French Government. This is a firmly rooted feeling, both in the nation and in the people, and it is represented that the influence of Spain will be permanently against the French movement in this country.

They say that Spain and the American Spaniards view the French movement in Mexico precisely as Americans would regard a similar movement of the French in the United States, and are actuated by the same feelings in their conduct in regard to it. The Mexican church has, in losing the great bulk of its property, parted with its political influence to an extent not wholly appreciated by the American people. This is said by the adherents of Cobos and Miramon, who are regarded, in the political parlance of the day, as reactionists, or adherents of the Spanish church.

I have information of a most direct character that an officer on board our fleet has given information directly to the rebel military authorities of such a character as to change somewhat my plans, and I shall, in consequence, make more preparation for the defense of this position than I had hitherto contemplated.

You will pardon me if I express the opinion, upon full consideration of all the circumstances of the case, that the flag of the American Government is raised at a most opportune moment. The crisis is upon us.

Whatever may be the views or plans of Cobos or the revolutionists, it cannot be doubted that this movement has been in contemplation for a long time, and that it is precipitated by the evacuation of the rebel forces and the occupation of the Rio Grande by our troops. If it fail, it will be in consequence of a want of time to perfect the arrangements necessary for its complete success. It is apparent that there was a most perfect understanding between the rebel leaders and the parties under Cobos, both in Brownsville and Matamoras.

Our unexpected arrival precipitated his movement before preparations were completed. It can hardly be doubted that, with his complete success, the French party would have been established in power in the State of Tamaulipas, the importance of which can be estimated when it is remembered that it extends from the mouth of the Rio Grande to Tampico on the Gulf coast, to Laredo on the Rio Grande, and covers the gap left in the French decree for the blockade of Mexico. *

I have the honor to be, with much respect, your-obedient servant,

N. P. BANKS,
Major-General, Commanding.

Maj. Gen. H. W. HALLECK,
General-in-Chief, U. S. Army, Washington, D. C.

[Inclosures.]

José Maria Cobos, general of division of the Mexican Army, to his companions in arms.

MATAMORAS, *November 6, 1863.*

The grave situation of the nation, in consequence of French intervention and the misfortunes which afflict the Republic through the ineffectual resistance of a Government whose existence is a calamity for the people, has caused you to take up arms, and to salute the morning of this day with the cry of independence and liberty, thus preparing yourselves to reconquer for the nation the precious boon lost under the rude blows of a tyrannical demagogue, and to come to its defense with the courage and decision which I recognize in you.

Marvelous in fact is the accumulation of outrages which are actually practiced upon the public destiny, and it is far better not to live at all if we must lose the hope of re-establishing the empire of the law, which brings with it individual guarantees and respect for property, attacked in all parts of the country by these satellites of a corrupt Government. I will aid you with all my might in the work of political regeneration to which you have invited me, and, notwithstanding we are but few, it matters not, for Mexico has many and good patriots to unite in saving our nationality.

My heart swells with gratitude for the honor you have done me in proclaiming me your chief, and if in so doing you have had in view my eighteen years of service in the army of the Republic, defending the good principles—for my desire has always been to see it happy—I promise you that in the future I will not disappoint by my actions the good opinion I have merited from you.

Soldiers of the country! In being faithful to your colors in defense of the national integrity, you will have fulfilled your duty, and on returning to your firesides you will present to your wives and children the laurels of victory, which I hope you will pursue like good Mexicans. I invite you, then, to continue with firmness and constancy in this holy cause, and we will march to the cry of Long live Independence! Long live Liberty!

JOSÉ MARIA COBOS.

MATAMORAS,
November 6; 1863.

Citizens of Matamoras:

I have come to occupy this city in answer to the call of Mexican patriots desirous of sacrificing themselves for the national independence, and to put myself at the head of this handful of braves in defense of a cause so sacred. I do no more than perform my duty and remain faithful to my well-known principles, since, at an epoch not far distant, I consecrated my days to combating the anarchy in which this unhappy Government of demagogy is founded, and establishing one consolidated by peace, advance prosperity; and make law to reign.

As a general of the Mexican army, and an adopted son of this magnanimous nation, I do not come to incite domestic insurrections, nor to dispute on local questions. Our standard is actually that of independence, in which is centered the happiness of the country. I know that you are groaning under an insupportable oppression, and that they have thought you docile to serve the caprice and will of a few, who, in this city, as well as in others of the State, absorb like bloodsuckers the public funds and the fruit of your labor. You will take account of these and their management, and they must answer before their judges for their conduct.

Matamorians! In addressing you, it gratifies me to promise you that to every citizen, of whatever class and condition, he will give the necessary guarantees, and that he will watch with the greatest zeal for the security of property and the order in the city.

JOSÉ MARIA COBOS.

HEADQUARTERS DEPARTMENT OF THE GULF,
Brownsville, Tex., November 7, 1863—8 p. m.

GENERAL: Another revolution occurred to-day in Matamoras. General Cortinas, having obtained evidence that Cobos and his partisans were plotting for a French supremacy in Tamaulipas, seized the reins of the government, arrested Cobos, and, after a trial occupying but a few minutes, condemned him and two of his companions to be shot. The execution took place about 10 o'clock, in the presence of all the people of Matamoras, in the outskirts of the city. Cobos was shot by a platoon of troops. Vila, one of his principal officers, was permitted to run the gauntlet, and was shot upon his flight. Vila was a revolutionist of Spain, compelled to abandon his country. He resided for several years in New York. It is probable he was in sympathy and communication with the French partisans of that city. Within a few months past he has been connected with Cobos in Brownsville, and went with him from this city to Matamoras to assist him in the revolutionary movement, which was probably to place the French in power.

His career was a short one. A third party (———) was shot outside the city later in the day. The partisans of Cortinas are still in pursuit of other leading members of the Cobos government.

Great consternation is manifested in Matamoras and Brownsville on the part of those who had been privy to the acts of Cobos. Governor Ruiz was immediately released upon the assumption of power by Cortinas, and issued a proclamation to the army and to the citizens of Matamoras, copies of which I herewith inclose. It was supposed by his friends that he was permanently invested with military power, and such was his own assumption in his proclamations.

At 4 o'clock, however, he was waited upon by Cortinas, who expressed to him a fear for his safety, and offered him a guard of 25 men to protect his retreat from the city.

Governor Ruiz interpreted this as an intimation of his own execution, and, without waiting for the guard, and not even obtaining permission from the American consul, according to regulations we had established, came to this city and demanded my protection, which was readily and cheerfully granted to him.

He still remains in this city. Cortinas has declared for the Governor of ——, who holds the position of Civil Governor of the State of Tamaulipas, coexistent and subordinate in the present condition of Mexico to the authority of the military government, which was the position held by Ruiz, who is succeeded by Cortinas as Military Governor *de facto.*

Great excitement existed in the city during the whole day among the partisans of the French, both the French residents and the Cobos party, and the sympathizers with the rebels against the American Government, and it was feared another revolution would occur to-night which might place the French party in power.

This fear was shared by all those whose sympathies were with the United States Government, and seems to indicate in the strongest manner the belief that this was the principal object of the Cobos movement.

At 5.30 p. m. I received a communication from the American consul, expressing strong apprehensions that his house would be among the earliest objects of attack. I immediately notified him that in case his apprehensions were verified, I would give him full protection. A copy of his letter, and my reply thereto, I herewith inclose.

My troops are under orders to be ready for movement at any moment during the night. I have directed a battery of artillery to take position on the bank of the river opposite Matamoras. The authorities of Matamoras have probably been notified by our consul of my purpose to protect the American flag. It is understood that Cortinas will declare for the restoration of Governor Serna. Serna, about ten years since, ran for the office of Governor, and the polls resulted in a tie. A new election was ordered, with great violence, which resulted in Serna's election. He was in sympathy with the Juarez Government. The military authorities of Matamoras, for local reasons, resisted his authority, and a siege occurred of nearly three months' duration, which ended in the defeat of Serna. A Military Governor *ad interim* was appointed, who held his office for several months, but discontents and disturbances arose, and he resigned his office, and was succeeded by Governor Ruiz, appointed by Juarez as Military Governor. Ruiz has held power until overthrown by Cobos.

The chief feature to be noticed in regard to Serna's politics is, that all parties represented by Ruiz, Cortinas, and Serna are Mexicans, thoroughly hostile to the French.

I have received information to day from a most intelligent man, who has been long connected with the steam navigation of the Rio Grande, who says that the French fleet has been waiting for a long time for a pronunciamento placing the French party in power in Tamaulipas.

I am confident that this statement is correct. It will explain that decree of the French Government establishing a blockade upon the Mexican coast up to a point 9 miles south of the Rio Grande. This gap was to be filled by the Governor of Tamaulipas. Tamaulipas extends from Tampico to Laredo on the Rio Grande, and, the French in possession, it would give them complete control of the right bank of that river.

I have the honor to be, with much respect, your obedient servant,
N. P. BANKS,
Major-General, Commanding.

Maj. Gen. H. W. HALLECK,
General-in-Chief, U. S. Army, Washington, D. C.

[Inclosure No. 1.]

Proclamation by the Citizen Manuel Ruiz, Brigadier-General, Governor and Military Commander of the State of Tamaulipas.

MATAMORAS, *November 7, 1863.*

Garrison of Matamoras:

SOLDIERS: You have won new laurels; you have added a new luster to the many already acquired; you have re-established order in a moment of terrible danger, and you have re-established the authority of the highest government of the nation, which is the authority of the Mexican people, for it is they who have constituted it. You have proved to me in a moment of terrible trial that I can depend upon you in all circumstances, as you may count upon me.

Soldiers, in the name of the Supreme Government, in the name of the nation, in the name of the Mexican people, I thank you, and I congratulate you upon your heroic conduct. Rest assured that I shall never forget the proofs of affection that you have given me, and I shall always speak of you as models of loyalty, of discipline, and patriotism.

MANUEL RUIZ.

[Inclosure No 2.]

Proclamation by the Citizen Manuel Ruiz, Brigadier-General, Governor and Military Commander of the State of Tamaulipas.

MATAMORAS, *November 7, 1863.*

Citizens of Matamoras:

Thanks to the infamy of a small number of traitors, an iniquitous party arrived in your beautiful city and overpowered it for twenty-four hours. But they quickly received the punishment they deserved, and the earth already covers their dead bodies. Before long the loyal will have received their recompense.

You have also acquired a new title of glory, and you have demonstrated that it is not in vain you bear upon your escutcheon the triple device of loyal, invincible, and heroic Matamoras.

Not for a single moment have I doubted your triumph, for I trusted in you.

Citizens of Matamoras, Long live Independence! Long live Liberty! Long live the National Guard! Long live Lieut. Col. Juan Nepomuceno Cortinas!

MANUEL RUIZ.

[Inclosure No. 3.]

UNITED STATES CONSULATE,
Matamoras, November ·7, 1863.

Major-General BANKS,
Commanding Department of the Gulf, Brownsville:

DEAR SIR: We anticipate a riot (or what is called, in Mexican phraseology, a revolution) to-night, and I am fearful that my house may be made a point of attack, judging from the appearance of the Frenchmen. However, Captain Bennett can better explain everything, as I have been very busy all day.

He brings two gentlemen with him; one, Signor Chapa, is one of our most eminent men, and very wealthy, and goes over for refuge.

, Very respectfully, &c.,

L. PIERCE, JR.,
United States Consul.

[Inclosure No. 4.]

HEADQUARTERS DEPARTMENT OF THE GULF,
Brownsville, Tex., November 7, 1863—5.30 p. m.

L. PIERCE, Jr.,
American Consul at Matamoras:

SIR: Your note of this date, expressing an apprehension of an attack upon the American consulate in Matamoras, is this moment received. If the American flag is assailed or your person threatened in the progress of such riot as you anticipate, and the authorities fail to protect you, you may rely upon protection, if notice is given to me. My artillery is placed in position where it will be effective.

I cannot believe the apprehension you express will be verified, but desire information of the fact if there be any substantial ground of apprehension of such an event.

I have the honor to be, &c.,

N. P. BANKS,
Major-General, Commanding.

—

HEADQUARTERS DEPARTMENT OF THE GULF,
Brownsville, Tex., November 9, 1863.

SIR : I am in occupation of Brazos Island, Point Isabel, and Brownsville. My most sanguine expectations are more than realized. Three revolutions have occurred in Matamoras, affecting the government of Tamaulipas. The first was adverse to the interests of Mexico and the United States. Everything is now as favorable as could be desired.

Very respectfully, your obedient servant,

N. P. BANKS,
Major-General, Commanding.

The PRESIDENT OF THE UNITED STATES.

—

HEADQUARTERS DEPARTMENT OF THE GULF,
Brownsville, Tex., November 9, 1863.

GENERAL: But little is to be added to the dispatches of the 6th and 7th instant. Affairs are quiet in Matamoras. Governor Ruiz is in Brownsville, Cortinas in power, and messengers have been dispatched for Governor Serna, who resides 200 miles distant. The friendship of the Cortinas party for the American Government has been signally manifested by his placing three Rio Grande steamers on this side of the river under our control. One of these, the Matamoras, is the only boat that can cross the bar.

General Dana arrived at Brownsville last evening. I shall remain here until our affairs are in a settled condition.

I repeat my representations to the Government, that a small force of effective men, in addition to the strength I have, will be of incalculable service in the restoration of Texas, which I think can be accomplished in a very brief period. Volunteers in New England and in the West, I am certain, could be readily obtained if the Government would authorize it. Five or ten thousand men is all that I will ask.

Our success, thus far, has exceeded my most sanguine expectations. The people on both sides the river are friendly to the Government, and if affairs are managed with any discretion, the cause of the Government will be greatly strengthened throughout the whole Southwest.

The Fifteenth Maine Volunteers is at Brazos; the Twentieth Wisconsin at Point Isabel. Two regiments of the Corps d'Afrique, the First and Sixteenth, occupy Brazos Island. The balance of the force connected with the expedition is *en route* for this point.

I have the honor to be, with much respect, your obedient servant,
N. P. BANKS,
Major-General, Commanding.
Maj. Gen. H. W. HALLECK,
General-in-Chief, U. S. Army, Washington, D. C.

—

HEADQUARTERS DEPARTMENT OF THE GULF,
Brownsville, Tex., November 9, 1863.

GENERAL : I have the honor to inclose copies of the proclamations issued this day (November 9). The signatures to the "acta" represent, as far as I can understand, the permanent officers of the military organization.

Governor Serna, it is supposed, will be heard from within two days, and it is believed that the prominent men of both parties will acquiesce in his government. However, everything is yet unsettled as to the future.

With much respect, your obedient servant,
N. P. BANKS,
Major-General, Commanding.
Maj. Gen. H. W. HALLECK,
General-in-Chief, U. S. Army, Washington, D. C.

[Inclosure No. 1]

MATAMORAS,
November 8, 1863.

To the Public:

The subscriber, feeling himself obliged to explain promptly to the nation, as well as the people of this heroic city and the armed garrison which he has the honor to command, the reason for the execution done at 8 o'clock yesterday morning on the person of Don José M. Cobos, and as neither time nor the demands of the service to which he is pre-eminently dedicated in order to maintain tranquillity and order among the people will permit him to make an elaborate explanation of what has taken place, he will merely say that the garrison agreed to proclaim the raising of the siege in Tamaulipas, thereby re-establishing constitutional order, as the situation was no longer endurable in the State, for reasons which he proposes to explain to the Supreme Government of the nation. Cobos assented to this idea, and, under its protection, he was able, only in appearance, to obtain the command of the soldiers, including him who subscribes himself their chief, all being Mexicans, belonging to the country, and, as Liberals, they are disposed to sacrifice themselves to sustain and protect the constitution of 1857, no less than the Government from which it emanates. He then made the first step toward discord, issuing a proclamation, in which he could not avoid showing the tendency of his ideas, contrary to the fundamental letter of the Republic, and of the legitimate Government established by virtue of it, crowning the work which he proposed to erect in Tamaulipas with the abortion of a plan, which, reduced to writing and signed, should take the place of that. What madness!

At this state of things it was necessary to work as became the defenders of the code of 1857. Consequently Cobos was shot. As for the rest, the garrison, with the people and the first *ayuntamiento* (common council) of this heroic city, have done away with the proclamation by raising the siege, and the consequent result by changing the face of the State, purely with the feeling that it enters upon constitutional order, under whose standard all citizens and inhabitants will have the guarantees stipulated by law, to whose preservation I have consecrated the arms of the faithful soldiery which are subservient to me.

JUAN NEPUMUSENO CORTINAS.

[Inclosure No 2.]

The plan which the former exposition contracts says thus:

In the heroic city of Matamoras, on the 7th day of November, 1863, the subscribers united themselves for the purpose of deliberating upon the situation in which the Republic finds itself, threatened on one side by the loss of her independence, and destroyed on the other in consequence of the demagogy represented by a mob of men who, renouncing the principles which constitute order and the guarantees of a free people, sustain their barbarous power by means of violence and terror which reflect the image of the dishonor of our country.

Considering that the Mexican nation neither can nor ought to abdicate its rights by allowing a minority to invest itself with the power of altering the fundamental form of our Government.

Considering that it is an imperious necessity to arrive at the important object of saving our independence and establishing peace, which our people so much desire, that in all points of the country the wretched constitution of '57, and the Government emanating from it, may cease, whose history of intolerance and repeated offenses against what is most respectable in our laws, institutions, and habits, calls for a speedy and effectual reparation.

Considering that by combining the means conducive to the ends of subduing the anarchy which afflicts the nation, and to give solidity to its future march toward peace and progress, it cannot accomplish it unless all patriotic and moral Mexicans, whatever may be the political party to which they have belonged, shall gather around the glorious national standard, not permitting powers which the national will has not sanctioned to organize under its shadow.

Considering that if upon the ruins which to-day it sees the edifice reduced, erected more than forty years ago at the cost of innumerable sacrifices of the lives of thousands of Mexicans, it be indispensable to construct anew our political regeneration under the legal protection and good faith of those nations which profess for us a loyal and disinterested friendship, it will never be admitted by the generality of Mexicans with the character and conditions which it now imposes on them.

PROCLAMATION.

ARTICLE 1. The constitution of 1854 shall cease to reign in the Republic of Mexico, and the Government emanating from it.

ART. 2. We proclaim the senior-general of division, Don José Maria Cobos, chief of the forces, to carry out this plan, who shall dictate the necessary means for making it generally adopted in the rest of the Republic.

ART. 3. In adhering to it, the people will transmit to the said chief the respective act of proclamation.

ART. 4. The aforesaid general-in-chief shall immediately convene a meeting of the people of Matamoras, which, upon voting, shall form a junta, composed of five individuals of wisdom and discretion, to propose without delay a plan which shall have for its object the constitution of a provisional government, which shall have the direction of public administration, and advance the necessary means for the defense of our venerated independence.

ART. 5. In the meantime the collection of taxes which may have been made, belonging to the public treasury, shall be placed in safe custody, taking only what may be necessary for the expenses of war and of office; they shall also reserve a corresponding portion for foreign contracts.

[Inclosure No. 3.]

ACT.

In the heroic city of Matamoras, on the 7th day of the month of November, 1863, the garrison of this place reunited themselves *en masse* under the command of Col. Juan N. Cortinas, chief of the armies, as well as the people convened to the effect.

In consideration that the State has long suffered and bewailed the effects of the declaration of siege in which the decree of January 4, 1862, has placed it, the more that it has failed to accomplish the object for which it was dictated, for the reason that the State and its sons have always contributed for the national defense, not stinting the Supreme Government either in men or means, yet it thinks it can do more under the influence of its tutelary institutions, as they are derived from the general constitution of 1857; they facilitate all the means which can be offered to meet a similar emergency, leaving to public and private citizens more liberty and desire to fulfill their obligations in accordance with its true wishes, which thus comes to destroy itself when it enters in a situation like that in which the said decree has placed the State by declaring it in a state of siege, as it already causes the suspension of some guarantees, and because the most disappear when authority has concentrated itself in the hands of functionaries who, in exercising it, bring upon themselves, almost without thinking of it, a general animadversion, whatever may have been the prudence and skill they have exercised in their official acts.

Considering that the State has never been really in a condition when it could with justice be declared in a state of siege, but at most in that of war, according to the opinion of distinguished public men, as the foreign invasion which threatened it before, and from which it actually suffers, does not pass, nor has it ever passed, one of its gates, as it notoriously has that of Tampico.

Considering that it was doubtless a similar circumstance that impelled the Supreme Governor to issue another decree on the 12th of May, raising the siege, and ordering that the Acting Governor shall dictate proper measures for re-establishing constitutional order in the State, unless he knows positively that its abolition has been suspended.

Considering, lastly, that Tamaulipas is passing through that restrictive position without all the benefits due it from the national cause, and greatly obstructing its local advancement, being all the time an exception in the Federal balance, where there is hardly another State which maintains the siege.

For similar public and notorious considerations, the armed garrison of this city and people respectfully and spontaneously agree upon the following articles for its prompt execution :

ARTICLE 1. *Be it enacted*, That the state of siege imposed by the decree of January 4, 1862, shall cease in the State, and consequently the Governor-elect, citizen Jesus de la Serna, shall be called to enter anew upon his functions, who, according to the constitution of the State, will arrange for suitably organizing and electing the other constitutional powers wherever they are incomplete through their term of duty having expired, or other causes.

ART. 2. The Governor and Military Commander, C. Manuel Ruiz, who actually exercised both commands in this heroic city, shall cease to exercise them from to-day.

ART. 3. The political authority of C. Juan Fernandez shall also cease, and, until some one be named in his place, this authority will be exercised by the citizen First Alcalde Rafael Quintero.

ART. 4. This resolution shall be communicated to the Supreme Governor, showing him forcibly that, being the spontaneous work of the most perfect unanimity, it is hoped he will give it his supreme approbation.

—

HEADQUARTERS DEPARTMENT OF THE GULF,
Flag-ship McClellan, off Aransas Pass, Tex., November 18, 1863.

GENERAL: I left Brownsville on the 13th, for the purpose of moving against the passes above Brazos Santiago. We completed the embarkation of troops at Brazos Island on the 15th, and sailed on the morning of the 16th for Corpus Christi. The troops on board were the Thirteenth and Fifteenth Maine, Thirty-fourth and Twenty-sixth Iowa, and the Eighth Indiana Regiments, and one battery of artillery, numbering in all about 1,500 men. We reached Corpus Christi the day before yesterday (16th), at 1 o'clock. We expected to be able to cross the bar at Corpus Christi with the Matamoras, one of the boats brought from the Rio Grande, and drawing 3½ feet of water, but we found the passage was impracticable, the bar being covered by only 2½ feet. We were, therefore, compelled to land our troops upon the coast. The disembarkation was superintended by Brigadier-General Ransom (who commanded the troops during the day), and was commenced immediately upon our arrival, and occupied the night. The troops, after landing, commenced a movement toward the upper end of the island, a distance of 22 miles. This march, performed immediately after effecting a most difficult landing by means of boats through the surf, reflects great credit upon the officers and troops engaged. The enemy was completely surprised by our arrival, having no intimation of our presence until the morning, when we presented ourselves. After skirmishing a couple of hours on the island, and some most effective and well-directed artillery fire from the gunboat Monongahela, the enemy surrendered. Lieutenant-Colonel ———— was in command, and we captured alto-gether 9 officers, 90 men, three heavy siege guns, a quantity of most excellent small-arms, 80 or 90 good horses, a schooner, nearly new, and considerable minor land and water transportation.

We shall move to-morrow against Pass Cavallo, the most important pass on the coast except Galveston. We shall have a sharper contest there than at Aransas, but are confident of success.

The success of our expedition will very likely transfer our operations to the coast. The best line of defense for Louisiana, as well as for operations against Texas, is by Berwick Bay and the Atchafalaya. To operate promptly and effectively on this line, we need light-draught sea boats, drawing 6 or 7 feet of water. A supply of these will be a measure of great economy to the Government. Larger ships are in great peril constantly, from their inability to escape the "northers" by entering the bays. We lost one excellent steamer, the Nassau, on the bar at Brazos from this cause. The steamers Saint Mary's, Clinton, Crescent, and others of that class, have been of the greatest service, and to them we owe the success of our expedition. It is of the utmost importance that this number should be increased. We need very much light-draught gunboats on the Atchafalaya, as, if this line is well pro-tected from Berwick Bay to the Red River, the enemy necessarily is thrown back from the Mississippi.

Admiral Porter informs me that he had received your orders to send boats down, but that he was unable to enter the Atchafalaya from Red River, owing to the low stage of the water, and that his boats could not pass by sea into Berwick Bay with safety. I am quite confident that, watching for fair weather, all his boats can be buoyed around with the assistance of steamers. The distance is only 40 miles and the sea is often quite smooth. We have frequently sent river boats around in that way. I respectfully request your attention to this subject.

I have the honor to be, with much respect, your obedient servant,*

N. P. BANKS,
Major-General, Commanding.

Maj. Gen. H. W. HALLECK,
  General-in-Chief, U. S. Army, Washington, D. C.

ADDENDA.

SPECIAL ORDERS, }   HDQRS. DEPARTMENT OF THE GULF,
  No. 284½.   }   *Brazos Santiago, Tex., November 15,* 1863.

I. Brig. Gen. T. E. G. Ransom is hereby assigned to the command of this post, including Brazos Island and Point Isabel. He will take charge of the troops now here, and prepare them for a movement up the coast this afternoon, in accordance with the verbal instructions already given.

*   *   *   *   *   *   *

V. The following are the directions for the expedition to Aransas Pass:

1. Brigadier-General Ransom will prepare all the troops at this post, except so many companies of the First and Sixteenth Corps d'Afrique as may be necessary to protect the stores at Brazos Island and Point Isabel, for the expedition, the general object of which is to obtain pos-

_____
* See Halleck to Banks, December, 7, p. 834, and Banks to Halleck, December 23, p. 871.

session of Aransas Pass, and, if possible, of Pass Cavallo. The force will enter Corpus Christi Pass with such boats as may be able to cross the bar at that point, and land upon Mustang Island, on the inner side. The rebel force at Aransas is supposed to be one light battery, with two or three companies of infantry and artillery, not more than 200 or 300 in number. Upon gaining Corpus Christi, the troops must be subject to the exigencies that may arise. The troops will move from this point in light marching order, their baggage to be sent to them after possession of the island is obtained. The boats adapted to the service are the Matamoras, Plauter, Bagaly, and two light-draught schooners, which will be designated. The Monongahela, and probably the Virginia, United States gunboats, will assist by an attack upon the force in front; the McClellan will sustain the fleet on the outside. All the disposable barges in possession of the fleet at Brazos, excepting such as are absolutely necessary, will be placed upon the boats that are designated for the expedition. Navy boat howitzers and two 20-pounder Parrotts will also be placed upon the boats that enter the bay. Should the battery from Brownsville fail to reach Brazos in season to depart with the fleet, the guns will be manned by a force extemporized from the gunboats and the transport vessels, with such as can be added from the infantry regiments. Fifteen days' rations should be provided, a sufficiency of water for the support of the troops one week, forage for 50 horses at least, and surplus ammunition for infantry and artillery.

2. Capt. R. M. Hill, ordnance officer, is placed in charge of the artillery, and will organize a sufficient force from the principal vessels and ships of war to man the guns, and will report to General Ransom.

3. Capt. J. P. Baker, engineer, is directed to accompany the expedition. If possible, the expedition will sail at 3 o'clock this afternoon.

By command of Major-General Banks:

AUGUSTUS W. SEXTON, JR.,
Acting Assistant Adjutant-General.

No. 2.

Reports of Maj. Gen. N. J. T. Dana, U. S. Army, commanding Thirteenth Army Corps.

HEADQUARTERS THIRTEENTH ARMY CORPS,
Brazos Santiago, November 7, 1863.

GENERAL: I leave now for Brownsville. I have just received dispatches from that place, from Major-General Banks, containing the following:

Steamers that can enter the Brashear should be sent forward as soon as possible for troops and artillery, with instructions to return to Brazos without delay.

The Saint Mary's will leave, to be followed by the Clinton and Crescent next day, each vessel capable of carrying 800 or 900 men, or 100 horses and 500 men.

I have the honor to be,

N. J. T. DANA,
Major-General.

Brig. Gen. CHARLES P. STONE,
Chief of Staff, New Orleans.

BRAZOS ISLAND,
November 7, 1863—8 p. m.

GENERAL: I have just received your dispatch of 10.30 a. m. of to-day. Brigadier-General Ransom has arrived, and I had intended to have relieved General Vandever and to have put him in his place, but I must for the present leave him here to push matters on.

The Twentieth are still on board the Scott, and I will remain here long enough to-morrow to see that they are sure to be landed, and to see that other things are so far progressed that General Ransom can understand them, but shall leave some time to-morrow.

Vandever's brigade, except the Fifteenth Maine, is on the march to Brownsville. The Twentieth Iowa, of Dye's brigade, is at Point Isabel. The Twentieth Wisconsin, of the same brigade, will march to-morrow for Brownsville.

I see no way immediately of sending the articles I have named in connection with the Scott, except on lighters which we expect from you by way of the mouth of the river. Will they be in danger by that route?

I shall send the Saint Mary's to Brashear at noon to-morrow. The Clinton and the Crescent will leave next day, unless otherwise directed.

I have the honor to remain, very respectfully,
N. J. T. DANA,
Major-General.

Major-General BANKS,
Brownsville.

BROWNSVILLE,
November 15, 1863—7 a. m.

GENERAL: I received last night your dispatch of 9 a. m. yesterday, and just before that I had written you by the sergeant commanding the escort which was furnished to Governor King. Nothing has occurred since then. The troops sent from here are the Thirteenth Maine, Thirty-fourth Iowa, and Battery F, First Missouri Light Artillery (six pieces), which, with the Fifteenth Maine, make about 1,100 men, 100 more than I understood you to have prepared.

The Twentieth Iowa is also at Point Isabel, 300 strong. I mention these things because you say in your communication "the Thirteenth Maine will probably be here to-night, and I think you should forward immediately the other regiments," and I am uneasy for fear you may be expecting more troops from here than I understood you to direct. I will wait to hear from you further before sending more.

I have the honor to be, very respectfully, your obedient servant,
N. J. T. DANA,
Major-General.

Major-General BANKS,
Brazos Island.

—

BROWNSVILLE, TEX.,
November 15, 1863—1 p. m.

GENERAL: I inclose notes from Colonel Davis and Mr. Gray,* on the subject of enlisting Texans for a term "during the campaign in Texas." From what you had said to me, I had decided, when Mr. Gray first applied to have a company of rangers mustered in that way, to order it to be done; but I then discovered that Gray had no authority

---

* Not found.

or commission from you, neither had he a company, but only 12 men to begin with, and expected to get others. Colonel Davis complains that some of these are his recruits, and that Gray, by holding out the inducement of short enlistment, influences men who have already offered to serve like the other old troops. He even asserts that Gray has been sworn in in his regiment himself. He thinks the interference of Gray has operated to check recruiting very much. As Gray had no authority from you, I decided to suspend any action till I could communicate with you; but I informed Colonel Davis that I had understood you to say you would authorize the acceptance of Texans for the term of "during the campaign in Texas" who would not otherwise enlist. I think the question involves difficulties, as it will, perhaps, operate to cause dissatisfaction among some old troops, especially in Davis' regiment.

Please accept my thanks for the papers you sent me. They are the only ones I have received.

It is superfluous to offer or express my best wishes for your new enterprise. I feel that it is already accomplished, and I have every confidence of hearing from you to that effect in a very few days.

With great respect, your obedient servant,

N. J. T. DANA,
Major-General.

Major-General BANKS,
Commanding Department of the Gulf.

[P. S.]—I have this moment received a message from Mr. Pierce, by one of my staff officers, to the effect that rumors were coming in that the French advance was falling back on Tampico, and preparations were making for the evacuation of Tamaulipas.

—

HEADQUARTERS THIRTEENTH ARMY CORPS,
Brownsville, November 16, 1863—7 p. m.

GENERAL: I have just received your dispatch of 2.30 p. m. of yesterday. This afternoon dispatches arrived here through Mr. Pierce, consul at Matamoras, from Mr. Kimmey, consul at Monterey, addressed to you, which I have taken the liberty of opening, owing to the supposition that they probably contained information from Eagle Pass or Franklin which ought to be acted on without delay. I inclose the packages.

In replying to Mr. Kimmey, I told him we were buying all the horses and mules which were presented, and would buy not less than 2,000 of both. I also informed him that if his mails were sent to our care at this place, via Brazos, we would deliver them to Mr. Pierce. I have sent Lieutenant Cushing into the interior of Mexico, 30 miles from Matamoras, to procure horses and mules; he will be gone two days. The fortifications were commenced to-day, and will be pressed forward. I have sent into the interior 30 miles for some cotton which was reported as approaching the river above here, and I also expect a couple of lots in from a point 70 miles from here on the King's ranch road. The teamsters came to ask permission to bring it in, and security that they might sell it. I offered them to pay their freight money ($4 per hundred) on their delivery of it if they would bring it in of their own accord. They consented, and have gone for it. The Thirty-fourth Iowa captured and delivered 39 bales on their march down to Point Isabel.

I have ordered a cavalry picket of 50 men, 40 miles from here, on the Corpus Christi road, beyond the Arroyo Colorado, at the point where the road crosses it at Taylor's Ferry. Also a picket at Rancho Rucia, on the Rio Grande, 27 miles above here, where the road to Las Animas leaves the river. Both pickets are ordered to keep out vedettes, and scout the country, &c. We shall keep our picket line vigilant and strong enough.

I have the honor to remain, with much respect, your obedient servant,

N. J. T. DANA,
Major-General.

Major-General BANKS,
Commanding Department of the Gulf.

[Inclosure.]

HEADQUARTERS THIRTEENTH ARMY CORPS,
Brownsville, November 16, 1863.

M. M. KIMMEY, Esq.,
U. S. Vice-Consul, Monterey, Mexico:

Your dispatch of the 11th instant, addressed to the major-general commanding the Department of the Gulf, was received here to-day, and, in his absence, I have opened and examined it. General Banks has gone up the coast, and I hope in two or three days to hear good news from him. We shall need many mules and horses for the army here, and are now buying all that are offered at fair prices. We shall need 1,000 of each very soon, and more after that.

In regard to your mails, it will give us great pleasure to serve you in that or any other way. If your mails are directed here, via Brazos Santiago, we will turn them over to Mr. Pierce at Matamoras for you. I send you the two latest papers I have, and am sorry I have no New Orleans papers.

Please accept our thanks for the information you give. It is to be hoped that our movements will leave * * * but little value * * * to Eagle Pass, in rebel estimation, before long. We are hoping soon to hear from General Carleton, through your agency, and shall depend a good deal on you to aid us with information.

Very truly, yours,

N. J. T. DANA,
Major-General.

—

HEADQUARTERS,
Brownsville, Tex., November 21, 1863—1 p. m.

GENERAL: I wrote my last dispatch on the 19th, and have not as yet heard from you since you left Brazos Island, except through Mexican reports, which have placed your advance as far as San Patricio. A rebel agent, who knows all about their train, and who manages most of them, told a friend of mine, whose relations with me are not known, that if you had landed at Corpus [Christi], and should march to San Patricio, you had force enough to take or compel them to destroy everything this side of there, and that he had one train this side of there loaded with blankets and clothing and other military supplies worth $300,000.

There was a cotton panic over the river yesterday; it was offered freely at 28 cents; everybody wanted to sell, but nobody would buy. People over there had all kinds of stories about it. Some said the consul had some secret instructions; some that there was to be an embargo.

To-day the rumor in Matamoras is that all foreigners are to be immediately prohibited from trading or doing business there. I have not
been able to give any satisfactory explanation to the numerous applications for information on the subject, nor can I offer you any other
solution than the one which will present itself to your own mind. The
rebels are reported to be fortifying at San Fernando Creek.

Colonel Davis left here this morning with 100 mounted men, two
howitzers, 100 infantry in wagons, and 150 [cavalry] and one howitzer,
on the Mustang. I instructed him to use his discretion in proceeding
as far as Rio Grande City. He expects to move 30 miles a day. His
condition, I regret to say, is just now discovered to be more deplorable
than ever. After repeated orders to hurry up his carbine ammunition
without loss of time from Brazos, and receiving no reply at all, I sent
down Colonel Sargent's stage by express for some yesterday, when I
discovered that there is not a carbine cartridge in Texas; they were all
sent back on the Peabody; she had of that description 180,000 rounds.

My last dispatch reported 114 bales of cotton since your departure.
Since then, that is, during two days, I have secured 268 bales more,
and I have the prospect of more work in that line than I can well attend
to. We have here and at Point Isabel now more than 500 bales. Some
horses begin to come in, and it is necessary Colonel Holabird should
without delay furnish more of both sorts of funds to Major Carpenter,
who is now here. To those who live over in Mexico, we can only pay
gold. I have paid none out yet, and we have enough now only for daily
wants—none for outstanding departments.

I have the honor to remain, with much respect, your obedient servant.

                                           N. J. T. DANA,
                                                  Major-General.
Maj. Gen. N. P. BANKS,
    Commanding Department of the Gulf.

—

                                           HEADQUARTERS,
                       Brownsville, November 27, 1863—7 a. m.

GENERAL: Herewith I inclose dispatches from the United States
consul at Monterey, of the respective dates 19th, 21st, and 22d instant.*
None of the refugees have as yet made their appearance. When they
arrive, I will issue rations to them until Mr. Braubach shall arrive and
organize them into a company, unless they are willing before his arrival
to attach themselves to Colonel Davis' command.

I am at a loss about supplying funds for the unusual expenses incurred by the consul and Mr. Braubach in raising, assisting, and forwarding these men, and for other expenses which he states in his dispatches he has incurred.

I have not the control of any funds which are applicable to such
objects, nor the authority to turn over funds to the consul, and therefore I hasten to address you this dispatch, and inclose copies of those
of the consul, in order that you may give me such orders and authority
as you think necessary, and order such funds sent here as are applicable
to the objects. I fear the consul will be embarrassed by advancing funds
himself.

I find that Colonel Holabird has left no special instructions with
Major Carpenter, nor supplied him with any contingent or secret fund

*Not found.

or any except the ordinary funds of the quartermaster's department, which, in the absence of extra authority, he has no right to expend except in the ordinary wants of the department.

I have the honor to remain, with much respect, your obedient servant,
                                                    N. J. T. DANA,
                                                         Major-General.
Maj. Gen. N. P. BANKS,
    Commanding Department of the Gulf.

—

No. 3.

Reports of Maj. Gen. Cadwallader C. Washburn, U. S. Army, commanding · First Division, of expedition against and capture of Fort Esperanza.

HEADQUARTERS UNITED STATES FORCES,
                    Cedar Bayou, November 25, 1863.

GENERAL: We are progressing fairly in crossing. The process is slow and tedious, but I will have all ferried over during the coming night. I will advance my headquarters to-morrow at least 15 miles, and will invest the fort the day after. I hope the gunboats may be in position by 10 a. m. on that day.

Please send me a signal officer.

The gunboat Granite City lies off this point, and has done so ever since my arrival, but I have not been able to communicate.

A rebel major was shot on the north side of the bayou on the day before yesterday.* His body was found this morning. He came down with a flag of truce. A sergeant from General Ransom's command swam over to him. He got into a dispute with the sergeant, and drew his pistol, and shot him, wounding him severely. Our soldiers, witnessing the struggle, fired, and the major was seen to limp away. His body was found a few hundred yards from the spot where he was struck. His inquiry was as to what had become of the Confederate troops that were on Mustang Island.

Respectfully, yours,
                                                C. C. WASHBURN,
                                                     Major-General.
Maj. Gen. N. P. BANKS,
    Commanding Department of the Gulf.

—

HEADQUARTERS GULF EXPEDITION,
        Matagorda Island, Tex., November 30, 1863—4 a. m.

GENERAL: The rebels evacuated Fort Esperanza at about 10 o'clock last night, and blew it up at 1 o'clock this morning. Our troops entered it at 2 o'clock. We captured ten guns, ranging from 24 to 128 pounders. Four magazines have already blown up, and there are three more which probably will blow up shortly, as a hot fire is raging within the fort. The fort contained about 1,000 men. Owing to the continuance of the norther, the gunboats could not move yesterday, but I continued at work without them. We drove them from all their outworks yesterday, and planted our field artillery at short range, and shelled them lively all day. Quite an amount of rations were found in the fort, which, if the fire does not consume, will prove a godsend, as we are entirely out.

---

* See Bee to Turner, November 24, 1863, Part II, p. 442.

The fort was a very large and complete one. Captain Baker will furnish plans as soon as possible. For the want of small boats, it was not possible for me to get round to McHenry Island, as I desired, to cut off their connections. I have sent a dispatch to Aransas to have all light-draught boats sent here, to enable me to move at once to Lavaca; also to have all troops sent up by water. They destroyed their means of communicating with the land, but I will get up a ferry·to-day, if I can, and shall follow them with as little delay as possible.

If you will send the Third Division, Thirteenth Army Corps, here, with that and the First, I will ask no more to go to Houston and take Galveston. I will move to Houston as soon as force enough is concentrated to make it prudent. For the past two days my men have suffered greatly from cold, and I shall expect much sickness growing out of the exposure on these islands. In the fight yesterday, we lost 2 men killed and 2 wounded. Please not forget to send me a battery of 20 or 30-pounder Parrotts. The First Wisconsin Battery, at Brashear City—four 30-pounders—I should like. They will be wanted at Galveston.

Respectfully, yours,

C. C. WASHBURN,
Major-General.

Major-General BANKS, *Comdg. Department of the Gulf.*

—

HEADQUARTERS COAST EXPEDITION,
Fort Esperanza, December 1, 1863.

GENERAL : I wrote you a brief dispatch.yesterday morning, informing you of the fall of this fort. The boat I intended to send it upon (the Crescent) I was afterward compelled to take to send to Aransas Pass for supplies, and to order up the light-draught boats there to enable me to move forward.

All the boats there, with one or two exceptions, are helpless for want of coal, as you will see by the inclosed note of Ensign Grinnell.* The Crescent has just returned, and the Saint Mary's, with troops and rations, is in the offing, and I hope will be able to cross the bar to-day. I have determined to move up the Matagorda Peninsula to the mouth of the Brazos River. There are two forts there which must be taken. If I have good luck, I will have that pass in one week. That will be my base of supply from which to move to Houston and Galveston. By the time that pass is in my possession, I shall hope to receive re-enforcements that will enable me to leave the coast and march on Houston. The latter point, I think, should be captured before moving against Galveston. The pass here is nearly 2 miles wide, and it is going to be a difficult job to ferry my wagons and artillery over to the peninsula, but it can be done. While waiting here for supplies yesterday, I thought it best to make a small demonstration toward Lavaca. We formed, and drove a company of mounted men, who were doing picket duty about 3 miles from here, in the direction of Lavaca. It is my intention to run the transports as far up Matagorda Bay as I can, to land supplies and troops, but, before doing so, I thought it best to have a gunboat reconnolter for rebel boats. I requested Captain Strong to send up his lightest draught boat, which he very readily did. She has not returned. Up to this time, no troops have joined me since I left Mustang Island. I have detailed the Twenty-third Iowa, Colonel Glasgow, to garrison this post.

---

* Not found.

My whole force with me is about 2,800, including the Twenty-third Iowa, but, with what are on the Saint Mary's and on the way by land, I expect my force will be increased to 4,000 and upward.

After writing you yesterday morning, my advance crossed over and took possession of a fort on Bayucos Island. One 24-pounder field gun was found in position, with about 100 rounds of ammunition, all in good order. Two other guns had been taken away. All the guns but one 24-pounder siege gun in Fort Esperanza were spiked. Five magazines were blown up, and two remain in good condition, with a good supply of ammunition. The ammunition for the large gun was not destroyed. It is needless for me to make any suggestions in regard to a supply of coal. A light-draught boat here now, with a supply of fuel, would be worth millions.

I am, general, your obedient servant,
C. C. WASHBURN,
Major-General.

Major-General BANKS,
Commanding Department of the Gulf.

—

HEADQUARTERS COAST EXPEDITION,
Fort Esperanza, December 1, 1863—6 p. m.

GENERAL: Your dispatch of the 26th instant [ultimo], directing me to remain here with the troops until further orders, in case I should capture the fort, is this moment received.

I had already crossed about 1,000 troops, which came on the Saint Mary's and Hussar, on to Matagorda Peninsula, and expected to have had my whole force, with artillery and wagons, over to-morrow, and ready to move the day following. I shall await here as you direct, but as the water here is bad, and no fuel, I will allow the troops on the peninsula to remain there, as they are in a perfectly safe position, and water and wood are to be had there.

As my men are without shelter, I was anxious to go ahead and get into some place less inhospitable, and with the troops I now have I should feel entirely safe so long as I kept along the coast and under cover of the gunboats.

Hoping that more troops may soon arrive, and that I may receive orders to advance, I remain, respectfully, your obedient servant,
C. C. WASHBURN,
Major-General.

Major-General BANKS,
Commanding Department of the Gulf.

—

HEADQUARTERS PASS CAVALLO EXPEDITION,
Fort Esperanza, Tex., December 6, 1863.

MAJOR: I herewith inclose reports of Brig. Gen. T. E. G. Ransom, commanding Third Brigade, Second Division, and Col. H. D. Washburn, commanding First Brigade, First Division, Thirteenth Army Corps, detailing the action of their respective brigades in the reduction of this fort.

I refer to these reports as containing most of the details pertaining to the expedition, and for the names of such persons as deserve specially to be honorably mentioned. On the 21st ultimo, I arrived at Aransas Pass, with the Thirty-third Illinois and part of the Eighteenth Indiana, on board steamer Clinton. On the 22d ultimo, I received your order to take command of an expedition up the coast, for the purpose of capturing this fort. On the same day, I proceeded to Saint Joseph's Island, and landed the troops and stores on board the Clinton by 12 m. On the 23d, I pushed forward same day to head of Saint Joseph's Island, 18 miles distant, having previously sent General Ransom in the advance, with instructions to bridge, if possible, the pass between Saint Joseph's and Matagorda Islands. On arriving at this pass (called Cedar Bayou), I discovered that to bridge would be impossible. With a width of nearly 300 yards, a strong current, and exposed to the terrible winds that here prevail, I saw that our only chance to get over was to ferry. Fearing that such would prove the case, I brought along on my wagons four yawl boats. By lashing together, I was able to take over my troops, wagons, and artillery. My horses and mules were swum across. On the 24th, a terrific norther sprung up, rendering it impossible to cross the pass, but on the following morning, the gale having subsided, the force commenced to cross, and by midnight were all over, and the rear went into camp, about 8 miles up the coast, at 3 a. m. On the 26th, marched over 20 miles, and encamped 10 miles from the fort, and on the 27th, at 11 a. m., came within range of the guns of the fort. Spent the rest of the day reconnoitering the position, the gunboats which were to co-operate not having come up. I soon discovered that the fort was a large and complete work, mounting heavy guns, and that all approaches were well guarded.

The country around was a level plain, and their outworks, which were of a most complete character, extended across from the Gulf to a lagoon connecting with the back bay. On the night after our arrival, a fierce norther sprung up, causing my men to suffer greatly, and rendering the prosecution of operations exceedingly disagreeable. The norther continued for two days, rendering it impossible for the gunboats to render us any assistance. I applied for launches, with which I intended to land troops on Bayucos Island and cut off their communication with the main [land], but the gale prevented their being furnished until too late.

The force within the fort was from 700 to 800, all of whom escaped under cover of night, excepting 6 belonging to their rear guard. The rebels left 1 man on the ground killed. If they had any wounded, they took them away. We lost 1 killed and 2 wounded. Lieutenant Fifer, a gallant young officer of the Thirty-third Illinois, was severely wounded in the breast. For a description of the fort, and the captures therein, I refer to the report of Captain Baker, engineer. We also captured a small fort on Bayucos Island, with one 24-pounder field gun. I cannot express in too strong language my admiration of the conduct of the officers and men engaged in this expedition. We left the foot of Saint Joseph's Island without transportation of any kind, except twelve wagons, which were used for transporting supplies. With this small train I had to supply 2,800 men, together with the animals belonging to the train, and horses for two batteries, nearly 60 miles from my base of supply.

The weather much of the time was very inclement, water very bad, and fuel scarce, but I never heard a complaint or murmur of any kind. The troops accompanying me were as follows, viz: Eighth Indiana Infantry, commanded by Major Kenny; Eighteenth Indiana, Lieutenant-Colonel Charles; Thirty-third Illinois, Col. C. E. Lippincott; Ninety-ninth Illinois, Colonel Bailey; Seventh Michigan Battery, Lieutenant Stillman, composing First Brigade; Twenty-third Iowa, Colonel Glasgow, of the Second Brigade, First Division, Thirteenth Army Corps, all commanded by Col. H. D. Washburn; and the Thirty-fourth Iowa,

Lieutenant-Colonel Dungan; Fifteenth Maine, Colonel Dyer; Thirteenth Maine, Colonel Hesseltine, and Foust's (Missouri) battery, of the Second Brigade, Second Division, Thirteenth Army Corps, commanded by Brigadier-General Ransom. It affords me great pleasure to state that the conduct of Brigadier-General Ransom and Col. H. D. Washburn, commanding brigades, was most prompt, gallant, and efficient, and deserves the highest praise. The navy has shown every disposition to co-operate in the most prompt manner, and to Captain Strong, of the Monongahela, commanding the fleet, and Captain Lamson, of the Granite City, I am under many obligations. Their failure to take part in the attack on the fort was attributable solely to the gale which at the time prevailed.

C. C. WASHBURN,
Major-General.

Maj. G. NORMAN LIEBER, *Assistant Adjutant-General.*

A D D E N D A.

HEADQUARTERS DEPARTMENT OF THE GULF,
New Orleans, December 5, 1863.

Maj. Gen. C. C. WASHBURN,
Commanding Forces on Matagorda Bay, Texas :

GENERAL: The major-general commanding the department has received with great satisfaction your report announcing the capture of the works of the enemy at Port Cavallo. You will be duly re-enforced and supplied. The Second Regiment Engineers, Corps d'Afrique, sails this p. m., with orders to report to you for duty on the fortifications, and troops of other arms will be forwarded as rapidly as practicable. Meantime the commanding general desires that you scout actively all the country in your front, and make such demonstrations in the direction of Indianola and Palacios as your means may allow, with a view to amuse and confuse the enemy as to your intentions, while you press your scouts in the direction of Coney Creek, and gain reliable information as to the roads, the present condition of the country, and the means that would be required to move a large force through it.

The major general commanding desires you to understand that an advance of your forces will bring down upon you the concentrated forces of the enemy; and that you must be largely re-enforced before such advance is made. Until such time you will be well employed in strengthening your present position, rendering your men as comfortable as possible, and preparing them for efficient service when the advance shall be ordered. Fuel has been ordered to you; also tents and lumber.

Very respectfully, I am, general, your obedient servant,
CHAS. P. STONE,
Brigadier-General, Chief of Staff.

No. 4.

Report of Col. Henry D. Washburn, Eighteenth Indiana Infantry, commanding First Brigade, of expedition against and capture of Fort Esperanza.

SALURIA, TEX., *December 3, 1863.*

MAJOR: I beg leave to submit the following report of the part taken by the First Brigade, First Division, Thirteenth Army Corps, in the reduction of Fort Esperanza, on Matagorda Island :

At midnight, November 25, I had succeeded, after much difficulty, in getting the whole of my force across Cedar Bayou, upon the island, and marched immediately to join General Ransom, some 8 miles in advance. After a few hours' rest, we moved up the island, making a very hard march through the sand of 23 miles; camped for the night, and moved in the morning for this place, my brigade, by your order, moving along the beach. About 12 o'clock we had advanced to the light-house, and in close proximity to the enemy's works. The main portion of the command was halted, and, by your order, I proceeded with one company from each of my regiments, under the command of Capt. Ira Moore, Thirty-third Illinois, a most excellent officer, supported by the Thirty-third Regiment Illinois Infantry, to reconnoiter, and endeavor to find the strength and position of the enemy. Moving cautiously up the beach, we soon drove in the enemy's picket, and our advance was safely lodged in a range of sand hills, within 300 yards of the outer work of the enemy—a heavy earthwork, extending from the bay to a lagoon running from the bay on the mainland side of the island. The work was regularly laid out, about 15 feet in thickness, and from 10 to 15 feet in height.

The enemy now opened upon us from Fort Esperanza with his 128-pounder and 24s, throwing shells, but with little or no effect. Having found out the position and apparent strength of the enemy, by your order I withdrew my advance. During the night, a heavy norther coming on, we were unable to do much the 28th. The night of the 28th, Captain McCallister, of the Eighth Indiana, and Captain Hull, of the Ninety-ninth Illinois, both of whom had had considerable experience in that line in the rear of Vicksburg, with a fatigue party from each of the regiments in the brigade, under cover of the darkness, dug a rifle-pit from the sand hills on the beach occupied by us the first day, and running parallel with the enemy's works, 210 yards in length, sufficient to cover a regiment. Sergeant Goodlander, of Company F, Eighth Indiana, with a small detail from the different regiments, was ordered to move at early dawn in advance of our rifle-pit, and endeavor to gain a position on the outer edge of the enemy's works. The Eighth Indiana was also moved out, and ordered to lie down in the open prairie, in order to take advantage of any lodgment our advance might make. Captain Hull, of the Ninety-ninth, volunteered, and accompanied the advance. The morning was bitterly cold, and our men suffered severely. Our advance moved up slowly and cautiously, took position on the outside of the work, the inside being controlled by the enemy in the sand hills between the work and the main fort, driving in a small picket force on the inside, the force for protection of the work having been driven by the weather to the sand hills. They endeavored to rally and drive our men back, but in vain. The Eighth Indiana was immediately sent forward in small detachments, so as to avoid the fire of the heavy guns of the fort, and gained a safe footing in our rifle-pit and on the enemy's work. Finding ourselves more successful than I had dared to hope, I returned to the main portion of my brigade, and immediately sent Colonel Lippincott with his regiment to the front, with instructions to take command of the force in front, and to advance as fast as prudence would allow, and to get, if possible, a position where our artillery might be made effective. Colonel Lippincott moved promptly with his command, and I soon had the pleasure of hearing from him that he had secured a good position for our artillery.

Adjt. W. W. Zener, of the Eighteenth Indiana, now on my staff, was ordered to bring up two pieces of the Seventh Michigan Battery, under command of Lieutenant Stillman, which he accomplished with dispatch.

The pieces were brought up and placed in battery under a heavy fire from the fort, fortunately not very accurate, and we soon had the pleasure of seeing our shells dropping in the enemy's stronghold, and driving them from their guns. Colonel Lippincott had very judiciously disposed of the two regiments, and had, previously to the arrival of the artillery, advanced several companies into the sand hills in our front, driving back the enemy nearer his main work. I also ordered possession to be taken of an old work several hundred yards in our front, and to the left and rear of the fort, which was gallantly done by Captain McCallister, Eighth Indiana, with his company. This enabled us to move our advance on the right nearer the fort. In the meantime I had ordered Lieutenant-Colonel Charles, Eighteenth Indiana, to move his regiment to the support of the Eighth and Thirty-third, in doing which he passed under a heavy fire of the fort, but fortunately for him the enemy threw nothing but solid shot, which, from their size, were easily avoided, and he gained his position with the loss of but 1 man.

Night coming on, found four companies of the Eighth Indiana and five companies of the Thirty-third Illinois in the sand hills near the fort (725 yards, as shown by measurement). Two companies of the Eighth Indiana held the old work to our front. The balance of three regiments held the outside of the new work. The men, although the night was raw and cold, remained upon the field and in their position. A fatigue party was detailed from the reserve regiments, and proceeded to move the four pieces of the Seventh Michigan Battery to the work occupied by our troops, and, by filling the ditch, placed them in a fine position. I also ordered a portion of the Eighteenth Indiana, under Captain Lowes, to re-enforce Captain McCallister, as I believed that to be an important point. The Ninety-ninth Illinois and Twenty-third Iowa, who were held in reserve, were to move at daylight to our position, while a general advance of the whole brigade was to take place. These arrangements were hardly completed when, about 12.30 o'clock, an explosion of gunpowder in the fort warned us that the enemy were on the move. I immediately ordered an advance of the skirmishers, and found that the enemy had fled, leaving behind him his stores and ammunition and the personal baggage of the officers. They had, however, piled a large quantity of cotton around the different magazines, after having scattered gunpowder around in different places.

The advance pushed on to the ferry, but were too late; the enemy had cut the rope, allowing the floating bridge to swing around upon the shore. They had also attempted to destroy it by piling cotton upon it and firing it, but our men were too close, and put out the fire. Six of the 8 men left by the enemy to fire the trains were captured.

At daylight I moved a small force across to McHenry Island, and took possession of a small earthwork containing one 24-pounder gun, considerable ammunition, and some garrison equipage. In Fort Esperanza we found one 128-pounder columbiad and seven 24-pounder siege guns. Two of the magazines were saved. Considerable camp and garrison equipage was in the fort, but, owing to the danger from the explosion, we failed to save it.

My total loss was 1 man killed and 10 wounded, among the latter Lieut. George H. Fifer, acting aide-de-camp, a gallant and brave officer, who fell, severely wounded, during our first reconnaissance. My officers and men behaved gallantly, showing that they had lost none of that coolness and bravery evinced by them upon the battle-fields of Pea Ridge, Fredericktown, Port Gibson, Champion's Hill, Black River Bridge, Vicksburg, and Jackson.

Colonel Lippincott, of the Thirty-third Illinois, rendered me great assistance in the advance upon the enemy's works, and displayed both courage and judgment.

Major Kenny, of the Eighth Indiana, though lately promoted to the position, proved by his courage and coolness that he was well worthy of the same.

Lieutenant-Colonel Charles, of the Eighteenth Regiment Indiana Volunteers, brought his regiment in fine style and good order through a heavy fire from the fort to the support of the two advance regiments.

Colonel Bailey, of the Ninety-ninth Illinois, and Colonel Glasgow, of the Twenty-third Iowa, who were held in reserve, were both anxious to be moved to the front, and, more by accident than anything else, were thrown into the reserve. Both regiments had already established their reputation as veterans in the well-fought fields of Mississippi. I am greatly indebted to Captain McCallister, Eighth Indiana, and Captain Hull, Ninety-ninth Illinois, for their assistance in the digging and laying out of their rifle-pit and placing of the battery.

Lieutenant Stillman, commanding Seventh Michigan Battery, rendered very efficient aid in discomfiting the enemy. Two guns of his battery were worked right under the fire of the guns of the fort.

My own staff discharged their duties with fidelity, courage, and ability. They are as follows: Maj. I. H. Elliott, Thirty-third Illinois, inspector and chief of staff; Capt. S. H. Dunbar, Eighth Indiana, acting assistant adjutant-general; Capt. John Ruess, Eighth Indiana, acting assistant commissary of subsistence; Lieut. and Adjt. W. W. Zener, Eighteenth Indiana, aide-de-camp and provost-marshal; Lieut. G. H. Fifer, Thirty-third Illinois, aide-de-camp; Lieut. J. G. Sever, Ninety-ninth Illinois, ordnance officer. Maj. Joseph H. Ledlie, Ninety-ninth Illinois, senior surgeon, was detailed on operating board.

I would also make especial mention of Sergt. John Goodlander, of Company F, Eighth Indiana, and Private Addison Hallenbeck, Company K, Eighteenth Indiana, who were the first to mount the enemy's works the morning of the 29th. In mentioning the above, I would not have it understood that any of my officers or men failed to do their duty, and their whole duty.

I am, very respectfully, your obedient servant,

H. D. WASHBURN,
Colonel, Comdg. First Brig., First Div., Thirteenth Army Corps.

No. 5.

Report of Col. [John] Charles Black, Thirty-seventh Illinois Infantry, First Brigade, Second Division, of expedition to Rio Grande City.

STEAMER MUSTANG,
December —, 1863.

MAJOR: I have the honor to submit the following report of the part borne by the Thirty-seventh Illinois Infantry in the late expedition to Rio Grande City, Tex.:

In pursuance to the instructions of the major-general commanding, I reported to Col. E. J. Davis for orders, November 22, and, in conformity therewith, embarked with seven companies of my command on board the steamer Mustang, at 12 m., November 23. The remaining three companies, under Major Payne, accompanied the land forces in wagons.

The trip up the river was devoid of incident, except that we found a very low stage of water, and were obliged to haul over several bad bars; the course of the river is extremely tortuous also, and these things in conjunction rendered it impossible to keep up with the land forces.

On the 26th day of November, I informed Colonel Davis, by express, that it was nearly impossible to proceed in anything like reasonable time, and that the steamer lay at the foot of a long reach or bar only 18 inches deep and 6 feet in length. He sent back word for me to await the arrival of the infantry and captured cotton where I was. The infantry reached us on the 28th, in company with the cavalry, which passed on. I awaited the arrival of the cotton impatiently for two days, and then sent out a detachment under Lieutenant Day, of Company E, to look for it. He found that part of the train had only come 8 miles from where it started. By dint of much exertion, he succeeded in reaching the boat with the cotton, 82 bales in all, about noon of the 1st of December, and the next morning at dawn he started on the return trip.

We have been so long in coming owing to the wretchedly poor stage of water. We have been aground every day, sometimes making but 10 miles in twenty-four hours, although every effort was made to hasten on.

My eight days' rations being exhausted while lying to for the cotton, I visited the town of Old Reynosa, on the Mexican side, to endeavor to obtain a fresh supply. In this I was unsuccessful, as there was no supply on hand.

I found the forces of the National Guard mustering to the number of some 200 men, under Don Florentino, the commandant of the post. This officer offered every courtesy possible to myself and officers during our visit. He complained to me that one John Travinio, a resident of the town of Edinburg, on the American side, had recently crossed over with a gang of some 15 armed men, committed depredations on the Mexican side, and then returned to Edinburg, and expressed a desire to concert some measure with the Federal commander to prevent the recurrence of a like offense. I determined to arrest Travinio, and did so on the 2d of December, since when he has been a prisoner in my hands. He is of a wealthy and influential family, a man of considerable attainments himself, and very much of a gentleman. I desire to submit his case to the proper authorities.

At Edinburg, I found a few days' rations awaiting my arrival, but have been very short all the way down, on half rations of bread-stuff, all except two days. I have hence been obliged to draw largely on the country for beef.

The officers of the steamer Mustang have afforded all possible comforts during the voyage. I desire to call the attention of the general to them as capable and accommodating gentlemen in their line of business.

There have been no casualties or losses sustained during the expedition. The health of the regiment continues good. The distance traveled by the regiment on water has been 360 miles; distance on land, 150 miles. Total distance, 510 miles.

I have the honor to be, very respectfully,

[JOHN] CHAS. BLACK,
Colonel Thirty-seventh Illinois, Commanding.

Maj. WILLIAM HYDE CLARK,
Asst. Adjt. Gen., Second Division, Thirteenth Army Corps.

No. 6.

Report of Maj. John Bruce, Nineteenth Iowa Infantry, Second Brigade, of the occupation of Brownsville, &c.

BROWNSVILLE, TEX.,
December 1, 1863.

GENERAL: I have the honor to submit to you an account of the part taken by my regiment in the expedition against Texas, which was under command of Major-General Banks and started from New Orleans on the 24th October, 1863.

On the 23d, my regiment embarked on the steamer General Banks. The entire fleet consisted of sixteen vessels and three gunboats, all loaded with troops, provisions, and munitions of war.

On the 27th, the fleet sailed through the Southwest Pass, and came to anchor outside the bar. Went to sea on the 29th. On the 30th, we encountered a severe storm from the north. Our ship being overloaded, as well as old and frail, labored and strained alarmingly. The sea striking very heavily under the guards and fan-tail, threatened to tear off the latter, rendering it necessary, in order to save life, to lighten the ship. This was at once done by heaving overboard 11 mules, one battery wagon, forage, &c., after which she rode easier, but her leakage constantly increased, requiring the unremitting working of the pumps.

On the 31st October, our fuel was nearly exhausted, and we were taken in tow by the Empire City.

On the 1st day of November, we came in sight of land, and at 6 p. m. came to anchor off the bar at the island of Brazos.

On the 2d November, we were the first of the fleet to cross the bar, and about noon effected a landing. The Nineteenth Regiment was the first command landed, and its colors the first that floated on the breeze of that desolate island. I was at once ordered out; moved 6 miles to the front, and held the advance for three days, until a large part of the force was landed and came up.

On the 6th of November, our orders were to move forward, and, after two days' march up the Rio Grande, crossing the battle-fields of Palo Alto and Resaca de la Palma, we entered Brownsville, Tex., on the 7th, without opposition.

The enemy had a small force, which evacuated the place on our approach. Previously, however, they fired the barracks of Fort Brown and many private buildings, which were smoldering ruins when we took possession of the town. We captured a large amount of cotton, and stopped a large trade going on between Mexico and the so-called Confederate States.

Col. William McE. Dye, of the Twentieth Iowa, commanding our brigade (Second Brigade, Second Division, Thirteenth Army Corps), was made commander of the post, and his brigade went into barracks in the town, where we still remain.

I am, very respectfully, your obedient servant,

JOHN BRUCE,
Major, Commanding Nineteenth Iowa Infantry.

N. B. BAKER,
Adjutant-General of Iowa.

No. 7.

Reports of Brig. Gen. T. E. G. Ransom, U. S. Army, commanding Third Brigade, of the capture of Confederate battery at Aransas Pass, and expedition against and capture of Fort Esperanza.

HEADQUARTERS UNITED STATES FORCES,
North end of Mustang Island, Texas, November 18, 1863.

SIR: I have the honor to report that, in obedience to Special Orders, No. —, dated Headquarters Department of the Gulf, Brazos Santiago, Tex., November 15, 1863, I embarked with the Thirteenth and Fifteenth Maine, Twentieth Iowa Infantry (two companies), First Engineers, Corps d'Afrique, and two boat howitzers, on the transports assigned by Colonel Holabird, assistant quartermaster, leaving orders for the Thirty-fourth Iowa Infantry and the battery, which were to arrive from Brownsville, to embark on the steamer Warrior and follow the expedition.

At sunset on the 16th instant, I disembarked the Thirteenth and Fifteenth Maine, Twentieth Iowa Infantry, and the two boat howitzers, through the surf near the south end of Mustang Island, and at once moved my force in a northerly direction up the beach, with a strong line of skirmishers in my front. Meeting no enemy, I moved rapidly, and by 4 a. m. on the morning of the 17th had made about 18 miles. I halted at this point, allowed the troops to rest until daylight, and again pushed forward.

The enemy's skirmishers made a faint show of resistance about 1 mile south of their camp, when I deployed the Thirteenth Maine, and, advancing in line, drove them to their camp on the north end of the island, where the garrison, consisting of 9 officers and 89 men, with a battery of three heavy guns, surrendered to me without further resistance, and unconditionally. I at once placed Col. Isaac Dyer, Fifteenth Maine Infantry, in command of the post, and made provision for the care of prisoners and captured stores, which consisted chiefly of three heavy guns, the small-arms of the prisoners, one schooner, and ten small boats, all in good condition.

I herewith forward descriptive lists of the prisoners and schedule of captured property.* There are about 140 horses and mules and 125 head of cattle on the island. Scarcity of forage has compelled me to let them run at large and subsist on the scanty growth of grass on the island.

Col. H. D. Washburn, Eighteenth Indiana Infantry, commanding the troops on the steamer Saint Mary's, disembarked a portion of his troops (Eighteenth Indiana) at the south end of the island, the remainder (Eighth Indiana) near the north end of the island, and, by a forced march, reached me at this point about two hours after the surrender.

After my forced night march of 22 miles up the beach, my command was completely exhausted and foot-sore. Both officers and men are entitled to great credit for their perseverance and zeal in accomplishing the march, and dragging the artillery by hand with them.

The co-operation of the United States naval forces, under Commander James H. Strong, in the Monongahela, merits and receives my entire approbation. He advanced soon after daylight, and searched for the enemy's works, making excellent practice with his guns, bursting 11-inch shell, as I afterward learned, in the enemy's camp. The conduct of the naval party, consisting of Acting Ensign H. W. Grinnell and 10 seamen of the Monongahela, in charge of two howitzers, in landing and accom-

---

* Omitted.

panying the expedition from Corpus Christi Pass, was of the most satis-factory character.

Capt. L. P. Griffin, naval aide to General Banks, afforded me much valuable assistance and advice. The sailing of the fleet was under his direction, and the plan of landing through the surf was adopted through his advice. I desire particularly to make honorable mention of Col. Isaac Dyer, commanding Fifteenth Maine Infantry, and Lieutenant-Colonel Hesseltine, Thirteenth Maine Infantry, who were untiring in their efforts to encourage their men and urge them forward. Lieutenant-Colonel Hesseltine was the first man to land through the surf and plant his colors on the island. Captain [Richard M.] Hill and Lieutenant Jackson, of General Banks' staff, volunteered much valuable assistance.

I regret to mention in this connection the unsoldierlike conduct of Major Thompson, commanding Twentieth Iowa Infantry, who constantly discouraged his men by complaining in their presence of the hardships of the march, and permitted them to scatter and straggle to the rear, losing more than half his men before he reached the north end of the island.

Lieut. Col. W. S. Dungan, Thirty-fourth Iowa, reported to me, shortly after the surrender, with his regiment and Battery F, First Missouri Light Artillery, on steamer Warrior. I caused the Thirty-fourth Iowa to be disembarked on Saint Joseph's Island, leaving the battery for the present on board.

T. E. G. RANSOM,
Brigadier-General of Volunteers.

Lieut. AUGUSTUS W. SEXTON,
Acting Assistant Adjutant-General, Department of the Gulf.

—

HEADQUARTERS THIRD BRIGADE, SECOND DIVISION,
Fort Esperanza, Tex., December 6, 1863.

MAJOR: I have the honor to report that, on the 22d ultimo, in obedi-ence to the order of Maj. Gen. C. C. Washburn, I moved my command (consisting of the Thirteenth and Fifteenth Maine and Thirty-fourth Iowa Infantry and Battery F, First Missouri Artillery) from Aransas Pass, 8 miles up Saint Joseph's Island, and encamped at a ranch for the night. Moved on the next morning, and reached Cedar Bayou about noon 23d ultimo, where my advance guard of mounted infantry, under command of Capt. C. S. Ilsley, Fifteenth Maine, had a slight skirmish with a scouting party of the enemy, in which Maj. Charles Hill, com-manding the rebel party, was killed, and Sergt. James Saunders, Com-pany F, Fifteenth Maine, was slightly wounded. I halted at this place, and commenced the construction of a ferry across Cedar Bayou.

On the 25th ultimo, I ferried my command across Cedar Bayou, and encamped about 7 miles up Matagorda Island, where I was joined by Colonel Washburn's brigade about midnight. On the 26th, I marched my command about 20 miles up the island, and encamped at a ranch about 10 miles from this point. On the morning of the 27th, I ad-vanced my brigade, under the direction of General Washburn, up the middle of the island, while Colonel Washburn moved his brigade in a parallel line up the Gulf beach. About 11 a. m. we met the advanced pickets of the enemy, and drove them into his works. After recon-noitering and ascertaining the location of the outer works and main fort of the enemy, I placed my command in an advanced position indicated by General Washburn, on the left of our line and under cover of a slight rise of ground. This afternoon and the following day were occupied in reconnoitering the approaches to the enemy's work, and was attended with occasional skirmishing and sharpshooting on both sides and occasional.artillery shots from the enemy.

On the night of the 28th, I threw up an earthwork in advance of my left, and on the opposite side of a salt lagoon which intervened between my position and the chief work of the enemy, where I placed Captain Foust's battery, supported by the Thirty-fourth Iowa Infantry, and opened fire on the fort at daylight on the 29th, continuing at intervals all day. In the meantime the Seventh Michigan Battery, of Colonel Washburn's brigade, had been advanced under cover of the sand hills on the beach, and opened upon the fort from the right of our line. No casualties occurred in my command. During the night of the 29th ultimo the enemy evacuated their works and retired, setting fire to their magazines and stores.

The whole of the troops of my command acquitted themselves creditably, and bore the hardships of the severe norther of the 28th and 29th on short rations with a cheerfulness scarcely to be expected from troops most of whom had never experienced a field campaign.

I am, very respectfully, your obedient servant,

T. E. G. RANSOM,
Brigadier-General of Volunteers.

Maj. WILLIAM H. MORGAN,
Assistant Adjutant-General, Coast Expedition.

No. 8.

Abstracts from " Record of Events" on the several returns of the Thirteenth Army Corps, for October, November, and December, 1863.

CORPS RETURNS.

November 15.—Part of the First Division, under command of General Washburn, embarked at Algiers, La., for Brazos Santiago, where it arrived on the 18th instant, but, in consequence of a strong wind, was unable to cross the bar.

November 20.—Orders were received from General Banks for the troops to be landed on Mustang and Saint Joseph's Islands, which was effected on the 21st and 22d.

November 23.—The troops, under command of General Washburn, moved against Fort Esperanza, at the head of Matagorda, and which the enemy evacuated on the 25th [29th] instant, after spiking their guns and blowing up all the magazines except one.

December 2.—The [Second] Division, excepting one regiment stationed at Aransas and a detachment under Brigadier-General Ransom, serving with First Division, continued to occupy Brownsville. During the month the remainder of the First Division, excepting four regiments at Plaquemine, La., and part of the Third and Fourth Divisions, were transported from Louisiana to Pass Cavallo, Texas.

RETURN OF FIRST DIVISION.

December 23.—The First Brigade left Saluria for Indianola, Tex., where they are now stationed. The Second and Third Brigades still remain at this (De Cros') Point.

RETURN OF SECOND BRIGADE, FIRST DIVISION.

November 17.—Early in the morning, broke camp at Berwick, La.; crossed Berwick Bay to Brashear City, where we took the cars for New Orleans, at which point we arrived the same night.

November 20.—In the afternoon, we left New Orleans on the steamship Thomas A. Scott, and went to sea.

November 22.—We arrived off the Rio Grande. A storm coming up, we had to put to sea. While at sea, spoke another steamer, and she ordered us up to Aransas, at which point we arrived on the 25th, where we landed.

November 28.—In the morning, started up Saint Joseph's Island.

November 30.—Reached the head of the island.

December 1.—Left the foot of Matagorda Island, and marched to Fort Esperanza, at the head of the island, arriving there on the 3d.

December 6.—Crossed to De Cros' Point, Matagorda Peninsula, and went into camp, where we now are.

RETURN OF SECOND DIVISION.

October 1.—The division was stationed at Morganza, La., until the 11th instant, when it embarked on transports and sailed for Carrollton.

October 12.—Arrived at Carrollton about 10 a. m., and went into camp, where it remained until the 22d instant, busily engaged in fitting out for a campaign in a new field.

October 21.—The Thirteenth and Fifteenth Maine Infantry were attached to the division by order of Major-General Banks, and the First Texas Cavalry, First Engineers, and Sixteenth Infantry, Corps d'Afrique, were ordered to report to Major-General Dana, commanding the corps and division, though not attached to the division.

October 23.—The division embarked on transports, and dropped down the river.

October 25.—Sailed for the mouth of the Rio Grande.

October 26, 27, 28, 29, 30, and *31* found them still in the Gulf, on board boats, *en route* to their destinations.

November 1.—This division, under the immediate command of Major-General Dana, was on transports, lying off the coast, awaiting an opportunity to land, a storm raging at the time.

November 3.—Commenced landing by lighters and small boats on Brazos Island, consuming several days, and losing two steamers and two schooners in so doing.

November 6.—The Second Brigade, excepting the Twentieth Iowa, marched on, and occupied Brownsville. On the same day, the Twentieth Iowa occupied Point Isabel. The First Brigade, excepting the Fifteenth Maine, which remained at Brazos, marched on same day toward Brownsville, encamped on the Rio Grande, and marched into Brownsville on the 8th. The First Texas Cavalry marched in detachments, as their horses were unloaded, for same point—a long and tedious process, consuming several days. The First Engineers and Sixteenth Infantry, Corps d'Afrique, left at Brazos.

November 13.—The Thirteenth Maine Infantry marched from Brownsville to Point Isabel.

November 14.—The Thirty-fourth Iowa and Battery F, First Missouri Light Artillery, marched from Brownsville to Point Isabel, and the Fifteenth Maine, having crossed to Point Isabel from Brazos, the Twentieth and Thirty-fourth Iowa, the Thirteenth and Fifteenth Maine, and

Battery F were placed under command of Brigadier-General Ransom, and proceeded up the coast by vessel, and landed on Mustang Island.

November 16.—Marched up the island, captured a small fort, with heavy guns, prisoners, &c., and proceeded to Saint Joseph's Island.

November 28.—Attacked a fort of the enemy, compelling them to abandon and destroy everything in it. This portion of the division is still absent, and no further reports have been heard from them.

November 20.—The First Texas Cavalry, the Thirty-seventh Illinois, and a section of Battery B marched on Ringgold Barracks, some 200 miles above the Rio Grande, where a force of rebels were said to be; and are at this date, November 30, still absent. The remainder of the troops are at Point Isabel and Brazos Island, engaged in fortifying and holding those posts. Health of the troops generally good. A large amount of cotton and valuable stores have been captured and turned over to the proper departments, for which the various staff reports will account.

RETURN OF SECOND BRIGADE, SECOND DIVISION.

November 3.—The Nineteenth Iowa, Thirteenth Maine, and Battery B, First Missouri Light Artillery, landed on Brazos Island, and the two regiments proceeded to the Boca Chica, where the Nineteenth Iowa encamped. The Thirteenth Maine crossed and moved down the coast to the mouth of the Rio Grande, and encamped.

November 4.—Received orders to land the brigade, and move at once with four days' rations to Brownsville, and occupy the place. The brigade commander landed with the Ninety-fourth Illinois, leaving orders to have the rations loaded and sent after him. Moved on the road to Brownsville, by way of the Rio Grande, passing the Nineteenth Iowa at the Boca Chica, who were ordered to wait for the artillery and rations, and come on with them. Found the Thirteenth Maine at the mouth of the Rio Grande, without rations, and also that the Twentieth Iowa and Twentieth Wisconsin had failed in the attempt to land, having drowned 3 or 4 men in the breakers and lost a number of arms, accouterments, knapsacks, &c. Pushed on for Brownsville, leaving the Thirteenth Maine to come on as soon as rations could be procured, and arrived in front of Brownsville with the Ninety-fourth Illinois, about 125 men, on the evening of the 5th.

November 6.—Moved in at 10 a. m. and took possession. At 4 p. m. the Thirteenth Maine arrived, and two pieces of Battery B.

November 7.—The Nineteenth Iowa arrived, and the Twentieth Wisconsin on the 10th. The Twentieth Iowa has not been heard from officially since landing. The Thirteenth Maine left this place on the 13th instant for Point Isabel, and has not been heard from officially since.

November 21.—One section of Battery B accompanied a scout to Ringgold Barracks.

RETURN OF FIRST BRIGADE, THIRD DIVISION.

December 19.—Left New Iberia, La., for Berwick Bay, La., arriving there on the evening of the 21st; distance marched, about 60 miles.

December 22, 23.—Crossed Berwick Bay, and took cars for Algiers, La., where we are still in camp, excepting the Thirty-fourth Indiana Infantry and four companies of the Forty-sixth Indiana Infantry, which have embarked for Texas.

RETURN OF FOURTH DIVISION.

During the month of December, the division marched from New Iberia, La., to Brashear City, where it took cars, and was transported to Algiers, from which place it was transported in vessels to this [Decros'] Point, arriving January 2, 1864.

RETURN OF FIRST BRIGADE, FOURTH DIVISION.

December 7.—This command was ordered to break camp by Major-General Franklin, and march to Berwick City, La.

December 10.—The command arrived at Berwick City.

December 11.—Was ordered by General Banks to report to Algiers, La.

December 12.—Arrived at Algiers.

December 16.—The Sixtieth and Sixty-seventh Indiana Regiments of this command embarked on the steamer Demale, and arrived on the 20th instant.

December 18.—The Nineteenth Kentucky and the Ninety-sixth Ohio embarked on the steamer George Peabody, and arrived here [Decros'] the 21st instant.

RETURN OF THE SECOND BRIGADE, FOURTH DIVISION.

December 7. —The brigade left New Iberia, and marched, via Franklin, to Berwick, La., where we encamped December 10.

December 11.—Proceeded by rail to Algiers, La., leaving one regiment (Seventy-seventh Illinois Volunteers) at Berwick, La.

December 13.—Embarked on the steam-transport Continental for Port Cavallo, Tex. Disembarked, and encamped at Decros' Point, Tex., 18th instant.

December 21.—The Seventy-seventh Illinois rejoined the brigade.

No. 9.

Reports of Maj. Gen. John B. Magruder, C. S. Army, commanding District of Texas, New Mexico, and Arizona.

HDQRS. DIST. OF TEXAS, NEW MEXICO, AND ARIZONA,
Houston, Tex., November 21, 1863.

GENERAL: I have the honor to transmit, for the information of the lieutenant-general commanding, copies of letters from Colonel Bradfute, announcing the capture of Aransas and Corpus Christi Passes, and from General Bee, relative to the plans of the enemy.

The orders of Lieutenant-General Smith to relieve the Confederate troops on the coast by State troops were being executed when the intelligence of the fall of Brownsville and the two passes arrived. It required much time to effect the change, as the State troops had to march a long distance, they having been massed, according to General Smith's previous orders, at points above the railroads, with the view of marching to Cotile. Nevertheless, I hope to be able to get troops west in time to save, if not Saluria, at least Velasco, at the mouth of the Brazos. It is highly probable, from the information received, that the enemy will attempt to take both of these places. I shall forward the information to Major-General Taylor, urging upon him the necessity of harassing the enemy in Lower Louisiana, as they may embark at any moment for the Texas coast, an event foreshadowed, I think, by their recent retreat toward Berwick Bay. I also forward for your information the organization of the Confederate troops under my command.

Very respectfully, your obedient servant,

J. BANKHEAD MAGRUDER,
Major-General, Commanding.

Brig. Gen. W. R. BOGGS,
Chief of Staff, Shreveport.

HEADQUARTERS DISTRICT OF TEXAS, &C.,
Houston, November 21, 1863.

GENERAL: Since writing to you in regard to the capture of Corpus Christi and Aransas, I received a telegram from Colonel [A.] Buchel, which I herewith inclose,* clearly indicating, I think, the embarkation of the enemy for the coast of Texas. Unless re-enforcements are sent me with the utmost dispatch, positions of vital importance may be lost. Upon the issue of the impending attack depends the fate of the heart of Texas, and I beg leave to most earnestly request the lieutenant-general commanding to order General Taylor to send to me, by rapid marches, such re-enforcements as he can spare from Louisiana. They can come most rapidly via Niblett's Bluff, and I shall have supplies of corn and provisions ready for them at that point and on the Calcasieu. I apprehend they [will] come too late, but no time should be lost.

Very respectfully, &c.,

J. BANKHEAD MAGRUDER,
Major-General, Commanding.

Brig. Gen. W. R. BOGGS,
Chief of Staff Shreveport, La.

No. 10.

Reports of Brig. Gen. Hamilton P. Bee, C. S. Army, commanding First Division, Army of Texas, of operations November 1-21.

HEADQUARTERS FIRST DIVISION, ARMY OF TEXAS,
Fort Brown, Tex., November 2, 1863.

SIR: I have the honor to inform the major-general commanding that I was advised by express from the mouth of the river this morning, at 3.30 a. m., that the enemy had made their appearance in seven steamers off the mouth of the Rio Grande at 7 p. m. yesterday. As they arrived just at dark, it was impossible to ascertain whether there were more in the offing. An express is expected every moment with additional news, and if it be of sufficient importance, I will dispatch another express to headquarters.

In the meantime I am forwarding everything that can be of value to

---

* Not found.

the Government up the river, and have sent out a detachment to turn back all cotton wagons *en route* for this place.

I shall hold the enemy in check as long as possible, with the small force now at my command, but shall feel sadly the want of artillery. My design is to retire slowly up the river, and continue to draw supplies from the Mexican side of the river. My movements, of course, will be governed by the operations of the enemy in the direction of Lavaca and Corpus Christi, with a design of cutting off my retreat from San Antonio.

I will continue to keep the major-general commanding fully posted as to my movements and those of the enemy.

With great respect, your obedient servant,

H. P. BEE,
Brigadier-General, Provisional Army, Confederate States.

Capt. EDMUND P. TURNER,
Assistant Adjutant-General, Houston.

—

HEADQUARTERS FORT BROWN,
November 2, 1863—3 p. m.

SIR: The enemy are in considerable force; fifteen vessels of all sizes, up to this time, are off the Brazos Santiago. Ten shells were fired this morning at the houses at the mouth. The weather is stormy, and I do not anticipate a landing before to-morrow. I have 150 of [James] Duff's cavalry, very much exhausted by a week's constant duty.

Respectfully,

H. P. BEE,
Brigadier-General.

Captain TURNER,
Assistant Adjutant-General, Houston.

—

LAS ÁNIMAS,
November 5, 1863.

So soon as Captain [Richard] Taylor was driven back to Palo Alto Prairie by the advance of the enemy's cavalry, I evacuated Fort Brown, destroyed the buildings and cotton, and am thus far on my route to King's ranch. My train is valuable and large, and I have made this distance in twenty-four hours. The enemy are in force. Brazos Island is covered with tents; six regimental flags were counted; twenty-six vessels, some of them very large. I think the expedition is from Fortress Monroe.

Duff's command is with me. I should have been sacrificed if I had had but one company. I shall await orders at King's ranch. My small command of 100 men are much exhausted, as we have been constantly on duty for ten days.

Respectfully,

H. P. BEE,
Brigadier-General.

Captain TURNER.

P. S.—I cannot go to Roma or up the river with so small a force, as the whole country will be against me. I received no assistance from Brownsville.

HEADQUARTERS FIRST DIVISION, ARMY OF TEXAS,
Santa Gertrudes, November 8, 1863.

SIR: I have the honor, in making my official report, to state, for the information of the general commanding, that on the morning of the 2d instant, at 3 a. m., I was advised that the enemy were in force off the Brazos Santiago Bar. In an hour afterward, I had dispatched Captain Taylor, Company A, Thirty-third Texas Cavalry, with 15 men, to the mouth of the Rio Grande, and Captain [Henry T.] Davis, Company F, same regiment, with the same number of men, to Point Isabel, with orders to give me constant information of the enemy's movements. The preparatory orders were also issued to evacuate the place. During the day I received constant information, and before night I knew the fact that the enemy was landing in force on the Brazos and Padre Islands.

Tuesday morning, I received a dispatch from Captain Taylor, stating that the enemy's pickets held the Boca Chica during the night, and had landed cavalry. Upon this information, orders were sent to both Captains Taylor and Davis to hold their posts of observation as long as possible, and then to fall back to where the main road from Brownsville to the Arroyo Colorado strikes the chaparral on the north side of the Palo Alto Prairie, and to join the train which would leave Brownsville at 2 o'clock that evening on that road.

On the 3d, Captain Taylor informed me that the enemy had crossed their cavalry over the Boca Chica, and that he was falling back up the river. I then determined to move down the river with all my available force, and, if possible, divert the attention of the enemy from the train which left Brownsville at 12 m., with no guard except 10 men sent with the 8 inch howitzer which accompanied the train, as I had no forces to send with it. To make this movement, I found that I had but 80 men, including officers. Just as I was starting, a courier came in from Captain Taylor with the information that the enemy's cavalry were on the Palo Alto Prairie, 200 strong, and in rapid pursuit of him, and, if I intended to evacuate Brownsville, no time was to be lost. I immediately ordered the garrison to be fired, and in person superintended the burning of all cotton which was liable to fall into the hands of the enemy. At 5 o'clock I left Brownsville, and overtook the train at 9 o'clock that night, and proceeded with it to the center of the sand desert, where, deeming it safe, I proceeded to this place to send you this dispatch. I wish that I could make you a more definite report of the number of and the strength of the enemy, but I had to choose to remain long enough to do so and risking the safety of the train, as the force of the enemy outnumbered mine perhaps 100 to 1, and as I could accomplish but the gratification of my personal feelings until they should come in force it was my duty to endeavor to save the latter.

I regret to say that the fire from the garrison extended to the town of Brownsville, and burned the block of buildings in front of the ferry. There were about 8,000 pounds of powder in the garrison, which had been condemned, and its explosion, though adding greatly to the terror and distress of the people, was of no loss to the Government. There were some commissary stores and a considerable amount of quartermaster's stores consumed, which it was impossible to save. Every wagon had been pressed into service, and large quantities had been reshipped across the river into Mexico, but there still remained a large amount which I could have wished was with the troops in the field. By daylight on the 4th, I was joined by Captains Taylor and Davis, and proceeded without interruption with the command to the point before stated.

My first intention was to fall back up the river to Roma, but, owing to the length of the train and the narrow and tortuous road through the chaparral along the river, every by-path of which was known to the Mexicans, and the impossibility of protecting the train with my small force, determined me to risk the effort to gain the more open country on the outside road, by the Arroyo Colorado and Las Animas. In connection with this, it is proper to state that I received no assistance from the citizens of Brownsville. The company of Captain Cummings, which had been mustered for six months, for special service, dissolved on the morning of the 3d, and disappeared. Out of the great number of Confederate citizens then in Brownsville, not more than a dozen would accompany me in my perilous effort to save the train. The movement of Vidal, I had become satisfied, was connected with Cortinas, and that the persistent efforts of the American consul in Matamoras were at last to be consummated. In a word, that peril was around me on all sides, and, as the regiment of Colonel Duff was, by reiterated orders from headquarters, ordered to Houston, thus leaving me with one company, I was satisfied that the position of Roma could not be held. I shall make my headquarters here until the general commanding can be heard from.

Captain [Thomas] Rabb's company, Thirty-third Texas Cavalry, is now in camp near King's ranch, having come across the country from Carrizo, on the Rio Grande; Captain [J. H.] Robinson's company, same regiment, was on the march from Rio Grande City to Fort Brown, and, if my couriers were not intercepted, he will join me here to-night or to-morrow. Captain Davis, the officer sent to Point Isabel, reports that twenty-six vessels, sail and steam, were landing troops. He counted six regimental flags at their evening parade on Brazos Island, and the decks of their transports were still crowded with troops, and large amounts of stores were being continually landed. My impression is, that the expedition is from the Atlantic coast, as the character of the vessels composing the fleet is different from those used in the Gulf. It is possible that the expedition which left Fortress Monroe early in October is the same now at Brazos Bar, and intend to occupy the line of the Rio Grande as a demonstration against the French in Mexico.

Colonel Duff's regiment must remain here for a few days, in order to let their horses recruit, as their duty has been very heavy. I bear testimony with great satisfaction to the good conduct of those troops—Companies A, B, D, and F. Their duty since the Vidal raid has been incessant and arduous, and not a single desertion has occurred.

The services rendered by Colonel Duff demonstrate him to be an accomplished soldier, and to him I am especially indebted for the good order and system which marked every movement of his small command during the exciting days which preceded the evacuation of Fort Brown, and on the march to this place. The country can rely on him for efficient service in any position in which he may be placed.

Lieutenant [James] Tucker, of [P.] Fox's battery, being in Brownsville on business connected with his battery, volunteered to take charge of the howitzer, and conducted it through the desert. Official reports will be forwarded as soon as they can be made out. I was accompanied to this place by Colonel Latham, the collector of the port of Brownsville.

I am, sir, very respectfully, your obedient servant,

H. P. BEE,
Brigadier-General, Commanding, &c.

Capt. EDMUND P. TURNER,
Assistant Adjutant-General, District of Texas, &c., Houston.

HEADQUARTERS FIRST DIVISION, ARMY OF TEXAS,
Santa Gertrudes, November 8, 1863.

SIR: The general commanding directs me to inform you of the evacuation of Brownsville by the Confederate forces, and the occupation of
that place by the enemy in large force. At 5 p. m. on the 1st instant,
the enemy made their appearance off the Brazos Bar with a fleet of
eleven vessels, which was increased to twenty-six transports and gunboats during the night. They effected their first landing on the evening
of the 2d, and, on the morning of the 3d, two large transports had entered the bay and landed five regiments of infantry and about 400 cavalry horses. On the evening of the 3d, about 100 of their cavalry ran
in our pickets at the mouth of the river.

The force of the enemy cannot be less than 8,000. Colonel Duff's
command will arrive at this point to-night.

I have the honor to be, very respectfully, your obedient servant,
E. R. TARVER,
Aide-de-Camp, and Acting Assistant Adjutant-General.
Lieut. Col. A. G. DICKINSON,
Commanding at San Antonio.

—

HEADQUARTERS FIRST DIVISION, ARMY OF TEXAS,
Corpus Christi, November 19, 1863.

SIR: I have the honor to state, for the information of the general commanding, that I was advised on the night of the 17th, at my camp on
the San Fernando, of the appearance of the enemy in force off Corpus
Christi Pass. They arrived in a fleet of nine vessels, six steamers and
three sail, from the direction of the Brazos Santiago, and before dark
that evening, the 16th, over 500 had landed on Mustang Island.

Immediately upon the reception of this news, I ordered my whole
force on the San Fernando to this place, where it arrived this morning.
The total aggregate of the troops now here amounts to 355 men—five
companies of the Thirty-third Cavalry, two companies State troops, one
company Eighth Infantry, and one company cadets.

I was surprised upon my arrival here to learn that no communication
whatever had been had with the troops on Mustang Island since the
enemy landed. Colonel [W. R.] Bradfute left this place at daylight on
the evening of the 18th, on the steamer Cora, with Captain [P. H.]
Breeden's company, Eighth Infantry, on board, with the intention, if
possible, to rescue the troops on Mustang, consisting of Captain [Will-
iam H.] Maltby's company, Eighth Infantry, and Captain Garrett's
Second Battalion [Third Regiment] State Troops. Shortly after the
steamer left, heavy firing was heard in the direction of Aransas Pass.
Captain [A. M.] Hobby, then commanding this post, dispatched, on the
evening of the 18th, a flag of truce by water to ascertain the fate of
Colonel Bradfute and his command, and at the same time a scout was
sent by land to Shell Banks on the like mission, and, I regret to say, up
to this late hour nothing has been heard. Should the general commanding not have been advised, via Indianola, before the reception of
this, of Colonel Bradfute's safe arrival at Saluria, the worst can be apprehended. This movement of the enemy has, of course, caused me
to abandon my intention of going to the Rio Grande, and, in consequence, Major [Santos] Benavides cannot be re-enforced.

I have news from Matamoras up to the 14th. Major [Charles] Russell
had been compelled to leave that city in order to save his life, so strong

was the feeling of the Cortinas party against the Confederates. I presume he is in Monterey by this time. The worst condition of affairs imaginable now exists on the Rio Grande.

I shall continue my headquarters at this place until the enemy's designs are more fully determined. Captain Townsend, of the State troops, withdrew his company from Padre Island on the 18th.

I am, very respectfully, your obedient servant,

H. P. BEE, .
Brigadier-General, Provisional Army.

Capt. EDMUND P. TURNER,
    Assistant Adjutant-General, Houston.

P. S.—Captain Townsend states that, to the best of his judgment, from 3,000 to 4,000 landed on the island.

—

HEADQUARTERS FIRST DIVISION, ARMY OF TEXAS,
Corpus Christi, Tex., November 21, 1863—8 a. m.

SIR: I presume you have been informed by Colonel Bradfute of his movements since he left Corpus Christi on the 18th, as I have ascertained that he passed safely to Saluria. There is no doubt of the loss of the little garrison on Mustang Island, but I have not been able to ascertain any of the particulars. A flag-of-truce boat sent down has not returned; probably detained by the enemy, to prevent communicating intelligence to me. The flag was sent by Colonel [A. M.] Hobby before my arrival. .

The force of the enemy on yesterday was two steamers inside and seven outside.

You are aware that from the position of Aransas Pass it is impracticable for me to obtain any information as to the movements of the enemy, as it is at least 5 miles from the nearest point that I can reach. There appeared to be no movements on yesterday.   ,

Major [L. M.] Rogers' battalion of State troops have reported, and been stationed in the vicinity of King's ranch, with orders to picket all the roads leading from Brownsville, and to execute your request as to the driving off the stock.

I regret to say that no reliance can be placed on the State troops from this vicinity, should I be obliged to fall back toward Goliad, or farther east. I am informed by their officers that they will not leave their families in their rear, and have no means of moving them. This feeling prevails to some extent among the Confederate troops, many of which are similarly situated as to their families. I am informed that there is a general feeling of alarm amongst the people of Western Texas, caused by the rumor that it is the intention of the general commanding to abandon the country to the Colorado. I would suggest that a call be made for all the fighting men west of the Colorado (except a home police), to report to me, and an assurance given that the advance of the enemy will be contested by the force which may be at my command, be it large or small, and that every soldier added to my ranks makes me the more able to contest the ground with the enemy.

This place is absolutely untenable for cavalry; there is neither water, grass, nor corn, and the camp must be made farther east. From the best information received, I will have to approach within a few miles of the San Antonio River to obtain grass, so barren and parched is the country. The point is on the Seco Creek, and is convenient to Saint

Mary's, Lamar, and Indianola, but about 50 miles from this place. I propose to establish a camp and call the people to me.

4 P. M.

Couriers from below represent the Yankees as quiet. I cannot fathom their movements, and cannot act until I do. They may seek to land a force at Lamar, and pass through Victoria to Indianola, thus turning Fort Esperanza. I am powerless to prevent it, but believe they will not move for some time.

8 P. M.

Letters from the Rio Grande. The expedition at Aransas Pass left the Brazos on Sunday, the 15th, 3,000 strong. The number of vessels correspond with those now known to be at the Pass. All of Kennedy and King's steamboats are in the possession of the enemy, and the Matamoras is with this expedition; she draws 3 feet water; 1,500 troops were to march to Ringgold. All else was quiet on both sides of the river.

With great respect, your obedient servant,

H. P. BEE,
Brigadier-General, Provisional Army.

Capt. EDMUND P. TURNER,
Assistant Adjutant-General, Houston.

—

HEADQUARTERS FIRST DIVISION, ARMY OF TEXAS,
Corpus Christi, Tex., November 21, 1863.

SIR: The general commanding directs me to state, for your information, that the enemy, who landed in force on Mustang Island on the 16th, captured two companies of our troops on the north end of that island, after a severe fight, which lasted more than half an hour, with small-arms. The gunboats in the Gulf shelled our forces from their guns before these troops, landed on the lower end of the island, came up, which was about 8 a. m. on the 19th. Major [George O.] Dunaway, of the State troops, is among the prisoners.

These facts are all ascertained from persons who witnessed the fight from the dredge-boat, about 6 miles distant from the island. Nothing is known as to the killed and wounded. The steamer Cora passed through safe, and is at Saluria. There are now three large steamers inside of Aransas Bar and five outside.

Nothing further from Brownsville since my last.

I am, colonel, your obedient servant,

[E. R. TARVER,]
Aide-de-Camp, and Acting Assistant Adjutant-General.

Lieut. Col. A. G. DICKINSON,
Commanding Post at San Antonio.

—

HEADQUARTERS FIRST DIVISION, ARMY OF TEXAS,
Corpus Christi, Tex., November 22, 1863.

His Excellency General SANTIAGO VIDAURRI,
Governor of the States of Nuevo Leon and Cohahuila:

SIR: My attention has been called to an official dispatch from General Ruiz, Governor of the State of Tamaulipas, to the Supreme Government of Mexico, at San Luis Potosi, dated Matamoras, November 4, 1863, in which he states that, after setting fire to the garrison of Fort Brown, soldiers were left by me to prevent the citizens from extinguishing the flames, which had spread to the city, and that they actually opened fire on them, &c.

As this statement, coming from such high authority, does me the greatest injustice, and may render my name odious as a vandal and a barbarian, I take the liberty of requesting that you will permit me to say that the statement is entirely false, and I much regret that the enlightened General Ruiz should have given credence to a report so monstrous, and which, as he was in Matamoras, he could not have known but from excited rumor.

I fired the buildings of the garrison, and burned such cotton as could not be saved, to prevent their use and appropriation by the enemies of my country, and in obedience to superior orders. It gave me great pain to hear that even a few houses in Brownsville were consumed; but that I left armed men to fire on the citizens, in the efforts to save their houses, is so horrible, in view of the civilized age in which we live, that I am surprised it could have been believed. I am incapable of such conduct.

If you will permit the insertion of this letter in your official journal, you will do me a great favor, for which I will be profoundly grateful.

I have the honor to be, with great respect, your obedient servant,

H. P. BEE,
Brigadier-General, Provisional Army.

No. 11.

Report of Col. James Duff, Thirty-third Texas Cavalry, of operations October 28–November 8.

CAMP ON SAN FERNANDO,
November 11, 1863.

CAPTAIN: I have the honor to make the following report of the operations of my command from the 28th of October ultimo to this date:

On the morning of the 28th of October, Companies B, E, and F, of my regiment, moved from Fort Brown *en route* to Houston, pursuant to orders from the major-general commanding the district. I remained with the commissioned and non-commissioned staff of the regiment at Fort Brown to close up the business of the quartermaster's and subsistence departments, intending to follow my command at an early hour on the morning of the 29th.

On the afternoon of the 28th, I dispatched Privates Litteral and [D. H.] Dashiell, of Company A, to the Boca Del Rio, with orders to Capt. A. I. Vidal, commanding a mounted company of six months' volunteers, stationed as a picket at that point, to move into Fort Brown with his company on the next day, and report for duty to the commanding officer of that post. At 8 o'clock of the same evening, the 28th, Litteral returned to the post, having been shot through both jaws by Vidal's men. He was unable to articulate, but communicated in writing the sad fact that Vidal and his company had evidently deserted their colors; had killed Dashiell, and had but narrowly missed killing him. This announcement caused every preparation to be made to resist the attempt which would doubtless be made to surprise the small garrison by Vidal, who it was supposed was acting in concert with the hundreds of renegades and deserters harbored on the other, side of the Rio Grande.

A detachment of 10 men of Company A, under Lieutenant [J. R.] Vinton, was immediately sent on the River road, to ascertain the where-abouts of Vidal and his party, with orders not to engage him, but to fall back and report. At 10 o'clock Lieutenant Vinton returned, and reported that he had been pursued by a party of at least 70 men to within half a mile of the post. I formed all the men under my command, and found the whole number not more than 30, exclusive of Captain Cummings' company of six-months' volunteers, in whom I had but little faith, and who were placed to watch the main ferry at the Garritta. Immediate steps were taken by the general, the major, and myself to get as many of the citizens of Brownsville under arms as possible, and in a short time they responded to the number of something more than 100, prominent among whom were several influential citizens from the interior.

In a short time arms were placed in the hands of all who were without any, ammunition was issued, the two siege guns were placed in position and manned, and a detachment was sent to watch the renegades at Freeport. All the cavalry were used in throwing a line of pickets around the town, and 3 different couriers were sent by different roads to overtake and order immediately back the three companies of my regiment that had moved that morning. Vidal and his party having ascertained that his approach was discovered, moved off, and, as was learned next morning, crossed the river into Mexico some 9 miles above town, after having committed several atrocious murders on unoffending citizens and soldiers.

In connection with the escape of Vidal, I would say that had the cavalry force, small as it was, been still in the garrison, he would certainly have been captured and his party annihilated. By daylight the three companies returned to the post, and were immediately dispatched in various directions to try and cut off Vidal, but, as already stated, without success. One of the scouts under Captain Taylor, arriving at the point at which he crossed within a few minutes after he had done so, evidence enough was there given to show that we could depend but little upon the assistance of the authorities of Tamaulipas, as Captain Taylor saw on the other bank a large body of cavalry, composed, as was afterward ascertained, of renegades and deserters from Bexar and other counties in Texas. Captain Taylor's party was entirely too small to attempt the crossing of the river in the face of this command, and he returned to the garrison.

Information having been received by the brigadier-general command-ing that an attempt would be made on the night of the 29th to capture the town and post of Fort Brown, by a combined movement on the part of all the Yankee sympathizers in and about Matamoras, the day of the 29th was spent in perfecting the arrangements to raise a force to meet the attempt, and that night the citizens again volunteered nobly, and by 10 o'clock my command was in position, and numbered, all told, about 300 men. Each man was eager for the fray, and had the authorities of Matamoras not prevented the crossing of the horde quartered in their city, I am satisfied the whole party would have been destroyed. During the succeeding days, the 30th and 31st October, and 1st November, citizens and soldiers were kept under arms; the whole country was in a state of excitement; Cummings' company showed that little or no dependence could be placed upon them, and I was satisfied that we were surrounded on all sides by a population quadrupling ours in numbers and bitterly hostile to us.

On the morning of the 2d, at 2.30 o'clock, an express from the mouth of the river gave the information that seven Yankee ships-of-war had arrived, and were lying off the Brazos Bar. At 4 o'clock I dispatched, in accordance with the general's order, a detachment of 15 men, under Captain Taylor, to the mouth, and a detachment of the same number of men, under Captain Davis, to Point Isabel, with the instructions, a copy of which is forwarded herewith. At noon of the same day, an additional party of 15 cavalry, under Lieutenant [Walter L.] Mann, First Texas Cavalry, accompanied by a party of 12 citizens, under Mr. Brady, of Houston, and composed of Mr. Darling, Colonel Walker, and other such gallant and patriotic citizens, were sent to Cobb's ranch, 7 miles above the mouth, with orders to ascertain the whereabouts of a party of guerrillas reported to be formed in that vicinity, and attack them, and also, if possible, to ascertain the whereabouts of a train reported to be loaded with arms for the Yankees, and, if possible, cross the river and capture or destroy the same. If neither of these objects could be attained, the party was ordered to join Captain Taylor, and act to the best advantage against any small parties that the enemy might throw out. Lieutenant Mann with the party of citizens returned the next morning before it was discovered that the enemy had crossed any of their number to the mainland.

Acting under instructions from the brigadier-general to make every preparation to evacuate Fort Brown and to save as much as was possible of the public property, I impressed, on the 2d, every available horse, mule, and wagon in the place, and, during the entire day and succeeding night, kept every man, not on picket, at work getting up trains and loading wagons.

On the evening of the 2d, I was much disappointed to find that few, very few, of the citizens would assist me—not more than 30, and those almost entirely men from the interior, would report or bear arms. A few honorable exceptions I must mention: Mr. Henry Seeligson neglected his own business entirely in the endeavor to raise men from his ward, and if he met with but little success, no less credit is due him. Mr. John Dunlevie was also on the ground, and, with his quiet energy. doing all that man could do. His honor the mayor was enthusiastic in, his efforts to get the citizens out, and deserves no small meed of praise; he was seconded promptly by the Hons. Judge Powers, Judge Bigelow, and a few other old Texans.

On the morning of the 3d, every effort was continued to load and dispatch wagons with clothing and other stores, and by 12 o'clock the last train was finally sent forward, consisting of forty-five wagons, part quartermaster's and part citizen teams, carrying the fixed ammunition that remained, camp and garrison equipage, and subsistence stores for thirty days for the command. This train was accompanied by Lieutenant Tucker, of Fox's battery, in charge of the 8-inch iron howitzer, drawn by impressed horses, driven by 5 soldiers of my regiment. The only guard furnished the train, with the exception of my acting assistant quartermaster and his sergeant, was 1 commissioned officer and 3 men. Captain [John S.] Greer, of the ordnance department, also accompanied the train, and was in charge of the ordnance stores; the assistant surgeon of my regiment, with the sick men, were also sent with the train.

Doubting the fidelity of Cummings' company, but desirous of giving them every opportunity of displaying their loyalty, I caused as many of the company to be gotten together as possible, and informed them that we were about to fall back, and asked such as were willing to share our fate to step to the front. With the exception of Lieutenant Burris, not one did so. I then directed all such as would not go—I was not in position to compel them—to stack their arms; all who had any did so, and the company disbanded, and doubtless two-thirds of their number are now actively opposed to us.

After the train moved off, I proceeded to ascertain the number of men left, and found the aggregate, including the brigadier-general and his staff, the commissioned and non-commissioned officers of my staff, the commissioned officers and men, to be 79. With this force we awaited the development of the plans of the enemy. At 3 p. m. an express from Captain Taylor announced the fact of from 200 to 300 horses having been crossed from Brazos Island to the mainland, and that a number of men accompanied them, the supposition being, of course, that there were as many men as there were horses. I immediately ordered "To horse," and the general readily and eagerly agreed to my proposition to proceed immediately to the mouth of the river and endeavor to capture or at least stampede the horses.

The general at once determined to head our small command, but, whilst engaged in giving directions to Major [Charles] Russell to destroy the buildings at Fort Brown in case we should not return by a certain hour, another express came galloping up with the information from Captain Taylor that the enemy's cavalry in force were rapidly advancing on Brownsville, and that not a moment's time was to be lost if we expected to evacuate, and that he had taken to the chaparral, and would meet the command toward the Arroyo Colorado. The information thus received being positive, the enemy being immensely superior to us in numbers, the whole country being disaffected and filled with hundreds and hundreds of our most bitter enemies, the order was immediately given to burn up the post and to destroy such cotton as could not be immediately floated across the Rio Grande. This was done; the buildings were burned; several hundred bales of cotton were thrown into the river, and were in the main floated across; and I burned about 200 bales in the yard near Freeport.

After this had been accomplished, under the groans and hisses of certainly not less than 400 renegades on the other side of the river, the command was formed at Freeport, where the general commanding, feeling and knowing that the several trains that had been sent forward by the Arroyo Colorado road would, if left unprotected, be certainly cut off and destroyed, determined upon that course which is always most bitter to the soldier, viz, a retreat without a fight, unless the latter could be obtained in the defense of our supplies. Strange to say, the enemy did not attempt to intercept us, although in our retreat we passed almost in sight of his legions, and were, as we now know, surrounded at all hours, day and night, by a hostile and ruthless foe numbering probably ten times our number.

In company with the brigadier-general commanding, we continued our march to this place, intercepting and turning back all trains loaded with cotton; destroying by fire, from each load, a sufficient number of bales to enable the teams to cross the sand with the balance. In performing this duty, my command was necessarily very much scattered, so as to cover the numerous roads leading across the desert. I am satisfied that but few teams evaded us. I arrived at Santa Gertrudes on the 8th. Since then, continual scouts have been kept out bringing up wagons and teams loaded with cotton, and the road has showed one continuous stream of trains. I have 1 picket stationed at La Para, 1 at the Bovida, and 1 at the Santa Rosa ranch. I am confident that every team is now within my picket, with the exception of such as were sent across the country to Roma from below the Las Animas. Since my arrival here, I have, under the orders of General Bee, sent all teams loaded with Government cotton to Laredo or Eagle Pass, and this fact has inspired the planters and others hauling private cotton with so much confidence that, with few exceptions, all teams west of the Nueces River have followed.

I cannot close this report without bearing testimony to the cheerfulness with which the officers and men of my command executed every order given to them, and although men and horses were incessantly on duty for eleven days and nights, without forage or grass for the latter, yet not a complaint or a murmur was uttered, and only one sad thought prevailed, that the circumstances under which we were placed, the paucity of our numbers, the immense value of the property we had to protect, and the immensely superior force of the enemy, had caused us to make a retreat without at least having one thrust or firing one shot at the invaders.

I have taken every step to call in the many detachments of my regiment on escort and other service, and hope that in a few days I will have sufficient men to obey any order that may be given as to its future movements.

I inclose herewith Captains Taylor's and Davis' reports; also a copy of the morning report of the command at Fort Brown on the 2d instant.

Since my arrival here, I have been joined by Captain Rabb's company (D), from Clareno, and I am momentarily looking for Captain Robinson's company (C), from Ringgold Barracks, which, without accident, ought to have been here two days ago.

I have the honor to be, respectfully, your obedient servant,

JAMES DUFF,
Colonel, Commanding Thirty-third Texas Cavalry.

Capt. E. R. TARVER,
Aide-de-Camp, and Acting Assistant Adjutant-General.

No. 12.

Report of Capt. Richard Taylor, Thirty-third Texas Cavalry, of operations November 2–3.

EN ROUTE FROM FORT BROWN,
November 3, 1863.

SIR: Pursuant to instructions received by me on the morning of the 2d instant, at 2 o'clock, I, at 4 o'clock of the same morning, with 15 men, proceeded to the mouth of the Rio Grande, to observe the movements of the Yankees' fleet, then supposed to be off the mouth of the river. On my arrival at the Boca Del Rio, I learned that the fleet was off Brazos Bar, and supposed to be unloading at the head of Brazos Island. Acting upon the information, I proceeded up the coast to within one-half mile of Boca Chica, and saw one large vessel at anchor off Boca Chica and several also inside of Brazos Bar.

At about 4 p. m. I returned to the mouth, and proceeded up the river to the crossing of the salt marshes. There left my main pickets, and, with 6 men, crossed on to the high land running up to the Boca Chica. Arrived within one-half mile of the shore about 6 o'clock, and discovered that the enemy had thrown on to the foot of the island about 100 men, and, immediately upon their arrival, the vessels stationed there raised anchor and sailed for the mouth of the Rio Grande.

I then withdrew, and camped on the ranch of Fermie Gonzales—one of the Vidal party—to watch the movement of a large life-boat on the Mexican shore. At daylight, with 5 men, I again crossed to the high point of land heretofore mentioned. Arriving within 1 mile of where I supposed the enemy would cross on to the mainland, I left 3 of my men, and, with the other 3, I cautiously moved up to within 300 yards of the enemy on the mainland. I discovered about 200 to 500 horses under herd of 2 soldiers, being covered with 25 mounted men armed and equipped.

Being unable to fight with the few men under me, I very quietly withdrew to the river, to watch their movements again at night. I encamped at noon at the Palmetto ranch, 9 miles above the mouth, and at 1.10 o'clock I discovered about one-half mile below, coming up the road, about 200 cavalry in full charge. I accordingly fell back to the chaparral, and made good my retreat, having expressed 2 men to your headquarters informing you of the rapid advance of the enemy on Brownsville.

I am, respectfully,

R. TAYLOR,
Captain, Commanding Pickets.

Col. JAMES DUFF,
Commanding Line of the Rio Grande.

No. 13.

Report of Capt. Henry T. Davis, Thirty-third Texas Cavalry, of operations November 2–3.

CAMP FRENCH,
November 11, 1863.

LIEUTENANT : In accordance with instructions from Col. James Duff, commanding line of Rio Grande, I proceeded on the morning of the 2d of November, 1863, with 19 of my company, to Point Isabel, to reconnoiter that country. I arrived at the Point about 9 a. m.; immediately proceeded to the light-house to take observations. I discovered that there were twenty-four vessels outside the bar, large and small. After looking at the fleet for a few minutes, I went down from the light-house; was not away but a short time when I heard firing at the Boca. I supposed them to be signal guns, as I perceived, when I went back to the light-house, that two vessels had crossed the bar and were inside, alongside Brazos Island, and were landing troops. I saw two regiments landed from those two vessels. In a short time troops were landing from a large vessel outside, besides a lot of stores. Two vessels during the evening moved off toward the Boca Del Rio. Nothing more of importance transpiring that evening, and it now growing late, and, for fear that myself and party should be cut off, I retired from the Point about 5 miles, and camped for the night. I discovered nothing to interrupt us during the night.

The next morning I returned to the Point, and, after placing my horses in a position that they could not be discovered by the enemy, I proceeded to the light-house to further observe the movements of the enemy. I discovered that two more vessels had come in during the night, and had discharged quite a lot of troops and stores. There were also several small boats running in and out, besides some few alongside the landing of Brazos, inside; there were also quite a number of tents up, but, owing to it being very smoky and some small crafts that intercepted the view, I could not tell the number. During my stay at the Point, four vessels came in from the direction of Corpus Christi, two transports and two gunboats; I could see no troops on either of the vessels. There were, in all the troops I saw landed, five regiments, four on Brazos, which moved in the direction of Boca Chica, and one regiment on Padre Island; there were also landed on Brazos about 100 head of horses and two pieces of artillery. I saw no cavalry on parade. A few minutes before I retired, I perceived that they were very busy landing their launches, evidently intending to land troops at the Point. When I left, there were twenty-six vessels inside and outside the bar, including nine gunboats, to say nothing of quite a number of small vessels. A majority of the vessels outside, except the gunboats, had troops on them.

Fearing that cavalry might be landed at Boca Chica to cut us off, and, having a very limited knowledge of the country surrounding the Point, I left, for Brownsville with my party; had proceeded about 5 miles when I met an express from Colonel Duff, ordering me to join the command, then en route for King's ranch, which I did forthwith.

Very respectfully, your obedient servant,

HENRY T. DAVIS,
Captain Company F, Thirty-third Texas Cavalry.

Lieut. GEORGE W. CALDWELL,
Adjutant, Thirty-third Texas Cavalry.

No. 14.

Reports of Col. W. R. Bradfute, C. S. Army, commanding Coast, of operations November 23–29.

LAVACA, TEX.,
November 24, 1863.

SIR: Inclosed please find a communication from Major Ireland, which gives the latest news received from Fort Esperanza.*

It is supposed the enemy's force numbers some 10,000 or 12,000, and, if this be so, we will need heavy re-enforcements.

I will send the troops under Col. S. H. Darden (three small companies) at once to Saluria, and shall call into service all the minute men in this vicinity, which will, perhaps, add to our strength some 75 or 100 men.

As I have not been informed that the major-general commanding intends to re-enforce the troops on this line, I am at a loss to know what to expect; but will avail myself of every means in my power, and make the best fight possible under the circumstances.

I am, captain, very respectfully, your obedient servant,

W. R. BRADFUTE,
Colonel, C. S. Army, Commanding Coast.

Capt. EDMUND P. TURNER,
Assistant Adjutant-General, Houston.

---

* See Ireland's report, p. 447.

HEADQUARTERS COAST COMMAND,
Fort Esperanza, November 27, 1863.

SIR: The enemy have appeared in considerable force some 2 miles below the fort. From the best information received, they number about 3,000, including probably some 200 cavalry. We had a slight skirmish with them this evening, and it is supposed a few of the enemy were killed and wounded. No casualties on our side. The skirmish occurred some mile below the fort. Our force was withdrawn, and the enemy retired some distance down the island and to the west side. Their intentions are not yet known, but, from their numbers, I suppose they will soon make a vigorous attack. Our force here is about 500 effective men.

I am, captain, very respectfully, your obedient servant,
W. R. BRADFUTE,
Colonel, C. S. Army, Commanding Coast.

Capt. EDMUND P. TURNER,
Assistant Adjutant-General, Houston.

—

MATAGORDA,
November 30, 1863.

SIR: I have the honor to inclose herewith a copy of a communication just received from Colonel Bradfute. I was preparing to embark the command at the time I received it, having arrived here this morning before daylight with my regiment and Colonel [P. C.] Woods', after a march of 40 miles yesterday.

I have concluded to move by land to Victoria, via Texana, as rapidly as I possibly can, as I do not deem it prudent to attempt to go to Lavaca by transports, in consequence of the enemy having possession of the bay. I will direct Colonel [A. W.] Terrell accordingly, who has not arrived here yet. I have sent dispatches to General Bee at Victoria, who, I suppose, will be there before I arrive, notifying him of this movement.

I have information that Colonel [T. J. M.] Richardson, with two companies of State troops, passed Texana yesterday, *en route* to Victoria.

Commodore [Leon] Smith will inform you by this courier about the particulars of the evacuation, &c., of Saluria.

Any dispatches for me will find me at Texana or *en route* to Victoria, at which place I will report to General Bee, should I not receive any instructions from the major-general commanding.

I am, sir, very respectfully, your obedient servant,
C. L. PYRON,
Colonel, Commanding, &c.

Capt. EDMUND P. TURNER,
Assistant Adjutant-General, Houston.

[Inclosure.]

POWDER HORN,
November 30, 1863—2 a. m.

Col. C. L. PYRON,
Or Officer Commanding Forces at Matagorda:

COLONEL: I have this moment arrived from Fort Esperanza. I am directed by Colonel Bradfute, commanding, to report to you that he evacuated the fort about 10 o'clock last night, after a severe shelling from the enemy all day. His movements after dark threatened communication with the mainland, and involved the necessity of a surrender to-day.

Colonel Bradfute directs that, if you are on shipboard with your command, you will proceed directly to Port Lavaca, or, if necessary for its safety, you will come to that point with as little delay as possible, in accordance with instructions you have previously received from the major-general commanding.

Captain Chesley, the bearer of this, will acquaint you with the causes of the evacuation. Be kind enough to report this disaster to General Magruder by earliest courier.

Respectfully, your obedient servant,

S. J. LEE,
Major, and Acting Assistant Adjutant-General.

P. S.—Colonel Bradfute will make a stand at Lavaca.

No. 15.

Report of Maj. John Ireland. Eighth Texas Infantry, of operations
November 23.

· FORT ESPERANZA,
November 23, 1863.

COLONEL: Captain Barden has just arrived. He left Cedar Bayou at 12 m. to-day, where he met the enemy, about 60 cavalry, about 300 infantry, and two pieces of artillery.

Major Hill was killed, and when Captain Barden left, the enemy were on this side of the bayou. He reports seventeen sail at Aransas. It appears from this that the enemy are advancing on this point.

This force is, I suppose, their advance guard. We want more men of every sort, and especially cavalry.

I am, very respectfully, your obedient servant,

' JNO. IRELAND,
Major, Commanding, &c.

Col. W. R. BRADFUTE,
Commanding Coast.

OCTOBER 28, 1863.—Mutiny of Vidal.

Reports of Brig. Gen. H. P. Bee, C. S. Army, commanding First Division, Army of Texas.

HEADQUARTERS FIRST DIVISION, ARMY OF TEXAS,
. *Fort Brown, Tex., October 28, 1863.*

The Commanding Officer, Ringgold Barracks :

SIR: I am directed by the brigadier-general commanding to inform you that the company of Capt. A. I. Vidal, led by him in person, have proved themselves base traitors, and have rebelled against the military and civil authorities of our country, and, after murdering several inoffensive citizens and 2 of their comrades, have passed up the river, forcing the rancheros on the roads into their ranks, and have raised once more the standard of the traitor Cortinas.

Under these circumstances, the brigadier-general commanding directs that you use your utmost endeavor to arrest their further progress, and, if possible, to capture them. Their numbers are supposed to be at present about 60. I am also further directed by the brigadier-general commanding to say that in case the companies of Captains Robinson and Rabb have left their stations, pursuant to late instructions, that you dispatch an express after them, with orders to countermarch immediately to this (Fort Brown) point, and, if practicable, to take the River road, and, if necessary and possible, act in conjunction with the troops from this point.

In conclusion, I am directed to remind you of the absolute necessity of prompt action in this matter, and that he expects vigilance and energy from all the officers and men of this command; that this attempt at insurrection may be speedily crushed out, and a proper punishment meted out to the traitors.

I have the honor to be, your obedient servant,

E. R. TARVER,

Aide-de-Camp, and Acting Assistant Adjutant-General.

—

HEADQUARTERS FIRST DIVISION, ARMY OF TEXAS,
Fort Brown, Tex., October 28, 1863.

SIR: I hasten to lay before the major-general commanding a history of the grave events which have kept the garrison and city under arms for two days and nights. I premise by saying that I was aware of a feverish state of public feeling on both sides of the river, arising from the local political questions in Matamoras as well as the question of French intervention, but I did not imagine that either of these ideas was used as a cloak by other parties to cover a design for the capture of this garrison.

You are aware that I have had a company of Mexican citizens, under command of Capt. Adrian I. Vidal, stationed at the mouth of the Rio Grande, which has done good service. Owing to the march of the Thirty-third Regiment and the light battery, it became necessary to order that company into Fort Brown, leaving only a picket of observation. On Tuesday [Monday], the 26th, the three companies of cavalry marched—the light battery having preceded it several days. Toward evening of that day, renewed orders were sent to Captain Vidal by Privates Dashiell and Litteral, of Company A, Thirty-third Regiment. Soon after dark, I was informed confidentially that I was to be attacked during the night by men from below, consisting of Vidal's company and renegades and deserters from Matamoras. In half an hour after, Litteral arrived at headquarters most grievously wounded (shot through the face), and informed me that about 14 miles below he met Captain Vidal with his whole company, some 60 men, and delivered his orders. The two men of Company A then countermarched with the command, which halted at a ranch some 2 miles on the march. Vidal there dismounted the command to get supper, when instantly a fire was opened on these two soldiers, killing Dashiell, and wounding, as stated, Litteral, who fortunately made his escape and reached me.

I found myself with but 19 men of Company A and a volunteer company of citizens, under Captain Cummings. Ten men of the cavalry were dispatched, under Lieutenant Vinton, to proceed on the road to the mouth of the river, and ascertain the truth of this statement. I then called on the citizens of Brownsville to rally to my aid, but before anything like an approximation to organization or order could be made, the pickets under Vinton were driven in to within 1 mile of the town.

Fully satisfied, then, that Vidal and his whole company were traitors, I, with the able assistance of Brigadier-General Slaughter, Colonel Duff,

Major [George A.] Magruder, jr., of the general's staff, and Captain Winston, was enabled, with the cordial assistance of the citizens, to get the two heavy guns into a favorable position, and something like order and organization among the men. Couriers were immediately sent to recall the three companies of cavalry encamped on Palo Alto Prairie, and the night passed off with every available man I could arm standing in line of battle. By 12 o'clock to-day I became satisfied that my enemy was Vidal's company alone, increased by a few rancheros from either side, and by this time the excitement has quieted down, although the citizens are all on duty to-night.

I regret to say that, as far as heard from, the following are the victims of this infamous young traitor: Dashiell, a gallant young soldier, the son of the respected and accomplished adjutant-general of the State of Texas; Captain King, who for many years lived at Galveston, and was incarcerated for months during this war at Fort Lafayette; Mr. Barthelow, former sheriff of Cameron County and a member of Captain Cummings' company; Mr. Cruz, a trustworthy friend of his country, much esteemed, and Litteral, wounded.

I promptly notified Governor Ruiz, of Tamaulipas, of this occurrence, and herewith inclose his reply, which I am sure will give pleasure to the general, as evincing prompt and cordial efforts to render us assistance. I am happy to state that Colonel Cortinas has up to this time captured 22 of Vidal's party, who had crossed the river, and has them prisoners.

I am confident that it was Vidal's determination to attack and plunder Brownsville, and I also believe that there existed a plan to aid the movement with the renegades and disaffected on both sides of the river, and that the plan was frustrated by the impetuosity of Vidal, who mistook by one day the departure of Duff's command. That it was settled to take advantage of the weak garrison and slaughter it, I have no doubt.

Under all these circumstances, I have taken the responsibility of retaining the companies of the Thirty-third ordered to the interior, and shall keep them here until I hear from the general commanding.

The fact that the warehouses are filled with valuable supplies for the army, awaiting transportation (all of which is used as fast as it comes); that the valuable trade in cotton would cease in a short time from the danger of its transportation on the adjacent roads, connected with the many elements of danger from the traitors in Matamoras and the disaffected on this side of the river, satisfies me that when the troops are removed the trade should also be removed, and that the commanding general can form no idea of the critical condition of things here. Owing to these causes, I have taken this responsibility with every confidence that I have done right.

I really had but 19 soldiers last night when my pickets were run in, and yet millions of property, invaluable to the soldiers of our army, and the plunder of the city was the stake for which Vidal played.

I am sustained in my action by the opinion of General Slaughter and the officers who have lately arrived from the interior, and trust it may meet the approval of the commanding general.

Prompt measures are being taken to follow Vidal, and crush this movement before it becomes an organization, and I hope to do it.

With great respect, your obedient servant,

H. P. BEE,
Brigadier-General, Provisional Army Confederate States.

Capt. EDMUND P. TURNER,
Assistant Adjutant-General, District of Texas, &c.

[Inclosures.]

HEADQUARTERS FIRST DIVISION, ARMY OF TEXAS,
Fort Brown, Tex., October 28, 1863.

His Excellency Brig. Gen. MANUEL RUIZ,
Governor of the State of Tamaulipas, Matamoras, Mexico:

SIR: I hasten to inform you of the occurrences of last night in this vicinity, believing, as I do, that they involve the peace of both sides of the river.

Capt. Adrian I. Vidal, who commanded a company at the mouth of the river, for reasons inexplicable to me, turned traitor to his country, and, at the head of his company, increased by additions from the lower ranches on both sides of the river, marched upon Brownsville, with the avowed intention of plunder and rapine. He passed within 1 mile of town about 3 o'clock this morning, and will seek, perhaps, to cross the river into Mexico. I have sent all my available cavalry in pursuit, and, with great respect, request that you will dispatch troops to intercept him, should he do so. I am satisfied that this movement is connected with incipient, or, perhaps, matured plans for a renewal of the scenes of which Matamoras was the victim two years ago. I am certain that one who would violate his allegiance, to plunder his own people, would not be likely to be more lenient in a foreign country, and the cause of humanity and justice both appeal for prompt and united action. I will cheerfully co-operate with you in this as every other occasion concerning the quiet of this frontier.

Since writing the above, I am informed that two parties of Americans left Matamoras early this morning, and took the direction of up the river. They are known to be men who were supported by the consul of the United States at Matamoras, and, although they may be engaged in their proper business, it is possible that they seek to violate the neutrality of Mexico by joining with Vidal for depredations on this side of the river. May I ask you to inquire into it?

With great respect, your obedient servant,

H. P. BEE,
Brigadier-General, Provisional Army Confederate States.

MATAMORAS,
October 28, 1863.

General H. P. BEE,
Fort Brown:

SIR: With much regret I am informed by your letter of to-day of the rebellion of Captain Vidal and his company, which took place last night at the mouth of the river. I at once gave orders that all the troops on the line should unite in pursuing the insurrectionists, and from this city will immediately set forth two detachments of cavalry to reconnoiter the left bank of the Rio Grande.

Do not doubt that I am resolved to sustain public order as the best means we can take on this frontier for the security of its inhabitants, following without resting all who seek to disturb it, and severely punishing them according to our laws.

Of all circumstances that transpire it will give me pleasure to inform you, and you will greatly oblige me by giving me prompt notice of what you may learn, that the combined effort of our forces may give the best results.

I am, general, with great respect and esteem, your obedient servant,

MANUEL RUIZ.

HEADQUARTERS FIRST DIVISION, ARMY OF TEXAS,
Fort Brown, Tex., October 30, 1863.

His Excellency Brig. Gen. MANUEL RUIZ,
Governor of the State of Tamaulipas, Matamoras, Mexico :

SIR: I am credibly informed that—thanks to the vigilance and activity of the troops under your command—a portion of the band of Vidal, which crossed into Mexico, have been captured.

I have the honor to inclose a summary of the investigations conducted before the mayor of the city,* and in the name of humanity, in the name of the desolate wives and orphan children that the desolating tracks of this vandal have caused, and especially in the name of the best interests of the people on both sides of the Rio Grande, do I ask that you will cause these murderers to be delivered up to me. The victims number at least 10, but so far there has been but time to examine into the causes of the deaths of King and Dashiell.

The list of names sent is necessarily imperfect, and should there be prisoners not on the list, I will furnish you the proofs of their complicity with Vidal, if you will send me their names. The papers herewith sent, being originals, I request will be returned after they have served their purpose.

It is reported that Vidal himself is in Matamoras. May I ask that you will cause him to be found, if there ?

I beg leave to express the thanks of the people of this city and myself for the cordial support which has been extended to me by you in this unfortunate affair, and, while I rely with confidence on a continuance of these good offices, I assure you of my earnest intention to shield and protect the innocent while I will punish the guilty.

With great respect, your obedient servant,

H. P. BEE,
Brigadier-General, Provisional Army Confederate States.

—

HEADQUARTERS,
Fort Brown, October 31, 1863.

SIR: The Vidalistas have dispersed; over 20 have been captured by Cortinas, under the orders of Governor Ruiz. Vidal himself is hiding in Matamoras. The danger of the effects of this outbreak has passed. I have offered a large reward for the capture of Vidal, which, I trust, the general will indorse, as the effect of his prompt punishment would be all-important. This outbreak has been potent in its lessons to us. I offer the following suggestions: That an order issue prohibiting the crossing of cotton at any point on the Rio Grande below Laredo—make it absolute; all goods now in Matamoras for Government account to be forwarded as rapidly as possible, and no more to be received there; make Eagle Pass the point of delivery; as soon as this can be done, withdraw the troops and guard the upper line. The road by King's ranch will be impracticable for ox-wagons after this month; it is even so now, as there is no grass. I shall act on these suggestions so far as the goods here are concerned, and hope in two weeks to be able to order the Thirty-third Regiment into the interior. This post can be defended against internal and external enemies, but, when the Yankees are added, the force will be destroyed. They will find an enemy in every thicket, and, therefore, the sooner they get away the better, as it is not in the power of the general to defend all of the State.

---

* Not found.

Brigadier-General Slaughter will leave to-day for Houston. He is well posted on all matters here, and will personally explain to the general commanding.

With great respect, .

H. P. BEE,
Brigadier-General.

Capt. EDMUND P. TURNER,
Assistant Adjutant-General.

NOVEMBER 9, 1863.—Skirmish near Bayou Sara, La.

Report of Col. Henry Maury, Fifteenth Confederate Cavalry.

MOBILE, ALA.,
November 12, 1863.

The following dispatch from Tunica, Miss., was received yesterday, dated 10th instant, from Col. Henry Maury, Fifteenth [Confederate] Cavalry Regiment:

We dashed in yesterday above Bayou Sara on a plundering party of Yankees, 300 strong; drove them to their iron-clads, with great slaughter. We brought off their wagon train and 25 prisoners from under the broadsides of their gunboats. Only 3 wounded of ours.

DABNEY H. MAURY,
Major-General.

General S. COOPER.

NOVEMBER 15–16, 1863.—Expedition from Vidalia to Trinity, La.

Report of Col. Bernard G. Farrar, Thirtieth Missouri Infantry.

POST OF VIDALIA, LA.,
November 18, 1863.

CAPTAIN: I have the honor to report the details of the expedition, made in obedience to your orders, into the enemy's lines on the west side of the Mississippi River.

Having obtained 18 mounted men and a single raft from Captain Lochbihler's Missouri company of pontoniers, in addition to 98 mounted men of the Thirtieth Missouri Volunteer Infantry and 14 mounted sergeants of the Second Mississippi (African descent) Volunteer Artillery, I started out from Vidalia at 3.30 o'clock on the 15th day of November, my whole force amounting to 8 officers and 140 enlisted men.

We crossed Cross Bayou on the Trinity road, and marched on that road to within 5 miles of Trinity. We then turned south on a plantation road, and kept such roads until we arrived at the banks of Black River, about 2½ miles below Trinity.

Here I ordered the horses and mules to be picketed, and left the pontoniers as guard over the same. In about a half hour the pontoon raft was placed in the river, and we commenced to cross afoot. At 4 o'clock an aggregate of 75 men had crossed, and the remainder of the men were missing, having either left to get fodder for their animals or shirked their duty at a time when they could not be hunted up. It being already 4 o'clock, and the object of the expedition (the capture of the camp on Colton's plantation, 6 miles distant from the river), being only attainable by a perfect surprise at night, I was forced either to march immediately, in order to arrive there before daybreak, with only 75 men, or to wait until a more fortunate opportunity was offered. To have pursued the first course would have been too hazardous, reliable report setting the number of rebels in the camp on Colton's plantation, at the least calculation, at 100 men. The last and most disagreeable alternative was unavoidable, under the circumstances.

In order to avoid having made an altogether fruitless expedition, it was determined upon to capture the picket station at Trinity, which was reported to be 1 captain and 17 men. I marched my command to within 500 yards of their barracks, and then went with a party of 20 men to capture them. Their 2 pickets were taken without firing a shot. Their barracks were then surrounded and 1 sergeant, 1 corporal, and 10 privates surrendered themselves prisoners of war. They belong to Major White's [?] First Louisiana Cavalry Battalion. In addition to the 14 prisoners and the arms that were thought fit to be brought along (7 muskets and 1 Colt's navy revolver), there were captured 10 horses and 6 bridles and saddles.

From the statement of the prisoners, it appears that the officer commanding the party had gone to headquarters in camp, Colton's plantation. After firing the barracks, I returned to our place of disembarkation and recrossed the river. After half an hour's rest, I ordered the line of march to be taken up, and arrived at Cross Bayou at noon.

While the main force had already recommenced its march, and the last load of the rear guard had but just crossed the bayou, a party of rebels fired upon them from ambush. The horses of my command being pretty well ridden down, and those of the enemy's fresh, I deemed it useless to recross the bayou and attack or pursue them, and I therefore ordered the rear guard to follow the main force.

I arrived at Vidalia, La., at 3.30 o'clock on the 16th day of November, having traveled 70 miles in twenty-four hours, and had no casualties in my command. The bearing of the officers and men who crossed Black River with me deserves my sincere commendation and approbation. The pontoniers were efficient in their duty and truly commendable for their soldierly behavior.

I remain, captain, most respectfully, your obedient servant,

BERNARD G. FARRAR,
Colonel, Commanding.

Capt. C. CADLE, Jr.,
Assistant Adjutant-General, Natchez, Miss.

NOVEMBER 18–21, 1863.—Operations against United States gunboats and transports near Hog Point, Mississippi River, La.

Reports of Capt. T. A. Faries, Louisiana Battery.

IN THE FIELD, NEAR HOG POINT,
Pointe Coupée Parish, La., November 18, 1863.

SIR: I have the honor to report that the following pieces were placed in position at Battery No. 1, Hog Point, 1 mile below Red River Landing, on the night of the 17th instant: One 12-pounder bronze field gun of Cornay's (Louisiana) battery, under Lieut. O. Berwick, in the upper gun-pit, sunk in the batture; two 3-inch Parrott rifles, of Daniel's (Texas) battery, on the lower end of platform, built in the angle of the levee for four field guns, forming a redoubt, with embrasures formed by gabions, all constructed by the company of engineers attached to the First Division, under the direction of Lieutenant [Alfonso] Buhlan, C. S. Engineers, by whom the river was triangulated and distances established from the batteries, diagrams of which were furnished the officers of artillery.

The two 3-inch rifled guns of Faries' battery occupied the upper end of platform in this redoubt, under First Lieut. J. R. Winchester.

At 7 a. m. this morning two solid shot were fired from the 12-pounder field gun of Lieut. O. Berwick's section at a Federal transport, bound down. The fog had not lifted sufficiently to make her out distinctly. She seemed to have grounded during the night. One shot missed, and the other, a ricochet shot, struck her; distance, about 1,000 yards. She got off, and disappeared in the fog immediately after the second shot was fired. The enemy replied to this fire from the 8-inch Parrott rifle on the barge anchored near the left bank of the river, opposite Red River Landing, but not until the fog had entirely lifted, two hours later. They fired shell, with 15-second fuse, but directed at Battery No. 3, some distance below me. These shell all passed to the right of Battery No. 3, and exploded in the woods in the rear of our line of batteries. I desire to say that no shell have been furnished for the heavy 12-pounder field gun of Cornay's (Louisiana) battery, rendering the fire from this gun much less effective. It is furnished with solid shot, spherical case, and canister, all good. The range of this piece, both above and below, is good.

At 3 p. m. to-day, the guns of the lower batteries, Nos. 2 and 3, opened on the Federal gunboat No. 8, bound up. The 12-pounder field gun, now under Lieut. O. H. Jones, of Cornay's (Louisiana) battery, fired six solid shot, of which four were hits, and three spherical case, two of which struck her.

One solid shot was fired from a 3-inch rifle of Lieut. J. R. Winchester's section at the No. 8, striking the iron covering of her boilers, but not penetrating; distance, 1,200 yards.

This boat seemed to be injured to some extent. She was laid up at the bank above the barge containing the heavy rifle Parrott guns, beyond the effective range of our guns, and, from the sound after dark, I concluded they were repairing her.

The enemy replied from a 200 pounder and 30-pounder, both Parrott rifles, on the barge above us; also from the iron-clad Choctaw, near Red River Landing, and the iron-clads Franklin and Carondelet from below, creating a cross-fire on the point where the redoubt was built. The Choctaw, during the firing, left her position above, and, passing down, delivered a very heavy fire from her bow, side, and stern guns, enfilading for a short time the four rifled guns in the redoubt. Captain [J. M.] Daniel, the senior officer present, two of whose guns occupied the redoubt, thought proper to order the four guns away from the platform in the redoubt. They were run down the ramp to the road below, and the cannoneers ordered to take shelter in the curves behind the levee. This will, I trust, account for the very limited number of shots fired by the guns usually under my immediate command. The firing by the enemy ceased about 5 p. m., the iron-clads taking their old position at anchor 1 mile above the redoubt at Battery No. 1. Two gunboats from above arrived at the anchorage above us about the time the three iron-clads reached there.

Most of the shell from the enemy's guns exploded in the immediate vicinity of the five pieces at the upper end of this battery.

I have no casualties to report.

I am, very respectfully, your obedient servant,

T. A. FARIES.
Capt., Comdg. Battery, First Brig., Louisiana Inf., Second Div.
Maj. T. B. FRENCH,
Chief of Artillery, (Walker's) First Infantry Division.

—

IN THE FIELD, NEAR HOG POINT,
Pointe Coupée Parish, La., November 21, 1863.

SIR: I have the honor to report the following shots fired from three pieces of Battery No. 1, at 4.30 p. m. this day, directed at the new Federal transport Black Hawk, bound down. She appeared to be well loaded with stores and material.

Piece No. 1, a 3-inch Parrott rifle of Faries' battery, two solid shot, both hits, fired from the lower embrasure of the first or upper gun-pit in the batture. She was not well under way until she had come in · range from the lower embrasure. Had she been fired upon from the upper embrasures, she could have returned to the cover of the iron-clads above, and waited until some time during the night, and made the passage of the batteries with less risk.

Piece No. 2, a 12-pounder bronze field gun, of Cornay's battery, under Lieut. O. H. Jones, fired six solid shot, four of which took effect. 'Ammunition good.

Piece No. 3, a 3-inch Parrott rifle, of Faries' battery, under Lieut. O. Berwick, of Cornay's battery, fired four shell (time-fuse), three of which took effect, one missing her. At least three more shots could have been fired from this piece, but for the failure of the friction primers, none of the same lot ever having failed before. With this exception, the ammunition of the 3-inch rifles is good.

The pieces under my command at Battery No. 1 were, in accordance with orders, withdrawn at sunset, and retired by the way of Red River Landing, under a very severe fire from all of the iron-clads and the heavy Parrott rifles on the barge anchored near the left bank of the river. I have learned since reaching camp that the steamer Black Hawk was discovered to be on fire as she passed Battery No. 3, and was run into the left bank below, where the most of her upper works were destroyed by the fire, her hull alone being visible.

I have no casualties to report.

I am, very respectfully, your obedient servant,

T. A. FARIES,
Captain, Comdg. Battery, First Louisiana Brigade, Second Div.
Capt. O. J. SEMMES, Commanding Batteries, Mississippi River.

———

DECEMBER 3, 1863.—Affair at Saint Martinsville, La.

Abstract from "Record of Events" on return of Cavalry Division, Department of the Gulf, for December, 1863.

Lieutenant [James S.] McHenry, Second Illinois Cavalry, with 17 men, charged upon an officer and 17 men of the enemy, and captured the officer and 16 of his men, on Petite Anse Bayou.

DECEMBER 9, 1863.—Mutiny at Fort Jackson, La.

Reports of Maj. Gen. Nathaniel P. Banks, U. S. Army, and record of Military Commission.

HEADQUARTERS DEPARTMENT OF THE GULF,
New Orleans, December 11, 1863.

GENERAL : An unpleasant affair occurred at Fort Jackson on the even-ing of the 9th instant. Lieutenant-Colonel Benedict, of the Fourth Regiment, Corps d'Afrique, having some difficulty with the troops there, struck and punished 2 soldiers with a whip.

This produced great excitement among the troops, who assembled on the parade grounds, in most violent excitement, and threatened the officers of the regiment. They fired their muskets in the air, and com-mitted other excesses, but without doing any injury to persons or prop-erty. This occurred about 6.30 o'clock. Colonel Drew, in command of the post, reports that the excitement continued about half an hour, when they were quieted, and at tattoo all were in their quarters. The next morning at reveille every man is reported to have answered to his name. The negroes have been constantly assured, whether engaging in labor or enlisting as soldiers, that under no circumstances whatever were they to be subjected to the degrading punishment of flogging. This has always been made a condition by them, and they have always received this assurance from the officers of the Government.

Lieutenant-Colonel Benedict, being ordered to report to these head-quarters, tendered his resignation, which was not accepted. A military commission, consisting of Major-General Herron, Col. Horace B. Sar-gent, and Capt. Stephen Hoyt, with Major Lieber as judge-advocate, has been appointed to make thorough investigation of all the facts con-nected with the affair. The order appointing the commission, with its instructions, are inclosed herewith.

The captain of the steamer Suffolk, lying near Fort Jackson, became greatly alarmed at the demonstrations made, and moved up to the Quarantine Station, sending from there exciting telegraphic dispatches to these headquarters.

It was difficult to get precise knowledge of affairs during the night, but, with a view of being on the safe side, Commodore [Henry H.] Bell was requested to send one or two more gunboats immediately to Fort Jackson. A regiment of troops was moved down during the evening and a battery of artillery in the morning. They proceeded no farther than Quarantine Station. Commodore Bell himself moved down the river with the Pensacola.

Many exciting rumors have been started in the city concerning this affair, and it is quite possible they may be reproduced in the north. It is proper for me to say, therefore, that however unfortunate the oc-currence may have been, and whatever guilt may be attached to the different parties concerned, there is nothing to excite apprehension or to suggest a doubt as to the perfect confidence which the Government may repose in troops of this class. There were no prisoners, either of the rebel or our own army, at Fort Jackson, and no inconvenience has been experienced, excepting that which arose from the imperfect knowl-edge of the events of the evening and the excitement produced by an occurrence of this character. Elsewhere in the department everything is quiet.

Inclosed I send copies of the various dispatches received and sent to the captain of the Suffolk and other officers at Quarantine Station, Fort

Saint Philip, and Fort Jackson, with a report of the affair from Col. Charles W. Drew, commanding the post of Fort Jackson.*

I have the honor to be, with much respect, your obedient servant,

N. P. BANKS,
Major-General, Commanding.

Maj. Gen. H. W. HALLECK,
General-in-Chief, U. S. Army.

———

HEADQUARTERS DEPARTMENT OF THE GULF,
New Orleans, December 17, 1863.

GENERAL: I have the honor to transmit the report of a commission appointed to investigate the occurrences at Fort Jackson on the evening of the 9th instant. The evidence is reported in full. Upon the conclusion of the report by the commission, a court-martial has been appointed consisting of the following officers: Col. F. S. Rutherford, Ninety-seventh Illinois Volunteers; Colonel Chickering, Third Massachusetts Cavalry; Lieut. Col. Richard Fitz Gibbons, Ninth Connecticut Volunteers; Major Maloney, First U. S. Infantry; Maj. Frederick Frye, Ninth Connecticut Volunteers; Lieutenant [Charles A.] Hartwell, Eleventh U. S. Infantry, colonel commanding Fifth Corps d'Afrique; Captain [John L.] Swift, Third Massachusetts Cavalry, judge-advocate.

Their session will commence immediately, at Fort Jackson, by a trial of all parties derelict in duty in this affair. Such measures will be taken as will prevent its repetition hereafter.† Upon full consideration of this matter in all its aspects, I am confirmed in the opinion I expressed to you upon my first report. There is nothing presented therein to impair the confidence of the Government in the efficiency and reliability of black troops. The conduct of the soldiers is inexcusable, and must be punished with such severity as to prevent its recurrence.

It is apparent, however, that the want of discretion, of a spirit of justice and of capacity to deal with men of this class manifested by some of the officers, whose conduct was the immediate cause of the outbreak, was such as could hardly be expected to produce any other result than that which occurred. The punishments to which the men were subjected for a considerable length of time before the revolt was contrary to the rules of war, and contrary to the orders constantly given in this department. They may justly be classed as among the cruel and unusual punishments interdicted by the Constitution.

The Fourth Regiment, Corps d'Afrique, stationed at Fort Jackson, was the first organized by me in this department. The commanding officer, Col. Charles W. Drew, was commissioned on the 29th of December, 1862, thirteen days after I assumed command. It has been among the best disciplined and the best instructed regiments of this class of troops. It was for a long time stationed at Baton Rouge, and received the commendation of all officers and citizens who had opportunity to witness its parades. Colonel Drew has been deemed an excellent officer, but it appears from the evidence reported by the commission that he has been derelict in reporting the conduct of some of his subordinate officers, and in giving full information of the condition and discipline of his command. We were unable to obtain from him full reports of this affair at the time of its occurrence. This is the only fault that appears in his official conduct. All the officers connected with this regiment

———

will be subjected to the examination of a competent court-martial, and such course pursued as will be justified by the facts.

All that I have known of the troops organized in this department in the Corps d'Afrique since the date mentioned of Colonel Drew's commission, now nearly a year, and covering periods of great exigency and difficulty, in which they have been exposed to all the trials to which any soldiers can be subjected, including the affair at Fort Jackson, which must be classed as a case of mutiny against official authority, I am gratified to be able to say that my confidence in their capacity for service is unimpaired. It must be considered, however, that they are unable immediately to comprehend to its full extent the necessity of strict military discipline; that a great many of the duties of citizens which are readily understood and accepted by white men are not by them understood and appreciated. A few months' instruction and discipline is not sufficient to enable them to comprehend all that is required of citizens or soldiers. All this will come in course of time, and much sooner than I should have anticipated, but for my experience in the organization of these troops. It is indispensable that the officers should be men of high character, able to appreciate the capacity as well as the deficiencies of the men placed in their charge.

We have organized from twenty-five to thirty regiments. It has been necessary to take a large number of officers from the regiments of the Thirteenth and Nineteenth Corps, upon very imperfect examination as to qualifications. Unfortunately, some officers, regarding the organization of the corps as of inferior character to that of white troops, and supposing that officers of inferior qualifications would be able to discharge the corresponding duty of officers in other branches of the service, have sometimes recommended men disqualified by want of character and capacity for the discharge of the humblest duties in the regiments to which they belonged, and others, seeking promotion for personal objects, indifferent to the success of the corps, have in some cases been appointed. A board of examiners was early organized for the investigation of the qualifications of officers who had been commissioned, as well as of those who applied for commissions, consisting of Col. C. C. Dwight, One hundred and sixtieth New York; Capt. J. S. Crosby, U. S. Army, and Capt. Samuel Hamblin, Eighth Regiment, Corps d'Afrique.

The examination by this board has been thorough, and officers receiving its approval have thus far appeared to be competent for the discharge of their duties. It is just to say, however, that the highest qualifications, physical and mental, are demanded for this command. The limitations in the number of men in each regiment to 500 works favorably; the troops are more quickly instructed and disciplined. It is approved by the experience of other nations in the organization of troops of a similar character; 1,000 men of such limited capacity, instruction, and self-possession is too strong a force for the officers provided by the Army Regulations for the command of a regiment. As soon, however, as the troops are completely disciplined, this number can be safely increased to the maximum by the addition of 50 or 100 at a time. By such a course, the men of the original regiment instruct their comrades.

Efforts have been made to instruct the troops in the normal branches of English education. An instructor has been authorized for each regiment, to be a part of the staff of its commander, with the rank of lieutenant, and a general instructor for the corps is authorized for the staff of the commanding officer. The chaplains have been efficient in the discharge of their professional duties, and have assisted greatly in most cases in the education of the men. Books have been supplied to them whenever requisition has been made, and orders have been issued that they shall be instructed in the Articles of War, and an edition of the Articles of War printed especially for the use of the men of this corps. It will be apparent that whatever soldierly qualifications may be ultimately found in these men, their full development requires time. The troops of other nations are such as have been made by military operations running through many centuries.

It is unreasonable to expect that men who have never handled a musket, who have never been admitted to civil or individual rights, can instantaneously become perfect soldiers. The organization in this department has proceeded upon the idea that it was a work of difficulty, requiring much time. Had instances of insubordination, of which this is the only one, been more frequent—had they signally failed in comprehending the routine duties of the soldier, or had they shrunk before the enemy in battle—it would have been no proof of their incapacity for war.

I have the honor to be, with much respect, your obedient servant,

N. P. BANKS,
Major-General, Commanding.

Maj. Gen. H. W. HALLECK,
  General-in-Chief, U. S. Army.

[Inclosure.]

Proceedings of a military commission convened at Fort Jackson, La., pursuant to the following order:

SPECIAL ORDERS, } HDQRS. DEPARTMENT OF THE GULF,
  No. 309.   }   *New Orleans, La., December* 11, 1863.

*   *   *   *   *   *   *

X. A military commission, to consist of Maj. Gen. F. J. Herron, U. S. Volunteers; Col. H. B. Sargent, First Massachusetts Cavalry; Capt. Stephen Hoyt, commissary of subsistence, and Maj. G. Norman Lieber, will assemble at Fort Jackson, La., to-morrow at 7 a. m., or as soon thereafter as practicable, to examine into and report upon the disturbance said to have occurred in the garrison of Fort Jackson on the 9th instant. The commission will investigate the cause, the course, and the termination of the disturbance, particularly the conduct of the commanding officer, officers and men of the garrison, and will sit without regard to days or hours, reporting to these headquarters by telegraph should it be deemed advisable. Maj. G. Norman Lieber, judge-advocate of the Department, will act as judge-advocate of the commission.

*   *   *   *   *   *   *

By command of Major-General Banks:

G. NORMAN LIEBER,
Acting Assistant Adjutant-General.

FORT JACKSON,
December 12, 1863—9 a. m.

The commission met pursuant to the foregoing order. Present, all the members. The order convening the commission was then read. The commission was then duly sworn by the judge-advocate, and the judge-advocate was duly sworn by the president of the commission.

Col. CHARLES W. DREW, Fourth Regiment Infantry, Corps d'Afrique, being duly sworn, testified as follows:

Question. Please state your name, rank, and the nature of your command.

Answer. My name is Charles W. Drew, colonel Fourth Regiment, Corps d'Afrique, and commanding the post which includes Fort Jackson and Fort Saint Philip.

Question. Were you in command on the 9th instant?

Answer. I was.

Question. Please state in detail what unusual events, if any, occurred on that day.

Answer. The first unusual event that I noticed occurred about 5 p. m. I saw Lieutenant-Colonel Benedict, of the Fourth Regiment Infantry, Corps d'Afrique, strike one of the drummers with a whip two or three times, at the same time reprimanding him. He made use of an expression like this: "I have had a great deal of trouble with you already, and I am going to stop it." He then walked off. I turned toward him when I saw him strike him, intending to reprimand him there, but he turned off, and I thought it best to delay it instead of reprimanding him in the presence of the men. I went to my quarters, and was sitting at my desk, as nearly as I can judge, about 6.30, when the adjutant, who had come into my room, said: "There is a disturbance among the men. I think they are taking their arms." I replied, "No, I think not." He then went to the door, and, upon opening it, ascertained that they were. I immediately went out into the parade, when they commenced firing into the air and shouting. I soon discovered from their language that it was in consequence of Lieutenant-Colonel Benedict's action. I immediately turned, and ordered him to his quarters, and, with my officers, who were all present, endeavored to quell the disturbance. I soon got enough of them quieted so that I could talk to them, and told them to go to their quarters and put up their guns, as I wished to talk to them, but would not do it whilst they had them. At this time I should think about 30 had gone outside the fort toward the river, continuing the firing. Nearly all those inside went to their quarters, and put up their guns upon my assuring them that I would see that justice was done them.

The firing had been going on then about half an hour. I formed the men into a hollow square, and had commenced talking to them, when some of those from outside the fort came in, saying, "Don't give up your guns," and demanding Lieutenant-Colonel Benedict, making so much disturbance that I directed the officers to form their companies in the company streets, as it was impossible to talk to them there. Very soon everything inside became quiet again. I should think that nearly one-half the regiment was engaged in the disturbance, the other half trying to quiet them. I had tattoo beaten, I think about 8 o'clock that night, much earlier than usual, when everything was quiet, and nearly all the men answered to their names at roll-call. I afterward discovered that Major Nye was missing, and while searching for him at about 9.30, perhaps a little later, some 8 or 10 men who were still on the levee fired off their guns and came in. I heard no more firing that night, and do not think there was any until after reveille the next morning, when some of the men, by my direction, came down to the levee and fired off their guns. Lieutenant-Colonel Benedict had been stationed at Fort Saint Philip, but came to Fort Jackson the day before, and was placed in command of the regiment by me, which at this time was all at Fort Jackson, numbering 500 men.

Question. You say that when you went out on the parade, during the disturbance, you soon discovered, from the language used, that the disturbance was in consequence of Lieutenant-Colonel Benedict's action in whipping a music boy? Please state what that language was.

Answer. It was language something like this: "Give us Colonel Benedict; we did not come here to be whipped by him. Kill Colonel Benedict; shoot him," and other language to the same effect.

Question. Were the guns fired aimed at any person?

Answer. I do not know of a single gun being aimed at any person. They were all apparently fired into the air. I heard one man, a soldier, cry out, "Kill all the damned Yankees."

Question. Were any of the guns—the artillery of the fort—fired off?

Answer. Not one.

Question. Were the muskets loaded when the men took them from their quarters, or did they load them afterward?

Answer. The men loaded them afterward. They were in the act of loading them when I arrived at the door of my quarters, coming out.

Question. How many shots do you judge were fired?

Answer. It is hard to judge. The firing continued indiscriminately for half an hour, some men discharging their guns three or four times; others only once.

Question. How many men do you suppose fired their guns?

Answer. About one-half of the regiment. About 250 men were under arms, but they did not all discharge their guns. About half of those who were under arms fired off their guns.

Question. Did you observe any men who took a prominent part in the disturbance and encouraged the others?

Answer. It being quite dark at the time, I could recognize but one. Company commanders inform me that they recognized the leaders. I have arrested one and ordered the arrest of another.

Question. Did you notice any men particularly prominent in the disturbance and leading the others?

Answer. I did; and I noticed the boy whom Lieutenant-Colonel Benedict whipped at the head of one squad.

Question. Did the disturbance seem to have any organization, or was it a mob raised without premeditation and plan?

Answer. So far as I know, it was raised on the spur of the moment. I have since understood that there was discontent with Lieutenant-Colonel Benedict by the men who were under him at Fort Saint Philip, part of whom had been transferred to Fort Jackson, and were in the disturbance.

Question. Was Lieutenant-Colonel Benedict's discipline at Fort Saint Philip severe? Did he employ the whip as a means of coercion? What was the state of his command there?

Answer. I never knew of Lieutenant-Colonel Benedict using the whip before. He was very strict, but I did not know of his being severe. His command was in good shape, and presented a fine appearance; so much so, that I remarked it when I visited Fort Saint Philip.

Question. Do you know of any other cause of discontent among the men at Fort Jackson or Fort Saint Philip?

Answer. None, other than their pay, which they spoke of on the evening of the disturbance.

Question. Had this anything to do with the disturbance on the 9th instant?

Answer. I think not, immediately, but I think it aggravated the matter.

Question. Please state more definitely the conduct of the men when you ordered them to·their quarters, and whether they refused or neglected to obey your orders.

Answer. When I first came into the parade, I immediately ordered them to stop firing and go to their quarters. Some of them stopped firing, and gathered around me, saying, "We don't want to hurt you; it is Colonel Benedict we are after;" while others replied, "We will not stop firing until we have him," and continued the firing. I then told them that Colonel Benedict had done wrong, but that was no excuse for their conduct. They must go to their quarters and put up their arms, and I would talk to them, and see that justice was done them. One of the officers came to me, and said that they thought I wanted them to put their guns away and turn the guns of the fort upon them. I took advantage of this information to tell them that if they would go to their quarters, I would take no further steps at that time, and most of them went to their quarters and put up their guns. Those who went outside the fort, violated the rules in doing so, and forced the guard. ·

Question. What did the officers under your command do during the disturbance?

Answer. The officers all did what they could to quell the disturbance. They were all present, and took an active part by going to the men and telling them to go to their quarters. Lieutenant-Colonel Benedict, Major Nye, and all the company officers were present. Some of the officers had their swords, others not. I did not have mine, as I thought it injudicious. The efforts of the officers in quelling the disturbance had the appearance of advice.

Question. Why did you order Lieutenant-Colonel Benedict to his quarters? Do you believe the men would have inflicted any injury upon him if he had remained upon the parade?

Answer. I thought his presence there did exasperate the men, and feared that they might injure him if he remained. I was satisfied that his presence would prolong the disturbance.

Question. You say half of your regiment were trying to appease the others. How and when did you know that half your command could be relied on to repress the mutiny?

Answer. I judged from appearances that about one-half could be relied upon. I judged so soon after I arrived upon the parade.

Question. You say that some men refused or neglected to obey your command. What motives restrained you from killing them or any violent ringleader on the spot? Were you armed?

Answer. I was not armed, and I think it would have been very injudicious to have fired a shot at that time.

Question. How strong was the guard on the day mentioned; what was their conduct and that of the officer of the day?

Answer. I think that the entire guard was 42 men. The sentinels all remained on post except where the tide in passing carried them away, but they returned again. The men who took part in the disturbance went to the guard-house and released some men confined there. The officer of the day did what the rest of the officers did. I think he was with the crowd, trying to quell the disturbance. I went to the guard-house once, thinking to blockade the entrance to the fort, the sallyport, with the guard, but concluded not to do so. The guard did not take any part in the riotous proceedings, but remained at their posts.

Question. Did you address the boy whom you say Lieutenant-Colonel Benedict whipped when you saw him leading a squad of the rioters? And, if so, what did you say to him?

Answer. As soon as I discovered that he was at the head of a squad of men, I immediately called for him, and said to him that Lieutenant-Colonel Benedict had done very wrong in whipping him, but that the men had done greater wrong in the steps which they had taken; that I was the proper person to settle the difficulty. I then told him to have the men put up their guns and come out on the parade, as I wished to talk to them, assuring him that I would see him protected in his rights, when he replied that he would do so, and set to work trying to quiet the disturbance, and it was quieted soon after.

Question. Has Lieutenant-Colonel Benedict been on duty since the disturbance, and what has been the conduct of the men toward him?

Answer. He has not been on duty since. The next morning I ordered him to proceed to New Orleans, and report to Colonel [Edward G.] Beckwith, commanding Defenses of New Orleans, to whom I forwarded a written report. Nothing was said, and no demonstration was made when he walked down to the boat.

Question. What has been the conduct of the men since the 9th instant?

Answer. Their conduct has been unexceptionable.

Question. Has there been any change in the discipline, rules, and regulations of the post since then?

Answer. There has not. I have taken especial pains to carry out all the rules established before. I had the prisoners, who were released by the rioters, rearrested, and arrested one of the men engaged in the riot. Upon going to the guard-house, he asked the men who arrested him what he was going for, and upon their declining to give him any answer, said he " would be damned if he would go until he knew what he was sent for." The officer of the day informed me that he remarked as he went into the guard house that he would come out of there or lose his life. I then instructed the officer of the day to confine him in the dungeon, which is reached by a door from the main guard-house, and take extra precautions that the prisoner did not escape.

Question. What was the cause of the arrest of the prisoner referred to ?

Answer. His captain, Capt. James Miller, reported to me on the night of the 9th that he, the prisoner, made an attempt to bayonet him. I then ordered his arrest, and directed the captain to prefer charges against him.

Question. What would be the effect if Lieutenant-Colonel Benedict was ordered back to the regiment ?

Answer. I think it would be very injurious to the regiment to have him returned. I do not think I should have any trouble in controlling the men; still, I think there would be a very discontented feeling among the men.

Question. Do not the men feel that they have carried their point in having Lieutenant-Colonel Benedict kept away from his post ?

Answer. I have heard no remarks to indicate their idea upon the subject, but my idea is that they feel so.

Question. Have the men ever made any complaints to you previous to the disturbance of the 9th instant ? And, if so, please state what they were, and how made.

Answer. I remember no complaints except in the case of pay. Their individual complaints I make them go to their company commanders with, and let them refer them to me. About the last of October, one company, immediately after being paid, turned out, and were coming toward my quarters, where the paymaster was. I ordered them to their quarters, and arrested two sergeants, who, I understood, were instrumental in starting the thing. I afterward sent for them, and told them the consequences that must follow from such action, and explained to them, as I had instructed the company officers to do before, that the amount of their pay was not definitely settled, and would not be until Congress convened. Upon the promise of future good behavior, I released them. Afterward the company sent me word that they were sorry, and such a thing should not occur again.

The commission then adjourned to meet again at 2 p. m.

G. NORMAN LIEBER,
Major and Judge Advocate.

—

FORT JACKSON, LA.,
December 12, 1863—2 p. m.

The court met pursuant to adjournment.

Examination of Col. CHARLES W. DREW resumed.

Question. How do you explain your opinion that the return of Lieutenant-Colonel Benedict would be injudicious if the men think they have gained their point ? How will the men be controlled if they gain their point?

Answer. I think it would be injudicious in this way : The feeling of hatred toward Lieutenant-Colonel Benedict would remain, though they would obey my orders without any difficulty.

Question. When you say that the men consider they have triumphed, is your opinion based upon what they have said or done ?

Answer. It is not. I have heard nothing that they have said or done that would make me think so. I only form that opinion as a natural consequence.

Question. Did any of the shots fired on the 9th instant strike the officers' quarters ?

Answer. I think some three or four shots struck them, but I do not think that they were aimed at them. It was the result, I think, of indiscriminate firing. The men being on the parade, and the officers' quarters on the parapet, it was natural that a few shots should take effect.

Question. What troops composed the garrison at Fort Saint Philip and Fort Jackson on the 9th instant?

Answer. The garrison at Fort Jackson was composed of the Fourth Infantry, Corps d'Afrique, 500 men. The garrison at Fort Saint Philip was composed of that portion of the Fourth Regiment Infantry, Corps d'Afrique, which had just been turned over to the Fifth Infantry, Corps d'Afrique, about 300 men, and Company A, First Regiment Artillery, Corps d'Afrique.

Question. If the men did not intend to fire at any officer, for what purpose, in your opinion, were they firing?

Answer. I judged that it was to make as much noise as possible, and to intimidate. I hardly think they had any definite object.

Question. Have you reason to suppose that any of the men were under the influence of liquor at the time of the disturbance ?

Answer. It did not occur to me at that time, but I have since learned that some liquor was brought into the garrison on that day. The amount reported to me was eight bottles of whisky.

The examination of Col. Charles W. Drew was then closed.

Maj. WILLIAM E. NYE, Fourth Infantry, Corps d'Afrique, was then duly sworn by the judge-advocate.

Question. Please state your name, rank, and regiment.

* Answer. William E. Nye, major Fourth Regiment Infantry, Corps d'Afrique.

Question. Where were you stationed on the 9th instant?

Answer. Fort Jackson.

Question. Please state in detail what unusual events, if any, occurred at Fort Jackson on the 9th instant.

Answer. About 6.30 p. m. on that day, whilst sitting in my quarters with Captain Merritt, I heard what sounded like blows and the cracking of a whip, and some one making a noise as if pleading. I stepped to my door, opened it, and discovered Lieutenant-Colonel Benedict in the act of whipping a man in front of the guard-house on the parade. I then closed the door, went back into my quarters, and sat down again. Lieutenant-Colonel Benedict then came in and sat down ; he then went to the door, opened it, and stepped out in front of the quarters. After a moment, he stepped back, taking his revolver from where it hung, and his bed, and stepped out again. I stepped out myself a moment after that, and saw a crowd of men on the opposite side of the parade. A portion of them had arms, and they were manifesting a good deal of confusion and noise. I started for the guard-house, and, seeing 2 or 3 officers, asked where the officer of the day was. Receiving no answer, I went to the guard-house, and, while ordering the guard to fall in, I discovered a large portion of the two companies that are quartered outside the fort in the act of loading their pieces. I stepped up to them, and asked by whose order they were loading. Receiving no satisfactory answers, I ordered them to their quarters. Their answers were, "I don't know ; I don't know what the trouble is," or words to that effect. In the meantime firing had commenced on the inside. Firing had commenced when I was going down to the guard-house. I do not know whether they were rifle or pistol shots. The men on the outside made a rush for the bridge, shouting as they went, "Kill him, shoot him; kill the son of a bitch," and other words of like meaning. While attempting to prevent them going outside the outer moat, I was caught hold of by a man grasping me by the coat collar and vest and tearing it down, and I partially fell. He then released his hold and mingled with the crowd, which was then apparently rushing for the levee. Judging from their movements and their language, I judged they were in pursuit of some one on the Suffolk, then tied up at the levee. During this time there was a good deal of yelling, swearing, cursing, and threatening, with, at the same time, considerable random discharging of pieces, apparently firing into the air without any object. I succeeded in turning back a few of them, but the larger and more noisy portion of them persisted in crowding their way to the levee. They approached the sentinel posted near the engineer's building, who made a feeble attempt to halt them, but there were several of them who stepped up to him, wrested his gun from him, and took off his cartridge-box, after which they went on down to the levee, still shouting and cursing, and the firing of pieces rather increasing. While on the levee, they arranged themselves in squads, not seemingly with any degree of order, but as a mob would collect. During this time my efforts to quiet them had aroused a sort of feeling against myself. Previous to this they had manifested no ill-will toward me, but had repeatedly said it was not me they wished to harm, but they would kill Lieutenant-Colonel Benedict if they could find him. At this time there was a portion of them who made a rush for the engineer's room. There were two or three shots fired which struck the building. I do not know whether they were aimed or not. Finding that my endeavors to quiet them were getting dangerous to my own person, as they were saying that they would interfere with no one else unless they stood in their way, and having been told by them that unless I let them alone they would bayonet me, at this time I stepped back off the levee, and a portion of the men started down the levee to the hospital. At this time the firing in the fort had nearly ceased; occasionally the report of a single gun could be heard. The crowd now seemed to divide, part going toward the hospital and part down the river. I then started back to the fort, and the sentinel at the outer end of the bridge refused to pass me without the countersign. I ordered him to call the corporal, which he did, but the call was not repeated, that I could hear, and the corporal did not come. He still refusing to pass me, I started back toward the stables, with the intention of waiting until the corporal or the officer of the day came. At this time all the firing had ceased. After waiting a few moments, I went to the hospital. While there, there were a few shots fired below the road, on the levee. These were the last shots that I heard fired. I waited awhile, watching for the relief or the officer of the day, that I might get into the fort. When I went into the fort, everything was quiet. This was after 8 o'clock.

Question. Was the guard paraded?

Answer. When I ordered them to turn out, there were 2 or 3 that started toward the line, but they did not turn out readily. By their actions they showed a stubbornness.

Question. Do you know what was the cause of the disturbance?

Answer. I should judge it was the whipping of those men by Lieutenant-Colonel Benedict.

Question. What men do you refer to when you say "those men"?

Answer. I refer to the two drummer boys, named Harry Williams and Munroe Miller. I do not know whether the latter is the correct name. I only know him by that. He is the one I saw Lieutenant-Colonel Benedict whip. I did not see him whip Williams. I saw him strike Miller three or four times with—as nearly as I could judge from the distance—a mule whip, such as used on carts; a whip with a stock and lash. He did not strike very severely.

Question. What reason have you to suppose that this was the cause of the disturbance?

Answer. First, by my servant coming to me when I was leaving my quarters, and telling me that the boys were going to shoot Lieutenant-Colonel Benedict for whipping Harry, and from the remarks made by the men while endeavoring to quiet them.

Question. For what purpose did the men go out of the fort to the levee?

Answer. My impression is that they thought that Lieutenant-Colonel Benedict was either on the Suffolk, or would attempt to get there, and that they were after him. I think they would have killed him if they had caught him.

Question. Had you arms upon your person? What motive restrained you from killing the soldier who seized you?

Answer. I had no arms upon my person. Had I had arms, I would not have attempted to kill him, because I think it would have exasperated them.

Question. Were the officers armed?

Answer. Those that I saw go out on the parade were not.

Question. What was the firing at?

Answer. I think it was without object.

Question. Did you see Colonel Drew, and what was he doing during the disturbance ?

Answer. I saw Colonel Drew in the parade ground, near a crowd of men. I saw him only for a moment. When I saw him, he seemed to be endeavoring to quiet the men. He appeared to be talking to them.

Question. What has been the conduct of the men since Lieutenant-Colonel Benedict's departure ?

Answer. They seem to be the same as before, and obey the orders given them.

Question. What would be the result if he were ordered back ?

Answer. I do not think it would be prudent for him personally. I do not think the men would submit to be commanded by him with a good degree of discipline.

Question. Did the non-commissioned officers take part in the disturbance ? .

Answer. I think I saw two or three with chevrons on.

Question. Was there ill-feeling toward Lieutenant-Colonel Benedict before this?

Answer. My impression is that there was, but I do not know personally. I think it was on account of some punishment inflicted upon men.

Question. What are the punishments in your regiment? Do you punish without court-martial, and how ?

Answer. Confinement in the guard-house, carrying ball and chain, and in one in-stance a man was tied up by the thumbs. Unless charges are preferred within twenty-four hours, or before the next guard-mounting, the new officer of the day has orders to release him, the prisoner.

Question. Do you know of the men having any other subject of complaint ?

Answer. Personally I do not. I have heard so since the disturbance, but not from the men. It was in the case of two punishments at Fort Saint Philip.

Question. At the time you heard blows, you say you heard pleading. What was the nature of the pleading—for mercy, or that the person inflicting the blows would desist ?

Answer. It was using such words as, "Don't; I won't do it again."

Question. Were any of the officers or warrant officers ready and dis posed to repress the mutiny by shooting ? What is the general feeling on the subject ?

Answer. I think that it was the feeling of a portion of the officers that if it could not be quieted in any other way, they would resort to shooting. I do not think the non-commissioned officers would resort to those means.

The evidence of Major Nye was here closed.

Capt. JAMES MILLER, Fourth Infantry, Corps d'Afrique, was then duly sworn by the judge-advocate.

Question. Please state your name, rank, regiment, and what position you were filling on the 9th instant.

Answer. James Miller; captain Company D, Fourth Regiment Infantry, Corps d'Afrique; I was officer of the day at Fort Jackson on the 9th instant.

Question. Please state what unusual transactions, if any, took place at Fort Jackson on that day.

Answer. Everything passed off very quietly until 5.30 p. m., when Lieutenant-Colonel Benedict did take two acting musicians and flog them. During the time that he was flogging them, there was a crowd of unarmed men assembled at the sally-port. After flogging the men, Lieutenant-Colonel Benedict dispersed the men, and they went to their quarters, and appeared to be very quiet; they went to their quarters, and plotted among themselves for a general insurrection. At 6.45 they rose up in arms, and went to the center of the parade, and commenced firing into the air. They were about half the regiment. During the time I went to fall in my guard, they would not take part against their comrades, and from 5 to 8 of the guard joined the insurrectionists. The insurrectionists then scattered over the parade, and discharged their guns into the air and at the officers' quarters, crying out, "We know what General Grant told us," meaning Adjutant-General Thomas. They then went to the guard-house and released the prisoners, 3 or 4 in number. Even those who did not join the insurrectionists would not obey orders. They then went outside the fort, and returned in greater force. Colonel Drew made his appearance upon the parade, and ordered the well-disposed to fall in, and the company officers to march the companies on the parade in close column, then to form square. He got in the center of the square, and undertook to address them. I was in the square. One man, named Frank Williams, Company I, rushed up to me, exclaiming, "God damn you! I have been looking for you all night;" and made two thrusts at me with his bayonet, striking me on the belt-plate. Then Colonel Drew dismissed them, and they went to their quarters, and acted very peaceably. They were brought back to duty by coaxing. The reason that the men were displeased with Lieutenant-Colonel Benedict was because he formed a habit of going around at inspection, and if a man's dress did not please him, he would knock him about and hit him. I have seen him do this several times. I saw him whip two musicians on the 9th. He whipped them severely with what I took to be a rawhide. I was stationed at Fort Saint Philip when Lieutenant-Colonel Benedict was in command there, and there was a great deal of discontent among the men there on account of his severe treatment. The men were very much enraged on the 9th, and would undoubtedly have killed Lieutenant-Colonel Benedict if they had caught him.

Question. If officers had fired upon the men, what would have been the result?

Answer. I think they would have killed the officers. One officer took a rifle on the parade, and one of the men snapped his piece at him.

Question. What has been the conduct of the men since?

Answer. Perfectly quiet. The men think that they have gained their point in getting rid of Lieutenant-Colonel Benedict, and they are quite content.

Question. Were any of the men under the influence of liquor?

Answer. I don't think they were.

Question. What did Colonel Drew to quiet the men?

Answer. He told them to go to their quarters and be quiet; that Lieutenant-Colonel Benedict had done wrong, and that he would see justice done, and that if they did not go to their quarters they would get themselves into trouble. He was there from first to last, and was not in any way afraid of them.

The court then adjourned to meet to-morrow morning at 8 o'clock.

F. J. HERRON,
Major-General Volunteers, President Military Commission.
G. NORMAN LIEBER,
Major, and Judge-Advocate.

—

PORT JACKSON,
December 13, 1863—8 a. m.

The court met pursuant to adjournment.

Present, all the members. The proceedings of the previous day were then read and approved.

The examination of Capt. James Miller was then resumed.

Question. You say that the men said that they knew what General Grant said to them, meaning Adjutant-General Thomas, who made a

speech here to them. To what portion of the speech did they allude?
Can you give the words?

Answer. General Thomas addressed the officers, and told them how to treat the men.
He then addressed the men, and told them that if the officers maltreated them in any
way or struck them, he would dismiss them. The address was made at Fort Saint
Philip, in the presence of both officers and men. Lieutenant-Colonel Benedict was
not present on duty. He might have been present, not on duty. This was about the
first week in September.

Question. Did you see Major Nye during the evening of the 9th instant, and what part did he take in quelling the disturbance?

Answer. The major left his quarters about 6.45; I did not see him again until
about 10. Colonel Drew and I searched for him about an hour after the disturbance,
thinking he had been killed, but couldn't find him. About 10 o'clock Major Nye
returned to his quarters.

Question. Do you know where Major Nye was?

Answer. He was not inside the garrison, and nowhere to be found.

Question. What was the conduct of the other officers?

Answer. Very good, indeed. They used their utmost endeavors to put down the
mutiny, and finally succeeded. They endeavored to quiet the men by talking to them.
They did not use force; there was no opportunity to use force. Some of the men said
to me, " Go away; we didn't wish to hurt you, but if you don't go away we will kill
you."

Question. Have you ever seen Lieutenant-Colonel Benedict maltreat
any of the men besides whipping the two music boys?

Answer. I have seen him, in the month of August, at Fort Saint Philip, spread a
man out on his back, drive stakes down, and spread out his hands and legs, take off
his shoes, and take molasses and spread it over his face, hands, and feet. Lieutenant-
Colonel Benedict ordered this punishment, and was present part of the time. The
man lay there a whole day, and was put out again on the next day, though I do not
know how long he remained on the second day. I have seen him strike men on other
occasions. I have seen him strike men on parade without any cause whatever, while
under arms. It was a common thing.

Question. You say that the men fired at the quarters of the officers
while they were sitting in them. Do you mean to say that officers were
sitting in their quarters when the mutiny was going on?

Answer. I do not. The officers were alarmed by the firing. They were not aware
that anything of the sort would occur until the balls came through the quarters.

Question. Where did Lieutenant-Colonel Benedict remain during the
night, and were any extra precautions used to prevent the men from
getting hold of him?

Answer. He was in the quarters of Captain Merritt and Lieutenant Bebey until
about 10 o'clock; then went to his quarters, and he requested me several times to
take him outside of the fort to the Suffolk. I told him he was safer inside. He remained the rest of the night in his quarters, the major's quarters, and the adjutant's
office.

Question. What reason have you to suppose that Major Nye was at
the hospital?

Answer. Because we searched every place where officers are in the habit of resorting, except the hospital.

Question. Were you with the crowd of men who came down to the
levee?

Answer. I was not.

Question. Do you know that Major Nye was not with the crowd of
men who came down to the levee?

Answer. I do not. I know that he did not come back with them.

Question. Could Major Nye have gotten into the fort without difficulty without the countersign, and if the corporal of the guard could not be found?

Answer. He is supposed to have the countersign. My instructions to the sentinels were to pass officers without the countersign when recognized. When we searched for Major Nye, I asked the sentinel at Post No. 1 and the one at the sally-port if they had seen him, and they said they had not.

Question. Have you no other reason for supposing that Major Nye was at the hospital than that you could find him nowhere else?

Answer. Another reason is, that if Major Nye were outside the fort he could have returned had he desired to do so.

The evidence of Capt. James Miller was here closed.

First Lieut. GEORGE H. KIMBALL, regimental adjutant, Fourth Regiment Infantry, Corps d'Afrique, was then duly sworn by the judge-advocate.

Question. Please state your name, rank, and the position you held on the 9th instant.

Answer. George H. Kimball, first lieutenant and regimental adjutant, Fourth Infantry, Corps d'Afrique, detailed as post adjutant at Fort Jackson and Fort Saint Philip.

Question. How did the disturbances on that day begin?

Answer. The men fell in in front of their tents about 6.30, and commenced shouting and firing.

Question. What did Colonel Drew do?

Answer. He came out of his quarters; went down into the parade. I saw him about twenty minutes after, talking to the men, trying to quiet them. I stood on the platform of my quarters about ten minutes before I went down into the parade. The other officers were in the parade when I went down there, talking to the men; trying to get them to put their guns up.

Question. Did you see Major Nye?

Answer. Not until after the disturbance was stopped.

Question. Do you know what the cause of the disturbance was?

Answer. It was Lieutenant-Colonel Benedict's whipping two music boys.

Question. Did you see him whip them?

Answer. I saw him whip one, Harry Williams, with a large whip resembling a wagon whip. I saw him strike five or six blows severely. The boy had his coat off.

Question. How do you know that this was the cause of the disturbance?

Answer. Because in less than half an hour after it happened the men began to fall in, and we had never had any trouble before.

Question. Were any of the shots fired on that evening aimed as if intended to take effect?

Answer. I do not think they took any aim; some struck the officers' quarters; I saw the marks of two. I think these were accidental.

Question. Did you ever see Lieutenant-Colonel Benedict maltreat any men before that?

Answer. I never saw him.

Question. Have any men ever complained to you of his treatment of them?

Answer. Not to me.

Question. Do you know the names of any of the ringleaders ?

Answer. I have the names which the officers have given me. I could not distinguish them.

Question. Do you know where Major Nye was on that evening ?

Answer. I do not.

Question. Does Major Nye get the countersign ?

Answer. It was not sent to him. The field officers call and get it when they wish to go out. Major Nye did not get the countersign from me on that evening.

Question. Did the officers wear their side-arms when they came out on the parade ?

Answer. The larger portion of them did not.

Question. What reason have you to suppose that the shots which struck the officers' building were accidental ?

Answer. The flashes all seemed to go up into the air. I saw very few that were aimed low.

Question. Was there any disposition on the part of the officers to quell the disturbance by force ?

Answer. I did not see any.

Question. What was the appearance of Lieutenant-Colonel Benedict when you saw him ?

Answer. He appeared very much agitated.

The examination of Lieut. George H. Kimball was here closed.

Quartermaster's Sergt. GEORGE McFAUL, Fourth Regiment Infantry, Corps d'Afrique, was then duly sworn.

Question. Please state your name and rank.

Answer. George McFaul; quartermaster's sergeant, Fourth Regiment Infantry, Corps d'Afrique.

Question. What has been the conduct of Lieutenant-Colonel Benedict toward the men under his command ?

Answer. I should say rough.

Question. What reason have you for saying so ?

Answer. From his expressions and his acts.

Question. Did you ever see him maltreat any man; if so, when and where ?

Answer. I saw him whip Harry Williams, a drummer boy, on the evening of the 9th instant. I have never seen him whip anybody else, but I have seen him handle men very roughly at guard-mount; shaking them. He struck Harry Williams from fifteen to twenty times with an army wagoner's whip or an artillery driver's whip. The boy had his coat off. I do not know what offense the boy had committed.

Question. Did you see Capt. James Miller in the parade ?

Answer. I did not see him.

Question. What portion of the men took part in the disturbance ?

Answer. I should think there were at least three-fourths of the regiment not disposed to take part in the riotous proceedings.

Question. Did the officers have their side-arms on ?

Answer. Those that I saw had.

The examination of Quartermaster's Sergt. George McFaul was here closed.

Second Lieut. EDWARD D. MOONEY, Fourth Regiment Infantry, Corps d'Afrique, was then duly sworn by the judge-advocate.

Question. Please state your name and rank.

Answer. Edward D. Mooney, second lieutenant Company A, Fourth Infantry, Corps d'Afrique.

Question. Were you stationed at Fort Saint Philip; and, if so, during what time?

Answer. I was stationed there from the 23d day of August until the 8th of December.

Question. Who was in command during that time?

Answer. Lieutenant-Colonel Benedict part of the time and Captain Knapp part of the time.

Question. How did Lieutenant-Colonel Benedict treat the men under his command?

Answer. He treated them tolerably well, as a general thing. He might have been a little hasty sometimes.

Question. Were you ever, as officer of the day or guard, required by Lieutenant-Colonel Benedict to inflict any unusual punishment?

Answer. I was officer of the day once, and officer of the guard once, when I had to inflict, by Lieutenant-Colonel Benedict's order, a punishment that was unusual to me.

Question. What were those punishments?

Answer. On the 7th of August, at Baton Rouge, when officer of the guard, I was ordered by Lieutenant-Colonel Benedict to take 2 men, have their shoes and stockings taken off, and to lay them on the ground, straighten their legs and arms out, and stake them—tie them down. Then he told me to go to the commissary and get some molasses, and cover their faces, feet, and hands with molasses. He told me to keep them there during the day and night, and said he did not care if I kept them there until they died. They belonged to Company B, Fourth Infantry, Corps d'Afrique. I do not remember their names. Lieutenant-Colonel Benedict was commanding the regiment at that time. I understood him at the time that the men had been stealing some corn to roast, but I do not know certainly. They were kept tied down from 10 a. m. until 7 p. m. or 7.30 p. m. They were tied down again the next morning and I turned them over to the officer of the guard that relieved me.

On the 25th of August, I think, when at Fort Saint Philip, he had a man tied down in the same way. I saw him so tied down. He was tied down when I took charge of the guard, and remained so until between 2 and 3 that day. I do not know what his offense was. His face was not smeared with molasses.

Question. Did you know of any ill-feeling toward Lieutenant-Colonel Benedict existing among the men prior to the disturbance of the 9th instant?

Answer. Yes, sir, I do. When we came to divide the regiment, many asked to remain at Fort Saint Philip, so that they would not have to be under Lieutenant-Colonel Benedict.

Question. What was the cause of the ill-feeling?

Answer. His general ill-treatment of them—kicking and knocking them about.

Question. Where were you during the disturbance?

Answer. I was at my quarters at Fort Jackson. I was under arrest. I had been placed under arrest by Lieutenant-Colonel Benedict about two months previously.

Question. Have you ever heard any of the officers approve of the punishment referred to, spreading men out on the ground and smearing molasses on their faces?

Answer. I have not.

The examination of Second Lieut. Edward D. Mooney was here closed.

The commission then adjourned to meet again at 2 p. m.

FORT JACKSON,
December 13, 1863—2 p. m.

The court met pursuant to adjournment.
Present, all the members and the judge-advocate.

Col. C. A. HARTWELL, Fifth Regiment Infantry, Corps d'Afrique, was then duly sworn by the judge-advocate.

Question. Please state your name, rank, and command.

Answer. Charles A. Hartwell, colonel Fifth Regiment Infantry, Corps d'Afrique. I have been commissioned, though not mustered in as such. I am first lieutenant Eleventh Infantry. I command the garrison at Fort Saint Philip.

Question. When did you assume command of that post?

Answer. On Tuesday, the 8th instant, at 1 p. m.

Question. Whom did you relieve?

Answer. Lieutenant-Colonel Benedict, Fourth Infantry, Corps d'Afrique.

Question. Do you know how long previously Lieutenant-Colonel Benedict had been in command at Fort Saint Philip?

Answer. I saw an order dated in September assigning him to the command of that fort. I think it was September.

Question. When you assumed command of the fort, did you observe any dissatisfaction among the garrison toward Lieutenant-Colonel Benedict?

Answer. I did not.

Question. When the Fourth Regiment, Corps d'Afrique, was divided, was there any preference shown by the men as to whether they should stay at Fort Saint Philip or go to Fort Jackson?

Answer. I saw only three cases of preference, two for Fort Saint Philip and one for Fort Jackson. Many of them, however, spoke to my officers, asking to be detained on that side.

Question. Do you know what reason they assigned for this request?

Answer. Merely a preference to remain. I heard of no other reason assigned.

Question. Do you know whether Lieutenant-Colonel Benedict's treatment of the men was the cause of their making the request?

Answer. I do not.

Question. Please state what you know of the disturbances, if any, at Fort Jackson on the 9th instant.

Answer. The only thing that I actually observed was the musketry firing. The wind was blowing off shore, and I could hear only a very little of it, but I saw the flashes.

Question. Have the men under your command manifested any discontent since you assumed command of them?

Answer. Not the slightest that I can observe. My officers have told me that their sergeants told them that the men were ready to march to quell the disturbance.

Question. How long did the firing continue?

Answer. From about 6 until 7.30. I had no means of sending over to Fort Jackson or I should have done so.

The examination of Col. C. A. Hartwell was here closed.

Capt. WILLIAM H. KNAPP, Fourth Regiment, Corps d'Afrique, was then duly sworn by the judge-advocate.

Question. Please state your name and rank.

Answer. William Henry Knapp, captain Company A, Fourth Infantry, Corps d'Afrique. I am senior captain.

Question. Where were you on the 9th instant?

Answer. At Fort Jackson.

Question. How did the disturbances said to have occurred at Fort Jackson on that day begin?

Answer. They began by Lieutenant-Colonel Benedict whipping two of the men. I did not see him do it.

Question. How do you know that this was the beginning of the trouble?

Answer. I only judge from what I heard from the men at the time of the disturbance, and their conduct.

Question. What did you hear?

Answer. I heard a number say that he had been rawhiding two of the men, and they were bound to have revenge.

Question. Do you know that Lieutenant-Colonel Benedict ever inflicted any cruel and unusual punishment upon the men?

Answer. I do. I have seen him strike them in the face with his fist, kick them, and, in one instance, strike a man with his sword in the face. On the 19th of October, I was officer of the day; the guard was turned out for Lieutenant-Colonel Benedict, and one man, Private Francis, of my company, did not dress properly, and Lieutenant-Colonel Benedict took the sergeant's sword and struck him in the face. I have frequently seen him at Fort Saint Philip, at guard-mounting, strike men in the face with his fist and kick them because their brasses were not bright or their boots not polished. Men of my company have come to me in two or three instances and complained.

Question. Have the Rules and Articles of War been read to the men?

Answer. I have read them to my company twice, and they were read to the regiment once. I believe they have been read to the other companies.

Question. Were the officers on the parade on the evening of the 9th armed?

Answer. I think most of them wore their side-arms.

Question. Do you know the two music boys said to have been whipped by Lieutenant-Colonel Benedict, and how old are they?

Answer. I know them. Williams I should judge to be from eighteen to twenty-one, and Miller twenty-five or twenty-seven.

Question. How have the men behaved since?

Answer. Very well. I think I have noticed one or two instances where they behaved a little more impudently, but, as a rule, I have not noticed any difference.

The examination of Capt. William H. Knapp was here closed.

The commission then having been cleared, the judge-advocate submits the question, whether it is advisable and necessary to take the evidence of any of the enlisted men (colored) of the regiment; which was decided in the negative.

The commission was then opened, and Lieut. Col. AUGUSTUS W. BENEDICT, Fourth Infantry, Corps d'Afrique, was introduced, and duly sworn by the judge-advocate.

The commission was then cleared, and a member of the commission introduced the question whether Lieutenant-Colonel Benedict's evidence should be taken, in view of the fact that it must implicate himself; which was decided that it should.

The commission was then opened.

Question. Please state your name, rank, and the command you held on the 9th instant.

Answer. Augustus W. Benedict, lieutenant-colonel, commanding Fourth Regiment Infantry, Corps d'Afrique.

Question. Please state what steps were taken to quell the disturbance at Fort Jackson on the 9th instant.

Answer. As quick as the outbreak occurred, Colonel Drew and myself proceeded to the parade ground, and ordered the men to disperse and go to their quarters. They refused to do it, and we expostulated with them; tried to quell them by reasoning and talking with them. This failed for that instant, but finally succeeded. No force was resorted to. Nearly every officer in the regiment present was there. I can't say that there were any not there. They used the same means. I did not see Major Nye there. I saw Captain Miller, the officer of the day, I think, on the parapet.

Question. Do you think the outbreak could have been put down if force had been resorted to at the first commencement of it?

Answer. Not by any force that the white officers present could have used.

Question. Had you noticed any disposition among the men to mutiny previous to the disturbance on the 9th?

Answer. Not during the time I was in command. I was only placed in command the day before.

Question. Was there at Fort Jackson?

Answer. Not to my knowledge. There was certainly no manifestation of it.

Question. Did you ever have the Rules and Articles of War read to the men?

Answer. I have.

Question. Do you know whether the company commanders have ever done so?

Answer. I do not.

Question. Did you notice any men disposed to do right on the night of the disturbance?

Answer. I did.

Question. What proportion of the regiment do you suppose were disposed to do right?

Answer. I should think four-fifths, but I do not think they could have been relied upon in putting down the others.

Question. What did you say to the men on the parade to quiet them?

Answer. The only remark that called for an answer from me was: "We want to be treated as soldiers." I replied, "Those boys were bad boys, and I treated them as such," and they then cried, "Don't shoot; don't shoot."

Question. What offense had the two boys to whom you refer committed?

Answer. The immediate offense was going to a sentinel, and telling him the sergeant of the guard had permitted them to go out, and going out on that pretense.

The examination of Lieutenant-Colonel Benedict was here closed.

The commission then adjourned until 5 p. m.

' ON BOARD STEAMER SUFFOLK,
Mississippi River, December 13, 1863.

The commission met pursuant to adjournment. Present, all the members. The examination of the witnesses was then closed.

The commission, having maturely considered the evidence adduced, finds and reports as follows:

1. As regards the cause of the disturbance at Fort Jackson on the 9th instant, the commission finds that the immediate cause of the disturbance was the whipping with a rawhide, or cart-whip, on the afternoon of the 9th instant, by Lieutenant-Colonel Benedict, Fourth Regiment Infantry, Corps d'Afrique, of two drummer boys belonging to that regiment, aggravated by his previous conduct toward the men of the regiment, and the severe punishments to which he had been in the habit of resorting.

2. As to the course and termination of the troubles, the commission finds that the disturbance began about an hour after the whipping of the music boys referred to, by about half of the regiment rushing upon the parade with their arms, shouting, and discharging their pieces into the air. The shouting and threatening language used was directed against Lieutenant-Colonel Benedict. One man proposed to "kill all the damned Yankees." Part of the men rushed to the guard-house, forced the guard, and released the prisoners confined there. Others rushed toward the levee, discharging their pieces, probably under the impression that Lieutenant-Colonel Benedict was on board the Suffolk, lying at the levee, or would try to get there. The commission does not find that the shots fired were fired at any person, but that they were fired into the air, although a number of them took effect upon the quarters of the officers. The disturbance was not premeditated, but was a sudden outbreak, and was quelled by the officers going amongst the men, and pacifying them by assurances that justice should be done them. It lasted until about 7.30, when the last shots were fired. Soon after, tattoo was beaten, and the men retired to their quarters.

3. As to the conduct of the commanding officer and other officers, the commission finds that Colonel Drew, commanding the post, went on the parade as soon as he knew of the disturbance, and attempted to quiet the men by telling them that Lieutenant-Colonel Benedict had done wrong, but that they were doing a greater wrong, and that, if they would go to their quarters, justice should be done them. The other officers, with the exception of Major Nye, Fourth Infantry, Corps d'Afrique, behaved in a similar manner. Major Nye was not on the parade, and his absence has not been satisfactorily accounted for. Soon after the disturbance commenced, Lieutenant-Colonel Benedict was ordered by Colonel Drew to his quarters, and remained there and in the quarters of the other officers until the next morning, when he was sent to New Orleans. All the witnesses express a belief that an attempt to quiet the disturbance by force would have resulted fatally to the officers, and, upon the evidence, the commission is of opinion that the means resorted to were, perhaps, the best that could have been adopted under the circumstances, although leaving the troops under the ill-effects of such temporizing measures.

4. As to the conduct of the men, the commission finds that about half the regiment took part in the disturbance, and that the other half, though not taking part, showed no disposition to assist in quelling the outbreak. The commission is of opinion that the conduct of the men was more owing to an ignorance of their rights and the proper means of redress than to any preconcerted plan of revolt.

The commission then adjourned to meet to-morrow morning at 10 a. m.

F. J. HERRON,
Major-General of Volunteers, President of Military Commission.
G. NORMAN LIEBER,
Major and Judge-Advocate.

—

NEW ORLEANS,
December 14, 1863—10 a. m.

The commission met pursuant to adjournment.

Present, all the members.

The proceedings of the previous day were then read and approved, and, there being no further business before the commission, it adjourned *sine die.*

F. J. HERRON,
Major-General of Volunteers, President of Commission.
HORACE BINNEY SARGENT,
Colonel, and Acting Aide-de-Camp.
STEPHEN HOYT,
Captain, and Commissary of Subsistence.
G. NORMAN LIEBER,
Major, and Judge-Advocate.

ADDENDA.

GENERAL ORDERS, }   HDQRS. DEPARTMENT OF THE GULF,
No. 90.   }   *New Orleans, December* 30, 1863.

I. Before a general court-martial, convened at Fort Jackson, Louisiana, pursuant to Special Orders, Nos. 315, 316, and 317, of December 17, 18, and 19, and reconvened pursuant to Special Orders, No. 326, of December 30, current series, from these headquarters, and of which Col. F. S. Rutherford, Ninety-seventh Regiment Illinois Volunteers, is president, were arraigned and tried:

1. Musician Edward B. Smith, Company B, Fourth Infantry, Corps d'Afrique.

CHARGE.—Mutiny.
PLEA.—"Not guilty."
FINDING.—" Guilty."

And the court does, therefore, sentence him "to be imprisoned at hard labor for one year on such permanent fortification as the commanding general may direct."

2. Private Frank Williams, Company I, Fourth Infantry, Corps d'Afrique.

CHARGE.—Mutiny.
PLEA.—" Not guilty."
FINDING.—" Guilty."

And the court does, therefore, sentence him, Frank Williams, private Company I, Fourth Infantry, Corps d'Afrique, " to be shot to death with musketry, at such time and place as the commanding general may direct," it appearing, upon the reconvening of the court, that two-thirds of the members concurred therein.

3. Corpl. Lewis Cady, Company K, Fourth Infantry, Corps d'Afrique.

CHARGE.—Mutiny.
PLEA.—" Not guilty."
FINDING.—" Guilty."

And the court does, therefore, sentence him, Corpl. Lewis Cady, Company K, Fourth Infantry, Corps d'Afrique, " to be imprisoned for the term of two years, at hard labor, on such permanent Government fortification as the commanding general may direct, and to forfeit all pay and allowances, except for prison food and clothing."

4. Corpl. Henry Green, Company G, Fourth Infantry, Corps d'Afrique.

CHARGE.—Mutiny.
PLEA.—" Not guilty."
FINDING.—" Not guilty."

And the court does, therefore, acquit him, Corpl. Henry Green, Company G, Fourth Infantry, Corps d'Afrique.

5. Private Jacob Kennedy, Company D, Fourth Infantry, Corps d'Afrique.

CHARGE.—Mutiny.
PLEA.—" Not guilty."
FINDING.—" Not guilty."

And the court does, therefore, acquit him, Private Jacob Kennedy, Company D, Fourth Infantry, Corps d'Afrique.

6. Private Charles Taylor, Company K, Fourth Infantry, Corps d'Afrique.

CHARGE.—Mutiny.
PLEA.—" Not guilty."
FINDING.—" Guilty."

And the court does, therefore, sentence him, Private Charles Taylor, Company K, Fourth Infantry, Corps d'Afrique, " to be imprisoned at hard labor for the term of ten years, on such permanent Government fortification as the commanding general may direct."

7. Private Abraham Victoria, Company D, Fourth Infantry, Corps d'Afrique.

CHARGE.—Mutiny.
PLEA.—" Not guilty."
FINDING.—" Guilty."

And the court does, therefore, sentence him, Private Abraham Victoria, Company D, Fourth Infantry, Corps d'Afrique, " to be shot to death with musketry, at such time and place as the commanding general may direct," it appearing, upon the reconvening of the court, that two-thirds of the members concurred therein.

8. Private Abram Singleton, Company F, Fourth Infantry, Corps d'Afrique.

CHARGE.—Mutiny.
PLEA.—"Not guilty."
FINDING.—"Guilty."

And the court does, therefore, sentence him, Private Abram Single-ton, Company F, Fourth Infantry, Corps d'Afrique, "to be imprisoned at hard labor, for the term of ten years, on such Government fortifica-tion as the commanding general may direct, and to forfeit all pay and allowances, except for prison food and clothing."

9. Private Volser Verrett, Company D, Fourth Infantry, Corps d'Afrique.

CHARGE.—Mutiny.
PLEA.—"Not guilty."
FINDING.—"Not guilty."

And the court does, therefore, acquit him.

10. Private Willis Curtis, Company D, Fourth Infantry, Corps d'Afrique.

CHARGE.—Mutiny.
PLEA.—"Not guilty."
FINDING.—"Guilty."

And the court does, therefore, sentence him, Private Willis Curtis, Company D, Fourth Infantry, Corps d'Afrique, "to be imprisoned at hard labor, for the term of three years, on such permanent fortification as the commanding general may direct, and to forfeit all pay and allow-ances, except for prison food and clothing."

11. Private Julius Boudro, Company D, Fourth Infantry, Corps d'Afrique.

CHARGE.—Mutiny.
PLEA.—"Not guilty."
FINDING.—"Guilty."

And the court does, therefore, sentence him, Private Julius Boudro, Company D, Fourth Infantry, Corps d'Afrique, " to be imprisoned at hard labor, for the term of twenty years, on such permanent fortification as the commanding general may direct, and to forfeit all pay and allow-ances except for prison food and clothing."

12. Private James H. Moore, No. 2, Company F, Fourth Infantry, Corps d'Afrique.

CHARGE.—Insubordinate conduct, to the prejudice of good order and military discipline.
PLEA.—"Not guilty."
FINDING.—"Guilty."

And the court does, therefore, sentence him, Private James H. Moore, No. 2, Company F, Fourth Infantry, Corps d'Afrique, "to hard labor for one month under guard."

13. Private James Hagan, Company B, Fourth Infantry, Corps d'Afrique.

CHARGE.—Mutiny.
PLEA.—"Not guilty."
FINDING.—"Not guilty."

And the court does, therefore, acquit him, Private James Hagan, Company B, Fourth Infantry, Corps d'Afrique.

14. Lieut. Col. Augustus W. Benedict, Fourth Infantry, Corps d'Afrique.

CHARGE.—Inflicting cruel and unusual punishment, to the prejudice of good order and military discipline.
PLEA.—"Not guilty."
FINDING.—"Guilty."

And the court does, therefore, sentence him, Lieut. Col. Augustus W. Benedict, Fourth Infantry, Corps d'Afrique, "to be dismissed the service."

*   *   *   *   *   *   *

IV. The proceedings, findings, and sentences in the cases of Musician Edward B. Smith, Company B; Corporal Lewis Cady, Company K; Privates Charles Taylor, Company K; Abram Singleton, Company F; Willis Curtis, Company D, and Julius Boudro, Company D, Fourth Infantry, Corps d'Afrique, are approved. The sentences will be carried into execution at Fort Jefferson, Fla. The provost-marshal-general, Department of the Gulf, is charged with their execution.

The proceedings, findings, and sentences in the cases of Private Frank Williams, Company I, Fourth Infantry, Corps d'Afrique, and Private Abraham Victoria, Company D, Fourth Infantry, Corps d'Afrique, are approved; but the execution of the sentences is suspended until further orders, and they will be turned over to the provost-marshal general, Department of the Gulf, to be sent to Fort Jefferson, Fla., there to be kept in close confinement.

The proceedings and findings in the cases of Corporal Henry Green, Company G; Private Jacob Kennedy, Company D; Private Volser Verrett, Company D, and Private James Hagan, Company B, all of the Fourth Regiment of Infantry, Corps d'Afrique, are approved. They will be released from confinement, and returned to duty.

In the case of Private James H. Moore, No. 2, Company F, Fourth Infantry, Corps d'Afrique, the proceedings are disapproved, the evidence being conflicting and unsatisfactory. He will be released from confinement, and returned to duty.

In the case of Lieut. Col. Augustus W. Benedict, the proceedings, findings, and sentence are confirmed. He ceases from this date to be an officer in the military service of the United States.

*   *   *   *   *   *   *

V. The general court-martial of which Col. F. S. Rutherford, Ninety-seventh Regiment Illinois Volunteers, is president, is dissolved.

By command of Major-General Banks:

G. NORMAN LIEBER,
Acting Assistant Adjutant-General.

DECEMBER 29, 1863.—Skirmish on Matagorda Peninsula, Tex.

REPORTS.*

No. 1.—Maj. Gen. Cadwallader C. Washburn, U. S. Army, commanding detachment Thirteenth Army Corps.
No. 2.—Lieut. Col. Frank S. Hesseltine, Thirteenth Maine Infantry.
No. 3.—Capt. Edmund P. Turner, Assistant Adjutant-General, C. S. Army.
No. 4.—Col. A. Buchel, First Texas Cavalry.

No. 1.

Report of Maj. Gen. Cadwallader C. Washburn, U. S. Army, commanding detachment Thirteenth Army Corps.

HEADQUARTERS UNITED STATES FORCES,
Fort Esperanza, Tex., January 2, 1864.

GENERAL: In addressing you yesterday, I mentioned that I had sent an expedition up the peninsula. They returned all safely last night. The infantry, according to the programme, drove the enemy's pickets down the peninsula until they saw our mounted men advancing from below. The enemy then abandoned their horses and took to a boat. Two men and 13 fine horses were captured, and 11 men escaped. Just at this moment the enemy's cavalry were seen charging down on the rear of our little force, fully 1,000 strong. Our men, who were of the Thirteenth Maine, and commanded by Lieutenant-Colonel Hesseltine, prepared immediately to receive them. Retiring to the cover of some sand hills along the beach, they constructed of drift-wood and sand a hasty protection, where they resisted all attempts to dislodge them. The gunboat Granite City in the meantime poured 150 rounds into them with telling effect. Night found our men still besieged, and the rebels hung around until nearly morning, when they drew off and were seen no more.

Our men remained in their stronghold until about 2 p. m. the second day, when they marched down the beach when the gale so far moderated as to enable the gunboat to take them aboard. Soon after our men had evacuated their position, the rebel gunboat Carr came across from Matagorda, and commenced to shell the abandoned position. In the meantime the prevailing norther had increased to great violence, and drove the rebel boat ashore high and dry.

Captain [James H.] Strong, of the Monongahela, lay off opposite to her during the night, and represents that the next morning she had disappeared, though a wreck was seen where she lay. He is confident they burned her to prevent her from falling into our hands. I had made all my arrangements to go up to day, through Matagorda Bay, and capture her if still aground, but the information just sent me by Captain Strong, as well as the tempestuous day, have prevented the move. The first pleasant day I shall send up, and find out if she is actually destroyed or not. I very much hope that she is destroyed, for being so light draught, she can easily keep out of our way, and might do us on some occasion great harm. She is one of the boats that participated in the Galveston affair one year ago.

The enemy has or had four boats in the upper end of Matagorda Bay, above the reef, all of which, I learn from reliable citizens, they have been arming and clothing with cotton lately, and the people have been

---

* For report of Commander James H. Strong, U. S. Navy, see Annual Report of the Secretary of the Navy, December 5, 1864.

promised by Magruder that they should hear of another brilliant operation on the 1st of January. It is supposed that they intended to run down here some night, and sink and destroy such of our vessels as they should find inside. If the Carr is destroyed, that arrangement will be broken into, but I shall endeavor to keep a good lookout. My 30-pounder Parrotts I have ready to receive any visitor that may choose to come. The enemy boast that if we march up the peninsula they will be able to punish us badly with gunboats on the inside by shelling the peninsula. They have made up their minds that we mean to take that route.

On the day that I sent up the infantry on the Granite City, I directed General Ransom, after seeing them safely landed and on the way down under the guns of the Granite City, to proceed up the coast on the gunboat Sciota, and reconnoiter as far as the mouth of Brazos River. He did so, and found apparently a large force and strong works at Velasco and Quintana. On the fort at Valasco he could distinctly see seven large guns.

At the mouth of the San Bernard he also saw quite a large force, who appeared very busy fortifying there. They had no guns mounted, but had thrown up a good deal of earth there. They shelled them and drove them away.

I have requested Captain Strong to keep a gunboat there, and prevent fortifying as far as possible.

It is probable that they intend to fight us near the mouth of the San Bernard, if we take the coast line, or at Hawkins' Ferry, if we leave the coast. I am satisfied that we shall have to fight the whole Texas force when we move.

I am, general, very respectfully, your obedient servant,

C. C. WASHBURN,
Major-General.

Maj. Gen. N. P. BANKS,
Commanding Department of the Gulf.

No. 2.

Report of Lieut. Col. Frank S. Hesseltine, Thirteenth Maine Infantry.

HEADQUARTERS UNITED STATES FORCES,
Decrow's Point, Tex., January 6, 1864.

Brig. Gen. CHARLES P. STONE, *Chief of Staff:*

GENERAL: I inclose herein report of Lieutenant-Colonel Hesseltine, Thirteenth Maine Infantry, in regard to an expedition on the Matagorda Peninsula. The conduct of Colonel Hesseltine and his men is deserving of great praise.

Captain Strong, of the gunboat Monongahela, reports that the rebel cotton-clad gunboat Carr was burned by the enemy to prevent her from falling into our hands.

Respectfully, your obedient servant,

C. C. WASHBURN,
Major-General.

[Inclosure.]

'FORT ESPERANZA, TEX., *January* 1, 1864.

GENERAL: I have the honor to report that, in accordance with the instructions received through you from the major-general commanding coast expedition, I embarked on the evening of the 28th ultimo with

31 R R—VOL XXVI, PT I

100 men of my regiment on the gunboat Granite City, and proceeded·
that night outside of Matagorda Peninsula to a point 7 miles from the
head of it. In the morning we landed in small boats through the surf
on a reconnaissance, intending to return on board when our object was
obtained, but shortly after our debarkation the surf was so increased
by a strong southerly wind as to cut off all communication with the
gunboat.

A detachment under Lieutenant Ham having returned from a scout
up the ·peninsula, I deployed a line of skirmishers nearly across, and
moved down under convoy of the Granite City, driving back the rebel
pickets cut off by our line. Our progress was so impeded on the right
by bayous from the lake, that·by 2 p. m. we had advanced but 7 or 8
miles, and were obliged to shorten the line of skirmishers. At this time
I was warned by the whistle of our convoy, and then shell from her
30-pounder Parrott, of an enemy in the rear. Soon, by the aid of my
glass, I was able to discern the head of a body of cavalry moving down
the peninsula. Under a heavy fire from the gunboat their line stretched
steadily toward us, and, without seeing the last of it, I made out a force·
of from 800 to 1,000 cavalry.

Throwing the reserve in the advance of the skirmishers, we moved
forward as before. In half an hour their skirmishers were swarming
close up to mine, slightly heeding the shell and shrapnel, which, by
reason of the heavy sea, only now and then emptied a saddle for them.
Having toled them to within good rifle-shot by allowing them to "pep-
per" away at us liberally, at command, half of the skirmishers faced
about and gave them a volley, with apparently good effect, as it sent
them, some hugging their horses, others being supported, out of range;
they all hastily chose the other side.

Having reached a narrow neck, some 200 yards wide, made by a bayou
from the bay, as the boys were anxious to see the parade, I assembled the
skirmishers, and, countermarching so as they could face the foe, formed
line of battle across· the neck. I knew my men ; they were cool, and determined rather than the rebels should meet the first encouragement
of this campaign that they would die there with as many of their foes
lying around them. They would not meet us in front; they were ford-
ing the bayou and gaining our rear. I gave orders to move back quick-
time, and rode ahead to select another spot for a stand. They were
closing around us. Hastily communicating to the officers my plan to
throw up, from the drift branches, logs, and stumps, a barricade, first a
face to the enemy and then on each flank, I wheeled the company in on
the beach. As if by magic, and while the enemy were forming their line
for attack, there arose with gnarled roots and branches projecting, a
rough, ugly looking redan, its *pan coupé* on a sand ridge, its gorge out
in the surf.

They formed, advanced, hesitated, halted; a party rode up to reconnoiter, and rode back with Minie balls to report. They moved stronger
to the right, to charge obliquely the left face, which speedily looked
too bad for them. While they deliberated, darkness came with a heavy
mist. For a ruse or threat, we sung out three hearty cheers and a
"tiger." Two fires on each flank gave our position to the gunboat
Sciota, which came in from a reconnaissance up the coast. The Granite ·
City goes to send re-enforcements. With the expectation of an attack,
the men were kept at the barricade all night. Their scouts approached,
to learn from our rifles that we were awake. Soon after midnight the
picket fired, and ran in to report a strong body moving to the left on to
the beach. This force came up, but a sharp fire sent them to the rear,

as the gunboat Sciota, which had slipped her anchor, ran round, and poured in a broadside. They retired for the night.

The morning was very foggy. Bodies of cavalry were occasionally seen, and about 10 a. m. a considerable force was seen on the right, but made no demonstration. As it was uncertain what more the enemy might bring, the work was further strengthened by digging pits with bayonets and wooden spades and filling the barricades. Blankets were used for sand bags. By noon it cleared away, and the rebel gunboat John F. Carr ran down inside, opposite our work, and commenced shelling it with her 20-pounder Parrott, making some very good shots, but injuring no one.

At 3 p. m., the men being without food and water, the gunboats expected to our relief having failed by reason of the fog to find us, and concluding that the enemy had driven back our re-enforcements, after some hesitation we moved secretly out, to cut our way down the peninsula. The rebel boat shelled the abandoned work, and, as they report from the Sciota, kept back a body of their own cavalry. Our advance skirmishers drove before us a few of the enemy's scouts. Night came with a heavy fog, and we advanced cautiously. At 10 p. m. the severest norther of the winter struck us. At 1 a. m. bivouacked for the night. The next day, at 2 p. m., 20 miles below our work, we were discovered from the Sciota, and with great difficulty taken on board.

On the march, the sick and exhausted soldiers had been nobly aided by their comrades, so that not a man, musket, or equipment was left for the enemy. The rebel gunboat John F. Carr was driven ashore in the norther, and Captain Strong, of the Monongahela, who came to relieve us, reports she was abandoned and destroyed. The loss of this boat, the information secured concerning the enemy and peninsula, already given you verbally, with the lesson taught our enemies, make the reconnaissance not altogether valueless.

To the officers with me, First Lieut. John S. P. Ham, commanding Company C; Second Lieut. Robbins B. Grover, commanding Company H; Second Lieut. Augustus C. Myrick, Company C, and Second Lieut. John D. Felton, commanding Company K, the highest credit is due for the energy and pluck they manifested, aiding and arousing their men to endure and die sooner than surrender. I would respectfully suggest that they are worthy of some notice, as a mark that the country honors those of her sons who are valiant in upholding her honor.

Captain [George H.] Perkins, of the Sciota, excited my admiration by the daring manner in which he exposed his ship through the night in the surf till it broke all about him, that he might, close to us, lend the moral force of his 11-inch guns and howitzers, and by his gallantry in bringing us off during the gale.

To Captain [Charles W.] Lamson, of the Granite City, great credit is due for his exertion to retard and drive back the enemy. By the loss he inflicted upon them, it is clear but for the heavy sea he would have freed us from any exertion. Information comes in that the attacking force was Green's cavalry, and from 1,200 to 1,500 strong. I have allowed myself to be too minute in this report that you may understand exactly how 100 of our Yankees baffled, beat back, and eluded so large a body of rebels and rebel gunboat without loss.

I have the honor to be, sir, very respectfully, your obedient servant,

FRANK S. HESSELTINE,
Lieutenant-Colonel, Commanding.

Brig. Gen. T. E. G. RANSOM,
Comdg. 3d Brig., 2d Div., 13th Army Corps, Ft. Esperanza, Tex.

No. 3.

Reports of Capt. Edmund P. Turner, Assistant Adjutant-General, C. S. Army.

BUCHEL'S CAMP,
December 30, 1863—7.30 a. m.

GENERAL: I have the honor to inclose to you a copy of a dispatch * just received from Lieutenant Forsgard, signal officer at mouth of Caney, stating that enemy has landed at Old Cedar Lake; numbers or movement not known, on account of darkness. I beg to suggest, if you will permit, that you send a portion of your force to mouth of Bernard at once, and also send to the west of Bernard, near Churchill's Ferry, the remainder of the force you have, to be thrown on the enemy should he attempt to hold a point on its coast.

You are acquainted with the country below the Caney and Bernard, and know whether or not artillery can be used with safety on the enemy. The enemy is heard firing at or in direction of Matagorda. This may be a real movement up the peninsula.

If the enemy has landed, as reported, he will move up the beach against the works at mouth of Bernard, or down against works at Caney, to get these positions.

Very respectfully, your obedient servant,

E. P. TURNER.

Brigadier-General BEE.

———

HEADQUARTERS, &C.,
Camp Wharton, December 30, 1863—5 p. m.

CAPTAIN: I have the honor to state that, on my return from the mouth of the San Bernard, on yesterday, the 29th instant, at 6 p. m., I received an official dispatch from Colonel [A.] Buchel, inclosing a report from the signal operator at the mouth of the Caney. From these dispatches it appeared that the enemy had landed, between 200 and 300 strong, at a point about 7 miles below the mouth of the Caney, on the Gulf shore of the Matagorda Peninsula. Colonel Buchel informed me that he had ordered down [R. R.] Brown's regiment and his own, with the view of expelling or capturing the enemy's forces. Thinking that I might reach there in time to be of some assistance, I left immediately. On arriving at the mouth of the Caney, we learned that Colonel Buchel, with about 300 men of his command, had passed down the beach about 2 p. m.

The enemy landed at 7 a. m., and no information was received by Colonel Buchel concerning the movement until yesterday at about 1 p. m. The enemy, having the start, and moving rapidly down the Gulf shore, could not be overtaken until quite late in the night (say 9 or 10 p. m.), when, halting under the protection of their ships (three in number), they collected the driftwood, and erected a hasty breastwork, behind which they formed and cheered lustily. Not arriving in time, we met Colonel Buchel with his command, returning about 10 miles up the beach from the point at which the enemy had lodged. He informed us that the enemy had availed himself of a position having a morass just in his front and large quantities of driftwood thrown upon the shore near by as a breastwork. A few shots were exchanged, the enemy firing several rounds. The numerical force of Colonel Buchel's command was small, many men having fallen into the rear and been lost sight of by the

———
* Not found.

impracticability of portions of the ground, and having broken down their horses by the fatigue of the journey.

The enemy's shipping had shelled them all the way down, moving *pari passu*, but without damage. Colonel Buchel informs me that he did not attempt to dislodge the enemy for the reason that his efforts would have been attended with very heavy loss (say 100 men), and the advantage to be gained by a successful effort not being in his opinion commensurate with the sacrifice. The scouts from the peninsula had not reported at my departure this morning from Colonel Buchel's command, which was hurried by the report from the signal officer at the mouth of the Caney, received at 5 a. m., that the enemy had landed a force on the Gulf shore, near the extremity of Cedar Lake. We went down immediately, and found the report to be incorrect, having arisen from the beaching of a Confederate States vessel, consigned to Messrs. Ball, Hutchings & Co., laden with Mexican blankets, salt, and sundries. The vessel will be lost. The cargo is saved, and has been removed by my orders.

The vessel was overhauled by the Yankees, and had all her passengers removed. During the examination of her papers, the captain took · advantage of the occasion under cover of the darkness and put directly to the shore, beaching her about 5 miles from the mouth of the Bernard, on the Gulf shore. She was from Tampico, and brings no arms or ammunition; nothing but the above-mentioned articles. Every article of value was being removed when I left. She will be dismantled at once.

It seems that the object of the enemy was clearly indicated, by their moving rapidly down the beach, to be the cutting off and capturing of Captain Henderson's company of exempts, who had been engaged for several days previous in scouting far down on the peninsula. This conclusion is the more apparent, as he landed about 300 men at Dutch Town, just below the point at which the company was engaged in scouting the day previous. This company, however, I am informed by Captain [E. S.] Rugeley, made their escape by passing in boats to Matagorda. Nothing is said of their horses, the inference, of course, being that they fell into the enemy's hands. None of the enemy's forces were captured, and we suffered no loss. Several of Colonel Buchel's command were absent from roll-call this morning, but are presumed to have straggled.

Communications from Colonel [James] Duff and Colonel [John S.] Ford have been sent forward to you to-day. Nothing later of importance is received from any source.

I am, captain, very respectfully, your obedient servant,

E. P. TURNER,
Assistant Adjutant-General.

Capt. W. A. ALSTON, *Assistant Adjutant-General.*

No. 4.

Report of Col. A. Buchel, First Texas Cavalry.

HEADQUARTERS SECOND BRIGADE, SECOND DIVISION,
Camp near P. McNeel's Plantation, December 31, 1863.

SIR : I have the honor to report that, on the morning of the 29th instant, I received intelligence of the arrival of two or three gunboats near the works being erected at the mouth of the Caney, and of the landing of a force of men 12 miles below on the peninsula. I immediately started with the two regiments under my command for the works, on arriving at which I left the left wing of my regiment for its defense, and proceeded with the right wing and Brown's regiment down the peninsula, for the purpose of saving Captain Henderson's squad of exempts and my scouts, as I had no doubt that these men had been landed with a view to cut them off and capture them. I proceeded in a trot and gallop until I had overtaken the enemy, who were about 300 strong, and who had moved down the peninsula from the place of landing about 8 miles. The gunboat which accompanied them awaited our approach about 2 miles below where they had landed, and, when within shelling distance, she opened on us with shell, rifle shot, and spherical case shot, firing about 200 rounds at us during the afternoon, always in easy range. After overtaking the enemy, they took a position behind a marsh, and began to make breastworks of the logs, which were profusely strewed along the beach, and were soon re-enforced by the arrival of two other gunboats. I immediately sent a courier to Williams' place to notify Captain Henderson of my arrival, with orders for him to join me. During five hours I kept the enemy invested in their breastworks, until the return of my courier.

As the forces were about equal when we were dismounted, and the enemy were behind a marsh, and under the protection of three gunboats, I thought the risk too great and the enterprise too hazardous to attack them in their breastworks, as their capture would not compensate for the loss of life which we must necessarily have sustained.

The courier returned with the report that Captain Henderson and his squad had left in a boat for Matagorda. My scouts, who were also below, have arrived via the peninsula. Captain Henderson has since reported to me in person, and states that he escaped with all his men, but lost his horses.

I am happy to state that, notwithstanding the heavy firing to which the men were subjected, and the volleys of infantry fire at our scouts, only 2 men were wounded (slightly) and 2 horses disabled, and that both officers and men behaved with coolness and bravery.

Very respectfully, your obedient servant,

A. BUCHEL,
Colonel, Commanding.

Capt. L. G. ALDRICH,
Asst. Adjt. Gen., Eastern Sub-District, Velasco, Tex.

CORRESPONDENCE, ORDERS, AND RETURNS RELATING TO OPERATIONS IN WEST FLORIDA, SOUTH ALABAMA, SOUTH MISSISSIPPI, LOUISIANA, TEXAS, AND NEW MEXICO, FROM MAY 14 TO DECEMBER 31, 1863.

UNION CORRESPONDENCE, ETC.

SPECIAL ORDERS, } HDQRS. DEPT. OF THE GULF, 19TH A. C.,
No. 116.   }   *Alexandria, La., May* 14, 1863.
       *   *   *   *   *   *   *

IV. Brig. Gen. Godfrey Weitzel is relieved from the operation of Paragraph III of yesterday's Special Orders, No. 115, assigning him to the temporary command of the Third Division, and will resume the command of his own brigade and Dwight's, together with the cavalry and artillery temporarily attached to the latter.

V. The Third Division will march at 4 o'clock to-morrow morning, and move by the Bayou Huffpower road to Simsport, where it will find these headquarters and receive further orders.

VI. Brigadier-General Weitzel, commanding his own and Dwight's brigade, will hold Alexandria until the 17th instant, when he will march to the intersection of the Bayou Huffpower road and the road to Opelousas, and there take post, and await further orders from these headquarters, which will be at Simsport. General Weitzel will draw his supplies from Simsport. He will to-day relieve the present provost-guard at Alexandria.

By command of Major-General Banks:

RICH'D B. IRWIN,
Assistant Adjutant-General.

GENERAL ORDERS, } WAR DEPARTMENT, ADJT. GEN'S OFFICE,
No. 128.   }   *Washington, May 15, 1863.*

I. Before a military commission, which convened at New Orleans, La., November 6, 1862, pursuant to Special Orders, No. 408, dated Headquarters Department of the Gulf, New Orleans La., September 25, 1862, and of which Col. William K. Kimball, Twelfth Maine Volunteers, is president, was arraigned and tried Charles H. Harris, of New Orleans, La.

CHARGE.—*Guilty of high crimes and misdemeanors.*

Specification.—For that the said Charles H. Harris, late of said New Orleans, on the 1st day of November current, he being then and there a soldier belonging to and serving in the Crescent City Regiment, a regiment duly organized, enrolled, enlisted, and in the service of the Confederate States, and then and there in open rebellion against the said United States, did then and there willfully, secretly, traitorously, and as a spy, in the clothing and garb of a citizen and not of a soldier, come within and was then and there found inside the lines of said forces and army of the United States, lurking about, secretly bringing information, knowledge, and intelligence to the traitorous enemies of said United States at said New Orleans; and while within said lines did secretly, covertly, and of design gather together, collect, and husband information and knowledge of the army and authorities of said United States, and of all loyal citizens of New Orleans; for the purpose and with the intent of communicating, transmitting, and conveying the same to the enemies of the said United States traitorously, unlawfully, and without right, as a spy and an enemy in open rebellion against the said United States Government, its laws and authority, did come and abide, and between said 1st day of November, and for a year prior thereto, did at divers days and times come within and present himself to the enemies of said United States, and did to the extent of his ability aid and assist the enemies of said United States at said New Orleans, contrary to the law, peace, and dignity of said United States and the law martial.

To which charge and specification the accused, Charles H. Harris, late of New Orleans, La., pleaded "Not guilty."

FINDING.

The commission, having maturely considered the evidence adduced, finds the accused, Charles [H.] Harris, late of New Orleans, La., as follows:

Of the *Specification.*—" Guilty."

․ Of the CHARGE.—" Guilty of being a spy."

SENTENCE.

And the commission does, therefore, sentence him, Charles H. Harris, late of New Orleans, La., "to be hung by the neck until he be dead, at such time and place as the commanding general shall direct."

II. In compliance with the fifth section of the act approved July 17, 1862, the proceedings in the foregoing case have been submitted to the President of the United States, who directs that the sentence "to be hung by the neck until he be dead" be commuted to confinement at hard labor on Ship Island, or some other military prison, for during the war.

The commanding general of the Department of the Gulf will designate the military prison to which the prisoner will be sent.

By order of the Secretary of War:

E. D. TOWNSEND,
Assistant Adjutant-General.

HEADQUARTERS DEPARTMENT OF THE GULF,
Sims' Plantation, opposite Simsport, La., May 17, 1863—9 p. m.

Maj. Gen. N. P. BANKS, *Commanding Department:*

GENERAL: I thank you for your note of yesterday, received this morning. The Sachem is just in, with dispatches from General Dwight of 8.30 last night, brought to the mouth of Red River by the Albatross. I inclose a copy.* The Laurel Hill arrived at 1 p. m., from below: Grover's division reported this morning, and is encamped at Simsport, on the other side. Emory's division encamped this evening 7 miles back of Simsport. The Bee will take these dispatches. The Laurel Hill will be used to cross both divisions, that no time may be lost in that way. We need another steamer to go up for the raft.

Commodore Palmer, who came down yesterday expecting to see you, fully agrees in the necessity of taking Port Hudson, and he will remain for the purpose. General Andrews thinks the information obtained by General Dwight as to the amount of the enemy's force at Port Hudson is not to be relied on, and that we should make our calculations for a larger force. But, however that may be, it does not materially affect our movements. In either case we must now move on Port Hudson at once. These are the most important things:

1. General Andrews urges you to return at the earliest possible moment.

2. The navy must have coal, hard coal especially, at once. No coal has come. If it is left to the quartermaster at Brashear, none will come. Without it we can do nothing. Please insist on the coal being sent immediately, in large quantity, and at any cost. The iron-clads are reported to have received a load of soft coal from above.

3. To get steamers up here. The Laurel Hill is alone available to cross the entire command.

4. To order General Augur to move in force in the direction of Port Hudson, to ascertain the enemy's strength, if nothing else. It will take a very long time to cross this command on the Laurel Hill alone. There is another consideration in regard to boats—the falling of the river will soon begin to reduce the number of boats capable of ascending it. Low water should find them above and not below, since we are to operate above.

---

* Not found; but see Irwin to Banks, p. 489.

General Sherman should be ordered to hold all his disposable force in readiness to join us at Port Hudson after its occupation. If necessary, he can spare us two brigades, but easily one. If only one brigade comes, it had better be the First, which is at the parapet, leaving General Dow there, and giving the command to the senior officer, Colonel Clark, Sixth Michigan.

I have the honor to be, very respectfully, your obedient servant,

[RICH'D B. IRWIN,]
Assistant Adjutant-General.

HDQRS. DEPT. OF THE GULF, NINETEENTH ARMY CORPS,
Sims' Plantation, May 17, 1863—9 p. m.

Maj. Gen. N. P. BANKS, *New Orleans:*

Dispatch from General Dwight, dated Grand Gulf, May 16, 8.30 p. m., just received, states that Grant occupies Jackson. Promises to secure the co-operation desired, but urges you not to wait for it. General Dwight says he is confident, from information from various sources, that there is only a brigade at Port Hudson. Grover is here; Emory's division 7 miles back. Troops begin to cross to-morrow morning on Laurel Hill. The vital points are, first, coal for the navy immediately, certainly, and at any cost; secondly, steamboats to move the command; thirdly, prompt movement. General Andrews and I both write by the messenger who takes this down.

Very respectfully, your most obedient servant,

[RICH'D B. IRWIN,]
Assistant Adjutant-General.

HDQRS. DEPT. OF THE GULF, NINETEENTH ARMY CORPS,
Simsport, La., May 17, 1863—9 p. m.

Maj. Gen. N. P. BANKS,
Commanding Department:

GENERAL: I have the honor to inform you of the receipt of a dispatch from General Dwight, copy of which Lieutenant-Colonel Irwin will send you herewith, and to report as follows: I propose to send Harwood to make a reconnaissance of the road to Morganza and the ferry opposite Bayou Sara, and no farther at present. I propose to retain the Laurel Hill here, and cross the Third and Fourth Divisions to this side as rapidly as possible. I propose to send the first transport that arrives to tow the raft down here. The Bee was sent for this purpose to-day, but got off too late to accomplish anything. General Weitzel should be at Bayou Huffpower to-morrow night, 40 miles from here, where he awaits orders. In the uncertainty about Colonel Chickering's movements, I do not like to send an order to General Weitzel to move farther until I hear from you. It will take about two days for him to reach this place from Bayou Huffpower.

I would suggest that General Sherman be directed to send a brigade of infantry and a battery of field artillery to re-enforce General Augur, and the latter (General Augur) be directed to move at once with his whole force, excepting one regiment of infantry (colored) and the Twenty-first Indiana Artillery, which mans the heavy guns, to the rear of Port Hudson. At least he can safely move up to Barnes' house, 14 miles from Baton Rouge, at the cross-road to Springfield Landing, and send his cavalry up in rear of Port Hudson. General Dwight's information as to the number of troops in Port Hudson may or may not be correct, and a rebel brigade is by no means a constant quantity, and may mean from 4,000 men, upward or downward, but it appears to me that we should move with all speed to the rear of Port Hudson. From the numerous details that have been made, and the large number sick, it is difficult to estimate accurately our strength and the precise disposition of our forces, but it is not far from the following:

Location.	Infantry.	Cavalry.	Artillery.	Total.
At Simsport, Third Division and Fourth Division	5,200	400	600	6,200
With Weitzel	3,200	300	300	3,800
With Chickering and below Opelousas	2,800	......	40	2,840
Total	11,200	700	940	12,840

The above does not include the troops at Brashear and Butte-à-la-Rose (two regiments). The total number of pieces of artillery is fifty, viz, thirty-two here at Simsport, sixteen with Weitzel, and two with Chickering. By sending up at once all the available transports, I think the force we now have here could be landed at Bayou Sara within four or five days. The most expeditious way of doing this appears to me to be to cross over the artillery first, with enough infantry to protect it; next cross over the baggage, and send it down the road toward Morganza as soon as circumstances will permit; meanwhile to send up all transports available, use in addition the gunboats, and, taking on board all the infantry and two batteries of artillery, with a supply of rations, land them directly at Bayou Sara; then cross over the rest of the artillery and the baggage train from the ferry, landing opposite Bayou Sara. In order, however, for the commodore to co-operate, some hard coal must be sent up immediately. If you should order Chickering's force to guard the train at Brashear, some order will have to be sent to Hill at Barre's Landing, directing what shall be done with the reserve ammunition which is there. Probably it will have to be sent here by transports, and the wagons designed to carry it sent to Brashear; this would, however, deprive us of their use in the field. The intention was to have had the ammunition escorted here by Chickering's force, via Holmesville. I can only cross over the forces from Simsport to this side as rapidly as possible, and improve the means of crossing until I hear from you. I trust you will return speedily.

I am, general, very respectfully, your obedient servant,

[GEO. L. ANDREWS,]
Brigadier-General of Volunteers, and Chief of Staff.

HDQRS. DEPT. OF THE GULF, NINETEENTH ARMY CORPS,
Sims' Plantation, May 17, 1863.

Commodore JAMES S. PALMER,
Commanding, &c., Flag-ship Hartford:

COMMODORE: In the absence of the general commanding, I have the honor to inclose for your information the copy of a dispatch received to-night by the Sachem from General Dwight.*

---

* Not found; but see Irwin to Banks, p. 489.

This dispatch will be forwarded to the general .early in the morning. At daylight we shall begin to cross the divisions of Grover and Emory. The former is at Simsport, the latter 7 miles back. There is only the Laurel Hill to do the work. General Andrews and I have both written to the commanding general, strongly urging the vital importance of coal, steamboats, and prompt movement. The quartermaster at Brashear has also been urged and directed to forward coal immediately. If you receive coal, the commanding general will probably request your assistance in the transportation of his infantry to Bayou Sara.

I have the honor to be, sir, very respectfully, your obedient servant,

[RICH'D B. IRWIN,]
Assistant Adjutant-General.

SPECIAL ORDERS, }   HDQRS. DEPT. OF THE GULF, 19TH A. C.,
No. 118.   } *Sims' Plantation, opposite Simsport, May* 17,1863.

*   *   *   *   *   *   *

III. During the absence of these headquarters from New Orleans, the troops serving in the district of La Fourche, under the command of Col. C. E. L. Holmes, Twenty-third Connecticut, consisting of his own regiment and the One hundred and seventy-sixth New York, will be reported to Brig. Gen. Thomas W. Sherman, commanding the Defenses of New Orleans.

*   *   *   *   *   *   *

By command of Major-General Banks:

[RICH'D B. IRWIN,]
Assistant Adjutant-General.

HEADQUARTERS DEPARTMENT OF NEW MEXICO,
Santa Fé N. Mex., May 17, 1863.
Brig. Gen. JOSEPH R. WEST,
Hart's Mills, Tex.:

GENERAL: My opinion is that no 4,000 men will make a demonstration on this country from Texas, at least until the growing crops are ripe. It is possible, perhaps probable, that half that number may soon attempt a raid into the country, some across the Llano Estacado (see the accompanying letter*) and some via Fort Davis. But, admitting that you are menaced by 4,000 men, a contingency alluded to in your letter of the 8th instant, there is not force enough in New Mexico safely to spare you 2,000 men, and the only light battery in the Territory for the defense of Hart's Mills and environs, without so weakening vital points as to make it too hazardous to do so. Everything must not be trusted upon one card, with the chances even then of 2,000 against 4,000. It is made in the right spirit, this offer of yours, and with California troops to stand by you, you could but come out of the battle with glory whatever might be the result. But, suppose for a moment that you have gathered this force there. Now contemplate the board! If you were at Hart's Mills, could he not amuse you by cavalry demonstration, while his main force could march on the Magoffin Salt Lake road to San Augustine Spring, and come into Doña Aña in spite of you, and thus get between you and your source of supplies? Could you help his doing this and still yourself hold Hart's Mills and defend the Mesilla

---

* Not found.

Valley? Perhaps I have as much repugnance to falling back as you may have, but if by falling back I risk less ultimately, would it not be wise to do so? We cannot afford to put our main strength at Hart's Mills, away from our supplies, and 450 miles away from the whole year's supplies now *en route* from the States, and this with many chances for an enemy, an active enemy, to get between us and those supplies, which would result in his having the whole country as well as ourselves at his mercy.

If you have 1,000 troops in hand, you will be likely to draw him into the Valley of the Rio Grande. It was not intended that you should then retire to Fort Craig without striking a blow. Even if he be 4,000, you will fight him whenever and wherever you can; provided, always, that you keep between him and Fort Craig, your source of supplies. To that point you will retire, disputing the ground inch by inch, and falling back no faster than you are driven by actual force. In this connection, I would suggest your having some half dozen water-tanks made for the crossing of the Jornada.

Besides the 1,000 men I hope to be able to spare you, if Bowie ever gets up from the Desert, you will organize guerrilla parties, and arm them with the arms I sent you for this purpose last winter. These will make fine auxiliaries to hover around the enemy, to watch his movements from mountain-tops, and communicate to you, by smokes in the daytime and fires by night, his movements; fine auxiliaries to fire into his camps at night; to run off his stock; to lay the country in waste in his front. They shall have all they can take. This will be a great incentive to the Mexican population in addition to their patriotism, and the knowledge that the Texans will come to live upon them without pay. Messrs. Mills, Jenkins, Lemmon, and others whom you know, together with the best Mexicans, will make splendid guerrillas, partisans, and spies.

How long can 4,000 men live in the Mesilla Valley, if they depend solely upon what they can get there and (without much money) from Chihuahua? You are authorized to call in Fritz's and French's companies, leaving McCleave 20 cavalry and two companies of infantry at Fort West for the present. This is under the supposition that you hear beyond a doubt that a force of rebels is advancing upon you.

I am, general, very respectfully, your obedient servant,

JAMES H. CARLETON,
Brigadier-General, Commanding.

HEADQUARTERS DEPARTMENT OF THE GULF,
New Orleans, La., May 18, 1863.

Major-General HALLECK,
Commander-in-Chief, U. S. Army:

GENERAL: Grover's division left Alexandria on the 14th; is now at Simsport. Emory's division marched on the 16th, and is 7 miles to-day from Simsport. Weitzel probably marched on the 17th, and will reach Simsport by the 20th, making a concentration of all our forces at that point. We shall move across the Mississippi, without delay, against Port Hudson, with the best chances of success, and join Grant immediately after. A communication received to-night informs me that this is satisfactory to him, and that he will send re-enforcements to us as proposed earlier, for which, however, we shall not wait.

Between 3,000 and 4,000 men, from the incessant labor of the last six weeks, have become disabled. The balance of the army is in good condition and fine spirit. I shall withdraw all the troops possible from New Orleans, and strengthen Augur's division at Baton Rouge, effecting a junction with him in the rear of Port Hudson.

General Emory, who is unable to resume his services in the field, will be left in command of New Orleans, for which he is competent, and General Sherman will be assigned to the command of his division.

General Augur's forces will move to-morrow toward Port Hudson. Admiral Farragut's fleet is now concentrated at that point.

I hope to send you further advices of our movements before the steamer sails, which is on Thursday next, 21st.

I have the honor to be, with much respect, your obedient servant,

N. P. BANKS,
Major-General, Commanding.

HDQRS. DEPT. OF THE GULF, NINETEENTH ARMY CORPS,
Sims' Plantation, opposite Simsport, May 18, 1863.

Commodore PALMER,
Commanding Fleet:

COMMODORE: I would respectfully inform you that I send to-day Lieutenant Harwood, of the U. S. Engineers, with an escort, to make a reconnaissance of the roads leading from this place to Morganza and the ferry opposite Bayou Sara, and a further reconnaissance, if practicable, of the roads from Morganza to Rosedale post-office, on the Grossetête Bayou; thence to a point opposite Baton Rouge, to open communications with General Augur. The escort will consist of five companies of cavalry, to be followed by a regiment of infantry and a section of artillery. The infantry and artillery will halt at or near Morganza, to secure the retreat of the cavalry from the operations beyond that place. The cavalry will probably reach Morganza to-night, the infantry and artillery to-morrow before night. The whole movement will probably occupy four or five days.

If you can co-operate in this movement, by sending a gunboat below Morganza, it will greatly tend to the security of the troops engaged therein. I send to-day by the Laurel Hill an order to have coal sent up here from Brashear City immediately; it will, however, probably take two or three days at least to get it here.

I am, commodore, very respectfully, your obedient servant,

[GEO. L. ANDREWS,]
Brigadier-General of Volunteers, and Chief of Staff.

SIMS' PLANTATION,
Simsport, May 18, 1863—10 p. m.

Maj. Gen. N. P. BANKS,
Commanding Department:

GENERAL: I have the honor to report as follows: The Union and Empire Parish arrived here to-day, loaded with ammunition and subsistence stores, and the latter vessel towing a schooner loaded with coal for the fleet, which is much needed. The Estrella and Switzerland also arrived here to-day from Alexandria, which they left at 12 m. on the 17th. A dispatch from General Weitzel has been received this evening. He is now at junction of Huffpower and Bayou Bœuf, awaiting orders. His rear guard had neither seen nor heard anything of the enemy. On Thursday last, two companies of his cavalry had a skirmish with the enemy on Cotile Bayou, they having been sent out to reconnoiter, on account of a report that the enemy were constructing breastworks of cotton at Judge Boyce's bridge. It was found that the enemy had about 1,000 dismounted cavalry and several pieces of light artillery. We had 1 man wounded and several horses killed. Three dead bodies of the enemy were found on the field and buried.

On the following day the whole cavalry force was sent out, with 200 infantry and one piece of artillery, on the gunboat Switzerland, to attack the enemy, who fled, on the appearance of our force, in three directions, closely pursued by our cavalry. He then took position at Cane River, and only a few of his pickets had since ventured down to Cotile Bayou. Six prisoners were captured who belonged to Colonel [W. P.] Lane's Texas cavalry, which left Texas two weeks since. Letters found in the mails seized indicate that there is but a small force at Mobile, much of it having been sent to re-enforce Johnston.

The indications respecting Port Hudson are that the garrison there has been much diminished, but how much is uncertain; probably the garrison does not now exceed 4,000 men. Four hundred head of beef-cattle were sent to Port Hudson from this side about a week ago. It is reported that they have only a picket at Bayou Sara.

Lieutenants Hill and Whitside arrived here to-day from Barre's Landing. They report about 1,000 bales of cotton still at Barre's Landing.

It seems that the enemy must be concentrating everything available on Rosecrans in the west, and he is probably doing the same against Hooker in the east—wise course.

General Grover's division crossed to this side to-day, and General Emory's division will cross to-morrow. I propose to send down the Sixth New York Regiment to Brashear and thence to New Orleans on the first opportunity, probably day after to-morrow. The Union leaves to-morrow morning with sick, contrabands, and mules for Brashear.

I do not quite like the intelligence from Hooker's army, but hope for better luck next time.

I am, general, very respectfully, your obedient servant,

[GEO. L. ANDREWS,]
Brigadier-General of Volunteers, Chief of Staff.

HEADQUARTERS OF THE ARMY,
Washington, D. C., May 19, 1863.

Major-General BANKS,
New Orleans, La.:

GENERAL: I learn from the newspapers that you are in possession of Alexandria, and General Grant of Jackson. This may be well enough so far, but these operations are too eccentric to be pursued. I must again urge that you co-operate as soon as possible with General Grant east of the Mississippi. Your forces must be united at the earliest possible moment. Otherwise the enemy will concentrate on Grant and crush him. Do all you can to prevent this. I have no troops to re-enforce him. Both Burnside and Rosecrans are calling loudly for re-enforcements. I have none to give either.

I have strongly urged the Navy Department to send the monitors to the Mississippi River, but I am answered that they can do nothing against Vicksburg and Port Hudson.

We shall watch with the greatest anxiety the movements of yourself and General Grant. I have urged him to keep his forces concentrated as much as possible, and not to move east till he gets control of the Mississippi River.

Very respectfully, your obedient servant,

H. W. HALLECK,
General-in-Chief.

HDQRS. DEPT. OF THE GULF, NINETEENTH ARMY CORPS,
' Sims' Plantation, opposite Simsport, May 19, 1863—8 p. m.

Maj. Gen. N. P. BANKS,
Commanding Department:

GENERAL: I have the honor to report as follows: Lieutenant [Franklin] Harwood reports from Morganza that the road along the river to that place is practicable for all arms. About 200 of the enemy's cavalry were in his front yesterday, but none to be seen to-day; they signaled along his front. A paroled soldier reported to him that there were only 2,000 men in Port Hudson. Commodore Palmer says that a dispatch from Admiral Porter states that the enemy are said to be evacuating Vicksburg.

Intercepted letters from Mobile show that there is but a small force there. Everything appears to have been sent to re-enforce Johnston in front of Rosecrans. An intercepted letter from a captain in the rebel army, under Johnston, represents his force at about 55,000 men, date April 16. Another intercepted letter from Richmond, date April 8, states that there are at least 50,000 men in that army; this letter is written by H. L. Clay, who appears to be connected with the office of the rebel Adjutant-General. He further intimates that the question of subsistence is the doubtful one with them. The letter is directed to Dr. S. A. Smith, Alexandria.

Several of the letters recently found in the intercepted mails are of considerable importance. One of them refers to the construction in England of iron-clads for the Emperor of China, and states that one of them is to be commanded by an officer whom he names, and who is certainly not a Chinaman. Both Grover's and Emory's divisions and most of their trains are now on this side. We are well supplied with ammunition, and have about twenty-five days' rations (partial rations) on hand. We shall need forage for the horses, this section of the country appearing to be pretty well stripped. Major Carpenter has applied to have some sent up, but I believe forage is rather short at Brashear. I propose to send down to Brashear to-morrow the Laurel Hill, and probably the Empire Parish, with the Sixth New York Regiment, which is to be sent to New York to be mustered out, and a load of prisoners, sick, contrabands, and mules, &c., getting rid of as much *impedimenta* as possible. Dr. Bacon is on the Laurel Hill. The raft is not here yet, but the Estrella has gone for it.

The rebels are evidently massing their western forces against Rosecrans, and very wisely, too. Grant should at once re-enforce Rosecrans to the utmost, leaving only enough before Vicksburg to mask its garrison. We should take Port Hudson and then re-enforce Grant before Vicksburg, enabling him still further to re-enforce Rosecrans. This should doubtless have been arranged earlier, but it is not too late to give Rosecrans the superiority in time, at least, to prevent serious disaster. I hope the Government appreciates the importance of Rosecrans' position and is acting accordingly, or else that I do not correctly appreciate it.

I am, general, very respectfully, your obedient servant,

GEO. L. ANDREWS,
Brigadier-General of Volunteers, Chief of Staff.

HDQRS. DEPT. OF THE GULF, NINETEENTH ARMY CORPS,
Sims' Plantation, opposite Simsport, La., May 19, 1863.

Col. E. D. TOWNSEND,
Assistant Adjutant-General, Washington:

MY DEAR COLONEL: I am one of the last men in the world to violate the official unities, but the following information, obtained while the commanding general was in New Orleans, may not keep until, on his return, he can communicate it officially:

1. For about a week we have taken every rebel mail intended for Alexandria, the former headquarters of Lieut. Gen. E. Kirby Smith, and the distributing office for Texas and Western Louisiana. Here are the results, mainly from official sources ::

2. Bragg was, "more than a fortnight since" (April 8), ordered to Richmond "for consultation." "Johnston, who has assumed immediate command of the Army in Tennessee, has surely 50,000 troops." Beauregard has more than 30,000 troops. (Private letter from Maj. H. L. Clay, assistant adjutant-general, on duty in the Adjutant and Inspector General's Office at Richmond, to his friend, Sarg. S. A. Smith, of E. K. Smith's staff, at Alexandria, dated April 8.) Major Clay is, I think, a relative of C. C. Clay, of Alabama. Incidentally, he mentions taking breakfast with Mr. Davis. At the close of a long and free letter, he says: "In many respects my position with General Cooper is more than agreeable. I seem to have his confidence in the fullest official sense."

3. One of Bragg's inspectors-general (J. P. Baltzell), writing from Tullahoma, April 11, says:

He has 60,000 infantry; that the whole army took four hours to march in review past General Johnston in column of companies.

(At the great review at Munson's Hill, seven divisions of the Army of the Potomac, lacking three brigades, and estimated at 65,000 men, took three hours and twenty minutes to march in review past General McClellan, formed in double column at half distance, except Porter's division, which took wheeling distance, of course.)

4. Capt. C. F. Sanders, of the Buckner Guards, writing from Tullahoma, April 15, to his brother, says the army consists of—

Hardee's corps: Breckinridge's division (19,000)—Adams', Brown's, Preston's, and B. H. Helm's brigades; Cleburne's division—Lucius [E.] Polk's, Liddell's, Johnson's, and Wood's brigades.

Polk's corps: Cheatham's division—McCown's and Withers' brigades. Total strength of the two corps 35,000 or 40,000 effective infantry. Hardee at Tullahoma, Polk at Shelbyville. Cavalry: [John H.] Morgan, with 6,000 or 8,000 at McMinnville; [John A.] Wharton, "north [toward Murfreesborough], with about 2,000 at Beach Grove;" Forrest and Van Dorn at Columbia, with about 10,000, "operating against Nashville and its environs." There are four regiments—Second, Fourth, Sixth, and Ninth Kentucky—in Helm's brigade. The captain belongs to Cleburne's division, and asks to have his letter directed to that general's care.

5. The enemy had about 5,000 or 6,000 men of all sorts in Mobile. At least one brigade has gone to Tullahoma, the Second Brigade, commanded by Brig. Gen. Alfred Cumming. There remained at Mobile, April 15, five regiments and a battery, viz, the Nineteenth Louisiana, First Georgia, Twenty-eighth, Thirty-sixth, and Fortieth Alabama, and [W. H.] Fowler's battery. Part of these are said to have gone to Tennessee since.

6. Mr. Ed. Eberstadt, a contractor for 50,000 suits of army clothing, writes from Columbus, Ga., April 6, having returned from Richmond the night before:

Two iron-clads are pretty soon [to be] ready again in Richmond. * * * In Wilmington, N. C., a large iron-clad vessel will be done in a few weeks. Here one iron-clad vessel is now in construction and several contracted for. In Selma, Ala., more are in construction, and one sea-going frigate, to carry fifty guns. Two iron-clads, which were built in Selma, are now in Mobile, ready to give the enemy a becoming reception.

There is no doubt in the minds of any of us—it is shown by hundreds of the letters in these captured mails; it is proved by every indication—that the rebels are now straining every nerve to crush Rosecrans. They have taken troops from Charleston, where you see they had 30,000, a brigade and more from Mobile, 7,000 from Port Hudson, where they had 16,000. To-day the army before Rosecrans is stronger, by certainly 30,000 effective men, than it was a month ago.

If Grant is at Jackson, as we hear and believe he is, and in sufficient force to whip the enemy, every man from Vicksburg will go to Tullahoma. We shall gain Vicksburg and Port Hudson before many days, but if Rosecrans is defeated the fruits of our victory will turn to ashes on our tongues.

I am, colonel, as ever, very truly, yours,

RICH'D B. IRWIN,
Assistant Adjutant-General.

NEW ORLEANS,
May 20, 1863.

Major-General BANKS:

The force proposed to be left here is very small; in my opinion, inadequate.

The forced emigration and the enlistment of negroes in the parishes declared slave by the President's proclamation, have made the population here very unsettled.

If a raid from Mobile or elsewhere should be made, the consequences might be disastrous. Could not another brigade be left here?

W. H. EMORY,
Brigadier-General, Commanding.

SPECIAL ORDERS, }   HEADQUARTERS AUGUR'S DIVISION,
    No. 20.   }   *Baton Rouge, La., May* 20, 1863.

*   *   *   *   *   *   *

VIII. During the temporary absence of the general commanding, the charge of the town and the troops therein will devolve upon Captain [Luther] Goodrich, provost-marshal.

*   *   *   *   *   *   *

Colonel Drew, Fourth Louisiana Native Guards, will move his regiment into Fort Williams to-day, and take command of the garrison. He will

not permit the camps or property of the troops now absent to be interfered with. The officer commanding the First Louisiana Native Guards
will hold his regiment in readiness to move at a moment's notice with
two days' cooked rations.

By command of Major-General Augur:

GEO. B. HALSTED,
Assistant Adjutant-General.

HDQRS. DEPT. OF THE GULF, NINETEENTH ARMY CORPS,
Simsport, La., May 21, 1863.

Major-General HALLECK,
Commander-in-Chief, U. S. Army, Washington, D. C.:

GENERAL: Recent occupation of this country as far as Natchitoches
gives us reason to believe that at no distant day it can be permanently
occupied and held with a small force, controlling substantially the entire northern part of the State. With the aid of transports and gunboats of light draught, this could be done without difficulty. This,
apart from other considerations, makes the railway communication in
this portion of the State a matter of increased importance.

The railway is now in operation as far as Brashear City, a distance
of 80 miles. It is vigorously managed, has plenty of business, and is
run for the profit of the Government. There are great quantities of the
staple products of the country still remaining in the northern part of
the State. If they are not destroyed by the advancing cavalry force of
the enemy, which follows our movements toward the Mississippi, these
products will all be transported to New Orleans, or a greater part by
railroad.

This Opelousas Railroad is intended to reach Alexandria; from this
northwardly to ———, and westwardly to the principal towns in Texas.
The grade is complete and perfect as far as from Berwick Bay to
Opelousas, the bridges mostly built, and ties prepared and on the
ground, the iron rails only wanting. We have labor enough, with the
negro regiments, to complete this work, if it is to be done by the Government. In the case of the reoccupation of this country, or the restoration of this State to the Union, it would be advisable that this road
should be completed either by the Government or by private parties.
I think I can say that at no distant day the country east of the Missis-
sipi, extending as far as and into the State of Mississippi, and covering
the line of railroad from Jackson to Mobile, will be held. This road,
following the tendency of the time, has been destroyed to an unnecessary degree by our troops, but we can easily repair it. The two lines
together make a very important railway interest for this department.
I have no complaint to make of its management, and no fear as to its
efficiency hereafter; but there is not that responsibility and accountability in the management of so large an undertaking which should be
established, both for the protection of the officers of this department
and the Government.

I desire very earnestly that General [Daniel C.] McCallum, or the
chief of the Railway Bureau, may send to this department a competent officer, who will understand enough of railway management to
organize the different departments of a railway bureau, so that each
department may operate as a check upon the others, and thus by a report of the superintendent present to the Government not only an accurate but a responsible statement of all the operations of the road
—the receipts and the expenditures and the responsibilities which

ought to attach to each of the departments of such bureau. General Haupt would be the best man for this purpose, if he could be spared, and this part of it would occupy him but a short time.

A great quantity of the staple products that must necessarily pass over these roads in the occupation of this country make it very important as a financial matter. The military movements, necessarily requiring great celerity and secrecy, considering our small force, will give us an interest in the efficient organization of this branch of business, and on every consideration I desire that the whole affair shall be placed under the direction of the Railway Bureau at Washington. This is said without any purpose of making a complaint of what has been done, but with a view to secure full accountability and responsibility in the transaction of the increased labor likely to devolve upon it.

I have the honor to be, with much respect, your obedient servant,

N. P. BANKS,
Major-General, Commanding.

U. S. FLAG-SHIP HARTFORD,
Off Red River, May 21, 1863.

[General BANKS:]

GENERAL: I inclose you the following extracts taken from a letter I received from the commanding naval officer at Bayou Sara, this morning:

· Picked up two deserters from Port Hudson that have been hidden in a swamp for several days, waiting for one of our vessels to come down. They say that there may be about 2,500 or 3,000 in Port Hudson, and many more beyond the place, but they do not know the force. Say that the batteries are well manned, and the guns still there; heard of no intended evacuation when they left. * * * The cavalry surprised everybody along the river banks. The officer in command did not stop to communicate. I, however, stopped one of his officers, and learned that they were going to Waterloo. Went down with Albatross, and met them returning from the spot where our mails went across to the lower fleet. They brought back 2 killed and 1 wounded, and, as they had no medical officer, I took him on board; had they told me where they were going, I could have saved them their loss, for I visited those woods and burned dwellings only the evening before, and heard that there was a force of cavalry and infantry opposite Port Hudson. I could have shelled them when drawn out by our cavalry. The number of men on both sides were the same. Anchored at Waterloo, and remained by the cavalry all night. * * * From Bayou Sara we still hear that Port Hudson has but a very small force—a brigade and a half.

J. S. PALMER, ·
Commodore.

SPECIAL ORDERS, ⎱ HDQRS. DEPT. OF THE GULF, 19TH A. C.,
    No. 122.   ⎰   *Simsport, May 21, 1863.*

I. The Third Division will move on Morganza at 8.30 a. m. In addition to the regiment now on the other side of the Atchafalaya, which will remain where it is, Colonel Paine will detail one regiment of infantry and one battery to remain at this post, and will order the commanding officer at once to report in person at these headquarters for instructions.

*   *   *   *   *   *   *

III. General Grover will, as speedily as practicable, proceed to place two batteries on board the steamers Empire Parish and Saint Maurice, with as large a part of his infantry as the two steamers can carry, in addition to the batteries. Six days' rations will be taken. The re-

mainder of General Grover's command will proceed on board other transports as soon as they can be furnished. The wagons will move in rear
of General Paine's command, under a proper guard. General Paine
moves on Morganza at 8.30 a. m. to-day.

IV. Brigadier-General Weitzel will march on Simsport to-morrow'
morning, cross the river, and await further orders on this side.

V. So much of Paragraph I of Special Orders as directs the commander of the Third Division to detail one battery of artillery to remain at this post, is hereby countermanded.

    ＊   ＊   ●   ＊   ＊   ＊

By command of Major-General Banks :
                              [RICH'D B. IRWIN,]
                              Assistant Adjutant-General.

GENERAL ORDERS, ⎰   HDQRS. DEFENSES OF NEW ORLEANS,
    No. 1.   ⎱   *New Orleans,* May 21, 1863.
I. The undersigned assumes temporary command of the Defenses of
New Orleans.*
II. Lieut. Col. W. D. Smith, One hundred and tenth New York Vol-
unteers, is temporarily appointed acting assistant adjutant-general.
                              W. H. EMORY,
                              Brigadier-General.

                              WASHINGTON,
                              May 23, 1863.
Major-General BANKS,
    New Orleans :
GENERAL : Your dispatches, dated Opelousas May 2 and 4,† are just
received.

I regret to learn from them that you are still pursuing your divergent
line to Alexandria, while General Grant has moved on Jackson, instead
of concentrating with him on the east side of the Mississippi, as you
proposed in your previous dispatch, and as I have continually urged.
If these eccentric movements, with the main forces of the enemy on the
Mississippi River, do not lead to some serious disaster, it will be because
the enemy does not take full advantage of his opportunity. I assure
you the Government is exceedingly disappointed that you and General
Grant are not acting in conjunction. It thought to secure that object
by authorizing you to assume the entire command as soon as you and
General Grant could unite. The *opening of the Mississippi River* has
been continually presented as the *first* and *most important* object to be
attained. Operations up the Red River, toward Texas, or toward Alabama, are only of secondary importance, to be undertaken *after* we get
possession of the river, and as circumstances may then require. If we
fail to open the river, these secondary operations will result in very little
of military importance. I have continually urged these views upon
General Grant, and I do hope there will be no further delay in adopting them.

If Grant should succeed alone in beating the enemy and capturing
Vicksburg, all will be well, but if he should be defeated and fail, both
your armies will be paralyzed and the entire campaign a failure. I can

------

* Relieving Brig. Gen. T. W. Sherman, who had been in command since January
10, 1863.
† See Series I, Vol. XV, pp. 305, 306,

well understand that you have had great obstacles to overcome, with inadequate means; but you have had all the means we could possibly give you, and, if you succeed, the glory will be so much the greater.

Very respectfully, your obedient servant,

H. W. HALLECK,
General-in-Chief.

HEADQUARTERS SECOND DIVISION,
Near Port Hudson, May 23, 1863.

Brigadier-General ANDREWS,
Chief of Staff, Nineteenth Corps:

GENERAL: Your dispatch of to-day was received. Arriving with my command at General Augur's headquarters yesterday, I was directed to take position on the Bayou Sara road, just below his position, but to-day, by his orders, moved to a position on the Western Port Hudson road, in the vicinity of the school-house, about 4 miles from Port Hudson. I could not occupy a position farther in advance to-day without going too far. We occupy the road to-night by our pickets up to within sight of his rifle-pits, a line of works supposed to be about 2½ miles from the town. Our cavalry picket has been exchanging shots with the enemy this afternoon, but they do not appear to be in much force behind their first line of works. I have been engaged to-day in repairing the bridges on this road, in order to make them practicable to the Springfield Landing, which are now reported practicable.

To close up on Port Hudson on this side, it is probable that we shall first have to carry the line of rifle-pits, and, unless I see some good reason hereafter to let them alone until the decided movement is made in the other portions of the line, I will carry them to-morrow. This would give me sufficient room to act further, and ground to occupy.

I have had the country on my front and flanks reconnoitered as far as our small cavalry force (only about 20 men) and our time have permitted. There are no means of immediate connection with General Augur, in consequence of a dense wood between us, but I have found a blind road leading from just above my present position, and cutting his road about 2 miles from the town, which cannot be used as a communication yet, and probably not at all for artillery.

Our means of transportation and pioneers' tools are very scant, but we are getting along as well as we can.

Very respectfully, your obedient servant,

T. W. SHERMAN,
Brigadier-General, Commanding.

HEADQUARTERS UNITED STATES FORCES,
Simsport, Lā., May 23, 1863.

Lieut. Col. RICHARD B. IRWIN,
Assistant Adjutant-General, Department of the Gulf:

SIR: I have the honor to report that I arrived here this morning, and am now crossing the trains and spare horses which I intend to send to Bayou Sara by land, together with all the cavalry force as a guard.

Two of Lieutenant [F.] Perkins' men were killed by guerrillas yesterday while in search for horses. The enemy has not been seen in our march to-day.

In your dispatch of yesterday, it was stated that the One hundred and seventy-third New York was to be a guard on both sides of this bayou.

The quartermaster here and chief of ordnance have an order to send this regiment with the ammunition. These orders are conflicting. I have directed the One hundred and thirty-first New York, of Dwight's brigade, to go with the ammunition. Shall I send the One hundred and seventy-third New York with the remainder of Dwight's brigade?

The river has fallen considerably, and the people here tell me that all the different roads here are now passable. I am told that there is not a single gunboat in the Atchafalaya.

The Quinnebaug, which was passed yesterday afternoon at 4 o'clock, about 15 miles below here, has not arrived, and has not been heard from. I have sent the Saint Charles with a guard to see about her.

As there is a good road from the Opelousas country to the junction of Bayou Rouge and the Atchafalaya, and as the country has been abandoned by us, and as the enemy has a force of cavalry, at least, throughout the country, I have been led to believe some accident has befallen the Quinnebaug.

Unless the Atchafalaya is held at the present stage of water with gunboats, the enemy can cross infantry and cavalry to the banks of the Mississippi, attack the baggage train and cavalry on its way to Bayou Sara, and even afford the garrison at Port Hudson a chance to escape in this direction.

Captain [Richard] Barrett, when surrounded, as mentioned in my last dispatch, himself escaped; his men were taken.

Does it not seem that the enemy, not having followed me, may be after Chickering? If so, would it not be well to advise him?

I shall cross my whole force here and await further orders. Perkins has taken 179 horses. There is no fuel here for any transports but the General Banks; hence the transports are unserviceable.

I am, sir, very respectfully, your obedient servant,

G. WEITZEL,
Brigadier-General, Commanding United States Forces.

P. S.—The Saint Charles has just returned. The Quinnebaug is following her.

HERMITAGE,
Sunday, May 24, 1863.

Lieut. Col. RICHARD B. IRWIN, *Assistant Adjutant-General:*

COLONEL: Yesterday we captured the rebel signal corps, and last evening took Lieutenant [John] Barthelemy, Twentieth Louisiana Regiment, who had just crossed from Port Hudson. No information of any consequence was obtained from any of the parties.

I took the position I was directed by order of 23d to assume, and am confident that no forces can be thrown across and escape by the roads indicated by Lieutenant Harwood. To-day I shall examine the country to the interior, and close any roads I may find.

In the hurry of our embarkation, we did not supply ourselves with rations. Captain Dunham was advised of the deficiency, and promised that we should be supplied to-day. We want coffee, hard bread, and pork for 350 men.

Will you oblige me by sending down my servant, Frank, with baggage which I need?

I send you the signal corps flag. Possibly it may be of use.

Very respectfully,

LEW. BENEDICT,
Colonel, Commanding.

HEADQUARTERS SECOND DIVISION,
May 24, 1863—11 p. m.

Brigadier-General ANDREWS,
    Chief of Staff, Nineteenth Army Corps :

GENERAL: Our line is now formed on the line of rifle-pits, and our line of skirmishers occupy the opposite edge of the wood, about three-fourths of a mile in advance. This line looks upon an open space nearly half a mile in width, on the opposite side of which is the enemy's second line of works.

We have not been able to reconnoiter on account of night, but shall feel them before morning.

The approaches to these works appear of some difficulty; the only avenue over which artillery can be taken having its bridges burnt, we are rebuilding them. The communication to the river is difficult, and the distance by the road about 3 miles. Here, however, appear in sight works that are said to be their only line at that point. But it was so dark we were unable to examine them.

A further reconnaissance will be made in the morning.

Very respectfully, &c.,

T. W. SHERMAN,
Brigadier-General, Commanding.

WASHINGTON,
May 25, 1863.

Maj. Gen. N. P. BANKS,
    Commanding, &c., New Orleans :

GENERAL: Your further dispatches of May 4 are just received.* Those relating to trade in cotton, &c.; and the disposition to be made of Ex-Governor Marston [Mouton?], have been delivered to the Secretary of War, to be submitted to the President.

More recent information respecting the operations of General Grant upon Vicksburg would indicate that he is likely to succeed in capturing that place without the assistance of your army. Nevertheless the Government is exceedingly uneasy at your separation. The success of such important operations on the Mississippi River should not be put in peril by the diversion of troops upon secondary operations. But I have so often called attention to this matter that it seems useless to repeat it.

As soon as I receive the orders of the Secretary of War in relation to cotton trade, &c., I will communicate them. I, however, regard that matter as of insignificant importance in comparison with your military operations on the Mississippi River.

Very respectfully, your obedient servant,

H. W. HALLECK,
General-in-Chief.

HDQRS. DEPT. OF THE GULF, NINETEENTH ARMY CORPS,
Riley's, before Port Hudson, May 25, 1863—8.30 a. m.

Commodore J. S. PALMER,
    Commanding, &c., Flag-ship Hartford :

COMMODORE: Having abandoned the Atchafalaya, and ordered the evacuation of Butte-à-la-Rose, the commanding general directs me to

----

* See Series I, Vol. XV, p. 309.

inform you that he will no longer need the Estrella at the Courtableau Junction. ´ He respectfully requests that you will order her and another gunboat, if possible, to hold and observe closely the head of the Atcha.-falaya, and prevent the enemy from attempting to cross near Simsport. We can furnish you a detachment of sharpshooters for service on the boats if you desire it. If you send a gunboat down to order up the Estrella, please send word to the commander at Butte-à-la-Rose that no more transports are to be permitted to pass up.

Our lines closed in upon Port Hudson yesterday. We occupy the enemy's advanced rifle-pits on our left, and on the center are within musket-range and in plain view of the work at the crossing of the Jackson road. Everything looks favorable.

We are in easy communication with Baton Rouge, and by telegraph and signals from our left to the admiral, who, as I presume you are informed, has his flag on the Monongahela. I shall be happy to send anything for you to New Orleans.

I have the honor to be, commodore, very respectfully, your obedient servant,

[RICH'D B. IRWIN,]
Assistant Adjutant-General.

HDQRS. DEPT. OF THE GULF, NINETEENTH ARMY CORPS,
Riley's, before Port Hudson, May 25, 1863—12 m.

Rear-Admiral D. G. FARRAGUT, *Flag-ship Monongahela:*

ADMIRAL: The commanding general is at the front. I will forward your dispatch to him immediately; meanwhile I take the liberty of stating our position early this morning.

Sherman on the left, in advance of the enemy's first line of rifle-pits, having his pickets at the front edge of a skirt of woods, separated from the enemy's main line of works by an open plain. His position is in front of the school-house.

Augur, next on the road from the Plains to Port Hudson, and well advanced. Grover, on the Jackson road, holding the front edge of a wood which is within from 250 to 400 yards of the apparent center of the works, and in plain sight and easy range of them.

Weitzel, with his own brigade, Dwight's, and Paine's (Emory's) division, reduced to about a brigade, on the right, near where the Telegraph road from Port Hudson to Bayou Sara crosses the Big Sandy Creek.

This morning everybody except Grover has closed up, and Grover cannot close up without taking the works in front of him. Thus the place is completely invested. I understand that it is the commanding general's intention to make the decisive attack to-morrow morning, but upon this point I do not speak officially or decidedly, as everything, of course, depends upon circumstances, which an hour might totally change.

I have the honor to be, sir, with great respect, your most obedient servant,

[RICH'D B. IRWIN,]
Assistant Adjutant-General.

HDQRS. DEPT. OF THE GULF, NINETEENTH ARMY CORPS,
Riley's, before Port Hudson, May 25, 1863—1 p. m.

Commodore JAMES S. PALMER, *U. S. S. Hartford:*

It is important that the gunboats should shell the point of land between Thompson's Creek and the Mississippi from a position a little above the turn of the river at midnight precisely. If the enemy attempts an escape, it will be across Thompson's Creek, between the creek and Fancy Point. This will probably occur, if at all, to-night. Grierson's cavalry is over the crest of Thompson's Creek. You will take the range of Port Hudson, covering Fancy Point about on the line marked on the inclosed sketch,* from the position marked on the river thus;

Very respectfully, your obedient servant,

N. P. BANKS,
Major-General, Commanding.

HDQRS. SECOND DIVISION, NINETEENTH ARMY CORPS,
May 25, 1863—1 p. m.

Brigadier-General ANDREWS,
Chief of Staff, Headquarters Nineteenth Army Corps:

GENERAL: Last night we failed to draw any artillery fire from the works in our immediate front. Nothing but picket firing ensued. I have reason to believe that there is no heavy artillery in our immediate front; but on a reconnaissance made by myself this morning on a road leading from our left to the left of the enemy's works, I drew the fire of three pieces of artillery, which exploded their shells with much accuracy immediately over our heads. I understand there are three more guns on the enemy's right of those, a portion of the parapet forming the extreme right of their line. I have ascertained to considerable certainty that the work now before us is the enemy's main line of defense; that is, that there is no other line behind it. This is confirmed by the citizens and by intelligent contrabands. This work is continuous from the bluffs on the river to the main road on which we were yesterday. It all seems to be occupied to a certain extent. The enemy are on the *qui vive* throughout the line, but do not venture out of it, excepting where there are thickets to offer them protection.

I am not entirely through with our reconnaissances on the extreme left. When they are completed, I can best see what should be done. The roads out there seem to be complicated. Our line is of great extent, and the general must not think we are dilatory. It is best to see exactly what is before us before we take decisive action. I hope to have many uncertainties removed this evening.

Can I obtain artillery ammunition, if I require it, from Springfield Landing?

We are now finely off for subsistence supplies.

Very respectfully, your obedient servant,

T. W. SHERMAN,
Brigadier-General, Commanding.

HDQRS. DEPT. OF THE GULF, NINETEENTH ARMY CORPS,
Riley's, before Port Hudson, May 25, 1863—4.15 p. m.

Brig. Gen. G. WEITZEL,
Commanding, &c.:

GENERAL: The commanding general directs that you assume command of the right wing of the forces before Port Hudson, including the

---

* Sketch not found.

Third Division, under Colonel Paine, and your own and Dwight's brigade and Prince's cavalry.

Very respectfully, your most obedient servant, .

RICH'D B. IRWIN,
Assistant Adjutant-General.

[MAY 25, 1863.—For Grant to Banks, in relation to 'co-operation of forces, see Series I, Vol. XXIV, Part III, p. 346.]

SPECIAL ORDERS, }   HDQRS. OF ARMY, ADJT. GEN.'S OFFICE,
No. 234.   }   *Washington, May 25, 1863.*
* * * * *
III. Brig. Gen. W. F. Smith, U. S. Volunteers, will repair immediately to New Orleans, La., and report for duty to Maj. Gen. N. P. Banks, commanding Department of the Gulf.*

By command of Major-General Halleck:

E. D. TOWNSEND,
Assistant Adjutant-General.

HDQRS. DEPT. OF THE GULF, NINETEENTH ARMY CORPS,
Riley's, before Port Hudson, May 26, 1863—1 a. m.

Admiral D. G. FARRAGUT, *Commanding, &c., Flag-ship Monongahela:*

ADMIRAL: Colonel Irwin informed you of our position early this morning. To-day we concentrated Paine's (Emory's) division, reduced to about a brigade, and the brigades of Weitzel and Dwight, all under General Weitzel's command, on the right; turned the head of Big Sandy Creek, and pushed through the woods on that part of the line, up to the abatis which continues the enemy's line of defense toward his left.

During the afternoon he made quite a determined attack on our right. For a short time the action was brisk, but the enemy was soon driven back in considerable confusion, and at dark we held the ground I have indicated on our right, and on the rest of the line the same general position indicated in Colonel Irwin's dispatch.

Colonel Prince, with the Seventh Illinois Cavalry and a section of the First Illinois Battery, was sent down and across Thompson's Creek, to destroy the enemy's means of transportation, with the view of frustrating the probable attempt to escape at this point. Colonel Prince took the large steamers Starlight and Red Chief, and a small flat, being the only means of transportation on the creek, and, finding the south bank overflowed and the steamers in good order, very properly decided to hold the boats instead of burning them, and only to destroy them in the last resort.

We are now everywhere close upon the works. To-day our artillery will be placed in position. We shall bring about ninety guns to bear upon the enemy. We shall replenish exhausted ammunition, bring up that which we need for the work before us, and prepare everything for the assault. At daylight to-morrow (27th), unless something unexpected occurs, I shall order the works to be carried by assault.

---

* Before General Smith had complied with this order, he was, by Special Orders, No. 268, War Department, Adjutant-General's Office, June 17, 1863, directed to report to General Couch, commanding Department of the Susquehanna, for temporary duty.

Please let the mortars destroy the enemy's rest at night. I will try to communicate with you and Commodore Palmer frequently by signals.

I have the honor to be, very respectfully, your obedient servant,

N. P. BANKS,
Major-General, Commanding.

HDQRS. DEPT. OF THE GULF, NINETEENTH ARMY CORPS,
Riley's, before Port Hudson, May 26, 1863—Midnight.

Admiral D. G. FARRAGUT,
Commanding, &c., Flag-ship Monongahela:

SIR: I have ordered the light artillery to open fire on the enemy's works at daybreak to-morrow morning, and the heavy batteries concentrated on the left center to open at 6 a. m.

The division commanders will dispose their infantry so as to seize any advantage and to carry the works at the earliest moment. They will be taken during the day.

Your fire should cease as soon as you observe our artillery cease its fire, which will probably be about 10 o'clock, though the time is of course dependent on circumstances.

I have the honor to request that you will communicate the contents of this by signals to Commodore Palmer.

Very respectfully, your obedient servant,

N. P. BANKS,
Major-General, Commanding.

(Same to Commodore Palmer, commanding, &c., flag-ship Hartford.)

FLAG-SHIP MONONGAHELA,
Below Port Hudson, May 26, 1863.

Major-General BANKS,
Commanding Department of the Gulf:

DEAR GENERAL: Your dispatch of this morning is duly received. I am glad to find that all is going on as well as you desire. I shall continue to harass the enemy occasionally day and night. He was pretty well exercised last night, both by the Hartford and the mortars. I am trying to get the range on the upper battery now. We have moved the mortar-boats up half a mile nearer, and the ships will be ready to open the moment you give us notice, or we judge you to be making the grand artillery attack. It seems to me that you have only to make the assault and they must fall. We will aid you all we can, but I am so anxious about the troops that I fear I will not do as much as I might if I knew exactly where they were; but I will not hurt your men, as that is my whole study.

The enemy have not replied to our fire this morning. I am glad your officer did not burn the steamers; they can be brought out easily at any time.

I shall be on the watch to aid you whenever I can, and with my sincere wishes for your success, I remain, very truly, yours,

D. G. FARRAGUT,
Rear-Admiral.

HEADQUARTERS,
Port Hudson, La., May 26, 1863.
Commanding Officer U. S. Forces, near Port Hudson, La.:

SIR: I have some United States prisoners of war within my line of fortifications that I am willing to release on parole if you will authorize them to give their parole and receive them. I will send them on the road leading to the Plains Store to-night, at 10 o'clock, if it meets with your approval.

I find myself constrained to mention that some of your troops have violated the rights of the flag of truce in making use of it to pick up killed and wounded in front of the breastworks. I request that orders be given to prevent the like occurring again, or otherwise I will be compelled to fire upon the flag used for such purposes.

I am, sir, very respectfully, your obedient servant,
FRANK. GARDNER,
Major-General, Commanding C. S. Forces.

CIRCULAR.]   HDQRS. DEPT. OF THE GULF, 19TH A. C.,
Riley's, before Port Hudson, May 26, 1863.
Brigadier-General SHERMAN:

SIR: The commanding general directs that no flags of truce be sent to the enemy without orders from these headquarters, and that in all cases the flag shall not be used to cover anything except the special object for which it is sent.

General Gardner complains that some of our men have used a flag, sent for a different purpose, to cover the burial of the dead in front of the enemy's breastworks.

Very respectfully, your obedient servant,
RICH'D B. IRWIN,
Assistant Adjutant-General.

(Copies sent to Major-General Augur and Brigadier-Generals Weitzel and Grover.)

SPECIAL ORDERS, } HDQRS. DEPT. OF THE GULF, 19TH A. C.,
No. 123.   }   *Riley's, before Port Hudson, May 26, 1863.*

*   *   *   *   *   *

II. Arrangements for to-morrow, May 27, 1863:

1. General Grover will order a battery, preferably of Napoleon guns, to report to General Sherman to-night.

2. Brigadier-General Arnold, chief of artillery, will take charge of all heavy artillery not now assigned to divisions or brigades. The light artillery as assigned to divisions by existing orders (including this order) will be under the direction of the respective division commanders, to be used according to circumstances.

III. Generals Augur and Sherman will open fire with their artillery upon the enemy's works at daybreak. They will dispose their troops so as to annoy the enemy as much as possible during the cannonade, by advancing skirmishers to kill the enemy's cannoneers and to cover the advance of the assaulting column. They will place their troops in position to take instant advantage of any favorable opportunity, and will, if possible, force the enemy's works at the earliest moment.

IV. General Augur will cause the heavy artillery under him to be supported by one regiment of infantry. General Sherman will see that all the artillery in his front is properly supported.

V. General Weitzel will, according to verbal directions already given him, take advantage of the attacks on other parts of the line to endeavor to force his way into the enemy's works on our right.

VI. General Grover will hold himself in readiness to re-enforce within the right or left, if necessary, or to force his own way into the enemy's works. He will also protect the right flank of the heavy artillery, should it become necessary.

VII. Generals Augur, Sherman, Grover, and Weitzel will constantly keep up their connection with the commands next them, so as to afford mutual aid and avoid mistakes.

VIII. The fire of the heavy artillery will be opened by General Arnold at as early an hour as practicable, say at 6 a. m.

IX. Commanders of divisions will provide the necessary means for passing the ditch on their respective points of attack.

X. All the operations herein directed must commence at the earliest hour practicable.

XI. Port Hudson must be taken to-morrow.

By command of Major-General Banks:
[RICH'D B. IRWIN,]
Assistant Adjutant-General.

FLAG-SHIP MONONGAHELA,
Below Port Hudson, May 27, 1863.

Maj. Gen. N. P. BANKS,
Comdg. Department of the Gulf, before Port Hudson:

DEAR GENERAL: I heard your firing last evening, and fear you have sustained some losses, but feel assured that the enemy must have suffered much more. Trust that you will be able to carry out your designs of to-day with ease. · I wish it was in my power to aid you more, but I kept up a heavy fire on them during the night, and will open upon them again with you and cease with your artillery. Such have been my orders heretofore.

Wishing you all success, I remain, truly yours,
D. G. FARRAGUT,
Rear-Admiral.

May 27, [1863]—10.40 a. m.
General WEITZEL:

Grover will re-enforce you with his whole force, excepting one regiment (1,300 men). Augur and Sherman will attack at once.
N. P. BANKS,
Major-General, Commanding.

MAY 27, [1863]—1.45 p. m.
General WEITZEL:

General Sherman has failed utterly and criminally to bring his men into the field. At 12 m. I found him at dinner, his staff officers all with their horses unsaddled, and none knowing where to find their command. I have placed General Andrews in command, and hope every moment to learn that he is ready to advance with Augur, who waits for him. Together they have 5,000 men. I should have sent Augur to you, but thought that Andrews could join sooner than he could reach you. We hear you are supporting your position successfully, and hope it is so. I shall forward another messenger the moment I hear from Andrews.

N. P. BANKS,
Major-General, Commanding.

————

MAY 27, [1863]—2.15 p. m.

General WEITZEL:

Augur's and Sherman's columns are now (2.15 p. m.) moving on the enemy's works, prepared to make the assault, and say they will cut their way through.

N. P. BANKS,
Major-General, Commanding.

————

MAY 27, [1863]—4.30 [p. m.].

General WEITZEL:

Augur's troops are all close up to the enemy's works, but cannot go in because the force behind is too heavy. General Andrews sends word this moment from Sherman's division that General Sherman and General Dow were wounded and carried off the field; that Dow's brigade was repulsed and had fallen back to this morning's position; that General Nickerson, it was said, had got one of his regiments in, and that he (General Andrews) would reform Dow's brigade and renew the attack.

Just before this (4 p. m.) General Banks ordered General Sherman to carry the works at all hazards. Loss very heavy.

By command of Major-General Banks:

RICH'D B. IRWIN,
Assistant Adjutant-General.

————

BEFORE PORT HUDSON,
May 27, 1863—7 p. m.

Col. S. B. HOLABIRD,
Chief Quartermaster:

We attacked the enemy to-day, and, having kept up a heavy artillery fire upon him all day, assaulted the works early in the afternoon. Sherman's division, on the left, was repulsed; Dow's brigade in some disorder, but holds, in tolerable strength, a position close to the works.

General Augur's men reached the ditch, but the fire of grape and musketry was too strong for them, and they did not get in. They are now close up to the works, and keep down the fire of the enemy's artillery by skirmishers.

A storming party from General Grover reached and retain a position against the parapet.

General Weitzel, commanding the right wing, including your division, and his own and Dwight's brigades, carried the heights before him; holds a position close to the works, and thinks he can go in to-night or in the morning.

The loss is very heavy. Generals Sherman and Dow are wounded. Colonels Chapin, Rodman, and Cowles killed; Colonels Holcomb, Bartlett, and Abel Smith wounded. It is thought that General Sherman's wound will prove mortal.

Send transportation to the point for Benedict's command, and communicate to Colonel Benedict the commanding general's order that he report to General Weitzel on the right at the earliest possible moment.

Clear out from Bayou Sara everything that we do not absolutely need there.

Very respectfully, your obedient servant,

[RICH'D B. IRWIN,]
Assistant Adjutant-General.

HEADQUARTERS DEPARTMENT OF THE GULF,
Before Port Hudson, May 28, 1863.

Admiral D. G. FARRAGUT:

DEAR SIR: I have received your several letters. We made a general attack upon the works yesterday, at 2.15 o'clock, advancing up to the breastworks on all sides, and many of our men were upon the parapets; but the enemy was too strong in numbers and the works too formidable to admit our full success, and we hold this position at this time: On the right, the opposing forces are separated only by a few feet, and no man on either side can show himself without being shot. On the left, the main force has fallen back, but the position is held by skirmishers as yesterday. We shall hold on to-day, and make careful examinations with reference to future operations. It is the strongest position there is in the United States, and the enemy is in stronger force than we have supposed. I can increase my force some 5,000 in three days, and it is not impossible that Grant may send us assistance. We may reasonably expect it, if he is fortunate. Our men fought with the utmost possible bravery, but I regret to say our losses have been very severe, indeed. A large number of officers have been killed and wounded. I have asked for a suspension of hostilities until 2 o'clock, that the dead and wounded may be brought in. They are within our lines, but cannot be removed without being fired upon, as they are mainly in the immediate vicinity of the fortifications.

I have the honor to be, admiral, very respectfully, your obedient servant,

N. P. BANKS,
Major-General, Commanding.

HDQRS. DEPT. OF THE GULF, NINETEENTH ARMY CORPS,
Before Port Hudson, May 28, 1863.

Admiral D. G. FARRAGUT:

DEAR SIR: We mean to harass the enemy night and day, and to give him no rest. I desire to establish a system of signals with you night and day, by which we can make instant communication. This can be done by means of rockets at night and with a signal flag, which, I think, we can accomplish in the day. I shall want you to shell the town at night unceasingly. I think if you can get the range of the center of the town, and then drop the shells on the right and left, front and rear, for the space of half a mile from the town, that it will harass the enemy without injury to us. A trial of the experiment can be made, so that

you can have immediate notice of its effect, and may extend your operations in the direction where it may be possible without injury. I will
communicate to-day upon the subject of signals. An examination of
the works when we reached them show them to be very formidable, and
the country in which they are placed is a perfect labyrinth. One is
unable to comprehend the lay of the land even after having traveled
through it. Ravines, woods, and obstructions of every sort disconcert
the movement of troops and break up the lines. A portion of these difficulties will disappear as we get acquainted with the ground, but at first
encounter they are very formidable. I want you to send to me 500 hand-
grenades. Let them be accompanied, if you please, by an officer who
can explain to our men their proper management. I desire, if possible,
that some means may be devised by which the steamers may be brought
out of Thompson's Creek. If you can suggest anything upon this subject I should like it. I did not receive your letter of the 20th until last
night, but most of the suggestions contained therein had been complied
with.

I have the honor to be, admiral, very respectfully, your obedient
servant

N. P. BANKS,
Major-General, Commanding.

FLAG-SHIP MONONGAHELA,
Port Hudson, May 28, 1863—11.30 a. m.

[Major-General BANKS:]

DEAR GENERAL: Your two dispatches, by Captain [Charles A.]
Hartwell, have this moment been received, and I am delighted to find
that you maintain so good a position. I thought Weitzel had been
driven back by the heavy bombardment in the night. I can but think
that one of the best points of approach is on the water front. Captain
Hoffman came down here opposite the Essex day before yesterday, and
knows the way. It is not over 1½ miles to the citadel, where they commenced fire on us this morning; we drove them out of it.

If you would come down abreast the Essex, and march up under the
support of her and other vessels of the fleet, it seems to me that we
could put you within the lines. The only thing I don't understand is
the exact character of the land along the shore ; your engineer officers
must look at it.

We have no hand-grenades ; they are not in use in the navy ; why, I
cannot tell, for we esteemed them highly during the war of 1812, and
I still think highly of them.

If you can furnish pilots and engineers, the steamers can come out
of Thompson's Creek at any time, and run up to the Hartford. As to
the enemy's forces, we had a runaway yesterday who said there were
between 4,000 and 5,000. They must work them very severely day and
night, but they work on a small radius and back and forth. You must
overcome them by a little perseverance. I will shell them, but I do not
believe it does much good, as they are not where we can throw our shell.
They go back to the line at night, but we will shell them any time they
show themselves and at night also. They have been very lavish of
their ammunition yesterday and to-day; the deserter said they had not
much of it on hand.

Wishing you every success. I remain truly yours,

D. G. FARRAGUT,
Rear-Admiral.

HEADQUARTERS UNITED STATES FORCES,
Before Port Hudson, May 28, 1863—6 a. m.

Maj. Gen. FRANK. GARDNER,
' *Commanding C. S. Forces at Port Hudson:*

GENERAL : I have the honor to request that there may be a suspension of hostilities until 2 o'clock this afternoon, in order that the dead and wounded may be brought off the field.

I have the honor to be, general, very respectfully, your most obedient servant,

N. P. BANKS,
Major-General, Commanding.

———

HEADQUARTERS,
Port Hudson, La., May 28, 1863—7.30 a. m.

Maj. Gen. N. P. BANKS,
Commanding U. S. Forces near Port Hudson:

GENERAL : I will consent to a suspension of hostilities until 2 p. m. for the purpose of allowing you to send to pick up your killed and wounded, provided you withdraw your entire force to a distance of not less than 800 yards from my lines, and send in only unarmed parties for that purpose. I cannot consent to a suspension of hostilities as long as your sharpshooters occupy such a near proximity.

I shall expect you to indicate to me your decision on this matter, and immediately give the necessary orders; also that the fleet withdraw to its original position.

I am, general, very respectfully, your obedient servant,

FRANK. GARDNER,
Major-General, Commanding C. S. Forces.

———

HDQRS. DEPT. OF THE GULF, NINETEENTH ARMY CORPS,
Before Port Hudson, May 28, 1863—8.30 a. m.

Maj. Gen. FRANK. GARDNER,
Commanding C. S. Forces at Port Hudson, La.:

GENERAL : Your note, dated at 7.30 a. m., is this moment received. The wounded men to whom my letter refers are on our left, upon the ground, as I understand, occupied by my men. The favor I solicit is that hostilities may be suspended until these wounded men can be withdrawn. I desire to take no advantage of such suspension of hostilities, except that of providing for suffering men. I cannot comply with your request to withdraw my entire force to a distance of not less than 800 yards from your lines. I should cheerfully consent to the condition that unarmed parties only should be charged with the duty of removing the dead and wounded. It is unnecessary for me to refer to your suggestion in regard to the fleet, as I am compelled to decline compliance with a similar request in regard to the forces wholly under my own command.

I have the honor to renew my request for a general suspension of hostilities, until such an hour as you shall name, for the purpose of withdrawing wounded men from this portion of the line, consenting to

your suggestion as to the parties who will be charged with the execution of this duty.

I am, general, with much respect, your most obedient servant,
                                        N. P. BANKS,
                              Major-General, Commanding

                                        HEADQUARTERS,
                              Port Hudson, La., May 28, 1863.
Maj. Gen. N. P. BANKS,
     Commanding U. S. Forces near Port Hudson:

Your note, dated at 8.30, has just been received. As a matter of
humanity, I will comply with your request to permit unarmed parties
to pick up the killed and wounded, if you will give orders that your
skirmishers shall not make any advance toward my breastworks. I am
compelled to make this request or condition, because your entire line
moved somewhat forward yesterday afternoon under white flags displayed, and it is also reported to me that a column of infantry was
seen moving forward at the same time.

The fleet is still firing, and your skirmishers on my left also. I must
request that hostilities shall entirely cease to carry out the object you
desire.

I will fix the time until 2 o'clock this afternoon, which can be further
extended at that time, if desired. I also have to request that I may be
permitted to send unarmed parties into the woods on my left, to pick up
such of the killed as may not have been buried, and such wounded as
may not have been previously picked up.

I am, general, very respectfully, your obedient servant,
                                        FRANK. GARDNER,
                              Major-General, Commanding C. S. Forces.

HDQRS. DEPT. OF THE GULF, NINETEENTH ARMY CORPS,
              Before Port Hudson, May 28, 1863—10 a. m.
Maj. Gen. FRANK. GARDNER,
     Commanding C. S. Forces at Port Hudson, La.:

GENERAL: I have received your note in reply to my communication
of 8.30 this morning. I inadvertently stated in my note that the dead
and wounded referred to were only on the left. I have been informed
that there are also some dead and wounded on my right. I accept the
conditions you propose, which is that unarmed parties will be permitted
to pick up the killed and wounded, and that my skirmishers shall not
make any advance toward your breastworks, and that the firing shall
cease.

I transmit to you a note to Admiral Farragut, with the request that
it may be forwarded to him from your position, notifying him of the
fact that I have consented to a suspension of hostilities, and requesting
him to suspend firing until the time appointed.

I have given orders to suspend firing from this moment, and I am
confident the men of my command will not continue it. If fired upon,
they are instructed to report the fact to these headquarters. I have
also given orders that no flag of truce shall be used without authority
from these headquarters. If any incident like that which you refer to

has occurred, it is through misunderstanding on the part of those who have used the flag, and will not be permitted.

You will be allowed, in accordance with your request, " to send unarmed parties into the woods on your left, to pick up such of the killed as may not have been buried, and such of the wounded as may not have been previously picked up." Notice of this has been sent to the commander of the troops on my right. It is my desire to take no advantage of any arrangements which may be consented to on your part tending to mitigate the horrors of war.

I am, general, with much respect, your most obedient servant,

N. P. BANKS,
Major-General, Commanding.

P. S.—I have ascertained that a white flag was in fact improperly used on my right yesterday. It was displayed by an inexperienced officer, without the knowledge of his commanders, and the flag which you displayed in acknowledgment gave them the first information of its existence. I need hardly say that I regret the circumstance exceedingly, as I have taken great pains to enforce the observance of the usages of war in regard to such flags within my command.

CIRCULAR.]   HDQRS. DEPT. OF THE GULF, 19TH ARMY CORPS,
Before Port Hudson, May 28, 1863.

· There will be a suspension of hostilities until 2 o'clock, and the time may be further extended by agreement, for the purpose of collecting the killed and wounded. This is to be done by unarmed parties, and no advance toward the breastworks is to be made by our skirmishers.

General Gardner has permission to send unarmed parties to our exterior lines, to receive his killed and wounded on our right, in the woods. General Grover will give orders to have a thorough search made of the woods on the right, and all the enemy's dead yet unburied, and all his wounded who have not been sent to the rear, to be delivered to these parties at our exterior lines.

By command of Major-General Banks:

RICH'D B. IRWIN,
Assistant Adjutant-General.

HEADQUARTERS,
Port Hudson, La., May 28, 1863.

Maj. Gen. N. P. BANKS,
Commanding U. S. Forces near Port Hudson:

GENERAL: I am informed that your troops are erecting a battery within easy range on my left. As this work could be materially interfered with if I should open on them, I consider it a violation of the truce.

I respectfully return your communication to Admiral Farragut, which the short time before 2 o'clock will not allow sufficient time for my boat to return.

I am, general, very respectfully, your obedient servant,

FRANK. GARDNER,
Major-General, Commanding C. S. Forces.

HDQRS. DEPT. OF THE GULF, NINETEENTH ARMY CORPS,
Before Port Hudson, May 28, 1863—1.10 p. m.
Maj. Gen. FRANK. GARDNER,
Commanding C. S. Forces at Port Hudson:

GENERAL: It was my intention, in proposing a suspension of hostilities for the purpose of relieving the wounded, to cease all offensive operations, and I have given orders to this effect, wherever and whenever any violation of this duty has been made known to me. I shall still do so until your answer to my last communication is received.

I have sent a staff officer to my left to ascertain if work is being done of the character you describe; and, if so, to suspend it.

Several complaints of infringements of the well-understood rights of the parties during a negotiation of this character, by your command, have been made to me, but I have considered them, if correctly stated, to have been unauthorized, and have forbidden my men to return them in kind. The duty of relieving wounded men from unnecessary suffering is a mutual one, all the obligations of which I shall fulfill with pleasure, and I think a common humanity requires that all incidental considerations should be held subordinate to this. To transfer wounded or dead men to the party to which they may belong, seems to me the best and least objectionable course that can be adopted. I will respectfully request an answer to this proposition.

I am, general, respectfully, yours, &c.,
N. P. BANKS,
Major-General, Commanding.

———

HEADQUARTERS, *Port Hudson, May 28, 1863—3 p. m.*
Major-General BANKS,
Commanding U S Forces near Port Hudson:

GENERAL: Your communication of 1 o'clock has just been handed me. I fully appreciate your motives in the care of the wounded, and I am willing to extend every proper facility for that purpose.

You apparently had not received my reply concerning sending your wounded within your lines. I have not ambulances sufficient for that purpose, and therefore wrote to you that I would willingly consent to extend the truce to allow you the opportunity to send for your wounded, and I now consider the truce as existing for the four additional hours you proposed, which will extend it to 6 p. m. If that is not sufficient, I request you to name a particular hour at which you wish to discontinue it.

I have also ordered that nothing shall be done that could be considered a violation of the truce, and I hope to be able to prevent any occurrence that could be so construed.

I am, general, very respectfully, your obedient servant,
FRANK. GARDNER,
Major-General, Commanding C. S. Forces.

———

HDQRS. DEPT. OF THE GULF, NINETEENTH ARMY CORPS,
Before Port Hudson, May 28, 1863—3 p. m.
Maj. Gen. FRANK. GARDNER,
Commanding C. S. Forces at Port Hudson:

GENERAL: Your communication of 1 o'clock is received. I regret that I misunderstood its purport. I will give directions immediately to forward all the dead and wounded of your command that are within my lines or in my front to your lines, and I will avail myself of your permission to send out unarmed men to pick up the killed and wounded of my command that are in the front of your lines. I will use every endeavor to restrain all persons from any improper advantage given by this arrangement.

If you please, I will ask that the time may run four hours from 3 o'clock, and issue my orders accordingly.

. Accept my thanks for your courtesy.

I am, general, very respectfully, your obedient servant,
N. P. BANKS,
Major-General, Commanding.

HEADQUARTERS,
Port Hudson, La., May 28, 1863—3.50 p. m.

Maj. Gen. N. P. BANKS,
Commanding U. S. Forces near Port Hudson:

GENERAL: I am just in receipt of your communication of 3 o'clock, and in reply I have to state that I will cheerfully extend the time of the truce, "that the time may run four hours from 3 o'clock," as you propose, and your litter and ambulance parties, unarmed, will be permitted to approach to pick up your killed and wounded. This fixes the time at 7 p. m.

My own killed and wounded outside of my lines were mostly on my left, to the distance of about three-quarters of a mile. If you can conveniently send them in, I will feel under obligations. I will send a party, to meet them, to your lines in that direction.

I am, general, very respectfully, your obedient servant,
FRANK. GARDNER,
Major-General, Commanding C. S. Forces.

HDQRS. DEPT. OF THE GULF, NINETEENTH ARMY CORPS,
Before Port Hudson, May 28, 1863.

Maj. Gen. FRANK. GARDNER,
Commanding C. S. Forces at Port Hudson:

GENERAL: Having received your communication withdrawing your consent to the suspension of hostilities, I respectfully withdraw my request.

In order to avoid all difficulties presented on this subject, I will agree to send all the killed and wounded of your command that are within my lines or on my front to your lines, by unarmed parties, if you will consent to send the killed and wounded of my command within your lines or on your front to my exterior lines, by unarmed parties.

And for this purpose I will agree that hostilities be suspended for four hours.

I have the honor to be, general, very respectfully, your most obedient servant,

N. P. BANKS,
Major-General, Commanding.

HEADQUARTERS SECOND DIVISION,
In the Field, near Port Hudson, May 28, 1863.
Col. RICHARD B. IRWIN,
   Asst. Adjt. Gen., Headquarters Department of the Gulf:

COLONEL: I have been informed this morning by a member of General Banks' staff that, pending the negotiations for cessation of hostilities, all firing on our part should cease. I have given orders to this effect. The enemy, however, are at work repairing damages sustained yesterday on their works in our front. Otherwise all is quiet.

Please inform me at the earliest moment of the conditions in relation to the truce; also any other matters to enable me to act more understandingly.

Very respectfully, your obedient servant,
F. S. NICKERSON,
Brigadier-General, Commanding Second Division.

CIRCULAR.] HDQRS. DEPT. OF THE GULF, 19TH ARMY CORPS,
Before Port Hudson, May 28, 1863—3.30 p. m.

A suspension of hostilities until 7 p. m. is just agreed on.
The conditions are:
1. Total suspension of hostilities.
2. We are to send the enemy's killed, who have not been buried, and his wounded not picked up and sent to the rear, to the enemy's lines, by unarmed parties.
3. We are to send unarmed parties to pick up our own killed and wounded before the works.
4. Our skirmishers are not to advance during the armistice.
These conditions will be strictly observed.
By command of Major-General Banks:
RICH'D B. IRWIN,
Assistant Adjutant-General.

U. S. FLAG-SHIP MONONGAHELA,
May 28, 1863.
Maj. Gen. N. P. BANKS:

DEAR GENERAL: I deeply sympathize with you in your losses and failures to carry the works of the enemy. I know nothing of the arrangements of their works, and consequently have no judgment in the case. When I saw General Weitzel open his batteries on the extreme right, I thought we were all right; but when the forts silenced his fire, I feared again that all was lost, and that he had retired.

In their exultation this morning, they opened upon us; we returned their fire, and continued to shell them until we silenced their guns. I now feel anxious to know what will be your next move in the case, so as to know how to co-operate with you.

I sent General Sherman and some of the wounded down to New Orleans last night in our tug, and have this morning sent three medical officers down to Springfield Landing to assist your surgeons, and I only desire to know in what other way I may assist you.

When you have made up your mind as to your next move, please let me know, that I may govern myself accordingly.

In the meantime, I remain, very sincerely, yours,
D. G. FARRAGUT,
Rear-Admiral.

HEADQUARTERS U. S. FORCES,
Trudeau's Landing, May 28, 1863—3.30 p. m.

Brigadier-General ANDREWS,
Chief of Staff, Nineteenth Army Corps:

GENERAL: A report reached me this morning that a force of 500 cavalry, which followed Weitzel's march from Alexandria, was advancing on to this place, and had reached Morganza last evening. I this morning sent out a cavalry squad above Waterloo to gain information, which has not yet returned. About an hour since, Lieutenant Harney, of the cavalry, reported to me that he learned from Mr. Hobdell (who has General Augur's permission to trade in cotton, and is a New Yorker by birth and residence until a few years since), that it was currently reported that Kirby Smith was advancing toward Port Hudson with a large force of infantry and cavalry. Several negroes have reported that they were on their route to Bayou Sara last evening with some forty wagons, when they were attacked by some 15 to 20 cavalry (men on horseback, armed), and they fled, and supposed the cavalry had taken the balance of the negroes.

Under these circumstances (though not crediting the report fully, and deeming it to be compounded of rebel hope, loyal apprehension, and a mixture of guerrilla), I have considered it my duty to withdraw half of my picket force on the levee opposite Port Hudson, and post them in my rear, to advise Commodore Palmer of the case, and to dispatch you this note.

As we have no forces in the rear, it may be that the rebels have acquired confidence on learning that our whole army is before Port Hudson. I shall attempt to hold this position against any force. By retreating to the river, I can secure the aid of the Hartford and the Albatross.

I am, very respectfully,

LEW. BENEDICT,
Colonel, Commanding.

HEADQUARTERS DEFENSES OF NEW ORLEANS,
May 28, 1863—9.15 p. m.

Lieutenant-Colonel IRWIN,
Asst. Adjt. Gen., General Banks' Headquarters:

The following-named troops are about to leave here for Springfield [Landing], in the steamer Fulton: Twenty-second Maine, Twenty-sixth Maine, Fifty-second Massachusetts (four companies detached), and a number of stragglers.

The Cahawba will carry the balance of the troops intended for that point to-morrow morning when they get up from Brashear City.

W. H. EMORY,
Brigadier-General, Commanding.

HDQRS. DEPT. OF THE GULF, NINETEENTH ARMY CORPS,
Before Port Hudson, La., May 28, 1863.

Major-General GRANT,
Commanding U. S. Army at Jackson, Miss.:

GENERAL: Upon the receipt of the report of General Dwight, who visited you recently, my command moved from Simsport for Port

Hudson, landing at Bayou Sara at 2 o'clock on the morning of the 22d. We reached Newport on the 23d, and moved upon Port Hudson.

Several combats were had with the enemy, in which we were success- ful. Outside of his intrenchments he has no power, and yesterday we made a combined assault upon his works. They are more formidable than have been represented, and his force stronger. The fight was very bitter and our losses severe. The enemy's losses are large, but not in comparison with ours. On either side we pushed our troops close to the line of his fortifications, and on the right our forces occupied the opposite faces of the same parapet with the enemy. But we have not strength enough yet to carry their works. There are 5,000 troops that I can bring to my support in three days. It is necessary that the enemy should be prevented from re-enforcing the garrison. I hope that he will be so occupied as to make it impossible for him to do so. Next to that it is essential that you should assist us if you can. We have ammunition, provisions, artillery, and cavalry, and want nothing but the men. We shall be grateful for any aid, however slight. Our solicitude for your safety is tempered with the strongest hopes that your good fortune and signal ability will establish the perfect success of all your plans.

The garrison of the enemy is 5,000 or 6,000 men. The works are what would ordinarily be styled "impregnable." They are surrounded by ra- vines, woods, valleys, and bayous of the most intricate and labyrinthic character, that make the works themselves almost inaccessible.. It re- quires time even to understand the geography of the position. They fight with determination, and our men, after a march of some 500 or 600 miles, have done all that could be expected or required of any similar force. I send this by an officer of my staff, and hope that information may be received from you without delay.

I have the honor to be, general, very respectfully, your obedient servant,

N. P. BANKS,'
Major-General, Commanding.

P. S.—With the gunboat that takes this communication to you, I send back the steamers Forest Queen and Moderator, that you sent for the transportation of my troops. If it be possible, I beg you to send to me at least one brigade of 4,000 or 5,000 men. This will be of vital importance to us. We may have to abandon these operations without it.

[MAY 29, 1863.—For Banks to Grant, in relation to affairs at Port Hudson, see Series I, Vol. XXIV, Part III, pp. 359, 360.]

FLAG-SHIP MONONGAHELA,
May 29, 1863—10.30 p. m.

Major-General BANKS,
Commanding Department of the Gulf, before Port Hudson:

DEAR GENERAL: Lieutenant Harcourt delivered your dispatch at this moment; hence you see it was too late for any of the purposes of which you speak, except the firing during the night, which we commence every night from 10 to 12, and shell all night. We shelled all the after- noon, but we cannot reach beyond the second battery. They cut up the mortar-boats and the Essex yesterday or last night, so that they had to drop down half a mile. Lieutenant Harcourt informs me that a gunboat cannot get into Thompson's Creek, nor can the Hartford shell the batteries without great exposure and risk of getting on shore.

Mr. Harcourt will show us the signal station in the morning, as well as the other points.

I have written to Porter for some hand-grenades, as I understand he has plenty in his fleet.

Very truly, yours,

D. G. FARRAGUT,
Rear-Admiral.

HDQRS. DEPT. OF THE GULF, NINETEENTH ARMY CORPS,
Before Port Hudson, May 29, 1863.

Admiral D. G. FARRAGUT:

DEAR SIR: We have a battery of four Dahlgren guns, for which I am providing platforms. I should be glad if you could detail, without detriment to your service, a sufficient number of marines to strongly man these guns with expert men. It will render us a material service.

Everything looks well for us. The rebels attempted a sortie upon our right last evening upon the cessation of the armistice, but were smartly and quickly repulsed. You must have heard the firing; but 4 of our men were wounded.

I have the honor to be, very respectfully, your obedient servant,

N. P. BANKS,
Major-General, Commanding.

HDQRS. DEPT. OF THE GULF, NINETEENTH ARMY CORPS,
Before Port Hudson, May 29, 1863—10 p. m.

Rear-Admiral D. G. FARRAGUT, U. S. Navy,
Commanding, &c., Flag-ship Monongahela:

ADMIRAL: Our general position is unchanged to-day. The enemy took advantage of the armistice yesterday to move the commissary stores from the store-house on our right, which was under our fire, and to mass new guns against us in that quarter. He is evidently very tender there. I wish you would continue to harass him; at night especially. We will keep him attentive during the day and occasionally at night also.

We are endeavoring to complete the telegraph line to Springfield Landing, and hope by to-morrow night to be in immediate communication with you by telegraph and signals. We can then inform you from time to time of the effect of your fire and measurably direct it.

Very respectfully, your obedient servant,

N. P. BANKS,
Major-General, Commanding.

HDQRS. DEPT. OF THE GULF, NINETEENTH ARMY CORPS,
Before Port Hudson, May 29, 1863—9 a. m.

Col. L. BENEDICT,
Commanding U. S. Forces opposite Port Hudson:

COLONEL: I am directed by the commanding general to acknowledge the receipt of your dispatch of yesterday. The commanding general approves your dispositions. It is not credited here that Kirby Smith is advancing with any large force. Still, you should be on your guard against surprise. The enemy may very possibly have crossed some cavalry over the Atchafalaya River.

A general assault upon the works here was made on the 27th instant. Our men fought bravely, drove the enemy into their works, and reached the parapet, close to which some of our sharpshooters now are, preventing the enemy from using his guns. But they were unable to pass the parapet under the severe fire of the enemy. Our loss is considerable, though much less so than was at first apprehended. We have lost several valuable officers. General Sherman is severely wounded. We still hold our position close to the enemy's works, and are making new preparations for a still more powerful attack.

We shall probably have to call upon you for assistance, and you will be in readiness to move to this place if ordered to do so.

I am, colonel, very respectfully, your obedient servant,

CHAS. P. STONE,
Brigadier-General of Volunteers, and Chief of Staff.

HDQRS. DEPT. OF THE GULF, NINETEENTH ARMY CORPS,
Before Port Hudson, May 29, 1863—9 a. m.

Commodore JAMES S. PALMER,
Commanding Fleet above Port Hudson:

COMMODORE: By direction of the commanding general, I have the honor to communicate to you the following:

A dispatch was received last evening from Col. L. Benedict, commanding United States forces on the point opposite Port Hudson, in which it states that it is reported that Kirby Smith is advancing with considerable force. This is not credited here, but it is very possible that a force of cavalry may have been sent across the Atchafalaya by the enemy. The gunboats, of course, prevent their crossing at Simsport. Colonel Benedict has been directed to guard against surprise, and will have, in any event, a safe retreat under the protection of your fleet. A general assault of the enemy's works here was made last Wednesday (27th instant). Our men behaved most gallantly, drove the enemy into his works, and followed him close up to the parapet, where some of our sharpshooters still remain, picking off the enemy's gunners and preventing him from serving his guns. But we were unable to pass the parapet under the severe fire of the enemy. Our loss is considerable, as might have been expected, but much less than was at first apprehended. The enemy's loss must be heavy. We are collecting reenforcements, and making preparations for a new and more formidable attack. General Sherman was badly wounded in the leg by a shell. General Dow was slightly wounded. We have lost several valuable officers. General Grover again opened fire on the enemy last evening, which provoked a sortie on the part of the enemy, which was promptly and easily repulsed.

I am informed by Colonel Irwin that Lieutenant [Stephen M.] Eaton, the signal officer, has been sent to you. Colonel Holabird, chief quartermaster, has been directed to carry out your wishes respecting the two schooners which brought coal for the fleet. I trust this has all been done to your satisfaction.

I am, commodore, very respectfully, your obedient servant,

[CHAS. P. STONE,]
Brigadier-General of Volunteers, and Chief of Staff.

HEADQUARTERS DEFENSES OF NEW ORLEANS,
May 29, 1863.

Lieut. Col. RICHARD B. IRWIN,
Port Hudson:

The Ninetieth New York, Fifty-second Massachusetts, and One hundred and fourteenth New York, three regiments, left here for Springfield Landing at 6 p. m., on steamer Cahawba.

W. H. EMORY,
Brigadier-General, Commanding.

HEADQUARTERS DEFENSES OF NEW ORLEANS,
May 30, 1863.

Lieutenant-Colonel IRWIN:

The Crescent City left at 6 p. m., with a detachment of the Thirteenth Connecticut and the Forty-first Massachusetts.

W. H. EMORY,
Brigadier-General, Commanding.

FLAG-SHIP MONONGAHELA,
Off Port Hudson, May 30, 1863.

Major-General BANKS,
Commanding Department of the Gulf:

DEAR GENERAL: I send you Lieutenant-Commander Terry, for the purpose of arranging the affair of the navy battery of 9-inch guns. Captain Alden very promptly said he would furnish the officers and men to work the guns. Lay the platforms with a slight inclination, so as to make it easy to run the battery and check the recoil. Separate the guns, so as not to expose too much to chance shot. Lieutenant-Commander Terry is an intelligent officer, and will do justice to the country and all concerned.

Respectfully and truly,

D. G. FARRAGUT,
Rear-Admiral.

HDQRS. DEPT. OF THE GULF, NINETEENTH ARMY CORPS,
Before Port Hudson, May 30, 1863.

Maj. Gen. D. HUNTER,
Commanding Department of the South:

GENERAL: I have just received your letter of the 2d instant, asking that the troops at Key West may be ordered to join you. In reply, I have the honor to state that these troops, though nominally a part of the Tenth Army Corps, actually formed the garrisons of Key West and the Tortugas. Those posts having been transferred to the Department of the Gulf, it is impossible, especially in view of the present exigencies of the service in this department, to relieve the garrisons.

I have the honor to be, general, very respectfully, your most obedient servant,

N. P. BANKS,
Major-General, Commanding.

HDQRS. DEPT. OF THE GULF, NINETEENTH ARMY CORPS,
Before Port Hudson, May 31, 1863.

Maj. Gen. H. W. HALLECK,
General-in-Chief, Washington, D. C.:

SIR: I beg to invite the special attention of the General-in-Chief and the War Department to the valuable services rendered to me by that excellent officer, Col. B. H. Grierson, Sixth Illinois Cavalry, and the Sixth and Seventh Regiments of Illinois Cavalry under his command, since, by the most brilliant expedition of the war, they joined the forces under my command.

The moral effect of that remarkable expedition upon a wavering and astonished enemy, and the assistance rendered us in breaking up the enemy's communications, in establishing our own, and in covering the concentration of our forces against this place, can hardly be overestimated.

Their timely presence has supplied a want which you will remember I have frequently represented was crippling all our operations.

I trust the services of Colonel Grierson and his command will receive at the hands of the Government that acknowledgment which they so eminently deserve.

I have the honor to be, general, very respectfully, your obedient servant,

N. P. BANKS,
Major-General, Commanding.

HDQRS. DEPT. OF THE GULF, NINETEENTH ARMY CORPS,
Before Port Hudson, May 31, 1863.

Brig. Gen. W. H. EMORY,
New Orleans:

The commanding general desires that General Ullmann will send forward to Port Hudson immediately all the colored troops which he has raised, whether armed or unarmed, and that he will report the number of each class and the regiments to which they belong. Request General Ullmann to press forward the organization of his troops, as they are much needed here.

Very respectfully, your obedient servant,

[RICH'D B. IRWIN,]
Assistant Adjutant-General.

FLAG-SHIP MONONGAHELA,
Port Hudson, May 31, 1863.

Maj. Gen. N. P. BANKS,
Comdg. Department of the Gulf, in front of Port Hudson:

DEAR GENERAL: We had 2 prisoners sent aboard to us, to be sent to headquarters for your examination, yesterday evening. The doctor appears to me to be a very suspicious character. I take him to be both a spy and an incendiary, torpedo-maker, or something of the kind. The soldier (officer) was no doubt on his way for re-enforcements, although it is strange that he should have crossed the river under the belief that we had no one on that side, when they have fired at our people there so frequently; but you will dispose of them according to your own judgment. I send the papers found on the doctor.

We had 3 deserters last night from Port Hudson. They gave a good account of things there; they say you destroyed a large amount of their commissary stores day before yesterday; that you killed a great many of their men in the fight, and kill some every day; that the hospitals are full of wounded; that they are on one-quarter of a pound of meat per day; they have a few beeves and some sheep; but, unless re-enforcements arrive, they cannot hold out three days longer; that they are worked all the time, and have no rest; they have no cavalry; it is cut off outside. The officers tell them that Johnston is coming to their aid, but if he does not come soon they will have to surrender; they have plenty of powder, but no shot; they dig up our shot whenever they can find them; they have some grape and canister, which they also make of everything. They say also that the mortar-boats kill some three or four every night.

The news from Grant is that he is mining the upper fort, and has the lower one. Warrenton is the base of operations; is pressing Pemberton in every quarter; has him in his inside works.

The enemy in their last sortie against you (as I learned from the deserters), which was for the purpose of *capturing your batteries* instead of *breaking through your lines*, suffered very heavy losses in *person* as well as in commissary stores.

Truly, yours,

D. G. FARRAGUT.
Rear-Admiral.

HDQRS. DEPT. OF THE GULF, NINETEENTH ARMY CORPS,.
Before Port Hudson, May 31, 1863.

Rear-Admiral D. G. FARRAGUT,
U. S. S. Richmond:

My DEAR SIR: Thanks for your note and the cheering report of the deserters. We are closing in upon the enemy, and will have him in a day or two. Can you spare to us the 32-pounder guns on board the mortar-boats, with men to man them? They will do us great service. General Grant's success is glorious.

Very truly, yours,

N. P. BANKS,
Major-General, Commanding.

NEAR VICKSBURG, MISS.,
May 31, 1863.

Maj. Gen. N. P. BANKS,
Commanding Department of the Gulf:

Your letters of the 28th and 29th instant, by Colonel Riggin, have just been received. While I regret the situation in which they left you, and clearly see the necessity of your being re-enforced in order to be successful, the circumstances by which I am surrounded will prevent my making any detachments at this time.

Concentration is essential to the success of the general campaign in the west; but Vicksburg is the vital point. Our situation is for the first time, during the entire western campaign, what it should be. We have, after great labor and extraordinary risk, secured a position which should not be jeopardized by any detachments whatever. On the contrary, I am now and shall continue to exert myself to the utmost to concentrate. The enemy clearly see the importance of dislodging me at all hazards. General Joe Johnston is now at Canton, organizing his forces and making his dispositions to attack me. His present strength is estimated at 40,000, and is known to be at least 20,000. The force he took from Jackson was 8,000; Loring's division, which has joined him since the battle of Champion's Hill, 3,000; General Gist, from South Carolina, 6,000; stragglers from Pemberton, 2,000; troops from Mobile, number not known. Besides this, Major-General Hurlbut writes me he is reliably informed that Bragg has detached three divisions from his army to report to Johnston. Pemberton has himself 18,000 effective men. I have ample means to defend my present position, and effect the reduction of Vicksburg within twenty days, if the relation of affairs which now obtains remains unchanged. But detach 10,000 men from my command, and I cannot answer for the result. With activity on the part of the enemy, and any increase of his present force, it becomes necessary for me to press my operations with all possible dispatch.

I need not describe the severity of the labor to which my command must necessarily be subjected in an operation of such magnitude as that in which it is now engaged. Weakened by the detachment of 10,000 men, or even half that number, with the circumstances entirely changed, I should be crippled beyond redemption. My arrangements for supplies are ample, and can be expanded to meet any exigency. All I want now is men.

U. S. GRANT,
Major-General.

Abstract from return of the Department of the Gulf (Nineteenth Army Corps), Maj. Gen. Nathaniel P. Banks, U. S. Army, commanding, for the month of May, 1863; headquarters, before Port Hudson, La.

Command.	Present for duty.		Aggregate present.	Aggregate present and absent.	Aggregate last return.	Pieces of artillery.	Remarks.
	Officers.	Men.					
Department staff	28	....	28	29	30	......	Port Hudson, La.
First Division (Augur):							
Staff	9	....	9	9	9	......	Port Hudson, La.
Infantry	222	4,365	5,724	6,769	6,769	......	Do.
First, Third, and Fourth Louisiana Native Guards.	70	2,022	2,252	2,338	2,338	......	Do.
Cavalry	27	468	549	816	816	......	Do.
Artillery	30	609	679	797	797	32	Do.
Total First Division	358	7,464	9,213	10,729	10,729	32	
Second Division (T. W. Sherman):							
Staff	7	....	9	9	9	......	Port Hudson, La.
Infantry	283	5,974	8,478	10,024	10,024	......	Do.
Artillery	6	201	256	429	429	16	Do.
Other troops in this command	62	2,622	3,143	3,419	3,419	......	New Orleans, La.
Total Second Division	358	8,797	11,886	13,881	13,881	16	
Third Division (Emory):							
Staff	10	....	10	10	10	......	Port Hudson, La.
Infantry	293	6,213	8,170	10,045	10,045	......	Do.
Artillery	4	106	124	136	136	18	Do.
Total Third Division	307	6,319	8,304	10,191	10,191	18	

Abstract from return of the Department of the Gulf, &c.—Continued.

Command.	Present for duty.		Aggregate present.	Aggregate present and absent.	Aggregate last return.	Pieces of artillery.	Remarks.
	Officers.	Men.					
Fourth Division (Grover):							
Staff	5	....	5	5	5	......	Port Hudson, La.
Infantry	235	4,731	5,511	9,387	9,387	......	Do.
Artillery	9	322	352	418	406	18	Do.
Total Fourth Division	249	5,053	5,868	9,810	9,798	18	
Second Brigade, First Division (Weitzel):							
Staff	10	....	·10	10	10	......	Port Hudson, La.
Infantry	157	4,014	4,933	5,721	5,721	......	Do.
Cavalry	6	229	266	297	297	......	Do.
Artillery	7	272	301	371	371	18	Do.
Total Second Brigade First Division.	180	4,515	5,510	6,399	6,399	18	
District of Pensacola (Holbrook)	80	1,437	1,872	1,945	1,945	12	
Ship Island, Miss. (Daniels)	22	502	637	679	679	......	
Key West and Tortugas (Woodbury).	......	....	1,512	1,565	1,565	......	
Grand total	1,582	34,087	44,830	55,228	55,217	114	

Abstract from tri-monthly return of the Department of the Gulf (Nineteenth Army Corps), Maj. Gen. Nathaniel P. Banks, U. S. Army, commanding, for May 31, 1863; headquarters, before Port Hudson, La.

Command.	Present for duty.		Aggregate present.	Aggregate present and absent.	Aggregate last return.	Pieces of artillery.	Remarks.
	Officers.	Men.					
Department staff	28	....	28	29	29	......	Front of Port Hudson.
First Division (Augur):							
Staff	8	....	8	8	8	......	Front of Port Hudson.
Infantry	189	4,196	5,915	6,809	6,809	......	Do.
First, Third, and Fourth Louisiana Native Guards.	68	1,993	2,502	2,654	2,654	......	Do.
Cavalry	6	141	167	191	191	......	Do.
Artillery	12	470	575	633	633	34	Do.
Total	283	6,800	9,167	10,295	10,295	34	
Second Division (Sherman):							
Staff	7	....	9	9	9	......	Front of Port Hudson.
Infantry	316	6,584	8,817	9,651	9,651	......	Do.
Artillery	5	259	317	529	529	20	Do.
Other troops in command	88	2,789	3,386	3,627	3,173	24	Do.
Total	416	9,632	12,529	13,816	13,362	44	
Third Division (Emory):							
Staff	10	....	10	10	10	......	Front of Port Hudson.
Infantry	173	3,439	3,980	9,819	9,819	......	Do.
Cavalry	18	231	314	403	403	......	Do.
Artillery	8	302	313	432	432	18	Do.
Total	209	3,972	4,617	10,664	10,664	18	

Abstract from tri-monthly return of the Department of the Gulf, &c.—Continued.

Command.	Present for duty. Officers.	Present for duty. Men.	Aggregate present.	Aggregate present and absent.	Aggregate last return.	Pieces of artillery.	Remarks.
Fourth Division (Grover):							
Staff	5	....	5	5	5	......	Front of Port Hudson.
Infantry	328	6,253	7,561	9,603	8,839	......	Do.
Cavalry	3	78	82	83	....	......	Do.
Artillery	7	262	288	419	421	18	Do.
Total	343	6,593	7,936	10,110	9,265	18	
Second Brigade, First Division (Weitzel):							
Staff	11	....	11	13	13	......	Front of Port Hudson.
Infantry	121	2,496	2,717	3,964	3,964	......	Do.
Cavalry	.3	136	155	189	189	6	Do.
Artillery	6	212	232	285	285	12	Do.
Other troops formerly in the command.	74	1,172	1,471	1,765	1,765	......	Opelousas R. R. and Brashear City.
Total	215	4,016	4,586	6,216	6,216	18	
Key West and Tortugas (Woodbury).	58	1,050	1,478	1,525	1,525	......	
Pensacola (Dyer)	80	1,437	1,872	1,945	1,945	......	
Ship Island (Daniels)	20	471	612	663	663	......	
Total Department of the Gulf.	1,652	33,971	42,825	55,263	53,964	132	

Abstract from the several returns of the Department of the Gulf, and subordinate commands, for the month of May, 1863.*

Command.	Present for duty. Officers.	Present for duty. Men.	Aggregate present.	Aggregate present and absent.	Pieces of artillery.	Remarks by the compiler.
Department staff	28	....	28	29	....	Department return.
First Division (Augur)	538	11,979	14,723	17,128	32	Including Weitzel's brigade.
Second Division (Dwight)	296	6,175	8,743	10,462	16	Troops at New Orleans dropped.
Third Division (Paine)	307	6,319	8,304	10,191	18	Department monthly return.
Fourth Division (Grover)	233	4,062	4,824	8,999	18	Division return.
Cavalry (Grierson)	......	....	....	....	....	Cannot be separated from the four divisions; the Sixth and Seventh Illinois probably not accounted for at all.
Defenses of New Orleans (Emory)	239	6,516	8,216	9,039	...	Return of the Defenses.
District of Key West and Tortugas (Woodbury).	34	709	1,043	1,084	....	District return.
District of Pensacola (Dyer)	51	986	1,285	1,359	12	District return.
Ship Island, Mississippi (Daniels)	22	502	637	679	...	Department monthly return.
Total	1,748	37,248	47,803	58,970	96	

* None of the returns account for the Corps d' Afrique, under Brigadier-General Ullmann's command.

Organization of the troops in the Department of the Gulf (Nineteenth Army Corps), Maj. Gen. Nathaniel P. Banks, U. S. Army, commanding, May 31, 1863.

FIRST DIVISION.

Maj. Gen. CHRISTOPHER C. AUGUR.

First Brigade.	*Second Brigade.*
Col. CHARLES J. PAINE.	Brig. Gen. GODFREY WEITZEL.*
2d Louisiana, Lieut. Col. Charles Everett.	12th Connecticut, Lieut. Col. Frank H. Peck.
21st Maine, Col. Elijah D. Johnson.	75th New York, Col. Robert B. Merritt.
48th Massachusetts, Col. Eben F. Stone.	114th New York, Col. Elisha B. Smith.
49th Massachusetts, Maj. Charles T. Plunkett.	160th New York, Lieut. Col. John B. Van Petten.
116th New York, Capt. John Higgins.	8th Vermont, Lieut. Col. Charles Dillingham.

Third Brigade.

Col. NATHAN A. M. DUDLEY.

30th Massachusetts, Lieut. Col. William W. Bullock.
50th Massachusetts, Col. Carlos P. Messer.
161st New York, Col. Gabriel T. Harrower.
174th New York, Maj. George Keating.

Artillery.

1st Indiana Heavy (seven companies), Col. John A. Keith.
1st Maine Battery, Lieut. John E. Morton.
6th Massachusetts Battery, Lieut. John F. Phelps.
12th Massachusetts Battery (one section), Lieut. Edwin M. Chamberlin.
18th New York Battery, Capt. Albert G. Mack.
1st United States, Battery A, Capt. Edmund C. Bainbridge.
5th United States, Battery G, Lieut. Jacob B. Rawles.

Miscellaneous.

1st Louisiana Engineers, Corps d'Afrique, Col. Justin Hodge.
1st Louisiana Native Guards, Lieut. Col. Chauncey J. Bassett.†
3d Louisiana Native Guards, Col. John A. Nelson.†
4th Louisiana Native Guards,‡ Col. Charles W. Drew.
1st Louisiana Cavalry, Maj. Harai Robinson.
2d Rhode Island Cavalry, Lieut. Col. Augustus W. Corliss.

SECOND DIVISION.

Brig. Gen. WILLIAM DWIGHT.§

First Brigade.	*Third Brigade.*
Col. THOMAS S. CLARK.	Brig. Gen. FRANK S. NICKERSON.
26th Connecticut, Lieut. Col. J. Selden.	14th Maine, Col. Thomas W. Porter.
6th Michigan,‖ Lieut. Col. E. Bacon.	24th Maine, Col. George M. Atwood.
15th New Hampshire, Col. John W. Kingman.	28th Maine (detachment¶), Col. Ephraim W. Woodman.
128th New York, Lieut. Col. James Smith.	165th New York, Capt. Felix Agnus.
162d New York, Lieut. Col. Justus W. Blanchard.	175th New York, Maj. John Gray.
	177th New York, Col. Ira W. Ainsworth.

* Weitzel was assigned, May 14, to command a provisional division consisting of his own and the First (Dwight's) Brigade, Fourth Division. Col. Stephen Thomas succeeded Weitzel as brigade commander.
† Probably in actual command.
‡ Reported as at Baton Rouge, La.
§ Upon Brig. Gen. Thomas W. Sherman being wounded, May 27, Brig. Gen. George L. Andrews, chief of staff, assumed command of this division. Nickerson succeeded him May 28, and Dwight (assigned May 29) assumed command May 30, Col. Lewis Benedict commanding at Trudeau's Landing. The Second Brigade serving in the Defenses of New Orleans.
‖ Temporarily with Third Brigade.
¶ Companies A, D, E, and parts of F, H, and I.

*Artillery.**

Capt. WILLIAM ROY.

1st Indiana Heavy (one company), Capt. William Roy.
21st New York Battery, Capt. James Barnes.
1st Vermont Battery, Capt. George T. Hebard.

.THIRD DIVISION.

Brig. Gen. HALBERT E. PAINE.†

First Brigade.‡

Col. TIMOTHY INGRAHAM.

4th Massachusetts, Col. Henry Walker.
16th New Hampshire, Col. James Pike.
110th New York, Col. Clinton H. Sage.

Second Brigade.

Col. HAWKES FEARING, Jr.

8th New Hampshire, Capt. William M. Barrett.
133d New York, Col. Leonard D. H. Currie.
173d New York, Capt. George W. Rogers.
4th Wisconsin, Col. Sidney A. Bean.

Third Brigade.

Col. OLIVER P. GOODING.

31st Massachusetts (seven companies), Lieut. Col. W. S. B. Hopkins.
38th Massachusetts, Maj. James P. Richardson.
53d Massachusetts, Col. John W. Kimball.
156th New York, Lieut. Col. Jacob Sharpe.

Artillery.

Capt. RICHARD C. DURYEA.

4th Massachusetts Battery, Lieut. Fred. W. Reinhard.
1st United States, Battery F, Capt. Richard C. Duryea.
2d Vermont Battery, Capt. Pythagoras E. Holcomb.

FOURTH DIVISION.

Brig. Gen. CUVIER GROVER.

First Brigade.§

Col. JOSEPH S. MORGAN.

1st Louisiana, Col. Richard E. Holcomb.
22d Maine, Col. Simon G. Jerrard.
90th New York, Maj. Nelson Shaurman.
91st New York, Col. Jacob Van Zandt.
131st New York, Lieut. Col. Nicholas W. Day.

Second Brigade.

Col. WILLIAM K. KIMBALL.

24th Connecticut, Col. Samuel M. Mansfield.
12th Maine, Lieut. Col. Edward Ilsley.
41st Massachusetts, Lieut. Col. Lorenzo D. Sargent.
52d Massachusetts, Col. Halbert S. Greenleaf.

Third Brigade.

Col. HENRY W. BIRGE.

13th Connecticut, Capt. Apollos Comstock.
25th Connecticut, Lieut. Col. Mason C. Weld.
26th Maine, Col. Nathaniel H. Hubbard.
159th New York, Lieut. Col. Charles A. Burt.

---

* As indicated by the division special orders.
† Assigned to command May 2. Brigadier-General Weitzel was assigned to command May 13, but order was revoked next day. Paine commanding since May 14.
‡ The Twenty-eighth Connecticut, Col. Samuel P. Ferris, assigned to this brigade June 2. The Sixteenth New Hampshire detached, guarding ammunition depot. The One hundred and sixty-second New York assigned May 31 to First Brigade, Second Division.
§ The Sixth New York ordered home for muster-out, on expiration of service.

Artillery.

Capt. HENRY W. CLOSSON.

2d Massachusetts Battery, Capt. Ormand F. Nims.
1st United States, Battery L, Capt. Henry W. Closson.
2d United States, Battery C, Lieut. Theodore Bradley.

Cavalry.

14th New York (one company).

CAVALRY.

Col. BENJAMIN H. GRIERSON.

6th Illinois, Lieut. Col. Reuben Loomis.
7th Illinois, Col. Edward Prince.
1st Louisiana* (detachment).
2d Massachusetts Battalion.*
14th New York* (detachment).

CORPS D'AFRIQUE.†

Brig. Gen. DANIEL ULLMANN.

6th Infantry.
7th Infantry.
8th Infantry.
9th Infantry.
10th Infantry.

DEFENSES OF NEW ORLEANS.‡

Brig. Gen. WILLIAM H. EMORY.§

23d Connecticut, Col. Charles E. L. Holmes.
1st Indiana Heavy Artillery, Company I, Capt. Richard Campbell.
1st Louisiana Native Guards Artillery, Company B, Capt. Loren Rygaard.
1st Louisiana Native Guards (detachment).
2d Louisiana Native Guards (detachment), Lieut. Col. Alfred G. Hall.
12th Maine, Company D, Capt. Elisha Winter.
13th Maine, Col. Henry Rust, jr.
12th Massachusetts Battery,‖ Capt. Jacob Miller.

13th Massachusetts Battery, Capt. C. H. J. Hamlen.
31st Massachusetts (three companies), Maj. Robert Bache.
14th New York Cavalry (three companies), Capt. John Ennis.
25th New York Battery, Capt. John A. Grow.
26th New York Battery, Lieut. George W. Fox.
176th New York, Col. Charles C. Nott.
1st Texas Cavalry (three companies), Col. Edmund J. Davis.
4th Wisconsin, Company G, Capt. James Keefe.

Second Brigade, Second Division.

Col. THOMAS W. CAHILL.

9th Connecticut, Lieut. Col. Richard Fitz Gibbons.
28th Maine (four companies), Maj. Joseph D. Bullen.
26th Massachusetts, Col. Alpha B. Farr.
42d Massachusetts, Lieut. Col. Joseph Stedman.
47th Massachusetts, Col. Lucius B. Marsh.

---

*Transferred from Grover's and Weitzel's commands, May 31.
† The officers of these regiments were mustered into service at New York City in February and March, 1863, but the regiments were not fully organized until August and September of that year. See Irwin to Emory, May 31, p. 524.
‡ Troops at Brashear City, Donaldsonville, Forts Jackson, Macomb, Pike, and Saint Philip, in New Orleans, at Pass Manchac, and at Ship Island.
§ Relieved Brig. Gen. T. W. Sherman May 21.
‖ Detachment at Port Hudson, La.

DISTRICT OF KEY WEST AND TORTUGAS.

Brig. Gen. DANIEL P. WOODBURY.

47th Pennsylvania (five companies), Col. Tilghman H. Good, Key West.
47th Pennsylvania (five companies), Lieut. Col. George W. Alexander, Tortugas.

DISTRICT OF PENSACOLA.*

Col. ISAAC DYER.

15th Maine, Lieut. Col. Benjamin B. Murray, jr.
7th Vermont, Lieut. Col. David B. Peck.
2d U. S. Artillery, Battery H, Capt. Frank H. Larned.
2d U. S. Artillery, Battery K, Capt. Harvey A. Allen.

SHIP ISLAND.

2d Louisiana Native Guards (seven companies), Col. Nathan W. Daniels.

HEADQUARTERS UNITED STATES FORCES,
Trudeau's Landing, June 1, 1863.

Brigadier-General ANDREWS,
Chief of Staff, Nineteenth Army Corps:

GENERAL: Since my last dispatch we have had many rumors of advancing forces and gathering guerrilla bands, but my cavalry scouts have been unable to verify any such intelligence, although the country has been scoured as far as the Grossetête on the one side and Morganza on the other. Occasionally we hear of small parties of our stragglers and guerrillas levying contributions on quiet people. These I have used every endeavor to arrest, and have doutless secured some of them, although unable to fix their crimes on them. In such cases, if enemies, I have paroled them, and expressed my determination to punish them, if found from home at night, or acting or being confederated with others.

This parish is full of loyal creoles and French. Large numbers have taken the oath. Daily I am in receipt of intelligence from them, not of much intrinsic value, but good evidence of honest intention.

This point was the cattle depot for the supply of Port Hudson. Large supplies were collected here and carried over as they were wanted. Many of them have been reclaimed (upon your advance) and driven into the interior some 10 or 12 miles.

I have taken and paroled many prisoners. They, with scarcely an exception, seem glad to get out of the army, both volunteer and conscript.

Dr. Charles Smith was sent to the lower fleet yesterday with the implicating papers found on him. To-day I have sent the Confederate money ($700) taken from him, and a copy of the order to send him to General Bowen, New Orleans, to the admiral:

Very respectfully,

LEW. BENEDICT,
Colonel, Commanding.

---

*The Twenty-eighth Connecticut, Colonel Ferris, embarked May 10 for Barre's Landing, La. Colonel Dyer in command, according to district return. The department return reports Col. William C. Holbrook as commanding at this date.

HEADQUARTERS DEFENSES OF NEW ORLEANS,
June 2, 1863.
.General ULLMANN:

The general commanding desires me to say he has received the following telegram from Lieut. Col. R. B. Irwin.

CAMP HEADQUARTERS,
—— —, 1863.
Brig. Gen. W. H. EMORY: \

The general commanding directs that General Ullmann forward to this point immediately all the troops which he has raised, whether armed or unarmed, and that the regiments be recruited to the standard fixed by General Orders, No. 4, viz, 500 men each.

RICH'D B. IRWIN,
Assistant Adjutant-General.

To which I have replied as follows:

All Ullmann's troops are *en route* for Port Hudson, armed and unarmed. Fourteen hundred will be in Algiers to-day, and leave in the Fulton about 4 o'clock. The order in cipher will be immediately communicated.

Very respectfully, your obedient servant,

W. D. SMITH,
Lieutenant-Colonel, and Acting Assistant Adjutant-General.

FLAG-SHIP MONONGAHELA,
Port Hudson, June 2, 1863.
Maj. Gen. N. P. BANKS,
   Commanding Department of the Gulf:

GENERAL: I have received your telegram, but cannot think it advisable to put guns in front. Their shell would reach our forces. I am now afraid to fire except on the flank.

I was afraid my shell reached your forces yesterday, but it annoyed the enemy so as to stop his firing, and I now give orders to open on him the moment he opens on your forces; that is, on the 10-inch columbiad in their middle battery, which generally annoys Weitzel. I am glad to hear that you are preparing for a final assault; all I think you need is concert of action and you must succeed. Let me know in time to give you my assistance.

Very truly and respectfully,

D. G. FARRAGUT,
Rear-Admiral.

GENERAL ORDERS, } HDQRS. DEPT. OF THE GULF, 19TH A. C.,
No. 45. }   *Before Port Hudson, June 2*, 1863.

A military court, to be known as the provost court of the Department of the Gulf, is hereby constituted, for the purpose of hearing, deciding, and passing judgment upon—*

I. All cases of violations of general or special orders, violations of the Rules and Articles of War, violations of the recognized laws of war, or other offenses arising under the military jurisdiction, where the offender is not in the military service of the United States, and where the penalty does not extend to loss of life.

II. All civil crimes against the persons or property of the inhabit-

---

* See General Orders, No. 52, of July 20, p. 649.

ants, committed by any person in the military service of the United States, where the penalty does not extend to loss of life or the dismissal of a commissioned officer.

III. All other cases arising under the military jurisdiction which may be specially referred to the court by the commanding general or the provost-marshal-general of the department.

This court will exercise original and exclusive jurisdiction in all the above cases, and will hold its sessions at the city of New Orleans, or such other point as may from time to time be designated in orders.

Col. Charles C. Dwight, One hundred and sixtieth New York, is appointed judge of the court hereby authorized and established, and will enter upon his duties immediately.

By command of Major-General Banks:

RICH'D B. IRWIN,
Assistant Adjutant-General.

HEADQUARTERS DEFENSES OF NEW ORLEANS,
June 3, 1863—10 a. m.

Lieutenant-Colonel IRWIN,
Assistant Adjutant-General:

The Fulton left at 9 o'clock last evening with 1,200 of Ullmann's troops. Baggage, which was left against orders, will follow in the Sallie Robinson. Iberville left here at 10 for Springfield [Landing] with orders. A tug, with the prison-ship in tow, left at 5 p. m.; prison-ship to be used as a wharf, at Springfield Landing. The Cahawba left for Fort Monroe at 9 p. m. yesterday, with Sixth New York and captured officers.

All quiet here.

W. H. EMORY,
Brigadier-General, Commanding.

WASHINGTON, D. C.,
June 3, 1863.

Maj. Gen. N. P. BANKS,
New Orleans:

GENERAL: I have just received your letters of May 5, 13, and 19.* In your dispatch of the 13th you speak of one of the 12th, which has not been received.† I cannot ascertain from your letters whether you propose to re-enforce General Grant at Vicksburg or not. The newspapers state that your forces are moving on Port Hudson, instead of co-operating with General Grant, leaving the latter to fight both Johnston and Pemberton. As this is so contrary to all your instructions, and so opposed to military principles, I can hardly believe it true.

I have so often pointed out what I thought ought to be done, and the peril of separate and isolated operations, that it would be useless to repeat them here.

Very respectfully, your obedient servant,

H. W. HALLECK,
General-in-Chief.

---

* For letters of May 5 and 13, see Series I, Vol. XV, pp. 311, 318.
† See Series I, Vol. XV, p. 317.

WASHINGTON, D. C.,
June 4, 1863.
Major-General BANKS,
  Commanding New Orleans:
  GENERAL: After writing my letter of yesterday, I received your letters of May 8, 11, 12 (four letters), 18, and 19. These fully account for your movement on Port Hudson, which before seemed so unaccountable. General Grant was probably drawn so far north in the pursuit of the enemy that he found it necessary to connect himself with his supplies above Vicksburg. As at Alexandria you were almost as near to Grand Gulf as to Port Hudson, we thought it exceedingly strange that you and General Grant should move in opposite directions to attack both places at the same time. I hope that you have ere this given up your attempt on Port Hudson and sent all your spare forces to Grant. The moment Vicksburg falls there will be no serious difficulty in taking Port Hudson. Moreover, both your armies can be supplied from the Upper Mississippi.
  If I have been over-urgent in this matter, it has arisen from my extreme anxiety lest the enemy should concentrate all his strength on one of your armies before you could unite, whereas, if you act together, you certainly will be able to defeat him. Your letter in regard to P. Soulé has been referred to the Secretary of War.
  Very respectfully, your obedient servant,
                              H. W. HALLECK,
                                  General-in-Chief.

HDQRS. DEPARTMENT OF THE GULF, 19TH ARMY CORPS,
                  Before Port Hudson, June 4, 1863. .
Major-General HALLECK,
  Commander-in-Chief, U. S. Army:
  GENERAL: Your letter of May 19, referring to my occupation of Alexandria, I received yesterday. I marched to Alexandria for the double purpose of dispersing the rebel army said to be concentrating there under Kirby Smith, and destroying the materials upon which an army could be organized or supported in that country. In both objects I succeeded. The enemy was driven into the pine woods more than 70 miles above Alexandria, and the destruction of foundries and shops, and the seizure of horses, carts, &c., throughout the whole of that district, the advantage of which I am now reaping, has made it impossible to organize and supply a large force from that country.
  Besides, my arrangement with Major-General Grant, upon his own proposition, was that I should join a corps of his force in the reduction of Port Hudson on May 25. I reached this place on the 23d, and a part of my force was earlier prepared for the attack. It was only at Alexandria that I learned that General Grant had been diverted from his original plan.
  The course to be pursued here gives me great anxiety. If I abandon Port Hudson, I leave its garrison, some 6,000 or 7,000 men, the force under Mouton and Sibley now threatening Brashear City, and the army of Mobile, large or small, to threaten or attack New Orleans. If I detach from my command in the field a sufficient force to defend that city, which ought not to be less than 8,000 or 10,000, my assistance to General Grant is unimportant, and I leave an equal or larger number of the enemy to re-enforce Johnston. If I defend New Orleans and its adjacent territory, the enemy will go against Grant. If I go with a

force sufficient to aid him, my rear will be seriously threatened. My force is not large enough to do both. Under these circumstances, my only course seems to be to carry this post as soon as possible, and then to join General Grant. If I abandon it, I cannot materially aid him.

I have now my heavy artillery in position, and I am confident of success in the course of a week. We can then render efficient aid to the army at Vicksburg. Every possible effort is being made to expedite and insure success.

The separation of the two armies is occasioned by the departure from the original plan of operations. I came here finally, after the failure of the first plan, upon the assurance of General Grant, brought by an officer specially sent to him (Brigadier-General Dwight), that he could still probably aid us by a small force, not so large as first contemplated, but sufficient for our purpose. I believe General Grant to be still of opinion as he was then, that an abandonment of Port Hudson would relieve as strong a force of the enemy to re-enforce Johnston as it would bring to his aid.

I earnestly hope for a successful solution of the difficulties by which I am surrounded by an immediate reduction of the enemy's works here, for which we shall use every possible means in our power. I need not say what I have so many times urged, that the force placed at my disposal is inadequate to the duty imposed upon me, and yet I appreciate the impossibility of re-enforcing my command.

I am, general, with much respect, your obedient servant,

N. P. BANKS,
Major-General, Commanding.

HDQRS. SECOND DIVISION, NINETEENTH ARMY CORPS,
Before Port Hudson, June 4, 1863.

Lieutenant-Colonel IRWIN,
Assistant Adjutant-General:

COLONEL: I have the honor to forward to headquarters 3 deserters, who came in this morning, with their statements, taken down by me. These men appear to have come in voluntarily, and to have mentioned their intention to some of their friends, who did not betray them. They desire to be sent to New York.

Respectfully, your obedient servant,

WILLIAM DWIGHT,
Brigadier-General, Commanding.

[Inclosure.]

Statements of deserters.

MIKE WELSH, *private in Captain [A. J.] Lewis' detached [Mississippi] company.*—Deserted last night; came in along the river's edge. Picket saw him, but said nothing. Five thousand effective men in Port Hudson. Beall's brigade, Miles' Legion (700 strong), and some detached companies. Very few sick. Equally distributed along the breastworks. One company cavalry. Rations, half pound meat, half pound meal. Four light batteries; 40 or 50 Federal prisoners. Officers think place can be defended; men differ; think we mean to starve them out. Reported that there is meal enough to last till the 16th. We damaged their mill. They are short of caps. A general order has been issued upon the subject. Have plenty of ammunition. Have thirteen guns upon the river; three can be turned inland.

JAMES FIELD, *sergeant in [Twelfth Battalion] Louisiana Heavy Artillery.*—Battery No. 4, in center, on river. Two guns, one 10-inch, one 8-inch columbiad, traverse on pivot, and fire inland. Have moved two 24-pounder, Coffin's, two Tennessee 24-pounders, and two 12-pounder Blakely guns to the breastworks. One Blakely has been disabled, and one Coffin gun has been dismounted. [W. N.] Coffin's guns are behind Beall's headquarters, near Slaughter's field. The Tennessee guns are beside the railroad, where it crosses the breastwork. Five thousand men in Port Hudson. Beall's brigade and Miles' Legion (500 strong) and detached companies. Think they can hold out till re-enforcements arrive. Rations issued 1st June for ten days. Very little meal left. Twenty-five thousand bushels corn and plenty of beef, and plenty of sugar and molasses. Troops mostly natives. Four batteries light artillery. Plenty of ammunition except caps. Muskets are altered to Springfield and Austrian and Belgian. There is a light ordnance work-shop near the commissaries.

Sergt. B. BATTELL, *detached company.*—Made a coat for Major [J. L.] Stockdale, chief of subsistence. Major's brother showed him the figures for issue of rations before the battle of Plains Store. Rations issued to 6,420 men. There were 500 killed and wounded. There are about 5,000 men now in the works. There are two classes of men; the largest desire to go home. The others are sanguine of defeating us.

Drew ten days' rations 1st of June. Said to have 40,000 pounds of meal left, being six days' rations. Mill injured; stones broken. Will move engine, &c., to grind in a hollow. Our captain made a speech on the day of the first attack, and said it would be over that night. We (Federals) could have gone in on our right that night. The works on the right may have been strengthened, but a man who saw them yesterday said it had not been done. Artillery would knock them down. Breastworks have been built on the right. They are nothing but rail fence and mud, and no ditch. Works on our (United States) left are the strongest; deep ditch and high works.

Many of their guns have been broken up, and some hid in hollows. They can only bring against us (in case of our advance) a part of the guns they brought the other day. Many dare not bring their guns to the parapet. They may fight in the woods a little, but the plan is to go to the water batteries, turn the guns on us, and kill all they can of us, and then surrender.

They have no exterior line of defense, and will not make any but on the right, where they have always expected us. Will fight from redoubt to redoubt which are detached.

Some guns in the woods and ravines inside. Sentiment the other day that we should take the place; now, that we have a small force and cannot. Their fire is intended to strike the earthworks we are supposed to be erecting.

——————

U. S. S. HARTFORD,
June 4, [1863]—8 p. m.

[General N. P. BANKS :]

GENERAL : I am just in receipt of your note. I sent Colonel Ellet up to you yesterday, and informed you that Simsport was in possession of the enemy, and the banks of the Atchafalaya were filled with their sharpshooters. This I presume he did, and told you how heavy the fire was.

Now, I question whether any gunboat could get down the Atchafalaya, owing to want of water, and there ought at least two or three be sent down to hold their own against the enemy.

We have scarcely coal enough to enable the gunboats to do their necessary police work up and down the river. This Bayou Sorrel, which I cannot find on the map, leads, I believe, out into the Mississippi near Plaquemine.

I will notify the admiral of your request, and see if he can't get the information you desire by way of Plaquemine.

I am sorry I did not know before of these vessels being in this dangerous situation, as the Estrella, when she last came up, about ten days ago, might have given them warning.

Very truly, yours,

J. S. PALMER,
Commodore.

HDQRS. DEPT. OF THE GULF, NINETEENTH ARMY CORPS,
Before Port Hudson, June 4, 1863.
Admiral D. G. FARRAGUT,
U. S. S. Richmond:

SIR: I beg you to bring your mortars to bear immediately while daylight lasts. Your mortars to bear upon a circle of 200 yards diameter, the center about 800 yards south of the church.

The magazine is about 800 yards almost due south of the church. Let the mortar shells fall in a circle of 200 yards diameter in that vicinity. One shell near this point will destroy their magazine. It is just in rear of first clump of trees looking up toward the town from your position.

Very respectfully, your obedient servant,

N. P. BANKS,
Major-General, Commanding.

SPECIAL ORDERS, }   HDQRS. DEPT. OF THE GULF, 19TH A. C.,
No. 131.   }   *Before Port Hudson, June* 4, 1863.

*   *   *   *   *   *

IV. Col. Lewis Benedict, One hundred and sixty-second New York, will turn over the command of the troops at Fausse Point to Col. Clinton H. Sage, One hundred and tenth New York, or the senior officer present, and will at once rejoin his proper regiment.

*   *   *   *   *   *

By command of Major-General Banks:

RICH'D B. IRWIN,
Assistant Adjutant-General.

HDQRS. DEPT. OF THE GULF, NINETEENTH ARMY CORPS,
Before Port Hudson, June 6, 1863.
Rear-Admiral D. G. FARRAGUT,
U. S. S. Monongahela, Commanding, &c.:

SIR: The shelling of the mortar-boats on Thursday night is reported to have seriously inconvenienced the enemy. Beef-cattle killed, several men wounded, and a regimental camp rendered untenable. The bulk of the early fire passed a little to the left of and beyond the main magazine. The sleep of half the garrison was prevented.

.   Very respectfully, your obedient servant,

N. P. BANKS,   ·
Major-General, Commanding.

GENERAL ORDERS, ∤HDQRS. DEPT. OF THE GULF, 19TH A. C.,
 , No. 47.   ∫   *Before Port Hudson, June 6, 1863.*

I. The regiments of infantry of the Corps d'Afrique, authorized by General Orders, No. 44 [No. 40], current series, will consist of ten companies, each having the following minimum organization : 1 captain, 1 first lieutenant, 1 second lieutenant, 1 first sergeant, 4 sergeants, 4 corporals, 2 buglers, 40 privates. To the above may be added hereafter, at the discretion of the commanding general, 4 corporals and 42 privates, thus increasing the strength to the maximum fixed by law for a company of infantry. The regimental organization will be that fixed by law for a regiment of infantry.

II. The commissary .and assistant commissaries of musters. will muster the second lieutenant into service as soon as he is commissioned; the first lieutenant when 30 men are enlisted, and the captain when the minimum organization is completed.

III. The First, Second, Third, and Fourth Regiments of Louisiana Native Guards will hereafter be known as the First, Second, Third, and Fourth Regiments of Infantry of the Corps d'Afrique.

IV. The regiment of colored troops in process of organization in the District of Pensacola will be known as the Fifth Regiment of Infantry of the Corps d'Afrique.   •

V. The regiments now being raised under the direction of Brig. Gen. Daniel Ullmann, and at present known as the First, Second, Third, Fourth, and Fifth Regiments of Ullmann's brigade, will be respectively designated as the Sixth, Seventh, Eighth, Ninth, and Tenth Regiments of Infantry of the Corps d'Afrique.

VI. The First Regiment of Louisiana Engineers, Col. Justin Hodge,. will hereafter be known as the First Regiment of.Engineers of the Corps d'Afrique.   ·   .

By command of Major-General Banks :.   .
RICH'D B. IRWIN,
Assistant Adjutant-General.

SPECIAL ORDERS, ∤ HDQRS. DEPT. OF THE GULF, 19TH A. C.,
 No. 133.   ∫   *Before Port Hudson, June 6, 1863.*

I. Maj. Gen. C. C. Augur is assigned to the command of the left wing of the forces before Port Hudson, including his own and the Second Division.

*   *   *   *

By command of Major-General Banks:
RICH'D B. IRWIN,
Assistant Adjutant-General.

HEADQUARTERS DEFENSES OF NEW ORLEANS,
June 7, 1863.
General THOMAS,
 Adjutant-General, U. S. Army:
 GENERAL: I am directed to send you the following. The George Washington having sailed, I send it by telegraph to the Southwest Pass, in hopes it will intercept.
 The enemy in some force are now threatening Brashear City, and I am doing all I can to re-enforce it.
W. H. EMORY,
Brigadier-General, Commanding.

[Inclosure.]

General W. H. EMORY,
 Commanding:
 Please inform the General-in-Chief by the George Washington as follows:
 The heavy guns and mortars will be all ready to open on Tuesday morning.
 The enemy has withdrawn his guns from the front of our right wing, apparently to an interior line of defenses. Many deserters report the enemy much shaken by the constant bombardment, but holding out firmly in the hope of re-enforcements. Brigadier-General Paine was sent out on the 5th to Clinton, to disperse the gathering force of the enemy in that quarter. We should hear from him this morning.
RICH'D B. IRWIN.

HEADQUARTERS DEFENSES OF NEW ORLEANS,
June 7, 1863.
Lieutenant-Colonel IRWIN,
 Assistant Adjutant-General:
 Persons having reached this city, who pretend to be well informed, represent that Taylor's and Mouton's forces near Pattersonville amount to about 1,800; that they are mostly cavalry, without artillery. At last accounts we had 1,500 convalescents at Brashear City. I have directed these to be armed and prepared to defend the place. If Lieutenant-Colonel Stickney turns out to be a proper commander, as I have no doubt he will, he ought to be able to hold the place. I do not, however, feel quite so sure that some damage may not be done to the railroads by raids through the La Fourche district. I propose to hold four or five companies, which is all I can spare, in reserve at Algiers, with a special train to send to any point of the road threatened.
W. H. EMORY,
Brigadier-General, Commanding.

HEADQUARTERS DEFENSES OF NEW ORLEANS,
June 7, 1863.
Lieutenant-Colonel IRWIN:
 Upon the authority of the medical director, Dr. [George M.] Sternberg, I telegraphed to you this a. m. that there were 1,500 convalescents at Brashear City whom I should arm for the defense of the place. The commanding officer there has this moment telegraphed me that he has sent

them all away, and that 600 left there this a. m.　He sends them away the moment that he writes me he is threatened with an attack.　Such conduct is incomprehensible, but if I can get hold of the 600, I will send them back until the emergency is passed.　I have sent a new commander down by a special train.

> W. H. EMORY,
> *Brigadier-General, Commanding.*

HEADQUARTERS DEFENSES OF NEW ORLEANS,
June 7, 1863.

Lieutenant-Colonel IRWIN:

I have received the following telegram from Colonel Stickney, the new commander whom I sent to Brashear City.　The 400 men whom he speaks of I have sent back to Brashear City.　The general will be gratified to see that Colonel Stickney looks upon affairs at Brashear City with less apprehension than his predecessor.

> W. H. EMORY,
> *Brigadier-General, Commanding.*

[Inclosure.]

Lieut. Col. W. D. SMITH,
　Acting Assistant Adjutant-General:

There is no one here who knows how many men we have exactly. I have seen nearly everything, and think there can be no danger here.

I shall send this evening two companies to Bayou Bœuf, as the danger is greatest there.　Four hundred men left here this morning, by whose order I cannot find out.

> STICKNEY,
> *Lieutenant-Colonel.*

HEADQUARTERS DEFENSES OF NEW ORLEANS,
June 8, 1863.

Lieutenant-Colonel STICKNEY,
　Brashear City:

In relation to convalescents, do as you think best.　If not required for the defenses of the place, send them on to their respective regiments. You are aware of the fact that convalescents are the only re-enforcements I can send you.　If you send them away, I cannot send you any but convalescents.

> W. D. SMITH,
> *Lieutenant-Colonel, and Acting Assistant Adjutant-General.*

HDQRS. DEPT. OF THE GULF, NINETEENTH ARMY CORPS,
Before Port Hudson, June 8, 1863—1.30 a. m.

Brig. Gen. C. GROVER,
　Commanding Right Wing:

GENERAL: Admiral Farragut, in a dispatch this moment received from him, states that heavy hammering has been heard on the Hartford for the last two nights (6th and 7th), supposed to be in or at the entrance of Thompson's Creek into the Mississippi, near the upper or first battery of the enemy. From Colonel Sage, at Fausse Point, there is a report that his men have observed persons during the moonlight bringing large logs or pieces of timber down to the water. The admiral's impression is that the enemy is building either a bridge or a raft to enable him to escape. The commanding general desires that · you will immediately ascertain and report whether this hammering has been heard upon your lines, and whether it was not possibly the noise made in constructing our own batteries upon the extreme right of our line. The commanding general considers it important that you should ascertain the truth, the exact truth, as to the matter, with the least possible delay.

Very respectfully, your obedient servant,

[RICH'D B. IRWIN,]
·   Assistant Adjutant-General.

HDQRS. DEPT. OF THE GULF, NINETEENTH ARMY CORPS,
Before Port Hudson, June 8, 1863—10 p. m.

Rear-Admiral D. G. FARRAGUT, U. S. Navy,
Comdg. West Gulf Squadron, Flag-ship Monongahela:

ADMIRAL : Matters are now approaching a crisis. All the guns will be ready to open to-morrow. The mortars on the right opened fire this afternoon for a short time to get the ranges, and succeeded in doing so very satisfactorily. To-morrow we shall open from all the batteries, and fire slowly, to get good ranges and to induce the enemy to develop his fire in response. I am well satisfied with the condition of affairs, and feel confident that the enemy cannot hold out beyond Thursday. It will be necessary for you now to keep a bright lookout to prevent any attempt at escape by crossing the river. Our rear is now clear of the enemy, so that we do not apprehend his presence in any force within two days' march. Nor do we hear anything definite of the arrival of re-enforcements, concerning which the enemy keeps up so many reports.

I am disposed to think that the hammering heard on the Hartford was either the sound of our own work in constructing batteries on the right, or the noise of the enemy doing the same thing opposite. I have, however, sent a party to make a thorough examination of the approaches near the mouth of Thompson's Creek. Two weeks ago they were impassable.

I inclose a copy of telegram sent to you last night.

Very respectfully, your most obedient servant,

N. P. BANKS,
Major-General, Commanding.

[JUNE 8, 1863.—For Schofield to Carleton, in relation to re-enforcements for Department of New Mexico, see Series I, Vol. XXII, Part II, p. 313.]

HDQRS. DEPT. OF THE GULF, NINETEENTH ARMY CORPS,
Before Port Hudson, June 9,. 1863—5.30 p. m.

Rear-Admiral D. G. FARRAGUT, Monongahela:

SIR: Opened fire at 11 a. m. from the heavy guns and mortars, and fired slowly during the day, with good ranges and excellent effect, driving the enemy away from the parapet. Our fire was, except in one or two instances, unanswered. The heavy guns were admirably served. Please keep up your mortar fire during the whole of this night. We shall fire slowly all night. Will send you a report of the operations at the mouth of Thompson's Creek this evening.

Very respectfully, your obedient servant,

N. P. BANKS,
Major-General, Commanding.

BEFORE PORT HUDSON,
June 9, 1863.

Brig. Gen. W. H. EMORY,
New Orleans:

GENERAL: Your three telegrams received. Send guns and ammunition to Brashear City. Your instructions as to steamboats Sykes, Segur, and Southern Merchant are approved. Shall send down some troops on Thursday. The gunboat should be sent to Brashear, as you propose.

Very respectfully, your obedient servant,

N. P. BANKS,
Major-General, Commanding.

HEADQUARTERS DEFENSES OF NEW ORLEANS,
June 9, 1863.

Commodore [HENRY W.] MORRIS:

I have just learned that Brashear City is threatened by a formidable force. Have you a gunboat you can send around there? If so, oblige me by sending it off with all possible dispatch. With the aid of a gunboat, I do not doubt the place can be held. There are so many sick, it cannot be abandoned without time and loss.

I have the honor, sir, to be, your obedient servant,

W. H. EMORY,
Brigadier-General, Commanding.

HEADQUARTERS DEFENSES OF NEW ORLEANS,
June 9, 1863.

Lieutenant-Colonel IRWIN:

A telegram this moment received from Colonel Stickney will be transmitted as soon as possible. Notwithstanding his telegram of the day before yesterday that he did not consider the place in danger, he now telegraphs me that he is to be attacked, and expresses great apprehensions for the safety of the place. Captain Shunk tells me neither the guns nor the ammunition which were ordered to be sent yesterday are here to send. I shall send him the re-enforcements and the field pieces which he asks for in to-day's dispatch.

The commanding general himself can judge whether he can spare any force from above to defend this post.

W. H. EMORY,
Brigadier-General, Commanding.

HEADQUARTERS DEFENSES OF NEW ORLEANS,
June 9, 1863.
Colonel IRWIN:

I send by Captain [Thomas S.] Dennett, assistant quartermaster, copies of telegraphic dispatches sent you this morning.

From these and from the testimony of Lieutenant Francis, who escaped from Franklin, I am quite sure the enemy intend to avail themselves of the present state of things to attack Brashear City. You will know my helpless condition here in regard to troops, and the limited aid I can give.

I have requested Commodore Morris to send a gunboat there. I have received no answer from him; but I am quite sure that the answer will be that he has none to send. Cannot one be detached, if only for a day or two, from the fleet above? It would, in my opinion, if done promptly, save the place and divert the attack.

I am, very respectfully, your obedient servant,
W. H. EMORY,
Brigadier-General, Commanding.

HEADQUARTERS DEFENSES OF NEW ORLEANS,
June 9, 1863.
Lieutenant-Colonel IRWIN:
Assistant Adjutant-General:

Commodore Morris has promised me to send the Hollyhock gunboat round to Brashear City as soon as he can obtain a pilot.
W. H. EMORY,
Brigadier-General, Commanding.

HEADQUARTERS DEFENSES OF NEW ORLEANS,
June 9, 1863.
Lieutenant-Colonel IRWIN:
Assistant Adjutant-General:

COLONEL: Yours received. All quiet at Brashear City. The guns and ammunition have reached there. The Hollyhock left here at 5 o'clock this evening. Nothing from the boats in the Plaquemine.
W. H. EMORY,
Brigadier-General, Commanding.

BRASHEAR CITY,
June 9, 1863.
Lieut. Col. W. D. SMITH,
Acting Assistant Adjutant-General:

I must have by the afternoon train to-day three or four light pieces of some kind. An attack was intended last night, I am sure, and the Confederate officers say they will surely have this place by Saturday. I have a mob, officered by fools, but I have put them into some shape, and, with three or four light pieces, I can show fight well. They are going to attack from the southern side of the city, and it is wholly unprotected. The battery will not help us; they will keep clear of that. There is nothing whatever to hinder their shelling the city, and they have artillery; I can't yet find how much. Can't I have for a few days Company G, of Forty-second. Massachusetts, and enough men to make it 100 strong? With that and the light guns, I feel sure. I must have the guns, anyway. I have Bayou Bœuf safe, I think. I ran down a howitzer and 50 men after midnight this morning. The men have returned. I shall throw up to-day a rifle-pit sufficient to help in working small guns.

I have just received the dispatch, dated last evening. The guns must come up in the afternoon train, and, with 100 good men for a day or two, I feel safe. I have not sent any force across the river, for my men are all too tired, and I must save them for to-night, and I know what they are going to try. I have only about 200 men that I can depend on. I am afraid they will take Fort Chêne. It is of no use now, and, were it not for the guns, I would take away the men. The convalescents I cannot depend on to-night, for they never were made to give in morning reports even, and were in utter confusion. I can have 100 useful men to-morrow, and perhaps more.

ALBERT STICKNEY,
Lieutenant-Colonel, Commanding Post.

WASHINGTON, D. C., June 10, 1863.

Major-General BANKS,
      New Orleans, La:

GENERAL: Your dispatches of May 21 and 30 are received.

In regard to the railroad superintendence, the Secretary of War informs me that he has already sent an agent to examine into the matter.

Your account of the bravery and good conduct of your troops at Port Hudson has given great satisfaction, and it is hoped that you will succeed in capturing the place. Nevertheless, there is much anxiety on the subject, and much annoyance at the simultaneous attack on Port Hudson and Vicksburg, when it was expected that you and General Grant would act in conjunction.

Very respectfully, your obedient servant,

H. W. HALLECK,
General-in-Chief.

HDQRS. DEPT. OF THE GULF, NINETEENTH ARMY CORPS,
Before Port Hudson, June 10, 1863—6 p. m.

Rear-Admiral D. G. FARRAGUT,
      Flag-ship Monongahela, via Springfield Landing:

SIR: Colonel Prince reports no rafts being built at the mouth of Thompson's Creek, and no indications there of any effort on the part of the enemy to escape. The ground on the west bank is very swampy, and can only be traversed by men on foot. A reconnoitering party sent down the east bank went as far as the mouth of Sandy Creek, which is 340 yards above the mouth of Thompson's Creek, but met no pickets.

Colonel Prince saw our camp at Fausse Point, and thinks the commanding officer there would be able to observe everything transpiring at the mouth of Thompson's Creek. Please request him to see if he can do so.

Very respectfully, your obedient servant,

N. P. BANKS,
Major-General, Commanding.

HEADQUARTERS DEPARTMENT OF THE GULF,
Before Port Hudson, June 10, 1863.
Brig. Gen. W. H. EMORY,
New Orleans :

GENERAL: Your dispatch in regard to removing the guns from Fort Chêne received. The commanding general wishes you to urge upon Commodore Morris the necessity of sending the gunboat at once. If it is necessary, however, you can order the removal of the guns. Please report when the boat will go around.

Very respectfully, your obedient servant,
RICH'D B. IRWIN,
Assistant Adjutant-General.

HEADQUARTERS DEFENSES OF NEW ORLEANS,
June 10, 1863.
Lieutenant-Colonel IRWIN:

I send you the last telegram from Colonel Stickney, which is just received. It may be more satisfactory to the general to have the telegram itself than any synopsis of it. I have sent 100 men to Bonnet Carré, to feel the force of the raid reported there.

I feel uneasy about the Hollyhock reaching Brashear. Commodore Morris, after promising that she should be there to-day at 5 p. m., gave her orders to go by Pass à l'Outre, and look after the tug-boat Boston, which was captured last night by the rebels. But for this I should feel entirely secure about Brashear.

W. H. EMORY,
Brigadier-General, Comm'nding.

SPECIAL ORDERS, ⎱ HDQRS. DEPT. OF THE GULF, 19TH A. C.,
No. 137.   ⎰   *Before Port Hudson, June* 10, 1863.

I. The commanding general directs that the following preparations for an attack upon the enemy's works be made as speedily as practicable to-day:

1. Bags filled with cotton, fascines, or other similar preparations will be made for filling the ditch at three principal points, of which one is on the front opposite General Augur's command.

2. Pioneers will be detailed, provided with the necessary implements for opening a way for artillery into the enemy's works, and will be instructed in their duties.

3. Storming parties and parties to carry the cotton bags or fascines will be detailed, and the necessary instructions given.

4. Major Houston, chief engineer, will provide from the pontoon train as many bridges as may be deemed necessary, not exceeding two for each point of attack, for which parties will be detailed and instructed.

5. Brigadier-General Arnold, chief of artillery, will see that the artillery, heavy and light, is fully supplied with ammunition and whatever is necessary for its efficiency, and will see that it is so disposed as to produce the greatest possible effect.

6. Generals Augur and Grover will see that their respective commands are fully provided with ammunition and other necessary supplies, and that their respective commands are fully instructed, in proper time, in their duties. They will also cause their subordinates to be in-

formed of the requirements of this order, so far as may be necessary to secure the prompt execution of the same.

II. 7.45 *p. m.*—The commanding general directs as follows:

With the view of harassing the enemy, of inducing him to bring forward and expose his artillery, acquiring a knowledge of the ground before the enemy's front, and of favoring the operations of pioneers who may be sent forward to remove obstructions, if necessary, Generals Augur and Grover will at once make arrangements to advance a line of skirmishers along their respective fronts, who shall cover themselves and open a fire upon the enemy. This fire will open at 12 o'clock midnight this day. The batteries, under the direction of General Arnold, chief of artillery, will take advantage of any opportunity that may be offered to dismount the guns of the enemy, or otherwise annoy him. The signal for the opening of the fire of the skirmishers will be three signal rockets thrown up in succession from the 24 pounder battery on the road leading by General Augur's headquarters. In cases in which natural covers cannot be found for the skirmishers, such artificial covers may be carried by the skirmishers, as Generals Augur and Grover may designate. The skirmishers should be thrown out along nearly the entire front.

8.30 *p. m.*—So much of the above orders as relates to throwing up rockets, and to opening the fire of the skirmishers at midnight, is countermanded. The advance of the skirmishers will take place at midnight without any general signal.

By command of Major-General Banks:

RICH'D B. IRWIN,
Assistant Adjutant-General.

HDQRS. DEPT. OF THE GULF, NINETEENTH ARMY CORPS,
Before Port Hudson, June 11, 1863.

Maj. Gen. C. C. AUGUR,
Commanding, &c.:

GENERAL: You will make preparations for a feigned attack by skirmishers similar to that made last night. Further orders respecting the hour and other details will be sent you.

Very respectfully, your obedient servant,

RICH'D B. IRWIN,
Assistant Adjutant-General.

(Copy to General Grover.)

FLAG-SHIP MONONGAHELA,
Below Port Hudson, June 11, 1863.

Maj. Gen. N. P. BANKS,
Commanding Department of the Gulf:

DEAR GENERAL: Your several dispatches were duly received yesterday, and all the shot and shell were sent down with all possible dispatch to Springfield Landing by the tug, and I then sent her down to Baton Rouge, to telegraph to Commander Morris to send me more 9-inch shells.

Your last dispatch, asking me to continue to bombard all night, arrived about 2.30 a. m. You must remember we have been bombarding this place five weeks, and we are now upon our last 500 shells, so that it will not be in my power to bombard more than three or four hoürs each night, at intervals of five minutes. I hope you will be able to take it before they give out, for although I have sent north for more, I do not know when they will arrive. I am told that the enemy has nearly all his men concentrated at the upper or northern side of his defenses, calculating on the assault being made there. They say the deserters say there are very few in the lower defenses.

I was under the impression that our shelling only served two purposes—to break their rest and silence their guns, when they opened in our sight; the last he has ceased to.do, and they have now become indifferent to the former. After the people have been harassed. to a certain extent, they become indifferent to danger, I think, but we will do all in our power to aid you.

It appears that the Arizona has gone to Natchez to look after Kirby Smith, and break up all boats and flats, and when she returns· the sharpshooters will be sent forward to you; they are very few.

Very truly, yours,

D. G. FARRAGUT,
Rear-Admiral.

HDQRS. DEPT. OF THE GULF, NINETEENTH ARMY CORPS,
Before Port Hudson, June 11, 1863.

Lieutenant-Colonel IRWIN,
Assistant Adjutant-General:

COLONEL: I have the honor to forward 13 prisoners to headquarters. Three of these are deserters; 1 came in last night and 2 this morning. The other 10 were captured on picket, on our extreme left, by Lieutenant Craig, Sixth Michigan Volunteers, with about 30 men of his company. He made a detour through the woods, came in on their rear, and cut off their retreat, capturing the whole picket without loss, with the exception of the lieutenant commanding the rebel picket, Lieutenant Taylor, who was shot in the leg in attempting to escape.

Very respectfully, your obedient servant,
WILLIAM DWIGHT,
Brigadier-General, Commanding.

P. S.—Lieutenant Craig went round the picket on the right; not by the river bank.

SPECIAL ORDERS, } HDQRS. DEPT. OF THE GULF, 19TH A. C.,
No. 138.   }   *Before Port Hudson, June* 11, 1863.

I. 9 *a. m.* The following will be the general order of each column of attack, assumed to consist of 2,000 men :

1. Three hundred men skirmishing and covering the storming party.

2. Seventy pioneers, carrying 35 axes, 18 shovels, 10 pickaxes, 2 hand-saws, 2 hatchets.

3. Storming party, 300 men, carrying cotton bags.

4. Thirty-four men, to carry balks and chesses of bridges.

5. Main assaulting column, marching in lines of battle as far as the ground will permit, and the firing should be, if possible, confined to the skirmishers and artillery until the works are carried. The light artillery should accompany the columns, and each battery be provided with pioneers. The advanced skirmishers, pioneers, and storming party, and bridge builders, should be of the best troops. The advance skirmishers and storming party might be each a well-tried regiment, or volunteers ·

may be called for. The pioneers and bridge-carriers should be picked men or volunteers. The details should be made at once, and the men be drilled both in their duties and the order of march.

*   *   *   *   *   *

By command of Major-General Banks:

RICH'D B. IRWIN,
Assistant Adjutant-General.

SPECIAL ORDERS, } HDQRS. SECOND DIV., 19TH ARMY CORPS,
No. 32.   }   *Before Port Hudson, June 11, 1863.*

The following is the order of the attack upon the enemy's works by this division:

1. Bags filled with cotton and fascines will be prepared and placed at or near the covered way at the white house mortar battery.

2. General Nickerson will detail 200 men to carry these bags, to be closely followed by 100 more to pick up those which may be dropped. A detail of the First Louisiana Engineers will carry the fascines.

3. The troops will be held well in hand, and prepared to move immediately to such point of assault as the brigadier-general commanding shall designate.

4. General Nickerson and Colonel Clark will each detail 50 men, under competent officers, to act as pontoniers. These men will provide themselves with tools, and make it their special duty to open a way for our artillery into the enemy's works.

5. Colonel Clark will detail 50 picked men of the Sixth Michigan Volunteers, under command of Captain Stark, for a sudden attack upon the headquarters of Major-General Gardner. These men will press forward at all hazards. They will establish themselves in the house, and hold it until relieved. The names of these men will be published in general orders, and they will be promoted, if successful.

6. Colonel Clark will also detail 200 men of the same regiment, under the senior captain, for an important and decisive movement. These parties will be supported by the One hundred and twenty-eighth New York Volunteers.

7. With the exception of the picked men who shall be detailed as stormers, the nine-months' troops of this command will lead the advance in the attack.

8. The officers designated by General Nickerson and Colonel Clark for the above special duties will report to-day at 2 p. m. at these headquarters.

9. The officers commanding the brigades will see that there is abundant ammunition on hand.

By order of Brigadier-General Dwight:

WICKHAM HOFFMAN,
Assistant Adjutant-General.

SPECIAL ORDERS, } HDQRS. SECOND DIV., 19TH ARMY CORPS,
No. 34.   }   *Before Port Hudson, June 11, 1863.*

Special Orders, No. 32, from these headquarters, are hereby modified, in pursuance of orders from headquarters department, as follows:

1. General Nickerson will detail 300 men instead of 200, to carry the cotton bags, and will prepare that number of bags.

2. General Nickerson and Colonel Clark will each detail 150 picked men to act as skirmishers, covering the storming party.

3. General Nickerson and Colonel Clark will each detail 35 men instead of 50 as pontoniers; each party will carry 17 axes, 11 shovels, 5 picks, 1 handsaw, and 1 hatchet.

4. Colonel Clark will detail 34 men to carry the balks and chesses of a bridge.

5. These details will be made at once, and the men drilled both in their duties and in the order of march.

By order of Brigadier-General Dwight:

WICKHAM HOFFMAN,
Assistant Adjutant-General.

HDQRS. DEPT. OF THE GULF, NINETEENTH ARMY CORPS,
Before Port Hudson, June 12, 1863.

Maj. Gen. C. C. AUGUR,
Commanding, &c.:

GENERAL: Instead of a feigned attack by skirmishers similar to that of last night, you will cause the regiments detailed for the purpose of supporting the field batteries to be constructed to-night to intrench themselves, under the direction of the engineer officers. You will also have proper dispositions made to promptly repel a sortie, should one be attempted by the enemy, with the intention of interrupting the working parties. Firing should only be resorted to when rendered necessary by the action of the enemy. The fire of the heavy batteries will be continued as usual. The approaches for General Grover being in front of Colonel Dudley, the latter has been directed to provide the necessary supports.

By command of Major-General Banks:

RICH'D B. IRWIN,
Assistant Adjutant-General.

HDQRS. DEPT. OF THE GULF, NINETEENTH ARMY CORPS,
Before Port Hudson, June 12, 1863.

Rear-Admiral D. G. FARRAGUT,
Commanding, &c.:

MY DEAR SIR: Your dispatches were duly received. We will give you notice of our assault, as you wish, and desire your participation in the work. The suggestion as to continuance of the fire of the fleet was made in consequence of a report from Colonel Benedict, that you understood that we requested a discontinuance of your fire. This was not so. Some suggestion may have been made as to ranges, but nothing more. We are ready for the assault to-morrow, but may postpone it till next day; we shall carry the works without fail when we attempt it.

There are some guns on the lower river front that are terribly destructive and as yet out of our reach. Will you not land two or three of your heavy Parrotts on the west side of the river, abreast your ship, and out of range of the enemy's batteries, to dismount them? It can be done effectually and in a few hours. The levee affords protection that can soon be made perfect. I send an officer to confer with you, and who will construct the works; we shall ask of you only the guns and men to man them.

Very truly, yours,

N. P. BANKS,
Major-General, Commanding.

FLAG-SHIP MONONGAHELA, *June* 12, 1863.

General N. P. BANKS, *Commanding Department of the Gulf:*

DEAR GENERAL: Your note of 8 a. m. to-day is received by Captain Baker, respecting the battery on the point opposite Port Hudson. I assure you, general, that no gun on the river front fires at the army; the 10-inch gun has done so once or twice at night, perhaps, without our seeing it, but my orders are to open on it the moment it fires a shot, and we silence it in five minutes. We lie in easy range of our Parrott guns and mortars, but we can see nothing of the guns to which you allude that annoy you in the rear; if we could, I would open immediately, but we can see nothing in that direction. We can send for the guns at New Orleans, and, if you wish, plant them and fire them, but if you think we can fire toward the rear, it is entirely different from all they have been saying to us. Your shells fall in the river, and it is certain that ours will go farther than yours. I fear it will be wrong, but I am ready for anything.

Yours, truly,

D. G. FARRAGUT.

HDQRS. SECOND DIVISION, *Before Port Hudson, June* 12, 1863.

Lieutenant-Colonel IRWIN, *Assistant Adjutant-General:*

COLONEL: I have the honor to forward 4 more deserters to headquarters department.

I have derived from Corpl. Aug. Meterne, Company H, Miles' Legion, a very intelligent man, the following information: He heard Lieutenant-Colonel Brand, of his legion, say that there were about 4,000 men in Port Hudson, composed about as follows: Miles' Legion, 250; Ninth Battalion [Louisiana Partisan Rangers], 150; two Tennessee regiments, consolidated, 800; First Alabama, 500; Forty-seventh [Forty-ninth] Alabama, 500; First and Fifty-ninth [Thirty-ninth] Mississippi, 500; Tenth and Fifteenth Arkansas, say 500; infantry, 3,200.

Twelfth Louisiana Battalion Artillery, on the river; Mohawk Battery, also called Red Shot; Boone's artillery, six 6-pounders; Seven Stars Battery, four 6-pounders; Cornay's ——, one 24-pounder, and two or three more batteries on our right; in all about 800; total, 4,000.

Caps are scarce; ammunition, as far as he knows, abundant.

Captain [R. M.] Boone, of Boone's battery, was killed yesterday by a shot from our battery on the left. There is no more meal. Corn was issued this morning. There is about five days' beef; plenty of peas, plenty of corn. The Mississippi regiment drove about 50 head of cattle out of the works about a week ago. The troops generally wish to surrender, and despair of relief.

WILLIAM DWIGHT,
Brigadier-General, Commanding.

HDQRS. UNITED STATES FORCES,
Fausse Point, opposite Port Hudson, La., June 12, 1863.

Lieutenant-Colonel IRWIN, *Assistant Adjutant-General:*

DEAR SIR: I have the honor to report that under [Special] Orders, No. 131,* from your headquarters, I assumed command of the forces at

---

* Of June 4. See p. 538.

this Point—my six companies of the One hundred and tenth New York State Volunteers, Second Rhode Island Cavalry, and two pieces of artillery.

We have rumors of enemy's forces in Bayou Fordoche and upper part of Pointe Coupée; do not credit the report, but think this point can be held by the present force. I have taken 11 prisoners, who were escaping from Port Hudson; also 18 from Fausse Island, who claimed to be conscripts, and had deserted from the rebel army; also 2 artisans, who were from the Webb, and had passes to Port Hudson; also one Major Vigne, who is represented as a man of influence, as having taken active part in the rebellion, drilling and forcing conscripts into service; also reported as one of the committee of cotton-burners for this parish.

Sent the prisoners to commanding officer of lower fleet.

Most respectfully, your obedient servant,

C. H. SAGE,
Colonel, Commanding.

———

HDQRS. DEPT. OF THE GULF, NINETEENTH ARMY CORPS,
Before Port Hudson, June 13, 1863—7.30 a. m.

Rear-Admiral D. G. FARRAGUT, *Flag-ship Monongahela:*

ADMIRAL: I shall open a vigorous bombardment at exactly a quarter past eleven this morning, and continue it for exactly one hour. I respectfully request that you will aid us by throwing as many shells as you can into the place during that time, commencing and ceasing fire with us. The bombardment will be immediately followed by a summons to surrender. If that is not listened to, I shall probably attack to-morrow morning; but of this I will give you notice.

Very respectfully, your obedient servant,

N. P. BANKS,
Major-General, Commanding.

———

HDQRS. DEPT. OF THE GULF, NINETEENTH ARMY CORPS,
Before Port Hudson, June 13, 1863—9 p. m.

Rear-Admiral D. G. FARRAGUT, *Flag-ship Monongahela:*

SIR: I have just sent you the following message by signals:

Please send us as much shrapnel as you can spare for the 9-inch navy guns. Please commence firing vigorously with mortars only at 11 p. m., and cease at exactly 2 a. m. Throw your shells as nearly as possible in the center of the work.

We shall attack Port Hudson at daybreak.

Very respectfully, your obedient servant,

N. P. BANKS,
Major-General, Commanding.

———

HDQRS. DEPT. OF THE GULF, NINETEENTH ARMY CORPS,
Before Port Hudson, June 13, 1863.

Maj. Gen. FRANK. GARDNER, C. S. Army,
Commanding Port Hudson:

SIR: Respect for the usages of war, and a desire to avoid unnecessary sacrifice of life, impose on me the necessity of formally demanding the surrender of the garrison of Port Hudson. I am not unconscious in making this demand that the garrison is capable of continuing a vigorous and gallant defense. The events that have transpired during the pend ng investment exhibit in the commander and garrison a spirit of constancy and courage that, in a different cause, would be universally regaided as heroism. But I know the extremities to which they are reduced. I have many deserters and prisoners of war. I have captured the couriers of the garrison, and have in my possession the secret dispatches of the commander. I have at my command a train of artillery seldom equaled in extent and efficiency, which no ordinary fortress can successfully resist, and an infantry force of greatly superior numbers, and most determined purpose, that cannot fail to place Port Hudson in my possession at my will. To push the contest to extremities, however, may place the protection of life beyond the control of the commanders of the respective forces. I desire to avoid unnecessary slaughter, and I therefore demand the immediate surrender of the garrison, subject.to such conditions only as are imposed by the usages of civilized warfare.

I have the honor to be, sir, very respectfully, your most obedient servant,

N. P. BANKS,
Major-General, Commanding.

HEADQUARTERS,
Port Hudson, La., June 13, 1863.
Maj. Gen. N. P. BANKS:
Commanding U. S. Forces near Port Hudson:
SIR: Your note of this date has just been handed to me, and in reply I have to state that my duty requires me to defend this position, and, therefore, I decline to surrender.

I have the honor to be, sir, very respectfully, your most obedient servant,

FRANK. GARDNER,
Major-General, Commanding C. S. Forces.

[FLAG-SHIP MONONGAHELA,
Below Port Hudson, June 13, 1863.]
Maj. Gen. N. P. BANKS, *Commanding:*
DEAR GENERAL: I will be ready for the bombardment at the time specified.

I [think] there is but little use in the demand for surrender. Although some think they may, I do not—that is, General Gardner will not. The men would be very willing.

Yours, truly,

D. G. FARRAGUT,
Rear-Admiral.

HDQRS. DEPT. OF THE GULF, NINETEENTH ARMY CORPS,
Before Port Hudson, June 13, 1863.
Rear-Admiral D. G. FARRAGUT, *Flag-ship Monongahela:*
ADMIRAL: General Gardner answers that his duty requires him to defend the place, and, therefore, he declines to surrender.

Very respectfully, your obedient servant,

N. P. BANKS,
Major-General, Commanding.

HEADQUARTERS BEALL'S BRIGADE,
Port Hudson, La., June 13, 1863.

Brig. Gen. W. DWIGHT:
  Commanding U. S. Forces in front of Beall's Brigade:

GENERAL: Your request to be permitted to carry off some of your dead and wounded that are in my front is granted, with the understanding that they will be moved by unarmed men, and that your sharp-shooters will not advance.

Accept, general, my best regards.

I am, very respectfully, your obedient servant,
  W. N. R. BEALL,
  Brigadier-General, Provisional Army, Confederate States.

SPECIAL ORDERS, }   HDQRS. DEPARTMENT OF THE GULF,
    No. 140.   }   *Before Port Hudson, June* 13, 1863.

*   *   *   *   *   *   *

VIII. 4.30 *p. m.*—Col. B. H. Grierson, Sixth Illinois Cavalry, commanding cavalry, will at once send the companies of the First Louisiana Cavalry and unattached Massachusetts cavalry (Magee's and Perkins') under his command to report to Brig. Gen. William Dwight, commanding Second Division.

IX. 4.30 *p. m.*—After establishing a line of pickets, only covering the roads leading from the rear to Port Hudson, Colonel Grierson will detach Col. Edward Prince, Seventh Illinois Cavalry, with 300 cavalry and the pieces of artillery belonging to the Cavalry Brigade, and order him to take post in the field in rear of the colored troops under Colonel Nelson, on our right, to prevent the escape of the enemy through the space between the right of General Grover and the left of Colonel Nelson.

X. Colonel Grierson, having made the details and established the picket line directed by Paragraphs VIII and IX of this order, will report at these headquarters with the remainder of his command at 7 o'clock this evening.

XI. Division commanders will at once see that a sufficient reserve of ammunition for the infantry and light artillery of their divisions is not only provided, but also placed where it can be readily reached and issued when needed.

XII. 8.45 *p. m.*—Col. N. A. M. Dudley, commanding Third Brigade, First Division, will detail one regiment of infantry to proceed at once to the headquarters of the Second Division, and report for temporary duty to Brig. Gen. William Dwight, commanding the division.

XIII. 8.45 *p. m.*—Major-General Augur will order the Forty-eighth Massachusetts, Colonel Stone, to proceed at once to the headquarters of the Second Division, and report for temporary duty to Brig. Gen. William Dwight, commanding the division.

XIV. 8.45 *p. m.*—Col. N. A. M. Dudley, commanding Third Brigade, First Division, will report for orders with two regiments of his brigade to Brigadier-General Grover, commanding right wing, to support his attack.

XV. 11.30 *p. m.*—A general assault upon the works of the enemy at Port Hudson will be made to-morrow morning, 14th instant. The following directions will be observed, and the following information is given for the benefit of those principally concerned: General Grover, with his command, including two regiments of Colonel Dudley's brigade, under Colonel Dudley, will make a vigorous and determined assault at the point in front of Colonel Dudley's present position, already indicated to him. The artillery cross-fire in front of this point of attack will commence at 3 a. m., and, excepting such as may have been placed under his direction, will cease only on intimation from General Grover to these headquarters that he desires it to cease. The attacks by skirmishers will commence at 3.30 a. m., or as soon thereafter as General Grover may find best. A detachment of the First Louisiana Engineers, under Captain Jones, has been directed to report to General Grover, with intrenching tools and sand bags, to take position, unless otherwise ordered by him, near the 12-pounder rifle battery. General Augur will, in pursuance of orders already given, detail two regiments of Colonel Dudley's brigade, under Colonel Dudley, to report to General Grover, and two regiments, as already ordered, to report to General Dwight. With the remainder of his command, General Augur will make a feigned attack on the part of the works in front of Holcomb's battery and slaughter-house, to be made vigorously, and converted into a real attack should circumstances favor it. He will also hold his command in readiness to support either General Grover or General Dwight, in pursuance of orders that may be given from these headquarters. A heavy fire of artillery will open on this point of attack at 2.45 a. m. At 3.15 a. m. the attack by skirmishers will be briskly made. An officer, to be designated by Colonel Hodge, will report to General Augur, with a detachment of the First Louisiana Engineers, and with intrenching tools and sand bags, to take position, unless otherwise ordered by General Augur, near Holcomb's battery, on the road leading from his headquarters to Port Hudson. General Dwight, with his command, including two regiments to be sent him by General Augur, will make an attempt to gain an entrance to the enemy's works on our extreme left. Should this attempt fail, it will be properly reported to these headquarters, and the same will be done in case of its success. In the former case, the command will be held in readiness to move promptly to re-enforce at other points, in pursuance of orders that may be given from these headquarters. A detachment of the First Louisiana Engineers, provided with intrenching tools and sand bags, will report to General Dwight, and take position, unless otherwise ordered by him, on the road on our extreme left leading to Port Hudson, as near the works as cover may be found, General Dwight to move at such time after 3.30 a. m. to-morrow as he may deem most expedient. Generals Augur, Grover, and Dwight will not wait for signals, but act at the times specified herein without further orders. The standard is the telegraph time at these headquarters. General Arnold will have charge of all artillery in position excepting such as he may have placed under the direction of division commanders. A reserve of engineer troops, under Colonel Hodge, with tools and sand-bags, will be stationed near General Augur's headquarters. General Banks' headquarters will be during the action at the barn near the naval battery.* All applications for re-enforcements will be made to these headquarters. Either of the three commanders of a point of attack is authorized to order the fire of artillery near him to cease if he finds it inconveniencing his troops or movements. He will report his act to these headquarters.

*   *   *   *

By command of Major-General Banks:

[RICH'D B. IRWIN,]
Assistant Adjutant-General.

HEADQUARTERS DEFENSES OF NEW ORLEANS,
June 13, 1863.

Commodore MORRIS:

I have the honor to receive your letter of this date, and in reply thereto I have to state that I do consider the necessity still exists for a gunboat at Brashear City.

I regret to be compelled to make this request of you, but I consider the safety of the place in a great measure depends upon the presence of a gunboat there.

Very respectfully, your obedient servant,

W. H. EMORY,
Brigadier-General, Commanding.

HDQRS. DEPT. OF THE GULF, NINETEENTH ARMY CORPS,
Before Port Hudson, June 14, 1863.

Rear-Admiral D. G. FARRAGUT,
Commanding, &c., Flag-ship Monongahela:

ADMIRAL: As you will have readily perceived, the attack did not succeed, though the merest accident separates success from failure.

We hold advanced positions, and shall intrench them to-night. The enemy made one or two attempts on the center and right to open with his artillery, but was almost instantly silenced. It required a little longer to silence some troublesome guns on the left, but it was done. We shall hold the advanced positions we now have, and throw up rifle-pits to cover them to-night. I believe our loss has not been heavy, excepting in officers, and the men are in tolerable good spirits. I am still confident of the final result.

Very respectfully, your obedient servant,

N. P. BANKS,
Major-General, Commanding.

HDQRS. DEPT. OF THE GULF, NINETEENTH ARMY CORPS,
Before Port Hudson, June 14, 1863.

Colonel PRINCE,
Commanding, &c.:

SIR: By the direction of the commanding general, I have the honor to inform you that General Paine, who was wounded to-day, and left on the field for several hours, reports movements of heavy bodies of the enemy's troops toward our right. This, with what is known of the condition of the enemy's troops, supplies of provisions and ammunition, is taken as an indication of an attempt to be made by him to escape by breaking through on our right. You will, therefore, be vigilant, and attack the enemy at once on his making such attempt, sending prompt notice to these headquarters and to the nearest commander of infantry. General Grierson has been ordered to send you a re-enforcement of 300 men, and a section of the Fourth Massachusetts Battery has been directed to report to you at once.

Very respectfully, your obedient servant,

[D. S.] WALKER,
Assistant Adjutant-General.

SPECIAL ORDERS, } HDQRS. DEPT. OF THE GULF, 19TH A. C.,
   No. 141.   }   *Before Port Hudson, June* 14, 1863.

I. 11.05 *p. m.*—One section of the Fourth Massachusetts Battery will report, without delay, to Colonel Prince, commanding Seventh Illinois Cavalry. An orderly from these headquarters will guide the section to Colonel Prince's position.

II. 11.10 *p. m.*—General Grierson will immediately send to Colonel Prince a re-enforcement of 300 men of his command, and will hold the remainder of his command in readiness to move at short notice.

By command of Major-General Banks:

.   RICH'D B. IRWIN,
                         Assistant Adjutant-General.

             HEADQUARTERS UNITED STATES FORCES,
                 Before Port Hudson, June 15, 1863.
Maj. Gen. FRANK. GARDNER,
   Commanding C. S. Forces, Port Hudson:

SIR: I have the honor to request your permission to send a small quantity of medical and hospital supplies within your works, for the comfort of my wounded in your hands and of such of your own as you may desire to use them for.

Very respectfully, your most obedient servant,

                         N. P. BANKS,
                    Major-General, Commanding.

                    HEADQUARTERS,
         Port Hudson, La., June 15, 1863.
Maj. Gen. N. P. BANKS,
   Commanding U. S. Forces near Port Hudson, La.:

SIR: In reply to your note of this date, I have the honor to state that I will send out to meet any party you may wish to send in with such medicines and hospital supplies as you may desire to send for your wounded in my possession.

I take the liberty to inform you (deeming that you are probably ignorant of the fact) that there are a few of your dead and wounded in the vicinity of my breastworks, and I have attempted to give succor to your wounded, but your sharpshooters have prevented it.

I am, sir, very respectfully, your obedient servant,

                      FRANK. GARDNER,
              Major-General, Commanding C. S. Forces.

   HDQRS. DEPT. OF THE GULF, NINETEENTH ARMY CORPS,
                Before Port Hudson, June 15, 1863.
Rear-Admiral D. G. FARRAGUT,
   Commanding Fleet, &c.:   .

ADMIRAL: Major-General Banks desires me to inform you that a negro has just arrived in camp who reports that he left Simsport on Tuesday last, and that Kirby Smith was then there with considerable force. The man says that he ran away that night, and joined our gunboats at the mouth of Red River the following morning; that the commander of the gunboat (which he thinks was the Lafayette) took him on board and proceeded at once to Simsport, shelled the rebels there, burned the town, and returned on Thursday morning to the mouth of the river.

Major-General Banks requests to know if the statement of the negro is confirmed by reports from the gunboats.

Very respectfully, I am, admiral, your most obedient servant,

[CHAS. P. STONE,]
Brigadier-General.

FLAG-SHIP MONONGAHELA,
Port Hudson, June 15, 1863.

Brig. Gen. CHARLES P. STONE:

DEAR GENERAL: Please inform General Banks that all of the negro's report, except Kirby Smith being there, is substantially true.

The gunboats went to Simsport, and drove them away, and burned or destroyed all the flats and boats there, but the water is now, or will soon be, so low that they can occupy the place with impunity to us.

Our boats have been compelled to come out of the Red River for want of water to pass the bar; but the enemy cannot come down to the Mississippi River, and, if they do, they have no means of crossing it.

A negro came in, reporting that a large force was crossing the Red River and some bayou, on cotton bales placed on a raft in a shallow part of the stream, and that Magruder was said to be at their head; but, as my informant told me that Colonel Sage had been informed of it, I did not send you word, as you were just then in your troubles. I took it for granted that Colonel Sage would know if there was any truth in the report before he sent you word.

I sincerely hope that your losses were not great yesterday, and that all may yet be well with us. I took 5 prisoners this morning, whom I send down to Springfield Landing. They say that Weitzel was driven back from all the ground that he had gained, and they report their killed, as reported, to be very few, but I cannot believe it.

Very respectfully,

D. G. FARRAGUT,
Rear-Admiral.

U. S. S. HARTFORD,
Above Port Hudson, June 15, [1863]—11 a. m.

General N. P. BANKS:

GENERAL: The officer in command of your troops on the Point has just sent me word that the enemy from Grossetête are advancing in considerable force toward the point opposite Port Hudson, our cavalry scouts having last night [captured] 2 of their pickets. Colonel Sage informs me he will retire under the protection of the lower fleet. Can you spare a force sufficient to prevent their occupation of the Point, and to re-enforce Colonel Sage?

Yours, respectfully,

J. S. PALMER,
Commodore.

HDQRS. DEPT. OF THE GULF, NINETEENTH ARMY CORPS, .
Before Port Hudson, June 15, 1863.

Col. CLINTON H. SAGE, *Commanding at Fausse Point:*

SIR: The commanding general being informed by Commodore Palmer that you propose to abandon your position and retire under the protection of the lower fleet, in consequence of a report that the enemy is advancing upon you in force from Grossetête, sends Lieut. Charles A. Hartwell, aide-de-camp, to you, to ascertain the exact condition of affairs at Fausse Point, and the extent to which these reports are to be credited. If the enemy is really advancing upon you, we can send you a small re-enforcement; but the importance and defensive character of your position require that you should not retire from it until actually forced to do so. You can communicate with these headquarters by signal from the Richmond.

Very respectfully, your obedient servant,
RICH'D B. IRWIN,
Assistant Adjutant-General.

LOWER FLEET,
June 15, 1863—6 p. m.

Lieut. Col. RICHARD B. IRWIN, *Assistant Adjutant-General:*

SIR: Yours of to-day is just received. I have the honor to report that, in consequence of reports received from my cavalry and from contrabands sent in by Mr. Parlange, and others from the Fausse River, and from two of the enemy's pickets taken prisoners by my cavalry, I thought it advisable to move my command to this point. The enemy's forces would, I was fearful, cut off my communication with the country and the lower fleet by the road, thus affecting my supplies.

My cavalry this morning burned a bridge, which delayed the enemy. I have also received reports during the day from my cavalry that they were skirmishing with the advance pickets of the enemy 6 miles out. I could have held the point where I was encamped to-night, but I could not have thrown out the usual pickets on the river. I can throw out as many posts of pickets from this point along the river bank with my command as I could from the post where I was stationed with the same force.

Most respectfully, your obedient servant,
C. H. SAGE,
Colonel, Commanding.

HDQRS. DEPT. OF THE GULF, NINETEENTH ARMY CORPS,
Before Port Hudson, June 15, 1863.

Brig. Gen. C. GROVER, *Commanding, &c.:*

GENERAL: The Carter House Hospital and the camp of the Fourteenth New York Cavalry were taken by the rebel cavalry in its dash, but were almost instantly retaken by Colonel Grierson, who reports a number of the horses of the cavalry and all their tents were left untouched, and that the infantry guard at the hospital had quietly stacked their arms and surrendered at the request of an overwhelming force, consisting of 4 of the enemy. What regiment is the guard from?

Very respectfully, your obedient servant,
[RICH'D B. IRWIN,]
Assistant Adjutant-General.

HEADQUARTERS DEFENSES OF NEW ORLEANS,
June 15, 1863.

Lieutenant-Colonel IRWIN, *Assistant Adjutant-General:*

Mouton's forces still threaten Brashear City and the Opelousas road. They are estimated at 2,000, and their plan has been to get through the lake in small detachments, and burn the bridges at Bayou Bœuf and La Fourche Crossing. They have been foiled in that by free use of the convalescents, who have been kept on this road and at the crossings in large numbers. I have only been awaiting the arrival of a gunboat at Brashear City to send these convalescents to join their regiments. The gunboat, I fear, is not able to cross the bar at Berwick Bay. I will, however, if you are in want of them, send forward these and all other convalescents.

I have not been able to make a personal inspection of the defenses, as I am still unable to ride without inconvenience, but I have caused thorough inspection by staff officers at every point excepting Ship Island. Everything is in a good state of preparation, excepting the numerical force. That, as you know, is very deficient, and I consider it necessary that one of two things shall be done—that I should be re-enforced by four or five regiments, or if, as is probable, that cannot be done, transports should be held ready at Springfield [Landing] to re-enforce me in case of a raid on the city. The city was never more quiet than at this time, but I learn the rebel sympathizers confidently anticipate a movement of Buchanan's fleet in this direction, to cover a landing in Lake Borgne. At present they have little or no land force at Mobile, but, in case of a reverse to our arms at Vicksburg or Port Hudson, they can put a force in Mobile by railroad in a few hours.

The Creole is in, but brings no late news.

Respectfully, your obedient servant,

W. H. EMORY,
Brigadier-General, Commanding.

GENERAL ORDERS, ⎱ HDQRS. SECOND DIV., 19TH ARMY CORPS,
No. 4.   ⎰   *Before Port Hudson, June 15, 1863.*

The brigadier-general commanding the division congratulates the troops on the brave advance they made yesterday, and the ground they gained from the enemy, which they now hold.

Every such approach toward the enemy must discourage and distress the rebel force; but to do this, it is important that not a step of ground be lost; that from every ravine, and every artificial cover our riflemen shall annoy and destroy the rebels within their works. It is important, then, that our soldiers shall get such advanced positions that the enemy cannot move about within their works in safety.

The brigadier-general commanding the division has to complain that regimental commanders do not keep their men well enough in hand, and that line officers do not keep the soldiers in ranks with sufficient strictness. These faults must be corrected. No soldiers can march to an assault who fail to preserve their formation strictly; no advance can be well held when soldiers are suffered to leave ranks; no sharpshooters or skirmishers can be effective unless controlled by their line officers.

Regimental commanders do not preserve control over their regiments when they allow their soldiers to mingle with the soldiers of other regiments on the battle-field. The proper intervals of regiments must, under all circumstances, be preserved. When regiments are crowded, they are inefficient, and sometimes uselessly exposed.

By order of Brigadier-General Dwight:

WICKHAM HOFFMAN,
Assistant Adjutant-General.

SPECIAL ORDERS,) HDQRS. SECOND DIV., 19TH ARMY CORPS,
No. 39.   )   Before Port Hudson, June 15, 1863.

All orders heretofore issued from these headquarters for the temporary organization of the brigades of this division are hereby revoked.

The First and Third Brigades will remain as organized by orders from headquarters department.

A temporary Second Brigade will be formed, to consist of: One hundred and sixty-second New York Volunteers, Emory's division; One hundred and seventy-fifth New York Volunteers, Emory's division; Twenty-eighth Maine Volunteers, Second Brigade, Second Division; to be commanded by Colonel Benedict, One hundred and sixty-second New York Volunteers.

By order of Brigadier-General Dwight:

WICKHAM HOFFMAN,
Assistant Adjutant-General.

U. S. FLAG-SHIP HARTFORD,
Above Port Hudson, June 16, 1863—4 p. m.
Maj. Gen. N. P. BANKS,
Commanding Nineteenth Army Corps, before Port Hudson:

GENERAL: As far as I can learn from the 2 captured pickets of the enemy, whom Colonel Sage has sent me for safe-keeping, their force consists of between 400 and 500 men, all cavalry, badly armed; not a private among them having a saber; have been only three months in the service, and have never been even in a skirmish. They have two light pieces of artillery with them; all from Texas, commanded by Colonel [B. W.] Stone.

Yesterday afternoon Colonel Sage sent me word that the enemy were so near him that he should defend himself where he was, and asked me to render him assistance. I immediately placed two gunboats to command the levee, and offered him 100 men and a field piece to aid in his defense, but it seems he changed his plan, deeming it more prudent to change his position where he always could retire upon the lower fleet, and be secure of his supplies. This information you probably have received before this. I have seen nothing of your staff officer which you mention in your note of yesterday having sent.

Communication can always be had with me from your headquarters in three and a half hours, across Thompson's Creek, and the road is tolerably good. Owing to the falling of the waters, I can no longer signalize to the admiral across the Point. Your shortest way of communicating with Fausse Point is through me.

The transports are all down here, being alarmed, by the proximity of the guerrillas, which they say are hovering about Bayou Sara. If that is the case, the road between you and Bayou Sara is not safe. If you see no necessity of protection at Bayou Sara, I will withdraw the two gunboats I now have there.

I have no later news from Vicksburg. As soon as I have, I will send you the information. I am afraid matters are not progressing there as favorably as we could wish, or we should have had good news before this. The defenses of Port Hudson are, it seems, far more formidable than any of us have imagined. What are our present hopes of success?

Very respectfully, your obedient servant,
J. S. PALMER,
Commodore.

P. S.—I have just learned that a fight has ensued between part of the crew of the gunboat Arizona and about 100 cavalry at Pointe Coupée. Her commander was imprudent enough to send his sailors on shore to, engage them. He lost several men, and had several taken prisoners.

HDQRS. DEPT. OF THE GULF, NINETEENTH ARMY CORPS,
Before Port Hudson, June 16, 1863.
Col. CLINTON H. SAGE,
One hundred and tenth New York, Comdg. at or near Fausse Point:
SIR : The commanding general directs that you at once return with your command to the position which you have just abandoned, and that you hold it until actually forced to quit it.

The commanding general learns, with surprise, that you have felt yourself at liberty, without orders, without asking for aid, to desert the important position in which your command was placed, and in which you could successfully have withstood a vastly superior force, and that you committed this grave error upon mere rumors, without even feeling the enemy.

The commanding general desires an immediate explanation in writing of this extraordinary proceeding.

The other four companies of your regiment will be sent you to-day.
Very respectfully, your obedient servant,
RICH'D B. IRWIN,   .
Assistant Adjutant-General.

HEADQUARTERS UNITED STATES FORCES,
Fausse Point, opposite Port Hudson, June 16, 1863.
Lieut. Col. RICHARD B. IRWIN, *Assistant Adjutant-General:*
SIR: I have the honor to report, in explanation of my move of yesterday, that on the night of the 13th a colored man came in from the Fausse River, about 12 miles distant, and stated that all the negroes in the vicinity were being collected to construct crossings on Bayou Grossetête for the enemy to cross. On the night of the 14th, my cavalry scouts came on the enemy's pickets on Fausse River, 12 miles out; we took two of the cavalry pickets prisoners. I have for one week had in arrest at this point one of the enemy's cavalry. On the arrival of the two last prisoners, this one stated he belonged to a command of five companies, who were in this vicinity a week previous; that Colonel Stone was in command of a force of one full regiment and the five companies, and that they were moving down upon us.

By moving my command to the lower fleet, I could picket the levee in front of Port Hudson equally as well as from this Point, and be better protected by the gunboats, as these here do not keep steam up, and I should be in communication with the Point, from which we get all our supplies.

I have received no direct orders as to what I should do here. I had supposed I was to protect this Point, and not allow any crossing to or from Port Hudson. I have aimed to do what seemed for the best.

I have returned to my old position. My cavalry report the enemy repairing a bridge destroyed yesterday, 6 miles out. Some report 500, some 3,000 as the number of their forces.

Most respectfully, your obedient servant,
C. H. SAGE,
Colonel, Commanding.

SPECIAL ORDERS, } HDQRS. DEPT. OF THE GULF, 19TH A. C.,
No. 144.   }   Before Port Hudson, June 17, 1863.

*   *   *   *   *   *   *

II. Maj. D. C. Houston, chief engineer, being on account of sickness disabled for active duty in the field, is, at his own request, temporarily relieved from duty with the forces now in the field, and will proceed to New Orleans without delay, to attend to the business of his department there.

III. Capt. J. C. Palfrey, engineer, will, until further orders, act as chief engineer of the army before Port Hudson.

*   *   *   *   *

By command of Major-General Banks:

RICH'D B. IRWIN,
Assistant Adjutant-General.

HEADQUARTERS DEPARTMENT OF NEW MEXICO,
Santa Fé, N. Mex., June 17, 1863.

Brig. Gen. LORENZO THOMAS,
Adjutant-General, U. S. Army, Washington, D. C.:

GENERAL: Inclosed herewith please find an order organizing an expedition against the Navajoes, and likewise a request from Colonel Carson, the designated commander of the expedition, asking authority to employ 100 Ute Indians to act as auxiliaries to his force. I beg respectfully to submit, with my approval, this request to the Adjutant-General, for the consideration of the War Department, believing the money expended in the employment of these Indians for the purpose indicated will be profitably laid out.

The Utes are very brave, and fine shot, fine trailers, and uncommonly energetic in the field. The Navajoes have entertained a very great dread of them for many years. I believe 100 Ute Indians would render more service in this war than more than double their number of troops. They could be mustered as a company, or, preferably, could be employed as spies and guides.

It is important, if the employment of these Indians be authorized, that I be so informed at the earliest practicable date.

I have the honor to be, general, very respectfully, your obedient servant,

JAMES H. CARLETON,
Brigadier-General, Commanding.

HDQRS. DEPT. OF THE GULF, NINETEENTH ARMY CORPS,
Before Port Hudson, June 18, 1863.

Maj. Gen. H. W. HALLECK,
General-in-Chief, Washington, D. C.:

GENERAL: I respectfully request that I may be informed by return mail what is the decision of the War Department on the question when the terms of service of the nine-months' regiments expire. These regiments originally claimed that their term of service expired by companies. They now understand that the term of the whole regiment expires with that of the last company; and the Governor of Massachusetts has distributed [notices] to that effect to the regiments from that State. But, in the absence of instructions, I shall decide that their term is to be reckoned, first, from date of muster of the regiment as a regiment; secondly, if no such formal muster was ever made, from the date of muster-in of the field and staff. As this decision is likely to create considerable feeling among this class of troops, many of whom think they have already exceeded the period for which they enlisted, I urge that the matter be settled at once by higher authority.

Very respectfully, your obedient servant,

N. P. BANKS,
Major-General, Commanding.

HDQRS. DEPT. OF THE GULF, NINETEENTH ARMY CORPS,
Before Port Hudson, June 18, 1863.

Major-General HALLECK,
Commanding Army of the United States:

GENERAL: I have the honor to acknowledge the receipt of your dispatches of June 3 and 4, which reached me yesterday. Since I have been in the army, I have done all in my power to comply with my orders. It is so in the position I now occupy. I came here not only for the purpose of co-operating with General Grant, but by his own suggestion and appointment. Before I left Brashear City, he sent me information, by a special messenger from the fleet, that he would send to me, by Black River, a corps of 20,000 men, to aid in the reduction of Port Hudson, preliminary to an attack upon Vicksburg. Later, while at Opelousas, I received from him a dispatch, in cipher, referring to the assistance promised, and naming the 25th of May as the day when his force would join me. I replied that I would be at Port Hudson on that day. I reached Bayou Sara on the 23d of May, and advanced immediately. A few days previous I received from the general information that, in consequence of a successful engagement with the enemy near Grand Gulf, he had moved to Jackson, and doubted if he could aid me, and requested me to join him. It was out of my power as I was then situated, having no communication, excepting by the Atchafalaya, with New Orleans, and no transportation, excepting that which came that way, to do so, and I immediately answered him that it would be impossible for me to transport my troops there in season to aid him.

The next day, however, desirous to do all I could to bring our forces together, I informed him that I would send to him all the troops I could, and sent my dispatch by Brigadier-General Dwight, who knew well my situation, and adding to my communication that, if I had 5,000 men to aid me in reducing Port Hudson, I could join him at once with all my forces. General Dwight returned with an answer from General Grant that I should move against Port Hudson at once, and that he would send me the troops I wanted, but desired I should not wait for them. It was upon this statement of his purpose that I moved to Port Hudson. Copies of all these dispatches have been sent to your headquarters.

It was not until after my assault on the works, the 27th of May, that I learned from Colonel Riggin, his aide-de-camp, who brought his message, that he could not spare the troops. It seemed to all my officers that the speedy reduction of the post was certain. It seemed so to Colonel Riggin, who thought that Port Hudson should be first reduced, and that we were holding in this locality, inside and outside of the Port, more of the enemy's troops than we could carry of our own to General Grant. My officers and troops all believed our success was certain and immediate. · They knew it would be a source of great danger to New Orleans to leave a garrison of 5,000 men at Port Hudson, as many at Mobile, and a larger number in the Teche country. They knew also that, if we withdrew from the attack here, with the low water of this month and the summer, it would be impossible to return to New Orleans by the Atchafalaya and the Grand Lake, and unless it was certain that Vicksburg should fall, and General Grant's army return with us, that we could not again reach New Orleans. New Orleans has no garrison for its defense under such circumstances, and it could not but stand in great peril. It seemed to me that it was absolutely necessary that I should complete my work here. It is now, we believe, certain to be done.

The reduction of Port Hudson has required a longer time than at first supposed. First, because it is a stronger position. Secondly, because a large part of my force consists of nine-months' men, who openly say they do not consider themselves bound to any perilous service. It is this wholly unexpected defection that has prevented our success, but it cannot defeat us. I do not hesitate to say that the opinion was universal among our troops and those of the enemy that the work must fall. In proof of this I have only to say that, in the assault of Sunday, two companies of the Fourth Wisconsin Regiment went over the works and were captured, because the column did not follow, for the reason I have stated. The troops near the end of their enlistments say they do not feel like desperate service; the men enlisted for the war do not like to lead where the rest will not follow. I can also say, with certainty, that the removal of my command, or a considerable portion of it, to Vicksburg, would enable the rebel troops to join their forces on either side of the river, and place New Orleans in immediate peril. The fleet can destroy but it cannot defend the city. The dispatches inclosed will inform you of the movements of the enemy on the river below, even when Port Hudson is invested and the enemy divided by the river.

I came here by express appointment of General Grant. It did not seem possible, and it does not now seem possible, to withdraw from this post, since the first assault, without doing great injury to the Government, far more than counterbalancing the good rendered General Grant. My force is not more than 14,000 effective men, if so much, including the nine-months' men. I could not, in the present condition of things, carry to him more than 8,000 men without infinite danger to the department.

The loss or the great peril of New Orleans will be an irreparable calamity to the Government, and ought to be avoided.

I hope to effect an immediate reduction of Port Hudson, and to transport all my force to Vicksburg.

I have the honor to be, with much respect, your obedient servant,
N. P. BANKS,
Major-General, Commanding.

HEADQUARTERS RIGHT WING, UNITED STATES FORCES,
Before Port Hudson, La., June 18, 1863.

Lieut. Col. RICHARD B. IRWIN,
Assistant Adjutant-General, Nineteenth Corps :

SIR: Two cavalrymen have just come in, and report [J. L.] Logan with a large force of cavalry at Bayou Sara. Negroes report they intend attacking us, with the intention of burning the boats. Major

Sawtell asks for 50 cavalrymen to be sent him.   Can you furnish them?
If so, please send them at once.

I am, sir, very respectfully, your obedient servant,

C. GROVER,
Brigadier-General, Commanding.

FLAG-SHIP MONONGAHELA,
Port Hudson, June 18, 1863.

Maj. Gen. N. P. BANKS,
Commanding Department of the Gulf:

GENERAL: I herewith send you two documents received from Commodore Palmer and Lieutenant-Commander Cooke.   You will be able to give them a more correct value than I can, but I do not believe that Kirby Smith or Mouton are there.

The Texas prisoners I sent you yesterday said they had not heard of any general in this part of the country, and only knew Colonel Jones, of their regiment.

I will send a vessel down to Donaldsonville, although I have very few.   I had to send my last gunboat down to cruise off the mouth of the Mississippi for these pirates who are running off with our tug-boats. I do believe, however, that all that affair was concocted in New Orleans, and by a scoundrel by the name of Duke, who was the captain of a vessel we captured running the blockade with cotton.   We kept him as long as we could, for I thought he was a daring scamp, nor would I be surprised to find that the merchants interested were in the secret.

I was thinking of going down to New Orleans for a few days, and leaving Captain Alden, of the Richmond, in command here.   I know he will do all that is required, and with a zeal and cheerfulness not to be surpassed.   My affairs require looking after below; but a few days will make no matter.   If you see any prospect of being able to do anything this week, I will put off my visit below.

They appear to be getting along well on the left, in putting up batteries.   If I can be of any service, let me know.   I must look out for fresh supplies, mortar shell particularly.   I expect they are on their way, but know nothing of them.

Very respectfully,

D. G. FARRAGUT,
Rear-Admiral.

[Inclosure.]

U. S. S. HARTFORD,
Wednesday evening, June 17, 1863.

ADMIRAL: I inclose you a letter just received from Lieutenant-Commander Cooke.   There is no doubt that Kirby Smith is in this vicinity, and, from reliable source obtained from Bayou Sara to-day, I learn that it is his intention to join General Mouton and capture Donaldsonville, so as to intercept General Banks' supplies from New Orleans.   The rebel cavalry, which have been hovering in this neighborhood all the morning, have suddenly disappeared, and have taken the road to Grosse-tête.

There was a party of about 100 with two field pieces close by me this morning at Waterloo, and I learned that it was their intention to-night to fire upon the transports which were anchored just ahead of me. I accordingly have dropped them down under my lee, and my intention was to have shelled them as soon as it became dark, but, on sending a scout on shore late this afternoon to get more particularly their exact locality, I found they, too, had disappeared.

The enemy are evidently mustering in force for some purpose, whether to drive our friend Colonel Sage into the Mississippi, and then run supplies into Port Hudson, or go down to Donaldsonville, I am uncertain, but one of the two is evidently their object.

The 2 cavalrymen belong to Banks, who, with their horses, the Bee has brought down, I shall turn over to Colonel Sage as a re-enforcement.

Respectfully, your obedient servant,

JAS. S. PALMER,
Commodore.

P. S.—I sent over to you this morning an Irishman, who deserted from the rebels, and who cheerfully took the oath of allegiance, and the 2 Texas cavalry pickets captured by Colonel Sage, whom I paroled.

[Sub-Inclosure.]

U. S. GUNBOAT ESTRELLA,
Above Morganza, June 17, 1863.

Commodore JAMES S. PALMER,
　　U. S. S. Hartford:

SIR: The Estrella and Arizona got under weigh this morning from Pointe Coupée, and went to Morganza to communicate with the enemy in reference to the fate of Captain Upton's men.

They were all captured, 12 in number, and are now in the enemy's hands. We can obtain no reliable information. They say that General Kirby Smith is below Pointe Coupée; that General Mouton is also in this vicinity. Nothing said about the strength of their force. The Arizona and this vessel are both short of fuel, and are at present wooding above Morganza, on the opposite side.

I send down by the Bee 2 cavalrymen, who came down to the bank and reported that they were a portion of the rear guard of a foraging party sent out from Port Hudson yesterday, and were cut off by the enemy's cavalry. The Bee has been detained wooding.

Very respectfully, your obedient servant,

A. P. COOKE,
Lieutenant-Commander.

BATON ROUGE,
June 18, 1863.

Lieut. Col. RICHARD B. IRWIN,
　　Assistant Adjutant-General:

COLONEL: Captain McCarty, of the Southerner, reports the Anglo-American, Sykes, and two other small boats burned at Plaquemine this morning. Planter reports that they have 2,000 infantry, 500 cavalry, and two field pieces, and intend marching on Donaldsonville. Some cavalry appeared in sight.

Gunboat No. 2 has gone down.

CHAS. W. DREW,
Colonel, Commanding.

NEW ORLEANS,
June 18, 1863.

Colonel IRWIN,
   Assistant Adjutant-General:
   I have this moment received the following, and suggest that gunboat be run down to Plaquemine immediately, to shell the rebels out:

    •   DONALDSONVILLE, LA:, *June* 18, 1863.

General EMORY:
   We left New Orleans at 7 o'clock yesterday for Springfield Landing.
   At Plaquemine we found the steamers Sykes and Anglo-American on fire. Negroes report that all our men are either shot or taken prisoners. We are now at Donaldsonville; have on board 350 convalescents, mostly unarmed. What shall we do? Negroes report 500 to 1,000 rebels at Plaquemine.

M. CLAPP,
   - *Lieutenant in Command.*

   The convalescents are on their way to join their regiments at headquarters. Will remain for the present at Donaldsonville.

W. H. EMORY,
Brigadier-General, Commanding.

HEADQUARTERS DEFENSES OF NEW ORLEANS,
June 18, 1863.

Lieutenant-Colonel IRWIN:
   I have just received the following telegram from Donaldsonville.*
   These are the chaps who started from Brashear, and have now come in by the Plaquemine.
   I have sent up the gunboat Kineo, and a transport with 200 infantry and one piece of artillery; all I could spare. You might send another gunboat from above.

W. H. EMORY,
Brigadier-General, Commanding.

HEADQUARTERS DEFENSES OF NEW ORLEANS,
June 18, 1863.

Commodore MORRIS:
   I have this moment received a telegram from Donaldsonville, by which you will see that the gunboat is really required at Donaldsonville. I hope the Kineo has started.
   I have the honor to be, your obedient servant,

W. H. EMORY,
Brigadier-General, Commanding.

HEADQUARTERS DEFENSES OF NEW ORLEANS,
June 18, 1863.

Lieutenant-Colonel STICKNEY:
   The enemy have crossed at Plaquemine, and are marching to Donaldsonville. They may go down the La Fourche, to attack your rear.

* See Clapp's dispatch, above.

Keep your pickets at La Fourche on the lookout.   Keep all your force in hand to resist an attack at that quarter. ·
By command of W. H. Emory, brigadier-general commanding:

W. D. SMITH,
Lieutenant-Colonel, and Acting Assistant Adjutant-General.

WAR DEPARTMENT,
Washington City, June 18, 1863.

The SECRETARY OF STATE,
Washington, D. C.:

SIR: I have the honor to transmit a copy of a correspondence between the commandant of the French corvette La Tisiphone and the general in command of the United States forces at New Orleans, and to suggest that the high appreciation of the President and of the Department for this prompt and generous consideration for our wounded at that place may be communicated to Captain Marivault through the French minister.

· Very respectfully, your obedient servant,

EDWIN M. STANTON,
Secretary of War.

[Inclosure No. 1.]

CORVETTE LA TISIPHONE,
Port de Nouvelle-Orléans, 30 *Mai,* 1863.

Mons. GÉNÉRAL: J'ai l'honneur de vous offrir les services des deux chirurgiens de La Tisiphone qui pourraient se rendre régulièrement à des heures qui seraient réglées selon vos convenances, dans un des hôpitaux de la ville où se trouvent des blessés parlant Français, quelle que soient d'ailleurs la provenance et la couleur de ces blessés.

Je suis avec respect, Général, votre très humble serviteur, le capitaine de frégate, commandant la corvette de S. M. I. La Tisiphone,

V. DE MARIVAULT.

Mons. LE GÉNÉRAL COMMANDANT
LA PLACE DE LA NOUVELLE-ORLÉANS.

[Inclosure No. 2.]

HEADQUARTERS DEFENSES OF NEW ORLEANS,
May 30, 1863.

CAPTAIN: I have the honor to receive your communication of this date, tendering the services of the two surgeons of the frigate La Tisiphone to aid in attending the wounded who speak French.

Nothing could be more timely or courteous than your kind offer, and I hasten to communicate it to the medical director of the forces here, who informs me he will gladly avail himself of their services.

I shall take pleasure in communicating to my Government this noble act of humanity, which adds to the respect entertained for the nation you represent, and consideration for yourself personally, whose deportment throughout the trying times which have surrounded your official position here has secured to you the esteem of the military and the affection of all the citizens of this community.

I have the honor to be, sir, respectfully, your obedient servant,

W. H. EMORY,
Brigadier-General, Commanding.

Captain MARIVAULT,
Commanding His Imperial Majesty's Corvette Tisiphone.

ADDENDA.

HEADQUARTERS DEFENSES OF NEW ORLEANS,
June 1, 1863.
General THOMAS, *Adjutant-General, U. S. Army:*

I have the honor to inclose you a correspondence between Captain Marivault, the commander of the French naval forces, and myself. It will be seen I have accepted the generous proposition of the French commander, and his surgeons are now actually engaged in the work of dressing our wounded.

It has occurred to me that the authorities at Washington might desire to make some official acknowledgment of this act through the foreign department, and I take the liberty of sending information of it direct to the Department, as the commanding general is now absent in the field.

I have the honor to be, your obedient servant,
W. H. EMORY,
Brigadier-General, Commanding.

—

DEPARTMENT OF STATE, *Washington, June* 19, 1863.
[Hon: WILLIAM L. DAYTON:]

SIR: The Secretary of War has submitted to the President a correspondence which has lately been held between Viscount de Marivault, captain of the French corvette La Tisiphone, and William H. Emory, the general in command of the United States military forces at New Orleans, on the occasion of a tender by the former and an acceptance by the latter of the services of the medical men of the French vessel for the care and relief of the sick and wounded soldiers of the United States.* The President is deeply affected by this generous and humane conduct on the part of the French officers on the occasion thus made known to him, and he has requested me to communicate his high appreciation of it to the Government of His Imperial Majesty. I am unable, however, to find for the performance of this duty any language more just and natural than that which General Emory has employed in his letter which closes the correspondence to which I have referred. I have, therefore, to request you to place a copy of this letter in the hands of Mr. Drouyn de l'Huys, and inform him that it gives a just expression of the sentiments of the President of the United States on an occasion which he is sure will be regarded as an incident in the present unhappy civil war equally interesting in its character and honorable to the French people.

I am, &c.,

WM. H. SEWARD,
[*Secretary of State.*]

—

FLAG-SHIP MONONGAHELA,
Donaldsonville, June 19, 1863.
[Maj. Gen. N. P. BANKS:]

GENERAL: I arrived at Plaquemine at 8 p. m., hearing all the way that both Donaldsonville and Plaquemine were in the possession of the enemy; that they had a force of 2,000 infantry and 600 cavalry, and many field pieces; all of which I found to be false.

---

* See Secretary of War to Secretary of State, June 18, p. 569.

About 100 of the Texas cavalry made a raid upon Plaquemine, and burned the steamers that were there, and captured some of the provost pickets, but they lost some of their number, and were shelled by the gunboat Winona, which arrived there two or three hours after they attacked the town. They also burned about 40 bales of cotton. I found your ammunition on board the Time and Tide, waiting for convoy, and sent her forward under protection of the Winona.

I also received some mortar shell for the mortar-boats, which will help us very much. I hope to be back in time to see Port Hudson fall.

The rebel papers say that Grant has Pemberton in a circumference of 1,200 yards, but that Johnston is coming in his rear with 70,000 men, and Kirby Smith is with a force at Milliken's Bend. This last is not credited by our side.

We saved 15 out of 21 of the provost picket at Plaquemine, and may recover more of them.

Major Bullen feels no uneasiness about Donaldsonville so long as he has a gunboat, which I shall leave.

Wishing you early success, I remain, very truly,

D. G. FARRAGUT,
Rear-Admiral.

HDQRS. DEPT. OF THE GULF, NINETEENTH ARMY CORPS,
Before Port Hudson, June 19, 1863.

Brig. Gen. W. H. EMORY, *New Orleans:*

GENERAL : A few days ago there were 300 cavalry hovering around Colonel Sage at Fausse Point. They went toward Plaquemine. To-day a quartermaster's clerk, taken prisoner at Plaquemine, says the enemy's force at that place was two regiments of cavalry, one of infantry, and six pieces of artillery. The reports began with 500, and have reached 5,000, but the lower number is probably the nearest to the truth. Donaldsonville is in no danger. The admiral has gone down with a gunboat. Make the transports come up. The fears of steamboatmen and provost-marshals will do more than the enemy can to interrupt the communications of this army.

By command of Major-General Banks:

RICH'D B. IRWIN,
Assistant Adjutant-General.

HEADQUARTERS DEFENSES OF NEW ORLEANS,
June 19, 1863.

Lieutenant-Colonel IRWIN :

The gunboat Princess Royal has just arrived at Southwest Pass from Philadelphia, and Commodore Morris has kindly consented to let her go up the river to aid in repelling the enemy at Plaquemine and opening the navigation.

W. H. EMORY,
Brigadier-General, Commanding.

HEADQUARTERS DEFENSES OF NEW ORLEANS,
June 19, 1863.

Commodore MORRIS :

I have just learned that Admiral Farragut is on his way down, and may be expected either to-night or to-morrow morning. The information he will have about the state of the river and the enemy's force at Plaquemine may suggest whether or not it is necessary to send the Princess Royal to support the Kineo.

I have the honor to be, commodore, very respectfully, your obedient servant,

W. H. EMORY,
Brigadier-General, Commanding.

DEPARTMENT OF STATE,
Washington, June 20, 1863.

Hon. E. M. STANTON, *Secretary of War:*

SIR: I have the honor to acknowledge the receipt of your letter of the 18th instant, transmitting a copy of a correspondence between Captain Marivault, of the French corvette La Tisiphone, and General Emory, commanding at New Orleans, and to inform you that your suggestion on the subject has been executed.

I have the honor to be, sir, your obedient servant,

WM. H. SEWARD,
[*Secretary of State.*]

HDQRS. DEPT. OF THE GULF, NINETEENTH ARMY CORPS,
Before Port Hudson, June 20, 1863.[*]

Maj. Gen. H. W. HALLECK,
General in-Chief, Washington:

GENERAL: The terms of service of the regiments of nine-months' volunteers, twenty-two in number, now serving in this department, will begin to expire in a few days, and by the end of August will all have expired. Some of these regiments claim to be already entitled to discharge, and every few days will add to the number of those who make such a claim. If the Government decides that their term is to be reckoned from the date of muster-in of the last company, as claimed, we shall lose them much sooner than I have stated. On this point I have asked for instructions.

When these regiments leave us, there will remain in my command thirty-seven regiments of three-years' infantry, averaging, at the outside, but 350 effective men each. Of these I must, in any event, leave one regiment at Key West and the Tortugas, one at Pensacola, one at Forts Jackson and Saint Philip, four at New Orleans, supposing my main force to be covering and in supporting distance of that city, and a very much larger force if we operate in a remote quarter. My movable force of infantry can, therefore, in no case exceed 10,000, and for any operations which uncover that city would be but half that number.

We shall be powerful in artillery, and our cavalry force, organized almost entirely here, will be respectable in numbers, though lacking in efficiency, owing to defective organization and discipline and want of instruction.

The control of the Mississippi, when gained, as I feel confident it will be, by hard struggles and great sacrifice, may be again wrested from our grasp if some provision is not made to repair the losses from the casualties of active service, from the diseases of the climate, and from the exodus of the nine-months' regiments.

I think it of the utmost importance for the interest of the Govern-

---

[*] This letter also appears in the files as of June 22 and 29.

ment that the ranks of our three-years' regiments should be filled up immediately, and that the nine-months' regiments should be replaced.

I ought, perhaps, to add that the organization of the colored troops is progressing steadily and as rapidly as the absorbing nature of our present operations will permit. We have four full regiments of infantry, reporting over 900 effective men each, in the field and in garrison'; one engineer regiment of three battalions, nearly full and actually in the field; two batteries of heavy artillery in garrison, one regiment in process of organization at Pensacola, and the five regiments of Ullmann's brigade, now in the field, being filled up as fast as circumstances permit.

Every negro within the present lines of this department, or within reach of them, without distinction of age, sex, or condition, is in the service of the Government, either in the army or in producing food for the army and its dependents.

Very respectfully, your most obedient servant,
N. P. BANKS,
Major-General, Commanding.

HEADQUARTERS UNITED STATES FORCES,
Fausse Point, June 20, 1863.

Lieut. Col. RICHARD B. IRWIN, *Assistant Adjutant-General:*

SIR: I have the honor to report everything quiet at this point. The forces that were threatening us in the rear are reported to have moved south, to the section of country known as Grossetête.

I had hoped to have been able to have reported something more definite of the enemy's doings on Fausse River and Island. A person who has gone through that section of country to obtain information has not yet returned.

Four companies of my regiment joined me here on Wednesday last. Under suggestions of General Stone, I am strengthening this point.

No attack is at present apprehended.

Most respectfully, your obedient servant,
C. H. SAGE,
Colonel, Commanding.

HDQRS. DEPT. OF THE GULF, NINETEENTH ARMY CORPS,
Before Port Hudson, June 20, 1863.

Col. EDWARD PRINCE, *Seventh Illinois Cavalry:*

COLONEL: The commanding general directs that you report your command to Brig. Gen. Benjamin H. Grierson, commanding cavalry, but remain in your present position, discharging your present duties, until further orders from him.

Very respectfully, your obedient servant,
RICH'D B. IRWIN,
Assistant Adjutant-General.

HDQRS. DEPT. OF THE GULF, NINETEENTH ARMY CORPS,
June 20, 1863—9.30 p. m.

Brig. Gen. B. H. GRIERSON, *Commanding Cavalry:*

SIR: The commanding general directs that you at once put your whole disposable force of cavalry, after arranging to picket our rear, in readiness to march, with two days' rations, and that you have it all at Newport by 1 a. m.

You will immediately report in person at these headquarters for instructions.

You have, of course, received the copy of an order placing Colonel Prince under your control.

Very respectfully, your obedient servant,

RICH'D B. IRWIN,
Assistant Adjutant-General.

HDQRS. DEPT. OF THE GULF, NINETEENTH ARMY CORPS,
Before Port Hudson, June 20. 1863.

Maj. Gen. C. C. AUGUR,
Commanding, &c.:

GENERAL: The volunteers for the storming party will assemble at 9 a. m. to-morrow, at the headquarters of the right and left wings, respectively, whence they will be conducted by orderlies to the camp of the stormers. They should have two days' rations, shelter-tents cooking utensils, &c.

Very respectfully, your obedient servant,

RICH'D B. IRWIN,
Assistant Adjutant-General.

(Same to Brigadier-Generals Grover and Dwight.)

HEADQUARTERS DEFENSES OF NEW ORLEANS,
June 20, 1863—2 a. m.

Lieutenant-Colonel IRWIN:

Captain Cole, of the Anglo-American, and Captain Eddy, of the Sykes, have arrived here, and give the information that the enemy, in large force, have passed the Plaquemine toward the La Fourche Crossing.

I am aware of the importance of this on your present operations, and have informed Captains Eddy and Cole they will be hung if false.

The force actually passed is one regiment of cavalry, fourteen pieces of artillery, two regiments of infantry.

W. H. EMORY,
Brigadier-General, Commanding.

HDQRS. DEPT. OF THE GULF, NINETEENTH ARMY CORPS,
Before Port Hudson, June 20, 1863.

Brig. Gen. W. H. EMORY,
New Orleans:

GENERAL: The commanding general directs that you leave a guard of two companies at Brashear City, and at once concentrate the whole of the remainder of the force on the Opelousas Railway at La Fourche Crossing; also that you immediately send to the same point the Twenty-sixth Massachusetts and Ninth Connecticut Volunteers, with such artillery and cavalry as you have disposable.

Direct the commanding officer to defend the position at all events, and, if he is strong enough, to attack and disperse the enemy.

The best information we have of the enemy's force indicates two regiments of cavalry, one of infantry, and one battery, under Col. J. P. Major. Please acknowledge.

By command of Major-General Ranks:
RICH'D B. IRWIN,
Assistant Adjutant-General.

HEADQUARTERS DEFENSES OF NEW ORLEANS,
June 20, 1863—2 a. m.

Lieutenant-Colonel STICKNEY:

The enemy are crossing at the La Fourche Crossing in some force. Leave the gunboat to guard Brashear City. Concentrate all your force at La Fourche Crossing, and defend it to the last extremity.

By command of W. H. Emory, brigadier-general, commanding:
W. D. SMITH,
Lieutenant-Colonel, and Acting Assistant Adjutant-General.

HDQRS. DEPT. OF THE GULF, NINETEENTH ARMY CORPS,
Before Port Hudson, June 20, 1863.

Brig. Gen. W. H. EMORY,
New Orleans:

GENERAL: If the gunboat is at Brashear, the two companies that went there can escape on her. What became of the guns at Brashear? The commanding general directs me to inform you that it is impossible for him to spare any force from here at present. He relies upon your doing the best you can with the small force at your disposal.

Very respectfully, your obedient servant,
RICH'D B. IRWIN,
Assistant Adjutant-General.

HEADQUARTERS DEFENSES OF NEW ORLEANS,
June 20, 1863.

Commanding Officer of military and naval forces at Donaldsonville:

The enemy, in considerable force, has crossed the Plaquemine at Indian Village, and passed down the La Fourche, to attack the Opelousas Railroad and Brashear City.

I do not think Donaldsonville in any immediate danger. What force can be spared should be sent down to Algiers, to be placed on the railroad.

Communicate this to Admiral Farragut.

By command of Brigadier-General Emory:
[F. W. LORING,]
Aide-de-Camp.

LA FOURCHE,
June 20, 1863.

Brigadier-General EMORY:

We have been attacked. We have repulsed them once. We do not know where they will appear again.

ALBERT STICKNEY.

LA FOURCHE,
June 20, 1863.

Brigadier-General EMORY:

Thus far we have repulsed them. We do not know their force in our front.

ALBERT STICKNEY,
Lieutenant-Colonel.

HEADQUARTERS DEFENSES OF NEW ORLEANS,
June 20, 1863.

Lieutenant Colonel IRWIN:

If a division could be spared to Donaldsonville, and march on the trail of the enemy, now ascertained to be 4,000, they would be captured. The gunboat at Brashear will keep them from crossing. But it must be done quickly, or Brashear falls.

W. H. EMORY,
Brigadier-General, Commanding.

HEADQUARTERS DEFENSES OF NEW ORLEANS,
June 20, 1863.

Lieutenant-Colonel STICKNEY:

Colonel Cahill, with strong re-enforcements of infantry and artillery, is now getting ready to support you. Hold the enemy in check, and fight him boldly. He is not as strong as you estimate.

W. H. EMORY,
Brigadier-General, Commanding.

LA FOURCHE,
June 20, 1863.

Brigadier-General EMORY:

We are all ready for fighting when they come. I shall feel easy when the re-enforcements come. We can give them a good fight, and, if we have enough men, can whip them thoroughly. They captured toward 100 men, convalescents, I think, at Thibodeaux. I don't know who was to blame; some one.

Respectfully,

ALBERT STICKNEY,
Lieutenant-Colonel.

HEADQUARTERS DEFENSES OF NEW ORLEANS,
June 20, 1863.

Lieutenant-Colonel STICKNEY:

Have you the Bayou Bœuf road and crossing well guarded? The enemy may come down on that road. Your scouts at Napoleonville should be able to notify you.

Keep your train all ready to defend either point.

By command of W. H. Emory, brigadier-general commanding:

W. D. SMITH,
Lieut. Col., and Acting Assistant Adjutant-General.

HEADQUARTERS DEFENSES OF NEW ORLEANS,
June 20, 1863.

Colonel CAHILL:

Stickney has been attacked, and repulsed the enemy at La Fourche. Hurry forward to his support; he does not know where they will appear next.

W. H. EMORY,
Brigadier-General, Commanding.

HEADQUARTERS DEFENSES OF NEW ORLEANS,
June 20, 1863.

Lieutenant-Colonel IRWIN:

You have underrated the force which has passed in your front and is now marching on La Fourche. Everything has been put forward to meet them, but the force is inadequate. Colonel Stickney telegraphs me from La Fourche the enemy numbering several thousand and approaching him.

Colonel Cahill, with the Ninth Connecticut and Twenty-sixth Massachusetts and a battery of artillery, has gone to his support.

This leaves this city and the public property here very unsafe.

W. H. EMORY,
Brigadier-General, Commanding.

HEADQUARTERS DEFENSES OF NEW ORLEANS,
June 20, 1863.

Lieutenant-Colonel IRWIN:

The enemy have attacked Stickney at La Fourche Crossing, and the enemy have been repulsed. We do not know where they will appear next. The train from Terre Bonne was charged by the cavalry, and just escaped.

W. H. EMORY,
Brigadier-General, Commanding.

HEADQUARTERS DEFENSES OF NEW ORLEANS,
June 20, 1863.

Lieut. Col. RICHARD B. IRWIN:

Your countermand of the order making the disposition of troops arrived too late. Two companies ordered back to Brashear, and I am afraid they are cut off.

W. H. EMORY,
Brigadier-General, Commanding.

HEADQUARTERS DEFENSES OF NEW ORLEANS,
June 20, 1863.

Admiral FARRAGUT:

Your telegram received. Enemy have approached at La Fourche Crossing, and were repulsed by Colonel Stickney. Our line is so long it is impossible to hold it with our force. They have already cut communication between La Fourche Crossing and Brashear. Urge Gen.

eral Banks to send a force to Donaldsonville to follow in their rear, and if the gunboat at Brashear does its duty, they cannot cross there, and must be caught. I have no more force left to send after them.

W. H. EMORY,
Brigadier-General, Commanding.

HEADQUARTERS DEFENSES OF NEW ORLEANS,
June 20, 1863.

Admiral FARRAGUT: ·

The railroad track at Terre Bonne is torn up. Communication with Brashear cut off.

It is idle to attempt to hold 90 miles of railroad with the small force I have. What portion is cut off by the Terre Bonne operation I cannot tell. I have at this moment but 400 men in the city, and I consider the o city and the public property very unsafe. The Secessionists here profess to have certain information that the forces are to make an attempt on the city.

W. H. EMORY,
Brigadier-General, Commanding.

HEADQUARTERS DEFENSES OF NEW ORLEANS,
June 20, 1863.

Lieutenant-Colonel IRWIN:

The railroad track at Terre Bonne is torn up. Communication with Brashear cut off.

What portion of Stickney's force is cut off by this operation I cannot tell. It is idle to attempt to hold this long road with the small force I have. After complying with your orders of this morning, I have left but 400 effective men in the city.

W. H. EMORY,
Brigadier-General, Commanding.

HEADQUARTERS DEFENSES OF NEW ORLEANS,
June 20, 1863.

Lieutenant-Colonel STICKNEY:

What force have you left at the fort? I begin to think, now, they will come down on the road direct from La Fourche to Brashear.

Hold everything in readiness to strike whenever they appear. If the fort and gunboat do their duty, the whole of the enemy's party, unless much stronger than I expect, must be captured, for we shall have a force down from above to aid.

W. H. EMORY,
Brigadier-General, Commanding.

HEADQUARTERS DEFENSES OF NEW ORLEANS,
June 20, 1863.

Lieutenant-Colonel STICKNEY:

Very much depends upon your cavalry. You must keep them posted so far in front that they may tell you whether the enemy will come on the La Fourche road or whether they will march on Brashear.

When you have ascertained the point they are going to attack, you will concentrate all your force there, and telegraph to Colonel Cahill to come to your support.

W. H. EMORY,
Brigadier-General, Commanding.

HEADQUARTERS DEFENSES OF NEW ORLEANS,
June 20, 1863.

Lieutenant-Colonel IRWIN:

The following dispatch* has been received from my aide-de-camp, Cooley. If the enemy are in this force, they must have crossed the Atchafalaya and Grossetête due west of Baton Rouge. Their object must be either New Orleans itself, or to go down the La Fourche and attack the Opelousas Railroad.

Upon whatever point the attack is developed, I shall concentrate all my force; but it must be apparent to you that I have nothing to resist a force like one described below. The truth of the report can be better ascertained from Port Hudson than from here, as the distance to Plaquemine there is three-fourths less than from here.

This force must have passed within one-half day's march of your pickets on the west side of the river. The transports sent to Springfield have refused to pass Plaquemine, and have dropped down under cover of the gunboat at Donaldsonville.

W. H. EMORY.
Brigadier-General, Commanding.

HEADQUARTERS DEFENSES OF NEW ORLEANS,
June 20, 1863.

Lieut. Col. RICHARD B. IRWIN:

Your telegram is received, and was so far anticipated that all the force from Brashear was concentrated at La Fourche early this morning, and all the available infantry held at Algiers, with a special train, ready to defend the point attacked. I still think this the best disposition to be made, as the enemy's pickets have passed Donaldsonville, and been reported within 23 miles of Fort Banks, and their point of attack is not yet developed.

Your order, however, shall be instantly obeyed, as I suppose your information is better than mine.

W. H. EMORY,
Brigadier-General, Commanding.

LA FOURCHE,
June 21, 1863.

Lieut. Col. W. D. SMITH, *Acting Assistant Adjutant-General:*

We have been attacked and suffered severely, but repulsed them. Send immediately 12-pounder howitzer canister, 6-pounder ammunition, Enfield rifle, caliber .57. Will send another dispatch soon for ammunition.

Respectfully,

ALBERT STICKNEY,
Lieutenant-Colonel.

---

* Not found.

LA FOURCHE,
June 21, 1863.
Lieut. Col. W. D. SMITH,
    Acting Assistant Adjutant-General:
    If I have three light pieces, with horses and ammunition, I can hold my position here and come through to New Orleans, I think, even if the railroad should be cut. I can retire to Des Allemands, if you think best; and now that the railroad is cut between here and Brashear, the value of this place is, of course, diminished. They can hold Brashear if they withdraw from Bœuf, and make good dispositions as long as their rations last. Major Anthony, in command there, is a good officer. Some scouts have just come in. No force this side of Thibodeaux, and don't think them well armed. Don't know about artillery.
    Respectfully,
                                        ALBERT STICKNEY,
                                            Lieutenant-Colonel.

_____

HEADQUARTERS DEFENSES OF NEW ORLEANS,
June 21, 1863.
Lieutenant-Colonel STICKNEY:
    Colonel Cahill, with two regiments of infantry and a battery of artillery, was ordered to support you. The infantry left early in the day, and the artillery at 1 o'clock last night. Colonel Cahill may have stopped at Boutte or Des Allemands, but his force must have joined you. As soon as it does, if strong enough, attack and disperse the enemy, and do something if you can to relieve Brashear.
    But, before doing anything, secure well your communication with Colonel Cahill at Boutte Station and Des Allemands.
                                        W. H. EMORY,
                                        Brigadier-General, Commanding.

_____

HEADQUARTERS DEFENSES OF NEW ORLEANS,
June 21, 1863.
Lieutenant-Colonel IRWIN:
    The force directed to be held at Brashear will no doubt hold that place for several days.
    Stickney was ordered to keep open the communication with Brashear, but the enemy have been too strong. All his re-enforcements have reached him by this time, and he is ordered to attack.
                                        W. H. EMORY,
                                        Brigadier-General, Commanding.

_____

HEADQUARTERS DEFENSES OF NEW ORLEANS,
June 21, 1863.
Lieutenant-Colonel IRWIN,
    Assistant Adjutant-General:
    At Brashear City there are five 24-pounders and 250 men, besides the guns in the fort, and over 300 convalescents, pronounced by surgeons fit to return to regiments. Another 24-pounder and howitzer at Bœuf. If they withdraw from Bœuf, with the gunboat covering their flanks, they can do it, and strengthen Brashear.

The enemy are between La Fourche and Brashear. Have cut the communication at Terre Bonne. The force at La Fourche is ordered, if possible, to restore the communication. Can't say the number of rations they have at Brashear City, but enemy can't subdue them while those rations last. I fear, however, that nothing can effectually relieve them but a strong force landed at Donaldsonville, and marching on the enemy's rear.

The enemy now threaten Des Allemands; in consequence, Colonel Cahill has stopped a smart force there.

W. H. EMORY,
Brigadier-General, Commanding.

HEADQUARTERS DEFENSES OF NEW ORLEANS,
June 21, 1863.

Lieutenant-Colonel STICKNEY:

In regard to whether you will attack the enemy and attempt to relieve Brashear City, or to fall back to Des Allemands, you must use your own discretion.

That must be decided on the ground, where you can judge the force of the enemy. Whatever you decide, telegraph me, and communicate with Colonel Cahill, at Boutte Station. Watch your trains, that none of them fall into the hands of the enemy.

W. H. EMORY,
Brigadier-General, Commanding.

HEADQUARTERS DEFENSES OF NEW ORLEANS,
June 21, 1863.

Commanding Officer at Brashear City:

SIR: The communication being cut at Terre Bonne by the enemy, I send round to you by sea, to direct you to hold on till the last extremity, and to say to you that I will communicate to you regularly by sea. Send me a full report of your condition and wants, if any. Any sick or wounded you may have, you can send round by the Saint Mary's, but you will give her immediate dispatch.

By command of W. H. Emory, brigadier-general, commanding:

W. D. SMITH,
Lieut. Col., and Acting Assistant Adjutant-General.

HEADQUARTERS DEFENSES OF NEW ORLEANS,
June 21, 1863.

Lieutenant-Colonel IRWIN:

The guns are at Brashear City; also a large number of sick, rolling-stock of the railroad, and a special train, which took off two companies.

I ordered Stickney, after repelling the attack at La Fourche, to go back to Brashear with the largest part of his force, but the enemy is so strong this would be only to isolate and probably lose his force.

Without aid from you, the force here cannot reoccupy Brashear. Therefore, the defense of this long line of road is impracticable, and should, in my opinion, be abandoned, and what we have left be with-

: drawn to the Des Allemands Bayou. ¡Shall I do this, or risk all by attempting to keep open the road to Brashear?

W.. H.. EMORY,
Brigadier-General, Commanding.

HDQRS. DEPT. OF THE GULF, NINETEENTH ARMY CORPS,
Before Port Hudson, June 21, 1863—2 p. m.
Brig. Gen. W. H. EMORY,
New Orleans:

GENERAL: Your dispatch in regard to Brashear, saying that you have sent round the Saint Mary's, is received. The commanding general does not regard it as important that we should run any great risk to save Brashear. He desires that you will send orders to Brashear to get off everything of value there and at Bayou Bœuf, including, especially, the guns, and, when pressed by the enemy, to retire on board the transports and proceed to New Orleans. The gunboat should remain in Berwick Bay, to prevent the enemy from crossing.

Very respectfully, your obedient servant,
[RICH'D B. IRWIN,]
Assistant Adjutant-General.

HEADQUARTERS SECOND BRIGADE, SECOND DIVISION,
Boutte Station, June 21, 1863—4 a. m.
Lieut. Col. W. D. SMITH,
Acting Assistant Adjutant-General, Defenses of New Orleans:

COLONEL: I have the honor to inform you that this command arrived here at 8.10 o'clock last night, and, in pursuance of instructions, I disembarked a portion of the troops, viz, 185 men, belonging to the Ninth Connecticut Volunteers. Of the remainder, three companies of the Twenty-sixth Massachusetts, under the command of Captain Annable, were left at Bayou Des Allemands, with instructions to guard the bridge and ascertain the character of approaching trains, and, in case the troops in front were forced to fall back, to cover the retreat by obstructing the track, and, if necessary, burning the bridge. I have communicated with them once during the night by means of a hand-car. This neighborhood all quiet.

I herewith transmit you a rough sketch of our position here,* as nearly as could be ascertained in the dark. The remaining portion of the command pushed on for the purpose of effecting a junction with Lieutenant-Colonel Stickney, which they accomplished about 12 last night. I have heard nothing from the cavalry force sent up the River road, and which left Algiers at 6 o'clock last night.

I have been unable to comply with your instructions in regard to keeping up constant communication with La Fourche, as I had no train at my disposal during the night, nor any means of communicating with the city. A telegraph operator with a field instrument is greatly needed at these headquarters. At present I am completely isolated, both from the city and from my command in front. The train by which I forward this dispatch brings down from La Fourche about 700 contrabands, mostly women and children, the able-bodied men being retained for intrenching purposes. Some of those on the train have the measles, and should be quarantined.

---

* Not found.

I also send you 8 suspicious persons, claiming to be refugees fleeing the guerrillas. They were apprehended at various points on the road between La Fourche and this place. I would respectfully suggest that they be put in confinement for the present, [to prevent] the dissemination of rumors which might cause disturbance in the city.

I also inclose to you a copy of the instructions issued to the engineers and conductors of trains approaching Des Allemands Bridge from the west.*

12 M.

Sir: I have heard nothing yet of the cavalry sent up the river. Lieutenant Reynolds, of the One hundred and fourteenth New York, district provost-marshal of Saint Charles, is now with me. He lives about 1 mile below the intersection of the road from this place to the river. He has seen or heard nothing of the cavalry. He is about 26 miles above Algiers.

So much was written when my outer picket reports the cavalry at the levee; they will report soon.

Lieutenant Reynolds informs me that on the 20th a sergeant, who is on a Government plantation called the Davis place, about 24 miles from Algiers, called upon him, and stated that the night before 8 guerrillas stopped at the place, inquired for the stock, and asked if it was a Government plantation; asked if there were any arms or ammunition there. This is a negro story. The sergeant did not see them, but said he heard the sound of their horses riding away. Lieutenant Reynolds does not place much reliance in the story. He had a letter from A. B. Triples, who is on the Webb plantation, 8 miles above where the road from Boutte Station strikes the river, say 34 miles above the city on this side, of the date of June 19. He makes no mention of any alarm up there. This officer states that he has not received the circular with reference to reports from your headquarters.

I propose to take some horses from the Government plantation, and mount a few men of a company I intend to send to the River road to act as vedettes, and I will then send the cavalry to the front as soon as their horses are fed and rested, as they are said to be very much fatigued. If it should be necessary, they can fall back on the company I shall have at the river, which it is true is only a small one, 28 men, but I consider it sufficient.

I respectfully suggest, that if the present position of our forces is to continue, it would be well to stop all travel or intercourse up along the river except to Government transports, as such intercourse may furnish the enemy with a knowledge of our very small force on the road, and encourage him to attack us. This might be done by the provost-marshal-general suspending passes for awhile, and so instructing his deputies. I allow no white person, excepting those employed on the road, to pass through my command. Negroes I allow to go to the city, but not out.

I consider my position a good one for the small force I have, as it will crowd the enemy if he comes down toward the river, and within reach of the gunboats. It is true I might be cut off by a force coming down the River road. Fifteen miles in my rear is the company canal, with a swing bridge, which canal is 30 feet wide, with a fine fortification on its lower bank, but I have not men enough to man it unless the whole force from La Fourche was brought in.

If I could be furnished with a field telegraphic instrument, I think I

---

* Not found.

could furnish an operator. Lieutenant Bonney, of the Twenty-sixth Massachusetts, who is at Des Allemands, was an operator before joining the service, and could use him, and thus be in constant communication. My objections to parties traveling out of the city will apply with particular force to passengers other than military on the railroad. I should think none such should be allowed going out, at least.

　I am, colonel, very respectfully,

THOS. W. CAHILL,
Colonel, Commanding Second Brigade. ·

HEADQUARTERS DEFENSES OF NEW ORLEANS,
June 21, 1863.

Colonel CAHILL, or
Lieutenant-Colonel STICKNEY:

I am afraid Brashear is gone. Do not let the enemy get between you and this place.

Keep everything prepared to fall back on the Des Allemands Bayou should your rear be threatened.

W. H. EMORY,
Brigadier-General, Commanding.

HEADQUARTERS DEFENSES OF NEW ORLEANS,
June 21, 1863—9 p. m.

Colonel CAHILL:

I have directed Colonel Stickney to attack the enemy to-morrow (Monday) at La Fourche Crossing, and I desire that you will move forward with your infantry on the railroad to support him.

Lieutenant-Colonel Stancel, of the Texas cavalry, is ordered to go to Boutte Station, to hold that position while you are gone, and to reconnoiter the country in advance as far as you consider necessary. The enemy's artillery has not yet reached Thibodeaux, and I wish Colonel Stickney to attack him at once before it arrives.

The attack made, the forces resume their former stations for the present, and the cavalry will be returned to this city.

By command of W. H. Emory, brigadier-general, commanding:

W. D. SMITH,
Lieut. Col., and Acting Assistant Adjutant-General.

HEADQUARTERS DEFENSES OF NEW ORLEANS,
June 21, 1863.

Colonel CAHILL:

You will go with your whole force immediately to support Colonel Stickney, who is engaged with the enemy at La Fourche Crossing.

The Texas cavalry will take your position, but you will not wait till they arrive. Secure Des Allemands as you pass.

By command of W. H. Emory, brigadier-general, commanding:

W. D. SMITH,
Lieut. Col., and Acting Assistant Adjutant-General.

HEADQUARTERS DEFENSES OF NEW ORLEANS,
June 21, 1863.

Lieutenant-Colonel STICKNEY:

Hold on bravely; I have ordered Colonel Cahill with all his forces to go to your support.

W. H. EMORY,
Brigadier-General, Commanding.

HEADQUARTERS DEFENSES OF NEW ORLEANS,
June 21, 1863—11.45 p. m.

Lieutenant-Colonel STICKNEY:

Train with ten cars this moment gone. Will reach Cahill in about an hour, and be with you in about another.

FRANK W. LORING,
Aide-de-Camp.

HEADQUARTERS DEFENSES OF NEW ORLEANS,
June 21, 1863.

Lieutenant-Colonel STICKNEY:

Use every effort to get a messenger through to Brashear City, with this message to the commanding officer at that place and to the gunboat:

Hold on firmly. Aid is coming to you by sea. Destroy everything you cannot protect.

Employ several messengers; you are authorized to pay any amount to get this through to him.

Answer if you receive this.

W. H. EMORY,
Brigadier-General, Commanding.

HDQRS. DEPT. OF THE GULF, NINETEENTH ARMY CORPS,
Before Port Hudson, June 21, 1863.

Maj. Gen. C. C. AUGUR,
Commanding, &c.:

GENERAL: The commanding general directs that you send the stormers to report at Colonel Birge's headquarters.

Very respectfully, your obedient servant,

RICH'D B. IRWIN,
Assistant Adjutant-General.

(Same to General Grover.)

HEADQUARTERS DEFENSES OF NEW ORLEANS,
June 22, 1863.

Lieutenant-Colonel IRWIN:

The Fifteenth Maine has this moment arrived, with a telegram from Cahill that the enemy are for the third time advancing to the assault. I send them immediately forward to La Fourche. We shall now beat the enemy back.

W. H. EMORY,
Brigadier-General, Commanding.

HEADQUARTERS DEFENSES OF NEW ORLEANS,
June 22, 1863.

Colonel CAHILL:

The Fifteenth Maine has just arrived, and I will send them to the La Fourche Crossing to support you at once. With this large **accession** of force, you can drive the enemy where you please. Hold on stoutly, and if the trains are all with you, send them back to bring up this regiment. More are coming.

By command of W. H. Emory, brigadier-general, commanding:

W. D. SMITH,
Lieutenant-Colonel, Acting Assistant Adjutant-General.

———

HEADQUARTERS DEFENSES OF NEW ORLEANS,
June 22, 1863.

Colonel CAHILL.

From the best information I can get, the enemy do not exceed 2,000 men between Plaquemine and the railroad, and eleven pieces of artillery. It appears to me they ought to be easily whipped with the force you have. They are mostly cavalry. I admit they cannot be caught without cavalry.

W. H. EMORY,
Brigadier-General, Commanding.

———

HEADQUARTERS DEFENSES OF NEW ORLEANS,
June 22, 1863.

Colonel CAHILL:

I do not believe the news you send me, but, if true, do exactly as you propose—retire the troops and all the trains to Algiers, leaving the cavalry at Boutte Station, to fall back slowly on the River road. But I do not believe the report is true. I have a telegram from Colonel Stickney at 8 o'clock, where he stated he had repulsed the enemy.

Respectfully,

W. H. EMORY,
Brigadier-General, Commanding.

———

HEADQUARTERS DEFENSES OF NEW ORLEANS,
June 22, 1863.

Lieut. PETER FRENCH, *Aide-de-Camp, Algiers:*

Go on and communicate with Colonel Cahill at La Fourche. Tell him to beat the enemy off, if he can; and, if he cannot, to do the best he can. The trains are all at his service. If you see the cavalry as you pass, hurry them forward to Boutte Station.

W. H. EMORY,
Brigadier-General, Commanding.

———

HEADQUARTERS DEFENSES OF NEW ORLEANS,
June 22, 1863.

Lieut. PETER FRENCH, *Aide-de-Camp:*

If the cavalry are there, and you can carry them without detention, do it. It was intended they should march by the river. Stickney telegraphs that he is closely pressed. Hurry Cahill forward to support, and withdraw him, if necessary.

By command of W. H. Emory, brigadier-general, commanding:

W. D. SMITH,
Lieutenant-Colonel, and Acting Assistant Adjutant-General.

HEADQUARTERS DEFENSES OF NEW ORLEANS,
June 22, 1863.

Lieutenant FRENCH,
Aide-de-Camp:

Go down in a special train to Colonel Cahill. Tell him he must go to the support of Stickney; that I have sent the trains down to be placed at his disposal, so that, if driven back, he can easily retire.

W. H. EMORY,
Brigadier-General, Commanding.

HEADQUARTERS DEFENSES OF NEW ORLEANS,
June 22, 1863.

Lieutenant-Colonel STICKNEY:

If you are compelled to withdraw from La Fourche, do you propose to do so by the railroad cars or by the road? If by the cars, I must have them organized for you.

By command of W. H. Emory, brigadier-general, commanding:

[FRANK W. LORING,]
Aide-de-Camp.

HEADQUARTERS DEFENSES OF NEW ORLEANS,
June 22, 1863.

Lieut.-Col. RICHARD B. IRWIN:

Colonel Stickney has twice repulsed the enemy at La Fourche Crossing. Colonel Cahill has since joined him.

W. H. EMORY,
Brigadier-General, Commanding.

HEADQUARTERS DEFENSES OF NEW ORLEANS,
June 22, 1863.

Admiral FARRAGUT:

Colonel Cahill has made a junction with Colonel Stickney at La Fourche. The enemy were repulsed by Stickney before the junction. If they attempt to move toward Brashear, I will order them to be attacked in the rear, so that I have no doubt we can keep them from Brashear long enough to enable a gunboat to get there, and if in the meantime Port Hudson falls, we will bag them or drive them into the lake.

Very respectfully, yours,

W. H. EMORY,
Brigadier-General, Commanding.

HEADQUARTERS DEFENSES OF NEW ORLEANS,
June 22, 1863.

Colonel CAHILL:

I have sent three companies of the Twenty-eighth Maine to Raceland, and all the cavalry to Boutte Station. You must judge of whether that is sufficient.

Unless you are strong enough to beat the enemy and reopen the communication to Brashear, there is not much use of being where you are, and you can fall back to Boutte Station, leaving your advanced guard at Des Allemands.

The whole matter must be left to your judgment, based upon a knowledge of the facts on the ground.

Unless you can reopen to Brashear, the only advantage gained by your present position is that you check the enemy in his attack on Brashear, and enable the gunboats to get there and prevent the enemy from escaping.

W. H. EMORY,
Brigadier-General, Commanding.

LA FOURCHE,
June 22, 1863.

Lieut. Col. W. D. SMITH,
Acting Assistant Adjutant-General:

Your telegram is just received. The men are in good spirits. The enemy are taking their dead under a flag of truce. I do not think I can compel the enemy to concentrate enough, so that I may act with effect against them with artillery or infantry. The front and right of our position is too open. It is open to the Brashear road, 4 miles in our front. What is to hinder them from striking the river by that road and cutting off our communication? The levee on the other side of the bayou can be made use of to enfilade our lines, as also can the railroad embankment. If they have artillery, they can shell us out of our position. The loss to the enemy last night was in consequence of their attacking us in the levee and railroad embankment, each being 16 feet high. We had also a slight intrenchment on one-third of our front. We have no means of protecting the line of railroad on our right for 4 miles to the swamp and to Des Allemands.

Colonel Stickney goes to the city to report in person this afternoon.

THOS. W. CAHILL,
Colonel, Commanding.

HEADQUARTERS DEFENSES OF NEW ORLEANS,
June 22, 1863.

Colonel CAHILL:

Why should Colonel Stickney leave his command at this time?

I must necessarily leave the question of remaining where you are or falling back to your own judgment, based upon a knowledge of the facts as you have them upon the ground.

If you cannot hold the place and keep open your communication, fall back.

W. H. EMORY,
Brigadier-General, Commanding.

NEW ORLEANS,
June 22, 1863.

Maj. Gen. N. P. BANKS,
Commanding Department of the Gulf:

GENERAL: I arrived at Plaquemine just in time to find that the gunboat Winona had shelled the enemy out of the town, and that the town had suffered also. The enemy burned two steamers, the Sykes and Anglo-American, the former being aground, and the latter trying to get her off.

I learn that there were 3,000 men in the raid, all Texans, and that they were going to Donaldsonville to get stores, &c. They have no baggage wagons, or only a few. They live on the country from day to day, and have only ammunition for a show fight (what they have in their boxes and caissons). They have fifteen 6 and 8 pounders and one 20-pounder Parrott. They say that they heard Taylor had 1,500 men below, who, I suppose, are now attacking the La Fourche Crossing, where our people have repulsed them twice. General Emory has sent re-enforcements.

I think, general, it is bad policy to have guns on the right bank of the river when there are not men enough to defend them. The enemy will certainly, if defeated at Brashear City (which they announced as their next place of attack, to procure ammunition and provisions), make an effort to obtain those supplies from Fort Banks or the fort at Donaldsonville. If they once get either of those works, they may capture transports, and do us much damage before we find it out and dislodge them. I have at Brashear City the only gunboat that can enter the bay, except those above Port Hudson.

These people may do us some damage, but if Port Hudson falls within a week, with 5,000 men you can capture every one by landing above and marching down upon them.

I will be up in a day or two, but I know that Captain Alden will do all that I could do if I was there.

I concentrated three or four gunboats at Donaldsonville in a few hours, which induced the rebels to give it up.

Wishing you every success, respectfully and truly, yours,

D. G. FARRAGUT,
Rear-Admiral.

GENERAL ORDERS, }   HDQRS. DEPT. OF THE GULF, 19TH A. C.,
No. 51.   }   *Before Port Hudson, June 22, 1863.*

I. Corpl. I. N. Earl, Company D, Fourth Wisconsin Volunteers, is hereby promoted to be first lieutenant of the same company and regiment, to date the 14th June, 1863, for gallant and meritorious conduct before Port Hudson, from the 1st to 14th June; for conspicuous gallantry in the assault upon the enemy's lines on the 14th, and for his subsequent zeal, daring, and good conduct. This appointment to be subject to the approval of the Governor of Wisconsin.

II. Col. S. G. Jerrard, Twenty-second Maine Volunteers, is hereby dishonorably dismissed the service of the United States, to take effect June 14, 1863, subject to the approval of the President,* for having, while temporarily in command of his brigade, when the column, of which his regiment formed a part, was ordered to take a portion of the enemy's

---
* Discharge confirmed by Special Orders, No. 302, Adjutant-General's Office, July 8, 1863.

works by assault, and when the column was at the foot of the parapet preparing for the assault, used discouraging and insubordinate language in the presence of a large number of officers and enlisted men, said language being in part to the purport that "rather than attempt to lead or put his command over that parapet, he would relinquish his command and go to the rear," or words to that effect; and, further, for using words to the same effect to a staff officer of Col. Joseph S. Morgan, Ninetieth New York Volunteers, commanding brigade, his superior officer, when ordered by the said Colonel Morgan, through the said staff officer, to assault the works. This order will be read to the delinquent in the presence of his regiment and of the brigade to which his regiment belongs.

III. This order will be read at the head of every regiment, battalion, and battery before Port Hudson, at retreat to-morrow.

By command of Major-General Banks:
RICH'D B. IRWIN,
Assistant Adjutant-General.

HEADQUARTERS DEFENSES OF NEW ORLEANS,
June 23, 1863.

Commanding Officer at Brashear City:

I have received the following dispatch from General Banks, which is sent you for your information, and that of the naval commander at Brashear City, to whom I will thank you to communicate a copy of these instructions.

If compelled to leave there, what public property you cannot bring off, destroy effectually. The steamer Crescent, which takes this, is sent to aid you in carrying out these orders.

If you do not require her services, send her immediately back with sick and public property not required at Brashear.

Very respectfully, your obedient servant,
W. H. EMORY,
Brigadier-General, Commanding.

[Inclosure.]

CAMP, *June 21—2* p. m.

General EMORY:

Your dispatch in regard to Brashear, saying that you have sent round the Saint Mary's, is received. The commanding general does not regard it as important that we should run any great risk to save Brashear. He desires that you will send orders to Brashear to get off everything of value there, and at Bayou Bœuf, including, especially, the guns, and, when pressed by the enemy, to retire on board the transports and proceed to New Orleans.

The gunboat should remain in Berwick Bay, to prevent the enemy coming across.
RICH'D B. IRWIN,
Assistant Adjutant-General.

HEADQUARTERS DEFENSES OF NEW ORLEANS,
June 23, 1863—9 p. m.

Lieutenant-Colonel IRWIN:

Your dispatch about Brashear was not received until 8 o'clock this evening. I have sent it around there by a steamer.

The fight is now going on at·Brashear. We hear their guns from La Fourche. Bridge at Bayou Chucahoula· burned by the enemy. Enemy left 200 ·wounded at ·Thibodeauxville. Their repulse at La Fourche is complete and disastrous to them.

W. H. EMORY,
Brigadier-General, Commanding.

HEADQUARTERS DEFENSES OF NEW ORLEANS,
June 23, 1863.

Colonel CAHILL :

I sent the steamer to Brashear City three days ago, directing them to hold out.

I now get a telegram from General Banks, telling me not to risk·too much to save Brashear City. You will, therefore, hold your reserves· on this side of the La Fourche, and send forward such relief to Brashear as will not risk your command.

W. H. EMORY,
Brigadier-General, Commanding.

HEADQUARTERS DEFENSES OF NEW ORLEANS,
June 23, 1863.

Colonel· CAHILL :

I am satisfied from dispatches from Donaldsonville that there is no enemy back of you, and that they are all between you and Brashear, and in no more force than you estimate. Therefore, push the repair of· the road, and get your advance on the enemy's rear as rapidly as pos-sible.

General Banks' dispatch to me, the substance of which I forwarded to you, is too late, and was written before he knew of our success.

The only chance of relieving Brashear is by attacking the enemy in the·rear.

W. H. EMORY,
Brigadier-General, Commanding.

HEADQUARTERS SECOND BRIGADE,
Boutte Station, June 23, 1863—11 p. m,

Lieut. Col. W. D. SMITH,
    Actg. Asst. Adjt. Gen., Defenses of New Orleans:

COLONEL : A train has just arrived at this place from La Fourche, and says all are killed or taken, and that both trains at that place have left: I will order one train in with this dispatch, as I do not know whether the news·has got to you by the wires or not. I shall retain one train here to await orders. Shall I make my way to the river and fall back, or remain here? Shall I burn the Des Allemands Bridge, and bring all the troops to the city? I await your orders by the train that takes this in.

2 P. M.

I have just returned from Thibodeaux, and your telegram of this a. m. received. That of 11.45 is so far complied with that I.have the Ninth Connecticut Volunteers forward this a. m. I am afraid the damage to the road is worse than reported, as I expected to hear from the bridge gang before this.

THOS. W. CAHILL,
Colonel, Commanding Second Brigade.

HEADQUARTERS DEFENSES OF NEW ORLEANS,
June 24, 1863.

Colonel CAHILL:

I have sent General Banks' instructions to Brashear City not to risk too much to hold the place, but come off in the transports.

Those instructions cannot reach there in time to change the result, but the commanding officer of the party which is sent to relieve that place should know they have been sent.

There will be a telegraphic station put up at Boutte to-day. Had you not better retire your reserve to that point? You can hold the train there without risk. Let me know exactly your plans.

W. H. EMORY,
Brigadier-General, Commanding.

HEADQUARTERS DEFENSES OF NEW ORLEANS,
June 24, 1863.

Colonel CAHILL:

I retract my suggestion of retiring your reserves to Boutte Station, and you will, as suggested in the previous telegram, hold your reserves for the present at La Fourche, and send forward a strong detachment, under the best officer you have, to attack the enemy in his rear at Brashear City.

Colonel Colburn goes down with a train of workmen to repair the bridge at Chucahoula. I will send a staff officer to Boutte Station to communicate any approach of the enemy that may be discovered by the cavalry up the river or on your flanks.

W. H. EMORY,
Brigadier-General, Commanding.

HEADQUARTERS DEFENSES OF NEW ORLEANS,
June 24, 1863.

Colonel CAHILL:

If the report of Major Morgan be true, it is your duty to retire to Boutte Station at once with all your force. Lose no time in the matter.

You might follow the track to Des Allemands, and telegraph the cars to meet you there.

W. H. EMORY,
Brigadier-General, Commanding.

HEADQUARTERS DEFENSES OF NEW ORLEANS,
June 24, 1863.

Colonel CAHILL:

If you believe the report to be true, you have no time to lose in getting away from where you are, leaving a strong guard and a light train at La Fourche.

If they really have 7,000 men coming down the bayou, Brashear is gone, and they will capture our trains there.

In that event it would be necessary to destroy the bridge at La Fourche Crossing, but if they have not that force, it would be an awful mistake to do so.

It is, however, a very small inconvenience to withdraw your forces to Boutte Station, even if the report is false.

W. H. EMORY,
Brigadier-General, Commanding.

HEADQUARTERS DEFENSES OF NEW ORLEANS,
June 24, 1863.

Colonel CAHILL:

Move at once your main force to Boutte. If you find you are deceived, you can move back again.

By command of Brigadier-General Emory:

[FRANK W. LORING,]
Aide-de-Camp.

HEADQUARTERS DEFENSES OF NEW ORLEANS.
June 24, 1863.

Lieutenant-Colonel IRWIN:

Saint Mary's has returned. Reports surprise and capture of Brashear City by forces which came across the lake. Nothing saved. The enemy in force are advancing down the La Fourche. Cahill is there with all his force, and has been ordered to fall back, but seems unable to do so. You must no longer be incredulous.

W. H. EMORY,
Brigadier-General, Commanding.

BEFORE PORT HUDSON,
June 24, 1863.

Brigadier-General EMORY:

Your telegram just received. Can you not send the gunboat to Brashear City and prevent their crossing guns? Why is Cahill unable to fall back?

N. P. BANKS,
Major-General, Commanding.

HEADQUARTERS DEFENSES OF NEW ORLEANS,
June 24, 1863.

Colonel CAHILL:

Do so, of course. Spike your guns, and retire your infantry by the railroad track, destroying the bridges as your rear guard passes them.

W. H. EMORY,
Brigadier-General, Commanding.

HDQRS. DEFENSES OF NEW ORLEANS, *June* 24, 1863.

Colonel CAHILL:

Why do you wait for the trains? Retire along the track of the railway with your infantry, if nothing else. Destroy your artillery, if necessary.

W. H. EMORY,
Brigadier-General, Commanding.

FLAG-SHIP, WEST GULF BLOCKADING SQUADRON,
New Orleans, June 24, 1863.

Captain [M. B.] WOOLSEY, *U. S. S. Princess Royal:*

Direct Captain Waters to drop down the river after daylight to the Red Church Landing, in front of Boutte Station, on the New Orleans and Opelousas Railroad, and watch there for the enemy, who may try to get over by a road running from the Mississippi River to Boutte Station.

D. G. FARRAGUT,
Rear-Admiral.

HEADQUARTERS DEFENSES OF NEW ORLEANS,
June 24, 1863—10 p. m.

Colonel CAHILL:

If you cannot bring your horses, kill every one on the spot. Kill them with a knife, so the enemy will not hear your guns. Don't let anything fall into their hands. Destroy all the bridges, including the one at La Fourche, after your rear has passed.

But do put Colonel Stickney or some man in command of your rear guard who will be cool and prompt. Destroy the telegraph office and all its records. Blow up your caissons, but make no fires until your main body is at least 10 miles off.

W. H. EMORY,
Brigadier-General, Commanding.

HEADQUARTERS DEFENSES OF NEW ORLEANS,
June 24, 1863—11.30 p. m.

Lieutenant-Colonel IRWIN:

Admiral Farragut has repeatedly informed me he can send no gunboat. The one there, unable to prevent the enemy crossing, retreated, and is now on its way here. The chances are that Cahill may get here. If he does not, it's his own fault. He has had every means of transportation, and his communications protected by every musket and saber at my disposal.

W. H. EMORY,
Brigadier-General, Commanding.

HEADQUARTERS DEFENSES OF NEW ORLEANS,
June 24, 1863—6 p. m.

Colonel CAHILL:

Why do you stay where you are if the enemy are advancing? You know that I have nothing to send you.

W. H. EMORY,
Brigadier-General, Commanding.

U. S. MILITARY TELEGRAPH OFFICE,
New Orleans (from Southwest Pass), June 24, 1863.

Brigadier-General EMORY :

DEAR SIR : The following is a copy of message just received from Southwest Pass :

Col. S. B. HOLABIRD, U. S. Army,
Quartermaster :

On arrival at Atchafalaya Bay, met gunboat Hollyhock and U. S. transport Kepper. They report the surprise and capture of Brashear City, morning of the 23d, at 5 a. m., by rebel forces. The attack was made by 10 more artillery from Berwick Bay, and a rebel force which effected a landing on the north side of the island; came across Flat Lake on rafts.

Nothing was saved. The provost-marshal and a few only escaped who were on board.

W. H. TALBOT,
U. S. Transport Saint Mary's.

Respectfully, yours,

H. STOUDER,
Operator.

[Indorsement.]

The above is the telegram which gives the only account I have of the Brashear affair, and is respectfully transmitted to headquarters.

W. H. EMORY,
Brigadier-General, Commanding.

SPECIAL ORDERS, } HDQRS. SECOND DIV., 19TH ARMY CORPS,
No. 47.   }   *Before Port Hudson, June 24,* 1863.

Colonel Benedict will advance his brigade as skirmishers at 2 a. m., capture the enemy's picket, and draw their fire. General Nickerson will support Colonel Benedict with one regiment upon his (Colonel Benedict's) left, acting in the same manner and for the same object.

The First Vermont Battery will open fire upon the enemy at 2 o'clock, and fire one-half hour, in such manner best calculated to annoy him. General Nickerson will personally see that the new battery is abundantly and fully supported against all possibility of attack from 2 o'clock in the morning until two hours after daylight.

By order of Brigadier-General Dwight:

WICKHAM HOFFMAN,
Assistant Adjutant-General.

HDQRS. DEPT. OF THE GULF, NINETEENTH ARMY CORPS,
Before Port Hudson, June 25, 1863.

Brig. Gen. C. GROVER,
Commanding Right Wing :

GENERAL: Direct Colonel Birge to organize the storming party immediately into two battalions, and to drill it for its work. Too great a proportion of officers ought not to be taken, but 4 may be allowed for each company.

Very respectfully, your obedient servant,

RICH'D B. IRWIN,
Assistant Adjutant-General.

HEADQUARTERS DEFENSES OF NEW ORLEANS,
June 25, 1863.·

Lieutenant COOLEY:

Send this to Cahill:

If you cannot get along on the train, march your men on the railroad track. Hurry your force to New Orleans, leaving one regiment at Boutte Station. Destroy track and bridges as you pass.

W. H. EMORY,
Brigadier-General, Commanding.

HEADQUARTERS DEFENSES OF NEW ORLEANS,
June 25, 1863—7.45 a. m.

Lieut. JAMES C. COOLEY:

Contrive to get this message to Colonel Cahill at any cost:

Hurry to this city with such force as you can bring. A gunboat lies at the red brick church, opposite to Boutte Station Landing.

By command of Brigadier-General Emory:
[FRANK W. LORING,]
Aide-de-Camp.

HEADQUARTERS DEFENSES OF NEW ORLEANS,
June 25, 1863.

Colonel CAHILL:

Send Colonel Dyer's regiment to Algiers. Leave one regiment at Boutte Station; if attacked, to fall back to the gunboat on the river. Bring all the rest of your force to New Orleans as rapidly as possible. Order the train to come to Algiers, and return at full steam.

W..H. EMORY,
Brigadier-General, Commanding.

HEADQUARTERS DEFENSES OF NEW ORLEANS,
June 25, 1863.

Colonel CAHILL:

I wish all the regiments, except that to be left at Boutte Station, when they return, to take as nearly as may be their old position. I wish no time to be lost in getting here.

I have decided not to burn Des Allemands Bridge at present; but you will leave a picket there to do so should it become necessary, for we shall take Port Hudson within three days, and then we shall take Brashear.

By command of W. H. Emory, brigadier-general, commanding:
[FRANK W. LORING,]
Aide-de-Camp.

HEADQUARTERS DEFENSES OF NEW ORLEANS,
June 25, 1863—9.45 a. m.

Major-General BANKS: .

Two regiments of Colonel Cahill's have at length reached Boutte Station. He is at Raceland with the balance of his force. His tardiness of movement is inexplicable.

W. H. EMORY,
Brigadier-General, Commanding.

HEADQUARTERS DEFENSES OF NEW ORLEANS,
June 25, 1863—10.20 a. m.

Lieutenant COOLEY:

The cavalry must be held at Boutte Station, to cover the River road leading to Boutte Station, as long as Boutte Station is occupied. I wish no artillery left there, as I do not intend to hold the place except with cavalry patrol on the River road. You know the enemy have half of our rolling-stock on the other end of the road, and Cahill must break up the communication in his rear as he comes along, particularly Des Allemands Bridge.

By command of Brigadier-General Emory:

[FRANK W. LORING,]
Aide de-Camp.

HEADQUARTERS DEFENSES OF NEW ORLEANS,
June 25, 1863.

Major-General BANKS:

The enemy's force at Brashear and on this side is known and ascertained to be at least 9,000, and may be more.

He has part of our rolling-stock, and is working this way. The city is quiet on the surface, but the undercurrent is in a ferment. The mystery to me is where the enemy got boats to cross Berwick Bay, and in face of the gunboat.

I still think you should have a brigade, at least, in reserve, with transports ready to move here at a moment's notice.

W. H. EMORY,
Brigadier-General, Commanding.

HEADQUARTERS DEFENSES OF NEW ORLEANS,
June 25, 1863.

Major-General BANKS:

Colonel Stickney has arrived, and reports Cahill's force all safe, and on its way to the city.

W. H. EMORY,
Brigadier-General, Commanding.

HEADQUARTERS DEFENSES OF NEW ORLEANS,
June 25, 1863.

Colonel CAHILL:

I will keep one regiment at Boutte, with a picket advance at Des Allemands, for the present, but I do not wish to keep many troops from this city until after your arrival here, when I will consult with you about it.

By command of Brigadier-General Emory:

W. D. SMITH,
Lieutenant-Colonel, and Acting Assistant Adjutant-General.

HEADQUARTERS DEFENSES OF NEW ORLEANS,
June 25, 1863.

Colonel CAHILL:

I have telegraphed you that the regiments would take the same places they had before, except the regiment left at Boutte.

I shall regret very much if the bridge is burned at Des Allemands, for the order was given upon your information of the approach of 7,000 of the enemy.

By command of Brigadier-General Emory:

[FRANK W. LORING,]
Aide-de-Camp.

___

HDQRS. DEPT. OF THE GULF, NINETEENTH ARMY CORPS,
Before Port Hudson, June 25, 1863.

Brig. Gen. W. H. EMORY, *New Orleans:*

SIR: Your dispatch is received. I have ordered transportation here, and will hold one brigade in readiness to move at call to your support. Two gunboats should be at once sent to Berwick Bay, to prevent the enemy from planting the heavy guns in the forts that protect the approaches to the bay from the Gulf. Brashear can be defended only by the navy. It is incredible that the gunboats should have allowed such a force as you describe to cross without notice, or that the Hollyhock should have left without taking off the garrison. We only want three days more here.

Very respectfully, your obedient servant,

N. P. BANKS,
Major-General, Commanding.

___

HDQRS. DEFENSES OF NEW ORLEANS, *June* 25, 1863.

Admiral FARRAGUT:

General Banks directs me to apply for two gunboats to go round to Brashear, "to prevent the enemy putting the guns in the forts that protect the approaches to the bay from the Gulf."

After your telling me a few days ago you had none of the right draught to send round there, I should not now make the application, excepting that I am directed to do so.

It is also proper to state that the general's directions to me were without any knowledge of what you had previously told me on the subject.

I herewith send inclosed some information * left at my office by the Hon. [Benjamin F.] Flanders, the member of Congress from this district.

I am, admiral, with high regard, your obedient servant,

W. H. EMORY,
Brigadier-General, Commanding.

___

HDQRS. DEFENSES OF NEW ORLEANS, *June* 25, 1863.

Admiral FARRAGUT:

There is a nest of smugglers on Lake Salvador or Onacha, which communicates with this by the Bayou Des Familles. If you could spare one or two launches to send in there, they would make a rich haul and do the Government much service.

These smugglers are now in direct communication with the enemy.

I have the honor to be, yours, &c.,

W. H. EMORY,
Brigadier-General, Commanding.

___

* Not found.

HEADQUARTERS DEFENSES OF NEW ORLEANS,
June 25, 1863.

Commanding Officer at Forts Jackson and Saint Philip :

You must be on the alert, and keep your posterns closed. It is rumored here that there is to be an attempt to surprise and capture you, as Brashear City has been, and by the same party. Answer when you receive this.

By command of Brigadier-General Emory:

W. D. SMITH,
Lieutenant-Colonel, and Acting Assistant Adjutant-General.

HEADQUARTERS DEFENSES OF NEW ORLEANS,
June 26, 1863.

Major-General BANKS:

Admiral Farragut informs me now, as he did before, that he has no gunboats of the proper draught to send round to Brashear.

The Hollyhock has returned. The captain reports that the enemy crossed to Brashear on rafts in the night, landing on Flat Island.

W. H. EMORY,
Brigadier-General, Commanding.

HDQRS. DEPT. OF THE GULF, NINETEENTH ARMY CORPS,
Before Port Hudson, June 26, 1863.

Capt. JAMES ALDEN, *U. S. S. Richmond, Commanding, &c.:*

DEAR SIR: The effect of the guns to-day was excellent, and leaves us in no doubt at all that the citadel can be destroyed. The premature explosion of the shells endangered the lives of our men in the fort and in the trenches. This is greatly to be regretted, because the fire of the mortars is most destructive to the enemy if the projectiles are well directed. I hope some means may be devised to make their fire effective and safe. Our pickets are in possession of the mound before the citadel, and we hope to run our trenches to the enemy's rifle-pits, and may, perhaps, assault the citadel itself. The fire will be sharp and constant to-night. Our men are greatly encouraged by this day's work. We shall continue the fire to-morrow at daybreak.

The suggestion in your note of this morning is excellent, but we scarcely have the troops to carry it into execution. With a sufficient number of thoroughly trained, thoroughly disciplined soldiers, enlisted for the war and desirous to bring it to an end, this would have been the surest and wisest policy. It ought to have succeeded on the 27th.

I send you copy of the dispatches containing the news brought by the steamer that left New York on the 20th instant. It is, as you will see, of great interest.

I have the honor to be, with much respect, your obedient servant,

N. P. BANKS,
Major-General, Commanding.

GENERAL ORDERS, } HDQRS. SECOND DIV., 19TH ARMY CORPS,
No. 5.   }   *Before Port Hudson, June 26,* 1863.

I. Lieutenant-Colonel Porter, Fourteenth Maine Volunteers, and Lieutenant-Colonel Bacon, Sixth Michigan Volunteers, are hereby placed in arrest, and directed to take up their quarters half a mile in rear of these headquarters. The limits of their arrest will extend one-quarter of a mile in every direction from the point at which they may be quartered.

II. These officers are arrested for speaking in a discouraging manner of the prospects of this army before Port Hudson, and for habitually using such language as is likely to discourage and dishearten the troops of this division in the event of an assault upon the enemy's works.*

III. The troops of this division will never be directed to perform any duty which should not be reasonably expected of good soldiers, and which is not only possible, but easy.

· The soldiers are cautioned not to listen to the voices of alarmists or to persons afflicted with diseased imaginations.

Such persons picture dangers which do not exist. All officers who indulge in such tone of remark will certainly be sent to the rear.

By order of Brigadier-General Dwight:

WICKHAM HOFFMAN,
Assistant Adjutant-General.

———

HEADQUARTERS DEFENSES OF NEW ORLEANS,
June 27, 1863—6 p. m.

Major-General BANKS:

I have just received the following communication from Boutte Station; the hour is not mentioned:

BOUTTE STATION,
June 27, 1863.

Colonel CAHILL:

From positive information, seven pieces of artillery passed the hospital at La Fourche Crossing last evening at 6.40, with a large force of cavalry *en route* to this place, which will be here, according to time and distance, at 4 p. m.

J. A. SAWTELL,
Lieutenant-Colonel Twenty-sixth Massachusetts.

W. H. EMORY,
Brigadier-General, Commanding.

———

HEADQUARTERS DEFENSES OF NEW ORLEANS,
June 27, 1863.

Commanding Officer at Boutte:

I am on my way with orders from General Emory for you to draw in your picket at Des Allemands, after destroying the bridge at that place, and to fall back with your infantry to Fort Banks. The cavalry will not fall back till driven back by the enemy, and then only step by step, disputing every inch of the way.

Please communicate this to Colonel Stancel, commanding cavalry. Please answer when this is received, and whether the commanding officer at Des Allemands has his instructions.

By command of Brigadier-General Emory:

W. D. SMITH,
Lieutenant-Colonel, and Acting Assistant Adjutant-General.

———

* No charges having been preferred against the officers named, they were, by General Banks' orders, released from arrest; both were promoted.

HDQRS. DEPT. OF THE GULF, NINETEENTH ARMY CORPS,
Before Port Hudson, June 27, 1863—11 p. m.

Capt. JAMES ALDEN, U. S. Navy,
Commanding Fleet :

SIR : Donaldsonville is threatened with an attack from the rebel forces under General Green. I would request that the Essex may be immediately sent to aid in the defense. The enemy is understood to have no other artillery than light field pieces, 6 and 12 pounders, probably.

Very respectfully, your obedient servant,

N. P. BANKS,
Major-General, Commanding.

HEADQUARTERS DEFENSES OF NEW ORLEANS,
June 27, 1863.

Commanding Officer at Donaldsonville :

Make a good fight. I will soon send gunboats to aid you.

By command of W. H. Emory, brigadier-general, commanding :

W. D. SMITH,
Lieutenant-Colonel, and Acting Assistant Adjutant-General.

HEADQUARTERS DEFENSES OF NEW ORLEANS,
June 27, 1863.

Major-General BANKS :

I have just received the following telegram* from commanding officer at Donaldsonville—Major Porter. I cannot say which is the real point of intended attack, this or Donaldsonville. Have shown this to Admiral Farragut, who has sent up an additional gunboat.

W. H. EMORY,
Brigadier-General, Commanding.

HEADQUARTERS DEFENSES OF NEW ORLEANS,
June 27, 1863.

Lieutenant-Colonel SAWTELL :

I believe the attack is at Donaldsonville. Don't you leave Boutte, and don't you burn the bridge at Des Allemands until your information is better, and don't burn Des Allemands Bridge until further orders.

By command of Brig. Gen. W. H. Emory :

W. D. SMITH,
Lieutenant-Colonel, and Acting Assistant Adjutant-General.

HEADQUARTERS DEFENSES OF NEW ORLEANS,
June 27, 1863.

Lieutenant-Colonel IRWIN :
Assistant Adjutant-General :

I have received the two following telegrams,† which I have forwarded to General Banks directly by telegraph, but I have received no acknowl-

---

* Not found.   † Not identified.

edgment of their receipt with the other telegrams notifying you of the fall of Brashear and the presence on this side the Atchafalaya of 9,000 of the enemy, and possibly more. These give information which you should possess, without trusting to the uncertainty of the telegraph. I need not remind the general of the total inadequacy of the force left to guard the vast public interest here, if the enemy's force should be turned toward New Orleans.

Both the following telegrams and all other information sent you have been communicated to Admiral Farragut as soon as received.

I have the honor to be, very respectfully, your obedient servant,

W. H. EMORY,
Brigadier-General, Commanding.

HDQRS. FIRST BRIG., FIRST DIV., 19TH ARMY CORPS,
Before Port Hudson, June 27, 1863—4 p. m.

Maj. GEORGE B. HALSTED,
     Assistant Adjutant-General :

MAJOR : I have to report that for the past twenty-four hours there has been at intervals artillery firing on the left. On my front there has been nothing unusual, excepting that between 8 and 9 last evening an advanced guard of the Twenty-first Maine, defending a breastwork at the end of a ravine on my left, was surprised by the enemy, and its commander, Lieutenant Bartlett, and 5 enlisted men were captured, the guard attempting no defense, alleging therefor Lieutenant Bartlett's order.

The enemy destroyed the breastworks, and were afterward driven back by Major Merry, Twenty-first Maine.

The Forty-eighth Massachusetts and two companies of One hundred and sixteenth New York support Holcomb's battery. The Forty-ninth Massachusetts supports the two batteries on my left. The Twenty-first Maine is on the road this side of and near Slaughter's burnt house. The Second Louisiana and eight companies of One hundred and sixteenth New York are near brigade headquarters.

Eight companies of One hundred and sixteenth New York will support Holcomb's battery to-night, relieving the troops now there.

I have the honor to be, with great respect, your obedient servant,

CHARLES J. PAINE,
Colonel, Commanding Brigade.

[Indorsement.]

HEADQUARTERS LEFT WING,
Before Port Hudson, June 28, 1863.

It appears that while the troops were under arms day before yesterday, Lieutenant Bartlett and 15 men were left to guard the work upon which Colonel Johnson is engaged ; that, before the regiment was relieved to return to the work in the evening, a sortie was made upon the guard, and the lieutenant and 5 men were taken, as also a number of sand bags. The men say that the lieutenant would not permit them to fire upon the advancing enemy.

C. C. AUGUR,
Major-General, Commanding.

WASHINGTON,
June 27, 1863.

Major-General BANKS, *New Orleans:*

' GENERAL: Your dispatches of the 18th are just received. The defection of your nine-months' men on the field of battle was a most criminal military offense, which should have been promptly and severely punished, in order to prevent a repetition of it by other troops. When a column of attack is formed of doubtful troops, the proper mode of curing their defection is to place artillery in their rear, loaded with grape and canister, in the hands of reliable men, with orders to fire at the first moment of disaffection. A knowledge of such orders will probably prevent any wavering, and, if not, one such punishment will prevent any repetition of it in your army. You will be fully sustained in any measures you may deem necessary to adopt to enforce discipline.

The reasons given by you for moving against Port Hudson are satisfactory. It was presumed that you had good and sufficient reasons for the course pursued, although at this distance it seemed contrary to principles and likely to prove unfortunate.

Your dispatch in regard to term of service of nine-months' men has been referred to the Adjutant- General for reply.

I regret exceedingly that we can get no more troops to send you. The discharge of nine-months' and two-years' men has so reduced our forces that we can hardly defend Washington and Baltimore. The effect of the Copperhead disaffection at the north has prevented enlistments, and the drafting has not yet been attempted. We have been forced to resort to State militia, most of whom refuse to be mustered into the service of the United States. Notwithstanding that Pennsylvania is invaded by a large army, the militia of that State positively refuse to be mustered. This is the work of the politicians.

Very respectfully, your obedient servant,

H. W. HALLECK,
General-in-Chief.

GENERAL ORDERS, }   HDQRS. DEFENSES OF NEW ORLEANS,
No. 16.   }   *June 28,* 1863.

I. His Excellency Governor Shepley, Military Governor of Louisiana, brigadier-general U. S. Volunteers, has authority to call into the service of the United States for sixty days one brigade of infantry, for service in defense of New Orleans. They will be organized into regiments and companies, in accordance with the laws and regulations governing the armies of the United States.

The command of this brigade is assigned to Governor Shepley.

*   *   *   *   *   *   ○

By command of W. H. Emory, brigadier-general, commanding:
[W. D. SMITH,]
Lieutenant-Colonel, and Acting Assistant Adjutant-General.

HEADQUARTERS STORMING COLUMN, *June* 28, 1863.

DUNCAN S. WALKER, *Assistant Adjutant-General:*

SIR: I have the honor to report that the volunteers for the storming column are organized in two battalions of eight companies each—strength of companies, about 50 enlisted men; 3, and in some cases 4, commissioned officers to a company. Battalion officers are to each, 1 lieutenant-colonel commanding, 2 majors or acting as such, 1 adjutant, 1 quartermaster. One surgeon (from One hundred and sixtieth New York), has reported. Present strength for duty is: Commissioned officers, 67; enlisted men, 826. Total, 893.

I am, captain, very respectfully, your obedient servant,
HENRY W. BIRGE,
Colonel, Commanding.

HEADQUARTERS DEFENSES OF NEW ORLEANS,
June 28, 1863.
Lieutenant-Colonel SAWTELL:

You will leave two companies of infantry at Jefferson Station, with orders to form a support for the cavalry in front, and, if driven from their position, to fall back on Fort Banks.

With the remainder of your regiment, you will proceed to Donaldsonville with all possible dispatch, to aid in the defense of that place. If, upon consultation with the navy officer there, you find that your presence is not very needed, which I doubt very much, you will return with all possible speed to this place. You will keep the boat with you for this purpose. You will take no baggage with you, nor leave any at Jefferson Station, but send it here. You will take with you your rations; chief quartermaster will furnish you the transportation.

By command of Brig. Gen. W. H. Emory:
W. D. SMITH,
Lieutenant-Colonel, and Acting Assistant Adjutant-General.

HEADQUARTERS DEFENSES OF NEW ORLEANS,
June 28, 1863.
Admiral FARRAGUT:

I understand, from a man whom I have no reason to doubt, that it is the plan of the enemy to cross above here about 18 miles night after to-morrow or Tuesday night. His main force is to cross there, while a detachment of 3,000 or 4,000 is to cross 4 miles below. I therefore respectfully suggest that you direct your gunboats to have all the schooners, sloops, and barges of every sort between here and Donaldsonville, and also for several miles below the town, brought to this side of the river. If necessary, I can order one or two of the river boats to aid in the operation.

I have the honor to be, admiral, your obedient servant,
W. H. EMORY,
Brigadier-General, Commanding.

HEADQUARTERS DEFENSES OF NEW ORLEANS,
June 28, 1863.
Lieutenant-Colonel SAWTELL:

Your order of this morning is so far modified that you will send two companies of your regiment to Donaldsonville by steamer Zephyr, which takes this up. You will hold the remainder ready to move at a moment's warning back to the corral where Colonel Dyer is stationed. These two companies will, upon arrival at Donaldsonville, report to

Major Bullen, commanding. Get up your telegraph as speedily as possible. Keep a train with you, fired up.

Notify Colonel Stancel by express to look out well to the front for the enemy, who may attempt to cross the river, and to give you the first information of any such attempts. Don't detain the Zephyr.

By command of Brig. Gen. W. H. Emory:

W. D. SMITH,
Lieutenant-Colonel, and Acting Assistant Adjutant-General.

HEADQUARTERS DEFENSES OF NEW ORLEANS,
June 28, 1863—9 a. m.

Lieut. Col. RICHARD B. IRWIN:

I inclose you the two following telegrams, which I received this morning from Donaldsonville. It is with great reluctance I detach any force from here, having already sent 250 men when the place was first threatened. I will send the Twenty-sixth Massachusetts or a part of it:

NEW ORLEANS, VIA DONALDSONVILLE, *June 28.*
(Received 8 a. m.)

General EMORY:

The enemy have attacked us and we have repulsed them. I want more men. I must have more men.

I am, sir, your obedient servant,

J. D. BULLEN,
Major, Commanding Post.

W. H. EMORY,
Brigadier-General, Commanding.

[Inclosures.]

HEADQUARTERS DEFENSES OF NEW ORLEANS,
June 28, 1863.

Maj. JOS. D. BULLEN:

The following telegram is just received:

CAMP NEAR BATON ROUGE.

Brigadier-General EMORY:

The First Louisiana Infantry and two sections of artillery have been ordered to Donaldsonville, and will arrive there at midnight. General Stone goes with them. Inform the commanding officer at Donaldsonville.

D. S. WALKER,
Assistant Adjutant-General.

By command of Brigadier-General Emory:

W. D. SMITH,
Lieutenant-Colonel, and Acting Assistant Adjutant-General.

HDQRS. DEPT. OF THE GULF, NINETEENTH ARMY CORPS,
Before Port Hudson, June 28, 1863.

Brig. Gen. W. H. EMORY,
● *New Orleans:*

GENERAL: The First Louisiana Infantry and two sections of artillery have been ordered to Donaldsonville, and will probably arrive there at midnight. General Stone goes with them. Please inform Colonel Beckwith and the commanding officer at Donaldsonville.

Very respectfully, your obedient servant,

RICH'D B. IRWIN,
Assistant Adjutant-General.

HEADQUARTERS DEFENSES OF NEW ORLEANS,
June 29, 1863.

Colonel CAHILL:

You will take all the infantry from the Metairie Race-Course, and all from the Cotton Press and United States barracks, and take them to the Algiers depot, where a train will be waiting to take them to the La Fourche Crossing.

You have already been notified to have 100 rounds ammunition and two days' cooked rations in readiness. You will send some reliable officer to take command of this force, and go to the crossing of the Des Allemands and La Fourche, where the enemy are expected in some force.

Colonel Stickney is ordered with his whole force to come to La Fourche Crossing.

By command of Brig. Gen. W. H. Emory:

W. D. SMITH,
Lieutenant-Colonel, and Acting Assistant Adjutant-General.

HEADQUARTERS DEFENSES OF NEW ORLEANS,
June 29, 1863.

Major-General BANKS:

I ordered a brigade formed of the unconditional Union men to be put under General [George F.] Shepley. Do you approve or disapprove? Please give me an answer before going too far. Something must be done for this city, and that quickly.

W. H. EMORY,
Brigadier-General, Commanding.

HDQRS. DEPT. OF THE GULF, NINETEENTH ARMY CORPS,
Before Port Hudson, June 29, 1863—10.30 a. m.

Brig. Gen. W. H. EMORY,
New Orleans :

GENERAL : The commanding general approves the organization of a brigade of the unconditional Union men of New Orleans, but it must be under your control, and not under that of General Shepley. Lieutenant Cooley just arrived.

Very respectfully, your obedient servant,
RICH'D B. IRWIN,
Assistant Adjutant-General.

HEADQUARTERS DEFENSES OF NEW ORLEANS,
June 29, 1863.

Commanding Officer at Bonnet Carré :

Three companies of rebels are reported on this side of the river, 20 miles above Bonnet Carré. Have you communicated with Read, at Humphrey's Station? Does he know the rebels are on this side? Make a brave stand. There will soon be a gunboat to aid you. Keep me constantly informed of what you hear of the enemy.

W. H. EMORY,
Brigadier-General, Commanding.

HEADQUARTERS DEFENSES OF NEW ORLEANS,
June 29, 1863.

Captain WATERS:

Rebel troops are reported on the east side the river, 20 miles above Bonnet Carré. Keep a sharp lookout on both sides the river.

D. G. FARRAGUT,
Admiral.

HEADQUARTERS DEFENSES OF NEW ORLEANS,
June 29, 1863.

Colonel COLBURN:

Have your force organized and in arms to-night, if possible. I am obliged to draw the force from the canal to this side.

By command of Brig. Gen. W. H. Emory:

W. D. SMITH,
· *Lieutenant-Colonel, and Acting Assistant Adjutant-General.*

HEADQUARTERS DEFENSES OF NEW ORLEANS,
June 29, 1863.

Colonel MARSH:

I hear of the enemy on this side and above Bonnet Carré. Keep your pickets on the *qui vive,* and all your force in hand. If your scouts give you any notice of the enemy and you communicate it to me in time, I have made all the arrangements, and can concentrate all my force for your support. Lieutenant French, aide-de-camp, has gone with a steamer to move the Fifteenth Maine Regiment over to the parapet.

By command of Brig. Gen. W. H. Emory:

W. D. SMITH,
· *Lieutenant-Colonel, and Acting Assistant Adjutant-General.*

HEADQUARTERS DEFENSES OF NEW ORLEANS,
June 29, 1863.

Colonel SAWTELL:

As the enemy approaches, I desire the cavalry to fall back slowly. You, with your infantry command, will at the same time fall back upon Fort Banks.

Telegraph to Algiers, and have brought to you a train, and keep it by you, with steam up.

W. H. EMORY,
Brigadier-General, Commanding.

WAR DEPARTMENT, ADJUTANT-GENERAL'S OFFICE,
Washington, D. C., June 29, 1863.
Maj. Gen. N. P. BANKS,
Commanding Department of the Gulf, via New Orleans:

GENERAL: I have the honor to acknowledge the receipt of your letter of the 18th [20th] instant, in reference to the expiration of service of the nine-months' regiments.

In reply, I am directed to inform you that the time of each regiment will expire in nine months from the date the last company of the regiment was mustered into the service of the United States. This is the rule which has been applied in all cases.

I am, general, very respectfully, your obedient servant,
THOMAS M. VINCENT,
Assistant Adjutant-General.

HEADQUARTERS UNITED STATES FORCES,
Fausse Point, June 29, 1863.
Lieut. Col. RICHARD B. IRWIN,
Assistant Adjutant-General:

SIR: I have the honor to report everything quiet in this vicinity.

It is reported, and, I think, from good authority, that three days ago a force about 3,000 strong crossed the Atchafalaya River and moved toward Plaquemine.

Most respectfully, your obedient servant,
C. H. SAGE,
Colonel, Commanding.

HEADQUARTERS DEFENSES OF NEW ORLEANS,
June 30, 1863.
Lieutenant-Colonel SAWTELL:

I have received your telegram and sent it to Admiral Farragut. If the enemy has only 2,500, I have no objection to fighting 40 or 50 miles above here.

But I take this force to be the advance of the army, and I can afford to send no more men from these defenses.

By command of Brig. Gen. W. H. Emory:
W. D. SMITH,
Lieutenant-Colonel, and Acting Assistant Adjutant-General.

HEADQUARTERS DEFENSES OF NEW ORLEANS,
June 30, 1863.
Major-General DIX,
Commanding Department of Virginia:

I have sent, under command of Colonel Davis, First Texas Cavalry, some 500 prisoners, who are not safe at this place, and who cannot be sent to Baton Rouge, where they would be less secure. The enemy are in considerable force between that place and this. Colonel Davis will give you the state of things here. The only guard I can afford is 100 convalescents taken from the hospital, commanded by Colonel Davis and several convalescent officers.

I request that steps be taken to keep this command together and returned to this department by the first transport from New York City.

I have the honor to be, your obedient servant,
W. H. EMORY,
Brigadier-General, Commanding.

HEADQUARTERS DEFENSES OF NEW ORLEANS,
June 30, 1863.

Major-General HALLECK,
Commander-in-Chief:

GENERAL: The enemy are in very considerable force on the west bank of the river, threatening General Banks' communication and this city.

On the 21st, we repulsed their advance guard at La Fourche, with great loss to the enemy, for the numbers engaged.

At Donaldsonville they attacked the redoubt yesterday morning with 5,000 men. They were repulsed, with the loss of 100 left dead upon the field, 120 prisoners, including several officers of rank; the force on one side in the fort consisting of only 150 men, but supported by three gun-boats.

The enemy's object is evidently to raise the siege of Port Hudson by attacking New Orleans. I have, of course, communicated everything to General Banks up to the time the telegraphic communication was cut, which was about 5 o'clock yesterday morning.

The land force in this city, and in the extensive lines of defenses contiguous to it, is less than a brigade. Should they succeed in cutting the communications of this army, I must look to the north for troops to defend this city, if they can be gotten here in time.

I have the honor to be, your obedient servant,
W. H. EMORY,
Brigadier-General, Commanding.

HEADQUARTERS OF BRIGADIER-GENERAL ULLMANN,
New Orleans, June 30, 1863.

The ADJUTANT-GENERAL, U. S. ARMY,
Washington, D. C.

SIR: I have the honor to report that all the forces under my command were ordered, as I have previously informed you, by Major-General Banks to Port Hudson. They have been employed there since the first days of June in digging. They have been of great service in this respect, the officers and men often passing twenty consecutive hours in the trenches. It has, however, entirely prevented my recruiting, excepting to a very limited degree. As soon as my officers can be relieved from this duty, I will proceed as rapidly as possible with the raising and organizing of my command.

I have the honor to be, general, your obedient servant,
DANIEL ULLMANN,
Brigadier-General, Commanding.

Abstract from return of the Department of the Gulf (Nineteenth Army Corps), Maj. Gen. N. P. Banks, U. S. Army, commanding, for the month of June, 1863; headquarters, before Port Hudson, La.

Command.	Present for duty.		Aggregate present.	Aggregate present and absent.
	Officers.	Men.		
Department staff	23	....	23	26
First Division (Augur):				
Staff	9	....	9	9
Infantry	292	6,387	7,976	9,107
Cavalry	27	468	549	816
Artillery	30	609	679	797
Total	358	7,464	9,213	10,729
Second Division (Dwight):				
Staff	7	....	9	9
Infantry	283	5,974	8,478	10,024
Artillery	6	201	256	429
Other troops in this command	62	2,622	3,143	3,419
Total	358	8,797	11,886	13,881
Third Division (Fearing):				
Staff	10	....	10	10
Infantry	323	6,213	8,202	10,091
Artillery	4	106	124	136
Total	337	6,319	8,336	10,237
Fourth Division (Grover):				
Staff	5	....	5	5
Infantry	179	3,582	4,496	8,110
Artillery	10	296	324	405
Total	194	3,878	4,825	8,520
Weitzel's brigade (Weitzel):				
Staff	10	....	10	10
Infantry	157	4,014	4,933	5,721
Cavalry*	6	229	266	297
Artillery	7	272	301	371
Total	180	4,515	5,510	6,399
District of Key West, &c. (Woodbury)	34	717	1,061	1,103
District of Pensacola (Holbrook)	44	884	1,136	1,206
Ship Island, Miss. (Daniels)	22	502	637	679
Grand total†	1,550	33,076	42,627	52,780

* But all the cavalry of Weitzel's command was assigned to Grierson, May 31.

† Does not account for the Corps d'Afrique under Ullmann's command; accounts in part only for troops in Defenses of New Orleans (see "Other troops, &c.," in Second Division), and in part only, if at all, for Grierson's cavalry command. See also abstract, following, from tri-monthly return for June 30,

Abstract from tri-monthly return of the Department of the Gulf (Nineteenth Army Corps), for June 30, 1863.

Command.	Present for duty.		Aggregate, present.	Aggregate present and absent.
	Officers.	Men.		
Department staff	23	....	23	26
First Division (Augur):				
Staff	8	....	8	8
Infantry	235	5,428	7,475	8,491
Cavalry	6	141	167	191
Artillery	12	470	575	633
Total	261	6,039	8,225	9,323
Second Division (Dwight):				
Staff	9	....	9	11
Infantry	133	2,980	3,831	5,109
Artillery	5	187	198	244
Total	147	3,167	4,038	5,364
Third Division (Fearing):				
Staff	9	....	9	9
Infantry	196	3,538	3,987	9,326
Cavalry	14	153	265	393
Artillery	9	300	314	430
Total	228	3,991	4,575	10,158
Fourth Division (Grover):				
Staff	5	....	5	5
Infantry	214	3,759	4,659	8,932
Cavalry	1	96	147	165
Artillery	6	237	250	417
Total	226	4,092	5,061	9,519
Weitzel's brigade (Weitzel):				
Staff	5	....	5	9
Infantry	106	2,294	2,584	3,922
Cavalry	5	173	194	278
Artillery	3	205	222	288
Total	119	2,672	3,005	4,497
Corps d'Afrique (Ullmann)	91	1,187	1,585	1,789
28th Connecticut (Ferris)	30	472	565	579
1st Indiana Heavy Artillery (Keith)	25	500	552	860
1st Louisiana (Hodge)	24	668	797	1,016
Baton Rouge (Drew)	43	1,746	3,145	3,215
Defenses of New Orleans (Emory)	231	5,680	8,270	9,315
District of Pensacola (Dyer)	59	966	1,282	1,349
District of Key West, &c. (Woodbury)	34	678	1,042	1,084
Ship Island, Mississippi (Daniels)	20	471	612	663
Grand total	1,561	32,329	42,777	58,757

Abstract from return of the Department of New Mexico, Brig. Gen. James H. Carleton, commanding,* for the month of June, 1863; headquarters, Santa Fé, N. Mex.

Command.	Present for duty.		Aggregate present	Aggregate present and absent	Aggregate present and absent last return.	Pieces of field artillery.
	Officers.	Men.				
Department staff..	16	....	16	19	18	......
Fort Marcy, N. Mex. (Capt. H. R. Selden), Fifth U. S. Infantry.	1	37	53	65	64	......
Fort Union, N. Mex. (Capt. P. W. L. Plympton), Fifth and Seventh U. S. Infantry.	5	95	171	179	430	......
Fort Union Depot, N. Mex. (Capt. W. R. Shoemaker, military storekeeper), company of ordnance.	......	15	15	15	15	......
Fort Sumner, N. Mex. (Capt. J. Updegraff), Fifth U. S. Infantry, Second Cavalry, California Volunteers.	5	83	115	142	143	......
Fort Stanton, N. Mex. (Maj. J. Smith), First New Mexico, Fifth Infantry, California Volunteers; First Cavalry, California Volunteers.	5	73	129	222	155	......
Fort Wingate, N. Mex. (Lieut. Col. J. F. Chaves), First New Mexico Volunteers.	10	215	313	344	348	......
Albuquerque, N. Mex. (Capt. W. H. Lewis), Third U. S. Artillery, Fifth U. S. Infantry.	4	128	172	182	173	4
Los Pinos, N. Mex. (Capt. S. Archer), Fifth U. S. Infantry.	5	63	90	94	95	......
Camp Easton, N. Mex. (Capt. E. H. Bergmann, First New Mexico Volunteers.	1	52	62	77	79	......
Fort Craig, N. Mex. (Col. E. A. Rigg), First and Fifth U. S. Infantry: First Cavalry, California Volunteers.	14	345	433	468	540	......
Franklin, Tex. (Col. George W. Bowie), Fifth U. S. Infantry; First Cavalry, California Volunteers.	15	236	326	386	459	......
Fort West, N. Mex. (Capt. V. Dresher), First Infantry, California Volunteers; First Cavalry, California Volunteers.	3	39	56	215	285	2
Fort Bowie, Ariz. (Capt. T. T. Tidball), Fifth Infantry, California Volunteers.	2	46	56	61	51	......
Tucson, Ariz. (Capt. William Ffrench), Fifth Infantry, California Volunteers.	4	63	94	121	119	......
Las Cruces, N. Mex. (Lieut. Col. W. McMullen), First and Fifth Infantry, California Volunteers.	3	108	156	163	311	......
Fort McRae, N. Mex. (Maj. A. Morrison), First New Mexico Volunteers.	1	43	92	101	104	......
En route, First U. S. Cavalry, First Infantry, California Volunteers.	......	......	......	......	103	......
En route, three companies First Infantry, California Volunteers.	9	225	234	234	....	......
In the field, New Mexico (Col. C. Carson), headquarters First New Mexico Volunteers, and four companies First New Mexico.	16	290	306	306	4	......
In the field, New Mexico. (Capt. C. R. Wellman), First Cavalry, California Volunteers.	2	70	72	72	....	......
Total	121	2,226	2,961	3,466	3,496	6

HEADQUARTERS DEFENSES OF NEW ORLEANS,
July 2, 1863.

Commodore MORRIS:

Some apprehensions are entertained that vessels may be sent from this city up the river to aid the rebels. I have given orders that no steamer or other vessel not on Government service be allowed to pass up the river, except by special authority from these headquarters.

I have, therefore, respectfully to suggest, if you can conveniently do so, that you will station a vessel at the parapet, with orders to let no vessel pass unless she is on Government service or has a permit from these headquarters.

I have the honor to be, commodore, your obedient servant,
W. H. EMORY,
Brigadier-General, Commanding.

* Brig. Gen. Joseph R. West, commanding District of Arizona.

HEADQUARTERS DEFENSES OF NEW ORLEANS,
July 2, 1863.

Lieutenant-Colonel IRWIN:

I have received the following dispatch from Major Bullen, in command at Donaldsonville.

I have already sent him two separate re-enforcements, one of 150 men and another, consisting of two companies of the Twenty-sixth Massachusetts, numbering 90 men; making in all 240 men.

The attempt to raise a brigade here from amongst the loyal and unconditional Union men is a failure, and must not be depended upon.

I have a report that the enemy are on the Vacherie road in force, and are repairing it. I have also a report of the enemy's pickets at Des Allemands Bayou.

W. H. EMORY,
Brigadier-General, Commanding.

SPECIAL ORDERS, }   HDQRS. DEPT. OF THE GULF, 19TH A. C.,
No. 158.   }   *Before Port Hudson, July 2, 1863.*

I. The commanding general cannot too warmly thank the officers and men of the Fiftieth Massachusetts Volunteers for their prompt and patriotic offer of the service of that regiment until the 14th instant, for two weeks beyond the period when they deem that their term of enlistment expires. This prompt decision reflects honor upon the gallant officers and men of this regiment, and will be in future their proudest title to the gratitude of their countrymen and the esteem of their comrades, with whom they will share the coming triumph and divide its glory.

II. Colonel Hodge, First Louisiana Engineers, will detail 100 men, with their officers, provided with 25 axes, 25 shovels, and 25 picks, to report to Lieutenant Hanman, assistant to chief of artillery, at General Nickerson's headquarters, at 6 a. m. to-morrow.

By command of Major-General Banks:

[RICH'D B. IRWIN,]
Assistant Adjutant-General.

HDQRS. DEPT. OF THE GULF, NINETEENTH ARMY CORPS,
Before Port Hudson, July 2, 1863—10.50 a. m.

Brig. Gen. W. DWIGHT, *Commanding, &c.:*

GENERAL: Colonel Dudley is ordered toward the church with two regiments and a battery, to intercept the enemy and recapture the train. The commanding general directs that you immediately report whether you had relieved the One hundred and sixty-second New York from duty at Springfield Landing; and, if so, when.

Very respectfully, your obedient servant,

RICH'D B. IRWIN,
Assistant Adjutant-General.

HDQRS. DEPT. OF THE GULF, NINETEENTH ARMY CORPS,
Before Port Hudson, July 3, 1863.

Major-General GARDNER, *Commanding at Port Hudson:*

GENERAL: I have the honor to request that a quantity of hospital stores may be distributed among the wounded men of my command now within Port Hudson, and to other wounded men to whom they may be acceptable. Especial interest is felt in the case of a wounded prisoner belonging to the Fourth Wisconsin Volunteers, who received a shot through the thigh. Will you please order to his use such of the accompanying stores as his case may require?

I acknowledge with satisfaction the attention and kindness which my wounded men have received at the hands of the surgeons of your command.

I have the honor to be, with respect, &c.,

N. P. BANKS,
Major-General, Commanding.

SPECIAL ORDERS, } HDQRS. DEPT. OF THE GULF, 19TH A. C.,
No. 159. } *Before Port Hudson, July* 3, 1863.

Hereafter during the operations before Port Hudson there will be detailed daily one brigade commander to act as general of the trenches. He will be relieved at 12 m. daily, and will, before withdrawing from the trenches, turn over to the new general of the trenches the orders and instructions which have been given to him relative to the works.

The duties of the general of the trenches will be to superintend the operations, to dispose the guards of the trenches, to repulse sorties, and protect the works; to take command of the guards of the trenches in repelling sorties, to see that the details of guards of the trenches and of the working parties report promptly at the designated hour; to see that no time is lost, but that the work is pressed forward as rapidly as possible. The officers in command of the guards of the trenches and of the working parties will be under the command and direction of the general of the trenches.

The character of the works to be constructed, their direction, and the manner of constructing them, will be indicated by the chief engineer, and the works will be laid out by his assistant, under his directions. The chief engineer will see that the general of the trenches is furnished with all information concerning the troops necessary to enable him to perform his duties understandingly. The tour of duty for the general of the trenches will be twenty-four hours, during which he will not be absent from the trenches, except in case such absence shall be absolutely necessary in the performance of his duties; and he shall make such arrangements as to enable any officer connected with the works to readily find him at any hour.

The general of the trenches and the chief engineer will each make a written report to these headquarters at 9 a. m. of the day following the one for which the report is made. The report of the chief engineer will show the progress made for the day, and what is proposed to be done during the day on which the report is sent in, accompanying his report with the necessary drawings. The general of the trenches will, in his report, state the nature of the operations during his tour, remarkable occurrences, the progress made on each part of the work, stating the number of feet in length by which the saps are advanced under each officer in charge of a working party, and such suggestions as may occur to him. A record will be kept by the general of the trenches, showing the progress made by each officer in charge of a working party, to be turned over successively to the new general of the trenches, and to be made known to the officers in charge of working parties. The assistant adjutant-general at these headquarters will see that the working parties called for by the chief engineer are duly detailed, and will furnish the general of the trenches with a statement of such details.

The chief engineer will hereafter make his requisitions for working parties and guards upon the assistant adjutant-general at these head-quarters. The provisions of this order, so far as the general of the trenches is concerned, will not apply to the works on our left.

By command of Major-General Banks:

RICH'D B. IRWIN,
Assistant Adjutant-General.

HEADQUARTERS DEFENSES OF NEW ORLEANS,
July 3, 1863.

Commodore MORRIS:

Our transports have been fired into at College Point, and one of them, the Iberville, badly disabled.

I find it necessary to send a dispatch to General Banks. Can you furnish convoy to the steamer which takes it as far as College Point?

Some of the gunboats at Donaldsonville should be concentrated at that Point and at Bonnet Carré.

If you have any dispatches to send, I shall be happy to send them by this boat.

I have the honor to be, your obedient servant,

W. H. EMORY,
Brigadier-General, Commanding.

HEADQUARTERS DEFENSES OF NEW ORLEANS,
July 3, 1863.

Colonel SAWTELL,
Jefferson:

If at any time you are forced to fall back, in place of falling back to Fort Banks, as directed, fall back to the line of earthworks at the company canal.

I shall have a steamboat ready to re-enforce you heavily.

W. H. EMORY,
Brigadier-General, Commanding.

GENERAL ORDERS, } HDQRS. DEFENSES OF NEW ORLEANS,
No. 18. } *July 3,* 1863.

Hereafter no public assemblages, excepting for public worship, under a regular commissioned priest, will be allowed in the city for any purpose or under any pretense whatever by white or black, without the written consent of the commander of the Defenses of New Orleans, and no more than three persons will be allowed to assemble or congregate together upon the streets of the city. Wherever more than that number are found together by the patrol, they shall be ordered to disperse, and, failing to do so, they shall be placed in arrest.

All bar-rooms, coffee-houses, stores, and shops of every description will be closed at 9 p. m.

All club rooms and gambling houses are hereby closed until further orders.

No citizen or other persons, excepting the police and officers in the United States service, or soldiers on duty or with passes, are to be allowed in the streets after 9 p. m.

By command of Brigadier-General Emory:

[W. D. SMITH,]
Lieutenant-Colonel, and Acting Assistant Adjutant-General.

GENERAL ORDERS, }   HDQRS. DEFENSES OF NEW ORLEANS,
No. 20.   }   *July 4, 1863.*

General Orders, No. 18, is not intended to apply to physicians visiting patients nor to persons going after physicians. Persons not included in the above order, desiring passes, must apply to the provost-marshal-general.

By command of Brigadier-General Emory:

[W. D. SMITH,]
Lieutenant-Colonel, and Acting Assistant Adjutant-General.

CIRCULAR.]   HEADQUARTERS DEFENSES OF NEW ORLEANS,
                                         July 4, 1863.

General Orders, No. 18, having just been published, and this being the anniversary of our American Independence, the order will not be enforced by the police or patrol this day,

By command of Brigadier-General Emory:

[W. D. SMITH,]
Lieutenant-Colonel, and Acting Assistant Adjutant-General.

HEADQUARTERS DEFENSES OF NEW ORLEANS,
July 4, 1863.

Admiral FARRAGUT:

The paroled prisoners have come in. The estimate I made of the strength of the enemy before you left here is fully confirmed. They are estimated at 13,000, with numerous artillery. They are slowly but steadily advancing on this place, making strong fortifications at all the passes.

I am, very respectfully, your obedient servant,

W. H. EMORY,
Brigadier-General, Commanding.

HEADQUARTERS DEFENSES OF NEW ORLEANS,
July 4, 1863.

Major-General HALLECK,
    Commander-in-Chief:

GENERAL: I have information, which I think reliable, that the enemy, from 10,000 to 15,000 strong, are marching on this city, by the line of the La Fourche. I have notified General Banks, but he is not in a condition to detach any re-enforcements to me.

My force here is wholly inadequate, but with the check I gave them at La Fourche Crossing, and the decided repulse I gave them at Donaldsonville, aided by the gunboats, I may be able to hold them in check till re-enforcements come from some quarter.

I think the circumstances justify me in asking you to send me re-enforcements here with all possible dispatch.

Very respectfully, your obedient servant,

W. H. EMORY,
Brigadier-General, Commanding.

[JULY 4, 1863.—For Grant to Banks, announcing the surrender of Vicksburg, see Series I, Vol. XXIV, Part III, p. 470.]

HEADQUARTERS,
Port Hudson, La., July 5, 1863—6 p. m.

Maj. Gen. N. P. BANKS,
Commanding U. S. Forces near Port Hudson:

GENERAL: Your note of the 3d instant has just been handed to me, and in reply I have the honor to state that I will send a party outside the breastworks to receive such hospital supplies as you may desire to send in to your wounded. It is scarcely necessary to assure you that every care will be continued to alleviate the sufferings of your wounded that circumstances will permit. The supplies you send will be applied as you request. There is no prisoner from the Fourth Wisconsin Regiment shot through the thigh, but there is one of the Zouaves shot as you mention, named J. K. P. Edward. He receives every care possible.

I have the honor to be, with respect, &c.,

FRANK. GARDNER,
Major-General, Commanding C. S. Forces.

FLAG-SHIP TENNESSEE,
Port Hudson, July 5, 1863.

Brigadier-General EMORY,
Commanding U. S. Forces, New Orleans:

DEAR GENERAL: Your note is duly received. I understand the play of the rebels, and think we can foil them. I have ample force on the river to keep them in check. They are on the west bank, from Donaldsonville down about 12 or 15 miles, and a picket of 200 or 300 extending down as far as Bonnet Carré. Waters shelled them the other night as I came up. I have two boats at Donaldsonville and one below, to convoy the transports.

The Quartermaster-General ought to be very particular in the captains of his steamers, as a rebel will run in and surrender if he has half a chance.

I had a long letter from Porter to-day by the Arizona. He says it is reported that Vicksburg will surrender to-day. They had pride in not surrendering until after the Fourth of July.

I shall go to see General Banks to-morrow. You have plenty of force at New Orleans—two sloops of war and three or four other vessels there, whose guns are as good as ever, and, even if their steam is not available, they can shell the city.

It is most important to have the gunboats watch the rebels on the river.

Porter writes me that they are playing the same game with him in trying to cut off supplies. They are 2,000 or 3,000 strong up there.

Very respectfully,

D. G. FARRAGUT,
Rear-Admiral.

NEW ORLEANS,
July 6, 1863.

Commanding Officer [Donaldsonville, La.]:

Send at once by any steamer now at Donaldsonville notice to General Banks and Admiral Farragut that the enemy are advancing in force on you from both directions.

By command of Brigadier-General Emory:

FRANK W. LORING,
Aide-de-Camp.

HEADQUARTERS U. S. FORCES AT DONALDSONVILLE, LA.,
Fort Butler, July 6, 1863—3 p. m.

Lieutenant-Colonel IRWIN:

SIR: There is a large force of the enemy around in the vicinity of this post. It has been reported as high as 18,000. I think, from the information I have received, there may be 10,000 or 12,000. Sixteen pieces of artillery are reported to have arrived. They are evidently making preparations to attack me.

WM. E. HADLOCK,
Lieut. Col. Twenty-eighth Maine Volunteers, Commanding.

HDQRS. DEPT. OF THE GULF, NINETEENTH ARMY CORPS,
Before Port Hudson, July 6, 1863.

Brig. Gen. B. H. GRIERSON,
Commanding Cavalry:

SIR: Information has been received that the enemy's cavalry has concentrated at Jackson with a battery of artillery, and that they intend to make a dash upon our rear at several different points to-morrow or the next day, in the morning.

The commanding general wishes you to have your command well in hand, to be prepared to prevent this attempt, and to endeavor to ascertain something more definite of the enemy's movements.

Your most obedient servant,

RICH'D B. IRWIN,
Assistant Adjutant-General.

GENERAL ORDERS, }   HDQRS. DEFENSES OF NEW ORLEANS,
No. 21.   }   *July 6, 1863.*

So much of General Orders, No. 18, as prohibits peaceable citizens from being out after 9 o'clock p. m. is hereby rescinded, provided they are not in parties of more than three.

By command of Brigadier-General Emory:

[W. D. SMITH,]
Lieutenant-Colonel, and Acting Assistant Adjutant-General.

WASHINGTON,
July 7, 1863.
Brig.-Gen. W. H. EMORY,
New Orleans :

Your dispatch of June 30 is this moment received.

General Grant has been urged to send all possible assistance to General Banks.   General Gillmore, commanding Department of the South, was ordered, on the 5th instant,* to send all his available forces to New Orleans.   All drafted men in the Eastern States have been ordered to New Orleans as fast as they can be collected.   The law of the draft is so complicated and defective, and the machinery of enrollment so cumbersome, that it works slowly.

Very respectfully, your obedient servant,
H. W. HALLECK,
General-in-Chief.

————

HDQRS. DEPT. OF THE GULF, NINETEENTH ARMY CORPS,
Before Port Hudson, July 7, 1863.
Brig. Gen. W. H. EMORY,
Commanding Defenses of New Orleans :

SIR : I am directed by the commanding general to inclose to you the copy of a dispatch from Major-General Grant, announcing the surrender of Vicksburg on the morning of the 4th instant.† The operations here will be pushed as rapidly as possible.   Donaldsonville can be strengthened somewhat by the army and navy.

The commanding general appreciates the power of the enemy to annoy us on the river and in the country west of the river, but does not apprehend immediate danger to the city of New Orleans.   He desires me to say that it cannot be many days before this command is relieved from its duty here.

Very respectfully, your most obedient servant,
RICH'D B. IRWIN,
Assistant Adjutant-General.

————

HDQRS. DEPT. OF THE GULF, NINETEENTH ARMY CORPS,
Before Port Hudson, July 7, 1863—11 a. m.
Maj. Gen. U. S. GRANT,
Commanding at Vicksburg :

MY DEAR GENERAL : Your most gratifying dispatch [4th instant] has just been received, announcing the surrender of Vicksburg.   I beg you to accept my hearty congratulations.   It is the most important event of the war, and will contribute most to the re-establishment of the Government.

The freedom of the Mississippi puts an end to the rebellion, so far as an independent Confederacy is concerned.·   There is no room for an independent government between the Mississippi and the Atlantic.

Port Hudson will be in our possession before the close of this week.   The Army of the Gulf sends its congratulations to the gallant and successful troops of your command.   Salutes will be fired at noon from the

———————
* See Series I, Vol. XXVIII.   † See Series I, Vol. XXIV, Part III, p. 470.

batteries on the right, left, and center of our lines, in honor of the fall of Vicksburg.

I have the honor to remain, general, with the highest respect, your obedient servant,

N. P. BANKS,
Major-General, Commanding.

———

FLAG-SHIP TENNESSEE,
Below Port Hudson, July 7, 1863.

Maj. Gen. N. P. BANKS,
Commanding:

GENERAL: I was aroused this morning by 4 a. m. with a dispatch, which I sent you. The letter of Colonel Holabird* was dated June 30, but I will go down to look after this blockade of the river below. I have four gunboats between Plaquemine and College Point. But I desired to stay here, to suggest going up with a flag of truce to-morrow to demand the surrender of Port Hudson. They will, no doubt, surrender to the navy more willingly than the army, on account of the negro question, and I thought if it would save the effusion of blood, it would be well to try it. I will go down this evening and be up to-morrow, if all is right below.

Very truly, yours,

D. G. FARRAGUT,
Rear-Admiral.

[Inclosure No. 1.]

HEADQUARTERS,
Donaldsonville, July 4, 1863.

Captain WOOLSEY:

DEAR SIR: My pickets were approached by those of the enemy last evening at about 11 o'clock. One of the enemy was in advance of the rest; my picket halted him, and ordered him to surrender, which he refused to do, when my picket fired on him, and then retired, sending me information of the transaction. This morning we found the man whom the picket fired at last night, badly wounded. He is a captain of one of the Texas companies; says only the advanced brigade attacked the fort on Sunday a. m.; that there were many wounded; that he was hot in the fight; that Colonel Phillips and the other field officers of his regiment were killed or captured.

A negro man came in this morning from Thibodeaux; says there is a rebel force at Thibodeaux; that there are wounded soldiers there; that there are three camps between Napoleonville and Donaldsonville; that they have artillery; that they brought four pieces of artillery from Berwick Bay; that they are repairing the railroad at La Fourche Crossing; that he heard them talking about going to New Orleans; that some of them left Napoleonville Thursday, and said they were coming to Donaldsonville to take the fort. Says General Mouton is in command. The wounded captain says there are 18,000 troops between Napoleonville and Donaldsonville. All of which I submit to you. My impression is that they mean to try us once more.

I am, sir, yours, respectfully,

J. D. BULLEN,
Major, Commanding Post.

———

* Not found.

[Inclosure No. 2.]

U. S. S. PRINCESS ROYAL,
Off Donaldsonville, La., July 5, 1863.

Rear-Admiral D. G. FARRAGUT,
Commanding West Gulf Blockading Squadron:

SIR: The Kineo returned from College Point this morning, convoying the Sallie Robinson. The latter vessel was fired into as she passed that point. I have directed Lieutenant-Commander Waters to make a report. I sent the Winona down to convoy up another boat which was expected. The North America is waiting the return of the Winona to convoy her down, and the Kineo will convoy the Sallie Robinson above Doyle's plantation and return. I find it necessary to keep a gunboat down about College Point to convoy vessels up, as the enemy has a field battery and sharpshooters there, and fires upon every transport that passes. We need all the force we can get here. The fort has been reenforced by men, but no more pieces. I respectfully inclose the copy of a note which I have just received from Major Bullen.

From the best information we can gain from spies, deserters, and prisoners, the rebel force is from 15,000 to 18,000. Major commanding the post thinks there are about 10,000. They are the united forces of Mouton, Green, and Taylor.

The report gives them twenty pieces of artillery. Last night their pickets were inside of ours, and they were within three-quarters of a mile of the post.

I am, most respectfully, sir, your obedient servant,

M. B. WOOLSEY,
Commander.

[Sub-Inclosure.]

HEADQUARTERS,
Donaldsonville, July 5, 1863.

Captain WOOLSEY:

DEAR SIR: So far as I can learn, the position of the enemy remains unchanged from yesterday. The pickets were thrown out nearer our lines than ever—up nearly to the town on the east side of the bayou.

The North America brought down six companies of Twenty-eighth Maine, and I am relieved by Lieut. Col. W. E. Hadlock.

I am, sir, yours, respectfully,

J. D. BULLEN,
Major Twenty-eighth Maine Regiment Volunteers.

[Inclosure No. 3.]

U. S. S. PRINCESS ROYAL,
Below Donaldsonville, La., July 6, 1863.

Rear-Admiral D. G. FARRAGUT,
Commanding West Gulf Blockading Squadron, Port Hudson:

SIR: It becomes my painful duty to report to you that Major Bullen, of the Maine Volunteers, and late commander of Fort Butler, was murdered in cold blood late last night by a private of the First Louisiana Volunteers. His body is now on board the Cornie, awaiting a convoy down to New Orleans.

The murderer is in double irons, under a guard, on board this vessel.

I am, most respectfully, sir, your obedient servant,

M. B. WOOLSEY,
Commander.

[Inclosure No. 4.]

HDQRS. FORT BUTLER, _Donaldsonville, July_ 6, 1863.
Commander WOOLSEY, _Gunboat Princess Royal:_

SIR: Accompanying this communication are two colored boys, who report that they were taken prisoners at Berwick Bay by the Confederate force at that place. They left the rebel camp, 7 miles down the coast, at Madame Winchester's plantation, last evening at 8 o'clock. They state the force there to be about 10,000, under command of Colonel [W. P.] Lane, with eight rifles and two smooth-bores; that their object is to cause a diversion of the gunboats from this post down the river, in order to make a raid on the fort, with the intention of capturing it. It is Colonel Hadlock's wish that you receive them, and proceed down the river to the point designated, and give them a shell or two; at the same time to convoy the steamer Cornie down below the point mentioned, with the remains of Major Bullen on board. The two colored boys are desirous of joining the Twenty-first Indiana Battery, now stationed at New Orleans, and Colonel Hadlock requests that you would exercise your own judgment in regard to them.

I am, sir, very respectfully, your obedient servant,
H. KEMBLE OLIVER,
Lieutenant, and Post-Adjutant.

[P. S.]—Colonel Hadlock has also received information that the enemy were moving down the road about a mile in rear of the fort with sixteen pieces of artillery; caliber not known. The force accompanying the artillery not stated. The above are stated to be three siege pieces, four brass smooth[-bores], and nine rifled, the siege guns drawn by sixteen horses.

HDQRS. DEPT. OF THE GULF, NINETEENTH ARMY CORPS,
Before Port Hudson, July 7, 1863.
Brig. Gen. C. GROVER,
Commanding, &c.:

GENERAL: The commanding general directs that the following be communicated for your information and guidance:

General Gardner has just requested the commanding general to give him "official assurance" whether Vicksburg has surrendered or not; and, if true, he asks a cessation of hostilities, to enable him to consider terms for surrendering Port Hudson.

The commanding general has replied that a cessation of hostilities is impossible, but nevertheless he desires that all active demonstrations on your part shall cease until further [orders] from these headquarters.

Very respectfully, your obedient servant,
[CHARLES A. HARTWELL],
Lieutenant, and Aide-de-Camp.
(Copy to General Dwight.)

HDQRS. DEPT. OF THE GULF, NINETEENTH ARMY CORPS,
Before Port Hudson, July 8, 1863.
Rear-Admiral D. G. FARRAGUT, U. S. Navy,
Commanding Lower Fleet:

SIR: I have the honor to inform you that General Gardner has offered to surrender, and that at his request a commission, to consist of 3 officers designated by me, will meet a similar commission on his part, at our lines at 9 a. m. to-day, to draw up the terms of surrender.

I have directed that active hostilities shall entirely cease until further orders for this purpose.

Very respectfully, your obedient servant,

N. P. BANKS,
Major-General, Commanding.

(Copy to Commodore Palmer, U. S. Navy, U. S. S. Richmond.)

Hᴅǫʀs. Dᴇᴘᴛ. ᴏꜰ ᴛʜᴇ Gᴜʟꜰ, Nɪɴᴇᴛᴇᴇɴᴛʜ Aʀᴍʏ Cᴏʀᴘs,
Before Port Hudson, July 8, 1863—6 a. m.
Admiral D. G. Fᴀʀʀᴀɢᴜᴛ,
Commanding Fleet, &c.:

Sɪʀ: General Gardner has made known his willingness to surrender, and officers meet at 9 a. m. to agree upon terms. An unconditional surrender will be required. It is important that our troops in force should first carry the news to New Orleans. I congratulate you upon the freedom of the Mississippi.

Very truly, yours,

N. P. BANKS,
Major-General, Commanding.

Hᴅǫʀs. Dᴇᴘᴛ. ᴏꜰ ᴛʜᴇ Gᴜʟꜰ, Nɪɴᴇᴛᴇᴇɴᴛʜ Aʀᴍʏ Cᴏʀᴘs,
Before Port Hudson, July 8, 1863.
Rear-Admiral D. G. Fᴀʀʀᴀɢᴜᴛ,
Commanding Fleet, &c.:

Mʏ Dᴇᴀʀ Sɪʀ: To intercept the rebel force now infesting the river and the La Fourche country, it is necessary that the gunboats should move at once to Berwick Bay. All the light-draught boats should be ordered down at once—the Arizona, Estrella, Hollyhock, Calhoun, and Sachem. I hope Captain Wiggin and Captain Perkins may be put in command, as they know the localities and are energetic in action. If the boats can proceed to the bay at once, we shall intercept and capture the force. Our troops move at 5 o'clock for Donaldsonville, and we shall press them with all vigor. Please inform me if it is possible to accomplish this. If we cut off this army, no other troops can be raised south of Red River.

Port Hudson surrendered to-day, substantially without conditions. We shall be compelled, however, to parole the greater part of the men. They call for 6,000 rations. The ceremony of rendition takes place at 7 to-morrow morning.

I am, very truly, yours.

N. P. BANKS,
Major-General, Commanding.

Cɪʀᴄᴜʟᴀʀ.]   Hᴅǫʀs. Dᴇᴘᴛ. ᴏꜰ ᴛʜᴇ Gᴜʟꜰ, 19ᴛʜ A. C.,
Before Port Hudson, July 8, 1863—2 p. m.

Sɪʀ: The articles of surrender are signed at 2 p. m.:

1. The enemy surrenders everything.
2. We respect private property.

3. Officers and soldiers not paroled.
4. We take care of the sick.
March in at 5 p. m.
Very respectfully, your obedient servant,
RICH'D B. IRWIN,
Assistant Adjutant-General.

HDQRS. DEPT. OF THE GULF, NINETEENTH ARMY CORPS,
Before Port Hudson, July 8, 1863.
Brig. Gen. W. DWIGHT,
Commanding, &c.:
GENERAL: Please designate two regiments of your division to go in with the occupying force at 5 o'clock, and order them to report immediately at the opening in front of General Augur's. Keep the rest of your command in hand, encamp it comfortably, and take stringent measures to repress straggling.
Very respectfully, your obedient servant,
RICH'D B. IRWIN,
Assistant Adjutant-General.

HDQRS. DEPT. OF THE GULF, NINETEENTH ARMY CORPS,
Before Port Hudson, July 8, 1863.
Maj. Gen. U. S. GRANT,
    Commanding Department of the Tennessee, Vicksburg:
GENERAL: The Mississippi is opened. I have the honor to inform you that the garrison of Port Hudson surrendered unconditionally this afternoon. We shall take formal possession at 7 o'clock in the morning.
Very respectfully, your most obedient servant,
N. P. BANKS,
Major-General, Commanding.

BEFORE PORT HUDSON, LA.,
July 8, 1863.
Major-General GRANT:
MY DEAR GENERAL: It gives me pleasure to inform you that Port Hudson surrendered this day. We are unable to determine the number of prisoners or the extent of the armament. The commissioners ask for 6,000 rations. The surrender is in effect unconditional. I declined to stipulate for the parole of officers or men, but necessity will compel me to parole at once a considerable portion of the prisoners, selecting those representing States mainly in our control, as Louisiana, Arkansas, &c.
About 12,000 or 15,000 of the enemy have been threatening my communications, and have occupied the La Fourche districts. I shall move against them forthwith.
My disposable force is about equal to their number if I detain General Grierson's cavalry. This I hope to do for a term of not more than two weeks, when I will return him in good condition to your camp. He has been of infinite service, and I know not in what way we could have supplied his place. My thanks are due to Lieutenant [H. A.] Ulffers for

valuable services. He is a patient, sound, intelligent, and patriotic officer. He returns with Colonel [T. K.] Smith.

The enemy in my rear disposed of, I earnestly desire to move into Texas, which is now denuded of troops. The enemy here is largely composed of Texans. We hope to capture them. Will it be possible for you to spare me for this expedition, which should be closed in two months from this date, a division of 10,000 or 12,000 men? I know the claims upon your force. I see that you will hope to strengthen our armies in the east, and propose my request with hesitation, but there is no point where the same number of men could do so much good. I want Western men. It was my hope to join you in the contest for Vicksburg, and strengthen your command with what force I have, but it was impossible.

Colonel Smith, who brought me the welcome message from you, has remained at my command to convey to you in return the news of the surrender or capture of Port Hudson, which could not have been deferred longer than to-morrow. His visit has given me the greatest pleasure. His effective destruction of the boats and other means of crossing the Mississippi which the enemy possessed has been of the greatest service to us and the cause. I hope he may return safely to you.

I am, general, with great respect, your obedient servant,

N. P. BANKS,
Major-General, Commanding.

HEADQUARTERS DEPARTMENT OF THE GULF,
Before Port Hudson, July 8, 1863—5 a. m.

Brig. Gen. B. H. GRIERSON, *Commanding Cavalry:*

SIR: General Gardner has offered to surrender.

A commission will meet at 9 o'clock to draw up the terms.

The commanding general desires that you will keep your command well in hand, and be more than usually watchful for our rear during the day.

Very respectfully, your obedient servant,

RICH'D B. IRWIN,
Assistant Adjutant-General.

HEADQUARTERS DEPARTMENT OF THE GULF,
Before Port Hudson, July 8, 1863.

General B. H. GRIERSON, *Commanding Cavalry:*

SIR: The commissioners have agreed to occupy the place at 7 o'clock to-morrow morning, instead of 5 this evening.

Very respectfully, your most obedient servant,

RICH'D B. IRWIN,
Assistant Adjutant-General.

HEADQUARTERS DEPARTMENT OF THE GULF,
Before Port Hudson, July 8, 1863.

Brig. Gen. C. GROVER, *Commanding, &c.:*

GENERAL: Please designate two regiments of your own division and two of the Third Division to go in with the occupying force at 5 o'clock to-day, and order them to report immediately in front of General Augur's. Order the stormers to report at the same place immediately. Keep the rest of your command in hand, encamp it comfortably, and take stringent measures to repress straggling. Don't forget Nelson.

Very respectfully, your obedient servant,
RICH'D B. IRWIN,
Assistant Adjutant-General.

BEFORE PORT HUDSON,
July 8, 1863.

[General WEITZEL:]

MY DEAR SIR: The officers to meet those appointed by General Gardner upon the subject of the terms of surrender were necessarily named as soon as his communication was received, otherwise I should have very gladly acted upon your suggestion. Unless a different course is suggested by the officers representing the garrison, I shall designate you as the officer to receive the surrender of General Gardner. I will notify you of the result as soon as it is ascertained.

I shall expect your brigade to move at once to La Fourche. I will review the troops in Port Hudson to-day, and then prepare for the close of the campaign, which has lasted without intermission for four months from this day. It began the 8th March.

Very truly, yours,
N. P. BANKS,
Major-General, Commanding.

[P. S.]—I shall name of the most deserving regiments eight or ten to occupy and garrison the forts as soon as surrendered. Will you name some most entitled to honor in your division?

BEFORE PORT HUDSON,
July 8, 1863—2.30 p. m.

General WEITZEL:

DEAR GENERAL: I am sorry that you do not accept the surrender. You seemed to be more closely identified with the whole campaign than any other officer.

The articles are signed—

1. The enemy surrendering everything.
2. We respect private property.
3. Officers and soldiers not paroled.

The regiments asked for are only as witnesses to the act of rendition. The transports will be ready to take your troops to-night to Donaldsonville. You will lead the advance. Nine-months' regiments only will remain. I shall be glad to see you this evening. It is reported from the upper fleet that Hooker is superseded by General Meade. No enemy between this and Baton Rouge.

Very truly, yours,
N. P. BANKS,
Major-General, Commanding.

SPECIAL ORDERS, }   HDQRS. DEPT. OF THE GULF, 19TH A. C.,
No. 164.   }   *Before Port Hudson, July* 8, 1863.

I. The following-named regiments, having but a brief time to serve, are detached from the divisions to which they belong; will concentrate in front of General Augur's position on the main road; march into Port Hudson at 9 o'clock to-morrow morning, and report to the commanding officer of the post. They will, for the present, constitute part of the garrison for that post.

From the First Division, Fiftieth Massachusetts; from the Second Division, Twenty-sixth Connecticut, Twenty-fourth Maine; from the Third Division, Fourth Massachusetts; from the Fourth Division, Twenty-second Maine, Fifty-second Massachusetts, Twenty-sixth Maine.

II. Major-General Augur will begin to embark his division, excepting the two regiments detailed to accompany the occupying force, on the transports at Point Pleasant*Landing at 5 o'clock to-morrow morning, with two days' rations in haversacks, and three days' additional, and a full supply of ammunition. The two regiments detailed to accompany the occupying force will go fully prepared to embark on transports as soon as the ceremony of rendition is over.

Brigadier-General Grover will send a brigade to Plains Store to-night, to relieve Colonel Dudley's brigade. Colonel Dudley will take up the line of march at 4 a. m.

Brigadier-General Arnold, chief of artillery, will designate the batteries to accompany the division, including Weitzel's brigade.

The embarkation will be completed as rapidly as possible. General Augur will immediately report in person to the commanding general for special instructions.

III. Brigadier-General Weitzel, commanding Second Brigade, First Division, will report to Major-General Augur with his brigade, excepting the regiment detailed to accompany the occupying force, at 4 o'clock to-morrow morning, with two days' rations in haversacks and three days' additional, and a full supply of ammunition, ready to proceed to Point Pleasant Landing and embark as above directed. The regiment detailed to accompany the occupying force will go in fully prepared to embark on transports as soon as the ceremony of rendition is over.

IV. Brigadier-General Grover, commanding right wing, and Brigadier-General Dwight, commanding Second Division, will be careful so to extend their lines as to cover the whole ground occupied by the troops withdrawn from the lines by these special orders, Paragraphs II and III.

V. The following-named batteries belonging to the First Division have been designated by the chief of artillery to accompany the division in its movement, as directed by these special orders, viz, Bainbridge's battery (A, First Artillery); Carruth's (Sixth Massachusetts) battery; Holcomb's [Bradbury's] (First Maine) battery. They will be put in movement accordingly by the division commander. All other batteries temporarily assigned to the First Division are relieved from duty therewith, and their commanders will to-morrow morning report in person to the chief of artillery for instructions.

By command of Major-General Banks:

RICH'D B. IRWIN,
Assistant Adjutant-General.

HEADQUARTERS DEFENSES OF NEW ORLEANS,
July 8, 1863.

Commodore MORRIS:

I communicated to you yesterday morning that the enemy were building a battery on the river opposite Bonnet Carré. I now have to com-

municate that I have learned, through a refugee of unquestionable ve-
racity, that the enemy, 3,000 strong, are moving through the lakes, by
way of Barataria, with the intention of interrupting our communication
between this city and the mouth of the river.

The expectation of the enemy is that as soon as they cut the communication below, as they have that above, the city will rise; and, in my
opinion, nothing will prevent such an enterprise but the glorious news
of the fall of Vicksburg.

I have communicated already to General Banks and Admiral Farragut the imminent danger in which I consider the city has been left by
withdrawing the forces from here. I now have no means whatever of
communicating with either, but although I have given them full information, and they are aware that this city is open to the force of the
enemy approaching from Brashear City, I nevertheless think it is due
to both of them that they should, with as little delay as possible, receive
the information contained in this letter, and would, therefore, thank you
to forward it to them, as I have no means of communicating with them
except by gunboat, and I do not think a communication of this character should go by any other mode of conveyance.

It is proper to state that the 3,000 coming in through the lakes to
occupy the bank of the river below, as far as I am informed, are no part
of the forces under General Taylor, estimated at 13,000, operating between General Banks and this city, but are composed of watermen,
fishermen, and irregular forces from the lagoons and bayous of Southern
Texas and Louisiana.

A prisoner just in informs me that the enemy have completed the reconstruction of the Opelousas Railroad, and are running cars as far as
Raceland, at which point they are throwing up breastworks.

Everything is doing by me that it is possible to strengthen our position, and I have expressed to those most concerned my determination
to hold the city to the last extremity, even if it involves its destruction.
What I am most concerned about is the scattered disposition of our
stores and armament, and the demoralization from the presence of 12,000
or 15,000 paroled prisoners, and 4,000 or 5,000 men—convalescent, sick,
and wounded.

I inclose herewith a telegram* this moment received from my cavalry
patrol, on the east bank of the river, containing information of two formidable batteries, one opposite College Point and one opposite a point
about 2 miles above Humphrey's Station. These batteries should be
shelled out before the works are perfected.

I am, commodore, your most obedient servant,

W. H. EMORY,
Brigadier-General, Commanding.

DEPARTMENT OF STATE, *Washington, July 9*, 1863.

Hon. E. M. STANTON, *Secretary of War:*

SIR: I have the honor to communicate for your information a copy
of a letter of the 13th ultimo, addressed to this Department by Henry
Connelly, esq,, the Governor of the Territory of New Mexico.

I have the honor to be, your obedient servant,

WILLIAM H. SEWARD,
Secretary of State.

---

* Not found.

[Inclosure.]

EXECUTIVE DEPARTMENT,
Santa Fé, June 13, 1863.

Hon. W. H. SEWARD, *Secretary of State, Washington, D. C.:*

SIR: I have the honor to inform you that on the 22d ultimo I arrived at this city. I had some detention on the road at the different military posts in changing escorts, whose company I found very necessary from the danger of Confederate bushwhackers near the frontier of Missouri, and a banded set of robbers and murderers that were infesting the roads and mountain districts between here and Fort Lyon, on the Arkansas.

Since I left the Territory, in October last, there has occurred nothing of a nature to excite alarm as respects another Texan invasion. There was a Confederate force of 500 or 600 men at Fort Davis, nearly 500 miles south of this place, of which some fears were entertained, as the advance guard of a large number, but it seems they were only stationed there temporarily as a protection to the trains that were transporting pro-visions from the State of Chihuahua by way of the Presidio del Norte, on the Rio Grande. I learn now that the whole force has left for San Antonio.

We are now at liberty to make a campaign against our fearful enemy, the Navajo Indians. Preparations for this have been making for some time, and now a regiment, under Colonel Carson, will be able to leave in a few days.

It is to be hoped that better success will attend this campaign than has attended others that have been made against that tribe, at such enormous expense and loss of stock to the Government. This is the only tribe that is hostile to our people, and the only one from which we have suffered any loss for a number of years. They are insignificant in numbers, and their only defense when invaded is in flight, with their immense amount of stock, beyond the reach and range of our troops, leaving but few of their men in sight, and they mounted on the best of their horses, rendering all pursuit fruitless in the country they inhabit.

General Carleton has reduced the whole Mescalero Apache tribe to a state of peace, and has them now living at Fort Sumner, on the Pecos River, in the immediate presence of the troops, with orders that not one be permitted to leave under penalty of being taken and treated as an enemy.

We have had the most seasonable rains this spring, such as hereto-fore have never visited this Territory in May and June. This has given us great hopes of a bountiful harvest and the earliest and most luxuri-ant growth of grass with which we have been blessed for a number of years. This will be quite a relief to the ravaged and desolate situation of the Territory, for such has been the desolation caused by the Texan invasion and the Indians, together with an unusual rise in the Rio Grande last year, that two of the lower counties, Valencia and Socorro, are kept from suffering with hunger by subscription from the people of the more fortunate counties more remote from the theater of the late Texan raid and Indian depredations, and where lands were more favor-ably situated on the river, and avoided the destruction of crops caused by the unusual and unexpected rise of that stream. In fact, everything now wears a cheerful appearance, and if we remain secure from further Texan and Indian depredations, will soon forget our past misfortunes.

Very respectfully, your obedient servant,

HENRY CONNELLY,
Governor of New Mexico.

HEADQUARTERS UNITED STATES FORCES,
Fausse Point, July 9, 1863.

Lieut. Col. RICHARD B. IRWIN, *Assistant Adjutant-General:*

SIR: I have the honor to report all quiet here.

The artillery on the levee opposite Port Hudson has left. There seems to be no further necessity for pickets on the levee or the river.

A negro brings information of a force of the enemy in camp, 30 miles up the river, of about 6,000.

Most respectfully, your obedient servant,

C. H. SAGE,
Colonel, Commanding.

———

HEADQUARTERS DEFENSES OF NEW ORLEANS,
July 10, 1863.

Major-General HALLECK, *Washington, D. C.:*

GENERAL: I have the honor to inclose you copy of dispatch received from Major-General Banks, announcing the surrender to him of Port Hudson, July 8, and also several papers showing the particulars of the surrender.

The enemy are in considerable force on the west side of the river, threatening General Banks' communication and this city. They have temporary possession of the right bank of the river, some 8 miles below Donaldsonville to Bonnet Carré, but the news of the surrender of Port Hudson relieves this city from all apprehensions, and I shall order my force, small as it is, to resume the offensive.

Before receiving the news of the fall of Port Hudson, I was compelled to call into the service two regiments for a period of sixty days. I regret to state to you that Major Bullen, of the Twenty-eighth Maine, who made such a heroic defense at Donaldsonville, was murdered by a soldier of the First Louisiana Regiment.

I have not been directed to forward these papers to you in relation to Port Hudson, but my adjutant-general, Captain Walker, who brought them down, informs me that he has no dispatches for the steamer about sailing, and I therefore send you copies of those sent me, though it is probable you will receive the news by way of Vicksburg much sooner than these.

Very respectfully your obedient servant.

W. H. EMORY,
Brigadier-General, Commanding.

·[Inclosure.]

HDQRS. DEPT. OF THE GULF, NINETEENTH ARMY CORPS,
Port Hudson, July 9, 1863.

Brig. Gen. W. H. EMORY, *Commanding Defenses of New Orleans:*

GENERAL: I have the honor to inform you that Port Hudson surrendered yesterday morning without conditions.

We took formal possession at 7 o'clock this morning.

The number of prisoners and guns is unknown as yet, but estimated at about 5,000 prisoners and fifty pieces.

General Weitzel, with the First Division, moves to Donaldsonville this morning.

The commanding general directs me to explain, as an apology for this late communication, that he regarded it as a matter of prime importance that the troops should precede the news to Donaldsonville.

Please have all the transportation that is available sent up here immediately.

The admiral has been requested to send all the light-draught gunboats to Brashear.

Very respectfully, your obedient servant,

RICH'D B. IRWIN,
Assistant Adjutant-General.

HDQRS. DEPT. OF THE GULF, NINETEENTH ARMY CORPS,
Port Hudson, July 10, 1863.

Brig. Gen. GEORGE L. ANDREWS,
    Commanding Post of Port Hudson:

GENERAL: The commanding general directs that all the enlisted men and citizens, employés of the enemy's forces captured at this post, be released upon giving their parole in triplicate upon the inclosed forms.

One copy of the individual parole, signed by the man himself, his regimental commander, and the paroling officer of our army, will be delivered to the regimental commanders at the time of parolement, for distribution to the men. One copy of the consolidated parole-rolls, signed by each man, by Major-General Gardner, and by the paroling officer, will be retained, and transmitted by you to these headquarters. One copy of the consolidated rolls, similarly signed, to be handed to General Gardner. The consolidated lists to be verified by roll-call. The Louisiana troops will be paroled first in order, furnished with five days' rations, and permitted to march out of our lines under escort and go to their homes. The other troops will be paroled as rapidly as possible, and disposed of as may be hereafter directed.

Very respectfully, your obedient servant,

RICH'D B. IRWIN,
Assistant Adjutant-General.

[JULY 10, 1863.—For Grant to Banks, in relation to re-enforcements for Port Hudson, &c., see Series I, Vol. XXIV, Part III, p. 492.]

HDQRS. DEPT. OF THE GULF, NINETEENTH ARMY CORPS,
Port Hudson, July 10, 1863.

Col. JOSEPH S. MORGAN,
    Commanding First Brigade, Fourth Division:

SIR: The commanding general directs as follows: Having embarked your command on board the steamer Laurel Hill, you will proceed to Donaldsonville, La. On your arrival there, you will, in case Brigadier-General Weitzel should be present, report to him in person, and receive his orders before disembarking. Should General Weitzel have moved with his forces before your arrival, you will at once send forward a courier to inform that commander of your presence at Donaldsonville, your strength in infantry and artillery, and, disembarking your command, will await General Weitzel's orders. The steamboat Laurel Hill will be ordered back to this point as soon as your command shall have landed, and it is deemed important that her return shall be prompt.

Very respectfully, your obedient servant,

RICH'D B. IRWIN,
Assistant Adjutant-General.

SPECIAL ORDERS,) HDQRS. DEPT. OF THE GULF, 19TH A. C.,
No. 166.   )   Port Hudson, July 10, 1863.
*   *   *   *   *   *   *

V. Brig. Gen. Daniel Ullmann will assume command of his brigade, consisting of the Sixth, Seventh, Eighth, Ninth, and Tenth Regiments of Infantry of the Corps d'Afrique, and will report for duty to Brig. Gen. George L. Andrews, commanding the corps at Port Hudson.
*   *   *   *   *   *   *

VIII. 9.30 *p. m.*—Brig. Gen. C. Grover, commanding right wing, will order the First Brigade of his own division and Nims' (Second Massachusetts) battery to march into Port Hudson immediately, prepared to embark on the steamer Laurel Hill by midnight, if possible, with five days' rations, 100 rounds of ammunition per man for the infantry, and the battery complement for the artillery. The brigade commander, after putting his brigade in march, and leaving it orders to march with celerity, will report in person at these headquarters for instructions.

IX. Brig. Gen. C. Grover, commanding right wing, will be prepared to move himself with the remainder of his own division, including the two three-years' regiments sent in with the column of occupation at 6 a. m. to-morrow, with five days' rations, 100 rounds of ammunition per man for the infantry, a full complement for each battery, and a full reserve supply. Marching orders will be given hereafter.

Before leaving, General Grover will make all necessary arrangements for picketing his present front.
*   *   *   *   *   *   *

By command of Major-General Banks:
RICH'D B. IRWIN,
Assistant Adjutant-General.

———

GENERAL ORDERS,) HEADQUARTERS UNITED STATES FORCES,
No. 1.   )   Port Hudson, July 10, 1863.

In compliance with Special Orders, No. 165, Headquarters Department of the Gulf, the undersigned hereby assumes command of the Corps d'Afrique and of the post at Port Hudson.
GEORGE L. ANDREWS,
Brigadier-General of Volunteers, Commanding.

———

Reorganization of the Third Division, Nineteenth Army Corps, under Paragraph XV, Special Orders, No. 166, Headquarters Department of the Gulf, July 10, 1863,* Brig. Gen. William Dwight commanding.

First Brigade.	Second Brigade.
Brig. Gen. FRANK S. NICKERSON.	[Senior colonel present.]
	28th Connecticut, Col. Samuel P. Ferris.
14th Maine, Col. Thomas W. Porter.	8th New Hampshire, Col. H. Fearing, jr.
110th New York, Col. Clinton H. Sage.	15th New Hampshire, Col. John W.
162d New York, Col. Lewis Benedict.	Kingman.
165th New York, Capt. Felix Agnus.	133d New York, Col. L. D. H. Currie.
177th New York, Col. Ira W. Ainsworth.	173d New York, Col. Lewis M. Peck.
	4th Wisconsin,† Lieut. Col. Frederick A. Boardman.

———

* Which, "in consequence of the expiration of the term of service of several of the nine-months' regiments," transferred the First and Third Brigades, Second Division, to the Third Division, and assigned Brigadier-General Dwight to the command. He assumed command July 12. Col. Hawkes Fearing, jr., appears to have commanded the division June 15–July 6.
† Detached for mounted service July 11.

*Third Brigade.**

Col. OLIVER P. GOODING.

31st Massachusetts, Lieut. Col. W. S. B. Hopkins.
38th Massachusetts, Col. Timothy Ingraham.
53d Massachusetts, Col. John W. Kimball.
128th New York, Col. James Smith.
156th New York, Lieut. Col. Jacob Sharpe.
175th New York, Col. Michael K. Bryan.

Artillery.†

Capt. RICHARD C. DURYEA.

4th Massachusetts Battery, Capt. George G. Trull.
1st United .States (Battery F), Capt. Richard C. Duryea.
1st Vermont Battery, Capt. George T. Hebard.

[JULY 11, 1863.—For Grant to Banks, conveying congratulations on the fall of Port Hudson, see Series I, Vol. XXIV, Part III, p. 499.]

HDQRS. DEPT. OF THE GULF, NINETEENTH ARMY CORPS,
Port Hudson, July 11, 1863.
Brig. Gen. GEORGE L. ANDREWS,
Commanding Port Hudson :
SIR : The commanding general directs as follows :˙ The demolition of all the batteries and works of approach constructed by the United States forces for the recent reduction of Port Hudson will be commenced without delay, and carried as rapidly as practicable to completion, under the direction of the commanding officer of the place. Such of the materials as may be found serviceable will be saved, brought into Port Hudson, and turned over to the proper staff officers, who will account for them on their property returns. To enable the commander to commence this important work without delay, the First Regiment Engineers, Corps d'Afrique, will be placed under his orders.
Very respectfully, your obedient servant,
RICH'D B. IRWIN,
Assistant Adjutant-General.

HDQRS. DEPT. OF THE GULF, NINETEENTH ARMY CORPS,
Port Hudson, July 12, 1863.
Brig. Gen. GEORGE L. ANDREWS,
Commanding Post at Port Hudson :
SIR : The commanding general is informed that the Confederate officers find great difficulty at the post commissary depot, and much delay, in obtaining rations on provision returns, and that, in consequence thereof, some have undergone considerable suffering. The commanding .

---

* Ordered to Baton Rouge, La., July 11.
† The other batteries of the Second and Third Divisions (apparently the First Maine and the Eighteenth and Twenty-first New York) directed by same˙order to report to Brigadier-General Arnold, chief of artillery.

general desires that you will give your attention to this matter, apply the proper corrective, and report the cause of the difficulty.
Very respectfully, your obedient servant,
RICH'D B. IRWIN,
Assistant Adjutant-General.

PORT HUDSON,
July 12, 1863.
Lieut. Col. RICHARD B. IRWIN,
Assistant Adjutant-General :
SIR: In reply to your communication respecting the rations of Confederate officers, I have to state that I have already given my attention to this matter; that as to the causes of the difficulty, Captain [Eugene E.] Shelton reports that he has had great difficulty in obtaining a sufficient quantity of rations in proper time, which is owing in part, at least, to the present embarrassment of the transportation caused by the movement of troops and stores. Concerning this point, Lieutenant-Colonel Chandler can, no doubt, give the necessary explanations. Captain Shelton further reports that much delay and annoyance is caused by the manner in which the Confederate officers draw their rations, in small quantities, for 5 or 6 officers or less at a time; the supply on hand only admitting of the issue of one or two days' rations at a time.
The proper corrections would seem to be—
1. Captain [Henry D.] Woodruff to see that sufficient supplies are promptly forwarded to this post.
2. The Confederate officers to consolidate their provision returns as much as practicable, and send them in at such an hour as may be indicated by Captain Shelton.
In regard to Captain Shelton, I have to state that he has labored faithfully and ably, and that I believe he has done, and is doing, all in his power to supply the Confederate officers and enlisted men with rations. His exertions, I fear, have not been appreciated by some of the Confederate officers, to judge from the discourteous remarks made by them to him.
Very respectfully, your obedient servant,
GEORGE L. ANDREWS,
Brigadier-General of Volunteers, Commanding.

HDQRS. DEPT. OF THE GULF, NINETEENTH ARMY CORPS,
Port Hudson, July 12, 1863.
Maj. Gen. FRANK. GARDNER,
C. S. Army :
GENERAL: I have the honor to acknowledge the receipt of your note of the 11th instant. The paroled troops will be conducted past the lines of this army, with such supplies as may be deemed necessary for their use. Their destination must be determined by themselves. It is not deemed expedient to enter upon any stipulation as to the course to be pursued by the Government in case any of the paroled prisoners should hereafter choose to remain within the lines of the army of the United States.
Very respectfully, your most obedient servant,
N. P. BANKS,
Major-General, Commanding.

HEADQUARTERS UNITED STATES FORCES, ·
Donaldsonville, La., July 12, 1863.
Lieut. Col. RICHARD B. IRWIN,
   Assistant Adjutant-General, Nineteenth Army Corps:

I have the honor to report that I arrived here at 9 p. m. last evening, and my division is now debarked.

Reports from different sources lead to the belief that the enemy are throwing up rifle-pits at Paincourtville; it is thought more for the purpose of retarding our advance than with a view to making a stand.

At Labadieville, however, they are fortifying more strongly, and have three or four 24-pounders in position. The enemy's pickets are within about 2 miles of here, but in no force. The enemy is evidently making preparations to escape if pursued by a strong force, or to resist a small one. Our gunboats can hardly be expected at Brashear City for some days, and it is evidently injudicious to press them until their retreat is cut off. I shall advance a brigade on each side of the bayou this afternoon, to act as advance guards, and to give us more country from which to obtain forage.

I think it of some little importance to have the Bayou Plaquemine guarded at Indian Village, to prevent guerrilla operations between Plaquemine and here, and also any escape in that direction. A small force with a section of artillery would be sufficient.

I am, colonel, very respectfully, your obedient servant,
                    C. GROVER,
                 Brigadier-General, Commanding.

HDQRS. DEFENSES OF NEW ORLEANS, *July* 12, 1863.
Lieut. Col. RICHARD B. IRWIN: ₓ

I omitted in my letters to General Banks to mention that when the force interposed between him and myself and this city was threatened, I found it absolutely necessary to have an officer of experience not only in command of the parapet, but also in command of the troops upon the west side of the river.

I therefore appointed Major Houston, chief engineer Department of the Gulf, acting brigadier-general, and placed him in command of the parapet and all the troops and laborers there engaged, and I appointed Captain [Alexander N.] Shipley, quartermaster U. S. Army, acting brigadier-general, and placed him in command of all the troops on the west side of the river, with orders to take up his quarters at the earthworks on the company canal, at which point all the new levies of troops have assembled.

Both these appointments were indispensable to the efficiency of the defense of this city, as things then stood, and the officers are still in the discharge of the duties assigned them.

I hope the appointments will be approved by the general commanding. If they cannot be, no bad consequences can result, but the country will have gained the services of these gentlemen at what threatened to be a very critical period.

I have the honor to be, your obedient servant,
                    W. H. EMORY,
                Brigadier-General, Commanding.

[JULY 12, 1863.—For Banks to Grant, in relation to re-enforcements, see Series I, Vol. XXIV, Part III, p. 504.]

HEADQUARTERS OF THE ARMY,
Washington, July 13, 1863.
Major-General BANKS,
Department of the Gulf, New Orleans:

GENERAL: I inclose herewith a copy of my letter to General Grant in regard to future operations on the Mississippi River, on the supposition that Port Hudson is already in our possession, or soon will be.* I sincerely hope that no serious disaster has resulted from leaving an insufficient garrison at New Orleans. General Emory's last dispatch was not encouraging. But long ere this you will have been so re-enforced as to be able to recover whatever you may have lost.

Very respectfully, your obedient servant,
H. W. HALLECK,
General-in-Chief.

———

HEADQUARTERS OF THE ARMY,
Washington, July 13, 1863.
Major-General EMORY,
New Orleans:

GENERAL: Your dispatch of July 4 is received.

No troops could possibly be spared from the north. General Gillmore, at Port Royal, was directed to send every man he could spare to New Orleans. General Grant was also directed some time since to re-enforce General Banks. As Vicksburg surrendered on the 4th, he ought certainly to have re-enforced him on the 7th. You have, therefore, been relieved long before this reaches you.

Very respectfully, your obedient servant,
H. W. HALLECK,
General-in-Chief.

———

HDQRS. DEPT. OF THE GULF, NINETEENTH ARMY CORPS,
Port Hudson, July 13, 1863.
Brig. Gen. W. DWIGHT,
Commanding Third Division:

SIR: The commanding general instructs me to say that the Second Division having been broken up, and the regiments composing it transferred to the Third Division, to the temporary command of which you are assigned, the permanent staff of the Third Division, as announced in the orders of its permanent commander, General Emory, continues to constitute the staff of the division. The staff officers of the Second Division may be assigned to fill vacancies, but all supernumerary staff officers formerly attached to the Second Division you will order to report in person to the chiefs of their proper staff departments at these headquarters. In regard to your Special Orders, No. 3, I am directed by the commanding general to inform you that Surgeon Hartwell is the designated medical director of the Third Division.

Very respectfully, your obedient servant,
RICH'D B. IRWIN,
Assistant Adjutant-General.

———

* See Halleck to Grant, July 11, Series I, Vol. XXIV, Part III, p. 497.

HEADQUARTERS DEFENSES OF NEW ORLEANS,
July 13, 1863.

Brigadier-General GROVER,
Donaldsonville:

Supposing a movement had been commenced down the La Fourche, I sent what little available force I have forward on the railroad to reconstruct the railroad bridges, so as to be able to supply the troops by rail when they reach La Fourche Crossing, and at the same time make a diversion in your favor; but the moment they pass Boutte Station they are liable to be cut off, unless acting in co-operation with the force from Donaldsonville down the La Fourche. Therefore, I request you will inform me when the movement takes place.

The enemy are in very considerable force.

Respectfully, your obedient servant,

W. H. EMORY,
Brigadier-General, Commanding.

HEADQUARTERS DEFENSES OF NEW ORLEANS,
July 13, 1863.

Lieutenant-Colonel IRWIN,
Assistant Adjutant-General, Port Hudson:

The Cromwell is in, with dates to the 4th, and the latest news we have from Gettysburg, July 3, 1 p. m., Meade had driven the enemy 4 miles north and west. Meade appeared to be driving the rebels. Longstreet reported killed. Jeff. Davis reported at Greencastle, Pa. Richmond closely invested by General Dix.

The news in this vicinity: The rebels are withdrawing from my front on the west bank. I have sent forward Stickney, with 300 infantry and all the cavalry, to press toward La Fourche, and reconstruct the bridges on the Opelousas Railroad.

W. H. EMORY,
Brigadier-General, Commanding.

HEADQUARTERS DEFENSES OF NEW ORLEANS,
July 13, 1863.

Lieutenant-Colonel IRWIN,
Assistant Adjutant-General, Port Hudson:

The lines made for the defense of this city were planned for the river at the flood and the marshes full of water. Now that the river is fallen and the marshes dry, these lines could have been turned in a number of places.

We have a force of at least 1,000 men repairing these defects, under Acting Brigadier-General Houston.

Although the emergency is passed which caused me to commence the work, it is my opinion, and General Houston's also, that we should go on and complete it, and also make an inclosed work which shall command the city independent of the navy. Shall we go on?

W. H. EMORY,
Brigadier-General, Commanding.

HEADQUARTERS DEFENSES OF NEW ORLEANS,
July 13, 1863.
Lieutenant-Colonel SAWTELL,
Jefferson Station:
Communicate this at once by express to Lieutenant-Colonel Stickney:

Be very cautious how you advance. There is a report Weitzel has been repulsed on the La Fourche. Hold your force in readiness to fall back on Jefferson Station, leaving the cavalry where you found it.

W. H. EMORY,
Brigadier-General, Commanding.

ENGINEER OFFICE,
Port Hudson, July 13, 1863.
Brig. Gen. CHARLES P. STONE:

GENERAL: With reference to the engineer organization in this department, I have the honor to submit the following report:

These troops, I understand, to be under the immediate command of the chief engineer: Company K, Forty-second Massachusetts (detached), Lieutenant Harding commanding, pontoniers; Company K, Fifty-third Massachusetts (detached), Captain Breman commanding, pioneers; First Louisiana Engineers (colored), Col. J. Hodge commanding, civil and engineer assistants.

The pontoniers (about 30 men for duty) have a pontoon bridge of about 100 feet, with rigging, &c., complete, in wagons furnished by the quartermaster. They are under orders to join General Weitzel, with 200 feet of bridge, and turn over the rest to Col. J. Hodge, First Louisiana Engineers. Their time of service expires this week. After the present expedition, I intend to appoint the company of Louisiana Engineers commanded by Captain Smith pontoniers in their stead, and transfer the bridge and train to them.

The pioneers (about 80 men for duty) have about two wagon-loads of tools and materials, forming part of their train of six 4-horse wagons. They are usually kept with the advanced guard for repairing roads, bridges, &c., under the direction of the engineer's assistants. I understand they have proved very useful in this capacity, including many mechanics among them. They are at Mount Pleasant Landing, awaiting transportation to join General Grover. I believe their term of service expires in August.

The First Louisiana Engineers (colored) number about 800 men for duty, the colonel reports. They are organized for three battalions of 600 men each. They are well supplied with intrenching tools, and have also a fair supply of other engineer materials, such as rope, nails, spikes, chests of tools, &c., for all of which the colonel is responsible, and issues to engineer assistants and general officers on their receipts, by order of the chief engineer. I intend they shall remain here for the present, unless otherwise ordered by Major Houston, and have ordered them to collect all engineer property in the trenches, and then to furnish General Andrews any tools, materials, and working parties he may apply for, till further orders.

The engineer assistants are Captain Long, First Louisiana Engineers, and Sergeant Nutting, Rhode Island Cavalry (detached); 1 surveyor, 2 topographical engineers, and 2 photographers. Captain Long will accompany headquarters, to direct the pioneers in their duties, assisted by Sergeant Nutting. The 2 topographical engineers will also move with headquarters, to make and plot reconnaissances. The surveyor will remain here, to begin a survey of our lines and the enemy's. I have asked Major Houston to send other surveyors from New Orleans to assist him. One photographer will remain here, to take the views already ordered, and the other will probably go to New Orleans, to print the impressions with greater facility.

There is also an engineer quartermaster who draws, by order of the chief engineer, all necessary articles from the quartermaster's department, and receipts and accounts for them.

Respectfully submitted.

JOHN C. PALFREY,
Captain, U. S. Engineers.

HEADQUARTERS DEFENSES OF NEW ORLEANS,
July 14, 1863.

Colonel SAWTELL,
        Jefferson:

Forward this to Colonel Stickney by express:

The forces from Donaldsonville are not yet ready to move down the La Fourche. I do not intend you to move until they move. I will notify you as soon as I get notice when they move.

W. H. EMORY,
Brigadier-General.

HEADQUARTERS DEFENSES OF NEW ORLEANS,
July 14, 1863.

Brigadier-General GROVER,
        Donaldsonville:

The following information received from my advance at Boutte Station may be of some service to you. I have ordered Stickney not to commencé reopening the road until I hear from you.

W. H. EMORY,
Brigadier-General, Commanding.

[Inclosure.]

BOUTTE STATION, VIA JEFFERSON,
July 14, 1863.

[Brigadier-General GROVER:]

I sent out a squad of cavalry this morning, who returned a short time since, bringing 2 prisoners from [E.] Waller's battalion of Texas cavalry. From the prisoners, examining them separately, I find that they keep a picket of about 25 men at the other end of Des Allemands Bridge, and have had a small post of 6 or 8 men a mile or two this side.

Between Des Allemands and Raceland there is nothing till you get close to Raceland, where the Waller battalion is stationed, about 250 men, with two pieces of artillery.

There is no artillery at Des Allemands, the two pieces there having been withdrawn. Our party went just over the bridge and got these 2 prisoners there. The balance retreated. Infantry can cross Des Allemands Bridge in single file; horses cannot cross the bridge.

Mouton is at Thibodeaux. There is a small force at La Fourche Crossing. Their force at Raceland is designed merely as a strong outpost. Their main force on Bayou La Fourche is above Thibodeaux.

These men first heard of the fall of Port Hudson last night. From these facts, I cannot think it possible that they will venture an attack here. I can leave here at any time if you think it necessary for any reason.

I shall immediately throw out a picket at this side of Des Allemands Bridge, if their pickets have not recrossed, and, at any rate, very near to the bridge.

Very respectfully,

ALBERT STICKNEY,
Lieutenant-Colonel, Commanding.

HEADQUARTERS UNITED STATES FORCES,
Donaldsonville, La., July 14, 1863.

Lieut. Col. RICHARD B. IRWIN,
Assistant Adjutant-General, Nineteenth Army Corps:

I asked the question of re-enforcement from above merely as a matter of news. I have no reason to believe that the enemy has over 7,000 or 8,000 men within striking distance of us. It was reported by a rebel, under a flag of truce, while collecting the wounded yesterday, that Magruder was in our front. I think, however, had that been true I should have heard it from other sources. I do not think, therefore, that we need re-enforcements until it is intended to march upon the enemy down the bayou. In order to do that, we ought to have, I think, all the available force in the department. The force against us will undoubtedly be considerably larger than it was in the Teche country. The reverse of yesterday was entirely due to the disobedience of orders, drunkenness, and misbehavior before the enemy of Colonel Morgan, commanding brigade. I wish that he may have a speedy trial by court-martial. It is due to the troops engaged that he be tried as soon as possible.

I am, colonel, very respectfully, your obedient servant,

C. GROVER,
Brigadier-General, Commanding.

HDQRS. DEPT. OF THE GULF, NINETEENTH ARMY CORPS,
Port Hudson, July 14, 1863.

Rear-Admiral D. G. FARRAGUT,
New Orleans:

SIR: Please let me know immediately and positively whether you can send the Sachem, Estrella, Arizona, Clifton, Calhoun, Hollyhock, or any other boats to Berwick Bay immediately, to cut off the retreat of the enemy. The garrison should be back to-day. I can add nothing to the strength of my former request that these vessels should be sent, but, if they cannot be, please let me know immediately, so that I may order the troops to attack the enemy without further delay, instead of waiting for the gunboats to cut off his retreat.

Very respectfully, your obedient servant,

N. P. BANKS,
Major-General, Commanding.

HDQRS. DEPT. OF THE GULF, NINETEENTH ARMY CORPS,
Port Hudson, July 14, 1863.

Brig. Gen. W. H. EMORY,
    Commanding Defenses of New Orleans:

GENERAL: The officers—prisoners sent to New Orleans—had their side-arms returned to them, after unconditional surrender, in consideration of their gallant defense. They are not paroled, and it was not intended that they should wear their arms. The major-general commanding desires that they be kept under guard in some comfortable house or houses which you may select, and that, while keeping them in safe custody, you cause them to be made as comfortable as practicable.

Very respectfully, your obedient servant,
                RICH'D B. IRWIN,
                    Assistant Adjutant-General.

HDQRS. DEPT. OF THE GULF, NINETEENTH ARMY CORPS,
Port Hudson, July 14, 1863—9 p. m.

Brig. Gen. GEORGE L. ANDREWS,
    Commanding Post, Port Hudson:

SIR: The commanding general has just gone to New Orleans for a day or two; directed me before his departure to inform you of the fact, and that he leaves Brigadier-General Stone as the senior officer present, in temporary command of the forces in this vicinity. The commanding general further desired me to communicate to you his direction that hereafter no citizen be allowed to enter our lines under any circumstances whatever; that all citizens now within our lines be given forty-eight hours from to-morrow morning to decide whether they will depart beyond our lines or remain within them unconditionally, and that, after the expiration of that time, no citizen be permitted to go beyond our lines under any circumstances whatever. The commanding general further directed that no more permits to go beyond the fortifications be granted to any of the Confederate officers, prisoners of war. All non-commissioned officers and privates of the Confederate army, who, having been paroled, return to our lines, will be sent under guard to the provost-marshal, who will send them to the provost-marshal-general at New Orleans.

Very respectfully, your obedient servant,
                RICH'D B. IRWIN,
                    Assistant Adjutant-General.

PORT HUDSON, LA.,
July 15, 1863.

Lieut. Col. RICHARD B. IRWIN,
    Assistant Adjutant-General:

SIR: In reply to the communication from department headquarters, relative to paroled prisoners who have returned to our lines, I have to state:

1. That I have received no directions to have the oath administered, but, on the contrary, was verbally informed by General Banks that it was not expedient to administer the oath at present.

2. That I communicated the order received from department headquarters relative to the disposition to be made of the paroled prisoners who returned to our lines, and I am informed by Colonel Chickering

that he has complied with the order from the time he received it, but had sent away one squad of such paroled prisoners before he received the order.

Respectfully, your obedient servant,

GEORGE L. ANDREWS,
Brigadier-General of Volunteers, Commanding.

HDQRS. DEPT. OF THE GULF, NINETEENTH ARMY CORPS,
Port Hudson, July 15, 1863.

Maj. Gen. N. P. BANKS,
Commanding Department of the Gulf:

GENERAL: All the enlisted men captured in this place have been paroled; all, excepting the sick and wounded and nurses in the hospital, have been sent out of our lines. Forty officers left for New Orleans on the steamboat I. M. Brown at 3.30 p. m. to-day. The total number of enlisted men paroled is stated to be 5,935; the total number of officers (not paroled) is stated at 405; aggregate of prisoners taken, 6,340.

Very respectfully, your obedient servant,

[CHAS. P. STONE,]
Brigadier-General.

HDQRS. DEPT. OF THE GULF, NINETEENTH ARMY CORPS,
Baton Rouge, July 15, 1863.

Col. O. P. GOODING,
Commanding United States Forces at Baton Rouge:

SIR: The commanding general directs that you at once forward to General Grover, at Donaldsonville, the troops—infantry, artillery, and cavalry—which have recently come to Baton Rouge from Port Hudson. The quartermaster's department will furnish the necessary transportation.

Very respectfully, your obedient servant,

[C. EMERSON,]
Second Lieutenant 174th New York Vols., Actg. Asst. Adjt. Gen.

SPECIAL ORDERS, }   HDQRS. DEPT. OF THE GULF, 19TH A. C.,
No. 171.   }   *Port Hudson, July* 15, 1863.

*   *   *   *   *   *

IX. Leave of absence for twenty days, on surgeon's certificate, with permission to apply to the Adjutant-General of the Army for an extension of 40 days, is granted to Maj. Gen. C. C. Augur, U. S. Volunteers.*

*   *   *   *

By command of Major-General Banks:

RICH'D B. IRWIN,
Assistant Adjutant-General.

---

* General Augur being assigned to duty elsewhere, did not return to the Department of the Gulf.

GENERAL ORDERS, }   HDQRS. DEFENSES OF NEW ORLEANS,
 No. 26.   }   *New Orleans, July 15, 1863.*

So much of General Orders No. 18, as directs that coffee-houses, stores, and shops of every description will be closed at 9 p. m., is for the present suspended, and they may be kept open, as was the case before this order was issued.

By command of Brigadier-General Emory:

            [W. D. WOOD,]
  Lieutenant-Colonel, and Acting Assistant Adjutant-General.

[JULY 16, 1863.—For two letters from Grant to Banks, in relation to affairs at Vicksburg, see Series I, Vol. XXIV, Part III, pp. 518, 519.]

  HDQRS. DEPT. OF THE GULF, NINETEENTH ARMY CORPS,
            Port Hudson, July 16, 1863.
Maj. Gen. U. S. GRANT,
 Commanding Department of the Tennessee, Vicksburg:

GENERAL: By the steamboat Planet I send a large number of Confederate officers, prisoners captured at this place (189, according to the list inclosed). These officers have not been paroled, and are placed under the escort of a battalion of General Grierson's cavalry, returning to rejoin your command. General Grierson, with the remainder of his cavalry, will probably leave this post to-morrow on the steamboat Imperial, having in charge Brigadier-General Beall and certain field and staff officers. May I ask of you, on the part of Major-General Banks, who is temporarily absent, to forward these prisoners to the proper destination in the north? Yesterday brought us the welcome intelligence of the occupation of Natchez by General Ransom, of your command; and two transports, laden with beef-cattle, captured by him, have since been received here. The arrival of this beef is most opportune and acceptable.

There is nothing especially interesting to communicate concerning operations in this region since the last communication of the major-general commanding.

I am, general, very respectfully, your most obedient servant,

            [CHAS. P. STONE,]
             Brigadier-General.

SPECIAL ORDERS, }   HDQRS. DEPT. OF THE GULF, 19TH A. C.,
 No. 172.   }   *Port Hudson, July 16, 1863.*

 *   *   *   *   *   *   *

II. All the Confederate officers, prisoners, destined north, excepting Brigadier-General Beall and staff, will be sent on board the steamer Planet to-day before 2 p. m. Careful lists of these officers must be prepared and furnished to these headquarters before sailing. A battalion of Grierson's cavalry will be ordered on board as escort.

 *   *   *   *   *   *

By command of Major-General Banks:

         RICH'D B. IRWIN,
          Assistant Adjutant-General.

HDQRS. DEPT. OF THE GULF, NINETEENTH ARMY CORPS,
Port Hudson, July 17, 1863.
Surg. THOMAS J. BUFFINGTON,
In Charge C. S. Army Hospital, Clinton, La. :
SIR : Your letter by flag of truce has been received. Your proposition to receive the sick and wounded of the late garrison of this place,
and to provide for them at Clinton, has received my respectful attention, and it has been discussed with Surgeon Russell, C. S. Army, now
in charge of those sick and wounded. Dr. Russell agrees with me that
it would be dangerous to move most of these men, and that the remainder
need certain medicines and supplies which are more easily obtained
here than they would be in Clinton. While it is the desire of the United
States authorities to do that which will most conduce to the speedy recovery of these men, it is believed that the course proposed of removing
them at this time would not be the best for attaining that end. These
sick and wounded are paroled and sent to their homes as fast as they
become able to journey.
Very respectfully, your obedient servant,
[CHAS. P. STONE,]
Brigadier-General.

HEADQUARTERS TROOPS WEST BANK MISSISSIPPI,
Company Canal, July 18, 1863.
Brigadier-General EMORY,
Commanding Defenses at New Orleans :
SIR : I have the honor to report that at 8 o'clock this a. m., a man,
who came down the canal from the neighborhood of Thibodeaux, 44
miles above here, assures me that Major-General Mouton, of the rebel
army, has his headquarters at that place, together with 25,000 men and
nine batteries of artillery.
That this may not be true, I am not prepared to deny; however, I
would respectfully suggest that with one or two good scouts I can ascertain the exact number and locality of the enemy should he be near us.
I am, general, with much respect, your obedient servant,
M. W. PLUMLY,
Commanding Troops West Bank Mississippi, at Company Canal.

HDQRS. DEPT. OF THE GULF, NINETEENTH ARMY CORPS,
Port Hudson, July 18, 1863.
Maj. Gen. U. S. GRANT,
Comdg. Department of the Tennessee, Vicksburg, Miss.:
GENERAL : During the temporary absence of the major-general
commanding, I have had the honor to receive Colonel Lagow, of your
staff, who arrived here this morning with a steamboat-load of sick and
wounded prisoners. He was immediately dispatched to New Orleans,
where he will doubtless receive all facilities for transporting his charge
to Mobile, according to your wishes.
A portion of Grierson's cavalry has doubtless arrived to-day at your
headquarters, having been sent on the Steamer Planet the day before
yesterday. General Grierson himself, with most of the remainder of his
command, leaves to-day on the steamer Imperial. By the same steamer,
and under the escort of Grierson's cavalry, are sent 22 commissioned

officers of the rebel army, prisoners, including Brigadier-General Beall and staff. A list is inclosed.*

You will greatly oblige Major-General Banks by forwarding these prisoners up the river to such point as may have been designated by the War Department. A steamboat laden with cattle arrived here this , morning from Natchez, forwarded by Brigadier-General Ransom. Our forces here are engaged in destroying the works of attack recently constructed for the reduction of the place, and in putting the lines in a state of defense, so that a smaller force can maintain the position.

· Hoping to soon receive cheering accounts of success on General Sherman's line of operations, and congratulating you most sincerely on the recent mark of recognition of your services by the Government, I have the honor to be, general, very respectfully, your obedient servant,

CHAS. P. STONE,
Brigadier-General.

SPECIAL ORDERS, }   HDQRS. DEPT. OF THE GULF, 19TH A. C.,
No. 174.   }   *Port Hudson, July 18, 1863.*

*   *   *   *   *   *   *

-XII. Brig. Gen. Benjamin H. Grierson, commanding cavalry, will proceed with the Sixth and Seventh Regiments of Illinois Cavalry, and the First Illinois Battery, under his command, to Vicksburg, and will there report to Major-General Grant for duty in the Department of the Tennessee. It is with extreme regret that the major-general commanding sees this gallant officer and his brave cavalry leave this department, in which they have rendered such brilliant and useful service, but it is due both to commander and command that they should be no longer detained absent from their comrades of the Department of the Tennessee.

The major-general commanding, while tendering to General Grierson and his troops the thanks of the Nineteenth Corps, wishes for them in each future field of duty opportunities for maintaining the reputation they have so justly won, and for rendering to the Republic services which shall add new luster to her arms.

*   *   *   *

By command of Major-General Banks:

[RICH'D B. IRWIN,]
Assistant Adjutant-General.

HEADQUARTERS DEFENSES OF NEW ORLEANS,
July 18, 1863.

Brigadier-General GROVER,
Commanding at Donaldsonville :

My advance is at Des Allemands Bayou, finishing the rebuilding of the bridge.

· My pickets report that the enemy are intrenching at La Fourche Crossing.

W. H. EMORY,
Brigadier-General, Commanding.

[JULY 18, 1863.—For Banks to Grant, in relation to affairs in the Department of the Gulf, see Series I, Vol. XXIV, Part III, pp. 527.]

---

* Omitted.

HDQRS. DEPT. OF THE GULF, NINETEEENTH ARMY CORPS,
New Orleans, July 19, 1863.

Major-General HALLECK,
    Commander-in-Chief, &c.:

GENERAL: I left Port Hudson Wednesday, the 15th instant, reaching this city on the 18th, for the purpose of expediting the movements of the gunboats into Berwick Bay. They sail to day, not in season, I fear, to prevent the enemy's passage across the bay with whatever material he may have in his possession. It is reported, and I believe correctly, that they were crossing as early as Wednesday, having brought two or three steamers from Red River to aid them. It was impossible to prevent this, excepting by the occupation of the bay by the gunboats, and Admiral Farragut assures me that he has made every effort to facilitate their movement; but it has been unavailing till now. We have but four boats that can cross the bar at the present low stage of water, and these were so much out of repair, after long service, that they could not be at once moved.

Everything remains quiet at Port Hudson. The troops are stationed at that point, at Baton Rouge, and at Donaldsonville. We shall soon reoccupy the La Fourche district.

The nine-months' regiments will be sent home at once by sea, the expense to the Government being much less that way.

The officers of the garrison at Port Hudson are in confinement here. The men have been paroled.

The city of New Orleans is perfectly quiet, and has been in no danger whatever during the campaign, notwithstanding the representations made to the public. The departure of so many troops leaves my force quite small, and I hope the Government may now be able to re-enforce the army here, where it is so much needed.

The news of the repulse of Lee's army up to the 7th has filled us all with joy, and we believe that if the victories of the east are confirmed the war must be considered near its end. I have the honor to acknowledge the receipt of your letter covering intercepted dispatches from Jefferson Davis.

I have the honor to be, with much respect, your obedient servant,

N. P. BANKS,
    Major-General, Commanding.

HEADQUARTERS DEFENSES OF NEW ORLEANS,
July 20, 1863.

Maj. Gen. N. P. BANKS:

GENERAL: In the absence of your [chief of] staff, I take the liberty of addressing you directly upon a subject which I think of sufficient interest to present directly to your attention without passing it through the adjutant-general's office, still at Port Hudson.

The defenses of this city are essentially those projected by the enemy, and are based upon three considerations, none of which exist at this time.

1. Upon the presence of a large defending force, say, at least, 10,000 men.

2. Upon a population supposed to be in the main friendly, if not wholly so.

3. Upon a high stage of water and the filling of the swamps, which at that season are impassable.

The consequence of this condition of things is that when it was nec- essary to leave but a small force for the defense of the city, which the casualties of the service may again at no very distant time render im- perative, these lines of defense were absolutely an embarrassment, so great was their extent, and so easily could they be turned on both sides of the river by going through the swamps, which are now perfectly dry and passable for both footmen and artillery.

Now, what I have to propose is that these defenses shall be so ar- ranged as to conform to the real condition of things which has hap- pened and may happen again, that is to say, for a small garrison, a hostile population, and a dry season.

Very considerable progress has already been made in one branch of this work; that is, adapting the defenses to the present state of water. This has been done by cutting down trees and making abatis from the flanks of the parapet to the lakes on either side.

What is most wanted is a citadel, or a place of arms, occupying some central point which shall overlook the city, render it independent of the presence of a naval force, and which shall at the same time be a rendezvous for the reserves and a safe place of deposit for arms, am- munition, and commissary stores.

The selection of the site of this fortress or citadel will involve a great many considerations, and its construction be attended with some expense.

I therefore respectfully suggest that if the general commanding has not already determined in his own mind where this point should be, that he will either select it himself, or institute a board to make the selection of the site and determine upon the extent and trace of the work, so that the force which we now have employed in strengthening the old rebel lines at the parapet and at the company canal, may be, when their work is done with, which will be in a few days, placed upon this new work.

I have the honor to be, general, very respectfully, your obedient servant,

W. H. EMORY,
Brigadier-General, Commanding.

HEADQUARTERS DEFENSES OF NEW ORLEANS,
July 20, 1863.
Maj. Gen. N. P. BANKS:

GENERAL: Recent events have shown that the establishment of civil power in this State is, I think, premature, and wholly inconsistent with the interests of the United States.

Without for a moment intending to cast a reflection on the probity of those having supervision of the internal commerce, under this system supplies have been put in the La Fourche district which have enabled the enemy, who were in very considerable force, to subsist there for the last month. The supplies captured by them at Brashear were very few, and they have subsisted almost entirely upon the supplies which were sent from this city under the ægis of the civil authority for the use of the plantations. The same has been the case with the planta- tions below this city on the west bank of the river.

The enemy have drawn supplies from them through the lakes and various little canals tapping this river below this city to a very consid- erable amount.

It is impossible for these civil officers to know what is right unless they remain in the adjutant-general's office and make themselves familiar with all the movements of the enemy, and I respectfully suggest that all power to give permits to trade, or for provisions to be taken into either insurrectionary or what are called non-insurrectionary districts be placed exclusively in the hands of the military authorities.

I have found it necessary to assume this authority for a short time, and to stop all intercourse with those districts, but do not feel at liberty to continue this restriction on the action of these officers of the customs without referring the matter to you.

I have the honor to be, general, very respectfully, your obedient servant,

W. H. EMORY,
Brigadier-General, Commanding.

HDQRS. DEPT. OF THE GULF, NINETEENTH ARMY CORPS,
Port Hudson, July 20, 1863.

Maj. Gen. N. P. BANKS,
Commanding Department of the Gulf, New Orleans:

GENERAL: I inspected the camps, hospitals, kitchens, &c., of Ullmann's brigade this morning. They are getting into a pretty good state of police generally. Large mortality from dysentery and measles.

There is very considerable disaffection in some of the nine-months' regiments. Most of them think of nothing but getting home, without any regard to want of transportation. To-day one company of the Fiftieth Massachusetts mutinied and refused to do duty. The mutineers were promptly put under guard, and I have directed Brigadier-General Andrews to send them under guard to-day to New Orleans, to be sent to Ship Island for hard labor during the war, subject to your approval. At the same time I have selected the Fifty-second Massachusetts Regiment, in which there has been no instance of refusal to do duty, or of insubordination, for immediate shipment north, and, without any publication of the fact, have allowed it to be understood that the regiments are to be shipped in such order as to leave those who behave badly to go last. Most of Ullmann's brigade are unarmed. Shall the arms and accouterments of the nine-months' men be taken for them?

Very respectfully, your obedient servant,
[CHAS. P. STONE,]
Brigadier-General.

HDQRS. DEPT. OF THE GULF, NINETEENTH ARMY CORPS,
Port Hudson, July 20, 1863—4 p. m.

Maj. Gen. N. P. BANKS,
Commanding Department of the Gulf, New Orleans:

GENERAL: The mutineers of Fiftieth Massachusetts Regiment having made their submission, Brigadier-General Andrews has restored them to duty. While I would not recommend such a course at this time, I do not deem it proper to change the order.

Very respectfully, your obedient servant,
[CHAS. P. STONE,]
Brigadier-General.

GENERAL ORDERS, } HDQRS. DEPT. OF THE GULF, 19TH A. C.,
No. 52.   }   July 20, 1863.

General Orders, No. 45, current series, headquarters Department of the Gulf,* is hereby amended to read as follows:

A military court, to be known as the provost court of the Department of the Gulf, is hereby constituted, for the purpose of hearing, deciding, and passing judgment upon—

1. All cases of violations of general or special orders, violations of the Rules and Articles of War, violations of the recognized laws of war, or other offenses arising under the military jurisdiction, where the offender is not in the military service of the United States.

2. All civil crimes against the persons or property of the inhabitants, committed by any person in the military service of the United States.

3. All other cases, arising under the military jurisdiction, which may be specially referred to the court by the commanding general or the provost-marshal-general of the department.

The court will exercise original and exclusive jurisdiction in all the above cases, but when the penalty extends to loss of life or the dismissal of a commissioned officer, the sentence of the court shall be subject to the approval of the major-general commanding the department.

The court shall have power to bring before it, and to examine into the cause of confinement of any person held imprisoned within the department, provided that, upon the application of the person so held imprisoned, it shall be made to appear that he is not undergoing the sentence of any court of competent civil or military jurisdiction, nor awaiting trial in such court, nor confined by order of the major-general commanding the department, or of the commander of the Defenses of New Orleans in his absence. And the court, upon such examination, shall have power to discharge the prisoner from confinement, or to make such other order or decision as the justice of the case may require.

The sessions of the court will be held at the city of New Orleans, or such other point as may from time to time be designated in orders.

Col. Charles C. Dwight, One hundred and sixtieth New York, is appointed judge of the court hereby authorized and established, and will enter upon his duties immediately.

By command of Major-General Banks:

RICH'D B. IRWIN,
Assistant Adjutant-General.

HDQRS. DEPT. OF THE GULF, NINETEENTH ARMY CORPS,
Port Hudson, July 21, 1863.

Maj. Gen. N. P. BANKS,
Commanding Department of the Gulf, New Orleans:

GENERAL: Brigadier-General Andrews has sent a small cavalry force to the opposite side of the Mississippi River, along the Fausse River, with orders to collect all the able-bodied black men and bring them here. I regard this as a false military move. The district opposite is one containing a large number of small farmers, the best disposed to the Government I have seen in this State. Their negroes are few, and are reported to be contented and quiet. If they are forcibly taken from their homes and put into the ranks, we shall gain a few worthless soldiers and have on our hands hundreds of their families to feed, and shall

* Of June 2, p. 533.

at the same time make hostile a region now friendly. This region is one, too, which, from its position, it is important to have some friends in. Now the inhabitants freely bring information to us; if robbed, they will become a set of spies for the enemy, and that in a dangerous position. I do not feel at liberty to countermand General Andrews' order, as he quotes your authority, but were I in command I should not hesitate to do so, as a measure of military policy.

Very respectfully, your obedient servant,

CHAS. P. STONE,
Brigadier-General.

HEADQUARTERS DEFENSES OF NEW ORLEANS,
July 21, 1863.

Admiral FARRAGUT:

Referring to our conversation last evening, and the newspaper complaint of injustice done to the navy at the defense of Donaldsonville, I desire to send you extracts of the only reports I have been able to make upon the subject, and beg, if you think it of sufficient importance, that you will communicate it to the brave officers who commanded the gunboats on that occasion, and will say to them that the reason why I have made no report is that Major Bullen never made any report to me, except his short telegraphic announcement of the repulse of the enemy, and the reason of his making no report was that he was murdered by a miscreant a few days after the battle.

If any other reports than these have been made to headquarters, they have been made irregularly and without due authority. I only regret the sad event which has deprived me so far of the pleasure of making a detailed report of the brilliant affair at Donaldsonville.

If I should have that opportunity, I shall not fail to signalize the officers and ships that played so important a part in it.*

I have the honor to be, admiral, your obedient servant,

W. H. EMORY,
Brigadier-General, Commanding.

HDQRS. DEPT. OF THE GULF, NINETEENTH ARMY CORPS,
Port Hudson, July 22, 1863.

Maj. Gen. N. P. BANKS,
Commanding Department of the Gulf, New Orleans:

GENERAL: Col. F. E. Claiborne, of Pointe Coupée Parish, is anxious to go to New Orleans, to have an interview with you for the purpose of arranging matters in his parish. He is frank and explicit, and states his conviction of the utter hopelessness of further resistance to the power of the Government; is ready to make his submission, and hopes to make such arrangement as shall save the parish from total and lasting destruction, while the Government shall be firmly established over the State. Shall I give him and a merchant of the same district who came with him a pass to you? The merchant's name is Hermann. Colonel Claiborne was a member of the Legislature, but declined to act as in longer opposition to the Government; was offered the nomination for Governor, but declined. I would respectfully recommend the inter-

----

* See Emory to Farragut, July 26, p. 656.

view, as I believe you could through him produce a large and lasting impression on the people of this State and on those adjacent.

Very respectfully, your obedient servant,

[CHAS. P. STONE,]
Brigadier-General.

HDQRS. DEPT. OF THE GULF, NINETEENTH ARMY CORPS,
New Orleans, July 23, 1863.

Maj. Gen. H. W. HALLECK,
Commander-in-Chief, U. S. Army, Washington, D. C.:

GENERAL: Since my last dispatch, our troops have taken possession again of Brashear City. There is now no enemy between the river and Berwick Bay. It is a mistake to suppose that we have lost the country this side of the Red River, as represented in the public prints. We do not occupy it, it is true, but, with the repossession of the Mississippi, the Atchafalaya, and Berwick Bay, we have control of it precisely the same as if our troops were there. None of the advantages gained by our campaign have been lost to the Government. It is a misfortune that we could not have captured the force of the enemy that invaded the La Fourche country, but the limited force of the navy and the army, and the complete exhaustion of both, made it impossible to prevent their escape. They have, however, done no harm, except the devastation of a few plantations and the capture of some convalescents who remained at Brashear, chiefly by their own fault, and without the knowledge of the military authorities. It was not intended that any force should remain at Brashear, and it was ordered that all supplies should be removed from there as speedily as possible when we left the line of the Teche. Disobedience of orders occasioned the slight loss we suffered at Brashear.

Preparations are making for the immediate return of the nine-months' men. Of these there are twenty-two regiments in number. A portion will go by the river and a part by sea. It is represented by the quartermaster's department that the expenses will be about the same on each line. The departure of these regiments will reduce my effective force to about 12,000 men. I trust that the defeat of Lee's army may enable the Government to strengthen my force without delay. There is still strength at Mobile and in Texas, which will constantly threaten Louisiana, and which ought to be destroyed without delay. The possession of Mobile and the occupation of Texas would quiet the whole Southwest, and every effort ought to be made to accomplish this. Its importance can hardly be overestimated. A large number of wounded and sick officers and privates will be sent north upon furlough, upon the recommendation of the medical director, a change of climate being essential to their recovery.

The general condition of the army is good. No contagious diseases exist, and the chief cause of sickness is exhaustion and climatic affections. The city of New Orleans was never healthier than this season, and never more cleanly or quiet. My forces are stationed on the river at Donaldsonville, Baton Rouge, and Port Hudson. As soon as they can be reorganized, I shall place them in healthy locations for the summer. Brashear will be held by a small force, and possibly some detachments may patrol the river above Port Hudson.

It is reported to us from Alexandria that the rebel troops there, expecting a movement from Port Hudson, and learning that the gunboats

were ascending Red River, had abandoned the place and retreated to
Natchitoches. The inhabitants were making preparations to leave
town.

I have the honor to be, with much respect, your obedient servant,
N. P. BANKS,
Major-General, Commanding.

HDQRS. DEPT. OF THE GULF, NINETEENTH ARMY CORPS,
Port Hudson, July 23, 1863.

Maj. Gen. N. P. BANKS,
Commanding Department of the Gulf, New Orleans:

GENERAL: A Frenchman, just arrived from the vicinity of Alexandria, reports that the rebel troops there, expecting troops from here, and
learning that the gunboats were ascending the Red River, had abandoned the place and retreated to Natchitoches; that the gunboats had
gone up as far as the mouth of the Black River; that the inhabitants
of Alexandria were packing up to flee; that Texas cavalry was patrolling the Atchafalaya, opposite this. Thinking his statements will be
interesting, I shall send him to you.

Very respectfully, your obedient servant,
[CHAS. P. STONE,]
Brigadier-General.

SPECIAL ORDERS, } HDQRS. DEPT. OF THE GULF, 19TH A. C.,
No. 179.   {   *Port Hudson, July 23, 1863.*

I. Forty of the sick and wounded prisoners now in hospital at this
place, reported able to travel in ambulance, will be sent to-morrow under
a flag of truce to Clinton, La., and turned over to the surgeon in charge
of the Confederate hospital there.

The train will be accompanied by a Confederate medical officer, and
will be supplied with three days' rations and such medicines as may be
deemed necessary by the medical director.

The flag will be escorted by a detachment of 12 men from Battery G,
Fifth Artillery, under the command of Lieutenant Rawles of that company.

*   *   *   *   *

By command of Major-General Banks:
[RICH'D B. IRWIN,]
Assistant Adjutant-General.

WASHINGTON, D. C.,
July 24, 1863.

Major-General BANKS,
New Orleans, La.:

GENERAL: I have nothing from you since the 8th. I suppose the
first thing done by your army after the fall of Port Hudson was to clean
out the Teche and Atchafalaya countries. That being accomplished,
your next operations must depend very much upon the condition of
affairs.

Texas and Mobile will present themselves to your attention. The
navy are very anxious for an attack upon the latter place, but I think
Texas much the most important. It is possible that Johnston may fall
back toward Mobile, but I think he will unite with Bragg.

While your army is engaged in cleaning out Southwestern Louisiana, every preparation should be made for an expedition into Texas. Should Johnston be driven from Mississippi, General Grant can send you considerable re-enforcements. The organization of colored troops should be pushed forward as rapidly as possible. They will serve as part of the garrisons of the forts on the river and interior posts, and some of the older regiments will do well in the field. Your water transportation should be increased. Many of your supplies can be now obtained from Saint Louis and the West.

I inclose herewith a copy of my dispatches of July 22 to General Grant.*

Very respectfully, your obedient servant,

H. W. HALLECK,
General-in-Chief.

[JULY 25, 1863.—For Banks to Grant, in relation to re-enforcements, see Series I, Vol. XXIV, Part III, p. 551.]

BRASHEAR CITY,
July 25, 1863.

Lieutenant-Colonel IRWIN:

SIR: I have the honor to report that I arrived at this post this morning at 10 o'clock. Captain Wiggin, of the navy, reached here on the 22d without opposition. The enemy were compelled to leave behind nine pieces of heavy artillery; they burned the carriages, but the guns are not materially injured. The ruins of fifty-two railroad cars and two engines lie upon the track. I shall commence removing the *débris* and relaying the track to-morrow morning.

The docks and landings are undisturbed; no buildings of consequence are destroyed. The defensive works, nearly completed, are of the strongest character. I find some 200 head of beef-cattle and a small quantity of other supplies.

I am, sir, your obedient servant,

FRANK H. PECK,
Lieutenant-Colonel, Commanding Detachment.

WASHINGTON, D. C.,
July 26, 1863.

Major-General BANKS,
New Orleans, La.:

GENERAL: Your dispatch of the 19th is just received. My dispatches to General Grant, copies of which have been sent to you, will inform you that he has been requested to give you such re-enforcements as may be necessary to enable you to clean the enemy out of Southwestern Louisiana. In a dispatch to me, he proposed to do this immediately. You cannot expect any re-enforcements from the north at present. Our army here is greatly reduced by the discharge of nine-months' and two-years' troops, and, as yet, we have received no drafted men to supply their places.

This reduction comes just at a time to prevent us from profiting by

---

* See Series I, Vol. XXIV, Part III, p. 542.

recent victories, and Copperhead Secessionists at the north seem determined to do all in their power to discourage and prevent the draft.
Very respectfully, your obedient servant,

H. W. HALLECK,
General-in-Chief.

_____

HEADQUARTERS DEPARTMENT OF THE CUMBERLAND,
Winchester, Tenn., July 26, 1863.

Maj. Gen. H. W. HALLECK, General-in-Chief:

GENERAL: I send you herewith, by Colonel [Joseph C.] McKibbin,
a map of Mobile and its fortifications, with a memorial in regard to
the same, the information contained in which I consider of great importance to the Government.

The importance of the last clause, in regard to the manner of preventing a junction between the forces of Johnston and Bragg, is obvious.

Very respectfully, &c.,

W. S. ROSECRANS,
Major-General, Commanding.

[Inclosure.]

HEADQUARTERS DEPARTMENT OF THE CUMBERLAND,
July 25, 1863.

Major-General ROSECRANS, Comdg. Army of the Cumberland:

The accompanying map of Mobile* and the information following
were obtained from Capt. J. H. Bunch, of the Ninth Tennessee Volunteer Cavalry. Captain Bunch was seized in East Tennessee while
trying to escape to our lines, and was conscripted into an Alabama
regiment. This regiment was for a long time the garrison of Mobile,
but afterward it was sent to Bragg. On Bragg's retreat from Tullahoma, Captain Bunch managed to escape into our lines, and he immediately raised a company in the Ninth Tennessee Cavalry. He seems
to be a reliable man, and of an observing turn of mind. He has good
natural ability and has apparently received a good education.

A serious attack on Mobile should be made from Pascagoula, 43
miles distant. The road from Pascagoula is sandy and good until
within 8 or 10 miles of Mobile; here it becomes somewhat clayey. The
road passes through open piney woods as far as Dog River; here the
pines are mingled with thick water-oaks. This is the first place at
which the rebels can attempt a stand. There are about 50 yards of
marshy ground in the road and some rising ground on the north side.
Between Dog River and the works are roads in all directions and many
ditches and hedges. These afford excellent rifle-pits to either party.
The forts inside of the line are in the suburbs of the city, and there
are brick walls, houses, ditches, and hedges in close proximity.

The guns in the vicinity of Mobile are mostly 8 and 10 inch columbiads, obtained from Pensacola after the evacuation by the rebels.
When Captain Bunch left, there were no guns mounted in the forts,
but they were hauling some from the wharves.

Up the Alabama River are several forts—one at Irving Bluff, one at
Choctaw Bluff, one at Mount Vernon Arsenal. There is a ram at
Mobile and one ram and four gunboats at Selma. These latter have
never been at Mobile.

_____

* Not found.

CAVALRY RAID FROM PENSACOLA.

The communications between Alabama and Mississippi are by three routes: a new one from Montgomery west by rail, from Montgomery by water to Selma, and thence by rail, and by rail from Montgomery to Tensas, and thence by water to Mobile.

The first route was once finished, and a train passed over it. Soon after, the Alabama rose and washed away miles of the track. Running through a very low and swampy country, it was found impossible to keep the road in running order, and it was abandoned.

The route by Selma is scarcely ever used, as there are but few boats on the Alabama River and very little rolling-stock on the railroad from Selma. Moreover, this road runs through very marshy country, and, being carelessly built, the bridges and trestles are continually being washed away.

The main transportation route is by rail from Montgomery, through Pollard to Tensas Station or Tensas River, thence by boat 26 miles to Mobile. Pollard is the junction of the Montgomery and Pensacola Railroad with the Mobile and Great Northern Railroad. The actual junction is 1 mile below Pollard. The track from Pollard to Pensacola is torn up. Between Pollard and Tensas are many bridges and long trestles. Tensas Station is built on piles, and thence to the first firm land is 3 miles of trestle-work. The destruction of this would be almost irreparable in the present state of the rebels.

From Pollard to Tensas is 60 miles, and from Pollard to Pensacola is the same distance. There are many bridges near Tensas and about midway between Tensas and Pollard, the road having to cross many small streams, bayous, and marshes. The largest bridge is 32 miles from Tensas. It is one-half mile long, and is approached by trestle-work on both sides, so that the entire length of bridge and trestle is $1\frac{1}{4}$ miles. The road is protected by one regiment of infantry (Seventy-ninth Alabama) and three companies of cavalry. The latter are conscripts, and of very little use. These men have the entire 60 miles to guard. There are no block-houses or earthworks along the line anywhere. The proper place to strike first would be at Tensas Station, as that would prevent troops from Mobile from coming up.

It would be well, however, to strike near Pollard at the same time, and have the two detachments meet in the center of the road, after destroying its entire length, and return together to Pensacola. The enemy having so little cavalry in the vicinity would be unable to interfere. Four good companies of cavalry could destroy the road, but a regiment would be better. Such a command, secretly embarked at New Orleans, as if for Texas or other out of the way place, could suddenly land at Pensacola and destroy the road before the rebels could suspect their presence. The road from Pensacola to the Tensas River is through open piney woods; is sandy and well watered. There is a deficiency of forage, though plenty of coarse grass for cattle. The latter are plentiful in that region. The importance of destroying this route may be judged from the fact that Bragg's whole army passed over it when moving up into Tennessee and Kentucky. From the time a cavalry regiment left New Orleans until its return to the same place, after destroying this railroad, need not be over two weeks.

Respectfully submitted.

WM. E. MERRILL,
Captain of Engineers.

HEADQUARTERS DEPARTMENT OF THE CUMBERLAND,
July 26, 1863.

General HALLECK, *General-in-Chief:*

GENERAL: I have the honor herewith to transmit for the use of your headquarters a map of Winchester and vicinity, of Hillsborough and Pelham, and of Chattanooga.*

All these maps were compiled in the field from information in advance of the movements of the army, and printed in the field by Capt. William C. Margedant's process. They fit each other, and are on the uniform scale of 1 inch to the mile. I also send a local map of Manchester, Jasper, and vicinity, and the defenses of Mobile.* The Manchester map is from survey, and the other two are from information. A memoir accompanies the latter.

I should be glad to know exactly what maps are in your office from this army, that I may supply the deficiency. The records of my office do not show what were issued prior to my incumbency.

Respectfully, your obedient servant,
WM. E. MERRILL,
Captain of Engineers.

_____

HEADQUARTERS DEFENSES OF NEW ORLEANS,
July 26, 1863.

Admiral FARRAGUT:

I send you, with the consent and approval of the general commanding this department, a copy of the report made by me,† inclosing one made by Major Porter,‡ of the fight made by the United States forces at Donaldsonville.§

I send this in consequence of complaints having been made that the official reports did not properly recognize the important part taken by the gunboats in this affair. If other reports have been sent to headquarters, they have been sent irregularly and without my knowledge.

I am, very respectfully, your obedient servant,
W. H. EMORY,
Brigadier-General, Commanding.

_____

[JULY 27, 1863.—For Grant to Banks, in reference to movement of troops, see Series I, Vol. XXIV, Part III, p. 553.]

_____

DEPARTMENT OF STATE,
Washington, July 28, 1863.

Hon. E. M. STANTON, *Secretary of War:*

SIR: I have the honor to inclose for your information a copy of a dispatch of the 4th ultimo from M. M. Kimmey, esq., United States vice-consul at Monterey, Mexico.

I am, sir, very respectfully, your obedient servant,
WILLIAM H. SEWARD.

[Indorsement.]

Referred to General-in-Chief by Secretary of War.

_____

* Omitted; unimportant.   ‡ See p. 202.
† See pp. 187-191.   § See also Emory to Farragut, July 21, p. 650.

[Inclosure.]

UNITED STATES CONSULATE,
Monterey, Mexico, June 4, 1863.
Hon. WM. H. SEWARD,
Secretary of State, Washington, D. C. :

SIR : I learn from some refugees, just in from Texas, that several guerrilla companies are being organized in that State, to operate on the frontiers of Kansas and Missouri. One of these companies is to be commanded by a notorious Missourian. My informant had forgotten his name. Since the successes of General Banks in Louisiana, all the troops from the western frontier of Texas have been ordered east. The line of the Rio Grande is now nearly deserted by the rebels.

General Magruder has removed all restrictions on the exportation of cotton and allowing all the liberty of shipping. The rebels are getting all they need from Mexico in the way of army supplies. What they lack from Mexico is landed directly on their coast, at the mouth of the Rio Grande. By the last mail from Matamoras, I learn that a steamer had just arrived there, loaded with goods for the rebels.

I am seldom without some Texas refugees on my hands. They come to me destitute of money and often nearly naked.

I sent off to Matamoras last week 10 men, who made their escape from the mountains and cedar brakes near Austin. Some of these had not been with their families for over a year. They were dressed in buckskin, having shot the deer, tanned the hide, and cut and made it into clothing.

They report several hundred Union men hid in the same mountains. By a letter from a friend at Piedras Negras, I learn that 64 more had passed over the river and were on their way here.

Without any provision being made by the United States Government, I am unable to bear personally the expenses of so large a party. I have sent from here over 270 destitute Union men, of which the majority are [in] the regiments of Texas cavalry at New Orleans. Without a regular appointment as consul, and only acting under an appointment from C. B. H. Blood, I feel powerless to use the seal of the office, though I have done so in a few cases where a refusal would have been a serious injury to the party applying.

The commanding general of the Department of New Mexico and Arizona is depending on me for information as to the movements of the Confederates in Texas. I have just written him a letter of eight pages.

The French forces have taken Puebla, and with it 18,000 Mexican prisoners. They are supposed to be now on the march toward the city of Mexico.

Your most obedient servant,

M. M. KIMMEY,
Acting Consul.

———

SPECIAL ORDERS, } HDQRS. DEPT. OF THE GULF, 19TH A. C.,
No. 183.   }   *New Orleans, July 28,* 1863.

I. A board, to consist of Maj. Gen. W. B. Franklin, U. S. Volunteers, Brig. Gen. C. P. Stone, U. S. Volunteers, Brig. Gen. W. H. Emory, U. S. Volunteers, Brig. Gen. G. Weitzel, U. S. Volunteers, and Maj. D. C. Houston, chief of engineers, will assemble in this city to-day at 10 a. m., to take into consideration the best mode of defense for the city of New

Orleans, the defensive works proper to construct on the Mississippi and Red Rivers within the limits of the department, with reference to the present war, and report fully its opinions on these subjects, as well as upon the proper positions for depots of ammunition and material, and the points most advantageous to be held in the event of war with a foreign naval power.

* * * * * * *

II. Maj. Gen. William B. Franklin, U. S. Volunteers, is assigned to the command of the First Division, headquarters at Baton Rouge.

The Second Brigade, First Division, will immediately take post at Thibodeauxville.

The Third Brigade, First Division, and the Third Brigade, Third Division, both now near Donaldsonville, will proceed without delay to Baton Rouge, and take post at that place.

The Fourth Division, now near Donaldsonville, will, with the exception of the First Regiment Louisiana Volunteers, be transferred to Camp Kearny, Carrollton, La., and be reported to Brig. Gen. W. H. Emory for duty in the Defenses of New Orleans. The First Regiment Louisiana Volunteers will occupy the post at Donaldsonville.

* * * * * *

By command of Major-General Banks:

RICH'D B. IRWIN,
Assistant Adjutant-General.

WASHINGTON, D. C., *July* 29, 1863.

Maj. Gen. N. P. BANKS, *New Orleans, La.*:

GENERAL: I inclose herewith an extract from dispatch No. 113, from United States consul at Liverpool. The contents are important, and should receive your immediate attention.

. It occurs to me that the most proper defense against these rams would be earthen batteries, erected near Fort Jackson or Fort Saint Philip, and armed with heavy ordnance brought down from Vicksburg and Port Hudson.

Very respectfully, your obedient servant,

H. W. HALLECK,
General-in-Chief.

[Inclosure.]

DEPARTMENT OF STATE,
Washington, July 29, 1863.

Hon. E. M. STANTON, *Secretary of War:*

SIR: I have the honor to call your attention to an extract from a very important dispatch, No. 113, received from the United States consul at Liverpool, in regard to the rebel rams now building at Liverpool, and which, it is said, are intended for an attack on New Orleans.

I have the honor to be, sir, your obedient servant,

WILLIAM H. SEWARD.

[Sub-Inclosure.]

UNITED STATES CONSULATE, LIVERPOOL,
July 17, 1863.

Hon. WM. H. SEWARD, *Secretary of State:*

SIR: You will recollect the boy Robinson, from whom we obtained much information in the case of the Alabama.

Everything he told us about that vessel proved to be true. He is from New Orleans. His father and all his relations are from the South. They are now trying to procure him a berth as midshipman on one of the rams building by the Lairds. He is constantly with the Southerners here, and hears their talk. In one of their conferences yesterday, he heard them say that the first thing that was to be done after they got the rams out was to attack and retake New Orleans. This seemed to be a well-understood thing with them, and was to be done immediately. I give you this for what it is worth. There is no doubt but what that is now contemplated by those over here, but the programme may be entirely changed at Richmond before they sail from here.

If these vessels get out, they will give us much trouble. I regard them as the most formidable and dangerous vessels afloat. No time should be lost in making preparations to meet them. They will be fast sailers, making 13 knots per hour, armed with the heaviest and most improved guns, and almost, if not quite, invulnerable. The collector told me day before yesterday that the contract price for building each of them was £225,000 sterling. This he no doubt got from the Lairds themselves, as he sees and talks with them, at least I infer so from the way he talks to me.

*　　　*　　　*　　　*

I am, sir, your obedient servant,

T. H. DUDLEY.

[Indorsement.]

Referred to the General-in-Chief, to be communicated to Major-General Banks with such instruction as he deems proper.

EDWIN M. STANTON,
Secretary of War.

EXECUTIVE MANSION,
Washington, July 29, 1863.

Hon. SECRETARY OF WAR:

SIR: Can we not renew the effort to organize a force to go to Western Texas?

Please consult with the General-in-Chief on the subject.

If the Governor of New Jersey shall furnish any new regiments, might not they be put into such an expedition? Please think of it.

I believe no local object is now more desirable.

Yours, truly,

A. LINCOLN.

OFFICE CHIEF OF ARTILLERY, HDQRS. DEPT. OF THE GULF,
New Orleans, July 29, 1863.

General STONE, Chief of Staff:

GENERAL: I would respectfully recommend the following disposition of the heavy and light artillery, with a view of bringing the batteries under their proper commanders, as well as the best dispositions for re-equipment and drill for future operations:*

1. First Indiana [Heavy] Artillery and the Sixth Regiment Michigan Volunteers to remain at Port Hudson.

------

* These recommendations were embodied in Special Orders, No. 184, Headquarters Department of the Gulf, July 29, 1863.

2. *First Division.*—Company A, First United States Artillery, Captain Bainbridge, Baton Rouge; First Maine Battery, Lieutenant Bradbury, Baton Rouge; Eighteenth New York Battery, Captain Mack, Baton Rouge; Sixth Massachusetts Battery, Captain Carruth, Thibodeaux.

3. *Third Division.*—Company F, First Artillery, Captain Duryea, Port Hudson; Fourth Massachusetts Battery, Captain Trull, Port Hudson; First Vermont Battery, Captain Hebard, Port Hudson.

4. *Fourth Division.*—Company L, First Artillery, Captain Closson, Camp Kearny; Company C, Second Artillery, Captain Rodgers, Campi Kearny; Second Massachusetts Battery, Captain Nims, Camp Kearny.

Battery G, Fifth Artillery, Second Vermont Battery, Twenty-first New York Battery, and Thirteenth Massachusetts Battery to remain for the present at Port Hudson as the light artillery of General Andrews' command.

Twefth Massachusetts Battery, Fifteenth Massachusetts Battery, Twenty-fifth New York Battery, and Twenty-sixth New York Battery to remain as at present distributed by General Emory until the changes ordered in Department Special Orders, No. 183, are executed; then to be subject to such changes as may be deemed expedient by the chief of artillery, in co-operation with the commanding officer of the Defenses of New Orleans.

I am, general, very respectfully, your obedient servant,
RICHARD ARNOLD,
Brigadier-General, Chief of Artillery.

U. S. FLAG-SHIP HARTFORD,
New Orleans, July 29, 1863.
Col. ALBERT J. MYER,
Chief Signal Officer, U. S. Army, Washington, D. C.:

SIR: I desire to express to you my appreciation of the services of the Army Signal Corps, of which I learn you are the chief. The rapidity and accuracy with which signals are communicated have exceeded any impression I had hitherto formed.

I commend to your most favorable notice Lieutenant Eaton, of that corps, who has served with me during the long period I commanded above Port Hudson. To his zeal, energy, and ability I am indebted for most valuable assistance. His gentlemanly and officerlike deportment has won for him my esteem, and that of all the naval officers with whom he has been associated.

Respectfully, your obedient servant,

J. S. PALMER,
Commodore.

GENERAL ORDERS, }   HDQRS. DEPT. OF THE GULF, 19TH A. C.,
No. 54.   }   *New Orleans, July 29,* 1863.

I. Brig. Gen. Charles P. Stone is announced as chief of staff at these headquarters from the 25th instant.

＊   ＊   ＊   ＊   ＊

By command of Major-General Banks:
RICH'D B. IRWIN,
Assistant Adjutant-General,

SPECIAL ORDERS, }   HDQRS. DEPT. OF THE TENNESSEE,
*No. 205.   }   *Vicksburg, Miss., July* 29, 1863.

I. The Thirteenth Army Corps, Maj. Gen. E. O. C. Ord commanding, will be held in readiness to move to and take post at Natchez, Miss., as soon as transportation can be furnished.

On the arrival of one division of the Thirteenth Army Corps at Natchez, the troops now there will return to Vicksburg.

The commander at Natchez will be charged with keeping the river open to navigation from Rodney, Miss., to the Louisiana and Mississippi State line.

*   *   *   *

By order of Maj. Gen. U. S. Grant:

T. S. BOWERS,
Acting Assistant Adjutant-General.

HDQRS. DEPT. OF THE GULF, NINETEENTH ARMY CORPS,
New Orleans, July 30, 1863.
Maj. Gen. H. W. HALLECK,
     Commander-in-Chief, U. S. Army:

GENERAL: I have satisfactory information that the rebels have abandoned the country as far north as Alexandria, with the exception of a small corps of observation near Franklin. Our forces took possession of Brashear City some days since. There is no enemy of any force now in the department south of Alexandria. It is believed that the force which has occupied the La Fourche district is moving northward and westward toward Natchitoches or Shreveport, with a view of joining Kirby Smith at that place. A small force, with a few light-draught gunboats, will be able to keep this district clear. The navigation of the river has been undisturbed this side of Port Hudson. A few guerrillas are heard of above, but nothing to obstruct the successful navigation of the river for our transport vessels. The nine-months' regiments are being transported to the north by sea and by river as rapidly as our transportation will admit. We lose twenty-two regiments, leaving about 12,000 effective men in this department.

Information from Mobile leads us to believe that the force at that point is now about 5,000, engaged industriously on the land side in strengthening the position. My belief is that Johnston's forces are moving to the east, and that the garrison will not be strengthened unless it be by paroled men from Vicksburg or Port Hudson. While the rebel army of the east is occupied at Charleston and at Richmond by our forces, it would be impossible for them to strengthen Mobile to any great extent. It seems to be the favorable opportunity for a movement in that direction. The attack should be made by land. Troops can be transported up the river to Mobile, with the intervention of a march of 25 miles from Portersville on the west side of the bay to the rear of the city. We have outlines of their works, and can estimate very well their strength. I am confident a sudden movement, such as can be made with 20,000 or 25,000 men on this point, will reduce it with certainty and without delay. The troops of the west need rest, and are incapable of long or rapid marches. It is, therefore, impracticable to attack Mobile except by the river and Mississippi Sound. A portion of General Grant's force could be transported there with but little labor to themselves and with very little loss of time. The place would be invested before the enemy could anticipate our movement.   •

The city of New Orleans is perfectly quiet, the people well disposed, and the city itself was never so cleanly nor so healthy. The negro regiments are organizing rapidly.

I have the honor to be, with much respect, your obedient servant,

N. P. BANKS,
Major-General, Commanding.

SPECIAL ORDERS, ⎰ HDQRS. DEPT. OF THE GULF, 19TH A. C.,
No. 185. ⎱   *New Orleans, July 30, 1863.*

*   *   *   *   *   *   *

III. Col. S. B. Holabird, chief quartermaster of the department, is authorized and directed to appropriate to the use of the public schools of the city of New Orleans, as a foundation for public-school libraries, to be devoted to the exclusive use of teachers and pupils, all books and engravings suitable for this object which may come into the possession of the military authorities of the United States. The chief quartermaster of the department, the superintendent of public schools, and the judge of the military court for the time being, are hereby constituted a board for the organization of one or more public-school libraries, with authority to establish all necessary rules and regulations for their use and preservation. This order will be executed without delay.

*   *   *   *   *   *   *

By command of Major-General Banks :•
RICH'D B. IRWIN,
Assistant Adjutant-General.

BRASHEAR CITY, LA.,
July 30, 1863.

Lieut. Col. RICHARD B. IRWIN,
Assistant Adjutant-General:

I have the honor to report everything quiet at this post; I send by dispatch boat and hand-car daily to La Fourche. .

The enemy are in considerable force a few miles from here. Semmes' battery is near Pattersonville, another is a few miles beyond, and between Franklin and this point are the commands of General Green and Colonel Major. Deserters come in daily, and from them, paroled prisoners, and negroes I learn that after the fall of Port Hudson and Vicksburg, the enemy, anticipating an attack from above, hastened their cavalry and a strong artillery detachment to Vermillion Bayou, intending to make a stand at the bridge. After the occupation of Berwick Bay by our gunboats, the greater part of their cavalry was sent back to cover the rear of their column. A strong picket is in plain sight on the opposite side of the bay, and small parties have several times crossed to this side through Lake Palendre. Since we have been in occupation here, a party of 15 or 20 have been seizing conscripts in our rear, not 6 miles from us, and, three nights ago, 5 men were carried, tied hand and foot, across the lake. About Bayou Long these acts have been frequent. With infantry alone, I am unable to do anything. I therefore request that a detachment of cavalry, and, if convenient, a section of artillery, may be sent to this post.

Parties are at work upon the bridge at Bayou Ramos; the track is nearly cleared, and, from the scattered parts of the demolished locomotives, a few skillful mechanics have made a new one, which is now running between here and Bayou Ramos.

I have the honor to be, sir, your obedient servant,

FRANK H. PECK,
Lieutenant-Colonel, Comdg. U. S. Forces at Brashear City, La.

[Indorsements.]

HEADQUARTERS DEPARTMENT OF THE GULF,
New Orleans, August 4, 1863.

Respectfully referred to Brigadier-General Weitzel for his information; to be returned.

The naval forces ought to prevent any of the depredations by the enemy mentioned in this report. Railroad communication will be open with Brashear in the course of next week, and then better arrangements can be made by me.

G. WEITZEL,
Brigadier-General.

GENERAL ORDERS, }   HDQRS. UNITED STATES FORCES,
'No. 12.   }   *Port Hudson, La., July* 30, 1863.

The commanding general of this post has been informed of the abuse of colored soldiers, and disregard of their authority as sentinels, on the part of some of the other troops of this command, and on the part of some persons not in the military service. He takes this opportunity to correct certain erroneous impressions, and to announce to all concerned that this course of conduct must cease at once and entirely.

The Government having decided upon the employment of colored troops, it is the imperative duty of all officers and soldiers to acquiesce fully and promptly in this decision, for which they are in no wise responsible. The colored soldier employed as such is entitled to respect and consideration, and to the protection and support of his military superiors, particularly when performing any duty which has been imposed upon him.

While engaged in carrying out the orders he has received, he is but the agent or instrument of his commanding officer. Any opposition to him or abuse of him while so engaged is not disobedience of his orders nor contempt of his authority, but is nothing less than disobedience of the orders and contempt of the authority of the commanding general, neither of which will be tolerated under any circumstances in this command. Abuse of the colored soldier, or opposition to him in the discharge of his duty in this command, will be punished with unrelenting severity, not only for the protection of the colored soldier, who is justly entitled to it, and shall have it, but because such conduct is grossly insubordinate to lawful authority.

All discussions of the subject of employing colored soldiers, all remarks disparaging them, and any course of conduct tending to create ill-feeling between the colored troops and other troops of this command, are most strictly prohibited.

All soldiers of this command are exhorted to the prompt, cheerful, soldierlike performance of military duties. The exhibition of high soldierly qualities by them in the camp, on the march, and on the battle-field, will leave neither time nor inclination for vexatious discussions of a subject with which as soldiers they have no concern.

By command of Brig. Gen. George L. Andrews:

GEO. B. HALSTED,
Captain, and Assistant Adjutant-General.

WASHINGTON,
July 30, 1863—4.30 p. m.

Major-General GRANT,
Vicksburg, Miss.:

You will send Major-General Banks a corps of 10,000 or 12,000 men, to report at such point as he may designate; probably at New Orleans.

H. W. HALLECK,
General-in-Chief.

WAR DEPARTMENT,
Washington, July 31, 1863—5 p. m.

Major-General BANKS,
New Orleans, via Cairo and Vicksburg :

General Grant has been ordered to send you a corps of 10,000 or 12,000 men for operations west. Get everything ready. We are only waiting for your answer to my dispatch of the 24th.

H. W. HALLECK,
General-in-Chief.

WASHINGTON,
July 31, 1863.

Major-General BANKS,
New Orleans, La.:

GENERAL: Your dispatch of July 23 is just received. It is impossible at present to send you a single man from the north. We must wait the enforcement of the draft. General Grant has been directed to send you a corps of 10,000 or 12,000 men. As soon as the expedition now in Arkansas occupies Arkansas River, more troops can be sent to you or to Red River.

It is important that we immediately occupy some point or points in Texas. Whether the movement should be made by land or water is not yet decided. We shall wait your answer to my dispatch of the 24th. In the meantime every preparation should be made. If by water, Admiral Farragut will co-operate.

The Navy Department recommends Indianola as the point of landing. It seems to me that this point is too distant, as it will leave the expedition isolated from New Orleans. If the landing can be made at Galveston, the country between that place and New Orleans can be soon cleaned out, and the enemy be prevented from operating successively upon these places. In other words, you can venture to send a larger force to Galveston than you can to Indianola.

I merely throw out these suggestions without deciding upon any definite plan till I receive your answer to the former dispatch.

Very respectfully, your obedient servant,

H. W. HALLECK,
General-in-Chief.

Abstract from return of the Department of the Gulf (Nineteenth Army Corps), Maj. Gen. N. P. Banks, U. S. Army, commanding, for the month of July, 1863; headquarters, New Orleans.

Command.	Present for duty.		Aggregate present.	Aggregate present and absent.	Pieces of artillery.	
	Officers.	Men.			Heavy.	Field.
Department staff..	24	....	24	27	....	......
First Division (Weitzel).................................	193	4,642	5,506	9,489	....	......
Third Division (Dwight)	221	4,047	5,619	8,619	....	......
Fourth Division (Grover)	111	2,622	3,304	5,254	....	16
Baton Rouge, La. (Woodman)...........................	48	1,385	2,906	3,406	....	......
Defenses of New Orleans (Emory)	163	6,927	9,233	10,312	24	43
Port Hudson* (Andrews).................................	381	8,250	11,865	14,197	....	53
District of Key West, &c. (Woodbury)	36	727	1,069	1,104	....	......
District of Pensacola (Holbrook).......................	34	460	624	673	....	......
Ship Island, Miss. (Daniels)	22	502	637	679	....	......
Grand total..	1,233	29,562	40,787	53,760	24	112
Grand total, according to tri-monthly department return for July 31.	1,201	27,423	38,273	52,048	....	......

Abstract from return of Herron's division, Army of the Tennessee, Maj. Gen. Francis J. Herron, U. S. Army, commanding, for July 31, 1863; headquarters, Port Hudson, La.

Command.	Present for duty.		Aggregate present.	Aggregate present and absent.	Pieces of field artillery.
	Officers.	Men.			
Staff..	9	....	9	9	......
First Brigade	93	1,547	2,875	3,707	12
Second Brigade	92	1,796	2,575	3,003	6
Cavalry	4	64	97	125	......
Total...	198	3,407	5,556	6,844	18

Composition of division commanded by Maj. Gen. Francis J. Herron, U. S. Army, July 31, 1863.†

First Brigade.

Brig. Gen. WILLIAM VANDEVER.

37th Illinois, Col. John Charles Black.
26th Indiana, Col. John G. Clark.
20th Iowa, Col. William McE. Dye.
34th Iowa, Col. George W. Clark.
38th Iowa, Col. D. Henry Hughes.
1st Missouri Light Artillery, Battery E, Capt. Nelson Cole.
1st Missouri Light Artillery, Battery F, Capt. Joseph Foust.

Second Brigade.

Brig. Gen. WILLIAM W. ORME.

91st Illinois, Col. Henry M. Day.
94th Illinois, Col. John McNulta.
19th Iowa, Maj. John Bruce.
20th Wisconsin, Col. Henry Bertram.
1st Missouri Light Artillery, Battery B, Capt. Martin Welfley.

Cavalry.

15th Illinois, Company F, Capt. Joseph Adams.
36th Illinois, Company A, Capt. George A. Willis.

---

* Does not include Herron's division, for which see following table.
† Transferred from Vicksburg, Miss., to Port Hudson, La., July 24–25.

HDQRS. DEPT. OF THE GULF, NINETEENTH ARMY CORPS,
Vicksburg, Miss., August 1, 1863.
Maj. Gen. H. W. HALLECK,
General-in-Chief, U. S. Army :

GENERAL: I have the honor to acknowledge the receipt of your telegram of the 27th July, transmitted to me by General Grant. I have already informed you of the condition of this department. The views I expressed in reference to other movements are strengthened by the occurrences of the day. The advantage of immediate operations against Mobile consists in the fact that its fortifications thus far are upon the Gulf and the bay. The rear of the city is unprotected except by a line of incomplete works, with few guns mounted, and is unprepared for an assault on the land side. In a short time these works will be completed, the guns mounted, the city provisioned, and the garrison strengthened.. The army and people are now in such panic from the fall of Vicksburg and Port Hudson, that if attacked on the land side, where assault is not anticipated, and re-enforcements are not sent from the east at once, the place will probably be surrendered without serious contest. The approach by land from Portersville, on Mississippi-Sound, is 25 miles; from Pascagoula, 65 miles. The country to Mobile is level and sandy. Roads can be made in any direction without labor.

From Pensacola the way is open to the rear of Mobile, from which all supplies can be cut off. The condition of troops on the Mississippi is such that rapid or long marches are impracticable. The movement against Mobile can be made by water, except a single march of 25 miles. Attacked from land, the water defenses are unavailable, and the forts will fall with the city.

The co-operation of the naval force now here is all that is required. Twenty-five thousand men, one corps of General Grant's army, with the available forces at New Orleans, are sufficient for the work. It is believed that Western Louisiana is free from any considerable force of the enemy.

The possession of Mobile gives the Government the control of the Alabama River and the line of railways east and west from Charleston and Savannah to Vicksburg, via Montgomery, and places the whole of Mississippi and Southern Alabama in position to resume at will their place in the Union. If the rebel Government loses this position, it has no outlet to the Gulf except Galveston. The operation need not last more than thirty days, and can scarcely interfere with any other movements east or west. I understand it to meet with General Grant's approval, if it be consistent with the general plans of the Government, upon which condition only I urge it. I send this from Vicksburg, having arrived here at 9 o'clock this morning, and return to New Orleans this evening.

I have the honor to be, with respect, your obedient servant,
N. P. BANKS,
Major-General, Commanding.

HDQRS. DEPT. OF THE GULF, NINETEENTH ARMY CORPS,
New Orleans, August 1, 1863.
Commanding Officer at Baton Rouge :

SIR: General Emory directs that you send the Fourth Wisconsin across the river to drive off and disperse some 200 of the enemy's cavalry, said to be at Madame Seager's plantation, 14 miles above Donaldsonville. Colonel Dudley, commanding at Donaldsonville, has been directed to send a regiment of infantry to encamp at the same place. If you have no means of transportation, call upon General Andrews, at Port Hudson, for it. Acknowledge.

Very respectfully, your obedient servant,
RICH'D B. IRWIN,
Assistant Adjutant-General.

HDQRS. DEPT. OF THE GULF, NINETEENTH ARMY CORPS,
New Orleans, August —, 1863.

Col. N. A. M. DUDLEY,
Baton Rouge:

SIR: The commanding general desires you to exercise your discretion in regard to sending re-enforcements to Madame Seager's. Send them, if it is necessary, but the moment that the withdrawal will not have the appearance of a retreat or an attempt to avoid the enemy, the commanding general directs that you have the troops at Madame Seager's, including the Fourth Wisconsin Cavalry, concentrated at Plaquemine. The order directing the Fourth Wisconsin Cavalry to concentrate at Baton Rouge may be regarded as modified to this extent.

Very respectfully, your obedient servant,
[RICH'D B. IRWIN,]
Assistant Adjutant-General.

HEADQUARTERS UNITED STATES FORCES,
Donaldsonville, La., August 2, 1863.

Lieut. Col. RICHARD B. IRWIN,
Assistant Adjutant-General, Nineteenth Army Corps:

I have the honor to report for the information of the commanding general that, in compliance with instructions received from headquarters, the following distribution of troops lately occupying this point has been made; the last battery will embark to-morrow:

General Grover's division, Carrollton, La., Colonel Birge commanding; General Weitzel's brigade, First Division, with Carruth's battery and four companies Louisiana cavalry, Thibodeaux, Colonel Merritt commanding; Paine's brigade, First Division, Colonel Love commanding, and Dudley's brigade, First Division, Colonel Harrower commanding, at Baton Rouge; Gooding's brigade, Emory's division, Colonel Sharpe commanding, Baton Rouge; One hundred and twenty-eighth New York Volunteers, Colonel Smith, Madame Seager's plantation, Mississippi River; Bainbridge's, Mack's, and Bradbury's batteries, Baton Rouge; Twenty-first Indiana Heavy Battery, Captain McLaflin, Port Hudson.

First Louisiana Volunteers, Colonel Fiske, remains at Donaldsonville, with Trull's battery, engineer and pioneer corps. The pontoon bridge across the Bayou La Fourche I directed to be taken up to-day, and the officer in charge directed to report to the chief of engineer corps for instructions.

I would respectfully suggest that the men temporarily assigned to the pioneer corps be ordered to join their several regiments. Most of them are nine-months' men. There is a signal party of 1 non-commissioned officer and 6 men here waiting orders.

I deem it my duty to call the attention of the general to the fact that there are several Government plantations in this vicinity stocked with negroes, from 100 to 250 each, that are without overseers, destitute of subsistence, and doing no work. These negroes, in some instances having procured mules and horses, ride from one plantation to another, threaten the lives of the few white inhabitants that remain, and commit various depredations, in some instances of a serious character.

There is a very large amount of ammunition here, for both artillery and small-arms, awaiting the orders of the ordnance officer, and for which there is no proper place of storage.

Very respectfully,

N. A. M. DUDLEY,
Colonel, and Acting Brigadier-General, Comdg. U. S. Forces.

HDQRS. DEPT. OF THE GULF, NINETEENTH ARMY CORPS,
New Orleans, August 4, 1863.

Commodore H. H. BELL,
U. S. Navy, Commanding, &c.:

COMMODORE: I have the honor to inform you that I hear through many sources that the enemy at Mobile intend making a sudden and vigorous attack on Ship Island. I am satisfied that there is good ground to apprehend such a movement, and will at once send two additional regiments of infantry there.

I respectfully request that you will lend us your aid in that quarter as may be in your power, and would suggest sending a light-draught iron-clad into the lake, where it will be held in readiness to act very promptly.

Very respectfully, your most obedient servant,

N. P. BANKS,
Major-General, Commanding.

U. S. STEAM-SLOOP PENSACOLA,
Off New Orleans, August 4, 1863.

Maj. Gen. N. P. BANKS,
U. S. Army:

GENERAL: I have the honor (at 3 p. m.) to receive your letter of this date, informing me of the probability of an immediate attack being made on Ship Island by the enemy from Mobile.

I have no iron-clad of light-draught at my disposal, but will immediately dispatch one or more efficient vessels to act in the sound. In the course of two or three days I expect to have two small vessels capable of acting in the lake.

We shall meet them in the sound, and defeat them if they come.

I have the honor to be, your obedient servant,

H. H. BELL,
Commodore, Comdg. West Gulf Blockading Squadron, pro tempore.

BRASHEAR CITY, LA.,
August 4, 1863.

Lieut. Col. RICHARD B. IRWIN,
Assistant Adjutant-General:

SIR: I have information, which I deem reliable, that the enemy's force this side of New Iberia are about concentrating at Camp Bisland.

It consists substantially of the old command of General Mouton, increased by conscription, and probably amounts to 2,000 infantry troops and four or five batteries of light artillery. The cavalry brigade of Colonel Major is also under his command. It consists of four small regiments of Texans, who are chiefly employed upon outpost duty. I crossed the Berwick this morning to examine the fort built there, and learned that large numbers of negroes have been seized within a few days to work upon the fortifications at Camp Bisland. The fort at Berwick, prepared for eight guns, I think I shall destroy, unless otherwise ordered.

They are also fortifying at Irish Bend. Through deserters, who are arriving constantly, much information in regard to the movements of the enemy reaches me, not of great military importance, but personally interesting. If desired, detailed reports can be furnished.

I respectfully repeat my application that a few pieces of light artillery may be sent to this post.

I am, sir, your obedient servant,

FRANK H. PECK,
Lieutenant-Colonel, Commanding United States Forces.

[Indorsement.]

HDQRS. SECOND BRIGADE, FIRST DIVISION,
Camp Hubbard, La., August 5, 1863.

Respectfully forwarded, and for the information of the commanding general I add the following, which was communicated to me by the colonel of the Seventh Louisiana Volunteers:

The parish priest of La Fourche yesterday told Captain Silvey, provost-marshal, that he has received information, through a channel which he could not disclose, that 2,000 rebel cavalry were massed in the vicinity of the Teche, for the purpose of a raid on this post.

I entertain no fears, but have made dispositions accordingly.

I am, colonel, very respectfully, your obedient servant,

ROBERT B. MERRITT,
Colonel, Commanding Brigade.

NAVY DEPARTMENT,
August 5, 1863.

Hon. E. M. STANTON,
Secretary of War:

SIR: I have the honor to inclose to you the copy of a letter, dated the 24th ultimo, from Acting Rear-Admiral Bailey, and also the copy of a paper transmitted by him, signed by George S. Denison, who calls himself "special agent of the Treasury Department and acting collector of customs," authorizing Brott, Davis, and Shonn to bring cotton from the rebel region, and whose vessel, the Sea Lion, was captured coming out of Mobile.

The particulars of this extraordinary proceeding will be ascertained from a perusal of Acting Rear-Admiral Bailey's letter. As regards Mr. Denison and his license to trade with rebel enemies, or any assumed authority to evade or violate the blockade, they cannot be recognized, nor am I aware that General Banks has power to issue an order for such purpose, if he has done so.

I have deemed it proper to communicate the facts to you; which are, as you will perceive, wholly inconsistent with the maintenance and enforcement in good faith of the blockade.

    Very respectfully, &c.,
                              GIDEON WELLES,
                                  Secretary of the Navy.

[Indorsement.]

                                            AUGUST 8, 1863.

Respectfully referred to Major-General Banks, to return with report.*
                              H. W. HALLECK,
                                  General-in-Chief.

[Inclosure.]

                          U.-S. FLAG-SHIP SAN JACINTO,
                                  Key West, July 24, 1863.
Hon. GIDEON WELLES,   ·
    Secretary of the Navy:

    SIR: The schooner Sea Lion was lately captured coming out of the port of Mobile, loaded with cotton, and sent to this port for adjudication. She exhibited at the time of her capture a license to bring cotton to New Orleans from a Mr. Denison, who appears to be a special agent of the Treasury Department. I send herewith inclosed a copy of this paper. I am credibly informed that Mr. Denison has answered, in reply to the question whether this license was intended to apply to blockaded ports as well as to bringing the cotton through the military lines by land, that the license was granted in pursuance of an order of General Banks, and that he did not think it necessary to inquire how the property should come to New Orleans. Under this license, it seems the favored parties at New Orleans sent their agent to Mobile, bought the cotton, had it shipped in the name of a Mobile firm, and consigned by the papers to a Mobilian at Havana. When captured, it was claimed that the vessel was really going to the mouth of the Mississippi River, or to New Orleans, for the orders of Brott, Davis, and Shonn, the parties named in the license.   ·
    This is not only trading with the enemy pure and simple, but it is trading with the enemy through a closely blockaded port. It seems to me that, if this action is sustained, it amounts to a virtual abandonment of the blockade of all the ports to which these or other favored parties may choose to trade, and that it possibly has some importance in connection with our foreign relations. I have thought it a matter proper to be referred to you.
    I am, very respectfully, your obedient servant,
                              THEODORUS BAILEY,
        Acting Rear-Admiral, Comdg. East Gulf Blockading Squadron.

[Sub-Inclosure.]

                          CUSTOM-HOUSE, COLLECTOR'S OFFICE,
                                  New Orleans, February 16, 1863.
    The United States military and other authorities at New Orleans permit cotton to be received here from beyond the United States military lines, and such cotton is exempt from seizure or confiscation. An order is in my hands from Major-General Banks, approving and directing this policy. The only condition imposed is that cotton or other

---

* See Banks to Halleck, August 29, p. 702.

produce must not be bought with specie. All cotton or other produce brought hither from the Confederate lines by Brott, Davis, and Shonn will not be interfered with in any manner, and they can ship it direct to any foreign or domestic port.

GEORGE S. DENISON,
Special Agent of Treasury Dept., and Acting Collector of Customs.

Approved:

D. G. FARRAGUT,
Rear-Admiral.

I, Abel Dreyfous, notary public, duly commissioned and sworn, for the parish of Orleans and city of New Orleans, therein residing, certify the foregoing to be a true, faithful, and literal copy of the original document exhibited to me by Mr. Brott, and which I have signed and paraphed *ne varietur*, to identify it with the foregoing copy.

In testimony whereof I have granted this certificate, under my signature and the impress of my seal of office, at New Orleans, this 9th of March, 1863.

[SEAL.]   ABEL DREYFOUS,
Notary Public.

GENERAL ORDERS, }   HDQRS. DEPT. OF THE GULF, 19TH A. C.,
No. 57.   }   *New Orleans, August 5, 1863.*

The commanding general takes great pleasure in communicating to the troops of this department the contents of the following dispatch this day received from the General-in-Chief:

HEADQUARTERS OF THE ARMY,
Washington, July 23, 1863.

Major-General BANKS,
New Orleans:

GENERAL: Your dispatches of July 8, announcing the surrender of Port Hudson, are received. I congratulate you and your army on the crowning success of the campaign. It was reserved for your army to strike the last blow to open the Mississippi River. The country, and especially the great West, will ever remember with gratitude their services.

Very respectfully, your obedient servant,

H. W. HALLECK,
General-in-Chief.

By command of Major-General Banks:

RICH'D B. IRWIN,
Assistant Adjutant-General.

HDQRS. DEPT. OF THE GULF, NINETEENTH ARMY CORPS,
New Orleans, August 5, 1863

Brig. Gen. W. H. EMORY,
Commanding Defenses of New Orleans:

GENERAL: The major-general commanding desires that you designate two regiments of the Fourth Division to proceed to Ship Island for temporary duty. The first regiment will be sent to-morrow morning on board the steamer Crescent, now near the foot of Jackson street wharf. The second regiment will be sent as soon as the quartermaster's department shall have transportation prepared.

Very respectfully, your most obedient servant,

[CHAS. P. STONE,]
Brigadier-General, and Chief of Staff.

WAR DEPARTMENT,
Washington, August 6, 1863—12.30 p. m.

Major-General BANKS,* *New Orleans, La.:*

There are important reasons why our flag should be restored in some point of Texas with the least possible delay. Do this by land at Galveston, at Indianola, or at any other point you may deem preferable. If by sea, Admiral Farragut will co-operate. There are reasons why the movement should be as prompt as possible.

H. W. HALLECK,
General-in-Chief.

(Copy by mail.)

———

PORT HUDSON,
August 6, 1863.

Colonel FEARING, *Commanding Third Division:*

SIR: Lieutenant-Colonel Sargent, Third Massachusetts Cavalry, reports that 200 to 300 of the enemy (mounted) are now between the Bayou Sara and Jackson roads, about 1 mile from our advanced post. Lieutenant-Colonel Sargent is ordered to report to you, and, if you find on examination that his report is correct, you will make arrangements to attack and disperse or destroy the enemy to-morrow morning as early as practicable, sending me notice of your proposed arrangements and what information you have. Meantime you will have the position of your pickets changed, and caution them to be vigilant and to be prepared for an attack on the part of the enemy. The infantry of your command will be prepared to form line at short notice, and the pickets will be ready to start to their arms at once. Frequent patrols will be sent out from 3 to 7 a. m. to-morrow. You will not fail to take sufficient force to make success certain, if you attack, and on no account allow yourself to be surprised by an attack from the enemy. If the enemy is found to be in force, do not fail to inform me at once, making, meantime, active preparations to meet him. Keep patrols observing the enemy to-night. I think it not improbable that he is only reconnoitering, and that he will disappear before morning. However, be prepared for him in any event.

Respectfully, your obedient servant,

GEO. L. ANDREWS,
Brigadier-General of Volunteers, Commanding Post.

———

SPECIAL ORDERS, }   HDQRS. DEPARTMENT OF THE GULF,
No. 191.   }   *New Orleans, August* 6, 1863.

*   *   *   *   *   *   *

XIV. The regiments and companies called into the service of the United States for sixty days, by order of Brig. Gen. William H. Emory, commanding the Defenses of New Orleans, will be immediately disbanded and mustered out of service.

*   *   *   *   *

By command of Major-General Banks:

RICH'D. B. IRWIN,
Assistant Adjutant-General.

———

* Sent through Major-General Grant, Vicksburg, who was requested to give all assistance necessary to execution of the order. See Series I, Vol. XXIV, Part III, p. 578. See also Banks to Halleck, August 15, 1863, p. 682.

[AUGUST 7, 1863.—For Grant to Banks, in reference to transfer of Thirteenth Army Corps to Department of the Gulf, see Series I, Vol. XXIV, Part III, p. 580.]

WASHINGTON, D. C., *August* 10, 1863.

Maj. Gen. N. P. BANKS, *Commanding Department of the Gulf:*

GENERAL: In my dispatch to you of the 6th instant, sent by the direction of the Secretary of War, it was left entirely to your own discretion to select any point for occupation in Texas, either on the seaboard or in the interior, the only condition imposed being that the flag of the United States should be again raised and sustained somewhere within the limits of that State.

That order, as I understood it at the time, was of a diplomatic rather than of a military character, and resulted from some European complications, or, more properly speaking, was intended to prevent such complications.

The effect and force of that order are left precisely as they were at its issue. The authority conferred on you by it is not in the slightest degree changed.

You will, therefore, consider the following remarks as suggestions only, and not as instructions.

In my opinion, neither Indianola nor Galveston is the proper point of attack. If it be necessary, as urged by Mr. Seward, that the flag be restored to some one point in Texas, that can be best and most safely effected by a combined military and naval movement up Red River to Alexandria, Natchitoches, or Shreveport, and the military occupation of Northern Texas. This would be merely carrying out the plans proposed by you at the beginning of the campaign, and, in my opinion, far superior in its military character to the occupation of Galveston or Indianola. Nevertheless, your choice is left unrestricted.

In the first place, by adopting the line of the Red River, you retain your connection with your own base, and separate still more the two points of the rebel Confederacy. Moreover, you cut Northern Louisiana and Southern Arkansas entirely off from supplies and re-enforcements from Texas. They are already cut off from the rebel States east of the Mississippi.

If you occupy Galveston or Indianola, you divide your own troops, and enable the enemy to concentrate all of his forces upon either of these points or on New Orleans.

I write this simply as a suggestion and not as a military instruction.

Very respectfully, your obedient servant,

H. W. HALLECK,
General-in-Chief.

HDQRS. DEPT. OF THE GULF, NINETEENTH ARMY CORPS,
New Orleans, August 10, 1863.

Maj. Gen. U. S. GRANT, *Commanding, &c., Vicksburg, Miss.:*

GENERAL: I have the honor to acknowledge the receipt of your letter, dated the 7th of August, by the hand of Captain [Peter] Hudson.

General Ord has reported to me, and I have directed his corps to be camped near the city of New Orleans. I think he will find everything to his satisfaction, and I do not anticipate any important movements which will put his men to great labor. His transportation will be used to bring his command here, and will be returned immediately for the troops he has left behind.

I have read General Halleck's dispatch with attention. Some information has been received at Washington in regard to the sailing of the iron-clads from Liverpool. The conversation of Southern men overheard in the ship-yards indicated that their destination will be the southwest, and a possible attack on New Orleans. I do not apprehend any danger from this source, but the Government deems it worthy attention, and the positions indicated will be strengthened. It is quite possible the movement of troops, not having reference to your dispatch or to my own, might have been caused by the information received.

I have the honor to inclose to you some memoranda concerning Mobile.* I still think it of the utmost moment that that port should be in our hands. Except for Johnston's army, we should have no difficulty. He seems to occupy a position intended to cover Mobile, and if he is in force, 30,000 or 40,000 strong, as I suppose, he could embarrass operations against that point very seriously. I am unable, however, to see how he can hold his position in the southwest, with Rosecrans' army pressing down upon the rebel center. A line extending from Mobile to Richmond, in the present shattered condition of the rebel armies, the right, center, and left having all been disastrously defeated, it seems to me impossible that they can maintain their positions, if Rosecrans, with a heavy force, pushes down upon their center, or if Charleston shall fall into our hands through the operations of the fleet and army combined. A successful movement in either direction from Charleston, or by Rosecrans, will cut their center, and place Bragg and Johnston, with their forces, between the troops under Rosecrans, your own, and mine at New Orleans. I do not believe that that condition of things can be maintained. All the information we receive here points to a change in their operations. For instance, we hear that the guns are removed from the forts at Mobile to the town. This indicates that their ordnance is deficient, or that they may be intending to remove them to a distance. The Catholic priests there write to their friends here that they are in daily anticipation of an order for the evacuation of the city. This is said with reference to the supply of provisions, and for the purpose of assuring the friends here that their supplies from the Government of the United States may be expected very soon. The Mobile papers, in speaking of Johnston's visit, though apparently denying the possibility of evacuation, actually evade the question. Johnston is made to say that if he had intended to evacuate, he should not have shown himself there; and, after an examination of the works, he is said to have pronounced the opinion that the post was one of the strongest on the rebel seaboard. This is undoubtedly true, but it does not affect the question of maintaining a line extending from Mobile to Richmond.

It is important that as much information as possible should be had of Johnston's movements. I shall be greatly indebted to you for any information you may gain upon this subject, and will also transmit to you without delay memoranda or information that may fall into our hands. Until we have further orders from the Government, active operations will, of course, be suspended.

I am greatly indebted to you for the promptness with which you have sent the re-enforcements to this department.

I have the honor to be, with much respect, your obedient servant,

N. P. BANKS,
Major-General, Commanding.

---

* Not found; but see Banks to Halleck, p. 666.

SPECIAL ORDERS, } HDQRS. DEPARTMENT OF THE GULF,
No. 196.   }   *New Orleans, La., August 11, 1863.*

*   *   *   *   *   *   *

XXII. The Defenses of New Orleans will continue to include Don-aldsonville, and will extend from that point down the La Fourche to Napoleonville and the canal leading from Bayou La Fourche at that point to Lake Venet, and from Algiers west to Bayou des Allemands. All that part of the La Fourche country south of Napoleonville and west of Bayou des Allemands will constitute the District of La Fourche, and will be under the command of the commander of the Second Brigade, First Division.

By command of Major-General Banks:

          RICH'D B. IRWIN,
           Assistant Adjutant-General.

           WASHINGTON, D. C.,
            August 12, 1863.

Maj. Gen. N. P. BANKS, *New Orleans, La.:*

 GENERAL: Your dispatches of July 30 and August 1 are just received. I fully appreciate the importance of the operation proposed by you in these dispatches, but there are reasons other than military why those heretofore directed should be undertaken first. On this matter we have no choice, but must carry out the views of the Government.

 Very respectfully, your obedient servant,

           H. W. HALLECK,
            General-in-Chief.

    HEADQUARTERS DEPARTMENT OF THE GULF,
        New Orleans, August 12, 1863.

Maj. Gen. H. W. HALLECK,
  General-in-Chief, Washington, D. C.:

 GENERAL: I have the honor to acknowledge the receipt of your let-ter referring to Forts Jackson and Saint Philip, and inclosing a copy of communication from England, relative to the possible operations of the enemy in this quarter. Immediate measures will be taken to carry into execution your instructions. Previous to the receipt of this letter, a commission, consisting of Major-General Franklin, General Stone, General Weitzel, and General Emory, instructed to take into consideration the whole subject of the defenses of New Orleans, visited Forts Jackson and Saint Philip on the 6th day of August, with a view of determin-ing what additional defenses were necessary at those points.

 I have the honor to inclose a copy of the report. It is believed that the conclusions arrived at by the commission will be substantially in conformity with the instructions contained in your letter. You may be assured that nothing will be omitted which is necessary for the perfect defense of that position. Requisitions have been made for the additional armament which is required, and sufficient labor will be employed to secure the early completion of the work. I need not say to you, however, that the defense of this department must be secured very largely by the co-operation of the naval forces. One or two iron-clads, at least, would be necessary for the defense of this point in case of immediate danger, and this portion of the river ought, under all circumstances, to be strongly protected by the naval forces. I earnestly recommend that measures be adopted to secure this co-operation.

Previous to my assuming command of this department, very little had been done to complete or strengthen the national defenses since the evacuation of New Orleans by the Confederate army. Much labor and money were expended upon other public works, but the fortifications were, as a general thing, neglected. The small work at Donaldsonville is, perhaps, the only exception, which was just commenced, and has been completed under my authority. During my administration, all the public works have been greatly strengthened, and many have been added. The recent invasion of the enemy has renewed our attention to this subject, and some elaborate and extensive works have been projected, the outline of which is presented in the report of the commissioners.

The completion of this work requires much labor, and some provision must be made for defraying the expenses incident thereto. Hitherto the work has been done by hired men, working at the rate of $1.25 a day—men who were formerly paid $1.50. We have been obliged to employ this labor to a considerable extent upon the works commenced since the investment of Port Hudson, the negro troops being employed in the siege of that place. My belief is that negro troops can be usefully employed to a considerable extent in this kind of work, but that they ought not to be withdrawn altogether from the field. The regiments that have been organized will constitute a considerable part of our force, and I should reluctantly see them all drawn to any other duty. If we avail ourselves of their labor, it will be at considerable expense, and I hope that our requisitions upon the engineering fund may be honored, or that we may be permitted to apply property within the control of the Government here to works of that kind. Great dissatisfaction is occasioned by the employment of men without prompt payment.

Major-General Ord, of General Grant's command, reported here on the 10th instant. His corps, which consists of about 11,000 effective men, will be placed on the north side of Lake Pontchartrain. It will probably be increased by the return of absentees during the present month 2,000 or 3,000 men, making possibly 13,000 or 14,000 men.

The location is healthy, and the spirit and strength of his command will be much improved by the rest they may obtain in the position assigned to them.

I have the honor to be, very respectfully, your most obedient servant,

N. P. BANKS,
Major-General, Commanding.

[Inclosure.]

Proceedings of a board convened to take into consideration the best mode of defense for the city of New Orleans, by virtue of the following Special Orders, viz:

SPECIAL ORDERS, } HDQRS. DEPT. OF THE GULF, 19TH A. C.,
No. 183. } *New Orleans, July 27, 1863.*

I. A board, to consist of Maj. Gen. W. B. Franklin, U. S. Volunteers, Brig. Gen. C. P. Stone, U. S. Volunteers, Brig. Gen. W. H. Emory, U. S. Volunteers, Brig. Gen. G. Weitzel, U. S. Volunteers, and Maj. D. C. Houston, chief engineer, will assemble in this city to-day at 10 a. m., to take into consideration the best mode of defense for the city of New Orleans, the defensive works proper to construct on the Mississippi and Red Rivers, within the limits of this department, with reference to the present war, and to report fully its opinions on these subjects, as well as upon the proper positions for depots of ammunition and other material, and the points most advantageous to be held in the event of war with a foreign naval power.

The board will habitually. hold its sittings in the office of the chief of engineers of the department, but may, if deemed by the board desirable, visit any point within the department, to make examinations of positions.

The quartermaster will furnish all necessary transportation to the board while in discharge of its duties.

The junior member will record the proceedings of the board.

By command of Major-General Banks:

G. NORMAN LIEBER,

Acting Assistant Adjutant-General.

—

OFFICE OF CHIEF OF ENGINEERS,
July 27, 1863—10 a. m.

The board met and organized in pursuance of the above order. All the members were present except Brigadier-General Weitzel.

The session was occupied in a general discussion of the subject.

Adjourned to meet at 10 a. m., July 28.

—

OFFICE OF CHIEF OF ENGINEERS,
July 28, 1863—10 a. m.

The board met according to adjournment.

Present, all the members.

The board visited Algiers, the Chalmette fortifications, the company canal, Camp Parapet fortifications, and Fort Banks, to make examinations of positions.

Adjourned to meet at 10 a. m., July 29.

—

OFFICE OF CHIEF OF ENGINEERS,
July 29, 1863—10 a. m.

The board met according to adjournment.

Present, all the members.

It is the opinion of the board that the city of New Orleans snould be garrisoned by a force of 5,000 men.

Three redoubts should be constructed, respectively, at the termini of the Jefferson and Lake Pontchartrain Railroad, of the Bayou Saint John, and of the Pontchartrain Railroad, sufficiently large for a garrison of two companies each; and a redoubt of similar size on the Gentilly road, about 2 miles below the Pontchartrain Railroad. There should be a citadel large enough for a garrison of 5,000 troops, the line of parapet about 1,250 yards long, a field work of high relief, with a revetted scarf, the site to be chosen by the chief engineer, in the vicinity of the Chalmette line.

The works constructed by the rebels should be allowed to remain. The line along the company's canal, and the Camp Parapet fortifications, should be put into a state of defense, and all the guns mounted on siege or field carriages. The work, including the redoubts, now in process of construction for strengthening these lines, should be carried out.

A floating battery of at least ten heavy guns should be stationed in the river, in front of the city, at all times, and two floating batteries of light draught on Lake Pontchartrain. A road of communication should be made from the citadel to the Gentilly road.

Adjourned.

On the evening of July 29, the board started up the river to examine all the positions within this department proper to be defended, and returned August 2.

—

OFFICE OF CHIEF OF ENGINEERS,
August 4, 1863—10 a. m.

Board met according to adjournment.

All the members present.

In the opinion of the board, a permanent garrison of about 1,000 men at Baton Rouge will be sufficient, it being within supporting distance of Port Hudson.

At Port Hudson, the board recommend the construction of a system of detached works, connected by a line, the details to be arranged by the chief engineer of the department; the garrison to be 2,500. The hill at Tunica Bend to be garrisoned by about 400 men, and the work a redoubt sufficient for this garrison.

A strong regiment should hold Plaquemine and Donaldsonville. At Bayou Sara, a gunboat should be stationed in the river.

The board is of opinion that at least a division of the troops on the east side of the river, with two regiments of cavalry, should be stationed at Clinton. This would greatly lessen the garrisons required at the points above mentioned, and the concentration of the troops would add to their discipline.

Red River.—A work should be erected at the west end of Turnbull Island, and a garrison of 500 troops stationed there to command the entrance to the Atchafalaya and the mouth of Red River.

For the permanent control of the Mississippi River, the town of Alexandria should be occupied by a division of infantry, with a proper amount of cavalry and artillery, and an intrenched camp constructed, with a large supply of provisions constantly on hand.

Berwick Bay.—A small field work should be constructed on the north side of Bayou Bœuf, about a half mile from the, railroad depot, large enough for a garrison of 500 men. The system already adopted of stockades at all the crossings on the railroad should be carried out.

With reference to war with a foreign power, there should be a work at the mouth of the Atchafalaya River. The mouth of the Bayou La Fourche should be examined by the engineers, to ascertain whether works are necessary there. Fort Livingston should be armed and garrisoned.

It is also recommended that the work at Proctorville be completed, and a strong redoubt built on White Oak Ridge, about 800 yards east of it. Also a strong redoubt at Madame Ducro's sugar-house, about 4 miles from Proctorville, near the railroad, sufficient for a garrison of 1,000 men.

Adjourned.

—

August 6, 1863.

The board visited Forts Jackson and Saint Philip, for the purpose of examining them.

—

OFFICE OF CHIEF OF ENGINEERS,
August 7, 1863—10 a. m.

The board met according to adjournment. All the members present, excepting General Stone.

The board recommends that there be added to the armament of Forts

Jackson and Saint Philip ten rifled 30-pounders, ten rifled 100-pounders, and four 15-inch guns.

At Forts Pike and Macomb there should be two rifled 30-pounders each; at Ship Island, two rifled 100-pounders.

The board also recommends that the main depot for ordnance stores and other material be in the citadel at New Orleans, and secondary depots at Port Hudson and Baton Rouge.

The approaches to the city of New Orleans by water are so numerous that no system of defense can be complete without the co-operation of a large naval force.

Adjourned *sine die.*

D. C. HOUSTON,
Major, and Aide-de-Camp, Captain U. S. Engineers.
W. B. FRANKLIN,
Major-General of Volunteers.

———

PORT HUDSON,
August 13, 1863.

Lieut. Col. RICHARD B. IRWIN,
Assistant Adjutant-General:

COLONEL: With reference to the proposed fortifications at Port Hudson, I have the honor to submit the following statements and report:

I have been verbally authorized by General Banks to proceed to fortify the place according to my own judgment in the case. I have already given to General Banks, General Stone, and Major Houston an outline of my views on the subject. It appears to me that the opinion I have on the subject, after much consideration, and with very favorable opportunities for studying the ground, may not be without interest to the commanding general.

The plateau in the center of the present fortification is about 1,000 yards long, in a direction nearly parallel with the river bank, and about 650 yards wide from the edge of the river bank back. It is very irregular, being surrounded by a ravine with very crooked ———; so crooked that it is difficult to sweep them with artillery. I suppose the garrison would not ordinarily, at least, during the season of active operations be very large—perhaps two or three regiments and some artillery. When the garrison should be large, the present works, somewhat repaired, with the addition of some redoubts at the important points, would admit of a very good defense; but in the usual state of the garrison a smaller work of much stronger profile would be necessary. A line of detached works under these circumstances would not, it appears to me, be as strong as a single strong work. I would, therefore, respectfully recommend the construction of a work, of strong profile, of from 1,500 to 2,000 yards' length of interior crest, with a covered way of profile strictly necessary, made partly in excavation and partly in embankment, so arranged as to be completely under the fire of the main works. For the defenses of the ravine, I would recommend simple rifle-pits, placed along the crest of the ravine, with a few small redoubts in which to place field or siege artillery, the whole to be swept by the fire of the main works.

I would recommend for the armament, in addition to the smooth-bore guns which may be deemed necessary, from six to ten 30-pounder Parrott guns, to be used to dismount the enemy's guns in batteries which he may attempt to establish against the works.

I have thus given a hasty outline of my views, and respectfully sub.
mit the same to the commanding general.
Respectfully, your obedient servant,
GEORGE L. ANDREWS,
Brigadier-General of Volunteers.

HEADQUARTERS DEPARTMENT OF THE TENNESSEE,
Vicksburg, Miss., August 13, 1863.
Maj. Gen. N. P. BANKS,
Commanding Department of the Gulf:
GENERAL: The inclosed dispatch from the General-in-Chief of the
army is just received.* I send it to you in all haste.
Lack of boats prevents my getting the Thirteenth Corps to you
promptly. Can you not send me some boats from below for them ?
Call on me for anything it is possible to serve you in.
Very respectfully, your obedient servant,
U. S. GRANT,
Major-General.

STATE OF NEW HAMPSHIRE, EXECUTIVE DEPARTMENT,
Concord, August 14, 1863.
The PRESIDENT OF THE UNITED STATES:
SIR: It would be very gratifying to myself and the citizens of our
State if another effort could be made by the Government to relieve the
Union citizens of Texas by the re-appointment of General Hamilton as
brigadier-general and Military Governor, and the organization and de-
parture of a military force for that department sufficient to place the
State completely under the control of Union soldiers and citizens. My
knowledge of General Hamilton's sufferings and services for the Union
cause makes me feel very solicitous that, on his account, and on account
of those he represents, as soon as the military situation will admit, a
Texas military expedition may be set on foot and carried to a successful
consummation.
If any plan can be devised for raising troops specially for that service
in New England, I shall cheerfully and earnestly lend it my sympathy
and co-operation, and trust that the President will not fail to favor and
authorize it without delay as soon as the public service will justify it.†
I have the honor to be, very respectfully, your obedient servant,
J. A. GILMORE,
Governor.

HEADQUARTERS DEPARTMENT OF THE TENNESSEE,
Vicksburg, Miss., August 14, 1863.
Maj. Gen. N. P. BANKS,
Commanding Department of the Gulf:
GENERAL: General Ord is now here, and not having heard from his
family for forty days, and, when he did hear, they were among strangers,
his wife and two little children sick, he has asked me for permission to
go up the river to Cairo to learn something from them by telegraph if
he can, and, if not, he will go on or send an aide until something can

---

* See Halleck to Banks, August 6, 1863, 12.30 p. m., p. 672.
† Reply, if any, not found.

be learned. General Ord will not absent himself except in the most imperative necessity, and, in that case, will endeavor to return before any field operations can possibly take place with his corps.

Captain [Joseph C.] Audenried has just returned, bringing your dispatch of the 10th instant.

Johnston's forces, under the immediate command of Hardee, are still on the Southern Railroad; the cavalry at Brandon, principally, and the balance scattered from there to Enterprise, on the Mobile and Ohio Railroad; most of them, however, in one camp in the pine woods, 40 or 50 miles east of Jackson. Their principal occupation seems to be to collect deserters and conscripts. Johnston's force after his retreat from Jackson is said to have fallen off to 10,000 men, and. no doubt, they were so demoralized that half of their number could have put them to flight. Now, he must be better off, both as to numbers and *morale.* I do not believe, however, that he could get together 30,000 men, exclusive of the Mobile force.

Johnston's cavalry were to have crossed to the west side of Pearl River yesterday; probably did. Their object is to suppress a movement now being made by the citizens to bring the State back into the Union; to pick up deserters, and to run off negroes.

I have no cavalry force to operate with. My whole cavalry force with this army, including escort companies with general officers, and that belonging to the Thirteenth Corps going to your department, does not exceed 2,000 effective men, and 1,000 of them are penetrating the north, in co-operation with a force I ordered to be sent from La Grange, Tenn., for the purpose of collecting and saving, if possible, the rolling-stock cut off from the enemy by the destruction of the Big Black Bridge. They will go on through to Memphis, and will not probably return here for a month. I am much in need of cavalry, and regret exceedingly that I have not got more to send to you.

I am, general, very truly, your obedient servant,

U. S. GRANT,
Major-General.

GENERAL ORDERS, }   HDQRS. THIRTEENTH ARMY CORPS,
No. 24.   }   *Vicksburg, Miss., August 14, 1863.*

I. The divisions of this corps will hereafter be known as the First, Second, Third, and Fourth.

II. The division commanded by Maj. Gen. C. C. Washburn will be known, as heretofore, as the First Division, Thirteenth Army Corps.

III. The division known as the Army of the Frontier, Maj. Gen. F. J. Herron commanding, will henceforth be known as the Second Division Thirteenth Army Corps.

IV. The Twelfth Division, commanded by Brig. Gen. A. P. Hovey, will hereafter be known as the Third Division, Thirteenth Army Corps.

V. The Tenth Division, Colonel Landram commanding, will be known as the Fourth Division, Thirteenth Army Corps.

VI. The cavalry will form a separate brigade, under Col. John J. Mudd, chief of cavalry. All reports of escort companies or mounted orderlies at division, brigade, or other headquarters will henceforth be made through headquarters of the regiment to which the escort or orderlies may belong, or directly through Colonel Mudd.

By order of Maj. Gen. E. O. C. Ord:

WALTER B. SCATES,
Lieutenant-Colonel, and Asst. Adjt. Gen., Thirteenth Army Corps.

SPECIAL ORDERS, }   HDQRS. THIRTEENTH ARMY CORPS,
    No. 42½.   }   August 14, 1863.
*   *   *   *   *   *   *

II. Col. John J. Mudd, chief of cavalry, will move his cavalry to Carrollton, near New Orleans, by such steamers as he can procure. He will load them as quickly as possible, and report to these headquarters how much room there may be for the transportation of infantry and ordnance.

*   *   *   *

By order of Maj. Gen. E. O. C. Ord:
WALTER B. SCATES,
Lieutenant-Colonel, and Assistant Adjutant-General.

GENERAL ORDERS, }   HDQRS. 1ST DIV., AND OF U. S. FORCES
    }   IN AND AROUND BATON ROUGE,
    No. 1.   }   August 14, 1863.

In pursuance of Special Orders, No. 183, Extract 2, headquarters Nineteenth Army Corps, Department of the Gulf, I hereby assume command of the First Division and of the United States forces in and around Baton Rouge.

My staff is announced as follows: Capt. Wickham Hoffman, assistant adjutant-general; Capt. George S. Shaw, additional aide-de-camp; Capt. John P. Baker, First U. S. Cavalry, aide-de-camp; Lieut. David Lyon, Seventy-seventh New York Volunteers, aide-de-camp; Capt. George M. Franklin, Pennsylvania Volunteers, aide de-camp. They will be obeyed and respected accordingly.

Other staff officers will be announced as appointed.
W. B. FRANKLIN,
Major-General, Commanding.

NEW ORLEANS, LA., *August* 15, 1863,
VIA CAIRO, ILL., *August* 24.

Major-General HALLECK,
    General-in-Chief, Washington, D. C.:

GENERAL: Your dispatch of the 6th was received this morning at 9 o'clock. There will be no delay in the execution of your orders. I shall be ready to move as soon as General Grant's troops can reach this point, and hope to attain the object in view within a week or ten days at outside. I have forwarded a full statement of my purpose and plans by mail. I shall be greatly deficient in cavalry. If you can aid me in this, it will greatly facilitate my work. The duty assigned me is very satisfactory, and I hope to realize all your expectations.
N. P. BANKS,
Major-General.

HDQRS. DEPT. OF THE GULF, NINETEENTH ARMY CORPS,
New Orleans, August 15, 1863.

Major-General HALLECK,
    Commander-in-Chief, U. S. Army:

GENERAL: I have the honor to acknowledge the receipt of your dispatch (in cipher), a copy of which is inclosed as received.* It was re-

---

* See Halleck to Banks, August 6, 1863, 12.30 p. m., p. 672.

ceived this morning at 9.15 a. m. by telegraph from General Grant, and a duplicate of the same this evening by Colonel [T. K.] Smith, one of his aides-de-camp.

Measures have been already taken to carry into effect your orders. We shall plant the flag in Texas within a week, I hope. My plan has been to move against Galveston upon the land side, via the Sabine Pass, and from Berwick Bay, via Vermillionville and Niblett's Bluff, to Houston and Galveston, for the transportation and artillery. We shall be ready, I think, as soon as General Grant's corps can reach us. The route indicated is that followed by the Texans in their invasions of Western Louisiana.

We can move 8,000 men at once to the Sabine Pass, and thence concentrate rapidly on Galveston, fortifying and holding a position on the mainland or the island only, as may be deemed expedient. From thence operations are practicable in any direction to the interior or to the Rio Grande.

From Galveston, when strongly fortified, I would move a force of 5,000 or more to the Rio Grande, where one or more positions can be so fortified as to be held by a much less force, while we hold Galveston or the interior of the State. This has been my view of operations in Texas from the beginning.

Indianola is too far distant; does not command the important communications of the State, and, if occupied, would leave the forces of the enemy between us and New Orleans, which is to be avoided, if possible.

No movement can be made from the Gulf against Galveston with a certainty of success. Our naval forces are not strong enough, and the enemy's works are too extensive and thorough. The enemy fears only an attack from the land, via Niblett's Bluff, the route I propose, or Alexandria. From that point our success is certain. We learned this from intercepted letters while at Alexandria, in May.

I send a sketch of the fortifications at Galveston made at that time by one who was engaged upon them, with a description of the guns mounted.

If General Grant sends me 10,000 men, I can throw 20,000 immediately into Texas. The force should be larger, if possible. I urge strongly upon the Government, if possible, to fill up some of our old regiments with conscripts or volunteers. This would greatly relieve us. Officers have been sent north for this purpose.

I am very deficient in cavalry. I ought to have a few regiments from the west. General Grierson desires to join us in the expedition to Texas, and would render us infinite service. If possible, I hope he may be ordered to join us. Once in Texas, with a moderate cavalry force, we can mount our men rapidly.

I have organized about twenty regiments of the Corps d'Afrique, of 500 men each, besides a regiment of engineers of 1,200, and two regiments of infantry, of 800 each, numbering in all about 12,000. They are nearly ready for service. When in Texas, I shall fill these skeleton regiments to the number of 800 or 1,000 men each. These regiments will thus number, when full, 25,000 men. I want good officers. If you can send me 50 or 100, or more, good company officers, or for field and staff in fair proportions, I shall be glad.

I will report our progress daily, in preparation and movement.

I have the honor to be, with much respect, your obedient servant,

N. P. BANKS,
Major-General, Commanding.

SPECIAL ORDERS, }   HDQRS. DEPARTMENT OF THE GULF,
   No. 200.   }   *New Orleans, August* 15, 1863.

*   *   *   *   *   *   *

XXIV. Maj. Gen. W. B. Franklin is assigned to the command of the Nineteenth Army Corps; headquarters for the present at Baton Rouge.
By command of Major-General Banks:
                    RICH'D B. IRWIN,
                         Assistant Adjutant-General.

HEADQUARTERS DEPARTMENT OF THE GULF,
                         New Orleans, August 15, 1863.
Maj. Gen. N. P. BANKS,
        Commanding Department:
·GENERAL: In compliance with your direction, I have the honor to make the following report of the number of colored troops raised in this department:

1st Infantry, Corps d'Afrique, Colonel Stafford	696
2d Infantry, Corps d'Afrique, Colonel Daniels	637
3d Infantry, Corps d'Afrique, Colonel Nelson	816
4th Infantry, Corps d'Afrique, Colonel Drew	923
5th Infantry, Corps d'Afrique (no report).	
6th Infantry, Corps d'Afrique ⎫	
7th Infantry, Corps d'Afrique ⎪	
8th Infantry, Corps d'Afrique ⎬ Ullmann's brigade (no detailed report)	2,100
9th Infantry, Corps d'Afrique ⎪	
10th Infantry, Corps d'Afrique ⎭	
11th Infantry, Corps d'Afrique (no report).	
12th Infantry, Corps d'Afrique (no report).	
13th Infantry, Corps d'Afrique ⎫	
14th Infantry, Corps d'Afrique ⎪	
15th Infantry, Corps d'Afrique ⎬ Plumly's brigade (no report).	
16th Infantry, Corps d'Afrique ⎭	
17th Infantry, Corps d'Afrique, Colonel Goodrich	382
18th Infantry, Corps d'Afrique, Colonel Hanks	378
19th Infantry, Corps d'Afrique, Colonel Bostwick (no report).	
1st Engineers, Corps d'Afrique, Colonel Hodge	936
2d Engineers, Corps d'Afrique, Colonel Cobb	531
Companies A, B, and C, Heavy Artillery, about	300.
Total	7,699

The missing reports were called for as soon as I received your order, and the call for them has been renewed. The number of recruits for each of the eight regiments not reported may, I think, be safely estimated at 300 (or 2,400 in all), making a grand total of 10,099.
   Very respectfully, your obedient servant,
                    [RICH'D B. IRWIN,]
                         Assistant Adjutant-General.

GENERAL ORDERS, }   HDQRS. DEFENSES OF NEW ORLEANS,
   No. 35.   }   *New Orleans, August* 15, 1863.
Robberies on the highway and elsewhere having been committed by banditti in the uniform of the United States, who, upon being arrested, were discovered to be citizens, who are not now nor ever have been in the service of the United States, and who had assumed this garb to facilitate them in eluding the vigilance of the guard of police, it is hereby directed that every person, not an officer or an enlisted man in

the service of the United States, found in this dress, within the limits of this command, will be immediately arrested and confined in the provost prison.

By command of Brigadier-General Emory:

[D. S. WALKER,,
Assistant Adjutant-General.

HEADQUARTERS DEPARTMENT OF THE GULF,
New Orleans, August 16, 1863.

Maj. Gen. H. W. HALLECK,
General-in-Chief, Washington:

GENERAL: I have the honor to transmit herewith copies of Paragraphs XIX and XXIV,* of Special Orders, No. 200, of yesterday's date, from these headquarters, reorganizing the Nineteenth Army Corps, and assigning Maj. Gen. W. B. Franklin to the command.

The orders being rendered imperatively necessary by the arrival of the Thirteenth Corps in this department, and by the operations in view, I respectfully request that the assignment may be confirmed by the President, from its date.

I have, at the same time, the honor to inclose for your information a list of the regiments and batteries assigned to the Nineteenth Corps, showing the organization by brigades and divisions.†

Very respectfully, your most obedient servant,

N. P. BANKS,
Major-General, Commanding.

[Inclosure.]

SPECIAL ORDERS, }   HDQRS. DEPARTMENT OF THE GULF,
No. 200.   }   *New Orleans, August 15, 1863.*

*   *   *   *   *   *   *

XIX. The troops comprising the Nineteenth Army Corps will be organized as follows:

First Division, to be commanded for the present by Brig. Gen. Godfrey Weitzel.

First Brigade, to be commanded by Col. N. A. M. Dudley, Thirtieth Massachusetts, and to comprise the present First and Third Brigades of the First Division, as follows: Thirtieth Massachusetts, Colonel Dudley; Second Louisiana, Colonel Paine; One hundred and sixty-first New York, Colonel Harrower; One hundred and seventy-fourth New York, Colonel Parmele; One hundred and sixteenth New York, Colonel Love.

Second Brigade (the present Third Brigade, of the Third Division), under the command of Col. Oliver P. Gooding, Thirty-first Massachusetts.

Third (Emory's) Division, to be commanded for the present by Brig. Gen. F. S. Nickerson.

First Brigade (Nickerson's), as at present organized.

Second Brigade, to be commanded by Brig. Gen. James W. McMillan, and to be organized as at present, with the addition of the Twenty-sixth Massachusetts, Col. A. B. Farr, now serving in the Defenses of New Orleans.

---

* For Paragraph XXIV, see extract from Special Orders, No. 200, p. 684.
† See Special Orders, following.

Fourth (Grover's) Division, to be commanded for the present by Brig. Gen. W. H. Emory.

First Brigade, to be commanded by Col. Henry W. Birge, Thirteenth Connecticut, and to consist of the following-named regiments:

Thirteenth Connecticut, Colonel Birge; Ninetieth New York, Colonel Morgan; Ninety-first New York, Colonel Van Zandt; One hundred and fifty-ninth New York, Colonel Molineux; One hundred and thirty-first New York, Lieutenant-Colonel Day.

Second Brigade, to be commanded by Col. Thomas W. Cahill, Ninth Connecticut.

Ninth Connecticut, Colonel Cahill; Thirteenth Maine, Colonel Rust; Twelfth Maine, Colonel Kimball; Fifteenth Maine, Colonel Dyer; First Louisiana, Colonel Fiske.

The present Second Brigade of the First Division will be designated by its former title of the Reserve Brigade, will be commanded by the senior colonel, and will, for the present, be attached to the Defenses of New Orleans, occupying the District of La Fourche.

The commander of the Defenses of New Orleans will, for the present, continue to report direct to department headquarters.

The light artillery of the several divisions will continue as at present assigned, until further orders.

The cavalry of the Nineteenth Corps will be reported as follows:

The Third Massachusetts, now at Port Hudson, and Fourth Wisconsin, now at Baton Rouge and Plaquemine, to the corps commander; the First Louisiana, at Thibodeaux, Second Rhode Island, under orders to move from Baton Rouge to Thibodeaux, First Texas, at New Orleans, and Fourteenth New York, at New Orleans, to the commander of the Defenses of New Orleans; the Third Massachusetts, Fourth Wisconsin, and First Louisiana will be kept concentrated. All details for orderly duty will be furnished by General Emory from the Fourteenth New York Cavalry, in the proportion of 1 sergeant, 1 corporal, and 11 privates to each division, and such number for corps headquarters as the corps commander may call for.

*   *   *   *

By command of Major-General Banks:

RICH'D B. IRWIN,
Assistant Adjutant-General.

HDQRS. DEPT. OF THE GULF, NINETEENTH ARMY CORPS,
New Orleans, August 16, 1863.

Major-General GRANT,
Commanding Department of the Tennessee:

GENERAL: I have the honor to acknowledge the receipt of your letter, inclosing a dispatch from Major-General Halleck, by the hand of Col. Thomas Kilby Smith, last evening at 9 o'clock. Colonel Smith had considerately forwarded a copy of the dispatches from Port Hudson by telegraph, which were received at 9 a. m.

I beg you will accept my thanks for the tender of your assistance. I shall call upon you freely, assured as I am, from our intercourse since I have been in this department, that whatever you can you will do to assist us.

There will be no delay in making the movement suggested by the Government. As soon as General Ord's command can reach us, we shall be ready. I shall move, I hope, within a week.

I hope to concentrate, with your corps, 20,000 men. Our great want will be in cavalry. If you can send us any assistance in this, I shall be greatly indebted. General Grierson expressed a strong desire to join us in this expedition, but it opens sooner than either of us expected. If he can be spared, I hope he will be permitted to join us. I forward a dispatch to him by way of information. Cavalry is of the highest importance in the country to which we are ordered.

I am sorry that I cannot now send transports to expedite General Ord's movements. The steamers sent north have not yet returned. We have not one to send you, but, as soon as they arrive, will urge them forward.

The vessels fit for sea navigation only can be used by us in this expedition. If you can spare any of the tug-boats temporarily, I shall be greatly obliged, and will return them as soon as they can be spared. We shall be compelled to use sailing vessels, from the deficiencies of our transportation.

I will keep you advised of all our movements, and shall be indebted to you for any suggestions which you make upon the matter in hand.

I am, general, with regard, your obedient servant,

N. P. BANKS,
Major-General, Commanding.

[P. S.]—Light-draught tin-clads, of which there are many on the upper river, as I am informed by Commodore Graham, will be of great service to us in the waters connecting with New Orleans. If they can be spared, I beg you to send them to us without delay.

NEW ORLEANS, LA., *August* 16, 1863,
VIA CAIRO, ILL., *August* 24.

Major-General HALLECK,
General-in-Chief, U. S. Army:

It is necessary that three or four steamers should be sent us from New York without delay. If they are needed for public service, the steamers on the way to New York from New Orleans can be substituted for them. I beg you to give an order to the quartermaster at New York to that effect. We shall not await their arrival, but we shall need their assistance.

N. P. BANKS,
Major-General.

HDQRS. DEPT. OF THE GULF, NINETEENTH ARMY CORPS,
New Orleans, August 16 1863.

Admiral DAVID D. PORTER,
Or the Officer Commanding the Fleet at Vicksburg:

SIR: It is probable that a movement will be undertaken from New Orleans which will draw most of the forces from that city. To prevent an invasion of the Texas troops, it will be necessary that the Atchafalaya River and Berwick Bay should be patrolled by light-draught gunboats. If you have a half dozen light-draught tin-clads that you can send into these waters, it will be of great service to us. None of our gunboats will pass Lake Chicot, as they draw over 6 feet of water. If your boats could enter the Atchafalaya from the Red River, and patrol that river to Berwick Bay, it would effectually cut off any invasion of the enemy from that point. In view of the movements contemplated, it is probable that two or three boats would be sufficient for the purpose indicated, and they would at the same time prevent the incursions of guerrillas on the west bank of the Mississippi as far up as the mouth of Red River. This would be, perhaps, the most effective service to which this small force could be put.

I have the honor to be, &c.,

N. P. BANKS,
Major-General, Commanding.

HDQRS. DEPT. OF THE GULF, NINETEENTH ARMY CORPS,
New Orleans, August 16, 1863.

Maj. Gen. H. W. HALLECK,
General-in-Chief, U. S. Army:

GENERAL: In the event of the movements contemplated in my dispatch of this date, it will be necessary that the Atchafalaya River and Berwick Bay should be patrolled by light-draught gunboats, to prevent the invasion of the La Fourche district by the enemy. If Admiral Porter can send three of his light-draught tin-clads down the Atchafalaya into Berwick Bay from the Red River, it will effectually accomplish this object, and at the same time prevent the incursion of guerrillas upon the west bank of the Mississippi below the mouth of Red River.

This will be the most effectual service that these boats could possibly render in this quarter. I respectfully, but earnestly, recommend that such an order be given. It is impossible to protect Brashear City and the La Fourche district, except by the aid of gunboats. It was their absence that enabled the enemy to capture Brashear, and to escape across the bay upon our return from Port Hudson.

I have addressed this request to Admiral Porter or the officer commanding the fleet at Vicksburg.

I have the honor to be, &c.,

N. P. BANKS,
Major-General, Commanding.

HDQRS. DEPT. OF THE GULF, NINETEENTH ARMY CORPS,
New Orleans, August 17, 1863.

ABRAHAM LINCOLN,
President of the United States of America:

SIR: From a private note to one of the editors of the Era, I learn that some interest was manifested by you concerning the organization of the negro troops in this department, and especially with reference to General Ullmann's brigade. I have purposely avoided the publication of information respecting the organization of that class of soldiers. General Ullmann has now five regiments nearly completed, numbering about 2,500 men, or 500 to each regiment. I have twenty-one regiments nearly organized, three upon the basis of 1,000 men to each, and eighteen of 500 men, making in all, 10,000 or 12,000 men. There are also batteries of artillery and companies of cavalry in process of organization. These embrace all the material for such regiments that is within my command at the present time. It is necessary to possess ourselves of other portions of country within the control of the enemy to increase this strength.

When I first assumed command in this department, I found three regiments in existence. They were demoralized from various causes, and engaged in controversy with white troops to such an extent that the white officers of these regiments, as well as the colored men who were in commission, believed that it was impracticable for them to continue in service. This difficulty was caused in a great degree by the character of the officers in command. They were unsuited for this duty, and have been most of the time, and some are still, in arrest upon charges of a discreditable character.

The reorganization of these three regiments by the appointment of white officers, and the organization of two other regiments of infantry and a regiment of engineers, were among the first acts of my administration in this department. They embraced all the material then within the control of the Government for regiments of this class. On the opening of the Teche country, in April, a large acquisitior of recruits was obtained. The whole of these were appropriated to the organization of General Ullmann's brigade. The siege of Port Hudson has largely increased our material, and enabled us to complete the force that I have described. The regiments recently organized are limited to the number of 500 for the following reasons:

First. The speedy instruction and discipline of these troops makes it necessary that the officers should have the most complete control over them, and this is obtained by the smaller number much more certainly and efficiently than it would with the maximum number of men allowed.

Second. The skeleton organizations of 500 well-disciplined men enable us to add to the number whenever recruits may offer, and we have these regiments constantly in hand to receive any that may present themselves within or from beyond our lines. It was the practice in the organization of the conscripts of France, when they were required for immediate service, to limit the battalions to 300 or 400 men, instead of 1,000, which was the maximum number. There is certainly reason for such limitation, and I am sure that it will be found to be the only successful method of organization under the present circumstances. Should our armies get possession of Mobile or of Texas, these regiments can be filled without delay, and we shall have a force in the department of at least 25,000 good men. It is impossible to raise negro regiments except we get possession of the country where negroes are. This is a fact overlooked by many persons who are greatly interested in the success of these organizations. The regiments raised thus far have been of great service in this department. I think it may be said with truth that our victory at Port Hudson could not have been accomplished at the time it was but for their assistance.

The number recruited could not have been increased materially up to this time. The movement now contemplated will enable me to carry out my original plan. The command of white troops is for the reason I have stated preliminary to the organization of black troops.

I hope my command may be enlarged by filling up the regiments now in this department with conscripts or volunteers. My cavalry is deficient, and should be at once increased.

Fifty or 100 officers for the Corps d'Afrique would be of the greatest service, if they could be sent at once.

I have the honor to be, with much respect, your most obedient servant,

N. P. BANKS,
Major-General, Commanding.

HDQRS. DEPT. OF THE GULF, NINETEENTH ARMY CORPS,
New Orleans, August 17, 1863.
Maj. Gen. H. W. HALLECK,
    General-in-Chief, U. S. Army:

GENERAL: I think it my duty to represent that among the French residents of this city there is evidently an expectation of some assistance from the Government of France. This comes informally from the conversation of the French residents here, but too frequently to leave room for doubt that they have some reason upon which to ground the remarks that are commonly made. This is undoubtedly the conversation of the officers of the French frigate Catinet, which has recently arrived at this port. I do not think that it is more than mere surmise on their part, but have thought it worth while to direct the provost-marshal-general of the department to investigate the subject and to report the facts as they are, of which I will give you due notice.

    I have the honor to be, with much respect, your obedient servant,
                              N. P. BANKS,
                             Major-General, Commanding.

HDQRS. DEPT. OF THE GULF, NINETEENTH ARMY CORPS,
New Orleans, August 17, 1863.
Maj. Gen. H. W. HALLECK,
    General-in-Chief, U. S. Army:

GENERAL: The departure of many regiments of nine-months' troops, and the organization of many regiments of the Corps d'Afrique, with a large number of detachments occupying outposts, and the sick in the hospitals, confuse somewhat the statements embraced in the monthly report of the 31st July. I shall, in a day or two, as soon as an exact statement can be prepared, give you a better idea of our forces here than can be obtained from the examination of that report. Our effective force of white troops does not exceed 10,000 or 12,000. I am reluctant to call upon you for re-enforcements from the north, but if these regiments could be filled by men obtained by the draft or conscription, it would aid us very much indeed. I am very confident that the authorities of most of the States would be glad to send them to this department.

If we expect to succeed in the movements referred to in my dispatches of this date, it will be indispensable that our military force should be increased beyond what can be obtained by the enrollment of negroes. The letter addressed to the President, a copy of which I send to you,* as well as the reference to this subject in my dispatch addressed to you, will show what we have done in this respect. I can assure the Government that nothing will be omitted that is calculated to strengthen this arm of the service, but before we can successfully organize the negroes of this country we must obtain control of the States where they are by means of white troops.

The want of cavalry is the greatest deficiency we suffer. It is indispensable in any movement in Texas that we should be strong in this arm. All the Texas troops are mounted men; their movements are rapid, and their concentration effective and powerful. We must meet them in the same way, and I earnestly urge upon the Government the necessity of strengthening us in that arm. We also want horse

---

* See p. 688.

equipments, carbines, and sabers for the negroes who will be enlisted in this service. Once in Texas, mules and horses will be abundant, but the equipments are indispensable.

I have the honor to be, &c.,

N. P. BANKS,
Major-General, Commanding.

OFFICE CHIEF OF ARTILLERY,
New Orleans, August 17, 1863.

Captain SHUNK,
Chief of Ordnance:

CAPTAIN : I have the honor to forward you a list of the light batteries of the Thirteenth Army Corps that have already arrived at Carrollton, with the number of rounds of ammunition on hand with each piece.

In regard to the English rifle, caliber 3.50, there are, I believe, but eight in the country, and all the ammunition that there is for them is at Saint Louis Arsenal. The officers who have used the James rifle complain very much of the James projectile, but have found no trouble with the Hotchkiss, and very much prefer the latter.

As soon as the remaining batteries of the corps arrive, I will furnish you with a list of guns and the amount of ammunition.

Very respectfully, your obedient servant,

RICHARD ARNOLD,
Brigadier-General, Chief of Artillery.

[Inclosure.]

Light batteries in the Thirteenth Army Corps, now at Carrollton, with the number of rounds of ammunition on hand with each.

HERRON'S DIVISION.

Battery F, First Missouri Artillery : Four English rifles (iron), caliber 3.50; two James rifles (bronze), caliber 3.80; 320 rounds to each of the English rifles ; 120 rounds to each of the James rifles.

Battery E, First Missouri Artillery: Four 10-pounder Parrotts ; two English rifles (iron), caliber 3.50; 303 rounds to each Parrott; 200 rounds to each English rifle.

Battery B, First Missouri Artillery : Four 12-pounder howitzers; two 12-pounder guns ; 70 rounds to each howitzer ; 128 rounds to each 12-pounder gun.

WASHBURN'S DIVISION.

Seventh Michigan Battery: Six 3-inch ordnance guns ; 144 rounds to each gun.

LEE'S DIVISION.

Battery A, First Missouri Artillery : Three 12-pounder howitzers ; one 12-pounder Napoleon; two 6-pounder guns; 67 rounds for each howitzer; 103 rounds for the Napoleon gun ; 191 rounds for each 6-pounder gun.

Second Illinois Battery : Three 6-pounder guns ; one 12-pounder howitzer; 200 rounds to each 6-pounder gun ; 128 rounds to the 12-pounder howitzer.

Second Ohio Battery: Four James rifles, caliber 3.50; two 12-pounder howitzers (bronze); 187 rounds to each rifle; 132 rounds to each howitzer.

HEADQUARTERS DEPARTMENT OF THE GULF,
New Orleans, August 19, 1863

Maj. Gen. WILLIAM B. FRANKLIN,
Commanding Nineteenth Army Corps, Baton Rouge :

SIR: The commanding general directs that you place your corps in readiness for immediate service. The convalescents and non-effective men will be separated from the effective force, organized into companies and battalions, and enrolled for service in the Defenses of New Orleans. You will have the officers and men required by existing orders to be transferred to the invalid corps so transferred without delay, and concentrated and organized subject to future orders. The troops will be put in the lightest possible marching order, taking only shelter-tents for the men, and the smallest possible number of tents for the officers.

In the movement, three days' cooked rations will be taken.

No baggage will be transported, but will be forwarded to the troops after they reach their destination.

Please acknowledge the receipt of these orders and report their execution.

The foregoing is communicated by order of Major-General Banks.

Very respectfully, your most obedient servant,
RICH'D B. IRWIN,
Assistant Adjutant-General.

(Copy to Maj. Gen. E. O. C. Ord, or commanding general Thirteenth Army Corps, Carrollton.)

HEADQUARTERS DEPARTMENT OF THE GULF,
New Orleans, August 19, 1863.

Brig. Gen. RICHARD ARNOLD,
Chief of Artillery :

SIR : I have the honor to communicate, by direction of the major-general commanding, the following orders for your guidance :

Brig. Gen. Richard Arnold, chief of artillery, Col. S. B. Holabird, chief quartermaster, and Maj. D. C. Houston, chief engineer, are hereby appointed a board to consider and arrange transportation for an immediate movement of the troops. The board will enter upon its duties at once, and will meet at such time and place as the senior member may indicate.

Very respectfully, your obedient servant,
RICH'D B. IRWIN,
Assistant Adjutant-General.

WASHINGTON, D. C.,
August 20, 1863.

Maj. Gen. N. P. BANKS,
New Orleans :

GENERAL: Your dispatch of the 12th instant is just received. The report on the Defenses of New Orleans, said to have been transmitted with it, is not received.

My dispatches to you will show that no movement on Mobile is at present contemplated, nor can any iron-clads be now detached from Charleston or other points for the defense of New Orleans.

Mexican and French complications render it exceedingly important that the movement ordered against Texas be undertaken without delay.

Very respectfully, your obedient servant,

H. W. HALLECK,
General-in-Chief.

GENERAL ORDERS, }   HDQRS. NINETEENTH ARMY CORPS,
No. 1.   }   *Baton Rouge, La., August* 20, 1863.

In pursuance of Special Orders, No. 200, Extract 24, Headquarters Department of the Gulf, the undersigned hereby assumes command of the Nineteenth Army Corps.

His staff is announced as follows: Capt. Wickham Hoffman, assistant adjutant-general; Lieut. Col. J. G. Chandler, assistant quartermaster; Capt. William Scheffler, adjutant, aide-de-camp, and commissary of musters; Capt. George S. Shaw, adjutant, and aide-de-camp; Capt. John P. Baker, First U. S. Cavalry, aide-de-camp; Lieut. David Lyon, Seventy-seventh New York Volunteers, aide-de-camp; Capt. George M. Franklin, One hundred and twenty-second Pennsylvania Volunteers, aide-de-camp; Surg. John H. Rauch, U. S. Volunteers, medical director.

They will be obeyed and respected accordingly.

Other staff officers will be announced as appointed.

W. B. FRANKLIN,
Major-General, Commanding.

HEADQUARTERS POST,
Natchez, August 22, 1863.

Maj. Gen. E. O. C. ORD,
Commanding Thirteenth Army Corps, New Orleans:

GENERAL: 1 have information this a. m. from Alexandria; the parties are reliable, and report General Walker's division, 8,000 to 10,000 strong, passed through Alexandria last week. They were several days in getting through Alexandria, and reported to be *en route* for Berwick Bay.

Kirby Smith was said to have passed through, for same place, some ten days before. Walker's force was nearly all infantry, very little artillery, and no cavalry. Only two companies of cavalry garrisoning Alexandria at present.

Very respectfully, your obedient servant,

T. E. G. RANSOM,
Brigadier-General of Volunteers.

U. S. S. DE SOTO,
Gulf of Mexico, August 22, 1863.

Commanding Officer, U. S. Naval Forces, off New Orleans:

SIR: Within the last few days we have captured a steamer from Havana, bound to Mobile, with a cargo of salted beef and pork for the Confederate Government.

The fact that steamers, at great cost, with all the attendant risk, are so employed, is the most conclusive evidence I have yet had of the scarcity of supplies in the Gulf States, and I deem the fact of sufficient importance to make it known to you, and to suggest that it be communicated to the commanding general.*

I am, sir, respectfully, very hastily, your obedient servant,
W. M. WALKER,
Captain, U. S. Navy.

WASHINGTON, D. C.,
August 24, 1863.

Major-General BANKS, *New Orleans, La.:*

GENERAL: I have just received a duplicate of your letter of the 12th instant, inclosing a copy of the report of a board of defense.

The Engineer Department will furnish funds so far as it may be able; beyond that we shall be obliged to resort to the Quartermaster's Department, &c.

I fear the Ordnance Department may not be immediately able to fill your requisitions for heavy ordnance. You must supply the deficiency by taking large guns from Port Hudson and Vicksburg. I think General Grant can also spare some from Island No. 10, as that place has now become unimportant. It is hoped that no time will be lost in occupying some point or points in Texas, as directed in my previous dispatches.

Very respectfully, your obedient servant,
H. W. HALLECK,
General-in-Chief.

WAR DEPARTMENT,
Washington City, August 24, 1863.

Brigadier-General SHEPLEY,
Military Governor of Louisiana:

GENERAL: You are authorized to grant passes to such persons as you see fit, to travel within or without the lines of the army. Wherever officers are appointed by you to discharge the functions of any civil office, thenceforth the authority of provost-marshals and assistant provost-marshals in relation to the same subject, under the Provost-Marshal-General, will be confined to persons connected with the army and to military and political offenses.

Yours, truly,
EDWIN M. STANTON,
Secretary of War.

WAR DEPARTMENT,
Washington City, August 24, 1863.

Brig. Gen. GEORGE F. SHEPLEY,
Military Governor of Louisiana:

GENERAL: Information has reached this Department that the loyal citizens of Louisiana desire to form a new State constitution, and to re-establish civil government in conformity with the Constitution and laws of the United States. To aid them in that purpose, the President directs the following instructions to be given you:

1. You will cause a registration to be made in each parish in the

---

* Original found in the files of Department of the Gulf.

State of Louisiana of all the loyal citizens of the United States in the parish, as soon as it can conveniently be done after the people are relieved from the presence of the rebel troops, and included within the lines occupied by the armies of the United States. This registration to include only such as shall have taken or shall take an oath of allegiance to the United States, accompanied by a declaration that the oath was taken freely and voluntarily for the purpose of reorganizing a State government in Louisiana loyal to the United States.

2. When this registration is made as far as practicable, you will order an election to be held on a day fixed, not less than thirty days from the date of the proclamation of such election, for delegates to a convention of the loyal people of the State, for the purpose of forming a constitution and re-establishing a civil government in the State, loyal to the United States, and in conformity with the Federal Constitution and laws, and for the passage of all needful ordinances and laws.

3. This convention will be called on a basis of representation which shall allow one delegate for every 2,500 of the loyal citizens aforesaid in each parish, as shown by the census of 1860, giving at least one delegate to each parish; and one delegate for each fraction of people in any parish over 1,250.

4. You are authorized to appoint the officers necessary to complete such registry, to preside at the elections, to receive, sort, count, and make returns to you of the votes and of the persons elected. The returns will be opened by you, and you will make proclamation of the persons elected, notifying them to appear at the time and place of holding the convention.

5. Further instructions will be given, if required, in the course of these proceedings.

EDWIN M. STANTON,·
Secretary of War.

SPECIAL ORDERS, }　　HDQRS. DEPARTMENT OF THE GULF,
No. 210. 　　　}　　　　　New Orleans, August 25, 1863.

* 　　 * 　　 * 　　 * 　　 *, 　　 * 　　 *

XVIII. The services of Brig. Gen. William H. Emory being required with troops preparing for field service, he is hereby relieved from the command of the Defenses of New Orleans, and will report to the commander of the Nineteenth Army Corps, by whom he will be assigned to a command.

Col. E. G. Beckwith, U. S. Army, is assigned to the command of the Defenses of New Orleans, and will relieve Brigadier-General Emory.*

* 　　 * 　　 * 　　 * 　　 * 　　 * 　　 *

By command of Major-General Banks:

RICH'D B. IRWIN, ·
Assistant Adjutant-General.

HDQRS. DEPT. OF THE GULF, NINETEENTH ARMY CORPS,
New Orleans, August 26, 1863.

Major-General HALLECK,
　　Commander-in-Chief, Washington, D. C.:

GENERAL: The steamer Hudson, arrived yesterday, brought duplicate copy of the order of August 6, received earlier by telegraph from

---

* Colonel Beckwith assumed command August 26.

General Grant, and also your letter of the 10th instant upon the sub-ject of the expedition into Texas.

I have made all possible exertions to get a sufficient force into the field to execute the order, but encounter serious difficulties in the prep-aration. General Ord's *corps d'armée* has not yet arrived. The last division will be here at the close of this week. The sickness and ab-sence of officers delays seriously our preparations for movement.

There is very great deficiency of transportation for movement by water, either by sea or the river. The river boats sent up with the nine-months' troops are detained above, and return slowly. By the Gulf we are able to move, after all possible exertions, but one-third of our forces at one time. This is a serious misfortune, as it costs us most valuable time and gives the enemy opportunity to anticipate our plans and concentrate his forces against us. I hope, however, to be able to execute your orders without further material delay.

The considerations embraced in your letter of the 10th, duplicate copies of which I have received, have been carefully weighed. To enter Texas from Alexandria or Shreveport would bring us at the nearest point, Hemphill, in Sabine County, or Marshall, in Harrison, due west of Alexandria and Shreveport, respectively. These points are accessible only by heavy marches, for which the troops are illy pre-pared at this season of the year; and the points occupied would attract but little attention; and if our purpose was to penetrate farther into the interior, they would become exposed to sudden attacks of the ene-my, and defensible only by a strong and permanent force of troops. The serious objection to moving on this line in the present condition of the forces of this department is the distance it carries us from New Or-leans—our base of operations necessarily—and the great difficulty and the length of time required to return, if the exigencies of the service should demand, which is quite possible. In the event of long absence, Johnston threatens us from the east. The enemy will concentrate be-tween Alexandria and Franklin, on the Teche, until our purpose is de-veloped. As soon as we move any distance, they will operate against the river and New Orleans. It is true that we could follow up such a movement by falling on their rear, but that would compel us to aban-don the position in Texas, or leave it exposed with but slender defenses and garrison.

This view is based, as you will see, upon the impossibility of moving even to Alexandria, at the present low stage of the rivers, by water, and the inability of the troops to accomplish extended marches.

A movement upon the Sabine accomplishes these objects: First, it executes your order by planting the flag at a prominent and command-ing position in Texas; secondly, it is accomplished by water; thirdly, it is safely made with a comparatively small force, and without attract-ing the attention of the enemy until it is done; fourthly, it enables us to move against Galveston from the interior, destroying at the same time all the naval and transport vessels of the State between the Sabine and the Colorado; fifthly, to occupy Galveston Island with a small force of 2,000 or 3,000 only, and to push on to Indianola on the Rio Grande, or to return to the Mississippi, as the exigencies of the service may re-quire. If the enemy moves in force upon New Orleans, we can return from Sabine or Galveston in such time and in such strength as to cut off his retreat by the bay on the Atchafalaya.

The advantage to be gained by the destruction of the rebel boats on the Sabine, in Galveston Bay, and on the Trinity and Brazos Rivers would be very great. This can be effected only by a movement upon

Galveston from the Sabine by Beaumont, Liberty, and Houston. If the enemy is in such strength as to defeat this, by occupying a position between the Sabine and Neches, we shall make available the fortifications of the enemy at Orange, and be supported by the navy, whose light boats can run up to Orange or to Beaumont.

If the season were different, the northern line would be doubtless preferable on many grounds.

With much respect, I am, general, your obedient servant,

N. P. BANKS,
Major-General, Commanding.

HDQRS. DEPT. OF THE GULF, NINETEENTH ARMY CORPS,
New Orleans, August 26, 1863.
Major-General HALLECK,
Commander-in-Chief, U. S. Army, Washington, D. C.:

GENERAL: Your dispatch of the 12th instant, referring to the necessity of operations in Texas rather than against Mobile, was received by the Morning Star, arriving yesterday. Independent of any political or diplomatic considerations, Texas presents an arena as important as any portion of the country. The occupation of Galveston, if it could be accomplished by a dispersion or capture of any considerable portion of Texas troops, and the destruction of the rebel steamers in the central rivers emptying in the Gulf, would cripple beyond recovery the rebel forces of the southwest. The rebellion in Louisiana is kept alive only by Texas.

A considerable land force is requisite to accomplish this result, even with the co-operation of the navy, and protect at the same time New Orleans. The enemy has been very active in gathering up conscripts. There are about 15,000 between Natchitoches and Franklin. Kirby Smith has moved the forces at Shreveport westward to the terminus of the railway from Shreveport to Marshall, where a convocation of the Trans-Mississippi Governors and commanders was held on the 15th instant. The Governor of Texas has ordered the conscription of all men between sixteen and sixty years of age. General Magruder is at Galveston, with from 5,000 to 7,000 men. This will constitute a pretty formidable army if concentrated against us in Texas, or if thrown against New Orleans.

My disposable force is not over 20,000, but the deficiencies of transportation make it impossible to move at once more than one-third of this force by water. I have twenty negro regiments, numbering 500 each, or about 10,000 in all, but they are just organized, armed, and uniformed, and are available only for labor at the present moment. If New Orleans is attacked or threatened, the defense is in a very great degree dependent upon the navy. In the absence of the army, they must make it impossible for them to cross the Mississippi, and obstruct the passage of Berwick Bay or the Atchafalaya by any considerable military force. It is necessary the naval force should be strengthened for this purpose and to protect the river. The light-draught gunboats of the upper fleet would be of the greatest service, and I hope they may be ordered down, for temporary service, at least.

I renew most earnestly my request for the dispatch of sea steamers from New York for temporary service in this department. If our enterprise is successful, as I am confident it will be, it ought to be followed up closely, and with power. It will give us great military as well as diplomatic advantages.

The severity of the conscription, as well as the success of our arms, has led to demoralization, and, in some instances, to open revolt in the rebel districts. Deserters bring in a report to-day that a collision occurred between disaffected Texans and the troops under command of General Mouton near New Iberia, which resulted in the death of General Mouton. This is probably incorrect, but it is repeated in so many forms and from so many sources that the fact of disaffection or revolt can hardly be questioned.

I hope to move by Monday, at furthest. The first object will be quickly attained.

I have the honor to be, with much respect, your obedient servant,

N. P. BANKS,
Major-General, Commanding.

SPECIAL ORDERS, } WAR DEPARTMENT, ADJT. GEN.'S OFFICE,
No. 382.   }   *Washington, August 26, 1863.*

*   *   *   *   *   *   *

XXI. Maj. Gen. E. O. C. Ord, U. S. Volunteers, will proceed to join his corps in the Department of the Gulf without delay.

By order of the Secretary of War:

E. D. TOWNSEND,
Assistant Adjutant-General.

SPECIAL ORDERS, }   HDQRS. NINETEENTH ARMY CORPS,
No. 9.   }   *Baton Rouge, La., August 28, 1863.*

I. Brig. Gen. W. H. Emory having reported to these headquarters, in pursuance of orders from headquarters department, is hereby assigned to the command of the Third Division.

*   *   *   *   *   *   *

VII. Brig. Gen. F. S. Nickerson is hereby assigned to the command of the First Brigade, Third Division.

VIII. The following-named batteries will be immediately reduced to four-gun batteries, as enumerated below, in order to render them efficient for field service: Company A, First U. S. Artillery, two Napoleons and two 3-inch rifle guns; Company F, First U. S. Artillery, four Napoleons; Eighteenth New York, four 20-pounder Parrotts. The Eighteenth New York Battery will have 8 horses to each gun and caisson.

*   *   *   *   *   *

By order of Major-General Franklin:

WICKHAM HOFFMAN,
Assistant Adjutant-General.

WASHINGTON, D. C.,
August 28, 1863.

Maj. Gen. N. P. BANKS,
    New Orleans:

GENERAL: Your dispatches of the 15th and 16th are just received.

The Navy Department has been requested to direct Admiral Porter to send to the Atchafalaya the gunboats asked for.

General Grant was directed to give all the re-enforcements in his power; this, of course, includes cavalry. Cavalry equipments have been ordered both to New Orleans and Vicksburg for mounting infantry. No re-enforcements of any kind can possibly be sent to you from the Northeastern States at present. You will not base any calculation upon receiving any for some time to come.

Be cautious in moving on the Rio Grande. It should be your effort to get, between the armies of Kirby Smith and Magruder. Should they unite and get between you and Grant, or between you and New Orleans, they may give you much trouble.

Your note in regard to reports in New Orleans respecting French intentions only confirms what we have already received from other sources. While observing every caution to give no cause of offense to that Government, it will be necessary to observe the movement of its fleet, and to be continually on your guard.

You will readily perceive the object of our immediately occupying at least some part of Texas.

Very respectfully, your obedient servant,
H. W. HALLECK,
General-in-Chief.

HEADQUARTERS DEPARTMENT OF THE GULF,
New Orleans, August 28, 1863.
Rear-Admiral DAVID D. PORTER,
Commanding Mississippi Squadron :

ADMIRAL : I find it necessary to request you most earnestly to give me the assistance of some of your gunboats to keep up uninterrupted communication on the Mississippi River, and assist in keeping marauding bands and detachments of the enemy at a distance.

There is great need of patrolling boats along the river, from the mouth of the Red River to College Point, and urgent need of light-draught armed boats for the lakes and bayous in the country west of the Mississippi.

With a few of your tin-clads in these waters, I should be able to operate during impending movements of importance with much more freedom from anxiety and vastly less risk to the public service than I can without them.

I hope it may be in your power to comply with my request, and that with the promptitude which has always characterized your movements.

General Andrews, commanding at Port Hudson, was instructed yesterday to send you information concerning the movements of the rebels on the right bank of the Mississippi. From subsequent information, their force in that quarter is supposed to be considerable.

Very respectfully, I am, admiral, your most obedient servant,
N. P. BANKS,
Major-General, Commanding.

HEADQUARTERS DEPARTMENT OF THE GULF,
New Orleans, August 28, 1863.
Maj. Gen. H. W. HALLECK,
Commander-in-Chief, U. S. Army:

GENERAL: The great want of an increased cavalry force in this department, and the hope of organizing a sufficient number of regiments here as soon as we can get control of a portion of the country adjacent, compels me to request that an efficient cavalry officer may be detailed to take charge of that arm of the service.

I desire to name Col. Horace B. Sargent, of the First Massachusetts Cavalry, for that position, and earnestly request that he may be assigned to that duty. His regiment is now attached to General Gregg's division. If it be an objection that he is in command of a regiment, then I would request, on public and on personal grounds, that his regiment also be ordered to this department. The regiment commanded by Colonel Lowell, and numbered Second and Third of the cavalry of that State, was raised for this department. But for my personal exertions, it would not and could not have been organized at the time it was placed in the field. The city government of Boston honored me by calling a special meeting, that I might make known to the members the necessity of a participation in the western military movements, and the importance to the country, as well to the State, that the East should at least assist in the opening of the Mississippi. They appropriated large sums of money to complete the regiments, and at once removed all questions of controversy between the State and city governments upon the subject of volunteers. The most prominent merchants of the State gave up their time, contributed large sums of money, and assisted in the personal labor of raising recruits and organizing the companies in order that there should be no unnecessary delay in its taking the field.

With the exception of the squadron raised in California, which was equipped and paid by the Boston merchants, the regiment was raised in the manner I have stated. It would have been a poetic as well as a patriotic conception if California and Massachusetts, the Pacific and Atlantic coasts, could have struck hands together with the central sons of the great west for the perpetual freedom of the Mississippi. It was in this spirit that the organization was urged, and for this purpose that it was completed.

It was no sooner placed in the field than it was ordered to a different department. The object in view, however, has been accomplished. The Mississippi is free. The East and the central West unfurled their standards together. The shouts of victory rose from the armies in commingling harmonies. It is forever to be regretted—it is a national grief—that the Pacific coast should not have been represented with the Central Valley of the Mississippi and the old States of the Atlantic in the triumph that makes an independent confederacy impossible, and places the great contest of all times in such light that all nations can now see its end. It is too late, perhaps, to do this now; but I ask, nevertheless, that that regiment may be ordered to the department for which it was intended.

Failing in that, I ask urgently that Colonel Sargent may be ordered here with his regiment. Failing in that, I respectfully request that Colonel Sargent may be assigned to this department, to assist in organizing our cavalry. We are not pressing unduly the Government for aid, I am sure. We are helping ourselves—organizing the blacks, conscripting the whites, building steamers, and applying all material to the support of the army—but we are justly entitled to assistance. What we ask is our own. We only want that to get more. To get cavalry we must have cavalry. This is the universal law of increase.

With great respect, I am, general, your obedient servant,

N. P. BANKS,
Major-General, Commanding.

HDQRS. DEPT. OF THE GULF, NINETEENTH ARMY CORPS,
New Orleans, August 28, 1863.
Major-General GRANT,
Commanding Department of the Tennessee:

GENERAL: Your dispatch of the 14th instant I received to-day. The absence of General Ord has not delayed the reorganization of the Thirteenth Corps. General Washburn has been most assiduous in his attention to the troops, and they are daily improving. I reviewed General Herron's, General Lee's, and General ———'s divisions last week, and to-morrow a review of the corps is ordered. Their appearance is in the highest degree gratifying.

I regret that you are unable to strengthen our cavalry, but appreciate the heavy demands made upon this arm of the service. The deficiency of cavalry is the great misfortune of our army organization. I hope to correct it here, but want it much as a means of increasing this force.

A deserter from Mobile came in to-day. He reports the greatest confusion there, and much conflict among the troops. They are ill-fed and greatly discontented. The naval officers report the capture of one or two prizes, loaded with beef and pork, from which they conclude there is a greater scarcity of provisions than has been reported. General Johnston is reported above Mobile, with his force greatly weakened by desertion.

The enemy, under Taylor, in Western Louisiana, is reported in movement toward the Mississippi, about 8,000 strong. They are likely to debouch between Plaquemine and Morganza, possibly to attack our forces in the La Fourche District.

To defend this department we need light-draught gunboats. It is impossible for us to intercept the enemy and cut off his retreat excepting by naval occupation of Berwick Bay and the Atchafalaya. This is the best method of protecting the river. I beg you to urge upon Admiral Porter the necessity of assisting us in this, if it be only temporarily.

The first movement in the expedition before referred to will probably take place by Wednesday.

I am, very truly, yours,

N. P. BANKS,
Major-General, Commanding.

HEADQUARTERS DEPARTMENT OF THE GULF,
New Orleans, August 28, 1863.
Col. E. G. BECKWITH,
Commanding Defenses, New Orleans:

COLONEL: The major-general commanding deems it advisable to send immediately to Thibodeauxville an additional brigade. He suggests Birge's brigade, of the Fourth Division, and wishes that the movement be made with all possible dispatch.

Well authenticated reports show that the enemy have largely strengthened their forces in the direction of Berwick Bay, and have crossed some troops through Grand Lake.

Very respectfully, &c.,

CHAS. P. STONE,
Brigadier-General, Chief of Staff.

HDQRS. DEPT. OF THE GULF, NINETEENTH ARMY CORPS,
New Orleans, August 29, 1863.
Maj. Gen. H. W. HALLECK,
    General-in-Chief, U. S. Army:

GENERAL: I have the honor to acknowledge the receipt of a letter from the Secretary of the Navy to the Secretary of War, inclosing a letter of Rear-Admiral Bailey, with the indorsement by the Secretary of War and your own indorsement, transmitting to me the papers, and ask-ing a report.*

In answer to these several communications, I have only to say that I have no knowledge whatever of the transactions to which it refers, and have never given, in any manner or form or at any time, any authority for such proceedings. I have read the letter of Rear-Admiral Bailey with utter astonishment. I should as soon have proposed to sell New Orleans to the French Government as to participate in any movement having in view the violation of the blockade of the rebel ports. The only order that I have ever issued upon the subject of trade is that of January 12, 1863, a copy of which is inclosed.† The seventh and eighth paragraphs only relate to the subject of trade, and both are limited to operations in the vicinity of New Orleans, having not the slightest pos-sible reference to any trade with the enemy, or to any interference with the blockade. As you will see, the seventh paragraph simply gives au-thority to the planters to bring the products of the country to the city of New Orleans, for sale here, and to receive in limited quantities plan-tation supplies, to be transported within the lines of the army. It was never intended nor understood that this gave authority for any other transactions than the local business of this part of the country. I ask your special attention to all the provisions of this general order.

Upon my arrival here, many propositions were made to me to partici-pate in speculative movements, having in view the purchase and trans-port of cotton out of the rebel lines by the sea. I have no reason to doubt that an extensive movement of this kind had been prepared; on the contrary, I have every reason to believe that extensive arrangements had been made, in which prominent men in both Governments were in-terested, to obtain supplies of cotton by running it out of rebel ports and throwing it into the blockading squadron, then to be claimed by the parties owning it, with the understanding that it was to be delivered to them. I saw at once that this was a violation of the blockade, which would as effectually destroy it as if the squadron had been withdrawn. The whole of this arrangement was known to the officers of the rebel Government, and at the very first attempt to put it in operation it would have been published to the world by the Government as an in-vasion of the obligations due to other States. I declined participation in any operation of this kind, without hesitation or qualification, against the very strongest persuasions, remonstrances, and defamation. Dr. Perkins, the agent of the Confederate Government, who had obtained a contract for purposes thus indicated, called upon me in person to ex-plain his object and the practicability of the plan, to which he stated he had obtained the assent of the rebel Government. He presented an original contract made for the purpose specified, copies of which I in-closed to the Secretary of State at the time, and copies of which are herewith inclosed.‡ I immediately said to Dr. Perkins that it was im-possible for me to enter into any arrangements of this character with him, to which he replied that it was not only possible, but that I would

---

* See of August 5, p. 669.   † See Series I, Vol. XV, pp. 643, 644,   ‡ Not found.

do it. He was interrupted in the midst of a sentence by a citizen occupying a high position, who accidentally was a party to the conversation, and who, by private movements, led him to drop the subject, and took him out of my hands. From that day I heard nothing of him until I met him at Alexandria, when that city was in our possession. He asked of me a pass for a gentleman of his acquaintance, engaged in the collection of cotton in that neighborhood. Letters which had fallen into my hands showed that this gentleman for whom Dr. Perkins solicited a pass had been regularly appointed by the Confederate Government for the collection of cotton for its own purposes. I promised to give him a pass, but for some cause or other unexplained he did not apply for it. Had he done so, he would have been arrested.

This is a full statement of my action upon the subject of exporting cotton from the rebel States. Early in my administration, I was induced to allow a few schooners to cross the lake without supplies, for the purpose of bringing in cotton from the other side to the city of New Orleans, to be sold here for the currency of the United States. This was done in but few instances, and long since was suspended entirely.

Messrs. Brott, Davis, and Shonn, in the early part of my administration were constant and persistent in their applications for privileges and favors of this kind. I invariably refused them, and, after a short time, they ceased altogether their applications to me, and soon suspended their business in this city by a dissolution of their copartnership. It is impossible for me to believe that this would have occurred had I granted the numerous and important privileges that were persistently demanded. I do not remember that any favor whatever was granted to them by me. Certainly the affair in which they were engaged was without my knowledge, never received my sanction in the slightest degree, and would have been instantly prohibited had it come within my knowledge.

To show the connection of the rebel Government and those interested in these operations, I ask your attention to the letter of Major-General Pemberton, commanding at Vicksburg, who demanded the surrender of a schooner laden with cotton, which had been captured by our troops near Ponchatoula, and brought into this city, upon the ground that it had been shipped by his permission, and upon a pass granted by him. Of course, I declined to comply with his request. The cotton was sold in this market, and the proceeds paid over to the quartermaster's department. The British consul made application for the restoration of the value of this cotton to a merchant in this city, upon the plea that he was a British subject. I answered that it had been captured by our troops in the enemy's country, and was a prize of war, and that any claim they had to the possession of the cotton must be made to the Government of the United States. Copies of these papers were transmitted to Washington at the time. In my communication to the Secretary of State, and also to the War Department, I stated very fully the effect of all these operations carried on by collusion with the Confederate Government. The results were invariably detrimental to the interests of this Government. It was easy for the Confederate Government, or any parties interested in its success, to purchase, of Englishmen or Frenchmen, vessels of war or privateers for the destruction of American commerce, and to pay for the same by cotton that was to be shipped from the rebel States through New Orleans. I saw immediately, when the subject was presented to me, that this would be the effect, and notified the Secretary of State of the propositions which had been made, of the consequences which I thought would ensue, and of my disinclination to give official sanction to any of them. This is a full statement of my official action upon this subject.

I have the honor to be, with much respect, your obedient servant,

N. P. BANKS,
Major-General, Commanding.

GENERAL ORDERS, }   HDQRS. DEPARTMENT OF THE GULF,
No. 64.   }   *New Orleans, August* 29, 1863.

I. Col. John S. Clark, Maj. B. Rush Plumly, and Col. George H. Hanks, are hereby appointed a commission to regulate the enrollment, recruiting, employment, and education of persons of color. All questions concerning the enlistment of troops for the Corps d'Afrique, the regulation of labor, or the government and education of negroes, will be referred to the decision of this commission, subject to the approval of the commanding general of the department.

II. No enlistments for the Corps d'Afrique will be authorized or permitted, except under regulations approved by this commission.

III. The provost-marshal-general will cause to be enrolled all ablebodied men of color, in accordance with the law of conscription, and such number as may be required for the military defense of the department, equally apportioned to the different parishes, will be enlisted for the military service, under such regulations as the commission may adopt. Certificates of exemption will be furnished to those not enlisted, protecting them from arrest or other interference, excepting for crime.

IV. Soldiers of the Corps d'Afrique will not be allowed to leave their camps, or to wander through the parishes, excepting upon written permission, or in the company of their officers.

V. Unemployed persons of color, vagrants, and camp loafers will be arrested and employed upon the public works by the provost-marshal's department, without other pay than their rations and clothing.

VI. Arrests of persons and seizures of property will not be made by colored soldiers, nor will they be charged with the custody of persons or property, excepting when under the command and accompanied by duly authorized officers.

VII. Any injury or wrong done to the family of any soldier on account of his being engaged in military service will be summarily punished.

VIII. As far as practicable, the labor of persons not adapted to military service will be provided in substitution for that of enlisted men.

IX. All regulations hitherto established for the government of negroes, not inconsistent herewith, will be enforced by the provost-marshals of the different parishes, under the direction of the provost-marshal-general.

By command of Major-General Banks:

RICH'D B. IRWIN,
Assistant Adjutant-General.

NEAR CLINTON,
August 30, 1863.

Major-General FRANKLIN:

SIR: Rumors are in circulation that the Federal officers at Port Hudson have declared their purpose to make a general devastating raid through this part of the country. I do not know whether such rumors are well founded, but think it quite likely that they are, and that the purpose, if it exists at all in the minds of the Federal officers at Port Hudson, has been provoked by the actions of some parties, some of whom are regular Confederate troops, while others are of irregular formation; both of which, however, are pursuing a very irregular system of warfare. I wish to say to you that this system of warfare is not approved here, but that we are powerless to prevent it. These guerrillas, or whatever you may term them, are regarded universally with as much disapprobation by us as by you, and our people suffer much from their lawlessness. But we have neither the means of prevention nor redress, and remonstrance is of no avail. There is no Confederate officer of any considerable grade here, or near here, to control and direct the action of these men. I assure you that the universal sense of the people here is bitterly opposed to this system of irregular warfare. It is not only irregular as a system of warfare, but, as most necessarily the case, degenerates into a system of indiscriminate plunder, of which our people are victims to an extent which would surprise you.

But what can we do with a sparse population, without arms, quietly pursuing the occupations of a peaceful life? We can only deprecate what we cannot prevent.

No doubt the Federal officers, exasperated by the harassing of these irregular squads, entertain the conviction that they are upheld and sustained by the popular feeling and favor. I assure you that such is not the fact; directly the reverse is true.

While we are willing to see the war carried forward by legitimate means, and in accordance with the rules of civilized and decent warfare, and to bear the consequences which such a state of hostilities may carry along with it, we do not see the propriety of that system of action which we have occasion to deplore as much as yourself. It would be a harsh measure, general, not to say a cruel one, to visit an unoffending and helpless people with widespread and cruel devastation. While it would not remedy the evil, it would be, in fact, as it would appear to the world, an act of frenzied retribution upon the innocent, who deprecate the acts of the guilty as much as you can. Such an act would be as injudicious for your interest as it would be unjust to us, upon whom this plan of desolating vengeance would fall.

Not one of these guerrillas would be reached or affected by any devastation which you could inflict, nor would they care if you should lay the entire country in ashes. This must be evident, since men who had any interest at stake would not wantonly invite destruction as these men do. The people here take no part in these raids, and are bitterly opposed to the whole thing.

If the Federal officers have seriously entertained such a purpose, let me entreat you that it be reconsidered, and that a quiet and peaceable population shall not be made to suffer useless injury for what they cannot prevent.

I should like to have a personal interview with you, if I could be permitted to enter and depart from your lines without taking the oath of allegiance to your Government. There is much I could say to you which I do not wish to write.

I have been in the Confederate army, as you probably know, but am now disconnected with it, and expect to remain so. At all events, if I ever fight you, it will be in fair, open, and manly battle, unless a savage system of devastation should drive me to a desperation which I hope never to reach.

I have the honor to be, very respectfully, yours,

PRESTON POND, Jr.

[Indorsements.]

HEADQUARTERS DEPARTMENT OF THE GULF,
New Orleans, September 7, 1863.

Mr. Preston Pond, jr., in the name of the people of Clinton, protests against the irregular warfare pursued by men he calls guerrillas. He does not seem to be opposed to the war for the overthrow of the Government, at least his letter does not show that. Now, it is not material to the United States whether the war against its authority is pursued by regular or irregular courses or parties. Whoever they are, or in whatever form they appear, they must be overthrown, and the country that supports them put in resistance to them, or else disabled from providing them with supplies. It is very natural, when the commanding officer at Port Hudson finds that his position is threatened, and his men captured by men pursuing irregular courses of war, as is stated, that he should determine to make an invasion of the country where they are, and from which they get their supplies.

The remedy is for the people of this section to re-establish the government and to take arms for the defense of their own homes and their own property. Whenever they do that, the Government of the United States will not only assist them, but will give them the power, which Mr. Pond now thinks they do not possess, of accomplishing this result.

Until the inhabitants of the rebel districts assume this position, they must expect that the Federal troops will not only not protect, but they may look for the destruction of their property by them. It is impossible that we can allow officers and soldiers to be murdered by the men haunting these districts under the plea that the people of the country disapprove of the manner in which they wage war.

It is not known at these headquarters whether such a movement is in contemplation or not. It is not probable, however; but if there should be cause for it, I do not see that the commanding general can forbid its execution.

N. P. BANKS,
Major-General, Commanding.

HEADQUARTERS DEPARTMENT OF THE GULF,
New Orleans, September 7, [1863.]

Respectfully referred to commanding officer Port Hudson. Please see within indorsement.

By command of Major-General Banks:

G. NORMAN LIEBER,
Acting Assistant Adjutant-General.

HEADQUARTERS UNITED STATES FORCES,
Port Hudson, La., October 8, 1863.

Respectfully returned. I know nothing of the matter referred to by Mr. Pond. He has probably paid too much attention to unauthorized threats.

GEORGE L. ANDREWS,
Brigadier-General of Volunteers, Commanding Corps d'Afrique.

GENERAL ORDERS, }   HDQRS. DEPARTMENT OF THE GULF,
No. 65.   }   *New Orleans, August 31, 1863.*

I. The court of the city of New Orleans, styled the provost court, exercising the functions of a military court, and assuming jurisdiction over the persons of officers and soldiers of the United States, Judge

Hughes presiding, not having been established or recognized by the military authorities of this department, and not being consistent with the proper government of the army, nor conducted according to the principle of military law, is hereby abolished.

II. The provost-marshal-general is hereby directed to take possession forthwith of the records of said court, and to retain them in safe custody until further orders. He will, by himself or his deputies, dispose of all cases of arrest existing upon the receipt of this order, and take such measures as may be necessary to maintain the public peace.

III. Any officer or soldier of the army of the United States charged with any offense against the law or the public peace, and any other person charged with the violation of military orders, will, when arrested, be held for trial and sentence before the military court established by General Orders, No. 45, unless otherwise ordered.

By command of Major-General Banks:

RICH'D B. IRWIN,
Assistant Adjutant-General.

---

*Abstract from return of the Department of the Gulf, Maj. Gen. N. P. Banks, U. S. Army,
commanding, for the month of August, 1863. · ·*

Command.	Present for duty.		Aggregate present.	Aggregate present and absent.	Pieces of artillery.		Remarks.
	Officers.	Men.			Heavy.	Field.	
General headquarters	31	96	131	238	....	......	New Orleans, La.
Thirteenth Army Corps (Washburn)....	778	13,934	20,632	32,532	8	68	Carrollton. La.
Nineteenth Army Corps (Franklin).....	337	8,881	11,877	16,911	....	34	Baton Rouge, La.
Port Hudson, La. (Andrews)............	215	5,212	6,616	7,212	....	......	
Baton Rouge, La., Post of	54	1,574	2,789	3,517	....	......	
Defenses of New Orleans (Beckwith)...	270	7,333	9,594	11,940	....	......	
District of Key West and Tortugas (Woodbury).	35	717	1,053	1,096	....	......	'
District of Pensacola (Holbrook) .٠......	22	474	604	660	....	......	
Grand total	1,742	38,221	53,296	74,106	8	102	
Grand total according to tri-monthly return for August 31.	1,662	35,250	50,980	73,967	....	*121	

Organization of the Department of the Gulf, Maj. Gen. Nathaniel P. Banks, U. S. Army, commanding, August 31, 1863.[1]

GENERAL HEADQUARTERS.

Headquarters Troops, Capt. Richard W. Francis.

ENGINEER BRIGADE.[‡]

Maj. DAVID C. HOUSTON.

1st Engineers, Corps d'Afrique, Col. Justin Hodge.
2d Engineers, Corps d'Afrique, Col. John C. Cobb.
3d Engineers, Corps d'Afrique, Maj. George D. Robinson.

---

* Not classified.

† During the months of July and August, the following regiments (nine-months' men) left the Department for muster-out of service, viz: The Twenty-third, Twenty-fifth, Twenty-sixth, and Twenty-eighth Connecticut; the Twenty-first, Twenty-second, Twenty-fourth, Twenty-sixth, and Twenty-eighth Maine; the Forty-second, Forty-seventh, Forty-eighth, Forty-ninth, Fiftieth, Fifty-second, and Fifty-third Massachusetts; the Fifteenth and Sixteenth New Hampshire, and the One hundred and seventy-seventh New York.

‡ At Brashear City and New Orleans,

DEFENSES OF NEW ORLEANS.*

Col. EDWARD G. BECKWITH.

24th Connecticut, Col. Samuel M. Mansfield.
1st Louisiana Cavalry, Lieut. Col. Harai Robinson.
3d Massachusetts Cavalry, Company A, Lieut. Henry D. Pope.
12th Massachusetts Battery, Capt. Jacob Miller.
13th Massachusetts Battery, Lieut. Ellis L. Motte.
15th Massachusetts Battery, Lieut. James W. Kirke.
31st Massachusetts (three companies), Capt. Eliot Bridgman.
14th New York Cavalry (battalion), Capt. George Brenning.
176th New York, Maj. Morgan Morgan, jr.
1st Lousiana Native Guard Artillery (two companies), Capt. Loren Rygaard.
1st Infantry, Corps d'Afrique (detachment).
2d Infantry, Corps d'Afrique, Lieut. Col. Alfred G. Hall.
4th Infantry, Corps d'Afrique, Col. Charles W. Drew.
14th Infantry, Corps d'Afrique, Col. Mardon W. Plumly.
4th Division, 19th Army Corps, Col. Edward G. Beckwith.

PORT HUDSON.

Brig. Gen. GEORGE L. ANDREWS.†

1st Infantry, Corps d'Afrique, Lieut. Col. Chauncey J. Bassett.
3d Infantry, Corps d'Afrique, Capt. Charles W. Blake.
1st Michigan Heavy Artillery, Lieut. Col. Edward Bacon.
21st New York Battery, Capt. James Barnes.
5th U. S. Artillery, Battery G, Lieut. Jacob B. Rawles.
2d Vermont Battery, Capt. Pythagoras E. Holcomb.
3d Massachusetts Cavalry (ten companies), Lieut. Col. Lorenzo D. Sargent.

Ullmann's brigade, Corps d'Afrique.‡

Col. SAMUEL B. JONES.

6th Infantry, Maj. George Bishop.
7th Infantry, Maj. Cornelius F. Mowers.
8th Infantry, Lieut. Col. William S. Mudgett.
9th Infantry, Lieut. Col. Isaac S. Bangs, jr.
10th Infantry, Lieut. Col. Ladislas L. Zulavsky.

BATON ROUGE.§

1st Indiana Heavy Artillery, Col. John A. Keith.
2d Louisiana (detachment).
174th New York, Lieut. Col. Benjamin F. Gott.
4th Wisconsin Cavalry (ten companies), Maj. Webster P. Moore,

DISTRICT OF KEY WEST AND TORTUGAS.

Brig. Gen. DANIEL P. WOODBURY.

47th Pennsylvania (five companies), Col. Tilghman H. Good.
47th Pennsylvania (five companies), Lieut. Col. George W. Alexander.

DISTRICT OF PENSACOLA.

Col. WILLIAM C. HOLBROOK.

2d U. S. Artillery, Battery H, Capt. Frank H. Larned.
2d U. S. Artillery, Battery K, Capt. Harvey A. Allen.
7th Vermont, Capt. Salmon Dutton.

---

*Colonel Beckwith assumed command August 26, vice Emory, taking the field.
Troops at Bonnet Carré, Forts Bienvenue, Jackson, Macomb, Pike, and Saint Philip,
in the La Fourche District, at New Orleans, and on Ship Island. The Sixth and
Seventh Louisiana Regiments (sixty-days' men) mustered in and out in July and
August.

†Assigned to command of the post and the Corps d'Afrique July 9, 1863, by Special
Orders, No. 165, Headquarters Department of the Gulf.

‡ Brig. Gen. Daniel Ullmann was ordered, July 10, to assume command of this
brigade, but Col. John F. Appleton appears in command July 31, and Jones on
August 31.

§ Commanding officer of post not indicated on returns. The First and Third Divisions, Thirteenth Army Corps, were also in and about Baton Rouge.

THIRTEENTH ARMY CORPS.*

Maj. Gen. CADWALLADER C. WASHBURN.†

GENERAL HEADQUARTERS.

1st U. S. Infantry, Maj. Maurice Maloney.
Independent Company (Kentucky) Pioneer Corps, Capt. William F. Patterson.

FIRST DIVISION.

Brig. Gen. WILLIAM P. BENTON.

First Brigade.	*Third Brigade.*
Col. DAVID SHUNK.	Col. THOMAS W. BENNETT.
33d Illinois, Capt. Ira Moore.	118th Illinois, Capt. Arthur W. Marsh.
99th Illinois, Maj. Edwin A. Crandall.	49th Indiana, Lieut. George W. Riddle.
8th Indiana, Lieut. Col. Charles S. Parrish.	69th Indiana, Capt. Robert K. Collins.
18th Indiana, Col. Henry D. Washburn.	7th Kentucky, Col. Reuben May.
1st Indiana Battery, Lieut. Jacob Main.	120th Ohio, Maj. Willard Slocum.
	7th Michigan Battery, Capt. Charles H. Lanphere.

Second Brigade.	*Fourth Brigade.*‡
Col. SAMUEL L. GLASGOW..	Col. DANIEL W. LINDSEY.
21st Iowa, Lieut. Col. Salue G. Van Anda.	54th Indiana, Col. Fielding Mansfield.
22d Iowa, Maj. Ephraim G. White.	22d Kentucky, Lieut. Col. George W. Monroe.
23d Iowa, Lieut. Col. Charles J. Clark.	16th Ohio, Maj. Milton Mills.
11th Wisconsin, Lieut. Col. Luther H. Whittlesey.	42d Ohio, Col. Lionel A. Sheldon.
2d Illinois Light Artillery, Battery A, Capt. Peter Davidson.	114th Ohio, Lieut. Col. John H. Kelly.
	1st Wisconsin Battery, Lieut. Oscar F. Nutting.

SECOND DIVISION.

Maj. Gen. FRANCIS J. HERRON.

First Brigade.§	*Second Brigade.*‖
Col. WILLIAM McE. DYE.	Col. HENRY M. DAY.
37th Illinois, Col. [John] Charles Black.	91st Illinois, Col. Henry M. Day.
26th Indiana, Col. John G. Clark.	94th Illinois, Col. John McNulta.
20th Iowa, Col. William McE. Dye.	19th Iowa, Lieut. Col. Daniel Kent.
34th Iowa, Col. George W. Clark.	20th Wisconsin, Col. Henry Bertram.
38th Iowa, Maj. Charles Chadwick.	1st Missouri Light Artillery, Battery B, Capt. Martin Welfley.
1st Missouri Light Artillery, Battery E, Lieut. Joseph B. Atwater.	
1st Missouri Light Artillery, Battery F, Capt. Joseph Foust.	

---

* The Thirteenth Army Corps was transferred from Vicksburg, Miss., to Carrollton, La., August 10–26. On August 7, the Army of the Frontier was assigned to the corps as Herron's division, and the Fourth Division (formerly of Sixteenth Army Corps) was transferred to Seventeenth Army Corps. On August 14, the corps was reorganized, so that the Ninth and Fourteenth Divisions became the First Division ; Herron's division became the Second; the Twelfth the Third, and the Tenth the Fourth.

† Commanding in the temporary absence of Maj. Gen. E. O. C. Ord.

‡ Consolidated with Third Brigade, Brig. Gen. Michael K. Lawler to command, September 23, 1863.

§ Brig. Gen. William Vandever on detached service.

‖ Brig. Gen. William W. Orme on sick leave.

THIRD DIVISION.

Brig. Gen. ALBERT L. LEE.

First Brigade.

Brig. Gen. GEORGE F. McGINNIS.

11th Indiana, Col. Daniel Macauley.
24th Indiana, Col. William T. Spicely.
34th Indiana, Capt. Robert G. Morrison.
46th Indiana, Col. Thomas H. Bringhurst.
29th Wisconsin, Lieut. Col. William A. Greene.
2d Illinois Light Artillery, Battery E, Lieut. Emil Steger.
16th Ohio Battery, Lieut. R. P. Twist.

Second Brigade.

Col. JAMES R. SLACK.

87th Illinois, Col. John E. Whiting.
47th Indiana, Lieut. Col. John A. McLaughlin.
24th Iowa, Lieut. Col. John Q. Wilds.
28th Iowa, Col. John Connell.
56th Ohio, Col. William H. Raynor.
1st Missouri Light Artillery, Battery A, Lieut. Charles M. Callahan.
2d Ohio Battery, Lieut. A. Beach.

FOURTH DIVISION.

Brig. Gen. MICHAEL K. LAWLER.*

First Brigade. †

Col. THOMAS J. LUCAS.

16th Indiana, Maj. Robert Conover.
60th Indiana, Capt. Augustus Goelzer.
67th Indiana, Maj. Francis A. Sears.
83d Ohio, Col. Frederick W. Moore.
96th Ohio, Lieut. Col. Albert H. Brown.
23d Wisconsin, Capt. James M. Bull.
17th Ohio Battery, Lieut. Wm. Hunt, jr.

Second Brigade.

Lieut. Col. JOHN COWAN.

77th Illinois, Lieut. Col. L. R. Webb.
97th Illinois, Lieut. Col. L. D. Martin.
130th Illinois, Lieut. Col. J. H. Matheny.
19th Kentucky, Capt. Wm. T. Cummins.
48th Ohio, Capt. Isaac L. Tice.
Chicago Mercantile Battery, Capt. Patrick H. White.

CAVALRY BRIGADE.‡

Col. JOHN J. MUDD.

2d Illinois (seven companies), Maj. Hugh Fullerton.
3d Illinois (five companies), Capt. Robert H. Carnahan.
15th Illinois, Company C, Capt. Joseph Adams.
36th Illinois, Company A, Capt. George A. Willis.
1st Indiana, Company C, Capt. James L. Carey.
4th Indiana, Company C, Capt. Andrew P. Gallagher.
6th Missouri (seven companies), Maj. Bacon Montgomery.

NINETEENTH ARMY CORPS.§

Maj. Gen. WILLIAM B. FRANKLIN.

FIRST DIVISION. ‖

Brig. Gen. GODFREY WEITZEL.

First Brigade.

Col. GEORGE M. LOVE.

2d Louisiana, Maj. Alfred Hodsdon.
30th Massachusetts, Lieut. Col. William W. Bullock.
116th New York, Capt. John M. Sizer.

161st New York, Lieut. Col. William B. Kinsey.
174th New York, Lieut. Robert S. Vandenburgh.

---

* Commanding since August 15, *vice* Brig. Gen. A. J. Smith, assigned August 5 to command of the District of Columbus. Special Orders, No. 43, Headquarters Thirteenth Army Corps.
† Brig. Gen. S. G. Burbridge on sick leave.
‡ Organized August 14; detachment of Second Wisconsin Cavalry ordered same day to join the regiment, in Seventeenth Army Corps.
§ This corps was reorganized under Special Orders, No. 200, Headquarters Department of the Gulf, of August 15, Major-General Franklin being assigned to command. He assumed command August 20.
‖ On July 15, Major-General Augur (going on sick leave) was superseded in command of the old First Division by Brigadier-General Weitzel. On August 15, Weitzel was assigned to the division as reorganized; Col. Jacob Sharpe reported as in command of it August 20, and Weitzel does not appear to have assumed command earlier than September 1. The Third Brigade at Camp Hubbard, Thibodeaux; remainder of the division at Baton Rouge.

Second Brigade.*

Col. JAMES SMITH.

31st Massachusetts (seven companies), Lieut. Col. W. S. B. Hopkins.
38th Massachusetts, Maj. Chas. F. Allen.

128th New York, Capt. Francis S. Keese.
156th New York, Capt. Alfred Neafie.
175th New York, Capt. Chas. McCarthey.

Third (or Reserve) Brigade.†

Col. ROBERT B. MERRITT.

12th Connecticut, Lieut. Col. Frank H. Peck.
75th New York, Capt. Henry B. Fitch.
114th New York, Col. Samuel R. Per Lee.
160th New York, Lieut. Col. John B. Van Petten.
8th Vermont, Lieut. Col. Charles Dillingham.

Artillery.

Capt. EDMUND C. BAINBRIDGE.

1st Maine Battery, Capt. Albert W. Bradbury.
18th New York Battery, Lieut. George G. Curtiss.
1st United States, Battery A, Capt. Edmund C. Bainbridge.

THIRD DIVISION.‡

Brig. Gen. JAMES W. McMILLAN.

First (Nickerson's) Brigade.

Col. THOMAS W. PORTER.§

14th Maine, Col. Thomas W. Porter.
110th New York, Col. Clinton H. Sage.
162d New York, Col. Lewis Benedict.
165th New York, Capt. Felix Agnus.

Second (McMillan's) Brigade.

Col. ALPHA B. FARR.

26th Massachusetts, Maj. E. S. Clark.
8th New Hampshire, Capt. J. J. Ladd.
133d New York, Capt. James K. Fuller.
173d New York, Col. Lewis M. Peck.

Artillery.

4th Massachusetts Battery, Capt. George G. Trull.
1st United States, Battery F, Lieut. Hardman P. Norris.
1st Vermont Battery, Lieut. Edward Rice.

FOURTH DIVISION.‖

Col. EDWARD G. BECKWITH.

First Brigade.

Col. HENRY W. BIRGE.

13th Connecticut, Capt. A. Comstock.
90th New York (eight companies), Lieut. Col. Nelson Shaurman.
91st New York, Capt. John B. Collins.
131st New York, Maj. Willie M. Rexford.
159th New York, Col. E. L. Molineux.

Second Brigade.

Col. THOMAS W. CAHILL.

9th Connecticut, Lieut. Col. Richard Fitz Gibbons.
1st Louisiana, Col. William O. Fiske.
12th Maine, Col. William K. Kimball.
13th Maine, Col. Henry Rust, jr.
15th Maine, Col. Isaac Dyer.

---

*Formerly Third Brigade, Third Division.

†Formerly Second Brigade, First Division. On August 15 it was assigned as the Reserve Brigade to the Defenses of New Orleans, but was, on August 28, restored to the First Division.

‡Designated by Special Orders, No. 200, as Emory's division, Brig. Gen. Frank S. Nickerson being assigned temporarily to the command. McMillan assumed command August 29, and was relieved by Brig. Gen. William H. Emory September 4. Troops at and about Baton Rouge, La.

§ Brigadier-General Nickerson on detached service.

‖ Designated by Special Orders, No. 200, as Grover's division, Brigadier-General Emory being assigned temporarily to command. Colonel Beckwith assigned to command August 25. General Grover on leave of absence July 30 to October 2, when, upon reporting for duty, he was detached from the Fourth Division, and ordered to assume command of the Third Division. The First Brigade (formerly the Third), at Brashear City and Thibodeaux, and along the New Orleans, Opelousas and Great Western Railroad; the Second Brigade (formerly Second Brigade, Second Division) and the artillery, at New Orleans.

Artillery.

25th New York Battery, Capt. John A. Grow.
26th New York Battery, Capt. George W. Fox.
2d United States, Battery C, Lieut. Theodore Bradley.

CAVALRY.

3d Massachusetts (ten companies), Lieut. Col. Lorenzo D. Sargent (Port Hudson),
1st Texas (four companies), Col. Edmund J. Davis (New Orleans).
4th Wisconsin (ten companies), Maj. Webster P. Moore (Baton Rouge).

RESERVE ARTILLERY.*

2d Massachusetts Battery, Capt. Ormand F. Nims.
6th Massachusetts Battery, Capt. William W. Carruth.
1st United States, Battery L, Lieut. Franck E. Taylor.

Abstract from return of the District of Northeastern Louisiana, August 31, 1863, Department of the Tennessee, Brig. Gen. John P. Hawkins, U. S. Army, commanding, for August, 1863.

Command.	Present for duty.		Aggregate present.	Aggregate present and absent.	Remarks.
	Officers.	Men.			
District staff	4	....	4	4	Goodrich's Landing, La.
1st Arkansas, *a. d.*, Col. William F. Wood	21	521	641	661	Do.
8th Louisiana, *a. d.*, Col. Hiram Scofield ..	26	408	641	698	Milliken's Bend. La.*
10th Louisiana, *a. d.*, Col. Frederick M. Crandal.	21	654	755	803	Goodrich's Landing.
11th Louisiana, *a. d.*, Col. Edwin W. Chamberlain.	19	335	524	594	Transylvania, La.
1st Mississippi, *a. d.*, Lieut. Col. A. Watson Webber.	12	332	477	505	Goodrich's Landing.
3d Mississippi, *a. d.*, Lieut. Col. Orlando C. Risdon.	20	314	508	544	Milliken's Bend. *
Total	123	2,564	3,550	3,809	

* Under command of Brig. Gen. J. L. Kiernan.

OFFICE CHIEF OF ARTILLERY, DEPT. OF THE GULF,
New Orleans, September 2, 1863.

Captain SHUNK,
Chief of Ordnance:

The following-named batteries of the Thirteenth Army Corps are designated to take the field:

Captain Welfley's battery.—Six 12-pounders—four guns, old pattern, and two howitzers.

First Indiana Battery.—Six 12-pounders—four Napoleon and two howitzers.

First Missouri Battery.—One Napoleon 12-pounder, two howitzers, 12-pounders, and three 6-pounder smooth-bores.

Mercantile Battery.—Four rebel imitation Parrotts, caliber 2.90, and two Rodman rifles, caliber 3.

---

* At New Orleans, La.

Captain Foust, Company F, First Missouri.—Four English rifles, caliber 3.50, two 10-pounder Parrotts, caliber 2.90.

Foster's First Wisconsin Battery.—Four 30-pounder Parrotts.

If possible, I wish Company F, First Missouri, to turn in the two Parrotts, and take in their place two 12-pounder howitzers.

I have requested that the ordnance officer of the corps be directed to report to you, and state how much ammunition he will require from you to make up 200 rounds per gun, with the amount packed in the ammunition chests.

Very respectfully, your obedient servant,

RICHARD ARNOLD,
Brigadier-General, Chief of Artillery.

SPECIAL ORDERS, }   HDQRS. NINETEENTH ARMY CORPS,
No. 12.   }   *New Orleans, September 2, 1863.*

I. The First Brigade, First Division, with the light batteries already designated, will embark immediately on the transports now lying at Baton Rouge, as follows:

Steamer General Banks, One hundred and sixty-first New York Volunteers, and horses of officers entitled to draw forage; steamboat Arago, Thirtieth Massachusetts and Second Louisiana Volunteers; steamboat Iberville, One hundred and sixteenth New York and One hundred and seventy-fourth New York Volunteers.

At New Orleans, the troops on board the Arago and Iberville will be transferred to the transport Alexander.

Steamer Pocahontas, Third Division, First Brigade, One hundred and sixty-fifth New York Volunteers, and Battery F, First Artillery; steamer North America, Fourteenth Maine, One hundred and sixty-second New York, and One hundred and tenth New York.

Horses of officers entitled to draw forage, on steamer Belvidere; second Brigade, steamer Crescent, Twenty-sixth Massachusetts Volunteers and First Texas Cavalry; steamer Continental, Eighth New Hampshire, One hundred and thirty-third New York, and One hundred and seventy-third New York.

Horses of officers entitled to draw forage, on board Belvidere; steamer Exact, First Vermont Battery.

II. The troops will carry three days' cooked rations in their haversacks. Ten days' additional rations will be embarked on each boat, of which three days' rations must be easily accessible.

*   *   *   *   *   *

By order of Major-General Franklin:

WICKHAM HOFFMAN,
Assistant Adjutant-General.

SPECIAL ORDERS, }   HDQRS. THIRTEENTH ARMY CORPS,
No. 57.   }   *Carrollton, La., September 2, 1863.*

*   *   *   *   *   *

XVIII. The First and Second Brigades, First Division, will be prepared to embark from here on Friday morning by sunrise. Transports will receive them near the railroad depot. They will take one day's cooked rations in their haversacks. The wagons belonging to these two brigades will load early to-morrow with ten days' rations, and proceed to

New Orleans. They will there cross the river to Algiers. The rations will be loaded upon the cars to-morrow night, so as not to delay the troops on Friday morning. The wagons belonging to the two brigades will remain at Algiers for the return train, when they will be forwarded.

The First Wisconsin Battery will proceed to New Orleans to-morrow with twelve days' rations, two days' being cooked, and will cross to Algiers and load their guns on the cars to-morrow night, the horses on Friday morning. They will take 500 rounds of ammunition for their Parrott guns, and wagons enough to haul ten days' rations and their ammunition. Each brigade will take wagons at the rate of one wagon to 80 men.

*   *   *   *   ‡

By order of Maj. Gen. C. C. Washburn:

WALTER B. SCATES,
Lieutenant-Colonel, and Assistant Adjutant-General.

WASHINGTON, D. C.,
September 3, 1863.

Major-General BANKS,
New Orleans:

GENERAL: Your two dispatches of the 26th ultimo are just received. The sea-going steamers asked for some days ago were immediately ordered by General Meigs. The Navy Department was also requested to send you light-draught gunboats from the Upper Mississippi. General Grant has been directed to give you all the aid in his power. I have suggested to the Quartermaster's Department to ship horses to you down the Mississippi River.

In regard to absence of officers, of which you complain, the rule established here is to give no extensions unless especially recommended by the general commanding the department. In many cases you give leaves, with permission to apply to the Adjutant-General for an extension. This is not deemed a recommendation by you. I call your attention to this matter, as officers come north with a leave of twenty days, under the expectation of an extension. Hereafter no extensions will be given without your written recommendation. Too many officers are absent from their commands on private business. At this time all able to do duty should be in the field.

Very respectfully, your obedient servant,

H. W. HALLECK,
General-in-Chief.

HEADQUARTERS DEPARTMENT OF THE GULF,
New Orleans, September 3, 1863.

Major-General WASHBURN,
Commanding Thirteenth Army Corps, Carrollton, La.:

GENERAL: The major-general commanding the department desires that you dispatch as rapidly as practicable the First Division of the Thirteenth Army Corps to the point selected as a camping ground by Major [William H.] Morgan, of your staff, in the neighborhood of Brashear City. The troops will move in the light marching order directed in recent orders, and fully prepared for continued field service.

The major-general commanding also desires that the heavy battery, verbally ordered yesterday, shall immediately proceed to Brashear City, where it will remain for the present under the immediate orders of the commander of the Defenses of New Orleans. The movement of this battery had better precede that of the First Division.

The commander of the First Division, on his arrival at the camping ground selected, will put himself in communication with the command-ers at Brashear City and Thibodeauxville, but will not be considered as forming any portion of the forces of the Defenses of New Orleans, ex-cepting in case of emergency, when, of course, he would take such steps as the good of the service might seem to require.

The First Division will be regularly reported to you as commander of the corps.

Very respectfully, I am, general, your most obedient servant,

CHAS. P. STONE,
Brigadier-General, and Chief of Staff.

GENERAL ORDERS, }   HDQRS. DEPARTMENT OF THE GULF,
No. 66.   }   *New Orleans, September 3, 1863.*

I. The trade of the city of New Orleans with Cairo, Saint Louis, and the cities and towns of the Upper Mississippi, the Missouri, and Ohio Rivers is hereby declared free from any military restriction whatever. The trade of the Mississippi at intermediate points within the Depart-ment of the Gulf is held subject only to such limitations as may be necessary to prevent the supply of provisions and munitions of war to the enemies of the country.

II. The products of the country intended for general market may be brought into the military posts on the line of the Mississippi within the Department of the Gulf without restraint, viz, at New Orleans, Car-rollton, Donaldsonville, Baton Rouge, and Port Hudson.

III. Officers and soldiers of the army are hereby directed to transfer to the Hon. B. F. Flanders, agent of the Treasury Department of the United States, or his deputies, taking receipts therefor, all captured, abandoned, or sequestrated property not required for military purposes, in accordance with General Orders, No. 88, of the Department of War.

IV. The military court of this department is hereby invested with exclusive jurisdiction in all cases of extortion, excessive or unreasonable charges, or unjust treatment of officers and soldiers of the United States army by proprietors or agents of steamboats or other vessels in the navigation of the Mississippi or the Gulf; and upon conviction of any of the offenses herein described, the offender shall be held liable to fine, imprisonment, or confiscation of property.

By command of Major-General Banks:

G. NORMAN LIEBER,
Acting Assistant Adjutant-General.

U. S. S. CONESTOGA,
Mississippi River, September 4, 1863.

Maj. Gen. N. P. BANKS,
Commanding Department of the Gulf:

SIR: I have the honor to acknowledge the receipt of your communi-cation of the 28th ultimo. Admiral Porter, to whom I have forwarded it, is expected down daily, and I have no doubt will be able to afford you all the assistance necessary. The great obstacle at present is the bar at the junction of the Mississippi and Red Rivers, upon which there is not now more than 3 feet; but we can overcome this by lightening our vessels.

The admiral contemplates a secret expedition up the Red and Black Rivers, which will cut off any rebel transports destined for the Atchafalaya. This river is now divided into districts, under the control of regular naval officers. Lieut. Commander J. P. Foster commands the second division, within which lies the threatened district you mention. There are at present a considerable number of gunboats in the vicinity of Red River, so that a diversion of the enemy in that vicinity should be productive of little harm.

Our intelligence from Arkansas represents Price as ready to give battle behind intrenchments on the Bayou Meto, some 15 miles from Little Rock. His force is generally estimated at about 18,000 men and twenty-six pieces of artillery. His army, however, is not in a good fighting condition, his men constantly deserting. Our largely superior force of cavalry, under Davidson, harasses them extremely. General Steele is very confident of the final result, and was moving for the attack some three days ago. His force numbers about the same as the enemy, but greatly superior in artillery. Steele's base of operations is Devall's Bluff, on the White River, about 45 miles from Little Rock, his supplies being brought up the river about 120 miles. This service at present employs four light-draught gunboats. It would give more expedition were all communications addressed directly to Admiral Porter or the commanding officer at Vicksburg.

I have the honor to be, most respectfully, your obedient servant,

THOS. O. SELFRIDGE,
Lieutenant-Commander, U. S. Navy.

HEADQUARTERS DEPARTMENT OF THE GULF,
New Orleans, September 4, 1863.

Maj. Gen. F. J. HERRON,
Comdg. Second Div., Thirteenth Army Corps, Carrollton:

GENERAL: It is officially reported by the commander of the gunboat Neosho that a rebel force, numbering at least 900 men, is now at Morgan's Bend, on the Mississippi River, establishing four batteries of field artillery, for the purpose of annoying our transports.

You will please proceed with your division to a point some 10 miles below that occupied by the enemy, and sending thence notice of your presence for co-operation to the naval commander now watching that position as to the best means of capturing or destroying the rebel force there. You will carry this out with all possible dispatch.

Having accomplished this object, you will return to your present position, and report to the commander of the Thirteenth Army Corps for duty, reporting the result of your expedition to these headquarters.

[CHAS. P. STONE,]
Brigadier-General, and Chief of Staff.

HEADQUARTERS DEPARTMENT OF THE GULF,
New Orleans, September 5, 1863.

Maj. Gen. H. W. HALLECK,
General-in-Chief, U. S. Army, Washington, D. C.:

GENERAL: The inclosed memoranda embrace the chief points of information which have been received from Mississippi in relation to affairs of the Confederate States. They are reliable, so far as the information of the leading men at Mobile and in the State of Mississippi is concerned.

I have the honor to be, with much respect, your obedient servant,

N. P. BANKS,
Major-General, Commanding.

[Inclosure.]

A well-informed person, direct from Richmond, says that by the 1st of October six iron-clads will leave England, one of them a very powerful vessel, carrying 1,400 men, and of a formidable armament. Their guns and officers are in France, and will be put aboard at a point off the coast agreed upon.

He says Jefferson Davis is broken and desponding, but braving it out; that he feels his waning popularity, and is much affected by the desertions in the army.

Strong symptoms of disaffection manifested in the North Carolina regiments, and in that State especially.

Two thousand negroes are at work on the fortifications of Mobile. No soldiers there except city volunteers and militia. They rely entirely on Johnston's army.

Hardee has the command of the troops at Morton, Johnston devoting himself to the department generally.

Martial law very rigorous in Mobile and on our seaboard towns.

Confederate money rapidly depreciating there, at Richmond, and all along the route. People at Richmond sanguine of French armed intervention, but the newspapers asking only recognition and rejecting all idea of armed intervention.

Report says that Alabama Legislature, now sitting, has recommended the immediate employment of negro troops.

· Mr. Benjamin has very lately stated to a friend of mine that there would be peace in a few months. He bases his calculation chiefly on the disappointment of the Western States in regard to the river trade, to political reaction, &c.

It has leaked. out, likewise, that the late invasion of Pennsylvania was not a measure of Lee's or Davis', but had been insisted on by the Congress in recent session.

HEADQUARTERS DEFENSES OF NEW ORLEANS,
September 5, 1863.

Maj. Gen. N. P. BANKS,
Commanding, &c.:

GENERAL: I have the honor to acknowledge the receipt of your letter of this date, informing me that General Grant will send a regiment of cavalry into this department for service with the expedition, and that he will also send a full division of infantry to New Orleans, for the purpose of occupation and defense of the city during the absence of the main body of the army, and that this division will be placed under my command, and at such point between this city and Port Hudson as may be necessary; and you desire an expression of my views in regard to landing the infantry division, as has been suggested, in the vicinity of Bayou Sara, and marching it thence by the rear of Port Hudson to Baton Rouge, at once sweeping off the guerrilla bands in that neighborhood, and depriving them of military supplies, upon which they now subsist.

The suggestion, it seems to me, is a good one, and entirely practicable for this march; but, to make it effective for the indicated purpose, it should be accompanied by two light batteries, and a considerable cavalry force to scour the country considerably to the 'eastward of the direct road between Bayou Sara and Baton Rouge. Such cattle as may be found should be driven in for the use of the army, and receipts given by the chief commissary with the division to owners for them. To remove other stores would, however desirable, not be practicable to any considerable extent, perhaps, for want of transportation.

Should this division itself not be provided with the necessary artillery and cavalry forces to land with it, might not those at Port Hudson be used and returned from Baton Rouge at the end of the march?

An equally important march might, perhaps, be made, if for any reason this one should not be practicable or necessary, by landing near the same point, but on the opposite bank of the river, and sweeping it clean of guerrillas down to Plaquemine or Donaldsonville. The force in this case would, being for the most part near the river, be able to use boats for transporting its supplies.

I am, very respectfully, your most obedient servant,
E. G. BECKWITH,
Colonel, Commanding.

DEPARTMENT OF STATE,
Washington, September 5, 1863.
Hon. E. M. STANTON,
Secretary of War:
SIR: I have the honor to inclose a copy of a dispatch dated July 21 last, from L. Pierce, jr., esq., United States consul at Matamoras, and to request that the information given therein respecting the arrangements made by the rebel General Bee for obtaining cotton, to be sent to Europe in English vessels from that port, may be made known to Maj. Gen. N. P. Banks.

I have the honor to be, sir, your obedient servant,
WILLIAM H. SEWARD.

[Indorsement.]

SEPTEMBER 10, 1863.
Respectfully referred to Major-General Banks for his information.
H. W. HALLECK,
General-in-Chief.

[Inclosure.]

U. S. CONSULATE,
Matamoras, July 21, 1863.
The SECRETARY OF STATE,
Washington, D. C.:
SIR: On the 15th instant, the rebel General Bee, commanding Western Frontier of Texas, issued an order prohibiting any more cotton crossing the Rio Grande, at the same time calling a meeting of the owners, or agents of the owners, of all the cotton in Brownsville or its vicinity.

At the meeting, General Bee stated to the merchants that the Confederate Government had a large stock of cotton on the way out, but as it would not reach the frontier for some sixty days, and it was very necessary that they should have cotton to send to Europe immediately, that he would borrow one fifth of all that was in the vicinity of the crossing. The Texas merchants have submitted, and I believe that some of the foreigners have also.

To carry this cotton to Europe, the British steamers Sea Queen and Sir William Peel and the sailing ship Gladiator (also British) have been engaged, and are now loading.

All of these vessels were consigned to rebel agents in this city, and the larger part of their cargoes have been sent forward for rebel consumption. A great many army blankets, which were brought here in these steamers, are also stored here to be sent forward in the fall.

I am, sir, very respectfully, your most obedient servant,

L. PIERCE, JR.,
U. S. Consul.

WAR DEPARTMENT,
Washington City, September 7, 1863.

Hon. WM. H. SEWARD,
Secretary of State:

SIR: I have the honor to acknowledge the receipt of your note of the 5th instant, inclosing a copy of a dispatch, dated 21st of July last, from the United States consul at Matamoras, respecting arrangements made by the rebel General Bee for obtaining cotton to be sent to Europe in English vessels from that port, and to advise you that the same has been referred to the General-in-Chief.

I have the honor to be, sir, your obedient servant,

[EDWIN M. STANTON,]
Secretary of War.

WASHINGTON, D. C.,
September 8, 1863.

Major-General BANKS,
New Orleans:

GENERAL: Your letter of August 28, respecting your application for additional cavalry force, is just received. I have already informed you that General Grant would give you all the cavalry he could possibly spare, and that 8,000 horse equipments had been ordered to you and to him to mount infantry. It was also suggested to the Quartermaster's Department to send you as many horses as possible down the Mississippi River. General Meigs has gone west, and will give the matter his personal attention.

I have already stated to you that it would be impossible to send you any cavalry very soon from the north. The great losses in that arm in recent battles, and by the discharge of two-years' and nine-months' men, and the great difficulty in procuring cavalry recruits, places this matter beyond question or discussion. Requisitions are received almost simultaneously with yours from nearly every other department for additional cavalry, some 20,000 or 30,000 being urgently asked for, it being alleged in many cases that operations cannot be continued without them. Instead of 30,000, I have not a single man to supply these demands. You do not seem fully to appreciate the fact, general, that the loss in your army by expiration of terms of service has not been as great in proportion to numbers as in some others. As volunteering had virtually ceased, the only mode of supplying this loss was by the draft, which, as yet, has been almost entirely unproductive. We are, therefore, much weaker here than we were at this time last year, while Lee's army is probably as strong as before the battle of Gettysburg. Instead of sending any troops away, I have been strongly urged to bring re-enforcements from the Mississippi to protect Maryland and Pennsylvania from a threatened attack. I hope, however, that the necessity may not arise.

In regard to Colonel Lowell's regiment, I need simply to mention the fact that it is the only one we have for scouts and pickets in front of · Washington. If taken away, there is none to replace it.

I hope that in a few weeks more the draft will put a different face upon matters here.

Very respectfully, your obedient servant,

H. W. HALLECK,
General-in-Chief.

WASHINGTON, D. C.,
September 8, 1863.

Brig. Gen. JAMES H. CARLETON,
Santa Fé, N. Mex. :

GENERAL: Your letter of the 16th, asking for an additional regiment of cavalry, is just received.

You have already been informed that no more troops of any kind can now be sent to your department, and that you are authorized by the Secretary of War to raise in that department such number of troops, infantry or mounted, as you think the necessity of the service requires.

In this great war, when every resource of the Government must be employed upon the most important points, the commanders of frontier departments, remote from the more active theater of operations, must make every exertion to economize material and men. Everything possible should be spared to strike the enemy at the vital points.

The number of troops now stationed in the frontier departments and Territories is much larger than in time of peace, and yet nearly all the commanders are asking for large re-enforcements; both are entirely beyond the reach of the enemy; no extraordinary circumstances are known which require additional troops. New Mexico and Arizona, being near Texas, may be partial exceptions. But at this time there can be no reasonable apprehension of any invasion by the rebels from that State. They are likely to have sufficient occupation at home.

Under existing circumstances, I must strongly urge you to economize your force, and to limit your demands as much as possible. I am fully aware of the importance of exploring and opening up for mining and settlement that vast region of country that separates the Mississippi Valley from the Pacific States. But at the present time we have not the means of doing this. All the military forces we can possibly raise are required to operate against the rebel masses which are threatening the very existence of our Government. It is true that we have had great successes within the last two months, but the reduction of our armies by expiration of terms of service has prevented us from fully profiting by these successes. To detach more troops from these reduced armies, at present, to operate in the frontier Territories, and thus risk all we have gained, would expose the Government to severe and well-merited censure.

Very respectfully, your obedient servant,

H. W. HALLECK,
General-in-Chief.

OFFICE CHIEF OF ARTILLERY,
New Orleans, September 8, 1863.

[The following is a] list of batteries of artillery of the Nineteenth Army Corps, to accompany the expedition now organizing in this city:

Reserve Brigade.—Company A, First Artillery, two Napoleons and two 3-inch rifles.

First Division.—Company L, First Artillery, four Napoleons and two 10-pounder Parrotts; Sixth Massachusetts, four Napoleons; First Maine, four Napoleons.

Third Division.—Company F, First Artillery, four Napoleons; Fourth Massachusetts, four Napoleons and two 3-inch rifles; First Vermont, six 3-inch rifles.

Reserve Artillery.—First Indiana Artillery, four 30-pounder and four 20-pounder Parrotts; Eighteenth New York Battery, four 20-pounder Parrotts; Second Massachusetts (Horse Artillery), six 6-pounder rifles.

Recapitulation.—Twenty-two Napoleon guns, four 3-inch rifles, six 6-pounder rifles, two 10-pounder Parrotts, eight 20-pounder Parrotts, four 30-pounder Parrotts.

DEPT. OF THE GULF, U. S. MILITARY TELEGRAPH,
New Orleans, September 8, 1863.

Maj. Gen. N. P. BANKS,
Comdg. Department of the Gulf, New Orleans, La.:

GENERAL: I have the honor to report that since January 15, 1863, there has been constructed in this department 108 miles of telegraph line; of this, 14 miles, built for camp purposes before Port Hudson at the commencement of the siege, has been removed, leaving 94 miles of new line.

From December 15, 1862, to January 15, 1863, there was constructed 57 miles; including this, there has been constructed in this department, since you assumed command, 151 miles. In addition to the above, there has been 93 miles of old and partially destroyed lines repaired, amounting in the aggregate to 244 miles constructed, repaired, and working.

During this time the old lines have been thoroughly repaired, and insulation and instruments made more perfect.

The whole length of line in the department is 510 miles, connecting Carrollton, Bonnet Carré, Donaldsonville, Baton Rouge, Port Hudson, Pass Manchac, Lakeport, Fort Macomb, Fort Pike, Algiers, Quarantine, Fort Jackson, Southwest Pass, Boutte, La Fourche, Thibodeaux, Bayou Bœuf, Brashear City, and New Orleans. Twenty-three operators and assistants are employed in the above offices.

The city lines of New Orleans are repaired, in good condition, and working satisfactorily. The cost of working these lines has been decreased, and will be rendered still less expensive to the city as soon as practicable.

I have received 70 miles of new wire and 4,000 insulators; old material has been used for much of the construction and repairs.

New instruments have been furnished by the quartermaster's department only sufficient to open new offices and guard against accident or the destruction often caused by atmospheric electricity in this latitude.

I am, most respectfully, your obedient servant,

CHAS. S. BULKLEY,
Capt., and Asst. Quartermaster, Asst. Supt. U. S. Mil. Telegraph.

HEADQUARTERS DEPARTMENT OF THE GULF,
New Orleans, September 9, 1863.
Maj. Gen. H. W. HALLECK,
Commanding U. S. Army, Washington, D. C.:

GENERAL: I have the honor to state in reply to your letter of the — August, 1863, noticing my letter of August 16 ultimo, that the assignment of Major-General Franklin to the command of the Nineteenth Army Corps was intended to be only a temporary assignment, during the time of service of other army corps in this department, and especially during the present expedition. He is expected to have the staff of a major-general commanding a division in the field, with such additional staff officers as I can assign to him.

Very respectfully, I am, general, your most obedient servant,
N. P. BANKS,
Major-General, Commanding.

SPECIAL ORDERS, }   HDQRS. DEPARTMENT OF THE GULF,
No. 227.   }   *New Orleans, September 11, 1863.*

I. Brig. Gen. A. L. Lee, U. S. Volunteers, is hereby appointed chief of cavalry for the Department of the Gulf, and will report without delay in person at these headquarters.

*   *   *   *

By command of Major-General Banks:
G. NORMAN LIEBER,
Acting Assistant Adjutant-General.

SPECIAL ORDERS, }   HDQRS. OF ARMY, ADJT. GEN.'S OFFICE,
No. 409.   }   *Washington, September 11, 1863.*

*   *   *   *   *   *

III. Brig. Gen. P. St. George Cooke, U. S. Army, will report in person for duty to Major-General Banks, commanding Department of the Gulf.

By command of Major-General Halleck:
E. D. TOWNSEND,
Assistant Adjutant-General.

HDQRS. SECOND DIVISION, THIRTEENTH ARMY CORPS,
Morgan's Bend, La., September 12, 1863.
Brigadier-General STONE,
Chief of Staff, Department of the Gulf:

GENERAL: I am directed by the major-general commanding to forward you the inclosed letter, which has been received at these headquarters.

The general desires me to say that a portion of the division is at Morgan's Ferry, skirmishing with the enemy on the other side of the Atchafalaya River, while the balance of the command is on the road between here and the ferry.

· General Herron is still confined to his bed by sickness, and General Vandever is in immediate command of the troops.

· I am, general, very respectfully, your obedient servant,

J. D. BREWSTER,
Captain, and Aide-de-Camp.

[Indorsement.]

The inclosure was a letter from Colonel Claiborne, which is in the possession of the major-general commanding.

C. P. S. [STONE.]

HDQRS. 3D DIV., 19TH ARMY CORPS, *September* 14, 1863.

Captain HOFFMAN, *Asst. Adjt. Gen., Nineteenth Army Corps:*

It is my imperative duty to call attention to the condition of the part of this division now under my command, and to request that your inspector-general be sent here to look for himself.

It is utterly unfit to take the field as it now is, and something should be done at once to restore its numbers and efficiency.

The artillery horses, cooped up for the last twelve days aboard transports, are unable to drag the pieces 50 yards at a trot, and, unless allowed time to rest and recuperate, must all be lost. The battery wagon and forge and one section of guns of the First Vermont are at Baton Rouge, as before reported to you. The horses are foot-sore, and need shoeing, and it is essential that this forge and wagon should join its battery.

The First Brigade is in a state of destitution and demoralization; first, from the long-continued absence of any permanent brigade commander, and, secondly, from the absence of so many of the officers and men; thirdly, this brigade was not allowed any rest after the fall of Port Hudson, but was placed on picket duty in rear of Port Hudson, thence transferred directly on crowded transports, without change of clothing, and both officers and men are necessarily filthy beyond endurance, and utterly broken down; and all of the regiments, excepting the Twenty-sixth Massachusetts, are more or less in the same condition.

Two of the regiments, the One hundred and tenth and One hundred and sixty-second New York, are infected with the swamp fever, and are incapable at this time of any effort.

I desire that the general commanding will visit this division, or send some responsible inspector to see its condition. It is beyond my power to restore it except by time, and more power than I now possess to compel the return of absent officers and men, and the proper control over the material of the artillery.

I inclose a report of my acting chief of artillery,* and as soon as the division inspector can make out his reports, they will be forwarded.

I have the honor to be, your obedient servant,

[W. H. EMORY,]
Brigadier-General, Commanding.

HDQRS. DEPT. OF THE GULF, NINETEENTH ARMY CORPS,
New Orleans, September 15, 1863.

[Major-General HALLECK:]

GENERAL: The military operations require more troops. Assuming that we have sufficient force to cope with the enemy in Louisiana, if the

---
* Not found.

forces in Texas and Louisiana combine, they outnumber us largely. Our only hope of success is in preventing their junction.

As it is impracticable to obtain troops from the east, as far as possible the force on the Upper Mississippi, both naval and military, should be sent to New Orleans to strengthen offensive operations and to defend against attacks of the enemy.

Johnston is near Pascagoula, at Hall's Mills, in expectation of attack on Mobile, with 26,000 men; Taylor, between Pattersonville and Vermillion, with 15,000, and Magruder at Sabine Pass with such force as could be brought from Galveston. If we move east or we st toward Mobile or Galveston, one or the other of these forces threaten New Orleans in our absence.

The increase of the naval force is indispensable for the proper defense of the city on the lake (Pontchartrain) east by light draught gunboats; on the Atchafalaya by light-draught boats; and the mouth of the river, at the forts, by one or two iron-clads.

This increase of naval force, very little in itself, ought to be furnished without delay. It requires altogether but six or eight light-draught boats and two iron-clads. The upper river will furnish the first without difficulty.

It is reported to us to-day (the 21st), when I finish this letter, that the enemy is evacuating Little Rock and retreating toward Alexandria. If so, it is with a view of concentrating all the forces west of the river in Texas. Our forces should be directed to the same point without loss of time, either overland or by the river. I beg you will press upon the Government the necessity of strengthening the forces, temporarily at least, in Louisiana, until we can prevent the junction of the enemy's forces.

The temptations to contraband trade ought to be laid before the Government. All other considerations that require presentation are so well known to you that I need not refer to them. The chief object is to strengthen the naval and land forces for our temporary but most important duties.

Everything is pleasant and promising in the city. The concert in the square last evening was one of the most remarkable demonstrations of the season. There were as many young men in attendance as heretofore there have been women and children. The change was universally remarked.

September 22, 7 a. m.—The capture of another tow-boat, the Leviathan, at the Southwest Pass last night, shows the necessity of increasing the number of light gunboats in the lower river. This is the third or fourth of these invaluable boats that have been captured by the enemy for the want of some protection of this kind.

I desire it to be said that I believe these captures are arranged by collusion with parties in this city, who place these boats in positions where they can be captured when the enemy is ready for the descent, and that they are paid for by cotton passed through the hands of the officers of the Government. When the United States comes to a settlement with foreign nations for the pirate ships which are destroying American commerce, I believe it will turn out that they are paid for in this manner.

I am, very truly, yours, &c.,

N. P. BANKS,
Major-General, Commanding.

HDQRS. THIRD DIVISION, NINETEENTH ARMY CORPS,
Algiers, La., September 15, 1863.
Capt. WICKHAM HOFFMAN,
　　Assistant Adjutant-General:

　I must again call the attention of the general commanding to the gross neglect on the part of the commissaries assigned to the brigades of my division.

　My troops are positively suffering from their carelessness, inattention, and almost constant absence. They give as a pretext orders from the chief commissary of the army in the field, or of the corps, and in one case the commissary of the First Brigade produced such orders, a copy of which I have already sent you.

　Yesterday Battery F, First Artillery, was obliged to send to town to get rations. I respectfully suggest that the usages and the convenience of the service be followed, and that no orders be given to the commissaries and quartermasters of this division, unless they go through these headquarters. In this same connection I wish to state that one of these brigades has had no issue of fresh meat since the 23d of August.

　I am, very respectfully, your obedient servant,
　　　　　　　　　　　　　　[W. H. EMORY,]
　　　　　　　　　　Brigadier-General, Commanding.

HDQRS. THIRD DIVISION, NINETEENTH ARMY CORPS,
Camp at Algiers, September 15, 1863.
General McMILLAN,
　　Commanding Second Brigade:

　In accordance with instructions from corps headquarters, the commanding general directs that you move your brigade to-morrow morning to Brashear. The train will be ready for the baggage at 8 a. m., and for the troops shortly afterward.

　I am, very respectfully, your obedient servant,
　　　　　　　　　　　　　　[D. S. WALKER,]
　　　　　　　　　　Assistant Adjutant-General.

GENERAL ORDERS, ⎱　　HDQRS. DEPARTMENT OF THE GULF,
　　No. 68.　　 ⎰　　　*New Orleans, September 15, 1863.*

The mounted forces of this department will constitute a cavalry division, under command of Brig. Gen. A. L. Lee, chief of cavalry. He is charged with the efficiency and discipline of that arm of the service, and his orders will be respected and obeyed accordingly.

All regiments and detachments serving with other commands will be considered as but temporarily detached, and will, in due course, promptly forward to him reports required by existing orders and regulations, in addition to those required by their immediate commanding officers.

By command of Major-General Banks:
　　　　　　　　　　　　G. NORMAN LIEBER,
　　　　　　　　Acting Assistant Adjutant-General.

SPECIAL ORDERS, ⎱ HDQRS. THIRD DIV., 19TH ARMY CORPS,
   No. 53. ⎰ *Camp at Algiers, September* 16, 1863.

I. The Second Brigade, as directed last night, and the First Vermon Battery, will move at once to Brashear City by the Opelousas Railroad. The train is now ready to receive them.

II. The First Brigade and Battery F, First Artillery, will move to morrow at 7 a. m. over the same road and to the same place.

*   *   *   *   *   *

By command of Brigadier-General Emory :
                    [D. S. WALKER,]
                    Assistant Adjutant-General.

GENERAL ORDERS, ⎱ HDQRS. DEPARTMENT OF THE GULF,
   No. 69. ⎰ *New Orleans, September* 16, 1863.

During the temporary absence of Brig. Gen. James Bowen, the powers of provost-marshal-general of the department will be exercised by Col E. G. Beckwith, commanding Defenses of New Orleans.

By command of Major-General Banks :
                G. NORMAN LIEBER,
             Acting Assistant Adjutant-General.

SPECIAL ORDERS, ⎱ HDQRS. DEPARTMENT OF THE GULF,
   No. 231. ⎰ *New Orleans, September* 16, 1863.

*   *   *   *   *   *   *

XVIII. The first twenty regiments of infantry of the Corps d'Afrique will be at once organized by the commander of the corps into two divis- ions, of two brigades each.*

*   *   *   *   *

By command of Major-General Banks :
                G. NORMAN LIEBER,
             Acting Assistant Adjutant-General.

HDQRS. DEPT. OF THE GULF, NINETEENTH ARMY CORPS,
             New Orleans, September 17, 1863.

Capt. ROBERT T. DUNHAM,
    Assistant Adjutant-General :

CAPTAIN : You will please proceed to perform the following duty :

You will take the first steamer bound up the Mississippi River, and communicate as soon as practicable with Rear-Admiral Porter, U. S. Navy, commanding Mississippi Squadron, and with Maj. Gen. U. S. Grant, commanding the Department of the Tennessee.

To the former, you will represent the solicitude which I experience in view of the partially defenseless condition of the Lower Mississippi, which has not an iron-clad boat between New Orleans and the sea, nor a light-draught gunboat, either iron-clad or tin-clad, to patrol or to co- operate with the land forces in any expedition which the army may be required to set on foot.

---

* See organization of the Corps d'Afrique, under date of September 22, p. 733.

You will carry to him my earnest request that, if in his power, two or more good iron-clad gunboats and at least three or four of his tin-clads may be sent here for co-operation. At this moment, such an addition to our forces would be invaluable.

To Major-General Grant, you will present regards, and my hope that he is rapidly being restored from his late injuries, and will express my hope that he may be able to strengthen us promptly by the re-enforcement of cavalry and infantry proposed by him for this quarter, and will call his attention to the fact that my information, recently received, seems to show that the enemy are evacuating Southwestern and Central Arkansas, to strengthen Texas against any movement we may make against that section. In case such information should prove correct, a large force of our troops would be set free, under Generals Steele and Davidson, a large portion of which troops I would hope might be rapidly forwarded here to counterbalance the enemy's re-enforcements from that quarter against us.

If these views should coincide with those of Major-General Grant, you will please point out to him the importance of collecting a large amount of river transportation, to be ready at a convenient point of the river, for the rapid transfer from such point to this.

You will also request Major-General Grant to send to this place any heavy rifled guns, such as Parrott 100-pounders, which he can spare, for the more efficient armament of the forts on the various approaches to this city.

You will please be as expeditious as possible, and having properly represented these matters to the two commanders, and possessed yourself fully of their ideas upon them, will return, and report in person at these headquarters.

You will please report by letter during your absence, by every safe opportunity, giving account of your progress.

Very respectfully, I am, captain, your obedient servant,

N. P. BANKS,
Major-General, Commanding.

HEADQUARTERS DEPARTMENT OF NEW MEXICO,
Santa Fé, N. Mex., September 19, 1863.

Col. CHRISTOPHER CARSON,
Comdg. Expedition against the Navajoes, Fort Canby, N. Mex.:

COLONEL: By custom of service, no officer who is not competent to order a general court-martial can order a court of inquiry, excepting in the case of an enlisted man, when a colonel commanding a regiment may order the court (De Hart, 272, 273). You will, therefore, annul all proceedings of any such court in the case of Lieutenant Hodt.

Non-commissioned officers must not be reduced to the ranks within your regiment by any person's order but your own. The Regulations must be your guide in all such matters, or the discipline of your regiment will be bad.

I recommend, unless you can produce the same results by more gentle measures, that you seize 6 of the principal men of the Zuñi Indians, and hold them as hostages until all Navajoes in and near their village are given up, and all stolen stock surrendered. You will assure the Zuñi Indians that if I hear that they help or harbor Navajoes, or steal stock from any white men, or injure the person of any white man, I will as certainly destroy their village as that the sun shines.

I have received the report of your operations in the vicinity of Cañon de Chelly. If any Indians desire to give themselves up, they will be received and sent to Fort Wingate, with a request that from that post they be sent to Los Pinos. No Navajo Indians of either sex, or of any age, will be retained at Fort Canby, as servants, or in any capacity whatever; all must go to the Bosque Redondo.

You are right in believing that I do not wish to have those destroyed who are willing to come in. Nor will you permit an Indian prisoner once fairly in our custody to be killed, unless he be endeavoring to make his escape. There is to be no other alternative but this: say to them, "Go to the Bosque Redondo, or we will pursue and destroy you. We will not make peace with you on any other terms. You have deceived us too often, and robbed and murdered our people too long, to trust you again at large in your own country. This war shall be pursued against you if it takes years, now that we have begun, until you cease to exist or move. There can be no other talk on the subject." As winter approaches, you will have better luck. I send your reports to Washington.

I am, colonel, very respectfully, your obedient servant,
JAMES H. CARLETON,
Brigadier-General, Commanding.

HEADQUARTERS DEPARTMENT OF THE GULF,
New Orleans, September 19, 1863. .

Maj. Gen. WILLIAM B. FRANKLIN,
Brashear City:

SIR: Lieut. Col. J. G. Chandler is announced as chief quartermaster of the troops in the field during the existing campaign. He will continue to perform the duties of chief quartermaster Nineteenth Army Corps.

By command of Major-General Banks:
[G. NORMAN LIEBER,
Acting Assistant Adjutant-General.

HEADQUARTERS DEPARTMENT OF THE GULF,
New Orleans, September 20, 1863.

M. FAUCONNET, *Consul of France, New Orleans:*

SIR: I have the honor to acknowledge the receipt of your note of this day, requesting that the corvette Colbert, commanded by Captain Youbert, may be permitted to pass the quarantine station without detention. Receiving, as entirely correct, your statement that the vessel is without contagious disease, I am, nevertheless, obliged to decline compliance with your request. The preservation of the health of New Orleans is, in a military point of view, one of the most imperative duties, and this requires a strict observance of the quarantine regulations, and it is the more binding upon me now to insist upon their observance, and I have declined to English, Spanish, and American vessels permission to pass except upon full compliance therewith.

With sincere regret that I find myself unable to comply with your request, I remain, with high consideration, your obedient servant,
N. P. BANKS,
Major-General, Commanding.

HDQRS. SECOND DIVISION, THIRTEENTH ARMY CORPS,
Morganza, La., September 20, 1863.

Brig. Gen. CHARLES P. STONE,
Chief of Staff, New Orleans:

GENERAL: Matters in this section have not changed much in the past five days. General Green still holds his position at Morgan's Ferry, on the west side of the Atchafalaya, and has been re-enforced by the detachments from the direction of Opelousas, and a regiment from above Simsport on Red River. He has between 3,800 and 4,000 men for duty. I have been making every effort to draw the whole or a portion of his force to this side of the river, but without avail. Their location is such as to make it a difficult matter to cross the river in front of them; still, I think it could be done.

All detachments have been withdrawn from the east side of the Atchafalaya, excepting a small picket at mouth of Red River.

We keep up a continual skirmishing with them at the ferry, and yesterday, in an attempt to drive a party of my men from their position, the rebs were pretty severely handled.

Price has evacuated Little Rock, and the rumor among the secesh here is that his force is on its way to Alexandria.

Do you desire me to take more active steps against this force of Green's, or merely to carry out your last order and hold them where they are? Please advise me by telegraph. I brought the command away with only the clothing they had on, and they need a change badly. Will your plans justify my sending to Carrollton for it?

I sent down to-day some prisoners, and will send to-morrow, to the chief commissary, 200 head of fine cattle.

In connection with Captain [James P.] Foster, of the navy, I have arranged a plan to capture the band of marauders that make their headquarters at Bayou Sara.

I am, general, very respectfully, your obedient servant,

F. J. HERRON,
Major-General.

HEADQUARTERS DEPARTMENT OF THE GULF,
New Orleans, September 21, 1863.

Maj. Gen. H. W. HALLECK,
General-in-Chief, U. S. Army, Washington, D. C.:

GENERAL: I have the honor to report that the Nineteenth Army Corps crossed Berwick Bay on Saturday, and will have advanced as far as Franklin to-morrow.

The Thirteenth Army Corps, under General Franklin, is at Brashear, awaiting transportation. Owing to the low stage of water, we have been able to get but two steamers around to Brashear, and the crossing has been very slow in consequence of this deficiency. It adds another proof of the absolute necessity of light-draught boats for the service of the Government in the waters of this department.

Four or five boats, sent around to assist the troops in crossing, are aground on their way out.

Major-General Herron, with one division of the Thirteenth Army Corps, is between the Atchafalaya and Morganza, holding in check General Green, with about 3,000 of the rebel force now on the west bank of the Atchafalaya.

Reports reach us this evening that Price has evacuated Little Rock, and is moving toward Alexandria. If this prove to be true, it will show that they intend to concentrate their forces west of the Mississippi, in Texas.

It is greatly to be regretted that we failed to make a landing at Sabine City, which would have placed our forces in the very center of the circle upon which they operate, in such time and in such strength as to make their concentration impossible.

We shall endeavor, without loss of time, to compensate for this failure by the land movement. The troops are in good condition, improving in health and spirit.

I hope that orders may be given to Admiral Porter to furnish us some light-draught boats, now in the upper river. By the occupation of the Teche country, and the dispersion of the enemy in that quarter, we cover completely the west bank of the Mississippi, both from the rebel forces and the assaults of guerrillas.

The only danger to New Orleans must come from Johnston's army on the east. Two or three light-draught gunboats should be placed in Lake Pontchartrain, subject to the orders of the military commandant of this department. This is indispensable to protect the city from invasion from that quarter, and also to check contraband trading operations with the enemy.

I join my command as soon as the crossing of the forces can be effected.

I am glad to report every day an improvement in the condition of affairs in New Orleans. Business is progressing ; new establishments are opening daily for trade, and every manifestation of a better feeling on the part of all classes of society, and all phases of opinion, is shown. We have witnessed this evening an exhibition which has not been seen before—an assemblage of some thousands of persons, men, women, and children, representing all classes of citizens, in one of the public squares of the city, with every manifestation of good feeling and of satisfaction.

I have the honor to be, with considerations of high respect, your obedient servant,

N. P. BANKS,
Major-General, Commanding.

HEADQUARTERS DEPARTMENT OF THE TENNESSEE,
Vicksburg, Miss., September 21, 1863.

Maj. Gen. N. P. BANKS,
Commanding Department of the Gulf, New Orleans, La..

GENERAL: Capt. Robert T. Dunham, of your staff, has arrived, and has shown me his instructions. I regret to say that I am still confined on my back as much as when I left New Orleans, but hope for a permanent cure in the course of time.

The cavalry which I ordered from West Tennessee to this place before my departure for New Orleans has not yet arrived. It should have been here by the 3d of this month at the latest. Finding that it was not arriving as expected, my adjutant-general reiterated the order for this cavalry to be sent at once. I am now daily expecting it. Until it does arrive, it will be totally impracticable for me to spare from my command any cavalry. There is to my front a rebel cavalry force, under General Stephen D. Lee. To watch and counteract their movements, I have a cavalry force at present of scarcely 1,200 effective men. When my cavalry does arrive, I will endeavor to clean out the country east of

Pearl River and south of Bayou Pierre, as far south as Port Hudson, of all bands of rebel cavalry.

I have received official information from General Steele of the evacuation of Little Rock by the enemy. I don't think that this action of the enemy had any reference to your movements into Texas, but, no doubt, when your movements are discovered by them, they will abandon Arkansas and Northern Louisiana to concentrate against you. If my forces, with General Steele are returned to me, I could re-enforce you largely without interfering with my army corps that have been in the field. These forces, however, are operating in another department, and are for the present beyond my control. As it is, I will have to send you for the present emergency one division from the Seventeenth Army Corps. As it reduces this army corps very much to make this draft upon it, I hope this division will be returned as soon as the good of the public service will admit.

I find, on inquiry of my ordnance officer, that we have not got here the class of guns you desire. After supplying the forts at this place and at Natchez, I can spare you the following guns, to wit: Two 10-inch columbiads, three 10-inch sea-coast guns, seven 10-inch mortars, six 8-inch mortars, four 9-inch navy guns, two rifled guns, 6.50 caliber, and quite a large number of guns of a smaller caliber, some of which, I presume, are rifled. Anything you call for in this list will be promptly furnished.

As I am compelled to dictate for another writing, to which I am unaccustomed, I make my letter brief; should write more fully could I write myself.

Instead of sending you a division, as I spoke of in the first part of this letter, I will hold one in readiness here, with sufficient transportation and fuel, to send you on receipt of orders, in accordance with the understanding I had of our conversation in New Orleans.

Should you require them at once, please inform me. The division I desire to send you has not yet returned from Helena, where it was ordered to re-enforce the Little Rock expedition. Orders have gone for its return.

I am, general, very respectfully, your obedient servant,

U. S. GRANT,
Major-General.

————

HEADQUARTERS DEPARTMENT OF THE TENNESSEE,
Vicksburg, September 22, 1863.

Maj. Gen. N. P. BANKS,
Commanding Department of the Gulf:

GENERAL: I arrived at this point yesterday morning, after a slow and tedious ride of three days and a half on the steamer Welcome, and have the honor to report that I immediately communicated to Major-General Grant, commanding the Department of the Tennessee, your requests, as contained in my instructions, dated September 17, 1863. Inclosed herewith I have the honor to transmit Major-General Grant's reply * to the same.

Rear-Admiral Porter is nowhere in this neighborhood, but somewhere between here and Cairo. I shall at once proceed on up the river until I find him. Should he be at Cairo, it will take at least ten days to go and return. I will embrace every opportunity to keep you advised of my movements.

—————————————————————

* See letter immediately preceding.

Since writing the above, Major-General Grant directs me to say that he has received instructions (copies of which will be sent you) to re-enforce Major-General Rosecrans, and that he has telegraphed Major-General Halleck the number of troops he will send to Major-General Rosecrans, and, until further orders are received from Washington, it will be impossible to give you the division promised in the accompanying communication. I would account for my silence by saying that the boat bearing this dispatch is the first which has left this place since my arrival. Major-General Grant will keep you informed of all changes which take place during my absence up the river.

I have the honor to be, general, very respectfully, your most obedient servant,

R. T. DUNHAM,
Captain, and Assistant Adjutant-General.

HDQRS. SECOND DIVISION, THIRTEENTH ARMY CORPS,
Morganza, La., September 22, 1863.

Brig. Gen. CHARLES P. STONE,
Chief of Staff, New Orleans :

GENERAL: General Vandever has just returned from a thorough reconnaissance of the enemy's position, and brings in with him some prisoners. From one of them, I learn that great alarm existed in Green's camp on the 20th, caused by a report that our troops were approaching by way of Opelousas. One brigade was ordered to march, and did go half-way to that place, but was ordered back by General Taylor. Green has been re-enforced by a brigade of infantry and a battery. He has now two brigades of cavalry, one of infantry, and eighteen pieces of artillery (three four-gun batteries and one six). These brigades average 1,500 men each. All detachments through the country have been ordered in. There is one brigade of infantry at Vermillionville, and a small force at Washington, guarding ammunition and supplies. Kirby Smith has just arrived at Alexandria from Shreveport, and Taylor is at Washington. The movement from below has disconcerted them. The prisoners think, if it had not been made, they would have concentrated, crossed at Simsport and Morgan's Ferry, and attacked me.

I send below to-day for cavalry ammunition and a change of clothing for the men; also sending down the sick, and ordering up the convalescents from camp. In the meantime will make some arrangements for a crossing, and be ready for any movement. They are evidently afraid to go away, leaving my force in their rear; will keep a close watch on every movement.

Very respectfully, your obedient servant,
F. J. HERRON,
Major-General.

HEADQUARTERS DEPARTMENT OF THE GULF,
New Orleans, September 22, 1863—6.30 a. m.

Major-General FRANKLIN, *Berwick City :*

SIR: The tug Leviathan was captured by the rebels at 4 a. m. to-day at Southwest Pass. Look out for your boats in the bay and river.

Very respectfully, your obedient servant,
[CHAS. P. STONE,]
Brigadier-General, and Chief of Staff.

HEADQUARTERS DEPARTMENT OF THE GULF,
New Orleans, September 22, 1863—3 p. m.

Major-General FRANKLIN,
Berwick City:

SIR: The Leviathan, captured early this morning, has been recaptured by the Crescent and a gunboat, and is coming in.

Very respectfully, your obedient servant,

CHAS. P. STONE,
Brigadier-General, Chief of Staff.

Organization of the Corps d'Afrique, Brig. Gen. George L. Andrews, U. S. Army, commanding, September 22, 1863;* headquarters, Port Hudson.

FIRST DIVISION.

Brig. Gen. DANIEL ULLMANN.

First Brigade.	*Second Brigade.*
1st Infantry.	4th Infantry.
2d Infantry.	7th Infantry.
3d Infantry.	8th Infantry.
11th Infantry.	9th Infantry.
12th Infantry.	10th Infantry.

Artillery, attached.

5th United States, Battery G.

SECOND DIVISION.

[Commander not assigned.]

First Brigade.	*Second Brigade.*
5th Infantry.	6th Infantry.
13th Infantry.	17th Infantry.
14th Infantry.	18th Infantry.
15th Infantry.	19th Infantry.
16th Infantry.	20th Infantry.

Artillery, attached.

2d Vermont Battery.

HEADQUARTERS DEPARTMENT OF THE GULF,
New Orleans, September 24, 1863—6.30 p. m.

Major-General FRANKLIN,
Brashear City:

GENERAL: There is no occasion to advance the command to Franklin until you are ready to move on Vermillionville or the enemy's force, wherever it is, except so much as is necessary to protect and support the advance. Precaution ought to be taken against a surprise, as it is very likely to be attempted on any portion of our troops too much exposed.

---

*As announced by General Orders, No. 20, Headquarters Corps d'Afrique, of that date. See Special Orders, No. 231, Department of the Gulf, of September 16, p. 726.

Captain Bulkley has the material for blowing up the obstructions, and will go at once to Franklin if you desire it. Please answer.

Very respectfully, your obedient servant,

N. P. BANKS,
Major-General, Commanding.

HEADQUARTERS DEPARTMENT OF THE GULF,
New Orleans, September 24, 1863—8.15 p. m.

Major-General FRANKLIN, *Berwick City :*

GENERAL : Your two telegrams received. The major-general commanding desires that you use discretion about advancing your force until obstructions in Teche be removed and the troops under Washburn cross. While rapidity is desirable, the movement should be secure. Please inform me where your advance holds itself.

Very respectfully, your obedient servant,

[CHAS. P. STONE,]
Brigadier-General, Chief of Staff.

HEADQUARTERS DEPARTMENT OF THE GULF,
New Orleans, September 24, 1863.

Colonel FISKE,
Comdg. First Louisiana Volunteers and Donaldsonville :

COLONEL : Brig. Gen. S. G. Burbridge has been ordered to proceed with a force to a point on the left bank of the Mississippi River, a little above or opposite to your post, as may be deemed most advisable, with the object of dispersing any force of the enemy collected in that region. You will please give all possible assistance and information ; furnish him guides for the country in which he is to operate, and, in case of need, such force as you may be able to spare from Donaldsonville. It is supposed that you have many men in your regiment well acquainted with the country about Galveston and New River, and will be able to furnish good guides to General Burbridge's command.

It is the desire of the major-general commanding that you leave nothing undone which will forward the expedition.

Very respectfully, I am, colonel, your most obedient servant,

CHAS. P. STONE,
Brigadier-General, Chief of Staff.

SPECIAL ORDERS, ⎱   WAR DEPT., ADJT. GEN.'S OFFICE,
No. 427.   ⎰   *Washington, September* 24, 1863.

*   *   *   *   *   *   *

X. Brig. Gen. Fitz Henry Warren, U. S. Volunteers, is hereby relieved from duty in the Department of the Susquehanna, and will proceed without delay, at the expiration of his present leave of absence (10 days from the 28th instant), to Baton Rouge, La., and report in person to Major-General Banks, commanding Department of the Gulf, for duty. His adjutant-general will accompany him.

*   *   *   *   *   *

By order of the Secretary of War :

E. D. TOWNSEND,
Assistant Adjutant-General.

SPECIAL ORDERS, }   HDQRS. THIRTEENTH ARMY CORPS,
No. 79.   }   *Carrollton, La., September 24, 1863.*

I. Maj. Gen. F. J. Herron is relieved from the command of the Second Division, Thirteenth Army Corps. He will report in person to these headquarters.

II. Maj. Gen. N. J. T. Dana, having by virtue of orders from Washington reported for duty with the Thirteenth Army Corps, is assigned to the command of the Second Division, Thirteenth Army Corps.

*   *   *   *   *   *   *

By order of Maj. Gen. E. O. C. Ord:

WALTER B. SCATES,
Lieut. Col., and Asst. Adjt. Gen., Thirteenth Army Corps.

HEADQUARTERS DEPARTMENT OF THE GULF,
. *New Orleans, September 26, 1863.*
Maj. Gen. H. W. HALLECK,
General-in-Chief, U. S. Army, Washington, D. C.:

GENERAL: Major-General Franklin reports from Berwick Bay that Weitzel's and McMillan's divisions of the Nineteenth Army Corps will be at Bisland to-day (26th). The obstructions to the navigation of the Teche Bayou are being rapidly removed. The Thirteenth Corps is crossing the bay, and the troops will all be over to-night. As soon as the obstructions in the Teche Bayou can be removed, which will be speedily, we shall advance. General Taylor is represented to be between Opelousas and Bisland, with 10,000 to 15,000 men. I bear in mind constantly the instructions of the Government as to Texas, and shall lose no time in doing all that is required of me so far as the means in my hands render possible.

I have the honor to be, with much respect, your obedient servant,

N. P. BANKS,
Major-General, Commanding.

HEADQUARTERS DEPARTMENT OF THE GULF,
New Orleans, September 26, 1863.
Maj. Gen. H. W. HALLECK,
·   *General-in-Chief, U. S. Army, Washington, D. C.:*

GENERAL: I have the honor to call the attention of the Government to the subject of charities in this department. Upon my arrival here, I found, under the administration of General Butler, that nearly eleven thousand families were supported in great part by the Government.

Notwithstanding a very large increase of population and of soldiers, more or less of whom have destitute families, by very close examination into the disbursements of these charities, and the correction of all abuses, we have reduced the number from eleven thousand to about six thousand families, and ten large asylums. These probably include 24,000 persons.

By the general order of the War Department, all property has been turned over to the agents of the Treasury Department, and it will be impossible for me to continue the charities as heretofore.

They should be transferred to the Treasury Department with the transfer of confiscated or abandoned property, which ought to be applied to the great wants of the population of this department, so far as it is entitled to relief from the Government.

I desire immediate attention to this subject, as it will be impossible for me in the present condition of affairs to continue these charities, and some provision should be made for their transfer to the officers holding the property that might be applied to this purpose.

The winter is approaching, the charities and the number of families are rapidly increasing, and it will be impossible to discontinue them without creating great individual suffering and very great public disturbance. I earnestly ask attention and instructions.

With the establishment of the system of labor on the plantations, I have provided support for all the negroes of this department. They are upon the plantations where they have been accustomed to labor, or upon those carried on by the Government. Up to the time of the invasion of the rebels during the siege of Port Hudson, I had no difficulty in supporting, feeding, and clothing all the negroes here without public expense, and I should have been very glad at that time to have received any number in addition from other departments, as their labor compensated for all expenses incurred on their behalf.

The invasion of the rebels to the west bank of the river, occupying that country for a couple of weeks, necessarily much disturbed the relations of labor and laborers.

In addition to this, all the plantations have been turned over to the Treasury officers, and are worked upon Government account.

The support of destitute negroes, and those not in employment, should be charged to the plantation property, and I respectfully request that we may be relieved from the support of negroes not now employed, and that it may be charged to the property of this class in the hands of the Treasury agents; also that definite instructions be given me concerning the disposition to be made of this subject.

I cannot overestimate its importance, both to the people and the Government.

I have the honor to be, with much respect, your obedient servant
N. P. BANKS,
Major-General, Commanding.

OFFICE SUPERVISING SPECIAL AGENT, TREASURY DEPT.,
New Orleans, September 26, 1863.

Maj. Gen. N. P. BANKS,
    Commanding Department of the Gulf:

GENERAL: I exceedingly regret being compelled to lay before you an instance of flagrant violation of your order on the part of Colonel Kempsey, commanding Sixteenth Regiment, Corps d'Afrique. The accompanying papers will sufficiently explain the offense.

I cannot refrain, general, from availing myself of the present occasion to urge upon your consideration the vast importance of a strict enforcement of your former orders upon the subject. Both the State and the Government have a vital interest in the matter. If we lose the confidence of the negro, we shall labor in vain to secure his services in a profitable working of the plantations; the money already invested by the United States will be irretrievably lost, the great staples of Louisiana will be ruined, the internal revenue deprived of a fruitful source of income, and society itself be demoralized by rendering a large part of the population vagabond.

If negroes are to be impressed as described in the inclosed papers, they, have lost, not gained, by the proclamation of the President. They are nominally free, but, in reality, the most unprotected of serfs.

I invoke, general, your most efficient intervention in this matter. I beg that the wisdom which dictated your orders, giving assured protection to the negro, may have the largest and fullest operation. Touching the carts and mules, I will merely say that as they are my property, receipted for by me, I am confident that you will order their immediate restoration.

I have the honor to remain, general, very respectfully, your obedient servant,

BENJ. F. FLANDERS,
Supervising Special Agent, Treasury Department.

[Memorandum for the general.]

' Unless some stringent measures are adopted, the oppression of these negro recruiting officers will become insupportable by all classes. These cases of cruelty are reported daily.

C. P. S. [STONE.]

[Inclosure.]

OFFICE SUPERVISING SPECIAL AGENT, TREASURY DEPT.,
Plantation Bureau, New Orleans, September 26, 1863.

Hon. B. F. FLANDERS,
Supervising Special Agent, Treasury Department:

SIR: I desire to call your attention to the inclosed copies of letters received from the overseers on the Payne and Taylor plantations, worked by this department; nor are these acts confined to these places alone— the Le Blanc, Hermitage, Ashland, Point Houmas, and other Government places have suffered severely from having the able-bodied hands forced at the point of the bayonet from the plantations for conscription; mules and carts, which you receipted for, have also been taken by officers and soldiers without hesitation, notwithstanding the order issued by General Banks that property on those places should not be interfered with.

I dislike to complain, Mr. Flanders, but it will be impossible for us to take off and secure our crops if our mules, carts, and men are thus taken. The Government will thus entirely lose not only the thousands already furnished in supplies, but hundreds of thousands of dollars in prospect. If, as is the case on the Payne place, mules and carts are taken, we cannot get wood to take off our crops (as it is impossible to procure these things at any price), nor indeed can we cut the wood, as none but able-bodied hands can work in the swamps. Under these circumstances, I most respectfully ask you what I am to do.

Very respectfully,

G. W. COZZENS,
Superintendent of Plantations.

[Sub-Inclosures.]

PARISH OF SAINT CHARLES, LA.,
Mayronne Plantation, September 25, 1863.

Captain COZZENS:

My overseer on the Payne plantation reports to me this minute that Colonel Kempsey, of the Sixteenth Regiment, of colored population, last night, about 11 o'clock, took from the said place two carts and 6 mules and 22 men, and the overseer, Mr. Cozanah, did show the letter of August 15 of protection, but the said colonel said his orders were of later date. Now, this colonel was entreated not to take the said hands from Government place of protection. His headquarters are at Bonnet Carré Point, some 16 miles above this place. You will attend to this matter immediately, as the hands taken are men we cannot do without.

JNO. L. MURPHY,
Manager of Mayronne, Taylor, and Payne Places.

TAYLOR PLANTATION,
Parish Saint Charles, La., September 25, 1863—5 a. m.

Capt. G. W. COZZENS:

DEAR SIR: Last night about 8 o'clock a lieutenant, or captain, representing himself as colonel of the Sixteenth Regiment, Native Guards, took away 23 of our best men, two carts, and 6 mules from Payne plantation. He was intoxicated. When we showed him our protection, he cursed all the men represented therein. He has not left a man able to work on the plantation. We cannot do anything until we get them back. Let us know what to do in respect to this affair, and oblige, your obedient servant,

P. FLANIGAN.

HEADQUARTERS THIRTEENTH ARMY CORPS,
September 26, 1863.

Brig. Gen. CHARLES P. STONE,
Chief of Staff, Department of the Gulf:

SIR: I learn that, with about 6,000 men for duty, the Nineteenth Corps have three hundred and fifty wagons for the expedition.

I have 15,000 men for duty, 20,000, including sick, &c., and but four hundred wagons. My men have been accustomed in the sieges to fire away much ammunition, and I should like to carry 240 rounds of ammunition, at least, for infantry in wagons, and 400, all told, for artillery. To do this will take nearly all my wagons. With one hundred wagons from the Nineteenth Corps, leaving them two hundred and fifty, and giving me five hundred, I could manage the ammunition, excepting for the 30-pounders, and 200 rounds might do for them, and would then have a smaller proportion of wagons than the number of my men would entitle me to by one hundred and twenty-five wagons—that is, if the Nineteenth Corps has two hundred and fifty wagons for 6,000 men, I ought to have six hundred and twenty-five wagons. I beg to call attention to the unnecessary large number of wagons which the cavalry of my corps still have, considering the necessities of the infantry and cavalry.

Yours, respectfully, &c.,

E. O. C. ORD,
Major-General of Volunteers, Commanding.

OFFICE OF THE CHIEF OF ARTILLERY,
New Orleans, September 26, 1863.

I have the honor to furnish, for the information of the chief of ordnance, Department of the Gulf, the following list of the artillery of the Thirteenth Army Corps:

Command.	30-pounder Parrotts.	10-pounder Parrotts.	James guns.	English 3½-inch.	Rodman 3-inch.	12-pounder Napoleons.	12-pounders.	6-pounders.	12-pounder howitzers.	Total.
First Division:										
2d Illinois Artillery, Battery A*	4									4
1st Indiana Battery*					2		2		2	6
7th Michigan Battery					4					4
1st Wisconsin Battery*	4									4
Second Division:										
1st Missouri Artillery, Battery B					4				2	6
1st Missouri Artillery, Battery E		2		2					2	6
1st Missouri Artillery, Battery F			2	4						6
Third Division:										
2d Illinois Artillery, Battery E								3	1	4
1st Missouri Artillery, Battery A*						1		3	2	6
2d Ohio Battery			4						2	6
16th Ohio Battery			3			2	1			6
Fourth Division:										
Chicago Mercantile Battery						4				4
17th Ohio Battery		6								6
Total	8	8	9	6	10	7	3	6	11	68

* With the division; the other batteries of the corps are at Carrollton.

RICHARD ARNOLD,
Brigadier-General, and Chief of Artillery.

GENERAL ORDERS, }   HDQRS. THIRTEENTH ARMY CORPS,
No. 39.   }   *Carrollton, La., September 26, 1863.*

Major-General Herron, having received leave of absence some time since from the department commander, with the true spirit of a soldier, remained with his men as long as the special service intrusted to him required. That command being about to join the corps, the leave of absence takes effect.

In parting with General Herron, though but for a time, the general commanding deems it a fitting opportunity to thank him for the promptness and efficiency with which every order that carried him toward the enemy has been obeyed; and for the zeal and bravery displayed by his command during the rapid, difficult, frequent, and successful campaigns conducted by Major-General Herron in person.

By order of Maj. Gen. E. O. C. Ord:

WALTER B. SCATES,
Lieutenant-Colonel, and Assistant Adjutant-General.

HEADQUARTERS OF THE ARMY,
Washington, September 28, 1863.

Memoranda for Generals Banks, Grant, and Steele.

The rebel Secretary of War directs General Kirby Smith to break up all plantations within 8 or 10 miles of the Mississippi River, on west side, remove the negroes, and remove or destroy the cotton. He is also directed to organize batteries of artillery to operate on that shore.

and fire upon river boats. One object in breaking up the plantations is to prevent our receiving any information of rebel movements.

All persons in the Trans-Mississippi District who manifest any desire for reconstruction of the Union are to be severely punished.

Funds are to be sent via Havana and Matamoras, and thence to Arkansas, under military escort furnished by General Magruder. A million of dollars have been sent to Shreveport, La., and more will be forwarded across the Mississippi, as opportunities may occur.

The Postmaster-General establishes Shreveport and Camden as general mail depots west of the Mississippi, to and from which points the mails are to be sent across the river, as opportunities occur.

There are extensive powder mills at Arkadelphia, Ark. Niter beds and iron mines are to be extensively worked in Texas. Niter is scarce, but no complaints about sulphur. Iron for railroads and machinery scarce. All iron and iron mines and works to be hired, purchased, or impressed for the Government. Arms scarce in Arkansas.

It is said that the fall of Vicksburg and Port Hudson has been favorable to the rebel cause by the reaction of public feeling and a determination to avenge the loss. The rebel ranks are filling up much more rapidly than before.

[Indorsement.]

The foregoing memoranda are taken from intercepted official rebel dispatches, dated from August 1 to 18, 1863.

Very respectfully, your obedient servant,

H. W. HALLECK,
Major-General, Commanding.

GENERAL ORDERS, ¦   HDQRS. DEPARTMENT OF THE GULF,
No. 70.   ¦   *New Orleans, September 28, 1863.*

I. The heroic efforts of the Army of the United States have re-established the free navigation of the Mississippi and its tributaries. The vindication of the freedom of these waters by the iron hand of war, against a confederation of rebel States, is an event of equal import with their discovery and settlement, and makes the Union a nation. It is a baptism of blood. In a brief period of time, this vast and fertile valley will be opened to the peaceful commerce of the world.

Notwithstanding the ravages of war, the destruction of property, the dispersion of laborers, and the decimation of population, the inhabitable globe does not offer a nobler theater for intelligent enterprise than the Valley of the Mississippi. The cultivation of new products, the application of new elements and different systems of labor, the immediate reorganization of local governments, and the resistless energy of many millions of freemen, will create individual and national wealth such as the world has never seen. Never was a country better worth fighting for, better worth defending.

The highest duty of the people is to maintain and defend the freedom of the Mississippi, upon which depends the support of the present and the hope of the future. The Government is entitled to the armed assistance of all those who claim the right of citizens or seek to share their privileges. Those who covet the profits of trade, disclaiming citizenship and acknowledging allegiance to foreign nations only, remain here by permission and favor, and not of right.

In the performance of this duty, and to assist in maintaining the important advantages secured by free communication between the Valley of the Mississippi and the markets of the world, the citizens of the first and second congressional districts of Louisiana, liable to military duty, have been enrolled for general military service, in accordance with the provisions of the law of conscription, passed by Congress, so far as it may be applicable to this department. Proper publication will be hereafter made of the number of troops required for this purpose, and the time and manner of their selection. The conscription will not be held to embrace those well-disposed persons who, in the event of capture by the enemy, would not be entitled to the full immunity of soldiers of the United States.

II. The organization of one or more volunteer regiments, to be designated the "New Orleans Volunteers," whose services will be limited, by the terms of enlistment, to the protection and defense of New Orleans, is hereby authorized. Volunteers for this service will receive a bounty of $100, $25 of which, and one month's pay, will be advanced when the volunteer is mustered into service for the war. Capt. C. W. Kilborn, provost-marshal of the city of New Orleans, is charged with the immediate organization and command of the first regiment; Capt. R. W. Brown, provost-marshal of the parish of Jefferson, is authorized to organize and command the second regiment. The first regiment will be recruited and organized in the city of New Orleans, excepting the fourth district, and the second within the limits of the parish of Jefferson and the fourth district of New Orleans.

III. Able-bodied men of color between the ages of twenty and thirty years, employed upon Government or private plantations, will be detailed for military service in the Corps d'Afrique, upon order of the commission of enrollment. No officer or other person is allowed to recruit men for any special regiment of that corps, and every officer recruiting for this corps under this order will be required to exhibit authority for his acts, signed by the superintendent of recruiting, and approved by the commission of enrollments. Substitutes will be received in cases where the labor of the recruit is specially required, and exemptions allowed in cases of necessity, upon application to the commission of enrollment, but by no other person or authority. Arrangements will be made to secure the crops of the season, and laborers will be furnished, as far as practicable, to supply the vacancies occasioned by the execution of this order. The first duty of those engaged in the cultivation of the soil is to protect it from invasion, and those whose interests are inconsistent with a vigorous defense of the department, or who are indifferent to the invasions of a public enemy, can have no rights which the Government is bound to respect.

By command of Major-General Banks:

G. NORMAN LIEBER,
Acting Assistant Adjutant-General.

SPECIAL ORDERS, }   HDQRS. DEPARTMENT OF THE GULF,
     No. 244.   }   *New Orleans, September 29, 1863.*
          *   *   *   *   *   *

IV. Brig. Gen. Alexander Asboth, having reported at these headquarters, in compliance with Special Orders, No. 261, Headquarters Department of the Tennessee, is assigned to duty with the Thirteenth Army Corps, and will report in person to Major-General Ord.
          *   *   *   *   *   *

By command of Major-General Banks:

G. NORMAN LIEBER,
Acting Assistant Adjutant-General.

WASHINGTON, *September* 30, 1863.

Major-General BANKS, *New Orleans:*

GENERAL: Your dispatch of September 13 was received some days ago, and submitted through the Secretary of War to the President. It has not been returned, nor have I received any instructions in relation to it. The failure of the attempt to land at Sabine is only another of the numerous examples of the uncertain and unreliable character of maritime descents. The chances are against their success.

In regard to steamers, we sent you all the sea transports of light draught that could be procured. We also requested the Navy Department to send you, down the Mississippi River, the tin-clads which you asked for. This was done the moment your requisitions were received. Admiral Porter replied to the Navy Department that he would send you some gunboats, although he did not believe they could be used on account of the draught of water. Light river transports must be obtained on the Mississippi or western rivers; they cannot be sent from here. Were we to attempt this, probably three-quarters of them would founder at sea.

I do not regard Sabine City in the same light as you do. Instead of being " the very center of the circle" of the enemy's operations, it seems to me to be upon the very circumference of his theater of war west of the Mississippi. The center of this theater is some point near Marshall or Nacogdoches. The enemy's line extends from near Little Rock to the mouth of the Rio Grande. The occupation of Sabine City neither cuts this line nor prevents the concentration of all his forces on any point of it which he may select. Nevertheless, as the objects of your expedition are rather political than military, and do not admit of delay, you may be able to accomplish the wishes of the Government by the route you have chosen sooner than by any other.

There is no possible danger of New Orleans at the present time from Johnston's forces east of the Mississippi River. All these forces have been sent to Bragg, at Chattanooga.

General Steele is in possession of Little Rock, and it is reported that Price's army is retreating on Arkadelphia. Possibly they may fall back into Texas to re-enforce Magruder. Probably, however, they will not fall back farther than Shreveport, perhaps not as far, without water transportation to obtain supplies in that exhausted country.

I am very happy to receive such favorable accounts of affairs in New Orleans.

I must again call your attention to the fact that your communications sent by mail usually reach here two or three days before your bearers of dispatches. These bearers of dispatches seem to stop a day or two in New York to refresh themselves before coming to Washington. Are they not, except in extraordinary cases, a useless expense to the Government?

Very respectfully, your obedient servant,

H. W. HALLECK,
General-in-Chief.

————

DEPT. OF THE GULF, HDQRS. TROOPS IN WEST FLORIDA,
Barrancas, Fla., September 30, 1863.

Brig. Gen. CHARLES P. STONE,
Chief of Staff, New Orleans, La.:

SIR: I have the honor to report that on the 8th day of September, 1863, a scouting party from this command captured in the town of Pensacola, at the house of the Spanish consul, 2 rebel officers and 6 privates. As there has been considerable correspondence as to the legality of the capture, I herewith refer the matter, with the communications received at and those sent from these headquarters, for your consideration and orders thereon.

I have received from the Spanish consul two communications relating to the case, copies of which I inclose, marked A* and B. The first of these, marked A, I answered, a copy of which I inclose, marked C.

I have also received a letter from Maj. Gen. D. H. Maury, commanding Confederate forces at Mobile, Ala., a copy of which, as well as my answer thereto, I transmit, marked D and E. The affidavit and report of Captain Young and Lieutenant Parker, Seventh Vermont Regiment (the officer in charge of the scouting party), and that of Captain Campbell (rebel), I also forward, marked F, G, H, and I. From these statements, it appears that the rebels rode into the town without displaying a flag of truce, and were very particular to examine the hollow ways and bushes, to be sure that the enemy (Federals) were not secreted there. They then proceeded into the town, and rode to the consulate, as they habitually have, to gossip and obtain information. Captain [Thomas F.] Wade, of the U. S. bark Arthur, blockading off Pensacola, was ashore with an illegitimate flag of truce, and was indulging in a confab with the rebel officers, when suddenly, to the astonishment of all at the consulate, Captain Young and party suddenly turned a corner, and demanded the immediate surrender of the rebels, who very tamely submitted to be captured. All of the party excepting the two rebel officers were in the road. No hostile encroachment was made upon the premises of the Spanish consul. Captain Young, at this stage of the proceedings, was subjected to a tirade of obscene and ungentlemanly swagger from Captain Wade, whose conduct and language I have reported to the naval authorities.

The Spanish consul, at the time of the evacuation of Pensacola, declined to come with the troops to this place, although he was offered every facility for moving his effects. He is now within the enemy's lines, and undertakes to protect rebels in arms under the folds of the Spanish flag.

I refer you for the other particulars to the documents accompanying this statement.

I have the honor to be, sir, very respectfully, your obedient servant,

W. C. HOLBROOK,
Colonel, Commanding Troops in West Florida.

[Indorsement.]

Submitted to the general at the time of reception, and returned without action.

[Inclosure B.]

OFFICE OF SPANISH CONSULATE,
Pensacola, September 22, 1863.

Colonel HOLBROOK,
Commanding U. S. Forces, Fort Barrancas :

SIR: I have the honor to acknowledge the receipt of your communication of the 17th instant.

The main point to which, in my dispatch under date of the 8th instant,

---

* Inclosure A not found.

I intended to call your attention, was the violation of the sanctity of the Spanish flag, in the forcible taking from under its folds men who were on business with me at the time.

If Captain Young is under the impression that I did not claim that the men in question were under the protection of the Spanish flag, he must have been very inattentive to what I said, as I advised the men more than once, and in a voice which could hardly fail to be heard by all present, not to leave my premises, for that they were under my official protection. But, be this as it may, it does not affect the question, unless it can be deemed that the commander of the United States forces then present was unacquainted with my consular capacity, or character and authority, which is certainly not the fact. I have, however, referred the matter to the Spanish embassador at Washington, and have only to add that, in my official capacity, I can know no distinction between Federals and Confederates; they are alike entitled to protection when under my flag.

I have the honor to be, very respectfully, your obedient servant,

J. MORINO,
Vice-Consul of Spain.

[Inclosure C.]

HEADQUARTERS TROOPS IN WEST FLORIDA,
Barrancas, Fla., September 17, 1863.

J. MORINO,
Spanish and Mexican Consul, Pensacola, Fla.:

SIR: I have the honor to inform you that I am in receipt of your communication, dated "Office of the Spanish Consulate, Pensacola, September 8, 1863." I fully appreciate your courtesy in referring the matter to my consideration. I have fully considered the facts in the case of the capture of the Confederate cavalry by Captain Young, and I find that the party captured by Captain Young displayed no flag of truce, nor do they claim to have been under the protection of such flag.

They had no ostensible reason for coming into Pensacola, and I should judge visited that place, as they habitually have, to get information and for amusement.

I understand from Captain Young's statement that neither you nor the Confederate prisoners, at the time of the capture, claimed that they were under the protection of the Spanish or Mexican flag, nor do they claim so now, and that none of his command encroached on your premises with hostile intent, and that no force or violence was used in capturing the party aforementioned, they surrendering immediately.

I furthermore learn from officers who were present that the conduct and behavior of Captain Young and party was exceedingly polite and courteous to all at the consulate.

No flag of truce is legitimate unless the party bearing such flag has authority from his Government, or the commanding officer of an army, or detached post, or fleet, to communicate with the opposing Government forces or fleet in the immediate vicinity; then, and only then, is or can a flag of truce be sacred or respected. If the case were otherwise, any party might avail themselves of a flag of truce if in danger of capture, thereby abrogating its object and sanctity.

Any legitimate flag of truce I will respect with due deference, but in this case the party captured do not claim that protection. I should regret, sir, if any officer or soldier from my command had imposed on or insulted you or the Spanish or Mexican flag in any way, and if such is the case, such party or parties shall be brought to immediate punishment, and such reparation given you as the offense demands.

I have the honor to be, sir, very respectfully, your obedient servant,
W. C. HOLBROOK,
Colonel, Commanding.

[Inclosure D.]

HEADQUARTERS DEPARTMENT OF THE GULF,
Mobile, Ala., September 21, 1863.

Commanding Officer Federal Forces, near Pensacola, Fla.:

SIR: It has been reported to me that several officers and men of my command have been made prisoners by troops acting under your orders while in the house of the Spanish vice-consul, at Pensacola, and under the protection of the flag of Spain.

I protest against this act as a violation of the rules of civilized warfare, and demand the restoration of those officers to the lines of my army. I inclose a list containing their names.

I am, sir, respectfully, your obedient servant,
DABNEY H. MAURY,
Major-General.

[Inclosure E.]

DEPARTMENT OF THE GULF,
Barrancas, Fla., September 30, 1863.

Maj. Gen. DABNEY H. MAURY,
Commanding Confederate Forces, Mobile, Ala.:

SIR: I am in receipt of your communication dated "Headquarters Department of the Gulf, Mobile, Ala., September 21, 1863," and in reply I have the honor to state that a scouting party from my command captured the party at the place and time referred to in your letter.

At the time of the capture, neither the Spanish consul nor the party captured claimed that they (the Confederates) were under the protection of the Spanish or Mexican flag, nor do they (the Confederates) claim so now. I understand, however, that since the capture the Spanish consul makes some such claim as you refer to.

As soon as the Confederates were brought within my lines, I investigated thoroughly the facts in the case, and I find that they (the Confederates) rode into Pensacola without displaying a flag of truce, and they were very particular to examine the hollow ways and bushes, as though expecting to find an enemy concealed there; and finally, after a careful survey of the grounds, they repaired to the consulate, where they were captured. The commander of the captured party states that he had no ostensible business in Pensacola, but came in, as he expressed it, "for a ride, and to see how it looked about there."

Without entering into any argument as to the rights and privileges of a consul credited to the United States Government who persists in remaining within the lines of that (United States) Government's enemies, after having had extended to him every facility for moving within the United States lines, I shall respectfully decline complying with your demands, as I do not feel authorized nor can I assume the responsibility of giving up what I consider lawful prisoners of war. I will, however, refer the case to the consideration of the major-general commanding this department, for his orders thereon.

I have the honor to be, very respectfully, your obedient servant,
W. C. HOLBROOK,
Colonel, Commanding Troops in West Florida.

[Inclosure F.]

BARRANCAS, FLA.,
September 9, 1863.

Colonel HOLBROOK:

SIR: I have the honor to submit the following report of the proceedings of the recent scouting party to Pensacola under my command:

After leaving this place on the night of September 7, I proceeded direct to the vicinity of Pensacola. Arriving near there, I ordered Lieutenant Parker to go with the main body to the old Spanish fort, and remain
there, while I, with 4 men, proceeded to reconnoiter the city. Owing
to a misunderstanding of my order, Lieutenant Parker went to Fort
McClellan, instead of Spanish fort, and I did not discover him or his
party until after daylight, when it was too late to rectify the mistake.
Consequently I joined him there, where we secreted ourselves, and
awaited the approach of any scouting party of the enemy. About
12 m. we discovered 9 horsemen approaching on the Oakfield road.
They were armed with the common carbine, and appeared to be engaged
in the same kind of business that we were, viz, scouting.

They passed quite near us, but I did not deem it expedient to halt
them, for I concluded that, if I ordered them to stop, they would be
quite apt to put spurs to their horses, in which case I should have felt
bound to fire at them, to say the least; therefore, I allowed them to
pass by into the city. I immediately detached Lieutenant Parker with
15 men to the east part of the town, while I followed the enemy with
the remainder. They were not aware of my approach until I came upon
them suddenly at the house of Mr. Morino, where they were apparently resting their horses. As resistance would have been worse than
useless, they surrendered as soon as asked. The party consisted of 1
captain (Campbell), 1 lieutenant ([J. C.] Boylston), and 6 privates, all
of the Fifth Alabama Cavalry. After securing the prisoners, I returned
to camp with my party in good condition and the best of spirits.

At the house of Mr. Morino I met Captain Wade, of the bark Arthur,
and, as I considered myself and those who were with me grossly insulted
by him, I deem it necessary to make an affidavit of the facts in the case,
all of which is respectfully submitted.

I have the honor to remain, sir, most respectfully, yours, to command,

MAHLON M. YOUNG,
Captain Seventh Vermont Volunteers.

[Inclosure G.]

I, Mahlon M. Young, captain Company H, Seventh Vermont Volunteers, do make the following affirmation, viz:

By order of Colonel Holbrook, commanding troops in West Florida,
I proceeded to the vicinity of Pensacola, Fla., on the night of September 7, 1863, with a scouting party of 25 men. I reached Pensacola just
before daylight on the morning of the 8th, and concealed my party in
Fort McClellan, just outside the town. About 12 m. we observed a
party of rebel cavalry approaching; they passed quite near us, and
went into the city. I followed them with a part of my men; at the
same time I sent the remainder of my party, under Lieut. J. V. Parker,
Seventh Vermont Volunteers, to the east part of the city, for the purpose of cutting off their retreat. I found the enemy at the house of Mr.
Morino. I came upon them suddenly, ordering them to surrender,
which they immediately complied with. As I was securing the arms
of party, Captain Wade, of the bark Arthur, came out of the house at

the same time Lieutenant Parker joined me with his detachment. Captain Wade appeared much excited; inquired the strength of my party, and asked what business I had to come inside of the town with an armed party; said I was a damned coward for doing so; that I did not know the usages of war, and if he had a few marines he would protect the rebel party and drive me from the town. At the same time he gave orders to one of his men to go on board the Arthur and have the officer in charge send him 25 marines immediately, armed and equipped. After giving the order, he turned to me, saying, that if I took the men away it would be "over his corpse." I asked him if he had received a communication from Colonel Holbrook to the effect that he intended sending an armed party to Pensacola or vicinity upon that day. He replied that he had, but he wished me to inform Colonel Holbrook that he took no notice of his communication, nor did not recognize it. He frequently taunted myself and Lieutenant Parker with the epithet of coward, and his language when addressing either of us was as abusive as his demeanor was ungentlemanly.

MAHLON M. YOUNG,
Captain Seventh Vermont Volunteers.

BARRANCAS, FLA.,
September 9, 1863.

Then personally appeared the said Mahlon M. Young, captain Seventh Vermont Volunteers, and made oath and subscribed to the above.

GEO. W. SHELDON,
Acting Assistant Adjutant-General.

[Inclosure H.]

BARRANCAS, FLA.,
September 9, 1863.

I, Jackson V. Parker, first lieutenant Company B, Seventh Vermont Volunteers, do make the following affirmation, to wit:

By order of Col. William C. Holbrook, commanding troops District of West Florida, on the night of the 7th of September, 1863, in company with Capt. M. M. Young, Seventh Vermont Volunteers, and a scouting party of 25 men, proceeded to Pensacola, Fla., where we arrived about daybreak, September 8, 1863. We took possession of Fort McClellan, where we remained secreted until about 12 o'clock, at which time we saw 9 Confederate cavalrymen approaching, who passed by us into the city. As soon as said cavalrymen had gained the right position, I proceeded with a part of the force, by orders of Capt. M. M. Young, and took a position to cut off the retreat of said cavalrymen. Capt. M. M. Young, with the rest of his force, proceeded into the city in pursuit of the enemy; found and captured them in front of Mr. Morino's residence. I immediately joined him with my party; found Captain Wade, of the bark Arthur, at Mr. Morino's, and heard him make several unbecoming and indecent remarks to Captain Young, of the following character: "You are a damned coward; give my compliments to Colonel Holbrook, and tell him for me that you are all damned cowards; you should not take those men," referring to the cavalrymen; "I will protect them. I have sent for 25 marines, and if you take those men, you will have to do it over my dead body, and also over the dead bodies of 25 Jacks. I will show you that 25 marines can whip 30 army soldiers. You don't know the usages of war." He said to the rebel captain, "It matters not how this affair may terminate, one thing I wish you to bear in mind—if I had forces here, I would protect you."

J. V. PARKER,
First Lieutenant Company B, Seventh Vermont Volunteers.

BARRANCAS, FLA.,
September 10, 1863.

Then personally appeared the said J. V. Parker, first lieutenant Seventh Vermont Volunteers, and subscribed and made oath to the above.

GEO. W. SHELDON,
Acting Assistant Adjutant-General.

[Inclosure I.]

I, W. G. Campbell, Captain Fifth Regiment Alabama Cavalry, C. S. Army, do hereby make the following affidavit, to wit:

I came into Pensacola, Fla., September 8, 1863, and met Captain Wade, U. S. Navy, at the house of Mr. Morino, Spanish consul. Supposing myself to be on neutral ground, entered into conversation with said Captain Wade. While there, Captain Young, with a detachment of the Seventh Regiment Vermont Volunteers, U. S. Army, came upon my party, ordering me and my party to surrender as prisoners of war. Captain Wade went immediately out of the house, and protested against Captain Young taking me and my party prisoners, claiming that we were on neutral ground. The said Captain Wade appeared much excited, using violent and abusive language while addressing Captain Young. And I hereby further state that I did not hear Captain Young (or any of his party) use any ungentlemanly language, or in any way conduct himself otherwise than in a manner as becomes an officer and a gentleman, while at the house of the Spanish consul aforesaid.

W. G. CAMPBELL,
Captain Fifth Alabama Cavalry, C. S. Army.

Then personally appeared the above-named W. G. Campbell, captain Fifth Regiment Alabama Cavalry, C. S. Army, and subscribed to the foregoing statement before me, at Fort Pickens, Fla., this 16th day of September, 1863.

SAMUEL T. BUELL,
Lieutenant Seventh Vermont Volunteers, Adjutant of the Post.

Abstract from returns of the Department of the Gulf, Maj. Gen. N. P. Banks, U. S. Army, commanding, for the month of September, 1863.[*]

Command.	Present for duty.		Aggregate present.	Aggregate present and absent.	Pieces of artillery.	Remarks.
	Officers.	Men.				
General headquarters............	......	......	......	......	......	New Orleans, La.
Staff and escort	33	96	132	242	......	
Engineer troops	......	......	......	......	......	Not accounted for.
Total...............	33	96	132	242	......	

* Compiled from the department and subordinate returns.

Abstract from returns of the Department of the Gulf, &c.—Continued.

Command.	Present for duty.		Aggregate present.	Aggregate present and absent.	Pieces of artillery.	Remarks.
	Officers.	Men.				
Thirteenth Army Corps (Ord)	......	......	......	......	......	Carrollton, La.
Staff and pioneer corps	15	11	34	45	......	Do.
First Division (Washburn)	278	4,302	5,678	10,717	10	Brashear City, La.
Second Division (Dana)................	101	1,455	1,978	5,678	18	Morganza, La.
Third Division (McGinnis)	211	3,483	4,055	6,307	6	Berwick, La.
Fourth Division (Burbridge)	204	2,760	3,723	6,040	10	Carrollton, La.
Artillery detached....................	5	343	377	533	18	Do.
Total Thirteenth Army Corps	814	12,354	15,845	29,320	62	
Nineteenth Army Corps (Franklin).....	......	......	......	......	......	Near Bisland, La.
Staff and escort.....................	12	44	77	112	......	Do.
First Division (Weitzel)	123	3,150	3,773	6,372	10	Do.
Third Division (McMillan)	114	2,606	3,092	5,182	10	Do.
Reserve Artillery	3	133	143	196	6	Do.
Total Nineteenth Army Corps in the field.*	252	5,933	7,085	11,862	26	
Cavalry division (Lee)....................	......	......	4	5	......	In the field.
Staff	4	......	......	......	......	
First Brigade (E. J. Davis)............	36	802	891	1,100	......	Near Bisland, La.
Second Brigade (John J. Mudd).......	33	733	924	1,479	4	Near New Iberia, La.
Total cavalry in the field†........	73	1,53⁵	1,819	2,584	4	
Port Hudson (Andrews):						
Staff	10	......	10	10	......	
Corps d'Afrique (Ullmann).............	113	2,598	3,449	3,821	......	
Cavalry...............................	16	410	642	812	......	
Artillery..............................	17	392	555	701	14	
Total	156	3,400	4,656	5,344	14	
Baton Rouge (Gooding) :						
Staff.................................	2	......	2	2	......	
Second Brigade, First Division, Nineteenth Army Corps (Sharpe's).	53	665	2,226	3,059	......	
Cavalry...............................	16	363	467	610	......	
Artillery	14	613	800	1,137	......	Guns not reported.
Total	85	2,641	3,495	4,808	.....	
Defenses of New Orleans (Beckwith) :						
Staff.................................	8	......	8	8	......	
First Brigade, Fourth Division, Nineteenth Army Corps (Birge).	54	1,595	2,202	3,038	8	Brashear City and Thibodeaux, La.
Second Brigade, Fourth Division, Nineteenth Army Corps (Cahill).	95	2,390	3,266	4,062	12	New Orleans.
Other troops‡	98	2,821	3,536	4,075	......	
Total	255	6,806	9,012	11,183	20	
District of Key West and Tortugas (Woodbury).	35	690	1,028	1,088	......	
District of Pensacola (Holbrook)	22	451	596	666	......	
Grand total.....................:....	1,725	33,906	43,668	67,097	126	
Grand total according to department monthly return.	1,705	36,167	49,298	71,125	156	
Grand total according to department tri-monthly return for September 30.	1,718	35,357	49,274	71,174	153	

* The Second Brigade, Fourth Division, accounted for at Baton Rouge and the Fourth Division in Defenses of New Orleans.

† Exclusive of the Sixteenth Indiana Mounted Infantry at Carrollton ; the Third Massachusetts at Port Hudson ; the Fourteenth New York in the Defenses of New Orleans, and the Fourth Wisconsin at Baton Rouge.

‡ At New Orleans, Bonnet Carré, Carrollton, Forts Jackson, Macomb, Pike, and Saint Philip, and at Ship Island.

Abstract from returns of the Department of New Mexico, Brig. Gen. James H. Carleton, U. S. Army, commanding,* for the month of September, 1863; headquarters, Santa Fé, N. Mex.

Command.	Present for duty.		Aggregate present.	Aggregate present and absent.	Pieces of field artillery.
	Officers.	Men.			
Department staff	20	....	20	21	......
Fort Marcy, N. Mex. (Capt. H. R. Selden), Fifth U. S. Infantry.	1	45	60	65	......
Fort Union, N. Mex. (Lieut. Col. W. McMullen), Fifth U. S. and Seventh U. S. Infantry; First Infantry, California Volunteers; First Cavalry, California Volunteers.	6	167	260	318	....
Fort Union Depot, N. Mex. (Capt. W. R. Shoemaker, military storekeeper), company of ordnance.	......	15	15	15	......
Fort Sumner, N. Mex. (Capt. J. Updegraff), Fifth U. S. Infantry; Second Cavalry, California Volunteers.	4	75	109	137	.....
Fort Stanton, N. Mex. (Capt. E. B. Frink), Seventh U. S. Infantry; First Cavalry, New Mexico Volunteers; Fifth Infantry, California Volunteers.	4	37	85	194	......
Fort Wingate, N. Mex. (Capt. R. Chacon), First Infantry, California Volunteers; First Cavalry, New Mexico Volunteers.	6	136	189	329	......
Albuquerque, N. Mex. (Capt. W. H. Lewis), Third U. S. Artillery; Fifth U. S. Infantry.	4	69	101	173	4
Los Pinos, N. Mex. (Capt. S. Archer), Fifth U. S. Infantry	4	35	56	93	......
Fort Bascom, N. Mex. (Capt. P. W. L. Plympton), Seventh U. S. Infantry; First Cavalry, New Mexico Volunteers.	2	84	108	112	......
Fort Craig, N. Mex. (Col. Ed. A. Rigg), First and Fifth U. S. Infantry; First Cavalry, California Volunteers.	10	240	282	382	17
Franklin, Tex. (Col. George W. Bowie), Fifth Infantry, California Volunteers.	5	62	89	94	....
Fort West, N. Mex. (Capt. J. H. Whitlock), First and Fifth Infantry, California Volunteers.	3	100	128	200	......
Fort Bowie, Ariz. (Capt. T. T. Tidball), Fifth Infantry, California Volunteers.	2	40	56	56	2
Tucson, Ariz. (Lieut. Col. T. A. Coult), Fifth Infantry, California Volunteers.	4	40	95	120	......
Las Cruces, N. Mex. (Capt. T. P. Chapman), Fifth Infantry, California Volunteers.	1	60	110	210	.....
Fort McRae, N. Mex. (Capt. H. A. Greene), First Infantry, California Volunteers.	2	67	75	77	2
Fort Canby, N. Mex. Maj. F. P. Abreü), First Cavalry, New Mexico Volunteers.	11	335	379	687	......
En route to New Mexico, First Cavalry, California Volunteers; Fifth Infantry, California Volunteers (three companies).	6	223	229	229	......
Grand total	95	1,830	2,446	3,512	25

* Brig. Gen. Joseph R. West, commanding District of Arizona.

HEADQUARTERS DEPARTMENT OF THE GULF,
New Orleans, October 1, 1863.

Major-General FRANKLIN, *Camp Bisland:*

GENERAL: The within telegram* was received at 7 p. m. .
You will perceive that it was dated yesterday. I have answered that General Washburn reported himself to-day ready to move, and has been ordered to advance within half a day's march of the Nineteenth [Corps], and hold that distance, following Franklin's marches, unless otherwise ordered by Franklin, who, if he needs or wishes him nearer, can order it.

Very respectfully, your obedient servant,
[CHAS. P. STONE,]
Brigadier-General, and Chief of Staff.

* Not found.

HEADQUARTERS DEPARTMENT OF THE GULF,
New Orleans, October 2, 1863—3.50 p. m.

Major-General FRANKLIN,
    Camp Bisland:

GENERAL: The major-general commanding is very desirous that the advance should be made in time to prevent too much concentration of the enemy at Vermillionville. Washburn has been ordered to move up to-morrow, and the Fourth Division, Thirteenth Corps, leaves this for Brashear to-morrow.

Very respectfully, your obedient servant,
          CHAS. P. STONE,
      Brigadier-General, and Chief of Staff.

HEADQUARTERS DEPARTMENT OF THE GULF,
New Orleans, October 2, 1863—9 p. m.

Major-General FRANKLIN,
    Camp Bisland:

GENERAL: Your dispatch received. General Washburn telegraphs he will move early to-morrow. The absent men and officers of your corps will be sent forward as fast as found. Brigadier-General Grover leaves this to report to you to-morrow by early train.

Very respectfully, your obedient servant,
          CHAS. P. STONE,
      Brigadier-General, and Chief of Staff.

HEADQUARTERS DEPARTMENT OF THE GULF,
New Orleans, October 2, 1863—10.10 p. m.

Major-General FRANKLIN,
    Camp Bisland:

GENERAL: Your dispatch of 9.50 p. m. received. Good beginning. Has all the cavalry of the Thirteenth Army Corps reached you yet?

Very respectfully, your obedient servant,
          CHAS. P. STONE,
      Brigadier-General, and Chief of Staff.

HEADQUARTERS DEPARTMENT OF THE GULF,
October 2, 1863.

Maj. Gen. E. O. C. ORD,
    Commanding Thirteenth Army Corps:

GENERAL: The major-general commanding desires that you send forward as rapidly as possible the Fourth Division, Thirteenth Army Corps, to join the First and Third Divisions, now in the field, and that you proceed, as soon as you are satisfied with the completeness of the movement, to take personal command of those three divisions.

I have the honor to be, general, very respectfully, your most obedient servant,
          CHAS. P. STONE,
      Brigadier-General, and Chief of Staff.

GENERAL ORDERS, } HDQRS. DETACHMENT 13TH ARMY CORPS,
No. —. } Berwick, La., October 2, 1863.

The First and Third Divisions, Thirteenth Army Corps, with two days' rations in haversacks, will take up their line of march, the First at 6 a. m. and the Third at 8 a. m., on the 3d instant, in the order they are named. The troops will march in column, excepting when detachments may be made for special purposes. The desertion of the column on the march, or straggling for purposes of pillage and plunder, is an offense made punishable by death by the Articles of War, and will not be permitted. All officers, of whatever grade, who permit the men under their respective commands to leave the line of march or the camp without authority, will be reported to department headquarters for neglect of duty, with the recommendation that they be summarily dismissed the service. Property found in the country necessary for the support or comfort of the troops will be taken and distributed by the proper officers. Officers of divisions, brigades, and regiments are directed to place a guard, in charge of an efficient officer, in the rear of their respective commands, for the purpose of preventing straggling. When men are sick or foot-sore, they will, on the certificate of their surgeon, be allowed to ride in the ambulances so far as transportation of that kind can be furnished. The commissary and ammunition trains will follow in the rear of their respective divisions.

By order of Maj. Gen. C. C. Washburn:
WILLIAM H. MORGAN,
Major, and Assistant Adjutant-General.

GENERAL ORDERS, } HDQRS. DETACHMENT 13TH ARMY CORPS,
No. —. } Berwick, La., October 2, 1863.

The movement of the troops is postponed until Sunday, the 4th, when they will move at the time and in the manner specified for the 3d. The pioneer corps of each division will move in the rear of the regiment having the advance.

By order of Maj. Gen. C. C. Washburn:
WILLIAM H. MORGAN,
Major, and Assistant Adjutant-General.

GENERAL ORDERS, } HDQRS. DETACHMENT 13TH ARMY CORPS,
No. —. } Berwick, La., October 2, 1863.

The First and Third Divisions will march to-morrow (Saturday) morning, as ordered first. Instructions just received makes this imperative. The paymaster will follow.

By order of Maj. Gen. C. C. Washburn:
WILLIAM H. MORGAN,
Major, and Assistant Adjutant-General.

HEADQUARTERS DEPARTMENT OF THE TENNESSEE,
Vicksburg, Miss., October 3, 1863.

Maj. Gen. N. P. BANKS,
Commanding Department of the Gulf:

GENERAL: I regret that recent events in Northern Georgia, and consequent orders to me from Headquarters of the Army, prevent me entirely from keeping any portion of my promises to you in regard to furnishing you with further aid. I am left in a condition that I cannot even send the cavalry force which I intended to clear out the country between the Mississippi River and the New Orleans and Jackson road as far south as Port Hudson. The brigade which I ordered from West Tennessee never came, but, in lieu of it, General Hurlbut sent parts of three regiments, numbering about 1,000 men.

I have sent to Rosecrans' aid one entire army corps from here and a part of the Sixteenth from West Tennessee. This leaves me a force of little over 16,000 men of all arms to guard the whole country from Helena to your lines. I have in my immediate front four brigades of rebel cavalry that I know of, and some twenty or more pieces of artillery. I assure you, general, this is no less a disappointment to you than to me. I was anxious to give you the aid to make your expedition a certain success. But my orders from Washington were peremptory to send every man I could east from Corinth. I informed the General-in-Chief that you had made a call upon me to furnish one division more, but received no reply.

I am very glad to say that I have so far recovered from my injuries as to be able to move about on crutches. It will probably be some time yet before I will entirely recover.

I am, general, very respectfully, your obedient servant,

U. S. GRANT,
Major-General, Commanding.

HDQRS. SECOND DIVISION, THIRTEENTH ARMY CORPS,
Morganza, October 3, 1863.
Brig. Gen. CHARLES P. STONE,
Chief of Staff :

I have not been able to obtain any more information of the enemy than is contained in my dispatches to the headquarters of the Thirteenth Corps, copies of which I have presumed were sent to you.

My cavalry force is reduced below 100 effectives, and, considering the strength of the enemy and the number of his cavalry, it would require four times that many to enable me to scout well and command the country. I have found it necessary to be very strict in allowing access to my position, as I discover that the principal effect of free and easy passage to the " good and loyal citizens" through the lines has been to furnish the rebel commander with the minutest details of our force and its supplies and localities. I have reason to believe that rebel soldiers have very often, in the guise of citizens, been in our camp here, and have even broken bread with our men.

I send down to-day a lieutenant-colonel, who is communicative, and 10 soldiers, prisoners of war. You will find some of the men intelligent. The two citizens, Sweeny and Mulholland, whom I send, with papers and a package of gold taken from the latter, are a precious pair of scoundrels. I am more firmly convinced than ever that they are spies, or partake of that character. I find that they are well known to the rebel officers, and have been among them lately. A rebel officer, during the truce, stated " in his cups" that they, and other cotton-seekers, were " damned bores;" that they were very troublesome. He also stated that their orders were not to burn any more cotton, as they could do better with it.

My reconnaissance of yesterday appears to confirm the belief that the enemy is on the west of Atchafalaya, excepting between 300 and 400 cavalry. They have one or two small steamers and two scows. I think the report from Franklin's scouts, as to the arrival of Walker's division, correct. We had the arrival of that force reported as having occurred at Alexandria, four days since. Green expected them to have co-operated with him in his attack here, and was disappointed.

There is a large gunboat, drawing 9 feet, heavily clad, and pierced for sixteen guns, at Shreveport, waiting for her armament.

Walker's force is reported as being the advance of a force formed by the junction of his and Price's. Unless something occurs to change my intention, I expect to-morrow, under cover of a cavalry reconnaissance, to bring in all of Norwood's cotton which is ginned, and to burn the remainder.

I send down by the Iberville all the wounded of the affair at Fordoche; also the men belonging to the howitzers, and 26 head of beef-cattle collected in my reconnaissance of yesterday.

The effective strength of my command is, in round numbers, now 1,400 infantry, 225 artillery, and 100 cavalry.

Respectfully,

N. J. T. DANA,
Major-General, Commanding.

HEADQUARTERS THIRTEENTH ARMY CORPS,
Carrollton, October 3, 1863.

Maj. Gen. N. P. BANKS,
Comdg. Department of the Gulf, Headquarters, New Orleans:

GENERAL: My chief quartermaster and the one intrusted with charge of clothing, camp and garrison equipage, by my order, and under my special supervision, made out estimates and requisitions to replenish the corps supply with a good allowance of quartermaster's stores, mules, horses, clothing, camp and garrison equipage, &c., and I learned that it is expected these things will be taken from the corps and turned in to general depot here. The horses have nearly all been turned over to General Lee or his cavalry. I have no objection to sharing my supplies, when other quartermasters are accidentally out, with a fair prospect of the return of the favor; but, general, the staff of my corps and myself have taken great pains and trouble to get these articles, did so without the aid of any one, and now to have depots where we ought to get supplies taking ours is rather an encouragement to their omissions, and none to our providence.

I sent for these supplies nearly two months ago, and, had the quartermaster sent them promptly, would have been fit for the field without asking for a nail here.

I hope, general, you will leave orders that my staff be not called on to turn over these supplies.

Respectfully, yours, &c.,

E. O. C. ORD,
Major-General.

[Indorsement.]

If the views of Colonel Holabird are understood at these headquarters, he is desirous that the Thirteenth Army Corps should keep its own depots.

CHAS. P. STONE,
Brigadier-General, and Chief of Staff.

HEADQUARTERS DEPARTMENT OF THE GULF,
New Orleans, October 3, 1863—7.40 p. m.

Major-General FRANKLIN:

GENERAL: Your dispatch of 7 p. m. received. I congratulate you on the good conduct of the Nineteenth Corps, and hope it will continue. Fourth Division, Thirteenth Corps, moving to Brashear.

Very respectfully, your obedient servant,

CHAS. P. STONE,
Brigadier-General, and Chief of Staff.

SPECIAL ORDERS, }   HDQRS. THIRTEENTH ARMY CORPS,
No. 87.   }   *Carrollton, La., October 3, 1863.*

*   *   *   *   *   *   *

VI. Brig. Gen. A. Asboth will report forthwith in person to Major-General Banks, commanding Department of the Gulf, for orders.

*   *   *   *   *   *   *

By order of Maj. Gen. E. O. C. Ord:

WALTER B. SCATES,
Lieutenant-Colonel, and Asst. Adjt. Gen., Thirteenth Army Corps.

HEADQUARTERS DEPARTMENT OF THE GULF,
New Orleans, October 4, 1863.

Major-General FRANKLIN,
Saul's Plantation:

GENERAL: Dana reports that the enemy have one or two steamers on the Atchafalaya near him. Let them be watched if they attempt to come down.

Very respectfully, your obedient servant,

[CHAS. P. STONE,]
Brigadier-General, and Chief of Staff.

HEADQUARTERS DEPARTMENT OF THE GULF,
New Orleans. October 6, 1863.

Major-General FRANKLIN,
In the Field:

GENERAL: The major-general commanding desires that so soon as General Washburn's forces join you, you push on toward Vermillionville and feel the enemy.

The major-general commanding and staff leave this [place] to join you to-morrow morning at 9 o'clock.

Very respectfully, your obedient servant,

CHAS. P. STONE,
Brigadier-General, and Chief of Staff.

HEADQUARTERS DEPARTMENT OF THE GULF,
Mrs. Olivia's, October 8, 1863.
Major-General FRANKLIN,
Beyond New Iberia :

GENERAL : The major-general commanding and staff arrived at 5 p. m. The general intends to join you to-morrow. Please report to-day's results. Ord's corps moves forward to-morrow.
Very respectfully, your obedient servant,
[CHAS. P. STONE,]
Brigadier-General, and Chief of Staff.

SPECIAL ORDERS, }   HDQRS. DEPARTMENT OF THE GULF,
No. 252.   }   In the Field, October 8, 1863.

I. Brigadier-General Asboth, U. S. Volunteers, is assigned to the command of the troops in West Florida, headquarters Pensacola, and will proceed without delay to assume his command.

II. Brig. Gen. Philip St. George Cooke, U. S. Army, having reported for duty in this department, is assigned to the command of the troops at Baton Rouge, La., to which post he will proceed without delay, and enter upon the discharge of his duties. Brigadier-General Cooke will consider himself responsible for the good order of the district of country in the vicinity of Baton Rouge, and from that point to the vicinity of Donaldsonville.

III. The troops within the district embraced between the following limits, viz : The Bayou La Fourche from its mouth to Thibodeauxville ; thence north to the Mississippi River ; thence along the west bank of the Mississippi River to Donaldsonville and its immediate vicinity ; thence west to Grand River ; thence down the Grand River, Grand Lake, and the Atchafalaya River to the Gulf of Mexico, and thence to the mouth of the La Fourche, will comprise a separate command, under Brig. Gen. Henry W. Birge, U. S. Volunteers.*

*   *   *   *   *

By command of Major-General Banks :
G. NORMAN LIEBER,
Acting Assistant Adjutant-General.

NEW IBERIA, LA.,
October 9, 1863—10 a. m.
Maj. Gen. H. W. HALLECK,
General in-Chief, Washington, D. C.:

My advance, under Major-General Franklin, is near Vermillion Bayou to-day. It is believed that there are but 2,000 or 3,000 of the enemy on the other side. If this be so, it is probable they are moving in the direction of the Sabine, for the purpose of concentrating their forces there. I mourn our failure to get possession of Sabine Pass, which enables them to do this. If it prove true, I shall disperse them by a counter-movement, which has been in preparation for ten days. As soon as we

---

* This separate command was extended by Special Orders, No. 269, of October 28, to embrace "all troops stationed on the New Orleans, Opelousas and Great Western Railroad, as far as the Railroad des Allemands,"

cross the Vermillion Bayou, I will inform you of my plans. The new position of affairs seems to be among the most important developments of the war in this quarter.

I will explain to you more fully by letter. No time will be lost in raising the flag, as directed.

N. P. BANKS,
Major-General.

HEADQUARTERS DEPARTMENT OF THE GULF,
New Orleans. October 9, 1863.

Brig. Gen. CHARLES P. STONE,
  Chief of Staff :

GENERAL: When I arrived at Cairo, Rear-Admiral Porter informed me that he had already sent down three tin-clads, but said that he deemed it unnecessary as well as impracticable at the present time to send any iron-clads into this department, because of the low stage of the Mississippi. Lieutenant Ramsay leaves this morning for headquarters. I will forward dispatch by him, and start myself to-morrow morning.

Very respectfully, your obedient servant,

[R. T. DUNHAM,]
Captain, and Aide-de-Camp.

HEADQUARTERS DEPARTMENT OF THE GULF,
New Orleans, October 9, 1863

Senior Officer in Command, U. S. Squadron, at New Orleans:

SIR: I have the honor to inform you that I have just received a telegram from Brig. Gen. Charles P. Stone, chief of staff, to the effect that—

Should any tin-clad boats from Admiral Porter's fleet arrive, the major-general commanding desires that the commanders be requested to come around immediately to Berwick Bay, to co-operate with the army in present and impending operations.

I would respectfully request that you be kind enough to notify them of this request upon their arrival, so that no time may be lost.

Very respectfully, your obedient servant,

[J. SCHUYLER CROSBY,]
Acting Assistant Adjutant-General.

HEADQUARTERS DEPARTMENT OF THE GULF,
In the Field, October 9, 1863.

Maj. Gen. E. O. C. ORD,
  Commanding Thirteenth Army Corps:

GENERAL: The major-general commanding the department desires that you leave a good brigade of your corps at the town of Franklin, for the purpose of forming a point of support for trains and small bodies of troops along the line of operations.

The commander of the brigade should be instructed to keep his command perfectly in hand, and be very vigilant to prevent surprise by small guerrilla parties, which may be expected to attempt to annoy the line of communications.

Guards, under active and efficient officers, should be supplied from the brigade at Franklin to the steam transports navigating the Bayou Teche, these guards to be relieved each trip of the steamboats.

Very respectfully, I am, general, your obedient servant,

[CHAS. P. STONE,]
Brigadier-General, Chief of Staff.

VERMILLION,
October 9, 1863.

Colonel BECKWITH:

The Nineteenth Corps reached Vermillion Bayou this morning. The First Texas Cavalry and a regiment have already crossed; bridges are being constructed, and the force will cross to-night. There has been sharp skirmishing, which resulted in the retreat of the enemy. Some prisoners have been captured. Loss of the enemy not ascertained. Lieutenant-Colonel Cowan, of the Third Texas Cavalry, wounded in the leg, but not seriously. The Thirteenth Corps advances from New Iberia to-morrow. Send copy to Colonel Holabird.

N. P. BANKS,
Major-General, Commanding.

HEADQUARTERS DEPARTMENT OF THE GULF,
Bayou Vermillion, October 9, 1863.

Major-General ORD,
Commanding Thirteenth Army Corps:

GENERAL: The Bayou Vermillion has been crossed at two places by Franklin's troops, and our cavalry is reported skirmishing with that of the enemy at the town of Vermillionville. The major-general commanding desires that you advance with the troops about New Iberia, leaving one strong regiment and 100 of the cavalry now with you at the head of navigation, to cover the line of operation as much as practicable. You will please commence your movement at 6 o'clock to-morrow morning, and take the most direct route to the bridge at this place. You will please leave as many empty wagons as possible, to bring forward rations as fast as they arrive for your corps, and, having seen your command well started on the road, with a good rear guard to prevent straggling, will please come rapidly forward, and report in person to the major-general commanding.

Very respectfully, your obedient servant,

CHAS. P. STONE,
Brigadier-General, and Chief of Staff.

SPECIAL ORDERS, }   HDQRS. THIRTEENTH ARMY CORPS,
No. 92.   }   *Near New Iberia, La., October* 9, 1863.

*   *   *   *   *   *   *

VI. The portion of the Fourth Division (excepting the brigade detached*), under General Burbridge, and the Third Division, under General McGinnis, will move forward early to-morrow. The Fourth

---

* Landram's, directed to remain at Franklin.

started at 6 a. m. and the Third at 7 a. m., on the direct road for Vermillion Bridge.

*   *   *   *

By order of Maj. Gen. E. O. C. Ord:
WALTER B. SCATES,
Lieutenant-Colonel, and Assistant Adjutant-General.

HEADQUARTERS NINETEENTH ARMY CORPS,
Vermillion Bayou, La., October 10, 1863.

Brig. Gen. CHARLES P. STONE,
Chief of Staff, Department of the Gulf:

GENERAL: I have received your dispatch of this date. My advance will move to-morrow at 6.30 a. m.

.Shall I leave the pontoons here without any orders, presuming that they will be disposed of by direction from the commanding general, or shall I give them instructions?

Respectfully, your obedient servant,
W. B. FRANKLIN,
Major-General, Commanding Nineteenth Army Corps.

HEADQUARTERS DEPARTMENT OF THE GULF,
Vermillion Bayou, October 10, 1863.

Major-General FRANKLIN,
Commanding Nineteenth Army Corps:

GENERAL: The major-general commanding desires that you' take with you the portion of the pontoon train not in use in the bridges across the bayou, and instructions will be given for the remainder from these headquarters.

Very respectfully, general, your most obedient servan
CHAS. P. STONE,
Brigadier-General, and Chief of Staff.

HEADQUARTERS DEPARTMENT OF THE GULF,
In the Field, October 10' 1863.

Major-General ORD,
Commanding Thirteenth Army Corps:

GENERAL: Major-General Washburn took the road through Saint Martinsville yesterday, and, on his arrival at that place, found that a band of about 60 rebel cavalry (Second Louisiana) were hovering about that section. The major-general commanding desires that Colonel Mudd's cavalry, accompanying you, take the Saint Martinsville road, and scout thoroughly the roads leading from that town toward Opelousas for the distance of a few miles from Saint Martinsville, and then turn and take the Vermillion road to the bridge across the Vermillion Bayou, the present position of these headquarters. The remainder of your marching command will continue on the direct road to this place.

Our troops now hold the opposite side of the Bayou Vermillion and the outskirts of the town of Vermillionville.

Very respectfully, I am, general, your obedient servant,
CHAS. P. STONE,
Brigadier-General, and Chief of Staff.

HEADQUARTERS DEPARTMENT OF THE GULF,
Vermillion Bayou, October 11, 1863.

Brig. Gen. RICHARD ARNOLD,
Chief of Artillery, Department of the Gulf:

GENERAL: The major-general commanding, being very solicitous for the forts defending the approaches to New Orleans, and desiring that the new armament provided for the principal permanent works shall be promptly put in an efficient condition, directs that you proceed without delay to New Orleans, and thence to Forts Jackson and Saint Philip, there to superintend the mounting and equipping of the new heavy armament, and the providing and convenient arrangement of the proper amount of ammunition for the several classes of guns.

He directs that you shall also give such instructions as you may find necessary to the commanders of the forts concerning the instruction of their respective garrisons in artillery, and in the care and management of munitions and other material. These instructions will not, of course, be given without conference and agreement with the commander of the Defenses of New Orleans. You will also visit Forts Pike and Macomb, and perform the same duties in reference to them as to Forts Jackson and Saint Philip. The visit to Forts Pike and Macomb will succeed that to Jackson and Saint Philip.

You will please report frequently to these headquarters the progress of the work indicated, and make such suggestions as your professional experience may dictate. All work should be carried on in harmony with the officers of engineers and ordnance.

Very respectfully, I am, general, your obedient servant,
CHAS. P. STONE,
Brigadier-General, and Chief of Staff.

HEADQUARTERS DEPARTMENT OF THE GULF,
Vermillion Bayou, October 11, 1863.

Maj. Gen. E. O. C. ORD,
Commanding Thirteenth Army Corps:

GENERAL: The major-general commanding the department, having left the field for a few days, the command of the troops in this portion of Louisiana devolves temporarily upon you. Major-General Franklin holds at present the Opelousas Mail road, at the crossing of Carrion Crow Bayou, the whole of the Nineteenth Army Corps in the field being with him.

Very respectfully, your most obedient servant,
CHAS. P. STONE,
Brigadier-General, and Chief of Staff.

HEADQUARTERS NINETEENTH ARMY CORPS,
Carrion Crow Bayou, October 11, 1863—4.45 p. m.

Brig. Gen. CHARLES P. STONE,
Chief of Staff, Department of the Gulf:

GENERAL: I send to headquarters 3 men, who, I believe, are deserters from the rebel army, and have taken the oath of allegiance, and 1 man who was captured on the day we crossed Vermillion Bayou. I do not know whether the last is a spy or a legitimate prisoner of war, and can get no evidence against him. He ought, however, to be well looked after. The guard with these men will take them to New Iberia, and deliver them to the commanding officer there, if you think that course necessary, but I have thought that you could probably place them in charge of some men who would be going to New Iberia on other duty, so that my men may be returned.

Nothing has been heard or seen of the rebels since my dispatch of 12.30 p. m. General Taylor was with the other rebel generals whom I mentioned as being here last night.

My ammunition train has arrived, but provisions are getting scarce. I hear no loud complaints about water so far.

Respectfully, yours,

W. B. FRANKLIN.
Major-General, Commanding Nineteenth Army Corps.

[P. S.]—The signal officer informs me that he will have communication opened with headquarters of the major-general commanding in a few minutes.

HEADQUARTERS THIRTEENTH ARMY CORPS,
October 11, 1863.

General CHARLES P. STONE,
Chief of Staff, Department of the Gulf:

GENERAL: I learn that there is a mill here which can be used to grind meal for my men, and that the corn there is being taken for horses.

Some of my command have been out of rations and dependent on meal some days, and I now have not more than two days' rations, which, if possible, ought to be held in reserve, as the Red Chief brought up but little, and the flat stuck near Franklin. Shall I set the mill going, making meal?

Yours, truly,

E. O. C. ORD,
Major-General of Volunteers, Commanding Corps.

HEADQUARTERS DEPARTMENT OF THE GULF,
Vermillion Bayou, October 11, 1863.

General FRANKLIN:

Your dispatch from Carrion Crow Bayou, 12.30 p. m., has been received. The major-general commanding has no special instruction for you beyond what will naturally occur to you, viz, to hold your position in that quarter, and ascertain as much concerning the country in your front and on your flanks as possible, and to keep these headquarters well informed of what may transpire, with such suggestions as may occur to you.

Very respectfully, I am, general, your most obedient servant,

[CHAS. P. STONE,]
Brigadier-General, and Chief of Staff.

SPECIAL ORDERS, }   HDQRS. DEPARTMENT OF THE GULF,
No. 255.   }   *Vermillion Bayou, La., October* 11, 1863.

*   *   *   *   *   *   *

VI. 1. The Thirteenth Army Corps will move forward to within easy supporting distance of the Nineteenth Army Corps as soon as the condition of the supply departments will admit of such movement, and under the same circumstances the two corps will move forward to the vicinity of Washington, La., care being taken that the line of operations be not too long for safe supply before new water communication shall be established.

2. The chief quartermasters of the Thirteenth and Nineteenth Army Corps will immediately adopt measures, under the direction of the corps commanders, for seizing all the available horses suitable for cavalry or mounted infantry within the safe reach of the forces in the field. The seizures must be made by officers of the quartermaster's department, who will be held accountable to the corps commanders for all property seized for the use of the army, and receipts for the same will be furnished to the owners thereof.

By command of Major-General Banks:

J. SCHUYLER CROSBY,
Acting Assistant Adjutant-General.

HEADQUARTERS,
October 12, 1863.

General CHARLES P. STONE,
Chief of Staff:

GENERAL: I am quite indisposed to-day; feel feverish, &c., and will send all applications and other matters of importance which my staff cannot properly attend to to you for action. Will you please dispose of such? Will you please also notify General Franklin of the condition of affairs here and the prospect of our remaining a few days here? I will direct Colonels Lucas and Mudd to report to you. Please post them. Lucas has not come in. He reported to and remained with Franklin.

I have given Citizen Chargois permission to organize a patrol, and sent Maloney to town to see if more guard is required. Let me know if any important news comes from front or rear, and come and see me if you can.

Yours, &c.,

ORD.

HDQRS. SECOND DIVISION, THIRTEENTH ARMY CORPS,
Carrollton, October 12, 1863.

Lieut. Col. WALTER B. SCATES,
Assistant Adjutant-General, Thirteenth Army Corps:

I have to report the arrival of this division here yesterday morning. I am fitting it for field service as rapidly as possible. In nine regiments and three batteries we have only ten medical officers for duty to supply regiments, &c. And for the duties of medical director, &c., there are 5 medical officers of this division at the convalescent camp. This cripples us very much, and apparently places an unnecessary number there.

Can we not have those of ours sent back from there?

Respectfully,

N. J. T. DANA,
Major-General.

GENERAL ORDERS, }   HDQRS. THIRTEENTH ARMY CORPS,
No. 42.   }   Camp on Vermillion Bayou, October 12, 1863.

t Colonel [David] Shunk is hereby relieved from the command of his brigade * for failing to perform his duty and prevent marauding in his command. He will proceed to New Orleans, La., and report to the senior officer there, in arrest.†

Division commanders will cause this order to be read in each regiment on their parade to-day.

By order of Maj. Gen. E. O. C. Ord:

WALTER B. SCATES,
Lieutenant-Colonel, and Assistant Adjutant-General.

SPECIAL ORDERS, }   HDQRS. THIRTEENTH ARMY CORPS,
No. 94.   }   Vermillion Bayou, La., October 12, 1863.

*   *   *   *   *   *   *

IV. The citizens of Vermillionville, La., are authorized to organize themselves into a patrol, for the protection of themselves, their families, and personal property against marauders and thieves, white or black.

*   *   *   *

By order of Maj. Gen. E. O. C. Ord:

WALTER B. SCATES,
Lieut. Col., and Asst. Adjt. Gen., Thirteenth Army Corps.

VERMILLION BAYOU, October 13, 1863.

Maj. Gen. N. P. BANKS,
Commanding Department of the Gulf:

GENERAL: A citizen has just come in from the parish of Saint Landry, and has also traveled about 25 miles on our left flank; he reports that the enemy are between Washington and Holmesville. The most of their wagons and baggage have been sent on to Alexandria. He reports their force at about 10,000 men, under Generals Green, Walker, and Mouton; has seen no armed men on our left flank, and thinks their whole force intend to fall back, if pressed, to Alexandria. Until Sunday, the enemy have had a regular established line of couriers from Vermillionville and Opelousas to the Texas line. Reports that the Texans have driven almost every available negro into Texas. Kirby Smith is at Shreveport, and Governor Moore is also said to be there. Everything quiet in our front. A train of seventy-five wagons with supplies has arrived from below, all right.

Very respectfully, your obedient servant,

[J. SCHUYLER CROSBY,]
Acting Assistant Adjutant-General.

(Copies to Generals Franklin and Ord.)

GENERAL ORDERS, }   HDQRS. DEPARTMENT OF THE GULF,
No. 74.   }   New Orleans, October 13, 1863.

Col. Charles C. Dwight, One hundred and sixtieth New York Volunteers, is relieved from duty as judge of the provost court of the De-

---

* First Brigade, First Division.
† See Special Orders, No. 294, Department of the Gulf, November 25, 1863, p. 823.

partment of the Gulf, established by General Orders, Nos. 45 and 52, current series, from these headquarters, and will rejoin his regiment.

A. A. Atocha, esq., is relieved from duty as judge-advocate, and is appointed judge of the provost court.

By command of Major-General Banks:

G. NORMAN LIEBER,
Acting Assistant Adjutant-General.

HEADQUARTERS DEPARTMENT OF THE GULF,
New Orleans, October 15, 1863.

Maj. Gen. H. W. HALLECK,
General-in-Chief, U. S. Army, Washington, D. C.:

GENERAL: 1. Thus far in my administration I have not troubled the Government about negroes. When I arrived at New Orleans, I found many thousand negroes in idleness. I set them all to work, for wages, wherever they pleased to go. What with the system of compensated labor by the Government and by individuals universally adopted, and their enlistment as soldiers, they were all employed, and all supported by their labor. With the exception of a brief period, when the enemy occupied a portion of the country west of the Mississippi, there has not been a day when I would not have daily accepted 10,000, 20,000, or 50,000 negroes, in addition to those I found here, from any part of the country. We had estimated their labor on Government plantations at nearly a quarter of a million of dollars for the year. The condition is now changed. I have, in obedience to orders from the Government, turned over to the agents of the Treasury Department all plantations and plantation property. The disposition of this property that is made is a matter of public interest. Those who have leased them prefer, in working them, the able-bodied men and women to the disabled and infirm. They are daily sifting them out; placing the helpless on plantations, as I am informed, that are and have been uncultivated. I am officially notified of the fact that they are there. It is expected that the military authorities are to support them. To-day I received information that large numbers of negroes are coming into Brashear from the Teche country. They are, of course, nearly all incapable of providing for themselves. The rebels have run into Texas and Upper Louisiana all that are valuable. The Government finds itself in this position: the lessees of Government plantations, and the enemy, turned over to us all their helpless men, women, and children. We turn over very gladly all plantation property to the agents of the Treasury Department. Does the support of the infirm and poor negroes go with the property to which they naturally belong, or is it charged upon the army as military expenses, and fastened upon the War Department, and paid out of the war estimates and appropriations? If the latter, I desire an order to that effect, and means provided for defraying the cost. It is a pressing and important matter here, and increasing in magnitude daily. I beg instructions as to my course. The process pursued will bring us tens of thousands before the winter is over.

2. When I assumed command of this department, I found 11,000 families supported at the public expense. By exposing frauds and cutting off contributions to families of soldiers in the rebel army, who do not seem entitled to support at our hands, and requiring our soldiers, where they are regularly paid, to support their families, I have reduced the number of families receiving rations to 5,500, instead of 11,000, and

the number of rations from 143,000 to 72,250. The coming winter will, I fear, be one of terrible suffering here. The people are becoming poorer every hour, and some supplies, as coal and wood, are insufficient even for the wants of the Government, to say nothing of the people. Hitherto the expenses have been paid out of rents, contributions levied upon rebel property, &c. This property is now turned over to the Treasury officers. I do not complain of this. The administration of these charities, and providing for the increase, have been a labor of far greater intensity and suffering than the creation of an army and the conduct of campaigns. My inquiry is, ought not these charities to go with the only property out of which they can be properly paid? Ought the expense of supporting from 6,000 to 10,000 families, as will be this winter, be considered as part of my military expenses, and charged to war appropriations? If it be so, I request that orders may be given without delay to that effect, and means provided therefor. The calls upon us are very urgent, increasing in number, and coming from families hitherto beyond want.

A part of the anticipated increase in the number of families arises from the number that are evicted in the process of reducing the tenements to the possession of the Government.

I have the honor to be, &c.,

N. P. BANKS,
Major-General, Commanding.

VERMILLION BAYOU,
October 15, 1863.

Maj. Gen. N. P. BANKS,
. *Commanding Department of the Gulf, New Orleans :*

GENERAL : Captain Franklin, of General Franklin's staff, has just arrived from the front, and reports that the enemy drove in our pickets last night, and that heavy skirmishing was going on all along our lines when he left (at 8 a. m.). General Burbridge's division has just passed these headquarters to join General Franklin; also the One hundred and eighteenth Illinois Mounted Infantry has been sent forward. The telegraph wires were cut last night between here and New Iberia, but the communication is again resumed this morning.

Very respectfully, your obedient servant,
[J. SCHUYLER CROSBY,]
Acting Assistant Adjutant-General.

GENERAL ORDERS, }   HDQRS. DEPARTMENT OF THE GULF,
No. 75.   }   *New Orleans, October 15, 1863.*

Col. E. G. Beckwith, commanding Defenses of New Orleans, will detail such number of officers from the convalescent camp of the Thirteenth Army Corps as may be necessary for duty in the provost-marshal's department, and will relieve Captains Page and [Samuel A.] Walling, and, if necessary, any other officers now on duty in the department, and order them to rejoin their regiments.

To enable Captains [Curtis W.] Kilborn and [Eugene] Tisdale to devote their entire time to the important duties intrusted to them of raising troops, Colonel Beckwith will relieve them from duty in the provost-marshal's department as speedily as possible.

Officers doing duty in the provost-marshal-general's department, or under the provost-marshal of the State of Louisiana, at any military post, or in any military district in the Department of the Gulf, are not in any sense independent authorities, but are aides to the respective military commanders of such districts and posts, and are subject to their orders, supervision, and control, in a manner analogous to that of officers in any one of the staff departments proper of the army. Especially is this the case in the matter of granting permits for vessels to proceed to and touch at any except military posts, and to ship the products of the country to market from points heretofore designated in general orders; but, above all, no provost-marshal will presume to give a pass for any person or thing to pass beyond our military lines.

Commanders of troops are responsible for whatever or whoever passes their lines, and none but superior military authority (no matter by what branch of the Government it may be claimed) can relieve them from this responsibility; and they and the provost-marshal general alone will be permitted to exercise this authority, under the orders now in existence, and any instructions that may be hereafter given by the commanding general.

All permits granted prior to July 23, 1863, to keep arms in the parishes of Orleans and Jefferson, are hereby revoked, and such permits will hereafter be granted only by the provost-marshal-general.

By command of Major-General Banks:

G. NORMAN LIEBER,
Acting Assistant Adjutant General.

HEADQUARTERS DEPARTMENT OF THE GULF,
New Orleans, October 16, 1863.
Maj. Gen. H. W. HALLECK,
General-in-Chief, U. S. Army, Washington, D. C.:

GENERAL: I have the honor to inclose to you copies of General Orders, No. 70,* providing for the conscription of citizens of New Orleans, and the organization of two regiments of volunteers.

There are a large number of citizens here from the loyal States, engaged in speculation in various pursuits, who ought to be made to share the burden of the war, which they escape by leaving the States to which they belong. A considerable portion of the citizens of New Orleans will accept service without reluctance if they are required to do it. The occupation and means of support for themselves and families is a powerful incentive thereto, and the diminished confidence in the success of the rebel army tends in the same direction. But public opinion is so strong, and especially the influence of the female portion of the community so positive, that many persons will consent to that without reluctance which they will do only upon compulsion. We have in this department five regiments, three of cavalry and two of infantry, for general service. From the conscription I hope to get men enough to fill these regiments; they are among the best regiments in the department, and are now composed of the same class of men for which the regiments will be formed.

In reference to the organization of volunteer regiments of limited service in one respect only, I have to observe that the Government will find it necessary in all of these States, in order to pave the way for a participation of their citizens in the army, to organize them with

* See p. 740.

some changes in conditions of service. For example, there are no more loyal men in the country than the Union men of Texas, and no men so terribly embittered against the principles of secession and the leaders of the rebel army. But it is impossible to get these men to participate in the struggle in which we are engaged excepting for a reclamation of Texas. Every man looks to that end, and is unwilling to labor for any other. It will be very unwise for the Government to reject these men upon that ground. There are also numerous deserters from the rebel army, without means of support for themselves or families, who would gladly take service in our army. But it is impossible for them to do so, because, in the event of capture, to which all soldiers are liable, their fate would be that of deserters. We could not claim for them the immunities of the soldiers of the United States. These organizations open a door for them. From these two sources I hope to obtain from 4,000 to 5,000 men.

I cannot too strongly recommend to the consideration of the Government the fact that the amalgamation of the people of the rebel States with the army of the Union will be the first and the strongest proof of the restoration of the Government. This offers also an opportunity for stating more distinctly than it has been stated the true position of foreign citizens, and to declare that those who remain here, without intention to support the Government in its hour of trial, and seek to share the profits of re-established trade and the advantages of well-ordered society, which are the results of our victories, remain here by the favor and clemency of the Government and not of right.

I have the honor to be, with high respect, your obedient servant,

N. P. BANKS,
Major-General, Commanding.

HEADQUARTERS DEPARTMENT OF THE GULF,
New Orleans, October 16, 1863.

Maj. Gen. H. W. HALLECK,
General-in-Chief, U. S. Army, Washington, D. C.:

GENERAL: I have the honor to acknowledge the receipt of your communication of September 28, with accompanying memoranda of the movements of the enemy in Arkansas and the northern part of Louisiana.

The position of my forces at the present time, between Vermillionville and Opelousas, will preclude the operations contemplated by them on the Mississippi, as, from the mouth of the Red River, we shall cover it completely, and, as we move north, our protection will be extended above. The importance of Shreveport, as represented, is very great, and it confirms representations made to us. I had the strongest possible desire to reach Shreveport when in Alexandria in May, but the necessity of operations on the Mississippi prevented it.

There has been no such reaction in the public mind of this section as is represented to have existed upon the fall of Vicksburg and Port Hudson. They have been depressed rather than stimulated by such effects.

I have also the honor to acknowledge the receipt of your letter of the 30th September, by the river mail of yesterday. It was never our intention to make Sabine City the base of operations, but only to effect a landing at that point, or on the coast below. Had we been successful, I should have had in ten days an army of 20,000 at Houston, which commands all the prominent communications of the State of Texas, and will be the center of operations of the rebels when they are completely concentrated. This was the point of operation. It would have separated the rebel forces of Louisiana and Western Texas, and also those of Galveston, from the Arkansas army, and, although not geographically the center, it would have placed us in such a position as to have made impossible the concentration that is now contemplated. All our information here leads us to believe that there will be a concentration of the rebel forces in the State of Texas. They have upon their pay-rolls 55,600 men west of the Mississippi; so it is reported, but, I am sure, with exaggeration.

The movement upon Shreveport and Marshall is impracticable at present. It would require a march from Brashear City of between 400 and 500 miles. The enemy destroying all supplies in the country as he retreats, and the low stage of the water making it impossible for us to avail ourselves of any water communications, excepting upon the Teche as far as Vermillionville, it would require a communication for this distance by wagon trains. Later in the season, this can be done, making Alexandria the base of operations, but it could not be done now. The rivers and bayous have not been so low in this State for fifty years, and Admiral Porter informs me that the mouth of the Red River, and also the mouth of the Atchafalaya, are both hermetically sealed to his vessels by almost dry sand bars, so that he cannot get any vessels into any of these streams. It is supposed that the first rise of the season will occur early in the next month.

I am satisfied that if we could have placed our force at Houston, as contemplated, it would have prevented the concentration. Had the army relied upon itself exclusively, the failure at Sabine City would not have occurred. It was perfectly feasible to land below at any point on the coast between Sabine and Galveston Bay. The instructions of General Franklin contemplated this, but the naval officers were so perfectly confident in regard to their information of the fortifications at Sabine Pass, that their boats were disabled and in the possession of the enemy before any other course was contemplated. It was equally practicable to march from the coast, between the Sabine and Galveston, directly to Houston, as from Beaumont to Houston, and a landing could have been effected without difficulty. It would have been repeated immediately, but the failure had given to the enemy so much notice that he was able to concentrate his forces to prevent a landing at that point. It left me no alternative, therefore, but to move across Berwick Bay in the direction of Opelousas, for the purpose of taking a route westward to Niblett's Bluff, on the Sabine, or to advance north to Alexandria, Shreveport, and Marshall, in accordance with the suggestion which you have made both now and heretofore.

I make this explanation in regard to Sabine and Houston, as your letter implies that Sabine City was the contemplated position which we intended to assume. Sabine City did not enter into our original calculations at all, and was only contemplated by the navy as a point of landing.

The boats asked for have been received, and relieves us very much in the matter of transportation. I will pay attention to your suggestion in regard to official communications by mail, and avoid the expense incurred by special messenger, except in cases of great importance.

I have the honor to be, with much respect, your obedient servant,

N. P. BANKS,
Major-General, Commanding.

HEADQUARTERS DEPARTMENT OF THE GULF,
New Orleans, October 16, 1863.
Maj. Gen. E. O. C. ORD,
    Commanding Troops in the Field, Vermillion Bayou:
    GENERAL: Brigadier-General Lee, chief of cavalry, proceeds to-day
to the field to take command of the cavalry forces. He has caused to be
forwarded 300 sets of horse equipments and about the same number of
horses, for the purpose of mounting and equipping additional infantry.
The major-general commanding desires that you designate the infantry
to be temporarily mounted, and afford General Lee all possible facilities
for increasing the mounted force. Nims' Light Battery (horse artillery)
will be assigned to the cavalry command.
    Very respectfully, general, your most obedient servant,
                                        [CHAS. P. STONE,]
                            Brigadier-General, and Chief of Staff.

———

HEADQUARTERS NINETEENTH ARMY CORPS,
October 16, [1863]—8.30 p. m.
Maj. Gen. E. O. C. ORD,
    Commanding Thirteenth Army Corps:
    GENERAL: I understand from a negro who lately came into my lines
that there are a quantity of horses and mules in a bend of the Teche, between Breaux Bridge and Dr. Scott's plantation. I heard two or three
days ago that you were about to send there to drive out the guerrillas
who were said to be there. Has there been any such expedition? And
is it your intention to make one? My cavalry has so much picket duty
to do that it would be pretty hard work for it to go, but I think there
is no doubt that the thing should be done, if possible.
    I hold a line now nearly 2 miles deep by 1 broad. This extension is
necessary on account of the pertinacity of the enemy in trying to find
out what we want. There has been nothing heard from the enemy this
morning.
    Very respectfully, yours,
                                        W. B. FRANKLIN,
                    Major-General, Commanding Nineteenth Army Corps.

———

HEADQUARTERS NINETEENTH ARMY CORPS,
October 16, 1863.
Maj. Gen. E. O. C. ORD,
    Commanding Thirteenth Army Corps:
    GENERAL: I presume that you have, of course, seen Special Orders,
No. 255, Paragraph VI, Headquarters Department of the Gulf. I take
it for granted that under this order I will receive notice from you when
you are ready to move within "easy supporting distance."
    The actions of the enemy lead me to believe that he will try us every
day until our intentions are developed to him. But I consider the road
between here and Vermillion as rather unsafe now, and that it will become more unsafe every day.
    I shall be obliged to you if you will give me early information as to
when you will be ready to move up, and am in readiness to receive any
orders from you. But my supply train is not yet up, and I have not
wagons enough to carry the rations that were brought up last night. I
do not think it will answer to depend upon our communications with the

rear after we leave Vermillion with the rear of the column. The enemy showed himself in some force this morning, but with no result.

Very respectfully, yours,

W. B. FRANKLIN,
Major-General, Commanding Nineteenth Army Corps.

SPECIAL ORDERS, }   ': HDQRS. DEPARTMENT OF THE GULF,
No. 258½.   }   *New Orleans, October* 16, 1863.

*   *   *   *   * .   *   *

II. Brigadier-General Lee, chief of cavalry, will proceed without delay to Vermillion Bayou, or the headquarters of the troops in the field, and report to the senior major-general present, to take personal command of the cavalry forces serving with the Thirteenth and Nineteenth *Corps d'Armée.*

*   *   *   *   *

By command of Major-General Banks:

G. NORMAN LIEBER,
Acting Assistant Adjutant-General.

HDQRS. DISTRICT OF NORTHEASTERN LOUISIANA,
Goodrich's Landing, October 17, 1863.

Maj. Gen. J. B. MCPHERSON, *Vicksburg, Miss.:*

GENERAL: I have just sent you, by signal, a dispatch stating that information is received that the enemy soon design to make an attack on the troops in this district, and for this purpose are assembling their forces on the Bayou Macon; 3,000 are now reported this side of Bayou Macon. This is not a mere rumor. For several days matters have looked cloudy, and to-day appear to be assuming tangible shape. The troops for the defense of the district are much scattered, and entirely inadequate for the purpose, and not enough for self defense. They will sweep the district if they come with the force reported, and I respectfully request that re enforcements be sent without delay—2,000 infantry, 200 cavalry, and a battery of artillery. I have, since being in command here, on several occasions heard reports of forces, but none so well founded as this, and at those times wished for no re-enforcements, nor called for any. I hope, therefore, it will not now be thought that this is a stampede.

The forces under me, I have stated, are much scattered—one regiment at Milliken's Bend (small), two here (one weak), one at Transylvania. The one at Milliken's Bend, 15 miles, the one at Transylvania, 5 miles from here. I hope the re-enforcements may be sent me, and, if the enemy do not attack, I will attack him, if re-enforced.

Very respectfully, your obedient servant,

JOHN P. HAWKINS,
Brigadier-General, Commanding.

HEADQUARTERS DEPARTMENT OF THE GULF,
New Orleans, October 17, 1863—11.10 a. m.

Maj. Gen. E. O. C. ORD, *Vermillion Bayou:*

GENERAL: As you have doubtless been ere this strengthened in mounted force equal to Colonel Davis' regiment, the major-general commanding desires that he proceed to this point as rapidly as possible. You are desired to send notice to the quartermaster at Brashear of the time Davis' command will reach New Iberia, that steam transportation may be furnished.

Very respectfully, your obedient servant,

CHAS. P. STONE,
Brigadier-General, and Chief of Staff.

HEADQUARTERS DEPARTMENT OF THE GULF,
New Orleans, October 17, 1863.

Maj. Gen. E. O. C. ORD,
Vermillion Bayou:

GENERAL: The dispatch of Major-General Franklin of yesterday was received last night by the general commanding. The condition of the supply departments in the field being now good, the commanding general desires that, if practicable, a compact force be advanced against the present positions of the enemy; that his force be dispersed, and a point occupied which will give us access to Barre's Landing, establishing a new line of communications.

He desires that information be promptly communicated to these headquarters, and to the quartermaster at Brashear, of the time of occupation of such position, in order that a boat already laden and armed at Brashear may be promptly dispatched to the Courtableau. He also recommends a reconnaissance to the mouth of the Courtableau as soon as the advance of the troops will justify it, as a precautionary measure regarding the new line of communication.

Examinations of the route west should be continued when practicable.

Very respectfully, your obedient servant,

CHAS. P. STONE,
Brigadier-General, and Chief of Staff.

HEADQUARTERS DEPARTMENT OF THE GULF,
New Orleans, October 17, 1863.

Maj. Gen. W. B. FRANKLIN,
In the Field:

GENERAL: It is the desire of the major-general commanding that an advance should be made sufficiently to cover the Courtableau and insure the safety of Barre's Landing. That being accomplished, the base of supplies can be changed.

Very respectfully, your obedient servant,

CHAS. P. STONE,
Brigadier-General, and Chief of Staff.

NEW ORLEANS,
October 18, 1863.

Major-General FRANKLIN,
Commanding Troops in the Field:

GENERAL: Your dispatch of 16th, 3.40 p. m., was not received until this afternoon.

All that is desired at present is to hold firmly sufficient country in [your] region to secure the use of the Courtableau line of communication, and hold the country thus far occupied.

The general commanding deems it important to hold New Iberia strongly while getting possession of the other line. All necessary preparations must be made by your chief quartermaster for a long march, but he can have time to make them.

More mounted force has been sent you, and horses for mounting more still. The general commanding desires you, during the illness of General Ord, to give instructions such as you deem necessary to all the troops in the field, the object being to hold what we have got, and secure for the present the lines to New Iberia and Barre's Landing.

Very respectfully, your obedient servant,
CHAS. P. STONE,
Brigadier-General, and Chief of Staff.

———

HEADQUARTERS NINETEENTH ARMY CORPS,
October 19, 1863—11 a. m.
Brig. Gen. CHARLES P. STONE,
Chief of Staff:

GENERAL: Your dispatch of yesterday is received. As I understand the wishes of the commanding general, New Iberia is to be held, and Barre's Landing, between Opelousas and New Iberia, is to be let go. I shall, therefore, wait here until General Washburn is ready to start. I had ordered a reconnaissance to mouth of Courtableau, but countermanded it, so that it is to start on the day that we leave here, and could join us at Barre's Landing. If, however, the steamer has started for Barre's Landing, she ought to be sent back, or I must send the reconnaissance at once, showing our hands.

General Washburn is apparently not as nearly ready as he supposed, and I have not the means of determining the correctness of his statements, except by reports from the chief quartermaster, which, of course, I have not been entitled to receive until to-day.

I send a reconnaissance in some force (1,000 men) to vicinity of Opelousas to-day.

W. B. FRANKLIN.

———

NEW ORLEANS,
October 19, 1863.
Major-General FRANKLIN,
Headquarters Nineteenth Army Corps, via New Iberia:

GENERAL: Your dispatch of this date received. The steamer Red Chief has gone to the Courtableau, and cannot be stopped. My dispatch of yesterday cannot have got to you correctly, if you understand it that Barre's Landing is to be let go. It is exactly the wish of the commanding general that Barre's Landing shall be occupied.

The reconnaissance to Barre's Landing should be certainly made, or the steamer Red Chief will certainly be captured.

Have you been furnished with all the orders sent to General Ord? If not, send for them. They should have been sent to you if he was not well enough to command.

Very respectfully, your obedient servant,
CHAS. P. STONE,
Brigadier-General, Chief of Staff.

NEW IBERIA, *October* 19, 1863.

Major-General WASHBURN,

   Commanding Thirteenth Army Corps, Vermillion Bayou:

GENERAL: I have just received a dispatch from the Half-way House telegraph station, between this point and Vermillion, stating that a force of 40 guerrillas left Saint Martinsville in a northwesterly direction, to cut off our trains and pick up stragglers. Can you send a force to intercept them?

   Very respectfully, your obedient servant,

               [J. SCHUYLER CROSBY,]
               Acting Assistant Adjutant-General.

SPECIAL ORDERS, }   HDQRS. THIRTEENTH ARMY CORPS,
No. 101.   }   *Vermillion Bayou, La., October* 19, 1863.

*   *   *   *   *   *   *

II. Brig. Gen. M. K. Lawler will assume command of the First Division, Thirteenth Army Corps, until further orders.

III. The First Brigade, First Division, Thirteenth Army Corps, and the First Indiana Battery, will march to-morrow morning at 6 o'clock, with all their camp and garrison equipage and four days' rations, under the command of Col. H. D. Washburn.

*   *   *   *   *   *   *

   By order of Maj. Gen. C. C. Washburn:

               WALTER B. SCATES,
   Lieutenant-Colonel, and Asst. Adjt. Gen., Thirteenth Army Corps.

HEADQUARTERS NINETEENTH ARMY CORPS,
               October 20, 1863—9 a. m.

Brig. Gen. CHARLES P. STONE, *New Orleans:*

GENERAL: To-morrow morning I shall march the whole force now at Carrion Crow Bayou to Barre's Landing, if possible. This course I consider necessary on account of the departure of the Red Chief and the consequent reconnaissance. The enemy is in some force about 2½ miles this side of Opelousas.

I respectfully request instructions as to what I shall do in case the Red Chief does not arrive and my provisions begin to get low.

   Very respectfully, yours,

               W. B. FRANKLIN.

NEW ORLEANS, LA., *October* 20, 1863.

Maj. Gen. W. B. FRANKLIN,

   Commanding Troops in the Field:

GENERAL: Your dispatch of, 9 a. m. is received. The commanding general desires that in case the Red Chief should not arrive at her intended destination, you hold such positions and establish and retain such lines of communication as you shall deem best under the circumstances in which you find your command.

   Very respectfully, your obedient servant,

               CHAS. P. STONE,
               Brigadier-General, and Chief of Staff.

CAMP AT OPELOUSAS,
October 20, 1863.

Major HOFFMAN:

In reply to your communication of to-day, I have the honor to state that my position is a good one. Should it be necessary to meet any ordinary or probable force of the enemy, I do not anticipate being dislodged from it.

Should this possibly occur, I will bear in mind your instructions. I am unable to say what force there is now in front of my position. The enemy's pickets are still in view.

I am, sir, very respectfully, your obedient servant,
[C. GROVER,]
Brigadier-General, Commanding.

NEW ORLEANS,
October 23, 1863

Maj. Gen. W. B. FRANKLIN,
Commanding Troops in the Teche Basin:

GENERAL: The major-general commanding desires that two regiments of good troops be sent without delay to this city from the forces in the Teche Basin. They will be reported to the commander of the Defenses of New Orleans.

Very respectfully, I am, general, your obedient servant,
CHAS. P. STONE,
Brigadier-General, and Chief of Staff.

HEADQUARTERS TROOPS IN THE FIELD,
October 23, 1863.

Brig. Gen. A. L. LEE,
Commanding Cavalry, Department of the Gulf:

GENERAL: Information which I have received to-day induces me to believe that the enemy has retired from our immediate front. The cavalry with General Grover has been out 5 miles to the left of Opelousas and 3 miles to its front, and has seen no enemy. If, therefore, the roads are in condition to-morrow, I wish you to make a reconnaissance toward Washington, and as far as Montville, if possible, with all your available force, so as to demonstrate the fact. Leave only the pickets and reserves about your present position, and dispose of General Grover's cavalry by orders sent through him, leaving his pickets and reserves. After the reconnaissance is finished, send back his cavalry as soon as possible. Let me know the result as soon as any result is obtained.

Very respectfully, yours,

W. B. FRANKLIN,
Major-General, Commanding.

GENERAL ORDERS, }   HDQRS. NINETEENTH ARMY CORPS,
No. 18.   }   *October* 24, 1863.

The major-general commanding takes this opportunity publicly to express his thanks to Lieuts. R. H. Ryall, Sixth Missouri Cavalry, and George W. Naylor, Second Illinois Cavalry, for valuable services rendered by these officers on a reconnaissance upon the Courtableau River, under circumstances demanding unusual courage, caution, and intelligence. These officers, by their daring and energy, have fully determined a question upon which the commanding general had no reliable information, and of vital importance to the welfare and success of this command.

By order of Major-General Franklin:

WICKHAM HOFFMAN,
Assistant Adjutant-General.

HEADQUARTERS DEPARTMENT OF THE GULF,
New Orleans, October 25, 1863.

Major-General FRANKLIN,
Commanding Forces in Western Louisiana:

GENERAL: Your dispatch of yesterday afternoon is received, and is very satisfactory to the general commanding. Written instructions have been sent to you by two officers, both of whom have probably reached you before this time. You command all the troops west of Brashear.

By command of Major-General Banks:

CHAS. P. STONE,
Brigadier-General, and Chief of Staff.

HEADQUARTERS FORCES IN THE FIELD,
October 25, 1863—8.15 p. m.

Brig. Gen. A. L. LEE, *Commanding Cavalry:*

GENERAL: From a dispatch received from General Banks to-day, I am led to the inference that he thinks that the country between the Teche and Mississippi abounds in horses and mules, and ought to be swept of them and of negroes. I do not know whether this is the case or not, but it is our duty to find out whether it be so. I therefore request that you will, to-morrow, send out a force eastward from your present position, with orders to be gone two days, returning to your present position by a road different from that by which they go out, to bring in all horses and mules that they find, leaving only to physicians one good horse, to clergymen the same, and two mules to farmers, &c., for the purpose of grinding corn. Negroes without families, able-bodied, who will be of use to us as teamsters, should also be brought in. No women or children, and no negroes who have families dependent upon them for support, must be taken. I hardly think that the expedition will meet with resistance, but, for fear that it may, I suggest 300 men and two guns. I shall be glad to see you to-morrow morning.

Respectfully,

W. B. FRANKLIN,
Major-General, Commanding.

HEADQUARTERS OF THE ARMY,
Washington, October 26, 1863.

Major-General BANKS, *New Orleans:*

GENERAL: Your letter of October 15, inclosing one from Colonel Holabird, dated the 14th, has been received and submitted to the Secretary of War.

In regard to the helpless men, women, and children sent from plantations turned over to the agents of the Treasury Department to you for support, I am directed to say that you will make such orders and regulations as you may deem necessary to remedy the evil.

In regard to the support of the suffering families thrown upon your hands, the Secretary of War directs that you retain in your hands, or assume control over, all such plantations, houses, funds, and sources of revenue as you may deem most suitable for that purpose.

In regard to the complaints against the conduct of Mr. Jones, I am directed to say that you are authorized to assume control over any person, whatever be his official position in your department, whose course of conduct you deem prejudicial to the public service.

The employés of the civil departments of the Government should be permitted to exercise their official functions and to perform the duties assigned to them so long as they conform to the orders and regulations issued by you; but when they do not so conform, you have full authority to remove them from your command.

In other words, general, your military department is composed of States in rebellion, whose inhabitants are in arms against the Government—it is a theater of actual war—and all civil authorities of whatever character in that department must act in subordination to the general commanding. You will, therefore, enforce the laws of war against all classes of persons and all kinds of property within your command. Of course, all property used and all moneys expended under your orders must be expended and accounted for in accordance with law and regulations.

Very respectfully, your obedient servant,

H. W. HALLECK,
General-in-Chief.

HDQRS. DEPARTMENT OF THE GULF, *October 26, 1863.*
. (On board steamer McClellan, Mississippi River—5 p. m.)
Hon. E. M. STANTON,
Secretary of War, Washington, D. C.:

SIR: The number of black troops in this department is steadily increasing. I hope within a month or six weeks to add from 5,000 to 10,000 to their number. We are greatly in need of competent officers. If you can send me from 100 to 300 (chiefly company officers), I think I can give them employment. If the Ordnance Department be in such condition as to increase the number of muskets in this department, they will be of immediate service.

To-day (26th) at 12 m. we sailed for the Rio Grande. If a landing is effected, as I hope, at the Brazos Santiago, occupying the line of the river, we shall immediately effect a lodgment at Matagorda, and seize an interior position. This will inevitably give us a large accession to our negro troops. Officers and arms will be immediately indispensable. I hope you will give favorable consideration to both these suggestions.

I have the honor to be, with much respect, your obedient servant

N. P. BANKS,
Major-General, Commanding.

GENERAL ORDERS, }   HDQRS. THIRTEENTH ARMY CORPS,
No. 49.   } *Steamer McClellan, New Orleans, October 26, 1863.*

. I. The undersigned assumes command of the Thirteenth Army Corps, and will, at the same time, for the present retain the personal command of the [Second] division.

II. Lieut. Col. W. B. Scates, assistant adjutant-general, will report in person, with the corps staff, books, papers, &c., without unnecessary delay.

N. J. T. DANA,
Major-General.

NEW ORLEANS,
October 27, 1863.

Brig. Gen. P. ST. G. COOKE, U. S. Army,
Commanding District of Baton Rouge:

GENERAL: Your letter of the 23d instant, covering report of reconnaissance by Colonel Boardman, Fourth Wisconsin Cavalry, is this day received. Colonel Boardman reports that accounts agree in placing a large rebel force at Jackson, La.

This information is different from that previously in possession of these headquarters, and it is very desirable to know if any considerable force of the enemy is occupying a point so near our lines as Jackson, La.

If you can find means of getting accurate information, and of keeping yourself and these headquarters advised of the amount and character of any force of the enemy in that region, it will be very valuable, and money would be well spent in procuring it.

Up to this time we have been led to believe that there were in that region only small partisan bands, with a portion of Scott's cavalry.

Very respectfully, I am, general, your most obedient servant,

CHAS. P. STONE,
Brigadier-General, and Chief of Staff.

GENERAL ORDERS, }   HDQRS. DEPARTMENT OF THE GULF,
No. 77.   }   *New Orleans, October 27, 1863.*

I. All persons of color coming within the lines of the army, or following the army when in the field, other than those employed in the staff department of the army, or as servants of officers entitled by the regulations to have servants or cooks, will be placed in charge of and provided for by the several provost-marshals of the parishes, or, if the army be on the march or in the field, by the provost-marshal of the army.

II. The several provost-marshals of the parishes and of the army will promptly forward to the nearest recruiting depot all able-bodied males for service in the Corps d'Afrique.

III. Recruits will be received for the Corps d'Afrique of all able-bodied men from sections of the country not occupied by our forces, and beyond our lines, without regard to the enrollment provided for in General Orders, Nos. 64 and 70, from these headquarters.

IV. Instructions will be given by the president of the commission of enrollment to the superintendent of recruiting, to govern in all matters of detail relating to recruiting, and officers will be held to a strict accountability for the faithful observance of existing orders and such instructions; but no officer will be authorized to recruit beyond the lines without first having his order approved by the officer commanding the nearest post, or the officer commanding the army in the field, who will render such assistance as may be necessary to make the recruiting service effective.

By command of Major-General Banks:

G. NORMAN LIEBER,
Acting Assistant Adjutant-General.

WASHINGTON, *October* 28, 1863.

Major-General BANKS, *New Orleans:*

GENERAL: Rear-Admiral Porter has addressed a letter to the Navy Department, in which he says that by fortifying and occupying a narrow pass (A-B) between the Mississippi and Red Rivers, below Union Point, the enemy will be cut off from all access to the Atchafalaya. I inclose herewith a copy of his map,* which fully explains his views. The matter is left for such action as you may deem best.

Very respectfully, your obedient servant,

H. W. HALLECK,
General-in-Chief.

NEW ORLEANS, *October* 28, 1863.

Maj. Gen. W. B. FRANKLIN,
Commanding Troops in Western Louisiana:

GENERAL: Major-General Ord reported to the general commanding that during his stay at Vermillionville many white citizens came in, and, taking the oath of allegiance, desired to arm, to protect the country from further inroads on the part of the rebel forces. Major-General Ord thought he could have procured nearly 1,000 good men in that section with the aid of his scouts and of some Union citizens of influence who conversed with him. He mentioned the names of the following at Vermillionville: Honoré Béreaud, Joseph Boudreau, Zephraim Doucet, W. H. Hawkins.

There is also a man whom I think you have named O. Currier, west of Opelousas, who has raised men, and successfully resisted the enemy when attempting to enforce a draft. The major-general commanding is very desirous of raising a regiment of men in that region for the protection of the region, and desires that you make every effort practicable to do so.

You are authorized to offer commissions to men who are leaders, and those who enlist may be assured that their service shall be only in their own State, and habitually west of Berwick Bay, and in their own parishes. They would be most useful equipped as cavalry. Should you find the movement successful, you will spare no pains in rendering the corps quickly efficient, and to this end will please make the necessary requisitions for arms and equipments, and select good officers from among the natural leaders there and among the officers of the Thirteenth and Nineteenth *Corps d'Armée.*

Very respectfully, &c.,

CHAS. P. STONE,
Brigadier-General, and Chief of Staff.

P. S.—These men may be accepted in companies if a regiment cannot be raised, and liberal issues of provisions will be made to families in case you find the disposition to enlist is good.

NEW ORLEANS, *October* 28, 1863.

Maj. Gen. W. B. FRANKLIN,
Comdg. Troops in Western Louisiana, in the Field:

GENERAL: The major-general commanding sailed from the Southwest Pass of the Mississippi River, with the troops under command of

---

* Not found.

Major-General Dana, yesterday morning. Should he be successful in effecting a lodgment, as he desires, he will immediately dispatch steamers to Berwick Bay, to receive troops as re-enforcements to the coast expedition. He desires that the troops should, therefore, be so disposed as to enable the prompt shipment of as many as the available steamers can transport, say, 5,000 infantry, three or four batteries, and 200 cavalry. I am causing coal, &c., for the steamers to be transported to Brashear, and making other preparations for facilitating the shipment of troops at that point and Berwick City, should his movements require it.

It is the desire of the general commanding that Lieutenant-Colonel Chandler should be at Berwick or Brashear, to control the operations of the quartermaster's department. Two additional light-draught steamers will be in Berwick Bay, to add to the river transportation on the Teche. Troops can, therefore, be rapidly transported from New Iberia to Berwick. While such a force as that indicated should be held ready for prompt transfer from Berwick, it is desirable that the enemy should still regard the movement in your direction as the real one, and as much show as possible should be made of an intended push westward toward the Sabine, or northwesterly toward Alexandria. Again, it may become necessary to make the movement in one of those directions.

I inclose a letter from the commanding general.*

Very respectfully, your most obedient servant,

CHAS. P. STONE,
Brigadier-General, and Chief of Staff.

NEW ORLEANS, *October* 28, 1863.

Rear-Admiral D. D. PORTER, U. S. Navy,
Commanding Upper Mississippi Squadron:

ADMIRAL: By direction of the major-general commanding the department, I have the honor to inform you that he left the Southwest Pass yesterday morning, with a considerable transport fleet, to make a descent upon the coast of Texas. The force with the commanding general is well appointed, and composed of the three arms, and his transports are all armed. I shall expect to hear the result within ten or twelve days, and will immediately communicate it to you. By the latest account, all was quiet along the banks of the Mississippi River within the limits of this military department. There are some reports indicating an assemblage of force in rear of Plaquemine, but a force has been sent to that point, which, with a gunboat to patrol the river there, and a little above and below, will prevent all trouble in that region.

Very respectfully, I am, admiral, your most obedient servant,

CHAS. P. STONE,
Brigadier-General, and Chief of Staff.

NEW ORLEANS, *October* 28, 1863.

Brig. Gen. P. ST. G. COOKE, U. S. Army,
Commanding District of Baton Rouge:

GENERAL: The country west of the Mississippi River, and between that river and the Bayou Plaquemine and Grossetête, as far north as

---

* No inclosure found.

Lobdell's Landing, will be considered within the lines of your command. There are indications of the assembling of bands of guerrillas in that region, and, to prevent their making a descent upon the country below, the major-general commanding deems it proper that you should send a small force of infantry, a troop of cavalry, and, say, a section of artillery to Plaquemine, to guard the passage down the country.

Rodgers' (Regular) battery is ordered to report to you for duty without delay, and this will enable you to spare a section for that service. Brigadier-General Birge, commanding District of La Fourche, has been instructed to scout the country nearly up to Bayou Plaquemine, and his scouting parties will correspond with yours.

By command of Major-General Banks:

CHAS. P. STONE,
Brigadier-General, and Chief of Staff.

SPECIAL ORDERS, ¦   HDQRS. NINETEENTH ARMY CORPS,
No. 49.   ∫   *Bayou Barricroquant, La., October 28, 1863.*

*   *   *   *   *   *   *

V. In pursuance of authority from headquarters department, the batteries of this command are authorized to employ negroes as drivers of battery wagons, forges, and caissons.

The commanding officers of batteries may employ such number of negroes as may be necessary for this purpose, provided the number so employed does not exceed that of enlisted men allowed for the same purpose.

The chief quartermaster Nineteenth Army Corps is hereby authorized and directed to pay such drivers at the same rate and in the same manner as the teamsters employed in the quartermaster's department.

*   *   *   *   *   *   *

By order of Major-General Franklin:

WICKHAM HOFFMAN,
Assistant Adjutant-General.

NEW ORLEANS, *October 29, 1863.*

Maj. Gen. WILLIAM B. FRANKLIN,
Comdg. Troops in Western Louisiana, in the Field :

GENERAL: Your dispatch of October 26 instant is received this morning, by the hands of Lieutenant Craft.

In regard to supplies, the assistant quartermaster at Brashear reports that he had yesterday twelve days' supplies for your force at New Iberia. The wishes of the commanding general, expressed in my letter of yesterday, make it clear that you must not be incumbered with heavy supplies in your extreme front.

Very respectfully, I am, general, your most obedient servant,

CHAS. P. STONE,
Brigadier-General, and Chief of Staff.

NEW ORLEANS, *October 29, 1863.*

Brig. Gen. A. ASBOTH, *U. S. Volunteers :*

GENERAL : It has been represented that a regiment of cavalry could be easily raised in that portion of Florida to the command of which you have been assigned. You are authorized to take immediate steps for the enlisting of such a regiment on your arrival at Pensacola, and will please report as early as possible your opinion as to the practicability of the matter. Should you see clearly that a regiment or a strong battalion can be raised promptly, you will please make requisition for horses, equipments, arms, and ammunition, which will be at once filled. You will please recommend for appointment in said regiment such good cavalry officers of your acquaintance as can be approved, that the corps may be properly commanded.

Very respectfully, I am, general, your most obedient servant,
[CHAS. P. STONE,]
* Brigadier-General, and Chief of Staff.

HEADQUARTERS NINETEENTH ARMY CORPS,
Bayou Barricroquant, La., October 30, 1863.

Brig. Gen. CHARLES P. STONE, Chief of Staff, Dept. of the Gulf:

GENERAL: Having now been for some time in command of the forces of this department in the field, I have considered some changes of details which, in my opinion, should be made, and respectfully submit them, very generally, of course, for the consideration of the commanding general, not even knowing whether they can be legally made, but convinced that some change of the kind is required for efficient service.

In my opinion, the Thirteenth and Nineteenth Army Corps, so long as they serve together, should be embodied into one corps, by an intermixture of the two corps, forming brigades of, say, six or eight regiments, as nearly us possible three or four from the Western and three or four from the Northern and Eastern States, the brigades to be organized into divisions of three brigades each; the artillery to be distributed, as nearly as possible, equally among the divisions.

The corps thus formed should be allowed some time for this organization, and should be thoroughly drilled, whenever time or opportunity will permit.

The regiments now in garrison should be embodied in the organization, and the western regiments should form parts of the garrisons, as well as those of the Nineteenth Corps. In fact, as there are two corps of white troops in the department, the duty should be divided between them, as nearly equally as possible.

I believe that the plan now suggested will add much to the efficiency of the troops. I have seen great want of discipline, and a tendency to disobedience of general orders, caused by the fact that the two corps are from different sections of the country, do not know each other, and are consequently jealous of each other. I think that the combination of the two will, in a great degree, correct this, and that the experiment is worth trial. There is no doubt in my mind that, after the change, there will be a spirit of emulation in the performance of duty that must be beneficial to both bodies.

The legal objections to this combination may, perhaps, be insuperable, but, if it be possible to overcome them, I am convinced that the efficiency of the army in this department will be much increased. Some general and staff officers will be deprived of some rank and command, if the change be made, but I do not think that that consideration would actuate any of them in their opinions as to the propriety of the course which I now suggest.

Very respectfully, your obedient servant,
W. B. FRANKLIN,
Major-General, Commanding.

NEW ORLEANS,
October 31, 1863.

Maj. Gen. N. P. BANKS,
Commanding Department of the Gulf, in the Field:

GENERAL: The position of affairs in your rear is to-day as follows: New Orleans, all quiet and in good order.

Western Louisiana, General Franklin occupies the country near the Carrion Crow Bayou and all in rear.

New Iberia was occupied by Lawler's division, Thirteenth Army Corps.

Franklin is occupied by two regiments and a detachment of cavalry.

There are sufficient supplies with General Franklin's forces and at New Iberia for fifteen days, in provisions.

The transportation between Brashear and New Iberia is now ample, viz: Red Chief, J. M. Brown, A. G. Brown, and Louisiana Belle, with the Starlight on the way around.

In order to save coal, of which we are nearly destitute, I have ordered the purchase of wood on the Teche for the supply of the river steamers. When you left, there was no coal here in the quartermaster's department. Only 500 tons have since arrived, and no intimation was left by the chief quartermaster as to when or how much coal might be expected.

I have endeavored to borrow from the navy, and have procured all the commodore can spare—about 500 tons. Three hundred tons have been sent to Brashear, and more will be held ready to transfer by railroad at the first intimation received by telegraph of your success or wants. I am having the city coal yards examined, to secure a supply from them, if necessary, and we shall get some from the naval department, Pensacola.

Wagons are arriving, and mules from up the river, and horses from that source and New York. Forage on hand is very limited, while our animals are rapidly increasing in numbers.

Brigadier-General Ransom has reported for duty in the Thirteenth Army Corps, and goes on the Warrior to report to General Dana.

Brigadier-General Asboth has reported back, his order for Alton having been countermanded. He has been ordered to Pensacola, as before.

The commanding officer at Pensacola having reported that a regiment of white cavalry could be raised in Western Florida from among the refugees, I gave authority to Brigadier-General Asboth to proceed at once with the organization of one on his arrival.

From the nature of the reports about the country in rear of Plaquemine, I directed, as you intimated, General Cooke to send a regiment of infantry, a troop of cavalry, and a section of artillery to that point.

General Birge has been authorized to mount a company of infantry, to enable him to scout his district more thoroughly.

General Lee reports plenty of ponies brought in on the Teche, and has been authorized to mount the Thirtieth Massachusetts Volunteers.

Will you have the goodness to instruct me as to the extent to which you desire the mounting of infantry carried?

All is reported quiet at Baton Rouge and Port Hudson, with no large force of the enemy near. There were, however, vague rumors of a force of infantry at Jackson, La. They have not been confirmed.

CHAS. P. STONE,
Brigadier-General, and Chief of Staff.

Abstract from returns of the Department of the Gulf, Maj. Gen. N. P. Banks, U. S. Army, commanding, for the month of October, 1863.

Command.	Present for duty.		Aggregate present.	Aggregate present and absent.	Pieces of artillery.		Remarks.
	Officers.	Men.			Heavy.	Field.	
General headquarters...............	......	....	....	......	......	......	New Orleans, La.
Staff	28	....	28	31	......	......	New Orleans and on Rio Grande Expedition.
Headquarters troops...........	3	79	88	122	......	......	New Orleans, La.
Engineer troops (Houston)* ...	131	1,975	2,532	2,715	......	......	New Orleans and Brashear City.
Total......................	162	2,054	2,648	2,868		......	
Thirteenth Army Corps (Dana):							
Staff and pioneers	17	11	36	46	......	......	New Orleans, La.
First Division (Lawler)........	252	3,957	4,929	9,126	......	6	Near New Iberia, La.
Second Division (Dana)†	203	3,551	4,416	6,998	......	16	Rio Grande Expedition.
Third Division (McGinnis)....	207	3,174	3,679	5,525	......	6	Opelousas, La.
Fourth Division (Burbridge)...	210	2,831	3,607	5,851	......	10	About Opelousas, La.
Artillery detached.............	5	343	377	533	......	24	New Orleans, La.
Total Thirteenth Army Corps.	894	13,867	17,044	28,079	......	62	
Nineteenth Army Corps (Franklin):							
Staff and escort..................	12	40	84	117	......	......	Near Opelousas, La.
First Division (Weitzel)‡	138	2,934	5,728	6,366	......	12	Do.
Third Division (Grover	107	2,629	3,007	4,886	......	8	Opelousas, La.
Reserve Artillery..............	5	132	147	185	....	8	Near Opelousas, La.
Total in the field. §	262	5,735	8,966	11,554	......	28	
La Fourche District (Birge)¶	......	....	....	....	......	......	Thibodeaux.
First Brigade, Fourth Division, Nineteenth Army Corps.	48	1,430	1,994	2,702	......	......	
Other troops	35	786	936	1,137	......	12	
Total.......................	83	2,216	2,930	3,839	......	12	
Cavalry Division (Lee)............	......	......	......	......	......	......	In the field.
First Brigade (Fonda)	37	753	958	1,970	......	......	Do.
Second Brigade (Mudd)........	44	839	1,056	1,469	......	4	Do.
Other troops...................	66	1,106	1,298	1,922	......	6	Do.
Total in the field**..........	147	2,698	3,312	5,361	......	10	
Defenses of New Orleans (Beckwith): ††							
Second Brigade, Fourth Division, Nineteenth Army Corps (Cahill).	75	1,685	2,069	3,988	......	8	
Other troops....................	93	2,647	3,362	3,527	4	9	
Total......:	168	4,332	5,431	7,515	4	17	
Baton Rouge, La. (Cooke):							
Second Brigade, First Division, Nineteenth Army Corps (Gooding).	58	1,668	2,236	3,000	......	....	
Other troops	20	544	699	1,157	32	4	
Total......................	78	2,212	2,935	4,157	32	4	

* Includes the Fifteenth and Twenty-second Infantry Regiments, Corps d'Afrique.
† Including cavalry and engineer troops attached.
‡ Exclusive of Second Brigade, accounted for at Baton Rouge.
§ The Fourth Division accounted for in the La Fourche District and Defenses of New Orleans.
¶ Troops at Bayou Bœuf, Brashear City, Donaldsonville, Napoleonville, and Thibodeaux.
** Does not include the Third Massachusetts, at Port Hudson; First Texas, on Texas Expedition; and Fourth Wisconsin, at Baton Rouge.
†† Troops at New Orleans, Bonnet Carré, Donaldsonville, Forts Jackson, Macomb, Pike, and Saint Philip, and at Ship Island.

Abstract from returns of the Department of the Gulf, &c.—Continued.

Command.	Present for duty.		Aggregate present.	Aggregate present and absent.	Pieces of artillery.		Remarks.
	Officers.	Men.			Heavy.	Field.	
Port Hudson. La. (Andrews):							
Corps d'Afrique, (Ullmann)....	102	2,763	3,489	3,868	......	......	
Other troops	78	1,583	2,097	2,311	......	12	
Total......................	180	4,346	5,586	6,179	......	12	
District of Key West and Tortugas (Woodbury).	23	365	690	1,080	......	......	
District of Pensacola (Holbrook) ..	46	834	1,049	1,142	......	......	
Grand total.................	2,043	38,659	50,591	71,774	36	155	

ALGIERS, LA.,
November 1, 1863.

Maj. G. NORMAN LIEBER,
  Acting Assistant Adjutant-General :

SIR: With deep regret I have to inform you that a serious accident occurred this morning upon this railroad at a point known as "company canal," 8 miles distant from this station. A train, which left Brashear at 8.30 p. m., was obliged to stop at that point, owing to a defect in the engine, and send to this place for another engine.

As near as can be ascertained, the conductor of the train failed to take the usual precautions, as per rules and regulations, and just at daybreak another train, which was nearly or quite four hours behind the first, was thrown upon the rear of the train, crushing the cars in and upon each other.

The casualties among the troops which were being transported were 10 men killed, and between 60 and 70 wounded, many of the latter seriously.

These were principally men belonging to the Ninety seventh Illinois Regiment, and were upon the second train.

I very respectfully request that a board of inquiry may be appointed as soon as practicable to investigate the causes which led to this accident, and to fix the responsibility upon the proper parties.

Very respectfully, your obedient servant,

E. A. MORSE,
Captain, and Assistant Quartermaster.

GENERAL ORDERS, }   HDQRS. NINETEENTH ARMY CORPS,
    No. 24.   }   *Vermillion Bayou, La., November* 2, 1863.

Col. E. L. Molineux, One hundred and fifty-ninth New York Volunteers, acting assistant inspector-general at these headquarters, Nineteenth Army Corps, is hereby appointed acting provost-marshal general of all the forces in the field under command of Major-General Franklin, and is announced as such. He will be obeyed and respected accordingly. Colonel Molineux is authorized to call upon the assistant inspectors-general of divisions and brigades for such assistance as he may require.

By order of Major-General Franklin:

WICKHAM HOFFMAN,
Assistant Adjutant-General.

FLAG-SHIP McCLELLAN,
Off Brazos Santiago, November 3, 1863.

Brig. Gen. M. C. MEIGS,
Quartermaster-General, Washington, D. C.:

GENERAL: We have raised our flag in Texas again. Our troops occupy Brazos Santiago and the adjacent country. I hope to-morrow to be in possession of the Rio Grande.

The recent movements in Louisiana have drawn the whole force of the enemy to the Sabine. As soon as possible, I desire to get possession of the bays upon the coast up as far as Galveston.

The great difficulty we encounter is in a deficiency of light-draught boats. One or two tugs, drawing 6 and 7 feet of water, would be of infinite value to us.* Had we not been greatly favored by fortune, we should have lost several vessels at the Brazos. Those we have are much disabled. I feel confident that the Empire City, which goes to New York, can tow one or two of them safely to the Gulf, and I earnestly urge you to order them to us at once by telegraph to New York. Colonel Holabird writes you upon this subject also. It is impossible to spend money more advantageously than for this purpose.

I hope you will urge upon the Government the expediency of strengthening our forces here by a few thousand men at this time. We have great advantages in prospect, and ought not to peril them for want of small forces or supplies.

I remain, with much respect, your obedient servant,

N. P. BANKS,
Major-General, Commanding.

FLAG-SHIP McCLELLAN,
Off Brazos de Santiago, November 3, 1863.

Commodore H. H. BELL,
Commanding Blockade Squadron, New Orleans:

SIR: I have the honor to inform you that we reached Brazos de Santiago on Sunday, 1st of November, and, at meridian on the 2d, effected a landing on Brazos Island, which is now in our possession. We shall move for the Rio Grande as soon as the vessels too deep for the bar can be discharged. On the 30th, we encountered a severe gale from the north off Aransas, which scattered somewhat our fleet. The Virginia was disabled, and did not reach the Brazos until late Sunday evening. The Monongahela was separated from us, and has not yet reported. The Owasco arrived this morning, and reports that they have been at the rendezvous for three days.

At 10 a. m. the Monongahela is now in.

With much respect, your obedient servant,

N. P. BANKS,
Major-General, Commanding.

---

* See Thomas to Secretary of War, December 1, p. 829.

NEW ORLEANS, LA., *November* 3, 1863.

Brig. Gen. CHARLES P. STONE, *Chief of Staff:*

GENERAL: I have the honor to report that on yesterday I embarked for Pensacola on transport Suffolk. On crossing the bar at Pass à l'Outre, the mouth of the Mississippi, a short distance into the Gulf, the captain declared it necessary, on account of the heavy sea and weakness of the boat, to return into the mouth of the river. I requested two competent naval officers to examine the boat, and, as they reported her unsafe and unseaworthy, I directed the captain to return to New Orleans, and would respectfully request the necessary orders on the quartermaster's department for a seaworthy boat in place of the Suffolk.

I beg to inclose copies of the statement above alluded to, declaring the Suffolk unseaworthy, and also of my order given to the captain of the boat.

Very respectfully, general, your obedient servant,

ASBOTH,
Brigadier-General.

[Inclosure.]

U. S. STEAM TRANSPORT SUFFOLK,
November 3, 1863.

CAPTAIN: After crossing the bar at Pass à l'Outre this morning at 7 o'clock, with the U. S. steam transport Suffolk, you felt compelled to retire into the Mississippi River, considering it unsafe to continue with this boat longer in the open sea.

E. O. Adams, acting master, commanding U. S. schooner Orvetta, and Benjamin Thompson, master, U. S. ordnance ship Sportsman, practical seamen and officers of long experience, have, at my request, examined your boat, and they pronounce her in the inclosed certificate unsafe and unseaworthy.

Under these circumstances, I direct you, by authority given the senior officer upon transports by General Orders, No. 276, War Department, Adjutant-General's Office, Washington, D. C., August 8, 1863, to return with the steam transport Suffolk to New Orleans, for the transfer of its cargo to another boat better adapted to an ocean voyage.

Very respectfully, your obedient servant,

ASBOTH,
Brigadier-General.

[Sub-Inclosure.]

U. S. STEAM TRANSPORT SUFFOLK,
November 3, 1863.

We, the undersigned, officers and masters of the U. S. Navy, at the request of General Asboth, made the following report on the seaworthiness of the above-named steamer on her late passage toward Pensacola:

On crossing the bar at Pass à l'Outre, with a light sea on, she labored and strained heavily, making water forward and amidship freely. At 7 a. m., while rounding to, a sea struck under the starboard guard, lifting same 6 inches, and forcing water between the ends of the timbers and planks shear on to main deck and hold, and in our opinion, as practical seamen, consider her unsafe and unseaworthy as a sea-going vessel.

Very respectfully, your obedient servants,

E. O. ADAMS,
Acting Master, Commanding U. S. S. Orvetta.
BENJ. THOMPSON,
Master U. S. Ordnance Ship Sportsman.

FLAG-SHIP McCLELLAN,
Off Brazos Santiago, November 4, 1863.

Brig. Gen. CHARLES P. STONE,
New Orleans:

GENERAL: Our troops are nearly all landed. We have had great difficulty in getting horses and artillery ashore. The weather has greatly favored us. I shall send vessels to Brashear as soon as possible for troops—within a day or two at furthest. Let them be put in preparation, but do not withdraw the force so as to notify the enemy of our purpose. Rather let them threaten the Sabine from Vermillion-ville. This is important. Our chances are better than I had ever supposed, but we must have more troops, and especially more artillery. Artillery is of vital importance.

With much respect, your obedient servant,

N. P. BANKS,
Major-General, Commanding.

HEADQUARTERS THIRTEENTH ARMY CORPS,
Steamship McClellan, Brazos Santiago, November 4, 1863.

Captain STRONG,
U. S. Ship Monongahela, Commanding Naval Forces off Brazos:

I desire to express my sincere thanks to you and through you to your officers and men for the many services you have rendered this expedition, and particularly for the gallant service rendered by Captain [Edmund W.] Henry and the crew of the Owasco in saving the steam transport Zephyr from wreck during the late storm, and towing her to the rendezvous, and to you and your crew for assisting the steam transport Bagley, in distress; also especially for the signal gallantry of your brave tars in landing our soldiers through a dangerous surf yesterday at the mouth of the Rio Grande.

I wish also to mention for your special approval the names of Master's Mate [James H.] Rogers, Captains of Forecastle [David] White and [Guiseppi] Conte Modena, and Ordinary Seamen [Alonzo] Birt and [James] Hewes, of the Virginia, who, when a boat from this ship was capsized in the breakers on this bar at dusk last night, boldly pushed into the perilous place, and searched for the men all night.

You will oblige me now by bringing your ship to this anchorage when I will communicate with you in reference to future operations.

I have the honor to be, very respectfully,

N. J. T. DANA,
Major-General.

HEADQUARTERS TROOPS IN THE FIELD,
Vermillion, November 5, 1863.

Brigadier-General LAWLER,
Commanding Division, New Iberia:

GENERAL: The enemy, on account of the large booty at New Iberia, may think it worth while to attempt a raid from Opelousas, by way of the Teche, on your force. I have sent a mounted force 20 miles up to see if any such movement is on foot, but in the meantime please move your division to the intersection of the Saint Martinsville and Vermillion roads, posting your battery carefully, so as to command both roads.

The point is about 1 mile in front of New Iberia. Also look out well that your left flank may not be turned, supposing your front faces north. Make the movement as early as possible to-morrow morning.

W. B. FRANKLIN,
Major-General, Commanding.

BRAZOS SANTIAGO,
November 5, 1863.

General CARLETON,
Commanding U. S. Forces in New Mexico, Franklin, Tex.:

GENERAL: I have the honor to inform you that the forces of the United States occupy Brazos Island and Brownsville, upon the Rio Grande. It is our expectation that the flag will be permanently maintained here. I should be very glad to know the condition of forces in your department; whether it be practicable for you to co-operate with us in any movement in the direction of San Antonio.* The probability is that a successful movement in that direction will so cover New Mexico as to make an invasion of that territory impracticable for the enemy.

Any information or suggestions in regard to the forces in this part of the country which you may please to give me will be most gladly received. I will communicate to you early information of our future movements, until otherwise ordered, by Monterey and Chihuahua.

With much respect, your obedient servant,

N. P. BANKS,
Major-General, Commanding.

NEW ORLEANS,
November 5, 1863.

Maj. Gen. WILLIAM B. FRANKLIN,
Commanding Troops in Western Louisiana, Vermillion:

GENERAL: Your dispatch of 11.30 p. m. yesterday just received. Who commands on the part of the enemy? How strong do you consider him? It is important to retain as large a force of the enemy as possible in your front. Keep him amused. Advices from Brownsville, Tex., show that Magruder was withdrawing all the force from the Rio Grande, in order to concentrate in Northeastern Texas. The steamer Creole is in from New York, 28th. Nothing very important. Lee has again crossed the Rappahannock. Meade at Warrenton. Nothing new in Tennessee.

Very respectfully, your obedient servant,

CHAS. P. STONE,
Brigadier-General, and Chief of Staff.

BRAZOS SANTIAGO,
November 5, 1863.

Major THOMPSON,
Twentieth Iowa:

MAJOR: As early in the morning as the wind will permit, you will proceed with your regiment, on board the schooner Emma Amelia, to Point Isabel, and occupy that place. You will secure your position by

---

* See Carleton to Banks, December 25, 1863, p. 879.

strong pickets, and use every precaution to prevent surprise, collecting all possible information of the enemy, and send the same to these head-quarters. In order to keep up communication with this island, Major Carpenter, assistant quartermaster, will furnish a small boat and oars, to be kept under your charge. You will treat the people kindly, except-ing those against whom you may have positive information or suspicions of communicating with or aiding the enemy. All such you will take prisoners.

Collect all the means of transportation, horses, mules, cattle, and such property as may be useful or necessary for the public service, and have the same turned over to the proper officers. You will, under no circumstances, permit thieving, pillaging, or any depredations on the part of your troops, but will be careful to maintain proper discipline among them. There is a quantity of commissary stores on board the boat, for which you will cause your quartermaster to receipt to Capt. E. M. Emerson, commissary of subsistence of the division.

If all your command cannot be placed on the boat at once, you will use all possible dispatch in returning the boat and carrying over the rest, and, as soon as all are over, return the boat to Major Carpenter, assistant quartermaster.

You will be very economical of the water you may find on the island, as it will be very scarce.

By order of Maj. Gen. N. J. T. Dana:

WM. HYDE CLARK,
Assistant Adjutant-General.

BRAZOS SANTIAGO, *November* 5, 1863.

Brig. Gen. WILLIAM VANDEVER,
Commanding First Brigade :

GENERAL: The Twentieth Iowa Infantry, Major Thompson com-manding, has been ordered to proceed at an early hour in the morning to Point Isabel.

The major-general commanding directs that you move with your bri-gade at daylight in the morning to the point on the Rio Grande where the road from Boca Chica to Brownsville approaches nearest to or strikes the Rio Grande. It will be unnecessary to leave any troops at Boca Chica, and the regiment now there (Thirty-fourth Iowa, supposed to be) will be moved forward also.

You will collect all means of transportation, horses, mules, cattle, or whatever may be necessary or useful for the public service, but will treat the people you may meet kindly, allowing no pillaging or depre-dations to be committed by the men, and maintaining strict discipline amongst them, and enforcing obedience to orders.

I am, sir, your obedient servant,

WM. HYDE CLARK,
Assistant Adjutant-General.

MISSISSIPPI SQUADRON, FLAG-SHIP BLACK HAWK,
Cairo, November 5, 1863.

Maj. Gen. N. P. BANKS,
Commanding Department of the Gulf, New Orleans, La.:

GENERAL: I beg leave to acknowledge the receipt of yours of Octo-ber 17. I am glad to see your forces getting along so well in Louisiana.

I am now fitting out twelve gunboats, a little better than tin-clads, or at least with more iron on them, and by the time the water is high enough to operate you will have them with you. They will be armed with rifled guns and 24-pounder howitzers, and will not draw more than 30 inches.

This will give you twenty-two gunboats in your department with those now there, and I may be able to do more after we drive the rebels back from the Tennessee River.

The precarious position in which General Rosecrans' army was left after the battle of Chickamauga forced me to strain every nerve to endeavor to open communication with him up the Tennessee River, which was very low at the time, and I felt quite uneasy about General Sherman, who was advancing (by the way of Corinth) to his assistance. An unexpected rise swelled the river, and I got up a large fleet of gunboats and transports.

General Sherman arrived at Iuka at the same time, or a little before, and we ferried his army over in a very short time. That put matters straight, and we now command the position. Of course my whole mind was engrossed with this business, and I had to withdraw gunboats from every district to accomplish what was done, and, for moral effect, and to convoy transports, I have to keep them there. As soon as the water will permit, you will find me coming into the Atchafalaya or Bayou La Fourche with a good force.

I inclose you copy of a letter I wrote to the Secretary of the Navy, intended for General Halleck's inspection.* One of the gunboats captured two of General Dick Taylor's steamers, and burned them at the point A on the inclosed sketch.†

My letter to Mr. Secretary Welles will explain what I wished done. It would materially assist your operations.

Hoping soon to be able to supply your wants, I remain, very respectfully, your obedient servant,

DAVID D. PORTER,
Rear-Admiral.

NEW ORLEANS,
November 7, 1863.

Major-General FRANKLIN,
Comdg. Troops in Western Louisiana, Vermillion Bayou:

GENERAL: The movement of the major-general commanding has been a complete success.

You had better move a division promptly to Berwick Bay. Make provision for guarding your large supplies at New Iberia and covering your trains. More full particulars will come to-day.

Very respectfully, your obedient servant,

CHAS. P. STONE,
Brigadier-General, and Chief of Staff.

HEADQUARTERS DEPARTMENT OF THE GULF,
New Orleans, November 7, 1863.

Maj. Gen. WILLIAM B. FRANKLIN,
Vermillionville:

GENERAL: Your dispatch of this date received. One division at Berwick will be sufficient for some days. Please make as much show as

---

* See Report of the Secretary of the Navy for 1863, p. 546.   † Sketch not found.

possible of advance on the road to Sabine Pass. Use the mounted force freely in that direction and covering that road, and make all possible show of continued intention of passing that way.

Very respectfully, your obedient servant,

CHAS. P. STONE,
Brigadier-General, and Chief of Staff.

SPECIAL ORDERS, }   HDQRS. DEPARTMENT OF THE GULF,
No. 278.   }   *New Orleans, November 7, 1863.*

*   *   *   *   *   *

VII. Company C, First Louisiana Heavy Artillery, under command of Capt. Loren Rygaard, commanding battalion stationed at Camp Parapet, New Orleans, having been reported by the commander of the Defenses of New Orleans in such a state of insubordination as to indicate unmistakably the incapacity or criminal action of the officers of the company, and that the conduct and character of the company is such as to make the men composing it unworthy to bear arms, Capt. Loren Rygaard, commanding battalion, and the following-named officers composing Company C, First Louisiana Heavy Artillery, viz, Capt. N. L. Rich, Senior First Lieut. H. C. Rawson, Junior First Lieut. M. J. Kenyon, Junior Second Lieut. F. Walton, are hereby dismissed the service of the United States, and the company will be immediately disarmed and sent under guard to Port Hudson, where the men will be placed at hard labor on the public works, under the direction of the commanding officer of the post, until further orders.

The quartermaster's department will furnish the necessary transportation.

Senior Second Lieut. James M. Lawton, Company C, First Louisiana Heavy Artillery, not having served with the company during its insubordination, is honorably discharged the military service of the United States.

By command of Major-General Banks:

G. NORMAN LIEBER,
Acting Assistant Adjutant-General.

HEADQUARTERS DISTRICT OF NORTHEASTERN LOUISIANA,
Goodrich's Landing, La., November 9, 1863.

Maj. Gen. J. B. McPHERSON,
Vicksburg, Miss.:

GENERAL: Up to this day my information about the enemy was that Harrison, with 1,200 cavalry, was 2 miles west of Washita River, near Monroe, with two pieces of artillery. Parsons, with 1,000 cavalry, was 30 miles west of Washita, on Shreveport road. No knowledge concerning artillery.

This evening I have information from a negro, who left Floyd yesterday, that a considerable force of the enemy is 2 miles beyond Floyd, said to number 2,000 cavalry. He saw their artillery, and counted six pieces as it was traveling by him on the road. I was careful to learn from him that in numbering he did not count caissons as cannon. Harrison is in command of the force, and, from what I can learn, I presume that he and Parsons have united their forces and brought them into

Floyd, increased by McNeill's, Johnson's, and other companies. He learned also that Mr. Smith's (Kirby Smith's) command was expected to join from Bastrop. This is the direction, I presume, that troops would move from Arkadelphia. The last news I saw in the Northern papers was that not much more than a picket was left at the latter place, the remainder being withdrawn. I have no doubt as to the truth of the number of cannon seen and the number of cavalry reported. He (the negro) said, also, that he heard that they had two other pieces of artillery. The reported number of cavalry is sufficient to sweep over the district—not enough to hurt my command., What other force they may have in reserve to accomplish the latter, I have no other means of judging than is herein stated.

I am, general, very respectfully, your obedient servant,

JOHN P. HAWKINS,
Brigadier-General, Commanding.

HEADQUARTERS DEPARTMENT OF THE GULF,
New Orleans, November 10, 1863.

VICE-CONSUL OF FRANCE,
New Orleans :

Mr. CONSUL: Your respected letter of yesterday's date to the provost-marshal-general of the department has been this day referred to these headquarters. Therein you inform the provost-marshal-general that you have received a protest from several French subjects, passengers on board the schooner J. W. Wilder, which regularly cleared from the custom-house, on the 21st October, for the Mexican port of Matamoras, and which sailed the same day from New Orleans, was stopped lower down the river by superior authority, and, being without knowledge of any order, either from the Government at Washington or from the military authorities of this department, which could have induced such action, you ask the provost-marshal-general for information as to what may have been the reason for the adoption of a measure which, you state, will, if continued, be hurtful to the interests of your co-patriots.

In reply, I have the honor to inform you that said vessel was detained and prevented from making her intended voyage by command of the major-general commanding the department, for the reason that it was by him deemed necessary, as a military measure, to prevent, for a limited period of time, any communication between the port of New Orleans and that of Matamoras, Mexico.

The major-general commanding experienced a sincere regret that any interruption of lawful commerce should result from his operations, but deemed the measure referred to as one of absolute necessity to the good of the public service of the country.

With regard to the refusal of passes hence to Tampico and Vera Cruz, I would state that at this moment none can be granted, for good military reasons. The restrictions in this respect, as in the former, will doubtless soon be removed.

The letter of November 3 instant to the provost-marshal-general, of which you had the goodness to inclose a copy, having been referred to the proper office, will be duly answered on receipt of report.

With great respect, I have the honor to be, Mr. Consul, your most obedient servant,

CHAS. P. STONE,
Brigadier-General, and Chief of Staff.

NEW ORLEANS,
November 11, 1863.
Commodore H. H. BELL, U. S. Navy,
    Commanding West Gulf Squadron:
`COMMODORE`: A reconnaissance, made by order of Major-General Franklin toward the Mermeuton River, develops the fact that there are four blockade-running schooners in that river, discharging freight from New Orleans. Two of these are British schooners—the Adelaide, which cleared for Matamoras August 16, 1863, and sailed September 2, and the Derby, a British schooner, which cleared August 29, and sailed September 2 for Balize, Honduras, via Matamoras. Cannot these vessels be caught?
    Very respectfully, I am, commodore, your most obedient servant,
                                        CHAS. P. STONE,
                            Brigadier-General, and Chief of Staff.   .

———

NEW ORLEANS,
November 11, 1863
Hon. C. BULLITT,
    Collector of Customs, New Orleans:
SIR: As it appears from undeniable testimony that several vessels, cleared from this port within the past three months, wearing foreign flags and bound to foreign ports, have violated the blockade, and been found supplying the enemy with goods directly from New Orleans, I deem it my duty to inform you that orders have been given from these headquarters that hereafter no vessel cleared for a foreign port south of New Orleans will be permitted to sail unless furnished with a sufficient military pass. Will you have the goodness to notify this fact to all applicants for such clearances?
    Very respectfully, I am, sir, your most obedient servant,
                                        CHAS. P. STONE,
                            Brigadier-General, and Chief of Staff.

———

NEW ORLEANS,
November 12, 1863.
Maj. Gen. N. P. BANKS,
    Commanding Department of the Gulf, in the Field:
GENERAL: The steamer Alabama goes to you with a full battery of artillery and some convalescent officers of the Thirteenth Army Corps.
    Three schooners, which I have caused to be fitted up, will start to-morrow, to be towed to the Rio Grande. They will be loaded with extra artillery horses and forage.
    I am expecting the arrival of coal from Pensacola hourly, and will cause it to be forwarded as rapidly as possible.
    The Saint Mary's sailed from Brashear this afternoon with General Washburn on board. She takes two regiments and 30,000 rations. She was not fitted up for horses, and could not, therefore, take the battery which I had intended to send by her without great delay. I have ordered the steamer Kate Dale to be taken here; she is of light draught, and will be loaded to-morrow with wagons and mules, and sent to Brazos Island. She will carry about 40 wagons and 80 mules, and will carry forward some of Dana's convalescents.

In the destitution of the quartermaster's department here, I have been obliged to take all the soft coal in the private yards in the city, and, with this, hope to keep the transports going until coal shall arrive from up river.

The United States marshal, under the orders of the district judge of the United States, this morning took possession of the Alabama, and drove all the workmen and coalers off, saying he would teach the military authorities to respect the courts. As I had formally borrowed the Alabama, and had her in possession for thirty-six hours, it is difficult to see what could have been the object of such a violent proceeding on the marshal's part. As it was no time to wait, I immediately sent Colonel Abert on board with a detachment of the First Infantry, and arrested the deputy marshals on board, caused work to be resumed, and then wrote a respectful letter to the judge on the subject. The result of the marshal's proceedings was a delay of nearly a day in getting off the battery to you, and I informed him that a repetition of such interference with my forwarding re-enforcements to you would place him in close custody. General Thomas, Adjutant-General, fully approved all that was done in the premises.

Everything is quiet at Port Hudson and along the river. Port Hudson lines, interior and exterior, are expected to be completed before the end of the month. General Andrews reports them now fully in condition to hold with his present force.

General Franklin is at Vermillion, and has recently made heavy reconnaissances to Carrion Crow Bayou and in the Mermenton country. One regiment of Texas cavalry has appeared from Niblett's Bluff, and the force in his front seems to be increasing and waiting for something.

I do not think it will be well to weaken him materially beyond the withdrawal of the 5,000 already taken, until he can withdraw to a less extended line.

Very respectfully, I am, general, your obedient servant.

CHAS. P. STONE,
Brigadier-General, and Chief of Staff

NEW ORLEANS,
November 12, 1863

The Honorable Judge of U. S. District Court, New Orleans, La. :

YOUR HONOR: I am greatly concerned on learning that there is some difficulty about the steamer Alabama, a prize under adjudication in the court over which Your Honor so worthily presides. The day before yesterday I was officially informed that the steamer in question had been transferred to the Navy Department, and, as her services would be of incalculable advantage to the army at the moment, I addressed myself to the commodore commanding the West Gulf Squadron, asking for the use of her for one month. My request was immediately granted by the commodore, and the necessary repairs and preparations for service were commenced that night, and have been continued until the present time, when she is nearly ready for sea. It is of vital importance to the full success of military operations now prosecuting under the eye of the major-general commanding the department that the troops and supplies ordered on this steamer should reach him at once, and the vessel should sail without fail at the first moment practicable. The steamer must sail as soon as she can be prepared. The public service of the country requires it. I am ready to give any security which Your Honor may see fit to require, that no pecuniary loss shall result to the court, and I would not for any less reason than an imperative public necessity even seem to be disrespectful to Your Honor or your court.

I deeply regret that the marshal of the district should have taken violent measures to interrupt the occupation of the steamer ordered by me thirty-six hours since, in a way which I supposed to be perfectly consistent with Your Honor's orders concerning her. His violent measures, adopted without first referring to me, compelled me to use prompt and efficient measures to insure the prompt relief of the commander of the department.

With the highest respect, I have the honor to be, Your Honor's most obedient servant,

CHAS. P. STONE,
Brigadier-General, and Chief of Staff.

NEW ORLEANS,
November 12, 1863.

RUFUS WAPLES, Esq.,
 United States District Attorney:

SIR : I have just had the honor to receive your letter of this date, in reply to mine of even date to His Honor Judge Durell. As soon as the great pressure of business connected with transfer of troops and supplies to General Banks will permit, I will see that the requirements of His Honor are complied with. The violent measures adopted by the marshal, referred to in my letter, consisted in his going on board the steamer Alabama with a party of deputies, and suddenly arresting the work of preparation there in progress, and in his ordering all the military employés off the vessel, where they were busily at work, in pursuance of my orders. The action taken by the marshal will detain important reenforcements to General Banks probably one day; when his proper object (the securing of the rights of the honorable court he represented) could have been obtained in a five minutes' interview with me in my office.

I have honor to be, sir, very respectfully, your most obedient servant,

CHAS. P. STONE,
Brigadier-General, and Chief of Staff.

NEW ORLEANS,
November 12, 1863.

Maj. Gen. N. P. BANKS,
 Comdg. Department of the Gulf, in the Field :
  (Care of Lieutenant-Colonel Chandler, Brashear.)

GENERAL : The steamer Alabama will sail to-night to join you, carrying a battery of artillery, men, horses, and extra ammunition.

Schooners with 80 extra artillery horses will start this evening, to be towed to you; 100 extra artillery horses have been sent to-day to Brashear, to be shipped thence to you. All quiet up the river. The enemy shows strong force in front of Franklin's troops, and there has been heavy skirmishing between Vermillion and Opelousas. General Franklin all right, but should not be weakened much at present.

One of the small steamers of the enemy was captured yesterday in Bayou Long by Lieutenant-Colonel Tarbell.   All quiet in New Orleans.
    Very respectfully, your obedient servant,
                                    CHAS. P. STONE,
                .   Brigadier-General, and Chief of Staff.

                        NEW ORLEANS, LA., November 13, 1863.
                                VIA NEW YORK, November 20.
Major-General HALLECK, ·   .
        General-in-Chief:
    Major-General Banks was at Brownsville, Tex., on the 9th instant, with a good force of infantry, cavalry, and artillery.   There had been three revolutions in Matamoras.   His position highly satisfactory.
                                    CHAS. P. STONE,
                        Brigadier-General, and Chief of Staff.

            HEADQUARTERS DEPARTMENT OF THE GULF,
                        Brownsville, Tex., November 13, 1863.
L. PIERCE, Jr.,
        United States Consul, Matamoras:
    SIR: Recent events upon the western boundary of the United States make it necessary that the attention of Mexican authorities be called to the movements of men recently, and, we believe, still engaged in armed rebellion against the United States.   The rebels, impelled by military necessity to leave the State of Texas, have taken refuge in Matamoras and its vicinity.   They are making preparations, by the accumulation of stores adapted to the use of their army and the disposition of property transported from this State against law, to continue their hostile movements against the Government.   It is not my purpose to complain of any refuge or protection given by the authorities of the State of Tamaulipas to men lately engaged in rebellion who have suspended hostilities or laid down their arms.   Such protection is consistent with the magnanimous course of Mexico as of other States, and the Government of the United States would be the last to complain of any assistance accorded to men under such circumstances; but it must be admitted that the persistent continuation of hostile acts against the Government they have left, justly deprives them of both refuge and protection, and, under the general law of nations, as well as treaties of amity and friendship heretofore made between Mexico and the United States, such act or intention would justify a demand on the part of the latter, not only for the suspension of hostile purposes, but for their surrender to the Government against which their operations are directed.
    I appeal to you, as the representative of the United States in the State of Tamaulipas, to make known to its authorities the evidence in your possession in relation to the movements of men lately engaged in rebellion against the United States [who] are now prosecuting their hostile purposes in Matamoras and its vicinity, and I ask you to make official and earnest protest against their right to continue such hostilities or to make preparations in that State for future movements against the authorities of the United States, and, if such hostilities are still continued, to demand their surrender to the authorities of the United States.

I am persuaded that the Government of Mexico, hitherto manifesting so much friendship for the United States, and whose whole history has been distinguished by acts in the highest possible degree honorable to its people and to its rulers, will, upon full representation of the facts, admit the property of non-representatives and comply with the demands which international law and comity so clearly justify.

I respectfully call your attention to the fact that the law of blockade, hitherto respected by all nations, prohibits trade with the people of those States which have been in rebellion. So long as the boundary between Mexico and the United States was unprotected by force sufficient to maintain the blockade, no just grounds of complaint can be urged against that traffic which may have taken place over this border. The Government of the United States has now a sufficient force to maintain its rights under the blockade, and that force will be permanently maintained. I trust that you will urge upon the authorities of the State of Tamaulipas the duty of discountenancing preparations within its territory on the part of partisans of the rebel States for the interruption of the blockade which has been lawfully established. The complete enforcement of the rights of the Government under the blockade is the surest method of ending the controversy in which our Government is engaged, and it will soon restore the ancient commerce existing between the American and Mexican States.

This remonstrance should be directed against operations within Mexican territory in favor of rebel States or the people engaged in their service. You will understand the grounds upon which this remonstrance is to be enforced.

Recent events in this State call attention to another subject which affects the interests of the Government of the United States, and, in a very strong degree, the private rights of loyal people living under its authority, many of whom are of Mexican origin, and have strong claims upon the sympathy and protection of the Mexican people. Persons assuming to act by authority of the rebel States have, without law and without justice, taken property in large amounts from inoffensive and peaceful citizens of the State of Texas, under the pretext that such property was to be devoted to the use of the rebel Government.

Such pretext, it is believed, affords no justification for such seizures, but however that may be, it certainly does not justify such assumed agents in the appropriation of property so seized (ostensibly for the use of the rebel Government) to their own private and personal use; and it is manifest whenever such property may be found which has been seized in the name of the rebel authorities and applied by such agents to their own private and personal advantage, it ought to be returned to the persons from whom it had been taken. Property of very large amounts there seized under such unlawful pretensions, and fraudulently applied to private account of the agents or parties so seizing it, is now in the State of Tamaulipas. I respectfully ask you to call the attention of the Mexican authorities to the evidence and proof of such cases, and to demand—

1. That this property seized from peaceable and unoffending citizens in the State of Texas, either under the pretense that it was to be appropriated to the use of the rebel Government, or which may now stand in the name of private parties or individuals who have been connected with its seizure, may be returned to the lawful owners of the same, upon the presentation of the proofs of the title to the authorities in Mexico; or,

2. That this property may be detained by order of the authorities of Mexico until such time as evidence can be obtained for the proper,

equitable, and just disposition to be made of the same, in concurrence with the views of the Governments of the United States and Mexico.

These suggestions, briefly presented, embrace very important considerations, affecting materially the interests of the people of the two countries, between which, I am sure, strong friendship exists. They exhibit clearly the injustice of allowing insurrectionists to continue their operations against our Government upon Mexican soil, or to accumulate property against the law of blockade in Mexican territory, which is to be appropriated ultimately to the supply of munitions of war; and the purchase of armed vessels in foreign States for the purpose of driving from the seas or destroying American commerce may show in a still stronger degree the iniquity of allowing the fraudulent seizure of property of citizens, in great part of Mexican origin, under pretext of rebel authority, and the appropriation of the same to aggrandizement of the assumed agents who have been parties to the seizure. Such acts as these, persisted in, might be regarded as justifying the invasion of Mexican territory by the Government of the United States, upon the right, simply, of self-preservation. Such extreme claims will not, of course, be urged, but you will represent in the strongest manner the confidence that is felt in the justice of the Mexican authorities, and our confident belief that they will promptly enforce our rights and afford the redress which justice demands.

I have the honor to be, with high respect, yours, &c.,

N. P. BANKS,
Major-General, Commanding.

NEW ORLEANS,
November 13, 1863.

Maj. Gen. N. P. BANKS,-
Commanding Department of the Gulf, in the Field:

GENERAL: The steamers Crescent and Clinton have arrived here this morning, bringing your dispatches of November 9 instant.

I shall forward the dispatches by special messenger to Washington on the steamer of to-morrow.

Permit me to tender my congratulations on the great and most important success attained. Its results cannot fail to be appreciated by the country.

The Cresent and Clinton will, if possible, be gotten off on their return to-morrow, carrying 1,000 men of First Division, Thirteenth Army Corps, and wagons and mules for General Dana's division.

Colonel Beckwith has been directed to send an efficient commissary of subsistence.

After conversing with Major Houston, I shall probably be able to get one or two regiments of colored troops off to you as soon as transportation can be provided. As I understand your instructions, however, I shall first send "good troops."

Very respectfully, I am, general, your obedient servant,

CHAS. P. STONE,
Brigadier-General, and Chief of Staff.

P. S.—I have been this morning summoned to appear before the United States district court to show cause why I should not be fined and imprisoned for contempt of court, in having seized the steamer Alabama. I shall appear and treat the court with all respect, but if a disposition is shown to thwart military operations by these officers of the court, I shall arrest them.

NEW ORLEANS,
November 13, 1863.

Maj. Gen. WILLIAM B. FRANKLIN, *Vermillion :*

GENERAL: Your dispatch of this date just received, 3 p. m. Send in by all means for your overcoats and blankets. I have dispatches from General Banks to 9th instant. All well with him. I think you had better make such arrangements as you think will best secure the occupation of as much of the Teche country as your present force can hold. I do not think you will be materially weakened for some time to come. You were reported here this morning as killed.

Very respectfully, your obedient servant,

CHAS. P. STONE,
Brigadier-General, and Chief of Staff.

---

* HEADQUARTERS TROOPS IN THE FIELD,
Vermillion, November 14, 1863—3.15 p. m.

Brig. Gen. S. G. BURBRIDGE, *Commanding at New Iberia :*

If you get anything definite about Price and Magruder re-enforcing the rebels in my front, I shall be glad to know it. My position here is good against double my number. I have sent to see about the Abbeville Bridge, but I do not believe it. Perry's bridge is destroyed, to the best of my knowledge and belief. If the rebels get below you on the other side of the Teche in force, they will never get above you again.

Colonel Fournet, with Mr. D. Beraud, will see you to-morrow morning. I wish you to investigate the case of the former as soon as possible, letting me know the result. Major Cowan's papers ought to show whether he has authority to ship sugar. Demand to see them.

W. B. FRANKLIN,
Major-General.

HEADQUARTERS TROOPS IN THE FIELD,
Vermillion, November 15, 1863.

Brigadier-General McGINNIS, *Commanding Division :*

GENERAL: It is my intention to move this command to the vicinity of New Iberia to-morrow. I therefore request that you will quietly make such preliminary arrangements to-day as will enable you to be ready to march promptly at 7 o'clock in the morning. Your command will cross by the bridge which you have had made, and, after it has crossed, the bridge is to be thoroughly destroyed. The order of march will be sent you later in the day. Please say nothing about the movement until the order of march is received.

spectfully,

W B. FRANKLIN,
Major-General, Commanding.

GOODRICH'S LANDING, LA.,
November 15, 1863.

Maj. Gen. J. B. McPHERSON, *Vicksburg, Miss.:*

GENERAL: I have no further news or evidence of the troops reported in my last letter as being at Floyd. The last report is of quite a number of cavalry, infantry, and artillery in camp near Monroe, said to be 15,000. The number is doubtless exaggerated. Price's army was expected a few days since at Minden, between Monroe and Shreveport. Rations and forage were being collected there for it.

A gentleman, recently from Texas, says that everybody is being conscripted, and that Kirby Smith expects to have 75,000 men. Another, who has been beyond Bayou Macon, says his command is now reported to number that. Large numbers of negroes are being sent from Texas and Louisiana to Shreveport, to work on the fortifications. There is some talk of arming them there. There is also a report of the rebels fortifying the Washita at some point below Monroe.

Very respectfully, your obedient servant,
JOHN P. HAWKINS,
Brigadier-General, Commanding.

GOODRICH'S LANDING,
November 15, 1863.

Lieut. Col. W. T. CLARK,
Adjutant-General, Vicksburg:

COLONEL: Early in September I wrote to General Rawlins, requesting that Springfield (rifled) muskets might be substituted for the Austrian rifles now in the hands of my troops. The letter was referred to Lieutenant [Francis H.] Parker, chief of ordnance, who wrote me, telling me how it could be managed, to save delay, to send in an inspection report, showing condition of arms, organization, &c. The corps commander approving this report was to be warrant to allow a requisition to be made for arms.

The inspection report was made some time since, and I would respectfully request that the ordnance officer at Vicksburg be directed to estimate for the arms required for the troops mentioned in the inspection report. The Austrian rifle is not fit for a soldier. It is classed a third rate by the Ordnance Department, and I see very little wisdom in requiring voluminous reports and vexatious delays before replacing them with an arm that is known to be first class. Our present arms are constantly breaking and bursting, and their fire is very inaccurate. I could not go into a fight with much confidence in their efficiency. The men fear the effect on themselves of their own fire.

Very respectfully, your obedient servant,
JOHN P. HAWKINS,
Brigadier-General, Commanding.

NEW ORLEANS, LA.,
November 15, 1863.

Maj. Gen. N. P. BANKS,
Commanding Department of the Gulf, in the Field:

GENERAL: The steamer Clinton sails this afternoon, with Major-General Washburn on board, about 600 infantry, 100 horses, and wagons and ambulances.

I was informed that General Washburn had gone on the Saint Mary's, but he wisely concluded to go with the second detachment of his division.

I have ordered Brigadier-General Warren to go forward also, feeling that he would be useful with you.

Mr. Gallup, former proprietor of the Brownsville Flag newspaper, goes also.

General Cortes, of the Mexican army, envoy from Juarez to our Government, arrived here last Sunday from Washington, and I send him forward to Brownsville, where his knowledge of Mexican affairs and bitter opposition to the French can hardly fail to be of advantage to the cause, both on our side and on that of Mexico. You will find General Cortes highly intelligent, and devoted to the cause of Mexico against the invaders.

I have just received (11 a. m.) notice from Southwest Pass that the steamers Thomas A. Scott and Northerner have crossed the bar, and are on the way up the river. They will be immediately put in order, loaded, and sent off.

I have succeeded in borrowing from the navy 1,000 tons additional of coal, which relieves us much. The schooners from Pensacola have not yet reported.

All is quiet up the river. I sent a very intelligent spy last week through the country back of Baton Rouge and Port Hudson. He returned last night, having been beyond Clinton east and up to Woodville, where he was held prisoner two days by Scott's cavalry. He estimates the entire force within thirty-six hours' concentration distance of Clinton at 4,000, nearly all mounted; represents that there is no idea of attack on Baton Rouge or Port Hudson.

From General Franklin we have rather interesting news. The rebels seem to be concentrating against him, and it is rumored that Price and Magruder are marching to join the forces opposed to him. He received the intelligence about the same time that I did here. While neither of us place much reliance in the reports, yet I advised Franklin to concentrate more, and he will fall back on New Iberia and establish a strong line in that neighborhood.

The guerrillas, 75 strong, day before yesterday attacked a steamboat on the Teche, 10 miles below New Iberia. They were driven off by the guard of 30 colored troops of Frisbie's regiment, after a three hours' fight.

I learn that General Vandever is on his way up the river. This makes me more satisfied with the order to Warren. General Washburn thinks highly of General Warren, and is much pleased that he goes.

I have ordered by the Crescent, now nearly loaded, 1,500 sets cavalry equipments, and arms complete (uniform), and all the irregular horse equipments (about 300). Also, arms, accouterments, and ammunition for 2,000 infantry. More will go forward. Fifty thousand feet of lumber has also been ordered.

The district attorney and United States district marshal seem to have gone demented in your absence, and are cutting at everybody. Their last blow at the military was the affair of the Alabama. Since that they have thrown the whole town into confusion by a general seizure of cotton, which had already been overhauled by the internal revenue officials, and more excitement has been created by it than by anything I have seen here.

If much more confusion and trouble should ensue, I think these gentlemen will have to be arrested. Should I, after consultation with General Bowen and Colonel Beckwith, think it necessary to do anything of the kind, I shall do it as my own act, as senior military officer present here, so that you can repudiate the act on your return or confirm it, as may seem best for the public interest, and no odium or responsibility rest on you.

Of course, I shall take no step precipitately, or without being, fully impressed with the necessity, nor should I do it without full consultation with the officers mentioned, and the Adjutant-General, now here. I shall report again by the Crescent a few hours later.

Very respectfully, I am, general, your obedient servant,

CHAS. P. STONE,
Brigadier-General, and Chief of Staff.

———

GOODRICH'S LANDING, LA.,
November 16, 1863.

Maj. Gen. J. B. McPHERSON,
Vicksburg, Miss. :

GENERAL : A person who has been out on Joe's Bayou tells me that Mrs. ———, at whose house he staid over night, was informed through a rebel soldier that the rebels at Monroe were under marching orders to leave there last Friday. It was not stated in what direction they were to go, but the impression was conveyed that they were coming this way. Their reported strength is 15,000. From another party he got the report that they were coming this way; that they intended to wipe out the troops and plantations this side of the river. I hope a better gunboat will be sent me than the one now here. It is heavily loaded with ordnance stores, and would have to leave out of danger in case we are attacked by artillery. I understood Franklin is on his return march; so an officer from Vicksburg tells me. This will leave Price's hands free to operate in this direction. If this point and Milliken's have any strategic or other value, a large re-enforcement is required to assure their safety. If the value is small, the risk overbalances it; the play is not worth the candle, and your order for the abandonment would, in such case, be the better policy. So the question resolves itself, in my mind, into proper re-enforcement or abandonment.

I am, general, very respectfully, your obedient servant,

JOHN P. HAWKINS,
Brigadier-General, Commanding.

———

. GOODRICH'S LANDING, LA.,
November 16, 1863.

Maj. Gen. J. B. McPHERSON,
Vicksburg, Miss.:

GENERAL : The contingency of abandoning this place and Milliken's Bend, spoken of in my letter to you of this date, has been more fully thought over since that letter was written. There is a military consideration in keeping possession, and also the adherence to the Government policy with regard to the leasing of plantations and giving employment to the freed negroes. The question of retention or abandonment involves many nice points, which, in a war point of view, may be resolved into the question of strength at your command, inclining you to do the one or the other.

When the plantation policy was adopted, the Government had a large force near by, part of which might be diverted for its protection. That force is now much diminished. Is what remains sufficient to carry out the original intention in case of attack by a superior force? If it is, the policy can be carried out. If not, an abandonment of the district may become necessary, and giving up the plantation policy.

Very respectfully,

JOHN P. HAWKINS,
Brigadier-General, Commanding.

SPECIAL ORDERS, ⎫　　　　　　　NEW ORLEANS, LA.,
　　No. 102.　⎬　　　　　　　*November* 16, 1863.

I. So much of General Orders, No. 70, dated Headquarters Department of the Gulf, September 28, 1863, as prescribes that—

All able-bodied men of color employed upon Government or private plantations will be detailed for military service in the Corps d'Afrique, upon order of the commission of enrollment—

is hereby suspended.

II. No officer or other person will hereafter be permitted to recruit for any corps or regiment of colored troops from off the Government or leased plantations.

III. No negro will be recruited from off the plantations of private individuals until further orders, for the purpose of permitting planters to take off their present crop. This paragraph refers only to parishes in Louisiana exempted by the President in his proclamation of January 1, 1863.

The above order is issued by the undersigned in the absence of Maj. Gen. N. P. Banks, feeling assured that were that officer present, and cognizant of existing circumstances, he would issue orders to the same effect.

*　　　*　　　*　　　*　　　*　　　*

By order of the Secretary of War:

L. THOMAS,
Adjutant-General.

FLAG-SHIP McCLELLAN,
Off Aransas Pass, Tex., November 17, 1863.

Brig. Gen. CHARLES P. STONE,
Chief of Staff, Department of the Gulf:

GENERAL: It gives me pleasure to inform you of the capture of the works at Aransas Pass this day (17th). We have in our possession three heavy guns, 1 lieutenant-colonel, 9 officers, 90 men, between 80 and 90 horses, a quantity of small-arms, a schooner, and considerable transportation.

We arrived at Corpus Christi, from Brazos Santiago, yesterday about 2 p. m., and landed our troops during the night. It was supposed that the Matamoras, which we brought with us from the Rio Grande, would be able to cross the bar, but we found only $2\frac{1}{2}$ feet of water there, which made it impossible, and we were compelled to land our troops upon the coast by means of surf-boats. The landing occupied a greater part of the night. The troops reached Aransas Pass early this morning, taking the enemy completely by surprise. After skirmishing for a couple of hours on the island, and the firing of some most excellent shots from the Monongahela, they surrendered.

To-morrow we move against Pass Cavallo, where we shall have, perhaps, a more severe contest.

It is important, in reference to our future movements, that there should be one or two gunboats in Berwick Bay. I desire you to communicate with Commodore Bell upon this subject. Admiral Porter ought to send some of his gunboats, which were ordered here by the Government, to the mouth of the river and around by the coast. I am confident we could get them round safely by means of buoying them with the assistance of steamers, and watching closely for fair weather.

Captain Strong has been of great assistance to us in enabling us to land troops. His artillery practice against the enemy was most effective.

With much respect, your obedient servant,

N. P. BANKS,
Major-General, Commanding.

P. S.—Colonel Davis informs me that a sutler belonging to his regiment, Mr. H. C. Jordan, now in New Orleans, is thoroughly acquainted with the inland navigation at Matagorda. I desire that you will send him down here at the first opportunity.

FLAG-SHIP McCLELLAN,
Off Aransas Pass, Tex., November 17, 1863.

Commodore H. H. BELL,
Comdg. West Gulf Blockading Squadron, &c., New Orleans:

COMMODORE: It gives me pleasure to inform you of the capture of the works at Aransas Pass this day. We have in our possession three heavy guns, 1 lieutenant-colonel, 9 officers, 90 men, between 80 and 90 horses, a quantity of small-arms, and considerable transportation.

We arrived at Corpus Christi from Brazos Santiago yesterday about 2 p. m., and landed our troops during the night. It was supposed that the Matamoras, which we brought with us from the Rio Grande, would be able to cross the bar, but we found only 2½ feet of water there, which made it impossible, and we were compelled to land our troops upon the coast by means of surf-boats. The landing occupied a greater part of the night. The troops reached Pass Aransas early this morning, taking the enemy completely by surprise. After skirmishing for a couple of hours on the island, and the firing of some most excellent shots from the Monongahela, they surrendered.

To-morrow we move against Pass Cavallo, where we shall have, perhaps, a more severe contest.

It is important, in reference to our future movements, that there should be one or two gunboats in Berwick Bay. I hope you will send down one or two as soon as possible. Admiral Porter ought to send some of his gunboats, which were ordered here by the Government, to the mouth of the river, around by the coast. I am confident we could get them round safely by means of buoying them with the assistance of steamers, and watching closely for fair weather. The distance is about 40 miles. I wish you would communicate with him upon this subject.

Captain Strong has been of great assistance to us in enabling us to land troops.

The artillery practice against the enemy was most effective.

I have the honor to be, &c.,

N. P. BANKS,
Major-General, Commanding.

NEW ORLEANS,
November 17, 1863.
Brig. Gen. H. W. BIRGE, *Thibodeauxville:*
GENERAL: Look well to your right flank. There are movements reported up the Grossetête, which require care. Cavalry may come down from that direction in force. I have ordered the troops in Berwick to cross to Brashear.
Very respectfully, your obedient servant,
CHAS. P. STONE,
Brigadier-General, and Chief of Staff.

NEW ORLEANS,
November 17, 1863.
Commanding Officer, Donaldsonville:
SIR: Look sharp toward Bayou Grossetête. Caution commanding officer at Plaquemine to the same effect. You will both please report to me by telegraph whether or not there are signs of assemblage or movement of the enemy in that direction.
Acknowledge receipt of this dispatch promptly.
Very respectfully, your obedient servant,
CHAS. P. STONE,
Brigadier-General, and Chief of Staff.

NEW ORLEANS,
November 17, 1863.
Colonel FISKE, *Commanding at Donaldsonville:*
COLONEL: It is reported that the enemy have crossed the Atchafalaya back of Morganza, and that some have moved down the Grossetête. Be vigilant and report frequently. Establish couriers between your post and General Birge.
Very respectfully, your obedient servant,
CHAS. P. STONE,
Brigadier-General, and Chief of Staff.

NEW ORLEANS,
November 17, 1863.
Brigadier-General LAWLER, *Berwick or Brashear:*
GENERAL: Throw what troops you have at Berwick across to Brashear immediately, and report by telegraph what strength you have.
Very respectfully, your obedient servant,
CHAS. P. STONE,
Brigadier-General, and Chief of Staff.

NEW ORLEANS,
November 17, 1863.
Senior Naval Officer, near Donaldsonville:
SIR: Is there any gunboat at Plaquemine? If not, can one be sent there? There is information that the enemy are on the Grossetête, above that point.
Very respectfully, your obedient servant,
CHAS. P. STONE,
Brigadier-General, and Chief of Staff.

'NEW ORLEANS,
November 18, 1863.
Brigadier-General BIRGE,
Thibodeauxville :

GENERAL: Please re-enforce Donaldsonville 1,000 men, and call on General Lawler at Brashear for an equal number, if necessary. Plaquemine is said to be threatened heavily from above.
Very respectfully, your obedient servant,
CHAS. P. STONE,
Brigadier-General, and Chief of Staff.

———

NEW ORLEANS,
November 18, 1863.
Brigadier-General LAWLER,
Brashear :

GENERAL: Leave one regiment at Berwick to guard property. The remainder of your troops will remain on this side of the bay, ready to move, if necessary.
Very respectfully, your obedient servant,
CHAS. P. STONE,
Brigadier-General, and Chief of Staff.

———

WASHINGTON, D. C.,
November 19, 1863.
Maj. Gen. N. P. BANKS.
Commanding Department of the Gulf :

GENERAL: Your dispatch of the 4th instant, announcing the occupation of Brazos Island, Tex., is received. In regard to re-enforcing you, I can only repeat what I have previously written. All drafted men are assigned to regiments from their own States. Orders were issued some time ago to fill up your regiments, as far as possible, from the States to which they belong. Some progress has been made in this, but it is slow work.

We cannot send you other regiments at present without taking them from other generals in the field, who are as urgent as yourself for re-enforcements. Moreover, it is thought that your army is sufficiently strong for that against which you are operating. The enemy can defeat you only by concentrating all his forces against your separate and isolated columns.

The concentration of rebel forces in Northern Georgia has compelled us to send there everything available.
Very respectfully, your obedient servant,
H. W. HALLECK,
General-in-Chief.

———

THIBODEAUX, LA.,
November 19, 1863.
Maj. G. NORMAN LIEBER,
Acting Assistant Adjutant-General, Department of the Gulf :

MAJOR: I have the honor to report that the Seventh and Twenty-second Regiments Kentucky Volunteers, Forty-second and One hundred and twentieth Ohio Volunteer Infantry, and First Indiana Battery, four guns, all under command of Colonel Sheldon, Forty-second Ohio, and being a part of the First Brigade, Third Division, Thirteenth Army Corps, arrived at this post this morning at 9 a. m., and marched immediately for Donaldsonville, where they will probably arrive to-morrow. The strength of Colonel Sheldon's command is about 1,050 men.

I am, major, very respectfully, your obedient servant,

H. W. BIRGE,
Brigadier-General, Commanding.

HEADQUARTERS DEPARTMENT OF MISSOURI,
Saint Louis, Mo., November 19, 1863.

[Maj. Gen. N. P. BANKS:]

* * * * * * *

The General-in-Chief suggests that General Steele might now advance to Red River and form a junction with you, or at least hold that river while you operate in Texas. I am anxious to advance his force to Red River as soon as practicable. No doubt this will also strengthen you, and aid you to carry out your plans.

* * * * * * *

J. M. SCHOFIELD,
Major-General.

NEW ORLEANS, *November* 19, 1863.

ADJUTANT-GENERAL OF THE ARMY, *Washington, D. C.*:

GENERAL: I deem it my duty to report for the information of the War Department the recent action taken by the United States district court in this city in reference to the prize-steamer Alabama, now in the transport service of the army.

When Major-General Banks left this place, on the 26th ultimo, for the Rio Grande, he directed me to remain at these headquarters and carry out such directions as he had given and would give me.

Among the important duties with which I was charged was that of forwarding troops and supplies in case he should call for them.

On the arrival of the first return steamer from the expedition, I learned that artillery was greatly required, and while I had an excellent battery ready, I had no means of transporting it, with its men and horses.

On the 9th of November, I directed the quartermaster's department to purchase the prize-steamer Alabama, which I understood had been condemned and ordered sold. On the 10th instant, I was informed that the commodore of the West Gulf Squadron had secured her for the naval service. I immediately applied to Commodore Bell, asking him to lend her to the army for the period of a month, and during the evening of the 10th received an answer that he consented. Notwithstanding the consent of the commodore reached me only about nightfall, I caused workmen to be placed at once on board of her, and repairs and preparations were carried on uninterruptedly throughout the night of the 10th and the day and night of the 11th, and on the morning of the 12th she was nearly ready for sea, with boilers repaired, stalls for horses erected, coal partly on board, &c. She was expected to sail shortly after noon, and get over the [bar] of the river and to sea that night. Greatly to my astonishment and regret, a report was brought to me about 10 a. m. on the 12th that the United States marshal for the district of Louisiana had appeared on board of the steamer, accompanied by several deputies; had taken possession of the ship; ordered all work on her to cease, and driven off all the mechanics, officers, and coalers, using violent language against the military authorities, and saying he would teach these military men not to ride over the courts, &c.

Captain McClure, assistant quartermaster, went on board and found all work suspended and three deputy marshals in charge of the steamer. He requested permission to go on with the work, and was told that not a blow could be struck until the vessel was paid for.

Meantime the report having come to me, I deeply regretted any chance of collision with civil authorities, but deemed it necessary to push the re-enforcements forward to General Banks at all hazards, and, foreseeing great and perhaps disastrous delays in stopping to argue with excited civilian officers, I ordered a discreet officer (Lieutenant-. Colonel Abert, assistant inspector-general) to proceed to the steamer with a guard of 20 soldiers, to arrest any persons on board interfering with the preparations and repairs, and to restore the workmen to their duty. All this time I had supposed that the military authorities had lawful possession of the steamer, under the authority of Commodore Bell, from whom I had borrowed her, and with the consent of the court which had ordered her transfer to the navy.

Lieutenant-Colonel' Abert performed his duty satisfactorily, and arrested three deputy marshals, whom he brought to my office, after having re-established order and industry on the steamer.

Meantime I addressed a respectful letter to His Honor the judge of the district court, expressing my concern that there should have been any misunderstanding; informing him of the necessity which existed of the steamer's promptly leaving with the re-enforcements for General Banks; stating to him that I had been in peaceable possession of the vessel for more than thirty-six hours before the violent action of the marshal, and, as I supposed, with his full concurrence and approval; that nothing could be more regretted by the military authorities than a conflict with or a seeming disrespect to the honorable court, but that, under any circumstances, the steamer must remain in my possession, and go to sea with troops on board as quickly as possible. It was a case of necessity.

To this letter the honorable judge made no reply; but later, the United States district attorney wrote to me that the judge was ill, and that the steamer had not yet been paid for by the navy, and therefore was still in the custody of the court. To this letter I wrote a respectful reply.

The steamer, after a delay of one day, by reason of the interruption of the work of preparation, was duly dispatched to Brazos with the re-enforcements and supplies.

On the day following, I received a summons to appear before the honorable Mr. [Edward H.] Durell, United States district court judge, on the 18th of November instant, and show cause why I should not be fined and imprisoned for contempt of court in having seized said steamer from the custody of the marshal and arresting his officers.

On the 18th instant, I presented myself in court and made a statement of the facts as herein related; stated my responsibilities and the necessity of the action taken, and disclaimed any intent to be disrespectful to the honorable court. I regret to state that the course pursued in court by the district attorney was very far from conciliatory. He strained every point to make out a case of disrespect, while I constantly disclaimed for myself and the military authorities of the department any such attempt. He insisted upon calling testimony to prove the points admitted in open court by me, and although I represented that my time at that moment was valuable, and my absence from duty in my office was of so much detriment to the course of business, that only a desire to show perfect respect to the court could have induced me to be present myself even for a quarter of an hour, I was detained there two hours, and made to listen to a long argument from the district attorney, in the endeavor to fabricate a case of contempt. The honorable judge dismissed the case, after administering a long reprimand to me for my ignorance of the law and apparent desire to override the civil authority.

I made no answer, either to the long argument of the district attorney or the reprimand of the judge, being quite content, so far as the public service was concerned, that my action had caused the re-enforcements to go forward to the commanding general without any loss of time due to my action or want of action. I am constrained to say that the whole affair produced upon my mind the impression that the judge, district attorney, and marshal seemed more anxious to maintain a false appearance of maintaining dignity and making newspaper reputation for courage and eloquence than to strengthen and support the military power of the country, and to contribute to military success now so necessary to the country.

So strongly was this impression upon me, that had the commanding general himself been present, I should have felt myself constrained to advise him to ship the whole court to Washington.

I have the honor to be, general, very respectfully, your obedient servant,

CHAS. P. STONE,
Brigadier-General, Chief of Staff.

NEW ORLEANS,
November 19, 1863.
Col. W. O. FISKE, *Commanding at Donaldsonville:*

COLONEL: A battery or two batteries of field artillery will sail for Donaldsonville to-morrow morning.

Send by telegraph all reports you can get from Plaquemine. Advise the commanding officer there from me to intrench strongly and establish signals with the gunboat. Keep up couriers between yourself and him with regularity, and report all you hear. Reconnoiter well to the west and northwest.

Very respectfully, your obedient servant,

CHAS. P. STONE,
Brigadier-General, and Chief of Staff.

NEW ORLEANS, LA.,
November 19, 1863.
Maj. Gen. N. P. BANKS,
Commanding Department of the Gulf, in the Field:

GENERAL: I had the honor to report yesterday by the steamer Nathaniel P. Banks, which sailed from Brashear with a light load of subsistence stores. She would not have been safe in a sea-way with heavy load.

To-day the Thomas A. Scott sails with 600 infantry of First Division, Thirteenth Army Corps, under Colonel Harris. She also carries 50 tons subsistence stores. I am exceedingly anxious to forward troops and supplies with more rapidity, but the steamers do not come back as rapidly as might be wished, and as none come into Berwick Bay, where our stores have been collected, more difficulty is experienced in shipping than was expected.

When the Scott shall have left, we shall have no steamer which can cross the bar at Brazos Santiago.

The Corinthian draws too much water fully laden; she will be loaded light and sent.

I cannot report matters quiet up the river. Yesterday morning the steamer Emerald, loaded with recruits and returning men of Thirteenth Army Corps, was fired into at Hog Landing, just below mouth of Red River. The enemy seemed to have four 6-pounders. The firing damaged the boat somewhat, but no men were killed or wounded.

Green is reported to have crossed the Atchafalaya back of Morganza with a heavy force of cavalry and sixteen pieces of artillery. One report states his object to be to seize a steamboat, cross the river, and effect a junction with Logan at Clinton. The other report is that he intends a raid down the Grossetête, to cut the railroad. I do not believe he intends either, but think he wishes to blockade the river near Morganza.

I have, however, strengthened Donaldsonville, and promised that a gunboat shall remain off Plaquemine.

I shall send steamboats to Donaldsonville, so that, in case of need, Plaquemine can be re-enforced thence.

Logan has been re-enforced at Clinton, since Sunday last, by three small regiments from Alabama.

General Andrews thinks himself secure against Logan. Baton Rouge is doubtless strong enough also, if well defended, which I think it would be.

General Franklin is at New Iberia, the enemy showing considerable force at Camp Pratt. I have recommended him to make such a strong demonstration as to ascertain whether he has a mere shell or a solid force in front, and he replies that he shall do so to-morrow. His cavalry force is too much jaded to act to-day.

I am informed, from what I consider a reliable source, that Waul's Legion recently crossed the Mississippi River, near Romney, 1,000 strong, and got safely to the west bank. This would seem to indicate that the enemy propose fighting strongly west of the Mississippi.

Very respectfully, I am, general, your obedient servant,

CHAS. P. STONE,
Brigadier-General, and Chief of Staff.

NEW ORLEANS,
November 20, 1863.

Col. J. C. KELTON,
Assistant Adjutant-General, Headquarters of the Army:

COLONEL: In the absence of the major-general commanding, I have the honor to report the following for the information of the General-in-Chief:

On the 10th instant, the major-general commanding department was at Brownsville, Tex., with about 3,000 men and sixteen pieces of artillery. No known force of the enemy nearer than Corpus Christi, where there was but a handful, and San Antonio, whither Bee had retired with from 150 to 200 men.

Refugees and recruits are coming into our lines in great numbers, and the commanding general called on me for additional horse equipments and cavalry arms. The recruits bring their own horses. I have forwarded about 2,000 sets, with arms, for cavalry.

Brownsville was being put in defensible condition, and works were being constructed on Point Isabel and Brazos Santiago Island. It was supposed that Corpus Christi would be occupied and fortified by our troops.

During the past week I have, on the requisition of the commanding general, forwarded to the mouth of the Rio Grande 2,000 infantry, a battery of artillery, and 100 extra artillery horses. More troops, to the extent of 3,000 infantry of Thirteenth Army Corps, two regiments of the Corps d'Afrique, and two batteries of field artillery, are awaiting means of transportation to go forward.

Major-General Franklin is holding the Teche country, with his headquarters at New Iberia. The enemy has made considerable show of force in his front, and it has been reported that Magruder has joined General Dick Taylor from Niblett's Bluff, and a portion of Price's force from Shreveport, but neither General Franklin nor myself credit the report.

This morning General Franklin effected a surprise of the enemy's advanced force of cavalry (Sixth Texas Regiment), and captured all but 25 of it. The regiment was small. The captured amounted to 12 commissioned officers and 100 rank and file.

Up the river the enemy have shown some activity. Day before yesterday they came to the Mississippi River at Hog Landing, near the mouth of Red River, and fired upon a transport, coming down, with four pieces of field artillery. No lives were lost on the boat, and a gunboat at the point immediately commenced shelling the position. No further result reported as yet. The rebel General Green has crossed the Atchafalaya River back of Morganza with artillery and cavalry, and was yesterday reported as intending a raid down the Grossetête, to interrupt our line to Berwick Bay. To prevent mischief in that direction, I have sent re-enforcements to Donaldsonville and Plaquemine.

On the east bank of the river, Logan is reported as near Clinton, La., with from 3,000 to 4,000 men (much scattered), on Thursday of last week, and re-enforced last Monday at Clinton by three small regiments from Alabama, with promise of more, to threaten Port Hudson and Baton Rouge. Both these positions are well garrisoned and in good state for defense.

While writing, I receive information that a steamer is just coming up the river from the Texas expedition, and she reports by telegraph from the quarantine station that Corpus Christi was in possession of our forces when she sailed.

I would respectfully suggest that the heavy guns and ammunition called for by the chief of ordnance of the department by last steamer be sent forward as rapidly as possible, as they will be much needed in the positions which have been seized on the Texas coast.

I have the honor to be, colonel, very respectfully, your obedient servant,

CHAS. P. STONE,
Brigadier-General, and Chief of Staff.

NEW ORLEANS,
November 20, 1863.

Major-General FRANKLIN,
    New Iberia:

GENERAL: I congratulate you heartily on the success of this morning's work. A gentleman from Rapides Parish informs me that the whole force of enemy in Western Louisiana does not exceed 7,000 men. He thinks the movement made by Green across the Atchafalaya was necessary to the rebels, in order to raise the secessionists from the state of despair into which they were falling, and to gather up a few mules and conscripts. I am re-enforcing Plaquemine, however, to prevent chance of trouble below. I have received intelligence that Corpus Christi is in the commanding general's possession. No particulars.

Very respectfully, your obedient servant,   '
CHAS. P. STONE,
Brigadier-General, and Chief of Staff.

NEW ORLEANS,
November 20, 1863.

Colonel FISKE,
    Donaldsonville:

COLONEL: Two batteries have left this for Donaldsonville, one at 10 a. m., the other at noon. I have received no report from you to-day. If the same state of affairs as last reported still exists above you, Colonel Sheldon will, on the arrival of the batteries, embark his infantry on the steamers conveying them, and proceed without delay to Plaquemine, where he will disembark his infantry and the two batteries, and take such measures for securing that section of country as may be deemed by him necessary. You will please acknowledge receipt of this dispatch, and report by telegraph once in three hours until further orders.

Very respectfully, your obedient servant,
CHAS. P. STONE,
Brigadier-General, and Chief of Staff.

HEADQUARTERS FIRST DIVISION, ARMY OF TEXAS,
Corpus Christi, Tex., November 21, 1863.

Comdg. Officer of the U. S. Land or Naval Forces, Aransas Pass:

SIR: In response to the appeals made to me by the families of the soldiers of this army stationed on Mustang Island, I have the honor to send Lieut. Walter L. Mann, acting assistant adjutant-general of this division, under a flag of truce, with this communication.

In the name of humanity, I ask that you will inform me of the fate of those soldiers, that the families may be relieved from this state of suspense.

A flag-of-truce boat sent down by Colonel [A. M.] Hobby, of this command, before my arrival, has not returned; it was borne by Acting Sailing Master Neal; information as to its whereabouts is requested.

I have the honor to be, with great respect, your obedient servant,
H. P. BEE,
Brig. Gen., Provisional Army Confederate States.

NEW ORLEANS,
November 21, 1863.
Brigadier-General LAWLER, *Brashear:*
GENERAL: Send forward to Algiers as rapidly as possible 1,500 infantry.
Very respectfully, your obedient servant,
CHAS. P. STONE,
Brigadier-General, and Chief of Staff

———

NEW ORLEANS,
November 21, 1863.
Brig. Gen. A. ASBOTH, *Commanding Troops in West Florida:*
GENERAL: I have information, which seems to be reliable, that the rebel authorities intend making a serious attack on your position early the coming week.
Large bodies of troops are said to have been sent to Pollard by rail, for the purpose, and another force by way of Bonsecours Bay. I hope this intelligence will reach you in time to anticipate such movements, if really intended, and feel perfect confidence that in any case all will be done that can be to make the result disastrous to the enemy.
Very respectfully, I am, general, your most obedient servant,
CHAS. P. STONE,
Brigadier-General, and Chief of Staff.

———

PORT HUDSON, LA.,
November 22, 1863—8 p. m.
Brig. Gen. CHARLES P. STONE, *Chief of Staff, New Orleans:*
Captain Halsted crossed the river this morning; has just returned. Reports that rebel pickets are at Pointe Coupée, and stop all persons going up. Cannot learn the cause of the firing up river last evening which was heard here. It is and has been repeatedly reported that Taylor is this side the Atchafalaya with 12,000 or 14,000 men, marching on Plaquemine and Donaldsonville; is certain that straggling parties of rebels are below this post, on west bank. Three brigades are reported—Green's, Walker's, and [H. W.] Allen's—sixteen pieces of artillery. No new information from this side the river. Captain Halsted's information came from citizens. Taylor's present position reported on Grossetête. No informant had actually seen any considerable body of the enemy.
GEO. L. ANDREWS,
Brigadier-General of Volunteers, Commanding Post.

———

NEW ORLEANS,
November 22, 1863.
Maj. Gen. N. P. BANKS,
Commanding Department of the Gulf, in the Field:
GENERAL: The news of the occupation of Corpus Christi was brought night before last by the steamer Hussar, and was duly communicated by letter to the General-in-Chief by the mail steamer Washington, which sailed yesterday morning.

The steamer Saint Mary's passed by the bar yesterday morning, and news reached me at 10 a. m. from her that you had captured the garrison at Aransas Bay. I at once telegraphed to Fort Jackson, and had a telegraphic dispatch, announcing the success to General Halleck, placed on board.

Captain Dunham being convalescent, and recommended to go north by the medical officers, I had sent him on the Washington, charged with duplicates of your dispatches by the last steamer, and a short report on the occurrences of the week to the General-in-Chief and Adjutant-General.

The steamer Corinthian sails to-day, taking two Iowa regiments, 600 men.

The Saint Mary's will be sent to-morrow with about the same number and the transportation. I have ordered the purchase of three prize schooners for running stores to Aransas, and hope to get them off to-day laden with subsistence and ammunition.

I have ordered—have had a standing order with the quartermaster's department to get possession of any steamer and sailing vessels coming into port which can be used, and have dispatched them as fast as procured. The Nathaniel P. Banks was so strained getting around to Brashear that it was not deemed safe to send her to Texas. She will be used between this and Pensacola.

Yesterday I received very direct information that the rebels in Mobile were moving troops to Pollard and Bonsecours Bay, intending to attack Pensacola in both directions. I immediately wrote to General Asboth, warning him, and sent by the steamer George Peabody, which will probably reach him in time to prevent surprise. I have already informed you by the Scott of General Lee's handsome operation in capturing the Sixth Texas (rebel) Cavalry. It was a dashing and successful affair; only 25 escaped. Twelve officers and 100 men were captured. Plaquemine is now well fortified, and secure. Green has undoubtedly affronted [confronted] the Mississippi River, and no doubt intends to occupy a point to blockade the river. If the occupation should be at all serious, I shall send up a force to co-operate with the navy in capturing him. This can be done without interfering with the transportation of troops to your re-enforcement.

I would now recommend raising the embargo on Berwick Bay, as much suffering is caused by it within our lines on the Teche, and, if properly watched, no mischief can result from a judicious granting of passes for proper persons, and supplies to the people. Now we have to feed starving people from the army supplies, who could and would procure for themselves, if permitted. I intend to send, by next opportunity after the Saint Mary's, the Twenty-second Regiment, Corps d'Afrique, to Texas, as Major Houston represents the services of colored regiments much needed there.

Noon, 22d.—Your dispatch of 17th, dated off Aransas Pass, has just been received. I shall at once communicate with Admiral Porter and Commodore Bell on the subject of gunboats for Berwick Bay. If they cannot furnish any, I will make two for that service. I fear we shall have to do this, from the results we have had from former applications.

I have nothing new to communicate from up the river, although the telegraph is working well to Port Hudson, and General Andrews has instructions to report frequently. From this silence, I suppose there has been as yet nothing serious at Morganza.

Very respectfully, I am, general, your most obedient servant,

CHAS. P. STONE,
Brigadier-General, and Chief of Staff.

*DEPARTMENT OF STATE,
Washington, November 23, 1863.

Maj. Gen. N. P. BANKS,
Comdg. Department of the Gulf, Brownsville, Tex.:

GENERAL: I have received and have submitted to the President your three dispatches of the 6th, 7th, and 9th instant, respectively. I have great pleasure in congratulating you upon your successful landing and occupation upon the Rio Grande, which is all the more gratifying because it was effected at a moment of apparently critical interest to the national cause. You have already found that the confusion resulting from civil strife and foreign war in Mexico offers seductions for military enterprise. I have, therefore, to inform you of the exact condition of our relations toward that Republic at the present time. We are on terms of amity and friendship and maintaining diplomatic relations with the Republic of Mexico. We regard that country as the theater of a foreign war, mingled with civil strife. In this conflict we take no part, and, on the contrary, we practice absolute non-intervention and non-interference. In command of the frontier, it will devolve on you, as far as practicable consistently with your other functions, to prevent aid or supplies being given from the United States to either belligerent. You will defend the United States in Texas against any enemies you may encounter there, whether domestic or foreign. Nevertheless, you will not enter any part of Mexico unless it be temporarily, and then clearly necessary for the protection of your own lines against aggression from the Mexican border. You can assume no authority in Mexico to protect citizens of the United States there, much less to redress the wrongs or injuries committed against the United States or their citizens, whether those wrongs or injuries were committed on one side of the border or the other. If consuls find their positions unsafe on the Mexican side of the border, let them leave the country, rather than invoke the protection of your forces. These directions result from the fixed determination of the President to avoid any departure from lawful neutrality, and any unnecessary and unlawful enlargement of the present field of war. But at the same time you will be expected to observe military and political events as they occur in Mexico, and to communicate all that shall be important for this Government to understand concerning them.

It is hardly necessary to say that any suggestions you may think proper to give for the guidance of the Government in its relations toward Mexico will be considered with that profound respect which is always paid to the opinions which you express.

In making this communication, I have endeavored to avoid entering into the sphere of your military operations, and to confine myself simply to that in which you are in contact with the political movements now going on in Mexico.

I am, general, your obedient servant,

WILLIAM H. SEWARD.

PLAQUEMINE, LA.,
November 23, 1863—1 p. m.

Brig. Gen. CHARLES P. STONE,
Chief of Staff:

SIR: This morning I sent you a telegram, advising you of the state of affairs here. Nothing new has transpired. I am making a reconnaissance on the west side of Bayou Grossetête. As soon as the party returns, shall at once advise you of whatever I may learn.

Shall at once intrench myself, but think, however, I can successfully defend against any attacking force which will probably be sent against me.

I have sent Lieut. **A. J.** Dyer, acting quartermaster, for such things as are needed by the troops which came with me. I should have 50 boxes of ammunition, caliber .58.

The regiments have all their books and some camp equipage, together with clothing of officers, at Brashear City, under charge of officers and men belonging to the regiments.

Requisitions had been made for new tents, clothing, and a supply of camp and garrison equipage, but it had not reached them before ordered here, except the clothing, which was in the hands of the brigade quartermaster.

If consistent with military designs, I should like to send for the men and things at Brashear City.

It will probably be necessary for Lieutenant Dyer to procure new tents for the regiments I brought here, as those left in store at New Orleans were old and worn, and some of them have been taken from the place where stored by persons to whom they did not belong.

I have reported to General Cooke, but he has not sent me any instructions whatever.

There is some trade in cotton and sugar, as well as dry goods, &c., concerning which I have no instructions. I am not permitting anything to go out of the lines, but am allowing cotton and sugar and some other articles to be shipped to New Orleans.

Having reported myself to General Cooke without receiving any instructions, I take the liberty to address you so fully as I have.

Very respectfully,

L. **A.** SHELDON,
Colonel Forty-second Ohio Volunteers, Commanding Post.

SPECIAL ORDERS, } HDQRS. DIST. NORTHEASTERN LOUISIANA,
No. 43.   }   *Goodrich's ·Landing, La., November* 23, 1863.

I. On an expedition to Skipwith's Landing after corn, the detachment of troops from the First Arkansas (48 men) and Tenth Louisiana (57 men) committed depredations against E. L. Wade, by killing 1 cow, 5 hogs, and 2 pigs. The officers were Captain Berry and Lieutenant Hitchcock, Tenth Louisiana.

The commanders of these regiments will, together, assess the damages, and charge the same, to be collected at the pay-table, to reimburse Mr. Wade.

By order of Brig. Gen. J. P. Hawkins:

S. B. FERGUSON,
Assistant Adjutant-General.

PORT HUDSON,
November 23, 1863—8 a. m.

Brig. Gen. CHARLES P. STONE,
Chief of Staff, New Orleans:

The steamers National and Black Hawk passed down from above last night. The Black Hawk was fired into just below Red River. This was the firing Saturday afternoon. Our gunboats took part in the affair. Two prisoners, escaped from the rebels at Alexandria, report Taylor's force at 12,000 or 15,000; don't know where he is.

GEO. L. ANDREWS,
Brigadier-General of Volunteers, Commanding Post.

PORT HUDSON,
November 23, 1863—12 m.
Maj. G. NORMAN LIEBER,
Acting Assistant Adjutant-General, New Orleans:
Several officers of the Sixth Michigan, now at this post, have had much trouble in endeavoring to get mustered into the service. I respectfully request that Maj. J. Langdon Ward, commissary of musters at this post, be authorized to muster in officers of Sixth Michigan.

GEO. L. ANDREWS,
Brigadier-General of Volunteers, Commanding Post.

PORT HUDSON, LA.,
November 23, 1863.
Brig. Gen. CHARLES P. STONE,
Chief of Staff, New Orleans:
GENERAL: I have the honor to send you herewith a few of the letters captured in a rebel mail by our expedition to Tunica Bend.* There is little of importance in any of them. The following is a summary of what I have found in reading them, viz: From letter directed to Simsport, October 31, reported that articles are smuggled out of New Orleans; that negroes are dying fast, and coming back from the Yanks as fast as they went. Mobile, November 2: Prepared for attack, but no prospect of one at present. Northern elections overwhelmingly Abolition. News encouraging. Mobile, October 19, 1863: Families cannot live at less than $40 to $50 per day on the plainest food; are going to Lumpkin, Ga., where they can live for one-fourth of what it costs at Mobile. Bragg whipped Rosecrans, taking 7,000 and killing and wounding 20,000 to 25,000 more; rebel loss, 1,700 to 1,800 killed, and 12,000 to 15,000 wounded and missing. Reported that Lee cleaned out the Yankees again in Virginia last Thursday. Mobile, October 19, 1863: Glory over Taylor, Kirby Smith & Co. Everything is confident, hopeful, &c: Addressed to commander of C. S. steamer Cotton, at Shreveport. Richmond, October 31: Things awful high. (See price current inclosed. Boots, $250 per pair, &c.)

I am, general, respectfully, your obedient servant,

GEO. L. ANDREWS,
Brigadier-General of Volunteers, Commanding Post.

HEADQUARTERS DISTRICT OF PENSACOLA,
Barrancas, Fla., November 23, 1863.
Brig. Gen. CHARLES P. STONE,
Chief of Staff, Headquarters Department of the Gulf:
GENERAL: I have the honor to report, upon information received, that the nearest permanent rebel camps are at Pollard, Ala., and Camp

---

* No inclosures.

Hunter, Fla., 9 miles from that town, on the Mobile Railroad, with head-quarters of General [J. H.] Clanton, together about 3,000 strong, mostly mounted, with three smaller advanced camps, one between Escambia and Perdido Rivers, not far from Pensacola; one east of Escambia River, 7 miles above Florida Town; and the third, west of the Perdido River, near Neuneces Ferry, on the Blakely road. The encampment west of the Perdido, about 300 strong, is constantly scouting up and down the river, guarding all crossings and ferries, and aiding the rebel pirates, who captured, on the 14th instant, near the Perdido Bay, two of our coal schooners coming from New Orleans, and destroying one of them, the Norman, by fire. (See inclosed copy of my communication to Captain [Jacob] Mahler, assistant quartermaster of transportation, with several statements relating to it.*)

The encampment east of the Escambia River numbers only 120 to 140 cavalry, and has its pickets at Milton, Bagdad, Parces, and Florida Town, with the view to prevent the white and black refugees concealed in the woods from joining the Union forces.

I consider it most important to clear the Perdido and Escambia Bays, and break up and capture those three advanced rebel camps, but this can only be done successfully by boats.

My application for a light-draught side-wheel steamer, dated New Orleans, October 14, a copy of which is herewith inclosed,* was favor-ably indorsed at department headquarters, and I beg, therefore, to re-new my application, with request that, in consideration of circumstances above alluded to, instead of one, two steamers, of not more than 3½ to 4 feet draught of water, be ordered to this district.

I am confident that the result would be a success, securing our schooners in the Gulf against further annoyances, and enabling me to collect at once sufficient men for two Florida regiments, one white and the other colored.

It is essential that both expeditions, on the Perdido and Escambia, be started simultaneously, and, as my cavalry numbers only 40 men, I would respectfully request that on the two small steamers two compa-nies of cavalry be embarked, as a cavalry addition so much needed.

The re-occupation of Pensacola should be a consequence of those two expeditions. It would encourage and bring in the Union service many men from the interior neighboring country of South Alabama and West Florida, and would give me a better basis to start from against the Mobile, Pollard and Montgomery Railroad, which passes through the best cotton and corn lands of the State of Alabama, with large planta-tions, now almost exclusively engaged in raising corn for the Confed-erates.

This road has been and is the most important military road the rebels have in the Southwest, it being their only reliable speedy route in transporting troops from the Mississippi east and *vice versa*. It was over this road that the rebels were re-enforced at Corinth in 1862, and General Johnston passed lately over this road with 30,000 men to Bragg's assistance at Chattanooga.

Under those circumstances, the commanding general will excuse my request for two efficient white infantry regiments and one light battery. They will not be idle, but will do good work.

I am, general, very respectfully, your obedient servant,
ASBOTH,
Brigadier-General.

---

* Not found.

NEW ORLEANS,
November 24, 1863.

Major-General FRANKLIN,
New Iberia:

GENERAL: An intelligent scout, escaped from Texas, by way of Alexandria, says that Magruder crossed the Sabine at Niblett's Bluff about ten days or two weeks ago, to move toward Vermillionville his entire force, more than 20,000 of all kinds, volunteers, militia, and conscripts. That Kirby Smith has sent all his force from Shreveport to Dick Taylor excepting 500 retained by him at Shreveport. That Walker, Mouton, Green, and Maxwell [?] are trying to get in rear of Brashear; have crossed the Atchafalaya for that purpose, at the same time sending artillery to the mouth of Red River to annoy our transports. I shall send the scout to you to-morrow morning.

I have blocked the passage of any ordinary force at Plaquemine, and have ordered reconnaissance from Brashear to look at the Grand River road.

Very respectfully, your obedient servant,
CHAS. P. STONE,
Brigadier-General, and Chief of Staff.

PORT HUDSON, LA.,
November 24, 1863—10.30 a. m.

Brig. Gen. CHARLES P. STONE,
Chief of Staff, New Orleans:

Navigation appears to be interrupted above Natchez. The steamer Welcome was fired into above that place on her way down. Thirty women and children on board, including General Crocker's family. None of them hurt.

GEO. L. ANDREWS,
Brigadier-General of Volunteers, Commanding Post.

NEW ORLEANS, LA.,
November 25, 1863.

Maj. Gen. N. P. BANKS,
Commanding Department of the Gulf, in the Field:

GENERAL: Brigadier-General Lawler went forward to you yesterday, with 750 infantry of the Thirteenth Army Corps, on board steamer Saint Mary's.

Active and searching reconnaissances have been made from Plaquemine, Donaldsonville, and Napoleonville, westerly and northwesterly, without so far developing the enemy on the Grossetête or Grand River.

Boat and steamboat reconnaissances in Lake Verret and Bayou Long are not reported. General Birge is, of course, vigilant and efficient.

General Franklin, on receiving the information which was furnished you in my last letter of yesterday concerning the reported movement of Magruder toward Vermillionville, took immediate steps toward feeling the enemy there, and early this morning pushed out Lee with a heavy mounted force.

Lee's conduct is reported by Franklin as admirable. His cavalry came upon the enemy, and made handsome saber charges on him, pushed him across Vermillion Bayou, killed and wounded a number, and captured 5 officers and 68 men of the Fourth Texas and Second Louisiana (rebel) Cavalry.

He found only Bagby's and Major's brigades at Vermillion; the prisoners report Magruder as at Mermenton. General Franklin says these prisoners speak of Magruder only from hearsay, or that they have been stuffed. General Franklin's body-guard to-day captured 11 guerrillas.

All is quiet back of Port Hudson and Baton Rouge.

The Second Regiment Engineers, Corps d'Afrique, will be sent to, Texas, on recommendation of Major Houston.

An officer, writing a private letter from Washington to Lieutenant-Colonel Abert, says that he "is preparing to join Heintzelman's expedition to Texas."

If such an expedition has been in contemplation, I hope they will not fail to send you the troops intended for it.

Very respectfully, I am, general, your most obedient servant,
CHAS. P. STONE,
Brigadier-General, and Chief of Staff.

NEW ORLEANS, LA.,
November 25, 1863.

Brig. Gen. H. W. BIRGE,
Thibodeauxville:

GENERAL: Your dispatch without date received. Lieutenant-Colonel Chandler was yesterday ordered to have ready for you a suitable steamboat of light draught, which could take guns and proper guard on board for reconnaissance of Lake [Verret] and Bayou Long. When did you receive my dispatch ordering steamboat reconnaissance? Please date your dispatches by the hour, invariably.

Colonel Sheldon arrived at Plaquemine last Saturday evening, and has been strengthening himself there and reconnoitering northwest. He reported yesterday a line of rebel couriers running west of Grosse-tête Bayou, southerly.

Colonel Sheldon left his battery at Donaldsonville, where it can co-operate with Colonel Fiske, and Sheldon has been supplied with two field batteries from here.

Very respectfully, your obedient servant,
CHAS. P. STONE,
Brigadier-General, and Chief of Staff.

HEADQUARTERS DISTRICT OF PENSACOLA,
Barrancas, Fla., November 25, 1863.

Brig. Gen. CHARLES P. STONE,
Chief of Staff, Hdqrs. Department of the Gulf:

GENERAL: I have the honor to acknowledge the receipt of your communication of November 21, that the rebels intend to make a serious attack on my positions, and that large bodies of troops are said to have been sent to Pollard by rail for that purpose, and another force by way of Bonsecour Bay.

Reports from Pensacola received day before yesterday in the evening, and yesterday again, are of a similar nature, stating that rebel troops are returning from Chattanooga in considerable numbers, advancing from Pollard on the Pensacola Railroad, about 14 miles from Pensacola, and throwing up there extensive fortifications.

I am inclined to consider this movement more a defensive than offensive one, preparatory to an anticipated combined attack of the Union forces upon Mobile, and especially my advance upon the Mobile and Montgomery Railroad.

I made, however, proper preparations for a warm reception, and have secured the co-operation of the navy; but you are well aware, general, how very limited my forces are, and I respectfully request, in connection with my report of November 23 (No. 42), a speedy increase of my forces adequate to the present exigency, enabling me, not only to repulse an attack successfully, but assume the offensive before the new line of rebel fortifications is completed for the defense of Mobile, Pollard, Montgomery and Alabama Railroad, of so vital importance for the Confederacy.

· In regard to the Bonsecour Bay, I beg to state that it does not communicate with the Perdido Bay, and that the troops advancing by way of Bonsecour Bay would have to disembark on Bear Creek and make over 2 miles by land to Bay La Launch, communicating with Perdido Bay.

If my request for two small steamers is granted, as I confidently hope, the Perdido Bay will soon be cleared, and any approach of a larger rebel force in that direction made impossible.

Rebel cavalry visited Pensacola day before yesterday·with a flag of truce, and the night after some scouts were approaching our pickets from the Perdido.

My cavalry was out yesterday in that direction 5 miles beyond our pickets, discovering nothing.

I beg to inclose copy of general and special orders issued yesterday.

I am, general, very respectfully, your obedient servant,

ASBOTH,
Brigadier-General.

●   [Inclosures.]

GENERAL ORDERS, }   HDQRS. DISTRICT OF PENSACOLA,
    No. 5.   }   *Barrancas, Fla., November 24, 1863.*

Commanders of brigades and forts will report on the advantages as well as weak points of their respective positions, and give their suggestions as to improvements, with proper topographical illustrations. They will state how far the strength and organization of their forces are adequate to their present requirements, or what re-enforcements they need to make them so. They will also continually gather reliable information of the enemy's whereabouts, strength, movements, and, if possible, his intentions and plans, and keep the general commanding advised promptly, to enable him to meet every emergency in time.

In order to avoid alarms from unfounded rumors, and consequent fatigue for the troops, commanding officers of brigades and forts, as well as the district provost-marshal, will report daily, in writing, at noon, until further orders, whether all is quiet.

By order of Brigadier-General Asboth:

E. T. SPRAGUE,
Lieut. Eighth Wisconsin, and Actg. Assistant Adjutant-General.

SPECIAL ORDERS, }   HDQRS. DISTRICT OF PENSACOLA,
    No. 10.   }   Barrancas, Fla., November 24, 1863.

*   *   *   *   *   *.   *

V. Citizens from the direction of the Perdido River will not be permitted to pass the pickets either within or without our lines till further orders.

*   *   *   *   *   *

VIII. 1. Information having been received that the rebels intend making a serious attack on our positions, commanders of brigades and forts will hold their troops ready for action, and use all precautions usual in face of the enemy.

2. Commanders of regiments will inspect at once cartridge-boxes, see that they are filled, and that 100 rounds of ammunition per man is on hand, easily accessible.

3. Colonel Holbrook, commanding brigade, will divide his infantry as nearly as possible into three parts, to relieve each other every 24 hours. One-third will be posted along the intrenched line between Fort Barrancas, the redoubt, and the Bayou Grande, and along the bayou to picket-post No. 5, in adequate squads, in places easiest to be crossed or most exposed to an attack. One-third will rest on their arms in their respective camps, ready to join, in case of an alarm, the forces already posted, without waiting for orders, and strengthen our line of defense. The remaining third will be held as a reserve and camp guard.

4. The signal of alarm will be given by the firing of two blanks in rapid succession from any of the guns at Fort Barrancas or the redoubt, but only at the order of the respective commanding officer. At this signal, the forces resting on their arms in their camp will be marched to the respective posts along the intrenchment and Big Bayou, and the reserve will be formed and await orders.

5. The squads on duty on the intrenched and bayou line will stack arms and rest. Care will, however, be taken to post a sufficient number of sentinels in well-connected chain.

6. Colonel Holbrook will place two pieces of artillery in a proper position, between the redoubt and the Big Bayou, to assist the redoubt in controlling the crossing of the swamps, and two pieces at picket-post No. 5, to prevent the crossing of the narrow portion of the bayou, not sufficiently covered by the gunboats at the mouth of the bayou. The colonel will order a sufficient number of men of his own regiment to serve these guns efficiently, adding to them the required guard from the Fourteenth Regiment, Corps d'Afrique.

7. The cavalry will be divided into three squads, and, patrolling constantly by relief along the picket line, will communicate immediately anything of importance to Fort Barrancas or the redoubt, and to district headquarters.

8. The intrenched and stockade line between the sea-shore, Fort Barrancas, and the redoubt will be improved at once, and the opening near Fort Barrancas properly protected against a cavalry dash. Colonel Holbrook will have detailed 60 men as a working party, to work in squads of 20 men each, in charge of a commissioned officer, uninterruptedly day and night, relieving every six hours. They will have their arms stacked for immediate use in case of an alarm. Lieutenant [John Q.] Dickinson, acting assistant quartermaster, will furnish the required material, tools, and mechanics, and, during the day, 25 laborers, and Captain Larned, Second U. S. Artillery, commanding Fort Barrancas, will detail an officer to superintend the work properly.

9. The guard at district headquarters will be doubled during the night until further orders.

10. The commissary of subsistence and district quartermaster will keep all Government stores at Fort Pickens, and make their regular issues from there until further orders.

By order of Brig. Gen. A. Asboth:

E. T. SPRAGUE,
Lieut. Eighth Wisconsin, and Actg. Assistant Adjutant-General.

SPECIAL ORDERS, }　　HDQRS. DEPARTMENT OF THE GULF,
No. 294.　　　　}　　　*New Orleans, La., November 25, 1863.*

*　　　*　　　*　　　*　　　*　　　*　　　*

IX. Brigadier-General Benton, having reported from leave of absence, will rejoin his division in the field, and will at once assume command of that portion of the division now awaiting transportation.

X. No charges having been preferred against Colonel Shunk, Eighth Indiana, within the time prescribed by law, he is released from arrest, and will rejoin his command.*

*　　　*　　　*　　　*　　　　　*

By command of Major-General Banks:

G. NORMAN LIEBER,
Acting Assistant Adjutant-General.

HEADQUARTERS UNITED STATES FORCES,
Brownsville, Tex., November 26, 1863.

His Excellency JESUS DE LA SERNA,
Governor of Tamaulipas:

I have the honor to acknowledge the receipt of a letter from you last night, notifying me of your arrival at Matamoras as Governor of the State of Tamaulipas.

Please accept my thanks for your attention and for the gratifying expressions of friendship which you utter.

The interests of our respective nations are in many respects common, and occurrences in either must attract the lively sympathy of the other.

Let me assure you that nothing will be omitted on my part which shall tend to perpetuate the feelings of friendship and mutual regard now existing between our people.

With assurance of my highest respect and consideration, I have the honor be, Your Excellency's most obedient servant,

N. J. T. DANA,
Major-General.

HEADQUARTERS UNITED STATES FORCES,
Brownsville, November 27, 1863.

Mr. M. M. KIMMEY, *United States Consul, Monterey:*

Your several dispatches of the 19th, 21st, and 22d are received, and I have referred them to Major-General Banks, at Aransas, in order that he may give me the necessary authority regarding the supply of funds.

---

* See General Orders, No. 42, Thirteenth Army Corps, October 12, 1863, p. 763.

We are greatly indebted to you for the trouble you have taken in serving the country through your assistance to us, and we shall rely on you in the future as in the past to keep us informed. General Banks has not left me any authority to turn over funds, nor has he yet supplied me with any money to liquidate the claims for service which you have presented, but I have no doubt that, upon receipt of the dispatches I have sent him this morning, he will give me such authority as is neces-. sary, and, perhaps, send his chief quartermaster to settle all accounts.

None of the refugees you mention have as yet arrived, but when they reach here I will subsist them, and encourage them to organize as fast as they arrive. Meanwhile I hope they will very soon be cheered by good news from General Banks on the coast.

I presume you have heard of our capture of the fort at Aransas Pass and all the troops and material there.

Colonel Davis is at Rio Grande City, where I sent him with a force of infantry, cavalry, and artillery.

We are purchasing all the good horses and broken mules which offer, but are not paying as high as you mention. We have selected the best horses which the State of Tamaulipas raises, but have not paid to exceed $35 each. We are very desirous to get about 200 well-broken mules, and we will buy as many as 1,000 horses if we can get them at fair rates. Meanwhile we are having a good many brought down from New Orleans.

I have no papers later than those I sent last.

Hoping to hear frequently from you, and that we will be able often to send you cheering tidings for our stray friends and countrymen who are standing the test of patriotism during their long sufferings and privations, I remain, with much respect,

N. J. T. DANA,
Major-General.

NEW ORLEANS,
November 28, 1863.

Brigadier-General BENTON,
    Saint Charles Hotel, New Orleans:

GENERAL: You will please prepare the troops under your command at Algiers for transportation to Aransas Pass, Tex., and hold them ready for embarkation at 6 a. m. to-morrow, with twenty days' rations and their clothing and camp and garrison equipage.

Very respectfully, I am, general, your most obedient servant,

CHAS. P. STONE,
Brigadier-General, and Chief of Staff.

HEADQUARTERS DEPARTMENT OF THE GULF,
On Board the McClellan, off Pass Cavallo, November 28, 1863.

Major-General WASHBURN,
    Commanding, &c., Matagorda Island:

GENERAL: Your dispatch of this date was received at 4.30 p. m. this day. It is probable the Saint Mary's can land her rations to-night or in the morning. We will send you the boats you want immediately from the McClellan and the gunboats, probably five or six. There are also boats with the Matamoras and the Planter on their way to you. The Matamoras has five days' supplies for 3,500 men, and, unless some accident should intervene, must soon reach you. A signal officer is on board, and has instructions to report to you as soon as possible.

There are two 20-pounder Parrotts on field carriages and two on siege carriages at Aransas. These can be brought up immediately by boats or by land. They are equally effective with the 30-pounder Parrotts, which will be sent you as soon as possible from New Orleans. You may rely upon 20-pounder Parrotts producing as much effect as 30-pounders for your operations. There are no gunny-bags here; what were on board were left at Brazos. I will send some to you from New Orleans immediately. The navy will supply you with boat howitzers.

The gunboats will open at daylight to-morrow morning. A copy of your sketch has been furnished to Captain Strong, who will keep constant communication with you either by boats or by signal telegraph. Undoubtedly either to-night or to-morrow morning you will have smooth water, so as to make your communications constant. Send a strong force as quickly as you can on the other side of the fort to cut off their communications. Do not be in any hurry to reduce the fort, as time is in your favor and against the enemy. Captain Strong will receive instructions to open upon the camp of the enemy as indicated in your sketch.

The Hussar carried down to Aransas last night 250 men, with orders to join you. The Twenty-second Iowa, 200 strong, are at Aransas also. There are four companies, 200 strong, at Brazos, who will return in the Alabama, which went down day before yesterday. The Saint Mary's has 800, and two companies of the Twentieth Iowa are also at Brazos, making altogether 1,550 men who will immediately join your forces. The Scott also has 400 men, who were landed at Aransas City night before last at dark, and must join you by to-morrow. You should communicate, if possible, with the Matamoras and the Planter, that are upon the bay, inside.

The 20-pounder Parrotts, on siege carriages, are on board a sloop at Aransas. The Crescent is ordered to Aransas, to send forward the two schooners there, and the howitzers by the bay. If the Matamoras gets up to you, you will send her back for whatever may be needed. The floating battery, which Mr. Comstock reports as near the fort, is a poor attempt at an iron-clad. It has no guns and can do no harm.

Captain Strong has all the points suggested in your letter, and will put them in execution, communicating with you as soon as the weather will permit. He is confident his guns, if the sea is so he can approach, will reach the fort and camp of the enemy, and will furnish you with one or two 30-pounder Parrotts and men to man them.

With much respect, &c.,

N. P. BANKS,
Major-General, Commanding.

GENERAL ORDERS, }   HDQRS. NINETEENTH ARMY CORPS,
        No. 40.   }   *New Iberia, La., November* 29, 1863.

No cotton or sugar will be shipped hereafter from any point between this place and Brashear City without the written permission of Mr. G. P. Davis, Treasury agent at this post.

Assistant quartermasters and captains of steamers will see that this order is strictly enforced.

By order of Major-General Franklin:

WICKHAM HOFFMAN,
Assistant Adjutant-General.

Abstract from returns of the Department of the Gulf, Maj. Gen. N. P. Banks, U. S. Army, commanding, for the month of November, 1863. *

Command.	Present for duty.		Aggregate present.	Aggregate present and absent.	Pieces of artillery.		Remarks.
	Officers.	Men.			Heavy.	Field.	
General headquarters...............							New Orleans, La.
Staff......................	28	....	28	31	......	......	Do.
Headquarters troops (Francis).	3	71	90	120	......	......	Do.
Engineer Brigade (Houston) ...	77	1,278	1,664	1,834	......	.....	Do.
Total......................	108	1,349	1,782	1,985	......		
Thirteenth Army Corps (Dana):							
Staff and pioneer corps........	16	11	33	38	......		
First Division (Washburn)† ...	263	4,030	5,125	9,268	......	10	Matagorda Island, Tex.
Second Division (Dana)‡	232	3,764	4,883	8,453	......	8	Brownsville, Tex.
Third Division (McGinnis).....	213	3,443	3,951	5,408	......	6	Near New Iberia, La.
Fourth Division (Burbridge)...	158	2,203	2,871	5,765	......	11	Do.
Total......................	882	13,451	16,863	28,932	......	35	
Nineteenth Army Corps (Franklin).							New Iberia, La.
Staff............................	9	.*.....	9	11	......	......	Do.
First Division (Weitzel)	136	2,646	3,224	4,955	......	8	Do.
Third Division (Grover).......	126	2,800	3,290	4,756	......	8	Do.
Reserve Artillery	3	132	148	186	......	8	Do.
Total§	274	5,578	6,671	9,908	......	24	
Cavalry Division (Lee)...............							Near New Iberia, La.
First Brigade (Lucas)...........	47	1,150	1,384	1,926	......	......	Do.
Second Brigade (Fonda)........	31	644	921	1,277	......	......	Do.
Third Brigade (Paine)	38	653	864	1,623	......	4	Do.
Other troops in the field........	28	535	640	962	......	6	Do.
Total ‖.....................	144	2,982	3,809	5,788	......	10	
La Fourche District (Birge)........							Thibodeaux, La.¶
First Brigade, Fourth Division, Nineteenth Army Corps.	50	1,418	2,054	2,662	......	......	Do.
Other troops	35	894	1,020	1,251	4	17	Do.
Total.......................	85	2,312	3,074	3,913	4	17	
Defenses of New Orleans (Beckwith):							New Orleans, La.**
Second Brigade, Fourth Division, Nineteenth Army Corps (Cahill).	112	2,235	2,728	4,862	......	6	
Other troops	97	2,490	3,118	3,540	......	11	
Total.......................	209	4,725	5,846	8,402	......	17	
District of Baton Rouge (Cooke)...							Baton Rouge, La.
Second Brigade, First Division, Nineteenth Army Corps (Sharpe):	60	1,613	2,068	2,915	......	......	Do.
Detachment from First Division, Thirteenth Army Corps (Sheldon).	50	1,153	1,454	2,360	......	8	Plaquemine, La.
Other troops	48	1,105	1,380	1,987	......	8	Baton Rouge, La.
Total......................	158	3,871	4,902	7,262	......	16	

*Compiled, as far as practicable, from the subordinate returns.
†Portions of this division accounted for in the District of Baton Rouge.
‡Includes forces (First Texas Cavalry and Corps d'Afrique) attached.
§At and about New Iberia. The Second Brigade, First Division, and the Fourth Division, are accounted for in the Defenses of New Orleans and Districts of La Fourche and Baton Rouge.
‖The Third Massachusetts, First Texas, and Fourth Wisconsin accounted for at Baton Rouge, in Second Division, Thirteenth Army Corps, and at Port Hudson.
¶Troops at Brashear City, Donaldsonville, Napoleonville, and Thibodeaux, and along the New Orleans, Opelousas and Great Western Railroad.
**Troops at Bonnet Carré, Donaldsonville, Forts Jackson, Macomb, Pike, and Saint Philip, in New Orleans, and on Ship Island.

Abstract from returns of the Department of the Gulf, &c.—Continued.

Command.	Present for duty. Officers.	Men.	Aggregate present.	Aggregate present and absent.	Pieces of artillery. Heavy.	Field.	Remarks.
Port Hudson (Andrews):							
Corps d'Afrique (Ullmann).....	156	3,700	4,866	5,519	......	8	
Other troops	27	405	537	669	......	4	
Total......................	183	4,105	5,403	6,188	......	12	
District of Key West and Tortugas (Woodbury).	23	369	755	1,171	......	......	Key West, Fla.
District of Pensacola (Asboth)......	59	876	1,124	1,210	122	11	Barrancas, Fla.
Unattached troops:							
Brashear City (Corps d'Afrique).	55	895	1,072	1,087	......	......	
New Orleans (Corps d'Afrique).	25	672	771	789	......	......	
Total......................	80	1,567	1,843	1,876	.....	......	
Grand total................	2,205	41,185	52,072	76,635	126	142	
Grand total according to Department monthly return.	1,994	39,142	52,004	75,486	,154	162	

Abstract from returns of the Department of New Mexico, Brig. Gen. James H. Carleton, U. S. Army, commanding, for November, 1863; headquarters, Santa Fé, N. Mex. [*]

Command.	Present for duty. Officers.	Men.	Aggregate present.	Aggregate present and absent.	Aggregate last return.	Pieces of field artillery.
Department staff (Santa Fé)...........................	25	....	25	27	21	......
Fort Marcy, N. Mex. (Lieut. Samuel Ovenshine), Field, staff, and band, Fifth U. S. Infantry.	......	11	11	13	62	......
Fort Union, N. Mex. (Lieut. Col. W. McMullen), Fifth and Seventh U. S. Infantry; First Infantry, California Volunteers; First Cavalry, California Volunteers.	8	216	256	321	319	......
Fort Union Depot. N. Mex. (Capt. W. R. Shoemaker, military storekeeper), company of ordnance.	......	13	14	'14	14	......
Fort Sumner, N. Mex. (Maj. H. D. Wallen), Seventh U. S. Infantry; Second Cavalry, California Volunteers.	3	·75	115	147	135	......
Fort Stanton, N. Mex. (Maj. J. Smith), First Cavalry, New Mexico Volunteers; Fifth Infantry, California Volunteers.	5	28	93	147	194	......
Fort Wingate, N. Mex. (Capt. J. C. Shaw), First Cavalry, New Mexico Volunteers.	5	114	169	293	359	......
Albuquerque, N. Mex. (Capt. D. H. Brotherton), Third U. S. Artillery, Fifth U. S. Infantry.	3	82	129	157	158	4
Los Pinos, N. Mex. (Lieut. M. Mullens), Fifth U. S. Infantry.	3	48	76	86	90	......
Fort Bascom, N. Mex. (Capt. P. W. L. Plympton), Seventh U. S. Infantry; First Cavalry, New Mexico Volunteers.	4	72	96	110	109	......
Fort Craig, N. Mex. (Col. E. A. Rigg), First and Fifth U. S. Infantry; First Cavalry, California Volunteers.	9	182	238	311	312	17
Mesilla, N Mex. (Capt. J. S. Thayer), Fifth Infantry, California Volunteers; First Infantry, New Mexico Volunteers.	4	135	155	162	73	4
Franklin, Tex. (Col. G. W. Bowie), Fifth Infantry, California Volunteers.	6	74	93	94	94	......
Fort West, N. Mex. (Capt. J. H. Whitlock), First and Fifth Infantry, California Volunteers.	2	94	115	127	128	......

[*] Brig. Gen. Joseph R. West, commanding District of Arizona.

Abstract from returns of the Department of New Mexico, &c.—Continued.

Command.	Present for duty.		Aggregate present.	Aggregate present and absent.	Aggregate last return.	Pieces of field artillery.
	Officers.	Men.				
Fort Bowie, Ariz. (Capt. T. T. Tidball), Fifth Infantry, California Volunteers.	1	35	49	56	56	......
Tucson, Ariz. (Lieut. Col. T. A. Coult), Fifth Infantry, California Volunteers.	4	42	81	120	119	......
Las Cruces, N.,Mex. (Maj. W. McCleave) First Cavalry, California Volunteers; Fifth Infantry, California Volunteers.	6	127	179	211	214	......
Fort McRae, N. Mex. (Capt. H. A. Greene), First Infantry, California Volunteers	1	36	51	77	77	......
Fort Canby, N. Mex. (Maj. F. P. Abreü), First Cavalry, New Mexico Volunteers.	5	87	128	622	711	2
Fort Cummings, N. Mex. (Capt. V. Dresher), First Infantry, California Volunteers.	1	51	56	64	63	......
En route to New Mexico, Fifth U. S. Infantry; First New Mexico Volunteer Infantry; First Infantry, California Volunteers.	8	179	187	187	....	......
Valles Grandes, N. Mex. (Lieut. C. A. Custis), Fifth U. S. Infantry.	1	26	32	49	50	......
Camp Miembres, N. Mex, (Lieut. C. P. Nichols), First Cavalry, California Volunteers.	2	57	66	157	157	......
En route to Fort Whipple (Maj. E. B. Willis), First Infantry, California Volunteers.	7	132	139	139	69	......
Grand total.....................................	113	1,916	2,553	3,691	3,584	27

Organization of the Cavalry Division, Department of the Gulf, Brig. Gen. Albert L. Lee, U. S. Army, commanding, November 30, 1863.*

First Brigade.

Col. Thomas J. Lucas.

87th Illinois,† Lieut. Col. John M. Crebs.
16th Indiana,† Lieut. Col. James H. Redfield.
1st Louisiana, Lieut. Col. Harai Robinson.

Second Brigade.

Col. John G. Fonda.

2d Illinois (seven companies), Col. John J. Mudd.
3d Illinois (five companies), Capt. Robert H. Carnahan.
118th Illinois,† Lieut. Col. Thomas Logan.

Third Brigade.

Col. Charles J. Paine.

15th Illinois, Company F, Lieut. Peter Phillips.
1st Indiana, Company C, Capt. Elihu E. Rose.
4th Indiana, Company C, Capt. Andrew P. Gallagher.
2d Louisiana,† Maj. Alfred Hodsdon.
6th Missouri (seven companies), Maj. Bacon Montgomery.
14th New York (six companies), Maj. Abraham Bassford.

Not brigaded.

36th Illinois, Company A, Capt. George A. Willis.
3d Massachusetts,‡ Lieut. Col. Lorenzo D. Sargent.
Mounted Rangers, Company A, Capt. Samuel White.
75th New York,† Capt. Benjamin F. Thurber.
1st Texas,§ Col. Edmund J. Davis.
4th Wisconsin,‖ Col. Frederick A. Boardman.
2d Massachusetts Battery, Capt. Ormand F. Nims.

---

* Reorganized, as herein indicated, November 7. The troops, with exceptions indicated, at and about New Iberia, La.
† Mounted infantry.
‡ At Port Hudson, La.
§ On the Texas Expedition.
‖ At Baton Rouge, La.

Abstract from returns of the District of Northeastern Louisiana, Brig. Gen. John P. Hawkins, U. S. Army, commanding, for the month of November, 1863.

Command.	Present for duty.		Aggregate present.	Aggregate present and absent.	Pieces of field artillery.	Remarks.
	Officers.	Men.				
District staff*	5	....	5	6	......	Goodrich's Landing.
1st Arkansas, *a. d.*, Col. W. F. Wood....	17	522	620	641	......	Do.
10th Louisiana, *a. d.*, Col. F. M. Crandal..	25	660	766	791	3	Do.
11th Louisiana, *a. d.*, Col. Van E. Young .	23	424	495	544	......	Do.
3d Mississippi, *a. d.*, Col. R. H. Ballinger.	23	505	591	614	4	Milliken's Bend.
Total	93	2,111	2,477	2,596	7	

* Brig. Gen. James L. Kiernan absent with leave since November 10.

QUARTERMASTER-GENERAL'S OFFICE,
Washington, D. C., December 1, 1863.
Hon. E. M. STANTON,
Secretary of War, Washington, D. C. :

SIR : I have the honor to return herewith the letter of the Hon. S. Hooper, of Boston, dated the 24th ᵢnstant [ultimo], in relation to providing one or two steam tugs for the use of General Banks, in Texas, referred to me yesterday, and have to report that, immediately upon the receipt of General Banks' letter* at this office, a copy of which was submitted to you, a very superior and fast new tug, coppered, called the Perry, was purchased, fitted out in Philadelphia, and dispatched to New Orleans for service on the coast of Texas. She sailed on Monday, the 30th ultimo.

From the lists on file in this office, another suitable tug, the James Murray, has been selected, and will be dispatched forthwith from Fort Monroe. She will be ready this week.

To guard against accidents on the coast of Texas, and replace the tug I. W. Hancox, lost on the expedition, I have selected a third one, the Ajax, of 83 tons, which can be ready by Monday next.

In selecting these tugs, I have endeavored to be careful in procuring vessels suitable for the trying service they will be called upon to perform on that hazardous coast, and I trust I have succeeded in doing so.

From the foregoing, it will be seen that the tugs named by the Hon. Mr. Hooper are not needed unless more than three are required.

Very respectfully, your obedient servant,
CHAS. THOMAS,
Acting Quartermaster-General.

NEW ORLEANS, *December* 1, 1863.
Major-General FRANKLIN, *New Iberia :*

GENERAL : The major-general commanding expresses the greatest satisfaction with the condition of affairs in the region under your control.

Very respectfully, your obedient servant,
CHAS. P. STONE,
Brigadier-General, and Chief of Staff.

* Of November 3. See p. 785.

BROWNSVILLE, TEX.,
December 1, 1863.

L. PIERCE, Jr.,
    United States Consul, Matamoras:

I have nothing new as yet from General Banks, though I hope, now that we have a calm at last, that I shall receive some dispatches.

The fiction of our occupying Indianola was, like that of our landing at Corpus [Christi] and marching to San Patricio, probably founded on fact. Our forces in considerable strength, under Major-General Washburn and Brigadier-General Ransom, marched on the 21st from Aransas up the beach of Saint Joseph's Island to force a capitulation of the forts of Saluria and Pass Cavallo. I presume this was consummated on the 26th or 27th, and that is probably the foundation of the rumor of our occupying Indianola. Matters will soon come to a focus in that direction.

Davis advises me that Benavides escaped across the river to Reynolds with some 20 men. Now, is he a Mexican or a Texan? The authorities on your side must choose one position or the other. I am not disposed to play hide and seek with such cut-throats as he is. If he is a Texan, I shall demand him, as a renegade, for punishment. If he is a Mexican, it must be looked to that he answers properly to the Mexican authorities for his outrages against our laws. I have full confidence that our friends of the Mexican nation will not object to helping us in this matter as much as we have a right to demand, or else will not complain or feel unfriendly if we are compelled to help ourselves.

Can you, without inconvenience, send me a copy of our treaty with Mexico embracing the extradition clauses?

I have the honor to remain, most respectfully,
                                N. J. T. DANA,
                                    Major-General.

————

HEADQUARTERS,
Brownsville, December 2, 1863.

Brig. Gen. CHARLES P. STONE,
    Chief of Staff, New Orleans:

Colonel Davis returned with his cavalry and artillery last night. The infantry on the steamboat Mustang has not yet returned. The command went to Rio Grande City, and a small detachment was sent to Roma. No enemy whatever was encountered, and none could be heard of except the small force of Benavides, which had left Rio Grande City about a week before Davis' arrival. The country in the vicinity of Camargo is even more bare of supplies than that in this vicinity. What little corn was procured there was double the price it is here. Some 2,500 bales of cotton had been crossed over the river within the last two weeks, but that trade is about stopped now this side of the Laredo. About 80 bales were sent down by Davis. My accumulation now is about 800 bales. I must order some of it to be sold, to settle the freight due on it and to compensate the worthy men, according to the instructions of the commanding general.

The command here and at Point Isabel and Brazos will be out of rations and forage in three days, owing to the loads of subsistence stores having been carried back from Brazos. I shall be compelled to purchase supplies at Matamoras, should none arrive in that time. That can readily be done.

Vidal's command has been mustered in, armed, and equipped to the number of 89 men, for one year. One of them was killed yesterday in a brawl, and I propose to make an example of the murderer.

One hundred and fifteen recruits have been mustered in for the First Texas Cavalry, and 75 into the Second. Colonel Haynes has at Roma and Rio Grande City about 200 for the latter. Thirty-three men have been mustered in for the Twenty-sixth Regiment, Corps d'Afrique. About 175 men are employed daily on the defensive works here, and they are progressing well. About 200 horses have been purchased from the Mexican side of the river, and we expect 100 more in a couple of days. If it is thought desirable to send any of the Mustang breed to Louisiana, or any other department, I could procure 5,000 easily in a month. The price here would be about $45 a head. Good mules will cost $60; wild, unbroken ones, about $40.

A few of the refugees from Monterey sent by Braubach have arrived. When he comes, they expect to be mustered in "for the campaign in Texas."

I have the honor to remain, with great respect,

N. J. T. DANA,
Major-General.

HEADQUARTERS TROOPS IN WESTERN LOUISIANA,
New Iberia, December 2, 1863—8 p. m.

Brig. Gen. CHARLES P. STONE,
Chief of Staff, New Orleans, La.:

The enemy came down with a force of about 80 men on the pickets on the Saint Martinsville road to-day. I had already ordered an expedition in that direction to-morrow, and this fact makes its usefulness all the more likely. It starts long before light.

W. B. FRANKLIN,
Major-General, Commanding.

HEADQUARTERS TROOPS IN WESTERN LOUISIANA,
New Iberia, December 3, 1863—9.15 a. m.

Brig. Gen. CHARLES P. STONE,
Chief of Staff, New Orleans, La.:

The expedition to Saint Martinsville captured a major and 4 men, and is now on its way back. I have heard no details.

W. B. FRANKLIN,
Major-General, Commanding.

HEADQUARTERS TROOPS IN WESTERN LOUISIANA,
New Iberia, December 3, 1863—11.45 a. m.

Brig. Gen. CHARLES P. STONE,
Chief of Staff, New Orleans, La.:

Burbridge's division numbers for duty here 1,583 infantry, 131 artillery, and seven guns; at Franklin, 350 infantry, 92 artillery, and four guns.

W. B. FRANKLIN,
Major-General, Commanding.

SPECIAL ORDERS, } HDQRS. OF ARMY, ADJT. GEN.'S OFFICE,
 No. 537. }   *Washington, December* 3, 1863.

  *   *   *   *   *   *   *

X. The Secretary of War directs that Maj. Gen. J. J. Reynolds re-, pair, without the least possible delay, to New Orleans, and assume, command of the troops at that place and in the vicinity, reporting to Major-General Banks. Brig. Gen. C. P. Stone will be relieved from all command at New Orleans, and directed to report in person to General Banks.

 By command of Major General Halleck :

       E. D. TOWNSEND,
        Assistant Adjutant-General.

    HEADQUARTERS DEPARTMENT OF THE GULF,
       New Orleans, December 4, 1863.

THE PRESIDENT OF THE UNITED STATES:

 SIR: Your letter, bearing date———, was presented to me by General Hamilton the 13th October. It gave me pleasure to assure him of my desire to comply with your instructions, and to assist him in the performance of his official duties in the State of Texas. We were then upon the eve of our departure for Texas, delayed for some days by a violent storm beyond the day appointed. I gave him an outline of my purposes, with which he expressed himself entirely satisfied, but advised him to remain in New Orleans until the practicability of re-establishing the flag of the Union in Texas could be determined. He adopted this course.

 Advised of our success by the officer charged with the execution of my orders at New Orleans, he immediately left New Orleans, and met me at Aransas Pass, on the central coast of Texas, on the 25th November. Our positions on the coast, constantly changing by our advances, and being inclement and uncomfortable, in consequence of the sterility of the soil and the violence of the northers, I advised him to make his headquarters at Brownsville, where our position would be permanent, and his official communication with the interior of the State uninterrupted and easy. He adopted this course, and sailed for Brownsville on the 26th of November in the steamer Alabama. He had the pleasure of receiving at Aransas an official letter from the rebel officers, granting permission to his family to remove to Brownsville and thence to New Orleans. This was dated October 26, the day of the departure of my force from New Orleans, and he hoped to meet his family upon his arrival.

 General Hamilton expressed unqualified satisfaction with the success which had been attained, and said that the occupation of Matagorda Bay placed in the control of. the Government the entire State of Texas.

 We have received news to-day of the capture of the fortifications at Pass Cavallo, which gives us the entire control of Matagorda Bay and every important position on the coast, except Galveston and the Sabine, which will follow Galveston.

 I have the honor to be, with high respect, your obedient servant,

        N. P. BANKS,
        Major-General, Commanding.

HEADQUARTERS DEPARTMENT OF THE GULF,
New Orleans, December 4, 1863.

THE PRESIDENT OF THE UNITED STATES:

SIR: Dispatches received from the Southwest Pass, by the U. S. gunboat Bermudas, report the capture of the works at Pass Cavallo without loss. The Pass was defended by very strong works, an armament of twelve heavy guns, and a garrison of 1,000 men. We have no particulars of the affair. This gives us possession of the Bay of Matagorda, which enables us to control the State at our pleasure, and the occupation of every important point on the coast, excepting Galveston.

It has been impossible, within any reasonable time, to gain a foothold in Texas, excepting by the sea, at this season. The march by Louisiana, either to the Sabine or by Alexandria or Shreveport, would cover from 300 to 500 miles to any important point in Texas, over a country without water or supplies of any kind; without other transportation, in the present stage of the rivers, than that of wagon trains, and against the constantly retreating, but steadily concentrating forces of the enemy, who could not fail, by their superiority in numbers of mounted troops, to inflict upon our columns, trains, and communications serious and irreparable injury.

I appreciated the perils of coast descents in winter; but after the failure to effect a landing on the Sabine coast, which would have enabled me to place a force of from 15,000 to 17,000 men at Houston, in the very center of all the rebel forces of Louisiana and Texas, there was nothing left but a failure to re-establish the flag in Texas or an effort to occupy the western coast of the State. The results of the expedition thus far have been communicated to you at earlier dates; other important results will follow immediately.

Appreciating the great exigencies of the Government, I am ashamed to ask for increased forces; but it seems to me that our regiments from the East and the Northwest, depleted by constant and perilous service on sea and land, ought to be filled up by drafted men or volunteers. I would be satisfied with this.

I have the honor to be, with high respect, your obedient servant,

N. P. BANKS,
Major-General, Commanding.

———

HEADQUARTERS DISTRICT OF PENSACOLA,
Barrancas, Fla., December 5, 1863.

Brig. Gen. CHARLES P. STONE,
Chief of Staff, Headquarters Department of the Gulf:

GENERAL: I have the honor to submit, in connection with my report of November 25 (No. 48), that, after careful combination of all the different conflicting reports received, I feel daily more confirmed in my opinion, already given, that the lively movements of rebel forces on the Mobile and Pensacola Railroad are at present defensive only, and that the larger portion of the troops collecting at Pollard were forwarded by rail to Chattanooga, to re-enforce Bragg, who was, according to rebel papers, severely punished, and is continually hard pressed by General Grant's army.

On the 27th of November, I visited Pensacola on the steamer George Peabody, she having discharged her cargo, and the heavy guns not being ready on the wharf for loading.

Having placed in town three companies of infantry, I started with a cavalry escort to examine the fortified line and reconnoiter the neighboring country. The position is a favorable one, elevated and surrounded in half circle by swamps connecting with the bay in front of the town ; the woods all cleared to proper distance. The only disadvantage to the present fortifications is a hill, called the Old Spanish Fort, commanding Fort Arnold.

On the bay two of the wharves are destroyed, and only one can be used, with proper caution.

The houses are nearly all deserted, and deprived not only of their furniture, but mostly of doors and windows, the streets covered with high weeds and bushes.

I visited Mr. Morino, the Spanish consul; he is the father-in-law of Mallory, the Secretary of the Navy at Richmond ; has two sons in the rebel army; contributed $25,000 to Jeff. Davis' Cabinet, and claims Pensacola as neutral ground, against which I politely protested.

The other inhabitants, very few in number, also strongly sympathize with the rebellion, and require a more vigilant control than heretofore given.

General Clanton, commanding at Pollard, was at Pensacola with 300 men in October, and Major [E. A.] McWhorter came in with 150 cavalry two days after my visit there, but generally their scouting parties do not number more than 10 to 15 men.

Reports concur that they have a regiment of infantry and some cavalry at Fifteen-Mile Station, on the Pensacola Railroad, and are fortifying that point; cavalry pickets on both flanks as before. (See report of November 23, No. 42.)

Deserters are constantly coming in, taking the oath of allegiance. Fifteen young men have enlisted in my cavalry company.

One officer of the Confederacy, Lieutenant Howard, reported also voluntarily with valuable information and took the oath.

Several contrabands, who succeeded in reaching our lines, were added to the Fourteenth Regiment, Corps d'Afrique. One of them came in with a heavy iron bar on his leg, wandering with it three weeks through woods and swamps.

The practice of allowing citizens to come in from beyond our lines and go out again with provisions I have suspended, and a schooner coming from Milton? Fla., under a similar pretext, was confiscated by my order.

Not knowing whether my report of November 25 (No. 48) has safely reached the department headquarters, I beg to inclose a copy of it, * requesting the commanding general's decision and orders.

Very respectfully, general, your obedient servant,

ASBOTH,
Brigadier-General.

WASHINGTON, D. C.,
December 7, 1863.

Major-General BANKS,
    Commanding Department of the Gulf, New Orleans, La.:

GENERAL: I have just received your letter of November 18, "off Aransas Pass."† In this you say the "best line of defense for Louisiana, as well as for operations against Texas, is by Berwick Bay and the Atchafalaya." I fully concur with you in this opinion. It is the line which

------

* See p. 820.   † See Rio Grande Expedition, etc., p. 409.

I advised you from the beginning to adopt. In regard to your Sabine and Rio Grande expeditions, no notice of your intention to make them was received here till they were actually undertaken. The danger, however, of dividing your army, with the enemy between the two parts, ready to fall upon either with his entire force, was pointed out from the first, and I have continually urged that you must not expect any considerable re-enforcements from other departments.

Your communications in regard to light-draught sea-going vessels have been referred to the Quartermaster-General, who has uniformly answered that he had given you all such vessels that were available, there being only a small number that could be procured. His attention will be again called to the matter to-day.

In regard to gunboats for your department, we must rely upon the Navy. Admiral Porter has been requested to give you all possible assistance in this matter. You may not be aware that by a law of last Congress, the building, purchasing, and commanding of gunboats are placed exclusively under the Navy Department. I will again ask that admirals commanding in the Gulf and in the Mississippi be directed to co-operate with you and render you all the aid in their power. You will also communicate with them, asking their assistance in any way you desire.

The Secretary of War has directed Maj. Gen. J. J. Reynolds to repair immediately to New Orleans, and assume command at that place in your absence, reporting to you.

Very respectfully, your obedient servant,
H. W. HALLECK,
General-in-Chief.

HEADQUARTERS TROOPS IN WESTERN LOUISIANA,
New Iberia, December 7, 1863.
Brig. Gen. CHARLES P. STONE,
Chief of Staff, New Orleans, La.:

I sent out some 350 cavalry last night to capture some 70 or 80 rebels, said to have been near Abbeville; but our information was incorrect; none were found.

The Eighth New Hampshire Regiment left this morning, and Burbridge's command this afternoon. There has been some picket skirmishing toward Saint Martinsville, but nothing important. The negotiations for the exchange of prisoners have commenced. Those at New Orleans for exchange should be prepared for transportation at short notice.

W. B. FRANKLIN,
Major-General, Commanding.

SPECIAL ORDERS, } HDQRS. 19TH A. C., AND U. S. FORCES,
No. 85.   } *New Iberia, La., December* 7, 1863.

I. The Fourth Division, Thirteenth Army Corps, will march this day at 1 p. m. They will proceed to Berwick City; arriving there, the commanding officer will report by telegraph to headquarters Department of the Gulf, New Orleans.

*   *   *   *   *   *

By order of Major-General Franklin:
WICKHAM HOFFMAN,
Assistant Adjutant-General.

HEADQUARTERS,
Baton Rouge, December 8, 1863.
Brig. Gen. CHARLES P. STONE,
Chief of Staff, Department of the Gulf, New Orleans:

GENERAL: Amongst a number of refugees who came in the other day, are 4 deserters from Ninth Louisiana Battalion Partisan Rangers, probably conscripts. Shall they be released on taking the oath ?

Am I to understand your telegram of 3d instant, that hereafter landings of supplies on the river plantations are to be authorized on simple Treasury permits ?

Ten prisoners from the enemy were taken yesterday morning by Lieutenant Earl, Fourth Wisconsin, 22 miles from here.

Very respectfully, your obedient servant,
P. ST. GEORGE COOKE,
Brigadier-General, U. S. Volunteers.

HEADQUARTERS DEPARTMENT OF THE GULF,
New Orleans, December 9, 1863.
Maj. Gen. H. W. HALLECK,
General-in-Chief, U. S. Army, Washington, D. C.:

GENERAL: I beg leave to submit upon the subject referred to in the accompanying papers * relating to the detention of the British vessel H. G. Berry, the following report:

All the facts stated therein were within my knowledge, excepting that which relates to the information being conveyed by the schooner, but of this I have no doubt whatever. The time and circumstances of the arrival of that vessel make it impossible that the information could have been otherwise conveyed.

A full statement of the vessel's forces, guns, &c., the losses sustained on the voyage, was sent to a rebel officer in Matamoras, and received there on the evening of the day that my troops occupied Brownsville.

Of this fact I have positive knowledge. Had it been received earlier by the rebels, it would have prevented their evacuation, and might have defeated our landing at Brazos Santiago. If this had occurred, the expedition would have failed. The person who gave this information called upon me as a Texas refugee, and offered to procure information in regard to the armament and defenses of Fort Brown. The circumstances detailed to me at Matamoras make this certain. The information as to our forces was conveyed to the rebels by this schooner, either by passenger or letter, and her detention by my order caused the delay in its transmission which enabled the forces of the United States to occupy the position in advance of the reports of this spy. The information in regard to our fleet and forces was obtained at New Orleans, the report of our losses at the Rio Grande. Of these facts I have no doubt whatever. It is not probable that the owners of the vessel were parties to the treason.

I have the honor to be, with much respect, your obedient servant,
N. P. BANKS,
Major-General, Commanding.

----

* Not found.

HEADQUARTERS DEPARTMENT OF THE GULF,
New Orleans, December 9, 1863.
Major-General FRANKLIN,
Comdg. Troops in Western Louisiana, New Iberia :

GENERAL: As soon as General Weitzel can be spared, please send him to New Orleans, to report at these headquarters for special temporary duty in the. north.* General Emory will join you in a few days.
Very respectfully, your obedient servant,
[CHAS. P. STONE,]
Brigadier-General, and Chief of Staff.

WAR DEPARTMENT,
Washington, December 10, 1863.
Maj. Gen. JOSEPH J. REYNOLDS,
Louisville, Ky., or Cairo, Ill. :

Directions were given to General Banks to remove the large guns from Port Hudson, not required for the land defenses of that place, to the Defenses of New Orleans. It is reported that this has not been done, and that the guns in the water batteries of Port Hudson are liable to fall into the enemy's hands. That place will be included in your command, in General Banks' absence, and you will carry out the above instructions. Call upon Major-General McPherson for such assistance and co-operation as he may be able to give you. Acknowledge receipt.
H. W. HALLECK,
General-in-Chief.

HEADQUARTERS DEPARTMENT OF THE GULF,
New Orleans, December 10, 1863.
Maj. Gen. C. C. WASHBURN,
Commanding Troops near Matagorda Bay, Tex.:

GENERAL: The steamers Saint Mary's and Fair Haven leave this day for your station, with the Forty-ninth Indiana Volunteers and supplies on board. Additional troops and material will be forwarded as fast as transportation can be furnished. The Fourth Division, Thirteenth Army Corps, will soon be with you. The major-general commanding desires me to say to you that the movement indicated will be made as soon as sufficient force and material shall be concentrated with you, but that much more of both are necessary to insure success. He desires that while these preparations are in progress you should make it appear that your intentions are to take up a line of operations toward San Antonio, yet not wasting any time, but securing means of occupying the Peninsula of Matagorda, and learning the facilities and difficulties of a movement along it by water and by land. The necessary material for bridging rivers is being rapidly prepared, and will be soon completed. Proper trains of artillery are also prepared for shipment, and by the time the necessary troops can be concentrated with you, this material can also be sent to you. Scouts and pilots should be secured for all directions, and no pains spared to learn the force, positions, and intentions of the enemy, and the natural and artificial difficulties to be met and overcome in the march really proposed. I should feel personally obliged

---

* So ordered by General Franklin same day. General Emory was assigned, December 13, 1863, to command of the First Division, Nineteenth Army Corps.

if you would cause to be sent to me, by each steamer leaving your post, a short, concise statement of your force at the time and of the condition of your supplies of all kinds.

· Very respectfully, I am, general, your most obedient servant,
CHAS. P. STONE,
Brigadier-General, and Chief of Staff.

HDQRS. FIRST DIVISION, THIRTEENTH ARMY CORPS,
New Orleans, December 10, 1863.
Brig. Gen. CHARLES P. STONE,
Chief of Staff, Department of the Gulf:

GENERAL: I have the honor to report to you my departure this morning on the steamship Saint Mary's, with all the troops of the First Division at this place excepting the train guards and two mounted companies, containing, respectively, 36 and 42 men. These two companies of mounted infantry were mounted by General Washburn, in the Teche country, on the native ponies. My own judgment is, with our limited transportation, it would be better to turn these ponies over and get others at Matagorda. But, from a profound respect for General Washburn, I have not issued the order. I prefer to leave the companies for the present, and report the fact to the general on my arrival.

I am, most respectfully, your obedient servant,
WM. P. BENTON,
Brigadier-General.

HEADQUARTERS THIRTEENTH ARMY CORPS,
Brownsville, Tex., December 10, 1863.
L. PIERCE, Jr.,
United States Consul, Matamoras:

Your dispatch of this date is this moment received. Every protection in my power will be thrown around every loyal American and his property. I would not be justified in bringing a force into the city of Matamoras to defend it against the Federal forces of President Juarez. The Federal Government of Mexico is on terms of intimate friendship with ours. It seems to me, if your danger is imminent, you should remove more under my protection with your property and money. The folds of the Star-Spangled Banner are large enough to cover every loyal American and every friendly foreigner who has not forfeited its protection by acts of alliance with rebels, aiding them to cut our throats, and the strong arms of the citizen soldiers here will protect them against all comers.

To the loyal and true, I say freely, "Come ; come one, come all!" But to the assassins in Matamoras, who have disgraced the American name, I can only say, "Come as prisoners of war." Should any loyal man so far forget himself in a misplaced sympathy as to attempt to secure the property of a rebel or disloyal man by bringing it here in a loyal name, he will certainly suffer the consequences. I extend to you a hearty welcome, if you come. and ask you to command me personally or officially.

I am your friend and servant,
N. J. T. DANA,
Major-General.

HEADQUARTERS THIRTEENTH ARMY CORPS,
Brownsville, Tex., December 10, 1863.

His Excellency Don JESUS SERNA,
Governor of Tamaulipas.

I was informed the day before yesterday that the British schooner Nancy Dawson, with an assorted cargo of military supplies, including 10,000 muskets, had anchored off the mouth of the Rio Grande, and that she was consigned to the firm of Hale & Co., who are doing business in Matamoras. I have reason to know that these supplies are for the use of the enemies of the United States—the rebels and traitors who have for two years held high carnival in the State of Texas. For this reason I sent a dispatch yesterday, requesting any naval vessel near Brazos Santiago, or the mouth of the river, to seize the Nancy Dawson as a prize. I am now informed that the arms from the Nancy Dawson have been landed in Mexico, and are on the way to Matamoras. Confidently relying on your feelings of friendship for my Government, and on the intimate relations which are existing between our two nations, and in the knowledge that Your Excellency is fully informed of the barbarities and enormities which have been and are being committed on loyal citizens and their families by the atrocious villains who are waiting for the safe delivery of these arms and other military supplies, I request that they may be immediately seized and turned over to me, unless Your Excellency has reasons, after seizing them, to retain them as forfeited by their owners for your own use.

Protesting to Your Excellency the sincerity of my good feeling and my distinguished consideration, I have the honor to remain, your most obedient servant,

N. J. T. DANA,
Major-General.

.WASHINGTON, D. C., *December* 11, 1863.

Major-General BANKS, *Commanding Department of the Gulf:*

GENERAL: I inclose herewith a copy of memorandum from the Navy Department to the Secretary of War in regard to guns left at Port Hudson.*

In my dispatch to you of August 24, it was directed that the fortifications at New Orleans should be supplied by removing to that place the heavy ordnance at Port Hudson and Vicksburg. It appears from Admiral Porter's dispatch that this has not been done, and that there is danger of the water batteries at Port Hudson falling into the hands of the enemy. Major-General Reynolds has been directed, in your absence, to remove these water batteries to New Orleans. As we control the waters of the Mississippi River, we require only land batteries on its banks between New Orleans and Memphis, especially in places which are liable to fall into rebel hands.

General Steele reports that Price, with a portion of the Texas troops, is moving toward Little Rock. If your forces are operating up the Atchafalaya, as stated in your last dispatch, they will be likely to check Price's advance. If your forces operate together on the line proposed, you will be strong enough to resist anything the enemy can bring against you, but the division of your army and the occupation of so many points in Western Texas cause serious apprehensions that the enemy may concentrate and overwhelm some one of your isolated detachments.

------

* Not found.

A regiment of cavalry is being sent from Baltimore to your command. In the present condition of affairs in the West and on the Mississippi River, it will not be possible to immediately re-enforce you from that quarter. I hope, however, that General Grant may be able to spare some troops from his line. But, as I have stated, you must make your dispositions with regard only to the troops of your own army, and not so divide it as to render re-enforcements necessary for your own security.

Contingencies may arise elsewhere which will render it impossible to give you more troops at the time you ask for them.

Very respectfully, your obedient servant,

H. W. HALLECK,
General-in-Chief.

HEADQUARTERS DEPARTMENT OF THE GULF,
New Orleans, December 11, 1863.
Maj. Gen. H. W. HALLECK,
General-in-Chief, U. S. Army, Washington, D. C.:

SIR: I have the honor to acknowledge the receipt of a dispatch from the Secretary of State,* indorsed by the Secretary of War,† stating the relations which it is desirable that this Government should maintain with the Mexican Government and the French authorities in Mexico. I am confident there will be no departure from the line of policy indicated on the Rio Grande. Major-General Dana, a discreet and able officer, is in command at Brownsville, and has been instructed that it is the purpose of this Government to avoid all complications beyond the limits of this country. I have forwarded to him a copy of the dispatch for his guidance.

I have the honor to be, with much respect, your obedient servant,

N. P. BANKS,
Major-General, Commanding.

HEADQUARTERS DEPARTMENT OF THE GULF,
New Orleans, December 11, 1863.
Maj. Gen. H. W. HALLECK,
Commander-in-Chief, U. S. Army, Washington, D. C.:

GENERAL: At the date of my departure from Brownsville, information had been received in Mexico by Governor Ruiz up to the 24th of October. It is probable later dates have been received by the Government at Washington.

It was represented at that time that the citizens were manifesting great energy in the defense of their country against the French invaders, military preparations being limited to the movements of State troops rather than extending to national organizations.

The French had moved from Mexico with a force of about 12,000. An equal force representing the Juarez government was between San Luis and Mexico, acting with great energy and spirit against the advanced columns of the French, and harassing them on all sides. Between the city of Mexico and Vera Cruz there was an irregular force of 6,000 Mexicans, for the purpose of attacking the communications of the French army with the coast. It was reported from San Luis that the towns which had declared for the French intervention acknowledged their adherence only so long as the French troops occupied them, and that

---

* Of November 23, p. 815.   † For indorsement, see p. 846.

the moment they left, the people resumed their allegiance to the Mexican authorities.

Governor Serna, the civil governor of the State of Tamaulipas, who was elected two years since by a vote of the people, but had been unable in consequence of political disturbances to take his seat, and who was restored by the revolution headed by Cortinas, arrived at Matamoras on the 22d of November. All parties appeared to acquiesce cordially in his government, and a spirit of earnest friendship for the Government of the United States prevailed in that city.

I have the honor to be, with much respect, your obedient servant,

> N. P. BANKS,
> *Major-General, Commanding.*

HEADQUARTERS DEPARTMENT OF THE GULF,
New Orleans, December 11, 1863.

Maj. Gen. H. W. HALLECK, *General-in-Chief, U. S. Army:*

GENERAL : Upon the occupation of Brownsville by the troops of the United States, it was found that large quantities of cotton had been transported across the river to the city of Matamoras. Representations were made by prominent citizens of Texas that a very large portion of this property was owned by the rebel Government, and was to be used for purposes hostile to the United States; that other portions of the property were owned by prominent rebel officers, many of whom were in Matamoras supervising its disposition for their individual benefit; also that a large part of the property so held by the rebels had been stolen from the citizens of Texas. I felt it my duty to call the attention of the American consul at Matamoras to this subject, and to request him to bring it to the attention of the representatives of the Mexican Government, and ask that the property so taken from the United States should be returned to the persons from whom it was taken, or that it should be held by the Mexican authorities until proper investigation could be made of the facts connected with it and satisfactory assurances given that it was not to be used to aid the rebellion against the United States.

A large number of rebel officers were known to be in Mexico engaged in movements hostile to the United States. I requested him to present these facts to the Government, with such proofs as were in his possession, and to ask that such officers should be required to suspend all acts of hostility to this Government, or that they might be surrendered to this Government. My communication to the consul is inclosed herewith; it bears date of the day of my departure from Brownsville. I have no communication from him upon this subject. At Aransas Pass, however, I received information from General Dana stating that much excitement had occurred in Matamoras among the cotton traders; that it was understood that foreigners had been interdicted the privilege of trade by the Mexican authorities, and that in consequence the price of cotton in Matamoras had fallen to 25 or 28 cents a pound, and great efforts were being made at that time to transfer it from the owners to the citizens of Mexico. An extract from General Dana's letter is herewith inclosed.* The rebels probably felt its effect.

I have the honor to be, with much respect, your obedient servant,

> N. P. BANKS,
> *Major-General, Commanding.*

---

* Not found.

BROWNSVILLE,
December 11, 1863—11 a. m.

Brig. Gen. CHARLES P. STONE,
 Chief of Staff:

I have the honor to acknowledge the receipt of the dispatch of the major-general commanding, dated 3d instant, and to report that nothing of great interest has occurred here since my last dispatch.

I think proper to mention my conviction that this country being purely under martial law, I have supreme command, but I understand that General Hamilton will organize a court of some kind here, and I have heard one of his staff officers say this morning that a citizen here, whom I have been pursuing for evidence against him, would be punished by General Hamilton, in case he should get the same evidence against him, by a fine or otherwise, &c.   I have also discovered in two or three instances that matters which I have been occupied with were at the same time engaging the same attention from him, as, for instance, the procurement by demand from the Mexican authorities of the 2 men who stole the county records from here, also the records which are supposed now to be in Matamoras—a matter upon which my provost-marshal has been engaged, under my orders, in getting such testimony as will enable me to make a demand.   I understood only by hearsay to-day that General Hamilton has made a demand on Governor Serna for the men, which may, I fear, lose the records.

I mention these things merely to show the commanding general the danger of a clash of authority.   I shall not hesitate to act promptly according to my convictions of duty, but I would like to have the general's views and instructions.   It is my opinion that General Hamilton can only act here under my authority, and if he should, in interfering in matters with which I, as commander here, am occupied, by any means gather any piece of public information or evidence which would be of use to the public service, and which has not come to my knowledge, he should promptly furnish it to me, with his views and opinions, if necessary, so that I may execute the duties of commanding general here, in a country wholly under martial law, advisedly.   Day before yesterday, having heard that a British schooner had anchored at the mouth of the river with 10,000 stand of arms for the rebels, consigned to Hale & Co., of Matamoras, I immediately sent a dispatch to whatever naval officer might be near, that the vessel might be seized; but the arms were landed on the Mexican side before the matter was accomplished. I then made a demand of Governor Serna that the supplies should be seized and turned over to me, or kept by himself, with the certainty of never reaching their rebel owners.

I have received a satisfactory reply from the Governor, informing me that the seizure had been made and the property confiscated, and would be used by his Government, and he gives me the assurance that the rebels or our enemies shall not receive any part of it.

I discovered, after acting in this matter, that it also had engaged the attention of General Hamilton.

I send a Matamoras paper to the general to-day, which gives an account of a reception given General H[amilton] on Sunday last, wherein he is reported to have promised the aid of himself and his force to the Mexican Government against the French.

My position here is being made strong by the new fortifications, and I have at present no detachment out except the Thirty-seventh Illinois Infantry, which went up the river on the Mustang when Colonel Davis went up by land. The boat is somewhere between here and Edinburg, having a hard time on account of low water. They are fully able to protect themselves.

Next week I propose to send out a detachment of cavalry by each road, to meet at King's ranch, and may send a piece of artillery with them. I have sent two spies there. I shall follow the general's instructions and cautions, and will run no risks. My picket line is kept strong and alert, and I have spurred Colonel Hodge, at Point Isabel, to active vigilance. My trains go with small escorts of infantry.

The health of the troops is good. The cavalry is increasing, but the horses improve hardly any. We ought to have oats. We have purchased about 600 horses (mustang), and brought in about 125 from Stillman's and Latham's ranches, besides 100 head of beef-cattle and 700 sheep. Stillman appears to have some friends and sympathizers here among the Government officials, one of whom (Mr. Brackenridge) brought him over and introduced him to me the day after he (Brackenridge) arrived.

I have thought proper this morning to send him back; he is only here to accomplish his own selfish ends.

The Matamoras has not reported at Brazos yet. I was compelled to send the Hale there, but it is not safe for her to remain there, and I propose to relieve her on the arrival of the Matamoras.

No carbine ammunition has, as yet, arrived here, although every effort has been made to have a duplicate supply sent. If any was on the schooner which brought Davis' equipments, it is gone, as she went to pieces on the bar. We ought to have it at once, of both kinds of Sharps carbines, and Davis very much wants 300 sets of cavalry equipments of the regular pattern, inasmuch as what is here is of citizen's pattern. Davis remembers with hope the assurance he had from the general that he should have an outfit of American horses. They ought to come on either the Clinton, Crescent, or Saint Mary's, with a light load.

Information from the interior of this State, via Monterey, is to the effect that the rebel troops are leaving their ranks rapidly by every opportunity, regiments which two months ago numbered 500 men being able to muster now only 150 or 200. The company of 40 Mexicans they had stationed near Eagle Pass revolted, as reported, and attacked the custom-house, carrying off all the supplies found stored there, and left for some point lower down on the Rio Grande, where they said they intended to join the Union forces. I captured, near King's ranch, a few days ago, about 8,000 yards of English cloth, gray and blue, on its way to the Confederate army, and ordered it to be turned over to Mr. Brackenridge. Great quantities of cotton and military supplies are crossing the river at Laredo and Eagle Pass, and I have accepted the services of a refugee, by the name of McManus, who has offered to go there, collect 30 refugees, and destroy everything he cannot run over the river and get a Mexican custom-house receipt for in the name of the United States. I have furnished him with a little money and some pistol cartridges, and he has gone. I think he will be successful. I have given him orders to put everything near the river in the Mexican custom-house, and to kill, burn, and destroy everything else, with the object of getting up a panic about the danger of the roads and of breaking up the trade. I have also given authority to one Webber, a very loyal friend of ours between this and Roma, to make the roads in his neighborhood difficult and hazardous for rebels, and the Jews and speculators who are furnishing them.

The French army has marched from Queretaro in two divisions—one for Guanaxuato, the other for San Luis Potosi—General Bazaine in command. Not a man has been sent to San Luis from either Nuevo Leon or Tamaulipas.

Ruiz is marching on Matamoras with 800 men. There is great panic and confusion there, and an attack hourly expected. Stillman & Co.'s cotton is in the barricades. Serna will offer to leave the settlement of the question to Juarez, and wait, and says if that is not conceded by Ruiz, he will fight it out. The consul wrote me yesterday, saying he feared pillaging by a mob, and had large amounts of treasure in his keeping, and asked advice. I urged him to bring all our friends over here, under our protection, and to notify rebels that, if their lives were in danger, they would be welcome here as prisoners of war.

Very great apprehensions are felt for the safety of the Union men in Texas. No one is permitted to leave the State without a pass, and passes are not given to any one fit for service, or suspected of Union sentiments. Impressment is the order of the day. In Dallas County, the farmers are said to have banded themselves together, resisting the impressment of wheat, and civil war is threatening.

Please excuse my prolixity, and believe that I remain, with great respect,

N. J. T. DANA,
Major-General.

SPECIAL ORDERS, }   HDQRS. DEPARTMENT OF THE GULF,
No. 309.   }   *New Orleans, December* 11, 1863.

*   *   *   *   *   *   *

XIV. Brig. Gen. R. A. Cameron will proceed to Indianapolis, Ind., and there confer with the Governor of the State on the subject of filling the regiments from that State now serving in this department, making such suggestions as may be for the benefit of the recruiting for their regiments and the manner of forwarding the recruits to the department. Having accomplished this duty, Brigadier-General Cameron will return to New Orleans, and report for duty with his brigade.

*   *   *   *   *   *   *

By command of Major-General Banks :
G. NORMAN LIEBER,
Acting Assistant Adjutant-General.

FORT SUMNER, N. MEX.,
December 11, 1863.

Brig. Gen. JAMES H. CARLETON,
Commanding Department of New Mexico :

MY DEAR GENERAL: Your letter of the 29th ultimo came safely to hand. I am pleased to inform you that everything at the post is working to my entire satisfaction. I had anticipated your wishes in reference to Cremony's company, an order having been given him before the reception of your letter, and he is now off on a thirty days' scout, with all the disposable men of his company. I will adopt your suggestion about keeping our own stock well in hand, and having them carefully guarded.

The Navajoes, under the escort of Captain Calloway's company, arrived yesterday, and I assure you the meeting between those here and the new arrivals was truly affecting. Many tears were shed on both sides. I have encamped them adjoining those already at the post, and only about 75 yards from the extreme right of my camp. They are comfortably quartered in old Sibley tents, and have had their sick cared for by the attending surgeon. Many of the little ones required medical treatment. I have just had a favorable interview with the leading men of the Navajoes, just arrived, and they (four of them, with the interpreter) express the desire to leave here in five or six days, to return to their own country and bring others in. I have already heard from you on the subject of granting passes to four of the Navajoes and the interpreter. There are now so many of this tribe collected at the Bosque Redondo that I deem the presence of their agent here of paramount importance. They are just like children, requiring some one constantly to look after their wants, and to direct them in their farming pursuits. The subject of huts for the Indians will command my attention at an early date.

I am much gratified at your sending Calloway's company to this station. It is a valuable acquisition to my force, and I needed more troops. Company I, First Infantry, California Volunteers, I know well, having inspected them several times. I don't want any better men or soldiers than they are.

I have submitted Agent Labadie's views in reference to the reduction of the ration now issued to the Apaches for your consideration. He seems to take a sensible view of the subject, and, with your approbation, I will continue to issue the ration as before, viz, 1 pound of flour, $1\frac{1}{4}$ of meat, a little salt, and sugar and coffee in addition to the above, to the eight chiefs or principal men. I do not think the Indians residing here are at all disposed at present to give any trouble. Should they become troublesome, such summary measures will be taken as, in my judgment, will quell any disturbance. I beg to bring to your notice the destitute condition of the Navajoes just arrived, in point of clothing. The others have received presents of blankets, clothes, &c., and these expect the same treatment. I regret much the absence of the superintendent of Indian affairs from the Territory at this particular juncture, as his presence at Santa Fé would doubtless insure to these poverty-stricken Navajoes the same consideration as the others, who acknowledge themselves chastised and conquered, and justly so, by the policy you are pursuing at present in the department.

Next week the widening, deepening, and lengthening of the azequia madre is to be commenced; immediately after, the land for the separate farms (the one for the Apaches and the other for the Navajoes) will be broken up, as next summer it is the intention of the agent to produce large crops. The Navajoes tell me they intend to beat the Apaches in their crops, as they know all about planting and the use of the azequias. They all, Apaches and Navajoes, appear contented and happy, and speak with pleasure of their prospective crops.

Very truly, yours,

H. D. WALLEN,
[*Major Seventh U. S. Infantry, Commanding.*]

NEW ORLEANS, *December* 12, 1863.

Maj. Gen. H. W. HALLECK,
General-in-Chief, U. S. Army, Washington, D. C.:

GENERAL: Your dispatch, calling my attention to the importance of the command of New Orleans, is received. In reply, I have the honor to state that Col. E. G. Beckwith, chief commissary of the department, is temporarily in command of the defenses of this city.

After the campaign of the Mississippi, a large number of general officers were necessarily absent upon leave, in consequence of sickness, exhaustion, and a pressure of private business. The entire disposable force of the department, under orders from the Government at Washington, was in the field, preparatory to a movement into Texas. In the absence of so many general officers for the reasons stated, all who were competent for duty were required in the field. There were very few in the department who understood the character of its defenses, which are extended and complicated, and it became necessary, in the absence of so large a portion of the military force from the neighborhood of the city, that some one should be in charge who was familiar with them. Colonel Beckwith was at that moment, considering all the circumstances, the best able to perform the duty required, and was temporarily appointed for that purpose. It is my intention to place a major-general in command, and my attention was directed to Major-General Herron as a suitable officer for that position. If this be inconsistent with the views of the Department, I should be very glad to receive information, and will await your reply.

I have the honor to be, with much respect, your obedient servant,

N. P. BANKS,
Major-General, Commanding.

DEPARTMENT OF STATE,
Washington, December 12, 1863.

Maj. Gen. N. P. BANKS, *New Orleans:*

GENERAL: I inclose a copy of the letter of the 23d ultimo,* addressed to you by this Department, and will thank you to communicate the same to Mr. [Andrew J.] Hamilton, the Military Governor of Texas, for his information in regard to the matters to which it relates. You will at the same time inform him that the President expects that all such intercourse as must necessarily arise out of the war with the insurgents in that State or with the Government of Mexico or any Mexicans, should be carried on by yourself alone, on whom the exclusive responsibility has been devolved. You are further authorized to suspend the Military Governor from his command if the public interest should at any time seem to require it, but not otherwise.

I am, general, your very obedient servant,

WILLIAM H. SEWARD.

[Indorsement.]

WAR DEPARTMENT,
December 14, 1863.

The foregoing instructions having been submitted to this Department, are approved, and Major-General Banks is directed to observe them. In case he should find it necessary at any time to suspend the functions of the Military Governor of Texas, he will immediately report his action to this Department, with the reasons and facts upon which it is predicated.

EDWIN M. STANTON,
Secretary of War.

---

* See p. 815.

HEADQUARTERS DEPARTMENT OF THE GULF,
New Orleans, December 12, 1863.

Maj. Gen. H. W. HALLECK,
General-in-Chief, U. S. Army, Washington, D. C.:

GENERAL: Major-General Washburn's dispatches from Pass Cavallo, Tex., are inclosed herewith.* He is instructed not to move farther up the coast, but to maintain his position either on the island or at a secure point inland, either at Indianola or Lavaca. He has from 5,000 to 6,000 men, and can defend himself against any force it is possible for the enemy to concentrate against him. A movement upon the Brazos, which he suggests, would unquestionably lead to an immediate engagement with the forces under Magruder, and I have thought it unsafe to take that position until we are strong enough to insure success. My desire is to occupy Galveston Island, if it can be done within reasonable time. This will give us the entire coast, and relieve the blockading squadron, which numbers now over thirty war vessels, enabling us to direct this naval force against the enemy on the Mississippi or any other part of the Gulf coast. If this can be accomplished, it will be of very material advantage. If we move in that direction, I shall concentrate on the Brazos all the disposable force at my command for a decisive and very short campaign. Eastern Texas offers us recruits, horses, forage, and supplies of every kind. All other parts of this department have been stripped by the two armies of everything necessary for their support. If this movement is made, the force under General Franklin on the Teche will be withdrawn and concentrated in Texas. I do not intend to divide my forces by the occupation of numerous positions. With the exception of Brazos Santiago, it will be unnecessary to hold any other post, except it be upon Matagorda or Galveston Bay. Either of these positions will be sufficient for the permanent occupation of the coast, and for an entrance into the interior whenever it shall be deemed expedient. So far as the occupation of the State is concerned, Matagorda Bay, which is now in our possession, gives us the key to the greater part of it, which we can occupy whenever we please.

Accompanying this letter is a chart of the coast of Texas, showing by flags the positions we occupy on the Rio Grande and the coast, the route pursued by the expedition to the Rio Grande, and the losses sustained by the sea.†

Colonel Davis is at Ringgold Barracks.

I have the honor to be, with much respect, your obedient servant,

N. P. BANKS,
Major-General, Commanding.

HEADQUARTERS TROOPS IN WESTERN LOUISIANA,
New Iberia, December 12, 1863.

Brig. Gen. CHARLES P. STONE,
Chief of Staff, New Iberia [*New Orleans, La.*]:

I have sent 2 scouts into Vermillion to learn whether there is still a force of the enemy there, the rumors being that there are very few there. They are said to be in some force on Bayou Fusilier, to the right of Grand Coteau. This is not unlikely, as there is nothing for either horses or men in the vicinity of Vermillion.

---

* Not found.　　　　　　　　　† For chart, see Atlas.

Taylor writes, by flag of truce received to-day, that part of our pris-oners are at Shreveport and part at Tyler, Tex., so that some delay will occur in getting them back. I hear that Red River has risen 2½ feet. Do not know the authority. ˊ

W. B. FRANKLIN,
. *Major-General.*

HEADQUARTERS DEPARTMENT OF THE GULF,
New Orleans, December 12, 1863.

Brig. Gen. G. WEITZEL, *U. S. Volunteers :*

GENERAL : The major-general commanding desires that you proceed to the State of Ohio and have conference with the Governor of the State on the subject of promptly filling up the regiments from that State now serving in this department, of which a list is inclosed herewith.* He de-sires that you should represent to His Excellency the admirable service already rendered by these regiments and batteries, their present de-pleted condition, and the importance to the State and to the country of having their ranks soon filled to the maximum. This action alone on the part of States represented in this department will give to its commander the means of insuring the success of the Union cause within the limits intrusted to his command.

The commanding general will hand you a letter to His Excellency the Governor of Ohio. He desires that you use all possible dispatch in your movements, and return to the department as soon as you feel that your mission has been accomplished.

Wishing you an agreeable and safe journey, and in the hope of seeing you soon again on duty in this department, I have the honor to be, general, very respectfully, your most obedient servant,

[CHAS. P. STONE,]
Brigadier-General, and Chief of Staff.

HEADQUARTERS DEPARTMENT OF THE GULF,
. *New Orleans, December 13, 1863.*

Brig. Gen. W. DWIGHT, *U. S. Volunteers, New Orleans :*

GENERAL : By special order of this date, you have been assigned to duty at Fort Jackson, La., for temporary command. Recent occur-rences at that station, which have been fully mentioned to you in con-versation to-day, make it necessary, in the opinion of the major-gen-eral commanding, that an officer of high rank and good judgment should be charged with the command. He recommends to you the greatest discretion, with the greatest firmness, in the administration of affairs at Fort Jackson, and recommends also that, as soon as you shall be fur-nished with fresh troops, the present garrison be relieved from all duties which involve the safety of the post. The measures which will in future be adopted with reference to that garrison will depend much upon the nature of the reports he may receive from you. You will please keep these headquarters constantly advised of the condition of affairs in your command.

Very respectfully, I am, general, your most obedient servant,

CHAS. P. STONE,
Brigadier-General, and Chief of Staff.

---

* Not found.

HEADQUARTERS UNITED STATES FORCES,
Fort Esperanza, Tex., December 13, 1863.

Brig. Gen. CHARLES P. STONE, *Chief of Staff:*

GENERAL: Yours of the 10th is received. I regret to see so poor a prospect of speedily concentrating men and munitions of war at this point to justify a forward movement. I should await with great patience were it not that on this island there is neither wood, wholesome water, nor forage. The necessities of my position have compelled me to occupy the southern point of Matagorda Peninsula, where we find drift-wood comparatively plenty, with fair water, and a little very poor grass. The position is entirely secure, and I shall land all troops and stores that arrive there, thus saving the very tedious job of ferrying from this island when we are ready to move. The troops which captured this island I shall retain here until a forward movement is ordered. I do not know what amount of force the commanding general will consider necessary before a forward movement can be safely made.

The time that has already elapsed since we came here has enabled General Magruder to collect all his available force to oppose our march.

From 6 refugees from Matagorda that came in this morning, I hear that Magruder is collecting troops on the Caney, between Matagorda and Brazoria. There are no natural obstacles of a serious character to marching an army along the beach to the mouth of the Brazos River.

On the Caney are large plantations, plenty of corn, sugar, and mules. Our animals are dying here from starvation at the rate of 8 or 10 a day. The importance of reaching a country where we can obtain forage you will readily see. I do not want a large wagon train. One hundred wagons is all I want for 10,000 men, and twenty-five ambulances. There is good water on the bar at the mouth of Brazos River, from 8 to 9 feet. Taking that point, we shall have a good base, near Houston and Galveston. Boats that can cross the bar can go to Brazoria. Having that point, we can supply an army as far as Houston with a small train, and, if we can once reach the inland, we can no doubt press many teams. To send a large number of mules here to starve seems unnecessary.

There seems to be great fault somewhere in regard to sending out coal. The steamer Blackstone arrived off the bar last night, and sends me word that she is out of coal. The steamers Planter and Matamoras at last accounts were aground in Espiritu Santo Bay, without fuel. I have sent a small schooner-load of 10 tons to them, obtained from the McClellan.

Respectfully,

C. C. WASHBURN,
Major-General.

P. S.—We shall need cavalry greatly, as soon as we can get where it can be subsisted. A squadron or two we ought to have at once.

I send you a few secesh papers.

HEADQUARTERS UNITED STATES FORCES,
Saluria, Tex., December 13, 1863.

Brig. Gen. CHARLES P. STONE, *Chief of Staff:*

GENERAL: Last night, just before sunset, a small schooner, flying a white flag, was seen approaching from the direction of Matagorda. I sent out a small boat to meet her, and she was stopped and brought to anchor about 1 mile above Decrow's Point. Two officers of General Magruder's staff were found on board, bearing the inclosed dispatch from General Magruder. I returned a reply, of which I inclose a copy. There can be no doubt but their real object was to ascertain the amount of our force and its destination when we shall move from here. They return no wiser than they came.

I have the honor to be, your obedient servant,

C. C. WASHBURN,
Major-General.

[Inclosure No. 1.]

HDQRS. DISTRICT OF TEXAS, NEW MEXICO, AND ARIZONA,
Matagorda, Tex., December 10, 1863.

Maj. Gen. N. P. BANKS, U. S. Army,
Or officer in command of U. S. Forces at or near Saluria, Tex.:

SIR: Brigadier-General Bee informs me that you deemed his sending a flag of truce to inquire as to the fate and condition of the garrison captured by your forces at Aransas improper, and had therefore detained his messenger. I have also received information, which seems to be reliable, that 2 men, citizens of Texas, or residents within her limits, were seen a few days since hanging in the rigging of one of the small sail craft taken possession of by your command in Matagorda Bay.

I am also informed that citizens of Texas have been captured on the Matagorda Peninsula, and have been assured that on the arrival of the permanent commanding officer in that quarter they will be made to take the oath of allegiance to the United States Government, and that if they attempt previously to escape they will be shot.

In reference to the above, I have the honor to state that the sending of flags of truce to inquire as to the state and disposition of prisoners of war is in accordance with the usages of civilized warfare; that it has been practiced frequently by the commanding officer of the United States naval forces in their intercourse with me during the early part of this year, and more recently for this precise purpose after the repulse of your forces at Sabine Pass, and that all such communications have been answered by me and the officers under my command with promptness, courtesy, and truth. I shall, therefore, expect a like course on the part of yourself and your officers under similar circumstances. With regard to the reported hanging and the alleged threat of death to our citizens. I have to inform you that the citizens of Texas have had their remembrance of the massacres of Goliad and the Alamo kept fresh in their minds by the atrocities of the savage Indians with whom they are constantly at war; that they are quite willing to trust to their own bravery in battle for the safety of their lives, and that if the act alleged to have been done by you or your officers be true, and the threats alleged to have been made be carried out, no earthly power can prevent such retaliation as will astonish the world. Up to this time, in this part of the country, the war has been conducted by me strictly in accordance with the rules of civilized warfare.

Those bearing flags of truce have been treated with courtesy and dispatched promptly. No prisoner of war has ever received even a momentary insult, and all have been cared for as well as the circumstances of the country would permit. It is my desire to do this in future, and I am determined that the civilized world shall know that the black flag and its horrors cannot, with truth, be attributed to me. Should they occur, they will result from the views you are said to entertain, and the responsibility will rest with you and your Government alone.

In this connection I have the honor to remind you that I have several hundred prisoners of war in my hands, including officers of the rank of colonel in the army and lieutenant-commander in the navy of the United States, and that my treatment of these prisoners will be rigorously and mercilessly regulated by your adherence to or departure from the known laws of civilized warfare.

I have the honor to be, very respectfully, your obedient servant,

J. BANKHEAD MAGRUDER,
Major-General, Commanding District of Texas, &c.

[P. S.]—This communication will be borne by Maj. William Kearny and Lieut: J. Adair Murray, members of my staff.

Two men who accompanied Lieutenant Mann did not leave the island and return with him. If this be so, I request, as they are citizens, that they be permitted to leave the island and return to their homes.

[Inclosure No. 2.]

HEADQUARTERS UNITED STATES FORCES,
Saluria, Tex., December 13, 1863.

Maj. Gen. J. B. MAGRUDER,
Commanding District of Texas, &c.:

SIR: Your communication, dated the 10th instant, addressed to Major-General Banks, or the officer in command of United States forces at or or near Saluria, Tex., has been received.

As to the course that may have been pursued by Major-General Banks in regard to flags of truce said to have been sent to him by Brigadier-General Bee, I have no knowledge whatever. His action was—I have no doubt that it was—strictly proper, and such as the circumstances fully justified.

The reliable information you have received in regard to the hanging of two men, citizens of Texas, in the rigging of one of the small sail craft, taken possession of by this command in Matagorda Bay, is entirely destitute of truth, but is not more false than your information in regard to citizens captured on Matagorda Peninsula. I am not aware that any such persons have been captured, but had they been, no one knows better than you (and that, too, without sending a flag of truce to inquire) that they would receive the treatment that a powerful and humane Government has always extended to its prisoners, and you have evidently been hard pressed for an excuse to send within my lines. If you have none better to offer than those contained in your communication, I should be fully justified in detaining the bearer of your dispatch, as its object is too transparent.

Your threat of "merciless retaliation," and the disclosure of your intention to raise the black flag, I do not deem it important to advert to, neither to the general tone and temper of your dispatch.

The desperate fortunes of a bad cause induce me to pardon much which, under other circumstances, would not be lightly passed over.

In conclusion, I beg to say that flags of truce will always be recognized by me when made use of for a legitimate purpose, and such as the usages of war recognize, but I notify you now that if any more are sent that the usages of war do not justify, I shall detain the bearer as a prisoner of war.

I have the honor to be, respectfully, your obedient servant,

C. C. WASHBURN,
Major-General, Commanding.

P. S.—The two men that accompanied Lieutenant Mann, I am informed, were allowed to return home.

PORT HUDSON, LA., *December* 13, 1863.

Brig. Gen. CHARLES P. STONE, *Chief of Staff, New Orleans:*

Major Ward has just returned, and brings from Captain Foster, of the gunboat Lafayette, the following information:

Foster had just returned from mouth of Red River. He writes me as follows: Forces operating near mouth of Red River, 6,000, change positions continually. Colonel Carpenter, of Jessie Scouts, reports the entire force between Shreveport and Bayou Sara, 25,000. Force at present near the river, opposite Bayou Sara, is 15,000 men, who are felling timber, to cross the river on rafts, it is supposed. Firing on transports is doubtless for the purpose of diverting the attention of gunboats, while they attempt to cross below. They rigidly exclude intercourse within their lines, and conceal their timber operations; their object evidently is to cross the river, and probably attack Port Hudson or Baton Rouge. Principal part of their force is gradually moving southward; they feign movements against our forces south. General Dick Taylor has made some movements of this kind, with ostentation, but has used every effort to conceal his designs, if any, to cross the river. The enemy is now sufficiently concentrated to be formidable, if he can succeed in crossing the river, but he will hardly accomplish his purpose in any considerable number. The force west of the river is under the command of Kirby Smith; his brigadiers are Taylor, Mouton, Green, Major, Maxwell [Maxey?], and Walker. On east bank of river, 2,000 or 3,000 men, under General [Col. F. P.] Powers, headquarters at Woodville. An Alabama regiment encamped within 7 miles of Bayou Sara for some time, but, like most of rebel forces, are migratory. General Mouton is in immediate command of the forces on the west side of river. There is now 10 feet water on the bar, at mouth of Red River. Foster thinks the rise is back water caused by rise in the Mississippi. The above is the substance of Foster's information.

I do not see how they can have so large a force. The operation of crossing so large a force seems to me very hazardous. The timber cutting may be only what is necessary for fuel and shelter. However, I would recommend an increase of the gunboat force between here and Red River temporarily. The gunboats now on this station are nearly out of coal.

GEO. L. ANDREWS,
Brigadier-General of Volunteers, Commanding Post.

SPECIAL ORDERS, }   HDQRS. DEPARTMENT OF THE GULF,
No. 311.   }   *New Orleans, December* 13, 1863.
*   *   *   *   *   *   *

II. The post of Fort Jackson, La., is hereby constituted a separate command, and, until further orders, the garrison will be reported directly to these headquarters.

III. Brig. Gen. William Dwight, U. S. Volunteers, is assigned to duty at Fort Jackson, to which post he will proceed without delay, and assume command.

By command of Major-General Banks:

G. NORMAN LIEBER,
Acting Assistant Adjutant-General.

HEADQUARTERS UNITED STATES FORCES,
Fort Esperanza, Tex.. December 14,.1863.

Brig. Gen. CHARLES P. STONE,
Chief of Staff:

GENERAL: I report that yesterday I sent Brigadier-General Warren, with a regiment of troops, up to Indianola on the steamer Alabama. They drove the enemy's pickets out of town, and took possession, and raised the Stars and Stripes. After remaining a few hours, they returned. The inhabitants were much frightened when the troops arrived, as great pains have been taken by General Magruder to impress upon them the idea that our troops would burn, ravish, and destroy wherever they go, and, acting upon their fears, is endeavoring to induce them to flee from the coast and destroy their property. Before our troops left, their minds were disabused, and they showed considerable friendly feeling.

Respectfully, yours,

C. C. WASHBURN,
Major-General.

PORT HUDSON,
December 14, 1863—7 p. m.

Brig. Gen. CHARLES P. STONE,
Chief of Staff, New Orleans:

It is rumored among citizens outside my lines that Powers has 3,000 men near Woodville. Negroes from Bayou Sara state that they have been with the rebels, and they had not more than 500 or 600. I can learn nothing further about the forces on the west bank of the Mississippi.

GEO. L. ANDREWS,
Brigadier-General of Volunteers, Commanding Post.

SPECIAL ORDERS, }   HDQRS. DEPARTMENT OF THE GULF,
No. 312.   }   *New Orleans, December* 14, 1863.

*   *   *   *   *   *   *

XXXIV. Mr. E. Whittemore and associates, having tendered their resignations as president and officers of the commission of relief, will, on the 15th instant, turn over all the stores and property then remaining in their hands pertaining to this commission—also all the records, books, and papers of the office of the commission—to Lieutenant-Colonel Van Petten, One hundred and sixtieth New York; Capt. John L. Swift, Third Massachusetts Cavalry; Capt. J. B. Nott, commissary of subsistence; and submit to these headquarters their final report and accounts as the commission of relief.

The officers above named will for the present constitute the commission of relief, and conduct its business in compliance with Special Orders, No. 66, of March 7, 1863, from these headquarters, and the following instructions:

First. There being no funds applicable to the purchase of provisions exclusively for this commission, they will be temporarily supplied by the commissary of subsistence in charge of the principal commissary depot in this city, at present Capt. A. J. McCoy, commissary of subsistence, volunteers, upon requisitions signed by the president of the commission of relief, and ordered from these headquarters semi-monthly for the half-month next succeeding, for which the president of the commission will receipt to the commissary furnishing the provisions, who shall, at the expiration of each month, make a correct abstract of the same, which shall be compared with the original returns by the chief commissary of subsistence, or other officers designated from these headquarters, and certified by him, when correct, to serve as vouchers for the issue of these provisions. These certified abstracts shall also be made by the chief commissary for all provisions issued in this manner since the 31st of October, 1863, when the last payment was made for provisions for this commission. The orphan asylum and charitable institutions will continue to be furnished by the depot commissary, on orders signed by the chief commissary, as heretofore, and the stores issued on these orders will be included in the abstracts, named above, of issues to asylums and the destitute poor of New Orleans.

Second. A new, thorough, and complete canvass of the necessities of all persons now receiving aid from the commission shall be at once made by the commission and its assistants; and the most stringent examination in all cases of new applications, to discover and prevent all distributions of provisions to any but the actually destitute, as pointed out in Special Orders, No. 66, above cited. The chief paymaster of the department, when applied to by the president of the commission, shall furnish him with a complete list of companies or regiments raised prior to August 12, 1863, if any remain, who have not been paid or received bounty, to enable the commission to judge of the validity of claims of soldiers' families under Special Orders, No. 209, of July 21, 1862, the authority to make such promises to soldiers having been revoked since August 12, 1863. Abuses, if any can be discovered, will be at once corrected by the commission, which is expected to reduce the amount of these temporary but unavoidable charities to the lowest possible amount consistent with a just regard to humanity.

By command of Major-General Banks:

G. NORMAN LIEBER,
Acting Assistant Adjutant-General.

GENERAL ORDERS, }   HDQRS. NINETEENTH ARMY CORPS,
No. 45.   }   *New Iberia, La., December 14,* 1863.

I. Some few officers and more than 50 men of this command have been taken prisoners by the enemy while outside of the picket lines straggling. stealing, and robbing, going upon unauthorized expeditions or upon expeditions sent by regimental commanders, without authority and without proper escort.

II. When the time arrives for exchange, these men are a source of vexation and delay, preventing or delaying the exchange of good soldiers, who have done their duty to their country and-have been captured in battle, in some cases compelling us to leave such soldiers in the enemy's hands, or procuring their release on parole alone, thus losing their valuable services to the country.

III. The commanding general therefore announces to this command that he shall keep accurate lists of all men captured in the disgraceful manner referred to, and that he shall notify the enemy's commissioner of exchange that he will not exchange such men until all others have been exchanged, nor receive them on parole under any circumstances. He has already informed the commanding officer of the enemy that it is his wish that any soldier of this command found robbing outside our lines should be treated like other robbers.

IV. This order is applicable to all arms, but applies more directly to the mounted men, whose conduct in straggling, stealing, and maltreating women is a disgrace to the name of American soldier. The officers who permit it are more criminal than the men who perpetrate the crime, and, were proper discipline enforced, would expiate their crime in a prison.

V. The commanding general believes that there is yet self-respect enough among the officers of this command to force them to put a stop to these daily outrages. He calls upon them to exercise their authority to its fullest extent, and assures them that they will be fully upheld by him. He directs their attention to the fact that the harm done to the enemy by these outrages is as nothing compared with the injury done to the discipline and efficiency of our own troops.

VI. This order will be read to every company of this command.

By order of Major-General Franklin:

WICKHAM HOFFMAN,
Assistant Adjutant-General.

HEADQUARTERS DISTRICT OF KEY WEST AND TORTUGAS,
Key West, Fla., December 14, 1863.

Brig. Gen. CHARLES P. STONE,
Chief of Staff, New Orleans, La.:

GENERAL: It has been reported to me from time to time by refugees from the State of Florida, that deserters from the rebel army and men hiding to avoid conscription were lurking in the woods between Charlotte Harbor and Lake Okeechobee, in numbers variously estimated from 200 or 300 to 700 or 800, and that many of these men would join the forces of the United States should a military post be established in their neighborhood.

I propose to establish a small post on Charlotte Harbor to enlist the men above referred to, as many as possible, to break up or check the cattle-driving business in that part of the State, and to extend operations according to circumstances. Nineteen men, refugees from the State of Florida, now residing at this place, have recently enlisted in the service of the United States, and as many more will probably enlist unconditionally, but with the understanding that their first service shall be in the State of Florida.

As we have but one regiment of troops in this district, the Forty-seventh Pennsylvania, divided between Key West and Tortugas, it will, of course, be impossible to detach any considerable force. I propose to detach one company only of the Forty-seventh Pennsylvania to act in conjunction with the native troops. The native troops propose to take the name of the Florida Rangers.

I have appointed, subject to the approval of Major-General Banks and of the President of the United States, Enoch Daniels captain, and Zachariah Brown first lieutenant of the first company to be raised.

I don't know that this enterprise will result in anything of importance, but it can hardly result in much loss, and I have thought it my duty to undertake it.

As our mails are exceedingly irregular, I shall not wait for an answer, but commence as soon as possible.

I respectfully request the approval of the commanding general of the Department of the Gulf of the appointments above made.

I also request authority to operate on the coast of Florida at my discretion, and should be glad to receive re-enforcements, say 1,000 men, from the north.

Respectfully,

D. P. WOODBURY,
Brigadier-General.

HEADQUARTERS THIRTEENTH ARMY CORPS,
Brownsville, December 15, 1863.

Brig. Gen. CHARLES P. STONE,
Chief of Staff:

I have the honor to inclose copies of a correspondence between Brigadier-General Hamilton and myself on the subject of powers conferred by the extradition treaty with Mexico, &c., for the information and orders of the commanding general. I ask an attentive consideration of them, in connection with page 1200, Vol. XII, U. S. Statutes at Large.

I hope General Hamilton will not force any collision of authority under a vague suspicion of a "jealousy on the part of military men," as expressed by him in conversation during an interview with me at my request. I feel that it would not be complimentary to the major-general commanding to enter into any disclaimer on my part of any such unworthy and ungenerous feeling.

Whilst I refrain from an active interference with General Hamilton, who announces his determination to pursue his course until my power is used to restrain him, the general will readily preceive the new position I shall be placed in when a case shall arise under the fourth article of the treaty. Mr. Brackenridge, the special agent of the Treasury Department, on the 12th instant, made a demand, in accordance with the instructions of the Treasury Department of September 11, and General Orders, No. 88, of the War Department, for all captured and abandoned property, and I have ordered it all turned over.

Should it be disapproved by the major-general commanding, I will take it all back. I was compelled to sell 100 bales of cotton to raise gold to pay for 300 horses, which Fenn was in trouble about, and of which I advised you.

I have also been obliged to sell 150 more to purchase a brig-load of corn, oats, and hay, at the mouth of the river—oats, $2.50 per sack of 70 pounds; corn, $10 per cargo of 312 pounds; and hay at $75 per ton, all in gold.

The Matamoras has not yet arrived.

The Mustang, with the Thirty-seventh Illinois, arrived Saturday night. She is now raising a siege piece which we have discovered in the river.

To-morrow I send out a reconnaissance of 60 cavalry 40 miles beyond the Arroyo Colorado, and, on their return and the return of a spy, whom

I have sent to San Fernando, I have the intention of occupying King's ranch.

Matters are fast coming to a crisis in Matamoras. All compromises appear to-day to have failed, and it appears certain there will be a fight.

I have the honor to remain, &c.,

N. J. T. DANA,
Major-General.

[Inclosure No. 1.]

STATE OF TEXAS, EXECUTIVE DEPARTMENT,
December 14, 1863.

Maj. Gen. N. J. T. DANA, *Headquarters:*

GENERAL: Having been informed that a young man, now in this city (Mr. Pendergrast), had witnessed the murder of Capt. William W. Montgomery near this place in March last, and that one of the party engaged in the murder was in Matamoras, I caused the said Pendergrast to come before me on the 11th instant, when, after hearing his statements, an affidavit, embracing the material facts, was drawn up, which was sworn to and subscribed by him (a copy of which you will find inclosed. On the same day I addressed to His Excellency the Governor of the State of Tamaulipas a communication, accompanied with a copy of the affidavit, demanding the body of the party, Dick Hamilton, under and 'by virtue 'of the extradition treaty of 1861, between the United States and Mexico.

Yesterday I was notified by the Governor of Tamaulipas that the party had been arrested under my requisition, and would be delivered to my order at 9.30 p. m.

I believe that you are already informed unofficially that he was delivered according to the understanding had with Governor Serna.

I now have the honor to give this official information, and to say that I propose to turn the party over to your hands, to be dealt with as justice may demand. He is doubtless a proper subject for trial by either a civil or military tribunal, but inasmuch as Captain Montgomery was in the military service of the United States at the time of his murder, and his murderers in the rebel service, it seems to me there would be a fitness in having him tried by the latter.

I herewith send inclosed a copy of my commission as Military Governor of Texas, and instructions from the Secretary of War, &c.,* as I promised yesterday evening.

I have the honor to be, your obedient servant,

A. J. HAMILTON,
Military Governor of Texas.

[Sub-Inclosure.]

THE STATE OF TEXAS,
County of Cameron, ss:

Personally appeared before me, J. B. McFarland, provisional judge, Richard Pendergrast, a citizen of Brownsville, Cameron County, who deposes and says that on or about the — day of ———, A. D. 1863, he witnessed in the said county the murder of Capt. William W. Montgomery by a band of armed men, numbering some 7 men, among whom was one Dick Hamilton, who is now, or was a day or two past, in the city of Matamoras, Mexico. The murder of said Montgomery was effected by

---

* To be published in Series III.

hanging him by the neck with a rope to a mesquite tree. Deponent saw the said Montgomery captured or kidnapped on the Mexican side of the Rio Grande on the morning of the day that he was murdered by the persons who hung him, together with others. Deponent saw the body of said Montgomery still hanging to the mesquite tree four days after the murder.

RICHARD PENDERGRAST.

Sworn to and subscribed before me this 11th day of December, 1863.

J. B. McFARLAND,
Judge of Provisional Court at Brownsville.

STATE OF TEXAS,
    County of Cameron, ss :
I certify that the above affidavit is a true copy of the original now on file in my office.

A. G. BUDINGTON,
Clerk of Provisional Court at Brownsville, Tex.

[Inclosure No. 2.]

HEADQUARTERS THIRTEENTH ARMY CORPS,
Brownsville, December 15, 1863.

Brig. Gen. **A. J. HAMILTON,**
    Military Governor of Texas:
Within the limits of this command we have not among its officers persons suitable and proper to conduct a delicate trial in a criminal case, when the evidence is scant and not apparently overwhelming.

I consider it very essential that Judge McFarland should act as judge-advocate, or Government prosecutor, on the trial of Hamilton. You will readily appreciate the necessity of it.

I request that he be made available for that purpose, and ask that you request him to call on me, that I may fully understand the matter.

I have the honor to remain, with much respect, your obedient servant,

N. J. T. DANA,
Major-General.

[Inclosure No. 3.]

HEADQUARTERS THIRTEENTH ARMY CORPS,
Brownsville, Tex., December 15, 1863.

Brig. Gen. **A. J. HAMILTON,**
    Military Governor of Texas :
I have the pleasure of acknowledging your letter of yesterday, which was received in the afternoon, and which inclosed copies of your commission and your instructions from the honorable Secretary of War, in accordance with my request made of you day before yesterday.

I have attentively read those papers, and have also weighed your arguments which you used during the interview which I had the pleasure to have with you at the time above indicated with that respect and consideration which I surely feel not only for your personal standing and position, and the services you have rendered, but for the exalted station you occupy by appointment of the War Department, and I feel bound by my obligations of duty frankly to say to you that I am still of opinion (referring to the second and fourth articles of the treaty with Mexico of December 11, 1861, commonly known as the extradition treaty) that by the presence of this invading force, under my orders, martial law alone prevails here, and that, therefore, the "civil authority" of this " State " is " suspended ;" and as I am the senior officer in the State and as the treaty reads that requisitions for criminals shall be made, when the civil authority is suspended, "through the chief military officer in command of such State or Territory," that I am the only one empowered to make such requisitions.

The only doubt existing in my mind regarding it arises from the fact that my immediate commander, Major-General Banks, commanding the Department of the Gulf, at New Orleans, may decide that he alone can make requisitions under the treaty as commander of the department, and that I cannot make them.

Considering our great distance from New Orleans, and greater from Washington, I am more than anxious that no collision of authority here should cause inconvenience to the public service during the time which would elapse for the proper reference of a case, and my inclinations, as well as my duty, urge me to avoid any by using all means within my power, and by waiving all questions which can be waived without a culpable neglect of my official obligations; but I hope you will secure from the War Department, or from our military superiors, such instructions and orders as may settle matters which may arise in question, and as may avoid the danger of confusing the ideas of the powers in Mexico, with whom we are in communication, and thereby causing them to refuse action which they might otherwise be willing to take.

In the case of the man Hamilton, whether you or I are decided to be right, or are sustained in the opposite opinions we entertain on this matter, he is in our hands. I have received him into custody, in accordance with your request, and in the same spirit will try him according to law, and punish him according to his findings and sentence.

In conclusion, I will say that in this case, as in any others that may arise, my feelings of satisfaction will amount to almost delight to bring to a merited punishment any and all persons who may be convicted of having been engaged among the band of cut-throats and assassins who have persecuted to death, and driven from their homes and from the domains their country has given them, the loyal men of Texas.

I have the honor to remain, with great respect, your obedient servant,

N. J. T. DANA,
Major-General.

HEADQUARTERS UNITED STATES FORCES,
Fort Esperanza, Tex., December 15, 1863.

Brig. Gen. CHARLES P. STONE,
Chief of Staff:

GENERAL: The First Indiana Battery, belonging to the First Division, Thirteenth Corps, is a fine battery, and I am anxious to have it sent here, if possible. I learn that two sections of it were sent up to Donaldsonville. The remaining section, I suppose, is at Algiers. I shall also be very glad to have the First Wisconsin Battery, consisting of four 30-pounder Parrotts, sent out, or, if a battery of 20-pounder Parrotts can be had, they would be preferable, on the score of easier transportation. In reducing the works of Quintana and Velasco, some heavy guns will very likely be required. The First Wisconsin is a good battery, and has seen a good deal of service; has good guns and good horses.

The last information I have in regard to the force of the enemy is that he has about 3,000 men on the Caney River. I should mention, if I have not already done so, that we cannot go up Matagorda Bay with boats drawing over 3 feet for a greater distance than about 20 miles, so that water communication after leaving here will be of little use. At the proper time I will make a demonstration in the direction of San Antonio, and shall endeavor to convey the idea, so far as I can, that we intend to move in that direction.

Respectfully, yours,

C. C. WASHBURN,
Major-General.

HEADQUARTERS UNITED STATES FORCES,
Fort Esperanza, December 15, 1863.

Brig. Gen. CHARLES P. STONE,
Chief of Staff :

GENERAL : I inclose report of the strength of this command.* You will observe that I have 6,321, or, exclusive of the colored regiment, 5,865. That you may fully understand with what rapidity men and supplies are being concentrated here, I would say that in the last thirteen days 380 soldiers of the Forty-ninth Indiana have arrived here, also the Engineer (colored) Regiment. We have also received in the same time 10 wagons and about 150 mules and horses, also about two days' forage. We have on hand about eight days' rations.

Respectfully, yours,

C. C. WASHBURN,
Major-General.

HEADQUARTERS,
Fort Jackson, December 15, 1863.

Brig. Gen. CHARLES P. STONE,
Chief of Staff, &c. :

SIR : In compliance with the orders you handed me, I have assumed this command. I found on my way here the steamer Empire Parish, near the quarantine, having on board Major Maloney's command of the First U. S. Infantry. I directed Major Maloney to move down to this fort, and the Empire Parish is now about a quarter of a mile above the usual landing for the fort, with Major Maloney's command still on board. There are no quarters for that command within this fort, and only a small detachment could be placed here if they had their own tents. The ground outside the fort is not fit to encamp upon.

I do not find this garrison in a state of insubordination. The minds of the greater part of the soldiers here are in a healthy state; they know a great military crime has been committed, and they expect the guilty to suffer. This crime should be promptly punished ; the example should be immediate and of the severest character. Until that punishment is inflicted, it will be well for Major Maloney's command to remain where it now is; but after that, the presence of white troops here does not appear to me necessary. The late affair is a warning against trusting foolish and passionate officers in high command over these black troops. But the details of the affair do not prove to my mind that these soldiers cannot be trusted. On the contrary, this occurrence may be made such an example of discipline as will render these soldiers more than ever trustworthy. It shows that great care must be taken in the selection of officers who are to be trusted in command of these soldiers when a regiment is separated from the corps to which it belongs.

---

* Omitted.

It seems to me of great importance that no white troops shall be garrisoned with these black ones, at least for the present; that it shall not be acknowledged that the black soldiers are unfit to be trusted, and the appearance of garrisoning white soldiers with them to enforce discipline should be, if possible, avoided. If any white soldiers are to be sent here, it seems to me that one or the other of the forts should be wholly garrisoned with whites. But I think it better to avoid even this concession to the riot of the other evening.

I would most respectfully recommend that this case be dealt with as follows:

1. That Lieutenant-Colonel Benedict be dishonorably dismissed the service for whipping with his own hands two negro drummers. It appears from evidence here that this is not the first time Lieutenant-Colonel Benedict has found it necessary, in his own judgment, to raise his hands in violence against soldiers. Such judgment is so bad as to unfit an officer for command.

2. That at least three of the ringleaders, in the use of fire-arms and in inciting disturbance in the late affair, be shot in the presence of this garrison; that the remaining leaders be sent to Ship Island for hard labor during life; that a military commission decide who shall be so executed and so transported. If this action is taken immediately, I believe it will have the greatest effect on the discipline of the negro soldiers of this department. As a punishment and example, it will have greater weight and force than would have resulted from prompt action on the part of the officers on the night of the riot. Now the punishment will be free from passion, and come from the highest authority; it will be military justice, not the exasperation of officers threatened with violence by their soldiers. It is important that this act of discipline shall be executed by the soldiers of this command; they should be compelled to execute the sentence against their guilty companions. I believe that this can be done, and that it will end forever insubordination among the black troops in this department. The moral effect will be greater if this matter be settled without white troops, and it be shown that these soldiers can be trusted to enforce the severest tests of military discipline. In regard to this whole matter of riot and mutiny, if the commanding general will give me authority to act, I will undertake to find and execute the proper persons with the promptness the case deserves. I should like three intelligent officers for a military commission, to act under my instructions, Colonel Hartwell and some of his officers, for instance.

The condition of things here can be greatly improved, but, I repeat, insubordination is at an end; the evils which exist can be corrected by a proper administration of affairs.

I have the honor to be, sir, most respectfully, &c.,

WILLIAM DWIGHT,
Brigadier-General, Commanding.

HEADQUARTERS DEPARTMENT OF THE GULF,
New Orleans, December 15, 1863.

Rear-Admiral DAVID D. PORTER, U. S. Navy,
Commanding Mississippi Squadron .

ADMIRAL: It gave me very great satisfaction to receive, on my return from Texas, your letter of November 5, with copy of your letter to the honorable the Secretary of the Navy, inclosed.

I was especially gratified to know that I might expect to hear of your gunboats in the Atchafalaya and on Berwick Bay as soon as the rise in the former would permit, and that you intended to provide so efficient an addition to that portion of your fleet serving within the limits of this. department as that which you mention. That number of gunboats of such class as you mention will very greatly facilitate all operations in this region, and will render it impossible for the enemy to annoy us as they have heretofore done, by using against us the wonderful network of navigable waters west of the Mississippi River.

At this moment a large force of the enemy is established between the Atchafalaya and the Mississippi River, near Morgan's Ferry, and the mouth of Red River. The recent rise in the latter renders it and the Atchafalaya navigable by the gunboats, and, should they arrive soon, a little active work of the navy, in co-operation with the land forces at my disposition, will place that force at our mercy.

I earnestly hope that you will find it convenient to dispatch the intended re-enforcements without delay, and that another fortnight may witness the capture or dispersion of the rebel forces now so seriously impeding the navigation of the Mississippi.

Very respectfully, I am, admiral, your obedient servant,
N. P. BANKS,
Major-General, Commanding.

SPECIAL ORDERS, }   HDQRS. DEPARTMENT OF THE GULF,
No. 313.   }   *New Orleans, December 15,* 1863.

*   *   *   *   *   *   *

XII. The First Brigade, Fourth Division, Thirteenth Army Corps, will proceed without delay to Fort Esperanza, Pass Cavallo, Tex., and be reported to Maj. Gen. C. C. Washburn, U. S. Volunteers, for duty. The brigade will take twenty days' rations and ten days' forage for such animals as can be taken on the transports with the troops. The quartermaster's department will furnish the necessary transportation.

*   *   *   *   *   *   *

By command of Major-General Banks:
G. NORMAN LIEBER,
Acting Assistant Adjutant-General.

HEADQUARTERS DEPARTMENT OF THE GULF,
New Orleans, December 16, 1863.

Maj. Gen. N. J. T. DANA,
Commanding Thirteenth Army Corps, Brownsville, Tex.:

GENERAL: Your letter of the 2d instant has been this day received, and laid before the major-general commanding. He directs that you dispose of as much of the cotton collected as may be necessary for defraying the expenses of collection and such extraordinary expenditures as the exigencies of the service may require, and that you hold the remainder subject to the order of the chief quartermaster of the department, who will make such disposition of it as may be directed from these headquarters. He further directs that you shall have authority to give provisional appointments as officers for the newly raised troops in your vicinity to such persons as you may deem best fitted for such commissions; such appointments being subject to his approval.

Should you need subsistence stores at Brownsville during the season when it is so difficult to land them at Brazos Santiago, you are, of course, authorized to purchase them at Matamoras, and pay for them from proceeds of cotton in your possession. The chief quartermaster will correspond with you in reference to purchase of animals. I think it will be impracticable to furnish cavalry horses from this depot for Texas.

The commanding general expresses his satisfaction with all that has been done at Brownsville during your occupation.

Very respectfully, I am, general, your most obedient servant,

CHAS. P. STONE,
Brigadier-General, and Chief of Staff.

PORT HUDSON, LA.,
December 16, 1863.

Brig. Gen. CHARLES P. STONE,
Chief of Staff, New Orleans:

Two deserters from the rebels this morning report the rebels as having mostly left this side the Atchafalaya. It would seem from all reports that their whole force was 10,000 men. Their artillery is stated as very numerous, sixty to seventy pieces, mostly field, but poorly horsed. Movement across Atchafalaya ordered December 7. Captain Foster is here. His information seems now to agree pretty well with that brought by the deserters. Taylor and Green are said to have gone toward New Iberia. Kirby Smith said to be at Washington.

GEO. L. ANDREWS,
Brigadier-General of Volunteers, Commanding Post.

HEADQUARTERS,
Fort Jackson, December 17, 1863.

Brig. Gen. CHARLES P. STONE,
Chief of Staff, &c.:

GENERAL: Major Maloney's command moved from the position in which I had placed it, and steamed up the river yesterday afternoon without notifying me. I understood from you that that force constituted a portion of my command. I stated in my last communication that I recommended that some white troops should remain in this vicinity until the leaders in the late mutiny shall be punished.

While I do not anticipate any trouble here, for the leaders in the late mutiny were all arrested day before yesterday, and this command is quiet and orderly, and while I believe that if the most severe punishment known to military law cannot be inflicted on these leaders in mutiny by the regiment to which they belong, colored troops are utterly untrustworthy, and therefore worthless, still, I think it wise to have some white troops at hand until the case is established.

It seems to me quite as important to know whether these soldiers are equal to the highest efforts of discipline as it was to know whether they would fight. From the telegram which I received yesterday from the commanding general, I was in hopes that the boats which arrived here last night would have the members of the commission on board. Forty-eight hours seems to me long enough for men to live after their arrest for a mutiny so palpable. For such an offense, a swift and terrible punishment alone is effective.

I have the honor to be, general, very respectfully, your obedient servant,

WILLIAM DWIGHT,
Brigadier-General, Commanding.

SPECIAL ORDERS, } HDQRS. DIST. NORTHEASTERN LOUISIANA,
No. 48.   }   *Goodrich's Landing, La., December* 17, 1863.

I. Mr. J. C. Horn, a citizen of Carroll Parish, Louisiana, is hereby ordered to proceed at once beyond the limits of this district, for offering a bribe to the general commanding to confirm him in the possession of a certain lot of cotton. He will not return again under penalty of imprisonment.

By order of Brig. Gen. J. P. Hawkins:

S. B. FERGUSON,
Assistant Adjutant-General.

HEADQUARTERS THIRTEENTH ARMY CORPS,
Brownsville, December 18, 1863.

Brig. Gen. CHARLES P. STONE,
Chief of Staff:

I have nothing of much importance to report since my last dispatch.

No forage having arrived, and our animals constantly increasing, I have been compelled to procure a supply from day to day, at high prices, from Matamoras, or from bottoms which entered there, and pay specie, and, not having money, I have converted the great staple into gold to pay the bills.

Braubach has not yet returned, but I have information that he arrived at Piedras Negras on the 27th ultimo. A few of his men have arrived, but not many. I have notice, besides the call made by the consul at Monterey for funds, about which I wrote the general, that bills will come in immediately on the arrival of the men for transportation and supplies from Piedras Negras here. I wish the general would send me orders regarding these things.

One hundred Texas Rangers have arrived at Eagle Pass from San Antonio, to take the place of the Mexican company which revolted there. Information from the interior states that a force of 1,200 mounted men from Eastern Texas have been sent to keep open the line from San Antonio to Eagle Pass and Laredo. The importance of keeping this line open is fully appreciated in Texas, especially among officers who have large amounts of cotton on the road. Very many supplies go through Eagle Pass to Texas. Monterey is now the rebel headquarters on this frontier, and many officers are there, including some of Kirby Smith's staff. No new movement of the French from Queretaro. The citizens of that place had been required by General Bazaine to register themselves for or against the French. General Uraga had succeeded Comonfort, and had 8,000 men in the neighborhood of Guanaxuato.

I have two small reconnoitering parties out toward King's ranch, one of 60 men, the other of 35 men. Our horses are in bad condition. General Garcia, with about 400 men, arrived at Matamoras from before Tampico yesterday. Ruiz is still at San Fernando. Matters are very unsettled there. Ruiz appears hardly strong enough to attack. I understand unofficially that, in event of an attack, I shall be called on to send force to protect the consulate and the property of loyal Americans. Rebel officers are getting frightened at the prospect, and are leaving.

I have the honor to remain, with great respect,

N. J. T. DANA,   •
Major-General.

HEADQUARTERS THIRTEENTH ARMY CORPS,
Brownsville, December 18, 1863.

M. M. KIMMEY,
United States Consul, Monterey, Mexico:

SIR: I have the pleasure to acknowledge your dispatch of the 13th instant, and again express thanks for your attention and kindness.

We have not received anything from New Orleans for twelve days, but I hope very soon to receive instructions regarding the funds for your expenses. Braubach's men come in very slowly; very few have arrived yet. I will take care of them as fast as they come. I believe some of them are getting into the First Texas Cavalry.

I have given a special mission to Mr. McManus. Please keep me advised regarding his movements. I mean to stand by him and support him, if he is useful.

I desire to make the road from San Antonio to Eagle Pass and Laredo so perilous that neither Jew nor Gentile will wish to travel it. Please make this known, confidentially only, to good, true, and daring men. I wish to kill, burn, and destroy all that cannot be taken and secured.

I presume Mr. McManus has spoken freely to you. I am sorry the company of Rangers arrived so soon at Eagle Pass.

Notwithstanding all the rumors of rebel forces moving this way, I do not think there is anything worth regarding this side of the Nueces.

I have the honor to remain, your obedient servant,

N. J. T. DANA,
Major-General.

STATE OF TEXAS, EXECUTIVE DEPARTMENT,
Brownsville, December 19, 1863.

Hon. E. M. STANTON,
Secretary of War, Washington, D. C.:

SIR: I arrived here on the night of the 1st instant. When General Banks left New Orleans with the expedition which resulted in the capture and occupation of this and other points on the coast of Texas, he suggested to me that there had occurred one or two failures by the forces of the Government on the Texas coast which had greatly encouraged the enemy and depressed the loyal citizens, and that, if another failure should happen, it would be magnified if I were known to have been with it. He thought it better that I should remain at New Orleans until the expedition was heard from, which I consented to do. While in New Orleans, I employed myself in relieving the wants of refugees from Texas, to the extent of my private means, and in acquiring such information as they could give me of the real condition of things in Texas and the tone and sentiment of the people.

After the news of the capture of this place reached New Orleans, I availed myself of the earliest transportation, and arrived, as stated, on the 1st instant. There are here some hundreds of refugees from the interior of the State, most of whom have traveled hundreds of miles, and have arrived destitute. I have been constantly surrounded with them since my arrival, advising and assisting them. To all who are able-bodied, I say, " If you are not willing to fight to reclaim your home, then you deserve no aid, and will get none." There are many, however, who are old and otherwise physically unfit for the service; to them I have extended relief.

So far this has been done without using the money of the Government. The voluntary contributions of a few generous men have, up to this time, sufficed to prevent any suffering, and, to meet increasing demands for aid, I propose, through the municipal authorities of the city, to levy such license tax upon certain avocations that need regulation as will afford the necessary means.

The money which I received from the Government ($2,000) has not yet been touched. I have kept it in reserve for some emergency, such as has not yet occurred. I have found opportunity to send messages to my friends in many portions of the State, and am preparing an address to the people of the State, a copy of which I will forward to you, together with a full and formal report, by the next mail after this. There will be no difficulty in introducing throughout the State any communication which I may choose to make, and I am happy to be able to say that all of my information is to the effect that the people are preparing to be conquered. I feel very confident that if our arms are successful in the first general engagement had in Texas, it will end the campaign and reclaim the State.

We have the information from so many refugees just from the interior, and it is so uniform and consistent, one story with another, that there can be no doubt of the fact that the rebel commanders have abandoned all idea of defending the country west of the Colorado River. When the advance upon the interior commences, if the force is adequate, say 25,000 effective men, two months will settle the fate of Texas. The utmost confidence is felt in the result of the campaign by the loyal men of the country, and the prisoners whom I have seen and conversed with admit the despondency of the rebels.

General Banks has been most successful in his operations upon the coast. His position on Matagorda Bay I have always regarded as the key to the heart of the interior.

I am laboring under the most painful apprehensions for my family. I received, a day or two past, from Monterey, Mexico, a letter from the American consul, who states that on the 24th of October Governor Vidauri obtained from General Magruder an order for my family to pass into Mexico, and that on the next day he wrote Mrs. Hamilton, inviting her to enter Mexico, and kindly tendering the hospitalities of his capital; but, from refugees from the vicinity of my home one month past, I learn that my family were still there, and asking in vain for permission to leave. May God protect them.

There will certainly be much need of a court here, if for no other purpose, to settle questions arising under the act of Congress providing for the confiscation of the property of persons engaged in the rebellion. This, however, I will embrace fully in the report which I am preparing, and which I will have the honor to submit in a few days.

Sincerely hoping that the news which reached us yesterday of a great victory by General Grant over General Bragg may be true, and that your health may be preserved, I have the honor to be, very truly and respectfully, your obedient servant,

A. J. HAMILTON,
Brigadier-General, and Military Governor of Texas.

———

HEADQUARTERS DEPARTMENT OF THE GULF, ·
New Orleans, December 19, 1863
Maj. Gen. C. C. WASHBURN,
U. S. Vols., Comdg. Troops on Bay of Matagorda, Tex.:

GENERAL: The steamer Clinton leaves to-morrow morning, taking a complete battery of 30-pounder Parrotts, well manned by First Indiana Heavy Artillery, and stores and supplies called for in your dispatches by Captain Stone.

The Fourth Division, Thirteenth Army Corps, is now *en route* for Pass Cavallo, with orders to report to you for duty. Other troops of infantry and artillery are now awaiting transportation to you, and will be rapidly forwarded.

I inclose to you a slip containing the message and proclamation of the President.*

Very respectfully, I am, general, your most obedient servant,

CHAS. P. STONE,
Brigadier-General, and Chief of Staff.

———

SPECIAL ORDERS, ⎱   HDQRS. DEPARTMENT OF THE GULF,
No. 317.   ⎰   *New Orleans, December* 19, 1863.
*   *   *   *   *   *   *

XII. Lieut. Col. George W. Stipp, U. S. Army, having reported at these headquarters, in compliance with Paragraph II, of Special Orders, No. 440, from the War Department, Adjutant-General's Office, is announced·as medical inspector of this department.

*   *   *   *   *   *

By command of Major-General Banks:

G. NORMAN LIEBER,
Acting Assistant Adjutant-General.

———

HEADQUARTERS,
Fort Jackson, December 20, 1863.
Brig. Gen. CHARLES P. STONE,
Chief of Staff, &c.:

GENERAL: Affairs at this post are in much the same condition as when I last had the honor of addressing you. No progress has been made in dealing with the mutineers. The orders which I have received for the assembling of a court-martial for the trial of Lieutenant-Colonel Benedict and of the mutineers are not in accordance with what I had been led to expect and hope from the telegram of the commanding general. That telegram spoke of a "military commission," and of immediate action.

The change from a "military commission," which should summarily dispose of this flagrant case, to a regularly constituted court-martial,

———
* Omitted.

with the delays inseparable from it, will deprive the service of the benefit of moral effect, which must have followed a speedy and terrible punishment.

Lieutenant-Colonel Benedict is not at this post. Who shall make the charges against him? The troops at this post are quiet and attentive to duty, but the soldiers show an unwillingness to testify of the occurences at the mutiny; they refuse to remember when questioned. This is passive mutiny; it directly aids the mutineers; it is the most potent means remaining to these soldiers to resist authority, and shows them how much they can do in contempt of that military power which they lately actively resisted. If there were any white soldiers here, and if I had the necessary authority to deal with this case, I should exercise that power, if necessary using the most extreme means to compel these men to speak; that as they are about to learn the result of active mutiny, they might also know the meaning of passive mutiny. Unfortunately, I have neither the power nor the means.

It should be remembered that nothing has been done as yet to quell the mutiny which occurred; that the quiet and order which now exist result from no exercise of authority, no use of force. From active mutiny this command relapsed into its present state. Precisely what that state is can hardly be known. Its appearance is that of entire submission to authority. It is an unquestioning submission, but it demands to be as unquestioned as it is unquestioning. These men are ignorant and cunning; they are silent and submissive; they know the meaning only of force and power, and these, unfortunately, they have not yet felt. Many of them are well disposed, and desire to see the guilty punished, but there are some who mutter, and still put on threatening looks.

A soldier arrested since my taking command, said, pointing to an officer, "There is a man who ought to be put out of the way," with other threatening words; this was said three days after the mutiny. All this shows me the need of the greatest activity and energy in dealing with this case—an activity and energy I am far from seeing in the present progress of affairs or method of dealing with these mutineers. If any unfortunate or inadequate results shall follow, I wish this opinion on record, not that I wish to excite any alarm, for I feel none; all is profoundly quiet, but it seems to me that the possibility of misfortune can and should be avoided.

I shall have occasion in a day or two to express to you my ideas of what should be done at once to put this post in a condition creditable to the Government of the United States. There is so much in disorder that it is difficult to determine where it is most essential to begin. I have ordered a minute inspection, to find out exactly what is going on in the way of work, and what every man is doing.

I forward some requisitions for lumber and material, which should be filled immediately.

There is much iron and other material about this post which ought to be protected from the weather. Temporary quarters for officers must be erected at once. Permanent quarters for the whole garrison of this post should be erected as soon as possible. The casemates cannot be used; they often have much water in them. I have again to ask for two good-clerks.

I have the honor to be, general, very respectfully, your obedient servant,

WILLIAM DWIGHT,
Brigadier-General, Commanding.

HEADQUARTERS DEPARTMENT OF THE GULF,
New Orleans, December 21, 1863.
Maj. Gen. C. C. WASHBURN,
Commanding Troops near Matagorda Bay, Tex. :

GENERAL: Your letters of the 13th, 14th, and 15th instant are this day received; also your inclosures of letter from Major-General Magruder, C. S. Army, and your reply thereto. All have been laid before the major-general commanding, who expressed his satisfaction with your course.

In regard to the artillery you ask for, I have the honor to state that a perfectly appointed battery of four 30-pounder Parrotts has been forwarded on the steamer Clinton, which will probably arrive at your station to-morrow.

The Chicago Mercantile Battery, 6 guns, in complete order, sails to-morrow. The First Indiana Battery is now here, being refitted and put in perfect order. Either that or one of the batteries of the Fourth Division, Thirteenth Army Corps, will follow in two days, and other artillery and cavalry will follow as rapidly as transportation can be procured for the horses.

It is very desirable that the steamers should be sent back as promptly as possible. The Warrior should be towed back, and the Planter sent here, if practicable. A tug-boat, for a dispatch boat, has been ordered to you.

The commanding general hopes that you will be able to make such safe demonstrations in the direction of San Antonio as will induce the enemy to at least divide his forces and not concentrate fully in the Caney Bottom.

The "secesh papers" you mention did not reach me.

Very respectfully, I am, general, your most obedient servant,
CHAS. P. STONE,
Brigadier-General, and Chief of Staff.

HEADQUARTERS,
Fort Whipple, Ariz., December 21, 1863.
[Capt. BEN. C. CUTLER:]

CAPTAIN: After leaving Navajo Springs with my command on the 21st ultimo, I found a good road and plenty of feed at most points, but water rather scarce, until I reached the Little Colorado River on the 25th. The road follows this river about 60 miles, crossing it nearly middle way. The water and feed is abundant, but very alkaline, affecting the stock very much. At the San Francisco Mountain, I divided the train in three parts, the watering places not affording sufficient water for the large amount of stock at one time. The weather here was extremely cold, there usually being 8 to 10 inches of ice on the water-holes. About half way from the mountain to this point, the road became so extremely rough, that, to avoid breaking my wagons to pieces, I made a depot, leaving about one-third of my loading. It will take a week to send out and get this in here.

I have had no trouble whatever with Indians; after leaving Colorado River, I saw no signs of any until we met the Tonto Apaches at this place.

The last of the three trains, under Captain Benson, arrived here safely this evening. Captain Enos starts to-morrow for the Colorado River.

It is very doubtful if he will be able to find a wagon road to that river below Fort Mojave. Six wagons have already come here from that point, and report a good road.

I judge the number of miners is about the same as that last summer, when General Clark was here; probably more of them Americans than at that time. Large numbers have come here from California, and returned, not being able to procure provisions. The trains with us sell their loading readily and at good prices. There is no flour here excepting what they bring. It sells at $30 per hundred.

There is great scarcity of water in the mining districts, having had no rain as yet. Those having claims think they will do well if they get water.

The Tonto Apaches have stolen a number of horses from the miners the past two weeks. I apprehend some trouble with them on account of it. Ten men of Captain Hargrave's company (C), First California Volunteers, were left at Fort Wingate, they being at the time of our departure on escort duty at Fort Canby. I would respectfully request that they may be ordered to join their company as soon as practicable.

I am, sir, very respectfully, your obedient servant,

EDWARD B. WILLIS,
Major First California Infantry.

HEADQUARTERS DEPARTMENT OF THE GULF,
New Orleans, December 22, 1863.

Maj. Gen. WILLIAM B. FRANKLIN,
Commanding Troops in Western Louisiana, New Iberia:

GENERAL: The major-general commanding directs me to inform you that assurances may be given to such of the regiments as re-enlist as veterans that they shall be permitted to go home and have a furlough of thirty days in their States within their present term of service, and that these furloughs to a regiment in a body will commence immediately, and be continued at the rate of at least two regiments every thirty days.

Blanks have been prepared here, and will go up to you to-morrow.

Very respectfully, your obedient servant,

[CHAS. P. STONE,]
Brigadier-General, and Chief of Staff.

HEADQUARTERS DEPARTMENT OF THE GULF,
New Orleans, December 22, 1863.

Maj. Gen. WILLIAM B. FRANKLIN,
Commanding Troops in Western Louisiana, New Iberia:

GENERAL: Colonel Molineux is appointed commissioner for Major-General Banks, to meet commissioner of Major-General Taylor at Red River Landing on the 1st of January, 1864, or as soon thereafter as practicable to both commissioners.

Very respectfully, your obedient servant,

[CHAS. P. STONE,]
Brigadier-General, Chief of Staff.

SPECIAL ORDERS, }   HDQRS. DEPARTMENT OF THE GULF,
No. 320.   }   *New Orleans, December* 22, 1863.

*   *   *   *   *   *   *

II. Officers of the Coast Survey, serving with the army in this department, will have the assimilated rank of captain, and will be obeyed and respected accordingly.

*   *   *   *

By command of Major-General Banks:

G. NORMAN LIEBER,
Acting Assistant Adjutant-General.

HEADQUARTERS DEPARTMENT OF THE GULF,
New Orleans, December 23, 1863.
Maj. Gen. H. W. HALLECK,
General-in-Chief, U. S. Army, Washington, D. C.:

GENERAL: Your dispatch of December 9 [7] I received yesterday. My orders from the Department were to establish the flag of the Government in Texas at the earliest possible moment. I understood that the point and the means were left to my discretion. It was implied, if not stated, that time was an element of great importance in this matter, and that the object should be accomplished as speedily as possible. In addition to the instructions received from your Department upon this subject, the President addressed me a letter, borne by Brigadier-General Hamilton, Military Governor of Texas, dated September 19, 1863, in which he expressed the hope that I had already accomplished the object so much desired. In the execution of this order, my first desire was to obtain possession of Houston, and the expedition which failed to effect a landing at the Sabine was designed to secure that object. The failure of that expedition made it impossible to secure a landing at that point. I immediately concentrated all my disposable force upon the Teche, with a view to enter Texas by the way of Niblett's Bluff, on the Sabine, or by Alexandria, at some more northern point.

The low stage of the water in all the rivers, and the exhaustion of supplies in that country, made it apparent that this route was impracticable at this season of the year—I might say it was impossible, within any reasonable time—and it would be accompanied by imminent peril, owing to the condition of the country, the length of march, and the strength of the enemy. Making this certain by thorough reconnaissances of the country, but without withdrawing my troops, I concluded to make another effort to effect a landing at some point upon the coast of Texas, in the execution of what I understood to be imperative orders. For this purpose, I withdrew a small force, stationed at Morganza, on the Mississippi, which had been under command of General Herron, and was then under Major-General Dana, and put them in a state of preparation for this movement. Assisted by the commander of the naval forces, Commodore Bell, I directed a reconnaissance of coast of Texas as far as Brazos Santiago, making my movements entirely dependent upon that report.

A return from this reconnaissance was made October 16, and my troops being in readiness for movement somewhere, without the delay of a single day, except that which the state of the weather made necessary, I moved for the Brazos. You will see from these facts that it was impossible for me to give you sufficient notice of this intention, to receive instructions from you upon this subject; but as soon as I had received the information necessary, and arrived at the determination to land at the Brazos, I gave you full information of all the facts in the case. It is my purpose always to keep you informed of all movements that are contemplated in this department, but it did not seem to me to be possible to do more in this instance; and, upon a review of the circumstances, I cannot now see where or when I could have given you more complete and satisfactory information than my dispatches conveyed.

I repeat my suggestion that the best line of defense for Louisiana, as well as for operations against Texas, is by Berwick Bay and the Atchafalaya, and I also recall the suggestions made by you upon the same subject; but that line was impracticable at the time when I received your orders upon the subject of Texas. I ought to add that the line of the Atchafalaya is available for offensive or defensive purposes only when the state of the water admits the operations of a strong naval force. At the time I made this suggestion to you, it was impossible to get a boat up the Atchafalaya, either from the Red River or from the Gulf, owing to the low stage of the water, and there were very few, if any, boats on the Mississippi or in this Department that could have navigated these waters at that time. It was, therefore, impossible to avail myself of this natural line; first, for the reason that we had not sufficient naval force for this purpose, and that the navigation was impossible. As soon as the Mississippi and Red River shall rise, the Government can make available the advantages presented by this line of water communication.

I recognize the embarrassments under which the Government labors in regard to re-enforcements in this department, yet as my lines are continually extending, I thought it to be my duty to renew the suggestion which I had formerly made in regard to the strength of my command and the many imperative demands made upon it. This is in the way of information, and not of complaint. I do not think my dispatches will show unreasonable urgency in this regard. I do not intend unnecessarily to divide my forces. I shall keep them concentrated as far as it is possible to do so. You may be sure that your suggestions upon this subject will receive due consideration. I know there is great difficulty in obtaining light-draught sea-boats, yet, from the necessities of the service, I feel called upon to urge, as far as may be proper, the want of vessels of this character. We have had very serious difficulty in obtaining the use of such vessels when in this department and in the possession of the Government. I am very glad that you have called the attention of Admiral Porter again to the subject of light-draught boats for the Atchafalaya and Berwick Bay. He has promised that as soon as the state of the water will admit the passage of his boats, he will send some of them into that river. I was not aware of the existence of the law to which you refer, but I appreciate the embarrassment which it throws upon the administration of the War Department. I will, as you suggest, communicate with the naval authorities, and request their assistance in all enterprises which I may undertake.

I have the honor to be, with much respect, your obedient servant,

N. P. BANKS,
Major-General, Commanding.

HEADQUARTERS DEPARTMENT OF THE GULF,
New Orleans, December 23, 1863.

Maj. Gen. WILLIAM B. FRANKLIN,
Commanding Troops in Western Louisiana, New Iberia:

GENERAL: I suppose the gunboat Arizona has reported, in compliance with a request of the commanding general to the commodore that one or two gunboats of light draught should be kept constantly in Berwick Bay. When the water rises, she can enter Grand Lake and the Atchafalaya.

Very respectfully, your obedient servant,

[CHAS. P. STONE,]
Brigadier-General, and Chief of Staff.

ADQUARTERS DEPARTMENT OF THE GULF,
New Orleans, December 23, 1863.

Maj. Gen. WILLIAM B. FRANKLIN,
Commanding Troops in Western Louisiana, New Iberia:

GENERAL: The order has been given respecting veterans. Two regiments from each corps are to go home in a body every thirty days; corps commanders to recommend the order in which regiments shall leave, having due regard in these recommendations to the age of the regiment in service and the promptness with which they enroll.

Very respectfully, your obedient servant,

[CHAS. P. STONE,] ·
Brigadier-General, Chief of Staff.

HDQRS. DISTRICT OF KEY WEST AND TORTUGAS,
Key West, Fla., December 23, 1863.

Brig. Gen. CHARLES P. STONE,
Chief of Staff, New Orleans, La.:

GENERAL: Referring to my letter of the 14th instant, I have now to report that on the 17th instant I sent a small detachment to Charlotte Harbor, to commence a nucleus of operations in that neighborhood. I inclose a copy of my instructions to the officer in charge.

I propose in a few days to go up with one company of the Forty-seventh Pennsylvania, and establish, if practicable, a lodgment on the mainland.

Two thousand head of cattle are reported to be driven out of Florida every week for the use of the rebel armies. Probably half of these cattle are driven from Middle and Lower Florida.

In a Florida newspaper of November 7, I find printed official "Instructions to commissary officers and agents;" an interesting document, giving, among other things, detailed instructions for driving cattle and taking care of them. I insert a single extract:

> The utmost promptness, energy, and industry are required of every agent and his assistants to secure all the surplus supplies of the country; otherwise the armies in the field cannot be fed. As Florida is now, next to Georgia, the most productive State remaining to the Confederacy, much depends upon the activity of the Government agents within her bounds.

After more observation, I have come to the conclusion that Enoch Daniels is not a proper man to command the enlisted men of Florida, though qualified for subordinate command. I therefore ask the commanding general of the department to suspend his provisional appointment as captain, if already made. I recommend in his place, as a proper person to command all the refugees who can be enlisted in the State of Florida, Henry A. Crane, acting master's mate, who enjoys the full confidence of Admiral Bailey and of all the naval officers who have had occasion to notice him during the past year.

I inclose a copy of a letter of Admiral Bailey relative to his charac-ter and services. He is an educated man, edited a newspaper at Tampa at the outbreak of the rebellion, and as agent, guide, and soldier has served in almost all parts of Florida.

I respectfully request the commanding general to appoint him pro-visionally as captain, the appointment to take effect as soon as he has raised 80 men. He has already been transferred by Admiral Bailey to my command.

It has been customary, for obvious reasons, to apply directly to Washington and New York for supplies of all sorts, and for the means of transportation required for this district.

I should be glad to receive the approbation of the commanding gen-eral of the proposed undertaking in Florida, so that I may be justified in making the necessary requisitions upon the north.

Respectfully,

D. P. WOODBURY,
Brigadier-General, Commanding.

[Indorsement.]

HEADQUARTERS DEPARTMENT OF THE GULF,
New Orleans, January 4, 1864.

The movement referred to by General Woodbury is an advantageous and proper one, but great care should be taken to avoid any surprise by the enemy. Any movement should be of a temporary character. If the supply of beef in Florida be of importance to our army, a force should be sent there sufficiently large to scour the country. This will be done as soon as the operations of the army will admit. Any in-formation upon this point will be of service.

In the meantime the general can pursue any operations that he may consider safe, but under no circumstances should he place his command where it can be surprised or overpowered.

N. P. BANKS,
Major-General, Commanding.

[NOTE.—The foregoing indorsement communicated to General Wood-bury by letter dated January 5, 1884, with information that "the com-mission of captain of Second Regiment, Florida Rangers, has been ordered for Mr. Crane, and will be forwarded to you."]

[Inclosure No. 1.]

HEADQUARTERS DISTRICT OF KEY WEST AND TORTUGAS,
Key West, Fla., December 17, 1863.

Lieut. James F. Meyers, of the Forty-seventh Pennsylvania, tempo-rarily detached from his company (A) and regiment, will proceed to Charlotte Harbor, in charge of 29 newly enlisted men, mostly refugees from the State of Florida, and of 1 sergeant and 6 privates of the Forty-seventh Pennsylvania. He will camp on one of the islands in Charlotte Harbor, and enlist as many more men as possible.

Enoch Daniels will accompany the expedition as guide, and as soon as 80 men have been enlisted, will probably be appointed captain or first lieutenant of the Florida Rangers, subject to the approval of the Presi-dent of the United States.

Captain Daniels will be allowed to communicate freely with people living on the mainland, for the purpose of effecting more enlistments, and will be allowed to take with him such men from the detachment as he may choose. These men must go armed, and must be cautioned to act with prudence and circumspection. The objects of the expedition are—

1. To afford Union men in the State of Florida. an opportunity to enlist in the service of the United States.

2. To break up or check the cattle-driving business in the neighborhood of Charlotte Harbor and as far north as practicable.

3. To procure able-bodied negroes for the service of the United States.

4. To obtain cattle for the use of the United States.

It is hoped that the force will soon become large enough to act with efficiency. It is understood that but few or no regular rebel troops are now to be found in that part of Western Florida which lies south of Tampa Bay, but that guerrillas and unauthorized men calling themselves regulators occasionally scour the country to drive away cattle and to enforce.the conscription. The troops in all their operations must be governed by the laws of war and by the regulations of the War Department. Lieutenant Meyers will provide himself with copies of the printed general orders of the War Department, and, if practicable, of the Department of the Gulf, and cause the more important of these orders to be read to the officers and men of the detachment.

The property of men in arms against the United States may be confiscated for the use of the United States, whether these men be in the regular service or not. Peaceable citizens must not be injured in person or property. Women and children must not be disturbed. The interest of the United States alone must be consulted on all occasions. Nothin ·ust be done to avenge old wrongs.

D. P. WOODBURY,
Brigadier-General.

[Inclosure No. 2.]

U. S. FLAG-SHIP DALE,
Key West, December 18, 1863.

Brig. Gen. D. P. WOODBURY, U. S. Army,
     Comdg. Dist. of Key West and Tortugas:

SIR: Agreeably to your request, I have ordered Acting Master's Mate Henry A. Crane to report to you for such duty connected with the army as you may assign him.

I would take this occasion to state that ·Mr. Crane is a refugee from Florida, of a far superior stamp to the greater part of those who have come over to us; he, together with seven others, who were voluntarily subordinate to him, offered their services to the vessel on blockade at Indian River nearly a year ago, and were received on board as supernumeraries. They proved to be of great service to us, from their knowledge of the country, their zeal, and their exemplary conduct during a series of operations along the coast, and Mr. Crane was distinguished among them for his superiority in all these qualities, in consequence of which he was induced to remain with us in his present capacity, and would have been advanced to a higher grade if he had been more of a seaman. He has been variously employed as an officer, guide, and pilot on the vessels and expeditions about Charlotte Harbor and Tampa Bay; has assisted greatly in several captures and in some small skirmishes with the enemy, and has always shown the utmost zeal, coolness, and gallantry. I understand also that he has had some military training; that he has been a colonel in the Florida militia, and that he was offered a commission as lieutenant-colonel by the rebel Government; he is well known and popular among the people of Lower Florida, and will, no doubt, be useful in recruiting.

I would recommend him most highly to your favorable consideration.

Respectfully,

THEODORUS BAILEY,
Acting Rear-Admiral, Comdg. East Gulf Blockading Squadron.

HEADQUARTERS THIRTEENTH ARMY CORPS,
Brownsville, December 24, 1863.

Maj. Gen. N. P. BANKS,
Commanding Department of the Gulf:

I have the honor to acknowledge receipt of your dispatch of the 17th instant.

The newspapers you were so good as to send me have reached me, and were a great gratification. When those which you forward to the consuls arrive, I will take care to forward them.

The quarrel on the Mexican side is not yet settled, and many foolish plans have been laid by our filibuster friends on them to draw us into it. Their principal anxiety is to have our flag among them on any pretext. They went even so far as to concoct a plan to seize the consulate, supposing I would come over and retake it. Pierce got frightened, and let me know it, and I immediately notified Serna, through his advisers, that it was too delicate a matter to trifle with, and I would have no "understanding" whatever, but should act according to circumstances, and the plan was given up. Notice was given me that Juarez was going to Durango, and my advice was asked. I strongly deprecated such a move, on the ground that it would be tantamount to a notice to the world that he had abandoned his cause and was about to fly. I urged his coming to Tamaulipas, as he would then have the Sierra Madre between him and the French, and his friends at his back.

Nothing new from interior Texas. Vidal with his scouting party has returned. Captain Speed and his 60 men are still out. His orders were to go about 70 or 80 miles. I have heard to-night that he was at Las Animas Monday, and intended going to King's ranch. I hope it is not so, as I do not consider it safe for his strength.

The mustang horses which we have bought are a very poor shift. The want of hay and grass, and the experiment to teach them to eat corn, are a bad combination of circumstances for them. General Hamilton has gone to Pass Cavallo for a few days, when he will return here.

I have the honor to remain, with much respect,

N. J. T. DANA,
Major-General.

HEADQUARTERS THIRTEENTH ARMY CORPS,
Brownsville, December 24, 1863—12 m.

Brig. Gen. CHARLES P. STONE,
Chief of Staff:

I hope it will not be considered officious if I advance my opinions, uncalled for, to the commanding general regarding the present arrangement of the troops on this frontier.

The movement to this point has had its full effect. It has entirely cut off the immense trade which has heretofore been carried on with the rebels by this route, and has occasioned them very serious losses, and compelled them to direct their trade now to points high up the river, known as Eagle Pass and Laredo, where they are crossing large quantities of supplies, the trade being mostly carried on with Monterey. The distance from here to Laredo is 235 miles, and to Eagle Pass 345 miles. The country is almost barren of supplies and forage, and there is little, if any, grass. Our horses being in poor condition, owing to the scarcity of grass in this region, will not stand such long marches and be of any service at the end of them; whereas the animals of the enemy, coming from a good grazing country, are in good condition. The water in the Rio Grande is so low that it cannot be relied on for supplies, with the means at our disposal. The Mustang, recently sent to Roma, 120 miles, could not reach there, but was occupied three weeks in incessant toil in arriving at a point 30 miles below there, and returning, with only 180 men on board.

The distance from here to San Antonio is over 200 miles, and from that place to Eagle Pass only 150 miles; consequently, with the rebel facilities for obtaining information, they can always learn by courier on the Mexican side of any movement on our part. By sending a force to Eagle Pass sufficiently large to defend itself, it is possible it might be scantily subsisted from the State of Nuevo Leon, but it would be at very great expense, and subject to interruptions by the whims of the officials of a peculiarly revolutionary people.

In fact, looking as I do only to our front against rebeldom, the occupation of the immense line of the frontier of the Rio Grande, so as effectually to stop communication between the rebels and Mexico, would require an expenditure of force and resources seemingly to me unjustifiable, if there is any cheaper way of accomplishing the same end.

From my spies, I am pretty well satisfied that there is now in the vicinity of King's ranch a body of 150 well-armed and well-mounted Texans. Their horses are in fine condition, and they are on the other side of the sand desert, which is 30 miles wide and devoid of water. They are very much on the alert, and scout actively, besides having spies between them and us, with orders to signalize our approach by smokes or otherwise.

Considering the poor condition of our cavalry and the rebel facilities of information and the nature of the country, it is hardly possible to surprise or capture them. We could easily drive them away, but they could as readily return unless we remained there with cavalry in some force. Should we do that, we would be compelled, from this base, to haul forage and supplies 120 miles, over a barren road, with great scarcity of water, whereas with Corpus Christi as a base, the distance to a point in that vicinity, should it then be thought advisable to occupy it, would be only 40 miles, with good water and grass. With Corpus Christi as a base of supplies, the Nueces River Valley would furnish abundance of water and grass, and our cavalry would rapidly recruit. We could occupy and threaten much more readily than from here all the roads leading from San Antonio to Mexico.

The respective distances from it are: To Eagle Pass, 200 miles; to Laredo, 135 miles; to Roma, 145 miles; to San Antonio, 135 miles; to Goliad, 60 miles; to Fort Ewell, the point where the San Antonio and Laredo road crosses the Nueces, 120 miles. The produce of the country, which has not yet been seized, and which has been arrested on its transit by our presence here, could be more readily reached from there, and our force there would be more menacing to the enemy and more inviting to our friends who now remain in the interior, too distant to reach either this place or Saluria with safety.

The above principal reasons, in connection with many other minor ones which might be mentioned, have led me, after much hesitation, to offer the above suggestions.

I would propose to leave here a garrison of about 500 men and six companies of the Corps d'Afrique at Point Isabel and four companies at Brazos. I would place in the works here the two 20-pounder Parrotts, the captured 24-pounder, and a section of one of the batteries here. I would march all the cavalry, six pieces of artillery, 500 infantry, and all the transportation overland to Corpus Christi, and would transport the remainder by water from Point Isabel, and I should ask for this purpose one of Morgan's steamships, the Matamoras, now at Pass Cavallo, and one other boat of not over 5 feet draught, with two light schooners, and one load of coal.

I have the honor to remain, with great respect,

N. J. T. DANA,
Major-General.

HEADQUARTERS UNITED STATES FORCES,
Fort Esperanza, Tex., December 24, 1863.

Brig. Gen. CHARLES P. STONE, *Chief of Staff:*

GENERAL: I have reliable information that the rebels are in considerable force at Velasco and Quintana, under General [P. N.] Luckett. They have two strong forts there, the one at Velasco having eight or ten large siege guns, and that at Quintana something less. I am also informed that some of the guns captured on the Clifton and Sachem, at Sabine Pass, are mounted at Velasco. From information I have, I judge that they have not less than three regiments at these forts. They have also two steamboats there, one of which is supposed to be a gunboat. My information is as recent as yesterday.

I report the arrival and landing of the 30-pounder Parrott battery. I regret that the public service in Louisiana would not justify the sending the First Wisconsin Battery, which is thoroughly drilled and practiced as heavy artillerists, having worn out in the service one battery of 20-pounders. The battery sent is perfectly raw, having never fired a shot at friend or foe. I request that, while our animals are dying daily for forage, you would put a stop to sutlers monopolizing the transportation. The Jews have already appeared in force.

Respectfully, yours,

C. C. WASHBURN,
Major-General.

P. S.—Yesterday General Warren occupied Powderhorn (Indianola) with the First Brigade, First Division. They will reconnoiter to-morrow as far as Lavaca. I have visited Palacios; also stirred them up at the head of the peninsula.

[Inclosure.]

[The following is an] extract from communication from Major [William G.] Thompson. commanding at Mustang Island, dated December 22, 1863:

I have information from a reliable man, direct from Corpus Christi (with whom I have frequently communicated verbally), that all the forces in the State of Texas, west, are ordered to rendezvous at Columbia, on the Brazos River, about 30 miles from Galveston; that many of the Confederate troops have deserted, and that several companies refuse absolutely to go, and that hundreds are now hiding around Corpus Christi, and waiting the coming of our forces.

HEADQUARTERS DEPARTMENT OF THE GULF,
New Orleans, December 24, 1863.
Depot Quartermaster at Brashear:

SIR: The artillery of the Third Division, Thirteenth Army Corps, will be transported to Algiers by rail as soon as practicable. Let all the infantry of that division and the Ohio battery ordered by the chief of artillery precede the artillery of the division.

Very respectfully, your obedient servant,
[CHAS P. STONE,]
Brigadier-General, and Chief of Staff.

SPECIAL ORDERS, }   HDQRS. DEPARTMENT OF THE GULF,
No. 322.   }   New Orleans, December 24, 1863.
*   *   *   *   *   *

IV. Maj. Gen. Francis J. Herron, U. S. Volunteers, will proceed without delay to Brownsville, Tex., and report to Maj. Gen. N. J. T. Dana, U. S. Volunteers, to take command of the Rio Grande frontier of Texas. On the arrival of Major-General Herron at Brownsville, Major-General Dana will proceed to Fort Esperanza, Pass Cavallo, Tex., and assume immediate command of the troops on the coast of Texas.
*   *   *   *   *   *

VI. The Fourth Division, Thirteenth Army Corps, will proceed without delay to Fort Esperanza, Pass Cavallo, Tex., and be reported for duty to the major-general commanding the forces of the United States in that vicinity. The quartermaster's department will furnish the necessary transportation.
*   *   *   *   *   *

By command of Major-General Banks:
G. NORMAN LIEBER,
Acting Assistant Adjutant-General.

HEADQUARTERS DEPARTMENT OF NEW MEXICO,
Santa Fé, N. Mex., December 25, 1863.
Maj. Gen. N. P. BANKS,
Commanding Department of the Gulf, Brownsville, Tex.:

GENERAL: On the 24th instant, I had the honor to receive your letter of the 5th ultimo, dated at Brazos Santiago. I beg to congratulate you on your foothold upon the soil of Texas. There can be no doubt but that the flag will be permanently maintained, not only where you are, but at every new and advanced point where you may plant it. It will be out of my power to send any troops from New Mexico toward San Antonio to co-operate with you in your contemplated advance upon that city—

1. For lack of force over and above what is absolutely necessary here to carry on the existing war against the Navajoes and Apaches.

2. For lack of means of transportation to move over the 700 miles of nearly a desert from the Rio Grande to San Antonio.

From information derived from Union refugees from Western Texas, there will be thousands of loyal hearts who will gather around the colors as you advance, and so that you have arms and material for them

you can hardly fail to have an army of Texans even; and you will receive from them, as you move along, information as to the country and
its resources, as to the temper of the people, and as to the actual
strength and whereabouts of all who oppose you, which will be of the
greatest value.

I only wish it were my lot to be with you and serve under you.
Please keep me informed of your movements and successes. That God
may continue your good fortune, for your own sake and for the glory of
the country, is the earnest prayer of, very respectfully, your obedient
servant,

JAMES H. CARLETON,
Brigadier-General, Commanding.

HEADQUARTERS DEPARTMENT OF THE GULF,
New Orleans, December 25, 1863.
Maj. Gen. F. J. HERRON, *New Orleans, La.:*

GENERAL: When assuming command of the forces of the United
States on the Rio Grande, in accordance with your instructions,* you
will bear in mind it is the interest of the Government you represent to
avoid all complications or difficulties with any foreign power. The immediate purpose of the occupation of the Rio Grande was the restoration of the flag of the Union in Texas. The Rio Grande was selected as
the most practicable opening for that purpose presented at the time
when our orders were received, earnest efforts to secure a position in any
other part of the State having failed. I am confident you will find the
Mexican authorities to be friendly to the Government and the people of
the United States, and you will, of course, feel it to be your duty to cul-
tivate such feeling in your intercourse with them.

General instructions were given to General Dana upon this subject,
which will, doubtless, be turned over to you. I have also the honor to
inclose to you a copy of instructions received from the Secretary of
State,† indorsed by the Secretary of War,‡ upon the subject of our relations with Mexico, and suggesting the course of conduct to be pursued
by the officers representing the Government on the Rio Grande.

You will find preparations have been made for the enlistment of recruits
for the army of the United States from the citizens of Texas, and also from
the citizens of Mexico. The Texans entering the service have insisted
upon their term being limited to the campaign in Texas, and a general
assent has been given to their request in that respect. In all other respects the condition of their service is the same as that of volunteers in
other States. It is of the utmost importance that our army be increased
as far as possible by recruits in that country, and I earnestly commend
this subject to your immediate and favorable consideration.

The river has been occupied as far as Rio Grande City by the cavalry
under Colonel Davis. It is desirable that we should keep a close watch
upon the river as far north as possible, and that communication may be
established with General Carleton, who is in command of our forces in
New Mexico, and whose advance guard hold position at Franklin, the
northwestern point of Texas.

The immediate point of interest in connection with him is to ascertain
in what way our forces can best co-operate in some future general opera-

---

* See Special Orders, No. 322, p. 879.
† See p. 815.
‡ For indorsement of the Secretary of War, see p. 846.

tions against the rebel army in Texas. You will, of course, feel it your duty, by the employment of scouts, to obtain all possible information of the movements of the rebel army, or of the enemies of the country in Mexico, and to make frequent reports to these headquarters. The difficulties of communication with the commanding officer of the Thirteenth Corps, who, under present instructions, is likely to occupy a position on the central coast or the interior of Texas, will be so great as to make that impracticable, and we cannot rely upon receiving information from you by that route. You will, therefore, make reports directly to these headquarters, sending duplicate copies of such papers as may be necessary to Major-General Dana, in command of the Thirteenth Army Corps.

I inclose a letter of introduction to Mr. L. Pierce, jr., American consul at Matamoras,* upon whom you can rely for any important information in that quarter affecting the interests of your command or the Government.

I inclose also a letter of introduction to a citizen of Matamoras—Mr. Galvan*—who rendered us very important services during the early occupation of the river, and who, I doubt not, will be ready to continue his favors.

With much respect, your obedient servant,

N. P. BANKS,
Major-General, Commanding.

HEADQUARTERS DEPARTMENT OF THE GULF,
New Orleans, December 26, 1863.

Col. E. G. BECKWITH,
Commanding Defenses of New Orleans:

COLONEL: The major-general commanding the department directs that you occupy the country in the vicinity of Madisonville, La., with all the available force at your disposal, provided, from your information, you have sufficient force to insure success.

Col. D. J. Keily, commanding Second Louisiana Cavalry, will order to report to you a force of 60 cavalry with 3 good officers.

Very respectfully, I am, colonel, your most obedient servant,

CHAS. P. STONE,
Brigadier-General, and Chief of Staff.

HEADQUARTERS DEPARTMENT OF THE GULF,
New Orleans, December 26, 1863.

Maj. Gen. WILLIAM B. FRANKLIN,
Commanding Troops in Western Louisiana, New Iberia:

GENERAL: The agent of the State of Connecticut is here, and offers to pay at once to every Connecticut volunteer who enlists as a veteran $300 on his being mustered in. This refers only to men who come from Connecticut.

Very respectfully, your obedient servant,

[CHAS. P. STONE,]
Brigadier-General, and Chief of Staff.

---

* Not found.

HEADQUARTERS THIRTEENTH ARMY CORPS,
Brownsville, December 26, 1863.

M. M. KIMMEY,
United States Consul, Monterey, Mexico:

Your very welcome and interesting dispatch of the 17th instant has this moment reached me. As usual, I am greatly indebted to you for your information, and hope you will continue to supply. I have only time now to say that I send to Mr. Pierce, the American consul at Mata- moras, three large packages of files of papers for you to-day. If you will send me down vouchers for the amount of money you have disbursed by General Banks' request for sending expresses, recruits, supplies, &c., and have the receipts signed and forwarded to Mr. Pierce, or other persons whom you authorize to receive the money, I will try and have them paid. Please let the vouchers specify exactly how much in Treasury notes and how much in gold is paid in each instance.

I have the honor to remain, your most obedient servant,

N. J. T. DANA.

[P. S.]—Vouchers should be about as follows:

U. S. to A. B. C., Dr.

For ——

Then follows receipt in full. Let these vouchers be fully explained. There is no authority now to pay over money to anybody to disburse excepting a bonded officer of the quartermaster's department.

GENERAL ORDERS, }   HDQRS. DEPARTMENT OF THE GULF,
No. 87.   }   *New Orleans, December 26, 1863.*

Complaints having been made to these headquarters that peaceable private families are frequently annoyed by visits of unauthorized persons, officers and soldiers of the army, and civil employés of the Government, the commanding general directs that persons residing within the limits of this department shall not be disturbed in the possession of their houses without the exhibition of written orders from proper military authority, or from an authorized agent of the Treasury Department.

The provost-marshal-general is charged with the due execution of this order; and violations of its terms or spirit will be taken cognizance of by the provost courts.

By command of Major-General Banks:

G. NORMAN LIEBER,
Acting Assistant Adjutant-General.

HEADQUARTERS THIRTEETNTH ARMY CORPS,
Brownsville, December 27, 1863.

Brig. Gen. CHARLES P. STONE,
Chief of Staff:

At half past 12 o'clock on yesterday I received a communication from the United States consul at Matamoras, a copy of which is inclosed, marked No. 1.

I immediately addressed the *de facto* Governor of Tamaulipas, and inclose a copy of my dispatch, marked No. 2, and I ordered eight pieces of artillery, two squadrons of cavalry, and five battalions of infantry to get under arms, with ammunition and two days' rations.

At first, as I am informed by the staff officer by whom I sent the communication, the Governor was inclined to assume the position that "if American citizens did not like the laws of Mexico, they were at liberty to remain from its soil," and sent me that verbal message in reply, but it was scarcely spoken to the officer when a courier reached the chamber in great haste, with the report that I had taken possession of the ferry-boats. This cause great excitement, which resulted in His Excellency requesting the officer to wait a few moments and he would send a written reply. I inclose a copy of the translation of that reply, marked No. 3.

At 8 o'clock last evening, His Excellency did me the honor to call at my quarters, in company with Mr. Peeler, from the consulate, quite informally and unannounced. It was his first visit, and I received him with great courtesy and kindness. He remained some two hours, and the subject of our correspondence was not mentioned. Had I have entertained any doubt as to the propriety of the extreme tone of my dispatch at the moment it left my hands, that doubt was entirely dispelled within a very few minutes afterward by the receipt from the consul of the formal protest of Mr. Galvan.

The case was much more intolerable than had been represented to me, for he had not only been threatened, but was actually imprisoned and kept from any communication with the consul or any one else till the money was extorted.

The loyal Americans in Matamoras this morning have the proud satisfaction of being, as I am informed, the only exceptions to an arbitrary exaction which has been practiced on all other foreigners.

I have the honor, &c.,

N. J. T. DANA,
Major-General.

[Inclosure No. 1.]

UNITED STATES CONSULATE,
Matamoras, December 26, 1863.

Maj. Gen. N. J. T. DANA,
Commanding U. S. Forces, Brownsville, Tex.:

SIR: Yesterday several of the merchants of the city were invited to go to the Governor's room, and among them Mr. I. Galvan, and one or two other Americans. Upon their arrival, they were shown to an anteroom, and an officer sent to inform them that they must pay the amount of their respective quotas of a loan impressed by Governor Serna or go to prison. To get out, they promised to pay some, and to-day I am called upon by all our American citizens, and a great many foreigners, asking for protection, claiming that the act is illegal, for the reason that Serna has not been recognized by the President of the Republic as Governor, and demands this loan upon his own responsibility, to be returned again in duties at the custom-house, upon what are called those custom-house bonds, which, until the Governor is recognized by the President, are worthless, and the money thrown away. The amounts are very large, Mr. Galvan's quota being $10,000. My opinion is that Governor Serna has not the shadow of a right to collect the moneys. He says that it is for the protection of the town against the forces being brought against it, and, as the bonds will be of no account if their forces should succeed, he thus urges American citizens and others to take a part in a State revolution without consulting their interests in the least, and the opposing Governor would probably not only annul everything of the kind, but also impose another loan to pay off his own troops. In the interior States they collect such loans through mere force, but as I am urged strongly to lay the matter before you, I thought if you would demand Governor Serna's authority, for doing this, it would serve to stop it, as I consider it illegal and wrong in every respect.

All taxes and loans imposed by the Supreme Government have always been paid, but in this instance it is only the caprice of a man claiming to be the Governor of Tamaulipas.

I am, sir, very respectfully, your most obedient servant,

L. PIERCE, JR.,
United States Consul.

[Inclosure No. 2.]

HEADQUARTERS THIRTEENTH ARMY CORPS,
Brownsville, Tex., December 26, 1863—1 p. m.

His Excellency Don JESUS DE LA SERNA,
Governor of Tamaulipas :

I am this moment advised by the United States consul at Matamoras that on yesterday you notified the foreigners residing in your city of your purpose to imprison them unless they complied with a demand made upon them by you for considerable sums of money, under the pretext of paying the expenses of defending the town against an anticipated attack threatened by troops who claim to be the troops of the Federal and Supreme Government of Mexico.

I am now called on to protect the rights of American citizens, and I propose to do that which I can do for the entire safety of every loyal man, woman, and child of the United States.

The traitors and rebels, the cut-throats and assassins from this side of the river, who have found an asylum in the States of Tamaulipas and Nuevo Leon, not only for safety and protection to their persons, but to carry on a trade in cotton and military supplies which feed and keep alive a rebellion which is aiming to destroy a Government which is the best friend of Mexico, are excluded from and will not receive my protection.

I humbly trust the report I have received of Your Excellency's intentions will not be confirmed by events.

I do not imagine that all professions of friendship from Mexico toward the United States are to be considered merely as complimentary words.

Of one thing I will assure Your Excellency, that American citizens are secure from forced loans in their own country, and do not know how to submit to them from any other power on earth. At all events, it will be time for them to submit when they have not the power to protect themselves.

Should the fears of the Americans in Matamoras prove to be well founded, Your Excellency is certainly aware that, under the peculiar circumstances which now surround you, and considering the probability that your acts might not be guaranteed by the responsibility of the Mexican Government to mine in this instance, I could not remain here an idle or uninterested spectator, and I now make peremptory protest against any such action as a forced loan on loyal citizens of the United States.

I request of Your Excellency immediate information as to the right under which you claim to exercise any such arbitrary power over those who are under my protection and that of my nation; nay, more, I demand that, if any such measures have been commenced, that they be forthwith discontinued, so far as said citizens are interested.

I shall hold myself in instant readiness for Your Excellency's reply, and now reassure Your Excellency of my distinguished consideration.

N. J. T. DANA,
Major-General.

[Inclosure No. 3.]

MATAMORAS,
December 26, 1863.

Maj. Gen. N. J. T. DANA,
Commanding Thirteenth Army Corps:

In answer to your note, dated to-day, in which you refer to a forced loan made by this Government on American citizens, I have the honor to say that, it not being the desire of the Government to place any forced contributions on the American citizens, I have this moment given orders that in this respect, or anything else of the kind, there shall not be molested any citizens of the United States that shall be met with at this port.

Protesting to you the sincerity of my friendship, &c.,

JESUS DE LA SERNA.

———

HEADQUARTERS THIRTEENTH ARMY CORPS,
Brownsville, December 27, 1863.

Brig. Gen. CHARLES P. STONE,
Chief of Staff:

Lieutenant-Colonel Scates, with a portion of the staff of this corps, arrived here yesterday. I have the honor and gratification of acknowledging the receipt of full files of papers through the attention of the major-general commanding the Department of the Gulf, to whose kindness in this and other matters I am deeply sensible.

The packages for the consuls at Matamoras and Monterey were immediately forwarded. I have written to the latter to forward vouchers for his outlays on account of military affairs since our advent here, in order that I may see them paid.

The First Texas Cavalry is now about 460 strong (present), and the Second (Haynes') is 300. Braubach is here with about 50 men. Fenn's efforts to supply horses have not been attended with success. Very many of them are not able to stand a single day's march. I have been compelled to stop that source of supply, and now depend on what few of superior quality are offered.

Owing to the destitute condition of the First Texas Cavalry when they reached here, and the number of cavalry recruits who have been enlisted since our arrival, the supply of clothing which I brought down has been entirely exhausted, and the new recruits and many of the old men are now suffering for want of it. I ordered requisitions for 500 new suits, which went forward some time ago. but no supplies have yet been received. I have to-day approved requisitions for 1,000 suits more, and hope they will, by some peremptory means, be hurried forward.

One thousand suits of infantry clothing were also called for some time ago, and are greatly needed, but none have arrived. We have not the equipment to mount our cavalry. It will be remembered by the commanding general that I brought down here 1,000 sets of regulation cavalry equipments, which were all carried back to New Orleans without being landed. They have never been sent back. Since then, I have asked for a further supply of 300 of the same sort, but they have not arrived. The equipments of many of the First Texas Cavalry, as well as their arms and ammunition, were carried back at the same time, and since then a portion were sent back on a schooner, which was lost. We have, as yet, received no ammunition for Sharps carbines. The arms which the First Texas brought down with them are the old pattern Sharps carbine.

Those which we have brought and which are issued to the recruits of both regiments are Sharps' new pattern and Burnsides. The ammunition of each is different, and we must have the three kinds. I brought down 180,000 rounds of Sharps. It was all carried back, and, although frequent calls have been made, none has yet reached here, and the cavalry are without ammunition. We ought to have at once 60,000 rounds of each of the three sorts. The fortifications here are nearly complete.

We get little or no cotton now, as we have pretty well cleaned out the roads, and no new lots are started out.

Nothing new from Juarez or the French since last report.

I inclose the last rebel papers which I have, and, at the risk of repeating information which you may have received from our troops up the coast, I will report Magruder is fortifying Round Top, on the Brazos. Bee is at Victoria with a considerable force, reported at 4,000, probably militia and conscripts. One thousand negroes are at work on fortifications at San Antonio. The refugees have become bolder and more defiant in Northwestern Texas, and the road from San Antonio to Eagle Pass is not considered altogether safe. In fact, some raids are reported to have been committed on trains. Captain Speed has not yet returned, but I have no doubt he will be in in two days.

I have the honor to remain, your most obedient servant,

N. J. T. DANA,
Major-General.

HEADQUARTERS DISTRICT OF PENSACOLA,
Barrancas, Fla., December 27, 1863.

Brig. Gen. CHARLES P. STONE,
Chief of Staff, Headquarters Department of the Gulf:

GENERAL: I have the honor to report, in relation to the organization of cavalry, that I am daily more convinced that not only one but several regiments could be raised in Western Florida, by offering to all those who are anxious to enlist into the Union Army proper assistance to come within our lines.

The two small steamers and re-enforcements, for which I applied on the 23d and 25th ultimo (Nos. 42 and 48), and on the 5th instant (No. 110), would supply these wants, enabling me to enter the Escambia and Perdido Rivers, scout to the interior of the State, and, capturing the isolated rebel posts, with their horses. collect also the refugees and deserters secreted in the woods and islands.

I beg, therefore, to renew most respectfully my former request for two small steamers, of not more than 4 feet draught, and the combined brigade, so much needed.

I would also request instructions and orders regarding the payment of bounty to those white soldiers who are enlisting for three years.

Considering the general destitution of the people here, it would be an act of humanity, as well as good policy, to grant advance payment of bounty. There are funds to the amount of $2,000 in the hands of Lieut. J. C. Breckinridge, U. S. Army, at Fort Barrancas, sent to him to be disbursed in payment of bounties to recruits at Key West, this State, from the Enrolling Bureau, Washington, D. C., and I would respectfully request that, as a temporary measure, the necessary orders be issued by which these funds may be disbursed by him to the men enrolled here until proper appropriation could be made.

Having no steamer and no other vessel at my disposal to collect the refugees with, I have made use of a private schooner in charge of Captain Galloway, a most reliable, high-minded Union man, who has succeeded, in one trip to the East Pass of the bay, in bringing 25 able-bodied men—all his schooner could take. They enlisted at once, and, in addition to those, 33 more, who have found their way through the rebel pickets, at the risk of their lives; of those, 18 have enlisted in Company M, Fourteenth New York Cavalry, and 40 in the Florida regiment.

I have started Captain Galloway on a second trip, and as Captain Gibson, commander and senior officer afloat here, has, upon my request, ordered the small steamer Bloomer to assist Galloway in bringing down from the East Pass and Choctawhatchee Bay the refugees waiting transportation, I am confident that he will return in a few days with at least 200 recruits.

Rebel movements in my neighborhood are reported as follows by deserters who came in yesterday : They anticipated an attack from here upon Pollard on Christmas day. There are 2,000 men there, and 200 infantry and 100 cavalry were sent in addition to the former force to Fifteen-Mile Station, on the Pensacola Railroad. At Mobile there are two regiments of infantry and one of cavalry. It is generally understood that the men will refuse on New Year's day further service. More troops have been sent to Fort Morgan. The two companies of cavalry reported heretofore encamped above Florida Town have been withdrawn, as they made preparations to desert *en masse.*

From the Perdido, rebel cavalry are continually scouting, approaching our pickets.

Very respectfully, general, your obedient servant,

ASBOTH,
Brigadier-General, Commanding.

HEADQUARTERS OF THE ARMY,
Washington, December 28, 1863.
Maj. Gen. WILLIAM T. SHERMAN,
Commanding Department of the Tennessee, Cairo :

GENERAL: It will be seen by the inclosed extracts from letters of the Acting Quartermaster-General, and of quartermasters at New Orleans,* that stores sent from the Upper Mississippi to New Orleans have been stopped at Vicksburg and Natchez, and diverted from their proper destination. Such proceedings are not only culpably improper, but, if continued, will entirely disarrange our system of supplies, produce great suffering and losses, and defeat all plans of military operations.

The Secretary of War directs that you immediately issue the orders necessary to correct the evils complained of, and that you ascertain the

---

* Not found.

names of the guilty parties, and report them to these headquarters for dismissal. The evil is of such a nature as to require your prompt and summary action.

Very respectfully, your obedient servant,

H. W. HALLECK.

HEADQUARTERS DEPARTMENT OF THE GULF,
New Orleans, December 29, 1863.
Rear-Admiral DAVID D. PORTER,
Commanding Mississippi Squadron :

ADMIRAL : I am in receipt of a communication from the General-in-Chief of the Army, covering a copy of your dispatch of December 2, instant, to the honorable the Secretary of the Navy, concerning the guns mounted on the river front at Port Hudson.

These guns were long since ordered removed by me, and I am informed by the general commanding at that point that the removal has been effected.

At the risk of being deemed importunate, I must again respectfully call your attention to the importance of the prompt arrival in the Atchafalaya and Berwick Bay of some of your gunboats. From your intimate acquaintance with the country near the Mississippi River, you are aware of the extreme difficulty which must be experienced in conducting military operations in the Atchafalaya Basin without a perfect control of the water communications.

The river has now been in good navigable condition for several weeks, and I had been led to hope that the first rise would bring your light-draught boats to our assistance.

Very respectfully, I am, admiral, your most obedient servant,

N. P. BANKS,
Major-General, Commanding.

MEMPHIS, TENN.,
December 29, 1863—4.30 p. m.
Maj. Gen. H. W. HALLECK,
General-in-Chief :

Deserter just in from Mobile reports that rebels have six vessels—four iron-clads—with which Admiral Buchanan proposes to raise the blockade from the 1st to the 20th of January. Chief of these is the Tennessee, of twelve ports, six guns mounted, clad with 6-inch iron; makes about 8 knots. The others are slow—not over 5 knots. I think the attempt will be made about that time. I send the information as it is, for the Navy Department. Only three regiments at Mobile.

S. A. HURLBUT,
Major-General.

HEADQUARTERS DEPARTMENT OF THE GULF,
New Orleans, December 30, 1863.
Maj. Gen. H. W. HALLECK,
General-in-Chief, U. S. Army, Washington, D. C.:

GENERAL : Your dispatch of December 11, inclosing dispatch from Admiral Porter, was received on the 27th instant. Orders were given to Brigadier-General Andrews, long since, for the destruction of the river batteries at Port Hudson and the removal of the guns. There is no excuse for his neglect, as his attention has been repeatedly called to the subject. Since your dispatch was received, the guns have been removed and the works demolished.

In reference to the report made by General Steele, that General Price, with a portion of the rebel troops, was moving toward Little Rock, I beg to suggest that but a small force of Texas troops can be moving in that direction. The greater portion are in Texas or in Central Louisiana. A portion of my command is now on the Teche, but will probably be withdrawn. The rivers are not yet deep enough to enable us to advance toward the Red River, excepting by wagon communication, which is impracticable. The country is without supplies of any kind. It is my desire, if possible, to get possession of Galveston. This, if effected, will give us control of the entire coast of Texas, and require but two small garrisons, one on the Rio Grande and the other on Galveston Island, unless it be the wish of the Department of War that extensive operations should be made in the State of Texas. A sufficient number of men can probably be recruited in that State for the permanent occupation of these two posts. It would relieve a very large number of naval vessels, whose service is now indispensable to us on the Mississippi and in the Gulf. This can occupy but a short time, and, if executed, will leave my whole force in hand to move to any other point on the Red River or wherever the Government may direct. Once possessed of Galveston, and my command ready for operations in any other direction, I shall await the orders of the Government, but I trust that this may be accomplished before undertaking any other enterprise. It is impossible at this time to move as far north as Alexandria by water. The Red River is not open to the navigation of our gunboats, and it is commanded by Fort De Russy, which has been remounted since our occupation of Alexandria. This position must be turned by means of a large force on land before the gunboats can pass.

To co-operate with General Steele in Arkansas, or north of Red River, will bring nearly the whole rebel force of Texas and Louisiana between New Orleans and my command, without the possibility of dispersing or defeating them, as their movement would be directed south and mine to the north. It is necessary that this force should be first dispersed or destroyed before I can safely operate in conjunction with General Steele. Once possessed of the coast of Texas, and the naval and land forces relieved, I can then operate against the forces in Louisiana or Texas, and I can disperse or destroy the land forces in Louisiana, and safely co-operate with General Steele or with any other portion of the army of the United States. It was in this manner that we captured Port Hudson. It would have been impracticable to proceed against Port Hudson from the Mississippi without having first dispersed the army of Texas and Louisiana on the west of that river.

I bear in mind the danger consequent upon the division of forces, but must suggest to you that my department is extended, and many posts must be occupied; and while I would be very glad to keep my forces concentrated, it is impossible to do so. The orders of the Government seemed to be peremptory that I was to occupy a position in Texas, and those which I have in view, Brownsville and Galveston, required as little force as any other position in that State. To this fact may be added that there are supplies and recruits which cannot be found in any other portion of this department. In all my operations, you may rely upon the bulk of my forces being kept together, and prepared for any movements of the enemy. It is possible, but not probable, that they will make a successful assault upon some of the isolated positions. We shall endeavor to prevent this by all possible means. I repeat, that in any movements in which I engage, I shall concentrate the available forces of my command, and peril nothing by an unnecessary division.

I am very much gratified that the Third Maryland Cavalry is ordered to this department. It promises to become a fine regiment. From the nature of the country in which we operate, a strong cavalry force is indis-pensable, and I am endeavoring to convert infantry regiments into cav-alry as rapidly as possible, consistent with the service. The true line of occupation, in my judgment, offensive and defensive, for this department, is the Atchafalaya and the Mississippi. The Teche country, and that between the Atchafalaya and the Mississippi, can be defended only by the assistance of the navy. It is impossible for land forces to oper-ate on that line successfully without the assistance of gunboats. With their assistance, the advance is easy and certain. The best position that we could occupy will be to defend this line by the aid of a strong naval force of light and heavy draught gunboats for the different waters in which they may operate, and the disposable land forces so held as to be able to move from one point to another in a body. We should then have one complete line of water navigation from the Rio Grande to Alexandria or Shreveport during the winter and spring, and from the mouth of the Mississippi to Key West in the Gulf, and could throw our entire force against any point of the territory occupied by the enemy without the possibility of their anticipating our movement or purposes. I am endeavoring constantly to secure means for offensive and defensive war upon this place, and am confident that it can be very speedily accomplished.

I have the honor to be, with much respect, your obedient servant,

N. P. BANKS,
Major-General, Commanding.

HEADQUARTERS DEPARTMENT OF THE GULF,
New Orleans, December 30, 1863.
Maj. Gen. H. W. HALLECK,
General-in-Chief, U. S. Army, Washington, D. C.:

GENERAL: The signal corps has been of very essential service in this department in all our operations by land and water. In our re-cent movements upon the coast of Texas, it was the only means of com-munication between the inland bays and the coast, and, without the assistance of the signal officers, it seems as if we would sometimes have been deprived of the power of communication. The importance of its service in this case can hardly be overestimated.

The same is true of its services on land. I can state with entire con-fidence that a discontinuance of this means of communication would cause universal regret among all the officers of the Government, both naval and military. The gentlemen connected with the signal corps in this department are men of excellent character, great energy and courage, almost always in the front of the army, and in positions of danger, and undergo any amount of fatigue and trial without complaint, discharging all their duties to our entire satisfaction. I do not know that I have ever received a complaint of neglect of any duty by any signal officer. This communication is written upon the suggestion of the signal officer of the army, through the chief officer of the corps in this department, as an expression of opinion as to the value of the corps and the conduct of its officers in this department.

I wish to make my unqualified approval both of the utility of the corps and the conduct of its officers.

I have the honor to be, your obedient servant,

N. P. BANKS,
Major-General, Commanding.

MEMPHIS, TENN., *December* 30, 1863—4.30 p. m.

Hon. GIDEON WELLES, *Secretary of the Navy:*

The Tennessee, at Mobile, will be ready for sea in twenty days. She is a dangerous craft; Buchanan thinks more so than the Merrimac. She is a ram; makes 8 knots; armed with 10-inch columbiads, and has heavy Blakely guns. This news just received.

S. A. HURLBUT,
Major-General, Commanding Sixteenth Army Corps.

PORT HUDSON, LA., *December* 31, 1863.

Brig. Gen. CHARLES P. STONE, *Chief of Staff, New Orleans, La.:*

There are still parties of guerrillas on the west bank. A boat was fired into, with musketry only, by them this morning. Two deserters from the rebels, Marshall and Conner, this morning report not over 500 rebels anywhere in this vicinity. Principal rendezvous at white house, near Woodville. Most of the rebels are now said to be on furlough for the holidays, to concentrate on the 6th of January. I am improving the opportunity to forage.

GEO. L. ANDREWS,
Brigadier-General of Volunteers, Commanding Post.

---

*Abstract from returns of the Department of the Gulf, Maj. Gen. N. P. Banks, U. S. Army, commanding, for the month of December, 1863.**

Command.	Present for duty.		Aggregate present.	Aggregate present and absent.	Pieces of artillery.		Remarks.
	Officers.	Men.			Heavy.	Field	
General headquarters:							
Staff and headquarters troops....	32	79	125	162	......	......	New Orleans. La.
Engineer Brigade (Houston)......	76	1,401	1,810	1,980	......	......	Do.
Total......................	108	1,480	1,935	2,142	......	......	
Thirteenth Army Corps (Dana):							
Staff	17	....	17	24	......	....	Brownsville, Tex.
First Division (Benton)	246	3,552	4,068	6,370	8	18	Decrow's Point, Tex.
Second Division (Dana)	235	3,804	4,832	7,621	......	12	Brownsville, Tex.
Third Division (McGinnis).......	167	3,090	3,464	4,750	......	6	Algiers, La.
Fourth Division (Landram)......	117	1,795	2,208	5,405	......	11	Decrow's Point, Tex.
Detachments, Engineers, &c.....	91	1,755	2,115	2,655	......	......	Texas.
Total †......................	873	13,996	16,704	26,825	8	47	

* Compiled as far as practicable from the subordinate returns.
† See abstracts from the monthly returns of Washburn's command, Thirteenth Army Corps, and Second Division, Thirteenth Army Corps.

Abstract from returns of the Department of the Gulf, &c.—Continued.

Command.	Present for duty.		Aggregate present.	Aggregate present and absent.	Pieces of artillery.		Remarks.
	Officers.	Men.			Heavy.	Field.	
Nineteenth Army Corps (Franklin):							
Staff	10		10	12			New Iberia, La.
First Division (Emory)	148	2,819	3,459	4,870		8	Do.
Third Division (Grover)	104	2,138	2,580	3,500		4	Do.
Reserve Artillery (Closson)	3	139	151	180		8	Do.
Total*	265	5,096	6,200	8,562		20	
Cavalry Division (Lee):							
Staff	8		10	10			New Orleans, La.
First Brigade (Redfield)	61	1,436	1,736	2,508			Near New Iberia, La.
Second Brigade (Fonda)	23	398	526	776			Donaldsonville, La.
Third Brigade (Paine)	46	956	1,260	1,971		4	Near New Iberia, La.
Fourth Brigade (Dudley)	38	1,165	1,317	1,572			Carrollton and Franklin, La.
Detachments in the field	4	114	143	165			Near New Iberia, La.
Artillery	3	147	155	188		6	Do.
At New Orleans (detachments)	27	410	571	795			
Total†	210	4,626	5,718	7,985		10	
La Fourche District (Birge)							Thibodeaux, La.
First Brigade, Fourth Division, Nineteenth Army Corps (Birge).	58	1,511	2,061	2,616			
Other troops	35	814	936	1,111		14	
Total	93	2,325	2,997	3,727		14	
Defenses of New Orleans (Beckwith):							
Second Brigade, Fourth Division, Nineteenth Army Corps (Cahill).	39	827	1,123	4,151			New Orleans, La.
Other troops	161	3,818	4,537	4,957	4	6	
Total	200	4,645	5,660	9,108	4	6	
Fort Jackson, La. (Dwight)							Garrison not reported.
District of Baton Rouge (Cooke)							Baton Rouge, La.
Second Brigade First Division, Nineteenth Army Corps (Sharpe).	50	1,157	1,566	2,197			Do.
Post of Plaquemine (Sheldon)	54	1,191	1,554	2,328		8	
Other troops	38	767	977	2,084	13	8	Baton Rouge.
Total	142	3,115	4,097	6,609	13	16	
Port Hudson, La. (Andrews):							
Corps d'Afrique	193	3,422	4,596	5,212			
Other troops	38	496	687	842		12	
Total	231	3,918	5,283	6,054		12	
District of Key West and Tortugas (Woodbury).	26	571	999	1,242			Key West, Fla.
District of Pensacola (Asboth)	52	909	1,133	1,225	127	6	Barrancas, Fla.

* The Second Brigade, First Division, and the Fourth Division, elsewhere accounted for.

† The Third Massachusetts accounted for at Port Hudson ; the First and Second Texas with Second Division, Thirteenth Army Corps at Brownsville, and the Fourth Wisconsin at Baton Rouge.

Abstract from returns of the Department of the Gulf—Continued.

Command.	Present for duty.		Aggregate present.	Aggregate present and absent.	Pieces of artillery.		Remarks.
	Officers.	Men.			Heavy.	Field.	
Miscellaneous commands:							
Corps d'Afrique..................	48	858	1,052	1,073	......	......	Brashear City, La.
Corps d'Afrique..................	22	473	529	542	......	......	New Iberia, La.
Corps d'Afrique..................	20	92	124	127	......	......	New Orleans, La.
Total..........................	90	1,423	1,705	1,742	......	......	
Grand total	2,290	42,104	52,431	75,221	152	131	
Grand total according to department monthly return.	2,101	39,899	13,436	76,923	148	132	
Grand total according to department tri-monthly return for December 31.	2,106	39,689	53,423	76,965	......	......	

Abstract from returns of the United States Forces in Texas, commanded by Maj. Gen. C. C. Washburn, U. S. Army, for the month of December, 1863; headquarters, Decrow's Point, Tex.

Command.	Present for duty.		Aggregate present.	Aggregate present and absent.
	Officers.	Men.		
General headquarters...	7	14	21	21
First Division, Thirteenth Army Corps..................................	205	3,521	4,266	6,285
Third Brigade, Second Division, Thirteenth Army Corps...............	67	827	1,116	1,646
Fourth Division, Thirteenth Army Corps..............................	113	1,715	2,124	5,447
23d Iowa.	20	263	337	520
1st Kentucky Engineers...	2	20	23	33
2d Engineers, Corps d'Afrique	22	366	466	534
Artillery	12	302	329	549
4th Indiana Cavalry, Company C	......	......	......	63
Total...	448	7,028	8,682	15,098

Abstract from returns of the Thirteenth Army Corps, Maj. Gen. N. J. T. Dana, U. S. Army, commanding, for the month of December, 1863.

Command.	Present for duty.		Aggregate present.	Aggregate present and absent.	Pieces of artillery.		Remarks.
	Officers.	Men.			Heavy.	Field.	
Staff	17	......	17	24	......	......	Brownsville, Tex.
First Division......................	239	4,046	4,919	7,281	4	14	Matagorda Island, Tex.
Second Division....................	180	2,908	3,842	7,118	......	14	Brownsville, Tex.
Third Division.....................	214	3,734	4,276	6,637	......	16	New Iberia, La.
Fourth Division....................	156	2,170	2,829	5,697	......	11	Decrow's Pt., Tex.
1st and 2d Texas Cavalry..........	29	719	837	1,037	......	......	Brownsville, Tex.
1st Engineers and 16th Infantry, Corps d'Afrique.	43	722	866	946	......	......	Point Isabel, Tex.
2d Engineers, Corps d'Afrique	22	366	466	534	......	......	Matagorda Island.
Pioneers	2	20	22	33	......	......	Do.
14th Rhode Island Heavy Artillery ..	14	434	483	562	......	......	Ft. Esperanza, Tex.
Total....................	916	15,119	18,558	29,869	4	55	

Abstract from returns of the Second Division, Thirteenth Army Corps, and attached troops, Maj. Gen. N. J. T. Dana, U. S. Army, commanding, for the month of December, 1863.

Command.	Present for duty.		Aggregate present.	Aggregate present and absent.	Pieces of field artillery.	Remarks.
	Officers.	Men.				
Staff..........................	12	....	12	12	....	Brownsville, Tex.
First Brigade.....................	64	1,186	1,493	2,375	4	Do
Second Brigade..................	52	788	1,056	2,133	8	Do
Third Brigade...................	65	823	1,136	1,797	6	Matagorda Island, Tex.
Infantry detachments...........	3	125	144	174	....	Brownsville, Tex.
1st and 2d Texas Cavalry	29	719	837	1,037	....	Do
Corps d'Afrique (engineers and infantry).	10	159	216	244	....	Do
Engineer troops and attached infantry.	39	497	624	683	....	Point Isabel, Tex.
20th Iowa	10	213	277	580	....	Aransas Pass, Tex.
Total	284	4,510	5,795	9,035	18	

Organization of the troops in the Department of the Gulf, Maj. Gen. N. P. Banks, U. S. Army, commanding, December 31, 1863.

GENERAL HEADQUARTERS.

Headquarters troops, Capt. Richard W. Francis.
Signal Corps, Capt. William B. Roe.

ARTILLERY.*

Brig. Gen. RICHARD ARNOLD, chief.

2d Illinois, Light Battery A, Capt. Herman Borris.
16th Ohio Battery, Capt. Russell P. Twist.
14th Rhode Island (Colored), First Battalion, Maj. Joseph J. Comstock.
1st United States, Battery F, Lieut. Hardman P. Norris.

ENGINEER BRIGADE.†

Maj. DAVID C. HOUSTON.

3d Engineers, Corps d'Afrique, Col. George D. Robinson.
4th Engineers, Corps d'Afrique, Lieut. Col. Samuel B. Guernsey.
15th Infantry, Corps d'Afrique, Lieut. Col. Uri B. Pearsall.

DEFENSES OF NEW ORLEANS.‡

Col. EDWARD G. BECKWITH.

1st Indiana Heavy Artillery, Company B, Capt. James Grimsley.
1st Indiana Heavy Artillery, Companies G and M, Capt. Samuel A. Armstrong.
1st Indiana Heavy Artillery, Company K, Capt. Clayton Cox.

* See also the artillery assigned to the several commands. The Fourteenth Rhode Island ordered, December 30, from New Orleans to Texas. Brigadier-General Arnold chief of artillery since December 17, 1862.
† Headquarters at New Orleans; troops at Brashear City. The First and Second Engineer Regiments on detached service in Texas. Major Houston chief of engineers since December 17, 1862.
‡ Colonel Beckwith commanding since August 26. The Fifty-fourth Indiana mustered out December 8, upon expiration of service. The First and Second New Orleans Regiments not reported on returns. The One hundred and thirty-third and One hundred and seventy-sixth New York at Bonnet Carré, under command of Lieutenant-Colonel Hall. The Second Infantry, Corps d'Afrique, and Second U. S. Colored Troops reported at Ship Island, Miss.; the Fifth Infantry, Corps d'Afrique, at Fort Saint Philip, and the Twentieth Infantry, Corps d'Afrique, at Forts Pike, Macomb, and Bienvenue; Fort Jackson detached December 13,

DEFENSES OF NEW ORLEANS—Continued.

2d New Orleans Regiment, Col. R. B. Brown.
3d Massachusetts Cavalry, Company A, Lieut. Henry D. Pope.
15th Massachusetts Battery, Capt. Timothy Pearson.
133d New York, Capt. James K. Fuller.
176th New York, Lieut. Col. Alfred G. Hall.
1st U. S. Infantry, Maj. Maurice Maloney.
1st U. S. Artillery, Battery A, Lieut. Ballard S. Humphrey.
5th U. S. Artillery, Battery G, Lieut. Jacob B. Rawles.
1st Wisconsin Battery, Lieut. Daniel Webster.
1st Cavalry, Corps d'Afrique, Maj. Nathaniel C. Mitchell.
1st Heavy Artillery, Corps d'Afrique (one company), Lieut. Thomas McCormick.
2d Infantry, Corps d'Afrique, Col. William M. Grosvenor.
2d Infantry, U. S. Colored Troops, Lieut. Col. Stark Fellows.
5th Infantry, Corps d'Afrique, Col. Charles A. Hartwell.
20th Infantry, Corps d'Afrique, Col. Eliot Bridgman.
Second Brigade, Fourth Division, Nineteenth Army Corps, Col. Thomas W. Cahill.

DISTRICT OF BATON ROUGE.*

Brig. Gen. P. St. George Cooke.

Baton Rouge, La.

1st Indiana Heavy Artillery (detachment), Capt. Edward McLaflin.
18th New York Battery, Lieut. George G. Curtiss.
2d U. S. Artillery, Battery C, Lieut. John I. Rodgers.
4th Wisconsin Cavalry, Col. Frederick A. Boardman.
Second Brigade, First Division, Nineteenth Army Corps, Col. Jacob Sharpe.

Plaquemine, La.

Col. Lionel A. Sheldon.

7th Kentucky, Lieut. Col. John Lucas.
22d Kentucky, Col. George W. Monroe.
42d Ohio, Maj. Frederick A. Williams.
120th Ohio, Col. Marcus M. Spiegel.
2d Illinois Light Artillery, Battery E, Lieut. Emil Steger.
2d Ohio Battery, Lieut. William H. Harper.
4th Wisconsin Cavalry, Company A, Capt. Henry W. Ross.

DISTRICT OF LA FOURCHE.†

Brig. Gen. Henry W. Birge.

1st Louisiana, Col Willam O. Fiske.
1st Louisiana Cavalry, Company B, Capt. Richard Barrett.
22d Infantry, Corps d'Afrique, Col. Henry N. Frisbie.
1st Indiana Battery, Lieut. Lawrence Jacoby.
26th New York Battery, Capt. George W. Fox.
1st Vermont Battery, Capt. George T. Hebard.
First Brigade, Fourth Division, Nineteenth Army Corps, Brig. Gen. Henry W. Birge.

DISTRICT OF PENSACOLA.

Brig. Gen. Alexander Asboth.‡

14th New York Cavalry, Company M, Capt. Adolph Schmidt.
14th Infantry, Corps d'Afrique, Col. Mardon W. Plumly.
2d U. S. Artillery, Battery H, Capt. Frank H. Larned.
2d U. S. Artillery, Battery K, Capt. Henry A. Smalley.
7th Vermont (six companies), Col. William C. Holbrook.

---

* Brigadier-General Cooke assigned October 8. The infantry at Plaquemine was a detachment from the Third Brigade, First Division, Thirteenth Army Corps.
† Constituted under command of Brigadier-General Birge, October 8, and limits extended October 28; see p. 779. Troops at Brashear City, Donaldsonville, Fort Butler, Napoleonville, along the New Orleans, Opelousas and Great Western Railroad, and at Thibodeaux.
‡ Assigned to command by Special Orders, Nos. 252 and 269, October 8 and 28, Headquarters Department of the Gulf. Assumed command November 9. Colonel Holbrook commanding at Barrancas and Maj. Harvey A. Allen commanding at Fort Pickens.

DISTRICT OF KEY WEST AND TORTUGAS.

Brig. Gen. DANIEL P. WOODBURY.*

47th Pennsylvania (six companies), Col. Tilghman H. Good (Key West).
47th Pennsylvania (four companies), Lieut. Col. George W. Alexander (Tortugas).
Florida Rangers, Lieut. James F. Meyers (Charlotte Harbor).

FORT JACKSON, LA.†

Brig. Gen. WILLIAM DWIGHT.

83d Ohio,‡ Maj. Stephen S. L'Hommedieu, jr.
4th Infantry, Corps d'Afrique, Col. Charles W. Drew.

PORT HUDSON, LA. §

Brig. Gen. GEORGE L. ANDREWS.

3d Massachusetts Cavalry, Col. Lorenzo D. Sargent.
12th Massachusetts Battery, Capt. Jacob Miller.
1st Michigan Heavy Artillery, Lieut. Col. Edward Bacon.
21st New York Battery, Capt. James Barnes.
2d Vermont Battery, Capt. John W. Chase.

CORPS D'AFRIQUE.

Brig. Gen. GEORGE L. ANDREWS

FIRST DIVISION.

Brig. Gen. DANIEL ULLMANN.

First Brigade.	*Second Brigade.*
Col. CHAUNCEY J. BASSETT.	Col. CYRUS HAMLIN.
1st Infantry, Maj. Hiram E. Perkins.	7th Infantry, Col. James C. Clark.
3d Infantry, Col. Henry W. Fuller.	8th Infantry, Lieut. Col. William S.
11th Infantry, Maj. Jasper Hutchings.	Mudgett.
12th Infantry, Maj. Moore Hanham.	9th Infantry, Maj. John C. Chadwick.
	10th Infantry, Col. Ladislas L. Zulavsky.

SECOND DIVISION. ‖

Second Brigade.

Col. SAMUEL B. JONES.

6th Infantry, Capt. Philip S. Cottle.
17th Infantry, Capt. T. Scott De Wolfe.
18th Infantry, Lieut. Col. Robert F. Atkins.

WASHBURN'S COMMAND.

Maj. Gen. CADWALLADER C. WASHBURN.

First Division, Thirteenth Army Corps, Brig. Gen. William P. Benton.
Third Brigade, Second Division, Thirteenth Army Corps, Brig. Gen. T. E. G. Ransom.
Fourth Division, Thirteenth Army Corps, Col. William J. Landram.
1st Indiana Heavy Artillery, Company L, Capt. Isaac C. Hendricks.
Patterson's Independent Company (Kentucky), Capt. William F. Patterson.
19th Infantry, Corps d'Afrique, Col. Charles E. Bostwick.

---

*Assigned to command March 16, 1863.
† Separated from Defenses of New Orleans, and Brigadier-General Dwight assigned to command December 13.
‡ Assigned December 21.
§ Brigadier-General Andrews commanding post and Corps d'Afrique since July 10, 1863. Brigadier-General Ullmann assigned to command of First Division, Corps d'Afrique, September 22.
‖ The First Brigade disintegrated.

THIRTEENTH ARMY CORPS.

Maj. Gen. NAPOLEON J. T. DANA.

FIRST DIVISION.*

Brig. Gen. WILLIAM P. BENTON.

First Brigade.

Brig. Gen. FITZ HENRY WARREN.

33d Illinois, Lieut. Col. Leander H. Potter.
99th Illinois, Col. George W. K. Bailey.
8th Indiana, Col. David Shunk.
18th Indiana, Col. Henry D. Washburn.

Second Brigade.

Col. CHARLES L. HARRIS.

21st Iowa, Maj. William D. Crooke.
22d Iowa, Lieut. Col. Harvey Graham.
23d Iowa, Col. Samuel L. Glasgow.
11th Wisconsin, Lieut. Col. Luther H. Whittlesey.

Third Brigade.†

Col. JAMES KEIGWIN.

49th Indiana, Major Arthur J. Hawhe.
69th Indiana, Lieut. Col. Oran Perry.
16th Ohio, Lieut. Col. Philip Kershner.
114th Ohio, Lieut. Col. John H. Kelly.

Artillery.

7th Michigan Battery, Lieutenant George L. Stillman.

SECOND DIVISION.‡

Maj. Gen. NAPOLEON J. T. DANA.

First Brigade.

Col. [JOHN] CHARLES BLACK.

37th Illinois, Col. [John] Charles Black.
91st Illinois, Col. Henry M. Day.
26th Indiana, Col. John G. Clark.
38th Iowa, Maj. Charles Chadwick.

Second Brigade.

Col. WILLIAM McE. DYE.

94th Illinois, Col. John McNulta.
19th Iowa, Major John Bruce.
20th Iowa, Maj. William G. Thompson.
20th Wisconsin, Col. Henry Bertram.

Third Brigade.

Brig. Gen. THOMAS E. G. RANSOM.§

34th Iowa, Lieut. Col. Warren S. Dungan.
13th Maine, Lieut. Col. Frank S. Hesseltine.
15th Maine, Col. Isaac Dyer.

Artillery.

1st Missouri Light, Battery B, Capt. Martin Welfley.
1st Missouri Light, Battery E, Capt. Joseph B. Atwater.
1st Missouri Light, Battery F, Capt. Joseph Foust.

---

* The First Brigade at Indianola; the other troops at Decrow's Point, Tex. Brigadier-General Benton assumed command December 15; Brigadier-General Warren assigned to duty with Thirteenth Army Corps, November 14.

† Colonel Keigwin, commanding since December 23. The Seventh and Twenty-second Kentucky, and the Forty-second and One hundred and twentieth Ohio, of this brigade, at Plaquemine, La. The Forty-ninth Indiana probably at Algiers, La.

‡ Major-General Dana, commanding since September 28. Brigadier-General William Vandever, relieved November 11, at his own request, from command of First Brigade, and ordered to report to commanding general Department of the Tennessee. Division headquarters, the First and Second Brigades, the cavalry, and Batteries B and E, First Missouri Light, at Brownsville; the Third Brigade on Matagorda Island, and Battery F, First Missouri Light Artillery, at Decrow's Point.

§ Ordered by General Banks, October 30, to report for duty to Brigadier-General Dana.

Cavalry.

Col. EDMUND J. DAVIS.

1st Texas.
2d Texas, Capt. Clemente Zapata.
Partisan Rangers (one company).

Detachments at Brownsville, Tex.

1st Engineers, Corps d'Afrique (one company) ⎫ Maj. E. Manville Hamilton.
16th Infantry, Corps d'Afrique (two companies) ⎭
Pioneers (one company), Capt. Alden H. Jumper.
Provost-guard (one company), Capt. Charles Altman.

Troops at Point Isabel, Tex.

Col. JUSTIN HODGE.

1st Engineers, Corps d'Afrique, Lieut. Col. Arthur F. Wrotnouski.
2d Engineers, Corps d'Afrique, Col. John C. Cobb.
16th Infantry, Corps d'Afrique, Col. Matthew C. Kempsey.

THIRD DIVISION.*

Brig. Gen. GEORGE F. McGINNIS.

First Brigade.	*Second Brigade.*
Col. DANIEL MACAULEY.†	• Col. WILLIAM H. RAYNOR.
11th Indiana, Maj. George Butler.	47th Indiana, Maj. Lewis H. Goodwin.
24th Indiana, Maj. John F. Grill.	24th Iowa, Maj. Edward Wright.
34th Indiana, Col. Robert B. Jones.	28th Iowa, Col. John Connell.
46th Indiana (six companies), Col. Aaron M. Flory.	56th Ohio, Lieut. Col. Sampson E. Varner.
29th Wisconsin, Maj. Bradford Hancock.	

Artillery.

1st Missouri Light, Battery A, Lieut. Elisha Cole.

FOURTH DIVISION.‡

Col. WILLIAM J. LANDRAM.

First Brigade.	*Second Brigade.*
Lieut. Col. JOHN COWAN.	Maj. MEMOIR V. HOTCHKISS.‖
60th Indiana, Lieut. Col. Augustus Goelzer.	77th Illinois, Capt. Joseph M. McCollough.
67th Indiana, Maj. Francis A. Sears.	130th Illinois, Maj. John B. Reid.
19th Kentucky, Maj. Josiah J. Mann.	48th Ohio, Capt. John A. Bering.
83d Ohio,§ Maj. S. S. L'Hommedieu, jr.	
96th Ohio, Col. Joseph W. Vance.	
23d Wisconsin, Maj. Joseph E. Greene.	

Artillery.

Chicago Mercantile Battery, Capt. Patrick H. White.
17th Ohio Battery, Capt. Charles S. Rice.

---

* Brigadier-General McGinnis assigned to command, September 13, the division (excepting the Thirty-fourth and part of the Forty-sixth Indiana, already embarked), at Algiers, La., under orders to proceed to Fort Esperanza, Pass Cavallo, Tex.
† Commanding, vice Brig. Gen. Robert A. Cameron, detached on special service.
‡ Colonel Landram commanding, vice Brig. Gen. S. G. Burbridge, relieved by Special Orders, No. 83, Headquarters Nineteenth Army Corps and United States Forces, December 5, and granted leave of absence by Special Orders, No. 307, Department of the Gulf, December 9. The infantry of the division was reorganized, as herein indicated, by Special Orders, No. 70, Headquarters Nineteenth Army Corps, November 21, and the division ordered December 11, 15, and 16, from Algiers, La., to Fort Esperanza, Tex. (Special Orders, Nos. 309, 313, and 314, Department of the Gulf, of those dates), and reported December 31, both as *en route* to and at Decrow's Point, Tex.
§ At Fort Jackson, La., assigned to that post by Special Orders, No. 21, Department of the Gulf, December 21, 1863.
‖ Assigned to command December 5, vice Col. David P. Grier, ordered north on recruiting service.

NINETEENTH ARMY CORPS.*

Maj. Gen. WILLIAM B. FRANKLIN.

FIRST DIVISION.

Brig. Gen. WILLIAM H. EMORY.†

First Brigade.

Col. GEORGE M. LOVE.‡

Massachusetts, Maj. H. O. Whitte-
more.
New York, Lieut. Col. John Hig-
gins.
New York, Lieut. Col. William B.
Kinsey.
New York, Maj. George Keating.

Second Brigade.§

Col. JACOB SHARPE.

38th Massachusetts, Lieut. Col. James P.
Richardson.
128th New York, Maj. Francis S. Keese.
156th New York, Capt. Alfred Neafie.
175th New York, Capt. Charles McCarthey.

Third Brigade.

Col ROBERT B. MERRITT.‖

12th Connecticut, Lieut. Col. Frank H. Peck.
114th New York, Lieut. Col. Henry B. Morse.
160th New York, Maj. William H. Sentell.
8th Vermont, Maj. Henry F. Dutton.

Artillery.

1st Maine Battery, Capt. Albert W. Bradbury.
6th Massachusetts Battery, Lieut. Edward K. Russell.

THIRD DIVISION.

Brig. Gen. CUVIER GROVER.

First Brigade.

Col. LEWIS BENEDICT.

New York, Lieut. Col. Warren D.
Smith.
New York, Lieut. Col. Justus W.
Blanchard.
New York (six companies), Lieut.
Col. Goaverneur Carr.
New York, Col. Lewis M. Peck.

Second Brigade.

Brig. Gen. JAMES W. McMILLAN.

14th Maine, Col. Thomas W. Porter.
26th Massachusetts, Col. Alpha B. Farr.

Artillery.

4th Massachusetts Battery, Lieut. George W. Taylor.

---

ae corps, with exceptions indicated, at and about New Iberia, La., Major-Gen-
'ranklin commanding since August 20, 1863.
)mmanding since December 13, vice Weitzel, ordered to report in person at
·tment headquarters for orders by Special Orders, No. 87, Headquarters Nine-
h Army Corps, December 9, 1863.
)mmanding since July 24, 1863.
; Baton Rouge, La., Colonel Sharpe commanding since November —, 1863.
mmanding since July 10, 1863.

FOURTH DIVISION.

Col. EDWARD G. BECKWITH.

*First Brigade.**	*Second Brigade.†*
Brig. Gen. HENRY W. BIRGE.	Col. THOMAS W. CAHILL.
13th Connecticut, Col. Charles D. Blinn.	9th Connecticut, Lieut. Col. Richard Fitz
90th New York, Col. Joseph S. Morgan.	Gibbons.
91st New York, Lieut. Col. Jonathan	97th Illinois, Col. Friend S. Rutherford.
Tarbell.	1st Louisiana, Col. William O. Fiske.
131st New York, Capt. Francis A. Howell.	12th Maine, Col. William K. Kimball.
159th New York, Lieut. Col. Charles A.	
Burt.	

Artillery Reserve.

Capt. HENRY W. CLOSSON.

25th New York Light, Capt. John A. Grow.
1st United States, Battery L, Lieut. James A. Sanderson.

Unattached.‡

25th Infantry, Corps d'Afrique, Col. Simon Jones.

CAVALRY DIVISION.§

Brig. Gen. ALBERT L. LEE.

First Brigade.	*Third Brigade.*
Lieut. Col. JAMES H. REDFIELD.	Col. CHARLES J. PAINE.
	2d Illinois (seven companies), Col. John
87th Illinois,‖ Maj. George W. Land.	J. Mudd.
16th Indiana,‖ Capt. Charles T. Doxey.	4th Indiana, Company C, Capt. Andrew
1st Louisiana, Maj. Harai Robinson.	P. Gallagher.
75th New York,‖ Maj. Benjamin F. Thur-	2d Louisiana,‖ Maj. Alfred Hodsdon.
ber.	6th Missouri (seven companies), Capt.
	Sidney A. Breese.
Second Brigade.	14th New York (six companies), Col. Abra-
Col. JOHN G. FONDA.	ham Bassford.
	Fourth Brigade.
3d Illinois (five companies), Maj. James	Col. NATHAN A. M. DUDLEY.
H. O'Connor.	
118th Illinois,‖ Lieut. Col. Thomas Logan.	31st Massachusetts, Lieut. Col. William
	S. B. Hopkins.
	8th New Hampshire,‖ Col. H. Fearing, jr.

Unassigned.

15th Illinois Cavalry, Company F,¶ Lieut. Peter Phillips.
36th Illinois,‖ Company A, Capt. George A. Willis.
1st Indiana Cavalry, Company C,¶ Capt. James L. Carey.
2d Louisiana Cavalry (one company),¶ Col. Daniel J. Keily.
3d Maryland Cavalry (five companies),¶ Maj. Byron Kirby.
2d Massachusetts Battery, Capt. Ormand F. Nims.
Mounted Rangers, Company A, Capt. Samuel White.
Headquarters Cavalry, Company C,¶ Capt. F. Sayles.

---

* In the District of La Fourche, La.
† In the Defenses of New Orleans, La.
‡ At New Iberia, La.
§ Division headquarters at New Orleans. The First and Third Brigades, White's
Mounted Rangers, Company A, Thirty-sixth Illinois, and Nims' battery, in the field
near New Iberia, under command of Col. Thomas J. Lucas. The Second Brigade at
Donaldsonville, under orders for Port Hudson, and return of Third Massachusetts
Cavalry ordered to New Orleans. The Fourth Brigade being organized at New Or-
leans.
‖ Infantry, mounted.
¶ At New Orleans.

Abstract from returns of the Department of New Mexico, Brig. Gen. James H. Carleton,* U. S. Army, commanding, for the month of December, 1863; headquarters, Santa Fé, N. Mex.

Command.	Present for duty.		Aggregate present.	Aggregate present and absent.	Aggregate last return.	Pieces of artillery.	
	Officers.	Men.				Heavy.	Field.
Department staff...............................	24	....	24	26	27	......	......
Fort Marcy, N. Mex. (Capt. J. Updegraff), Fifth U. S. Infantry; First Infantry, New Mexico Volunteers.	3	47	58	87	13	......	......
Fort Union, N. Mex. (Lieut. Col. W. McMullen), Fifth U. S. and Seventh U. S. Infantry; First Infantry, and First Cavalry, California Volunteers; First Infantry, New Mexico Volunteers.	8	213	259	324	321	2	4
Fort Union Depot, N. Mex. (Capt. W. R. Shoemaker, military storekeeper), company of ordnance.	......	11	12	12	14	......	......
Fort Sumner. N. Mex. (Maj. H. D. Wallen), Fifth and Seventh U. S. Infantry; First Infantry, California Volunteers; Second Cavalry, California Volunteers.	4	102	161	219	147	......	......
Fort Stanton, N. Mex. (Maj. J. Smith), Fifth Infantry, California Volunteers; First Cavalry, New Mexico Volunteers.	2	23	72	145	147	......	......
Fort Wingate, N. Mex. (Capt. J. C. Shaw), First Cavalry, New Mexico Volunteers.	3	71	107	183	293	......	......
Albuquerque, N. Mex. (Capt. D. H. Brotherton), Third U. S. Artillery; Fifth U. S. Infantry; First Infantry, New Mexico Volunteers.	5	165	204	249	157	......	4
Los Pinos, N. Mex. (Lieut. M. Mullens), Fifth U. S. Infantry.	2	22	43	83	86	......	......
Fort Bascom, N. Mex. (Capt. E. H. Bergmann), Seventh U. S. Infantry; First Cavalry, New Mexico Volunteers.	3	40	85	110	110	......	......
Fort Craig, N. Mex. (Col. E. A. Rigg), First and Fifth Infantry, California Volunteers; First Cavalry, California Volunteers.	5	111	179	402	311	4	13
Mesilla, N. Mex. (Capt. J. S. Thayer), Fifth Infantry, California Volunteers; First Infantry, New Mexico Volunteers.	5	139	160	167	162	......	4
Franklin, Tex. (Col. G. W. Bowie), Fifth Infantry, California Volunteers; First Cavalry, California Volunteers.	7	126	148	157	94	......	......
Fort West, N. Mex. (Capt. J. H. Whitlock), First and Fifth Infantry, California Volunteers.	2	105	125	127	127	......	......
Fort Bowie, Ariz. (Capt. T. T. Tidball), Fifth Infantry, California Volunteers.	2	43	56	56	56	......	2
Tucson, Ariz. (Lieut. Col. T. A. Coult), Fifth Infantry, California Volunteers.	2	44	70	114	120	......	......
Las Cruces, N. Mex. (Maj. William McCleave), Fifth Infantry, California Volunteers.	5	79	112	142	211	......	......
Fort McRae, N. Mex. (Capt. H. A. Greene), First Infantry, California Volunteers.	1	37	55	77	77	......	......
Fort Cummings, N. Mex. (Lieut. S. R. De Long), First Infantry, California Volunteers.	......	44	51	63	64	......	......
En route to New Mexico, Fifth U. S. Infantry; First Infantry, California Volunteers; First Infantry, New Mexico Volunteers.	....	....	....	....	187	......	......
Valles Grandes, N. Mex. (Lieut. C. A. Curtis), Fifth Infantry, California Volunteers.	1	33	39	49	49	......	......
Camp Miembres, N. Mex. (Capt. C. R. Wellman), First Cavalry, California Volunteers.	2	59	76	154	157	......	......
En route to Fort Whipple (Maj. E. B. Willis), First Infantry, California Volunteers.	3	79	119	138	139	......	......
Fort Canby, N. Mex. (Col. C. Carson), First Cavalry, New Mexico Volunteers.	17	460	582	718	622	......	......
Total	107	2,053	2,797	3,802	3,691	6	27

*Brig. Gen. Joseph R. West commanding District of Arizona.

COLUMBUS, KY.,
January 6, 1864.

Major-General HALLECK,
General-in-Chief:

Package relating to complaint of the interruption of stores *en route* for General Banks is received, and shall receive my immediate attention. You know General McPherson well enough to agree with me that he would not do such a thing without some good reason, or in consequence of some mistake. I will assure General Banks that, instead of taking his provisions, we stand prepared at all times to share our own with him.

W. T. SHERMAN,
Major-General.

WAR DEPARTMENT,
Washington City, January 8, 1864.

SECRETARY OF STATE,
Washington, D. C.:

SIR: The Secretary of War instructs me to transmit for your information the inclosed copy of a letter of the 26th ultimo from Major-General Banks, commanding Department of the Gulf, on the subject of your dispatch to him of the 12th ultimo, with the approval of this Department thereon indorsed, giving him the control over all intercourse arising out of the war with the insurgents in Texas or with the Government of Mexico, or any of its citizens.

I have the honor to be, your obedient servant,

ED. R. S. CANBY,
Brigadier-General, and Assistant Adjutant-General.

[Inclosure.]

HEADQUARTERS DEPARTMENT OF THE GULF,
New Orleans, December 26, 1863.

Hon. E. M. STANTON,
Secretary of War, Washington, D. C.:

SIR: A dispatch from the Secretary of State, with your indorsement thereon, directing that a copy of the instructions upon the subject of our relations with Mexico be sent to Brigadier-General Hamilton, was this day received. The papers have been forwarded as directed.

Major-General Herron assumes command on the Rio Grande, in place of Major-General Dana, having left the city yesterday for this purpose. A copy of the dispatch was given him. He is an officer of rank, of excellent capacity and address, and will make every exertion to maintain undisturbed the present relations existing between all parties in interest in Mexico and this country. Major-General Dana will assume command of the Thirteenth Army Corps as soon as he is relieved by General Herron.

It gives me pleasure to say that my relations with General Hamilton are entirely satisfactory, and I have no doubt we shall be able to discharge the duties assigned to us without any unpleasant results.

I have the honor to be, with much respect, your obedient servant,

N. P. BANKS,
Major-General, Commanding.

NEW ORLEANS,
January 13, 1864.

Major-General WASHBURN:

GENERAL: The report of General Warren, dated December 11, 1863, gives a very satisfactory account of his march to Lavaca, and its influence cannot but be favorable both upon the troops and the people. These expeditions are productive of good results, but great care should be taken against surprise. The policy of Magruder will be to lie in wait with a large force to cut off detachments of our troops, and it is certain to succeed, except by extreme vigilance on our part in the execution of these expeditions.

I am very anxious that such fortifications may be constructed at Indianola as will enable us to hold that position with safety; and with the advantage which you describe as likely to be derived from it by our troops, their position will be greatly improved. I hope soon to be able to concentrate such a force there as to make our movement against Magruder's army a certain success. At present his army is stronger than ours. I beg you to convey my compliments to General Warren, and say that I am very glad of his success.

I have the honor to be, with much respect, your obedient servant,

N. P. BANKS,
Major-General, Commanding.

HEADQUARTERS DEPARTMENT OF THE TENNESSEE,
Vicksburg, January 29, 1864.

Col. J. C. KELTON,
Assistant Adjutant-General to the General-in-Chief:

SIR: On the 6th instant I acknowledged to General Halleck the receipt of his letter of December 28, 1863, inclosing copies of letters from Colonel Holabird and Captain Armstrong, of the quartermaster's department at New Orleans, and instructing me to report the facts in the case, and give such orders as would prevent a recurrence of the matters complained of. I have made the orders, and now inclose General McPherson's report of the facts, with inclosures.

I need add to General McPherson's report nothing but the renewal of my assertion, that we stand prepared to share with General Banks our supplies, but must take exception to the language and manner of Colonel Holabird in making his complaint.

I am fully aware of the scarcity of forage north, and have impressed on my command the necessity of fighting for our forage out of the abundant cornfields of the south.

I am, with great respect, your obedient servant,

W. T. SHERMAN,
Major-General, Commanding.

[Inclosure No. 1.]

HDQRS. 17TH ARMY CORPS, DEPT. OF THE TENNESSEE,
Vicksburg, Miss., January 20, 1864.

Maj. Gen. WILLIAM T. SHERMAN,
Commanding Army, Department of the Tennessee:

GENERAL: I have the honor to acknowledge the receipt of letter to you from the General-in-Chief, dated Washington, December 28, 1863, and inclosing extract of letter from Col. S. B. Holabird, chief quarter-master, Department of the Gulf, and Capt. W. B. Armstrong, acting quartermaster, in relation to the stopping of coal, forage, &c., in this district, which was *in transitu* from the Upper Mississippi to that department. In reply and explanation of the course pursued here, I inclose the following papers, viz:

1. Report from Capt. W. C. Hurlbut, depot quartermaster.
2. Report from G. L. Fort, master transportation.
3. Copy of letter to Capt. A. R. Eddy, Memphis.
4. Copy of letter from Capt. A. R. Eddy, Memphis.
5. Copy of letter to Major [E. D.] Osband, Skipwith's Landing.

From these reports you will see that no efforts have been spared to procure necessary supplies for my command, and that the only seizures made have been 7,218 sacks of grain and 8,660 bushels of coal; that the amounts of forage due on the estimates for October, November, and December are 16,405,024 pounds of grain and 32,013,291 pounds of hay; in other words, we have only received about one-half the grain called for, and one-fifteenth part of the hay, and that during the months of October and November we received only about one-fifth of the grain, and one-eleventh part of the hay estimated for.

The grain was stopped by my order, but not until every effort had been made to procure forage from the country, and then only after repeated reports from my chiefs of cavalry and artillery that their horses were starving, and the former declared his inability to go on scouts and expeditions owing to the reduced state of his animals, and that it would take thirty days to bring them back to anything like an effective condition, with rest and plenty of forage.

There is corn in this country, but at the time the seizure was made it was impracticable to get it out, owing to the low stage of water in the Yazoo, Mississippi, and their tributaries.

No officer in the Department of the Gulf reported, or even intimated, that their animals were suffering for want of forage. They had two routes open to them to receive supplies, and I did not imagine for a moment that they were in as straightened circumstances as we were here.

Before the receipt by me of the letter from the General-in-Chief, the steamer Northerner came up for forage, the officer in charge of her stating that the animals in the Department of the Gulf were badly off for want of it.

We had only a few days' supply on hand, but I directed the quartermaster to load the steamboat Pringle, which had just arrived with part of a cargo for this place, and send her to New Orleans, which was done, and she carried down 5,111 sacks.

Troops were put on board the Northerner, and she was sent up the river in the neighborhood of Greenville and Bolivar, the officer in command, Brigadier-General Leggett, being instructed to disperse the enemy, who were making demonstrations on the river in that vicinity, and, if possible, load the steamer with corn. The corn could not be obtained, and immediately on the return of the expedition, 2,107 sacks of grain were put on board, and she was sent down, thus balancing the grain account.

The last 2,107 sacks were sent after the receipt of the communications from Washington. The 8,660 bushels of coal were stopped, but it was distinctly stated that there was plenty of coal in New Orleans, and that the authorities were selling to private steamers, whereas we had none for our machine and repair shops. Furthermore, the agent who had it in charge stated it was private coal, which was to be sold in New Orleans at contract price, and he was desirous of leaving the whole of it here. The statements of Colonel Holabird and Captain Armstrong are not only reckless and unjust, but they are false in many particulars. When Colonel Holabird wrote his letter, not a pound of coal consigned to the Department of the Gulf had been stopped within the limits of my command; but, on the contrary, we had nearly stripped ourselves to send to them.

Captain Armstrong says orders have been issued at Vicksburg to stop all supplies, &c.; that we make no estimates, but leave others to do the work, and then piratically take the supplies without trying to obtain them in a legitimate manner.

No such order was ever issued, or thought of being issued, and estimates have been made out and forwarded promptly, as the accompanying papers show.

Instead of trying to impede or throw obstacles in the way of supplies going down, I have always endeavored to expedite matters, and have ever been willing to divide with them anything I had. We have taken mules out of our trains to send them, and have sent beef-cattle, when we had to go out the next day and forage through the country to get a supply for our own command.

The reckless, unscrupulous assertions of Colonel Holabird and Captain Armstrong are but a poor recompense for what we have endeavored to do to assist them, but only what might be expected from officers who look more to pomp and official dignity than the real interests of the service.

Very respectfully, your obedient servant,

JAS. B. McPHERSON,
Major-General.

[Sub-Inclosure No. 1.]

DEPARTMENT QUARTERMASTER'S OFFICE,
Vicksburg, Miss., January 20, 1864.

Maj. Gen. J. B. McPHERSON,
Commanding Seventeenth Army Corps:

GENERAL: My attention has been called to a communication addressed to the Quartermaster-General at Washington by Colonel Holabird and Captain Armstrong, assistant quartermaster, New Orleans, in which they have made a complaint, accusing us of seizing quartermaster's stores consigned to them.

During the time that I have discharged the duties of this office in the months of October, November, and December, 1863, the only seizures we have made are two consignments of grain, amounting to 1,081,558 pounds, and 8,660 bushels of coal.

To counterbalance the amount of grain taken, we have made two shipments to New Orleans, one of 5,111 sacks, amounting to 776,018 pounds, per steamer Pringle, and the other of 2,107 sacks, amounting to 305,540 pounds, per steamer Northerner.

No horses, mules, or any stores have been stopped here, with the exception of the above.

Stock arriving at this point consigned to New Orleans have invariably been out of forage, and we have always promptly furnished whatever amount was needed to sustain them to destination.

I would respectfully state that at the time the coal was seized the quartermasters at New Orleans had a large quantity on hand, whereas we had not received any for six months, although several estimates had been forwarded in tnat time.

We have also shipped to the Department of the Gulf 1,200 serviceable mules, of which 300 were sent from Natchez, and the remaining 900 from this place. Yet, in spite of all this, they have made representations to the authorities at Washington which are highly detrimental to us. I would respectfully state that numerous estimates for various supplies needed at this post have been forwarded to the proper officers, as also many duplicates to the same, to which, I am sorry to say, the necessary attention has not been given.

Respectfully submitting the foregoing for your consideration, I am, general, your most obedient servant,

W. C. HURLBUT,
Captain, and Assistant Quartermaster.

Report of amount of forage estimated for, and the amount received, for the months of October, November, and December, 1863.

Month.	Amount estimated for.		Amount received.	
	Grain.	Hay.	Grain.	Hay.
	Pounds.	*Pounds.*	*Pounds.*	*Pounds.*
October	12, 363, 720	14, 420, 740	2, 713, 988	77, 000
November	9, 102, 666	10, 213, 333	1, 645, 824	1, 556, 473
December	8, 560, 000	9, 750, 000	9, 261, 550	737, 309
Total	30, 026, 386	34, 384, 073	13, 621, 362	2, 370, 782
Amount due on estimates			16, 405, 024	32, 013, 291

[Sub-Inclosure No. 2.]

ASSISTANT QUARTERMASTER'S OFFICE,
Vicksburg, Miss., January 4, 1864.

Capt. SAMUEL TAGGART, *Assistant Adjutant-General:*

The steamer Collier has just arrived with a tow of nine barges of coal, estimated to contain 125,000 bushels of coal. I am informed by the captain of the boat that it is private coal, and is to be sold to the Government at a contract price on its arrival in New Orleans. The steamer Porter is still in port with about 25,000 bushels of coal belonging to the quartermaster's department, and this is also consigned to New Orleans. About 8,000 bushels of the original amount that the Porter had has been ordered to be detained.

We are in great need of coal, and thought best to notify you of the fact, so that you could take such measures as you think best.

G. L. FORT,
Captain, and Assistant Quartermaster.

ASSISTANT QUARTERMASTER'S OFFICE,
Vicksburg, Miss., January 16, 1864.

Colonel CLARK, *Assistant Adjutant-General:*

I have the honor to respectfully report that up to December 1, 1863, not one single bushel of coal which was *en route* to the Department of the Gulf was ever seized by Major-General McPherson or any other authority, or in any manner stopped or detained at Vicksburg, Miss., to my knowledge. And, having been in charge of river transportation at this post since the middle of August last, I certainly would have known if anything of the kind had been done. And since December 1, 1863, only about 7,000 or 8,000 bushels have been taken at this post, and that was when there was not a bushel of coal at the post, and was taken from fleets of coal-boats containing about 150,000 bushels.

I would further state that on the 2d day of September last, there then being less than 20,000 bushels of coal at this post, I was ordered to send and did send 15,000 bushels of that amount to New Orleans for the use of the Department of the Gulf, and at the same time had no coal under way for us, and expected none, and have received none, excepting what we raised and reclaimed from barges that had been sunk last winter.

The tow-boat with which I sent the 15,000 bushels was stopped at Port Hudson, and 2,500 bushels taken out, for which I had trouble and long delay in obtaining receipts.

Very little forage has been stopped here to my knowledge, I think only when further transportation could not then conveniently be furnished, and I am certain that far less has been stopped here than has been reshipped from here to the Department of the Gulf.

Very large quantities have been forwarded from time to time of the supplies for the forces at this place. The undersigned would take the present occasion to respectfully state that Major-General McPherson, commanding the Seventeenth Army Corps, has always not only been careful to avoid delay in the transportation of supplies to the Department of the Gulf, but in his orders and by his personal attention has directed that they should be forwarded with all possible speed, which has been done.

Our own steamers have been employed for that purpose even when they were needed in this department. And when our steamers have been sent down with supplies to that department, officers at New Orleans board them as soon as they land, and demand and collect freight on all private shipments, and passenger money, and will not allow any private freight to be shipped, or private citizen to take passage, until the money has been paid to them; and, upon application to have this money paid over to this department, as was done through Colonel Bingham, chief quartermaster, Department of Tennessee, in the case of the Clara Bell, payment or tranfer was refused.

The steamers of this department have been largely engaged in transporting supplies to that department, and their steamers have been cheerfully fueled, supplied, loaded, and sent forward, and in all this General McPherson has manifested the most cheerful good feelings, and a desire to aid in forwarding supplies to the Department of the Gulf, the same as in any other service to the common cause in which all the armies of the Government are engaged.

I have the honor to be, very respectfully, your obedient servant,

G. L. FORT,
Captain, and Assistant Quartermaster.

[Sub-Inclosure No. 3.]

HDQRS. 17TH ARMY CORPS, DEPT. OF THE TENNESSEE,
Vicksburg, Miss., November 16, 1863.

Capt. A. R. EDDY, Assistant Quartermaster, Memphis, Tenn.:

CAPTAIN: I beg respectfully to call your attention to the fact that, since the 1st day of October, this command has been without a supply of forage. The estimates have been promptly forwarded, but have not been filled.

There are over 3,000 animals in this command to-day, with not a spear of hay or a grain of oats for issue. I herewith inclose consolidated estimate for December.* Similar estimates have been forwarded for the month of November.

There is great carelessness or inefficiency somewhere; and the evil should be remedied forthwith, and thus prevent great loss to the Government and secure efficiency in this command.

No grain or forage of any kind can be procured from the country.

Very respectfully, your obedient servant,

JAS. B. McPHERSON,
Major-General.

—

[Sub-Inclosure No. 4.]

DEPOT QUARTERMASTER'S OFFICE,
Memphis, Tenn., November 25, 1863.

Maj. Gen. J. B. McPHERSON,
Commanding Seventeenth Army Corps, Vicksburg, Miss..

GENERAL: I have the honor to acknowledge the receipt of your letter of the 16th instant, in regard to the want of the necessary forage at Vicksburg, and in reply would state that this depot had been entirely destitute of a supply sufficient to feed the animals at this place, until, on the 19th instant, when I received five barges of hay. I turned over two barges for transportation to Captain Hurlbut, assistant quartermaster, and on yesterday sent 1,400 sacks of grain for same, the first grain I have had this month that could be sent.

I am advised from Saint Louis that the cause of the trouble has been occasioned by the immense amount required by the Army of the Cumberland; that the command has now been plentifully supplied, and that as soon as boats can be obtained, this depot will be supplied also.

I shall forward as rapidly as possible.

I am, general, very respectfully, your obedient servant,
A. R. EDDY,
Assistant Quartermaster.

[Sub-Inclosure No. 5.]

HDQRS. 17TH ARMY CORPS, DEPT. OF THE TENNESSEE,
Vicksburg, Miss., November 23, 1863.

Maj. E. D. OSBAND, *Commanding at Skipwith's Landing:*

MAJOR: This will be handed you by Captain [David H.] Gile, who returns on the boat for the purpose of procuring forage for our animals. The urgency is great and immediate.

We have over 3,000 animals here, and nothing for them to eat, and have not had for several days.

You will take corn wherever you can find it, as a military necessity, without reference to protection papers, giving proper receipts, so that those who are loyal can get their pay.

Your proper attention to this matter will be the means of saving the lives of many valuable horses and mules.

Very respectfully, your obedient servant,
JAS. B. McPHERSON,
Major-General.

---

* Omitted.

[Inclosure No. 2.]

ASSISTANT QUARTERMASTER'S OFFICE,
Memphis, January 21, 1864.

Maj. Gen. WILLIAM T. SHERMAN,
   Comdg. Department of the Tennessee, Memphis, Tenn.:

GENERAL: In reply to your inquiry of this morning, whether supplies destined for the army operating under Major-General Banks had ever been taken possession of or detained at this port, I have the honor to report that since the 13th day of July, 1863, I have had charge of the transportation from this port; that since then every facility has been afforded transports arriving here from above and destined for New Orleans with public property; that I am not aware of a single instance where such supplies have been diverted or a boat detained; that supplies have been forwarded from this depot to meet the demands of the army in the Department of the Gulf, as follows, when the Army of the Tennessee were in need of the same:

July 28, 1863, per steamer Continental, 3,932 bales (1,413,460 pounds) hay and 120,000 pounds oats; October 3, 1863, per steamer Home and barges, 3,562 bales (1,127,735 pounds) hay; December 21, 1863, per steamer Porter and barges, 50,613 bushels coal.

In consequence of the coal having been forwarded from here, I have not a single bushel for issue to-day, nor has there been any at the depot for about one week.

Very respectfully, your obedient servant,
J. V. LEWIS,
Captain, and Assistant Quartermaster.

[Inclosure No. 3.]

HDQRS. 17TH ARMY CORPS, DEPT. OF THE TENNESSEE,
Vicksburg, January 18, 1864.

Maj. Gen. J. B. MCPHERSON,
   Comdg. District of Northern Mississippi, Vicksburg, Miss.:

GENERAL: In respect to the amount of subsistence forwarded from the depot of this command, I have the honor to inclose herewith a letter from Capt. J. B. Gilpin, commissary of subsistence, which will explain the reason why a more detailed statement is impracticable at the present day.

The shipments mentioned by him were made by my order, and were intended to amount to 2,000 barrels of pork and 1,000,000 pounds of pilot bread. The order was given at the request of Col. T. J. Haines, chief commissary of subsistence at Saint Louis, Mo.

In conformity with what I knew to be your intentions, I have been careful to extend all facilities within my control to the command of the Department of the Gulf.

During the months of October and November last we were insufficiently supplied with fresh beef, and frequently were without any in the hands of the contractors, owing to the necessity of using all available transportation for the supply of other posts. For weeks at a time we were obliged to forage for our supplies in an almost exhausted section of country; yet during this time, and frequently, large cargoes of cattle passed by this post *en route* for the Department of the Gulf. Though I frequently was urged to detain here at least sufficient for the supply of our hospitals, I was so fully satisfied that you would not approve such action, that I never brought the subject to your notice, and while I thought our claims did not receive their due consideration, I got over the difficulty as best I could, without abridging the supplies in tended for the command below a particle. It is now and ever has been my object to assist in every possible manner within my authority any portion of the army that requires my duty.

Very respectfully, your obedient servant,

JOHN C. COX,

Lieut. Col., and Chief Commissary of Subsistence, 17th A. C.

OFFICE DEPOT COMMISSARY,
Vicksburg, Miss., January 18, 1864.

Colonel [Cox]:

I had placed to the order of Colonel Beckwith about 250,000 pounds pilot bread. I have had no order to ship it, however, and now our corps is living on the stock in hand, as per statement now furnished you.

I have sent to New Orleans as follows: Two steamboat-loads of pilot bread and meat. Captain [Richard E.] Davies has all the papers relating to said shipment, and I cannot give you the amount.

Respectfully, your obedient servant,

J. B. GILPIN,

Captain, and Commissary of Subsistence.

APPENDIX.

Embracing documents received too late for insertion in proper sequence.

·REPORTS, ETC.

Resolution of thanks of Congress to Maj. Gen. Nathaniel P. Banks, U. S. Army, and his command.

GENERAL ORDERS, } WAR DEPT., ADJT. GENERAL'S OFFICE,
No. 41. } *Washington, February* 1, 1864.

The following resolution of the Senate and House of Representatives is published to the Army :

I. PUBLIC RESOLUTION—NO. 7.

A RESOLUTION expressive of the thanks of Congress to Maj. Gen. Nathaniel P. Banks, and the officers and soldiers under his command, at Port Hudson.

Resolved by the Senate and House of Representatives of the United States of America in Congress assembled, That the thanks of Congress are hereby tendered to Maj. Gen. Nathaniel P. Banks, and the officers and soldiers under his command, for the skill, courage, and endurance which compelled the surrender of Port Hudson, and thus removed the last obstruction to the free navigation of the Mississippi River.

Approved January 28, 1864.

By order of the Secretary of War :

E. D. TOWNSEND,
Assistant Adjutant-General.

Reports of Col. John A. Keith, First Indiana Heavy Artillery.

HEADQUARTERS FIRST INDIANA ARTILLERY,
Port Hudson, July 14, 1863.

GENERAL: In compliance with your order to submit a report of the ordnance, ordnance stores, and horses captured by the enemy from our companies at Brashear City, with statement of officers and men taken, I have the honor to submit the following :

At the time we left Brashear City (May 20) the morning report shows a total of 75 enlisted men and 2 commissioned officers of Company F present. Of this number there were 5 sergeants, 8 corporals, and 62 privates. The 2 commissioned officers were Capt. Francis W. Noblet and James H. Brown, first lieutenant. Aggregate of Company F present, 77. Of Company H, there were left at Brashear City Second Lieut. Jacob F. Sherfey, Corpl. Nelson C. Duzan, and 9 privates ; aggregate, 11. Of Company A, 1 private ; of Company B, 1 private ; unassigned recruits designed for Company L, 46. Total officers and men left at Brashear, 136.

Of this number I am informed that Lieutenant Brown, with about 23 men of Company F, were not captured, he being in command of a light battery at La Fourche Crossing. Lieutenant Sherfey, with about 30 men, were, with two pieces of artillery, at Bayou Bœuf. Captain Noblet was attacked by the enemy from across the bay. While engaging them, and passing from the guns in position at the town to the fort, his horse was shot under him, and he made a prisoner. The place was surrendered, as I am informed, to the enemy by Major Anthony, of the Rhode Island Cavalry, and the men manning the guns in the fort were notified in person by the major of the fact. This was on the 23d day of June, instant. On the same day Lieutenant Sherfey was attacked by a force coming down the railroad. He repulsed them, was again attacked on the 24th by the same force in his front, at the same time by a force in his rear (the one that captured Brashear).

These facts I learn from privates who were captured at Brashear and paroled. I have no official notice of the facts stated. These companies were detached from my command at the time.

I herewith transmit an exact statement of the ordnance and ordnance stores left at Brashear. There never was an invoice made of them to me by Colonel McMillan, but from the best data I can get this is correct. (See exhibit marked A.*) For statement of quartermaster's stores, see exhibit B.*

I have the honor to be, general, your most obedient servant,

JOHN A. KEITH,
Colonel, Commanding.

HEADQUARTERS FIRST INDIANA ARTILLERY,
Port Hudson, July 16, 1863.

GENERAL: At your request I have reduced to writing and transmit herewith the statements of 3 men of my regiment of the surrender of Brashear City to the enemy, and the particulars so far as they knew. I have been unable as yet to learn how many of our men were captured. One officer, Capt. F. W. Noblet, was captured at Brashear. It seems that the detachment of Captain Noblet, which could not have numbered more than 30 men, and these were divided into squads of from 5 to 8 men. One detachment of about 8 men was at a small earth-work called Fort Buchanan; another of 5, with a gun, one-fourth of a mile to the left of the fort and toward the town; another in the town near the depot; another near the water-tank in the rear of the town, and about a half mile from it.

Lieutenant Sherfey had a command of about 20 or 30 men at Bayou Bœuf, who repulsed the enemy on the day of the capture of Brashear, but was compelled to surrender the next day.

Lieutenant Brown, with a detachment, was at Bayou La Fourche; had an engagement, in which he lost 1 man killed and 1 wounded. This command was not captured. These different detachments make up the 136 men detached from my command at Brashear.

I have the honor to be, general, very respectfully, your obedient servant

JOHN A. KEITH,
Colonel, Commanding First Indiana Artillery.

Brigadier-General ARNOLD,
Chief of Artillery, Nineteenth Army Corps.

* Omitted.

[Inclosure No. 1.]

Eli Nail, Company F, First Indiana Artillery, private, says:
About the 20th of June I was at Brashear City; belong to Captain Noblet's company, First Indiana Artillery. Our company was detached from regiment. We had four guns in the fort, two 42's and two 32's, and three 24's in position, one at the sugar-house and one at the depot. These were pointing across the river. One of the last named (24-pounder) was in position at the water-tank on the railroad (about 100 yards from), pointing to the rear. At this time Major Anthony, of the Second Rhode Island Cavalry, was in command of the post. There were two companies of the One hundred and seventy-sixth New York stationed at the fort; also about 50 of the Fourth Massachusetts; I think that in all there were at least 150 men in these three companies. I would say that there were representatives of at least thirty regiments in the place, principally convalescents. I myself was helping work again at the water-tank. About the time specified the gun that was at the depot was moved out to the water-tank. These guns were moved back there on hearing that the enemy intended attacking us in the rear.

Early on the morning of the 23d, the enemy opened on us from across the bay with 6-pounder guns, directing part of their fire at a small gunboat, the Hollyhock, and at the camps. One of these 24-pounder guns at the tank was then taken down to the upper end of the depot, and, after firing 6 or 8 rounds, succeeded in silencing their batteries.

Corporal Wayman was in command of the gun that I was at. About fifteen minutes after silencing the batteries, word was brought us to cease firing, as the place had surrendered. The enemy came in and took possession of the troops in town and at the fort, and then came out to our gun and took us prisoners at our gun. The Hollyhock mounted three small guns, but after firing a few shots ran off. The troops were not even called into line on the appearance of the enemy, and but very little preparation was made to receive him, although he had been expected for some days.

ELI NAIL.

[Inclosure No. 2.]

Thomas P. Burt, Company B, First Indiana Artillery, says:
There was a detachment of the First Indiana Artillery left at Brashear City to take charge of the heavy guns at the fort. At the time they were left there three of the guns were opposite Bayou Shaffer, and one in the fort above the town.

On or about the 13th of June, in anticipation of an attack from the rear, one 24-pounder gun was moved to the rear of the town, near the water-tank on the railroad, distant from the latter about 100 yards. There was, including the artillery, between 700 and 800 men able for duty, and who stood the march from Brashear City to New Orleans. There was not to exceed 30 of our regiment at Brashear City, the rest of the detachment being at Bayou Bœuf and La Fourche, on the morning of the 23d. There was from 150 to 200 men from the One hundred and seventy-sixth New York supporting the battery at the fort. I was in command of one of the guns.

On the night of the 22d the enemy threw their artillery into Berwick City, on the opposite side of the bay, and early in the morning of the 23d, between daylight and sunrise, they began shelling our camps. Not being able to reach the enemy from the fort, and having no mules to the guns, we took 2 mules from a wagon and hauled a 24-pounder down to the sugar-house, from whence we silenced the enemy's guns. Sergt. George Brown, Company F, was in charge of this gun. The Fourth Massachusetts, which was on picket about a mile to the right of the fort, on the approach of the enemy, hid themselves and their arms, and did not fire a shot to give us warning of their approach. This we got from the enemy, who said they first found the arms and then the men. (It should be stated that this was the force that came up in the rear, and not the force that was shelling us.) When we began firing there were no two guns together, or nearer than a quarter of a mile apart, and only 5 or 6 men in the detachment with each gun.

By the neglect of duty in the picket in not informing us of the presence of an enemy in the rear, they were enabled to pass through the woods and form just in the rear of the town and between the fort and the town. The sergeant in charge of the gun at the sugar-house discovered them, and brought his piece to bear on them and fired a shell in their direction. As soon as they found they were discovered they fired a volley, and then charged with a yell. The troops were not formed to resist an attack, nor was any disposition shown to do so. The detachment at the fort was ordered twice to haul down the flag before they did so. Lieutenant Sherfey, who was at Bayou Bœuf, was attacked at the same time, but repulsed the enemy, and was not attacked again until the next morning, when he was compelled, from overwhelming numbers, to surrender. Captain Noblet, in passing from his gun in town to those at the fort, had his horse shot from under him, and was made prisoner.

The statement of effective men does not include those at any other place. The whole number taken at Brashear City and Bayou Bœuf was something over 1,100. The estimated force of the enemy was 300. That is what they said themselves, and from what I saw think it correct.

We left Brashear City as paroled prisoners on the 27th instant, numbering in all about 1,000 effective men.

THOMAS P. BURT.

[Inclosure No. 3.]

Benjamin F. Smith, Company F, says:

For three or four days before the attack was made, we had been expecting an attack. Saw no preparation made to resist the expected attack until in the evening of the 22d or 21st, when some Enfield rifles were given out to some negroes. Major Anthony, of the Second Rhode Island Cavalry, was in command, but so far as I know made no disposition of the troops to meet the attack. Captain Noblet, I think it was, issued the rifles to the negroes. There were at the time between 700 and 800 men in the place able for duty, and if they had had officers to lead them could undoubtedly have whipped them, as the force which captured the post did not number more than 250 men, well armed and equipped. After the surrender the troops crossed from Berwick to Brashear City, and I would suppose that in all, when we left there, they had at least 5,000 men in around the place, on this side of the bay.

I can fully corroborate Thomas Burt's statement, as he describes the capture as I should.

BENJAMIN F. SMITH.

Resolution of thanks of the Confederate Congress to Capt. Frederick H. Odlum and Lieut. Richard W. Dowling.

JOINT RESOLUTIONS of thanks to Captain Odlum, Lieutenant Dowling, and the men under their command.

Resolved, That the thanks of Congress are eminently due, and are hereby cordially given, to Captain Odlum, Lieut. Richard Dowling, and the 41 men composing the Davis Guards, under their command, for their daring, gallant, and successful defense of Sabine Pass, Tex., against the attack made by the enemy, on the 8th of September last, with a fleet of five gunboats and twenty-two steam transports, carrying a land force of 15,000 men.

Resolved, That this defense, resulting, under the providence of God, in the defeat of the enemy, the capture of two gunboats, with more than 300 prisoners, including the commander of the fleet, the crippling of a third gunboat, the dispersion of the transports, and preventing the invasion of Texas, constitutes, in the opinion of Congress, one of the most brilliant and heroic achievements in the history of this war, and entitles the Davis Guards to the gratitude and admiration of their country.

Resolved, That the President be requested to communicate the foregoing resolutions to Captain Odlum, Lieutenant Dowling, and the men under their command.

Approved February 8, 1864.

UNION CORRESPONDENCE, ETC.

HEADQUARTERS DEPARTMENT OF THE MISSOURI,
St. Louis, September 12, 1863.
Maj. Gen. N. P. BANKS,
Comdg. Department of the Gulf, New Orleans:

GENERAL: A scout formerly employed by me—a very reliable man, and formerly a resident of Texas—has just returned, and reports that he left Houston, Tex., about the last of July; estimates the whole force the rebels had in the State at that time to be about 15,000 strong, of which there were 7,000 or 8,000 at Galveston, under Magruder; about two regiments as a guard at Sabine Pass, and about 2,000 men at Houston; the remainder are scattered throughout the State guarding different posts. The troops are much demoralized, and poorly armed, equipped, and paid. The people are dissatisfied, and anxious to see the Federal armies deliver them from their thraldom.

I have thought it best to send you this information, as it may prove serviceable.

Accept my warmest wishes for your success, and believe me to be, general, very respectfully, your obedient servant,

J. M. SCHOFIELD,
Major General.

SEPTEMBER 14, 1863.
(Received 3.30 p. m.)
General C. P. STONE,
Chief of Staff:

GENERAL: A man whom I sent across the bay at Brashear City to converse with the people, reports Dick Taylor at or near Patterson (6 miles above the bay) with 5,000 men, and in expectation of 3,000 more to join him under General Walker. Kirby Smith said to have been at Taylor's camp on Friday last.

He reports Mouton at La Fayette with 12,000 men, mostly conscripts from Louisiana, Texas, and Arkansas. They have seven steam-boats in the Teche, 85 miles above its mouth. (Last week five steam-boats were reported to me as somewhere up the Atchafalaya.)

The information about the Sabine River is simply that the enemy has a fort mounting fourteen guns a half mile from Sabine City, and another fort below. They have two gunboats and two steam-boats on Sabine River.

Very respectfully, your obedient servant,
E. G. BECKWITH,
Colonel, Commanding.

UNITED STATES CONSULATE AT MONTEREY, MEXICO,
October 14, 1863.

Brig. Gen. J. R. WEST,
Hart's Mills, Tex.:

Hoping to hear from General Banks at New Orleans, I have delayed writing you. I sent by the last two mails all the Texas papers I could get directed to Mr. Creel, with instructions to him to forward to you. You will see by them that an attempt has been made to land at Sabine Pass, Tex., which quite agrees with the information we get from late New York papers, an extract from one of which I inclose.

Large quantities of cotton are now crossing at Eagle Pass; in fact, more than at any time since the war began. The increase is on account of the danger in crossing at Brownsville and other points. Large lots of cotton have been seized at the latter place by the Confederates to pay for goods landed for them at Matamoras. Men from Western Texas are daily coming in here, all, with few exceptions, having crossed at Eagle Pass. They all report large quantities of cotton on the road to the river. The Texans are expecting a Federal force to occupy the State soon, and are consequently making all haste to get out their cotton, as they know their claim upon it will not be respected when once the United States gets possession of Texas.

All the cotton now coming out of Texas and the greater part of it still remaining there belongs to the Confederate Government, Confederate officers, and a few speculators.

Eagle Pass is the great crossing-place. You can at any time take enemy's cotton there to pay a year's expense of your command. The principal Confederate officers in Texas are sending cotton here and the money on deposit, expecting to make it useful when they shall be obliged in their turn to seek safety in Mexico. The present governor of Texas has a large deposit here, the proceeds of shipment of cotton. The taking of cotton from such men deserves an effort. The time is now past to enlist in your army the Texas refugees. You can rely upon the assistance of these men in case you should advance down the river.

We have an organization partly complete. About 250 men are in camp ready to join the first force coming to the Rio Grande. I am personally acquainted with the greater part of these men, and know them to be such as you can place the greatest dependence on. Should you decide to make an advance down the river it would be well to send me by express your full instructions in relation to these men, which you can rest assured will be carried out.

I can hear of no troops being sent by General Magruder to the Rio Grande, but, on the contrary, some have been ordered from there east.
Your obedient servant,

M. M. KIMMEY,
Vice-Consul.

CHIHUAHUA, *October* 16, 1863.
Brig. Gen. JAMES H. CARLETON,
   Commanding Department of New Mexico, Santa Fé:
DEAR SIR:

*   *   *   *   *   *   *

Since the occupation of Arizona by Federal troops, under the command of General West, no complaint has been made in this capital of disorders or outrages on this frontier, at the point of contact, proceeding from military authorities or soldiers in that district. So far as I am informed here everything on that frontier works smoothly and peaceably and to the satisfaction of this people. I have wished to be able to speak very positive on this point, and therefore visited the governor this morning and asked him if anything had occurred since the reoccupation of Arizona, which was the cause of complaint or dissatisfaction. He answered, "No;" on the contrary he was highly gratified that the transactions at the point of contact had been, up to this date, of the most pleasant and unobjectionable character. This was not always the case, general; in old times, before the rebellion, a great many things happened on that frontier which were construed by Mexican authorities, properly or improperly, to be gross outrages. And many expressions of bitterness were hurled against us for being as they said an overbearing and reckless people.

That things are now placed upon such a good footing so far as Chihuahua and Arizona are concerned, and that such good order and discipline prevail, should be the source of pride to the commanding officers, and it certainly is the source of esteem and respect toward them from this Goverment.

*   *   *

Very respectfully,

REUBEN W. CREEL.

UNITED STATES CONSULATE AT MONTEREY, MEXICO,
October 17, 1863.
Brig. Gen. J. R. WEST:

Since writing you on the 14th instant, I have received a letter from our consul at Matamoras. He says he has positive information that Texas is invaded from the east. He was expecting a force on the Rio Grande daily.

Late Texas papers have no news from Sabine Pass. The last mention of the attack on that place was that official dispatches had been received at Houston, but it was not considered proper to give them to the public.

I have made sufficient inquiries to satisfy me that J. R. Baylor is not intending to raid into New Mexico or Arizona. Baylor has been elected to the Confederate Congress and will consequently resign as commander of the Partisan or Ladies' Rangers. You are safe from any attempt on the part of the Texans to annoy you. Skillman with 14 men left San Antonio a few days since for El Paso. Skillman's object is to watch your movements.

I have gathered all possible information in regard to the crops on this frontier and in Western Texas. Corn on this side of the river in the region of Eagle Pass is an average crop. A few thousand bushels could be delivered across the river at from 14 cents to 16 cents per bushel. From San Antonio west to the Rio Grande no corn is raised, the country is deserted, but at San Antonio and east of it corn is abundant. Crop in Western Texas is good, better than it has been for years. The last rains in September which were too late for corn have made good pasturage over the whole country. Plenty of beef can be bought at Eagle Pass. Refugees coming in report the roads full of cotton leading to Eagle Pass. I have now no doubt the cotton that is being bought by Hart in Texas and forwarded to Mexico is the property of Jeff. Davis and his Cabinet. Hart, by documents from the rebel President at Richmond, controls all the Government cotton in Texas. He has for the last year employed all the transportation of Western Texas to bring cotton to the Rio Grande. A few weeks since when cotton was needed at Matamoras to pay for some goods bought for the Confederacy from England, only eighty bales were known to have been brought there by Hart for the Confederate Government.

Attempts have been made in Texas to investigate the doings of Hart, but his commission from Jeff. Davis gives him a superior rank to any Texan official. The cotton on the road to and at Eagle Pass is marked

C. S. A. S. ⟨H⟩ and ⟨H H⟩ when it is the property of Hart and his associates.

The Union men of Western Texas are organizing and will be able to assist a Union force coming to their relief.

Your obedient servant,

M. M. KIMMEY,
Vice-Consul.

UNITED STATES CONSULATE AT MONTEREY, MEXICO,
November 8, 1863.

R. W. CREEL, *Chihuahua:*

A force of 5,000 Federals were landing on the Texas side at the mouth of the Rio Grande on the 3d instant. By this time they should be in possession of Brownsville.

I sent an express to the commanding general last evening and intend sending another to-morrow. All is excitement here. General Bee, the rebel commander, ordered all the cotton at Brownsville sent across the river into Mexico. The last express from Matamoras reports Brownsville burning. General Bee had gone to Roma and had evacuated the place.

If General West could have moved on to Eagle Pass at the time I gave him the notice, much cotton could have been secured to the United States, and he would have occupied the Upper Rio Grande at the time when his services would have been needed. I have been expecting an express from the commanding officer of the United States forces with

dispatches to Generals Carleton and West.   Should it come I will im-
mediately forward it to you to be sent on.
No New York news of a late date.
Yours, truly,

M. M. KIMMEY,
Vice-Consul.

CHIHUAHUA, *November* 9, 1863.
Brig. Gen. J. R. WEST,
Commanding District of Arizona, Mesilla:
DEAR SIR: Yours of the 24th September, together with the package
directed to me from the Department of State, was received on the 2d instant.
The President has honored me with the appointment of United States
consul in Chihuahua, and I am now in possession of the consulate, but
on this occasion do not sign this letter officially, nor head it thus, because in that case I should have to keep copies of all the correspondence which I send above.   I have not time now to do all that.   Hereafter, when I am settled and have things in order, I will attend to
the formalities required by law.   For the generous assistance which
you offer, with the object of obtaining the confirmation in the Senate,
please accept my sincere thanks.
The prices of provisions, &c., are, in Chihuahua, at present as follows: Corn, fanega, $3.50; beans, $3.50; wheat, $4; flour (*despajada*),
$10 the cargo; common soap, 6 pieces for 12½ cents; sugar, white, $6.75
to $7.50 arroba; sugar, brown (*peloncillo*), $38 to $40 cargo; beef cattle,
$18 to $22 each; sheep, $1.75 to $2 each.   The crop is not good, and
prices will rise as soon as you create a demand on this frontier.   Sheep
are plentiful.   In the country towns which are near the line the quantity of grain for sale is not great.   The Presidio del Norte has already
sold off half its crop.   Coffee, $15 per arroba; tea, $3 to $4 per pound;
rice, $4 to $5 per arroba.   The prices of articles which are brought from
interior of Mexico are subject to great fluctuations on account of the
war.
I never converse with any person relative to military matters and
movements on the frontier.   Your caution counseling prudence and
silence will be obeyed.   I judge, from remarks contained in both of
Cuniffe's letters, that the political enemies of the governor, Terrazas,
are circulating in El Paso reports about "that powder" calculated to
create uneasiness in the minds of American officers and fling discredit
upon this Government.   If there be any person who hints to you or
others that any powder leaves this State for Texas or any other point
hostile to the United States, I hereby declare to you that no credence
should thereto be attached.   The whole report originates in malice
among Afrancesados, and is emphatically a lie.   I should be very sorry,
indeed, if such report should reach General Carleton.
In case you advance, is there a ready outlet for paper money at El
Paso?   Can people go up there and buy salable goods in quantity for
paper?   A great deal depends upon a ready outlet for the paper which
may enter this city; but on this point I have, some time back, fully expressed myself to General Carleton.   I refer you to the two letters to
General C., which go open.   I send all letters and Texas papers, and
Mexican also.
Your obedient servant,

REUBEN W. CREEL.

UNITED STATES CONSULATE AT CHIHUAHUA,
November 30, 1863.

Brig. Gen. J. R. WEST,
Commanding District of Arizona, Mesilla :

DEAR SIR: Having received letters from Matamoras by to-day's mail placing beyond all doubt the presence of our troops in Brownsville, I think it my duty to send you such documents as I have received by express.

The express receives $100 for his trip going and coming. He will remain in El Paso as many days as you choose to detain.

The letters will tell you all the news from below. The Mexican papers will give you some idea of what is doing in Central Mexico, but I am inclined to think that matters are much worse than they are represented. Chihuahua is doing nothing at all, the men at the head of this State being more interested in No. 1 than in the Republic. Very sorry to say so, but it is very true.

I send in favor of Cuniffe a draft for the $100, which please approve for payment.

Yours, respectfully and in haste,

REUBEN W. CREEL,
United States Consul.

NEW IBERIA, *December 22, 1863*—1 p. m.
(Received at New Orleans, 1.15 p. m.)

Brig. Gen. C. P. STONE,
Chief of Staff :

MacQuod, a scout who went into the enemy's lines from Vermillion about one month ago, returned this morning. He left Washington and Opelousas on Sunday, and came down by way of the Teche. Was imprisoned seventeen days as a spy at Opelousas. Reports that he was told on Sunday that Walker's division was at Simsport on Friday. A commissioned officer was his informant. He thinks it true. He confirms the report of Green's division having gone to Texas, but thinks part of Mouton's division is at Simsport. His estimate of the troops left in the State is 7,000. The accounts are all very conflicting as to the intentions of the enemy with regard to Walker and Mouton. MacQuod thinks they recrossed the Atchafalaya because they were afraid the driftwood would carry away their pontoon bridges, as the bayou rose very fast. May not the 125 row-boats at Alexandria be pontoon?

W. B. FRANKLIN,
Major-General, Commanding.

Abbay's (George F.) Artillery. See *Mississippi Troops, Confederate*, 1st *Regiment, Battery K.*

Abercrombie's (L. A.) Infantry. See *Texas Troops, Confederate*, 20th *Regiment.*

Adams' (Joseph) Cavalry. See *Illinois Troops*, 15th *Regiment.*

Adams' (William) Infantry. See *Iowa Troops*, 19th *Regiment.*

Agnus' (Felix) Infantry. See *New York Troops*, 165th *Regiment.*

Ainsworth's (Ira W.) Infantry. See *New York Troops*, 177th *Regiment.*

Alexander's (A. M.) Cavalry. See *Texas Troops, Confederate*, 34th *Regiment.*

Alexander's (George W.) Infantry. See *Pennsylvania Troops*, 47th *Regiment.*

Allen's (Charles F.) Infantry. See *Massachusetts Troops*, 38th *Regiment.*

Allen's (C. M.) Cavalry. See *Arkansas Troops, Confederate*, 2d *Regiment.*

Allen's (Harvey A.) Artillery. See *Union Troops, Regulars*, 2d *Regiment, Battery K.*

Angell's (Henry) Artillery. See *Thomas Gonzales' Artillery, post.*

Annable's (Thomas H) Infantry. See *Massachusetts Troops*, 26th *Regiment.*

Armstrong's (Samuel A.) Heavy Artillery. See *Indiana Troops*, 1st *Regiment, Batteries G and M.*

Atkins' (Robert F.) Infantry. See *Union Troops, Corps d'Afrique*, 18th *Regiment.*

Atwater's (Joseph B.) Artillery. See *Missouri Troops*, 1st *Regiment, Battery E.*

Atwood's (George M.) Infantry. See *Maine Troops*, 24th *Regiment.*

Ayres' (James B.) Cavalry. See *New York Troops*, 14th *Regiment.*

Bache's (Robert) Infantry. See *Massachusetts Troops*, 31st *Regiment.*

Bacon's (Edward) Heavy Artillery. See *Michigan Troops*, 1st *Regiment.*

Bagby's (A. P.) Cavalry. See *Texas Troops, Confederate*, 7th *Regiment.*

Bailey's (George W. K.) Infantry. See *Illinois Troops*, 99th *Regiment.*

Bainbridge's (Edmund C.) Artillery. See *Union Troops, Regulars*, 1st *Regiment, Battery A.*

Ballinger's (Richard H.) Infantry. See *Mississippi Troops, Union*, 3d *Regiment (Colored).*

Bangs' (Isaac S., jr.) Infantry. See *Union Troops, Corps d'Afrique*, 9th *Regiment.*

Barnes' (James) Artillery. See *New York Troops*, 21st *Battery.*

Barrett's (Richard) Cavalry. See *Louisiana Troops, Union*, 1st *Regiment.*

Barrett's (William M.) Infantry. See *New Hampshire Troops*, 8th *Regiment.*

Bassett's (Chauncey J.) Infantry. See *Union Troops, Corps d'Afrique*, 1st *Regiment.*

Bassford's (Abraham) Cavalry. See *New York Troops*, 14th *Regiment.*

Baylor's (George W.) Cavalry. See *Texas Troops, Confederate*, 2d *Regiment, Arizona Brigade.*

Beach's (Augustus) Artillery. See *Ohio Troops*, 2d *Battery.*

Bean's (Sidney A.) Cavalry. See *Wisconsin Troops*, 4th *Regiment.*

Benavides' (Santos) Cavalry. See *Texas Troops, Confederate*, 33d *Regiment.*

Benedict's (Lewis) Infantry. See *New York Troops*, 162d *Regiment.*

Bering's (John A.) Infantry. See *Ohio Troops*, 48th *Regiment.*

Bertram's (Henry) Infantry. See *Wisconsin Troops*, 20th *Regiment.*

---

* References, unless otherwise indicated, are to index following.

Birge's (Henry W.) **Infantry.** See *Connecticut Troops, 13th Regiment.*
Bishop's (George) **Infantry.** See *Union Troops, Corps d'Afrique, 6th Regiment.*
Black's (John Charles) **Infantry.** See *Illinois Troops, 37th Regiment.*
Blake's (Charles W.) **Infantry.** See *Union Troops, Corps d'Afrique, 3d Regiment.*
Blanchard's (Justus W.) **Infantry.** See *New York Troops, 162d Regiment.*
Blinn's (Charles D.) **Infantry.** See *Connecticut Troops, 13th Regiment.*
Blober's **Cavalry.** See *Louisiana Troops, Union, 1st Regiment.*
Boardman's (Frederick A.) **Cavalry.** See *Wisconsin Troops, 4th Regiment.*
Bolton's (William H.) **Artillery.** See *Illinois Troops, 2d Regiment, Battery L.*
Boone's (H. H.) **Cavalry.** See *Texas Troops, Confederate, 13th Battalion.*
Boone's (R. M.) **Artillery.** See *Louisiana Troops, Confederate.*
Borris' (Herman) **Artillery.** See *Illinois Troops, 2d Regiment, Battery A.*
Bostwick's (Charles E.) **Infantry.** See *Union Troops. Corps d'Afrique, 19th Regiment.*
Bradbury's (Albert W.) **Artillery.** See *Maine Troops, 1st Battery.*
Bradford's (J. L.) **Artillery.** See *Mississippi Troops, Confederate, 1st Regiment, Battery F.*
Bradley's (Theodore) **Artillery.** See *Union Troops, Regulars, 2d Regiment, Battery C.*
Breese's (Sidney A.) **Cavalry.** See *Missouri Troops, 6th Regiment.*
Brenning's (George) **Cavalry.** See *New York Troops, 14th Regiment.*
Bridgman's (Eliot) **Infantry.** See *Union Troops, Corps d'Afrique, 20th Regiment ;* also *Massachusetts Troops, 31st Regiment.*
Bringhurst's (Thomas H.) **Infantry.** See *Indiana Troops, 46th Regiment.*
Bristol's (Henry B.) **Infantry.** See *Union Troops, Regulars. 5th Regiment.*
Brown's (Albert H.) **Infantry.** See *Ohio Troops, 96th Regiment.*
Brown's (R. B.) **Infantry.** See *Louisiana Troops, Union, 2d New Orleans Regiment.*
Brown's (R. R.) **Cavalry.** See *Texas Troops, Confederate.*
Bruce's (John) **Infantry.** See *Iowa Troops, 19th Regiment.*
Bryan's (Michael K.) **Infantry.** See *New York Troops, 175th Regiment.*
Bryant's (George E.) **Infantry.** See *Wisconsin Troops, 12th Regiment.*
Buchel's (A.) **Cavalry.** See *Texas Troops, Confederate. 1st Regiment.*
Buehler's (Theodore E.) **Infantry.** See *Indiana Troops, 67th Regiment.*
Bull's (James M.) **Infantry.** See *Wisconsin Troops, 23d Regiment.*
Bullen's (Joseph D.) **Infantry.** See *Maine Troops, 28th Regiment.*
Bullock's (William W.) **Infantry.** See *Massachusetts Troops, 30th Regiment.*
Burdick's (James) **Artillery.** See *Ohio Troops, 15th Battery.*
Burrell's (Isaac S.) **Infantry.** See *Massachusetts Troops, 42d Regiment.*
Burt's (Charles A.) **Infantry.** See *New York Troops, 159th Regiment.*
Bush's (Daniel B., jr.) **Cavalry.** See *Illinois Troops, 2d Regiment.*
Butler's (George) **Infantry.** See *Indiana Troops, 11th Regiment.*
Cahill's (Thomas W.) **Infantry.** See *Connecticut Troops, 9th Regiment.*
Caldwell's (J. P.) **Artillery.** See *Watson Artillery, post.*
Callahan's (Charles M.) **Artillery.** See *Missouri Troops, 1st Regiment, Battery A.*
Calloway's (William P.) **Infantry.** See *California Troops, 1st Regiment.*
Campbell's (Richard) **Heavy Artillery.** See *Indiana Troops, 1st Regiment, Battery I.*
Carey's (James L.) **Cavalry.** See *Indiana Troops, 1st Regiment.*
Cargile's (C. M.) **Infantry.** See *Arkansas Troops, Confederate, 10th Regiment.*
Carnahan's (Robert H.) **Cavalry.** See *Illinois Troops, 3d Regiment.*
Carr's (Gouverneur) **Infantry.** See *New York Troops, 165th Regiment.*
Carruth's (William W.) **Artillery.** See *Massachusetts Troops, 6th Battery.*
Carson's (Christopher) **Cavalry.** See *New Mexico Troops, 1st Regiment.*
Chacon's (Rafael) **Cavalry.** See *New Mexico Troops, 1st Regiment.*
Chadwick's (Charles) **Infantry.** See *Iowa Troops, 38th Regiment.*
Chadwick's (John C.) **Infantry.** See *Union Troops, Corps d'Afrique, 9th Regiment.*
Chamberlain's (Edwin W.) **Infantry.** See *Louisiana Troops, Union, 11th Regiment (Colored).*

Chamberlin's (Edwin M.) **Artillery.** See *Massachusetts Troops, 12th Battery.*
Charles' (William S.) **Infantry.** See *Indiana Troops, 18th Regiment.*
Chase's (John W.) **Artillery.** See *Vermont Troops, 2d Battery.*
Chicago Mercantile **Artillery.** See *Charles G. Cooley's Artillery, post.*
Chinn's (T. B. R.) **Infantry.** See *Louisiana Troops, Confederate, 9th Battalion.*
Chisum's (Isham) **Cavalry.** See *Texas Troops, Confederate, 6th Regiment.*
Claiborne **Infantry.** See *A. J. Lewis' Infantry, post.*
Clark's (Charles J.) **Infantry.** See *Iowa Troops, 23d Regiment.*
Clark's (Eusebius S.) **Infantry.** See *Massachusetts Troops, 26th Regiment.*
Clark's (George W.) **Infantry.** See *Iowa Troops, 34th Regiment.*
Clark's (James C.) **Infantry.** See *Union Troops, Corps d'Afrique, 7th Regiment.*
Clark's (John G.) **Infantry.** See *Indiana Troops, 26th Regiment.*
Closson's (Henry W.) **Artillery.** See *Union Troops, Regulars, 1st Regiment, Battery L.*
Cobb's (John C.) **Engineers.** See *Union Troops, Corps d'Afrique, 2d Regiment.*
Coffin's (W. Norris) **Heavy Artillery.** See *Louisiana Troops, Confederate, 12th Battalion, Battery D.*
Cole's (Elisha) **Artillery.** See *Missouri Troops, 1st Regiment, Battery A.*
Cole's (Nelson) **Artillery.** See *Missouri Troops, 1st Regiment, Battery E.*
Coleman's (F. G. W.) **Artillery.** See *Seven Stars Artillery, post.*
Collins' (John B.) **Infantry.** See *New York Troops, 91st Regiment.*
Collins' (Robert K.) **Infantry.** See *Indiana Troops, 69th Regiment.*
Comstock's (Apollos) **Infantry.** See *Connecticut Troops, 13th Regiment.*
Comstock's (Joseph J.) **Heavy Artillery.** See *Rhode Island Troops, 14th Regiment (Colored).*
Conn's (J. D.) **Infantry.** See *Louisiana Troops, Confederate, 4th Regiment.*
Connell's (John) **Infantry.** See *Iowa Troops, 28th Regiment.*
Conover's (Robert) **Infantry.** See *Indiana Troops, 16th Regiment.*
Cook's (Joseph J.) **Heavy Artillery.** See *Texas Troops, Confederate, 1st Regiment.*
Cooley's (Charles G.) **Artillery.** See *Illinois Troops.*
Corliss' (Augustus W.) **Cavalry.** See *Rhode Island Troops, 2d Regiment.*
Cornay's (Florian O.) **Artillery.** See *Saint Mary's Cannoneers, post.*
Cottle's (Philip S.) **Infantry.** See *Union Troops, Corps d'Afrique, 6th Regiment.*
Cowan's (John) **Infantry.** See *Kentucky Troops, Union, 19th Regiment.*
Cowles' (David S.) **Infantry.** See *New York Troops, 128th Regiment.*
Cox's (Clayton) **Heavy Artillery.** See *Indiana Troops, 1st Regiment, Battery K.*
Crandal's (Frederick M.) **Infantry.** See *Louisiana Troops, Union, 10th Regiment (Colored).*
Crandall's (Edwin A.) **Infantry.** See *Illinois Troops, 99th Regiment.*
Crebs' (John M.) **Infantry.** See *Illinois Troops, 87th Regiment.*
Cremony's (John C.) **Cavalry.** See *California Troops, 2d Regiment.*
Crescent **Infantry.** See *Louisiana Troops, Confederate.*
Crooke's (William D.) **Infantry.** See *Iowa Troops, 21st Regiment.*
Cropsey's (John W.) **Cavalry.** See *New York Troops, 14th Regiment.*
Cummins' (William T.) **Infantry.** See *Kentucky Troops, Union, 19th Regiment.*
Cummings' (Franklin) **Infantry.** See *Texas Troops, Confederate.*
Currie's (Leonard D. H.) **Infantry.** See *New York Troops, 133d Regiment.*
Curtiss' (George G.) **Artillery.** See *New York Troops, 18th Battery.*
Cushman's (C. W.) **Infantry.** See *Louisiana Troops, Confederate, 30th Regiment.*
Daly's (Andrew) **Cavalry.** See *Texas Troops, Confederate.*
Daniel's (James M.) **Artillery.** See *Texas Troops, Confederate.*
Daniels' (Nathan W.) **Infantry.** See *Union Troops, Corps d'Afrique, 2d Regiment.*
Dashiell's (George R.) **Artillery.** See *Texas Troops, Confederate.*
Davidson's (Peter) **Artillery.** See *Illinois Troops, 2d Regiment, Battery A.*
Davis Guards, **Heavy Artillery.** See *Texas Troops, Confederate, 1st Regiment, Battery F.*

Davis' (Edmund J.) **Cavalry.** See *Texas Troops, Union, 1st Regiment.*
Davis' (Henry T.) **Cavalry.** See *Texas Troops, Confederate, 33d Regiment.*
Day's (Henry M.) **Infantry.** See *Illinois Troops, 91st Regiment.*
Day's (Nicholas W.) **Infantry.** See *New York Troops, 131st Regiment.*
De Baun's (J.) **Cavalry.** See *Louisiana Troops, Confederate, 9th Battalion.*
Debray's (X. B.) **Cavalry.** See *Texas Troops, Confederate, 26th Regiment.*
De Gournay's (P. F.) **Heavy Artillery.** See *Louisiana Troops, Confederate, 12th Battalion.*
De Wolfe's (T. Scott) **Infantry.** See *Union Troops, Corps d'Afrique, 17th Regiment.*
Dillingham's (Charles) **Infantry.** See *Vermont Troops, 8th Regiment.*
Dowling's (R. W.) **Heavy Artillery.** See *Texas Troops, Confederate, 1st Regiment, Battery F.*
Doxey's (Charles T.) **Infantry.** See *Indiana Troops, 16th Regiment.*
Drew's (Charles W.) **Infantry.** See *Union Troops, Corps d'Afrique, 4th Regiment.*
Dudley's (Nathan A. M.) **Infantry.** See *Massachusetts Troops, 30th Regiment.*
Duff's (James) **Cavalry.** See *Texas Troops, 33d Regiment.*
Dungan's (Warren S.) **Infantry.** See *Iowa Troops, 34th Regiment.*
Dupeire's (St. L.) **Infantry.** See *Louisiana Troops, Confederate.*
Duryea's (Richard C.) **Artillery.** See *Union Troops, Regulars, 1st Regiment, Battery F.*
Dutton's (Henry F.) **Infantry.** See *Vermont Troops, 8th Regiment.*
Dutton's (Salmon) **Infantry.** See *Vermont Troops, 7th Regiment.*
Dye's (William McE.) **Infantry.** See *Iowa Troops, 20th Regiment.*
Dyer's (Isaac) **Infantry.** See *Maine Troops, 15th Regiment.*
Elmore's (H. M.) **Infantry.** See *Texas Troops, Confederate, 20th Regiment.*
English's (George H.) **Infantry.** See *Illinois Troops, 32d Regiment.*
English's (Richard T.) **Artillery.** See *Mississippi Troops, Confederate.*
Ennis' (John) **Cavalry.** See *New York Troops, 14th Regiment.*
Everett's (Charles) **Infantry.** See *Louisiana Troops, Union, 2d Regiment.*
Faries' (T. A.) **Artillery.** See *Pelican Artillery, post.*
Farr's (Alpha B.) **Infantry.** See *Massachusetts Troops, 26th Regiment.*
Farrar's (Bernard G.) **Heavy Artillery.** See *Mississippi Troops, Union, 2d Regiment;* also *Missouri Troops, 30th Regiment.*
Fearing's (Hawkes, jr.) **Infantry.** See *New Hampshire Troops, 8th Regiment.*
Fellows' (Stark) **Infantry.** See *Union Troops, Colored. 2d Regiment.*
Ferris' (Samuel P.) **Infantry.** See *Connecticut Troops, 28th Regiment.*
Fisher's (James A.) **Heavy Artillery.** See *Tennessee Troops, Confederate, 1st Regiment, Battery G.*
Fiske's (William O.) **Infantry.** See *Louisiana Troops, Union, 1st Regiment.*
Fitch's (Henry B.) **Infantry.** See *New York Troops, 75th Regiment.*
Fitz Gibbons' (Richard) **Infantry.** See *Connecticut Troops, 9th Regiment.*
Flanders' (George A.) **Infantry.** See *New Hampshire Troops, 8th Regiment.*
Florida Rangers. See *Florida Troops, Union, 2d Regiment, Cavalry.*
Flory's (Aaron M.) **Infantry.** See *Indiana Troops, 46th Regiment.*
Flynn's Sharpshooters. Official designation not of record. See *Captain Flynn.*
Foster's (Jacob T.) **Artillery.** See *Wisconsin Troops, 1st Battery.*
Fournet's (V. A.) **Infantry.** See *Louisiana Troops, Confederate, 10th Battalion.*
Foust's (Joseph) **Artillery.** See *Missouri Troops, 1st Regiment, Battery F.*
Fowler's (Pleasant) **Infantry.** See *Arkansas Troops, Confederate, 14th Regiment.*
Fowler's (W. H.) **Artillery.** See *Alabama Troops.*
Fox's (George W.) **Artillery.** See *New York Troops, 26th Battery.*
Francis' (Richard W.) **Cavalry.** See *Headquarters Troops, Department of the Gulf.*
Frazer's (George M.) **Cavalry.*** See *Texas Troops, Confederate, 3d Regiment, Arizona Brigade.*

---

* Temporarily commanding.

French's (Albert H.) Cavalry. See *California Troops, 1st Regiment.*
Frisbie's (Henry N.) Infantry. See *Union Troops, Corps d'Afrique, 22d Regiment.*
Fritz's (Emil) Cavalry. See *California Troops, 1st Regiment.*
Fuller's (Henry W.) Infantry. See *Union Troops, Corps d'Afrique, 3d Regiment.*
Fuller's (James K.) Infantry. See *New York Troops, 133d Regiment.*
Fullerton's (Hugh) Cavalry. See *Illinois Troops, 2d Regiment.*
Gallagher's (Andrew P.) Cavalry. See *Indiana Troops, 4th Regiment.*
Garrett's (S.) Cavalry. See *Texas Troops, Confederate, 3d Regiment (State).*
Glasgow's (Samuel L.) Infantry. See *Iowa Troops, 23d Regiment.*
Godfrey's (J. Franklin) Cavalry. See *Louisiana Troops, Union, 1st Regiment.*
Goelzer's (Augustus) Infantry. See *Indiana Troops, 60th Regiment.*
Gonzales' (Thomas) Artillery. See *Texas Troops, Confederate.*
Good's (Tilghman H.) Infantry. See *Pennsylvania Troops. 47th Regiment.*
Goodrich's (Luther) Infantry. See *Union Troops, Corps d'Afrique, 17th Regiment.*
Goodwin's (Lewis H.) Infantry. See *Indiana Troops, 47th Regiment.*
Gott's (Benjamin F.) Infantry. See *New York Troops, 174th Regiment.*
Gould's (N. C.) Cavalry. See *Texas Troops, Confederate, 23d Regiment.*
Graham's (Harvey) Infantry. See *Iowa Troops, 22d Regiment.*
Gray's (E. F.) Infantry. See *Texas Troops, Confederate, 3d Regiment.*
Gray's (John) Infantry. See *New York Troops, 175th Regiment.*
Green's (Thomas) Cavalry. See *Texas Troops, Confederate, 5th Regiment.*
Greene's (Joseph E.) Infantry. See *Wisconsin Troops, 23d Regiment.*
Greene's (William A.) Infantry. See *Wisconsin Troops, 29th Regiment.*
Greenleaf's (Halbert S.) Infantry. See *Massachusetts Troops, 52d Regiment.*
Grier's (David P.) Infantry. See *Illinois Troops, 77th Regiment.*
Griffin's (W. H.) Infantry. See *Texas Troops, Confederate.*
Grill's (John F.) Infantry. See *Indiana Troops, 24th Regiment.*
Grimsley's (James) Heavy Artillery. See *Indiana Troops, 1st Regiment, Battery B.*
Grosvenor's (William M.) Infantry. See *Union Troops, Corps d'Afrique, 2d Regiment.*
Grow's (John A.) Artillery. See *New York Troops, 25th Battery.*
Guernsey's (Samuel B.) Engineers. See *Union Troops, Corps d'Afrique, 4th Regiment.*
Guppey's (Joshua J.) Infantry. See *Wisconsin Troops, 23d Regiment.*
Haley's (Eben D.) Artillery. See *Maine Troops, 1st Battery.*
Hall's (Alfred G.) Infantry. See *Union Troops, Corps d'Afrique, 2d Regiment;* also *New York Troops, 176th Regiment.**
Hamilton's (A. S.) Infantry. See *Mississippi Troops, Confederate, 1st Regiment.*
Hamilton's (Samuel M.) Artillery. See *James M. Daniel's Artillery, ante.*
Hamlen's (Charles H. J.) Artillery. See *Massachusetts Troops, 13th Battery.*
Hampton's (G. J.) Cavalry. See *Texas Troops, Confederate, 4th Regiment.*
Hancock's (Bradford) Infantry. See *Wisconsin Troops, 20th Regiment.*
Hanham's (Moore) Infantry. See *Union Troops, Corps d'Afrique, 12th Regiment.*
Hanks' (George H.) Infantry. See *Union Troops, Corps d'Afrique, 18th Regiment.*
Hardeman's (W. P.) Cavalry. See *Texas Troops, Confederate, 4th Regiment.*
Hargrave's (Joseph P.) Infantry. See *California Troops, 1st Regiment.*
Harper's (William H.) Artillery. See *Ohio Troops, 2d Battery.*
Harrison's (James E.) Infantry. See *Texas Troops, Confederate, 15th Regiment.*
Harrower's (Gabriel,T.) Infantry. See *New York Troops, 161st Regiment.*
Hartwell's (Charles A.) Infantry. See *Union Troops, Corps d'Afrique, 5th Regiment.*
Hawhe's (Arthur J.) Infantry. See *Indiana Troops, 49th Regiment.*
Haynes' (John L.) Cavalry. See *Texas Troops, Union, 2d Regiment.*
Headquarters Troops (Department of the Gulf), Cavalry. See *Louisiana Troops, Union.*

---

* Temporarily commanding.

Hebard's (George T.) **Artillery.** See *Vermont Troops, 1st Battery.*

Henderson's **Exempts.** Official designation not of record. See *Captain Henderson.*

Hendricks' (Isaac C.) **Heavy Artillery.** See *Indiana Troops, 1st Regiment, Battery L.*

Herbert's (P. T.) **Cavalry.** See *Texas Troops, Confederate, 7th Regiment.*

Herod's (A. J.) **Artillery.** See *Mississippi Troops, Confederate, 1st Regiment, Battery B.*

Hesseltine's (Frank S.) **Infantry.** See *Maine Troops, 13th Regiment.*

Higgins' (John) **Infantry.** See *New York Troops, 116th Regiment.*

Hodge's (Justin) **Engineers.** See *Union Troops, Corps d'Afrique, 1st Regiment.*

Hodsdon's (Alfred) **Infantry.** See *Louisiana Troops, Union, 2d Regiment.*

Holbrook's (William C.) **Infantry.** See *Vermont Troops, 7th Regiment.*

Holcomb's (Pythagoras E.) **Artillery.** See *Vermont Troops, 2d Battery.*

Holcomb's (Richard E.) **Infantry.** See *Louisiana Troops, Union, 1st Regiment.*

Holmes' (Charles E. L.) **Infantry.** See *Connecticut Troops, 23d Regiment.*

Hopkins' (William S. B.) **Infantry.** See *Massachusetts Troops, 31st Regiment.*

Howell's (Francis A.) **Infantry.** See *New York Troops, 131st Regiment.*

Hubbard's (Nathaniel H.) **Infantry.** See *Maine Troops, 26th Regiment.*

Hughes' (D. Henry) **Infantry.** See *Iowa Troops, 38th Regiment.*

Hughes' (D. M. C.) **Infantry.** See *W. R. Miles' Legion, post.*

Hume's (P. G.) **Artillery.** See *Valverde Artillery, post.*

Humphrey's (Ballard S.) **Artillery.** See *Union Troops, Regulars, 1st Regiment, Battery A.*

Hunt's (William, jr.) **Artillery.** See *Ohio Troops, 17th Battery.*

Hutchings' (Jasper) **Infantry.** See *Union Troops, Corps d'Afrique, 11th Regiment.*

Ilsley's (Edward) **Infantry.** See *Maine Troops, 12th Regiment.*

Ingraham's (Timothy) **Infantry.** See *Massachusetts Troops, 38th Regiment.*

Jacoby's (Lawrence) **Artillery.** See *Indiana Troops, 1st Battery.*

Jerrard's (Simon G.) **Infantry.** See *Maine Troops, 22d Regiment.*

Johnson's **Cavalry.** Official designation not of record. See ——— *Johnson.*

Johnson's (Ben. W.) **Infantry.** See *Arkansas Troops, Confederate, 15th Regiment.*

Johnson's (Elijah D.) **Infantry.** See *Maine Troops, 21st Regiment.*

Johnston's (Thomas H.) **Infantry.** See *Mississippi Troops, Confederate, 1st Regiment.*

Jones' (B.) **Infantry.** See *Arkansas Troops, Confederate, 1st [8th] Battalion.*

Jones' (Edward L.) **Engineers.** See *Union Troops, Corps d'Afrique, 1st Regiment.*

Jones' (O. G.) **Artillery.** See *Texas Troops, Confederate.*

Jones' (O. H.) **Artillery.** See *Saint Mary's Cannoneers, post.*

Jones' (Robert B.) **Infantry.** See *Indiana Troops, 34th Regiment.*

Jones' (Simon) **Infantry.** See *Union Troops, Corps d'Afrique, 25th Regiment.*

Jones' (William) **Infantry.** See *Indiana Troops, 53d Regiment.*

Jumper's (Alden H.) **Pioneers.*** See *Alden H. Jumper.*

Keating's (George) **Infantry.** See *New York Troops, 174th Regiment.*

Keefe's (James) **Cavalry.** See *Wisconsin Troops, 4th Regiment.*

Keese's (Francis S.) **Infantry.** See *New York Troops, 128th Regiment.*

Keigwin's (James) **Infantry.** See *Indiana Troops, 49th Regiment.*

Keily's (Daniel J.) **Cavalry.** See *Louisiana Troops, Union, 2d Regiment.*

Keith's (John A.) **Heavy Artillery.** See *Indiana Troops, 1st Regiment.*

Kelly's (John H.) **Infantry.** See *Ohio Troops, 114th Regiment.*

Kempsey's (Matthew C.) **Infantry.** See *Union Troops, Corps d'Afrique, 16th Regiment.*

Kenny's (Alexander J.) **Infantry.** See *Indiana Troops, 8th Regiment.*

Kent's (Daniel) **Infantry.** See *Iowa Troops, 19th Regiment.*

Kershner's (Philip) **Infantry.** See *Ohio Troops, 16th Regiment.*

Kimball's (John W.) **Infantry.** See *Massachusetts Troops, 53d Regiment.*

Kimball's (William K.) **Infantry.** See *Maine Troops, 12th Regiment.*

King's (W. H.) **Infantry.** See *Texas Troops, Confederate, 18th Regiment.*

---

* Improvised.

Kingman's (John W.) Infantry. See *New Hampshire Troops,* 15th *Regiment.*
Kingsley's (Thomas G.) Infantry. See *Connecticut Troops,* 26th *Regiment.*
Kinsey's (William B.) Infantry. See *New York Troops,* 161st *Regiment.*
Kirby's (Byron) Cavalry. See *Maryland Troops, Union,* 3d *Regiment.*
Kirke's (James W.) Artillery. See *Massachusetts Troops,* 15th *Battery.*
Knox's (S. L.) Infantry. See *Alabama Troops,* 1st *Regiment.*
Ladd's (Joseph J.) Infantry. See *New Hampshire Troops,* 8th *Regiment.*
Land's (George W.) Infantry. See *Illinois Troops,* 87th *Regiment.*
Lane's (W. P.) Cavalry. See *Texas Troops, Confederate,* 1st *Regiment, Partisan.*
Lanphere's (Charles H.) Artillery. See *Michigan Troops,* 7th *Battery.*
Larned's (Frank H.) Artillery. See *Union Troops, Regulars,* 2d *Regiment, Battery H.*
Lewis' (A. J.) Infantry. See *Mississippi Troops, Confederate.*
L'Hommedieu's (Stephen S., jr.) Infantry. See *Ohio Troops,* 83d *Regiment.*
Lindsey's (Joseph W.) Infantry. See *Ohio Troops,* 48th *Regiment.*
Lippincott's (Charles E.) Infantry. See *Illinois Troops,* 33d *Regiment.*
Lochbihler's (Christian) Pontoniers. See *Missouri Troops,* 35th *Regiment, Infantry.*
Locke's (M. B.) Infantry. See *Alabama Troops,* 1st *Regiment.*
Logan's (Thomas) Infantry. See *Illinois Troops,* 118th *Regiment.*
Loomis' (Reuben) Cavalry. See *Illinois Troops,* 6th *Regiment.*
Louisiana 1st Regiment Engineers. See *Union Troops, Corps d'Afrique,* 1st *Regiment.*
Louisiana Native Guards, 1st Regiment Heavy Artillery. See *Union Troops, Corps d'Afrique,* 1st *Regiment.*
Louisiana Native Guards, 1st Regiment Infantry. See *Union Troops, Corps d'Afrique,* 1st *Regiment.*
Louisiana Native Guards, 2d Regiment Infantry. See *Union Troops, Corps d'Afrique,* 2d *Regiment.*
Louisiana Native Guards, 3d Regiment Infantry. See *Union Troops, Corps d'Afrique,* 3d *Regiment.*
Louisiana Native Guards, 4th Regiment Infantry. See *Union Troops, Corps d'Afrique,* 4th *Regiment.*
Love's (George M.) Infantry. See *New York Troops,* 116th *Regiment.*
Lowell's (Charles R.) Cavalry. See *Massachusetts Troops,* 2d *Regiment.*
Lucas' (John) Infantry. See *Kentucky Troops, Union,* 7th *Regiment.*
Lucas' (Thomas J.) Infantry. See *Indiana Troops,* 16th *Regiment.*
Luckett's (P. N.) Infantry. See *Texas Troops, Confederate,* 3d *Regiment.*
Lyles' (O. P.) Infantry. See *Arkansas Troops, Confederate,* 23d *Regiment.*
Macauley's (Daniel) Infantry. See *Indiana Troops,* 11th *Regiment.*
McCarthey's (Charles) Infantry. See *New York Troops,* 175th *Regiment.*
McCollough's (Joseph M.) Infantry. See *Illinois Troops,* 77th *Regiment.*
McConnell's (David W.) Artillery. See *New York Troops,* 18th *Battery.*
McCormick's (Thomas) Heavy Artillery. See *Union Troops, Corps d'Afrique,* 1st *Regiment.*
McDade's (W. A.) Cavalry. See *Texas Troops, Confederate,* 13th *Battalion.*
McDermott's (George) Infantry. See *Union Troops, Regulars,* 5th *Regiment.*
Mack's (Albert G.) Artillery. See *New York Troops,* 18th *Battery.*
McLaflin's (Edward) Heavy Artillery. See *Indiana Troops,* 1st *Regiment.*
McLaughlin's (John A.) Infantry. See *Indiana Troops,* 47th *Regiment.*
McNeill's Cavalry. Official designation not of record. See —— *McNeill.*
McNeill's (H. C.) Cavalry. See *Texas Troops, Confederate,* 5th *Regiment.*
McNulta's (John) Infantry. See *Illinois Troops,* 94th *Regiment.*
McPhaill's (H. A.) Cavalry. See *Texas Troops, Confederate,* 5th *Regiment.*
Madison's (George T.) Cavalry. See *Texas Troops, Confederate,* 3d *Regiment, Arizona Brigade.*
Magee's (James M.) Cavalry. See *Massachusetts Troops,* 2d *Battalion.*

Main's (Jacob) **Artillery.** See *Indiana Troops, 1st Battery.*
Malloy's (Adam G.) **Infantry.** See *Wisconsin Troops, 17th Regiment.*
Maloney's (Maurice) **Infantry.** See *Union Troops, Regulars, 1st Regiment.*
Mann's (Josiah J.) **Infantry.** See *Kentucky Troops, Union, 19th Regiment.*
Mansfield's (Fielding) **Infantry.** See *Indiana Troops, 54th Regiment.*
Mansfield's (Samuel M.) **Infantry.** See *Connecticut Troops, 24th Regiment.*
Marland's (William) **Artillery.** See *Massachusetts Troops, 2d (B) Battery.*
Marsh's (Arthur W.) **Infantry.** See *Illinois Troops, 118th Regiment.*
Marsh's (Lucius B.) **Infantry.** See *Massachusetts Troops, 47th Regiment.*
Martin's (Lewis D.) **Infantry.** See *Illinois Troops, 97th Regiment.*
Matheny's (James H.) **Infantry.** See *Illinois Troops, 130th Regiment.*
Maury **Artillery.** See *Tennessee Troops, Confederate.*
May's (Reuben) **Infantry.** See *Kentucky Troops, Union, 7th Regiment.*
Merchant's (Anderson) **Artillery.** Official designation not of record. See *Anderson Merchant.*
Merrill's (George S.) **Infantry.** See *Massachusetts Troops, 4th Regiment.*
Merritt's (Robert B.) **Infantry.** See *New York Troops, 75th Regiment.*
Messer's (Carlos P.) **Infantry.** See *Massachusetts Troops, 50th Regiment.*
Meyers' (James F.) **Cavalry.*** See *Florida Troops, Union, 2d Regiment.*
Miles' (W. R.) **Legion.** See *Louisiana Troops, Confederate.*
Miller's (Jacob) **Artillery.** See *Massachusetts Troops, 12th Battery.*
Miller's (Jesse S.) **Infantry.** See *Wisconsin Troops, 11th Regiment.*
Mills' (Milton) **Infantry.** See *Ohio Troops, 16th Regiment.*
Mitchell's (Nathaniel C.) **Cavalry.** See *Union Troops, Corps d'Afrique, 1st Regiment.*
Molineux's (Edward L.) **Infantry.** See *New York Troops, 159th Regiment.*
Monroe's (George W.) **Infantry.** See *Kentucky Troops, Union, 22d Regiment.*
Montgomery's (Bacon) **Cavalry.** See *Missouri Troops, 6th Regiment.*
Moore's (Frederick W.) **Infantry.** See *Ohio Troops, 83d Regiment.*
Moore's (Ira) **Infantry.** See *Illinois Troops, 33d Regiment.*
Moore's (Webster P.) **Cavalry.** See *Wisconsin Troops, 4th Regiment.*
Morgan's (Joseph S.) **Infantry.** See *New York Troops, 90th Regiment.*
Morgan's (Morgan, jr.) **Infantry.** See *New York Troops, 176th Regiment.*
Morrison's (Robert G.) **Infantry.** See *Indiana Troops, 34th Regiment.*
Morse's (Henry B.) **Infantry.** See *New York Troops, 114th Regiment.*
Morton's (John E.) **Artillery.** See *Maine Troops, 1st Battery.*
Moseley's (William G.) **Artillery.** See *Texas Troops, Confederate.*
Motte's (Ellis L.) **Artillery.** See *Massachusetts Troops, 13th Battery.*
Mowers' (Cornelius F.) **Infantry.** See *Union Troops, Corps d'Afrique, 7th Regiment.*
Mudd's (John J.) **Cavalry.** See *Illinois Troops, 2d Regiment.*
Mudgett's (William S.) **Infantry.** See *Union Troops, Corps d'Afrique, 8th Regiment.*
Murray's (Benjamin B., jr.) **Infantry.** See *Maine Troops, 15th Regiment.*
Neafie's (Alfred) **Infantry.** See *New York Troops, 156th Regiment.*
Nelson's (John A.) **Infantry.** See *Union Troops, Corps d'Afrique, 3d Regiment.*
New Orleans **Infantry.** See *Louisiana Troops, Union.*
Nichols' (William H.) **Artillery.** See *Texas Troops, Confederate.*
Nims' (Ormand F.) **Artillery.** See *Massachusetts Troops, 2d (B) Battery,*
Noland's (Philip J.) **Artillery.** See *R. T. English's Artillery, ante.*
Norès' (J. E.) **Artillery.** See *Watson Artillery, post.*
Norris' (Hardman P.) **Artillery.** See *Union Troops, Regulars, 1st Regiment, Battery F.*
Nott's (Charles C.) **Infantry.** See *New York Troops, 176th Regiment.*
Nutting's (Oscar F.) **Artillery.** See *Wisconsin Troops, 1st Battery.*
O'Connor's (James H.) **Cavalry.** See *Illinois Troops, 3d Regiment.*
Osband's (Embury D.) **Cavalry.** See *Illinois Troops, 4th Regiment.*

---

* Temporarily commanding.

Paine's (Charles J.) Infantry. See *Louisiana Troops, Union, 2d Regiment.*
Parish's (W. N.) Infantry. See *Arkansas Troops, Confederate, 18th Regiment.*
Parmele's (Theodore W.) Infantry. See *New York Troops, 174th Regiment.*
Parrish's (Charles S.) Infantry. See *Indiana Troops, 8th Regiment.*
Patterson's (William F.) Engineers. See *Kentucky Troops, Union.*
Pearsall's (Uri B.) Infantry. See *Union Troops, Corps d'Afrique, 15th Regiment.*
Pearson's (Timothy) Artillery. See *Massachusetts Troops, 15th Battery.*
Peck's (David B.) Infantry. See *Vermont Troops, 7th Regiment.*
Peck's (Frank H.) Infantry. See *Connecticut Troops, 12th Regiment.*
Peck's (Lewis M.) Infantry. See *New York Troops, 173d Regiment.*
Peel's (M. C.) Infantry. See *Arkansas Troops, Confederate, 18th Regiment.*
Pelican Artillery. See *Louisiana Troops, Confederate.*
Perkins' (Hiram E.) Infantry. See *Union Troops, Corps d'Afrique, 1st Regiment.*
Perkins' (S. A.) Cavalry. See *Massachusetts Troops, 2d Battalion.*
Per Lee's (Samuel R.) Infantry. See *New York Troops, 114th Regiment.*
Perry's (Oran) Infantry. See *Indiana Troops, 69th Regiment.*
Phelps' (John F.) Artillery. See *Massachusetts Troops, 6th Battery.*
Phillips' (Joseph) Cavalry. See *Texas Troops, Confederate, 3d Regiment, Arizona Brigade.*
Phillips' (Peter) Cavalry. See *Illinois Troops, 15th Regiment.*
Pike's (James) Infantry. See *New Hampshire Troops, 16th Regiment.*
Plumly's (Mardon W.) Infantry. See *Union Troops, Corps d'Afrique, 14th Regiment.*
Plunkett's (Charles T.) Infantry. See *Massachusetts Troops, 49th Regiment.*
Pope's (Henry D.) Cavalry. See *Massachusetts Troops, 3d Regiment.*
Porter's (T. K.) Infantry. See *Louisiana Troops, Confederate, 30th Regiment.*
Porter's (Thomas W.) Infantry. See *Maine Troops, 14th Regiment.*
Potter's (Leander H.) Infantry. See *Illinois Troops, 33d Regiment.*
Powell's (John W.) Artillery. See *Illinois Troops, 2d Regiment, Battery F.*
Prince's (Edward) Cavalry. See *Illinois Troops, 7th Regiment.*
Provence's (David) Infantry. See *Arkansas Troops, Confederate, 16th Regiment.*
Pyron's (Charles L.) Cavalry. See *Texas Troops, Confederate, 2d Regiment.*
Rabb's (Thomas) Cavalry. See *Texas Troops, Confederate, 33d Regiment.*
Rawles' (Jacob B.) Artillery. See *Union Troops, Regulars, 5th Regiment, Battery G.*
Raynor's (William H.) Infantry. See *Ohio Troops, 56th Regiment.*
Redfield's (James H.) Infantry. See *Indiana Troops, 16th Regiment.*
Reid's (John B.) Infantry. See *Illinois Troops, 130th Regiment.*
Reid's (T. J., jr.) Infantry. See *Arkansas Troops, Confederate, 12th Regiment.*
Reinhard's (Fred. W.) Artillery. See *Massachusetts Troops, 4th (D) Battery.*
Rexford's (Willie M.) Infantry. See *New York Troops, 131st Regiment.*
Rice's (Charles S.) Artillery. See *Ohio Troops, 17th Battery.*
Rice's (Edward) Artillery. See *Vermont Troops, 1st Battery.*
Richardson's (James P.) Infantry. See *Massachusetts Troops, 38th Regiment.*
Richardson's (T. J. M.) Cavalry. See *Texas Troops, Confederate, 3d Regiment (State).*
Riddle's (George W.) Infantry. See *Indiana Troops, 49th Regiment.*
Risdon's (Orlando C.) Infantry. See *Mississippi Troops, Union, 3d Regiment (Colored).*
Ritter's (Richard) Infantry. See *Illinois Troops, 28th Regiment.*
Roberts' (Calvit) Artillery. See *Seven Stars Artillery, post.*
Roberts' (O. M.) Infantry. See *Texas Troops, Confederate, 11th Regiment.*
Robinson's (George D.) Engineers. See *Union Troops, Corps d'Afrique, 3d Regiment.*
Robinson's (Harai) Cavalry. See *Louisiana Troops, Union, 1st Regiment.*
Robinson's (J. H.) Cavalry. See *Texas Troops, Confederate, 33d Regiment.*
Rodgers' (John I.) Artillery. See *Union Troops, Regulars, 2d Regiment, Battery C.*
Rogers' (George W.) Infantry. See *New York Troops, 173d Regiment.*

Rogers' (L. M.) Cavalry. See *Texas Troops, Confederate, 3d Regiment (State)*.
Rose's (Augustine D.) Infantry. See *Indiana Troops, 26th Regiment*.
Rose's (Elihu E.) Cavalry. See *Indiana Troops, 1st Regiment*.
Ross' (Henry W.) Cavalry. See *Wisconsin Troops, 4th Regiment*.
Rountree's (L. C.) Infantry. See *Texas Troops, Confederate, 13th Regiment*.
Rowland's (Edward S.) Artillery. See *Missouri Troops, 1st Regiment, Battery E*.
Roy's (William) Heavy Artillery. See *Indiana Troops, 1st Regiment*.
Russell's (Edward K.) Artillery. See *Massachusetts Troops, 6th Battery*.
Rust's (Henry, jr.) Infantry. See *Maine Troops, 13th Regiment*.
Rutherford's (Friend S.) Infantry. See *Illinois Troops, 97th Regiment*.
Rygaard's (Loren) Heavy Artillery. See *Union Troops, Corps d'Afrique, 1st Regiment*.
Sage's (Clinton H.) Infantry. See *New York Troops, 110th Regiment*.
Saint Mary's Cannoneers, Artillery. See *Louisiana Troops, Confederate*.
Sanderson's (James A.) Artillery. See *Union Troops, Regulars, 1st Regiment, Battery L*.
Sargent's (Horace B.) Cavalry. See *Massachusetts Troops, 1st Regiment*.
Sargent's (Lorenzo D.) Cavalry. See *Massachusetts Troops, 3d Regiment*.
Saufley's (W. P.) Cavalry. See *Texas Troops, Confederate, 1st Regiment, Partisan*.
Sawtell's (Josiah A.) Infantry. See *Massachusetts Troops, 26th Regiment*.
Sayles' (Frank) Cavalry. See *Headquarters Troops, Department of the Gulf*.
Schmidt's (Adolph) Cavalry. See *New York Troops, 14th Regiment*.
Scofield's (Hiram) Infantry. See *Louisiana Troops, Union, 8th Regiment (Colored)*.
Scott's (E. A.) Cavalry. See *Louisiana Troops, Confederate, 9th Battalion*.
Sears' (Francis A.) Infantry. See *Indiana Troops, 67th Regiment*.
Seawell's (W. B.) Heavy Artillery. See *Louisiana Troops, Confederate, 12th Battalion*.
Selden's (Joseph) Infantry. See *Connecticut Troops, 26th Regiment*.
Semmes' (Oliver J.) Artillery. See *Confederate Troops, Regulars*.
Sentell's (William H.) Infantry. See *New York Troops, 160th Regiment*.
Seven Stars Artillery. See *Mississippi Troops, Confederate*.
Shannon's (D. W.) Cavalry. See *Texas Troops, Confederate, 5th Regiment*.
Sharpe's (Jacob) Infantry. See *New York Troops, 156th Regiment*.
Shaurman's (Nelson) Infantry. See *New York Troops, 90th Regiment*.
Shelby's (W. B.) Infantry. See *Mississippi Troops, Confederate, 39th Regiment*.
Sheldon's (Lionel A.) Infantry. See *Ohio Troops, 42d Regiment*.
Shoemaker's (William R.) Ordnance. See *Union Troops, Regulars*.
Shunk's (David) Infantry. See *Indiana Troops, 8th Regiment*.
Sizer's (John M.) Infantry. See *New York Troops, 116th Regiment*.
Slocum's (Willard) Infantry. See *Ohio Troops, 120th Regiment*.
Smalley's (Henry A.) Artillery. See *Union Troops, Regulars, 2d Regiment, Battery K*.
Smith's (Elisha B.) Cavalry. See *New York Troops, 114th Regiment*.
Smith's (James) Infantry. See *New York Troops, 128th Regiment*.
Smith's (Warren D.) Infantry. See *New York Troops, 110th Regiment*.
Spaight's (A. W.) Infantry. See *Texas Troops, Confederate*.
Sparrestrom's (Frederick) Artillery. See *Illinois Troops, 2d Regiment, Battery G*.
Spear's (Edward, jr.) Artillery. See *Ohio Troops, 15th Battery*.
Speight's (J. W.) Infantry. See *Texas Troops, Confederate, 15th Regiment*.
Spicely's (William T.) Infantry. See *Indiana Troops, 24th Regiment*.
Spiegel's (Marcus M.) Infantry. See *Ohio Troops, 120th Regiment*.
Stafford's (Spencer H.) Infantry. See *Union Troops, Corps d'Afrique, 1st Regiment*.
Stedman's (Joseph) Infantry. See *Massachusetts Troops, 42d Regiment*.
Steedman's (I. G. W.) Infantry. See *Alabama Troops, 1st Regiment*.
Steger's (Emil) Artillery. See *Illinois Troops, 2d Regiment, Battery E*.
Stillman's (George L.) Artillery. See *Michigan Troops, 7th Battery*.
Stone's (B. W.) Cavalry. See *Texas Troops, Confederate, 6th Regiment*.
Stone's (Eben F.) Infantry. See *Massachusetts Troops, 48th Regiment*.

Street's (T. A.) **Infantry.** See *Alabama Troops*, 49*th Regiment.*
Tarbell's (Jonathan) **Infantry.** See *New York Troops*, 91*st Regiment.*
Taylor's (Franck E.) **Artillery.** See *Union Troops, Regulars*, 1*st Regiment, Battery L.*
Taylor's (George W.) **Artillery.** See *Massachusetts Troops*, 4*th* (*D*) *Battery.*
Taylor's (Richard) **Cavalry.** See *Texas Troops, Confederate*, 33*d Regiment.*
Thomas' (S. M.) **Artillery.** See *R. M. Boone's Artillery, ante.*
Thompson's (William G.) **Infantry.** See *Iowa Troops*, 20*th Regiment.*
Thurber's (Benjamin F.) **Infantry.** See *New York Troops*, 75*th Regiment.*
Tice's (Isaac L.) **Infantry.** See *Ohio Troops*, 48*th Regiment.*
Tilghman's (Oswald) **Artillery.** See *Tennessee Troops, Confederate*, 1*st Regiment, Battery B.*
Toledano's (E. A.) **Artillery.** See *Watson Artillery, post.*
Townsend's (S.) **Cavalry.** See *Texas Troops, Confederate*, 3*d Regiment* (*State*).
Trull's (George G.) **Artillery.** See *Massachusetts Troops*, 4*th* (*D*) *Battery.*
Twist's (Russell P.) **Artillery.** See *Ohio Troops*, 16*th Battery.*
Valverde Artillery. See *Texas Troops, Confederate.*
Van Anda's (Salue G.) **Infantry.** See *Iowa Troops*, 21*st Regiment.*
Vance's (Joseph W.) **Infantry.** See *Ohio Troops*, 96*th Regiment.*
Vandenburgh's (Robert S.) **Infantry.** See *New York Troops*, 174*th Regiment.*
Van Petten's (John B.) **Infantry.** See *New York Troops*, 160*th Regiment.*
Van Zandt's (Jacob) **Infantry.** See *New York Troops*, 91*st Regiment.*
Varner's (Sampson E.) **Infantry.** See *Ohio Troops*, 56*th Regiment.*
Vaughan's (E. L.) **Infantry.** See *Arkansas Troops, Confederate*, 10*th Regiment.*
Vidal's (Adrian I.) **Partisan Rangers.** See *Texas Troops, Union;* also *Texas Troops, Confederate.*
Vincent's (W. G.) **Cavalry.** See *Louisiana Troops, Confederate*, 2*d Regiment.*
Walker's (Henry) **Infantry.** See *Massachusetts Troops*, 4*th Regiment.*
Waller's (E., jr.) **Cavalry.** See *Texas Troops, Confederate*, 13*th Battalion.*
Washburn's (Henry D.) **Infantry.** See *Indiana Troops*, 18*th Regiment.*
Watkins' (William L.) **Infantry.** See *New York Troops*, 174*th Regiment.*
Watson Artillery. See *Louisiana Troops, Confederate.*
Waul's (T. N.) **Legion.** See *Texas Troops, Confederate.*
Webb's (Lysander R.) **Infantry.** See *Illinois Troops*, 77*th Regiment.*
Webber's (A. Watson) **Infantry.** See *Mississippi Troops, Union*, 1*st Regiment* (*Colored*).
Webster's (Daniel) **Artillery.** See *Wisconsin Troops*, 1*st Battery.*
Weld's (Mason C.) **Infantry.** See *Connecticut Troops*, 25*th Regiment.*
Welfley's (Martin) **Artillery.** See *Missouri Troops*, 1*st Regiment, Battery B.*
West's (J. A. A.) **Artillery.** See *O. J. Semmes' Artillery, ante.*
White's (Ephraim G.) **Infantry.** See *Iowa Troops*, 22*d Regiment.*
White's (Patrick H.) **Artillery.** See *Charles G. Cooley's Artillery, ante.*
White's (Samuel) **Mounted Rangers.** See *Union Troops, Corps d'Afrique*, 1*st Regiment, Cavalry.*
Whiteside's (S. A.) **Improvised Infantry.** See *S. A. Whiteside.*
Whiting's (John E.) **Infantry.** See *Illinois Troops*, 87*th Regiment.*
Whitman's (Charles T.) **Infantry.** See *Louisiana Tooops, Confederate*, 4*th Regiment.*
Whittemore's (Horace O.) **Infantry.** See *Massachusetts Troops*, 30*th Regiment.*
Whittlesey's (Luther H.) **Infantry.** See *Wisconsin Troops*, 11*th Regiment.*
Wilds' (John Q.) **Infantry.** See *Iowa Troops*, 24*th Regiment.*
Williams' (Frederick A.) **Infantry.** See *Ohio Troops*, 42*d Regiment.*
Williams' (William H.) **Infantry.** See *Ohio Troops*, 42*d Regiment.*
Willis' (George A.) **Cavalry.** See *Illinois Troops*, 15*th Regiment.*
Wingfield's (J. H.) **Cavalry.** See *Louisiana Troops, Confederate*, 9*th Battalion.*
Winter's (Elisha) **Infantry.** See *Maine Troops*, 12*th Regiment.*

Wood's (William F.) **Infantry.** See *Arkansas Troops, Union, 1st Regiment (Colored).*

Woodman's (Ephraim W.) **Infantry.** See *Maine Troops, 28th Regiment.*

Woods' (P. C.) **Cavalry.** See *Texas Troops, Confederate, 36th Regiment.*

Wright's (Edward) **Infantry.** See *Iowa Troops, 24th Regiment.*

Wrotnouski's (Arthur F.) **Engineers.** See *Union Troops, Corps d'Afrique, 1st Regiment.*

Yeaton's (Reuben F.) **Cavalry.** See *Louisiana Troops, Union, 1st Regiment.*

Yellow Jacket Infantry. See *Louisiana Troops, Confederate, 10th Battalion.*

Young's (Mahlon M.) **Infantry.** See *Vermont Troops, 7th Regiment.*

Young's (Van E.) **Infantry.** See *Louisiana Troops, Union, 11th Regiment (Colored).*

Zapata's (Clemente) **Cavalry.** See *Texas Troops, Union, 2d Regiment.*

Zulavsky's (Ladislas L.) **Infantry.** See *Union Troops, Corps d'Afrique, 10th Regiment.*

INDEX.

Brigades, Divisions, Corps, Armies, and improvised organizations are "Mentioned" under name of commanding officer; State and other organizations under their official designation. (See Alternate Designations, pp. 921–932.)

Page.

Abandoned and Captured Property. Communication from Napoleon J. T. Dana 856

See also *order of Banks*, p. 715.

Abandoned Lands. See *Refugees, Abandoned Lands, etc.*

Abbott, Henry. Mentioned 64

Abbott, John C.

  Correspondence with

    Banks, Nathaniel P 103

    Eaton, Stephen M 88

  Mentioned 76, 77, 88, 91, 111, 112

  Report of siege of Port Hudson, La., May 21–July 8, 1863 78

Abercrombie, L. A. Mentioned 308, 310

Abert, William S. Mentioned 794, 808, 820

Abreü, F. P. Mentioned 25, 257, 750, 828

Adams, Daniel W. Mentioned 496

Adams, Edgar E. Mentioned 63

Adams, Edgar G. Mentioned 60

Adams, E. O. Mentioned 786

Adams, Henry S. Mentioned 61

Adams, Joseph. Mentioned 336, 665, 710

Adams, Merrill H. Mentioned 60

Adams, William. Mentioned 322, 326

Adelaide, Schooner. Mentioned 793

Adjutant-General's Office, U. S. A.

  Correspondence with

    Army Headquarters 272

    Banks, Nathaniel P 269, 272, 496, 608, 807

    Carleton, James H 232, 254, 260, 563

    Emory, William H 540, 570

    Rhode Island, Governor of 270, 271

    Ullmann, Daniel 609

  Orders, General, series 1863: **No. 41,** 911; **No. 128,** 487.

  Orders, Special, series 1863: **No. 382,** 698; **No. 427,** 734.

Adjutant and Inspector General's Office, C. S. A.

  Correspondence with

    Johnston, Joseph E 182

    Maury, Dabney H 452

    Smith, E. Kirby 209, 392

    War Department, C. S 385

A. G. Brown, Steamer. Mentioned 380, 782

Agnus, Felix. Mentioned 65, 529, 632, 711

Ainsworth, Ira W. Mentioned 529, 632

Page.

Ajax, Tug. Mentioned 829
Alabama, Steamer. Mentioned 658,793–795,798,801,807,832,853
Alabama Troops. Mentioned.
    Artillery, Light—*Batteries :* Fowler's, 497.
    Cavalry—*Regiments :* 5th,·746.
    Infantry—*Regiments :* 1st, 36, 37, 143, 147, 156, 157, 161, 163, 166, 551 ; 28th,
      36th, 40th, 497 ; 49th, 143, 147, 150, 551 ; 79th [?], 655·
Alazan. (Indian.) Mentioned 31,260,261
Albatross, U. S. S. Mentioned..................................... 4,88,92,108,499,519
Alden, James.
    Correspondence with
      Augur, Christopher C.. 84,107,112,113
      Banks, Nathaniel P...................... 80,82,101,·102,106,·117–119,599,601
      Caldwell, Charles H. B... 107
      Eaton, Stephen M.. 88–91
      Farragut, David G 89–92
      Grover, Cuvier... 79
      Main, John N 107
      Palmer, James S 82,92,93,95,108,109
      Rauch, John H 113
    Mentioned 76,111,142,523,566,589
Alexander, Steamer. Mentioned... 713
Alexander, Captain. Mentioned 184
Alexander, George W. Mentioned.. 896
Alexander, Thomas. Mentioned... 59
Allcot, John H. Mentioned.. 69
Allen, ——. Mentioned.. 317
Allen, Charles F. Mentioned 711
Allen, C. M. Report of scout near Lake Pontchartrain, La., Sept. 13–Oct. 2,
    1863 313
Allen, Franklin. Mentioned 62
Allen, Harvey A. Mentioned....................................... 532,708,895
Allen, H. W. Mentioned... 813
Allen, Timothy. Mentioned 58,66
Allyn, John. Mentioned... 197
Alriso, Jesus. Mentioned.. 258
Altman, Charles. Mentioned 898
Alton, Edward. Mentioned.. 58
Amacker, O. P. Mentioned.. 166
Amey, De Witt C. Mentioned... 65
Amite River, La. Expeditions to. See *New and Amite Rivers, La. Expedi-
    tions from Carrollton and Baton Rouge to, Sept.* 24–29, 1863.
Ammons, J. B. Mentioned... 185
Anderson, A. L. Mentioned 29
Anderson, Daniel. Mentioned 59
Anderson, George. Mentioned 66
Anderson, James. Mentioned 64
Anderson, S. S. For correspondence as A. A. G., see *E. Kirby Smith.*
Andrew, John A. Mentioned.. 563
Andrews, George L.
    Correspondence with
      Banks, Nathaniel P.. 489,
        493,495,631,633,634,641,679,706,813,816,817,819,852,853,863,891
      Fearing, Hawkes, jr... 672

Page.

Andrews, George L.—Continued.

Mentioned 68,

488, 489, 491, 510, 529, 632, 638, 648–650, 660, 665, 667, 699, 707, 708, 726, 733,
741, 749, 777, 784, 794, 803, 810, 811, 814, 826, 827, 878, 888, 892, 893, 896

Report of skirmish at Jackson, La., Aug. 3, 1863 238

For correspondence as Chief of Staff, see *Nathaniel P. Banks.*

Andrews, Oliver C. Mentioned 57

Andrews, Philo. Mentioned 58

Angell, Henry. Mentioned 222, 230

Angeley, J. D. Mentioned 35

Anglo-American, Steamer. Mentioned 46, 108, 113, 191, 567, 568, 589

Annable, Thomas H. Mentioned 582

Antelope, Steamer. Mentioned 344

Anthony, Robert C. Mentioned 193, 580, 912–914

Apker, Samuel R. Mentioned 278, 279

Apodaca, Agapito. Mentioned 27, 258

Appleby, Charles F. Mentioned 63

Appleton, John F. Mentioned 60, 708

Arago, Steamer. Mentioned 713

Aransas Pass, Tex. Capture of Confederate battery at, Nov. 17, 1863. See
Rio Grande Expedition, Oct. 27–Dec. 2, 1863. Reports of

    Banks, Nathaniel P.   Bee, Hamilton P.   Ransom, Thomas E. G.

Aransas Pass, Tex., U. S. Officer in Command at. Correspondence with
Hamilton P. Bee 812

Archer, S. Mentioned 612, 750

Archuleta, Antonio. Mentioned 25

Argust, Benjamin M. Mentioned 28, 30

Arizona. Operations in, Nov. 21–Dec. 20, 1863. Communication from Edward
B. Willis 869

Arizona, U. S. S. Mentioned 11, 80, 92, 94, 101, 106, 108, 110,
114, 117, 204, 288, 294–299, 301, 302, 308, 311, 548, 562, 567, 617, 623, 640, 872

Arkansas Troops. Mentioned. (Confederate.)

Cavalry—*Regiments:* **2d**, 313, 314.

Infantry—*Battalions:* **1st [8th]**, 17, 143, 147. *Regiments:* **9th**, 44; **10th**,
143, 147, 148, 158, 159, 161, 163, 551; **11th**, 44, 143; **12th**, 143, 147, 159, 164:
14th, 143, 157; **15th**, 13, 17, 143, 147, 156, 161, 163, 551; **16th**, 143, 147, 149;
17th, 143; **18th**, 143, 151, 157, 158, 161, 162; **23d**, 143, 147, 151, 157, 176.

Arkansas Troops. Mentioned. (Union.)

Infantry—*Regiments:* **1st** (*Colored*), 712, 816, 829.

Arms, Ammunition, etc. Supplies of, etc. See *Munitions of War.*

Armstrong, Captain. Mentioned 342

Armstrong, David H. Mentioned 64

Armstrong, George E. Mentioned 65

Armstrong, Samuel A. Mentioned 894

Armstrong, W. B. Mentioned 903–905

Army Corps, 13th.

Artillery of. List of 738

    *Asboth, Alexander, assigned to duty with 741

Assigned to Department of the Gulf 2

Dana, Napoleon J. T.

    Assigned to command of 2d Division of 735

    Assumes command of 3, 776

Designations of divisions announced 681

Page.

Army Corps, 13th.—Continued.

Herron, Francis J., relieved from command of 2d Division of.............. 735
Lawler, Michael K., assigned to command of 1st Division of 773
Light batteries in. List of.. 691
Ord, Edward O. C., resumes command of 2
Proposed consolidation of, with 19th Corps. Communication from William
 B. Franklin.. 781
Transferred from Vicksburg and Natchez, Miss., to Carrollton, La......... 2,673
Washburn, Cadwallader C.
 Assigned to command of.. 2
 Assumes command of... 3
  For orders, see *Gulf, Department of the.*

Army Corps, 19th.

Batteries to accompany the Sabine Pass Expedition. List of.............. 721
Condition of 3d Division of. Communications from William H. Emory. 723, 725
Emory, William H.
 Assigned to command of 3d Division of............................... 698
 Assigned to command of 4th Division of.............................. 686
 Assigned to duty with 695
Franklin, William B.
 Assigned to command of... 684
 Assigned to command of 1st Division of.............................. 658
 Assumes command of... 2,693
Itinerary, Oct. 1–Nov. 18, 1863 369
Nickerson, Frank S.
 Assigned to command of 1st Brigade, 3d Division of.................. 698
 Assigned to command of 3d Division of............................... 685
Proposed consolidation of, with 13th Corps. Communication from William
 B. Franklin.. 781
Reorganization of. Communication from Nathaniel P. Banks............. 685
Reorganization of 3d Division of. Communication from Nathaniel P.
 Banks 636
Weitzel, Godfrey. Assigned to command of 1st Division of 685
  For orders, see *Gulf, Department of the.*

Army Headquarters.

Correspondence with
 Adjutant-General's Office, U. S. A...................................... 272
 Banks, Nathaniel P.. 338, 396, 492, 494, 498, 500, 503, 524, 534, 535, 545, 563, 564,
  572, 603, 636, 646, 651–653, 658, 661, 664, 666, 670–673, 675, 682, 685, 687, 688,
  690, 692, 694, 695, 697–699, 702, 714, 716, 718, 719, 722, 723, 729, 735, 742, 756,
  764, 766, 767, 775, 778, 796, 806, 810, 834, 836, 839–841, 845, 847, 871, 888, 890
 Carleton, James H... 720
 Emory, William H................................... 609, 616, 619, 630, 636
 Grant, U. S 664
 Hurlbut, Stephen A... 888
 Merrill, William E 656
 Reynolds, Joseph J... 837
 Rosecrans, William S.. 654
 Sherman, William T 887, 902, 903
 War Department, U. S.................................... 271, 656, 659
Memoranda for Banks, Grant, and Steele 739
Orders, Special, series 1863: **No. 234,** 506; **No. 409,** 722; **No. 537,** 832.

Army Transportation. See *Munitions of War.*

Page.

Arnold, Richard.
Correspondence with
  Banks, Nathaniel P 659, 692, 760
  Bradley, Theodore 87, 98
  Shunk, Francis J 691, 712, 738
  Swann, Robert P 143
  Terry, Edward... 142
Mentioned.................. 81, 114, 141, 382, 508, 509, 546, 547, 555, 627, 633, 692, 894
Arthur, Steamer. Mentioned... 743, 747
Artin, Lewis. Mentioned 28, 253, 254
Asboth, Alexander.
Assignments to command 741, 755, 756
Correspondence with
  Banks, Nathaniel P........................... 780, 786, 813, 817, 820, 833, 886.
  Suffolk, Steamer, Captain of... 786
Mentioned............................. 380, 741, 755, 756, 782, 786, 814, 827, 892, 895·
Atchafalaya, La.
Skirmish at Morgan's Ferry, on the, Sept. 20, 1863* 2
Skirmish at the, June 4, 1863*... 1
Skirmishes on the, Sept. 8–9, 1863*.. 2
Atkins, Robert F. Mentioned 896
Atkinson, William C. Mentioned 30
Atocha, A. A. Mentioned 764
Atwater, Joseph B. Mentioned 398, 709, 897
Atwood, George M. Mentioned... 529
Atwood, Robert. Mentioned... 62
Audenried, Joseph C. Mentioned 681
Augur, Christopher C.
Assignment to command 539
Correspondence with
  Alden, James 84, 107, 112, 113
  Banks, Nathaniel P............................... 112, 547, 550, 574, 585, 602
  Benner, Milton.. 84
  Dudley, Nathan A. M 116
  Dwight, William.. 102
  Farragut, David G.. 113
  Grierson, Benjamin H.. 84
  Paine, Charles J 602
Mentioned 5, 12, 13, 43–45, 67, 76, 77, 82–84,
    92, 93, 103, 104, 108, 121, 129, 137, 138, 140, 142, 179, 488, 489, 493, 501, 504,
    508–510, 519, 526–529, 539, 546, 547, 554, 555, 610, 611, 624, 626, 627, 642, 710
Auguste, Jacques. Mentioned 59
Austin, George I. Mentioned... 58
Austin, John. Mentioned... 62
Autenreith, Christopher. Mentioned....................................... 63
Averill, Perry. Mentioned.. 57
Avery, J. Mentioned 395
Ayres, James B. Mentioned.. 335
Ayres, Henry. Mentioned... 64
Baca, L. M. Mentioned.. 30
Baca. Roman A. Mentioned.. 30
Bache, Robert. Mentioned... 531
Bacon. Edward. Mentioned.......................... 529, 599, 708, 896

* No circumstantial reports on file.

Page

Bacon, Francis. Mentioned 495
Bagaly, Steamer. Mentioned 411, 787
Bagby, A. P. Mentioned 331, 346, 347, 349, 352, 370, 385, 391, 393, 394, 820
Bailey, George H. Mentioned... 71, 311
Bailey, George W. K. Mentioned................................... 334, 419, 423, 897
Bailey, G. W. Mentioned 353
Bailey, Herman W. Mentioned 58
Bailey, Theodorus.
  Correspondence with
    Navy Department, U. S. 670
    Woodbury, Daniel P 875
  Mentioned... 669, 702, 873, 874
Bainbridge, Edmund C. Mentioned.................................. 529, 660, 711
Baker, Charles. Mentioned 58
Baker, John P. Mentioned 368, 411, 682, 693
Baker, Joshua D. Mentioned.. 63
Baker, J. S.
  Correspondence with David G. Farragut................................ 115
  Mentioned... 80, 115, 292, 417, 419, 551
Baker, Richard. Mentioned 65
Baldwin, Herbert C. Mentioned 58
Baldwin, Silas. Mentioned.. 361
Ball, Hutchings & Co. Mentioned.. 485
Ball, James. Mentioned 65
Balling, George M. Mentioned 57
Ballinger, R. H. Mentioned.. 829
Balshaw, Richard. Mentioned.. 58
Baltzell, J. P. Mentioned... 496
    For correspondence as A. A. and I. G., see *Braxton Bragg.*
Bancroft, Horatio. Mentioned... 24
Bandka, Frederick. Mentioned... 66
Bangs, Isaac S., jr. Mentioned.. 708
Bankhead, Smith P. Mentioned.. 304
Bankhead, Smith P., Mrs. Mentioned.. 304
Banks, Nathaniel P.
  Congratulatory Orders. Siege of Port Hudson, La., May 21–July 8, 1863. 56, 671
  Co-operation of James H. Carleton with 879
  Co-operation of U. S. Grant with............. 494, 500, 506, 534, 535, 564, 680, 731
  Correspondence with
    Abbott, John C 103
    Adjutant-General's Office, U. S. A.................. 269, 272, 496, 608, 807
    Alden, James.......................... 80, 82, 101, 102, 106, 117–119, 599, 601
    Andrews, George L.. 489,
      493, 495, 631, 633, 634, 641, 679, 706, 813, 816, 817, 819, 852, 853, 863, 891
    Army Headquarters. 338, 396, 492, 494, 498, 500, 503, 524, 534, 535, 545, 563, 564,
      572, 603, 636, 646, 651–653, 658, 661, 664, 666, 670–673, 675, 682, 685, 687, 688,
      690, 692, 694, 695, 697–699, 702, 714, 716, 718, 719, 722, 723, 729, 735, 742, 756,
      764, 766, 767, 775, 778, 796, 806, 810, 834, 836, 839–841, 845, 847, 871, 888, 890
    Arnold, Richard.. 659, 692, 760
    Asboth, Alexander............................... 780, 786, 813, 817, 820, 833, 886
    Augur, Christopher C 112, 547, 550, 574, 585, 602
    Baton Rouge, La., Commanding Officer at 666
    Beckwith, Edward G................................... 701, 717, 758, 881, 915
    Bell, Henry H 668, 785, 793, 804

Page.

Banks, Nathaniel P.—Continued.

Correspondence with

Benedict, Lewis.. 502, 519, 521, 532

Benton, William P.. 824, 838

Birge, Henry W... 603, 805, 806, 820

Brashear, La., Depot Quartermaster at............................ 879

Buffington, Thomas J.. 644

Bulkley, Charles S 721

Bullitt, C 793

Carleton, James H... 788, 879

Cooke, Philip St. George 777, 779, 836

Crosby, J. Schuyler... 338, 763, 765

Dana, Napoleon J. T.............. 411, 753, 830, 842, 856, 862, 864, 876, 882, 885

Donaldsonville, La., Senior Naval Officer at...................... 805

Drew, Charles W... 567

Dudley, Nathan A. M 667

Dunham, Robert T.. 726, 731

Durell, Edward H.. 794

Dwight, William... 101,
102, 117, 118, 126, 536, 548, 551, 574, 613, 622, 624, 636, 848, 860, 863, 867

Eaton, Stephen M 95, 109

Emory, William H.. 49-51,
497, 519, 523, 524, 533, 534, 540, 541, 543, 544, 546, 559, 568, 571, 574-582,
585, 587, 590, 593-601, 605, 606, 613, 619, 630, 635, 637, 641, 646, 647, 671

Farragut, David G................................ 51, 78-82, 84, 89, 90, 100-102, 105,
106, 109-111, 113-117, 120, 504, 506, 507, 509, 511, 512, 518, 520, 521, 523-525,
533, 538, 542, 545, 547, 550-553, 556-558, 566, 570, 589, 620, 622, 623, 640

Fiske, William O.. 734, 805, 809, 812

Flanders, Benjamin F.. 736

Franklin, William B... 389,
692, 728, 732-734, 750, 751, 755, 756, 759-761, 763, 771-775, 778, 780, 781,
788, 790, 799, 812, 819, 829, 831, 835, 837, 847, 870, 872, 873, 881, 920

Gardner, Franklin 52, 53, 508, 513, 517, 552, 553, 557, 613, 617, 634

Gooding, Oliver P... 642

Grant, U. S... 49, 53, 506, 519, 520,
525, 617, 619, 624, 631, 633, 635, 643-645, 653, 656, 673, 680, 686, 701, 730, 752

Grierson, Benjamin H.. 573, 618, 625

Grover, Cuvier................... 541, 547, 559, 565, 574, 585, 595, 622, 625, 635, 640

Hadlock, William E.. 618

Herron, Francis J... 716, 722, 729, 732, 880

Holabird, Samuel B 510

Holbrook, William C 742

Hunter, David 523

Irwin, Richard B.. 488, 489, 684

Lawler, Michael K 805, 806, 813

Lincoln, Abraham.. 396, 688, 832, 833

Magruder, John B.. 850

Matamoras, Mexico, U. S. Consul at................................ 404, 405, 796

Merritt, Robert B... 669

Morgan, Joseph S 631

Morse, Edmund A 784

New Orleans, La., Commanding Officer U. S. Squadron at............ 757

New Orleans, La., French Consul at................................ 728, 792

Page.

Banks, Nathaniel F.—Continued.
Correspondence with
   Nickerson, Frank S... 518
   Ord, Edward O. C................ 692, 738, 751, 754, 757–763, 769–771
   Paine, Halbert E.. 127
   Palfrey, John C 638
   Palmer, James S 93,
     95, 98, 99, 108, 109, 118, 119, 490, 493, 499, 503, 504, 507, 522, 537, 558, 561, 622
   Peck, Frank H 653, 662, 668
   Porter, David D.............................. 687, 699, 779, 789, 861, 888
   Prince, Edward 556, 573
   Quartermaster-General's Office, U. S. A 785
   Sage, Clinton H..................... 81, 551, 558, 559, 562, 573, 608, 630
   Schofield, John M 807, 915
   Selfridge, Thomas O.. 715
   Sheldon, Lionel A 815
   Sherman, Thomas W 501, 503, 505
   State Department, U. S... 815, 846
   Stone, Charles P 102,
     118, 396, 642, 648–650, 652, 737, 782, 787, 793, 795, 798, 800, 803, 809, 813, 819
   Waples, Rufus 795
   War Department, U. S 5, 776, 846, 902
   Washburn, Cadwallader C.. 420,
     481, 714, 773, 824, 837, 849, 853, 859, 860, 867, 869, 878, 903
   Weitzel, Godfrey............... 501, 505, 509, 510, 626, 663, 848
   Woodbury, Daniel P.. 855, 873, 874
Mentioned 3–5, 7, 54, 66, 67, 76,
   77, 84, 91–94, 99, 100, 104, 105, 107–109, 112, 113, 115, 116, 118, 119, 137, 138,
   141, 144, 169, 180, 181, 183, 186, 189, 191, 203, 206, 210, 213, 214, 217, 218, 270–
   272, 293, 294, 320, 338, 367, 381, 383, 388, 389, 391, 393, 398, 410, 411, 414, 425,
   428, 429, 431, 488, 490, 506, 510, 520, 526, 527, 529, 557, 558, 566, 567, 578, 590–
   592, 598, 600, 601, 609–611, 615–619, 628, 630, 631, 633, 635, 636, 641, 643, 645,
   653, 656, 657, 659, 664, 665, 669, 670, 672–674, 679, 680, 682, 707, 718, 722, 734,
   737, 748, 755, 775, 783, 788, 795, 796, 799, 803, 807, 808, 823, 824, 826, 829, 830,
   832, 837, 846, 851, 856, 859, 865, 866, 870, 882, 891, 894, 897, 902, 909, 911, 916
Orders in cases of
   Abandoned and captured property.................................... 715
   Colored troops. Recruitment and organization of.................... 726
   Company C, 1st Louisiana Heavy Artillery............................ 791
   Negroes.. 704, 777
   Second Rhode Island Cavalry... 269
   Trade and intercourse.. 715
Re-enforcements for. Communication from Army Headquarters............ 664
Reports of
   Fort Jackson, La. Mutiny at, Dec. 9, 1863 .... 456, 457
   Gulf, Department of the. Operations in, Dec. 16, 1862–Dec. 31, 1863.. 6
   Port Hudson, La. Siege of, May 21–July 8, 1863......... 43, 45, 46, 48, 52, 55
   Rio Grande Expedition, and operations on the coast of Texas, Oct.
     27–Dec. 2, 1863......................... 396, 397, 399, 402, 405, 406, 409
   Sabine Pass (Texas) Expedition, Sept. 4–11, 1863.............. 286–288, 290
   Stirling's Plantation, on the Fordoche, La. Action at, Sept. 29, 1863.. 320
Resolution of thanks of U. S. Congress to, and the officers and soldiers
   under his command.. 911
Staff. Announcement of 660

Page.

Banks, N. P., Steamer. Mentioned .·... 809, 814
Banneras, José. Mentioned..... 25
Barbey, Julius L. Mentioned 24
Barboncito (Indian.) Mentioned... 316
Barden, Captain. Mentioned 447
Bargie, L. A. Mentioned.. 23
Barker, George. Mentioned.. 209
Barker, James E. Mentioned. 65
Barker, J. T.
    Correspondence with David G. Farragut 80
    Mentioned 80, 411
Barnes, James. Mentioned 530, 708, 896
Barnett, J. Mentioned... 166
Barnett, J. R. Mentioned.. 147
Barnum, Zera. Mentioned 62
Barre's Landing, La.
    Operations near. See *Teche Road, La. Operations on the, between Barre's
        Landing and Berwick, May 21-26, 1863.*
    Skirmish at, Oct. 21, 1863. See *Opelousas and Barre's Landing, La.*
    Steamer Louisiana Belle attacked near. See *Louisiana Belle, Steamer. Attack
        on, near Barre's Landing, Bayou Teche, La., May 22, 1863.*
Barrett, Richard. Mentioned 39, 209, 502, 895
Barrett, William M. Mentioned 530
Barry, Robert C. Mentioned... 58
Barry, Thomas. Mentioned.. 65
Barthelemy, John. Mentioned.. 502
Bartlett, Ozias E. Mentioned.. 602
Bartlett, William H. Mentioned.. 71, 511
Barthelow, Jeff. Mentioned 449
Bassett, Chauncey J. Mentioned...................... 59, 398, 529, 708, 733, 896
Bassett, James W. Mentioned 62
Bassford, Abraham. Mentioned 828, 900
Baton Rouge, La.
    Expeditions from. See *New and Amite Rivers, La. Expeditions from Carrollton
        and Baton Rouge to, Sept. 24-29, 1863.*
    Operations in the vicinity of, Sept. 25, 1863*............................... 3
    Skirmish on the Greenwell Springs road, near, Sept. 19, 1863* 2
Baton Rouge, La., Commanding Officer at. Correspondence with Nathaniel
        P. Banks 666
Battell, B.
    Mentioned 537
    Statement of. Siege of Port Hudson, La., May 21-July 8, 1863 537
Battles, John. Mentioned 61
Baylor, George W. Mentioned 358
Baylor, John R. Mentioned 917, 918
Bayou Bœuf Crossing, La. Capture of Union forces at, June 24, 1863. See
    *Louisiana. Operations in, west of the Mississippi, June 7-July 13,
    1863, Reports of*

        Green, Thomas.   Mouton, Alfred.   Taylor, Richard.
        Major, James P.

---

*No circumstantial reports on file.

                                                                    Page.
Bayou Bourbeau, La.   '
  Engagement at, Nov. 3, 1863.   See *Teche Country, La.   Operations in the, Oct:*
    3-Nov. 30, 1863. *Reports of*
        Buibridge, Stephen G.   Guppey, Joshua J.   Robinson, Harai.
        Fonda, John G.   Marland, William.   Taylor, Richard.
        Franklin, William B.   Ord, Edward O. C.   Washburn, Cadwallader C.
        Green, Thomas.
  See also *Record of Events, 13th Corps,* p. 366; *Record of Events, Cav. Div.,*
                              p. 377.
  Skirmish at, Nov. 2, 1863.   See *Teche Country, La.   Operations in the, Oct. 3-*
    Nov. 30, 1863. *Reports of*
        Green, Thomas.   Taylor, Richard.   Washburn, Cadwallader C.
  See also *Record of Events, Cav. Div.,* p. 377.
Bayou Courtableau, La.   Skirmish at, May 22, 1863*.......................   1
Bayou Goula, La.   Raid on, June 19, 1863.   See *Louisiana.   Operations in, west*
    of the Mississippi, June 7-July 13, 1863.   Report of Major, p. 217.
Bayou Macon, La.
  Expedition from Goodrich's Landing to, Sept. 27-29, 1863*................   3
  Skirmish at, Aug. 24, 1863.   See *Monroe, La.   Expedition from Vicksburg, Miss.:,*
    to, including skirmishes (24th) at Bayou Macon and at Floyd, Aug.
    20-Sept. 2, 1863.
Bayou Portage, Grand Lake, La.   Affair at, Nov. 23, 1863.   See *Teche Country,*
    La.   Operations in the, Oct. 3-Nov. 30, 1863. ' *Reports of*
        Franklin, William B.   Lucas, Thomas J.   Paine, Charles. J.
        Lee, Albert L.
  See also *Record of Events, Cav. Div.,* p. 377.
Bayou Sara, La.   Skirmish near, Nov. 9, 1863.
  Communication from Dabney H. Maury....................................   452
  Report of Henry Maury...   452
Bayou Sara, La., Commanding Naval Officer at.   Correspondence with James
    S. Palmer...   499
Bayou Sara Road, La.   Operations on.   See *Merritt's Plantation, La.   Opera-*
    tions about, and on the Bayou Sara Road, La., May 18-19, 1863.
Bayou Tensas, La.   Skirmish at, Aug. 10, 1863*................................   2
Bayou Tunica, or Tunica Bend, La.   Skirmish at, Nov. 8, 1863*..............   3
Bay Saint Louis, Miss.   Skirmish at, Nov. 17, 1863*.......................   3
Bazaine, François Achille.   Mentioned................................ 844, 864
Beach, A.   Mentioned..   710
Beach, George W.   Mentioned..   140
Beall, William N. R.
  Correspondence with
    Dwight, William...   554
    Gardner, Franklin..   164
  Mentioned.............................. 9, 151, 169, 171, 172, 174, 536, 537, 643, 645
  Report of siege of Port Hudson, La., May 21-July 8, 1863 146-148
Bean, Sidney A.
  Mentioned 17, 39, 71, 530
  Report of skirmish at Boyce's Bridge, Cotile Bayou, La., May 14, 1863   36
Beane, Nelson.   Mentioned   64
Beaton, Charles H.   Mentioned   57
Beattie, Simon.   Mentioned   60
Beaucamp, Peter S.   Mentioned..   65
Beauman, Peter.   Mentioned...   60
Beaupre, William.   Mentioned   279

Beauregard, Fort. See *Fort Beauregard*. Page.

Beauregard, G. T. Mentioned 496
Beck, William Butler. Mentioned.. 121
Beckwith, Edward G.
    Correspondence with Nathaniel P. Banks 701, 717, 758, 881, 915
    Mentioned. 462, 605, 695, 707, 708, 711, 726, 749, 765, 783, 798, 801, 826, 846, 894, 900, 910
Bee, Steamer. Mentioned 488, 489, 567
Bee, Hamilton P.
    Correspondence with
        Aransas Pass, Tex., U. S. Officer in command at 812
        Nuevo Leon and Cohahuila, Mexico, Governor of...................... 438
        Ringgold Barracks, Tex., Commanding Officer at..................... 447
        Tamaulipas, Mexico, Governor of. (Manuel Ruiz)................ 450, 451
    Mentioned 185, 283, 399, 416, 431, 443. 446, 718, 719, 811, 850, 851, 886, 918
    Reports of
        Mier, Mexico. Affair with Zapata's banditti near, Sept. 2, 1863....... 284
        Rio Grande Expedition, and operations on the coast of Texas, Oct.
            27–Dec, 2, 1863 .... 432–43♦, 436–438
        Vidal, Adrian I. Mutiny of, Oct. 28, 1863........................ 448, 451
Beecher, Miles J. Mentioned.. 58
Belcher, Thomas. Mentioned.. 65
Belfast, Steamer. Mentioned.. 192
Bell, Clara, Steamer. Mentioned 907
Bell, Henry H.
    Correspondence with Nathaniel P. Banks...................... 668, 785, 793, 804
    Mentioned................ 285, 287, 289, 292, 298, 396, 456, 804, 807, 808, 814, 871
Belton, J. F. For correspondence as A. A. G., see *Theophilus H. Holmes.*
Belvidere, Steamer. Mentioned 293, 294, 298–300, 713
Benavides, Christobal. Mentioned 284, 285
Benavides, Refugio. Mentioned 284
Benavides, Santos.
    Mentioned 283, 284, 436, 830
    Report of affair with Zapata's banditti near Mier, Mexico, Sept. 2, 1863... 284
Benedict, Augustus W.
    Court-martial in case of. Mutiny at Fort Jackson, La., Dec. 9, 1863....... 479
    Mentioned 456, 460–475, 479, 861, 867, 868
    Testimony of. Mutiny at Fort Jackson, La., Dec. 9, 1863.............. 473, 474
Benedict, Lewis.
    Correspondence with Nathaniel P. Banks 502, 519, 521, 532
    Mentioned........... 78, 95, 114, 336, 511, 522, 529, 538, 550, 561, 595, 632, 711, 899
    Report of operations in the Teche Country, La., Oct. 3–Nov. 30, 1863 368
Benet, George A. Mentioned.. 62
Benjamin, Judah P. Mentioned 717
Benjamin, Nathan O. Mentioned.. 71
Bentley, Frank. Mentioned... 63
Benner, Milton.
    Correspondence with Christopher C. Augur 84
    Mentioned 103, 104, 112
    Report of siege of Port Hudson, La., May 21–July 8, 1863................ 82
Bennett, Major. Mentioned... 164
Bennett, John. Mentioned.. 58
Bennett, Joseph F. Mentioned 405
Bennett, Thomas W. Mentioned.. 709
Benson, Benjamin E. Mentioned 58
Benson, Henry M. Mentioned... 869

Page.

Benton, William P.
Correspondence with Nathaniel P. Banks 824, 838
Mentioned.................... 708, 709, 714, 715, 739, 810, 823, 838, 891, 893, 896, 897
Béreaud, Honoré. Mentioned 363, 778
Bergmann, E. H. Mentioned 25, 26, 612, 901
Bergtold, Jacob. Mentioned.. 63
Bering, John A. Mentioned.. 898
Bermudas, U. S. S. Mentioned.. 833
Berney, Joseph. Mentioned 2:17
Berry, Charles R. Mentioned. 816
Berry, H. G., Schooner. Mentioned 836
Berry, Henry S. Mentioned 60
Berry, William M. Mentioned 60
Bertram, Henry. Mentioned................................... 328, 398, 665, 709, 897
Berweeks, John W. Mentioned... 59
Berwick, La.
Operations near. See Teche Road, La. Operations on the, between Barre's
    • Landing and Berwick, May 21-26, 1863.
Skirmish at, June 1, 1863.
    Communications from
        Dennett, Thomas S.. 185
        Wordin, C. W.. 186
    Reports of William H. Emory..................................... 185, 186
Berwick, O. Mentioned 453-455
Bethum, Edward. Mentioned... 60
Betts, ——. Mentioned 24
Bevens, Chester. Mentioned 62
Bickham, A. C. Mentioned 165
Bickmore, Charles S. Mentioned... 60, 102
Bigelow, Judge. Mentioned 441
Bingham, Judson D. Mentioned.. 907
Birge, Henry W.
    Assignment to command... 756
    Correspondence with Nathaniel P. Banks...................... 603, 805, 806, 820
    Mentioned 46, 54, 70, 205,
        530, 595, 667, 686, 701, 711, 749, 756, 780, 782, 783, 805, 819, 826, 892, 895, 900
Birt, Alonzo. Mentioned 787
Bishop, George. Mentioned 708
Bishop, Isaac W. Mentioned.. 57
Bishop, William. Mentioned.. 57
Black, Andrew. Mentioned 57
Black, E. L. Mentioned 151
Black, John Charles.
    Mentioned.................................... 322, 324, 398, 665, 709, 894, 897
    Report of Rio Grande Expedition, and operations on the coast of Texas,
        Oct. 27–Dec. 2, 1863... 423
Black Hawk, U. S. S. Mentioned.. 455, 816
Blackman, Niram. Mentioned... 58
Blackstone, Steamer. Mentioned 849
Blackwell, Charles E. Mentioned 60
Blair, J. D. Mentioned.. 224
Blake, Charles W. Mentioned... 59, 708
Blake, John. Mentioned.. 58
Blake, Levi R. Mentioned.. 72

Page.

Blakely, Thomas R. Mentioned... 59
Blakeman, Edson V. R. Mentioned 63
Blakeney, Thomas J. Mentioned... 251
Blanchard, Justus W.
    Mentioned 73, 529, 899
    Report of siege of Port Hudson, La., May 21–July 8, 1863................. 126
Blanco, Ojo. Mentioned 31
Bleistein, Anton. Mentioned... 65
Blinn, Charles D. Mentioned 57, 900
Bliss, George S. Mentioned... 71
Blober, Charles. Mentioned... 193
Blodgett, George. Mentioned 60
Blood, C. B. H. Mentioned.. 657
Bloomer, Steamer. Mentioned 887
Boardman, Frederick A. Mentioned 632, 777, 828, 895
Board of Officers.
    Orders assembling, to consider defense of New Orleans, La 657
    Proceedings of 676–678
    Recommendations of 678
Bogart, James H. Mentioned... 71
Boggs, William R. Mentioned... 391
    For correspondence as Chief of Staff, see E. Kirby Smith.
Bogue, Edmund. Mentioned.. 58
Bohonnon, Clinton. Mentioned... 63
Bolan, Albion K. Mentioned 60
Bolan, Patrick. Mentioned.. 66
Bond, T. M. Mentioned 144, 167
Bonnet Carré, La., Commanding Officer at. Correspondence with William
            H. Emory 606
Bonney, Seth. Mentioned 61, 584
Boone, Elish W. Mentioned.. 259
Boone, H. H. Mentioned 216, 329–331
Boone, R. M. Mentioned 173, 551
Borden, James E. Mentioned... 65
Borris, Herman. Mentioned 334, 894
Borusky, Charles. Mentioned... 67
Boston, Tug-boat. Mentioned 114, 546
Bostwick, Charles E. Mentioned... 684, 896
Boudreau, Joseph. Mentioned.. 778
Boudro, Julius.
    Court-martial in case of. Mutiny at Fort Jackson, La., Dec. 9, 1863...... 478
    Mentioned.. 478, 479
Bourne, Edmund L. Mentioned... 141, 142
Boutte Station, La., Commanding Officer at. Correspondence with William
            H. Emory 600
Bowden, Wilson. Mentioned 60
Bowen, James. Mentioned.................................. 110, 114, 532, 726, 801
Bowie, George W. Mentioned.............................. 492, 612, 750, 827, 901
Bowles, Charles E. Mentioned... 63
Boyce, James. Mentioned... 61
Boyce, R. P. Mentioned... 224
Boyce, Simon P. Mentioned 62

Page.

Boyce's Bridge, Cotile Bayou, La. Skirmish at, May 14, 1863.
    Communication from George L. Andrews 493
    Reports of
        Bean, Sidney A 36
        Weitzel, Godfrey 35
Boyd, Francis E. Mentioned.. 61
Boylston, J. C. Mentioned 746
Boyne, Patrick. Mentioned.. 64
Brackenridge, George W. Mentioned.............................. 843, 856
Bracton, Robert. Mentioned.. 59
Bradbury, Albert W. Mentioned.............................. 336, 660, 711, 899
Bradford, Edward. Mentioned 60
Bradford, Henry. Mentioned... 59
Bradfute, W. R.
    Correspondence with Charles L. Pyron................................. 446
    Mentioned 431, 436, 437, 446, 447
    Reports of Rio Grande Expedition and operations on the coast of Texas,
        Oct. 27–Dec. 2, 1863.. 445, 446
Bradley, John W. Mentioned.. 58
Bradley, Theodore.
    Correspondence with
        Arnold, Richard.. 87, 98
        Slack, Charles B 87, 98
    Mentioned 531, 712
Brady, ———. Mentioned 441
Brady, James. Mentioned... 65
Brady, William. Mentioned.. 235
Bragg, Braxton. Mentioned........ 496, 526, 652, 654, 655, 674, 742, 817, 818, 833, 866
Braley, Lester E. Mentioned 57
Brand, Frederick B.
    Mentioned 173, 174, 551
    Report of siege of Port Hudson, La., May 21–July 8, 1863.............. 177, 178
Brand, John. Mentioned... 58
Branson, Charles. Mentioned 59
Brashear City, La.
    Capture of, June 23, 1863. See *Louisiana. Operations in, west of the Mis-*
        sissippi, June 7–July 13, 1863. Reports of

        Emory, William H.   Keith, John A.   Mouton, Alfred.
        Green, Thomas.   Major, James P.   Taylor, Richard.
        Hunter, Sherod.

        See also *Talbot to Holabird*, p. 595; *statements of Nail and Burt*, p. 913;
        Smith, p. 914.
    Reoccupation of, by Union forces, July 22, 1863. Communications from
        Banks, Nathaniel P 651
        Peck, Frank H... 653
    Skirmish at, June 21, 1863. See *Louisiana. Operations in, west of the Mis-*
        sissippi, June 7–July 13, 1863. Reports of Emory, p. 190; *Stickney*,
        p. 192.
Brashear City, La., Commanding Officer at. Correspondence with William
        H. Emory 581, 585, 590
Brashear, La., Depot Quartermaster at. Correspondence with Nathaniel P.
        Banks 879
Braubach, Philip. Mentioned 415, 831, 864, 865, 885
Brazier, James. Mentioned... 64

Page.

Brazos Island, Tex. Occupation of, by Union forces, Nov. 2, 1863. See *Rio Grande Expedition and operations on the coast of Texas, Oct. 27– Dec. 2, 1863. Reports of*

Banks, Nathaniel P.	Bruce, John.	Duff, James.
Bee, Hamilton P.	Davis, Henry T.	Taylor, Richard (Captain).

Breaux, Captain. Mentioned 322
Breckinridge, J. C. Mentioned 887
Breckinridge, John C. Mentioned 496
Breese, Sidney A. Mentioned 900
Breman, Samuel B. Mentioned 638
Brennan, James. Mentioned 64
Brennan, John. Mentioned 59
Brennan, Patrick. Mentioned 58
Brenning, George. Mentioned 708
Brewer, John B. Mentioned 41
Brewer, Sylvester. Mentioned 63
Brewster, J. D. For correspondence as A. D. C., see *Francis J. Herron.*
Bridgman, Eliot. Mentioned 708, 895
Brigaloa, Blass. Mentioned 25
Briggs, Joseph. Mentioned 58
Bringhurst, Thomas H. Mentioned 335, 371, 710
Bristol, Frank C. Mentioned 58
Bristol, Henry B. Mentioned 260, 261
Brooklyn, U. S. S. Mentioned 89, 185
Brooks, John D. Mentioned 66
Brotherton, D. H. Mentioned .... 827, 901 .
Brott, ———. Mentioned 669–671, 703
Brower, Charles. Mentioned 63
Brown, Steamer. Mentioned 328
Brown, A. G., Steamer. Mentioned 380, 782
Brown, Albert H. Mentioned 335, 358, 361, 365, 710
Brown, Edward. Mentioned 60
Brown, George. Mentioned 914
Brown, George E. Mentioned 61
Brown, I. M., Steamer. Mentioned 642
Brown, Jacob. Mentioned 58
Brown, James H. Mentioned 911, 912
Brown, James M. Mentioned 61
Brown, J. M., Steamer. Mentioned 782
Brown, John C. Mentioned 496
Brown, John H. Mentioned 60
Brown, John J. Mentioned 57
Brown, R. B. Mentioned 895
Brown, R. W. Mentioned 741
Brown, Valcour. Mentioned 59
Brown, Zachariah. Mentioned 856
Brownsville, Tex. Occupation of, by Union forces, Nov. 6, 1863. See *Rio Grande Expedition, and operations on the coast of Texas, Oct. 27–Dec. 2, 1863. Reports of Banks,* pp. 399, 405 ; *Bee,* p. 436.
Bruce, John.
  Mentioned 396, 665, 897
  Reports of
    Rio Grande Expedition, and operations on the coast of Texas, Oct. 27– Dec. 2, 1863 425
    Stirling's Plantation, on the Fordoche, La. Action at, Sept. 29, 1863.. 325

Page.

Brundage, Henry A. Mentioned 63
Brunson, Duff G. Mentioned... 278
Bryan, Michael K. Mentioned 71,633
Bryant, George E. ' Mentioned... 276
Buchanan, Franklin. Mentioned... 560,888,891
Buchanan, Thomas McK. Mentioned 4
Buchel, A.
    Mentioned 432,484,485
    Report of skirmish on Matagorda Peninsula, Tex., Dec. 29, 1863........... 485
Buck, Frederick. Mentioned... 62
Buehler, Theodore E. Mentioned 335,354,360
Buffington, Thomas J. Correspondence with Nathaniel P. Banks........... 644
Buhlan, Alfonso. Mentioned... 454
Bulkley, Charles S.
    Correspondence with Nathaniel P. Banks............................... 721
    Mentioned 16,78,83,380,734
Bull, James M. Mentioned 361,710
Bullen, Joseph D.
    Correspondence with
        Emory, William H... 605
        Woolsey, M. B 620,621
    Mentioned................... 15,47,50,190,202,531,571,605,613,621,622,620,650
Bullitt, C. Correspondence with Nathaniel P. Banks......................... 793
Bullock, William W. Mentioned............................... 121,335,529,710
Bunch, J. H. Mentioned.. 654
Burbridge, Stephen G.
    Correspondence with William B. Franklin 363,799
    Mentioned 319,335,343,354-358,364-367,374,382,394,
        428,431,710,734,739,749,751,755,758,765,783,826,831,835,837,867,898
    Reports of
        New and Amite Rivers, La. Expeditions from Carrollton and Baton
            Rouge to, Sept. 24-29, 1863...................................... 317
        Teche Country, La. Operations in the, Oct. 3-Nov. 30, 1863.... 359,362,363
Burdick, James. Mentioned 276
Burgess, Asa. Mentioned.. 63
Burke, George. Mentioned 59
Burke, John E. Mentioned 65
Burke, Joseph J. Mentioned 64
Burke, Michael. Mentioned 58
Burns, Harry A. Mentioned 24
Burnside, Ambrose E. Mentioned.. 494
Burrell, Isaac S. Mentioned... 4,6,7
Burris, B. Mentioned.. 442
Burris, William. Mentioned... 64
Burt, Charles A. Mentioned.................................... 262,530,900
Burt, Thomas P. Mentioned... 913,914
Bush, Daniel B., jr. Mentioned 336,379
Bush, Louis. Mentioned 216
Butler, Benjamin F. Mentioned.................................... 6,7,735
Butler, George. Mentioned.. 898
Butler, J. B. Mentioned 70
Butterfield, F. D. Mentioned 353
Buttle, Richard W. Mentioned... 64

Page.

Buzzard's Prairie, La. See *Bayou Bourbeau.*

Cadle, Cornelius, jr. Mentioned 275

Cadette. (Indian.) Mentioned 31,260,261

Cady, Lewis.
    Court-martial in case of. Mutiny at Fort Jackson, La., Dec. 9, 1863....... 477
    Mentioned 477,479

Cage, John J. Mentioned 59

Cahawha, U. S. S. Mentioned 298,519,523,534

Cahill, Thomas W.
    Correspondence with
        Emory, William H 189,577,582,584,586,588,591-594,596,597,606
        Sawtell, Josiah A 600
    Mentioned 102,118,187-189,197-200,529,531,576,
        577,579-581,585-587,593,594,596,597,686,711,749,783,826,892,895,900

Cailloux, Andrew. Mentioned 70

Caldwell, Charles H. B. Correspondence with James Alden................ 107.

Caldwell, J. P. Mentioned 160,161,165

Caldwell, William S. Mentioned... 61

Calhoun, U. S. S. Mentioned 623,640

California Troops. Mentioned.
    Cavalry—*Regiments:* **1st,** 24,492,612,750,827,828,901 ; **2d,** 31,261,612,750,
        827,844,901.
    Infantry—*Regiments:* **1st,** 24,28,31,258-260,316,612,750, 827, 828, 844, 845,
        870,901 ; **5th,** 23,612,750,827,828,901.

Call, William. Mentioned 58

Callahan, Charles M. Mentioned.. 335,710

Callanan, Patrick. Mentioned.. 64

Calvitt, Captain. Mentioned.. 332

Cameron, Charles. Mentioned 64

Cameron, Robert A. Mentioned..... 335,347,358,361,364,367,370,371,430,844,898

Campbell, James F. Mentioned 65

Campbell, Richard. Mentioned.. 531

Campbell, W. G.
    Deposition of. Illegal arrests.. 748
    Mentioned.. 743,746,748

Camp Hubbard, Thibodeaux, La. Mutiny at, Aug. 29-30, 1863.
    Communications from
        Adjutant-General's Office, U. S. A...................................... 269-272
        Army Headquarters.. 271
        Banks, Nathaniel P 269,272
        Rhode Island, Governor of 270
    Military Commission.
        Detail for... 262
        Order convening 262
        Proceedings, testimony, and findings 262-268
        Testimony of
            Hall, Edward B.. 265,266
            Irving, Sidney E... 267,268
            Ives, Francis M 264,265
            Mosicot, Jules A 266,267
            Robinson, Harai 262-264
            Walton, Charles 267

Camp Pratt, La.
Affair at, Nov. 25, 1863. See *Teche Country, La. Operations in the, Oct. 3–Nov. 30, 1863. Record of Events, Cav. Div.,* p. 377.
Skirmish at, Nov. 20, 1863. See *Teche Country, La. Operations in the, Oct. 3–Nov. 30, 1863. Reports of Franklin,* p. 346; *Lee,* p. 369. See also *Record of Events, 13th Army Corps,* p. 366; *Record of Events, Cav. Div.,* p. 377.
Canby, Edward R. S. Mentioned 251
For correspondence as A. A. G., see *War Department, U. S.*
Captured Property. See *Abandoned and Captured Property.*
Carey, Asa B. Mentioned 233, 234
Carey, James L. Mentioned 336, 377, 710, 900
Cargile, C. M. Mentioned 143
Carle, Henry. Mentioned...................................... 58
Carleton, James H.
Correspondence with
Adjutant-General's Office, U. S. A........................ 232, 254, 260, 563
Army Headquarters 720
Banks, Nathaniel P 788, 879
Carson, Christopher.. 727
Chihuahua, Mexico, U. S. Consul at 917
Schofield, John M.. 542
Wallen, Henry D.. 844
West, Joseph R 491
Mentioned.................. 414, 542, 612, 629, 750, 788, 827, 880, 901, 919
New Mexico, Department of. Synopsis of operations in, May 16–Dec. 29, 1863 .... 23, 33
Carle, Van Buren. Mentioned...................................... 61
Carlos, W. W. Mentioned...................................... 169
Carmouche, E. A. Mentioned 331
Carnahan, Robert H. Mentioned...................... 318, 336, 710, 828
Carnes, Patrick. Mentioned 62
Carondelet, U. S. S. Mentioned............................... 454
Carpenter, Colonel. Mentioned 852
Carpenter, Lewis E. Mentioned 383, 415, 495, 789
Carpenter, Seymour D. Mentioned................................. 66
Carr, Gouverneur. Mentioned............................. 336, 899
Carr, John F., C. S. S. Mentioned.................... 480, 481, 483
Carrington, D. C. Mentioned 224
Carrion Crow and Vermillion Bayous, La. Skirmishes at, Nov. 11, 1863. See *Teche Country, La. Operations in the, Oct. 3–Nov. 30, 1863. Reports of*

Benedict, Lewis.   Fonda, John G.   Franklin, William B.

See also *Itinerary of 19th Army Corps,* p. 369; *Record of Events, Cav. Div.,* p. 377.
Carrion Crow Bayou, La. Skirmishes at.
Oct. 14–15, 1863. See *Teche Country, La. Operations in the, Oct. 3–Nov. 30, 1863. Reports of Franklin,* p. 338; *Pigman,* p. 352. See also *Record of Events, 13th Army Corps,* p. 366; *Itinerary 19th Army Corps,* p. 369; *Record of Events, Cav. Div.,* p. 377.
Oct. 18, 1863. See *Teche Country, La. Operations in the, Oct. 3 Nov. 30, 1863. Record of Events, Cav. Div.,* p. 377.

Page.

Carrion Crow Bayou, La. Skirmishes at—Continued.
    Nov. 3, 1863. See *Teche Country, La. Operations in the, Oct. 3–Nov. 30,*
        1863. *Reports of*

> Burbridge, Stephen G.   Green, Thomas.   Washburn, Cadwallader C.
> Franklin, William B.   Marland, William.

See also *Record of Events, 13th Army Corps,* p. 366; *Record of Events, Cav.*
    Div., p. 377.
    Nov. 18, 1863* 333
Carroll, Thomas. Mentioned 66
Carrollton, La. Expeditions from. See *New and Amite Rivers, La. Expeditions*
    from Carrollton and Baton Rouge to, Sept. 24–29, 1863.
Carruth, William W. Mentioned.. 660, 712
Carson, Christopher.
    Correspondence with James H. Carleton 727
    Mentioned........................26–28, 30, 31, 232, 254, 563, 612, 629, 901
    Reports of operations against Navajo Indians in New Mexico.
        July 7–Aug. 19, 1863 233–236
        Aug. 20–Dec. 16, 1863... 250, 252, 255
Carter, C. Pembroke. Mentioned 60
Carter, Joseph. Mentioned 59
Carter, Joseph W. Mentioned.. 57
Cartwright, N. D. Mentioned 229
Carville, Charles R. Mentioned 71
Case, Isaac W. Mentioned... 61
Casey, William E. Mentioned.. 57
Cassidy, John. Mentioned... 65
Cassidy, Joseph O. Mentioned... 308
Casualties in Action. See *Confederate Troops* and *Union Troops.*
Catinet, Frigate. Mentioned... 690
Cavanagh, William F. Mentioned 61
Cavriere, José. Mentioned... 342
Cazainier, Camile. Mentioned.. 59
Cedar Bayou, Tex. Skirmish at, Nov. 23, 1863. See *Rio Grande Expedition,*
        Oct. 27–Dec. 2, 1863. Reports of Ransom, p. 427; *Ireland,* p. 447.
Centreville, La. Skirmish at, May 25, 1863* 1
Ceressolle, Octave. Mentioned... 58
Chacahoula Station, La. Skirmish at, June 24, 1863. See *Louisiana. Opera-*
        tions in, west of the Mississippi, June 7–July 13, 1863. Report of
        Fitz Gibbons, p. 201.
Chacon, Rafael.
    Mentioned 24, 27, 29, 260, 750
    Report of operations against Navajo Indians in New Mexico, Aug. 20–Dec.
        16, 1863 257
Chadwick, Charles. Mentioned 398, 709, 897
Chadwick, John C. Mentioned 896
Chadwick, Philander B. Mentioned... 62
Chamberlin, Edwin M. Mentioned 529, 712
Chambers, Alexander. Mentioned... 248
Champanel, Edmond. Mentioned.. 59
Chandler, J. G. Mentioned ...108, 113, 183, 339, 341, 342, 382, 383, 634, 693, 728, 779, 820
Chapa, ——. Mentioned.. 405
Chapin, Edward P. Mentioned... 17, 67, 71, 511

---

* No circumstantial reports on file.

	Page.
Chapman, Albert B. Mentioned	62
Chapman, Galen A. Mentioned	60
Chapman, T. P. Mentioned	750
Chargois, ———. Mentioned	762
Charles, Isidore. Mentioned	59
Charles, William S. Mentioned	334, 419, 422, 423
Chase, John W. Mentioned	896
Chasten, Joseph M. Mentioned	308
Chatard, Emile. Mentioned	59
Chaves, J. Francisco. Mentioned	24, 27, 315, 612
Chaves, José. Mentioned	25
Cheatham, Benjamin F. Mentioned	496
Cheneyville, La.	
Affair near, May 18, 1863. Report of Godfrey Weitzel.	38
Skirmish near, May 20, 1863. Report of Godfrey Weitzel.	39
Cherry, Peter. Mentioned	65
Cheshire, Jonas. Mentioned	64
Chesley, Captain. Mentioned	447
Chickering, Thomas E. Mentioned	40, 44, 61, 457, 489, 490, 502, 641
Chihuahua, Mexico, U. S. Consul at. Correspondence with	
Carleton, James H	917
Monterey, Mexico, U. S. Consul at	918
West, Joseph R	919, 920
Chinn, T. B. R. Mentioned	143
Chisum, Isham. Mentioned	221, 395
Choctaw, U. S. S. Mentioned	454
Choctawhatchie Bay, Fla. Descent upon Confederate salt-works in, Dec.	
10-19, 1863 *	3
Churchill, Theodore. Mentioned	65
Circassian, U. S. S. Mentioned	89
Clack, F. H. Mentioned	331
Claiborne, F. E. Mentioned	650, 723
Clancy, George. Mentioned	58
Clanton, James H. Mentioned	834
Clapp, Edward A. Mentioned	71
Clapp, M.	
Correspondence with William H. Emory	568
Mentioned	568
Clara Bell, Steamer. Mentioned	907
Clarey, Thomas. Mentioned	65
Clark, B. W. Mentioned	169, 175
Clark, Charles J. Mentioned	709
Clark, Eusebius S. Mentioned	190, 711
Clark, Frederick J. Mentioned	71
Clark, George W. Mentioned	398, 665, 709
Clark, James C. Mentioned	896
Clark, John G. Mentioned	398, 665, 709, 897
Clark, John N. Mentioned	252, 870
Clark, John S. Mentioned	9, 704
Clark, Theodore. Mentioned	131, 133
Clark, Thomas S.	
Mentioned	4, 9, 68, 102, 118, 125, 489, 529, 530, 549, 550, 561, 632
Report of siege of Port Hudson, La., May 21–July 8, 1863	122

---

*See Annual Report of the Secretary of the Navy, December 5, 1864.

Page.

Clark, William E. Mentioned 62

Clark, William Hyde. For correspondence as A. A. G., see *Napoleon J. T. Dana.*

Clark, W. T. For correspondence as A. A. G., see *James B. McPherson.*

Clarke, Samuel W. Mentioned.. 60

Clarkson, Arthur. Mentioned 64

Clay, C. C. Mentioned.. 496

Clay, H. L. Mentioned.. 495, 496

Cleburne, Patrick R. Mentioned 496

Clement, Joseph F. Mentioned... 60

Clifton, U. S. S. Mentioned........ 5, 288, 289, 292–301, 303, 305, 306, 308–311, 640, 878

Clinton, Steamer. Mentioned 410–412, 418, 419, 798, 800, 843, 867, 869

Clinton, James. Mentioned... 59

Clinton, La. Expedition to, June 3–8, 1863. See *Port Hudson, La. Siege of, May 21–July 8, 1863. Reports of*

    Grierson, Benjamin H.   Paine, Halbert E.   Richardson, James P
    Logan, John L.

    See also *Banks to Paine,* p. 127.

Clinton Road, La. Scouts on. See *Merritt's Plantation, La. Scouts from, on the Clinton Road, May 14, 1863.*

Closson, Henry W. Mentioned........ .... 87, 98, 336, 354, 531, 660, 892, 900

Clothing, Camp and Garrison Equipage. See *Munitions of War.*

Clough, J. P. Mentioned 224

Cobb, John C. Mentioned 684, 707, 898

Cobos, José Maria.

    Mentioned ....:.. 399–403, 406–408

    Proclamation to Army... 401

    Proclamation to citizens of Matamoras, Mexico 402

Coburn, James E. Mentioned.. 71

Cochen, Henry. Mentioned.. 71

Coffin, W. Norris. Mentioned.. 156

Cohn, Alexander. Mentioned... 57

Cojer, William J. Mentioned.. 58

Colbert, Steamer. Mentioned 728

Colburn, Ledyard.

    Correspondence with William H. Emory 607

    Mentioned 189, 592

Colby, Richard J. Mentioned... 60

Colby, Seth P. Mentioned 60

Cole, Captain. Mentioned 574

Cole, Albert. Mentioned 63

Cole, Andrew. Mentioned 61

Cole, David B. Mentioned 60

Cole, Elisha. Mentioned 898

Cole, James F. Mentioned 229

Cole, Nelson. Mentioned.. 665

Cole, Percy B. S. Mentioned.. 66

Coleman, F. G. W. Mentioned 143

Coleman, H. W. Mentioned... 171

Coleman, J. T. Mentioned 177–179

Coleman, William J. Mentioned.. 62

Coles, Seymour N. Mentioned.. 66

Collier, Steamer. Mentioned... 906

	Page.
Collier, Madison M. Mentioned	65
Collins, John B. Mentioned	711
Collins, Robert K. Mentioned	709
Colored Troops. Recruitment, organization, etc. Communications from	
Banks, Nathaniel P	688, 704, 776, 777
Irwin, Richard D	684
Colvin, Isaac. Mentioned	63
Come, Peter. Mentioned	62
Comonfort, Ignacio. Mentioned	864
Comstock, ———. Mentioned	825
Comstock, Apollos.	
Mentioned	57, 530, 711
Report of siege of Port Hudson, La., May 21–July 8, 1863	129
Comstock, Joseph J. Mentioned	894
Conchas Springs, N. Mex. Skirmish with Indians at, July 29, 1863*	2
Conduct of the War. Communications from	
Andrews, George L	706
Army Headquarters	652, 739
Banks, Nathaniel P	706, 716, 728, 792–795, 807, 836
Bee, Hamilton P	812
Dana, Napoleon J. T	838, 839
Emory, William H	569, 570
Holbrook, William C	742, 744, 745
Marivault, Viscount de	569
Maury, Dabney H	745
Morino, J	743
Pond, Preston, jr	704
State Department, U. S	570, 572, 846
Stone, Charles P	650, 800
War Department, U. S	569, 846
Washburn, Cadwallader C	849, 851
Young, Mahlon M	746
See also *Memoranda for Generals Banks, Grant, and Steele*, p. 739.	
Cone, Edward R. Mentioned	63
Confederate Troops.	
Casualties. Returns of.	
Bayou Bourbeau, La. Engagement at, near Grand Coteau, Nov. 3, 1863.	395
Donaldsonville, La. Attack on, June 28, 1863	230
Plains Store, La. Action at, May 21, 1863	144
Port Hudson, La. Siege of, May 21–July 8, 1863	144, 147
Stirling's Plantation, on the Fordoche, La. Action at, Sept. 29, 1863	332
Mentioned.	
Artillery, Light—*Batteries:* Semmes', 216, 218, 227, 323, 329, 330, 395, 662.	
For Volunteers, see respective States.	
Organization, strength, etc. See Part II.	
Congress, C. S. Resolutions of thanks of, to Frederick H. Odlum and Richard Dowling, and the men under their command	312
Congress, U. S. Resolutions of thanks of, to Nathaniel P. Banks and the officers and soldiers under his command	911
Conn, J. D. Mentioned	179

---

* No circumstantial reports on file.

Page.

Connecticut Troops. Mentioned.

Infantry—*Regiments:* 9th, 46, 197, 201, 202, 531, 574, 577,582,591,686,711, 900; 12th, 22, 39, 57, 67, 131–133, 335, 529, 711, 899; 13th, 22,57,70,129, 130, 523, 530, 686, 711,900; 23d, 46,190,193–196,199,491,531.707 ; 24th, 70, 133, 530, 708; 25th, 58, 70, 530, 707; 26th, 68, 122–125, 529, 627,707 ; 28th, 69,530,532,611,632,707.

Connell, John. Mentioned... 335,710,898

Connelly, Henry. Mentioned... 628

For correspondence, etc., see *New Mexico, Governor of.*

Connelly, Samuel. Mentioned.. 60

Conner, ——. Mentioned... 891

Conners, Daniel. Mentioned... 60

Conover, Robert. Mentioned... 710

Constantine, Charles J. Mentioned....................................... 57

Continental, Steamer. Mentioned....................................... 431,713,909

Converse, Edwin. Mentioned 57

Cook, Andrew. Mentioned... 63

Cook, Franklin. Mentioned 233,234

Cook, R. V. Mentioned.. 308

Cook's Cañon, N. Mex. Skirmishes with Indians at.

July 10, 1863*.. 2

July 24, 1863*.. 2

Cooke, A. P.

Correspondence with James S. Palmer 567

Mentioned 4,10,566

Cooke, Philip St. George.

Assignments to command 722, 756

Correspondence with Nathaniel P. Banks........................... 777, 779,836

Mentioned.................... 380, 722, 756, 782,783,816,826, 892, 895

Cooke, Thomas B. Mentioned... 144

Cooley, James C.

Correspondence with William H. Emory............................. 596,597

Mentioned... 579, 606

Cooneys, Russell W. Mentioned... 66

Cooper, Douglas H. Mentioned.. 304

Cooper, John. Mentioned.. 60

Cooper, Samuel. Mentioned... 385, 496

For correspondence, etc., see *Adjutant and Inspector General's Office, C. S. A.*

Cooper, William. Mentioned... 65

Copinggan. (Indian.) Mentioned....................................... 23

Coppernoll, Levi. Mentioned... 63

Cora, Steamer. Mentioned.. 436,438

Corbett, Peter. Mentioned 65

Corinthian, Steamer. Mentioned....................................... 810,814

Corliss, Augustus W.

Mentioned 529

Report of siege of Port Hudson, La., May 21–July 8, 1863......... 139

Cornie, Steamer. Mentioned 11, 100,105,621, 622

Corson, Joseph B. Mentioned.. 60

Cortes, General. Mentioned... 801

Cortina, Juan Nepumuceno.

Mentioned.................... 400, 402–405,408, 435, 437, 447,449,451,841

Proclamations of. Affairs at Matamoras, Mexico................. 406, 408

---

* No circumstantial reports on file.

	Page.
Cosgrove, James. Mentioned	58
Costello, Patrick. Mentioned	64
Cottle, Philip S. Mentioned	896
Cotton. Trade in. See *Trade and Intercourse.*	
Cotton, J. A., C. S. S. Mentioned	4, 8
Couch, Darius N. Mentioned	506
Coult, T. A. Mentioned	750, 828, 901
Courtney, Thomas. Mentioned	61
Courts-Martial.	
Charges, findings, and sentences in cases of	
Benedict, Augustus W	479
Boudro, Julius	478
Cady, Lewis	477
Curtis, Willis	478
Green, Henry	477
Hagan, James	479
Kennedy, Jacob	477
Moore, James H	478
Singleton, Abram	478
Smith, Edward B	476
Taylor, Charles	477
Verrett, Volser	478
Victoria, Abraham	477
Williams, Frank	476
Morgan, Joseph S. Case of. See *Joseph S. Morgan.*	
Covensparrow, Daniel. Mentioned	63
Cowan, Lieutenant-Colonel. Mentioned	758
Cowan, John. Mentioned	335, 710, 898
Cowan, Jonathan E. Mentioned	362, 363, 799
Cowles, David S. Mentioned	17, 68, 71, 125, 511
Cowles, Ethan H. Mentioned	62
Cowles, John R. Mentioned	62
Cox, Clayton. Mentioned	894
Cox, John C. Correspondence with	
Gilpin, Joseph B	910
McPherson, James B	909
Cox, William R. Mentioned	141
Cox's Plantation, La. See *La Fourche. Engagement on the, etc., July 12–13,* 1863.	
Coy, George E. Mentioned	61
Cozanah, ———. Mentioned	737
Cozzens, G. W. Correspondence with	
Flanders, Benjamin F	737
Flanigan, P	738
Murphy, John L	737
Craft, Elijah R. Mentioned	780
Craig, Fort. See *Fort Craig.*	
Craig, Seldon F. Mentioned	548
Craig, W. Mentioned	26
Crain, G. B. Mentioned	374
Crandal, Frederick M. Mentioned	712, 829
Crandall, Edwin A. Mentioned	709
Crane, Henry A. Mentioned	873–875
Crane, Rollin H. Mentioned	278, 279
Crawford, M. G. Mentioned	144

Page.

Crebs, John M. Mentioned 336, 828
Creel, Reuben W. Mentioned 916
   For correspondence, etc., see *Chihuahua, Mexico, U. S. Consul at.*
Cremony, John C. Mentioned 844
Creole, Steamer. Mentioned 560, 788
Crescent City, Steamer. Mentioned 109,
          293, 297, 299, 410–412, 417, 590, 671, 713, 733, 798, 801, 802, 825, 843
Crissey, Edwin. Mentioned 3
Crocker, Frederick.
   Mentioned 19, 287, 289, 294, 295, 298, 299, 303
   Report of Sabine Pass (Texas) Expedition, Sept. 4–11, 1863 301
Crocker, Marcellus M. Mentioned 275–277
   Reports of
     Harrisonburg, La. Expedition from Natchez, Miss., to, etc., Sept. 1–7,
       1863 273
     Vidalia, La. Attack on, Sept. 14, 1863 314
Crockett, Otis G. Mentioned 60
Croley, Richard. Mentioned 58
Cromwell, Steamer. Mentioned 637
Cronk, George. Mentioned 63
Crooke, William D. Mentioned 897
Cropsey, John W. Mentioned 336
Crosby, Henry. Mentioned 71
Crosby, J. Schuyler.
   Correspondence with
     Banks, Nathaniel P 338, 763, 765
     Stone, Charles P 757
   Mentioned 458
     For correspondence as A. A. A. G, see *Nathaniel P. Banks.*
Crowder, John H. Mentioned 70
Crowell, Charles S. Mentioned 60
Crowell, Warren T. Mentioned 60
Cruz, ——. Mentioned 449
Crydenwise, Henry M. Mentioned 63
Crymes, A. F. Mentioned 37
Cullen, John. Mentioned 65
Culver, Charles. Mentioned 58
Cumming, Alfred. Mentioned 497
Cummings, Franklin. Mentioned 448
Cummings, A. B. Mentioned 89
Cummings, Joseph. Mentioned 26, 235, 238
Cummins, William T. Mentioned 710
Cuniffe, ——. Mentioned 919, 920
Cunningham, E. Mentioned 214
Cunningham, John. Mentioned 60
Cupples, George. Mentioned 331, 395
Currie, Leonard D. H. Mentioned 336, 530, 632
Currier, O. Mentioned 778
Curtis, Elliot M. Mentioned 201
Curtis, Norman S. Mentioned 41
Curtis, Oscar. Mentioned 64
Curtis, Willis.
   Court-martial in case of. Mutiny at Fort Jackson, La., Dec. 9, 1863 478
   Mentioned 478, 479

Page.
Curtiss, George G. Mentioned... 711, 895
Cushing, James W. Mentioned.. 413
Cushman, C. W. Mentioned.. 179
Custis, C. A. Mentioned... 828, 901
Cutler, Benjamin C.
    Correspondence with Edward B. Willis.. 869
    Mentioned 234, 235
        For correspondence as A. A. G., see *James H. Carleton.*
Dacey, Daniel C. Mentioned... 63
Dailey, George W. Mentioned.. 62
Dailey, John. Mentioned.. 60
Dale, Kate, Steamer. Mentioned... 793
Dallis, William. Mentioned.. 59
Daly, Simon. Mentioned... 61
Dana, John W.
    Correspondence with Stephen M. Eaton..................................... 85–87, 94–96
    Mentioned.. 77, 92, 104, 120, 293, 294
    Report of siege of Port Hudson, La., May 21–July 8, 1863.................... 85
Dana, Napoleon J. T.
    Assignments to command.. 735, 879
    Assumes command of 13th Army Corps.. 776
    Correspondence with
        Banks, Nathaniel P............... 411, 753, 830, 842, 856, 862, 864, 876, 882, 885
        Hamilton, Andrew J.. 857, 858
        Matamoras, Mexico, U. S. Consul at.. 830, 838, 883
        Monterey, Mexico, U. S. Consul at... 414, 823, 865, 882
        Ord, Edward O. C... 762
        Ratliff, W. B... 323
        Strong, James H.. 787
        Tamaulipas, Mexico, Governor of... 823, 839, 884, 885
        Thompson, William G... 788
        Vandever, William... 789
    Mentioned.. 20, 292, 327,
        334, 341–343, 355, 367, 380, 397, 398, 406, 428, 429, 458, 735, 749, 755, 776, 779,
        782, 783, 793, 798, 810, 811, 819, 826, 840, 841, 871, 879–881, 891–894, 897, 902
    Reports of
        Rio Grande Expedition and operations on the coast of Texas, Oct. 27–
          Dec. 2, 1863.. 411–415
        Stirling's Plantation, on the Fordoche, La. Action at, Sept. 29,
          1863 .... 321, 324
Dana, William H. Mentioned.. 285
Dane, Henry C. Mentioned.. 104, 293, 294
Daniel, Henry D. Mentioned... 63
Daniel, J. M. Mentioned 454
Daniel, John W. Mentioned.. 331
Daniels, Charles. Mentioned 57
Daniels, Enoch. Mentioned.. 856, 873, 874
Daniels, Nathan W. Mentioned............................. 527, 528, 532, 610, 611, 665, 684
Darby, James A. Mentioned 229
Darby, William. Mentioned.. 60
Darden, S. H. Mentioned 445
Darling, ———. Mentioned 441
Darling, Henry A. Mentioned... 73

Page.

Dashiell, D. H. Mentioned 439, 448, 449, 451
Dashiell, George R. Mentioned 247
Daub, Philip. Mentioned 66
Dauterive, B. D. Mentioned.. 376
Davidson, John W. Mentioned... 716, 727
Davidson, Peter. Mentioned ....:................... 709
Davies, Richard E. Mentioned.. 910
Davis, ——. Mentioned.. 669–671, 703
Davis, Edmund J. Mentioned...... 284, 321, 338, 339, 377, 379, 381, 382, 384, 398, 412,
413, 415, 423, 424, 531, 608, 712, 749, 804, 824, 828, 830, 842, 843, 847, 880, 898
Davis, G. P. Mentioned.. 825
Davis, Henry T.
  Mentioned 434, 435, 441, 443
  Report of Rio Grande Expedition and operations on the coast of Texas,
    Oct. 27–Dec. 2, 1863.. 444
Davis, Horace F. Mentioned... 61
Davis, Jefferson.
  Correspondence with War Department, C. S............................... 210, 385
  Mentioned ....:............... .... 210, 312, 385, 392, 496, 637, 646, 717, 915, 918
Davis, Samuel. Mentioned 65
Davis, William R. Mentioned 61
Davison, Andrew H. Mentioned... 57
Dawson, John H. Mentioned... 64
Dawson, Nancy, Schooner. Mentioned..................................... 839
Day, Alfred E. Mentioned.. 62
Day, Henry M. Mentioned 313, 326–328, 398, 665, 709, 897
Day, James P. Mentioned 424
Day, Nicholas W. Mentioned... 530, 686
Dayton, William L. Correspondence with State Department, U. S........... 570
Dean, Chauncey C. Mentioned 76, 122, 209
Dean, Clement R. Mentioned... 63
De Baun, James. Mentioned.. 143, 161, 167
Debray, X. B.
  Mentioned.. 244–247
  Reports of mutiny at Galveston, Tex., Aug. 10–13, 1863................... 242–244
De Coster, Moses. Mentioned... 66
De Forrest, Cyrus. For correspondence as A. D. C., see *James H. Carleton.*
De Frate, Edwin. Mentioned... 63
De Gournay, P. F.
  Mentioned 143
  Reports of siege of Port Hudson, La., May 21–July 8, 1863............... 152–156
Degruy, Eugene. Mentioned 59
Deitrich. Eugene. Mentioned.. 65
Delamater, Edward. Mentioned.. 63
Delamater, John L. Mentioned 63
De La Paturelle, Honore. Mentioned.................................... 63
Delgadito. (Indian.) Mentioned... 261
De Long, S. R. Mentioned 901
Demale, Steamer. Mentioned 431
Demarquis, Leonard. Mentioned 58
Demerly, Jacob. Mentioned... 63
Deming, Burton D. Mentioned... 71
Denison, George S. Mentioned.. 669, 670

Page.

Dennett, Thomas S.
Correspondence with William H. Emory.. 185
Mentioned... 544
Denton, Benjamin F. Mentioned... 71
Derby, Schooner. Mentioned.. 344, 793
Derinsbourg, Frederick. Mentioned.. 59
Des Allemands, La. Skirmish at, July 18, 1863*.............................. 2
De Soto, Steamer. Mentioned... 8
Deus, Charles. Mentioned... 238, 253
Devine, Patrick. Mentioned... 59
De Wint, Arthur. Mentioned.. 125
De Witt, Edgar L. Mentioned... 65
De Wolfe, T. Scott. Mentioned... 896
Diana, U. S. S. Mentioned... 10
Dickey, George S. Mentioned... 27
Dickins, John W. Mentioned... 65
Dickinson, John Q. Mentioned... 822
Dickson, George T. Mentioned.. 57
Dicton, Silas. Mentioned.. 60
Diemert, Lewis. Mentioned... 58
Dillingham, Charles. Mentioned..................................... 529, 711
Dillon, James. Mentioned.. 58
Dillon, John. Mentioned... 58
Dix, John A.
Correspondence with William H. Emory...................................... 608
Mentioned.. 637
Dixon, Josiah C. Mentioned.. 65
Dolores, Private. Mentioned... 24
Donahue, Peter. Mentioned.. 61
Donaldsonville, La.
Affair opposite, Sept. 23, 1863.
Communication from William O. Fiske....................................... 317
Report of Warren D. Smith... 317
Attack on, June 28, 1863. See *Louisiana. Operations in, west of the Missis-sippi, June 7–July 13, 1863. Reports of*

Emory, William H.   Mouton, Alfred.   Taylor, Richard.
Green, Thomas.   Porter, Henry M.

See also *indorsement of Taylor*, p. 229; *Banks to Alden*, p. 601; *Emory to Commanding Officer at Donaldsonville, Banks*, and *Sawtell*, p. 601; *Bullen to Emory* and *Banks to Emory*, p. 605; *Emory to Farragut*, pp. 650, 656.
Donaldsonville, La., Commanding Officer at. Correspondence with William H. Emory.. 575, 601
Donaldsonville, La., Senior Naval Officer at. Correspondence with Nathaniel P. Banks.. 805
Donnelly, Peter. Mentioned.. 202
Donovan, James. Mentioned.. 59
Dornback, Otto. Mentioned.. 66
Dorr, Peter. Mentioned.. 62
Dorsette, John W. Mentioned... 32
Dorson, Jack. Mentioned... 59
Doucet, Zephraim. Mentioned.. 778

*No circumstantial reports on file.

Page.
Dougherty, ——. Mentioned 279
Dougherty, John. Mentioned.. 60
Douglas, H. T. Mentioned 388
Douglass, Benjamin, jr. Mentioned 60
Douglass, Isaac R. Mentioned 60
Douglass, William. Mentioned 61
Dow, Henry B. Mentioned.. 62
Dow, Neal. Mentioned............................. 68, 94, 124, 182, 489, 510, 511, 522
Dowley, George. Mentioned 62
Dowlin, Paul. Mentioned 29, 251, 256
Dowling, Richard W.
    Mentioned 303–306, 308–310, 312, 915
    Report of Sabine Pass (Texas) Expedition, Sept. 4–11, 1863............... 311
    Resolution of thanks of C. S. Congress to. Sabine Pass (Texas) Expedition,
        Sept. 4–11, 1863 312
Downing, Joseph M. Mentioned 63
Downs, Peter T. Mentioned.. 62
Doxey, Charles T. Mentioned.. 900
Doyle, Dennis. Mentioned.. 58
Draft. Ordered in Louisiana............ 740
Draner, Charles. Mentioned... 66
Dresher, V. Mentioned 26, 612, 828
Dresser, Edson T. Mentioned 62
Drew, Charles W.
    Correspondence with Nathaniel P. Banks 567
    Mentioned........ 456–458, 460, 463, 464, 466–470, 474, 475, 497, 529, 611, 684, 708, 896
    Testimony of. Mutiny at Fort Jackson, La., Dec. 9, 1863.............. 460, 464
Drey, Louis L. Mentioned 59
Dreyfous, Abel. Mentioned.. 671
Druckhammer, Gustav. Mentioned 65
Du Bois, Cesar. Mentioned.. 61
Duboise, Charles. Mentioned.. 57
Dudley, Nathan A. M.
    Correspondence with
        Augur, Christopher C 116
        Banks, Nathaniel P 667
        Holcomb, Pythagoras E...................................... 116
    Mentioned............... 67, 204, 529, 550, 554, 555, 613, 627, 658, 667, 685, 892, 900
    Reports of
        Louisiana. Operations in, west of the Mississippi, June 7–July 13,
            1863 207
        Merritt's Plantation, La.
            Operations about, and on the Bayou Sara road, May 18–19, 1863. 38, 39
            Scouts from, on the Clinton road, May 14, 1863 .... 34, 35
        Port Hudson, La. Siege of, May 21–July 8, 1863..................... 120
Dudley, T. H. Mentioned 658, 703
    For correspondence, etc., see *Liverpool, England, U. S. Consul at.*
Duff, James.
    Mentioned... 435, 444, 445, 448, 485
    Reports of
        Point Isabel, Tex. Affair at, May 30, 1863...................... 185
        Rio Grande Expedition and operations on the Texas coast, Oct. 27–Dec.
            2, 1863 439

Page.

Duff, Thomas. Mentioned 65
Duffy, Thomas. Mentioned 58
Dugal, Leonard L. Mentioned 58
Dugué, Charles. Mentioned 59
Duke, ———. Mentioned 566
Dumonteil, F. Mentioned.. 313
Dunaway, George O. Mentioned 438
Dunbar, S. H. Mentioned 423
Dungan, Warren S. Mentioned.......................... 420, 427, 897
Dunham, Robert T.
    Correspondence with
        Banks, Nathaniel P 726, 731
        Stone, Charles P 757
    Mentioned....................................... 11, 380, 383, 502, 730, 814
        For correspondence as A. A. G., see *Nathaniel P. Banks.*
Dunlay, Patrick. Mentioned 61
Dunlevie. John. Mentioned.. 441
Dunn, Daniel W. Mentioned... 65
Dunn, James. Mentioned 57
Dunn, J. B. Mentioned 166
Dunn, Michael. Mentioned 59
Dunn, Michael H. Mentioned 58
Dupeire, St. L. Mentioned...................... 347, 362, 370, 376, 377
Dupuy, Joseph. Mentioned.. 59
Durand, Charles. Mentioned 70
Durell, Edward H.
    Correspondence with Nathaniel P. Banks 794
    Mentioned....................................... 795, 808, 809
Duryea, Richard C. Mentioned 530, 633, 660
Dutton, Henry F. Mentioned.......................... 335, 899
Dutton, Salmon. Mentioned 708
Duzan, Nelson C. Mentioned 911
Duzenberry, Captain. Mentioned...................................... 220
Dwight, Charles C. Mentioned.......................... 458, 534, 649, 763
Dwight, William.
    Assignment to command 853
    Congratulatory Orders. Siege of Port Hudson, La., May 21–July 8, 1863.. 560
    Correspondence with
        Augur, Christopher C 102
        Banks, Nathaniel P....................................... 101,
            102, 117, 118, 126, 536, 548, 551, 574, 613, 622, 624, 636, 848, 860, 863, 867
        Beall, William N. R....................................... 554
    Mentioned 11–14, 45, 46, 68, 74, 77, 85,
        96, 102, 104, 117, 118, 132, 139, 214, 231, 383, 486–490, 502, 504, 506, 510, 519,
        528, 529, 536, 539, 554, 555, 564, 610, 627, 632, 633, 636, 660, 665, 853, 892, 896
Dye, William McE. Mentioned.......... 20, 327, 328, 394, 425, 429, 430, 709, 894, 897
Dyer, A. J. Mentioned 816
Dyer, Isaac. Mentioned..................... 420, 426, 427, 528, 532, 604, 611, 686, 711, 897
Dyer, Peter. Mentioned 62
Eager, Steamer. Mentioned 185
Earl, Isaac N. Mentioned.................................... 320, 589, 836
Eaton, Charles P. Mentioned.. 99

Page.

Eaton, Stephen M.
Correspondence with
Abbott, John C 88
Alden, James 88–91
Banks, Nathaniel P 95, 109
Dana, John W 85–87, 94–96
Farragut, David G. 89
Gabaudan, Edward C 90
Jackson, Amos M 91, 92
Morris, Henry W.. 89
Palmer, James S 94
Roe, William B 94, 96, 109
Sherman, Thomas W 88
Mentioned............................... 76–78, 85, 92, 293, 522, 660
Report of siege of Port Hudson, La., May 21–July 8, 1863 88
Eberstadt, Ed. Mentioned....................................... 497
Eddy, Captain. Mentioned...................................... 574
Eddy, Asher R.
Correspondence with James B. McPherson 907, 908
Mentioned 904
Edgar, J. C. Mentioned....................................... 256
Edrington, J. B. Mentioned 144
Edward, J. K. P. Mentioned 617
Edwards, Richard M. Mentioned 64
Egan, Walter. Mentioned...................................... 57
Ehrlacher, Edwin T. Mentioned 61
Eisele, William F. Mentioned................................. 65
Eisemann, John. Mentioned.................................... 46
Elders, James. Mentioned..................................... 60
Eldridge, John. Mentioned.................................... 59
Elfield, Albert. Mentioned............................... 383, 384
Elgee, C. Le Doux. Mentioned 211, 214
Ellen, Steamer. Mentioned.................................... 11
Ellet, Colonel. Mentioned.................................... 537
Elliot, G. D. Mentioned 296
Elliott, Isaac H. Mentioned 423
Elliott, Joseph. Mentioned................................... 61
Elliott, Thomas J. Mentioned................................. 361
Ellis, Captain. Mentioned.................................... 395
Ellis, Louis F. Mentioned 64
Ellison, Edward. Mentioned 58
Elmore, H. M. Mentioned 242
Emerald, Steamer. Mentioned 810
Emerson, Alva. Mentioned..................................... 60
Emerson, Charles.
Correspondence with Richard B. Irwin 82
Mentioned 65
Report of operations in Louisiana west of the Mississippi, June 7–July 13,
1863 203
For correspondence as A. A. G., see *Nathaniel P. Banks.*
Emerson, E. M. Mentioned..................................... 789
Emma Amelia, Schooner. Mentioned 788
Emmerich, Balthazar. Mentioned............................... 57

                                                                    Page.
Emory, William H.
Assignments to command...................................... 686, 695, 698
Assumes temporary command of the defenses of New Orleans, La......... 500
Correspondence with
    Adjutant-General's Office, U. S. A.................................... 540, 570
    Army Headquarters............................... 609, 616, 619, 630, 636
    Banks, Nathaniel P.. 49–51,
        497, 519, 523, 524, 533, 534, 540, 541, 543, 544, 546, 559, 568, 571, 574–582,
        585, 587, 590, 593–601, 605, 606, 613, 619, 630, 635, 637, 641, 646, 647, 671
    Bonnet Carré, La., Commanding Officer at............................. 606
    Boutte Station, La., Commanding Officer at........................... 600
    Brashear City, La., Commanding Officer at...............:...... 581, 585, 590
    Bullen, Joseph D............................:...................... 605
    Cahill, Thomas W 189, 577, 582, 584, 586, 588, 591–594, 596, 597, 606
    Clapp, M 568
    Colburn, Ledyard 607
    Cooley, James C 596, 597
    Dennett, Thomas S... 185
    Dix, John A 608
    Donaldsonville, La., Commanding Officer at 575, 601
    Farragut, David G.................... 577, 578, 587, 598, 604, 616, 617, 650, 656
    Forts Jackson and Saint Philip, La., Commanding Officer at.......... 599
    Franklin, William B 723, 725
    French, Peter.. 586, 587
    Grover, Cuvier.. 637, 639, 645
    Hadlock, William E... 618
    McMillan, James W 725
    Marivault, Viscount de... 569
    Marsh, Lucius B 607
    Morris, Henry W 543, 556, 568, 571, 612, 615, 627
    Plumly, M. W.. 644
    Sawtell, Josiah A 601, 604, 607, 608, 615, 638, 639
    Stickney, Albert.......... 541, 544, 568, 575, 576, 578–581, 584, 585, 587, 638, 639
    Stouder, H.. 595
    Ullmann, Daniel 533
    Wordin, C. W... 186
Mentioned 8, 10,
    12, 13, 44, 46–48, 52, 85, 88, 100, 105, 191, 199, 200, 203, 207, 293, 300, 336,
    389, 487–489, 491–495, 504, 506, 526–528, 531, 570, 572, 589, 600, 611, 636, 650,
    656–658, 660, 665, 666, 672, 675, 676, 685, 686, 695, 698, 708, 711, 837, 892, 899
Reports of
    Berwick, La. Skirmish at, June 1, 1863........................... 185, 186
    Louisiana. Operations in, west of the Mississippi, June 7–July 13,
      1863 .... 187, 188, 190
Emperor, John. Mentioned...................................... 58
Empire City, Steamer. Mentioned............................... 425, 785
Empire Parish, Steamer. Mentioned............................. 493, 495, 499, 860
Empress, Steamer. Mentioned 319
Engel, John. Mentioned.. 65
English, George H. Mentioned................................. 276
Ennis, John. Mentioned 531
Ennson, Eugene S. Mentioned................................. 65
Enos, Herbert M. Mentioned 869
Erwin, Timothy N. Mentioned.................................. 61

Page.

Esperanza, Fort. See *Fort Esperanza.*

Essex, U. S. S. Mentioned 88, 91, 103, 141, 155, 220, 222, 512, 520, 601

Estrella, U. S. S. Mentioned 92, 108, 493, 495, 504, 538, 567, 623, 640

Eugenie, Steamer. Mentioned 3

Evans, Clark. Mentioned 64

Evans, William J. Mentioned 373

Everett, Charles. Mentioned 122, 529

Everett, Eben. Mentioned .....: 251

Exact, Steamer. Mentioned 296, 713

Fagan, Christopher. Mentioned 57

Fagan, James F. Mentioned 392

Fagan, John. Mentioned 57

Fahy, John. Mentioned 58

Fair Haven, Steamer. Mentioned 837

Fales, Eugene H. Mentioned 64

Fancher, George E. Mentioned 57

Faneuf, George N. Mentioned 66

Faries, T. A. Reports of

    Hog Point, Mississippi River, La. Operations against U. S. gunboats and
        transports near, Nov. 18–21, 1863 .... 453, 455

    Louisiana. Operations in, west of the Mississippi, June 7–July 13, 1863. 220, 222

Farr, Alpha B. Mentioned 336, 531, 685, 711, 713, 726, 899

Farragut, David G.

    Correspondence with

        Alden, James 89–92

        Augur, Christopher C 113

        Baker, J. S 115

        Banks, Nathaniel P .....: 51, 78–82, 84, 89, 90, 100–102,
            105, 106, 109–111, 113–117, 120, 504, 506, 507, 509, 511, 512, 518, 520, 521, 523–
            525, 533, 538, 542, 545, 547, 550–553, 556–558, 566, 570, 589, 620, 622, 623, 640

        Barker, J. T 80

        Eaton, Stephen M 89

        Emory, William H 577, 578, 587, 598, 604, 616, 617, 650, 656

        Fisher, James C 81, 115

        Jenkins, Thornton A 140

        Navy Department, U. S 140

        Palmer, James S 78, 92, 93, 95, 107, 108, 566

        Porter, David D 91

        Sage, Clinton H 115

        Shipley, Alexander N 108, 113

        Stone, Charles P 111, 114

        Waters, John G 607

        Watters, John 109, 110, 114, 115

        Weaver, Aaron W 81, 115

        Weitzel, Godfrey 109, 120

        Woolsey, M. B 594, 621

    Mentioned 4, 6–8, 10, 11, 16, 19, 48, 82, 88, 92, 99, 103, 190, 191, 493, 514,
        515, 541, 542, 571, 575, 594, 599, 601, 602, 608, 618, 628, 646, 650, 656, 664, 672

Farrar, Bernard G.

    Mentioned 314, 315

    Report of expedition from Vidalia to Trinity, La., Nov. 15–16, 1863 452

Farrington, Seymour A. Mentioned 60

Farrow, Alonzo L. Mentioned 60

Page.

Fauconnet, M. For correspondence, etc., see *New Orleans, La., French Consul at.*

Fearing, Hawkes, jr.
    Correspondence with George L. Andrews 672
    Mentioned.. 69, 530, 610, 611, 625, 627, 632, 900
Fedick, Nicholas. Mentioned 63
Fee, John. Mentioned 58
Feighery, John. Mentioned... 65
Fellows, John R. Report of siege of Port Hudson, La., May 21–July 8, 1863.. 148
Fellows, Stark. Mentioned... 895
Felton, John D. Mentioned .... •483
Felts, Albert P. Mentioned 63
Fenn, F. F. Mentioned 856, 885
Feotish, Louis. Mentioned.. 58
Ferguson, William. Mentioned.. 65
Fernandez, C. Juan. Mentioned... 409
Fernandez, Francis. Mentioned 59
Pero, Daniel. Mentioned 62
Ferris, Eugene W. Mentioned 121
Ferris, Samuel P. Mentioned 69, 530, 532, 611, 632
Ffrench, William. Mentioned.. 612
Fialon, Joseph. Mentioned.. 31, 260, 261
Field, James.
    Mentioned 537
    Statement of. Siege of Port Hudson, La., May 21–July 8, 1863............... 537
Fifer, George H. Mentioned... 419, 422, 423
Fink, John. Mentioned... 152, 153
Fink, John D. Mentioned.. 64
Finick, William. Mentioned 59
Finley, Dennison H. Mentioned 57
Finn, Joseph. Mentioned... 64
Fish, Latham A. Mentioned.. 65
Fisher, Charles. Mentioned 63
Fisher, James A. Mentioned 143
Fisher, James C. Correspondence with David G. Farragut 81, 115
Fiske, Edward A. Mentioned... 61, 208, 209
Fiske, G. A., jr. For correspondence as A. D. C., see *William Dwight.*
Fiske, William O.
    Correspondence with
        Banks, Nathaniel P... 734, 805, 809, 812
        Smith, Warren D.. 317
    Mentioned 667, 686, 711, 820, 895, 900
Fitch, Charles H. Mentioned 29, 236, 250
Fitch, Frank. Mentioned 62
Fitch, Henry B. Mentioned... 335, 711
Fitch, Lewis E. Mentioned... 64
Fitz Gibbons, Richard.
    Mentioned 457, 531, 711, 900
    Report of operations in Louisiana west of the Mississippi, June 7–July 13,
        1863 201
Fitz Gibbons, Thomas. Mentioned.. 201
Fitzpatrick, Cornelius. Mentioned 63
Fitzpatrick, Patrick. Mentioned 57

Page.

Flanders, Benjamin F.
  Correspondence with
    Banks, Nathaniel P 736
    Cozzens, G. W 737
  Mentioned 111, 114, 598, 715, 737
Flanders, George A. Mentioned 336
Flanigan, P. Correspondence with G. W. Cozzens 738
Fleming, John. Mentioned... 65
Fleming, Solomon. Mentioned 59
Fletcher, Abner W. Mentioned 194
Fletcher, Thomas. Mentioned 66
Flint, Abner N. Mentioned... 66
Flint, Horace P. Mentioned 61
Florida, Steamer. Mentioned 90, 308
Florida, Southern. Operations in, Dec. 14–23, 1863. Communications from
  Banks, Nathaniel P 874
  Woodbury, Daniel P 855, 873, 874
Florida Troops. (Union.)
  Mentioned.
    Cavalry—*Regiments:* 1st, 887 ; 2d, 896.
  Recruitment of. Communication from Nathaniel P. Banks................ 780
Florida, Western.
  Asboth, Alexander, assigned to command of troops in 756
  Operations in, Nov. 21–Dec. 27, 1863. Communications from
    Asboth, Alexander 817, 820, 833, 886
    Banks, Nathaniel P 813
  Recruitment and organization of Union troops in. Communication from
    Alexander Asboth 886
Florentino, ——. Mentioned 424
Flory, Aaron M. Mentioned... 898
Floyd, La. Skirmish at, Aug. 24, 1863. See *Monroe, La. Expedition from Vicksburg, Miss., to, including skirmishes (24th) at Bayou Macon and at Floyd, Aug. 20–Sept. 2, 1863.*
Floyd, John B. Mentioned.. 791, 792
Flynn, Captain. Mentioned... 280
Fonda, John G.
  Mentioned 336, 354, 357, 358, 360, 361, 374, 378, 379, 826, 828, 892, 900
  Reports of operations in the Teche Country, La., Oct. 3–Nov. 30, 1863.... 372, 373
Ford, John S. Mentioned 485
Forest Queen, Steamer. Mentioned 520
Forrest, Nathan B. Mentioned 496
Forsgard, G. A. Mentioned... 484
Fort Beauregard, La. Capture of, Sept. 4, 1863. See *Harrisonburg, La. Expedition from Natchez, Miss., to, etc., Sept. 1–7, 1863. Reports of Crocker,* p. 273; *Logan,* p. 281.
Fort Craig, N. Mex. Skirmish with Indians near, July 4, 1863*............... 2
Fort Esperanza, Matagorda Island, Tex. Expedition against and capture of, Nov. 22–30, 1863. See *Rio Grande Expedition, Oct. 27–Dec. 2, 1863. Reports of*
    Bradfute, W. R.   Ransom, Thomas E. G.   Washburn, Henry D.
    Ireland, John.   Washburn, Cadwallader C.
    See also *Record of Events, 13th Army Corps,* p. 428.

---

* No circumstantial reports on file.

Page.

Fort Jackson, La. Mutiny at, Dec. 9, 1863.
Communications from William Dwight 860, 863, 867
Court-martial. Charges, findings, and sentences. 476
Military Commission.
    Detail for 459
    Findings and opinions... 475
    Orders convening 459
    Proceedings.. 459
    Reports of Nathaniel P. Banks 456, 457
    Testimony of
        Benedict, Augustus W 473, 474
        Drew, Charles W.. 460–464
        Hartwell, Charles A... 472
        Kimball, George H... 469, 470
        Knapp, William H... 473
        McFaul, George.. 470
        Miller, James 466, 469
        Mooney, Edward D.. 471
        Nye, William E... 464–466
Fort Jackson and Fort Saint Philip, La., Commanding Officer at. Correspondence with William H. Emory 599
Fort Morgan, Ala. Attack on blockade runner near, Oct. 12, 1863* 3
Fort Wingate, N. Mex. Scout from. See *Ojo Redondo (Jacob's Well), N. Mex.*
    Scout from Fort Wingate to, Sept. 15–Oct. 5, 1863.
Fort, Greenberry L.
    Correspondence with James B. McPherson................................. 906
    Mentioned 904
Foster, James P. Mentioned............................. 716, 729, 852, 863
Foster, William K. For correspondence as A. A. A. G., see *P. N. Luckett.*
Fouche, Otto. Mentioned...................................... 59
Fountain, Albert J. Mentioned.................................... 26
Fournet, V. A. Mentioned 40, 41, 362, 363, 799
Foust, Joseph. Mentioned.......................... 398, 665, 709, 897
Fowler, Pleasant. Mentioned..................................... 143
Fowler, Thomas. Mentioned 72
Fox, Steamer. Mentioned 110, 114
Fox, George W. Mentioned 531, 712, 895
Fox, Gustavus V. Mentioned.................................... 89
Fox, Lester. Mentioned 62
Francis, Lieutenant. Mentioned 544
Francis, Joseph L. Mentioned.................................... 473
Francis, Richard W. Mentioned 707, 826, 894
Franey, Patrick. Mentioned..................................... 57
Frank, Thomas. Mentioned..................................... 144
Franklin, U. S. S. Mentioned 454
Franklin, George M. Mentioned 682, 693, 765
Franklin, William B.
    Assignments to command...................................... 658, 684
    Assumes command of 19th Army Corps 693
    Correspondence with
        Banks, Nathaniel P.. 389,
        692, 728, 732–734, 750, 751, 755, 756, 759–761, 763, 771–775, 778, 780, 781,
        788, 790, 799, 812, 819, 829, 831, 835, 837, 847, 870, 872, 873, 881, 920
        Burbridge, Stephen G.. 363, 799

*See Annual Report of the Secretary of the Navy, Dec. 5, 1863.

Franklin, William B.—Continued.

Correspondence with

	Page.
Emory, William H	723, 725
Grover, Cuvier	774
Lawler, Michael K	787
Lee, Albert L	774, 775
McGinnis, George F	799
Ord, Edward O. C	769
Pond, Preston, jr	704
Itinerary of 19th Army Corps, Oct. 1–Nov. 18, 1863	369
Mentioned	5, 19, 21, 286, 289, 290, 293,

301, 302, 304, 334, 335, 338, 341–343, 352, 354, 355, 357, 364, 369, 377, 378, 380–
384, 386, 387, 389–391, 393, 397, 431, 458, 645, 657, 658, 675, 676, 684, 685, 693,
695, 707, 710, 721, 722, 729, 735, 738, 749, 750, 755, 756, 758, 760–762, 765, 768,
770, 771, 781–784, 793–795, 801, 802, 810, 811, 819, 820, 826, 837, 847, 892, 899

Orders. Operations in the Teche Country, La., Oct. 3–Nov. 30, 1863 354

Reports of

Sabine Pass (Texas) Expedition, Sept. 4–11, 1863	294, 298
Teche Country, La. Operations in the, Oct. 3–Nov. 30, 1863	337–352
Staff. Announcements of	682, 693
Frazer, George M. Mentioned	329
Frazer, John. Mentioned	65
Freeman, Baskin. Mentioned	65
Freeman, Frederick. Mentioned	263
French. A. H. Mentioned	24

French, Peter.

Correspondence with William H. Emory	586, 587
Mentioned	50, 607

For correspondence as A. D. C., see *William H. Emory.*

Freret, James. Mentioned	177
Frick, Joseph. Mentioned	59
Friedley, George W. Mentioned	319
Frink, E. B. Mentioned	750
Frisbie, Henry N. Mentioned	895
Frits, Jules. Mentioned	59
Fritz, Emil. Mentioned	25
Frost, Abram. Mentioned	59
Fry, John. Mentioned	59
Frye, Frederick. Mentioned	457
Fullager, Isaac W. Mentioned	64
Fuller, Archelaus. Mentioned	60
Fuller, Charles J. Mentioned	57
Fuller, E. W. Mentioned	88
Fuller, Henry W. Mentioned	896
Fuller, James K. Mentioned	64, 711, 895
Fullerton, Hugh. Mentioned	382, 710
Fulton, Steamer. Mentioned	519, 533, 534
Fulton, John C. Mentioned	71
Fusilier, Alfred. Mentioned	217

Gabaudan, Edward C.

Correspondence with

Eaton, Stephen M	90
Schley, W. S	90, 91
Mentioned	11, 88, 89
Gaffnay, Francis J. Mentioned	57

Page.

Gale, John H. Mentioned 64
Galice, Clement. Mentioned 59
Gallagher, Andrew P. Mentioned....................... 336, 710, 828, 900
Gallagher, Eugene. Mentioned.. 59
Gallagher, James. (3d Massachusetts Cavalry.) Mentioned............. 61
Gallagher, James. (116th New York.) Mentioned 63
Gallagher, William. Mentioned 59
Galloway, Captain. Mentioned... 887
Gallup, ———. Mentioned.. 801
Gallup, John J. Mentioned 66
Gallway, A. Power. Mentioned... 72
Galvan, I. Mentioned 881, 883
Galveston, Tex. Mutiny at, Aug. 10-13, 1863.
    Orders. Magruder... 246
    Reports of
        Debray, X. B... 242-244
        Gray, E. F 241
        Luckett, P. N 245
Gammons, Warren. Mentioned 57
Garcia, General. Mentioned... 864
Gardiner, William H. Mentioned 60
Gardner, Charles. Mentioned 66
Gardner, Franklin.
    Congratulatory Orders. Springfield and Plains Store roads, La. Skir-
        mishes on the, May 23, 1863 167
    Correspondence with
        Banks, Nathaniel P............. 52, 53, 508, 513, 517, 552, 553, 557, 613, 617, 634
        Beall, William N. R 164
        Girard, Louis J 145
        Smith, Marshall J 159
        Wingfield, J. H... 165
    Mentioned 14, 17, 39, 45, 46, 54-56, 80,
        101, 106, 117, 154, 163, 164, 169, 180-182, 508, 515, 553, 622, 623, 625, 626, 631
Gardner, Joseph A. Mentioned 58
Gardner, William C. Mentioned.. 130
Garrett, S. R. Mentioned 221, 223
Garrity, Patrick. Mentioned 59
Garvey, Thomas J. Mentioned 66
Gaudet, O. Mentioned... 221, 223
Gay, Charles. Mentioned... 64
Gay, James. Mentioned.. 58
Gay, Moses. Mentioned.. 58
General Banks, Steamer. Mentioned. 288, 294, 296, 298-302, 397, 425, 502, 713, 809, 814
General Price, U. S. S. Mentioned 53, 98, 119
Genesee, U. S. S. Mentioned 47, 76, 82, 91, 220, 222
Gentien, Peter. Mentioned.. 57
George Peabody, Steamer. Mentioned.................... 415, 431, 814, 833
George Washington, Steamer. Mentioned 540, 813, 814
Georgia Troops. Mentioned.
    Infantry—Regiments : 1st, 497.
Gibson, Alexander. Mentioned 887
Gibson, George W. Mentioned... 65
Giehl, George. Mentioned 64
Gila River, N. Mex. Skirmish on the, Nov. —, 1863 * 3

* No circumstantial reports on file.

Page.

Gile, David H. Mentioned.. 908
Gillen, Stephen. Mentioned...... 65
Gillis, Isaac. Mentioned..,.... 60
Gillmore, Quincy A. Mentioned.......... 619,636
Gilman, Lemuel O. Mentioned............................. 274,276
Gilmore, J. A. For correspondence, etc., see *New Hampshire, Governor of.*
Gilpatrick, Almon L. Mentioned....................................... 60
Gilpin, Joseph B.
    Correspondence with John C. Cox.. 910
    Mentioned 909
Ginety, Patrick. Mentioned..... 65
Girard, Louis J.
    Correspondence with Franklin Gardner...................................... 145
    Report of siege of Port Hudson, La., May 21–July 8, 1863 145
Gist, S. R. Mentioned... 526
Gitey, Joseph. Mentioned 65
Gladiator, Ship. Mentioned.. 719
Glasgow, Steamer. Mentioned.. 318,319
Glasgow, Samuel L. Mentioned 334, 417, 419, 423, 709, 713, 897
Glass, Sylvester. Mentioned... 63
Glover, Alfred R. Mentioned.. 71
Godfrey, John F. Mentioned 35, 121, 135, 136, 139
Goelzer, Augustus. Mentioned.................................... 335, 358, 710, 898
Gonzales, José Y. Mentioned 25
Good, Tilghman H. Mentioned...................................... 532, 708, 896
Good, W. S. Mentioned 304, 306, 308, 312
Goodell, Henry H. Mentioned 58
Gooding, Oliver P.
    Correspondence with Nathaniel P. Banks................................... 642
    Mentioned...... .... 69, 335, 530, 633, 658, 667, 685, 749, 783
    Report of expedition from Baton Rouge to Amite River. La., Sept. 28–29, 1863 320
Goodlander, John. Mentioned... 421, 423
Goodrich, Luther. Mentioned 497, 684
Goodrich's Landing, La.
    Attack on, June 30, 1863* 2
    Expedition from, to Bayou Macon, Sept. 27–29, 1863† 3
Goodwin, Lewis H. Mentioned 898
Gordon, Calvin S. Mentioned 60
Gordon, Henry. Mentioned... 59
Gordon, John T. Mentioned 57
Gordon, Louis C. Mentioned 60
Gorman, H. J. Mentioned.. 144
Gorman, John. Mentioned.. 66
Gorman, Thomas B. Mentioned............................... 356, 361, 374, 375
Gott, Benjamin F. Mentioned.. 121, 708
Goud, Frederic. Mentioned 61
Graham, Commodore. Mentioned 687
Graham, Harvey. Mentioned... 897
Granadino, Gros. Mentioned 61
Grand Coteau, La. Skirmishes at.
    Oct. 16, 1863 * 332
    Oct. 19, 1863. See *Teche Country, La. Operations in the, Oct. 3–Nov. 30, 1863.*
        Report of Taylor, p. 388.

---

* For report, see Series I, Vol. XXIV, Part II, p. 450.　　　† No circumstantial reports on file.

Page.

Granite City, U.S.S. Mentioned.... 288, 294–297, 299, 301, 302, 308, 416, 420, 480–482

Granniss, Samuel H. Mentioned.. 131

Grant, Joseph W. Mentioned 60

Grant, U. S.

  Co-operation of, with Nathaniel P. Banks.. 494, 500, 525, 534, 535, 564, 698, 726, 731

  Correspondence with

    Army Headquarters... 664

    Banks, Nathaniel P................................. 49, 53, 506, 519, 520,

      525, 617, 619, 624, 631, 633, 635, 643–645, 653, 656. 673, 680, 686, 701, 730, 752

  Mentioned 4, 5, 11–14, 18, 44, 48, 49, 52, 53, 80, 84,

    89–92, 94, 95, 99, 100, 107, 108, 110, 112, 114, 118, 119, 137, 138, 239, 290, 305,

    326, 328, 393, 467, 489, 492, 494, 495, 497, 500, 503, 506, 511, 520, 525, 534–536,

    545, 564, 565, 571, 617, 619, 631, 633, 635, 636, 643, 645, 653, 656. 661, 664, 666,

    672, 673, 682, 683, 694, 696, 699, 714, 717, 719, 726, 727, 731, 732, 833, 840, 866

Grass, A. Mentioned 192

Grawi, Christian. Mentioned... 63

Gray, E. F.

  Mentioned.. 245

  Report of mutiny at Galveston, Tex., Aug. 10–13, 1863..................... 241

Gray, Henry. Mentioned 330, 331

Gray, John. (Major.) Mentioned....................................... 529

Gray, John. (Sergeant.) Mentioned.................................... 66

Green, Henry.

  Court-martial in case of. Mutiny at Fort Jackson, La., Dec. 9, 1863 477

  Mentioned 477, 479

Green, Thomas.

  Correspondence with John L. Logan.................................. 183

  Mentioned 15, 17, 47, 182, 192, 202, 213–219, 222, 227, 229, 232, 313, 321, 323, 326,

    328, 329, 331, 337, 338, 339, 343, 346, 351, 352, 359, 365, 374, 375, 382, 384–389,

    391, 392, 483, 601, 621, 662, 729, 732, 754, 763, 810–814, 819, 852, 863, 920

  Reports of

    Louisiana. Operations in, west of the Mississippi, June 7–July 13,

      1863 .... 225–227, 230

    Stirling's Plantation, on the Fordoche, La. Action at, Sept. 29, 1863.. 329

    Teche Country, La. Operations in the, Oct. 3–Nov. 30, 1863.......... 393

Green, William. Mentioned 59

Greene, Henry A. Mentioned....................... 26, 28, 30, 31, 750, 828, 901

Greene, Joseph E. Mentioned.. 898

Greene, William A. Mentioned..................................... 335, 710

Greenleaf, Alfred. Mentioned 64

Greenleaf, Halbert S. Mentioned..................................... 530

Greenwell Springs Road, La. Skirmishes on the.

  Sept. 19, 1863, near Baton Rouge * 2

  Oct. 5, 1863 * 3

Greer, John S. Mentioned 441

Gregg, David McM. Mentioned.. 700

Gresham, Walter Q.

  Mentioned.. 273–275, 278, 315

  Report of expedition from Natchez, Miss., to Harrisonburg, La., etc., Sept.

    1–7, 1863.. 276

Grey, Daniel. Mentioned.. 65

Grier, David P. Mentioned 335, 898

* No circumstantial reports on file.

Page.

Grierson, Benjamin H.
Correspondence with
Augur, Christopher C.. 84
Banks, Nathaniel P.. 573, 618, 625
Mentioned.............................. 16, 17, 34, 70, 84, 93, 107, 108, 112, 126,
127, 179, 505, 524, 528, 531, 554, 556, 557, 559, 573, 610, 624, 643–645, 683, 687
Reports of siege of Port Hudson, La., May 21–July 8, 1863 .... 134, 137
Griffin, Chauncey. Mentioned.. 57
Griffin, Henry B. Mentioned.. 62
Griffin, L. P. Mentioned.. 427
Griffin, Thomas. Mentioned 58
Grill, John F. Mentioned... 898
Grimsley, James. Mentioned.. 894
Grinnell, H. W. Mentioned 417, 426
Grosvenor, William M. (Captain.) Mentioned 130
Grosvenor, William M. (Colonel.) Mentioned............................. 895
Grover, Cuvier.
Correspondence with
Alden, James 79
Banks, Nathaniel P........... 541, 547, 559, 565, 574, 585, 595, 622, 625, 635, 640
Emory, William H 637, 639, 645
Franklin, William B 774
Stickney, Albert 639
Mentioned............. 6, 10, 12–14, 44–46, 69, 75, 77, 84, 85, 88, 93, 102, 104, 107, 110,
112, 113, 117, 118, 120, 127, 141, 231, 336, 353, 354, 381, 488–492, 494, 495, 499,
500, 504, 508–510, 515, 522, 527, 528, 530, 531, 546, 547, 550, 554, 555, 610, 611,
627, 632, 638, 642, 658, 660, 665, 667, 671, 686, 711, 751, 774, 783, 826, 892, 899
Report of operations in Louisiana west of the Mississippi, June 7–July 13,
1863 204
Grover, Robbins B. Mentioned 483
Grow, John A.
Mentioned 195, 336, 531, 712, 900
Report of operations in Louisiana west of the Mississippi, June 7–July 13,
1863 197
Guernsey, Samuel B. Mentioned.. 894
Gulf, Department of the. (Union.)
Affairs in, generally. Communications from
Banks, Nathaniel P............................... 523, 645, 673, 810, 871
Stone, Charles P 813
Army Corps, 13th, assigned to, from the Department of the Tennessee 2
Asboth, Alexander, assigned to duty in 755
Cooke, Philip St. George, ordered to duty in 722, 756
Engineer troops in. Communication from John C. Palfrey............... 638
Lee, Albert L., announced as Chief of Cavalry 722
Movement of troops in. Communication from U. S. Grant 656
Operations in, May 14–Dec. 31, 1863.
Communications from
Army Headquarters.. 834, 839
Banks, Nathaniel P......................... 5, 6, 671, 723, 767, 888
Halleck, Henry W 3
Stone, Charles P 782
Summary of events during.. 1–3
Orders, Circulars, series 1863: **May 26**, 508; **May 28**, 515, 518; **July 8**,
623.

Gulf, Department of the. (Union.)—Continued. **Page.**

Orders, General, series 1863: **No. 45,** 533; **No. 47,** 539; **No. 49,** 56; **No. 51,** 589; **No. 52,** 649; **No. 54,** 660; **No. 57,** 671; **No. 64,** 704; **No. 65,** 706; **No. 66,** 715; **No. 67,** 205; **No. 68,** 725; **No. 69,** 726; **No. 70,** 740; **No. 74,** 763; **No. 75,** 765; **No. 77,** 777; **No. 87,** 882; **No. 90,** 476; *Army Corps:* 13th (*Ord*), **No. 24,** 681; **No. 39,** 739; **No. 42,** 763; **No. 49** (*Dana*), 776; Oct. 2 (*Washburn*), 752. 19th, **No. 1,** 693; **No. 18,** 774; **No. 22,** 354; **No. 24,** 784; **No. 40,** 825; **No. 45,** 854; **No. 1** (*1st Division*), 682; **No. 4** (*2d Division*), 560; **No. 5** (*2d Division*), 599. *Corps d'Afrique:* **No. 1,** 632; **No. 12,** 663.

Orders, General, series 1864: **No. 25,** 21.

Orders, Special, series 1863; **No. 116,** 486; **No. 118,** 491; **No. 122,** 499; **No. 123,** 508; **No. 131,** 127, 538; **No. 133,** 539; **No. 137,** 546; **No. 138,** 548; **No. 140,** 554; **No. 141,** 557; **No. 144,** 563; **No. 158,** 613; **No. 159,** 614; **No. 164,** 626; **No. 166,** 632; **No. 171,** 642; **No. 172,** 643; **No. 174,** 645; **No. 179,** 652; **No. 183,** 657, 676; **No. 185,** 662; **No. 191,** 672; **No. 196,** 675; **No. 200,** 684, 685; **No. 209,** 269, 270; **No. 210,** 695; **No. 227,** 722; **No. 231,** 726; **No. 244,** 741; **No. 252.** 756; **No. 255,** 761; **No. 258½,** 770; **No. 278,** 791; **No. 284½,** 410; **No. 294,** 823; **No. 309,** 459, 844; **No. 311,** 852; **No. 312,** 853; **No. 313,** 862; **No. 317,** 867; **No. 320,** 871; **No. 322,** 879. *Corps:* 13th (*Ord*), **No. 42½,** 682; **No. 79,** 735; **No. 87,** 755; **No. 92.** 758; **No. 94,** 763; (*Washburn*), **No. 57,** 713; **No. 101,** 773. 19th, **No. 9,** 698; **No. 12,** 713; **No. 49,** 780; **No. 85,** 835; **No. 20** (*1st Division*), 497; **No. 32** (*2d Division*), 549; **No. 34** (*2d Division*), 549; **No. 39** (*2d Division*), 561; **No. 47** (*2d Division*), 595; **No. 53** (*3d Division*), 726.

Organization, strength, etc., of Union Troops in.

May, 1863 526–532
June, 1863 610–612
June 10, 1863 .... 632, 633
July, 1863 665
Aug., 1863 707–712
Sept. 22, 1863 733
Sept., 1863 .... 748, 749
Oct., 1863 .... 398, 783, 784
Nov., 1863 826–829
Dec., 1863 891–900

Railroad construction in. Communication from Nathaniel P. Banks 498
Recruitment and organization of troops for service in. Communications
    from Nathaniel P. Banks 848, 880
Re-enforcements for. Communications from
    Army Headquarters 619, 636, 653
    Banks, Nathaniel P. 635, 653, 690
    Grant, U. S. 631, 752
Reorganization of 3d Division of 19th Corps. 632, 633
Report of Nathaniel P. Banks of operations in, Dec. 16, 1862–Dec. 31, 1863. 6
Reynolds, Joseph J., assigned to duty in 832
Smith, William F., assigned to duty in 506
Stipp, George W., announced as Medical Inspector of 867
Warren Fitz Henry, assigned to duty in 734

Gullen, Gilbert S. Mentioned 64

Gunboat No. 2. Mentioned 567

Page.

Guppey, Joshua J.
Mentioned.. 335, 354, 358, 359, 361, 363
Report of operations in the Teche Country, La., Oct. 3–Nov. 30, 1863...... 363
Guyot, Arthur. Mentioned.. 59
Hadden, Freeman. Mentioned.. 62
Hadlock, William E.
Correspondence with
   Banks, Nathaniel P... 618
   Emory, William H... 618
   Woolsey, M. B... 622
   Mentioned... 190, 621, 622
Haffkille, Adam. Mentioned.. 17, 70
Hagan, James.
Court-martial in case of. Mutiny at Fort Jackson, La., Dec. 9, 1863...... 479
Mentioned... 479
Hagar, John H. Mentioned.. 63
Hageman, Louis. Mentioned.. 65
Hagerty, George C. Mentioned.. 60
Hague, John N. Mentioned.. 63
Haindel, John. Mentioned.. 152, 153
Haines, T. J. Mentioned.. 909
Hale, Steamer. Mentioned.. 843
Hale & Co. Mentioned.. 839, 842
Haley, Eben D. Mentioned.. 208, 209
Haley, James. Mentioned.. 39
Hall, Alfred G. Mentioned.. 531, 708, 894, 895
Hall, Cyrus.
Mentioned... 273, 274, 277
Report of expedition from Natchez, Miss., to Harrisonburg, La., etc.,
   Sept. 1–7, 1863... 275
Hall, Edward B.
Mentioned... 263, 265, 267
Testimony of. Mutiny at Camp Hubbard, Thibodeaux, La., Aug. 29–30,
   1863... 265, 266
Hall, G. Mentioned.. 308
Hall, Samuel. Mentioned.. 59
Hall, Thomas S.
Mentioned... 77, 78, 92, 104, 111, 112
Report of siege of Port Hudson, La., May 21–July 8, 1863................. 100
Hall, Walter T. Mentioned.. 65
Halleck, Henry W.
Mentioned.................... 7, 9, 18, 41, 271–273, 290, 398, 410, 524, 540, 636, 659,
   670–672, 674, 680, 682, 686, 719, 732, 753, 790, 807, 810, 813, 814, 888, 903, 904
Report of operations in the Department of the Gulf, Dec. 16, 1862–Nov. 10,
   1863... 3
   For correspondence, etc., see *Army Headquarters.*
Hallenbeck, Addison. Mentioned... 423
Hallett, Joseph L.
Mentioned... 76, 77, 105, 112, 116, 353
Report of siege of Port Hudson, La., May 21–July 8, 1863......... 103
Halley, Eben. Mentioned.. 66
Halley, Lawrence. Mentioned.. 65
Halsted, George B. Mentioned.. 813
   For correspondence as A. A. G., see *Christopher C. Augur.*

Page.

Ham, John S. P. Mentioned 482, 483
Hambleton, Wade. Mentioned 59
Hamblin, Samuel. Mentioned 458
Hamel, George. Mentioned.. 64
Hamilton, Andrew J.
    Correspondence with
        Dana, Napoleon J. T 857, 858
        War Department, U. S 865
    Mentioned...................................... 6, 680, 832, 842, 846, 856, 871, 876, 902
Hamilton, Andrew J., Mrs. Mentioned...................................... 866
Hamilton, A. S. Mentioned 143
Hamilton, Dick. Mentioned.. 857–859
Hamilton, E. Manville. Mentioned.. 898
Hamilton, J. T. Mentioned 224
Hamilton, Samuel M. Mentioned 394, 395
Hamlen, C. H. J. Mentioned.. 531
Hamlin, Cyrus. Mentioned 398, 733, 896
Hammer, A. C. Mentioned 64
Hammond, George W. Mentioned 63
Hampton, G. J. Mentioned.. 215, 230, 231, 374
Hance, John T. Mentioned.. 25
Hancock, Bradford. Mentioned 898
Hancox, I. W., Steamer. Mentioned.. 381, 829
Hanham, Moore. Mentioned 238, 239, 896
Hanks, George H. Mentioned.. 684, 704
Hanman, Lieutenant. Mentioned.. 613
Hanns, Frederick. Mentioned.. 58
Hansell, Theodore. Mentioned 63
Hansler, Nicholas. Mentioned.. 64
Harcourt, William. Mentioned.. 520, 521
Hardee, William J. Mentioned.. 496, 681, 717
Hardeman, W. P. Mentioned.. 227, 228, 395
Harding, Henry A. Mentioned 638
Hargrave, Joseph P.
    Mentioned.. 27, 258, 259
    Report of operations against Navajo Indians in New Mexico, Aug. 20–Dec.
        16, 1863.. 259
Hark, Amos. Mentioned 64
Harmount, George A. Mentioned 57
Harney, Lieutenant. Mentioned 519
Harper, William H. Mentioned.. 335, 895
Harrell, Louis. Mentioned.. 59
Harriet Lane, U. S. S. Mentioned.. 4, 6, 344
Harrigon, Andrew. Mentioned 59
Harris, C. C. Mentioned.. 167
Harris, Charles. Mentioned 308
Harris, Charles H.
    Military Commission in case of.. 487
    Mentioned.. 487, 488
Harris, Charles L. Mentioned.. 334, 428, 810, 897
Harris, George H. Mentioned 62
Harris, Roswell C. Mentioned.. 77, 104, 120
Harris, W. A. Mentioned 353

Page.

arrison, Burton N. For correspondence as Private Secretary, see *Jefferson Davis.*

rrison, James E. Mentioned.................................. 329–331, 394, 395, 791

rrison, W. H. Mentioned.. 144

rrisonburg, La.

Expedition from Natchez, Miss., to, Sept. 1–7, 1863.

  Communication from Richard Taylor 281

  Reports of

    Crocker, Marcellus M... 273

    Gresham, Walter Q... 276

    Hall, Cyrus 275

    Logan, George W 281

    Malloy, Adam G... 278

    Randal, Horace 279, 280

Skirmish near, Sept. 4, 1863. See *Harrisonburg, La. Expedition from Natchez, Miss., to, etc., Sept. 1–7, 1863. Reports of*

    Gresham, Walter Q.   Malloy, Adam G.   Randal, Horace.

    Logan, George W.

rrower, Gabriel T. Mentioned 121, 207, 529, 667, 685

rt, Captain. Mentioned 395

rt, Steamer. Mentioned... 380

rt, Robert McD. Mentioned... 64

rt, Simeon. Mentioned 918

rtford, U. S. S. Mentioned.................................... 4, 76–78, 88, 91, 92, 94–96, 99, 109, 111, 120, 507, 512, 519, 521, 541, 542

rtwell, Charles A.

  Mentioned................................... 457, 472, 512, 559, 861, 895

  Testimony of. Mutiny at Fort Jackson, La., Dec. 9, 1863 472

artwell, Samuel C. Mentioned 636

arwood, Franklin. Mentioned 82, 489, 493, 495, 502

askins, R. F. Mentioned.. 285

assett, Martin. Mentioned 61

atfield, George W. Mentioned 64

aunaburgh, David H. Mentioned...................................... 63

aupt, Hermann. Mentioned... 499

awhe, Arthur J. Mentioned 897

awkins, Elli. Mentioned 61

awkins, John P.

  Correspondence with James B. McPherson.......... 770, 791, 799, 800, 802

  Mentioned... 712, 829

awkins, W. H. Mentioned 778

awkins, William R. Mentioned 60

ayden, Charles T. Mentioned 23

ayes, John. (Private.) Mentioned................................... 59

ayes, John. (Corporal.) Mentioned................................. 60

aynes, John L. Mentioned.. 831

ealey, Thomas. Mentioned 278

ealy, John G. Mentioned... 201

ealy, Thomas. Mentioned 201

eath, John E. Mentioned 60

ebard, George T. Mentioned 530, 633, 660, 895

ebe, Steamer. Mentioned... 82

ebert, Paul O. Mentioned 249, 283

	Page.
Hegany, Dennis. Mentioned	57
Heinrichs, William. Mentioned	66
Heins, Conrad. Mentioned	62
Heintzelman, Samuel P. Mentioned	820
Helm, Benjamin H. Mentioned	496
Hemingway, William. Mentioned	144
Hemstreet, William. Mentioned	66
Henderson, Captain. Mentioned	485, 486
Henderson, Thomas. Mentioned	29
Hendricks, Isaac C. Mentioned	896
Hendrickson, Alexander. Mentioned	65
Henry, Edmund W. Mentioned	787
Henry, W. Mentioned	59
Herbert, George R.	
Mentioned	76, 352
Report of siege of Port Hudson, La., May 21–July 8, 1863	105
Herbert, P. T. Mentioned	215, 227–231, 347, 395
Hererra, Natividad. Mentioned	285
Hermann, Simon. Mentioned	650
Herod, A. J. Mentioned	161
Heron, John. Mentioned	63
Herrera, Andres. Mentioned	30, 255
Herrick, Charles A. Mentioned	65
Herrman, Alex. Mentioned	65
Herron, Francis J.	
Assignment to command	879
Correspondence with	
Banks, Nathaniel P	716, 722, 729, 732, 880
Ratliff, W. B	322
Mentioned	286, 320–323, 325, 327, 328, 389, 390, 456, 459, 665, 681, 691, 701, 709, 722, 723, 729, 735, 739, 846, 871, 879, 902
Relieved from command of 2d Division, 13th Corps	735
Report of skirmish at Morgan's Ferry, on the Atchafalaya, La., Sept. 7, 1863	312
Hersey, A. J. Mentioned	72
Hesseltine, Frank S.	
Mentioned	398, 420, 427, 480, 481, 897
Report of skirmish on Matagorda Peninsula, Tex., Dec. 29, 1863	481
Hewes, James. Mentioned	787
Hewett, Michael. Mentioned	64
Hewett, Minot D. Mentioned	61
Hewitt, R. M. Mentioned	169, 177
H. G. Berry, Schooner. Mentioned	836
Hicks, J. B. Mentioned	245
Higdon, W. H. Mentioned	24, 25
Higgins, John. (Lieutenant-Colonel.) Mentioned	529, 899
Higgins, John. (Private.) Mentioned	61
Hilderbrand, Frederick. Mentioned	63
Hildman, Adolph. Mentioned	152, 153
Hill, Charles. Mentioned	427, 447
Hill, Edgar P. Mentioned	366
Hill, Martin V. B. Mentioned	71
Hill, Michael. Mentioned	64

Page.

Hill, Richard M. Mentioned 411, 427, 490, 494
Hillis, James. Mentioned... 66
Hinchman, Eugene A. Mentioned.. 64
Hinkley, John. Mentioned.. 24
Hiscock, Gustavus. Mentioned 61
Hitchcock, Charles N. Mentioned 816
Hitchcock, R. B. Mentioned... 90
Hoag, David D. Mentioned... 70
Hobbey, Robert. Mentioned 65
Hobbs, I. Frank. Mentioned. 60
Hobby, A. M. Mentioned... 436, 437, 812
Hobdell, ———. Mentioned 519
Hodge, Justin. Mentioned.... . 74, 398, 529, 539, 555, 611, 613, 638, 684, 707, 843, 898
Hodges, William T. Mentioned... 61
Hodinger, Henry. Mentioned... 64
Hodsdon, Alfred. Mentioned... 710, 828, 900
Hodt, Nicholas. Mentioned 29, 30, 253, 727
Hoffman, John. Mentioned.. 59
Hoffman, Wickham. Mentioned 512, 682, 693
    For correspondence as A. A. G., see *William B. Franklin.*
Hoffsletter, ———. Mentioned... 251
Hogan, Michael. Mentioned 64
Hog Point, Mississippi River. Operations against U. S. gunboats and trans-
        ports near, Nov. 18–21, 1863.
    Communications from
        Andrews, George L 816
        Stone, Charles P 809
    Reports of T. A. Faries.. 453, 455
Hogue, Bazel. Mentioned... 60
Hogue, William. Mentioned.. 62
Hohn, Jacob. Mentioned.. 64
Holabird, Samuel B.
    Correspondence with
        Banks, Nathaniel P 510
        Talbot, W. H... 595
    Mentioned............. 203, 341, 415, 426, 522, 620, 662, 692, 754, 758, 775, 785, 903–905
Holbrook, William C.
    Correspondence with
        Banks, Nathaniel P 742
        Maury, Dabney H... 745
        Morino, J 743, 744
        Young, Mahlon M... 746
    Mentioned................... 527, 532, 610, 665, 707, 708, 746, 747, 749, 784, 822, 895
Holcomb, Pythagoras E.
    Correspondence with Nathan A. M. Dudley..................................... 116
    Mentioned 116, 121, 530, 708
Holcomb, Richard E. Mentioned................................... 17, 70, 130, 511, 530
Holland, Dr. Mentioned 243
Hollinger, Robert. Mentioned 58
Hollister, Edward P. Mentioned.. 62
Hollyhock, U. S. S. Mentioned 46, 544, 546, 595, 598, 599, 623, 640, 913
Holmes, Charles E. L. Mentioned 186, 491, 531
Holmes, Frederick. Mentioned.. 71
Holmes, Theophilus H. Correspondence with John S. Marmaduke.......... 392

	Page.
Home, Steamer. Mentioned	909
Hooker, Joseph. Mentioned	494, 626
Hooper, S. Mentioned	829
Hopkins, Albert. Mentioned	58
Hopkins, William S. B. Mentioned	530, 633, 711, 900
Horn, J. C. Mentioned	864
Hosley, Luther T. Mentioned	71
Hotchkiss, Memoir V. Mentioned	898
Housen, John. Mentioned	66
Houston, David C. Mentioned	383, 384,
546, 563, 635, 637–639, 657, 676, 679, 692, 707, 783, 798, 814. 820, 826, 891, 894	
Hovey, Alvin P. Mentioned	681
Hovey, Samuel D. Mentioned	62
Howard, Lieutenant. Mentioned	834
Howard, Harry S. Mentioned	62
Howard, John. Mentioned	59
Howell, Francis A. Mentioned	900
Howell, Luther C. Mentioned	62
Howland, George W. Mentioned	58
Hoyt, E. W. Mentioned	24
Hoyt, Stephen. Mentioned	456, 459
Hubbard, Camp. See *Camp Hubbard.*	
Hubbard, Edwin N. Mentioned	62
Hubbard, John B. Mentioned	71, 94
Hubbard, Nathaniel H. Mentioned	530
Hubbell, C. M. Mentioned	32, 237, 253
Hudson, Steamer. Mentioned	695
Hudson, Peter. Mentioned	64, 673
Huff, Silas. Mentioned	60
Hughes, Augustus Berkeley. Mentioned	707
Hughes, D. Henry. Mentioned	665
Hughes, D. M. C. Mentioned	37
Hughes, James. Mentioned	61
Hughes, Thomas H. Mentioned	62
Hulbert, Henry S. Mentioned	71
Hull, Henry D. Mentioned	421, 423
Hull, Willoughby. Mentioned	57
Hume, P. G. Mentioned	394
Humphrey, Ballard S. Mentioned	895
Humphrey, Charles E. Mentioned	58
Hunnewell, Randall F. Mentioned	61
Hunt, James L. Mentioned	60
Hunt, John. (13th Connecticut.) Mentioned	58
Hunt, John. (1st Louisiana.) Mentioned	58
Hunt, John Dela. Mentioned	·279
Hunt, William, jr. Mentioned	710
Hunter, Colonel. Mentioned	320
Hunter, David.	
Correspondence with Nathaniel P. Banks	523
Mentioned	523
Hunter, Sherod.	
Mentioned	215–217, 224, 225
Report of operations in Louisiana west of the Mississippi, June 7–July 13, 1863	223

Page.

Hunter, Walter B. Mentioned 62
Huntley, William H. Mentioned 58
Hurd, Francis M. Mentioned 62
Hurlburt, Byron J. Mentioned 66
Hurlburt, Henry A. Mentioned 58
Hurlbut, Stephen A.
    Correspondence with
        Army Headquarters 888
        Navy Department, U. S 891
    Mentioned 138, 526, 753
Hurlbut, W. C.
    Correspondence with James B. McPherson 905
    Mentioned 904, 908
Hussar, Steamer. Mentioned 418, 813, 825
Hussey, Willard A. Mentioned 61
Hutchings, Ball & Co. Mentioned 485
Hutchings, Charles B. Mentioned 58
Hutchings, Jasper. Mentioned 896
Huxford, Francis. Mentioned 58
Huxford, William P. Mentioned 65
Huys, Drouyn de l'. Mentioned 570
Iberville, Steamer. Mentioned 49, 52, 216, 615, 713, 754
Icks, Louis. Mentioned 59
I. C. Landis, Steamer. Mentioned 294, 296, 298
Illinois Troops. Mentioned.
    Artillery, Light—*Batteries:* Cooley's, 335, 710, 712, 739, 869, 898. *Regiments:* 1st (*Batteries*), K, 506, 645; 2d (*Batteries*), A, 334, 709, 739, 894; E, 335, 691, 710, 739, 895; F, 273, 275; G, L, 248.
    Cavalry—*Regiments:* 2d, 322, 325, 336, 373, 374, 377–379, 710, 828, 900; 3d, 336, 373, 374, 378, 379, 710, 828, 900; 4th, 248, 319; 6th, 16, 70, 91, 134–136, 524, 528, 531, 645; 7th, 16, 70, 91, 103, 134–136, 139, 506, 524, 528, 531, 645; 15th,* 322, 336, 376, 665, 710, 825, 900.
    Infantry—*Regiments:* 11th, 315; 14th, 15th, 275; 28th, 32d, 276; 33d, 334, 418, 419, 421, 422, 709, 897; 37th, 322, 324, 327, 398, 423, 424, 430, 665, 709. 842, 856, 897; 46th, 76th, 275; 77th, 335, 431, 710, 898; 87th, 336, 378, 379, 710, 828, 900; 91st, 328, 398, 665, 709, 897; 94th, 328, 398, 399, 430, 665, 709, 897; 95th, 315; 97th, 335, 368, 710, 784, 900; 99th, 334, 419, 422, 423, 709, 897; 118th, 336, 361, 367, 372, 373, 379, 384, 709, 765, 828, 900; 130th, 335, 368, 710, 898.
Ilsley, C. S. Mentioned 427
Ilsley, Edward. Mentioned 530
I. M. Brown, Steamer. Mentioned 642
Imperial, Steamer. Mentioned 644
Indian Bayou, La. Skirmish near, Nov. 9, 1863† 3
Indiana Troops. Mentioned.
    Artillery, Heavy—*Regiments:* 1st,‡ 22, 68, 190, 195, 287, 294, 354, 489, 529, 530, 611, 622, 659, 667, 708, 721, 867, 895, 911–914; 1st (*Batteries*), A, 911; B, 894, 911; F, 911, 912; G. 894; H, 911; I, 531; K, 75, 894; L, 896, 911; M, 894.
    Artillery, Light—*Batteries:* 1st, 334, 709, 712, 739, 773, 806, 859. 869, 895.
    Cavalry—*Regiments:* 1st, 336, 376, 710, 828, 900; 4th, 336, 359, 376, 710, 828, 893, 900.

---

* Co. A, 36th Illinois, assigned to 15th Cavalry, May, 1863.
† No circumstantial reports on file.
‡ Sometimes called 21st Indiana.

Page.

Indiana Troops. Mentioned—Continued.

Infantry—*Regiments:* **8th,** 334, 409, 419, 421, 422, 426, 709, 897; **11th,** 335, 358, 710, 898; **16th,** 317, 319, 336, 378, 379, 710, 749, 828, 900; **18th,** 334, 418, 419, 422, 423, 426, 709, 897; **24th,** 335, 710, 898; **26th,** 321, 322, 324–328, 330, 398, 665, 709, 897; **34th,** 335, 430, 710, 898; **46th,** 335, 371, 430, 710, 898; **47th,** 335, 710, 898; **49th,** 334, 709, 837, 860, 897; **53d,** 276; **54th,** 367, 709, 894; **60th,** 335, 358, 359, 361, 364, 365, 394, 431, 710, 898; **67th,** 335, 358, 359–361, 364, 365, 394, 431, 710, 898; **69th,** 334, 709, 897.

Ingraham, Asahel. Mentioned 58

Ingraham, Timothy. Mentioned 69, 530, 633

Insley, Joseph S. Mentioned 64

Intercourse. See *Trade and Intercourse.*

Inwood, Henry C. Mentioned 65

Iowa Troops. Mentioned.

Infantry—*Regiments:* **19th,** 321, 324–328, 330, 398, 425, 430, 665, 709, 897; **20th,** 325, 327, 398, 412, 426, 427, 429, 430, 665, 709, 788, 789, 825, 894, 897; **21st,** 334, 709, 897; **22d,** 334, 709, 825, 897; **23d,** 334, 417–419, 422, 423, 709, 893, 897; **24th,** 335, 358, 710, 898; **26th,** 409; **28th,** 335, 359, 710, 898; **34th,** 327, 398, 409, 412, 413, 419, 426–429, 665, 709, 789, 897; **38th,** 326, 327, 398, 665, 709, 897.

Ireland, John.

Mentioned 445

Report of Rio Grande Expedition and operations on the coast of Texas, Oct. 27–Dec. 2, 1863 447

Irvin, F. A. Mentioned 352, 353

Irving, Sidney E.

Mentioned 267

Testimony of. Mutiny at Camp Hubbard, Thibodeaux, La., Aug. 29–30, 1863 .... 267, 268

Irwin, L. C. Mentioned 308

Irwin, Richard B.

Correspondence with

Banks, Nathaniel P 488, 489, 684

Emerson, Charles 82

Mentioned 54, 96, 488–490, 506, 522, 531, 533

Report of siege of Port Hudson, La., May 21–July 8, 1863 72

For correspondence as A. A. G., see *Nathaniel P. Banks.*

Ives, Francis M.

Mentioned 264

Testimony of. Mutiny at Camp Hubbard, Thibodeaux, La., Aug. 29–30, 1863 .... 264, 268

I. W. Hancox, Steamer. Mentioned 381, 829

Jackson, Lieutenant. Mentioned 427

Jackson, Amos M.

Correspondence with Stephen M. Eaton 91, 92

Mentioned 77, 91, 93, 103, 112, 120

Report of siege of Port Hudson, La., May 21–July 8, 1863 107

Jackson, C. M. Report of siege of Port Hudson, La., May 21–July 8, 1863 144

Jackson, Fort. See *Fort Jackson.*

Jackson, Joseph. Mentioned 24, 59

Jackson, La. Skirmish at, Aug. 3, 1863. Reports of

Andrews, George L 238

Logan, John L 240

Jacobs, Harvey F. Mentioned 71

Page.

Jacob's Well, N. Mex. See *Ojo Redondo.*
Jacoby, Lawrence. Mentioned... 334, 895
J. A. Cotton, C. S. S. Mentioned... 4, 8
James, Joseph A. Mentioned.. 328
James Murray, Tug. Mentioned... 829
Jefferson, Thomas. Mentioned... 59
Jemez, Governor of. Mentioned.. 27
Jencks, John F.
    Mentioned 78, 88, 103, 104, 107
    Report of siege of Port Hudson, La., May 21–July 8, 1863 112
Jenkins, ———. Mentioned.. 492
Jenkins, James H. Mentioned... 197
Jenkins, Thornton A. Correspondence with David G. Farragut............ 140
    For correspondence as Chief of Staff, see *David G. Farragut.*
Jenkins, William F. Mentioned.. 60
Jerrard, Simon G. Mentioned... 530, 589
Jesemaughn, Paul. Mentioned... 61
Jewell, James S. Mentioned... 61
Jewett, Oliver D. Mentioned.. 60
J. M. Brown, Steamer. Mentioned....................................... 782
John F. Carr, C. S. S. Mentioned...................................... 480, 481, 483
John, Richard. Mentioned... 59
Johnson, ———. Mentioned.. 792
Johnson, Benjamin. Mentioned... 59
Johnson, Benjamin W. Mentioned.................... 143, 145, 147, 160, 162
Johnson, Bushrod R. Mentioned... 496
Johnson, Edward. Mentioned.. 61
Johnson, Elijah D. Mentioned.. 75, 529, 602
Johnson, James R. Mentioned... 62
Johnson, Robert S. Mentioned.. 25
Johnson, Thomas. Mentioned 60
Johnson, William. Mentioned... 66
Johnston, Brent. Mentioned.. 121
Johnston, Joseph E.
    Correspondence with
        Adjutant and Inspector General's Office, C. S. A....................... 182
        Logan, John L.. 182
    Mentioned 16, 46, 48, 49, 84, 107, 112, 127, 181, 211, 214, 495, 496,
            525, 526, 534–536, 571, 652–654, 661, 674, 681, 696, 701, 717, 724, 730, 742, 818
Johnston, Thomas B. Mentioned... 61
Johnston, Thomas H.
    Mentioned 150
    Report of siege of Port Hudson, La., May 21–July 8, 1863.................. 164
Jolley, William. Mentioned... 64
Jones, ———. Mentioned... 776
Jones, Colonel. Mentioned... 566
Jones, Alexander. Mentioned... 59
Jones, Augustus. Mentioned 62
Jones, B. Mentioned... 143
Jones, David. Mentioned... 72
Jones, Edward L. Mentioned 555
Jones, Henry. Mentioned... 66
Jones, John B. Mentioned.. 331
Jones, O. G. Mentioned 242, 247

Page.

Jones, O. H. Mentioned 220–222, 454, 455
Jones, Robert B. Mentioned 335, 898
Jones, Rufus L. Mentioned... 63
Jones, Samuel B. Mentioned... 708, 733, 896
Jones, Simon. Mentioned.. 900
Jones, William. Mentioned 276
Jones, William W. Mentioned.. 57
Jordan, H. C. Mentioned... 804
Jordan, Jeremy T. Mentioned.. 58
Jornada del Muerto, N. Mex. Skirmish on the, June 16, 1863*........... 2
Joseph, George. Mentioned 59
Joseph, Joseph. Mentioned... 59
Jost, Frederick. Mentioned 63
Juarez, Benito Pablo. Mentioned 403, 801, 838, 844, 876, 883, 886
Judd, Isaac E. Mentioned... 71
Judge-Advocate-General's Office, U. S. A. Correspondence with Robert
    N. Scott 206
Jumper, Alden H. Mentioned.. 398, 898
J. W. Wilder, Schooner. Mentioned 792
Kalt, Leo. Mentioned 65
Kampmann, J. H. Mentioned 242
Kan-a-at-sa. (Indian.) Mentioned.. 234
Kanawha, U. S. S. Mentioned 3
Kansas Troops. Mentioned.
    Infantry—Regiments: 1st, 315.
Kate Dale, Steamer. Mentioned 793
Kathra, Henry. Mentioned... 58
Kean, R. G. H. For correspondence as A. D. C., see War Department, C. S.
Kearney, Michael. Mentioned.. 58
Kearny, William. Mentioned 851
Keating, George. Mentioned...................................... 207, 208, 529, 899
Keating, William. Mentioned.. 65
Keefe, James. Mentioned 531
Keese, Francis S.
    Mentioned... 63, 711, 899
    Report of siege of Port Hudson, La., May 21–July 8, 1863 125
Keigwin, James. Mentioned 334, 897
Keiley, George W. Mentioned... 65
Keily, Daniel J. Mentioned 881, 900
Keith, John A. Mentioned 529, 611, 708
Kelcher, William. Mentioned... 141
Kelley, John. Mentioned.. 62
Kelley, Theodore. Mentioned 64
Kelly, James G. Mentioned.. 64
Kelly, John. Mentioned... 61
Kelly, John H. Mentioned 709, 897
Kelly, William. Mentioned 62
Kelton, John C. For correspondence as A. A. G., see Army Headquarters.
Kemple, Joseph. Mentioned 58
Kempsey, Matthew C. Mentioned........................... 398, 736–738, 898
Kendall, Nathan W. Mentioned... 60
Kennedy, ——. Mentioned 438

* No circumstantial reports on file.

Page.
Kennedy, Jacob.
    Court-martial in case of. Mutiny at Fort Jackson, La., Dec. 9, 1863 477
    Mentioned 477, 479
Kennedy, William. •Mentioned 65
Kennett, Steamer. Mentioned 319
Kenney, John. Mentioned 66
Kenny, Alexander J. Mentioned 419, 423
Kenny, William. Mentioned 61
Kent, Daniel. Mentioned 709
Kent, Lenox. Mentioned 63
Kent, Silas. Mentioned 325
Kentucky Troops. Mentioned. (Confederate.)
    Infantry—*Regiments:* 2d, 4th, 6th, 9th, 496.
Kentucky Troops. Mentioned. (Union.)
    Engineers—*Companies:* Patterson's, 709, 893, 896.
    Infantry—*Regiments:* 7th, 334, 709, 806, 895, 897; 19th, 335, 431, 710, 898;
    22d, 334, 709, 806, 895, 897.
Kenyon, Martin R. Mentioned 71
Kenyon, M. J. Mentioned 791
Kepper, Steamer. Mentioned 595
Kershner, Philip. Mentioned 897
Kiah, Alexander. Mentioned 58
Kiernan, James L. Mentioned 829, 712
Kilborn, Curtis W. Mentioned 741, 765
Killed and Wounded. See *Confederate Troops* and *Union Troops. Returns of
    Casualties.*
Killough, Ira G. Mentioned 228
Kimball, George H.
    Mentioned 469, 470
    Testimony of. Mutiny at Fort Jackson, La., Dec. 9, 1863 469
Kimball, John W. Mentioned 530, 633
Kimball, William K. Mentioned 70, 487, 530, 686, 711, 900
Kimberly, Lewis A. Mentioned 90
Kimmey, Myndert M. Mentioned 413–415, 656, 866, 885
    • For correspondence, etc., see *Monterey, Mexico, U. S. Consul at.*
Kineo, U. S. S. Mentioned 191, 202, 568, 572, 621
King, ——. Mentioned 438
King, Captain. Mentioned 449, 451
King, Governor. Mentioned 412
King, Dana W. Mentioned 62
King, W. H. Mentioned 395
King, William M. Mentioned 97
Kingman, John W. Mentioned 529, 632
Kingsley, Thomas G. Report of siege of Port Hudson, La., May 21–July 8,
    1863 123
Kinney, John C. Mentioned 57
Kinsey, William B. Mentioned 64, 335, 710, 899
Kirby, Byron. Mentioned 900
Kirk, David N. Mentioned 66
Kirke, James W. Mentioned 708
Klein, John. Mentioned 57
Knapp, William H.
    Mentioned 471, 473
    Testimony of. Mutiny at Fort Jackson, La., Dec. 9, 1863 473

Page.

Knickerbocker, George. Mentioned 62
Knipe, Flemming. Mentioned 65
Knox, Samuel L. Mentioned 157, 161, 163
Kohler, George. Mentioned ....♦............... 57
Krafft, Theo. W. Mentioned 63
Kraher, Lewis. Mentioned ,... 64
Kriegelstein, Samuel. Mentioned 64
Kuhfuss, John G. Mentioned 66
Kuhlmann, Edward. Mentioned 66
Labadie, Lorenzo. Mentioned.. 31, 260, 261, 845
Lacraie, Louis. Mentioned 59
Lacy, Dennis. Mentioned.. 65
Ladd, Joseph J. Mentioned 62, 711
Ladiges, Julius. Mentioned 66
Lafayette, U. S. S. Mentioned... 557
La Fourche (Cox's Plantation, etc.), near Donaldsonville, La. Engage-
    ment on the, July 12–13, 1863. See *Louisiana. Operations in, west*
    of the Mississippi, June 7–July 13, 1863. Reports of
        Dudley, Nathan A. M.   Green, Thomas.   Taylor, Richard.
        Faries, T. A.   Grover, Cuvier.

        See also *Joseph S. Morgan. Court-martial in case of.*
La Fourche Crossing, La. Engagement at, June 20–21, 1863. See *Louisiana.*
    Operations in, west of the Mississippi, June 7–July 13, 1863. Reports of
        Emory, William H.   Major, James P.   Stickney, Albert.
        Grow, John A.

Lagow, C. B. Mentioned.. 644
Laing, John K. Mentioned... 60
Lairds, Messrs. Mentioned... 659
Lake Borgne, La. Affair on, Nov. 22, 1863*.................................. 3
Lake Pontchartrain, La. Scouting near, Sept. 13–Oct. 2, 1863. Report of C.
        M. Allen 313
Lake Providence, La.
    Action near, June 9, 1863†....................................... 2
    Skirmishes at Mound Plantation, and near, June 24, 1863*.............. 2
    Skirmish near, May 27, 1863*.. 1
Lake Saint Joseph, La. Affair at, June 4, 1863‡.......................... 1
Lamar, T. B. For correspondence as A. A. G., see *Joseph E. Johnston.*
Lambert, John. Mentioned.. 25
Lamson, Charles W. Mentioned.. 285, 420, 483
Lancaster, Morris. Mentioned... 65
Land, George W. Mentioned... 900
Land, W. S. Mentioned.. 228
Landis, I. C., Steamer. Mentioned 294, 296, 298
Landram, William J. Mentioned.... 335, 368, 431, 681, 758, 879, 891, 892, 893, 896, 898
Landt, Henry. Mentioned.. 65
Lane, Harriet, U. S. S. Mentioned 4, 6, 344
Lane, John. Mentioned.. 59
Lane, W. P. Mentioned............................ 218, 219, 222, 227, 228, 231, 622
Lange, Laurentz. Mentioned.. 65
Lanphere, Charles H. Mentioned 709

* No circumstantial reports on file.
† For reports, see Series I, Vol. XXIV, Part II, pp. 448, 449.
‡ For report, see Series I, Vol. XXIV, Part II, p. 457.

Page.

Lantry, Edward. Mentioned 57
Lape, Charles W. Mentioned.. 66
Laramore, George. Mentioned.. 65
Larned, Frank H. Mentioned 532, 708, 822, 895
Larock, David, jr. Mentioned.. 66
Larrabee, George N. Mentioned 60
Lasher, Henry D. Mentioned.. 66
Latham, F. W. Mentioned 435
Latimer, Elisha E. Mentioned 29, 261
La Tisiphone, Corvette. Mentioned................................... 569, 572
Laughlin, J. Mentioned.. 30
Laughtman, John. Mentioned 65
Laurel Hill, Steamer. Mentioned........ 296. 297, 299, 488, 489, 491, 493, 495, 631, 632
Lavary, Barney. Mentioned... 66
Lawler, Michael K.
   Assignment to command 773
   Correspondence with
      Banks, Nathaniel P................................... 805, 806, 813
      Franklin, William B... 787
   Mentioned.. 319,
      334, 335, 342, 357, 366, 367, 380, 382, 417, 709, 710, 773, 782, 783, 798, 806, 819
Lawson, James P. Mentioned... 41
Lawton, James M. Mentioned... 791
Leach, Patrick. Mentioned.. 58
Leake, Joseph B. Mentioned...., ... 322, 323, 325, 327
Leary, John. Mentioned 61
Le Bisque, Felix. Mentioned 156
Lebo, William B. Mentioned...............'................................ 361
Lederick, Theodore. Mentioned.. 59
Ledlie, Joseph H. Mentioned.. 423
Lee, Albert L.
   Announced as Chief of Cavalry, Department of the Gulf 722
   Correspondence with William B. Franklin............................ 774, 775
   Mentioned....... 336, 340, 343–346, 349, 353, 367, 368, 373–378, 381, 390, 691, 701. 708,
      710, 722, 725, 739, 749, 754, 769, 770, 782, 783, 814, 819, 820, 826, 828, 892, 900
   Reports of operations in the Teche Country, La., Oct. 3–Nov. 30, 1863.... 369, 370
Lee, Auguste. Mentioned... 59
Lee, Henry. Mentioned....'.. 59
Lee, Maurice. Mentioned... 62
Lee, Robert E. Mentioned......'.......................... 646, 651, 717, 720, 788, 817
Lee, S. J. For correspondence as A. A. A. G., see W. R. Bradfute.
Lee, Stephen D. Mentioned 730
Leggett, Mortimer D. Mentioned... 904
Legross, Ernest. Mentioned 59
Lehman, Henry von. Mentioned... 66
Leinrie, William L. Mentioned... 62
Lemmon, ——. Mentioned 492
Lenning. William. Mentioned.. 57
Leonhardt, August. Mentioned... 64
Leviathan, Tug.
   Capture of. Communication from Nathaniel P. Banks 732
   Mentioned 724, 732, 733
   Recapture of. Communication from Nathaniel P. Banks................... 733
Lewis, A. J. Mentioned... 143

Page.

Lewis, David. Mentioned 65
Lewis, G. W. Mentioned 166
Lewis, J. L. Mentioned 331
Lewis, John V. Correspondence with William T. Sherman 909
Lewis, Joseph. , Mentioned 59
Lewis, Philip. Mentioned 64
Lewis, Victor. Mentioned 59
Lewis, W. H. Mentioned 612, 750
L'Hommedieu, Stephen S., jr. Mentioned 896, 898
Liddell, St. John R. Mentioned 496
Lieber, G. Norman. Mentioned 456, 459
    For correspondence as A. A. A. G., see *Nathaniel P. Banks ;* also *Judge-Advocate-General's Office, U. S. A.*
Linahan, Timothy J. Mentioned 71
Lincoln, Abraham.
    Correspondence with
        Banks, Nathaniel P 396, 688, 832, 833
        New Hampshire, Governor of 680
        War Department, U. S 659
    Mentioned 206, 488, 497, 503,
      569, 570, 589, 680, 685, 690, 694, 737, 742, 803, 815, 846, 856, 867, 871, 874, 919
Lindsey, Captain. Mentioned 151
Lindsey, Daniel W. Mentioned 709
Lindsey, Joseph W. Mentioned 335
Linebits, Philip. Mentioned 63
Linguist, Gustavus F. Mentioned 65
Lippincott, Charles E. Mentioned 334, 419, 421–423
Litteral, Private. Mentioned 439, 448, 449
Little Foot. (Indian.) Mentioned 251, 254
Liverpool, England, U. S. Consul at. Correspondence with State Department, U. S 658
Lochbihler, Christian. Mentioned 314, 315
Locke, M. B.
    Mentioned 157, 163, 166
    Report of operations on west side of the Mississippi River, near Port Hudson, La., May 17, 1863 36
Lockhart, William. Mentioned 28
Locust Point, Steamer. Mentioned 114
Loder, Peter W. Mentioned 31, 261
Loeb, Abraham. Mentioned 66
Lofra, Massalla. Mentioned 59
Logan, George W.
    Mentioned 182, 275, 279–281, 283
    Report of expedition from Natchez, Miss., to Harrisonburg, La., Sept. 1–7, 1863 281
Logan, John L.
    Correspondence with
        Green, Thomas 183
        Johnston, Joseph E 182
    Mentioned 134, 138, 180, 181, 239, 240, 313, 317, 320, 565, 810, 811
    Reports of
        Jackson, La. Skirmish at, Aug. 3, 1863 240
        Port Hudson, La. Siege of, May 21–July 8, 1863 179–183
Logan, Levi A. Mentioned 62
Logan, Samuel T. Mentioned 60

Page.

Logan, Thomas. Mentioned 828, 900
Long, John. Mentioned.. 64
Long, Walter S. Mentioned.. 638
Longstreet, James. Mentioned 637
Loomis, Private. Mentioned... 40, 41
Loomis, Reuben. Mentioned... 531
Lopez, Jesus. Mentioned 25
Lord, Charles T. Mentioned.. 60
    For correspondence as A. D. C., see *William H. Emory.*
Loring, Seldon H. Mentioned 122, 209
Loring, William W. Mentioned 526
Losses in Action. See *Confederate Troops* and *Union Troops. Returns of Casualties.*
Lotsum, Robert. Mentioned 59
Louisiana.
    Affairs in, generally. Communications from
        Army Headquarters... 775
        Banks, Nathaniel P... 651
        Stone, Charles P 652
    Charities for destitute inhabitants of. Communication from Nathaniel P.
        Banks 735
    Conscription in. Communication from Nathaniel P. Banks............... 766
    Draft in, ordered 740
    Operations in, west of the Mississippi, June 7–July 13, 1863.
        Casualties. Returns of.
            Confederate Troops 230
            Union Troops 205
        Communications from
            Banks, Nathaniel P........................ 50, 51, 543, 546, 557,
                571, 574, 575, 582, 590, 593, 598, 601, 619, 623, 631, 640, 642, 646, 699, 701, 729
            Bullen, Joseph D 620, 621
            Cahill, Thomas W 582, 588, 591
            Clapp, M 568
            Cooke, A. P.. 567
            Drew, Charles W... 567
            Emory, William H.. 49,
                51, 540, 541, 543, 544, 546, 556, 559, 568, 571, 574–581, 584–588, 590–594,
                596–601, 604, 606–609, 612, 613, 615, 616, 618, 627, 635, 637–639, 645
            Farragut, David G..................... 558, 570, 589, 594, 607, 617
            Grover, Cuvier.. 635, 640
            Hadlock, William E...................................... 618, 622
            Palmer, James S 566
            Plumly, M. W 644
            Sage, Clinton H... 573, 608
            Sawtell, Joseph A.. 600
            Smith, E. Kirby... 209, 212
            Stickney, Albert 541, 544, 575, 576, 579, 580, 639
            Taylor, Richard... 217, 220, 224
            Weaver, Aaron W... 81
            Woolsey, M. B... 621
        Co-operation of U. S. Navy with Army.............................. 190
        Reports of
            Banks, Nathaniel P 6
            Dudley, Nathan A. M 207

Page.

Louisiana—Continued.
Operations in, west of the Mississippi, June 7–July 13, 1863.
 Reports of
  Emerson, Charles **203**
  Emory, William H 187, 188, 190
  Faries, T. A.. 220, 222
  Fitz Gibbons, Richard... **201**
  Green, Thomas... 225–227, 230
  Grover, Cuvier.. 204
  Grow, John A.. 197
  Hunter, Sherod 223
  Keith, John A... 911, 912
  Major, James P 217
  Mouton, Alfred... 215
  Porter, Henry M 202
  Stearns, Albert.. 191
  Stickney, Albert 192
  Taylor, Richard... 209–212, 214
Re-establishment of civil authority in. Communication from War Depart-
 ment, U. S.. 694

Louisiana, Eastern.
Operations in, Aug. 6–Sept. 5, 1863. Communications from
 Andrews, George L... 672
 Banks, Nathaniel P 777
 Beckwith, Edward G.. 717

Louisiana, Northeastern, District of.
Operations in, Oct. 17–Nov. 16, 1863. Communications from John P. Haw-
 kins 770, 791, 799, 802
Orders, Special, series 1863: **No. 43**, 816; **No. 48**, 864.
Organization, strength, etc., of Union Troops in, Nov., 1863 829

Louisiana, Western.
Operations in, June 4–Dec. 31, 1863. Communications from
 Andrews, George L....................................... 813, 852, 853, 863, 891
 Banks, Nathaniel P.................... 663, 734, 779, 805, 806, 809, 812, 813, 820
 Birge, Henry W... 806
 Dana, Napoleon J. T 753
 Dudley, Nathan A. M... 667
 Franklin, William B 835, 847
 Herron, Francis J.. 729, 732
 Merritt, Robert B 669
 Palmer, James S 537
 Peck, Frank H.. 662, 668
 Ransom, Thomas E. G... 693
 Sheldon, Lionel A.. 815
 Stone, Charles P.. 809
Recruitment in. Communication from Nathaniel P. Banks 778

Louisiana Troops—Mentioned. (Confederate.)
 Artillery, Heavy—*Battalions:* **12th**, 143, 152, 551; **12th** (*Batteries*), D, 147,
  537.
 Artillery, Light—*Batteries:* Boone's, 143, 168, 171, 174, 175, 177, 551; Peli-
  can, 220–223, 230, 331, 453–455; **Saint Mary's Cannoneers,** 220–222, 375,
  453–455, 551; **Watson,** 143, 147, 150, 156, 161, 164–166.
 Cavalry—*Battalions:* **9th**, 143, 146, 156, 161, 165–167, 176, 551, 777, 801, 836.
  Regiments: **2d**, 215, 225, 347, 349, 382, 759, 820.

Page.
Louisiana Troops—Mentioned. (Confederate)—Continued.

Infantry—*Battalions:* 9th, 143; 10th, 379; Dupeire's Zouaves, 370, 377, 378. *Regiments:* 4th, 143, 179; 19th, 497; 30th, 143, 179; Crescent, 487.

Miscellaneous—Miles' Legion, 37, 143, 155, 167, 168, 171, 536, 537, 551.

Louisiana Troops. Mentioned. (Union.)

Cavalry—*Companies:* Headquarters Troops (*Department of the Gulf*), 707, 894, 900. *Regiments:* 1st, 22, 35, 39, 68, 70, 121, 134–136, 193–195, 207, 209, 262–270, 336, 359–361, 372–375, 377, 379, 394, 529, 531, 554, 667, 686, 708, 828, 895, 900 ; 2d, 881, 900.

Infantry—*Regiments:* 1st, 22, 47, 58, 69, 205, 530, 605, 658, 667, 686, 711, 895, 900; 1st New Orleans, 894 ; 2d, 22, 58, 67, 121, 205, 336, 376, 378, 529, 602, 685, 708, 710, 713, 828, 900: 2d New Orleans, 894, 895 ; 6th, 7th (*Colored*), 708; 8th (*Colored*), 712; 10th (*Colored*), 712, 816, 829; 11th (*Colored*), 712, 829.

Louisiana Belle, Steamer.

Attack on, near Barre's Landing, Bayou Teche, La., May 22, 1863. Report of George S. Merrill.. 183

Mentioned 183, 782

Love, George M. Mentioned............... 287, 299, 300, 335, 667, 685, 710, 713, 899

Lowell, Charles R. Mentioned.. 700

Lower, John. Mentioned... 58

Lowes, Abraham B. Mentioned.. 422

Lubbock, Francis R. Mentioned 697

Lucas, John. Mentioned.. 334, 895

Lucas, Thomas J.

Mentioned........ 318, 319, 336, 356, 369–371, 378, 379, 383, 710, 762, 826, 828, 862, 900

Report of operations in the Teche Country, La., Oct. 3–Nov. 30, 1863 375

Luce, Captain. Mentioned.. 17

Luce, Lyman P. Mentioned 66

Lucero, José. Mentioned 25

Lucero, Juan. Mentioned 23

Luckett, P. N.

Correspondence with John B. Magruder................................... 244

Mentioned... 243, 244, 878

Report of mutiny at Galveston, Tex., Aug. 10–13, 1863 245

Ludden, Alonzo G. Mentioned... 66

Lull, Oliver W. Mentioned... 17, 71

Luna, Ramon. Mentioned 28

Lyles, O. P.

Mentioned... 143, 161, 162

Reports of siege of Port Hudson, La., May 21–July 8, 1863 150–152

Lyman, John N. Mentioned... 57

Lyon, David. Mentioned 682, 693

McAdoo, J. D. Mentioned... 307

McAnelly, Leander. Mentioned 183, 216, 219, 229, 332

Macauley, Daniel. Mentioned............................... 335, 710, 898

McBeth, James E. Mentioned 64

McBride, John W. Mentioned 62

McCabe, F. Mentioned............................ 235, 253, 256

McCain, E. Mentioned... 167

McCall, A. Dwight. Mentioned 57

McCall, James. Mentioned.. 65

Page.

McCallister, Lorenzo D. Mentioned 421–423
McCallum, Daniel C. Mentioned.. 498
McCarthey, Charles. Mentioned 711, 899
McCarty, ——. Mentioned 567
McCleave, William. Mentioned.. 492, 828, 901
McClellan, Steamer. Mentioned 411, 824, 849
McClellan, George B. Mentioned 496
McClelland, Thomas. Mentioned 23
McClosky, Barney. Mentioned 59
McClure, John W. Mentioned 808
McCollough, Joseph M. Mentioned.. 898
McCollum, James T. Mentioned 63
McConnell, D. W. Mentioned.. 121
McConnell, Thomas. Mentioned 65
McCormick, George A. Mentioned 66
McCormick, John. (Private.) Mentioned 63
McCormick, John. (Sergeant.) Mentioned 65
McCormick, Thomas. Mentioned 895
McCown, John P. Mentioned.. 496
McCoy, A. J. Mentioned 854
McCumber, William W. Mentioned 63
McCutcheon, William. Mentioned.. 61
McDade, W. A. Mentioned 224, 395
McDaniel, Loudon. Mentioned 60
McDermot, David A. Mentioned.. 91
McDermott, George. Mentioned 31, 260, 261
McDonald, John. Mentioned.. 65
McDowell, Jacob. Mentioned 64
McDowell, William. Mentioned 59
McFarland, J. B. Mentioned.. 857, 858
McFaul, George.
        Mentioned 470
        Testimony of. Mutiny at Fort Jackson, La., Dec. 9, 1863 470
McGahay, Francis. Mentioned.. 59
McGee, Thomas. Mentioned 58
McGinnis, George F.
        Correspondence with William B. Franklin.. 799
        Mentioned 335, 343,
                357, 358, 366, 417, 428, 710, 749, 751, 752, 758, 759, 783, 826, 879, 891, 893, 898
McGinniss, James. Mentioned.. 71
McGlaflin, Charles E. Mentioned 57
McGoffin, Major. Mentioned.. 220
McGraw, George. Mentioned 58
McGrew, Frederick. Mentioned 361
McHenry, James S. Mentioned.. 455
McIntyre, Henry F. Mentioned.. 64
Mack, Sergeant. Mentioned 179
Mack, Albert G. Mentioned 529, 660
Mack, William. Mentioned 59
McKennon, A. S. Mentioned.. 149, 150
McKenny, Hugh. Mentioned.. 64
McKeon, Francis. Mentioned.. 201
McKeon, John. Mentioned.. 58
McKernan, Michael. Mentioned.. 312
McKibbin, Joseph C. Mentioned.. 654

Page.

McKinney. George. Mentioned 65
McKinstry, James P. Mentioned 89
McKown, Charles W. Mentioned 63
McLaflin, Edward. Mentioned 667, 895
McLaughlin, John. Mentioned 65
McLaughlin, John A. Mentioned 335, 710
McManus, T. P. [?] Mentioned 843, 865
McMillan, James W.
   Correspondence with William H. Emory 725
   Mentioned 287, 300, 336, 685, 711, 721, 735, 749, 899, 912
McMullen, W. Mentioned 25, 612, 750, 827, 901
McNalley, John. Mentioned 141
McNamara, Martin. Mentioned 63
McNeill, ———. Mentioned 792
McNeill, H. C. Mentioned 395
McNulta, John. Mentioned 398, 665, 709, 897
McPhaill, H. A. Mentioned 231
McPherson, James B.
   Correspondence with
      Cox, John C 909
      Eddy, Asher R 907, 908
      Fort, Greenberry L 906
      Hawkins, John P 770, 791, 799, 800, 802
      Hurlbut, W. C 905
      Osband, Embury D 908
      Sherman, William T 903
   Mentioned 709, 710, 731, 837, 902, 903, 906, 907
McPhetres, Daniel. Mentioned 61
McQueen, M. Mentioned 166
MacQuod, Scout. Mentioned 920
McWhorter, E. A. Mentioned 834
Maddox, John. Mentioned 57
Madison, Ed. Mentioned 59
Madison, George T. Mentioned 395
Magruder, George A., jr. Mentioned 449
Magruder, John B.
   Congratulatory Orders. Sabine Pass (Texas) Expedition, Sept. 4–11, 1863.   306
   Correspondence with
      Banks, Nathaniel P 850
      Luckett, P. N 244
      Pyron, Charles L. 446
      Smith, E. Kirby 386
      Washburn, Cadwallader C 851
   Mentioned 20, 47, 187, 244, 286, 289, 346,
         348–350, 352, 362, 363, 386–388, 391, 447, 481, 558, 640, 657, 697, 699, 724, 740,
         742, 788, 799, 801, 811, 819, 820, 847, 849, 850, 853, 866, 869, 886, 903, 915, 917
   Orders. Mutiny at Galveston, Tex., Aug. 10–13, 1863 246
   Proclamation of, to men of Texas. Sabine Pass (Texas) Expedition, Sept.
         4–11, 1863 307
   Reports of
      Mier, Mexico. Affair with Zapata's banditti near, Sept. 2, 1863   283
      Rio Grande Expedition and operations on the coast of Texas, Oct. 27–
            Dec. 2, 1863 .... 431, 432
      Sabine Pass (Texas) Expedition, Sept. 4–11, 1863 302–305

Page.

Maguire, John. Mentioned..   57
Maher, Thomas. Mentioned...   263
Mahler, Jacob. Mentioned....................................   818
Mahoney, Patrick. Mentioned.....................................   58
Main, Jacob. Mentioned...   709
Main, John N.
   Correspondence with James Alden................................   107
   Mentioned.. 96,103,104,111
Main, Richard C. Mentioned....................................   66
Maine Troops. Mentioned.
   Artillery, Light—*Batteries:* 1st, 22, 68, 139, 205, 208, 209, 300, 336, 529, 627,
      633, 660, 667, 711, 721, 899.
   Infantry—*Regiments:* 12th, 22, 60, 70, 193, 530, 531, 686, 711, 900; 13th, 60,
      397–399, 409, 412, 420, 426, 427, 429, 430, 480–483, 531, 686, 711, 897; 14th, 22,
      60, 68, 122, 123, 300, 336, 529, 632, 711, 713, 899; 15th, 46, 189, 199, 397, 398,
      406, 409, 412, 420, 426, 427, 429, 532, 585, 586, 596, 607, 686, 711, 897; 21st, 60,
      67, 529, 602, 707; 22d, 61, 69, 132, 519, 530, 627, 707; 24th, 61, 68, 529, 627,
      707; 26th, 70, 195, 519, 530, 627, 707; 28th, 15, 46, 61, 68, 191, 529, 531, 561,
      588, 621, 707.
Major, James P.
   Mentioned...................... 15, 46, 187, 189, 210, 213, 215–217, 220, 226–231,
      281, 323, 329, 331, 337, 339, 349, 352, 374, 385, 390–394, 575, 662, 669, 820, 852
   Report of operations in Louisiana west of the Mississippi, June 7–July 13,
      1863..   217
Maker, Amos. Mentioned..................................   63
Mallory, ——. Mentioned............................   36
Mallory, S. R. Mentioned..................................   834
Malloy, Adam G.
   Mentioned.. 273, 274, 276, 277
   Report of expedition from Natchez, Miss., to Harrisonburg, La., etc., Sept.
      1–7, 1863...   278
Maloney, John. Mentioned................................   66
Maloney, Maurice. Mentioned............... 457, 709, 762, 860, 895
Maloney, Thomas. (49th Massachusetts.) Mentioned...................   62
Maloney, Thomas. (116th New York.) Mentioned..................   63
Manahan, James. Mentioned................................   58
Mann, Josiah J. Mentioned................................   898
Mann, Walter L. Mentioned............................ 441, 812, 851, 852
Mannelita. (Indian.) Mentioned................................   256
Mannering, Patrick. Mentioned..............................   66
Mansfield, Fielding. Mentioned............................ 367, 709
Mansfield, Samuel M. Mentioned........................... 530, 708
Margedant, William C. Mentioned............................   656
Mariano, Governor. Mentioned..............................   256
Mariano. (Indian.) Mentioned...............................   256
Mariner, James. Mentioned...............................   59
Marivault, Viscount de.
   Correspondence with William H. Emory.........................   569
   Mentioned.. 569, 570, 572
Markham, Frank. Mentioned..............................   66
Marland, William.
   Mentioned... 358, 361
   Report of operations in the Teche Country, La., Oct. 3–Nov. 30, 1863.....   371
Marmaduke, John S. Correspondence with Theophilus H. Holmes.........   392
Marques, Juan. Mentioned..................................   24, 25

Page.

Marquez, Jesus. Mentioned 32
Marrener, Edward. Mentioned.. 65
Marsh, Arthur W. Mentioned 336,345,373,379,709
Marsh, Lucius B.
  Correspondence with William H. Emory................................ 607
  Mentioned 531
Marshall, ——. Mentioned.. 891
Marshall, Luther H. Mentioned... 61
Marshel, Henry. Mentioned 59
Martiel, Pierre. Mentioned.. 59
Martin, José Ma. Mentioned... 32
Martin, Lewis D. Mentioned... 335,710
Martin, Peter A. Mentioned 62
Martin, William. Mentioned 63
Martines, Joseph. Mentioned 65
Martinez, Francisco. Mentioned 26
Mary, Philip. Mentioned 63
Maryland Troops. Mentioned. (Union.)
  Cavalry—*Regiments :* **3d,** 890,900.
Masicot, Jules A.
  Mentioned.'.. 264, 266
  Testimony of. Mutiny at Camp Hubbard, Thibodeaux, La., Aug. 29-30,
    1863 266,267
Mason, Samuel S. Mentioned 61
Massachusetts Troops. Mentioned.
  Artillery, Light—*Batteries :* **2d** (*B*), 22, 36, 40,70,127,134-136, 336, 357-361,
    366,370,371,373,378,381,531, 632, 660, 712, 721,769, 828, 900 ; **4th** (*D*), 22,
    69, 336, 368, 530, 556, 557, 633, 660, 667, 711, 721, 899 ; **6th,** 22, 68, 205,
    207-209, 336, 529, 627, 660, 667, 712, 721, 899 ; **12th,** 529, 531, 660, 708, 896 ;
    13th, 22, 61, 531, 660, 708 ; **15th,** 660, 708, 895.
  Cavalry—*Battalions :* **2d,** 36, 134-136, 531, 554. *Regiments :* **1st,** 700 ; **2d,**
    700, 720 ; **3d,*** 22, 40, 61, 70, 134, 184, 238, 239, 336, 378, 523, 530, 686, 700,
    708, 712, 749, 783, 826, 828, 892, 895, 896, 900.
  Infantry—*Regiments :* **4th,** 14, 69, 183-185, 530, 627, 913, 914 ; **26th,** 22, 46, 61,
    188, 195-197, 336, 531, 574, 577, 582, 604, 605, 613, 685, 711, 713, 723, 899 ; **30th,**
    22, 39, 61, 67, 121, 205, 207, 208, 335, 529, 685, 710, 713, 782, 899 ; **31st,** 22, 62,
    69, 139, 530, 531, 633, 708, 711, 900; **38th,** 22, 62, 69, 128, 129, 530, 633, 711, 899;
    42d, 4, 6, 7, 193, 195, 196, 531, 545, 638, 707 ; **47th,** 531, 707; **48th,** 62, 67,
    205, 529, 554, 602, 707 ; **49th,** 62, 67, 205, 529, 602, 707 ; **50th,** 62, 67, 529, 613,
    627, 648, 707 ; **52d,** 70, 519, 523, 530, 627, 648, 707 ; **53d,** 62, 69, 630, 633, 638,
    707.
Matagorda Peninsula, Tex. Skirmish on, Dec. 29, 1863.
  Communication from Cadwallader C. Washburn.......................... 481
  Reports of
    Buchel, A.. 485
    Hesseltine, Frank S 481
    Turner, Edmund P... 484
    Washburn, Cadwallader C.. 480
Matamoras, Steamer. Mentioned........ 411,438,803,804,824,825,843,849,856,878
Matamoras, Mexico.
  Act raising the siege of 408
  Affairs at. Communications from
    Banks, Nathaniel P... 405
    Matamoras, Mexico, U. S. Consul at............................... 404

————————————
* Originally 41st Massachusetts Infantry.

Page.

Matamoras, Mexico—Continued.
Forced loans from Americans in. Communications from
Dana, Napoleon J. T 884
Tamaulipas, Mexico, Governor of. (Jesus de la Serna)............. 885
Matamoras, Mexico, U. S. Consul at. Correspondence with
Banks, Nathaniel P 404, 405, 796
Dana, Napoleon J. T 830, 838, 883
State Department, U. S... 718
Matheny, J. H. Mentioned... 710
Matt, Joseph von. Mentioned... 64
Matthews, Patrick H. Mentioned..................................... 65
Matthies, George. Mentioned.. 64
Maury, Dabney H.
Correspondence with
Adjutant and Inspector General's Office, C. S. A.................... 452
Holbrook, William C.. 745
Mentioned 743
Maury, Henry.
Mentioned 452
Report of skirmish near Bayou Sara, La., Nov. 9 1863................ 452
Maxey, S. B. Mentioned... 852
Maxson, B. F. Mentioned.. 64
Maxson, Daniel B. Mentioned....................................... 72
May, Reuben. Mentioned.. 709
Maynard, William M. Mentioned..................................... 58
Mayo, Henry. Mentioned.. 58
Mayo, W. K. Mentioned... 3
Mead, Benjamin L. Mentioned....................................... 57
Mead, Henry W. Mentioned.. 65
Meade, George G. Mentioned............................ 626, 637, 788
Meadows, James D. Mentioned....................................... 157
Mealey, Michael. Mentioned.. 61
Meigs, Montgomery C. Mentioned........... 617, 714, 719, 835, 905
For correspondence, see *Quartermaster-General's Office, U. S. A.*
Meisden, S. W. Mentioned... 66
Meisner, Louis. Mentioned.. 57
Merchant, Anderson. Mentioned............................... 168, 176
Meredith, W. F. Correspondence with James S. Palmer.............. 99
Merinus, George. Mentioned... 66
Merrill, Ezra A. Mentioned.. 60
Merrill, George S. Report of attack on steamer Louisiana Belle, near Barre's
Landing, Bayou Teche, La., May 22, 1863......................... 183
Merrill, Melville. Mentioned....................................... 60
Merrill, William E. Correspondence with
Army Headquarters 656
Rosecrans, William S 654
Merrimac, C. S. S. Mentioned....................................... 891
Merriman, Harmon N. Mentioned.................................... 72
Merritt, Charles H. Mentioned..................................... 464
Merritt, Robert B.
Correspondence with Nathaniel P. Banks............................ 669
Mentioned........................ 287, 299, 300, 335, 529, 667, 710, 711, 721, 899
Merritt's Plantation, La.
Operations about, and on the Bayou Sara road, May 18–19, 1863. Reports
of Nathan A. M. Dudley 38, 39

Page.

Merritt's Plantation, La.—Continued.
Scouts from, on the Clinton road, May 14, 1863. Reports of Nathan A. M.
Dudley 34, 35
Merry, Benjamin G. Mentioned....................................... 602
Merryfield, William E. Mentioned................................... 60.
Meservey, Albert B. Mentioned 60
Messer, Carlos P. Mentioned....................................... 529
Messmer, Joseph. Mentioned 66
Mestas, José M. Mentioned... 24
Metcalf, Albert W. Mentioned...................................... 317
Meteor, Steamer. Mentioned 319
Meterne, Aug. Mentioned... 551
Metzel, George A. Mentioned....................................... 65
Mexico.
Affairs in, generally. Communication from Nathaniel P. Banks.......... 841
Relations with. Communications from
Banks, Nathaniel P 796, 840, 880, 902
Dana, Napoleon J. T 823, 838, 842, 856, 858, 876, 884
Hamilton, Andrew J 857
Matamoras, Mexico, U. S. Consul at................................. 883
State Department, U. S 815, 846
Tamaulipas, Mexico, Governor of.................................... 885
War Department, U. S 846, 902
Meyé, Arthur. Mentioned.. 59
Meyers, James F. Mentioned 874, 875, 896
Michigan Troops. Mentioned.
Artillery, Heavy—*Regiments :* **1st,*** 22, 62, 68, 122–124, 529, 548, 549, 659, 708,
817, 896.
Artillery, Light—*Batteries :* **7th,** 334, 419, 421–423, 428, 691, 709, 739, 897 ;
8th, 248.
Mier, Mexico. Affair with Zapata's banditti near, Sept. 2, 1863. Reports of
Bee, Hamilton P 284
Benavides, Santos... 284
Magruder, John B... 283
Mieres, ——. Mentioned... 149
Miles, Reuben. Mentioned 57
Miles, W. R.
Mentioned... 143, 146, 148
Reports of siege of Port Hudson, La., May 21–July 8, 1863 167–177
Military Commissions.
Camp Hubbard, Thibodeaux, La. See *Camp Hubbard, Thibodeaux, La. Mu-
tiny at, Aug.* 29–30, 1863.
Fort Jackson, La. Mutiny at. See *Fort Jackson, La. Mutiny at, Dec.* 9,
1863.
Harris, Charles H., Confederate spy. Case of. Charge, specification, and
finding 487
Miller, Charles. Mentioned.. 61
Miller, David H. Mentioned... 194
Miller, Henry C. Mentioned... 63
Miller, Henry W. Mentioned... 3
Miller, Jacob. Mentioned.............................. 531, 708, 896
Miller, James. (Captain.)
Mentioned 463, 466, 467, 469, 470, 474
Testimony of. Mutiny at Fort Jackson, La., Dec. 9, 1863............... 466–469

Page.

Miller, James. (Private.) Mentioned 62
Miller, Jesse S. Mentioned 334
Miller, Joseph. Mentioned 59
Miller, Maxamillian. Mentioned 65
Miller, Munroe. Mentioned.. 465, 473
Milliken's Bend and Young's Point, La. Attack on, June 7, 1863* 2
Milliman, Adam. Mentioned 66
Mills, ——. Mentioned.. 492
Mills, A. N. For correspondence as A. A. G., see John B. Magruder.
Mills, Milton. Mentioned.. 334, 709
Miner, W. P. Mentioned 353
Mink, J. Mentioned... 60
Miramon, Miguel. Mentioned 399, 400
Misher, Peter. Mentioned.. 60
Mississippi, U. S. S. Mentioned 4
Mississippi and East Louisiana, Department of.
    Orders, General, series 1863: No. 47 (Gardner), 167.
Mississippi River.
    Attack on Union gunboats and transports on the, July 7-10, 1863. See
        Louisiana. Operations in, west of the Mississippi, June 7-July 13,
        1863. Reports of Emerson, p. 203; Faries, p. 220.
    Operations on west side of the, near Port Hudson, La., May 17, 1863. Re-
        port of M. B. Locke... 36
Mississippi Troops. Mentioned. (Confederate.)
    Artillery, Light—Batteries: English's, 143, 156; Seven Stars, 143, 179, 551.
        Regiments: 1st (Batteries), B, F, K, 143, 147.
    Infantry—Companies: Lewis', 143, 156. Regiments: 1st, 143, 147, 148, 150,
        156, 164, 551; 39th, 143, 147, 156, 158, 161, 551.
Mississippi Troops. Mentioned. (Union.)
    Artillery, Heavy—Regiments: 2d (Colored), 314, 315, 452.
    Infantry—Regiments: 1st (Colored), 712; 3d (Colored), 712, 829.
Missouri Troops. Mentioned. (Union.)
    Artillery, Light—Regiments: 1st (Batteries), A, 335, 691, 710, 712, 739, 898;
        B, 328, 398, 399, 430, 665, 691, 709, 712, 739, 897; E, 322, 325, 327, 398, 665, 691,
        709, 739, 897; F, 398, 412, 420, 427-430, 665, 691, 709, 713, 739, 897.
    Cavalry—Regiments: 6th, 322, 325, 336, 376, 710, 828, 900.
    Infantry—Regiments: 30th, 314, 315, 452; 35th, 314, 452, 453.
Mitchell, Nathaniel C. Mentioned 895
Mobile, Ala.
    Contemplated operations against. Communications from Nathaniel P.
        Banks 661, 666
    Defenses of. Communication from William S. Rosecrans 654
    Rebel vessels at. Communications from Stephen A. Hurlbut 888, 891
Modena, Guiseppi Conte. Mentioned 787
Moderator, Steamer. Mentioned... 520
Mohoney, Cornelius. Mentioned 66
Mohren, John. Mentioned 57
Molineux, Edward L. Mentioned 262, 686, 711, 784, 870
Monks, Patrick J. Mentioned.. 61
Monongahela, U. S. S. Mentioned.. 4,
        47, 152, 216, 397, 410, 411, 420, 426, 480, 483, 504, 785, 803, 804
Monroe, George W. Mentioned 334, 709, 895

* For reports, see Series I, Vol. XXIV, Part II, p. 446 et seq.

Page.

Monroe, La. Expedition from Vicksburg, Miss., to, Aug. 20-Sept. 2, 1863, including skirmishes (24th) at Bayou Macon and at.Floyd. Report of John D. Stevenson.. 248

Montaño, Baltasar. Mentioned 28

Monterey, Mexico, U. S. Consul at. Correspondence with

Chihuahua, Mexico, U. S. Consul at... 918

Dana, Napoleon J. T... 414, 823, 865, 882

State Department, U. S.. 657

West, Joseph R 916, 917

Montgomery, Bacon. Mentioned 322, 326, 328, 336, 370, 377, 710, 828

Montgomery, William W. Mentioned............................... 857, 858

Montoya, D. Mentioned.. 31, 32, 256

Montoya, E. Mentioned 30

Mooney, Edward D.

Mentioned 471

Testimony of. Mutiny at Fort Jackson, La., Dec. 9, 1863.................. 471

Moore, Lieutenant. Mentioned 283

Moore, Charles D. Mentioned 61

Moore, Daniel. Mentioned 58

Moore, Frederick W. Mentioned.. 335, 710

Moore, Ira. Mentioned.. 421, 709

Moore, James H.

Court-martial in case of. Mutiny at Fort Jackson, La., Dec. 9, 1863...... 478

Mentioned 478, 479

Moore, John. (12th Connecticut.) Mentioned................................ 57

Moore, John. (14th Maine.) Mentioned.................................... 60

Moore, Milo P. Mentioned 63

Moore, Stephen H. Mentioned.. 63

Moore, Thomas O. Mentioned..................................... 11, 384, 763

Moore, Webster P. Mentioned.................................... 708, 712

Morang, James N. Mentioned.. 61

Morgan, Fort. See *Fort Morgan.*

Morgan, Andrew B. Mentioned 66

Morgan, Elijah D. Mentioned.. 63

Morgan, E. S. Mentioned.. 166

Morgan, John H. Mentioned 496

Morgan, Joseph S.

Correspondence with Nathaniel P. Banks.................................... 631

Court-martial in case of. Engagement on the La Fourche, La., near Donaldsonville, July 12-13, 1863..................................... 205

Mentioned 69, 130, 131, 204-208, 530, 590, 632, 640, 686, 900

Report of operations on the Teche road, La., between Barre's Landing and Berwick, May 21-26, 1863..................................... 40

Morgan, Morgan, jr. Mentioned......................... 189, 197, 200, 592, 708

Morgan, William H. Mentioned...................................... 714

Morgan's Ferry, on the Atchafalaya, La. Skirmishes at.

Sept. 7, 1863.

Communication from Nathaniel P. Banks.................................... 716

Report of Francis J. Herron... 312

Sept. 20, 1863*... 2

Morganza, La. Skirmish at Stirling's Plantation, near, Sept. 12, 1863*........ 2

Morino, J.

Correspondence with William C. Holbrook 743, 744

Mentioned 743, 746, 834

*No circumstantial reports on file.

	Page.
Morning Star, Steamer. Mentioned	697
Morrill, John B. Mentioned	61
Morris, Henry W.	
Correspondence with	
Eaton, Stephen M.	89
Emory, William H	543, 556, 568, 571, 612, 615, 627
Mentioned	81, 115, 188, 544, 546, 547, 571
Morris, Thomas. Mentioned	58
Morrison, Arthur. Mentioned	23, 24, 237, 612
Morrison, Robert G. Mentioned	710
Morse, Lieutenant. Mentioned	394
Morse, Andrew, jr. Mentioned	35
Morse, Edmund A. Correspondence with Nathaniel P. Banks	784
Morse, Henry B. Mentioned	899
Morse, Irvin. Mentioned	60
Morton, Henry. Mentioned	57
Morton, John E. Mentioned	529
Morton, Oliver P. Mentioned	844
Mosher, Joseph C. Mentioned	63
Mosherman, James. Mentioned	63
Motte, Ellis L. Mentioned	708
Moule, George H. Mentioned	61
Moulton, Joseph N. Mentioned	71
Mound Plantation, La.	
Skirmishes at, and near Lake Providence, June 24, 1863*	2
Skirmish at, June 29, 1863*	2
Moushaud, Joseph. Mentioned	59
Mouton, Alexander. Mentioned	503
Mouton, Alfred.	
Mentioned	4, 10, 185, 186, 213,
217, 219, 222, 227, 304, 323, 329–332, 337–339, 348, 355, 374, 382, 384, 386,	
535, 540, 559, 566, 567, 620, 621, 639, 644, 669, 698, 763, 819, 852, 916, 920	
Reports of	
Louisiana. Operations in, west of the Mississippi, June 7–July 13, 1863	215
Stirling's Plantation, on the Fordoche, La. Action at, Sept. 29, 1863..	328
Teche Country, La. Operations in the, Oct. 3–Nov. 30, 1863	393
Mowers, Cornelius F. Mentioned	708
Mudd, John J. Mentioned	336,
354, 356, 370, 373–378, 381, 383, 681, 682, 710, 749, 759, 762, 783, 828, 900	
Mudgett, William S. Mentioned	708, 896
Mulholland, ———. Mentioned	753
Mullen, Alonzo C. Mentioned	28
Mullen, John. Mentioned	57
Mullens, M. Mentioned	827, 901
Muller, William. Mentioned	60
Munitions of War.	
Detention of, at Vicksburg, Miss. Communications from	
Army Headquarters	887
Cox, John C	909
Eddy, Asher R	908
Fort, Greenberry L	906
Gilpin, Joseph B	910

* No circumstantial report on file.

Page.

Munitions of War—Continued.

Detention of, at Vicksburg, Miss. Communications from

Hurlbut, W. C 905

Lewis, John V 909

McPherson, James B 903, 907, 908

Sherman, William T 902, 903

Importation of. Communications from Napoleon J. T. Dana 839, 842

Supplies of, etc. Communications from

Andrew, George L 493

Army Headquarters 694, 714, 719, 742, 834, 837, 839

Banks, Nathaniel P 687, 697, 754, 769, 780, 810, 824, 837, 862, 867, 869, 884

Bradley, Theodore 98

Bulkley, Charles S 721

Dana, Napoleon J. T 413, 414, 788, 789, 823, 830, 842, 876, 885

Grant, U. S 730

Hawkins, John P 800

Irwin, Richard B 488, 489

Ord, Edward O. C 754

Palmer, James S 99

Quartermaster-General's Office, U. S. A 829

Sheldon, Lionel A 815

Shipley, Alexander N 108, 113

Stone, Charles P 782, 793, 795, 798, 800, 809

Walker, W. M 693

Washburn, Cadwallader C 849, 878

Woodbury, Daniel P 873, 874

Murch, Charles. Mentioned 63

Murch, Isaac. Mentioned 203

Murcur, Mahlon M. Mentioned 65

Murphy, Edward. Mentioned 65

Murphy, John. Mentioned 256

Murphy, John L. Correspondence with G. W. Cozzens 737

Murphy, Joseph H. Mentioned 66

Murphy, Michael. Mentioned 58

Murphy, Richard. Mentioned 263

Murray, Surgeon. Mentioned 312

Murray, Benjamin B., jr. Mentioned 398, 532

Murray, J. Adair. Mentioned 851

Murray, James, Tug. Mentioned 829

Mustang, Steamer. Mentioned 415, 423, 424, 830, 842, 856, 877

Mutiny. Fiftieth Massachusetts Infantry. Communication from Charles P.

Stone 648

Muzzey, David P. Mentioned 61

Myer, Albert J. Correspondence with James S. Palmer 660

Myrick, Augustus C. Mentioned 483

Nail, Eli. Mentioned 913

Nancy Dawson, Schooner. Mentioned 839

Nashold, Elias. Mentioned 66

Nassau, Steamer. Mentioned 103, 410

Natchez, Miss. Expeditions from, to

Harrisonburg, La., Sept. 1-7, 1863. See *Harrisonburg, La. Expedition
from Natchez, Miss., to, etc., Sept. 1-7, 1863.*

Red River, La., Oct. 16-20, 1863* 3

.... * No circumstantial reports on file.

Page.

National, Steamer. Mentioned... 816
Nava, Antonio. Mentioned.. 32
Navajo Indians. Operations against, in New Mexico.
    July 7–Aug. 19, 1863. Reports of Christopher Carson.................. 233–236
    Aug. 20–Dec. 16, 1863.
        Communications from James H. Carleton.......................... 254,260
        Reports of
            Carson, Christopher..................................... 250,252,255
            Chacon, Rafael 257
            Hargrave, Joseph P.................................... 259
            Wallen, Henry D 260
Navy, U. S. Co-operation with Army. Communications from
    Army Headquarters... 698,834
    Banks, Nathaniel P................... 51,668,687,688,699,726,861,872,888
    Bell, Henry H 668
    Dunham, Robert T....................................... 757
    Porter, David D.. 789
    Selfridge, Thomas O...................................... 715
    Stone, Charles P 757
    See also *Emory to Banks*, p. 190. Also *Port Hudson, La. Siege of, May 21–
        July 8, 1863. Reports of*

        Eaton, Stephen M.   Hallett, Joseph L.   Jencks, John F.
        Hall, Thomas S.   Jackson, Amos M.   Rundlett, James H.

Navy Department, U. S. Correspondence with
    Bailey, Theodorus....................................... 670
    Farragut, David G...................................... 140
    Hurlbut, Stephen A..................................... 891
    War Department, U. S.................................... 669
Naylor, George W. Mentioned............................... 774
Neafie, Alfred. Mentioned................................. 711,899
Neal, Sailing-master. Mentioned........................... 812
Neenan, Daniel. Mentioned 63
Negroes.
    Action touching. Communications from
        Alden, James 82,119
        Banks, Nathaniel P................................. 704,764,777
        Cozzens, G. W 737
        Flanders, Benjamin F.............................. 736
        Flanigan, P.. 738
        Franklin, William B 775
        Murphy, John L 737
        Stone, Charles P 649,737
    Employment of, as laborers. Communications from
        Franklin, William B 337
        Irwin, Richard B.................................. 72
    Enlistment of. Communication from William H. Emory 497
Neill, John. Mentioned.................................... 63
Neilson, Neil. Mentioned.................................. 64
Nelson, John A. Mentioned................... 59,529,554,626,684
Nelson's Bridge, near New Iberia, La. Affair at, Oct. 4, 1863. See *Teche
    Country, La. Operations in the, Oct. 3–Nov. 30, 1863. Report of
    Mouton*, p. 393.
Nesch, Ferdinand. Mentioned 64
Netterberg, Ivan. Mentioned.............................. 64

Page.

Neville, Captain. Mentioned... 376
Neville, John. Mentioned... 72
New and Amite Rivers, La. Expeditions from Carrollton and Baton Rouge
    to, Sept. 24-29, 1863.
    Itinerary of 1st Brigade, 4th Division, 13th Army Corps, Sept., 1863....... 319
    Reports of
        Burbridge, Stephen G.. 317
        Gooding, Oliver P... 320
Newberry, S. S. For correspondence as Assistant Chief of Artillery, see Rich-
    ard Arnold.
Newbold, Charles. Mentioned 31, 260, 261
New Hampshire, Governor of. Correspondence with Abraham Lincoln 680
New Hampshire Troops. Mentioned.
    Infantry—Regiments: 8th,* 22, 62, 69, 336, 530, 632, 711, 713, 835, 900; 15th,
    68, 122-124, 529, 632, 707; 16th, 63, 73, 530, 707.
New Iberia, La. Affair near, Oct. 4, 1863. See Nelson's Bridge.
New London, U. S. S. Mentioned 50, 221, 222
New Mexico.
    Affairs in, generally. Communications from
        Carleton, James H 491, 727
        New Mexico, Governor of.. 629
        State Department, U. S 628
    Operations in. Communication from Henry D. Wallen............... ... 844
        See also Navajo Indians. Operations against, in New Mexico.
New Mexico, Department of. (Union.)
    Operations in, Dec. 16, 1862–Nov. 10, 1863 5
        See also report of Halleck, p. 3.
    Orders, General, series 1864 : No. 3, 23.
    Organization, strength, etc., of Union Troops in.
        June, 1863 612
        Sept., 1863 750
        Nov., 1863.. 827
        Dec., 1863.. 901
    Re-enforcements for. Communications from
        Army Headquarters... 720
        Schofield, John M 542
    Synopsis of operations in the, May 16–Dec. 28, 1863 23-34
New Mexico, Governor of. Correspondence with State Department, U. S .. 629
New Mexico Troops. Mentioned.
    Cavalry—Regiments: 1st, 23, 25, 28, 29. 233, 234, 236-238, 250-259, 316, 612,
    750, 827, 828, 901.
    Infantry—Regiments : 1st, 827, 828, 901.
New Orleans, La.
    Affairs in, generally. Communication from Nathaniel P. Banks 690
    Defense of.
        Communications from
            Banks, Nathaniel P 606, 675, 845
            Emory, William H 606, 646
        Orders assembling board of officers to consider 657, 676
        Proceedings of board... 676-678
        Recommendations of board 678
New Orleans, La., Commanding Officer U. S. Naval Forces off. Corre-
    spondence with W. M. Walker 693

---

* Sometimes called 1st Cavalry.

Page.

New Orleans, La., Commanding Officer U. S. Squadron at. Correspond-
 . ence with Nathaniel P. Banks 757
New Orleans, La. Defenses of. (Union.)
 Emory, William H., assigned to temporary command of 500
 Orders, Circulars, series 1863: July 4, 616.
 Orders, General, series 1863: No. 1, 500; No. 16, 603; No. 18, 615; No.
  20, 616; No. 21, 618; No. 26, 643; No. 35, 684; No. 46, 262.
New Orleans, La., French Consul at. Correspondence with Nathaniel P.
  Banks 728, 792
Newsome, ——. Mentioned 331
New York Troops. Mentioned.
 Artillery, Light—Batteries: 18th, 22, 68, 75, 121, 128, 529, 633, 660, 667, 698,
  711, 721, 895; 21st, 22, 530, 633, 660, 708, 896; 25th, 22, 195–201, 336, 531,
  660, 712, 900; 26th, 531, 660, 712, 895.
 Cavalry—Regiments: 14th, 70, 134, 313, 317, 335, 336, 359, 361, 372, 373, 376,
  378, 531, 559, 686, 708, 749, 828, 887, 895, 900.
 Infantry—Regiments: 6th, 494, 495, 530, 534; 75th, 22, 36, 63, 67, 131, 133,
  299, 300, 335, 362, 529, 711, 828, 900; 90th, 22, 40, 41, 63, 69, 205, 523, 530,
  686, 711, 900; 91st, 22, 63, 69, 132, 133, 530, 686, 711, 900; 110th, 22, 69,
  300, 336, 368, 530, 552, 573, 632, 711, 713, 723, 899; 114th, 22, 67, 335, 523,
  529, 711, 899; 116th, 22, 63, 67, 205, 335, 529, 602, 685, 710, 713, 899; 128th,
  22, 63, 68, 122–125, 529, 549, 633, 667, 711, 899; 131st, 22, 64, 69, 131, 205,
  502, 530, 686, 711, 900; 133d, 22, 64, 69, 336, 530, 632, 711, 713, 894, 895;
  156th, 22, 64, 69, 530, 633, 711, 899; 159th, 22, 64, 70, 530, 686, 711, 900;
  160th, 22, 64, 67, 335, 529, 711, 899; 161st, 22, 64, 67, 121, 205, 207, 208,
  299, 335, 529, 685, 710, 713, 899; 162d, 22, 65, 68, 72–74, 126, 300, 336, 368,
  529, 530, 561, 613, 632, 711, 713, 723, 899; 165th, 22, 65, 68, 336, 368, 529,
  632, 711, 713, 899; 173d, 22, 65, 69, 336, 308, 501, 502, 530, 632, 711, 713,
  899; 174th, 22, 65, 67, 121, 205, 207, 208, 335, 529, 685, 708, 710, 713, 899;
  175th, 22, 40, 66, 68, 529. 561, 633, 711, 899; 176th, 22, 46, 193, 195–197,
  199, 491, 531, 708, 894, 895, 913; 177th, 66, 68, 529, 632, 707.
Nichols, Lieutenant. Mentioned....................................... 283
Nichols, Charles. Mentioned... 57
Nichols, C. P. Mentioned 828
Nichols, H. L. Mentioned 165
Nichols, Melvin. Mentioned.. 57
Nickerson, Frank S.
 Assignments to command.. 685, 698
 Correspondence with Nathaniel P. Banks................................ 518
 Itinerary of 1st Brigade, 3d Division, 19th Army Corps, Sept., 1863 300
 Mentioned.................... 4, 9, 68, 300, 510, 529, 549, 550, 561, 595, 632, 685, 698, 711
Niles, Abner. Mentioned... 66
Niles, Nathaniel. Mentioned... 335, 368
Nilsen, Frederick. Mentioned.. 66
Nims, Ormand F. Mentioned........................... 336, 531, 660, 712, 828, 900
Noblet, Francis W. Mentioned 911, 912, 914
Noland, Philip J. Mentioned 143
Norcross, Frederick M. Mentioned..................................... 122
Norcutt, George A. Mentioned... 63
Norés, J. E. Mentioned.. 150, 165
Norman, Schooner. Mentioned.. 818
Normann, Gustave. Mentioned.. 65
Norman, William F. Mentioned 57
Norris, Guide. Mentioned.. 279
Norris, Hardman P. Mentioned.......................... 336, 711, 894

Page.

North America, Steamer. Mentioned......................... 112, 300, 621, 713

Northeastern Louisiana. See *Louisiana, Northeastern.*

Northerner, Steamer. Mentioned................................. 8.1, 904, 905

Northrup, Edward. Mentioned... 64

Norton, Martin. Mentioned... 63

Nott, Charles C. Mentioned... 531

Nott, J. B. Mentioned....:.. 853

Nourse, Edmund. Mentioned... 65

N. P. Banks, Steamer. Mentioned.................... .... 809, 814

Nuevo Leon and Cohahuila, Governor of. Correspondence with Hamilton
     P. Bee... 438

Nugent, John. Mentioned.. 58

Nurmon, Frederick A. Mentioned ....:.................... 58

Nutting, George S. Mentioned...........................'.................... 638

Nutting, Oscar F. Mentioned.. 709

Nye, William B.
    Mentioned.................... .... 460, 462, 464, 466, 468–470, 474, 475
    Testimony of. Mutiny at Fort Jackson, La., Dec. 9, 1863................ 464–466

Oakley, Stephen C. Mentioned.....................'.......................... 72

O'Brien, James. Mentioned... 71

O'Callaghan, William. Mentioned.. 66

O'Connell, Timothy. Mentioned.. 58

O'Conner, John. Mentioned.. 66

O'Connor, Henry. Mentioned... 64

O'Connor, James. Mentioned... 64

O'Connor, James H. Mentioned.. 900

Odlum, Frederick H.
    Mentioned....................................... 303–306, 308, 311, 312, 915
    Report of Sabine Pass (Texas) Expedition, Sept. 4–11, 1863... 309
    Resolution of thanks of C. S. Congress to. Sabine Pass (Texas) Expedition,
      Sept. 4–11, 1863.. 312

O'Donnell, Edward J. Mentioned....:....................................... 63

O'Donnell, Richard. Mentioned... 58

Oedekoven, Charles F. Mentioned 58

Ogden, Isaac. Mentioned.. 64

O'Gorman, Richard. Mentioned.. 66

Ohio Troops. Mentioned.
    Artillery, Light—*Batteries:* 2d, 335, 692, 710, 7.9, 895 ; 15th, 273, 276 ; 16th,
      335, 710, 739, 894 ; 17th, 335, 358–361, 364, 366, 710, 739, 879, 898.
    Infantry—*Regiments :* 16th, 334, 709, 897 ; 42d, 334, 709, 806, 895, 897 ; 48th,
      335, 359, 710, 898 ; 56th, 335, 710, 898 ; 83d, 318, 335, 359–361, 364, 365, 394,
      710, 896, 898 ; 96th, 335, 358, 359, 361, 364, 365, 394, 431, 710, 898 ; 114th,
      709, 897 ; 120th, 334, 709, 806, 895, 897.

Ojo Blanco. (Indian.) Mentioned 260, 261

Ojo Redondo (Jacob's Well), N. Mex. Scout from Fort Wingate to, Sept.
      15–Oct. 5, 1863. Report of Edward B. Willis..................... 315

O'Lahey, John. Mentioned.. 64

Oliver, George. Mentioned 65

Oliver, H. Kemble. For correspondence as Post Adjutant, see *William E. Had-
    lock.*

Onderkirk, Samuel. Mentioned... 64

Opelousas, La.
    Affair near, Oct. 30, 1863. See *Teche Country, La. Operations in the,* Oct. 3–
      Nov. 30, 1863. *Record of Events, Cav. Div.,* p. 377.

Page.

Opelousas, La.—Continued.

Occupation of, by the Union forces, Oct. 21, 1863. See *Teche Country, La. Operations in the, Oct. 3–Nov.* 30, 1863. *Reports of Franklin,* pp. 339, 340; *Taylor,* p. 389.

Union forces retire from, to New Iberia, Nov. 1–17, 1863. See *Teche Country, La. Operations in the, Oct. 3–Nov.* 30, 1863. *Report of Taylor,* p. 391

Opelousas and Barre's Landing, La. Skirmishes at, Oct. 21, 1863. See *Teche Country, La. Operations in the, Oct. 3–Nov.* 30, 1863. *Reports of Franklin,* p. 339; *Taylor,* p. 389. See also *Record of Events, 13th Army Corps,* p. 366; *Itinerary 19th Army Corps,* p. 369; *Record of Events, Cav. Div.,* p. 377.

Ord, Edward O. C.

Correspondence with

Banks, Nathaniel P 692, 738, 751, 754, 757–763, 769–771

Dana, Napoleon J. T 762

Franklin, William B 769

Ransom, Thomas E. G 693

Mentioned 286, 317, 334, 338–340, 355, 364, 367, 380–384, 386, 388–391, 661, 673, 676, 680, 681, 685–687, 691, 692, 696, 698, 701, 709, 712, 716, 729, 735, 738, 741, 749, 751, 753, 754, 756, 758, 761, 765, 770, 772, 778, 781

Report of operations in the Teche Country, La., Oct. 3–Nov. 30, 1863 354

Resumes command of the 13th Army Corps 2

Ordway, Edwin. Mentioned 60

Organization, Strength, etc.

Confederate Troops. See Part II.

Union Troops.. 334–336, 398, 526–532, 610, 611, 665, 707–712, 748, 749, 783, 784, 826–828, 891–900

Orme, William W. Mentioned.................................... 665, 709

Ortiz, José M. Mentioned.. 32

Ortiz, Juan F. Mentioned 25

Osband, Embury D.

Correspondence with James B. McPherson 908

Mentioned 248, 904

Osier, Charles. Mentioned.. 31, 261

Osterhout, Cornelius. Mentioned.. 64

Ostrander, Freeman. Mentioned 63

Ovenshine, Samuel. Mentioned 827

Owasco, U. S. S. Mentioned.................................... 393, 785, 787

Owen, Richard.

Itinerary of 1st Brigade, 4th Division, 13th Army Corps, Sept., 1863 319

Mentioned 318, 319, 335, 357, 361, 431

Owen, W. F. Mentioned 162

Page, Collin. Mentioned.. 59

Page, Edward, jr. Mentioned.. 765

Paine, Charles J.

Correspondence with Christopher C. Augur 602

Mentioned .. 44, 67, 121, 208, 209, 336, 370, 371, 375, 376, 529, 667, 685, 826, 828, 892, 900

Report of operations in the Teche Country, La., Oct. 3–Nov. 30, 1863 376

Paine, Halbert E.

Correspondence with Nathaniel P. Banks 127

Mentioned 17, 45, 69, 85, 93, 127–129, 131, 136, 139, 148, 487, 489, 490, 499, 500, 504, 506, 528, 530, 540, 556

Report of siege of Port Hudson, La., May 21–July 8, 1863 126

Pais, Luciano. Mentioned 27

Palfrey, John C.

Correspondence with Nathaniel P. Banks 638

Mentioned 320,563

Reports of siege of Port Hudson, La., May 21–July 8, 1863 74,75

Palmer, James S.

Correspondence with

Alden, James 82,92,93,95,108,109

Banks, Nathaniel P.. 93,
95,98,99,108,109,118,119,490,493,499,503,504,507,522,537,558,561,622

Bayou Sara, La., Naval Officer Commanding at 499

Cooke, A. P.. 567

Eaton, Stephen M.. 94

Farragut, David G.......................... 78,92,93,95,107,108,566

Meredith, W. F 99

Myer, Albert J... 660

Mentioned................. 80,94–96,99–101,105,106,117,488,495,507,519,558,566

Parish, W. N. Mentioned... 143,151,157,161

Parker, Lieutenant. Mentioned.. 283

Parker, Francis H. Mentioned 800

Parker, Jackson V.

Deposition of. Illegal arrests 747

Mentioned 743,746–748

Parker, Joel. Mentioned.. 659

Parker, J. W. Mentioned.... 149

Parlange, ——. Mentioned.. 559

Parmele, Theodore W. Mentioned 685

Parrish, Charles S. Mentioned.. 334,709

Parsons, J. R. Mentioned... 58

Parsons, W. H. Mentioned... 791

Patterson, Frank. Mentioned.. 58

Patterson, Joseph, jr. Mentioned.. 59

Patterson, Joseph, sr. Mentioned 59

Patterson, William F. Mentioned....................................... 709,896

Paul, Leon. Mentioned 59

Paulin, Lewis. Mentioned 60

Payne, Addis E. Mentioned.. 201

Payne, Eugene B. Mentioned.. 423

Payne, Frederick C. Mentioned... 57

Payne, John. Mentioned... 308

Payne, Robert. Mentioned 62

Peabody, George, Steamer. Mentioned 415,431,814,833

Pearsall, Uri B. Mentioned 894

Pearson, Timothy. Mentioned... 895

Peck, David B. Mentioned 532

Peck, Frank H.

Correspondence with Nathaniel P. Banks.......................... 653,662,668

Mentioned 131,335,529,711,899

Report of siege of Port Hudson, La., May 21–July 8, 1863 132

Peck, Lewis M. Mentioned 336,632,711,899

Peel, Sir William, Steamer. Mentioned................................. 719

Peeler, ——. Mentioned.. 883

Pemberton, John C. Mentioned............................ 16,525,526,534,571,703

Pendergrast, Richard.

Affidavit of, in relation to the murder of William W. Montgomery 857

Mentioned 857

Page.

Penfield, Loren D. Mentioned.. 57
Penny, Captain. Mentioned... 320
Pennsylvania Troops. Mentioned.
    Infantry—*Regiments:* 47th, 532, 708, 855, 873, 874, 896.
Pensacola, U. S. S. Mentioned 50, 456
Pensacola, District of. (Union.)
    Orders, General, series 1863: No. 5, 821.
    Orders, Special, series 1863: No. 10, 822.
Pensacola, Fla. Proposed cavalry raid from. Communication from William
    E. Merrill... 654
Perkins, Dr. Mentioned 702, 703
Perkins, F. Mentioned... 502
Perkins, George H. Mentioned................................. 483, 623
Perkins, Hiram E. Mentioned..................................... 896
Perkins, James T. Mentioned 64
Perkins, Newton W. Mentioned 57
Perkins, Solon A. Mentioned.. .... 71, 135, 136
Per Lee, Samuel R. Mentioned................................. 335, 711
Perry, Tug. Mentioned 829
Perry, Oran. Mentioned 334, 897
Pethie, William P. Mentioned 61
Pfeiffer, Albert H. Mentioned........ 23, 24, 26, 27, 234, 236, 237, 250, 253, 256
Pfeiffer, Albert H., Mrs. Mentioned............................ 24
Pfieffer, F. F. F. Mentioned.................................... 58
Phelps, John F. Mentioned.................................... 207, 529
Phelps, John W. Mentioned...................................... 57
Philley, Luman. Mentioned 65
Phillips, Daniel M. Mentioned.................................. 60
Phillips, Joseph. Mentioned 191, 192, 216–219, 227–229, 620
Phillips, Peter. Mentioned 828, 900
Phinney, Henry E. Mentioned................................... 58
Pierce, Irvin. Mentioned 144
Pierce, Leonard, jr. Mentioned................................ 403,
    413, 414, 435, 450, 718, 719, 841, 864, 866, 876, 881, 882, 884, 885, 917
    For correspondence. etc., see *Matamoras, Mexico, U. S. Consul at.*
Pigeon, Patrick. Mentioned...................................... 66
Pigman, William A. Report of operations in the Teche Country, La., Oct.
    3–Nov. 30, 1863... 352
Pike, James. Mentioned 530
Pilcher, Edward. Mentioned...................................... 192
Piña, José. Mentioned... 23
Pinsaid, Victor. Mentioned...................................... 57
Pishon, Nathaniel J. Mentioned................................ 24, 252
Pitt, Nicholas. Mentioned....................................... 64
Pittman, J. M. Mentioned.. 149
Pittsburg, U. S. S. Mentioned................................. 92, 108
Plains Store Road, La.
    Action on the, May 21, 1863. See *Port Hudson, La. Siege of, May 21–July 8,*
      1863. Reports of
        Banks, Nathaniel P.   Grierson, Benjamin H.   Miles, W. R.
        Dudley, Nathan A. M.   Logan, John L.
    Skirmish on the, May 23, 1863. Congratulatory Orders. Gardner........ 167
Planet, Schooner. Mentioned.................................. 643, 644

Page.

Planter, U. S. S. Mentioned 411, 567, 824, 825, 849, 869
Plaquemine, La. Skirmish at, June 18, 1863. See *Louisiana. Operations in, west of the Mississippi, June 7–July 13, 1863. Reports of Stearns,* p. 191; *Major,* p. 217.
Platto, William. Mentioned 63
Plumly, B. Rush. Mentioned 704
Plumly, Mardon W.
  Correspondence with William H. Emory 644
  Mentioned 684, 708, 895
Plummer, Charles E. Mentioned 62
Plunkett, Charles T. Mentioned 529
Plympton, P. W. L. Mentioned 612, 750, 827
Pocahontas, Steamer. Mentioned 89, 300, 713
Podger, Samuel H. Mentioned 72
Point Isabel, Tex. Affair at, May 30, 1863. Report of James Duff 185
              See also *Brownsville, Tex.*
Pointoiseau, Oscar. Mentioned 59
Polk, Leonidas. Mentioned 496
Polk, Lucius E. Mentioned 496
Pond, Preston, jr.
  Correspondence with William B. Franklin 704
  Mentioned 706
Pontchartrain, Lake. See *Lake Pontchartrain.*
Pooler, Henry. Mentioned 66
Pope, Henry D. Mentioned 708, 895
Poree, Ferdinand C. Mentioned 61
Porter, Steamer. Mentioned 906, 909
Porter, Benjamin F. Mentioned 50
Porter, David D.
  Correspondence with
    Banks, Nathaniel P. 687, 699, 779, 789, 861, 888
    Farragut, David G 91
    Mentioned 11, 88, 91, 92, 99, 380, 410, 495, 521, 617, 618, 688, 698,
        701, 715, 716, 726, 730, 731, 742, 757, 768, 778, 804, 814, 835, 839, 872, 888
Porter, Fitz John. Mentioned 496
Porter, Henry M.
  Mentioned 191, 601, 656
  Report of operations in Louisiana west of the Mississippi, June 7–July 13,
    1863 202
Porter, T. K. Mentioned 143
Porter, Thomas W. Mentioned 102, 336, 529, 599, 632, 711, 713, 723, 726, 899
Porter, Tobias. Mentioned 62
Porter, William A. Mentioned 62
Port Hudson, La.
  Assaults on.
    May 27, 1863. See *Siege of, May 21–July 8,* 1863. *Reports of*

      Banks, Nathaniel P.   Kingsley, Thomas G.   Richardson, James P.
      Girard, Louis J.   Miles, W. R.   Selden, Joseph.
      Keese, Francis S.   Peck, Frank H.   Steedman, I. G. W.

    June 14, 1863. See *Siege of, May 21–July 8,* 1863. *Reports of*

      Banks, Nathaniel P.   Comstock, Apollos.   Peck, Frank H.
      Beall, William N. R.   Fellows, John R.   Richardson, James P.
      Clark, Thomas S.   Miles, W. R.   Terry, Edward.

Page.

Port Hudson, La.—Continued.

Capture of

    Confederate outposts, June 11, 1863. See *Siege of, May* 21–*July* 8, 1863.

        Reports of

          Banks, Nathaniel P.   Steedman, I. G. W.   Weitzel, Godfrey.

    Union outposts, June 26, 1863. See *Siege of, May* 21–*July* 8, 1863. *Report of Provence,* p. 149.

Operations against, May 17–July 8, 1863. Communications from

    Andrews, George L.. 489

    Banks, Nathaniel P 490, 493

Proposed fortifications at. Communication from George L. Andrews 679

Siege of, May 21–July 8, 1863.

    Abstract from muster-roll of 1st Alabama Volunteers, April 20–Nov. 30, 1863 163

    Articles of capitulation proposed between the commissioners on the part of the garrison and the U. S. forces.......................... 54

    Casualties. Returns of.

        Confederate Troops... 144, 147

        Union Troops 67–72

    Communications from

        Alden, James 80, 82, 92, 101, 102, 106–109, 113, 117, 118

        Andrews, George L... 634

        Army Headquarters.. 534, 535, 545, 603

        Arnold, Richard 87, 98, 142, 143

        Augur, Christopher C 84, 107, 112, 113, 602

        Baker, J. S... 115

        Banks, Nathaniel P 51, 53, 78–82, 84, 93, 95, 99–102, 105, 106, 109–111, 113, 114, 116–119, 503–507, 509–511, 513, 514, 516, 517, 519–522, 524, 525, 533, 538, 540–542, 545, 547, 550, 552, 553, 556–559, 562, 564, 574, 585, 595, 599, 613, 618, 619, 622, 631, 633, 634

        Barker, J. T 80

        Bayou Sara, La., Commanding Naval Officer at 499

        Beall, William N. R... 164, 554

        Benedict, Lewis... 502, 519, 532

        Birge, Henry W.. 603

        Bradley, Theodore 87

        Caldwell, Charles H. B... 107

        Dana, John W 85–87

        Dudley, Nathan A. M 116

        Dwight, William 102, 117, 118, 536, 548, 551

        Eaton, Stephen M 85–87, 94, 96, 109

        Emerson, Charles 82

        Emory, William H... 519, 523, 533, 534

        Farragut, David G.................. 78–81, 92, 100, 101, 105, 106, 108–110, 114–117, 120, 140, 507, 509, 512, 518, 520, 523, 524, 533, 547, 551, 553, 566, 620

        Fisher, James C.. 81, 115

        Gardner, Franklin 159, 508, 513–517, 553, 557, 617

        Grant, U. S 49

        Green, Thomas.. 183

        Grover, Cuvier.. 79, 565

        Holcomb, Pythagoras E 116

        Jackson, Amos M.. 92

        Jenkins, Thornton A... 140

        Nickerson, Frank S.. 518

Port Hudson, La.—Continued.

Siege of, May 21-July 8, 1863.

Communications from

  Page.

Paine, Charles J 602

Palmer, James S 92–94, 99, 107, 108, 558, 561

Sage, Clinton H 81, 115, 551, 559, 562, 630

Sherman, Thomas W 501, 503, 505

Smith, Marshall J 159

Stone, Charles P 102, 111, 114, 118

Terry, Edward 81, 114

Ullmann, Daniel 609

Watters, John 114, 115

Weaver, Aaron W 115

Weitzel, Godfrey 109, 120, 501

Confederate troops paroled at. Statement of 143

Congratulatory Orders.

Banks, Nathaniel P 56, 671

Dwight, William 560

Congress, U. S. Resolution of thanks to Nathaniel P. Banks and his

 command 911

List of officers and men who volunteered for storming party under

 General Orders, No. 49 57–66

Raid on the Union lines, June 16, 1863. See *Report of Logan*, p. 181.

Reports of

Abbott, John C 78

Banks, Nathaniel P 43, 45, 46, 48, 52, 55

Beall, William N. R 146–148

Benner, Milton 82

Blanchard, Justus W 126

Brand, Frederick B 177, 178

Clark, Thomas S 122

Comstock, Apollos 129

Corliss, Augustus W 139

Dana, John W 85

De Gournay, P. F 152–156

Dudley, Nathan A. M 120

Eaton, Stephen M 88

Fellows, John R 148

Girard, Louis J 145

Grierson, Benjamin H 134, 137

Hall, Thomas S 100

Hallett, Joseph L 103

Herbert, George R 105

Irwin, Richard B 72

Jackson, Amos M 107

Jackson, C. M 144

Jencks, John F 112

Johnston, Thomas H 164

Keese, Francis S 125

Kingsley, Thomas G 123

Logan, John L 179–183

Lyles, O. P 150–152

Miles, W. R 167–177

Paine, Halbert E 126

Page.

Port Hudson, La.—Continued.
  Siege of, May 21–July 8, 1863.
    Reports of
      Palfrey, John C.. 74, 75
      Peck, Frank H.. 132
      Prince, Edward .:.. 138, 139
      Provence, David.. 149, 150
      Richardson, James P 128
      Roe, William B 76
      Rundlett, James H... 116
      Russell, Edmund H 119
      Selden, Joseph.. 124
      Shelby, W. B 164
      Steedman, I. G. W... 156–163
      Terry, Edward... 141
      Toledano, E. A.. 165
      Weitzel, Godfrey.. 130, 131
      Wingfield, J. H.. 165–167
    Statements of Confederate deserters.
      Battell, B.. 537
      Field, James.. 537
      Welsh, Mike... 536
    Surrender of, July 8, 1863. Communications from
      Army Headquarters... 671
      Banks, Nathaniel P 623–626, 630
      Emory, William H 630
      Gardner, Franklin 52, 53
      Grant, U. S... 633
    See also *Reports of*
        Banks, Nathaniel P.   Jackson, C. M.   Richardson, James P.
      Also *Banks to Halleck*, p. 52; *Gardner to Banks*, pp. 52, 53; *Banks to
        Gardner*, p. 53; *Articles of Capitulation*, p. 54. Also *Halleck's re-
        port*, p. 5.
    Skirmish near, Nov. 30, 1863*.. 3
    For operations near, see *Mississippi River. Operations on west side of the,*
        May 17, 1863.
Portsmouth, U. S. S. Mentioned... 50
Postle, Robert. Mentioned... 28, 253, 254
Postley, De Van. Mentioned.. 205, 209
Potter, Leander H. Mentioned... 897
Powers, Judge. Mentioned 441
Powers, F. P. Mentioned.. 179, 313, 852, 853
Powers, James. Mentioned... 60
Pratt, George H. Mentioned.. 57
Pratt, John G. Mentioned 383
Pratt, Joseph H. Mentioned... 57
Preble, Joseph. Mentioned.. 60
Prescot, Albert D. Mentioned... 63
President, C. S. See *Jefferson Davis.*
President, U. S. See *Abraham Lincoln.*
Preston, William. Mentioned 496
Price, General, U. S. S. Mentioned 53, 98, 119
Price, James H. Mentioned 224

*No circumstantial reports on file.

Page.

Price, John. Mentioned 308

Price, Sterling. Mentioned...... 346, 362, 363, 716, 729, 742, 754, 799-802, 811, 839, 889

Priest, David O. Mentioned 60

Prince, Edward

    Correspondence with Nathaniel P. Banks 556, 573

    Mentioned.. .... 79, 110, 111, 113, 114, 506, 531, 545, 554, 557, 574

    Report of siege of Port Hudson, La., May 21-July 8, 1863 .... 138, 139

Princess Royal, U. S. S. Mentioned 47, 191, 202, 203, 571, 572

Prindle, George. Mentioned... 57

Pringle, Steamer. Mentioned... 904, 905

Prisoners of War. Treatment, exchange of, etc. Communications from

    Andrews, George L.. 641

    Banks, Nathaniel P... 55, 631, 634, 641, 643

    Cooke, Philip St. George.. 836

    Emory, William H 608

    Farragut, David G.. 111

    Franklin, William B 351

    Gardner, Franklin.. 508

    Stone, Charles P 642, 644

Proctor, James. Mentioned 63

Provence, David.

    Mentioned 143

    Reports of siege of Port Hudson, La., May 21-July 8, 1863............... 149, 150

Pruett, P. H. Mentioned 144

Pruett, William H. Mentioned 37

Pueblo Colorado, N. Mex. Skirmish with Indians at, Aug. 18, 1863 * 2

Purdy, C. R. Mentioned 178

Purvis, Captain. Mentioned 281

Putnam, William. Mentioned 57

Pyron, Charles L.

    Correspondence with

        Bradfute, W. R.. 446

        Magruder, John B... 446

    Mentioned 196, 218, 219

Quartermaster-General's Office, U. S. A. Correspondence with

    Banks, Nathaniel P 785

    War Department, U. S... 829

Queen, Jonathan. Mentioned.. 25

Queen of the West, U. S. S. Mentioned.......................... 4, 8, 10, 11, 88

Quinlan, Murty. Mentioned 61

Quinnebaug, Steamer. Mentioned.. 502

Quintana, Martin. Mentioned 257

Quintana, N. Mentioned 24

Quintero, Rafael. Mentioned.. 409

Ragsdale, D. H. Mentioned.. 229

Raince, John M. Mentioned 64

Ramsay, Frank M. Mentioned 313

Ramsay, J. Gales. Mentioned 383, 757

Rand, William A. Mentioned 63

Randal, Horace.

    Mentioned... 281, 282, 385

    Reports of expedition from Natchez, Miss., to Harrisonburg, La., etc., Sept.

        1-7, 1863 .... 279, 280

---

* No circumstantial reports on file.

Page.

Randall, Jedediah. Mentioned 71
Randall, Valorus. Mentioned... 71
Randolph, Perry. Mentioned... 59
Ransom, Thomas E. G.
  Assignment to command 410
  Correspondence with Edward O. C. Ord............................... 693
  Mentioned..... 20, 409–412, 418–421, 428, 430, 481, 643, 645, 782, 830, 893, 894, 896, 897
  Reports of Rio Grande Expedition and operations on the coast of Texas,
    Oct. 27–Dec. 2, 1863... 426, 427
Rapsher, William. Mentioned... 62
Ratliffe, Captain. Mentioned 219
Ratliff, W. B. Correspondence with
  Dana, Napoleon J. T 323
  Herron, Francis J 322
      For correspondence as A. A. A. G., see *Thomas Green.*
Rauch, John H.
  Correspondence with James Alden.. 113
  Mentioned 693
Rawles, Jacob B. Mentioned.................................... 121, 529, 652, 708, 895
Rawlins, John A. Mentioned 600
Rawson, H. C. Mentioned 791
Raynor, William H. Mentioned.................................... 335, 710, 898
Read, Abner. Mentioned.. 91, 606
Ready, Philip. Mentioned... 64
Reagan, Andrew. Mentioned... 58
Reaman, Joseph. Mentioned... 58
Reas, John. Mentioned 58
Rebel Rams. Building of, in England. Communications from
  Army Headquarters.. 658
  Liverpool, England, U. S. Consul at 658
  State Department, U. S.. 658
  War Department, U. S... 659
Recruitment, Organization, etc. See *Union* and *Confederate Troops* and *Colored Troops.* Also respective States.
Red Chief, C. S. S.
  Capture of, May 25, 1863. See *Port Hudson, La. Siege of, May 21–July 8,*
    1863. Report of Prince, p. 138.
  Mentioned................... 139, 339, 381, 389, 506, 761, 772, 773, 782
Red Chief and Starlight. Capture of Steamers. See *Starlight and Red Chief.*
  Capture of the Confederate steamers, May 25, 1863.
Redfield, James H. Mentioned................................... 828, 892, 900
Red River, La. Expedition from Natchez, Miss., to the, Oct. 16–20, 1863 * 3
Redwood, Thomas. Mentioned 59
Reed, Nathaniel K. Mentioned .... , ... 61
Refugees, Abandoned Lands, etc. Communications from
  Army Headquarters... 775
  Asboth, Alexander 886
  Banks, Nathaniel P 764
Reid, John B. Mentioned.. 335, 898
Reid, Robert W. Mentioned 64
Reid, T. J., jr. Mentioned... 143
Reinhard, Frederick W. Mentioned 530
Rexford, Willie M. Mentioned.................................... 262, 711

Page.

Reynolds, Charles. Mentioned ....: 202
Reynolds, Joseph J.
  Assignment to command 832
  Correspondence with Army Headquarters.............................. 837
  Mentioned.. 832, 835, 839
Reynolds, John C. Mentioned... 583
Rhoads, Charles W. C. Mentioned 61
Rhode Island, Governor of. Correspondence with
  Adjutant-General's Office, U. S. A ....: 270, 271
  War Department, U. S 270
Rhode Island Troops. Mentioned.
  Artillery, Heavy—Regiments: 14th (Colored), 893, 894.
  Cavalry—Regiments: 1st, 265, 271; 2d, 68, 73, 74, 139, 140, 262–265, 267–273,
    529, 552, 686; 3d, 265, 273.
Rhodes, Henry. Mentioned 62
Rhodes, Henry C. Mentioned... 30
Rhodes, Robert. Mentioned.. 302
Rice, Charles S. Mentioned... 335, 358, 361, 898
Rice, Edward. Mentioned.. 711
Rice, Edwin. Mentioned 59
Rice, John L. Mentioned 63
Rice, Thomas. Mentioned.. 63
Rich, ——. Mentioned... 94
Rich, N. L. Mentioned 791
Richards, James. Mentioned 59
Richards, W. H. H. Mentioned.. 61
Richardson, Charles B. Mentioned...................................... 61
Richardson, George W. Mentioned...................................... 361
Richardson, James P.
  Mentioned 530, 899
  Report of siege of Port Hudson, La., May 21–July 8, 1863 128
Richardson, Joel. Mentioned.. 60
Richardson, T. J. M. Mentioned.. 446
Richmond, U. S. S. Mentioned 4, 77–78,
    88, 93–95, 99, 103, 105, 107, 111, 112, 116, 120, 141
Richmond, Duncan. Mentioned 64
Richmond, La.
  Action near, June 15, 1863* 2
  Reconnaissance from Young's Point to, June 20, 1863 † 2
  Skirmish near, June 6, 1863 ‡ 1
Riddle, George W. Mentioned 709
Ridley, Alonzo. Mentioned 216, 229
Rigg, Edwin A. Mentioned 612, 750, 827, 901
Riggin, John. Mentioned 525, 564
Rinaldo, Steamer. Mentioned.. 274, 278
Riney, John. Mentioned... 62
Ring, John E. Mentioned 61
Ringgold Barracks, Tex., Commanding Officer at. Correspondence with
    Hamilton P. Bee 447
Rio de las Animas, N. Mex. Skirmish with Indians on the, July 19, 1863†.. 2
Rio Grande City, Tex. Expedition to, Nov. 23–Dec. 2. See Rio Grande Ex-
    pedition, Oct. 27–Dec. 2, 1863. Report of Black, p. 423.

---

* For reports, see Series I, Vol. XXIV, Part II, pp. 451–453.
† No circumstantial reports on file.
‡ For reports, see Series I, Vol. XXIV, Part II, pp. 447, 457.

Page.

Rio Grande Expedition, and Operations on the coast of Texas, Oct. 27–
　　Dec. 2, 1863.
　Abstracts from "Record of Events" on returns of the 13th Army Corps for
　　　Oct., Nov., and Dec., 1863 428
　Communications from
　　Army Headquarters.. 806
　　Banks, Nathaniel P 776,
　　　　　　778, 779, 785, 787, 788, 796, 803, 804, 810, 812, 824, 832, 833, 836
　　Bee, Hamilton P 812
　　Dana, Napoleon J. T 787–789
　　State Department, U. S 815
　　Stone, Charles P 798, 800, 813
　Organization, strength, etc., of Union Troops in 398
　Proclamations of
　　Cobos, José Maria... 401, 402
　　Cortina, Juan Nepumuceno 406, 408
　　Tamaulipas, Mexico, Governor of. (Manuel Ruiz) 404
　Reports of
　　Banks, Nathaniel P..................... 396, 397, 399, 402, 405, 406, 409
　　Bee, Hamilton P.......................... 432–434, 436–438
　　Black, John Charles.. 423
　　Bradfute, W. R 445, 446
　　Bruce, John... 425
　　Dana, Napoleon J. T 411–415
　　Davis, Henry T.. 444
　　Duff, James.. 439
　　Ireland, John... 447
　　Magruder, John B 431, 432
　　Ransom, Thomas E. G 426, 427
　　Taylor, Richard... 443
　　Washburn, Cadwallader C 416–418
　　Washburn, Henry D 420
Rio Hondo, N. Mex. Skirmish with Indians on the, July 18, 1863* 2
Risdon, Orlando C. Mentioned...................................... 712
Ritter, Richard. Mentioned 276
Roach, Michael. Mentioned.. 62
Robards, W. L. Mentioned.. 331
Robert C. Winthrop, Steamer. Mentioned 300
Roberts, C. M. Mentioned 352
Roberts, John W. Mentioned.. 325
Roberts, O. M. Mentioned 374, 394, 395
Robertson, Morant J. Mentioned 57
Robinson, ———. Mentioned 658, 659
Robinson, Charles. Mentioned.. 65
Robinson, George D. Mentioned............................... 707, 894
Robinson, Harai.
　Mentioned 39, 262, 264–269, 271, 336, 356, 358, 361, 370, 372, 529, 708, 828, 900
　Report of operations in the Teche Country, La., Oct. 3–Nov. 30, 1863 374
　Testimony of. Mutiny at Camp Hubbard, Thibodeaux, La. Aug. 29–30,
　　　1863 262–264
Robinson, Henry. Mentioned 58
Robinson, Sallie, Steamer. Mentioned 49, 534, 621
Robinson, Samuel. Mentioned 65

*No circumstantial reports on file.

Page.

Roche, Armand. Mentioned... 59
Roche, James D. Mentioned 131
Rocher, William. Mentioned... 59
Rodgers, John I. Mentioned 660, 895
Rodman, William L. Mentioned 17, 71, 128, 511
Roe, William B.
    Correspondence with Stephen M. Eaton............................ 94, 96, 109
    Mentioned...................................... 16, 78, 104, 112, 119, 352, 894
    Reports of
        Port Hudson, La. Siege of, May 21-July 8, 1863...................... 76
        Sabine Pass (Texas) Expedition, Sept. 4-11, 1863 293
Rogers, George W. Mentioned 530
Rogers, James H. Mentioned 787
Roleson, Benjamin F. Mentioned 60
Rolle, Ferdinand. Mentioned.. 61
Rollins, Benjamin C. Mentioned 59
Rolph, Joseph W. Mentioned.. 62
Romero, G. Mentioned... 25
Romero, José M. Mentioned 26, 32, 236
Romero, Miguel. Mentioned 29
Root, James E. Mentioned... 62
Root, Nelson. Mentioned 63
Rose, Augustine D. Mentioned.. 322
Rose, Elihu E. Mentioned... 828
Rosecrans, William S.
    Correspondence with
        Army Headquarters.. 654
        Merrill, William E 654
    Mentioned..................... 391, 494, 495, 497, 674, 732, 753, 790, 817
Ross, Henry W. Mentioned.. 895
Ross, Isaac. Mentioned 283
Ross, John. Mentioned 60
Rountree, L. C. Mentioned 330, 331
Rourke, Jerry. Mentioned... 58
Rowland, Edward S. Mentioned 322
Rowley, William W. Mentioned... 16, 76
Roy, William. Mentioned.. 530
Royce, Clark E. Mentioned 239
Ruess, John. Mentioned... 423
Rugeley, E. S. Mentioned 485
Ruggles, Sidney B. Mentioned 57
Ruiz, Manuel. Mentioned 399,
                 400, 402, 403, 405, 409, 438, 439, 449, 451, 840, 844, 864, 865
    For correspondence, etc., see *Tamaulipas, Mexico, Governors of.*
Rundlett, James H.
    Mentioned 104
    Report of siege of Port Hudson, La., May 21-July 8, 1863 .... 116.
Russell, Surgeon. Mentioned 644
Russell, Charles. Mentioned 436, 442
Russell, Edmund H.
    Mentioned 57, 77, 78, 94, 112
    Report of siege of Port Hudson, La., May 21-July 8, 1863................. 119
Russell, Edward K. Mentioned.. 336, 899
Russell, George C. Mentioned 58

Page.

Russell, P. A. J. Mentioned 28
Rust, Henry, jr. Mentioned.................................... 531, 686, 711
Rutherford, Friend S. Mentioned............................ 457, 476, 479, 900
Ryall, R. H. Mentioned.. 774
Ryan, Samuel. Mentioned.. 61
Rygaard, Loren. Mentioned................................... 531, 708, 791
Sabine Pass (Texas) Expedition, Sept. 4–11, 1863.
    Army Corps, 19th. List of batteries to accompany...................... 721
    Communications from
        Army Headquarters.... .... 694, 698, 742
        Banks, Nathaniel P 692, 695, 697
    Congratulatory Orders. Magruder 306
    Itinerary of 1st Brigade, 3d Division, 19th Army Corps, Sept., 1863........ 300
    Itinerary of 1st Division, 19th Army Corps, Sept., 1863.................... 299
    Proclamation to men of Texas. Magruder................................. 307
    Reports of
        Banks, Nathaniel P 286–288, 290
        Crocker, Frederick 301
        Dowling, Richard W 311
        Franklin, William B 294, 298
        Magruder, John B... 302–305
        Odlum, Frederick H.. 309
        Roe, William B 293
        Smith, Leon 307
        Weitzel, Godfrey.. 298
    Resolution of thanks of C. S. Congress to F. H. Odlum, R. W. Dowling,
        and Davis Guards... 312
    Sketches... 291, 296
Sachem, U. S. S. Mentioned.................................... 5,
    92, 94, 103, 108, 204, 288, 292, 303, 305, 306, 308–312, 488, 490, 623, 640, 878
Sadusky, Albert. Mentioned.. 59
Sage, Clinton H.
    · Correspondence with
        Banks, Nathaniel P.................. 81, 551, 558, 559, 562, 573, 608, 630
        Farragut, David G.. 115
    Mentioned................... 336, 530, 538, 542, 558, 561, 567, 571, 632, 711
Saint Charles, Steamer. Mentioned 294, 296, 298, 502
St. John, Charles. Mentioned.. 62
Saint Martinsville, La.
    Affair at, Dec. 3, 1863.
        Abstract from "Record of Events" on returns of Cavalry Division, De-
        partment of the Gulf, for Dec., 1863............................. 455
        Communication from William B. Franklin............................ 831
    Operations about, Nov. 12, 1863. See Teche Country, La. Operations in the,
        Oct. 3–Nov. 30, 1863. Report of Burbridge, p. 362.
Saint Mary's, Steamer.
    Attack on the, July 8, 1863. Report of Charles Emerson 203
    Mentioned .... 46, 82, 203, 410_
    412, 417, 418, 426, 581, 582, 590, 593, 793, 800, 814, 819, 824, 825, 837, 838, 843
Saint Maurice, Steamer. Mentioned.. 499
Saint Philip, Fort. See Fort Jackson and Fort Saint Philip.
Sallie Robinson, Steamer. Mentioned 49, 534, 621
Salmas, Monico. Mentioned...................................... 285

Page.

Salomon, Edward. Mentioned 589
Saltus, Edward. Mentioned 66
Salvadore, Governor. Mentioned 256
Salvadore. (Indian.) Mentioned 256
Sanborn, Orville S. Mentioned... 99
Sanders, C. F. Mentioned 496
Sanders, R. W. Mentioned 216
Sanderson, James A. Mentioned.. 900
Sanford, Bradford. Mentioned... 65
Sara, Bayou. See *Bayou Sara*.
Sargent, Charles S. Mentioned 382
Sargent, Horace B. Mentioned.. 456, 459, 700
Sargent, Lorenzo D. Mentioned 530, 672, 708, 712, 828, 896
Saufley, W. P. Mentioned.. 395
Saunders, Glosky. Mentioned.. 59
Saunders, Herman. Mentioned... 58
Saunders, James. Mentioned... 427
Sauter, E. Mentioned.. 58
Sawtell, Josiah A.
   Correspondence with
      Cahill, Thomas W.. 600
      Emory, William H........................... 601, 604, 607, 608, 615, 638, 639
   Mentioned 188, 195, 566
Sawyer, Horace. Mentioned.. 60
Sawyer, Thomas A. Mentioned... 65
Sayles, Frank. Mentioned 73, 900
Scates, Walter B. Mentioned.. 777, 885
   For correspondence as A. A. G., see *Edward O. C. Ord.*
Scheffler, William. Mentioned... 693
Schellhaas, Frederick. Mentioned 65
Schirmer, L. A. Mentioned 153, 155
Schleifer, George. Mentioned... 64
Schlesinger, Samuel. Mentioned.. 58
Schley, W. S.
   Correspondence with
      Gabaudan, Edward C.. 90, 91
      Terry, Edward 81, 114
   Mentioned 90
Schlosser, Anton. Mentioned.. 58
Schmidt, Adolph. Mentioned.., ... 895
Schmidt, Ernst. Mentioned......................,..........,................ 66
Schmidt, Louis. Mentioned.. 57
Schnack, Christian. Mentioned.. 64
Schofield, George W. Mentioned.. 64
Schofield, John M.
   Correspondence with
      Banks, Nathaniel P.. 807, 915
      Carleton, James H.. 542
   Mentioned 542
Schottler, Richard. Mentioned... 66
Schreiber, A. Mentioned... 216
Schriver, John R. Mentioned.. 63
Schue, Nicholas. Mentioned... 58
Schuh, Frederick. Mentioned.. 58

Page.

Sciota, U. S. S. Mentioned 481–483
Scofield, Hiram. Mentioned 712
Scott, D. D. Mentioned 279
Scott, Frank N. Mentioned 62
Scott, John S. Mentioned 313
Scott, Mortimer H. Mentioned 57
Scott, Robert N. Correspondence with Judge-Advocate-General's Office,
U. S. A 206
Scott, Thomas A., Steamer. Mentioned 412, 429, 801, 810, 814, 825
Scovell, Joseph A. Mentioned 58
Scurry, W. R. Mentioned 246
Seabury, Thomas S. Mentioned 293
Sea Lion, Schooner. Mentioned 669, 670
Sea Queen, Steamer. Mentioned 719
Sears, Francis A. Mentioned 710, 898
Seddon, James A. Mentioned 210, 305, 385, 739
    For correspondence, etc., see *War Department, C. S.*
Seeley, Robert R. Mentioned 64
Seeligson, Henry. Mentioned 441
Segur, Steamer. Mentioned 543
Selden, H. R. Mentioned 612, 750
Selden, Joseph.
    Mentioned 529
    Report of siege of Port Hudson, La., May 21–July 8, 1863 124
Selfridge, Thomas O. Correspondence with Nathaniel P. Banks 715
Sentell, William H. Mentioned 899
Serna, Jesus de la. Mentioned 403, 405, 406, 409, 841, 842, 844, 857, 876, 882–884
    For correspondence, etc., see *Tamaulipas, Mexico, Governors of.*
Servis, David H. Mentioned 62
Sever, J. G. Mentioned 423
Severin, Francois. Mentioned 59
Seward, William H. Mentioned 570, 673, 703, 840, 880, 902, 919
    For correspondence, etc., see *State Department, U. S.*
Seymore, George. Mentioned 59
Shaden, Martin J. Mentioned 58
Shannon, D. W. Mentioned 216, 227–229
Sharpe, Jacob. Mentioned 530, 633, 667, 710, 749, 783, 826, 892, 895, 899
Shattuck, James A. Mentioned 63
Shaurman, Nelson. Mentioned 530, 711
Shaw, Edwin A. Mentioned 65
Shaw, George S. Mentioned 682, 693
Shaw, J. C. Mentioned 827, 901
Shea, Morgan. Mentioned 71
Sheer, Martin. Mentioned 58
Shehan, James. Mentioned 60
Shelby, W. B.
    Mentioned 143, 157, 158, 160, 161
    Report of siege of Port Hudson, La., May 21–July 8, 1863 164
Sheldon, Lionel A.
    Correspondence with Nathaniel P. Banks 815
    Mentioned 334, 428, 709, 807, 812, 820, 826, 892, 895
Shelton, Eugene E. Mentioned 634
Shelton, S. M. Mentioned 163
Shepard, E. M. Mentioned 140–142

Page.

Shepard, Sylvester B. Mentioned...................................... 71
Shepley, George F.
    Correspondence with War Department, U. S........................... 694
    Mentioned... 603, 606
Sheppard, C. B. Mentioned.. 229, 332, 395
Sherfey, Jacob F. Mentioned.. 911, 912, 914
Sheridan, Terrance. Mentioned...................................... 201
Sherman, Charles E. Mentioned...................................... 57
Sherman, Thomas W.
    Correspondence with
        Banks, Nathaniel P 501, 503, 505
        Eaton, Stephen M... 88
    Mentioned..................................... 13, 17, 43, 44, 68, 84, 93,
            94, 113, 124, 125, 489, 491, 493, 500, 504, 508–511, 518, 522, 526, 527, 529, 531
Sherman, William T.
    Correspondence with
        Army Headquarters... 887, 902, 903
        Lewis, John V 909
        McPherson, James B 903
    Mentioned.. 645, 790
Shields, John M. Mentioned... 361
Shipley, Alexander N.
    Correspondence with David G. Farragut........................... 108, 113
    Mentioned... 207, 209, 635
Shoemaker, W. R. Mentioned... 612, 750, 827, 901
Shonn, ——. Mentioned... 669–671, 703
Shunk, David. Mentioned............................ 334, 709, 713, 763, 823, 897
Shunk, Francis J.
    Correspondence with Richard Arnold.............................. 691, 712, 738
    Mentioned... 543
Sibley, Henry H. Mentioned... 4, 10, 39, 535
Sidders, Charles. Mentioned.. 58
Siegle, Conrad. Mentioned.. 65
Signal Corps.
    Efficiency of. Communication from James S. Palmer............... 660
    Services of. Communication from Nathaniel P. Banks............. 890
Silvey, James. Mentioned... 669
Simmons, George F. Mentioned....................................... 63
Simmons, Thomas. Mentioned... 60
Simpson, Enoch T. Mentioned.. 62
Sims, George R. Mentioned.. 356, 361
Simsport, La. Engagement near, June 3, 1863 *...................... 1
Sinclair, William T. Mentioned..................................... 65
Singleton, Abram.
    Court-martial in case of. Mutiny at Fort Jackson, La., Dec. 9, 1863....... 478
    Mentioned... 478, 479
Sir William Peel, Steamer. Mentioned............................... 719
Sizer, John M. Mentioned... 335, 710
Sketches. Sabine Pass (Texas) Expedition, Sept. 4–11, 1863......... 291, 296
Skillman, Captain. Mentioned....................................... 918
Skinner, Lieutenant. Mentioned..................................... 122
Skinner, Freeman. Mentioned.. 63
Slack, Charles B. Correspondence with Theodore Bradley............. 87, 98

* For report, see Series I, Vol. XXIV, Part II, p. 445.

Page.

Slack, James R. Mentioned... 335, 358, 710
Slaughter, James E. Mentioned.. 448, 449, 452
Slocum, J. J. Mentioned 167
Slocum, Willard. Mentioned.. 334, 709
Small, Michael P. Mentioned... 382
Smalley, Henry A. Mentioned.. 895
Smith, Captain. Mentioned... 89
Smith, Abel, jr. Mentioned... 17, 72, 511
Smith, A. J. Mentioned 319, 710
Smith, Benjamin F. Mentioned.. 914
Smith, Charles. (Dr.) Mentioned... 532
Smith, Charles. (Private.) Mentioned 59
Smith, Charles M. Mentioned 66
Smith, Edward B.
    Court-martial in case of. Mutiny at Fort Jackson, La., Dec. 9, 1863...... 476
    Mentioned 476, 479
Smith, E. Kirby.
    Correspondence with
        Adjutant and Inspector General's Office, C. S. A...................... 209, 392
        Magruder, John B... 386
        Taylor, Richard.................... 212, 217, 220, 224, 227, 229, 232, 281, 283, 329
    Mentioned... 49, 94, 127, 146, 180,
        210, 212, 289, 304, 305, 384, 385, 387, 431, 496, 519, 521, 522, 535, 548, 557, 558,
        566, 567, 571, 661, 693, 697, 699, 732, 739, 763, 792, 800, 817, 819, 852, 863, 916
    Report of operations in the Teche Country, La., Oct. 3–Nov. 30, 1863....... 384
Smith, Elisha B. Mentioned... 72, 529
Smith, Henry. Mentioned... 59
Smith, J. (Major.) Mentioned.. 612, 827, 901
Smith, J. (Private.) Mentioned 60
Smith, James. (Colonel.) Mentioned........................... 122, 529, 633, 667, 711
Smith, James. (Private.) Mentioned... 58
Smith, James W. Mentioned.. 60
Smith, James Y. Mentioned.. 270, 272, 273
        For correspondence, etc., see Rhode Island, Governor of.
Smith, J. Baptiste. Mentioned.. 59
Smith, John J. Mentioned 638
Smith, John S. Mentioned... 60
Smith, Joseph. Mentioned... 23, 24
Smith, Leon.
    Mentioned 304, 306, 311, 312, 446
    Report of Sabine Pass (Texas) Expedition, Sept. 4–11, 1863............... 307
Smith, Marshall J.
    Correspondence with Franklin Gardner.. 159
    Mentioned 36, 158, 159, 173, 178
Smith, Martin L. Mentioned 212
Smith, Nathan G. Mentioned... 61
Smith, N. H. Mentioned 306, 308, 310, 311
Smith, S. A. Mentioned.. 495, 496
Smith, T. Kilby. Mentioned................... 48, 49, 98, 99, 119, 625, 683, 686
Smith, Warren D.
    Correspondence with William O. Fiske....................................... 317
    Mentioned 500, 899
    Report of affair opposite Donaldsonville, La., Sept. 23, 1863............... 317
        For correspondence as A. A. A. G., see William H. Emory.

Page.

Smith, W. F.
Assignment to command 506
Mentioned 506
Smith, William. Mentioned 58
Smith, William P. Mentioned 57
Snow, W. K. Mentioned 40
Soulé, Pierre. Mentioned 535
Southern Florida. See *Florida, Southern.*
Southern Merchant, Steamer. Mentioned 543
Southworth, Irving D. Mentioned 200
Spade, General. Mentioned 189
Spain, E. M. Mentioned 144
Spalding, Stephen F. Mentioned 71
Sparling, George W. Mentioned 62
Spaulding, Charles. Mentioned 65
Speed, Frederic. Mentioned 122, 209, 876, 886
Speight, J. W. Mentioned 189, 212, 323, 329–332, 385
Spicely, William T. Mentioned 335, 710
Spiegel, Marcus M. Mentioned 895
Spies, Christopher. Mentioned 57
Spink, Elon P. Mentioned 64
Spivey, W. F. Mentioned 331
Sprague, Homer B. Mentioned 57
Sprague, Otis. Mentioned 60
Sprague, Sewell. Mentioned 60
Springfield and Plains Store Roads, La. Skirmishes on the, May 23, 1863.
    See *Port Hudson, La. Siege of, May 21–July 8, 1863. Reports of
    Banks,* p. 5; *Wingfield,* p. 165. See also *General Orders, No. 47
    (Gardner),* p. 167.
Springfield Landing, La. Affair at, July 2, 1863. Communications from
    Dwight, William 126
    Logan, John L 182
    See also *Port Hudson, La. Siege of, May 21–July 8, 1863. Reports of*
      Blanchard, Justus W.   Irwin, Richard B.   Logan, John L.
      Corliss, Augustus W.
Squires, M. T. Mentioned 216
Stacey, George F. Mentioned 60
Stack, James. Mentioned 65
Stackhouse, George W. Mentioned 72
Stafford, Spencer H. Mentioned 684
Stall, Jacob. Mentioned 59
Stancel, Jesse. Mentioned 584, 600, 605
Stanford, Bernard. Mentioned 58
Stanford, George E. Mentioned 64
Stanley, Daniel C. Mentioned 366
Stanton, Edwin M. Mentioned 269, 503, 535, 545,
    570, 673, 702, 720, 742, 775, 776, 785, 832, 835, 839, 840, 857, 858, 880, 887, 902
    For correspondence, etc., see *War Department, U. S.*
Stanton, John L. Mentioned 70
Stark, Henry. Mentioned 549
Starlight, Confederate steamer.
    Capture of, May 25, 1863. See *Port Hudson, La. Siege of, May 21–July 8, 1863.
      Report of Prince,* p. 138.
    Mentioned 139, 506, 782

Page.

Starlight and Red Chief. Capture of the Confederate Steamers, May 25, 1863.
Communications from
Banks, Nathaniel P 506
Palmer, James S 93, 108
Scarnes, B. B. Mentioned 166
Starr, Frederick. Mentioned 197
State Department, U. S. Correspondence with
Banks, Nathaniel P 815, 846
Dayton, William L .... 570 ,
Liverpool, England, U. S. Consul at 658
Matamoras, Mexico, U. S. Consul at 718
Monterey, Mexico, U. S. Consul at 657
New Mexico, Governor of 629
War Department, U. S 569, 572, 628, 656, 658, 718, 719, 902
Stearns, Albert. Report of operations in Louisiana west of the Mississippi,
June 7–July 13, 1863 191
Stearns, Marcellus L. Mentioned 60
Steck, M. Mentioned 25–27
Stedman, Joseph. Mentioned 188, 531
Steedman, I. G. W.
Abstract from muster-roll of 1st Alabama Volunteers, April 20–Nov. 30,
1863. Port Hudson, La. Siege of, May 21–July 8, 1863 163
Mentioned 143, 163, 166, 170, 171
Report of siege of Port Hudson, La., May 21–July 8, 1863 156–163
Steele, Frederick.
Co-operation with Nathaniel P. Banks. Communications from
Banks, Nathaniel P 888
Schofield, John M 807
Mentioned 716, 727, 731, 742, 807, 839, 889
Steele, William. Mentioned 304
Steger, Emil. Mentioned 335, 710, 895
Stephens, ——. Mentioned 93
Sternberg, George M. Mentioned 540
Sternberg, Seigmund. Mentioned 66
Sterry, Abner N. Mentioned 58
Stevens, Benjamin. Mentioned 25, 30, 32
Stevens, Charles L. Mentioned 71
Stevens, Samuel H., jr. Mentioned 66
Stevens, William S. Mentioned 61
Stevenson, John A. Mentioned 313
Stevenson, John D. Report of expedition from Vicksburg, Miss., to Monroe,
La., Aug. 20–Sept. 2, 1863, including skirmishes (24th) at Bayou
Macon and at Floyd 248
Stewart, James M. Mentioned 62
Stickney, Albert.
Correspondence with
Emory, William H 541, 544, 568, 575, 576, 578–581, 584, 585, 587, 638, 639
Grover, Cuvier 639
Mentioned 15, 46, 187–191, 198,
199, 540, 541, 543, 546, 577, 578, 580–582, 584, 586–588, 594, 597, 606, 637–639
Report of operations in Louisiana west of the Mississippi, June 7–July 13,
1863 192
Stillman, ——. Mentioned 843
Stillman & Co. Mentioned 844
Stillman, George L. Mentioned 334, 419, 421, 423, 897

Page.

Stipp, George W.
Announced as Medical Inspector, Department of the Gulf.................. 867
Mentioned 867
Stirling's Plantation, on the Fordoche, La.
Action at, Sept. 29, 1863.
Abstracts from "Records of Events," 2d Division, 13th Army Corps, for
Sept., 1863...... 326
Casualties. Returns of.
Confederate Troops 332
Union Troops.. 325
Communications from
Dana, Napoleon J. T 323
Ratliff, W. B... 322
Taylor, Richard.. 329
Reports of
Banks, Nathaniel P... 320
Bruce, John.. 325
Dana, Napoleon J. T 321, 324
Green, Thomas 329
Mouton, Alfred... 328
Skirmish at, near Morganza, Sept. 12, 1863 * 2
Stockdale, J. L. Mentioned 537
Stokely, Q. T. Mentioned 144
Stone, B. W. Mentioned 218, 219, 561, 562
Stone, Charles P.
Announced as Chief of Staff, Department of the Gulf.................... 660
Correspondence with
Banks, Nathaniel P... 102,
118, 396, 642, 648–650, 652, 737, 782, 787, 793, 795, 798, 800, 803, 809, 813, 819
Crosby, J. Schuyler.. 757
Dunham, Robert T.. 757
Farragut, David G... 111, 114
Mentioned... 54, 86, 97, 318, 381, 383, 573, 605, 641, 657, 660, 675, 676, 678, 679, 757, 832
For correspondence as Chief of Staff, see *Nathaniel P. Banks.*
Stone, Eben F. Mentioned 529, 554
Stone, Joseph C. [?] Mentioned 867
Storey, John. Mentioned 58
Stouder, H. Correspondence with William H. Emory 595
Stratton, William. Mentioned 64
Strawn, Charles. Mentioned 64
Street, T. A. Mentioned 143, 150
Strength of Troops. See *Organization, Strength, etc.*
Strickland, Joseph. Mentioned.................................... 70, 130
Striclan, W. D. Mentioned 150
String, Benjamin. Mentioned... 59
Strong, James H.
Correspondence with Napoleon J. T. Dana 787
Mentioned *............................. 396, 417, 420, 426, 480, 481, 483, 804, 825
Stubbs, J. T. Mentioned... 37
Stump, Charles. Mentioned... 64
Sturgis, Frederick L. Mentioned.................................... 57

* No circumstantial reports on file.

Page.

Suarman, John. Mentioned.. 58
Subsistence Stores. Supplies of, etc. See *Munitions of War*.
Suffolk, Steamer. Mentioned 72, 73, 293, 296, 456, 464, 465, 468, 475, 786
Suffolk, Steamer, Captain of. Correspondence with Alexander Asboth..... 786
Sullivan, James. Mentioned... 59
Surget, E. Correspondence with Richard Taylor.................................. 386
    For correspondence as A. A. G., see *Richard Taylor*.
Susquehanna, U. S. S. Mentioned 90
Sutherland, George. Mentioned 61
Swann, Robert P.
    Correspondence with Richard Arnold 143
    Mentioned 89-91, 140-142
Sweeney, Osborn. Mentioned.. 62
Sweeny, ——. Mentioned 753
Sweeny, Patrick. Mentioned... 65
Swift, John L. Mentioned... 457, 853
Switzerland, U. S. S. Mentioned 36, 493, 494
Sykes, Steamer. Mentioned 46, 543, 567, 568, 589
Tafolla, Luis. Mentioned.. 30
Taft, Jerome K. Mentioned... 71
Taggart, Samuel. For correspondence as A. A. G., see *James B. McPherson*.
Taladrid, Damasio. Mentioned.................................... 235
Talbot, W. H. Correspondence with Samuel B. Holabird 595
Taller, John. Mentioned.. 60
Tamaulipas, Mexico, Governors of.
    Riuz, Manuel.
        Correspondence with Hamilton P. Bee........................... 450, 451
        Mentioned 403, 409
        Proclamations of, to
            Matamoras, Mexico, Citizens of.................................. 404
            Matamoras, Mexico, Garrison of.................................. 404
    Serna, Jesus de la. Correspondence with Napoleon J. T. Dana. 823, 839, 884, 885
Tarbell, Jonathan. Mentioned.................................... 262, 796, 900
Tarver, E. R. For correspondence as A. D. C. & A. A. A, G., see *Hamilton P. Bee*.
Taylor, Lieutenant. Mentioned 548
Taylor, Private. Mentioned 59
Taylor, Andrew M. Mentioned... 325
Taylor, Charles.
    Court-martial in case of. Mutiny at Fort Jackson, Ala., Dec. 9, 1863..... 477
    Mentioned..... .... 477, 479
Taylor, Franck E. Mentioned 712
Taylor, George E. Mentioned 61
Taylor, George W. Mentioned 899
Taylor, J. A. Mentioned.. 173
Taylor, John. Mentioned 64
Taylor, Joseph. Mentioned... 58
Taylor, Richard.
    Correspondence with
        Smith, E. Kirby................. 212, 217, 220, 224, 227, 229, 232, 281, 283, 329
        Surget, E 386
    Mentioned 4, 10, 11, 15, 17, 47, 48, 90, 180, 182, 189, 209, 210, 212, 215,
        282, 289, 304, 306, 325, 351, 375, 384-386, 388, 391, 392, 432-434, 440-443, 540,
        589, 621, 628, 701, 724, 732, 735, 761, 811, 813, 817, 819, 848, 852, 863, 870, 915

Page.

Taylor, Richard—Continued.
Reports of
Louisiana. Operations in, west of the Mississippi, June 7–July 13,
1863 .... 209–212, 214
Rio Grande Expedition and operations on the coast of Texas, Oct. 27–
Dec. 2, 1863 443
Teche Country, La. Operations in the, Oct. 3–Nov. 30, 1863 386–392
Taylor, Roswell. Mentioned 57
Taylor, Samuel. Mentioned 58
Teche Bayou, La. Skirmish on the, Oct. 3, 1863. See *Stirling's Plantation,
on the Fordoche, La. Action at, Sept. 29, 1863. Report of Banks,*
p. 320.
Teche Country, La. Operations in the. Oct. 3–Nov. 30, 1863.
Abstract from "Record of Events" of the Cavalry Division, Department of
the Gulf, for Oct. and Nov., 1863 377
Abstract from "Record of Events" of 13th Army Corps, for Oct. and Nov.,
1863 366
Casualties. Returns of.
Confederate Troops 395
Union Troops 359
Communications from
Banks, Nathaniel P 338,
389, 733, 735, 750, 751, 755–761, 770–775, 790, 793, 799, 819, 829
Crosby, J. Schuyler 338, 763, 765
Dana, Napoleon J. T 762
Franklin, William B 354, 363, 759, 760, 769, 772–774, 787, 799
Grover, Cuvier 774
Ord, Edward O. C 738, 761, 762
Stone, Charles P 793, 800, 819
Taylor, Richard 386
Daily memoranda for Adjutant-General's Office, Department of the Gulf,
Oct. 9–14, 1863 380
Itinerary of 19th Army Corps, Oct. 1–Nov. 18, 1863 369
Organization, strength, etc., of Union Troops in 334–336
Reports of
Benedict, Lewis 368
Burbridge, Stephen G 359, 362, 363
Fonda, John G 372, 373
Franklin, William B 337–352
Green, Thomas 393
Guppey, Joshua J 363
Lee, Albert L 369, 370
Lucas, Thomas J 375
Marland, William 371
Mouton, Alfred 393
Ord, Edward O. C 354
Paine, Charles J 376
Pigman, William A 352
Robinson, Harai 374
Smith, E. Kirby 384
Taylor, Richard 386–392
Washburn, Cadwallader C 355, 356
Teche Road, La. Operations on the, between Barre's Landing and Berwick,
May 21–26, 1863. Report of Joseph S. Morgan 40
Tennessee, C. S. S. Mentioned 888, 891

                                                                Page.
Tennessee, U. S. S. Mentioned   292

Tennessee, Army of the. (Union.) Organization, strength, etc., July 31,
       1863. Herron's division   665

Tennessee, Department of the. (Union.)
    Orders, Special, series 1863: **No. 205,** 661.

Tennessee Troops. Mentioned. (Confederate.)
    Artillery, Heavy—*Regiments:* **1st** (*Batteries*), **G,** 143, 147.
    Artillery, Light—*Regiments:* **1st** (*Batteries*), **B.** 143, 147 ; **Maury,** 143.
    Infantry—*Regiments:* **41st, 42d, 48th, 49th, 53d, 55th,** 143.

Tennessee Troops. Mentioned. (Union.)
    Cavalry—*Regiments :* **9th,** 654.

Tenney, Joseph F. Mentioned   76

Terrazas, Governor. Mentioned   919

Terrel, James. Mentioned   150

Terrell, A. W. Mentioned   446

Terrell's Texas Cavalry. Mutiny in, Sept. 11, 1863..................   2
                        See also Part II.

Terry, Edward.
    Correspondence with
        Arnold, Richard..   142
        Schley, W. S.. 81, 114
    Mentioned 140, 142, 523
    Report of siege of Port Hudson, La., May 21–July 8, 1863................   141

Texas.
    Affairs in, generally. Communications from
        Hamilton, Andrew J..   865
        Monterey, Mexico, U. S. Consul at.............................   657
        State Department, U. S ....   656.
        War Department, U. S...   656
    Operations on the coast of, Dec. 9–26, 1863. Communications from
        Banks, Nathaniel P.................................... 837, 847, 903
        Benton, William P   838
        Thompson, William G...   878
        Washburn, Cadwallader C.................... 849, 853, 859, 860, 878
                See also *Sabine Pass (Texas) Expedition.*

Texas, Western.
    Affairs in, generally. Communications from
        Banks, Nathaniel P..   880
        Dana, Napoleon J. T.................................... 842, 858
    Operations in, Dec. 18–24, 1863. Communications from Napoleon J. T.
        Dana 864, 865, 876
    Proposed expedition into. Communications from
        Army Headquarters..................................... 664, 672, 673, 675
        Banks, Nathaniel P.................................... 682, 686
        Lincoln, Abraham..   659
        New Hampshire, Governor of   680

Texas, New Mexico, and Arizona. District of.
    Orders, General, series 1863: **No. 139,** 246 ; **No. 154,** 306.

Texas Troops. Mentioned. (Confederate.)
    Artillery, Heavy—*Regiments:* **1st,** 243–245, 247 ; **1st** (*Batteries*), **F,** 304–306,
        308, 310–312, 915.
    Artillery, Light—*Batteries :* **Daniel's,** 394, 395, 454 ; **Dashiell's,** 247 ; **Gon-
        zales',** 222, 230, 303 ; **Jones',** 242, 244, 247, 303 ; **Moseley's,** 247 ; **Nichols',**
        215, 225, 303 ; **Valverde,** 215, 225, 374, 391, 394.

Page.

Texas Troops. Mentioned. (Confederate)—Continued.

Cavalry—*Battalions :* 13th, 39, 215, 216, 225, 329, 330, 332, 394, 395, 639. *Companies :* Daly's, 308; Vidal's, 439, 447–450. *Regiments :* Brown's, 484, 486; 1st, 303, 484–486; 1st Partisan, 36, 38, 39, 218, 227, 228, 230, 231, 395, 494; 2d, 196, 216, 218, 446; 2d *(Arizona Brigade)*, 215, 225, 230, 349; 3d *(Arizona Brigade)*, 217, 218, 227, 230, 329, 331, 349, 395; 4th, 215, 216, 227–231, 329, 330, 349, 374, 394, 395, 820; 5th, 215, 225, 227, 230, 231, 329, 330, 349, 379, 394, 395; 6th, 221, 227, 230, 349, 395, 811, 814; 7th, 215, 227, 228, 230, 231, 330, 346, 347, 349, 370, 378, 394, 395; 23d, 243, 303; 26th, 243, 245, 247; 33d, 185, 284, 285, 433–436, 439–445, 448, 449, 451; 34th, 212; 36th, 446.

Infantry—*Battalions :* Griffin's, 243, 303, 308, 310; Spaight's, 308. *Regiments :* 3d, 241–243, 245, 247, 303; 8th, 436; 11th, 393, 395; 13th, 329, 330, 332, 387; 15th, 394, 395; 18th, 393, 395; 20th, 242–245, 247, 303, 310.

Miscellaneous: Waul's Legion, 810.

State:

    Cavalry—*Regiments :* 3d, 436, 437, 446.

    Infantry—*Companies :* Cummings', 435, 440, 441, 448.

Texas Troops. Mentioned. (Union.)

Cavalry—*Companies :* Vidal's Partisan Rangers, 830, 898. *Regiments :* 1st, 284, 287, 336, 334, 377, 397, 398, 413, 429, 430, 531, 584, 686, 712, 713, 758, 770, 771, 783, 826, 828, 831, 865, 885, 886, 892–894, 898; 2d, 821, 885, 892–894, 898.

Thalmann, John G. Mentioned 65

Thayer, J. S. Mentioned 827, 901

Theale, Daniel. Mentioned 59

Thibodeaux, La. Capture of, June 20, 1863. See *Louisiana Operations in, west of the Mississippi, June 7–July 13, 1863. Reports of Grou,* p. 197; *Major,* p. 217.

Thing, Charles W. Mentioned 60

Thomas, Steamer. Mentioned................................ 296, 299, 300

Thomas A. Scott, Steamer. Mentioned.............. 412, 429, 801, 810, 814, 825

Thomas, Charles. Mentioned 785, 887

    For correspondence as Acting Quartermaster-General, see *Quartermaster-General's Office, U. S. A.*

Thomas, J. W. Mentioned 60

Thomas, Lorenzo.

    Mentioned........................... 6, 467, 468, 603, 642, 714, 794, 802, 814

    Orders in cases of negroes.. 803

    Orders, Special, series 1863: No. 102, 803.

    For correspondence, etc., see *Adjutant-General's Office, U. S. A.*

Thomas, S. M. Mentioned... 143, 176

Thomas, Stephen. Mentioned 67, 130, 529

Thominick E. Mentioned.. 59

Thompson, Albert F. Mentioned............................... 62

Thompson, Benjamin. Mentioned................................ 786

Thompson, Charles N. Mentioned 66

Thompson, Daniel. Mentioned.................................... 58

Thompson, E. B. Mentioned 161

Thompson, George W. Mentioned................................. 71

Thompson, John. Mentioned.............................. 32, 237, 253

Thompson, William G.

    Correspondence with•

      Dana, Napoleon J. T 788

      Washburn, Cadwallader C 878

    Mentioned 398, 427, 789, 878, 897

*Composed of infantry, cavalry, and artillery.

Page.

Thompson's Creek, La. Skirmish at, May 25, 1863. See *Port Hudson, La. Siege of, May 21–July 8, 1863. Report of Fellows*, p. 148.

Thorington, William. Mentioned 62
Thorp, John. Mentioned 64
Thurber, Benjamin F. Mentioned. 828, 900
Tibbets, Charles E. Mentioned 57
Tibbetts, Howard. Mentioned 285
Tibbetts, William N. Mentioned 60
Tice, Isaac L. Mentioned 710
Tickfaw Bridge, La. Skirmish at, May 16, 1863 * 1
Tidball, T. T. Mentioned 23, 27, 612, 750, 828, 901
Tiernon, Bartley. Mentioned 58
Tilghman, Oswald. Mentioned 143
Time and Tide, Steamer. Mentioned 571
Tinker, Sebree W. Mentioned 58
Tisdale, Eugene. Mentioned 765
Tod, David. Mentioned 848
Todd, Francis E. Mentioned 62
Toledano, E. A.
   Mentioned 143, 161, 164
   Report of siege of Port Hudson, La., May 21–July 8, 1863 165
Tompkins, Daniel D. Mentioned 28
Tompkins, Jeddiah. Mentioned 66
Tooker, Cyrus. Mentioned 64
Torres, Santiago. Mentioned 25
Toser, Bartholomew. Mentioned 64
Towey, George. Mentioned 61
Townsend, Captain. Mentioned 437
Townsend, Edward D. For correspondence as A. A. G., see *Adjutant-General's Office, U. S. A.*
Townsend, William C. Mentioned 60
Tracy, C. A. Mentioned 58
Trade and Intercourse. Communications from
   Army Headquarters 503, 670
   Bailey, Theodorus 670
   Banks, Nathaniel P 702, 715, 862
   Dana, Napoleon J. T 864, 882
   Denison, George S 670
   Emory, William H 598, 647
   Matamoras, Mexico, U. S. Consul at 718
   Monterey, Mexico, U. S. Consul at 657
   Navy Department, U. S 669
   State Department, U. S 718
   War Department, U. S 719
Trans-Mississippi Department. Promotions in. Communications from
   Adjutant and Inspector General's Office, C. S. A. 385
   Davis, Jefferson 385
   Smith, E. Kirby 392
   War Department, C. S 385
Transportation, Army. See *Munitions of War.*
Transportation. (Railroad and Water.) Communications from
   Asboth, Alexander 786
   Banks, Nathaniel P 498, 726, 785
Travinio, John. Mentioned 424

---

* No circumstantial reports on file.

Page.

Tresquez, José D. Mentioned 25
Trezquez, Antonio José. Mentioned 24
Trinity, La.
    Expedition from Vidalia to, Nov. 15-16, 1863. Report of Bernard G. Far-
        rar 452
      Skirmish at, Sept. 2, 1863. See *Harrisonburg, La. Expedition from Natchez,*
          Miss., to, Sept. 1-7, 1863. Report of Crocker, p. 273.
Triples, A. B. Mentioned 583
Trosclair, Paul E. Mentioned 59
Trudeau, James. Mentioned 355
Trull, George G. Mentioned 336, 368, 633, 660, 711
Tschole, Jacob. Mentioned 63
Tubbs, E. S. Mentioned 62
Tucker, Charles E. Mentioned 71
Tucker, Elias H. Mentioned 65
Tucker, James. Mentioned 435, 441
Tunica Bend, or Bayou Tunica, La. Skirmish at, Nov. 8, 1863* 3
Turner, Edmund P.
    Mentioned 416
    Report of skirmish on the Matagorda Peninsula, Tex., Dec. 29, 1863 484
       For correspondence as A. A. G., see *John B. Magruder.*
Turner, William. Mentioned 166
Tuttle, David W. Mentioned 205
Twiggs, Isaac. Mentioned 60
Twist, Russell P. Mentioned 335, 710, 894
Twitchell, George H. Mentioned 58
Tyler, George. Mentioned 59
Ulffers, Herman A. Mentioned 624
Ullmann, Daniel.
    Correspondence with
        Adjutant-General's Office, U. S. A 609
        Emory, William H 533
    Mentioned 16, 72, 524, 528, 531,
        533, 534, 539, 573, 610, 611, 632, 648, 683, 684, 688-690, 733, 749, 784, 827, 896
Ulrich, Charles F. Mentioned 58
Uncle Ben, C. S. S. Mentioned 308, 309, 311
Union, Steamer. Mentioned 103, 493, 494
Union Troops.
    Casualties. Returns of.
        Bayou Bourbeau, La. Engagement at, near Grand Coteau, Nov. 3,
          1863 359
        La Fourche, La. Engagement on the, near Donaldsonville, July 12-13,
          1863 205
        Plains Store, La. Action at, May 21, 1863 67
        Port Hudson, La. Siege of, May 21-July 8, 1863 67-72
        Stirling's Plantation, on the Fordoche, La. Action at, Sept. 29, 1863. 325
    Mentioned.
        Infantry—*Regiments:* 2d (*Colored*), 894, 895.
        Corps d'Afrique: †
        Artillery, Heavy—*Regiments:* 1st, 464, 531, 684, 708, 791, 895.
        Cavalry—*Regiments:* 1st, 828, 895, 900.
        Engineers—*Regiments:* 1st, 44, 68, 287, 342, 354, 397, 398, 406, 410, 426,
        429, 529, 539, 549, 555, 611, 633, 638, 684, 707, 893, 894, 898; 2d, 420, 684,
        707, 820, 860, 893, 894, 898; 3d, 707, 894; 4th, 894.

1032 INDEX.

Union Troops—Continued.

Mentioned.

Corps d'Afrique:

Infantry—*Regiments:* **1st,** 44, 59, 68, 239, 498, 526, 527, 529, 531, 539, 684, 708, 733, 896; **2d,** 531, 532, 539, 684, 708, 733, 894, 895; **3d,** 44, 59, 68, 239, 526, 527, 529, 539, 684, 708, 733, 896; **4th,** 457, 460–475, 497, 526. 527, 529, 539, 684, 708, 733, 896; **5th,** 464, 539, 684, 733, 894, 895; **6th,** 70, 239, 531, 539, 632, 684, 708, 733, 896; **7th, 8th, 9th, 10th,** 70, 531, 539, 632, 684, 708, 733, 896; **11th,** 684, 733, 896; **12th,** 238, 684, 733, 896; **13th,** 684, 733; **14th,** 684, 708, 733, 822, 834, 895; **15th,** 684, 733, 783, 894; **16th,** 397, 398, 406, 410, 429, 684, 733, 893, 898; **17th,** 684, 733, 896; **18th, 19th,** 684, 733, 896; **20th,** 733, 894, 895; **22d,** 783, 801, 814, 895; **25th,** 900; **26th,** 831.

Regulars.

Artillery, Light—*Regiments:* **1st** (*Batteries*), **A,** 22, 68, 74, 75, 299, 335, 529, 627, 660, 667, 698, 711, 721, 895; **F,** 22, 69, 128, 129, 336, 530, 633, 660, 698, 711, 713, 721, 725, 726, 894; **L,** 22, 47, 70, 300, 336, 531, 660. 712, 721, 900; **2d** (*Batteries*), **C,** 22, 70, 531, 660, 712, 780, 895; **H. K.** 532, 708, 895; **3d,** (*Batteries*), **A,** 612, 750, 827, 901; **5th** (*Batteries*), **G,** 22, 68, 121, 529, 652. 660, 708, 733, 895.

Cavalry—*Regiments:* **1st,** 612.

Infantry—*Regiments:* **1st,** 319, 612, 709, 750, 794, 827, 860, 863, 895; **5th,** 31, 260, 612, 750, 827, 828, 901; **7th,** 31, 260, 612, 750, 827, 901.

Ordnance—*Companies:* **Shoemaker's,** 612, 750, 827, 901.

For Volunteers, see respective States.

Organization, strength, etc................... 334–336, 398, 526–532. 610–612, 632, 633, 665, 707–712, 733, 748–750, 783, 784, 826–829, 891–901

Recruitment, organization, etc. Communications from

Adjutant-General's Office, U. S. A **608**

Banks, Nathaniel P.. 563, 572, 848, 880

Updegraff, J. Mentioned.. 612, 750, 901

Upton, Daniel P. Mentioned..................................... 11, 567

Uraga, General. Mentioned 864

Urlibarra, Pamblino. Mentioned 23

Urwiler, Jacob. Mentioned...................................... 62

Ute Indians. Employment of, as guides, etc. Communication from James H. Carleton 563

Valencia, José Ignacio. Mentioned.............................. 31

Valk, John H. Mentioned 65

Vallance, William H. Mentioned............................... 341

Valun, Peter. Mentioned 62

Van Anda, Salue G. Mentioned............................... 334, 709

Vance, Joseph W. Mentioned.................................. 898

Vance, Richard. Mentioned.................................... 361

Vandenbergh, James M. Mentioned............................ 209

Vandenburgh, Robert S. Mentioned 710

Van Deusen, William J. Mentioned............................ 64

Vandever, William.

Correspondence with Napoleon J. T. Dana..................... 789

Mentioned................... 205, 398, 412, 429, 665, 709, 723, 732, 801, 897

Van Dorn, Earl. Mentioned 496

Van Dousen, John. Mentioned 65

Van Petten, John B. Mentioned................. 64, 335, 529, 711, 853

Van Puyl, Benjamin T. Mentioned............................ 64

Page.

Van Slyck, Charles L. Mentioned 71,125
Van Vliet. John S. Mentioned 361
Van Wyck, John H. Mentioned 65
Van Zandt, Jacob. Mentioned. 530,686
Varner. Sampson E. Mentioned 898
Vass, Edward. Mentioned 65
Vaughan, B. L. Mentioned 161,163
Veliscross, John. Mentioned 61
Vermillion Bayou, La.
    Skirmishes at.
      ¨Oct. 9-10, 1863. See *Teche Country, La. Operations in the,* Oct. 3–*Nov.*
          30, 1863. *Itinerary of 19th Corps,* p. 369 ; *Record of Events, Cav.*
          Div., p. 377 ; *Stone's Memorandum,* p. 380 ; *report of Taylor,* p.
          386.
      Nov. 11, 1863. See *Carrion Crow and Vermillion Bayous, La.*
      Nov. 30, 1863. See *Teche Country, La. Operations in the,* Oct. 3–*Nov.*
         ' 30, 1863. *Report of Franklin,* p. 352.
    Skirmish near, Nov. 25, 1863. See *Teche Country, La. Operations in the,*
         Oct. 3–*Nov.* 30, 1863. *Report of Franklin,* p. 349 ; *Record of Events,*
         Cav. Div., p. 377.
Vermillionville, La. Skirmishes at.
    Nov. 5, 1863* 332
    Nov. 8, 1863* 332
Vermont Troops. Mentioned.
    Artillery, Light—*Batteries :* 1st, 22,68,125,530, 595, 633, 660, 711, 713, 721,
        723,726,895 ; 2d, 22, 38, 69, 121, 122, 238, 239,530,555,602,660,708,733,896.
    Infantry—*Regiments :* 7th, 532, 708, 746–748, 895 ; 8th, 22, 66, 67, 335, 529,
        711, 899.
Vero, William. Mentioned 65
Verrett, Volser.
    Court-martial in case of. Mutiny at Fort Jackson, La., Dec. 9, 1863 478
    Mentioned 478,479
Vicksburg, Miss.
    Affairs at. Communications from U. S. Grant 643
    Expedition from. See *Monroe, La. Expedition from Vicksburg, Miss., to,*
        Aug. 20–*Sept.* 2, 1863.
    Surrender of, announced. Communications from
      Banks, Nathaniel P 53
      Grant, U. S 53
Victoria, Abraham.
    Court-martial in case of. Mutiny at Fort Jackson, La., Dec. 9, 1863 477
    Mentioned 477,479
Vidal, Adrian I.
    Mentioned 435, 439, 440, 444, 447–451, 830, 876
    Mutiny of, Oct. 28, 1863.
      Communications from
        Bee, Hamilton P 447, 450,451
        Tamaulipas, Mexico, Governor of. (Manuel Ruiz) 450
      Reports of Hamilton P. Bee 448,451
Vidalia, La.
    Attack on, Sept. 14, 1863. Report of Marcellus M. Crocker 314
    Expedition from. See *Trinity, La. Expedition from Vidalia to, Nov.* 15–16,
        1863.

---

* No circumstantial reports on file.

Page.

Vidauri, S̈antiago. Mentioned... 866
    For correspondence, etc., see *Nuevo Leon and Cohahuila, Mexico, Governor of.*
Vifquain, Victor. Mentioned 361
Vigne, Major. Mentioned 552
Vila, ——. Mentioned.. 402
Villareal, Manuel. Mentioned... 285
Vincent, Platt F. Mentioned.. 63
Vincent, Thomas M. For correspondence as A. A. G., see *Adjutant-General's Office, U. S. A.*
Vincent, W. G. Mentioned... 389, 393
Viño, Guillermo. Mentioned... 285
Vinton, J. R. Mentioned.. 440, 448
Virginia, U. S. S. Mentioned....................................... 397, 411, 785
Voorhees, Albert. Mentioned.. 382
Vose, Josiah H. Mentioned.. 71
Wade, E. L. Mentioned... 816
Wade, Frank S. Mentioned.. 61
Wade, Henry F., jr. Mentioned 219
Wade, Thomas F. Mentioned..................................... 743, 746–748
Wadsworth, Benjamin. Mentioned...................................... 71
Waite, George W. Mentioned.. 65
Walker, Colonel. Mentioned... 441
Walker, Duncan S. Mentioned..................................... 57, 630
    For correspondence as A. A. G., see *Nathaniel P. Banks;* also *William H. Emory.*
Walker, Henry. Mentioned 530
Walker, J. G. Mentioned...: 211, 212, 278, 337, 343, 344, 374, 384, 693, 754, 763, 813, 819, 852, 916, 920
Walker, W. M.
    Correspondence with Commanding Officer U. S. Naval forces off New Orleans, La... 693
    Mentioned 92, 108
Wallace, Aaron W. Mentioned... 71
Wallace, Joseph C. Mentioned.. 63
Wallen, Henry D.
    Correspondence with James H. Carleton 844
    Mentioned 31, 254, 260, 827, 901
    Report of operations against Navajo Indians in New Mexico, Aug. 20–Dec. 16, 1863 260
Walling, Samuel A. Mentioned.. 765
Wallis, Joseph. Mentioned.. 71
Walse, Ralemy. Mentioned.. 59
Walsh, Thomas. Mentioned.. 24
Walton, Charles.
    Mentioned 267
    Testimony of. Mutiny at Camp Hubbard, Thibodeaux, La., Aug. 29–30, 1863 267
Walton, F. Mentioned 791
Waples, Rufus. Correspondence with Nathaniel P. Banks.............. 795
War Department, C. S. Correspondence with
    Adjutant and Inspector General's Office, C. S. A 385
    Davis, Jefferson... 210, 385

Page.

War Department, U. S. Correspondence with
Army Headquarters... 271, 656, 659
Banks, Nathaniel P 5, 776, 846, 902
Hamilton, Andrew J 865
Lincoln, Abraham.. 659
Navy Department, U. S.. 669
Quartermaster-General's Office, U. S. A.......................... 829
Rhode Island, Governor of.. 270
Shepley, George F 694
State Department, U. S 569, 572, 628, 656, 658, 718, 719, 902
Ward, Henry C. Mentioned....................................... 58
Ward, J. Langdon. Mentioned.............................. 817, 852
Warner, John V. Mentioned 61
Warren, Fitz Henry.
Assignment to command 734
Mentioned........................ 734, 800, 801, 853, 878, 897, 903
Warren, Silas E. Mentioned 65
Warren, Thomas A. Mentioned................................... 61
Warren, W. F. Mentioned 353
Warrior, Steamer. Mentioned 426, 427, 782, 869
Washburn, Cadwallader C.
Assignment to command 2
Assumes command of 13th Army Corps 3
Correspondence with
Banks, Nathaniel P.. 420,
    481, 714, 773, 824, 837, 849, 853, 859, 860, 867, 869, 878, 903
Magruder, John B 851
Thompson, William G... 878
Mentioned 20, 276, 334, 339, 340, 342,
    343, 353, 354, 359, 360, 367, 374, 381, 387, 389–391, 427, 428, 681, 701, 707, 709,
    734, 749–751, 755, 759, 772, 793, 800, 801, 826, 830, 838, 847, 862, 891, 893, 896
Reports of
Matagorda Peninsula, Tex. Skirmish on, Dec. 29, 1863 480
Rio Grande Expedition, and operations on the coast of Texas, Oct. 27–
    Dec. 2, 1863...................................... 416–418
Teche Country, La. Operations in the, Oct. 3–Nov. 30, 1863......... 355, 356
Washburn, Henry D.
Mentioned 324, 418–420, 426–428, 709, 773, 897
Report of Rio Grande Expedition, and operations on the coast of Texas,
    Oct. 27–Dec. 2, 1863 420
Washington, George, Steamer. Mentioned 540, 813, 814
Washington, George. Mentioned 60
Washington, La. Skirmishes at.
Oct. 24, 1863. See *Teche Country, La. Operations in the, Oct. 3–Nov. 30,*
    1863. Reports of
    Franklin, William B.   Taylor, Richard.   Washburn, Cadwallader C.
Oct. 31, 1863. See *Teche Country, La. Operations in the, Oct. 3–Nov. 30, 1863.*
    Record of Events, Cav. Div., p. 377.
Waterhouse, George. Mentioned 60
Waterloo, La. Demonstration on, June 16, 1863. See *Louisiana. Operations*
    in, west of the Mississippi, June 7–July 13, 1863. Report of Major,
    p. 217.
Waters, John G.
Correspondence with David G. Farragut............................ 607
Mentioned.. 191, 617, 621

Page.

Watkins, George W. Mentioned... 57
Watkins, Willard L. Mentioned... 62
Watkins, William L. Mentioned... 335
Watson, Andrew P. Mentioned... 60
Watson, Edward L. Mentioned... 25
Watson, John C. Mentioned... 90, 93
Watt, A. J. Mentioned... 216
Watters, John. Correspondence with David G. Farragut 109, 110, 114, 115
Wayman, Willet. Mentioned... 913
Weaver, Aaron W.
    Correspondence with David G. Farragut................................... 81, 115
    Mentioned................................... 191, 192, 203
Webb, C. S. S. Mentioned................................... 10, 552
Webb, Amaziah W. Mentioned................................... 61
Webb, L. R. Mentioned................................... 710
Webber, A. Watson. Mentioned................................... 712
Webber, Frederick. Mentioned................................... 63
Webster, Albert Mentioned................................... 60
Webster, Daniel. Mentioned................................... 334, 895
Webster, Samuel. Mentioned................................... 63
Weed, Francis E. Mentioned................................... 57
Weed, Theodore. Mentioned................................... 62
Weeks, Charles W. Mentioned................................... 64
Weisiger, R. N. Mentioned................................... 330
Weitzel, Godfrey.
    Assignments to command................................... 486, 685
    Correspondence with
      Banks, Nathaniel P 501, 505, 509, 510, 626, 663, 848
      Farragut, David G...................... 109, 120
    Itinerary of 1st Division, 19th Army Corps, Sept., 1863................... 299
    Mentioned................................... 4, 43,
      67, 77, 85, 92, 94, 109, 115, 119, 120, 163, 204, 207, 214, 222, 231, 287–289,
      293–295, 297–299, 335, 337, 354, 369, 381, 382, 389, 394, 486, 487, 489, 490, 492,
      493, 500, 504, 506, 509–512, 518, 519, 527–531, 533, 558, 610, 611, 627, 630, 631,
      638, 657, 658, 660, 663, 665, 667, 676, 677, 685, 710, 735, 749, 783, 826, 837, 899
    Reports of
      Boyce's Bridge, Cotile Bayou, La. Skirmish at, May 14, 1863........ .. 35
      Cheneyville, La.
        Affair near, May 18, 1863.................................. 38
        Skirmish near, May 20, 1863.. 39
      Port Hudson, La. Siege of, May 21–July 8, 1863 .... 130, 131
      Sabine Pass (Texas) Expedition, Sept. 4–11, 1863 293
Welch, John. Mentioned................................... 61
Welcome, Steamer.
    Attack on, near Natchez, Miss. Communication from George L. Andrews. 819
    Mentioned................................... 731, 819
Weld, Mason C. Mentioned................................... 530
Welfley, Martin. Mentioned................................... 398, 665, 709, 897
Weller, John. Mentioned................................... 60
Welles, Gideon. Mentioned................... 3, 90, 99, 285, 396, 480, 702, 790, 861, 888
    For correspondence, etc., see Navy Department, U. S.
Wellman, C. R. Mentioned................................... 612, 901
Wells, E. R. Mentioned................................... 332, 395
Wells, Frank. Mentioned................................... 57

Page.

Welsh, Mike.
Mentioned 536
Statement of. Siege of Port Hudson, La., May 21–July 8, 1863. 536
Wentlandt, Julius. Mentioned 60
West, J. A. A. Mentioned 218, 219, 330
West, Joseph R.
Correspondence with
Carleton, James H 491
Chihuahua, Mexico, U. S. Consul at 919, 920
Monterey, Mexico, U. S. Consul at 916, 917
Mentioned 612, 750, 827, 901, 917–919
Western, Charles B. Mentioned 64
Western Florida. See *Florida, Western.*
Western Louisiana. See *Louisiana, Western.*
Western Texas. See *Texas, Western.*
Westfield, U. S. S. Mentioned 4, 7
Wharton, John A. Mentioned 496
Wheaton, George H. Mentioned 262
Wheeler, Alonzo. Mentioned 57
Whitcomb, A. C. Mentioned 62
White, Private. Mentioned 59
White, David. Mentioned 787
White, Ephraim G. Mentioned 334, 709
White, Martin. Mentioned 59
White, Patrick H. Mentioned 335, 710, 898
White, Samuel. Mentioned 828, 900
Whiteside, S. A. Mentioned 143
Whitfield, J. F. Mentioned 157
Whiting, John E. Mentioned 710
Whitlock, J. H. Mentioned 27, 750, 827, 901
Whitman, Charles T. Mentioned 143
Whitmore, Samuel. Mentioned 63
Whitside, Samuel M. Mentioned 494
Whittemore, E. Mentioned 853
Whittemore, H. O. Mentioned 899
Whittemore, James B. Mentioned 30
Whittier, Francis H. Mentioned 122, 209
Whittlesey, Luther H. Mentioned 709, 897
Wiggin, George. Mentioned 623, 653
Wilcoxen, Mr. Mentioned 40, 41
Wilcoxen, Mrs. Mentioned 40
Wilder, J. W., Schooner. Mentioned 792
Wildman, William. Mentioned 61
Wilds, John Q. Mentioned 335, 710
Wiley, Edward J. Mentioned 63
Wilkerson, Charles. Mentioned 60
Wilkie, William. Mentioned 59
Wilkins, W. G. Mentioned 229
Wilkinson, Robert F. Mentioned 122
Williams, Private. Mentioned 60
Williams, Frank.
Court-martial in case of. Mutiny at Fort Jackson, La., Dec. 9, 1863 476
Mentioned 467, 476, 479
Williams, Frederick A. Mentioned 895
Williams, Harry. Mentioned 465, 469, 470, 473

	Page.
Williams, John. Mentioned	141
Williams, Thomas. Mentioned	66
Williams, William H. Mentioned	334
Williamson, James. Mentioned	71
Willis, Edward B.	
Correspondence with Benjamin C. Cutler	869
Mentioned	28, 828, 901
Report of scout from Fort Wingate to Ojo Redondo (Jacob's Well), N. Mex., Sept. 15–Oct. 5, 1863	315
Willis, George A. Mentioned	336, 665, 710, 828, 900
Willson, T. Friend. For correspondence as A. A. G., see *Franklin Gardner.*	
Wilson, Alexander. Mentioned	60
Wilson, August. Mentioned	58
Wilson, Charles P. Mentioned	63
Wilson, George. (3d Massachusetts.) Mentioned	61
Wilson, George. (90th New York.) Mentioned	63
Wilson, G. J. Mentioned	144
Wilson, James G. Mentioned	380
Wilson, John. Mentioned	61
Winchester, B. Felix. Mentioned	220–222
Winchester, J. Richard. Mentioned	454
Wingate, Fort. See *Fort Wingate.*	
Wingfield, J. H.	
Correspondence with Franklin Gardner	165
Reports of siege of Port Hudson. La., May 21–July 8, 1863	165, 167
Winona, U. S. S. Mentioned	47, 191, 192, 202, 203, 571, 589, 621
Winslow, George A. Mentioned	58
Winston, Captain. Mentioned	449
Winter, Elisha. Mentioned	531
Wintermeyer, Gustavus. Mentioned	71
Winthrop, Robert C., Steamer. Mentioned	300
Wisconsin Troops. Mentioned.	
Artillery, Light—Batteries: **1st,** 334, 417, 709, 713, 714, 739, 859, 878, 895.	
Cavalry—Regiments: **2d,** 710; **4th,*** 22, 36, 66, 69, 134, 135, 136, 336, 378, 530, 531, 565, 632, 666, 667, 686, 708, 712, 749, 783, 826, 828, 892, 895.	
Infantry—Regiments: **11th,** 334, 709, 897; **12th,** 276; **17th,** 273, 274, 276–279, 315; **20th,** 328, 398, 406, 412, 430, 665, 709, 897; **23d,** 335, 358, 359, 361, 363–366, 394, 710, 898; **29th,** 335, 358, 710, 898.	
Wisner, John H. Mentioned	62
Witham, C. H. Mentioned	191
Witham, Elliott. Mentioned	60
Withers, Jones M. Mentioned	496
Wolff, Francis J. Mentioned	57
Wood, Almon A. Mentioned	40, 41
Wood, Henry L. Mentioned	61
Wood, S. A. M. Mentioned	496
Wood, William. Mentioned	59
Wood, William F. Mentioned	712, 829
Woodbury, Daniel P.	
Correspondence with	
Bailey, Theodorus	875
Banks, Nathaniel P	855, 873, 874
Mentioned	527, 528, 532, 610, 611, 665, 707, 708, 749, 784, 827, 874, 892, 896

---

*Originally 4th Wisconsin Infantry.

Page.
Woodcock, Leander. Mentioned... 61
Woodman, Ephraim W. Mentioned............................ .... 529, 665
Woodrow, Howard C. Mentioned 51
Woodruff, Henry D. Mentioned... 634
Woodward, John P. Mentioned... 57
Woolsey, M. B.
  Correspondence with
    Bullen, Joseph D.. 620, 621
    Farragut, David G.. 594, 621
    Hadlock, William E.. 622
  Mentioned 191, 203
Wordin, C. W. Correspondence with William H. Emory..................... 186
Wright, Edward. Mentioned.. 898
Wright, William. Mentioned 201
Wrotnouski, Arthur F. Mentioned 898
Wrotnowski, L. A. Mentioned 17
Wyman, Thomas. Mentioned 61
Yeaton, Reuben F. Mentioned 135
Youbert, Captain. Mentioned 728
Young, John F. Mentioned.. 65
Young, Lewis. Mentioned 65
Young, Mahlon M.
  Correspondence with William C. Holbrook................................. 746
  Deposition of. Illegal arrests 746
  Mentioned 743, 744, 746-748
Young, Van E. Mentioned.. 829
Young's Point, La. See *Milliken's Bend, La.*
York, James. Mentioned 58
Zacharie, H. H. Mentioned.. 219
Zapata, Clemente. Mentioned 898
Zapata, Octaviano. Mentioned.................................... 283, 284, 285
Zapata's Banditti. Affair with. See *Mier, Mexico. Affair with Zapata's banditti near. Sept. 2, 1863.*
Zener, W. W. Mentioned 421, 423
Zengle, William. Mentioned 152, 153
Zephyr, Steamer. Mentioned.................................. 50, 604, 605, 787
Zulavsky, Ladislas L. Mentioned.. 708, 896
Zumstein, Jacob. Mentioned 63
Zuñi, Governor of. Mentioned... 252, 256

14 DAY USE

RETURN TO DESK FROM WHICH BORR

This book is due on the last date stamped be
on the date to which renewed.
Renewed books are subject to immediate